Mobil Travel Guide

D0940005

Northern Great Lakes

2006

Michigan

Minnesota

Wisconsin

ExxonMobil
Travel Publications

Acknowledgements

We gratefully acknowledge the help of our representatives for their efficient and perceptive inspections of the lodging and dining establishments listed; the establishments' proprietors for their cooperation in showing their facilities and providing information about them; and the many users of previous editions who have taken the time to share their experiences. Mobil Travel Guide is also grateful to all the talented writers who contributed entries to this book.

www.mobiltravelguide.com

Front cover photo: Point Betsie Lighthouse, Frankfort, Michigan

ISBN: 0-7627-3929-0

ISSN: 1550-0977

Manufactured in the United States of America.

10 9 8 7 6 5 4 3 2 1

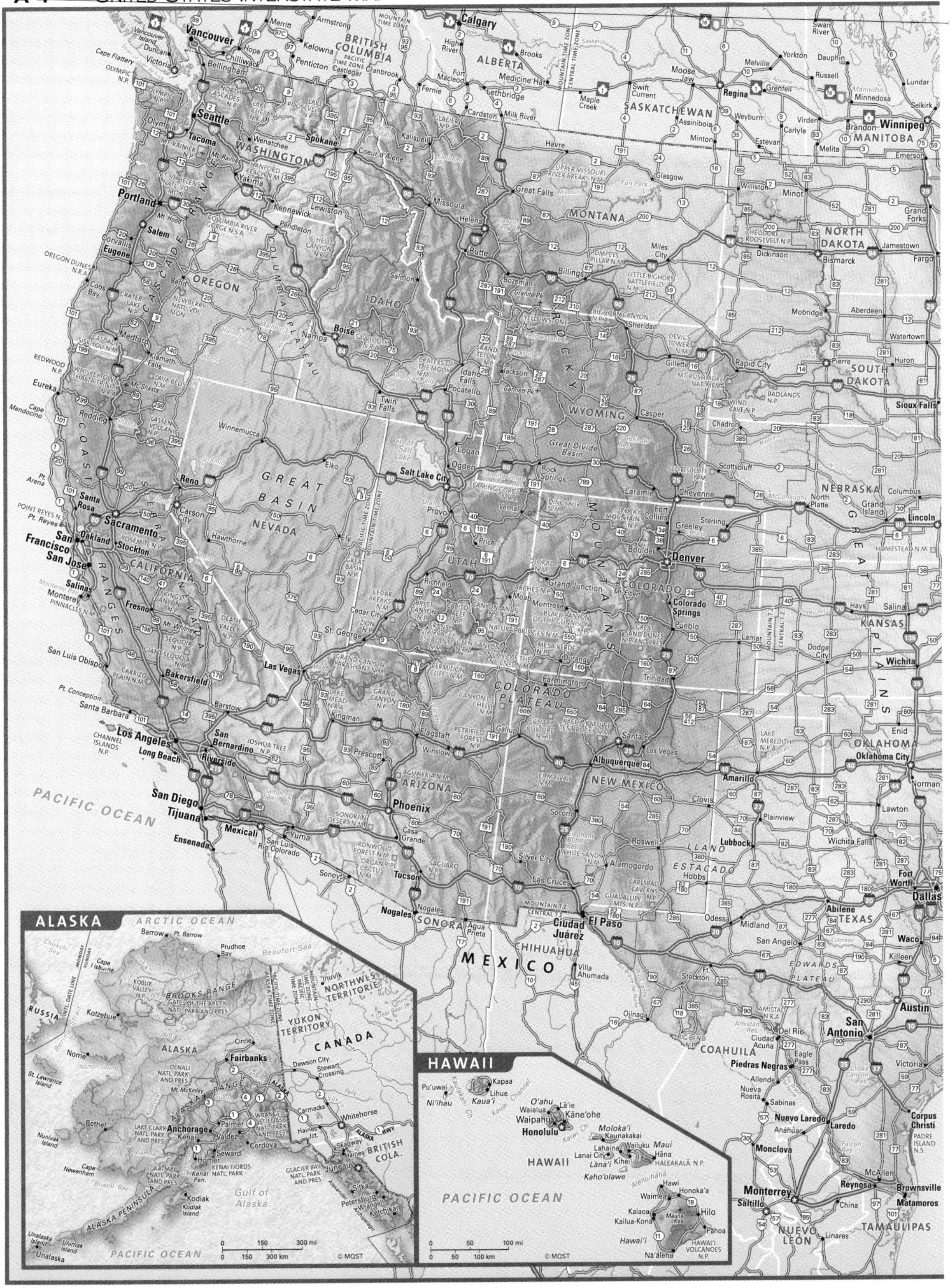
BRITISH COLUMBIA
ALBERTA
SASKATCHEWAN
MANITOBA
WASHINGTON
OREGON
IDAHO
MONTANA
WYOMING
NORTH DAKOTA
SOUTH DAKOTA
NEBRASKA
KANSAS
OKLAHOMA
TEXAS
NEW MEXICO
COLORADO
UTAH
ARIZONA
NEVADA
CALIFORNIA
MEXICO
SONORA
CHIHUAHUA
COAHUILA
NUEVO LEÓN
TAMAULIPAS
PACIFIC OCEAN
GREAT BASIN
COLORADO PLATEAU
COLUMBIA PLATEAU
ROCKY MOUNTAINS
GREAT PLAINS
LLANO ESTACADO
EDWARDS PLATEAU
Vancouver
Calgary
Seattle
Portland
Spokane
Boise
Salt Lake City
Denver
Sacramento
San Francisco
San Jose
Los Angeles
San Diego
Las Vegas
Phoenix
Tucson
Albuquerque
El Paso
Ciudad Juárez
Oklahoma City
Dallas
San Antonio
Austin
Monterrey
Winnipeg
Regina
ALASKA
ARCTIC OCEAN
BROOKS RANGE
Fairbanks
Anchorage
Juneau
CANADA
YUKON TERRITORY
NORTHWEST TERRITORIES
Gulf of Alaska
HAWAII
Honolulu
Hilo
© MQST

Contents

Maps

Northern Great Lakes

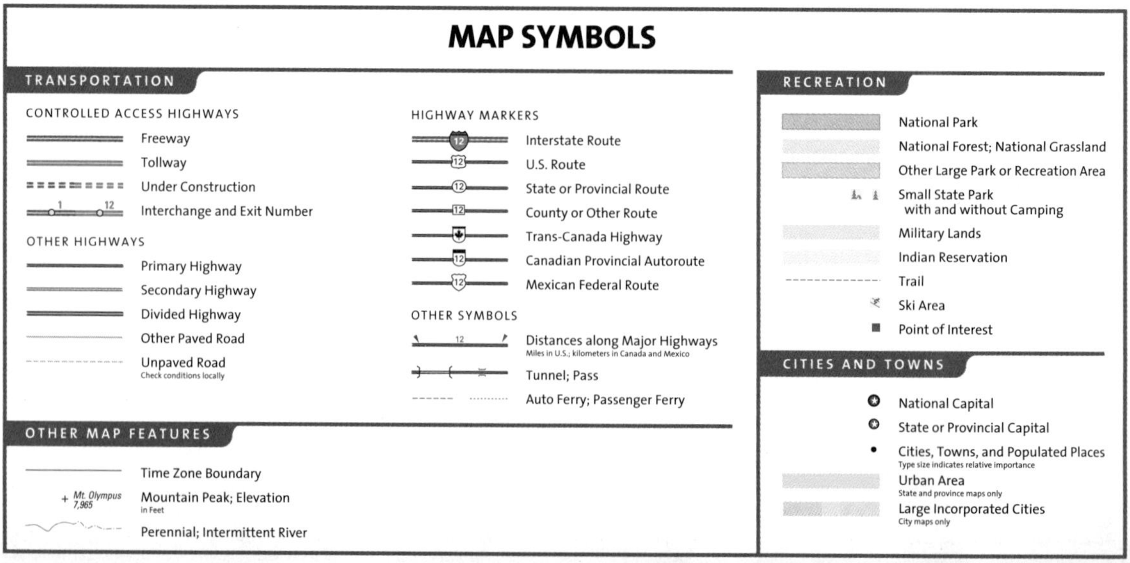

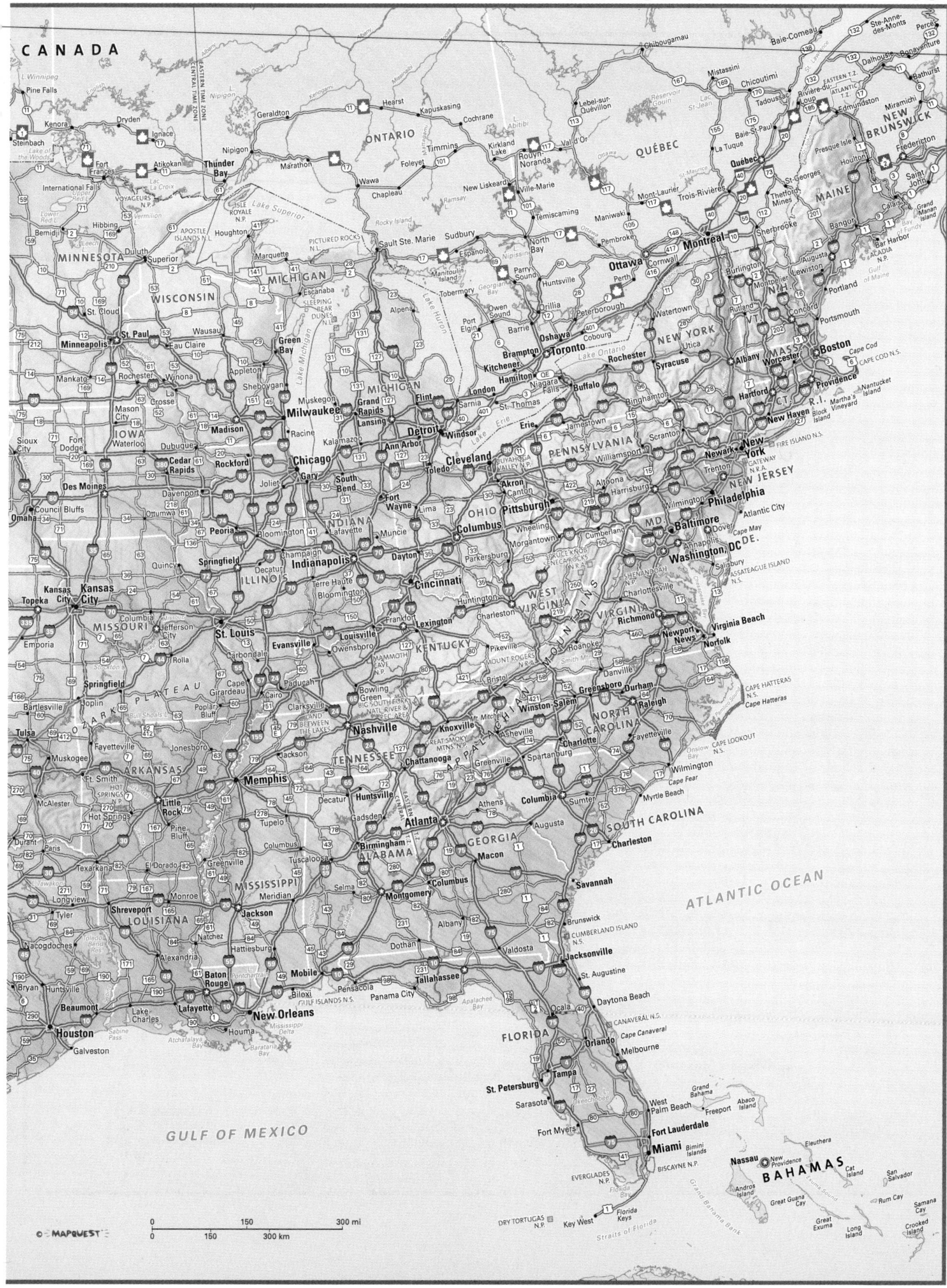
CANADA
ONTARIO
QUÉBEC
NEW BRUNSWICK
MAINE
NEW YORK
PENNSYLVANIA
NEW JERSEY
MINNESOTA
WISCONSIN
MICHIGAN
IOWA
ILLINOIS
INDIANA
OHIO
WEST VIRGINIA
VIRGINIA
KENTUCKY
MISSOURI
TENNESSEE
NORTH CAROLINA
SOUTH CAROLINA
ARKANSAS
MISSISSIPPI
ALABAMA
GEORGIA
LOUISIANA
FLORIDA
BAHAMAS
OZARK PLATEAU
APPALACHIAN MOUNTAINS
ATLANTIC OCEAN
GULF OF MEXICO
Lake Superior
Lake Michigan
Lake Huron
Lake Ontario
Lake Erie
Minneapolis
St. Paul
Milwaukee
Chicago
Detroit
Toronto
Ottawa
Montréal
Québec
Boston
New York
Philadelphia
Baltimore
Washington, DC
Pittsburgh
Cleveland
Columbus
Cincinnati
Indianapolis
St. Louis
Kansas City
Louisville
Lexington
Nashville
Memphis
Atlanta
Charlotte
Raleigh
Richmond
Virginia Beach
Norfolk
Jacksonville
Orlando
Tampa
Miami
Fort Lauderdale
New Orleans
Houston
Baton Rouge
Mobile
Birmingham
Little Rock
Tulsa
Des Moines
Omaha
Buffalo
Rochester
Syracuse
Albany
Providence
Hartford
Nassau
Key West
© MAPQUEST
0 150 300 mi
0 150 300 km

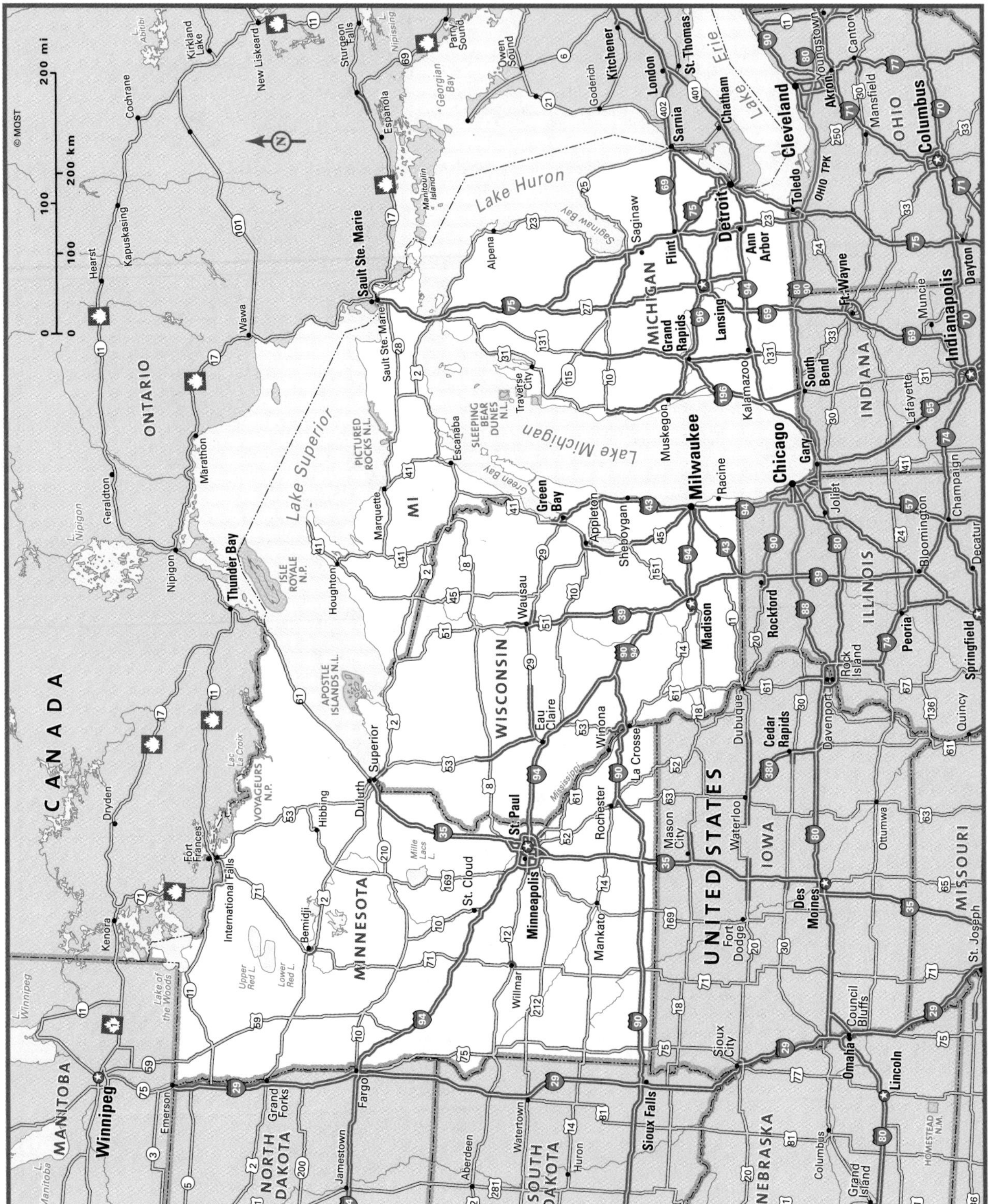

CANADA
ONTARIO
MANITOBA
UNITED STATES
MINNESOTA
WISCONSIN
MICHIGAN
MI
IOWA
ILLINOIS
INDIANA
OHIO
MISSOURI
NEBRASKA
NORTH DAKOTA
SOUTH DAKOTA
Lake Superior
Lake Michigan
Lake Huron
Lake Erie
Georgian Bay
Saginaw Bay
Green Bay
Lake of the Woods
L. Winnipeg
L. Manitoba
L. Nipigon
L. Abitibi
L. Nipissing
Upper Red L.
Lower Red L.
Mille Lacs L.
Lac La Croix
Mississippi
Manitoulin Island
ISLE ROYALE N.P.
APOSTLE ISLANDS N.L.
PICTURED ROCKS N.L.
SLEEPING BEAR DUNES N.L.
VOYAGEURS N.P.
HOMESTEAD N.M.
0 100 200 mi
0 100 200 km
© MQST
Winnipeg
Emerson
Kenora
Dryden
Fort Frances
International Falls
Thunder Bay
Nipigon
Geraldton
Marathon
Wawa
Hearst
Kapuskasing
Cochrane
Kirkland Lake
New Liskeard
Sturgeon Falls
Espanola
Parry Sound
Owen Sound
Goderich
Kitchener
London
St. Thomas
Sarnia
Chatham
Sault Ste. Marie
Grand Forks
Fargo
Jamestown
Aberdeen
Watertown
Huron
Sioux Falls
Bemidji
Hibbing
Duluth
Superior
St. Cloud
Minneapolis
St. Paul
Willmar
Mankato
Rochester
Winona
La Crosse
Eau Claire
Wausau
Houghton
Marquette
Escanaba
Green Bay
Appleton
Sheboygan
Milwaukee
Racine
Madison
Traverse City
Alpena
Muskegon
Grand Rapids
Kalamazoo
Lansing
Flint
Saginaw
Detroit
Ann Arbor
Toledo
Cleveland
Akron
Youngstown
Canton
Mansfield
Columbus
Dayton
Ft. Wayne
Muncie
Indianapolis
Lafayette
South Bend
Gary
Chicago
Joliet
Champaign
Bloomington
Decatur
Springfield
Peoria
Rockford
Rock Island
Davenport
Quincy
Dubuque
Cedar Rapids
Waterloo
Mason City
Fort Dodge
Des Moines
Ottumwa
Sioux City
Council Bluffs
Omaha
Lincoln
Columbus
Grand Island
St. Joseph
OHIO TPK

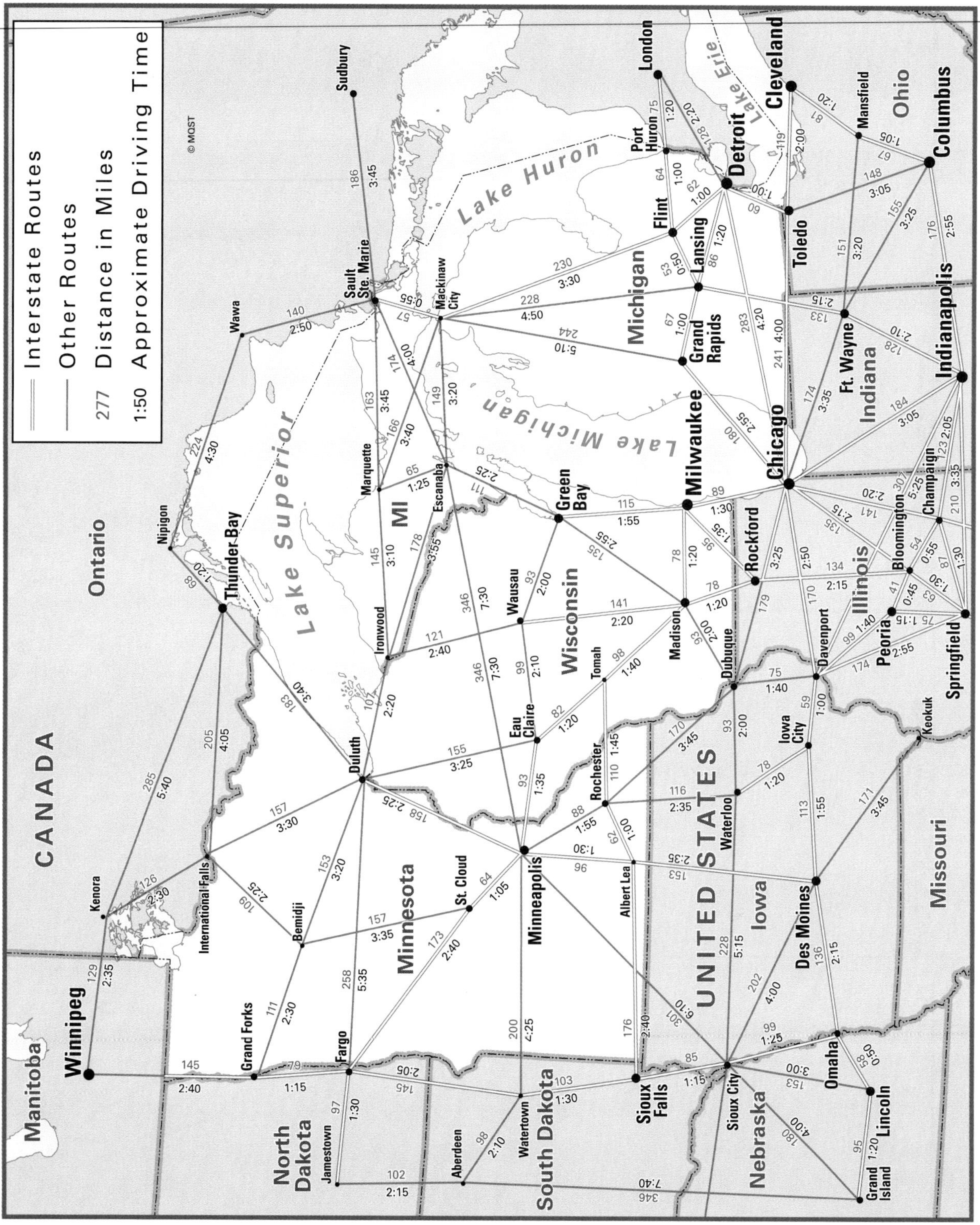
Interstate Routes
Other Routes
277 Distance in Miles
1:50 Approximate Driving Time
© MQST
CANADA
Ontario
Manitoba
UNITED STATES
Lake Superior
Lake Michigan
Lake Huron
Lake Erie
Minnesota
Wisconsin
Michigan
MI
Iowa
Illinois
Indiana
Ohio
Missouri
Nebraska
North Dakota
South Dakota
Winnipeg
Kenora
International Falls
Thunder Bay
Nipigon
Wawa
Sudbury
Sault Ste. Marie
Mackinaw City
Marquette
Escanaba
Ironwood
Duluth
Grand Forks
Fargo
Bemidji
St. Cloud
Minneapolis
Eau Claire
Wausau
Green Bay
Milwaukee
Madison
Tomah
Rochester
Albert Lea
Dubuque
Rockford
Chicago
Grand Rapids
Lansing
Flint
Port Huron
London
Detroit
Toledo
Cleveland
Mansfield
Columbus
Ft. Wayne
Indianapolis
Champaign
Bloomington
Peoria
Springfield
Davenport
Iowa City
Waterloo
Keokuk
Des Moines
Omaha
Lincoln
Grand Island
Sioux City
Sioux Falls
Watertown
Aberdeen
Jamestown

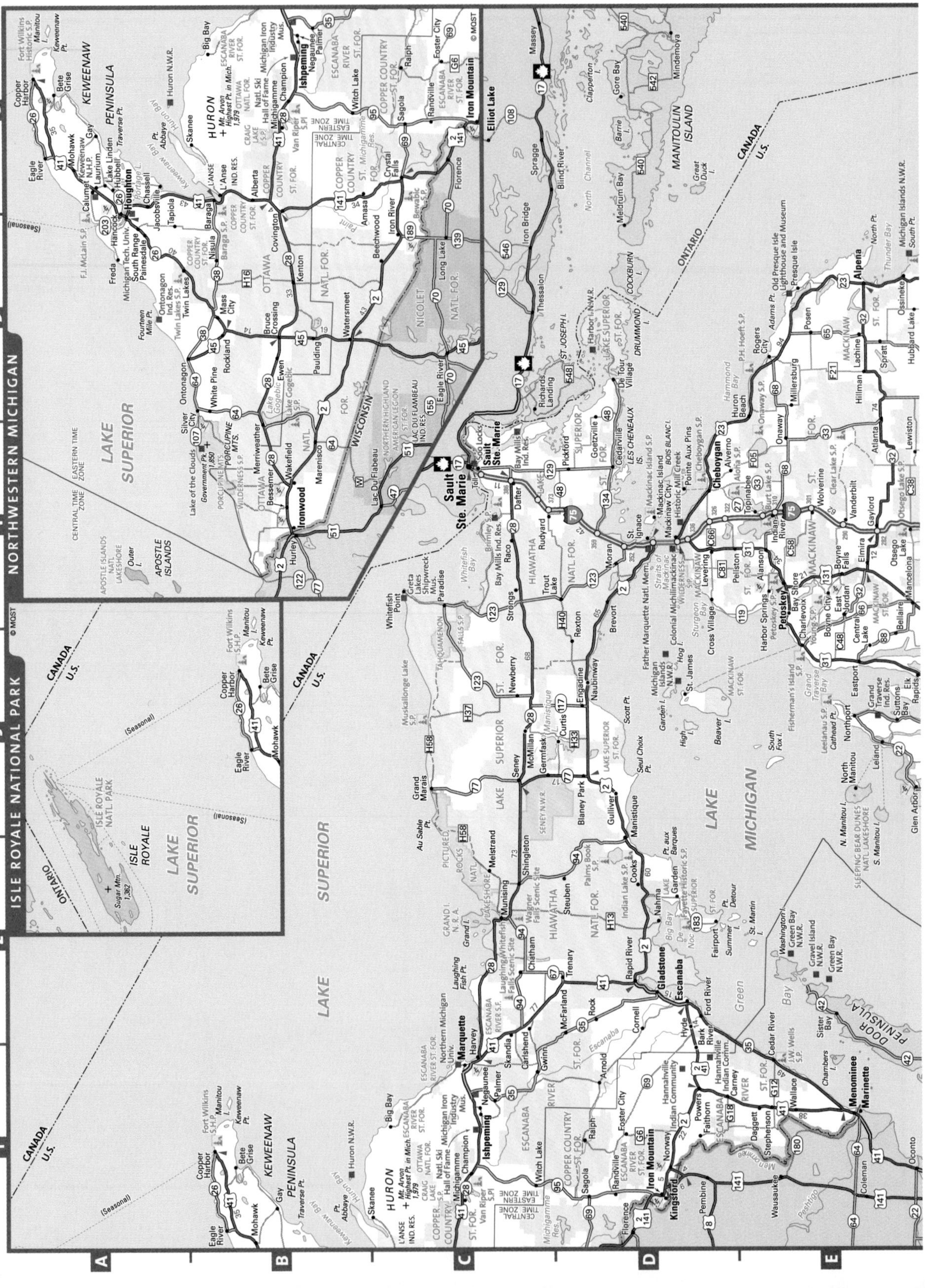
NORTHWESTERN MICHIGAN
ISLE ROYALE NATIONAL PARK
LAKE SUPERIOR
LAKE MICHIGAN
MANITOULIN ISLAND
KEWEENAW PENINSULA
ISLE ROYALE NATL. PARK
CANADA
U.S.
ONTARIO
WISCONSIN
Sault Ste. Marie
Marquette
Escanaba
Ironwood
Houghton
Cheboygan
Petoskey
Alpena
Menominee
Iron Mountain
Ishpeming
Munising
Manistique
Gladstone
St. Ignace
Mackinaw City
Newberry
Grand Marais
Gaylord
Marinette
Straits of Mackinac
© MOST

MICHIGAN

POP: 9,938,444, rank 8

AREA: 58,527 sq mi, rank 23

Adrian, 21574	K5
Albion, 9144	J4
Algonac, 4613	J6
Allegan, 4838	J3
Allendale, 11555	H3
Alma, 9275	H4
Almont, 2803	H6
Alpena, 11304	E5
Ann Arbor, 114024	J5
Bad Axe, 3462	G6
Battle Creek, 53364	J4
Bay City, 36817	G5
Belding, 5877	H3
Benton Harbor, 11182	K2
Big Rapids, 10849	G3
Birmingham, 19291	J5
Blissfield, 3223	K5
Boyne City, 3503	E4
Bridgeport, 7849	H5
Brighton, 6701	J5
Buchanan, 4681	K2
Burton, 30308	H5
Cadillac, 10000	F3
Carleton, 2562	K5
Caro, 4145	H5
Carrollton, 6602	H5
Cass City, 2643	G5
Cedar Sprs. , 3112	H3
Charlevoix, 2994	E3
Charlotte, 8389	J4
Cheboygan, 5295	D4
Chelsea, 4398	J5
Chesaning, 2548	H5
Clare, 3173	G4
Coldwater, 12697	K4
Coopersville, 3910	H3
Corunna, 3381	H5
Cutlerville, 15114	J3
Davison, 5536	H5
Dearborn, 97775	J5
Detroit, 951270	J6
De Witt, 4702	J4
Dorr, 2800	J3
Dowagiac, 6147	K3
Dundee, 3522	K5
Durand, 3933	H5
E. Grand Rapids, 10764	H3
E. Jordan, 2507	E4
E. Lansing, 46525	J4
E. Tawas, 2951	F5
Eaton Rapids, 5330	J4
Escanaba, 13140	D2
Essexville, 3766	G5
Fenton, 10582	J5
Ferrysburg, 3040	H2
Flat Rock, 8488	K5
Flint, 124943	H5
Flushing, 8348	H5
Fowlerville, 2972	J5
Frankenmuth, 4838	H5
Freeland, 5147	G5
Fremont, 4224	H3
Gaylord, 3681	E4
Gladstone, 5032	D2
Gladwin, 3001	G4
Grand Blanc, 8242	H5
Grand Haven, 11168	H2
Grand Ledge, 7813	J4
Grand Rapids, 197800	H3
Grandville, 16263	H3
Greenville, 7935	H3
Hancock, 4323	A5
Hastings, 7095	J3
Hillsdale, 8233	K4
Holland, 35048	J3
Holly, 6135	J5
Holt, 11315	J4
Houghton, 7010	A5
Houghton Lake, 3749	F4
Howell, 9232	J5
Hudson, 2499	K4
Hudsonville, 7160	H3
Imlay City, 3869	H6
Ionia, 10569	H4
Iron Mtn., 8154	D1
Iron River, 3386	C5
Ironwood, 6293	B4
Ishpeming, 6686	C1
Ithaca, 3098	H4
Jackson, 36316	J4
Jenison, 17211	H3
Kalamazoo, 77145	J3
Kentwood, 45255	J3
Kingsford, 5549	D1
Lake Orion, 2715	J5
Lambertville, 9299	K5
Lansing, 119128	J4
Lapeer, 9072	H5
Linden, 2861	J5
Livonia, 100545	J5
Lowell, 4013	H3
Ludington, 8357	G2
Manistee, 6586	F2
Manistique, 3583	D2
Marine City, 4652	J6
Marquette, 19661	C1
Marshall, 7459	J4
Marysville, 9684	H6
Mason, 6714	J4
Mattawan, 2536	K3
Menominee, 9131	E1
Michigan Ctr., 4641	J4
Middleville, 2721	J3
Midland, 41685	G4
Milan, 4775	K5
Milford, 6272	J5
Monroe, 22076	K5
Mt. Clemens, 17312	J6
Mt. Morris, 3194	H5
Mt. Pleasant, 25946	G4
Munising, 2539	C2
Muskegon, 40105	H2
Muskegon Hts., 12049	H2
Negaunee, 4576	C1
New Baltimore, 7405	J6
Newberry, 2686	C3
New Haven, 3071	J6
Niles, 12204	K2
N. Muskegon, 4031	H2
Norton Shores, 22527	H2
Norway, 2959	D1
Novi, 47386	J5
Okemos, 22805	J4
Otsego, 3933	J3
Owosso, 15713	H5
Oxford, 3540	J5
Paw Paw, 3363	J3
Petoskey, 6080	E4
Plainwell, 3933	J3
Pontiac, 66337	J5
Portage, 44897	K3
Port Huron, 32338	H6
Portland, 3789	H4
Richmond, 4897	J6
Rockford, 4626	H3
Rockwood, 3442	K5
Rogers City, 3322	E5
Romeo, 3721	J6
Romulus, 22979	J5
Saginaw, 61799	H5
St. Clair, 5802	H6
St. Helen, 2993	F4
St. Ignace, 2678	D4
St. Johns, 7485	H4
St. Joseph, 8789	K2
St. Louis, 4494	H4
Saline, 8034	K5
Sandusky, 2745	H6
Sault Ste. Marie, 16542	C4
Shields, 6590	H5
Skidway Lake, 3147	G5
S. Haven, 5021	J2
S. Lyon, 10036	J5
Sparta, 4159	H3
Springfield, 5189	J3
Sterling Hts., 124471	J6
Sturgis, 11285	K3
Swartz Creek, 5102	H5
Taylor, 65868	J5
Tecumseh, 8574	K5
Temperance, 7757	K5
Three Rivers, 7328	K3
Traverse City, 14532	F3
Troy, 80959	J6
Vassar, 2823	H5
Walker, 21842	H3
Warren, 138247	J6
Wayland, 3939	J3
Whitehall, 2884	H2
Whitmore Lake, 6574	J5
Williamston, 3441	J4
Wixom, 13263	J5
Wolf Lake, 4455	H3
Wyoming, 69368	H3
Ypsilanti, 22362	J5
Zeeland, 5805	J3

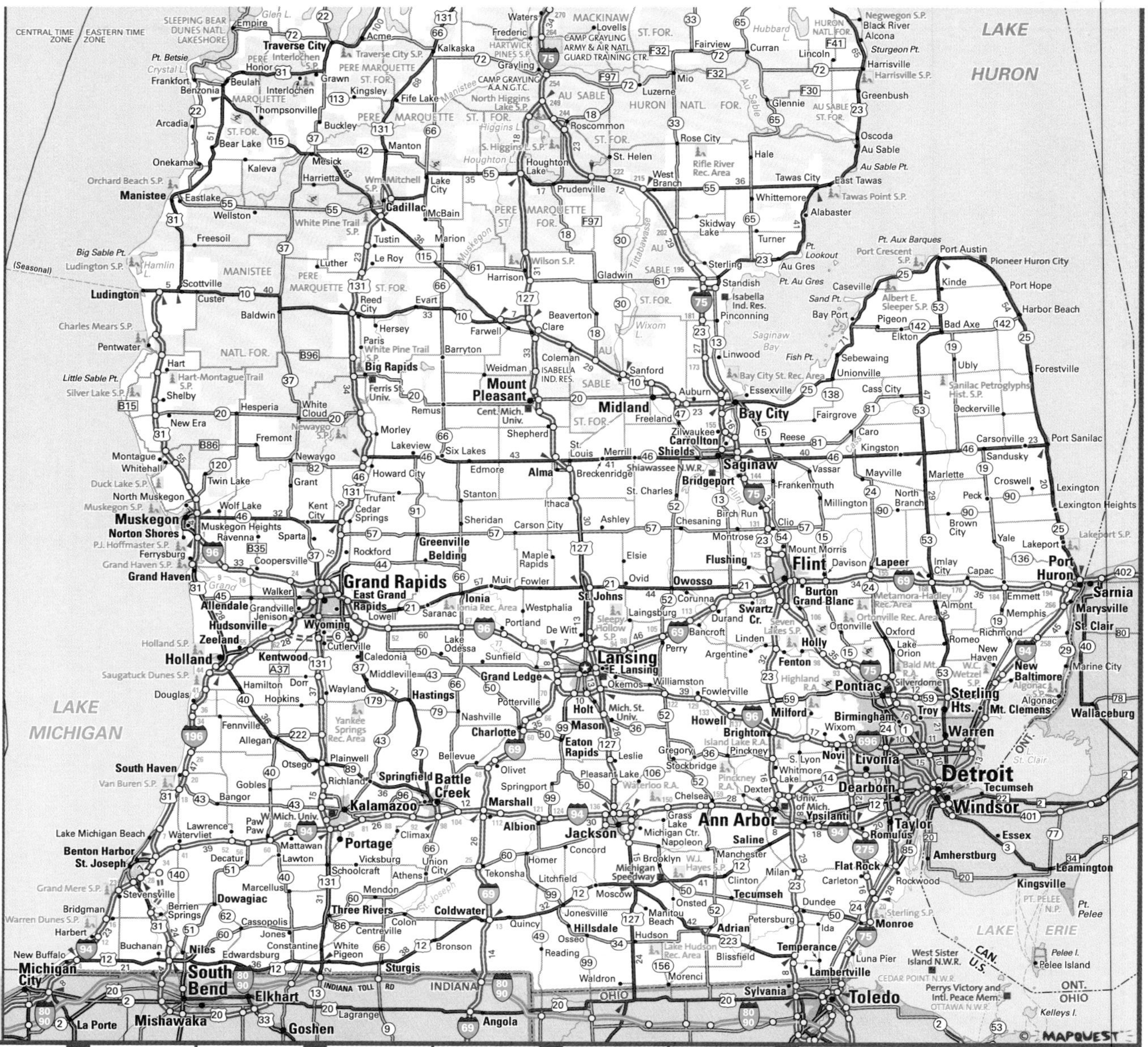

F G H J K

1 2 3 4 5 6

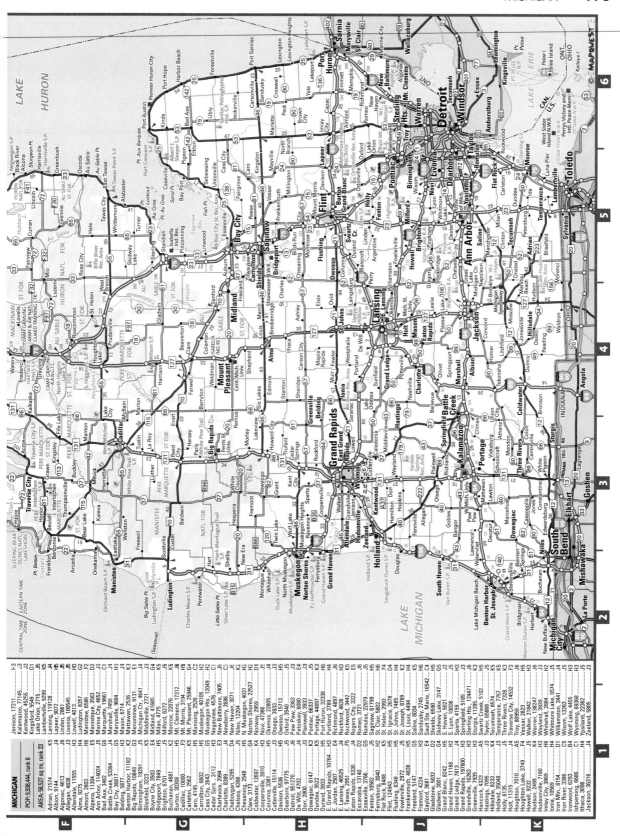

MINNESOTA

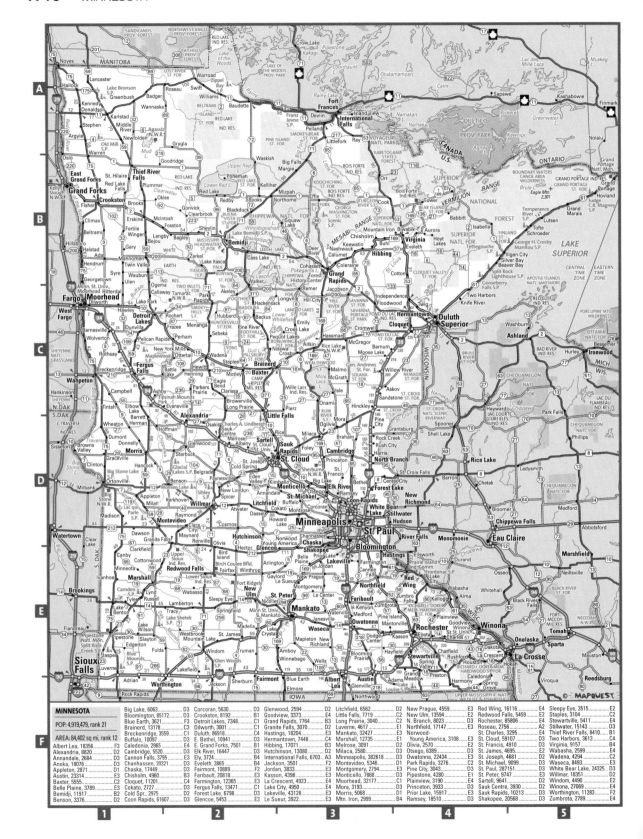

POP: 4,919,479, rank 21

AREA: 84,402 sq mi, rank 12

Albert Lea, 18356	F3
Alexandria, 8820	D2
Annandale, 2684	D3
Anoka, 18076	D3
Appleton, 2871	D1
Austin, 23314	E3
Baxter, 5555	C2
Belle Plaine, 3789	E3
Bemidji, 11917	B2
Benson, 3376	D2
Big Lake, 6063	D3
Bloomington, 85172	D3
Blue Earth, 3621	F3
Brainerd, 13178	C3
Breckenridge, 3559	C1
Buffalo, 10097	D3
Caledonia, 2965	E4
Cambridge, 5520	D3
Cannon Falls, 3795	E3
Chanhassen, 20321	D3
Chaska, 17449	D3
Chisholm, 4960	B3
Cloquet, 11201	C4
Cokato, 2727	D3
Cold Spr., 2975	D2
Coon Rapids, 61607	D3
Corcoran, 5630	D3
Crookston, 8192	B1
Detroit Lakes, 7348	C1
Dilworth, 3001	C1
Duluth, 86918	C4
E. Bethel, 10941	D3
E. Grand Forks, 7501	B1
Elk River, 16447	D3
Ely, 3724	B4
Eveleth, 3865	B4
Fairmont, 10889	F2
Faribault, 20818	E3
Farmington, 12365	E3
Fergus Falls, 13471	C1
Forest Lake, 6798	D3
Glencoe, 5453	E3
Glenwood, 2594	D2
Goodview, 3373	E4
Grand Rapids, 7764	B3
Granite Falls, 3070	D2
Hastings, 18204	E3
Hermantown, 7448	C4
Hibbing, 17071	B3
Hutchinson, 13080	D2
International Falls, 6703	A3
Jackson, 3501	F2
Jordan, 3833	E3
Kasson, 4398	E3
La Crescent, 4923	E4
Lake City, 4950	E4
Lakeville, 43128	E3
Le Sueur, 3922	E3
Litchfield, 6562	D2
Little Falls, 7719	C2
Long Prairie, 3040	C2
Luverne, 4617	E1
Mankato, 32427	E3
Marshall, 12735	E1
Melrose, 3091	D2
Milaca, 2580	D3
Minneapolis, 382618	D3
Montevideo, 5346	D1
Montgomery, 2794	E3
Monticello, 7868	D3
Moorhead, 32177	C1
Mora, 3193	D3
Morris, 5068	D1
Mtn. Iron, 2999	B4
New Prague, 4559	E3
New Ulm, 13594	E2
N. Branch, 8023	D3
Northfield, 17147	E3
Norwood-Young America, 3108	E3
Olivia, 2570	E2
Otsego, 6389	D3
Owatonna, 22434	E3
Park Rapids, 3276	C2
Pine City, 3043	D3
Pipestone, 4280	E1
Plainview, 3190	E4
Princeton, 3933	D3
Prior Lake, 15917	E3
Ramsey, 18510	D3
Red Wing, 16116	E4
Redwood Falls, 5459	E2
Rochester, 85806	E4
Roseau, 2756	A2
St. Charles, 3295	E4
St. Cloud, 59107	D3
St. Francis, 4910	D3
St. James, 4695	E2
St. Joseph, 4681	D2
St. Michael, 9099	D3
St. Paul, 287151	D3
St. Peter, 9747	E3
Sartell, 9641	D2
Sauk Centre, 3930	D2
Sauk Rapids, 10213	D3
Shakopee, 20568	D3
Sleepy Eye, 3515	E2
Staples, 3104	C2
Stewartville, 5411	E4
Stillwater, 15143	D3
Thief River Falls, 8410	B1
Two Harbors, 3613	C4
Virginia, 9157	B4
Wabasha, 2599	E4
Wadena, 4294	C2
Waseca, 8493	E3
White Bear Lake, 24325	D3
Willmar, 18351	D2
Windom, 4490	E2
Winona, 27069	E4
Worthington, 11283	F2
Zumbrota, 2789	E4

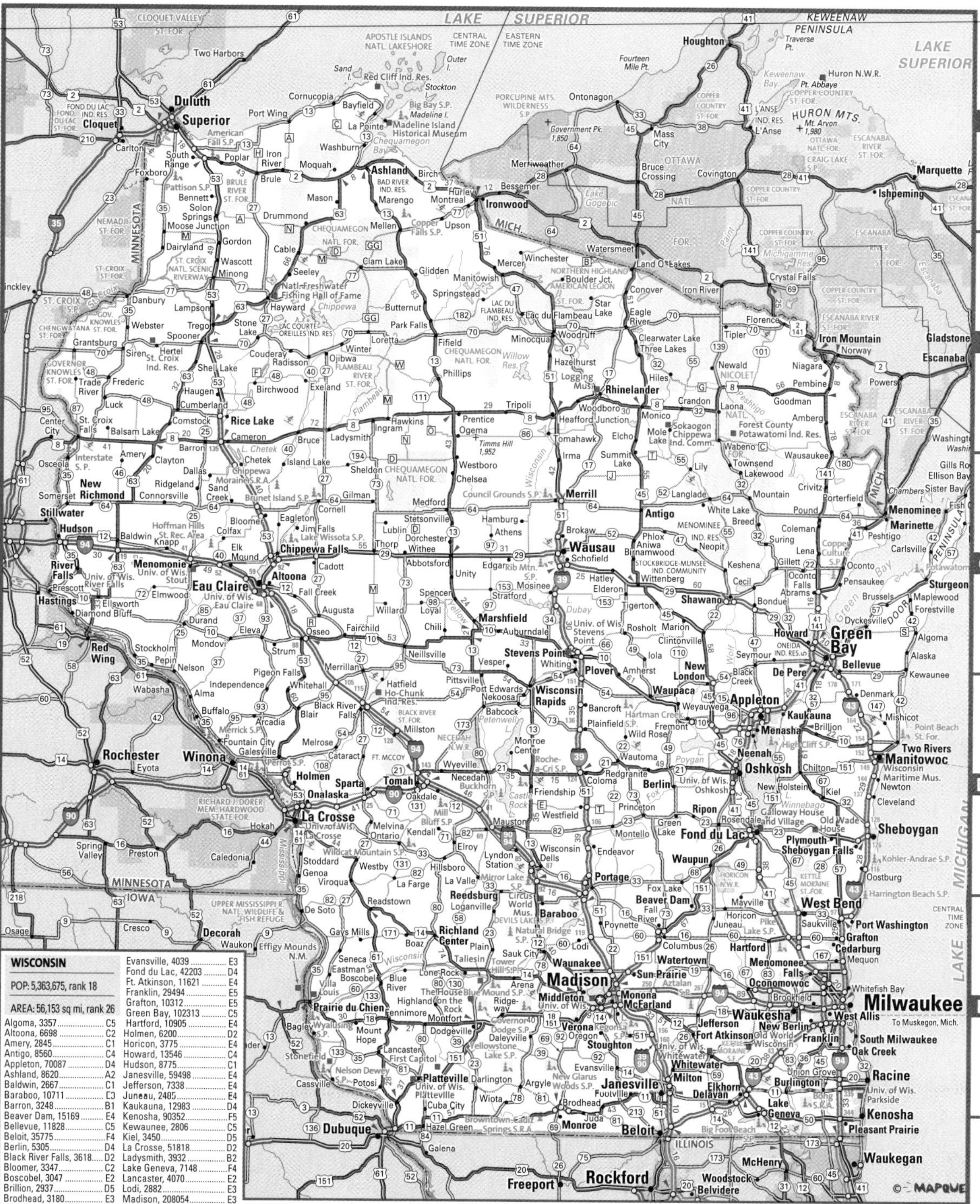

WISCONSIN

POP: 5,363,675, rank 18

AREA: 56,153 sq mi, rank 26

Algoma, 3357 ...... C5
Altoona, 6698 ...... C2
Amery, 2845 ...... C1
Antigo, 8560 ...... C4
Appleton, 70087 ...... D4
Ashland, 8620 ...... A2
Baldwin, 2667 ...... C1
Baraboo, 10711 ...... E3
Barron, 3248 ...... B1
Beaver Dam, 15169 ...... E4
Bellevue, 11828 ...... C5
Beloit, 35775 ...... F4
Berlin, 5305 ...... D4
Black River Falls, 3618 ...... D2
Bloomer, 3347 ...... C2
Boscobel, 3047 ...... E2
Brillion, 2937 ...... D5
Brodhead, 3180 ...... E3
Burlington, 9936 ...... E4
Cedarburg, 10908 ...... E5
Chilton, 3708 ...... D4
Chippewa Falls, 12925 ...... C2
Clintonville, 4736 ...... C4
Columbus, 4479 ...... E4
Delavan, 7956 ...... E4
De Pere, 20559 ...... D4
Dodgeville, 4220 ...... E3
Eau Claire, 61704 ...... C2
Elkhorn, 7305 ...... E4
Ellsworth, 2909 ...... C1
Evansville, 4039 ...... E3
Fond du Lac, 42203 ...... D4
Ft. Atkinson, 11621 ...... E4
Franklin, 29494 ...... E5
Grafton, 10312 ...... E5
Green Bay, 102313 ...... C5
Hartford, 10905 ...... E4
Holmen, 6200 ...... D2
Horicon, 3775 ...... E4
Howard, 13546 ...... C4
Hudson, 8775 ...... C1
Janesville, 59498 ...... E4
Jefferson, 7338 ...... E4
Juneau, 2485 ...... E4
Kaukauna, 12983 ...... D4
Kenosha, 90352 ...... F5
Kewaunee, 2806 ...... C5
Kiel, 3450 ...... D5
La Crosse, 51818 ...... D2
Ladysmith, 3932 ...... B2
Lake Geneva, 7148 ...... F4
Lancaster, 4070 ...... E2
Lodi, 2882 ...... E3
Madison, 208054 ...... E3
Manitowoc, 34053 ...... D5
Marinette, 11749 ...... C5
Marshfield, 18800 ...... C3
Mauston, 3740 ...... D3
Mayville, 4902 ...... E4
McFarland, 6416 ...... E3
Medford, 4350 ...... C3
Menasha, 16331 ...... D4
Menomonee Falls, 32647 ...... E4
Menomonie, 14937 ...... C1
Mequon, 21823 ...... E5
Merrill, 10146 ...... C3
Middleton, 15770 ...... E3
Milton, 5132 ...... E4
Milwaukee, 596974 ...... E5
Mondovi, 2634 ...... C2
Monona, 8018 ...... E3
Monroe, 10843 ...... F3
Mosinee, 4063 ...... C3
Neenah, 24507 ...... D4
Neillsville, 2731 ...... C2
Nekoosa, 2590 ...... D3
New Berlin, 38220 ...... E4
New Holstein, 3301 ...... D4
New London, 7085 ...... D4
New Richmond, 6310 ...... C1
Oak Creek, 28456 ...... E5
Oconomowoc, 12382 ...... E4
Oconto, 4708 ...... C5
Oconto Falls, 2843 ...... C4
Onalaska, 14839 ...... D2
Oostburg, 2660 ...... D5
Oregon, 7514 ...... E3
Oshkosh, 62916 ...... D4
Park Falls, 2793 ...... B3
Peshtigo, 3357 ...... C5
Platteville, 9989 ...... E2
Pleasant Prairie, 16136 ...... F5
Plover, 10520 ...... D3
Plymouth, 7781 ...... D5
Portage, 9728 ...... D3
Port Washington, 10467 ...... E5
Prairie du Chien, 6018 ...... E2
Prescott, 3764 ...... C1
Racine, 81855 ...... E5
Reedsburg, 7827 ...... E3
Rhinelander, 7735 ...... B3
Rice Lake, 8320 ...... B1
Richland Ctr., 5114 ...... E3
Ripon, 6828 ...... D4
River Falls, 12560 ...... C1
Sauk City, 3109 ...... E3
Saukville, 4068 ...... E5
Seymour, 3335 ...... C4
Shawano, 8298 ...... C4
Sheboygan, 50792 ...... D5
Sheboygan Falls, 6772 ...... D5
S. Milwaukee, 21256 ...... E5
Sparta, 8648 ...... D2
Spooner, 2653 ...... B1
Stevens Pt., 24551 ...... C3
Stoughton, 12354 ...... E4
Sturgeon Bay, 9437 ...... C5
Sun Prairie, 20369 ...... E4
Superior, 27368 ...... A1
Tomah, 8419 ...... D2
Tomahawk, 3770 ...... B3
Two Rivers, 12639 ...... D5
Union Grove, 4322 ...... E5
Verona, 7052 ...... E3
Viroqua, 4335 ...... D2
Watertown, 21598 ...... E4
Waukesha, 64825 ...... E4
Waunakee, 8995 ...... E3
Waupaca, 5676 ...... D4
Waupun, 10718 ...... D4
Wausau, 38426 ...... C3
W. Allis, 61254 ...... E5
W. Bend, 28152 ...... E4
Whitefish Bay, 14163 ...... E5
Whitewater, 13437 ...... E4
Wisconsin Rapids, 18435 ...... D3

A B C D E F

1 2 3 4 5

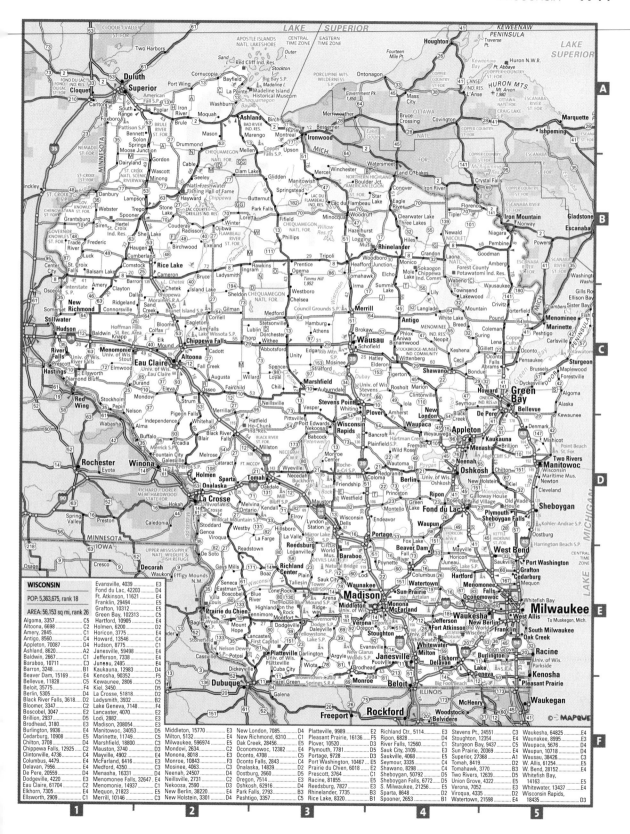

ALASKA
UNITED STATES
Anchorage
Fairbanks
Seward
Gulf of Alaska
PACIFIC OCEAN
YUKON TERRITORY
Dawson
Mayo
Carmacks
Faro
Ross River
Haines Jct.
Whitehorse
Skagway
Haines
Juneau
Sitka
Wrangell
Ketchikan
Watson Lake
Aklavik
Inuvik
Tuktoyaktuk
Tsiigehtchic
Fort McPherson
DEMPSTER HWY
MACKENZIE
Fort Good Hope
Norman Wells
Tulita
Déline
Great Bear Lake
NORTHWEST TERRITORIES
Wrigley
Rae Lakes
Wha Ti
Rae-Edzo
Yellowknife
Lutselk'e
Fort Simpson
Ft. Providence
Fort Liard
Hay River
Fort Resolution
Fort Smith
Great Slave Lake
NAHANNI NATL. PARK RESERVE
WOOD BUFFALO NATL. PARK
Banks Island
Sachs Harbour
Cape Bathurst
Amundsen Gulf
VICTORIA ISLAND
Melville Island
Bathurst Island
Cornwallis Island
Resolute
Devon Island
Byam Martin Island
Stefansson Island
Viscount Melville Sound
Prince of Wales Island
Somerset Island
Brodeur Peninsula
Boothia Peninsula
Gulf of Boothia
Taloyoak
Cambridge Bay
Kugluktuk
King William Island
Gjoa Haven
Coronation Gulf
Dease Strait
Queen Maud Gulf
Baker Lake
Chesterfield Inlet
Rankin Inlet
Whale Cove
Arviat
Churchill
WAPUSK NATL. PARK
PACIFIC TIME ZONE
MOUNTAIN TIME ZONE
CENTRAL TIME ZONE
BRITISH COLUMBIA
COAST MOUNTAINS
ROCKY MOUNTAINS
Stewart
Prince Rupert
Masset
Queen Charlotte Islands
Terrace
Kitimat
Smithers
Fort St. James
Prince George
Bella Coola
Williams Lake
Port Hardy
Vancouver Island
Port Alberni
Campbell River
Powell River
Nanaimo
Vancouver
Victoria
Kamloops
Merritt
Salmon Arm
Revelstoke
Kelowna
Penticton
Cranbrook
Castlegar
Fort Nelson
Fort St. John
Dawson Creek
Jasper
Hinton
ALBERTA
High Level
Rainbow Lake
Fort Vermilion
Peace River
Grande Prairie
Valleyview
Slave Lake
Fort McMurray
Whitecourt
Edmonton
Red Deer
Calgary
Banff
Drumheller
Brooks
Medicine Hat
Lethbridge
Lloydminster
SASKATCHEWAN
La Loche
La Ronge
Meadow Lake
North Battleford
Prince Albert
Saskatoon
Swift Current
Moose Jaw
Regina
Yorkton
Weyburn
Estevan
MANITOBA
Lynn Lake
Gillam
Thompson
Flin Flon
The Pas
Dauphin
Brandon
Portage la Prairie
Winnipeg
Kenora
Dryden
Fort Frances
UNITED STATES
WASH.
Bellingham
Seattle
Olympia
Tacoma
Wenatchee
Spokane
Yakima
Kennewick
Pendleton
Portland
Salem
Eugene
OREGON
Bend
Medford
Klamath Falls
Coeur d'Alene
Lewiston
Kalispell
Missoula
Helena
Great Falls
Havre
Glasgow
Butte
Bozeman
Billings
Miles City
MONTANA
IDAHO
Boise
Salmon
Idaho Falls
Pocatello
Twin Falls
Williston
Minot
NORTH DAKOTA
Dickinson
Bismarck
Jamestown
Fargo
Grand Forks
Bemidji
Duluth
MINNESOTA
Minneapolis
St. Paul
Rochester
SOUTH DAKOTA
Aberdeen
Watertown
Pierre
Rapid City
Sioux Falls
Sioux City
IOWA
WYOMING
Sheridan
Jackson
Casper
Rock Springs
Laramie
Cheyenne
NEBRASKA
UTAH
Ogden
Salt Lake City
Provo
NEVADA
Winnemucca
Elko
Ely
Reno
Carson City
CALIFORNIA
Redding
Sacramento
San Francisco

DISTANCES BETWEEN CITIES ARE COMPUTED IN KILOMETERS OVER MAIN HIGHWAYS AND INCLUDE FERRY DISTANCES

	BOSTON, MA	BRANDON, MB	CALGARY, AB	CHARLOTTETOWN, PE	CHICAGO, IL	DAWSON CREEK, BC	EDMONTON, AB	FREDERICTON, NB	HALIFAX, NS	KENORA, ON	MINNEAPOLIS, MN	MONTRÉAL, QC	NEW YORK, NY	NORTH BAY, ON	OTTAWA, ON	PRINCE GEORGE, BC	QUÉBEC, QC	REGINA, SK	ST. JOHN'S, NL	SASKATOON, SK	SAULT STE. MARIE, ON	SEATTLE, WA	THUNDER BAY, ON	TORONTO, ON	VANCOUVER, BC	VICTORIA, BC	WHITEHORSE, YT	WINDSOR, ON	WINNIPEG, MB
BANFF, AB	4434	1234	128	4681	2811	1001	412	4432	4802	1648	2156	3652	4104	3137	3500	637	3888	856	6032	729	2725	977	2105	3642	819	874	2219	3280	1429
BOSTON, MA		3220	4318	1049	1614	4950	4353	690	1149	2639	2280	504	346	1036	665	5093	634	3577	2379	3840	1572	4941	2187	917	5156	5235	6268	1181	3006
BRANDON, MB			1117	3468	1598	1749	1152	3217	3589	434	943	2438	2889	1923	2287	1894	2675	377	4817	639	1510	2041	892	2427	2016	2108	3067	2066	216
CALGARY, AB				4566	2696	885	296	4315	4686	1530	2041	3536	3986	3021	3384	755	3772	740	5914	613	2607	1093	1989	3524	900	991	2203	3162	1313
CHARLOTTETOWN, PE					2382	5198	4601	354	322	3035	3048	1030	1381	1574	1204	5341	819	3825	1376	4088	1997	5708	2583	1561	5924	6003	6516	1925	3241
CHICAGO, IL						3328	2731	2134	2504	1577	658	1353	1283	1138	1252	3471	1604	1955	3734	2216	896	3318	1521	821	3534	3613	4646	460	1384
DAWSON CREEK, BC							597	4947	5319	2165	2673	4168	4620	3653	4017	406	4405	1373	6548	1112	3241	1283	2622	4158	1184	1181	1318	3796	1946
EDMONTON, AB								4350	4722	1566	2076	3571	4022	3056	3420	740	3806	776	5950	513	2642	1308	2024	3560	1115	1207	1915	3198	1347
FREDERICTON, NB									452	2784	2797	779	1022	1323	953	5092	568	3574	1688	3837	1746	5457	2333	1310	5673	5752	6265	1674	2990
HALIFAX, NS										3156	3169	1151	1481	1695	1324	5462	940	3946	1402	4208	2118	5829	2704	1682	6045	6123	6637	2045	3362
KENORA, ON											668	2005	2622	1489	1854	2308	2240	792	4384	1052	1077	2456	459	1814	2432	2522	3483	1640	208
MINNEAPOLIS, MN												2020	1949	1802	1918	2816	2271	1299	4398	1561	1173	2662	547	1487	2877	2956	3989	1125	727
MONTRÉAL, QC													616	544	194	4311	250	2795	2379	3058	967	4678	1553	531	4894	4973	5486	895	2211
NEW YORK, NY														999	703	4764	838	3248	2710	3508	1545	4609	2171	816	4825	4905	5938	1001	2675
NORTH BAY, ON															364	3796	795	2280	2924	2541	423	4464	1072	336	3920	4012	4971	679	1696
OTTAWA, ON																4160	444	2644	2552	2906	787	4578	1401	431	4792	4873	5335	793	2060
PRINCE GEORGE, BC																	4548	1516	6691	1255	3384	922	2765	4302	778	821	1580	3940	2089
QUÉBEC, QC																		3032	2168	3293	1218	4929	1790	782	5143	5224	5723	1144	2448
REGINA, SK																			5176	261	1868	1664	1249	2786	1640	1732	2691	2424	573
ST. JOHN'S, NL																				5436	3346	7058	3933	2910	7272	7353	7866	3273	4590
SASKATOON, SK																					2129	1823	1511	3046	1630	1722	2430	2684	834
SAULT STE. MARIE, ON																						4223	649	674	3508	3598	4559	563	1283
SEATTLE, WA																							2913	4147	225	177	2504	3787	2237
THUNDER BAY, ON																								1355	2889	2980	3940	1699	665
TORONTO, ON																									4363	4443	5476	364	2213
VANCOUVER, BC																										93	2311	4001	2213
VICTORIA, BC																											2401	4081	2305
WHITEHORSE, YT																												5114	3264
WINDSOR, ON																													1852

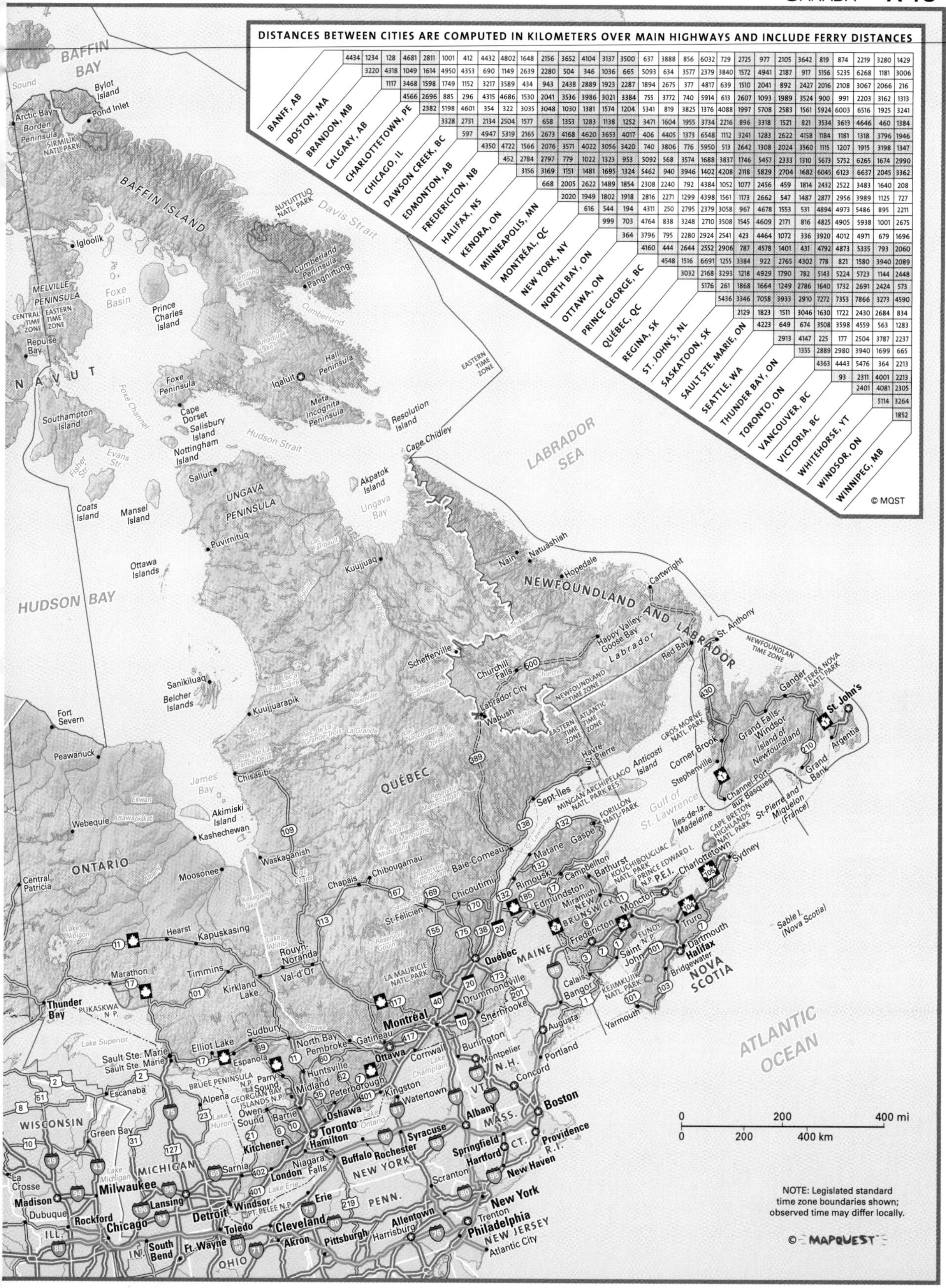

Distances in chart are in miles. To convert miles to kilometers, multiply the distance in miles by 1.609

Example:
New York, NY to Boston, MA = 215 miles or 346 kilometers (215 x 1.609)

	ALBUQUERQUE, NM	ATLANTA, GA	BALTIMORE, MD	BILLINGS, MT	BIRMINGHAM, AL	BISMARCK, ND	BOISE, ID	BOSTON, MA	BUFFALO, NY	BURLINGTON, VT	CHARLESTON, SC	CHARLESTON, WV	CHARLOTTE, NC	CHEYENNE, WY	CHICAGO, IL	CINCINNATI, OH	CLEVELAND, OH	DALLAS, TX	DENVER, CO	DES MOINES, IA	DETROIT, MI	EL PASO, TX	HOUSTON, TX	INDIANAPOLIS, IN	JACKSON, MS	KANSAS CITY, MO	LAS VEGAS, NV	LITTLE ROCK, AR	LOS ANGELES, CA	LOUISVILLE, KY
ALBUQUERQUE, NM		1490	1902	991	1274	1333	966	2240	1808	2178	1793	1568	1649	538	1352	1409	1619	754	438	1091	1608	263	994	1298	1157	894	578	900	806	1320
ATLANTA, GA	1490		679	1889	150	1559	2218	1100	910	1158	317	503	238	1482	717	476	726	792	1403	967	735	1437	800	531	386	801	2067	528	2237	419
BALTIMORE, MD	1902	679		1959	795	1551	2401	422	370	481	583	352	441	1665	708	521	377	1399	1690	1031	532	2045	1470	600	1032	1087	2445	1072	2705	602
BILLINGS, MT	991	1889	1959		1839	413	626	2254	1796	2181	2157	1755	2012	455	1246	1552	1597	1433	554	1007	1534	1255	1673	1432	1836	1088	965	1530	1239	1547
BIRMINGHAM, AL	1274	150	795	1839		1509	2170	1215	909	1241	466	578	389	1434	667	475	725	647	1356	919	734	1292	678	481	241	753	1852	381	2092	369
BISMARCK, ND	1333	1559	1551	413	1509		1039	1846	1388	1773	1749	1347	1604	594	838	1144	1189	1342	693	675	1126	1597	1582	1024	1548	801	1378	1183	1702	1139
BOISE, ID	966	2218	2401	626	2170	1039		2697	2239	2624	2520	2182	2375	737	1708	1969	2040	1711	833	1369	1977	1206	1952	1852	2115	1376	760	1808	1033	1933
BOSTON, MA	2240	1100	422	2254	1215	1846	2697		462	214	1003	741	861	1961	1003	862	654	1819	2004	1326	741	2465	1890	940	1453	1427	2757	1493	3046	964
BUFFALO, NY	1808	910	370	1796	909	1388	2239	462		375	899	431	695	1502	545	442	197	1393	1546	868	277	2039	1513	508	1134	995	2299	1066	2572	545
BURLINGTON, VT	2178	1158	481	2181	1241	1773	2624	214	375		1061	782	919	1887	930	817	567	1763	1931	1253	652	2409	1916	878	1479	1366	2684	1437	2957	915
CHARLESTON, SC	1793	317	583	2157	466	1749	2520	1003	899	1061		468	204	1783	907	622	724	1109	1705	1204	879	1754	1110	721	703	1102	2371	900	2554	610
CHARLESTON, WV	1568	503	352	1755	578	1347	2182	741	431	782	468		265	1445	506	209	255	1072	1367	802	410	1718	1192	320	816	764	2122	745	2374	251
CHARLOTTE, NC	1649	238	441	2012	389	1604	2375	861	695	919	204	265		1637	761	476	520	1031	1559	1057	675	1677	1041	575	625	956	2225	754	2453	464
CHEYENNE, WY	538	1482	1665	455	1434	594	737	1961	1502	1887	1783	1445	1637		972	1233	1304	979	100	633	1241	801	1220	1115	1382	640	843	1076	1116	1197
CHICAGO, IL	1352	717	708	1246	667	838	1708	1003	545	930	907	506	761	972		302	346	936	1015	337	283	1543	1108	184	750	532	1768	662	2042	299
CINCINNATI, OH	1409	476	521	1552	475	1144	1969	862	442	817	622	209	476	1233	302		253	958	1200	599	261	1605	1079	116	700	597	1955	632	2215	106
CLEVELAND, OH	1619	726	377	1597	725	1189	2040	654	197	567	724	255	520	1304	346	253		1208	1347	669	171	1854	1328	319	950	806	2100	882	2374	356
DALLAS, TX	754	792	1399	1433	647	1342	1711	1819	1393	1763	1109	1072	1031	979	936	958	1208		887	752	1218	647	241	913	406	554	1331	327	1446	852
DENVER, CO	438	1403	1690	554	1356	693	833	2004	1546	1931	1705	1367	1559	100	1015	1200	1347	887		676	1284	701	1127	1088	1290	603	756	984	1029	1118
DES MOINES, IA	1091	967	1031	1007	919	675	1369	1326	868	1253	1204	802	1057	633	337	599	669	752	676		606	1283	992	481	931	194	1429	567	1703	595
DETROIT, MI	1608	735	532	1534	734	1126	1977	741	277	652	879	410	675	1241	283	261	171	1218	1284	606		1799	1338	318	960	795	2037	891	2310	366
EL PASO, TX	263	1437	2045	1255	1292	1597	1206	2465	2039	2409	1754	1718	1677	801	1543	1605	1854	647	701	1283	1799		758	1489	1051	1085	717	974	801	1499
HOUSTON, TX	994	800	1470	1673	678	1582	1952	1890	1513	1916	1110	1192	1041	1220	1108	1079	1328	241	1127	992	1338	758		1033	445	795	1474	447	1558	972
INDIANAPOLIS, IN	1298	531	600	1432	481	1024	1852	940	508	878	721	320	575	1115	184	116	319	913	1088	481	318	1489	1033		675	485	1843	587	2104	112
JACKSON, MS	1157	386	1032	1836	241	1548	2115	1453	1134	1479	703	816	625	1382	750	700	950	406	1290	931	960	1051	445	675		747	1735	269	1851	594
KANSAS CITY, MO	894	801	1087	1088	753	801	1376	1427	995	1366	1102	764	956	640	532	597	806	554	603	194	795	1085	795	485	747		1358	382	1632	516
LAS VEGAS, NV	578	2067	2445	965	1852	1378	760	2757	2299	2684	2371	2122	2225	843	1768	1955	2100	1331	756	1429	2037	717	1474	1843	1735	1358		1478	274	1874
LITTLE ROCK, AR	900	528	1072	1530	381	1183	1808	1493	1066	1437	900	745	754	1076	662	632	882	327	984	567	891	974	447	587	269	382	1478		1706	526
LOS ANGELES, CA	806	2237	2705	1239	2092	1702	1033	3046	2572	2957	2554	2374	2453	1116	2042	2215	2374	1446	1029	1703	2310	801	1558	2104	1851	1632	274	1706		2126
LOUISVILLE, KY	1320	419	602	1547	369	1139	1933	964	545	915	610	251	464	1197	299	106	356	852	1118	595	366	1499	972	112	594	516	1874	526	2126	
MEMPHIS, TN	1033	389	933	1625	241	1337	1954	1353	927	1297	760	606	614	1217	539	493	742	466	1116	720	752	1112	586	464	211	536	1611	140	1839	386
MIAMI, FL	2155	661	1109	2554	812	2224	2883	1529	1425	1587	583	994	730	2147	1382	1141	1250	1367	2069	1632	1401	1959	1201	1196	915	1466	2733	1190	2759	1084
MILWAUKEE, WI	1426	813	805	1175	763	767	1748	1100	642	1027	1003	601	857	1012	89	398	443	1010	1055	378	380	1617	1193	279	835	573	1808	747	2082	394
MINNEAPOLIS, MN	1339	1129	1121	839	1079	431	1465	1417	958	1343	1319	918	1173	881	409	714	760	999	924	246	697	1530	1240	596	1151	441	1677	814	1951	711
MONTRÉAL, QC	2172	1241	564	2093	1289	1685	2535	313	397	92	1145	822	1003	1799	841	815	588	1772	1843	1165	564	2363	1892	872	1514	1359	2596	1446	2869	920
NASHVILLE, TN	1248	242	716	1648	194	1315	1976	1136	716	1086	543	395	397	1240	474	281	531	681	1162	725	541	1328	801	287	423	559	1826	355	2054	175
NEW ORLEANS, LA	1276	473	1142	1955	351	1734	2234	1563	1254	1588	783	926	713	1502	935	820	1070	525	1409	1117	1079	1118	360	826	185	932	1854	455	1917	714
NEW YORK, NY	2015	869	192	2049	985	1641	2491	215	400	299	773	515	631	1755	797	636	466	1589	1799	1121	622	2235	1660	715	1223	1202	2552	1262	2820	739
OKLAHOMA CITY, OK	546	944	1354	1227	729	1136	1506	1694	1262	1632	1248	1022	1102	773	807	863	1073	209	681	546	1062	737	449	752	612	348	1124	355	1352	774
OMAHA, NE	973	989	1168	904	941	616	1234	1463	1005	1390	1290	952	1144	497	474	736	806	669	541	136	743	1236	910	618	935	188	1294	570	1567	704
ORLANDO, FL	1934	440	904	2333	591	2003	2662	1324	1221	1383	379	790	525	1926	1161	920	1045	1146	1847	1411	1180	1738	980	975	694	1245	2512	969	2538	863
PHILADELPHIA, PA	1954	782	104	2019	897	1611	2462	321	414	371	685	454	543	1725	768	576	437	1501	1744	1091	592	2147	1572	655	1135	1141	2500	1175	2760	678
PHOENIX, AZ	466	1868	2366	1199	1723	1662	993	2706	2274	2644	2184	2035	2107	1004	1819	1876	2085	1077	904	1558	2074	432	1188	1764	1482	1360	285	1367	369	1786
PITTSBURGH, PA	1670	676	246	1719	763	1311	2161	592	217	587	642	217	438	1425	467	292	136	1246	1460	791	292	1893	1366	370	988	857	2215	920	2476	394
PORTLAND, ME	2338	1197	520	2352	1313	1944	2795	107	560	233	1101	839	959	2059	1101	960	751	1917	2102	1424	838	2563	1988	1038	1550	1525	2855	1590	3144	1062
PORTLAND, OR	1395	2647	2830	889	2599	1301	432	3126	2667	3052	2948	2610	2802	1166	2137	2398	2469	2140	1261	1798	2405	1767	2381	2280	2544	1805	1188	2237	971	2362
RAPID CITY, SD	841	1511	1626	379	1463	320	930	1921	1463	1848	1824	1422	1678	305	913	1219	1264	1077	404	629	1201	1105	1318	1101	1458	710	1035	1093	1309	1215
RENO, NV	1020	2440	2623	960	2392	1372	430	2919	2460	2845	2741	2403	2595	959	1930	2191	2262	1933	1054	1591	2198	1315	2072	2073	2337	1598	442	2030	519	2155
RICHMOND, VA	1876	527	152	2053	678	1645	2496	572	485	630	428	322	289	1760	802	530	471	1309	1688	1126	627	1955	1330	641	914	1085	2444	983	2682	572
ST. LOUIS, MO	1051	549	841	1341	501	1053	1628	1181	749	1119	850	512	704	892	294	350	560	635	855	436	549	1242	863	239	505	252	1610	416	1856	264
SALT LAKE CITY, UT	624	1916	2100	548	1868	960	342	2395	1936	2322	2218	1880	2072	436	1406	1667	1738	1410	531	1067	1675	864	1650	1549	1813	1074	417	1507	691	1631
SAN ANTONIO, TX	818	1000	1671	1500	878	1599	1761	2092	1665	2036	1310	1344	1241	1046	1270	1231	1481	271	946	1009	1490	556	200	1186	644	812	1272	600	1356	1125
SAN DIEGO, CA	825	2166	2724	1302	2021	1765	1096	3065	2632	3020	2483	2393	2405	1179	2105	2234	2437	1375	1092	1766	2373	730	1487	2122	1780	1695	337	1703	124	2144
SAN FRANCISCO, CA	1111	2618	2840	1176	2472	1749	646	3135	2677	3062	2934	2620	2759	1176	2146	2407	2478	1827	1271	1807	2415	1181	1938	2290	2232	1814	575	2012	385	2372
SEATTLE, WA	1463	2705	2775	816	2657	1229	500	3070	2612	2997	2973	2571	2827	1234	2062	2368	2413	2208	1329	1822	2350	1944	2449	2249	2612	1872	1256	2305	1148	2364
TAMPA, FL	1949	455	960	2348	606	2018	2677	1380	1276	1438	434	845	581	1941	1176	935	1101	1161	1862	1426	1194	1753	995	990	709	1259	2526	984	2553	878
TORONTO, ON	1841	958	565	1762	958	1354	2204	570	106	419	1006	537	802	1468	510	484	303	1441	1512	834	233	2032	1561	541	1183	1028	2265	1115	2538	589
VANCOUVER, BC	1597	2838	2908	949	2791	1362	633	3204	2745	3130	3106	2705	2960	1368	2196	2501	2547	2342	1463	1956	2483	2087	2583	2383	2746	2007	1390	2439	1291	2497
WASHINGTON, DC	1896	636	38	1953	758	1545	2395	458	384	517	539	346	397	1659	701	517	370	1362	1686	1025	526	2008	1433	596	996	1083	2441	1036	2702	596
WICHITA, KS	707	989	1276	1067	838	934	1346	1616	1184	1554	1291	953	1145	613	728	785	995	367	521	390	984	898	608	674	771	192	1276	464	1513	705

	MEMPHIS, TN	MIAMI, FL	MILWAUKEE, WI	MINNEAPOLIS, MN	MONTRÉAL, QC	NASHVILLE, TN	NEW ORLEANS, LA	NEW YORK, NY	OKLAHOMA CITY, OK	OMAHA, NE	ORLANDO, FL	PHILADELPHIA, PA	PHOENIX, AZ	PITTSBURGH, PA	PORTLAND, ME	PORTLAND, OR	RAPID CITY, SD	RENO, NV	RICHMOND, VA	ST. LOUIS, MO	SALT LAKE CITY, UT	SAN ANTONIO, TX	SAN DIEGO, CA	SAN FRANCISCO, CA	SEATTLE, WA	TAMPA, FL	TORONTO, ON	VANCOUVER, BC	WASHINGTON,DC	WICHITA, KS
ALBUQUERQUE, NM	1033	2155	1426	1339	2172	1248	1276	2015	546	973	1934	1954	466	1670	2338	1395	841	1020	1876	1051	624	818	825	1111	1463	1949	1841	1597	1896	707
ATLANTA, GA	389	661	813	1129	1241	242	473	869	944	989	440	782	1868	676	1197	2647	1511	2440	527	549	1916	1000	2166	2618	2705	455	958	2838	636	989
BALTIMORE, MD	933	1109	805	1121	564	716	1142	192	1354	1168	904	104	2366	246	520	2830	1626	2623	152	841	2100	1671	2724	2840	2775	960	565	2908	38	1276
BILLINGS, MT	1625	2554	1175	839	2093	1648	1955	2049	1227	904	2333	2019	1199	1719	2352	889	379	960	2053	1341	548	1500	1302	1176	816	2348	1762	949	1953	1067
BIRMINGHAM, AL	241	812	763	1079	1289	194	351	985	729	941	591	897	1723	763	1313	2599	1463	2392	678	501	1868	878	2021	2472	2657	606	958	2791	758	838
BISMARCK, ND	1337	2224	767	431	1685	1315	1734	1641	1136	616	2003	1611	1662	1311	1944	1301	320	1372	1645	1053	960	1599	1765	1749	1229	2018	1354	1362	1545	934
BOISE, ID	1954	2883	1748	1465	2535	1976	2234	2491	1506	1234	2662	2462	993	2161	2795	432	930	430	2496	1628	342	1761	1096	646	500	2677	2204	633	2395	1346
BOSTON, MA	1353	1529	1100	1417	313	1136	1563	215	1694	1463	1324	321	2706	592	107	3126	1921	2919	572	1181	2395	2092	3065	3135	3070	1380	570	3204	458	1616
BUFFALO, NY	927	1425	642	958	397	716	1254	400	1262	1005	1221	414	2274	217	560	2667	1463	2460	485	749	1936	1665	2632	2677	2612	1276	106	2745	384	1184
BURLINGTON, VT	1297	1587	1027	1343	92	1086	1588	299	1632	1390	1383	371	2644	587	233	3052	1848	2845	630	1119	2322	2036	3020	3062	2997	1438	419	3130	517	1554
CHARLESTON, SC	760	583	1003	1319	1145	543	783	773	1248	1290	379	685	2184	642	1101	2948	1824	2741	428	850	2218	1310	2483	2934	2973	434	1006	3106	539	1291
CHARLESTON, WV	606	994	601	918	822	395	926	515	1022	952	790	454	2035	217	839	2610	1422	2403	322	512	1880	1344	2393	2620	2571	845	537	2705	346	953
CHARLOTTE, NC	614	730	857	1173	1003	397	713	631	1102	1144	525	543	2107	438	959	2802	1678	2595	289	704	2072	1241	2405	2759	2827	581	802	2960	397	1145
CHEYENNE, WY	1217	2147	1012	881	1799	1240	1502	1755	773	497	1926	1725	1004	1425	2059	1166	305	959	1760	892	436	1046	1179	1176	1234	1941	1468	1368	1659	613
CHICAGO, IL	539	1382	89	409	841	474	935	797	807	474	1161	768	1819	467	1101	2137	913	1930	802	294	1406	1270	2105	2146	2062	1176	510	2196	701	728
CINCINNATI, OH	493	1141	398	714	815	281	820	636	863	736	920	576	1876	292	960	2398	1219	2191	530	350	1667	1231	2234	2407	2368	935	484	2501	517	785
CLEVELAND, OH	742	1250	443	760	588	531	1070	466	1073	806	1045	437	2085	136	751	2469	1264	2262	471	560	1738	1481	2437	2478	2413	1101	303	2547	370	995
DALLAS, TX	466	1367	1010	999	1772	681	525	1589	209	669	1146	1501	1077	1246	1917	2140	1077	1933	1309	635	1410	271	1375	1827	2208	1161	1441	2342	1362	367
DENVER, CO	1116	2069	1055	924	1843	1162	1409	1799	681	541	1847	1744	904	1460	2102	1261	404	1054	1688	855	531	946	1092	1271	1329	1862	1512	1463	1686	521
DES MOINES, IA	720	1632	378	246	1165	725	1117	1121	546	136	1411	1091	1558	791	1424	1798	629	1591	1126	436	1067	1009	1766	1807	1822	1426	834	1956	1025	390
DETROIT, MI	752	1401	380	697	564	541	1079	622	1062	743	1180	592	2074	292	838	2405	1201	2198	627	549	1675	1490	2373	2415	2350	1194	233	2483	526	984
EL PASO, TX	1112	1959	1617	1530	2363	1328	1118	2235	737	1236	1738	2147	432	1893	2563	1767	1105	1315	1955	1242	864	556	730	1181	1944	1753	2032	2087	2008	898
HOUSTON, TX	586	1201	1193	1240	1892	801	360	1660	449	910	980	1572	1188	1366	1988	2381	1318	2072	1330	863	1650	200	1487	1938	2449	995	1561	2583	1433	608
INDIANAPOLIS, IN	464	1196	279	596	872	287	826	715	752	618	975	655	1764	370	1038	2280	1101	2073	641	239	1549	1186	2122	2290	2249	990	541	2383	596	674
JACKSON, MS	211	915	835	1151	1514	423	185	1223	612	935	694	1135	1482	988	1550	2544	1458	2337	914	505	1813	644	1780	2232	2612	709	1183	2746	996	771
KANSAS CITY, MO	536	1466	573	441	1359	559	932	1202	348	188	1245	1141	1360	857	1525	1805	710	1598	1085	252	1074	812	1695	1814	1872	1259	1028	2007	1083	192
LAS VEGAS, NV	1611	2733	1808	1677	2596	1826	1854	2552	1124	1294	2512	2500	285	2215	2855	1188	1035	442	2444	1610	417	1272	337	575	1256	2526	2265	1390	2441	1276
LITTLE ROCK, AR	140	1190	747	814	1446	355	455	1262	355	570	969	1175	1367	920	1590	2237	1093	2030	983	416	1507	600	1703	2012	2305	984	1115	2439	1036	464
LOS ANGELES, CA	1839	2759	2082	1951	2869	2054	1917	2820	1352	1567	2538	2760	369	2476	3144	971	1309	519	2682	1856	691	1356	124	385	1148	2553	2538	1291	2702	1513
LOUISVILLE, KY	386	1084	394	711	920	175	714	739	774	704	863	678	1786	394	1062	2362	1215	2155	572	264	1631	1125	2144	2372	2364	878	589	2497	596	705
MEMPHIS, TN		1051	624	940	1306	215	396	1123	487	724	830	1035	1500	780	1451	2382	1247	2175	843	294	1652	739	1841	2144	2440	845	975	2574	896	597
MIAMI, FL	1051		1478	1794	1671	907	874	1299	1609	1654	232	1211	2390	1167	1627	3312	2176	3105	954	1214	2581	1401	2688	3140	3370	274	1532	3504	1065	1655
MILWAUKEE, WI	624	1478		337	939	569	1020	894	880	514	1257	865	1892	564	1198	2063	842	1970	899	367	1446	1343	2145	2186	1991	1272	607	2124	799	769
MINNEAPOLIS, MN	940	1794	337		1255	886	1337	1211	793	383	1573	1181	1805	881	1515	1727	606	1839	1216	621	1315	1257	2014	2055	1654	1588	924	1788	1115	637
MONTRÉAL, QC	1306	1671	939	1255		1094	1632	383	1625	1300	1466	454	2637	607	282	2963	1758	2756	714	1112	2232	2043	2931	2972	2907	1522	330	3041	600	1547
NASHVILLE, TN	215	907	569	886	1094		539	906	703	747	686	818	1715	569	1234	2405	1269	2198	626	307	1675	954	2056	2360	2463	701	764	2597	679	748
NEW ORLEANS, LA	396	874	1020	1337	1632	539		1332	731	1121	653	1245	1548	1108	1660	2663	1643	2431	1002	690	1932	560	1846	2298	2731	668	1302	2865	1106	890
NEW YORK, NY	1123	1299	894	1211	383	906	1332		1469	1258	1094	91	2481	367	313	2920	1716	2713	342	956	2189	1861	2839	2929	2864	1150	507	2998	228	1391
OKLAHOMA CITY, OK	487	1609	880	793	1625	703	731	1469		463	1388	1408	1012	1124	1792	1934	871	1727	1331	505	1204	466	1370	1657	2002	1403	1295	2136	1350	161
OMAHA, NE	724	1654	514	383	1300	747	1121	1258	463		1433	1228	1440	928	1561	1662	525	1455	1263	440	932	927	1630	1672	1719	1448	971	1853	1162	307
ORLANDO, FL	830	232	1257	1573	1466	686	653	1094	1388	1433		1006	2169	963	1422	3091	1955	2884	750	993	2360	1180	2467	2918	3149	82	1327	3283	860	1434
PHILADELPHIA, PA	1035	1211	865	1181	454	818	1245	91	1408	1228	1006		2420	306	419	2890	1686	2683	254	895	2160	1774	2779	2900	2835	1062	522	2968	140	1330
PHOENIX, AZ	1500	2390	1892	1805	2637	1715	1548	2481	1012	1440	2169	2420		2136	2804	1335	1308	883	2343	1517	651	987	358	750	1513	2184	2307	1655	2362	1173
PITTSBURGH, PA	780	1167	564	881	607	569	1108	367	1124	928	963	306	2136		690	2590	1386	2383	341	611	1859	1519	2494	2599	2534	1019	321	2668	240	1046
PORTLAND, ME	1451	1627	1198	1515	282	1234	1660	313	1792	1561	1422	419	2804	690		3223	2019	3016	670	1279	2493	2189	3162	3233	3168	1478	668	3301	556	1714
PORTLAND, OR	2382	3312	2063	1727	2963	2405	2663	2920	1934	1662	3091	2890	1335	2590	3223		1268	578	2925	2057	771	2322	1093	638	170	3106	2633	313	2824	1775
RAPID CITY, SD	1247	2176	842	606	1758	1269	1643	1716	871	525	1955	1686	1308	1386	2019	1268		1151	1720	963	628	1335	1372	1368	1195	1970	1429	1328	1620	712
RENO, NV	2175	3105	1970	1839	2756	2198	2431	2713	1727	1455	2884	2683	883	2383	3016	578	1151		2718	1850	524	1870	642	217	755	2899	2426	898	2617	1568
RICHMOND, VA	843	954	899	1216	714	626	1002	342	1331	1263	750	254	2343	341	670	2925	1720	2718		834	2194	1530	2684	2934	2869	805	660	3003	108	1274
ST. LOUIS, MO	294	1214	367	621	1112	307	690	956	505	440	993	895	1517	611	1279	2057	963	1850	834		1326	968	1875	2066	2125	1008	782	2259	837	441
SALT LAKE CITY, UT	1652	2581	1446	1315	2232	1675	1932	2189	1204	932	2360	2160	651	1859	2493	771	628	524	2194	1326		1419	754	740	839	2375	1902	973	2094	1044
SAN ANTONIO, TX	739	1401	1343	1257	2043	954	560	1861	466	927	1180	1774	987	1519	2189	2322	1335	1870	1530	968	1419		1285	1737	2275	1195	1714	2410	1635	624
SAN DIEGO, CA	1841	2688	2145	2014	2931	2056	1846	2839	1370	1630	2467	2779	358	2494	3162	1093	1372	642	2684	1875	754	1285		508	1271	2481	2601	1414	2720	1531
SAN FRANCISCO, CA	2144	3140	2186	2055	2972	2360	2298	2929	1657	1672	2918	2900	750	2599	3233	638	1368	217	2934	2066	740	1737	508		816	2933	2643	958	2834	1784
SEATTLE, WA	2440	3370	1991	1654	2907	2463	2731	2864	2002	1719	3149	2835	1513	2534	3168	170	1195	755	2869	2125	839	2275	1271	816		3164	2577	140	2769	1843
TAMPA, FL	845	274	1272	1588	1522	701	668	1150	1403	1448	82	1062	2184	1019	1478	3106	1970	2899	805	1008	2375	1195	2481	2933	3164		1383	3297	916	1448
TORONTO, ON	975	1532	607	924	330	764	1302	507	1295	971	1327	522	2307	321	668	2633	1429	2426	660	782	1902	1714	2601	2643	2577	1383		2711	563	1217
VANCOUVER, BC	2574	3504	2124	1788	3041	2597	2865	2998	2136	1853	3283	2968	1655	2668	3301	313	1328	898	3003	2259	973	2410	1414	958	140	3297	2711		2902	1977
WASHINGTON, DC	896	1065	799	1115	600	679	1106	228	1350	1162	860	140	2362	240	556	2824	1620	2617	108	837	2094	1635	2720	2834	2769	916	563	2902		1272
WICHITA, KS	597	1655	769	637	1547	748	890	1391	161	307	1434	1330	1173	1046	1714	1775	712	1568	1274	441	1044	624	1531	1784	1843	1448	1217	1977	1272	

Welcome

Dear Traveler,

Since its inception in 1958, Mobil Travel Guide has served as a trusted advisor to auto travelers in search of value in lodging, dining, and destinations. Now in its 48th year, the Mobil Travel Guide is the hallmark of our ExxonMobil family of travel publications, and we're proud to offer an array of products and services from our Mobil, Exxon, and Esso brands in North America to facilitate life on the road.

Whether you're looking for business or pleasure venues, our nationwide network of independent, professional evaluators offers their expertise on thousands of travel options, allowing you to plan a quick family getaway, a full-service business meeting, or an unforgettable Mobil Five-Star celebration.

Your feedback is important to us as we strive to improve our product offerings and better meet today's travel needs. Whether you travel once a week or once a year, please take the time to contact us at www.mobiltravelguide.com. We hope to hear from you soon.

Best wishes for safe and enjoyable travels.

Lee R Raymond

Lee R. Raymond
Chairman and CEO
Exxon Mobil Corporation

A Word to Our Readers

Travelers are on the roads in great numbers these days. They're exploring the country on day trips, weekend getaways, business trips, and extended family vacations, visiting major cities and small towns along the way. Because time is precious and the travel industry is ever-changing, having accurate, reliable travel information at your fingertips is critical. Mobil Travel Guide has been providing invaluable insight to travelers for more than 45 years, and we are committed to continuing this service well into the future.

The Mobil Corporation (known as Exxon Mobil Corporation since a 1999 merger) began producing the Mobil Travel Guide books in 1958, following the introduction of the US interstate highway system in 1956. The first edition covered only five Southwestern states. Since then, our books have become the premier travel guides in North America, covering all 50 states and Canada.

Since its founding, Mobil Travel Guide has served as an advocate for travelers seeking knowledge about hotels, restaurants, and places to visit. Based on an objective process, we make recommendations to our customers that we believe will enhance the quality and value of their travel experiences. Our trusted Mobil One- to Five-Star rating system is the oldest and most respected lodging and restaurant inspection and rating program in North America. Most hoteliers, restaurateurs, and industry observers favorably regard the rigor of our inspection program and understand the prestige and benefits that come with receiving a Mobil Star rating.

The Mobil Travel Guide process of rating each establishment includes:

- Unannounced facility inspections
- Incognito service evaluations for Mobil Four-Star and Mobil Five-Star properties
- A review of unsolicited comments from the general public
- Senior management oversight

For each property, more than 450 attributes, including cleanliness, physical facilities, and employee attitude and courtesy, are measured and evaluated to produce a mathematically derived score, which is then blended with the other elements to form an overall score. These quantifiable scores allow comparative analysis among properties and form the basis that we use to assign our Mobil One- to Five-Star ratings.

This process focuses largely on guest expectations, guest experience, and consistency of service, not just physical facilities and amenities. It is fundamentally a relative rating system that rewards those properties that continually strive for and achieve excellence each year. Indeed, the very best properties are consistently raising the bar for those that wish to compete with them. These properties proactively respond to consumers' needs even in today's uncertain times.

Only facilities that meet Mobil Travel Guide's standards earn the privilege of being listed in the guide. Deteriorating, poorly managed establishments are deleted. A Mobil Travel Guide listing constitutes a positive quality recommendation; every listing is an accolade, a recognition of achievement. Our Mobil One- to Five-Star rating system highlights its level of service. Extensive in-house research is constantly underway to determine new additions to our lists.

- The Mobil Five-Star Award indicates that a property is one of the very best in the country and consistently provides gracious and courteous service, superlative quality in its facility, and a unique ambience. The lodgings and restaurants at the Mobil Five-Star level consistently and proactively respond to consumers' needs and continue their commitment to excellence, doing so with grace and perseverance.
- Also highly regarded is the Mobil Four-Star Award, which honors properties for outstanding achievement in overall facility and for providing very strong service levels in all areas. These

award winners provide a distinctive experience for the ever-demanding and sophisticated consumer.

- The Mobil Three-Star Award recognizes an excellent property that provides full services and amenities. This category ranges from exceptional hotels with limited services to elegant restaurants with a less-formal atmosphere.
- A Mobil Two-Star property is a clean and comfortable establishment that has expanded amenities or a distinctive environment. A Mobil Two-Star property is an excellent place to stay or dine.
- A Mobil One-Star property is limited in its amenities and services but focuses on providing a value experience while meeting travelers' expectations. The property can be expected to be clean, comfortable, and convenient.

Allow us to emphasize that we do not charge establishments for inclusion in our guides. We have no relationship with any of the businesses and attractions we list and act only as a consumer advocate. In essence, we do the investigative legwork so that you won't have to.

Keep in mind, too, that the hospitality business is ever-changing. Restaurants and lodgings—particularly small chains and stand-alone establishments—change management or even go out of business with surprising quickness. Although we make every effort to double-check information during our annual updates, we nevertheless recommend that you call ahead to make sure the place you've selected is still open and offers all the amenities you're looking for. We've provided phone numbers; when available, we also list fax numbers and Web site addresses.

We hope that your travels are enjoyable and relaxing and that our books help you get the most out of every trip you take. If any aspect of your accommodation, dining, or sightseeing experience motivates you to comment, please drop us a line. We depend a great deal on our readers' remarks, so you can be assured that we will read your comments and assimilate them into our research. General comments about our books are also welcome. You can write to us at Mobil Travel Guide, 7373 N Cicero Ave, Lincolnwood, IL 60712, or send an e-mail to info@mobiltravelguide.com.

Take your Mobil Travel Guide books along on every trip you take. We're confident that you'll be pleased with their convenience, ease of use, and breadth of dependable coverage.

Happy travels!

How to Use This Book

The Mobil Travel Guide Regional Travel Planners are designed for ease of use. This book begins with a general introduction that provides a geographical and historical orientation to the state and gives basic statewide tourist information, from climate to calendar highlights to seatbelt laws. The remainder of the book is devoted to travel destinations within the state—mainly cities and towns, but also national parks and tourist areas—which are arranged in alphabetical order.

The following sections explain the wealth of information you'll find about those travel destinations: information about the area, things to see and do there, and where to stay and eat.

Maps and Map Coordinates

At the front of this book in the full-color section, we have provided state maps as well as maps of selected larger cities to help you find your way around once you leave the highway. You'll find a key to the map symbols on the Contents page at the beginning of the map section.

Next to most cities and towns throughout the book, you'll find a set of map coordinates, such as C-2. These coordinates reference the maps at the front of this book and help you find the location you're looking for quickly and easily.

Destination Information

Because many travel destinations are close to other cities and towns where travelers might find additional attractions, accommodations, and restaurants, we've included cross-references to those cities and towns when it makes sense to do so. We also list addresses, phone numbers, and Web sites for travel information resources—usually the local chamber of commerce or office of tourism—as well as pertinent statistics and, in many cases, a brief introduction to the area.

Information about airports, ground transportation, and suburbs is included for large cities.

Driving Tours and Walking Tours

The driving tours that we include for many states are usually day trips that make for interesting side excursions, although they can be longer. They offer you a way to get off the beaten path and visit an area that travelers often overlook. These trips frequently cover areas of natural beauty or historical significance.

Each walking tour focuses on a particularly interesting area of a city or town. Again, these tours can provide a break from everyday tourist attractions. The tours often include places to stop for meals or snacks.

What to See and Do

Mobil Travel Guide offers information about nearly 20,000 museums, art galleries, amusement parks, historic sites, national and state parks, ski areas, and many other types of attractions. A white star on a black background ★ signals that the attraction is a must-see—one of the best in the area. Because municipal parks, public tennis courts, swimming pools, and small educational institutions are common to most towns, they generally are not mentioned.

Following an attraction's description, you'll find the months, days, and, in some cases, hours of operation; the address/directions, telephone number, and Web site (if there is one); and the admission price category. The following are the ranges we use for admission fees, based on one adult:

- **FREE**
- **$** = Up to $5
- **$$** = $5.01-$10
- **$$$** = $10.01-$15
- **$$$$** = Over $15

Special Events

Special events are either annual events that last only a short time, such as festivals and fairs, or longer, seasonal events such as horse racing, theater, and summer concerts. Our Special Events listings also include infrequently occurring occasions that mark certain dates or events, such as a centennial or other commemorative celebration.

Listings

Lodgings, spas, and restaurants are usually listed under the city or town in which they're located. Make sure to check the related cities and towns that appear right beneath a city's heading for additional options, especially if you're traveling to a major metropolitan area that includes many suburbs. If a property is located in a town that doesn't have its own heading, the listing appears under the town nearest it, with the address and town given immediately after the establishment's name. In large cities, lodgings located within 5 miles of major commercial airports may be listed under a separate "Airport Area" heading that follows the city section.

LODGINGS

Travelers have different wants and needs when it comes to accommodations. To help you pinpoint properties that meet your particular needs, Mobil Travel Guide classifies each lodging by type according to the following characteristics.

Mobil Rated Lodgings

- **Limited-Service Hotel.** A limited-service hotel is traditionally a Mobil One-Star or Mobil Two-Star property. At a Mobil One-Star hotel, guests can expect to find a clean, comfortable property that commonly serves a complimentary continental breakfast. A Mobil Two-Star hotel is also clean and comfortable but has expanded amenities, such as a full-service restaurant, business center, and fitness center. These services may have limited staffing and/or restricted hours of use.
- **Full-Service Hotel.** A full-service hotel traditionally enjoys a Mobil Three-Star, Mobil Four-Star, or Mobil Five-Star rating. Guests can expect these hotels to offer at least one full-service restaurant in addition to amenities such as valet parking, luggage assistance, 24-hour room service, concierge service, laundry and/or dry-cleaning services, and turndown service.
- **Full-Service Resort.** A resort is traditionally a full-service hotel that is geared toward recreation and represents a vacation and holiday destination. A resort's guest rooms are typically furnished to accommodate longer stays. The property may offer a full-service spa, golf, tennis, and fitness facilities or other leisure activities. Resorts are expected to offer a full-service restaurant and expanded amenities, such as luggage assistance, room service, meal plans, concierge service, and turndown service.
- **Full-Service Inn.** An inn is traditionally a Mobil Three-Star, Mobil Four-Star, or Mobil Five-Star property. Inns are similar to bed-and-breakfasts (see below) but offer a wider range of services, most significantly a full-service restaurant that serves at least breakfast and dinner.

Specialty Lodgings

Mobil Travel Guide recognizes the unique and individualized nature of many different types of lodging establishments, including bed-and-breakfasts, limited-service inns, and guest ranches. For that reason, we have chosen to place our stamp of approval on the properties that fall into these two categories in lieu of applying our traditional Mobil Star ratings.

- **B&B/Limited-Service Inn.** A bed-and-breakfast (B&B) or limited-service inn is traditionally an owner-occupied home or residence found in a residential area or vacation destination. It may be a structure of historic significance. Rooms are often individually decorated, but telephones, televisions, and private bathrooms may not be available in every room. A B&B typically serves only breakfast to its overnight guests, which is included in the room rate. Cocktails and refreshments may be served in the late afternoon or evening.
- **Guest Ranch.** A guest ranch is traditionally a rustic, Western-themed property that specializes in stays of three or more days. Horseback riding is often a feature, with stables and trails found on the property. Facilities can range from clean, comfortable establishments to more luxurious facilities.

Mobil Star Rating Definitions for Lodgings

- ★★★★★ : A Mobil Five-Star lodging provides consistently superlative service in an exceptionally distinctive luxury environment, with expanded services. Attention to detail is evident throughout the hotel, resort, or inn, from bed linens to staff uniforms.
- ★★★★ : A Mobil Four-Star lodging provides a luxury experience with expanded amenities in a distinctive environment. Services may include, but are not limited to, automatic turndown service, 24-hour room service, and valet parking.
- ★★★ : A Mobil Three-Star lodging is well appointed, with a full-service restaurant and expanded amenities, such as a fitness center, golf course, tennis courts, 24-hour room service, and optional turndown service.
- ★★ : A Mobil Two-Star lodging is considered a clean, comfortable, and reliable establishment that has expanded amenities, such as a full-service restaurant on the premises.
- ★ : A Mobil One-Star lodging is a limited-service hotel, motel, or inn that is considered a clean, comfortable, and reliable establishment.

Information Found in the Lodging Listings

Each lodging listing gives the name, address/location (when no street address is available), neighborhood and/or directions from downtown (in major cities), phone number(s), fax number, total number of guest rooms, and seasons open (if not year-round). Also included are details on business, luxury, recreational, and dining facilities at the property or nearby. A key to the symbols at the end of each listing can be found on the page following the "A Word to Our Readers" section.

For every property, we also provide pricing information. Because lodging rates change frequently, we list a pricing category rather than specific prices. The pricing categories break down as follows:

- **$** = Up to $150
- **$$** = $151-$250
- **$$$** = $251-$350
- **$$$$** = $351 and up

All prices quoted are in effect at the time of publication; however, prices cannot be guaranteed. In some locations, short-term price variations may exist because of special events, holidays, or seasonality. Certain resorts have complicated rate structures that vary with the time of year; always confirm rates when making your plans.

Because most lodgings offer the following features and services, information about them does not appear in the listings:

- Year-round operation
- Bathroom with tub and/or shower in each room
- Cable television in each room
- In-room telephones
- Cots and cribs available
- Daily maid service
- Elevators
- Major credit cards accepted

Although we recommend every lodging we list in this book, a few stand out—they offer noteworthy amenities or stand above the others in their category in terms of quality, value, or historical significance. To draw your attention to these special spots, we've included the magnifying glass icon to the left of the listing, as you see here.

SPAS

Mobil Travel Guide is pleased to announce its newest category: hotel and resort spas. Until now, hotel and resort spas have not been formally rated or inspected by any organization. Every spa selected for inclusion in this book underwent a rigorous inspection process similar to the one Mobil Travel Guide has been applying to lodgings and restaurants for more than four decades. After spending a year and a half researching more than 300 spas and performing exhaustive incognito inspections of more than 200 properties, we narrowed our list to the 48 best spas in the United States and Canada.

Mobil Travel Guide's spa ratings are based on objective evaluations of more than 450 attributes. Approximately half of these criteria assess basic expectations, such as staff courtesy, the technical proficiency and skill of the employees, and whether the facility is maintained properly and hygienically. Several standards address issues that impact a guest's physical comfort and convenience, as well as the staff's ability to impart a sense of personalized service and anticipate clients' needs. Additional criteria measure the spa's ability to create a completely calming ambience.

The Mobil Star ratings focus on much more than the facilities available at a spa and the treatments it offers. Each Mobil Star rating is a cumulative score achieved from multiple inspections that reflects the spa management's attention to detail and commitment to consumers' needs.

Mobil Star Rating Definitions for Spas

- ★★★★★ : A Mobil Five-Star spa provides consistently superlative service in an exceptionally distinctive luxury environment with extensive amenities. The staff at a Mobil Five-Star Spa provides extraordinary service above and beyond the traditional spa experience, allowing guests to achieve the highest level of relaxation and pampering. A Mobil Five-Star spa offers an extensive array of treatments, often incorporating international themes and products. Attention to detail is evident throughout the spa, from arrival to departure.
- ★★★★ : A Mobil Four-Star spa provides a luxurious experience with expanded amenities in an elegant and serene environment. Throughout the spa facility, guests experience personalized service. Amenities might include, but are not limited to, single-sex relaxation rooms where guests wait for their treatments, plunge pools and whirlpools in both men's and women's locker rooms, and an array of treatments, including at a minimum a selection of massages, body therapies, facials, and a variety of salon services.
- ★★★ : A Mobil Three-Star spa is physically well appointed and has a full complement of staff to ensure that guests' needs are met. It has some expanded amenities, such as, but not limited to, a well-equipped fitness center, separate men's and women's locker rooms, a sauna or steam room, and a designated relaxation area. It also offers a menu of services that at a minimum includes massages, facial treatments, and at least one other type of body treatment, such as scrubs or wraps.

RESTAURANTS

All Mobil Star rated dining establishments listed in this book have a full kitchen and offer seating at tables; most offer table service.

Mobil Star Rating Definitions for Restaurants

- ★★★★★ : A Mobil Five-Star restaurant offers one of few flawless dining experiences in the country. These establishments consistently provide their guests with exceptional food, superlative service, elegant décor, and exquisite presentations of each detail surrounding a meal.
- ★★★★ : A Mobil Four-Star restaurant provides professional service, distinctive presentations, and wonderful food.
- ★★★ : A Mobil Three-Star restaurant has good food, warm and skillful service, and enjoyable décor.
- ★★ : A Mobil Two-Star restaurant serves fresh food in a clean setting with efficient service. Value is considered in this category, as is family friendliness.
- ★ : A Mobil One-Star restaurant provides a distinctive experience through culinary specialty, local flair, or individual atmosphere.

Information Found in the Restaurant Listings

Each restaurant listing gives the cuisine type, street address (or directions if no address is available), phone and fax numbers, Web site (if available), meals served, days of operation (if not open daily year-round), and pricing category. Information about appropriate attire is provided, although it's always a good idea to call ahead and ask if you're unsure; the meaning of "casual" or "business casual" varies widely in different parts of the country. We also indicate whether the restaurant has a bar, whether a children's menu is offered, and whether outdoor seating is available. If reservations are recommended, we note that fact in the listing. When valet parking is available, it is noted in the description. In many cases, self-parking is available at the restaurant or nearby.

Because menu prices can fluctuate, we list a pricing category rather than specific prices. The pricing categories are defined as follows, per diner, and assume that you order an appetizer or dessert, an entrée, and one drink:

- **$** = $15 and under
- **$$** = $16-$35
- **$$$** = $36-$85
- **$$$$** = $86 and up

Again, all prices quoted are in effect at the time of publication, but prices cannot be guaranteed.

Although we recommend every restaurant we list in this book, a few stand out—they offer noteworthy local specialties or stand above the others in their category in terms of quality, value, or experience. To draw your attention to these special spots, we've included the magnifying glass icon to the left of the listing, as you see here.

SPECIAL INFORMATION FOR TRAVELERS WITH DISABILITIES

The Mobil Travel Guide symbol indicates that an establishment is not at least partially accessible to people with mobility problems. When the symbol follows a listing, the establishment is not equipped with facilities to accommodate people using wheelchairs or crutches or otherwise needing easy access to doorways and rest rooms. Travelers with severe mobility problems or with hearing or visual impairments may or may not find the facilities they need. Always phone ahead to make sure that an establishment can meet your needs.

AMERICA'S BYWAYS™

Mobil Travel Guide is pleased to announce a new partnership with the National Scenic Byways Program. Under this program, the US Secretary of Transportation recognizes certain roads as National Scenic Byways or All-American Roads based on their archaeological, cultural, historic, natural, recreational, and scenic qualities. To be designated a National Scenic Byway, a road must possess at least one of these six intrinsic qualities. To receive an All-American Road designation, a road must possess multiple intrinsic qualities that are nationally significant and contain one-of-a-kind features that do not exist elsewhere. The road or highway also must be considered a destination unto itself.

America's Byways are a great way to explore the country. From the mighty Mississippi to the towering Rockies to the Historic National Road, these routes take you past America's most treasured scenery and enable you to get in touch with America's past, present, and future. Bringing together all the nationally designated Byways in the South, this bonus section of the book is a handy reference whether you're planning to hop in the car tomorrow or you're simply looking for inspiration for future trips. Look for it at the end of the front section, before page 1.

Understanding the Symbols

What to See and Do

★	=	One of the top attractions in the area
$	=	Up to $5
$$	=	$5.01 to $10
$$$	=	$10.01 to $15
$$$$	=	Over $15

Lodgings

$	=	Up to $150
$$	=	$151 to $250
$$$	=	$251 to $350
$$$$	=	Over $350

Restaurants

$	=	Up to $15
$$	=	$16 to $35
$$$	=	$36 to $85
$$$$	=	Over $85

Lodging Star Definitions

★★★★★ A Mobil Five-Star lodging establishment provides consistently superlative service in an exceptionally distinctive luxury environment with expanded services. Attention to detail is evident throughout the hotel/resort/inn from the bed linens to the staff uniforms.

★★★★ A Mobil Four-Star lodging establishment is a hotel/resort/inn that provides a luxury experience with expanded amenities in a distinctive environment. Services may include, but are not limited to, automatic turndown service, 24-hour room service, and valet parking.

★★★ A Mobil Three-Star lodging establishment is a hotel/resort/inn that is well appointed, with a full-service restaurant and expanded amenities, such as, but not limited to, a fitness center, golf course, tennis courts, 24-hour room service, and optional turndown service.

★★ A Mobil Two-Star lodging establishment is a hotel/resort/inn that is considered a clean, comfortable, and reliable establishment, but also has expanded amenities, such as a full-service restaurant on the premises.

★ A Mobil One-Star lodging establishment is a limited-service hotel or inn that is considered a clean, comfortable, and reliable establishment.

Restaurant Star Definitions

★★★★★ A Mobil Five-Star restaurant is one of few flawless dining experiences in the country. These restaurants consistently provide their guests with exceptional food, superlative service, elegant décor, and exquisite presentations of each detail surrounding the meal.

★★★★ A Mobil Four-Star restaurant provides professional service, distinctive presentations, and wonderful food.

★★★ A Mobil Three-Star restaurant has good food, warm and skillful service, and enjoyable décor.

★★ A Mobil Two-Star restaurant serves fresh food in a clean setting with efficient service. Value is considered in this category, as is family friendliness.

★ A Mobil One-Star restaurant provides a distinctive experience through culinary specialty, local flair, or individual atmosphere.

Symbols at End of Listings

- Facilities for people with disabilities not available
- Pets allowed
- Ski in/ski out access
- Golf on premises
- Tennis court(s) on premises
- Indoor or outdoor pool
- Fitness room
- Major commercial airport within 5 miles
- Business center

Making the Most of Your Trip

A few hardy souls might look back with fondness on a trip during which the car broke down, leaving them stranded for three days, or a vacation that cost twice what it was supposed to. For most travelers, though, the best trips are those that are safe, smooth, and within budget. To help you make your trip the best it can be, we've assembled a few tips and resources.

Saving Money

ON LODGING

Many hotels and motels offer discounts—for senior citizens, business travelers, families, you name it. It never hurts to ask—politely, that is. Sometimes, especially in the late afternoon, desk clerks are instructed to fill beds, and you might be offered a lower rate or a nicer room to entice you to stay. Simply ask the reservation agent for the best rate available. Also, make sure to try both the toll-free number and the local number. You may be able to get a lower rate from one than from the other.

Timing your trip right can cut your lodging costs as well. Look for bargains on stays over multiple nights, in the off-season, and on weekdays or weekends, depending on the location. Many hotels in major metropolitan areas, for example, have special weekend packages that offer leisure travelers considerable savings on rooms; they may include breakfast, cocktails, and/or dinner discounts.

Another way to save money is to choose accommodations that give you more than just a standard room. Rooms with kitchen facilities enable you to cook some meals yourself, reducing your restaurant costs. A suite might save money for two couples traveling together. Even hotel luxury levels can provide good value, as many include breakfast or cocktails in the price of a room.

State and city taxes, as well as special room taxes, can increase your room rate by as much as 25 percent per day. We are unable to include information about taxes in our listings, but we strongly urge you to ask about taxes when making reservations so that you understand the total cost of your lodgings before you book them.

Watch out for telephone-usage charges that hotels frequently impose on long-distance, credit-card, and other calls. Before phoning from your room, read the information given to you at check-in, and then be sure to review your bill carefully when checking out. You won't be expected to pay for charges that the hotel didn't spell out. Consider using your cell phone if you have one; or, if public telephones are available in the hotel lobby, your cost savings may outweigh the inconvenience of using them.

Here are some additional ways to save on lodgings:

- Stay in B&B accommodations. They're generally less expensive than standard hotel rooms, and the complimentary breakfast cuts down on food costs.
- If you're traveling with children, find lodgings at which kids stay free.
- When visiting a major city, stay just outside the city limits; these rooms are usually less expensive than those in downtown locations.
- Consider visiting national parks during the low season, when prices of lodgings near the parks drop by 25 percent or more.
- When calling a hotel, ask whether it is running any special promotions or if any discounts are available; many times reservationists are told not to volunteer these deals unless they're specifically asked about them.
- Check for hotel packages; some offer nightly rates that include a rental car or discounts on major attractions.

ON DINING

There are several ways to get a less expensive meal at an expensive restaurant. Early-bird dinners are popular in many parts of the country and offer considerable savings. If you're interested in visiting a Mobil Four- or Five-Star establishment, consider going at lunchtime. Although the prices are probably still relatively high at midday, they may be half of those at dinner, and you'll experience the same ambience, service, and cuisine.

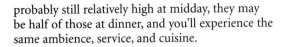

ON ENTERTAINMENT

Although many national parks, monuments, seashores, historic sites, and recreation areas may be visited free of charge, others charge an entrance fee and/or a usage fee for special services and facilities. If you plan to make several visits to national recreation areas, consider one of the following money-saving programs offered by the National Park Service:

- **National Parks Pass.** This annual pass is good for entrance to any national park that charges an entrance fee. If the park charges a per-vehicle fee, the pass holder and any accompanying passengers in a private noncommercial vehicle may enter. If the park charges a per-person fee, the pass applies to the holder's spouse, children, and parents as well as the holder. It is valid for entrance fees only; it does not cover parking, camping, or other fees. You can purchase a National Parks Pass in person at any national park where an entrance fee is charged; by mail from the National Park Foundation, PO Box 34108, Washington, DC 20043-4108; by calling toll-free 888/467-2757; or at www.nationalparks.org. The cost is $50.
- **Golden Eagle Sticker.** When affixed to a National Parks Pass, this hologram sticker, available to people who are between 17 and 61 years of age, extends coverage to sites managed by the US Fish and Wildlife Service, the US Forest Service, and the Bureau of Land Management. It is good until the National Parks Pass to which it is affixed expires and does not cover usage fees. You can purchase one at the National Park Service, the Fish and Wildlife Service, or the Bureau of Land Management fee stations. The cost is $15.
- **Golden Age Passport.** Available to citizens and permanent US residents 62 and older, this passport is a lifetime entrance permit to fee-charging national recreation areas. The fee exemption extends to those accompanying the permit holder in a private noncommercial vehicle or, in the case of walk-in facilities, to the holder's spouse and children. The passport also entitles the holder to a 50 percent discount on federal usage fees charged in park areas, but not on concessions. Golden Age Passports must be obtained in person and are available at most National Park Service units that charge an entrance fee. The applicant must show proof of age, such as a driver's license or birth certificate (Medicare cards are not acceptable proof). The cost is $10.
- **Golden Access Passport.** Issued to citizens and permanent US residents who are physically disabled or visually impaired, this passport is a free lifetime entrance permit to fee-charging national recreation areas. The fee exemption extends to those accompanying the permit holder in a private noncommercial vehicle or, in the case of walk-in facilities, to the holder's spouse and children. The passport also entitles the holder to a 50 percent discount on usage fees charged in park areas, but not on concessions. Golden Access Passports must be obtained in person and are available at most National Park Service units that charge an entrance fee. Proof of eligibility to receive federal benefits (under programs such as Disability Retirement, Compensation for Military Service-Connected Disability, and the Coal Mine Safety and Health Act) is required, or an affidavit must be signed attesting to eligibility.

A money-saving move in several large cities is to purchase a **CityPass.** If you plan to visit several museums and other major attractions, CityPass is a terrific option because it gets you into several sites for one substantially reduced price. Currently, CityPass is available in Boston, Chicago, Hollywood, New York, Philadelphia, San Francisco, Seattle, southern California (which includes Disneyland, SeaWorld, and the San Diego Zoo), and Toronto. For more information or to buy one, call toll-free 888/330-5008 or visit www.citypass.net. You can also buy a CityPass from any participating CityPass attraction.

Here are some additional ways to save on entertainment and shopping:

- Check with your hotel's concierge for various coupons and special offers; they often have two-for-one tickets for area attractions and coupons for discounts at area stores and restaurants.
- Purchase same-day concert or theater tickets for half-price through the local cheap-tickets outlet, such as TKTS in New York or Hot Tix in Chicago.
- Visit museums on their free or "by donation" days, when you can pay what you wish rather than a specific admission fee.

- Save receipts from purchases in Canada; visitors to Canada can get a rebate on federal taxes and some provincial sales taxes.

ON TRANSPORTATION

Transportation is a big part of any vacation budget. Here are some ways to reduce your costs:

- If you're renting a car, shop early over the Internet; you can book a car during the low season for less, even if you'll be using it in the high season.
- Rental car discounts are often available if you rent for one week or longer and reserve in advance.
- Get the best gas mileage out of your vehicle by making sure that it's properly tuned up and keeping your tires properly inflated.
- Travel at moderate speeds on the open road; higher speeds require more gasoline.
- Fill the tank before you return your rental car; rental companies charge to refill the tank and do so at prices of up to 50 percent more than at local gas stations.
- Make a checklist of travel essentials and purchase them before you leave; don't get stuck buying expensive sunscreen at your hotel or overpriced film at the airport.

FOR SENIOR CITIZENS

Always call ahead to ask if a discount is being offered, and be sure to carry proof of age. Additional information for mature travelers is available from the American Association of Retired Persons (AARP), 601 E St NW, Washington, DC 20049; phone 202/434-2277; www.aarp.org.

Tipping

Tips are expressions of appreciation for good service. However, you are never obligated to tip if you receive poor service.

IN HOTELS

- Door attendants usually get $1 for hailing a cab.
- Bell staff expect $2 per bag.
- Concierges are tipped according to the service they perform. Tipping is not mandatory when you've asked for suggestions on sightseeing or restaurants or for help in making dining reservations. However, a tip of $5 is appropriate when a concierge books you a table at a restaurant known to be difficult to get into. For obtaining theater or sporting event tickets, $5 to $10 is expected.
- Maids should be tipped $1 to $2 per day. Hand your tip directly to the maid, or leave it with a note saying that the money has been left expressly for the maid.

IN RESTAURANTS

Before tipping, carefully review your check for any gratuity or service charge that is already included in your bill. If you're in doubt, ask your server.

- Coffee shop and counter service waitstaff usually receive 15 percent of the bill, before sales tax.
- In full-service restaurants, tip 18 percent of the bill, before sales tax.
- In fine restaurants, where gratuities are shared among a larger staff, 18 to 20 percent is appropriate.
- In most cases, the maitre d' is tipped only if the service has been extraordinary, and only on the way out. At upscale properties in major metropolitan areas, $20 is the minimum.
- If there is a wine steward, tip $20 for exemplary service and beyond, or more if the wine was decanted or the bottle was very expensive.
- Tip $1 to $2 per coat at the coat check.

AT AIRPORTS

Curbside luggage handlers expect $1 per bag. Car-rental shuttle drivers who help with your luggage appreciate a $1 or $2 tip.

Staying Safe

The best way to deal with emergencies is to avoid them in the first place. However, unforeseen situations do happen, so you should be prepared for them.

IN YOUR CAR

Before you head out on a road trip, make sure that your car has been serviced and is in good working order. Change the oil, check the battery and belts, make sure that your windshield washer fluid is full and your tires are properly inflated (which can also improve your gas mileage). Other inspections recommended by the vehicle's manufacturer should also be made.

Next, be sure you have the tools and equipment needed to deal with a routine breakdown:

- Jack
- Spare tire
- Lug wrench
- Repair kit
- Emergency tools
- Jumper cables
- Spare fan belt
- Fuses
- Flares and/or reflectors
- Flashlight
- First-aid kit
- In winter, a windshield scraper and snow shovel

Many emergency supplies are sold in special packages that include the essentials you need to stay safe in the event of a breakdown.

Also bring all appropriate and up-to-date documentation—licenses, registration, and insurance cards—and know what your insurance covers. Bring an extra set of keys, too, just in case.

En route, always buckle up! In most states, wearing a seatbelt is required by law.

If your car does break down, do the following:

- Get out of traffic as soon as possible—pull well off the road.
- Raise the hood and turn on your emergency flashers or tie a white cloth to the roadside door handle or antenna.
- Stay in your car.
- Use flares or reflectors to keep your vehicle from being hit.

IN YOUR HOTEL

Chances are slim that you will encounter a hotel or motel fire, but you can protect yourself by doing the following:

- Once you've checked in, make sure that the smoke detector in your room is working properly.
- Find the property's fire safety instructions, usually posted on the inside of the room door.
- Locate the fire extinguishers and at least two fire exits.
- Never use an elevator in a fire.

For personal security, use the peephole in your room door and make sure that anyone claiming to be a hotel employee can show proper identification. Call the front desk if you feel threatened at any time.

PROTECTING AGAINST THEFT

To guard against theft wherever you go:

- Don't bring anything of more value than you need.
- If you do bring valuables, leave them at your hotel rather than in your car.
- If you bring something very expensive, lock it in a safe. Many hotels put one in each room; others will store your valuables in the hotel's safe.
- Don't carry more money than you need. Use traveler's checks and credit cards or visit cash machines to withdraw more cash when you run out.

For Travelers with Disabilities

To get the kind of service you need and have a right to expect, don't hesitate when making a reservation to question the management about the availability of accessible rooms, parking, entrances, restaurants, lounges, or any other facilities that are important to you, and confirm what is meant by "accessible."

The Mobil Travel Guide [D] symbol indicates establishments that are not at least partially accessible to people with special mobility needs (people using wheelchairs or crutches or otherwise needing easy access to buildings and rooms). Further information about these criteria can be found in the earlier section "How to Use This Book."

A thorough listing of published material for travelers with disabilities is available from the Disability Bookshop, Twin Peaks Press, Box 129, Vancouver, WA 98666; phone 360/694-2462; disabilitybookshop.virtualave.net. Another reliable organization is the Society for Accessible Travel & Hospitality (SATH), 347 Fifth Ave, Suite 610, New York, NY 10016; phone 212/447-7284; www.sath.org.

Border-Crossing Regulations

In addition to a photo ID, such as a driver's license or military ID, proof of citizenship—a passport or certified birth certificate—is required for travel into Canada for US citizens ages 18 and over. Children under age 18 traveling with their birth certificates are not required to have photo IDs, but it is highly recommended. A child under age 18 traveling to Canada without both legal guardians must have a notarized letter of consent from the nontraveling parent(s) granting permission for the child to travel. The notarized letter of consent is not waived even when the minor has his or her own passport.

For stays of up to 180 days, a visa is not required.

Each traveler may bring up to $800 worth of goods purchased in Canada back into the United States duty free. In addition, federal regulations permit each US citizen 21 years of age or older to bring back 1 liter of alcoholic beverage duty free in a 30-day period. Travelers are not permitted to bring in plants, fruits, or vegetables. State regulations vary, so check locally before entering Canada. New regulations may be issued at any time.

For more information about traveling to Canada, including safety information, look for the US State Department's Consular Information Sheet at travel.state.gov/canada.html, or request it by fax by calling 202/647-3000.

Important Toll-Free Numbers and Online Information

Hotels

Adams Mark . . . 800/444-2326
www.adamsmark.com
AmericInn . . . 800/634-3444
www.americinn.com
AmeriHost Inn . . . 800/434-5800
www.amerihostinn.com
Amerisuites . . . 800/833-1516
www.amerisuites.com
Baymont Inns . . . 877/229-6667
www.baymontinns.com
Best Inns & Suites . . . 800/237-8466
www.bestinn.com
Best Value Inn . . . 888/315-2378
www.bestvalueinn.com
Best Western . . . 800/780-7234
www.bestwestern.com
Budget Host Inn . . . 800/283-4678
www.budgethost.com
Candlewood Suites . . . 888/226-3539
www.candlewoodsuites.com
Clarion Hotels . . . 800/252-7466
www.choicehotels.com
Comfort Inns and Suites . . . 800/252-7466
www.comfortinn.com
Country Hearth Inns . . . 800/848-5767
www.countryhearth.com
Country Inns & Suites . . . 800/456-4000
www.countryinns.com
Courtyard by Marriott . . . 800/321-2211
www.courtyard.com
Cross Country Inns (KY and OH) . . . 800/621-1429
www.crosscountryinns.com
Crowne Plaza Hotels and Resorts . . . 800/227-6963
www.crowneplaza.com
Days Inn . . . 800/544-8313
www.daysinn.com
Delta Hotels . . . 800/268-1133
www.deltahotels.com
Destination Hotels & Resorts . . . 800/434-7347
www.destinationhotels.com
Doubletree Hotels . . . 800/222-8733
www.doubletree.com
Drury Inn . . . 800/378-7946
www.druryinn.com
Econolodge . . . 800/553-2666
www.econolodge.com
Embassy Suites . . . 800/362-2779
www.embassysuites.com
ExelInns of America . . . 800/367-3935
www.exelinns.com
Extended StayAmerica . . . 800/398-7829
www.extendedstayhotels.com
Fairfield Inn by Marriott . . . 800/228-2800
www.fairfieldinn.com
Fairmont Hotels . . . 800/441-1414
www.fairmont.com
Four Points by Sheraton . . . 888/625-5144
www.fourpoints.com
Four Seasons . . . 800/819-5033
www.fourseasons.com
Hampton Inn . . . 800/426-7866
www.hamptoninn.com
Hard Rock Hotels, Resorts, and Casinos . . . 800/473-7625
www.hardrock.com
Harrah's Entertainment . . . 800/427-7247
www.harrahs.com
Hawthorn Suites . . . 800/527-1133
www.hawthorn.com
Hilton Hotels and Resorts (US) . . . 800/774-1500
www.hilton.com
Holiday Inn Express . . . 800/465-4329
www.hiexpress.com
Holiday Inn Hotels and Resorts . . . 800/465-4329
www.holiday-inn.com
Homestead Studio Suites . . . 888/782-9473
www.homesteadhotels.com
Homewood Suites . . . 800/225-5466
www.homewoodsuites.com
Howard Johnson . . . 800/406-1411
www.hojo.com
Hyatt . . . 800/633-7313
www.hyatt.com
Inns of America . . . 800/826-0778
www.innsofamerica.com
InterContinental . . . 888/567-8725
www.intercontinental.com
Joie de Vivre . . . 800/738-7477
www.jdvhospitality.com
Kimpton Hotels . . . 888/546-7866
www.kimptongroup.com
Knights Inn . . . 800/843-5644
www.knightsinn.com
La Quinta . . . 800/531-5900
www.laquinta.com

Le Meridien 800/543-4300
www.lemeridien.com
Leading Hotels of the World 800/223-6800
www.lhw.com
Loews Hotels 800/235-6397
www.loewshotels.com
MainStay Suites 800/660-6246
www.mainstaysuites.com
Mandarin Oriental 800/526-6566
www.mandarin-oriental.com
Marriott Hotels, Resorts, and Suites 800/228-9290
www.marriott.com
Microtel Inns & Suites 800/771-7171
www.microtelinn.com
Millennium & Copthorne Hotels 866/866-8086
www.millenniumhotels.com
Motel 6 . . . . . 800/466-8356
www.motel6.com
Omni Hotels 800/843-6664
www.omnihotels.com
Pan Pacific Hotels and Resorts 800/327-8585
www.panpac.com
Park Inn & Park Plaza 888/201-1801
www.parkinn.com
The Peninsula Group . . . . . Contact individual hotel
www.peninsula.com
Preferred Hotels & Resorts Worldwide 800/323-7500
www.preferredhotels.com
Quality Inn 800/228-5151
www.qualityinn.com
Radisson Hotels 800/333-3333
www.radisson.com
Raffles International Hotels and Resorts . . . 800/637-9477
www.raffles.com
Ramada Plazas, Limiteds, and Inns 800/272-6232
www.ramada.com
Red Lion Inns 800/733-5466
www.redlion.com
Red Roof Inns 800/733-7663
www.redroof.com
Regent International 800/545-4000
www.regenthotels.com
Relais & Chateaux 800/735-2478
www.relaischateaux.com
Renaissance Hotels 888/236-2427
www.renaissancehotels.com
Residence Inn 800/331-3131
www.residenceinn.com
Ritz-Carlton 800/241-3333
www.ritzcarlton.com
RockResorts 888/367-7625
www.rockresorts.com
Rodeway Inn 800/228-2000
www.rodeway.com
Rosewood Hotels & Resorts 888/767-3966
www.rosewoodhotels.com
Select Inn 800/641-1000
www.selectinn.com
Sheraton 888/625-5144
www.sheraton.com
Shilo Inns 800/222-2244
www.shiloinns.com
Shoney's Inn 800/552-4667
www.shoneysinn.com
Signature/Jameson Inns 800/822-5252
www.jamesoninns.com
Sleep Inn 877/424-6423
www.sleepinn.com
Small Luxury Hotels of the World 800/525-4800
www.slh.com
Sofitel 800/763-4835
www.sofitel.com
SpringHill Suites 888/236-2427
www.springhillsuites.com
St. Regis Luxury Collection 888/625-5144
www.stregis.com
Staybridge Suites 800/238-8000
www.staybridge.com
Summerfield Suites by Wyndham 800/833-4353
www.summerfieldsuites.com
Summit International 800/457-4000
www.summithotels.com
Super 8 Motels 800/800-8000
www.super8.com
The Sutton Place Hotels 866/378-8866
www.suttonplace.com
Swissôtel 800/637-9477
www.swissotel.com
TownePlace Suites 888/236-2427
www.towneplace.com
Travelodge 800/578-7878
www.travelodge.com
Vagabond Inns 800/522-1555
www.vagabondinns.com
W Hotels 888/625-5144
www.whotels.com
Wellesley Inn and Suites 800/444-8888
www.wellesleyinnandsuites.com
WestCoast Hotels 800/325-4000
www.westcoasthotels.com
Westin Hotels & Resorts 800/937-8461
www.westin.com
Wingate Inns 800/228-1000
www.wingateinns.com
Woodfin Suite Hotels 800/966-3346
www.woodfinsuitehotels.com
WorldHotels 800/223-5652
www.worldhotels.com

Meet The Stars

Mobil Travel Guide 2006 **Five-Star** Award Winners

CALIFORNIA
Lodgings
The Beverly Hills Hotel, *Beverly Hills*
Chateau du Sureau, *Oakhurst*
Four Seasons Hotel San Francisco, *San Francisco*
Hotel Bel-Air, *Los Angeles*
The Peninsula Beverly Hills, *Beverly Hills*
Raffles L'Ermitage Beverly Hills, *Beverly Hills*
The Ritz-Carlton, San Francisco, *San Francisco*

Restaurants
Bastide, *Los Angeles*
The Dining Room, *San Francisco*
The French Laundry, *Yountville*
Gary Danko, *San Francisco*

COLORADO
Lodgings
The Broadmoor, *Colorado Springs*
The Little Nell, *Aspen*

CONNECTICUT
Lodging
The Mayflower Inn, *Washington*

DISTRICT OF COLUMBIA
Lodging
Four Seasons Hotel Washington, DC *Washington*

FLORIDA
Lodgings
Four Seasons Resort Palm Beach, *Palm Beach*
The Ritz-Carlton Naples, *Naples*
The Ritz-Carlton, Palm Beach, *Manalapan*

GEORGIA
Lodgings
Four Seasons Hotel Atlanta, *Atlanta*
The Lodge at Sea Island Golf Club, *St. Simons Island*

Restaurants
The Dining Room, *Atlanta*
Seeger's, *Atlanta*

HAWAII
Lodging
Four Seasons Resort Maui at Wailea, *Wailea, Maui*

ILLINOIS
Lodgings
Four Seasons Hotel Chicago, *Chicago*
The Peninsula Chicago, *Chicago*
The Ritz-Carlton, A Four Seasons Hotel, *Chicago*

Restaurant
Charlie Trotter's, *Chicago*

MAINE
Restaurant
The White Barn Inn, *Kennebunkport*

MASSACHUSETTS
Lodgings
Blantyre, *Lenox*
Four Seasons Hotel Boston, *Boston*

NEW YORK
Lodgings
Four Seasons, Hotel New York, *New York*
The Point, *Saranac Lake*
The Ritz-Carlton New York, Central Park, *New York*
The St. Regis, *New York*

Restaurants
Alain Ducasse, *New York*
Jean Georges, *New York*
Masa, *New York*
per se, *New York*

NORTH CAROLINA
Lodging
The Fearrington House Country Inn, *Pittsboro*

PENNSYLVANIA
Restaurant
Le Bec-Fin, *Philadelphia*

SOUTH CAROLINA
Lodging
Woodlands Resort & Inn, *Summerville*

Restaurant
Dining Room at the Woodlands, *Summerville*

TEXAS
Lodging
The Mansion on Turtle Creek, *Dallas*

VERMONT
Lodging
Twin Farms, *Barnard*

VIRGINIA
Lodgings
The Inn at Little Washington, *Washington*
The Jefferson Hotel, *Richmond*

Restaurant
The Inn at Little Washington, *Washington*

Mobil Travel Guide has been rating establishments with its Mobil One- to Five-Star system since 1958. Each establishment awarded the Mobil Five-Star rating is one of the best in the country. Detailed information on each award winner can be found in the corresponding regional edition listed on the back cover of this book.

Four-Star Establishments in Northern Great Lakes

Michigan

★★★★ Lodging

The Townsend Hotel, *Birmingham*

★★★★ Restaurants

The Lark, *West Bloomfield*

Tapawingo, *Ellsworth*

Wisconsin

★★★★ Lodgings

The American Club, *Kohler*

Canoe Bay, *Rice Lake*

America's Byways™ are a distinctive collection of American roads, their stories, and treasured places. They are roads to the heart and soul of America. In this section, you'll find the nationally designated Byways in Michigan, Minnesota, and Wisconsin.

Woodward Avenue (M-1)

MICHIGAN

The Motor City put the world on wheels, so welcome to Detroit's main drag: Woodward Avenue. Stretching out from the base of Detroit at the Detroit River, Woodward follows the pathway of growth from the heart of the city. Lined with history, cultural institutions, and beautiful architecture, Woodward Avenue travels through downtown Detroit, the Boston Edison neighborhood, past Highland Park, the Detroit Zoo, the delightful city of Birmingham, the Cranbrook Educational Community in Bloomfield Hills, and into the city of Pontiac. Nearly every mile of this Byway has historical sites to see that have shaped the industrial life of our nation. Perhaps the most famous are the Ford buildings that stand as monuments to the automobile revolution, although many other equally impressive automobile companies are still found along the Byway.

Woodward Avenue includes both landmarks of the past and monuments to the future. You can find one of the largest public libraries in the nation as well as one of the five largest art museums. From the Freedom Fireworks Display on the Detroit River to the annual Thanksgiving Day Parade to the phenomenal Woodward Dream Cruise, it's as if this street were meant to blend memories with the future.

QUICK FACTS

Length: 27 miles.

Time to Allow: 5 hours.

Best Time to Drive: The busiest months are August because of the Dream Cruise event and November because of America's Thanksgiving Day Parade.

Byway Travel Information: Detroit Metro Convention and Visitors Bureau: phone 313/202-1800; Byway local Web site: www.woodwardavenue.com.

Special Considerations: Because this Byway passes through downtown Detroit, avoid driving it during rush hour.

Bicycle/Pedestrian Facilities: Woodward Avenue has six major central business districts, three major cultural centers, and numerous other activity centers. The cultural centers in Detroit and Bloomfield Hills also allow for and encourage pedestrian travel. Many of the communities in the corridor are actively involved in the Walkable Communities program sponsored by the Southeast Michigan Council of Governments.

The Byway Story

Woodward Avenue tells cultural, historical, recreational, and scenic stories that make it a unique and treasured Byway.

CULTURAL

Much of the culture in southeast Michigan stems from the automobile and those who sacrificed much in its development. When visiting museums such as the Detroit Institute of Arts (DIA) and the Detroit Historical Museum, the impact of the automobile is evident. Your first steps into the DIA will take you to huge two-story murals painted by Diego Rivera that depict life on the assembly line. The Woodward Dream Cruise represents more popular culture and is included in the Library of Congress' permanent collection as a local legacy. The Woodward corridor is also onc of six arcas comprising thc Automobilc National Heritage Area (under the jurisdiction of the National Park Service).

Woodward Avenue is home to other major cultural institutions as well, including the Cranbrook Educational Community, Orchestra Hall, and the Detroit Public Library, which is among the top ten largest libraries in the nation.

The region's culture can also be defined by its faith. Traveling from Detroit to Pontiac, you pass by more than 50 churches, many of which are on national or state historic registers. Prominent among these is the National Shrine of the Little Flower in Royal Oak.

HISTORICAL

Woodward Avenue is the signature route for Detroit and southeast Michigan. The avenue gets its name from Judge Augustus B. Woodward, an early leader in the city's history.

Detroit is known internationally as the Motor City because of its role in the development of the automobile. This is the birthplace of the assembly line (Ford's 1913 Model T Plant on Woodward), a major technological innovation that made the automobile affordable to most families. Most people will agree that the assembly line had a major impact on American society and in the development of our urban areas.

The first people who may come to mind when talking about the automobile industry are the Fords, Chryslers, and Durants. But you should also remember the thousands of nameless autoworkers who, with blood and sweat, established the industry and carry on to this day—the United Automobile Workers (UAW). Henry Ford's $5-a-day wage attracted thousands to his factories, but the working conditions were brutal—this was true of all auto plants. In the late 1930s, the UAW was born and, with fair wages and better working conditions, auto workers and their families now enjoy a decent quality of life. Some of the former homes of early auto barons are located in historic neighborhoods, such as the Boston Edison Historic District.

RECREATIONAL

The city of Detroit and neighboring communities have worked hard and invested a lot of energy to develop safe, fun activities that the whole family can enjoy. It just so happens that a great majority of these activities are located on Woodward Avenue.

Some of the highlights found along this Byway include watching animals at the world-class Detroit Zoo, attending the Woodward Dream Cruise (where thousands from around the world gather to view hundreds of classic cars from around the country), touring historic homes and mansions, making maple syrup at the festival at Cranbrook, standing on the sidewalk during the famous America's Thanksgiving Day Parade, or watching the largest fireworks display in the nation that explodes over the shimmering Detroit River. This Byway, above most others in the nation, has such an abundance of activities and places to see that you could take part in different activities and visit various sites for months without repeating any of them.

SCENIC

A unique scenic quality of Woodward Avenue and the region is the geographic location of Detroit at the Canadian border. Driving southeast on Woodward from Pontiac, you conclude your journey at Hart Plaza, located on the Detroit River in Detroit's central business district. Approaching the plaza, the Windsor skyline unfolds in front of you. Noticeable at a closer distance are Belle Isle to the east and the Ambassador Bridge to the west. The Detroit/Windsor border is the only geographic location along the entire American-Canadian border (of the contiguous states) where the United States is north of Canada.

If you visit during the International Freedom Festival in July, you will notice hundreds of sail and power boats and get to enjoy the largest fireworks display in the country over the river. This fun-filled family event has a million people celebrating our nation's heritage, watching hundreds of exploding shells reflecting off the glass of the high-rise office buildings and the river.

The Detroit River is a major international waterway for commercial freighter traffic delivering goods to the world. Many of these vessels reach 1,000 feet in length. Detroit has also become an embarkation point for international cruise ships plying the Great Lakes.

Highlights

This Byway begins in Pontiac and ends in Detroit, where you can take the following downtown Detroit historical tour.

- The tour begins just south of Woodward Avenue at the **Detroit River,** a designated American Heritage River. It is the most frequently traveled major international boundary between Canada and the United States. It is also a major national and international waterway for the movement of freight and other commodities from the United States to foreign markets. In 1701, French explorer Antoine DeMothe Cadillac founded Detroit at the foot of the present-day Woodward at the Detroit River. In 2001, Detroit celebrated its 300th birthday.

- Located at the intersection of Michigan, Monroe, Cadillac Square, and Fort Street on Woodward Avenue, **Campus Martius** was part of the historic 1807 plan of Detroit by Judge Woodward. Today, it is being rebuilt as a public park and home to new office developments. This site includes the Michigan Soldiers' and Sailors' Monument of 1872.

- The next stop, the **Lower Woodward Historic District,** is located on Woodward north of State Street and south of Clifford. This district contains numerous former retail and office buildings constructed from 1886 to 1936. Significant loft development activity is underway in these buildings.

- **Woodward East Historic District (Brush Park)** is located east of Woodward, bounded by Watson and Alfred streets within the Brush Park neighborhood. Known for its high Victorian-style residences constructed for Detroit's elite in the late 1800s, it is the location of a major urban townhome development.

- The **Peterboro-Charlotte Historic District** is located on Peterboro at Woodward Avenue. The architecture represents a study in late 19th-century middle-class single-family dwellings and early 20th-century apartment buildings.

- Located in Detroit's Cultural Center at 315 E Warren, the **Charles Wright Museum of African American History** offers one of the United States' largest collections of African-American history and culture.

- The final stop, the **Detroit Historical Museum,** is located at 5401 Woodward in Detroit's Cultural Center. The museum specializes in telling the history of the Detroit area from its founding in 1701 to the present, including permanent exhibits, temporary exhibitions, programs, and events. It is especially noted for its Streets of Old Detroit exhibit.

Edge of the Wilderness

MINNESOTA

Celebrate northern hospitality, hometown pride, and the treasures of our natural heritage. Minnesota, midway between America's east and west coasts, is the home to 12,000 lakes. It is filled with beautiful country and all the pleasures of the four seasons. The Edge of the Wilderness is the rustic slice of this great state, with more than 1,000 lakes and one mighty river, the Mississippi, all in landscapes of remarkable natural beauty. There are still more trees than people here, offering classic North Woods seclusion.

The Edge of the Wilderness begins in Grand Rapids with meadows and lakes and winds through mixed hardwoods and stands of conifers and aspens in the Chippewa National Forest. Rounding bends and cresting hills, you will find breathtaking views that, during the fall, are ablaze with the brilliant red of sugar maples, the glowing gold of aspen and birch, and the deep bronze of oak.

The Edge of the Wilderness offers some of Minnesota's most popular sporting and resorting opportunities in its unique environment of clear lakes, vast shorelines, and hills blanketed in hardwood forests and northern pines. Recreation seekers will find hiking, camping, fishing, cross-country skiing, and snowmobiling within the Byway corridor. You will find that you are really living on the Edge.

Quick Facts

Length: 47 miles.

Time to Allow: 3 hours.

Best Time to Drive: Fall foliage season (end of September, beginning of October). High season includes July and August.

Byway Travel Information: Byway local Web site: www.scenicbyway.com.

Special Considerations: Highway 38 courses up and down and curves often—that's part of its charm. Locals named it Highway Loop-de-Loop in the early days. As you drive the Byway, be aware of the lower speed limits, other traffic on the highway, and weather conditions. This is a working roadway, with trucks carrying logs and other local products.

Bicycle/Pedestrian Facilities: Pedestrian and bicyclist facilities are not provided along the route. However, numerous hiking and mountain biking trails spur off the Byway. Facilities are available at the Scenic State Park near Bigfork, as well as a bike trail that runs from Gunn Park to Grand Rapids.

The Byway Story

Edge of the Wilderness tells historical, natural, recreational, and scenic stories that make it a unique and treasured Byway.

HISTORICAL

At the height of the Great Depression, President Franklin D. Roosevelt formed the Civilian Conservation Corps (CCC) to provide jobs and restore the environment. Nationally, the CCC program cost $3 billion. It removed 15 million families from the welfare rolls and employed 3 million young men. In Minnesota, $85 million was spent and 84,000 enrollees participated. Nationwide, CCC camp crews often were called the Tree Army. They were responsible for planting over 2 billion trees across the United States in nine years. Other tasks included road construction; site preparation; surveys of lakes, wildlife, and streams; and even rodent control.

The Day Lake CCC Camp was one of 20 camps established in Minnesota during the Great Depression. Its first enrollees were African Americans from Kansas and Missouri. Day Lake was the only camp in the forest to host African Americans in the segregated CCC program, where the men came in 1933 to work in Company 786. Day Lake CCC

Camp was one of only six that lasted past the CCC era; it became one of four camps in the Chippewa National Forest that housed German prisoners of war during World War II (1943-1945). As the Allied forces gained in the battles of North Africa, they shipped prisoners to the United States. The prisoners worked in local sawmills and for private logging firms. Their wages went to the US Army guards who were present. Security was minimal, and few escapes were reported.

Today, on the west side of Highway 38 are the remains of a concrete shower. East of the highway and up the hill can be seen the outside stone stairway and a chimney that are remnants of the camp mess hall. Many old camp foundations and sites are also visible. Ironically, after its closing, much of the Day Lake Camp was replanted with red pine, hiding many of the signs of this historical story.

NATURAL

Aspen, birch, pines, balsam fir, and maples blanket the rolling uplands of the forest along the Edge of the Wilderness Byway. In between these trees, water is abundant, with over 700 lakes, 920 miles of rivers and streams, and 150,000 acres of wetlands. The forest landscape is a reminder of the glaciers that covered northern Minnesota some 10,000 years ago. From the silent flutter of butterflies to the noisy squeal of wood ducks, and from the graceful turn of deer to the busy work of raccoons and beavers, this place of peace is bustling with activity. Many travelers try to identify the laugh of the loon, the honk of the goose, and the chorus of sparrows, red-winged blackbirds, goldfinches, and crickets.

Look skyward to glimpse an eagle, osprey, or turkey vulture. To distinguish among these three mighty birds, watch their manner of flight. The bald eagle has flat wings, the turkey vulture has upswept wings, and the osprey has a crook in its wings. There are more bald eagles on the Edge of the Wilderness than any other part of the lower 48 states. An eagle nest may measure up to 10 feet in diameter and weigh 4,000 pounds. Ospreys live in high nests in treetops, wintering as far away as South America but returning to the same nest year after year.

Minnesota has the greatest number of timber wolves in the lower 48 states as well. They are considered a threatened but not an endangered species in Minnesota. Less often seen but still present on the Edge of the Wilderness are coyotes, bears, and moose. White-tailed deer, ruffed grouse, and waterfowl offer good hunting and wildlife viewing opportunities as well.

During the autumn and spring, you see woody white strands of birch lacing the forest floor along the Byway. If you are a longtime resident or resort vacationer, you may no longer notice this phenomenon. But to newcomers, the question arises, "What happened to make all these trees fall to the ground?"

Paper birch trees, which live only 40 to 80 years, are found throughout Minnesota's northern woodlands. As late as the 1900s, Chippewa tribes in the north built birch bark canoes. They constructed canoes in the early summer when they could easily remove the lightweight bark. They also rolled up birch bark and lit it, creating a torch. Early settlers prepared birch for railroad ties for the trains that edged northward. In today's economy, birch is used as lumber and firewood and for veneers. Birch also contributes nutrients to the forest floor and has served as food for various insects. Stands of birch often begin to grow after a fire, windstorm, or timber harvest. Another reason so many birch trees lay on the ground is that birch loses out to the taller-growing aspen as both sun-loving species compete. Along the Highway 38 corridor, particularly at Pughole Lake, you can see how birch trees topple due to competition from other trees, diseases, and insects, as well as from northern Minnesota's light soils. A look across the lake shows how the pines and hardwoods are gradually taking over a notable birch stand.

RECREATIONAL

When the railroad was built, it brought tourists who were interested in fishing and hunting on the Edge of the Wilderness. It also brought the tools and supplies needed to begin the construction of Minnesota Highway 38 in the 1920s. The story of Camp Idlewild on North Star Lake is typical of Itasca County's early development. Two Indiana brothers and a friend, Walter and Lloyd Stickler and Phil Ernest, took the railroad as far as it went in 1907, then walked to what is now known as Camp Idlewild. They built a few guest cabins, and a magazine article was written about the camp. Soon a full-fledged resort was born, thanks to the magazine promotion.

Following World War II, northern Minnesota's tourist and resort industry grew rapidly. Itasca County had a peak of about 300 resorts in the 1940s and 1950s.

Today, there are approximately 100 resorts and vacation sites in the area, many vacationers returning year after year. North Star Lake—at more than 3 miles long and about 1/2 mile wide—is considered one of the best fishing and recreational lakes in the area. It is representative of many of the lakes on the Edge of the Wilderness, with its scenic beauty, islands and bays, clear waters, and recreational offerings. The still-visible remnants of the railroad trestle provide good habitat for the lake's many fish. The lake is 90 feet deep and is managed for muskie. Visitors also catch walleye (the state fish of Minnesota), northern pike, largemouth bass, smallmouth bass, bluegills, and crappies.

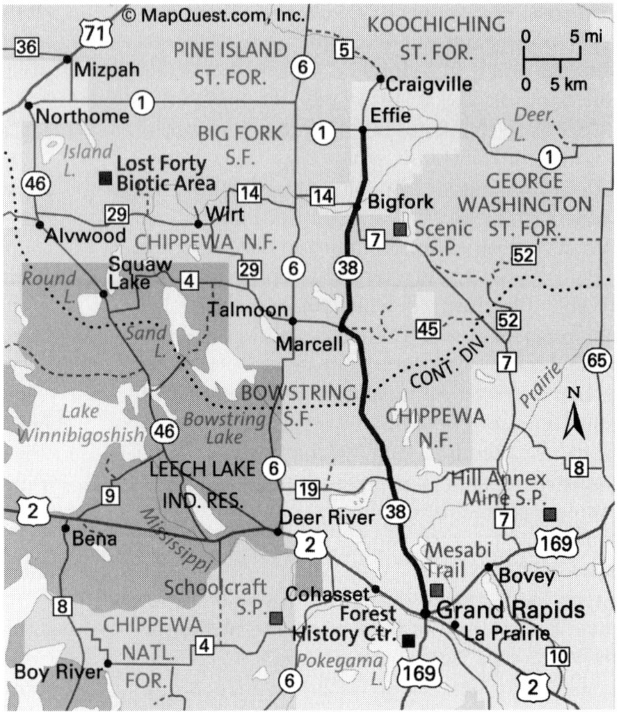

With a wingspan of over 6 feet, keen vision, and white head and tail feathers, the bald eagle is truly a magnificent bird. People often make a special trip to the Chippewa National Forest just to observe bald eagles. Spending time along the shorelines of the forest's larger lakes is the best way to treat yourself to the sight of an eagle in flight. The forest surrounding the Edge of the Wilderness supports the highest breeding density of eagles in the United States outside of Alaska. Large, fertile lakes; towering red and white pines; and remote areas provide an ideal nesting and feeding habitat. Nesting birds return in late February and early March, although a few birds spend the entire winter in the forest. Eggs are laid in early April, and the young leave their lofty nests in mid-July. Eagles occupy their breeding areas until the lakes freeze over in November or December.

The best opportunity for viewing bald eagles is from a boat; in fact, one of the best opportunities to see eagles is to canoe down the Mississippi River between Cass Lake and Lake Winnie. You can search the lakeshore with binoculars to spot eagles that are eating fish on the beaches. These birds of prey often perch in trees found around the larger lakes, such as Winnie, Cass, Leech, and Bowstring. The Bigfork and Leech rivers are also favorite eagle areas. However, if you do not have a boat, you can simply find an area along the beach with a good panoramic view of the lake. Campgrounds, picnic areas, and boat landings are good places to visit. Eagles also frequent Leech Lake Dam and Winnie Dam, particularly in the spring before the lake ice goes out.

SCENIC

What makes the Edge of the Wilderness truly unique is its rich and wide variety of upper Minnesota terrain, vegetation, wildlife, and history. While some elements are fairly common in other areas, no other route exposes travelers to so much variety in such a short distance along such a beautiful and accessible corridor. The Edge of the Wilderness is definitely a road to take slowly in order to enjoy the scenery of forests and meadows.

On the outskirts of Grand Rapids, the corridor begins to hint at the landscape to come. At first, the route is flat and flanked by mixed lowland meadows, swamps, and lakes. Very quickly, however, the corridor leaves most signs of the city and begins its rolling journey through mixed hardwoods and stands of conifers with aspen. With so many curves and hills, the corridor hides from view many memorable scenes until the traveler is upon them. Seemingly innocent turns in the road yield eye-popping surprises. The terrain continues in this way for half its length until the town of Marcell, where the terrain flattens slightly and offers more conifers. Between Bigfork and Effie, the corridor's terminus, the landscape introduces lowland wetlands, a flatter landscape that served as the bed of glacial Lake Agassiz thousands of years ago. Surrounding forests continue to contain aspen and lowland conifers such as jack pine and spruce.

A visitor to the Edge of the Wilderness could simply travel the route without stopping to take advantage of its recreational and interpretive opportunities, yet still leave with many vivid memories of the corridor. The Byway hugs the terrain, rising above lakes and then sloping down to meet their shores before rising up again through the trees and down into wetlands. Throughout the southern half of the route, maples, paper birch, and quaking aspen branches provide a canopy that envelops travelers in the lush forest. During the fall color season, the corridor displays bright red sugar maples, warm gold birch and aspens, and maroon red oaks. After the leaves have fallen and the ground is covered with snow, the forest opens up and offers new opportunities to see the terrain and spy on wildlife.

Highlights

For your convenience, the Edge of the Wilderness has milepost markers that guide you on your tour. The Byway officially begins at Grand Rapids, Minnesota. Designated as milepost 0, the Byway proceeds north with sites of interest marked consecutively as follows:

- **Mile 0:** Grand Rapids, a historic logging and paper-making region
- **Mile 3.4:** Lind-Greenway Mine, a historic iron mine
- **Mile 8.5:** Black Spruce/Tamarack Bog Habitat, one of the largest and most mature bogs in the area
- **Mile 12.6:** Trout Lake and Joyce Estate, an impressive estate created in the 1920s
- **Mile 13.4:** Birch Stand at Pughole Lake, an excellent place for viewing wildlife
- **Mile 19.0:** Day Lake CCC Camp, which has a long and varied history of use as both a Depression-era work camp and a German POW camp during World War II
- **Mile 20.9:** Laurentian Divide
- **Mile 23.5:** White Cedar Stand, an important habitat area for indigenous wildlife
- **Mile 24.5:** Scenic overlook at North Star Lake
- **Mile 27.7:** Marcell, a historic logging and rail town
- **Mile 28.7:** Chippewa National Forest Ranger Station, which offers information and displays
- **Mile 30.5:** Gut and Liver Line, the historic railway that once hauled logs and supplies for the area's inhabitants
- **Mile 40.0:** Bigfork, a small logging community
- **Mile 47.0:** Effie, a small agricultural community

The Grand Rounds Scenic Byway

MINNESOTA

Offering a unique Byway experience, the Grand Rounds Scenic Byway is a continuous course of paved pathways. It encompasses more than 50 miles of parks, parkways, bike paths, and pedestrian paths that encircle the Byway's host city, Minneapolis. The system includes the Chain of Lakes, Lake Nokomis, Lake Hiawatha, and the Mississippi River, as well as Minnehaha, Shingle, and Bassetts Creek. Currently, the Byway is divided into seven main sections: the Downtown Riverfront, the Mississippi River, Minnehaha Park, Chain of Lakes, Theodore Wirth, Victory Memorial District, and the Northeast District.

Quick Facts

Length: 52 miles.

Time to Allow: 3 to 4 hours.

Best Time to Drive: Spring through fall. High season is summer.

Byway Travel Information: Minneapolis Park & Recreation Board: phone 612/661-4800; Byway local Web site: www.mnmississippiriver.com.

Special Considerations: No significant or unusual seasonal accessibility limitations apply to the Grand Rounds Scenic Byway. With only a few exceptions, the route is generally above local flood plains. During the winter, in addition to the roadway surfaces, a single paved trail is plowed throughout the system for shared use by pedestrians and cyclists.

Restrictions: Truck traffic is prohibited from using all but several short segments of the Byway.

Bicycle/Pedestrian Facilities: Throughout the entire Grand Rounds Scenic Byway System, paved pedestrian trails (45 miles) and bicycle trails (43 miles) are separated from the adjacent parkway road surfaces. The entire route is designed and maintained for passenger vehicles, bicycles, and pedestrians. The 8-foot-wide paths are designed for two-directional travel, with one exception: the bike path around the Chain of Lakes. When on the paths, please obey the 10 mph speed limit, be considerate of others, keep to the right side of all paths, sound off when passing, and observe all current bike regulations.

Parks, recreation centers, historic districts, and lakes are all defining characteristics of the Grand Rounds Scenic Byway. Depending on the season, you interact with a landscape encompassing combinations of natural areas, historical features, and cultural amenities. The Grand Rounds Scenic Byway has been the crème de la crème of urban Byways for more than a century, being the longest continuous system of public urban parkways and providing motorists with access to an unprecedented combination of intrinsic qualities of the highest caliber. So spend a day in the park and enjoy the best of Minneapolis.

The Byway Story

The Grand Rounds Scenic Byway tells archaeological, cultural, historical, natural, recreational, and scenic stories that make it a unique and treasured Byway.

ARCHAEOLOGICAL

Recent archaeological digs occurring in the old milling district of Minneapolis have revealed artifacts from the time when Minneapolis was a milling capital. Excavations of this area have allowed archaeologists to uncover pieces of the past that indicate the way ordinary people in the milling districts lived and worked. Visitors can explore the way life used to be in Minneapolis at the newly constructed Mill Ruins Park. This park is a restoration of original walls, canals, and buildings of the West Side Milling District. Another of the archaeological features along the Grand Rounds Scenic Byway in Minnesota is the Winchell Trail. Located on the Mississippi River, this trail preserves an original Native American trail that linked two celebration sites.

CULTURAL

An urbanized culture originating in the early 1800s is what visitors to the Grand Rounds Scenic Byway will experience. However, amid this urban culture is a prominent appreciation for nature and the arts. This can be seen in the beautiful parkways, lakes, and parks on the Grand Rounds. These places that combine nature with art and architecture are the clearest picture of Minneapolis culture today. They represent the earliest residents of this area—Native American cultures that are responsible for many of the names and legends visitors find all along the Byway. Hiawatha Avenue and Minnehaha Park are examples of remnants of a culture that held a great respect for the waters of Minnesota.

Architectural styles ranging from fine to functional exist all along the Byway. Unique bridges hold views to the old milling district of the city, where settlers made a living working in the sawmills. Modern art of a more recent period can be found in the uptown area of the Byway as well as in the lakeside areas. In addition to the present city, this art represents the contribution of a culture that has evolved from all the previous inhabitants of the Minneapolis area.

HISTORICAL

The Grand Rounds Scenic Byway is one of the nation's longest and oldest connected parkway systems owned entirely by an independent park board. This road has many historical qualities. For example, the Stone Arch Bridge found along the Byway is a National Civil Engineering Historical Landmark Site. Minnehaha Falls, also found along the Byway, is immortalized in Longfellow's epic poem "The Song of Hiawatha." The fine craftsmanship is a significant element of the beauty of the Grand Rounds Scenic Byway, while other forms of architecture are being brought to the surface again. The St. Anthony Heritage Trail offers a look at Minneapolis from a perspective that explores the many highlights in the city's history.

NATURAL

With the Mississippi running through it and lakes scattered all around it, it's no wonder the Grand Rounds is a scenic attraction for nature lovers. In very few other urban places in the world is nature so artfully integrated with the city. The Grand Rounds is centered around several parks and parkways that bring the best of nature to the fingertips of urban life. St. Anthony Falls is the only natural waterfall and gorge along the entire 2,350-mile course of the Mississippi River; Minnehaha Park contains one of the most enchanting waterfalls in the nation; and the Chain of Lakes is a place on the Byway to enjoy the lake shore or sail a boat onto the water. All in all, the Grand Rounds Scenic Byway connects nine lakes, three streams, two waterfalls, the Mississippi River, and surrounding nature to travelers.

At the Eloise Butler Wildflower Garden, you will find hundreds of plants and flowers native to Minnesota. Eloise Butler feared that Minnesota's natural characteristics would be lost with urban development, so she did some development of her own. The garden she created displayed plants and flowers from many different habitats. The garden has expanded into a preserve that is also home to many birds. Nearly all the parks on the Grand Rounds offer a garden of some type. A rose garden is located on Lake Harriet Parkway, while at Minnehaha Park, the Pergola Garden displays native wildflowers. Theodore Wirth Park includes a section known as Quaking Bog. This 5-acre bog is covered in moss and tamarack trees. Exploring these parks and gardens will give you a taste of the best of nature.

RECREATIONAL

With such widely varied attractions in one city, you'll find many places to see and different activities to do at each of those places. Outdoor recreation is not out of reach, while touring historical buildings and parks is a possibility as well. Sailboats and canoes are seen every day on the Chain of Lakes, while bikers and hikers have miles of roads to enjoy. The Grand Rounds is one of the nation's first park systems to create separated walking and biking paths. The Byway is also host to many national running events; for example, the Twin Cities Marathon on the Grand Rounds was named "the Most Beautiful Urban Marathon in the Country." Four golf courses can be found on the Grand Rounds Scenic Byway, each one with its own beautiful and challenging terrain.

If recreation needs to be more thought-provoking, be sure to tour some of the more unusual places on the Byway. Sculpture gardens in uptown Minneapolis offer displays of creativity that will capture your imagination. The St. Anthony Heritage Trail offers a place for touring the historic districts of Minneapolis. When you've read all the informational signs, stop at a café or restaurant for a bite to eat and a bit of ambience. Rumor has it that the Nicolette Island Inn has the best desserts in town!

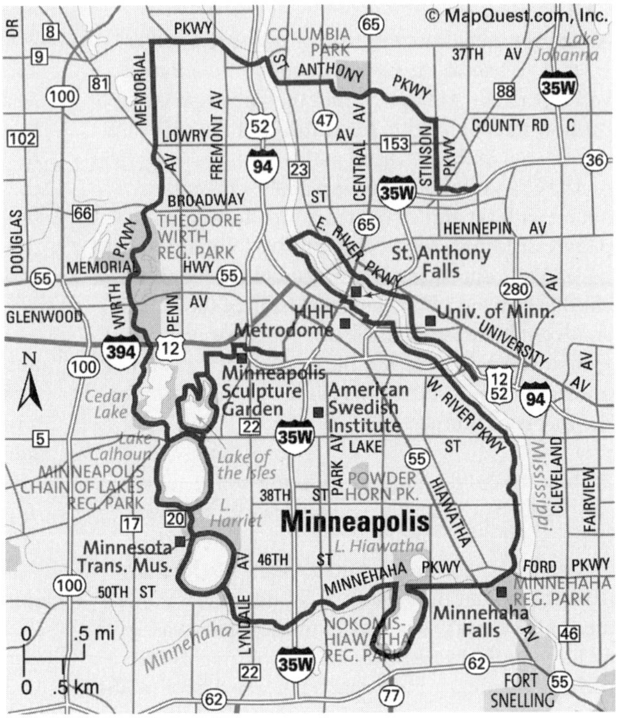

SCENIC

The scenes of the Grand Rounds vary greatly, but they are the city of Minneapolis at its finest. The architecturally diverse Minneapolis skyline is visible from nearly every portion of the Grand Rounds. Watch the buildings sparkle in the daylight or see them silhouetted by a Minnesota sunset. The heart of Minneapolis keeps the entire city healthy with growing prosperity and scenic style. The familiar view of the Stone Arch Bridge leads travelers to the historic district of Minneapolis with brick streets and flour mills. The sight of Minnehaha Falls is also a view linked directly to the ideals that embody Minneapolis. The falls have been admired for years, and their beauty is continually preserved. Landmarks like these characterize Minneapolis as a unique city in the United States.

Within a 50-mile drive, motorists witness diverse landscape settings, including natural, urban, historical, and ethnic settings, all from a unified Byway. The Grand Rounds Scenic Byway also includes outdoor sculptures, fountains, and public gardens that have been created by world-renowned artists. Where else can you find such a creative rendition of a giant cherry captured by an equally giant spoon? Fountains and sculptures of Minneapolis are the jewels of the city that set it apart from other urban sections of the country.

Often, the landmarks and artwork of Minneapolis lead visitors to the scenic trails of the St. Anthony Falls or Minnehaha Park. If you want to get a closer look at the Mississippi, follow the River Gorge hiking trail, which offers a natural setting right in the middle of the city. In the fall, these tree-lined trails are painted all the colors of autumn. Deep oranges and yellows are splattered about, creating a natural work of art that visitors can walk through. The lakes and rivers of Minneapolis are treasured, and there is something exhilarating about driving along the shores of sparkling blue water. Perhaps you will catch a glimpse of a sailboat gliding serenely along the water or a canoe passing by an inlet near the shore. And when the water is calm, the city skyline is mirrored in the water to create a perfect picture of symmetry. Trees and buildings line the lakes of Minneapolis, making this Byway the perfect combination of man and nature.

Highlights

Drive the Grand Rounds and you will see virtually all of the following sites.

- Beginning at the northeastern terminus of the Grand Rounds on Highway 35 W, travel west and follow the Byway as it winds around to **Theodore Wirth Park.** This park is well worth the visit and includes the **Eloise Butler Wildflower Garden,** with its spectacular display of wildflowers and other flowering plants.

- Returning to the Byway, follow it around **Cedar Lake** to **Lake Calhoun.** Here, turn northeast and travel around **Lake of the Isles** to **Loring Park.** Loring Park is home to the well-known **Sculpture Garden.** With its impressive display of sculpture and fanciful artwork, the Sculpture Garden is one of the highlights of the Grand Rounds.

- Return in the direction you came, only continue to wind around Lake Calhoun to **Lake Harriet** to visit the **Lake Harriet Refectory,** another popular site along the Grand Rounds.

- Continue following the Byway as it turns and travels east to **Minnehaha Park,** where you may view the falls, and **Lake Hiawatha,** immortalized by Longfellow's poem, "The Song of Hiawatha."

- From here, follow the Byway north to its terminus at **Nicollet Island** and **Boom Island.** Both are interesting places to visit in downtown Minneapolis if you have the time. Otherwise, you are pretty much right back where you started!

The Great River Road

MINNESOTA

Part of a multistate Byway; see also WI.

The Great River Road offers the best of Minnesota. The route encompasses the banks of the Mississippi River, 10,000 lakes, beautiful bluff lands, and a variety of outdoor recreation and wildlife. Brilliant wildflowers, evergreen forests, colored autumn leaves, rainbows, snowflakes, migrating birds, and waving fields of grain make this Byway a photographer's paradise.

Recreational spots have taken over the land of the lumberjack, where Paul Bunyan and his blue ox, Babe, used to roam freely. State parks and lakeside resorts are all part of the fun that visitors will find on the Great River Road today. And then there is the river itself. Minnesota is where the mighty Mississippi begins. Its meanderings make up a trail of cultural, historical, natural, recreational, and scenic sites. Whether camping in the forested areas of the north or relaxing in a Minneapolis hotel, you will find accommodations in the perfect setting.

The Great River Road is an adventure along a myriad of quaint towns and urban cities. The Twin Cities metropolitan area offers the hustle and bustle of a city that is rich in history, culture, and recreational opportunities. Deep wilderness surrounds the river towns of Minnesota and offers relaxation and privacy.

Quick Facts

Length: 575 miles.

Time to Allow: 2 days or longer.

Best Time to Drive: Anytime during the summer; fall leaf color is spectacular.

Byway Travel Information: Mississippi River Parkway Commission of Minnesota: phone 763/212-2560; Byway local Web site: www.mnmississippiriver.com.

Special Considerations: Several portions of the northern part of the road have a gravel surface. The speed limit on the Byway varies, but generally it is 55 mph in the country and 30 mph through towns. During the winter, you may find some icy patches in the rural parts of the roadway.

Bicycle/Pedestrian Facilities: Beautiful hiking, skiing, and snowmobiling trails exist all along the Byway. Catering to cyclists, the Great River Road provides easy access to a slew of biking trails along the way.

The Byway Story

The Great River Road tells cultural, historical, natural, recreational, and scenic stories that make it a unique and treasured Byway.

CULTURAL

The Great River Road in Minnesota takes you along the southeast end of the state, providing a look at the culture that began and continued on the banks of the Mississippi. This is where you find the source of the Great River and the source of the development of civilization in Minnesota. It began with the Indian tribes of the Sioux and Chippewa, who lived in the area for many years before they began to interact with the Europeans in fur trade. When wildlife grew scarce, new settlers began a new industry of logging, which forced native tribes out of the area so that logging could proceed.

The European settlers along the Great River Road brought a culture of farming and logging and their own style of folklore. The many lakes in Minnesota have been attributed to the legend of Paul Bunyan and his blue ox, Babe. According to legend, this lumberman of grand proportions was a hero in the area, and the hoof prints of his ox created the lakes that are scattered all over the state.

When tourism became a viable industry, it was time to nurse the forests back to health. Although many people initially came to the area for jobs in the logging industry, the tourism industry was blossoming as people traveled to see the beautiful Minnesota forests. In the 1930s, people began to restore the once-great forests of giant red and white pines. An appreciation of nature is still part of the Byway culture today.

Cultures of the past have left traces of the past. Native American languages can still be found in names like Lake Winnibigoshish and Ah-Gwah-Ching (Leach Lake), while the heritage of the European settlers resounds in the names of communities all along the road. You will also find more recent pieces of American culture in Lindbergh State Park and the Lindbergh home, a memorial and a glimpse at the past of the famous pilot Charles Lindbergh.

The civilizations of Minnesota society burst in full glory on the Great River Road in the cities of Minneapolis and St. Paul. Parks and parkways, bridges, and buildings are all part of the scenery that you experience throughout this Byway. But even with the great developments and changes of the present time, visitors and native dwellers all along the Great River Road can be seen returning to a culture of an earlier time—a culture of canoeing on the river and enjoying the wildlife and natural wealth of the area.

The Great River Road communities in Minnesota offer many festivals that celebrate the legends, products, immigrant culture, and art found along the Byway. For example, as you travel from Itasca to Bemidji, you can experience the Annual Ozawindib Walk, the Annual International Snowsnake Games, and the Lake Itasca Region Pioneer Farmers Reunion and Show. You can also enjoy the Annual Winter Bird Count, Art in the Park in July, and the People's Art Festival in November. Finally, you can visit the Paul Bunyan and Babe the Blue Ox statues that were erected in 1937 for a winter carnival.

As you travel the route from Little Falls to Brainerd, be sure to visit the Minnesota Fishing Museum in the Northern Pacific Depot, the Arts and Crafts Fair that takes place downtown the weekend after Labor Day, and the Antique Auto Show that takes place the weekend after Labor Day. Also, the Great River Arts Association sponsors exhibits and performances throughout the year, including Sunday afternoon concerts in Maple Island Park. The Heartland Symphony Orchestra performs in both Little Falls and Brainerd, and the Stroia Ballet Company offers performances throughout the year, including *The Nutcracker* each Christmas. Other things to see include the Morrison County Fair, held just east of Little Falls off of Highway 27, and the Little Falls House Concerts that feature folk musicians performing at a variety of venues. Also, Camp Ripley (Highways 371 and 115) contains the Minnesota Military Museum (open to the public) and the Historic Fort Ripley site (by appointment only). Finally, the Little Elk Heritage Preserve is located 2 miles north of Little Falls. This archaeological preserve has old fur-trading sites.

In the Minneapolis to St. Paul area of the Byway, you can experience 1840s food, dining, and preparation. Special events include Children's Day, Historic Mendota Days, the Mill City Blues Festival, the Capital City Celebration, and a New Year's Eve party. Also, visit the Taste of Minnesota, the Minneapolis Aquatennial, the St. Paul Winter Carnival, and La Fete de Saint Jean-Baptiste. From Red Wing to Winona, stop and visit the Red Wing Shoe Museum, located at 315 Main Street. Also found along the route is the Goodhue County Historical Society, located at 1166 Oak Street. Some of the events that occur along this part of the Byway include a Music Festival, a powwow, River City Days, and an Antique and Classic Boat Rendezvous.

HISTORICAL

When Henry Rowe Schoolcraft identified the true source of the Mississippi as the crystal-clear waters that flow from Lake Itasca, the final boundaries of the Louisiana Purchase were set. The Mississippi River, however, was important to Native Americans centuries before the Europeans arrived. In fact, the name Mississippi was an Algonquin name that, when applied to rivers, meant Great River (hence the name Great River Road). During the 1820s and 1830s, Fort Snelling and Grand Portage (on Lake Superior) were the focal points of Euro-American activity in the region. Strategically located at the confluence of the Mississippi and Minnesota rivers, Fort Snelling served as the first US military outpost in the area.

The Great River Road traces the river through the Chippewa National Forest, created by Congress in 1902. Although originally only small areas of pines were preserved, now more than 600,000 acres of land are managed by the National Forest Service. In this forest is historic Sugar Point on Leech Lake, another of the Mississippi River reservoirs. You can also visit Battleground State Forest, the site of the last recorded Indian battle with the US government, and Federal Dam, one of six dams constructed in the area between 1884 and 1912 to stabilize water levels on the Mississippi downstream. The legacies of the great pine forests along the Mississippi live in the majestic trees that remain. In Bemidji, the most recognizable landmark is the 1937 colossal statues of Paul Bunyan and Babe the Blue Ox, located on the shore of Lake Bemidji. The legend of the giant lumberjack illustrates the importance of the lumber industry for many northern Minnesota towns.

Due to its closeness to the river, St. Paul became a transportation hub for opening up the upper Midwest. It also became Minnesota's state capital, and Minneapolis became the nation's main flour-milling district. St. Anthony Falls and the locks and dams provide testimony to man's success at harnessing the power of the river to create a thriving urban center. Flour, beer, textiles, and lumber were produced and successfully transported to the nation and the world through the lock-and-dam system that begins here. In the early 1900s through the 1930s, the Cuyuna Iron Range produced over 100 million tons of ore that was used to build the US military machines of the great world wars. In Crosby, travelers visit the Croft Mine Historical Park—this mine operated between 1916 and 1934 and produced the richest ore found on the Cuyuna Range, with a composition of 55 percent iron. Portsmouth Lake in Crosby, once the largest open pit mine on the Cuyuna Range, is now one of the deepest lakes in Minnesota at 480 feet.

Camp Ripley, a Minnesota National Guard facility, tells two stories: the history of Minnesota soldiers from the Civil War to the present and the development of the weapons of war.

In Little Falls, the Great River Road follows Lindbergh Drive to the boyhood home of Charles Lindbergh, pilot of the first solo flight across the Atlantic Ocean. The evolution of the United States can be traced along the Great River Road on the Ox Cart trail, still visible through Schoolcraft and Crow Wing state parks. Across the river from the Great River Road, Elk River's most noted resident, Oliver H. Kelley, founded the Patrons of Husbandry (popularly known as the Grange), a group that evolved into the Democratic Farmer Laborer, or DFL, party. Today, the Oliver H. Kelley Farm is a 189-acre living-history farm operated by the Minnesota Historical Society. This historic site explores the life and lifestyle of the Kelleys, who lived here in the late 1800s. Byway travelers also learn through excellent interpretation about the historic importance of the Great River Road and the river as transportation routes and vital links among Mississippi River communities.

NATURAL

One of the most naturally diverse sections of the Great River Road can be found in Minnesota. Travelers are beckoned to the Great River Road to enjoy a multitude of lakes, native wildlife, and rugged river bluffs. If you seek outdoor beauty, you will find what remains of the once-abundant pine forests that have been drawing travelers to Minnesota for over 100 years. Visitors never tire of seeing the lakes along the Great River Road in Minnesota, and there are plenty to see. Nearly every town has its own lake along the road, and when the lakes end, the vastness of the Mississippi River is just beginning. Natural wildlife abounds in the marshes and prairies along the road. Visitors will pass a major roosting site for bald eagles and wildlife habitats for deer, waterfowl, turkeys, and pheasants.

Between the many lakes, streams and rivers flow, urging travelers on. The landscape along the route is the handiwork of a crowd of glaciers that meandered through the area, leaving pockets and creases for rivers and lakes. Large hills were smoothed into the rolling landforms that visitors can see along the road. The great Mississippi River bluffs are present on the Byway, evidence of a notable geological past. This past combined with a present of hardwood forests, lakes, and wildlife creates a beautiful natural setting that will tempt you to leave your car throughout your journey on the Great River Road.

RECREATIONAL

From the headwaters to the Iowa border, Minnesota's portion of the Great River Road allows visitors to partake in a vast variety of recreational opportunities along its route. No matter what the itinerary or expectation, there is something to suit every taste on the Great River Road. And the fun and adventure continues throughout all four of Minnesota's very distinct seasons.

The water itself creates a large amount of the recreational draw to the Great River Road. A taste of the recreational possibilities that are available on the water include swimming, sunning, fishing, boating, jet skiing, sailing, canoeing, kayaking, and water-skiing—just to name a few. Strung along the edge of the river are plenty of things to do as well—particularly for outdoor enthusiasts. One of six state parks may be the perfect stop after a drive on the Byway. At parks like Itasca State Park, visitors can enjoy hiking or biking the trails, picnicking, or even bird-watching. The northern part of the Byway provides a haven for hunters and fishermen. The wilderness in this area is home to a great deal of wildlife.

Winter weather is no excuse to stay indoors in Minnesota. Several places along the Byway offer miles of cross-country skiing and snowmobiling. Visitors also find places for downhill skiing. But if moving through the snow doesn't sound appcaling, perhaps drilling through the ice does. Ice fishing is a popular pastime for visitors to the Great River Road; ice-fishing resorts, services, and house rentals can be found from one end of the Great River Road to the other. And large catches from icy waters are not uncommon and are a well-known secret among residents of the state.

SCENIC

As you travel along the Great River Road, you can look upon pristine lakes, virgin pine forests, quaint river towns, and a vibrant metropolis. You can see eagles, loons, and deer, as well as blazing hardwood forests and hillsides fluttering with apple blossoms. Experience the awesome power of locks and dams, imagine a longshoreman's life as barges glide past, recall Mark Twain's time on paddlewheelers, feel the wind that pushes the sailboats, and watch water-skiers relive the sport's Mississippi birth.

Travelers along the Great River Road are witnesses to a river that is constantly changing. It first evolves from a clear, shallow stream into a meandering, serpentine watercourse. It then changes into vast marshes and later becomes a canoe route. After this, the waterway becomes a rolling river that powers dams and mills as it squeezes its way past the only gorge on the river. It then passes over large waterfalls, through the first locks, past tall sandstone bluffs, and finally into a mile-wide river that is surrounded by a vast and fruitful valley.

The literary legend Mark Twain described the beautiful scene when he said, "The majestic bluffs that overlook the river, along through this region, charm one with the grace and variety of their forms, and the soft beauty of their adornment. The steep verdant slope, whose base is at the water's edge, is topped by a lofty rampart of broken, turreted rocks, which are exquisitely rich and mellow in color—mainly dark browns and dull greens with other tints. And then you have the shining river, winding here and there and yonder, its sweep interrupted at intervals by clusters of wooded islands threaded by silver channels; and you have glimpses of distant villages, asleep upon cares; and of stealthy rafts slipping along in the shade of the forest walls; and of white steamers vanishing around remote points."

Highlights

The following must-see tour of the Great River Road's northern section gives you a sample itinerary to follow, if you so choose.

- The Great River Road begins at **Itasca State Park.** Covering about 32,000 acres, the park embraces the headwaters of the Mississippi River and 157 lakes, the foremost of which is Lake Itasca, the source of the great river. Site of the University Biological Station, the park has stands of virgin Norway pine and specimens of nearly every kind of wild animal, tree, and plant native to the state. Camping and hiking, as well as historic sites, are abundant here. Itasca Indian Cemetery and Wegmann's Cabin are important landmarks in the area.

- Leaving Itasca State Park, the Great River Road heads northeast toward the **Chippewa National Forest** and **Lake Bemidji State Park.** Just 31 miles north of Itasca State Park along Highway 71, the Bemidji area is rich in diverse activities. Stopping at Lake Bemidji State Park provides a lot of fun, including the 2-mile **Bog Walk,** a self-guided nature trail. A $4 fee per car (per day) applies when visiting the park.

- Outside the park, along the shores of Lake Bemidji, lie several historic sites, including the famous statues of **Paul Bunyan and Babe the Blue Ox** and of **Chief Bemidji.** The **Carnegie Library Building,** on the National Register of Historic Places, is also located here. You'll find many campgrounds and resorts in the area for staying the night.

- **Cass Lake** is the next stop along the tour of the Great River Road. It's a popular stop for fishing and camping. This lake is unique, though: **Star Island,** in Cass Lake, is an attractive recreation area because it contains an entire lake within itself. Other fabulous lakes in the area are worth visiting as well.

- Enjoy the scenery of northern Minnesota as you follow the GRR signs into the city of **Grand Rapids.** The city offers many activities, including the **Forest History Center,** a logging camp that highlights the logging culture of Minnesota.

- Heading south out of **Grand Rapids,** follow the signs toward Brainerd. On the way to **Brainerd,** be sure to stop at **Savanna Portage State Park,** with its 15,818 acres of hills, lakes, and bogs. The **Continental Divide** marks the great division of water—where water to the west flows into the Mississippi River and water to the east runs into Lake Superior. Be sure to walk along the **Savanna Portage Trail,** too, a historic trail traveled by fur traders, Dakota and Chippewa Indians, and explorers more than 200 years ago. A $4 fee per car (per day) applies when visiting the park.

- The town of Brainerd is a great place to stop for lunch. Many lake resorts nearby offer camping, hiking, and fishing. After Brainerd and south of **Little Falls,** just off of Highway 371, is **Charles A. Lindbergh State Park.** Look for bald eagles here when visiting in the spring or fall. During your visit, stop in at the historic home of Charles A. Lindbergh, Sr., father of the famous aviator. The home is operated by the Minnesota Historical Society and is adjacent to the park. A $4 fee per car (per day) applies when visiting.

- Once in the city of **St. Cloud,** the **Munsinger and Clemens Gardens** offer a relaxing end to this portion of the Great River Road. The nationally known gardens are located near Riverside Drive and Michigan Avenue, right in town. One of the treats of the gardens are the antique horse troughs filled with unique flowers. The gardens are popular but spacious, so they're hardly ever noticeably crowded.

The southern tour continues from this point all the way through Minneapolis and St. Paul and along the Mississippi River and Wisconsin border, down to the border of Minnesota and Iowa.

Historic Bluff Country Scenic Byway

MINNESOTA

Follow the panoramic Root River Valley to the Mississippi River. The scenery along the western end of the Byway showcases Minnesota's rich and rolling farmland, while the eastern part of the route winds toward the Great River Road along a beautiful trout stream and canoe route through spectacular tree-covered bluffs featuring limestone palisades and the rich hardwoods found in this area.

Quick Facts

Length: 88 miles.

Time to Allow: 3 hours.

Best Time to Drive: Summer and fall.

Byway Travel Information: Byway local Web site: www.bluffcountry.com.

Special Considerations: An extremely scenic route through the Yucatan Valley, the segment between Houston and Caledonia to the south curves frequently and climbs many steep grades in response to the area's topography. When traveling the Bluff Country, be careful of the wildlife inhabiting the area. Rattlesnakes are occasionally found on rock outcrops and on river bottoms.

Bicycle/Pedestrian Facilities: Shoulders are very narrow (2 feet) and do not support bicyclist or pedestrian use. The Historic Bluff Country Scenic Byway is unique, however, in that a parallel bicycle and pedestrian facility, the Root River Trail, is provided between Fountain and Houston. Many visitor facilities and interpretive opportunities are located at trailheads for this facility, providing similar experiences for bicyclists and motorists alike. You can ski, hike, and bike at the Root River State Trail, but other trails are available off the Historic Bluff Country Scenic Byway. You can find hiking and cross-country trails at Historic Forestville State Park. Between Houston and Rushford, you'll find the Wetbark Trail. And in towns like Rushford, Preston, and Fountain, trails are also available.

This valley was untouched by the glaciers and has weathered gradually over time to create a magnificent pastoral setting dotted with small towns, quaint and historic lodgings, and a recreational bike and hiking trail. Whether you come to Historic Bluff Country for the recreational opportunities or for the culture you'll find all along the Byway, you won't be disappointed. Day trips along and adjacent to the Historic Bluff Country Scenic Byway take you back to days when the horse and buggy dominated travel, while sights of places known only in history books are before your very eyes.

The Byway Story

The Historic Bluff Country Scenic Byway tells archaeological, cultural, historical, natural, recreational, and scenic stories that make it a unique and treasured Byway.

ARCHAEOLOGICAL

The Huta Wakpa and the Cahheomonah people who were native to the Driftless Area along the Byway realized its virtues as they found good hunting ground and resources for making tools. As a result, many Native American settlements, structures, and sites were once located all along the Byway. Now, many of these sites have been lost by time and nature, but they once represented the complex seasons and lifestyles of the people who first lived there.

Still in existence today is the Grand Meadow Quarry Site. This natural bed of chert provided materials for Native American arrowheads and tools for 10,000 years. Archaeological interpretation for visitors is limited to stories of the past and the occasional piece of chert that might be discovered in the forest.

CULTURAL

Among the small, historic Minnesota communities of the Historic Bluff area, a trail to the past defines today's cultures. Some of these cultures, like the Old Order Amish population, have changed little since first settling here. Others have evolved with the rest of America and yet keep a firm hold on their heritage. The descendents of Norwegians and Germans still celebrate many of the same events that their ancestors did 150 years ago.

Little is left, however, of the Native American culture that once dominated the lands along the Byway. At one time, the Winnebago and the Dakota developed celebrations and rituals around the Root River. The few tribes that still survive appreciate cultural sites and sacred places in Bluff Country, and archaeological sites provide a look at places that were important to these cultures. Above all, harmony with the land was a part of life for these people. Europeans who eventually took over the river and bluffs have their own appreciation for the lands they settled. Names like Spring Grove and Grand Meadow reflect the natural beauty of the past that can still be visited today on the Byway.

The settlers who built the towns in Bluff Country were industrious. Towns flourished, and their downtown sections contained splendid architecture that can still be observed today. The attitude of growth amid small-town life is still present in Byway towns today. Meanwhile, the past is still untouched in Amish communities, where people live without electricity, automobiles, and many of the cultural ideals that most Americans hold. Amish buggies can be seen near Harmony, Preston, and Lanesboro; the occupants may be traveling to a local store to sell homemade baked goods and crafts. Furniture created by Amish craftsmen can be found at shops in Byway towns.

HISTORICAL

Bluff Country is a unique place where modern ways of life have not entirely overshadowed memories of the past. Historic sites and districts are still evident throughout this historic Byway. Towns along the route were built on a very successful agricultural past. The agricultural society that developed in southeastern Minnesota in the 1800s flourished for many years and then evolved with the coming and going of the railroad. Barns, mills, and silos stand as evidence of the past in many different places along the Byway. Historic centers in Houston, Lanesboro, and Fillmore County display other parts of the past along the Byway.

When southeastern Minnesota was settled, little towns sprang up as the centers of agricultural trade and social activity. Farmers congregated to sell their crops and buy needed supplies, while grain was stored in silos or grain elevators like the one in Preston that once belonged to the Milwaukee Elevator Company. This grain elevator is now a rest stop for travelers along the Root River Trail. The towns profited from agricultural success, and now many of them display historic districts and buildings with elaborate architecture. Many of the buildings, including churches, libraries, and banks, are available to travelers as they explore history on the Byway.

As a result of a successful farming industry, mills began to appear in Bluff Country. In Lanesboro, a dam on the river provided power for three flour mills. The commercial district thrived there from the 1860s through the 1920s, and visitors today can tour these brick buildings and the shops and restaurants inside them. Towns along the Byway also benefited from the coming of the railroad. The entire town of Wykoff was platted and settled when the railroad passed through. The old Southern Minnesota Depot in Rushford now serves as a trail center. When the railroad left, the tracks lay in disrepair for many years until they were converted to the Root River Trail.

NATURAL

Readily accessible at every turn, the nature of Historic Bluff Country is available at overlooks, parks, riverbanks, and vistas. Deep river valleys, sinkholes, caves, and bluffs are all natural features of the Byway that travelers will want to explore. Bluff Country is part of the Driftless Area left untouched by the glaciers that once covered most of Minnesota and Wisconsin. The Root River flows along the Byway, calling to explorers from a tree-lined bank. The Byway celebrates its natural qualities with trails, parks, and places to stop and learn more about Byway surroundings.

Because of the unique situation of Bluff Country's natural history, unique habitats are found throughout the area. Labeled as Scientific and Natural Areas,

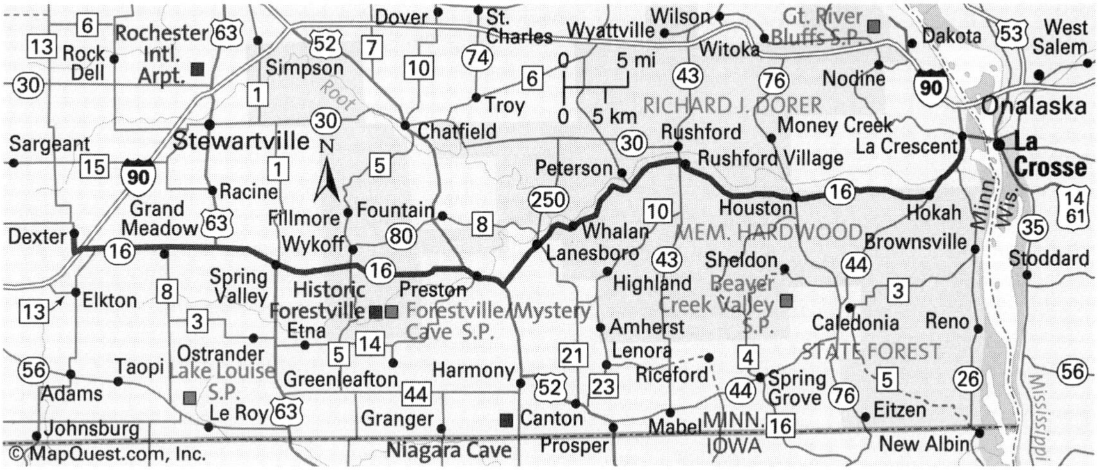

these places often support unusual plant and animal species, because natural features of the land remained unchanged during the time that the rest of the state was changed by glaciers.

The caves and underground streams along the Byway are a result of karst terrain, which is created when rainwater is absorbed into the ground to dissolve the calcite limestone beneath the ground. As this thick layer of limestone weakens, sinkholes form. Streams that continue to flow through the dissolved limestone create caves and caverns. The Mystery Cave and Niagara Cave are two places where you can see the results of a few streams and a little rainwater. You may also want a good look at a sinkhole. The nearby city of Fountain is known as the Sinkhole Capital of the United States. Here, you find more evidence of the unique geological features along the Byway.

If you like to get out of the caves and enjoy nature above ground, the Byway offers forests, rivers, and bluffs. The Root River and the Richard J. Dorer Memorial Forest provide places to enjoy the greenery of trees and the sunlight as it sparkles on moving water. Maple, oak, and birch create a setting for bird-watching, and in the fall, their colors draw audiences from miles around. As the Root River flows along the Byway and separates into two branches, canoe access points allow you to get a closer look. And of course, the natural feature for which the Byway was named is prevalent along the way. Travelers drive over and next to bluffs on the Byway. In the city of Hokah, a bluff known as Mount Tom stands over Como Park, where you can see the enchanting Como Falls.

RECREATIONAL

The forests, the trails, and the river are the central places for recreation on the Byway. And because most of the Byway goes through these places, recreation is never far away. State parks and natural areas provide places for hiking, camping, and exploring. With two caves within the Byway vicinity, spelunking is a skill that every traveler will want to develop. Driving through friendly towns, beautiful river valleys, and the bluff-covered countryside, you will certainly find a place to stop and have some fun. Classic outdoor recreational opportunities are around every corner.

Most travelers like to explore places with unique names and histories. The Forestville/Mystery Cave State Park has both. Not only do visitors have the opportunity to go spelunking in the Mystery Cave, but they also are able to explore the town site of one of Minnesota's oldest communities, Forestville. For visitors who want to continue spelunking, one of the largest caves in the Midwest, Niagara Cave, is located south of Harmony. You can camp among the forests and bluffs at Beaver Creek Valley State Park.

Two state trails on the Byway are the perfect place for bikers, hikers, and, in wintertime, cross-country skiers. The Root River State Trail and the Preston-Harmony Valley State Trail connect to provide miles of scenic trail for visitors to enjoy. Along the way, signs provide information about the surrounding area. When you visit the Richard J. Dorer Memorial Harwood Forest, you will be pleased to find trails for hiking, horseback riding, and off-road vehicles.

Perhaps the most inviting trail on the Byway is one made of water. The Root River is perfect for an afternoon or a day in a canoe. Several branches and tributaries give you the chance to get to know Bluff Country a little better. The Root River is not just a waterway, but also home to a population of trout. Anglers enjoy the wooded atmosphere of the Root River as they try to tempt a prize-winning fish. On the banks of the river, picnickers enjoy the shade of a maple tree and the peaceful sound of flowing river water. The Root River is central to many of the activities along the Byway, but even if you stray from the riverside, you'll be sure to find something to do.

SCENIC

Bluff Country is a land of rolling hills, pastoral fields, and scenic rivers. Several places along the way highlight the beauty of a river valley or a hardwood forest. The colors of the landscape change with each season to provide rich greens, beautiful golds, and a winter white. Each season has its own spin on the scenery, but you'll find the same scenic place whenever you drive the Historic Bluff Country Scenic Byway. And when you aren't enjoying the scenery from your car, you can be out on the Byway experiencing it.

From the car, you'll find dramatic views of steep river bluffs, or you can watch the Root River as it flows alongside the Byway. As the Byway parallels the river, enjoy the tree-lined banks of the river and the occasional tuft of wildflowers growing nearby. Of course, there are places to stop along the way and get a closer look at the river. The trail that parallels the river provides visitors with a scenic hike along the Byway.

Historic buildings, bridges, and walls along the Byway only enhance the scenery, making the Byway one of the most picturesque corners of the country. As civilization has developed in this natural prairie, industrious cultures and families left churches, homes, and parks for future generations to enjoy. Their efforts create an added sense of pastoral perfection along the Byway as the fields and forests are accented with classic buildings that continue to stand the test of time.

In addition to historic buildings, the Byway features a number of historic waysides and parks. These parks feature inviting picnic areas with beautiful overlooks. At Magelssen Park, you will find yourself at the top of a bluff overlooking Rushford. The fifth-largest tree in the state, a Burr Oak tree, is one of the sights you will want to look for in the park. At many of the parks and waysides, you can enjoy an afternoon walk along one of the quaint stone walls.

Minnesota River Valley Scenic Byway

MINNESOTA

The Minnesota River flows gently between ribbons of oak, elm, maple, and cottonwood trees. The Minnesota River Valley Scenic Byway, which follows the river, wanders past rich farmland and through towns steeped in Minnesota history. Passing through rolling farmland and woodlands bordering the river between Belle Plaine and Browns Valley—300 miles of highways and gravel roads—is a scenic, historical, and cultural experience.

Several sites tell the story of the Dakota Indians who lived here, the pioneers who settled here, and the tragic conflict between the two communities. Overshadowed by the Civil War, the struggle that occurred along the river valley in 1862 resulted in thousands of lost lives. Although struggles of the past have not been entirely forgotten, the Minnesota River Valley has been able to move on to form a new culture and way of life. Today, the production of agricultural products and the distribution of these products help to feed the nation.

Quick Facts

Length: 287 miles.

Time to Allow: 7 days.

Best Time to Drive: Fall, due to changing leaf colors.

Byway Travel Information: New Ulm Chamber of Commerce: phone toll-free 888/463-9856; Byway local Web site: www.mnrivervalley.com.

Bicycle/Pedestrian Facilities: The Byway's roadways are not conducive to quality bicycle travel because of the variety of surface types, widths, shoulder characteristics, and high commercial vehicle use in certain areas. The roadways are, however, generally low-volume roadways, and many of the local roads will be quite peaceful if you have a bicycle that accommodates both gravel and paved surfaces.

Winding through the countryside between Mankato and Faribault is the 39-mile, newly paved Sakatah Singing Hills Bike Trail. The trail passes through a state park of the same name and through the village of Elysian, where a train depot serves as a wayside rest for the trail. The lakes in the area around Waterville are popular for fishing, and there are several lakeside resorts and campgrounds.

The Byway Story

The Minnesota River Valley Scenic Byway tells cultural, historical, natural, recreational, and scenic stories that make it a unique and treasured Byway.

CULTURAL

The Minnesota River Valley is a productive land, and as a result, people have been living here for hundreds of years. They thrive on the land and develop rich cultures to complement their successful lifestyle along the Minnesota River. In every town and stop along the Byway, travelers have the opportunity to discover the industrious society that has made this land thrive. Towns and historic districts provide a peek at past successes and failures. Festivals and monuments define each community and store the memories that make the culture along the Byway unique.

The Dakota people share their regional history and thriving modern-day culture through festivals, museums, restaurants, hotels, casinos, and trading posts. European pioneers left their mark as well, and their strong ties to their European heritage remain and are celebrated today. Residents of New Ulm welcome visitors to numerous celebrations, shops, restaurants, and lodging, all of which focus on their unique German heritage. Milan residents are likewise proud of their Norwegian heritage, and their community festivals focus on the food, crafts, and traditions of those ancestors. Many other communities on or near the Byway demonstrate their proud heritage through festivals, events, museums, and residents.

The development of the railroad, the river, and the highways allowed more access into the western frontier. It also brought new developments to improve traditional agriculture. Some farmers tend land today that has been passed down from generation to generation for over a century. Their success over the years can be seen in ornate historic buildings and today's thriving communities. In Le Sueur, the museum features an exhibit on the Green Giant Company, which started in the Minnesota River Valley. For a look at past agriculture, the Olof Swensson Farm Museum is a great place to examine the culture that influenced today's lifestyle on the Byway. The traditions of agricultural life made this region what it is today, and much of the economy is still based on the rich soils of the river valley.

HISTORICAL

Once a wild and untamed river valley, the land of the Minnesota River Valley Scenic Byway used to belong solely to the Dakotas. As with many places in the country, this area was a region of great conflict between the native people and the settlers dreaming of a new life in the Midwest. Despite conflict and tensions, the land allowed its inhabitants to prosper and become one of the main food-producing areas of the country.

The land was rich and fertile and seemed ripe for the picking, yet struggles erupted during the same years that the Civil War was raging. In 1862, the largest and bloodiest Indian war in the history of the United States occurred. The Dakota people who once lived along the river in peace were threatened by the coming of new settlers from the east. For ten years, the land was divided and the first reservations were developed, but the Dakota eventually wanted their land and their way of life back. The result was a six-week war in which many settlers and Dakotas were killed. When the war was over, Abraham Lincoln pardoned 262 of the 300 Dakota men who were going to be hanged. The remaining 38 men became part of the largest mass execution in United States history. Other Dakota men, women, and children were taken to a prison camp at Fort Snelling and later sent west.

Today, visitors can visit the historic sites and communities that were caught up in turmoil. The Lower Sioux Agency Historic Site and the Fort Ridgely State Historic Site provide a closer look into the changes that were occurring across Minnesota at that time. Museums and historic buildings provide further insight into the characteristics of early settlements on the Byway.

NATURAL

When you aren't driving through enchanting towns and pastoral fields, you see that the land is overtaken by nature and the wilderness that's native to Minnesota. Prairies and woodlands combine to form natural areas full of plants and animals. The natural areas along the Byway are perfect places to see the Minnesota River Valley's natural ecosystems.

The Minnesota River is now gentle and calm. However, the river valley was once filled by the Glacial River Warren. The glacial river carved the valley down into ancient bedrock and exposed outcrops of gneiss. Visitors can see this bedrock throughout the valley and at the Gneiss Outcrop scientific and natural area. The valley topography varies from 1 to 5 miles in width and from 75 to 200 feet deep. The Minnesota River flows from the Hudson/Mississippi Continental Divide in Browns Valley through the steep bluffs and low floodplain area that characterize one of the most impressive landscapes in Minnesota.

The array of landscapes in the river valley boasts a large variety of wildlife and plant life. Wooded slopes and floodplains of willow, cottonwood, American elm, burr oak, and green ash rise into upland bluffs of red cedar and remnant tall grass where preserved tracts of prairie remain for public use and appreciation. Prairie chickens, turkeys, white-tailed deer, coyotes, foxes, beavers, and many species of fish and birds live here, as does the bald eagle.

RECREATIONAL

The Minnesota River is one of the great tributaries to the Mississippi River. It flows across Minnesota, providing some of the best recreational opportunities in the upper Midwest. Outdoor recreation abounds, including bird-watching, canoeing, hiking, trail riding, fishing, hunting, camping, boating, snowmobiling, cross-country skiing, and golfing. State parks and recreation areas combine outdoor recreation with opportunities to discover history along the Minnesota River Valley. Monuments and historic buildings commemorate the events of the past. An excursion to a lake or a museum can be equally enjoyable on the Byway, which successfully showcases both types of attractions.

All of these activities can be found along the Byway at the six state parks, at scientific and natural areas, at wildlife management areas, or at the local parks or waysides. Camping along the Byway is one of the best ways to experience the nature of the river valley. Spending time near the river, you can better enjoy the beautiful scenery at one of the Byway's lakes or take a stroll along the Minnesota River itself. Big Stone Lake was one of the earliest places for travelers to visit. At the turn of the century, visitors came to enjoy steamboat rides on the lake, as well as to spot wildlife.

Uncovering the history of the valley at the numerous historic sites and museums is another activity that many travelers enjoy. The museums and monuments are preserved and displayed by each of the Byway communities as they tell visitors the story of the valley. Historic homes and districts reveal opportunities for touring and shopping. Browsing the many unique gift and specialty shops and attending festivals and special events in the small towns along the Byway should not be missed.

SCENIC

The Minnesota River Valley Scenic Byway showcases a variety of scenic elements. The route brings travelers along the river and through prairies, farmland, cities, woodlands, and wetlands. Vistas from high upon the bluffs of the river let your eyes wander over the landscape, just as bald eagles, which are so commonly seen here, would do. Some roads along the river bottom bring you right up to the river, where your senses enjoy the sights, sounds, and smells of the river valley. Along the way, you'll find magnificent farmsteads of today and yesterday, bustling communities, tremendous historical sites, wildlife, and some of the most unspoiled prairie in the Midwest—all of which entice you to stop and enjoy them.

North Shore Scenic Drive

MINNESOTA An All-American Road

The North Shore of Lake Superior, the world's largest freshwater lake, is 154 miles of scenic beauty and natural wonders. It has what no other place in the Midwest can offer—an inland sea, a mountain backdrop, an unspoiled wilderness, and a unique feeling all its own.

QUICK FACTS

Length: 154 miles.

Time to Allow: 1 day.

Best Time to Drive: Late spring through late fall.

Byway Travel Information: Minnesota Office of Tourism: phone 612/296-5027; Grand Portage Traveler Information Center: phone 218/475-2592; Byway local Web site: www.superiorbyways.org; Byway travel and tourism Web sites: www.northshorescenicdrive.com, www.lakecnty.com.

Special Considerations: The weather along the shore can be quite cool at times, so a jacket is recommended even in summer. Each town along the Byway offers plenty of visitor services, including gasoline and lodging.

Restrictions: The North Shore Scenic Drive can be traveled year-round. At times in winter, snowfall is heavy. However, because homes and businesses exist along the route, the plowing of this road is a priority.

Bicycle/Pedestrian Facilities: The North Shore Scenic Drive has sidewalks and 6- or 8-foot shoulders in places along the route that provide safe biking and pedestrian opportunities. Most pedestrian traffic concentrates around the various state parks. Trails and pedestrian warning signs and crossings are in place. Be aware that this route is a major transport route to and from the Canadian border, so large semi trucks and other similar vehicles are frequently seen along the Byway.

The North Shore Scenic Drive runs from Duluth to the Canadian border. The drive along the lakeshore is rich with the history of Native Americans, French and British explorers, lumbering, and iron-ore mining. On one side of the highway, Superior National Forest, one of the great wilderness areas of the United States, carpets the hills of the Sawtooth Mountains with balsams, birch, and pine. On the other side, Lake Superior offers spectacular views from the rocky shore. Each of the eight state parks has beautiful trails, and the 200-mile Superior Hiking Trail provides the chance to experience this magnificent landscape firsthand. For those who want to get out on the lake, there are charter fishing, sailing, kayaking, and excursion boats.

The North Shore also has a rich history deeply rooted in its plentiful natural resources. The Grand Portage National Monument features a reconstructed NorthWest Company fur-trading post. Grand Marais is a quaint harbor town that is the entrance to the Gunflint Trail, a paved trail leading inland to the Boundary Waters Canoe Area Wilderness. Giant ore boats pull up to the docks at Two Harbors, and the much smaller, 100-year-old tugboat the *Edna G.* is displayed here. Small museums in Two Harbors and Tofte, as well as interpretive programs at the state parks, tell the story of this area. Whether you are looking for a wilderness expedition or the comforts of a modern lodge, the lofty pines of the Superior National Forest and crashing waves of Lake Superior seem to have a magic that whispers, "Come back."

The Byway Story

The North Shore Scenic Drive tells historical, natural, recreational, and scenic stories that make it a unique and treasured Byway.

HISTORICAL

The North Shore Scenic Drive includes the rich and colorful heritage of settlers who were attracted to the area's bounty of natural resources. Many examples of this heritage can be found along the route, from the Voyageur era at Grand Portage National Monument to more recent times at the Split Rock Lighthouse State Historic Monument or the Edna G. Steam Tug Boat National Monument in Two Harbors. A host of interpretive resources and festivals keep this heritage alive, allowing you to experience the story of the North Shore's legacy.

It is believed that the first people to settle the North Shore region arrived about 10,000 years ago. These Native Americans entered the region during the final retreat of the Wisconsin glaciation. Many waves of Native American people inhabited the North Shore prior to European contact.

The first Europeans, French explorers, and fur traders reached Lake Superior country around AD 1620. By 1780, the Europeans had established fur-trading posts at the mouth of the St. Louis River and at Grand Portage. During the fur-trading days, Grand Portage became an important gateway into the interior of North America for exploration, trade, and commerce. The trading post came alive for a short time each summer during a celebration called the Rendezvous, when voyageurs and traders from the western trading posts met their counterparts from Montreal to exchange furs and trade goods. Grand Portage is now a national monument and an Indian reservation. At this national monument, some of the original structures of the fur-trading days have been reconstructed.

In 1854, the Ojibwe signed the Treaty of La Pointe, which opened up northeastern Minnesota for mineral exploration and settlement. The late 1800s saw a rise in commercial fishing along the North Shore. Some of the small towns along the North Shore, such as Grand Marais and Little Marais, were first settled during this period. Many of the small towns still have fish smokehouses, thus keeping the fishing heritage alive. The North Shore Commercial Fishing Museum in Tofte interprets this period.

Lumber barons moved into the region between 1890 and 1910, and millions of feet of red and white pine were cut from the hills along the North Shore. Temporary railroads transported the logs to the shore, where they were shipped to sawmills in Duluth, Minnesota, and Superior, Bayfield, and Ashland, Wisconsin. Today, many of those old railroad grades are still visible, and some of the trails still follow these grades.

Miners digging for high-grade ore from the Iron Ranges in northeastern Minnesota established shipping ports like Two Harbors in 1884. With the rise of taconite in the 1950s, they developed shipping ports at Silver Bay and Taconite Harbors along Superior's shores. These harbors are still in use, and visitors driving the route may see large 1,000-foot-long ore carriers being loaded or resting close to shore. The shipping history and Lake Superior's unpredictable storms have left the lake bottom dotted with shipwrecks, which now provide popular scuba diving destinations.

With the completion of the North Shore highway in 1924, tourism became an important industry along the shore. However, even earlier (in the 1910s), Historic Split Rock Lighthouse attracted tourists who arrived by sailboat. Split Rock Lighthouse is still the best-known North Shore landmark. Visitors who explore the North Shore today will come to know not only this landmark, but also many others that point to past times in this area of Minnesota.

NATURAL

The North Shore Scenic Drive allows you to experience a number of unique natural and geological features. The Byway follows the shoreline of the world's largest freshwater lake, Lake Superior, which contains 10 percent of the world's freshwater supply. This Byway is a marvelous road to travel, never running too far from the lakeside and at times opening out onto splendid views down the bluffs and over the blue water. This allows visitors a chance to experience a landscape that has seen little alteration from its original state. During the winter, the many parks and hundreds of miles of groomed trails draw outdoor enthusiasts for cross-country skiing, snowshoeing, and snowmobiling. Lutsen Mountain is the largest and highest downhill ski area in the Midwest.

The North Shore's spectacular topography originated a billion years ago, when molten basalt erupted from the mid-continental rift. The Sawtooth Mountains,

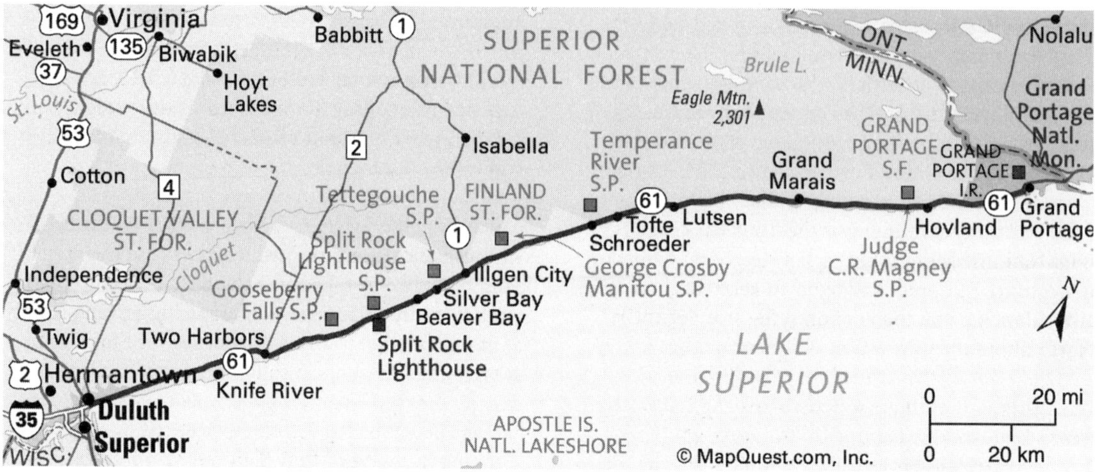

which frame the North Shore, are remnants of ancient volcanoes. The glaciers that descended from Canada 25,000 years ago scoured the volcanic rock into its current configuration. Cascading rivers coming down from the highlands into Lake Superior continue to reshape the landscape today. Northeastern Minnesota is the only part of the United States where the expansive northern boreal forests dip into the lower 48 states. The Lake Superior Highlands have been identified to be of great importance for biodiversity protection by the Minnesota Natural Heritage Program and the Nature Conservancy. This landscape contains significant tracts of old-growth northern hardwood and upland northern white cedar forest.

The natural environment along the corridor supports a number of wildlife species. Wildlife that may be observed from the road or at the state parks adjacent to the road include beaver, otter, timberwolf, white-tailed deer, coyote, red fox, black bear, and moose. Federally listed threatened species of bald eagle, gray wolf, and peregrine falcon also have populations here. Northeastern Minnesota is recognized as one of the better areas in the nation for viewing rare birds. Diversity of habitat, geography, and proximity to Lake Superior combine to attract a variety of bird life that draws bird-watchers from around the world. In the fall, hawks migrating along the shore of Lake Superior number in the tens of thousands. Winter is an excellent time to see northern owls, woodpeckers, finches, and unusual water birds.

Besides the state parks, a number of scientific and natural areas have been set aside along the route. These sites were selected because they contain excellent examples of the area's geologic history or harbor unique plant communities. Due to the unique geography of the landscape and climate changes during the ice ages, remnant species of arctic plants can be found along the shore. Examples of rare alpine plants that can also be found along the shore include butterwort, northern eyebright, alpine bistort, small false asphodel, and moonwort.

RECREATIONAL

Imagine yourself nestled next to a fireplace in the lodge after a long day of skiing or drying out next to a campfire from an afternoon of kayaking on a Minnesota river. The North Shore is one of the primary destinations for recreational activities in the Midwest, as well as recreational driving. It also features areas with well-developed facilities for outdoor activities that include camping, hiking, biking, skiing, snowmobiling, fishing, canoeing, and other water-related activities. The impressive scenery and natural beauty of the North Shore has been an attraction for tourists since the completion of Highway 61 in the early part of this century. The North Shore is dotted with innumerable points of interest, giving visitors a reason to come back again and again. The businesses along the corridor are set up to easily accommodate travelers from short weekend trips to multiple-week family vacations. They work together as partners to make this a quality recreational experience.

The North Shore Scenic Drive is home to one of the greatest trail systems in the nation. The Superior Hiking Trail stretches 200 miles from Two Harbors to the Canadian border, connecting the eight state parks and giving travelers an opportunity to enjoy the natural beauty and vistas from the highlands and the cliffs. The trail system is well signed and offers unlimited opportunities ranging from day hikes to multiple-week treks through a rugged wilderness setting. The trail is designated as a National Recreation Trail by the US Forest Service. A shuttle service offers transportation between trail heads. The Lake Superior Water Trail allows visitors to travel the coastline of Lake Superior by kayak. The trail uses public land for designated rest areas and will eventually be part of the Lake Superior Water Trail encircling all of Lake Superior. The Gitchi-Gami Trail is planned to accommodate bicyclists, pedestrians, and in-line skaters following the right of way of the North Shore Scenic Drive.

And when you're ready for a break from outdoor excitement, try touring some of the classic historical sites in the area. The Minnesota Historical Society takes care of the Split Rock Lighthouse site and provides interpretive programs. The Lake County Historical Museum, which is housed in the old Duluth & Iron Range Railway Depot, contains excellent exhibits on the region's history. In Two Harbors, you can tour an operating lighthouse and the *Edna G.*, which was the last steam tug to work the Great Lakes. So pack up your sled or your river raft and try them out in northeastern Minnesota, and be sure to bring your camera, because there are memorable sights to be seen!

SCENIC

One of the main draws of the North Shore is its reputation as one of the most scenic drives in the United States. The route offers splendid vistas of Lake Superior and its rugged shoreline, as well as views of the expansive North Woods. The road crosses gorges carved out by cascading rivers, offering views of waterfalls and adding diversity to the landscape. The attraction of the falls at Gooseberry State Park makes this the most visited state park in Minnesota. Different seasons and changes in weather continually alter the landscape's appearance, keeping the route fresh and interesting. During the fall, the corridor displays bright-red sugar maples and warm gold birch and aspens. The vibrant colors attract many day and weekend travelers to the North Shore. After the leaves have fallen and the ground is snow covered, new views of the lake open up with opportunities to spy wildlife like deer, moose, and wolf that use the frozen lakeshore as a way to travel. Spring ice break-up offers another fascinating scene as glimmering mountains of ice are driven up the shore. In summer, the lake, with an average water temperature of 40 degrees, offers a welcome breeze to cool down the summer heat.

A few charming towns dot the shoreline. Most started out as small fishing and harbor towns, shipping ore and timber. These towns still have a distinct sense of connection with the lake. For many travelers, the quaint town of Grand Marais is as far as they will go; however, the scenery becomes even more spectacular as you continue driving north toward the Canadian border. For long stretches, there is nothing alongside the road but trees, cliffs, beaches, and the whitecap-crested lake. The Byway ends at Grand Portage. Here, a national monument marks the beginning of a historic 9-mile portage trod by Indians and Voyageurs. A few miles farther at Grand Portage State Park, you can view the High Falls. At 120 feet, these are the highest waterfalls in Minnesota. The falls' magnificence is a fitting end to a trip up the North Shore.

Highlights

The North Shore Scenic Drive is comprised of the northern 150 miles of Minnesota Trunk Highway 61, from Duluth to Two Harbors all the way to Grand Portage near the US/Canadian border.

- Begin your experience on the North Shore Scenic Drive in **Canal Park** in Duluth. Follow Canal Park Drive over Interstate 35 to Superior Street.

- Take a right on Superior Street and follow this road through a portion of historic **downtown Duluth** and past the refurbished **Fitger's Brewery Complex,** with its many fine shops and restaurants.

- To continue along the Byway, take a right onto London Road. This intersection is at 10th Avenue East and Superior Street. Follow London Road for the next 5.4 miles, driving past **Leif Erikson Park,** which contains the **Rose Garden,** a popular attraction for visitors.

- To continue on the route, follow the signs for the North Shore Scenic Drive. The route proceeds along the lake, passing through small settlements and stunning lake vistas. There are no less than six rivers that cross under the Byway during this 19-mile segment to Two Harbors.

- Connect with the Byway loop in downtown **Two Harbors** by turning right onto Highway 61 just west of town. Follow Highway 61 to 6th Street (Waterfront Drive), where you take a right and pick up the Byway once again.

- Follow 6th Street to South Avenue, where you take a left. Prior to taking a left, be sure to stop at the **3M Museum.** As you drive down South Avenue, you can begin to see the massive ore docks that extend from the waterfront.

- Continue on the route by taking a left onto First Street (Park Road) and following it to Highway 61. First Street takes you past hiking trails that line the shoreline and the peaceful setting of **Burlington Bay,** the second of the two harbors that gives the community its name.

- Taking a right on Highway 61 and continuing on that route will lead you along the remainder of the North Shore Scenic Drive, which ends approximately 122 miles later at the Canadian border.

The Great River Road

WISCONSIN

Part of a multistate Byway; see also MN.

Wisconsin's Great River Road flanks the majestic and magnificent Mississippi River as it leisurely winds its way along 250 miles of Wisconsin's western border. Along the way, the road is nestled between the river on one side and towering bluffs on the other, becoming one of the most scenic drives in mid-America. Most of the time, the road parallels the river, but when the road does meander a short way from the river, it treats its guests to vistas of rolling farmland, as well as beautiful forested valleys and coulees.

The 33 quaint river towns along this Byway proudly reveal their culture and heritage through their festivals and the 19th- and 20th-century architecture of their homes, business blocks, storefronts, mansions, and more. The corridor is rich in history, and Great River Road travelers can learn about the early Native American occupants, the French fur traders and explorers, the lead mining boom, the steamboat era, and the lumber barons. Travelers can stop at the 30 or more state historical markers and archaeological sites and at the many local museums.

Recreational opportunities await you around each bend of the Great River Road at more than 50 local parks and beaches, in addition to 12 state and three national recreational resources. Observation decks at four lock and dams provide the opportunity to watch the barges and riverboats pass through. You may even see steamboats like the *Delta Queen* cruise by.

Quick Facts

Length: 249 miles.

Time to Allow: 10 hours.

Best Time to Drive: The Great River Road is a delight to drive in any season. High season is summer.

Byway Travel Information: La Crosse Area Convention and Visitor Bureau: phone toll-free 800/658-9480; Byway local Web site: www.wigreatriverroad.org.

Special Considerations: Fuel stations and food services are available in the 33 river towns along the Byway. These towns are found on average about every 10 miles.

Restrictions: No seasonal road closures are anticipated.

Bicycle/Pedestrian Facilities: Nearly 217 miles of the Wisconsin Great River Road make up the on-road portion of the bikeway. This portion has been rated as acceptable for accommodating cyclists.

Travel the Wisconsin Great River Road. It is a marvelous mix of natural beauty and history and is an area to be enjoyed by all ages—leisurely. In the new-green brilliance of spring or the white mantle of winter, in the summer sunlight or the amber hues of autumn, Wisconsin's Great River Road is a delight in any season.

The Byway Story

The Great River Road tells archaeological, cultural, historical, natural, recreational, and scenic stories that make it a unique and treasured Byway.

ARCHAEOLOGICAL

Based on many archaeological studies, it is estimated that Wisconsin was inhabited by people nearly 12,000 years ago, who hunted prehistoric animals like mammoths and mastodons. The primitive cultures of the Wisconsin Great River Road developed and evolved to leave behind many artifacts and monuments to the past—not the least of which were the great mounds of grand designs and animal shapes. Today, Wisconsin archaeologists research these ancient cultures, as well as the not-so-ancient cultures of the first explorers and traders who came to settle along the Wisconsin Great River Road.

The Wisconsin Great River Road runs through an area called the Driftless Area because it was not covered by glaciers during the last ice age. Because of this, many exposed rocks gave ancient inhabitants of the area an opportunity to create rock art that is still being discovered today. In caves and outcroppings, petroglyphs and pictographs have been found as displays of a way of life long forgotten. Designs of animals and people are left behind in the rocks for archaeologists to study.

Archaeological displays can be found in many local museums. You can view mound groups and village sites at Wyalusing State Park, Diamond Bluff, La Crosse, Prairie du Chien, along Lake Pepin, and at Trempealeau in Perrot State Park. In the city of La Crosse, archaeological enthusiasts can view displays at the Riverside Museum that catalog the earliest times in Wisconsin to the present. The Archaeology Center of the University of Wisconsin-La Crosse offers a closer look at artifacts from recent investigations, as well as detailed information about archaeology in Wisconsin. As the headquarters for the Mississippi Valley Archaeology Center, the University of Wisconsin-La Crosse Archaeology Center offers you an opportunity to view displays explaining techniques and prehistory.

Archaeological resources are plentiful along the entire length of the Wisconsin Great River Road corridor. There are 33 archaeological sites that are currently listed in the National Register of Historic Places. Excavations in the corridor have revealed pottery, ceramics, arrowheads, and tools, while burial mounds are prevalent throughout the corridor, ranging from individual sites to large groups. In Onalaska, an entire prehistoric village was uncovered, revealing structures and artifacts that indicated the lifestyle of the earliest inhabitants of the area. At Prairie du Chien, archaeologists have uncovered an American military garrison that was established in 1829. Visiting Trempealeau and Perrot State Park, you'll find remaining ancient mounds in the shapes of animals. With so many sites like these along the Wisconsin Great River Road, travelers develop a sense of respect for those who have come before to the mighty Mississippi.

CULTURAL

The varied past and present cultures of the corridor are recorded and revealed in the 33 river towns, the many state historical markers, and the archaeological sites found along the Byway. The residents of the corridor take pride in preserving their heritage, as evidenced by the many festivals. Some of these festivals include La Crosse's Riverfest and Octoberfest, Villa Louis's Carriage Classic, Prairie du Chien's Fur Trade Rendezvous, Alma's Mark Twain Days, and Pepin's Laura Ingalls Wilder Days. Travelers lucky enough to encounter one of these festivals get a taste of the true flavor of Wisconsin's Great River Road.

Well-maintained early architecture of homes and storefronts is evident throughout the corridor as well. Architecture from the 19th and 20th centuries is scattered throughout the towns and cities of the Byway; many of them reflect the varied architectural trends of the early days of settlement. Greek Revival, Italianate, and Queen Anne are just some of the styles you'll notice as you drive the Byway. As you watch for unique architecture, you will also want to notice the mail-order houses that were constructed in a matter of days after arriving by train. Today, unique buildings and art forms continue to surface on the Great River Road. At Prairie Moon Sculpture Garden, for example, a unique form of art typical to the Midwest is displayed.

HISTORICAL

Indians were the first people to live in this region, as evidenced by artifacts from archaeological sites and the presence of burial mounds—many of which survive today. European explorers and missionaries arrived in 1673. This area was first claimed by the French, and then later by the British. The United States gained control of the Northwest Territory in 1794, but many British traders maintained their lucrative posts until after the War of 1812. You can stop and ponder this area's history at the 30-plus historical markers found along the Byway, such as Fort Antoine, the Battle of Bad Ax, and the War of 1812. You also learn more at the Fur Trade Museum and Villa Louis in Prairie du Chien.

If you're a history hunter driving the Byway, you may notice evidence of a culture very different from America's present culture. Thousands of mounds can be found throughout the area that display the culture of the Hopewell Indians who once lived here. The culture of this people evolved over the years, and they began to establish large, permanent villages. Known as the Oneota people, they were able to farm the river valley using hoes made from bison shoulder blades.

The way of life these people developed can be seen in the many museums along the road that display tools and artwork of past cultures. By the time the first Europeans arrived, this culture had disappeared, replaced by a group of Sioux.

French missionary Jacques Marquette and explorer Louis Jolliet were the first Europeans to come through the area. They were searching for a waterway that would connect the Atlantic Ocean and the Gulf of Mexico. Later, French forts were established, and commerce and trade between the European and native cultures ensued. The area changed hands from the Indians to the French to the British and finally to the Americans, but not without struggle. From the beginning, Native Americans fought to retain their ancestral lands, but to no avail. Settlement began in Wisconsin soon after the Black Hawk War between the Sauk Indians and American troops. In 1848, Wisconsin became a state.

Wisconsin thrived as a state for lumbering and sawmills. Because the Mississippi flows alongside it, Wisconsin was in a good position for the steamboat industry to develop. Steamboat races and wrecks were as legendary then as they are today. Remnants of the new Mississippi culture can be seen along the Great River Road: abandoned quarries and old building ruins are just some of the things you may spot that remind you of an earlier day. Although the cities and communities have grown and changed, Mississippi River heritage remains.

NATURAL

Many natural wonders are found along this Byway. For example, the Mississippi River/Wisconsin Great River Road corridor incorporates four national features: the Upper Mississippi River National Wildlife and Fish Refuge, the Trempealeau National Wildlife Refuge, the Genoa National Fish Hatchery, and the St. Croix River National Scenic River. There are also 12 state-recognized natural areas featuring state parks and wildlife areas, as well as 17 state-designated scientific areas located along the corridor.

RECREATIONAL

Every season offers spectacular recreational opportunities on the Upper Mississippi River along the Wisconsin Great River Road. The upper Mississippi River provides excellent boating and sailing, and there are over 50 local parks, beaches, recreational areas, and water access sites along the route. On Lake Pepin, a huge lake in the Mississippi River, boaters have access to numerous boat landings, marinas, and docking. Fishing is a favorite activity because of the variety of fish species, ranging from catfish to walleye. The sandbars along the river provide places for public camping, picnicking, or just getting off the road.

Bird-watchers enjoy seeing bald eagles as the magnificent birds catch their dinners. Berry-picking and mushroom-hunting are also popular activities, and many travelers choose to experience a farm vacation by milking a cow. Shopping and antique hunting in quaint river towns may be of interest to shoppers, while golfers will find enticing, scenic golf courses.

The Wisconsin Great River Road provides safe accommodations for bikers—with alternate choices of separate bike trails and local roads or streets. Depending on the cyclist's preference and skills, the rider has a choice of touring the Great River Road on-road or off-road. Canoe and bike rentals are available so that every visitor may enjoy these forms of recreation.

Winter in Wisconsin provides ice fishing and wind sailing on the river. Many travelers prefer cross-country or downhill skiing, snowshoeing, and snowmobiling through deep valleys and scenic bluffs. Summertime is excellent for dinner cruises on the river, or you can rent a houseboat and explore on your own. The river valley features hiking and biking trails, picnic areas, and camping opportunities in the numerous parks and campgrounds located along the Byway.

SCENIC

Wisconsin's Great River Road meanders through the Mississippi River corridor. This corridor forms the southern half of the state's western border. The corridor's dramatic landscape was created by the melting ice age glaciers, which carved the magnificent river valley.

Many segments of the Wisconsin Great River Road parallel the Mississippi River, some of which gracefully snuggle between the bluffs and the river. You're afforded numerous vistas of the mighty Mississippi and its valley and vast backwaters. You are also accommodated by 20-plus waysides, scenic overlooks, and pull-out areas. Travel the Great River Road during all four seasons to experience its different year-round splendors.

Highlights

The following is an itinerary for the Victory to Bridgeport section—which is only one portion—of Wisconsin's Great River Road.

- You begin your tour in **Victory.** This small settlement along the Great River Road has a picturesque setting: snuggled next to the river on one side, with bluffs acting as a backdrop on the other. Five settlers laid out this village in 1852 and named it Victory to commemorate the final battle of the Black Hawk War fought south of the village 20 years earlier. Victory prospered during the wheat boom of the 1850s, but today, it is only a remnant of its past.

- The village of **De Soto** is 4 miles south of Victory. This river town has the distinction of being named after the famous Spanish explorer Fernando de Soto, the first European to see the Mississippi River. It was platted in 1854 on the site of a small outpost of the American Fur Company. Today, this community is a shadow of its past, when it peaked with sawmills, grain dealers, blacksmiths, dressmakers, breweries, and hotels. Learn from the locals how the wing dams constructed in the Mississippi diverted the river closer to their community.

- Eight miles south of De Soto lies **Ferryville.** This little river town clings to the bluffs along the river and is the longest one-street village in the world. It was first called Humble Bush but was renamed Ferryville when platted in 1858. The name reflects the founder's intentions to establish ferry service across the Mississippi to Iowa. In 1878, after being devastated by a tornado, it was written that "today a passerby can see no evidence of a village . . ." Ferryville still clings to the bluffs and portrays a true river town experience to its visitors.

- Your next stop, **Lynxville,** is 8 miles past Ferryville. Because of the stable depth of the river at Lynxville, it was a reliable and popular landing during the steamboat era of the mid- to late 1800s. Although the steamboats are gone, this quaint little river town remains as the host community to Lock and Dam 9.

- With about 6,000 residents, **Prairie du Chien** is the largest town on your tour. Stop at the Wisconsin Tourist Information Center to find out about the many area attractions of this second-oldest settlement in Wisconsin. It became a trade center as early as the 1670s with the arrival of Marquette and Jolliet. Hercules Dousman built **Villa Louis,** now owned and operated by the State Historical Society, an opulent 1870s estate with one of the nation's finest collections of Victorian decorative arts. The Villa Louis Historical Marker at this site provides an overview of the origin and history of this luxurious mansion. Medical history from the 1800s and an exhibit of medical quackery is displayed at the **Fort Crawford Medical Museum.** Some warehouses built in the early 19th century by the American Fur Company still survive on historic St. Feriole Island, as do remnants of the old American Fort built to protect this outpost. Tour the town in a horse and carriage or view the Mississippi aboard an excursion boat.

- Driving 7 miles southeast of Prairie du Chien, you arrive in **Bridgeport.** The name of this village is most fitting. In the late 1800s, a ferry carried grain and other farm products across the Mississippi River to a railroad in Minnesota. Today, Bridgeport is near the highway bridge crossing the Wisconsin National Scenic River and the gateway to Wyalusing State Park and Sentinel Ridge, where the Woodland Indians left behind hundreds of earthen mounds.

Michigan

Michigan has a mighty industrial heritage and is well known as the birthplace of the automobile industry, but rivaling the machines, mines, and mills is the nearly $13 billion-a-year tourist industry. The two great Michigan peninsulas, surrounded by four of the five Great Lakes, unfold a tapestry of lakeshore beaches, trout-filled streams, more than 11,000 inland lakes, nearly 7 million acres of public hunting grounds—and the cultural attractions of Detroit, Ann Arbor, Grand Rapids, Interlochen, and other cities.

Population: 9,295,297
Area: 56,954 square miles
Elevation: 570-1,980 feet
Peak: Mount Arvon (Baraga County, Upper Peninsula)
Entered Union: January 26, 1837 (26th state)
Capital: Lansing
Motto: If You Seek a Pleasant Peninsula, Look Around You
Nickname: Wolverine State
Flower: Apple Blossom
Bird: Robin
Tree: White Pine
Fair: Late August-early September in Detroit
Time Zone: Eastern and Central (Menominee, Dickinson, Iron, and Gogebic counties)
Web Site: www.michigan.org
Fun Facts:

- Forty of the state's 83 counties adjoin at least one of the Great Lakes. Michigan is the only state that touches four of the five Great Lakes.
- Michigan was the first state to guarantee every child the right to a tax-paid high school education.

Michigan has a geographically split personality linked by a single—but magnificent—5-mile-long bridge. The Upper Peninsula faces Lake Superior on one side and Lake Michigan on the other. It revels in its north-country beauty and ruggedness. The Lower Peninsula has shores on Lakes Michigan, Huron, and Erie. Its highly productive Midwestern-style farmland is dotted with diversified cities. In total, Michigan has more shoreline than any of the other lower-48 states.

Michigan is a four-season vacationland, with the tempering winds off the Great Lakes taming what might otherwise be a climate of extremes. In a land of cherry blossoms, tulips, ski slopes, and sugar-sand beaches, you can fish through the ice, hunt deer with a bow and arrow, snowmobile on hundreds of miles of marked trails, follow the trail of a bobcat, rough it on an uncluttered island, trace Native American paths, or hunt for copper, iron ore, and Lake Superior agates or Petoskey stones. One of the country's finest art museums is in Detroit, and Dearborn's The Henry Ford (formerly Henry Ford Museum and Greenfield Village) attracts visitors from all over the world. Shopping and casino gambling are popular attractions, and Michigan has an increasing array of challenging resort golf courses as well as more than 750 public courses, more than any other state. Ann Arbor, East Lansing, and Houghton offer outstanding universities that host exciting football, basketball, and hockey contests.

A world center for automobile manufacture, Michigan leads in the production of automobiles and light trucks. More than two-thirds of the nation's tart red cherries are harvested here; Traverse City hosts the National Cherry Festival each July. This state is also one of the nation's leading producers of blueberries and dry, edible beans. Wheat, hay, corn, oats, turkeys, cattle, and hogs are produced in vast quantities. The Soo Locks at Sault Ste. Marie

Calendar Highlights

January

Ice Sculpture Spectacular *(Plymouth). Kellogg Park. Phone 734/453-1540.* Hundreds of ice sculptures line the streets and fill Kellogg Park as professional and student chefs compete with each other carving huge blocks of ice. Sculptures are lighted at night.

May

Tulip Time Festival *(Holland). Phone 616/396-4221 or toll-free 800/822-2770. www.tuliptimes.org.* A celebration of Dutch heritage: 1,800 klompen dancers, three parades, street scrubbing, Dutch markets, entertainment, and millions of tulips.

June

Bavarian Festival *(Frankenmuth). Heritage Park. Phone 989/652-8155 or toll-free 800/228-2742.* www.bavarianfestival.com. Celebration of German heritage. Music, dancing, parades, and other entertainment; food; art demonstrations and agricultural displays.

Cereal City Festival *(Battle Creek). On Michigan Ave. Phone toll-free 800/970-7020.* Children's parade, Queen's Pageant, arts and crafts exhibits; also the world's longest breakfast table.

International Freedom Festival *(Detroit and Windsor, ON). Phone 313/923-7400.* Joint celebration with Detroit and Windsor; nearly 100 events, including fireworks.

July

National Cherry Festival *(Traverse City). Phone 231/947-1120. www.cherryfestival.org.* More than 150 activities, including pageants, parades, concerts, road race, fireworks, air show, Native American powwow and crafts, children's contests.

Sailing Races *(Mackinac Island). Phone 810/985-7101 for Port Huron race; 312/861-7777 for Chicago race.* Port Huron to Mackinac and Chicago to Mackinac.

Street Art Fairs *(Ann Arbor). Contact the Convention and Visitors Bureau, phone 734/994-5260 or toll-free 800/888-9487.* Nearly 1,000 artists and craftspeople display and sell works.

August

Michigan State Fair *(Detroit). Michigan Exposition and Fairgrounds. Phone 313/369-8250.*

Upper Peninsula State Fair. *(Escanaba). Upper Peninsula State Fairgrounds. Phone toll-free 888/335-8264.*

September

Historic Home Tour *(Marshall). Phone 616/781-5163 or toll-free 800/877-5163.* Informal tours of 19th-century homes, including Honolulu House, Governor's Mansion, and Capitol Hill School.

Mackinac Bridge Walk (*Mackinaw City and St. Ignace). Phone 231/436-5574, 517/347-7891 or toll-free 800/666-0160.* Approximately 70,000 participants take a recreational walk across Mackinac Bridge (some lanes open to motor vehicles).

December

Dickens Christmas *(Holly). Phone 248/634-1900.* Re-creates the Dickensian period with carolers, town crier, strolling characters, skits, bell choirs, street hawkers, carriage rides. Thanksgiving weekend through the weekend before Dec 25.

boast the two longest locks in the world, which can accommodate superfreighters 1,000 feet long.

French missionaries and explorers, namely Marquette and Joliet, were the first known Europeans to penetrate the lakes, rivers, and streams of Michigan. In their wake came armies of trappers eager to barter with the natives and platoons of soldiers to guard the newly acquired territory. Frenchmen and Native Americans teamed to unsuccessfully fight the British when Ottawa chief Pontiac banded together with other tribes in a bold attempt to overtake Fort Detroit, Fort Michilimackinac, and ten other British forts. The British, in turn, were forced to retreat into Canada after the American colonies successfully revolted. The British briefly forged into Michigan again during the War of 1812, retreating finally to become Michigan's good neighbors in Canada.

There has been a wavelike pattern to Michigan's economic development. First there were the trees that created a great lumber industry. These were rapidly depleted. The copper and iron-ore mines followed. They also are now mostly inactive, although the discovery of new copper deposits is leading to renewed activity. Finally, the automobile industry, diversified industries, and tourism have become successful. Today, the St. Lawrence Seaway makes the Michigan international port cities and the state's future a prosperous one.

When to Go/Climate

Long, hard winters and cool summers are common both in Michigan's Upper Peninsula and in the northern Lower Peninsula. In the southern Lower Peninsula, winters are more moderate and summers are warm. Brilliant fall foliage spreads southward from the Upper Peninsula beginning in September.

AVERAGE HIGH/LOW TEMPERATURES (° F)

Detroit

Jan 30/16	**May** 70/47	**Sept** 74/63
Feb 33/18	**June** 79/56	**Oct** 62/41
Mar 44/27	**July** 83/61	**Nov** 48/32
Apr 58/37	**Aug** 81/60	**Dec** 35/21

Houghton

Jan 22/8	**May** 62/41	**Sept** 63/46
Feb 25/9	**June** 71/49	**Oct** 52/36
Mar 34/18	**July** 76/55	**Nov** 37/25
Apr 47/30	**Aug** 74/55	**Dec** 26/14

Traverse City

Jan 27/14	**May** 67/42	**Sept** 70/50
Feb 30/14	**June** 77/52	**Oct** 58/40
Mar 40/22	**July** 81/58	**Nov** 44/31
Apr 53/32	**Aug** 79/57	**Dec** 32/21

Parks and Recreation

Water-related activities, hiking, horseback riding, various other sports, picnicking, and visitor centers, as well as camping, are available in many of Michigan's parks. Motor vehicle permits are required to enter parks: $4 per day (excluding Warren Dunes, $5 per day for nonresidents); annual sticker: $20. From May through September, about 80 percent of the campsites in each park are available by reservations for stays of 1-15 nights. The fee is $9-$23 per night. Pets on leash only. For reservations, phone toll-free 800/447-2757. For reservations, applications, and further information about state parks, contact the Department of Natural Resources, Parks and Recreation Division, PO Box 30257, Lansing 48909-7757; phone 517/373-9900. For information on state forests, contact the Department of Natural Resources, Forest Management Division, PO Box 30452, Lansing 48909; phone 517/373-1275.

FISHING AND HUNTING

In the 1960s, coho and chinook salmon were transplanted from the Pacific Northwest into the streams feeding into Lake Michigan and subsequently into Lakes Huron and Superior. The success of the program was immediate and today salmon fishing, especially for chinook, is a major sport. Chinook fishing is good throughout the summer in the Great Lakes and through the early fall during the spawning season in the rivers; the fish may weigh as much as 45 pounds. Information on charter boat fishing can be obtained from Travel Michigan, PO Box 3393, Livonia 48151; phone toll-free 888/784-7328; or visit the Web site at www.travel.michigan.org.

Nonresident restricted fishing licenses: annual $34; all-species fishing including spike, salmon, and brook and brown, rainbow, and lake trout: $42. A fishing license for all waters is required for everyone 17 years of age and older. Resident and nonresident 24-hour fishing license: $7.

Small game, deer, elk, and bear hunting are tremendously popular in Michigan, especially in the northern Lower Peninsula and the Upper Peninsula. In fact, the state's largest tourist attraction is the massive Cabela's hunting and fishing store in Dundee, where more than 6 million visitors shop each year for camouflage clothing, guns and ammunition, and beef jerky.

Nonresident season-long hunting licenses: small game $69; deer $138; bear $150; archery (deer only) $129. Three-day licenses are also available for some species. For further information about hunting and fishing, write to the Department of Natural Resources, Retail Sales Section, PO Box 30181, Lansing 48909; phone 517/373-1204.

Driving Information

Safety belts are mandatory for all persons in the front seat of a vehicle. Children ages 4-16 must be in approved passenger restraints anywhere in a vehicle. Children ages 1-4 may use regulation safety belts in the back seat, but must use approved safety seats in the front seat of a vehicle. Children under age 1 must use approved safety seats anywhere in a vehicle. For additional information, call the Office of Highway Safety Planning at 517/336-6477.

INTERSTATE HIGHWAY SYSTEM

The following alphabetical listing of Michigan towns in this book shows the cities that are within 10 miles of the indicated interstate highways. Check a highway map for the nearest exit.

Highway Number	Cities/Towns within 10 Miles
Interstate 69	Coldwater, Flint, Lansing, Marshall, Owosso, Port Huron.
Interstate 75	Bay City, Birmingham, Bloomfield Hills, Cheboygan, Dearborn, Detroit, Flint, Frankenmuth, Gaylord, Grayling Holly, Mackinaw City, Monroe, Pontiac, Saginaw, Sault Ste. Marie, St. Ignace, Warren.
Interstate 94	Ann Arbor, Battle Creek, Dearborn, Detroit, Jackson, Kalamazoo, Marshall, Mount Clemens, Port Huron, St. Clair, St. Joseph, Warren, Ypsilanti.
Interstate 96	Detroit, Grand Haven, Grand Rapids, Lansing, Muskegon.

Additional Visitor Information

Travel Michigan, PO Box 30226, Lansing 48909; phone toll-free 888/784-7328; www.travel.michigan.org, distributes publications including an annual travel planner, seasonal travel guides and calendars of events, and directories of lodgings, campgrounds, golf courses, and charter boat and canoe companies. Travel counselors are available (daily) to assist in planning a Michigan getaway.

There are 13 Welcome Centers in Michigan, open daily; visitors who stop will find information, brochures, and an extensive database of lodging facilities and attractions helpful in planning stops at points of interest. Their locations are as follows: Clare, off Hwy 27; Coldwater, off I-69; Dundee, off Hwy 23; Iron Mountain, off Hwy 2; Ironwood, off Hwy 2; Mackinaw City, off I-75; Marquette, off Hwy 41; Menominee, off Hwy 41/35; Monroe, off I-75; New Buffalo, off I-94; Port Huron, off I-94; St. Ignace, off I-75; and Sault Ste. Marie, off I-75.

THE KEWEENAW PENINSULA

The drive up the Keweenaw (KEY-when-awh) Peninsula is Michigan's most popular road trip–and with good reason. This route offers everything you could ever want in a driving tour: awe-inspiring waterfalls, amazing coastal scenery, colorful history, sunny beaches, and picturesque towns. Surrounded on three sides by spectacular Lake Superior, the Keweenaw Peninsula also offers visitors the rare treat of watching the sun rise and set over the same body of water.

No visit to the Keweenaw, often referred to as "Copper Country," would be complete without exploring the history of its days as a copper mining boom town. Quincy Mine, located in the town of Hancock, offers guided copper mine tours, as well as a passenger cog rail tram. The nearby town of Houghton was runner-up in the Chicago Tribune's "Best Little Town in the Midwest" contest and is well worth a visit. Houghton also offers seasonal ferry service to Isle Royale National Park, the United States's most isolated national park and an amazing wilderness experience that outdoor enthusiasts won't want to miss. Advance reservations are required. Isle Royale can also be accessed by seaplane. Just 11 miles north of Hancock/Houghton is Calumet, an almost perfectly preserved mining town, replete with flagstone streets and entire districts of restored dwellings. Keweenaw National Historic Park, located here, features a self-guided walking tour commemorating the history of copper mining in the area. From Calumet, head north on Route 26 to Eagle River, pausing at Eagle River Falls for a look at the beautiful scenery and a photograph or two. Route 26 between Eagle Harbor and Copper Harbor is Brockway Mountain Drive, believed by some to be the most beautiful road in the state. This 9-mile drive is the highest above-sea-level road between the Rockies and Alleghenies–the views are superlative from this commanding height! Fall paints this route with an amazing palate of colors; spring brings the migration of hawks and eagles. Whatever the season, Brockway Mountain is an ideal place to watch the sunset over Lake Superior–the perfect end to a perfect day in the Keweenaw Peninsula.

If you have more than one day–and we hope you do because there is so much yet to see–spend a day exploring attractions in and around Copper Harbor. Take the 20-minute boat ride out to Copper Harbor Lighthouse for a guided tour of one of the oldest lighthouses on Lake Superior. Visit Delaware Mine for a copper mine tour that will take you 110 feet down a mine shaft. Stop at Estivant Pines, located a few miles south of Copper Harbor, to see some of the oldest trees in Michigan. Scuba dive at the Keweenaw Preserve to explore the eighteen shipwrecks submerged there (note: it is illegal to remove anything from the wrecks). Whatever you choose to see and do, you are sure to enjoy your time in the Keweenaw Peninsula! **(Approximately 45 miles)**

Alma (H-4)

See also Clare, Mount Pleasant

Population 9,034
Elevation 736 ft
Area Code 989
Zip 48801
Information Gratiot Area Chamber of Commerce, 110 W Superior St, PO Box 516; phone 989/463-5525
Web Site www.gratiot.org

Home of Alma College and the Michigan Masonic Home, Alma is a pleasant stopping point while driving Highway 127 north from Lansing.

What to See and Do

Alma College. *614 W Superior St, Alma (48801). Phone 989/463-7111. www.alma.edu.* (1886) (1,400 students) On 87-acre campus. Campus tours. Includes a 190,000-volume library. Frank Knox Memorial Room in Reid-Knox building has mementos of former secretary of the Navy (by appointment).

Special Event

Highland Festival & Games. *Bahlke Field at Alma College, 614 W Superior St # 1, Alma (48801). Phone 989/463-8979. www.almahighlandfestival.com.* Piping, drumming, fiddling, Ceilidh, dancing; caber toss, sheaf toss, hammer throw competitions; art fair, parade. Memorial Day weekend.

Limited-Service Hotel

★ ★ **COMFORT INN.** *3110 W Monroe Rd, Alma (48801). Phone 989/463-4400; toll-free 877/424-6423; fax 989/463-2970. www.comfortinn.com.* 87 rooms, 2 story. Complimentary continental breakfast. Check-in 3 pm, check-out 11 am. Restaurant, bar. Indoor pool, whirlpool. **$**

Alpena (E-5)

See also Oscoda

Population 11,354
Elevation 593 ft
Area Code 989
Zip 49707
Information Convention and Visitors Bureau, 235 W Chisholm St, PO Box 65; phone 989/354-4181 or toll-free 800/425-7362
Web Site www.oweb.com/upnorth/cvb/

The largest city in northeastern Michigan, Alpena (al-PEE-na) has more than 20 miles of shoreline along Thunder Bay, notorious for shipwrecks. Once a major commercial fishing and lumber center, Alpena is today a resort community where fishing is one of the main attractions, as is diving among the 88 shipwrecks in the bay. The town has retained its late-1800s feel, and restored mansions still stands among newer houses.

What to See and Do

Dinosaur Gardens Prehistorical Zoo. *11160 Hwy 23, Ossineke (49766). 10 miles S. Phone 989/471-5477.* Authentic reproductions of prehistoric birds and animals. (Mid-May-mid-Oct: daily 10 am-6 pm) **$$**

Island Park and Alpena Wildfowl Sanctuary. *Hwy 23 N and Long Rapids Rd, Alpena (49707).* Wildfowl sanctuary and self-guided nature trails, fishing platforms, and picnic area.

Jesse Besser Museum. *491 Johnson St, Alpena (49707). 2 blocks E off Hwy 23. Phone 989/356-2202. www.bessermuseum.org.* Historical exhibits feature agricultural, lumber, and early industrial era; reconstructed avenue of 1890 shops and businesses; restored cabins, Maltz Exchange Bank (1872), Green School (1895). Jesse Besser exhibit. Science exhibits include geology, natural history, and archaeology displays. Also planetarium, shows (Sun; fee). Museum (Tues-Sat 10 am-5 pm, Sun noon-4 pm; closed Mon; holidays). **$**

Old Presque Isle Lighthouse and Museum. *5295 Grand Lake Rd, Presque Isle (49777). 20 miles N via Hwy 23 at Presque Isle Harbor. Phone 989/595-2787.* Pronounced presk-EEL. Spiral staircase; nautical instruments, marine artifacts, and other antiques housed in lighthouse and keeper's cottage (1840). Antiques from mid-1800s. (May-mid-Oct, daily) **$**

Special Events

Alpena County Fair. *Alpena County Fairgrounds, 10118 Spruce Rd, Alpena (49766). Phone 989/356-1174.* First week in Aug.

Art on the Bay–Thunder Bay Art Show. *Bay View Park, 313 N 2nd Ave, Alpena (49707). Phone 989/356-6678.*

The original artwork at this show includes quilting, crafts, jewelry, pottery, sculpture, stained glass, and painting. Third weekend in July.

Brown Trout Festival. *235 W Chisholm St, Alpena (49707). Phone 989/354-4181; toll-free 800/425-7362. www.alpenami-browntrout.com.* Third full week in July.

Limited-Service Hotels

★ BEST WESTERN OF ALPENA. *1286 Hwy 32 W, Alpena (49707). Phone 989/356-9087; toll-free 800/780-7234; fax 989/354-0543. www.bestwestern.com.* 40 rooms, 2 story. Complimentary full breakfast. Check-in 1 pm, check-out 11 am. Restaurant, bar. Children's activity center. Indoor pool, whirlpool. **$**

★★ HOLIDAY INN. *1000 Hwy 23 N, Alpena (49707). Phone 989/356-2151; toll-free 800/465-4329; fax 989/358-6732. www.holiday-inn.com.* 148 rooms, 2 story. Pets accepted, some restrictions. Check-in 2 pm, check-out noon. Restaurant, bar. Children's activity center. Fitness room. Indoor pool, whirlpool. **$**

Ann Arbor (J-5)

See also Dearborn, Detroit, Dundee, Jackson, Ypsilanti

Settled 1823
Population 109,592
Elevation 840 ft
Area Code 734
Information Convention & Visitors Bureau, 120 W Huron, 48104; phone 734/995-7281 or toll-free 800/888-9487
Web Site www.annarbor.org

Arguably the hippest town in Michigan, Ann Arbor is the home of the University of Michigan, which mingles its campus buildings with city attractions. The university, one of the largest in the United States, brings a cultural and artistic bent to the area, where galleries and museums abound. The downtown area offers exceptional shops, including the flagship Borders bookshop, as well as a variety of eateries. While summer months are usually quiet in Ann Arbor, for four days in July, the city closes off downtown streets and welcomes tens of thousands of visitors for the Street Art Fair, where artisans and craftspeople set up displays and sell works of art. City parks provide opportunities for outdoor activities, including walking, hiking, and cycling.

What to See and Do

Huron-Clinton Metroparks. *17845 Savage Rd, Belleville (48111). Phone toll-free 800/477-3191. www.metroparks.com.* A regional park system with 13 recreation areas located along the Huron and Clinton rivers in southeast Michigan. A motor vehicle entry permit, which is good at all metroparks, is required (free on Tuesday). (Also see FARMINGTON, MOUNT CLEMENS, ROCHESTER)

Delhi. *3780 W Delhi Rd, Dexter (48130). 5 1/2 miles NW on Delhi Rd, near Huron River Dr. Phone 734/426-8211; toll-free 800/477-7756.* On this 53-acre site are the Delhi Rapids. Fishing, canoeing, rentals (May-Sept); hiking trails, cross-country skiing, picnicking, playground.

Dexter-Huron. *6535 Huron River Dr, Ann Arbor (48103). 7 1/2 miles NW along Huron River Dr. Phone 734/426-8211; toll-free 800/477-3191.* Fishing, canoeing; hiking trails, cross-country skiing, picnicking, playground.

Hudson Mills. *8801 N Territorial Rd, Dexter (48130). 12 miles NW on N Territorial Rd. Phone 734/426-8211; toll-free 800/234-6534.* More than 1,600-acre recreation area; fishing, boating, canoe rentals; hiking, bicycle trail (rentals), 18-hole golf, cross-country skiing (winter), picnicking, playground, camping, activity center.

Kempf House Center for Local History. *312 S Division, Ann Arbor (48104). Phone 734/994-4898.* (1853) Unusual example of Greek Revival architecture, restored structure owned and maintained by the city of Ann Arbor. Antique Victorian furnishings; displays of local historical artifacts. Tours (Sun afternoons; closed Jan and Aug). **$**

★ University of Michigan. *530 S State St, Ann Arbor (48109). Phone 734/764-4636. www.umich.edu.* (1817) (36,000 students) Established here in 1837, after having moved from Detroit where it was founded. One of the largest universities in the country, it makes significant contributions in teaching and research. Points of particular interest are

Exhibit Museum of Natural History. *1109 Geddes Ave, Ann Arbor (48109). Phone 734/764-0478.* Anthropology, Michigan wildlife, geology, and prehistoric life exhibits.(Mon-Sat 9 am-5 pm, Sun noon-5 pm; closed holidays) **DONATION**

Gerald R. Ford Presidential Library. *1000 Beal Ave, Ann Arbor (48109). N campus. Phone 734/205-0555.* Research library that houses Ford's presidential, vice-presidential, and congressional documents. (Mon-Fri 8:45 am-4:45 pm; closed holidays) **FREE**

Kelsey Museum of Ancient and Medieval Archaeology. *434 S State St, Ann Arbor (48109). Phone 734/764-9304.* Museum houses more than 100,000 objects from the civilizations of the Mediterranean. (Tues-Fri 9 am-4 pm, Sat-Sun 1-4 pm) **FREE**

Law Quadrangle. *S State St and S University Ave, Ann Arbor (48109). Phone 734/764-9322.* Quadrangle includes four beautiful Gothic-style buildings. The law library, with an underground addition, has one of the nation's most extensive collections.

Matthaei Botanical Gardens. *1800 N Dixboro Rd, Ann Arbor (48105). 3 miles NE of campus. Phone 734/998-7061.* Approximately 250 acres, including greenhouses (daily; closed holidays). Seasonal exhibits. Grounds (daily). **$$**

Michigan Stadium. *101 Stadium Blvd, Ann Arbor (48104). Phone 734/747-2583.* Dubbed "The Big House," Michigan Stadium is the largest in the US, seating over 110,000. Tickets may be difficult to obtain through the U of M ticket office, but scalpers sell tickets on the street—and the better the game, the higher the price, sometimes reaching several hundred dollars. The two hottest games of the season are with Michigan State (MSU) and Ohio State: MSU is Michigan's biggest intrastate rival, while the Ohio State game, always the last of the season, often determines the Big Ten championship. **$$$$**

Museum of Art. *S State St and S University Ave, Ann Arbor (48109). Phone 734/764-0395.* (Tues-Sun) **DONATION**

Nichols Arboretum. *1610 Washington Heights, Ann Arbor (48104). Phone 734/998-9540.* Approximately 125 acres. (Daily) **FREE**

North Campus. *2 miles NE of central campus.* Contains research areas; School of Music designed by Eero Saarinen; School of Art and Architecture with public art gallery (Mon-Sat); School of Engineering.

Power Center for the Performing Arts. *121 S Fletcher, Ann Arbor (48109). Phone 734/763-3333.* A 1,414-seat theater houses performances of drama, opera, music, and dance.

Special Events

Ann Arbor Summer Festival. *120 W Huron St, Ann Arbor (48103). Phone 734/647-2278.* A performing arts festival of mime, dance, theater, and music; also lectures, films, and exhibits. June-early July.

Street Art Fair. *450 S Main St, Ann Arbor (48104). Phone 734/994-5260; toll-free 800/888-9487.* Nearly 1,000 artists and craftspeople display and sell works. Four days in mid-July.

Limited-Service Hotels

★ ★ BELL TOWER HOTEL. *300 S Thayer St, Ann Arbor (48104). Phone 734/769-3010; toll-free 800/562-3559; fax 734/769-4339. www.belltowerhotel.com.* This elegant boutique hotel boasts a perfect location on the University of Michigan-Ann Arbor's campus. Guests can take in concerts, theater productions, and shops on or near university grounds. After a long day, come back to plush surroundings and special details like down comforters and pillows in guest rooms. 66 rooms, 4 story. Complimentary continental breakfast. Check-in 4 pm, check-out noon. Restaurant. **$$**

★ RESIDENCE INN BY MARRIOTT. *800 Victors Way, Ann Arbor (48108). Phone 734/996-5666; toll-free 800/331-3131; fax 734/996-1919. www.residenceinn.com.* Ideal for longer stays, this hotel features studios, one- and two-bedroom suites, and bilevel penthouses. The rooms have been organized with separate living and sleeping areas. The hotel is located only 3 miles from downtown Ann Arbor. 114 rooms, 3 story. Pets accepted; fee. Complimentary full breakfast. Check-in 3 pm, check-out noon. Fitness room. Outdoor pool, whirlpool. **$$**

Full-Service Hotels

★ ★ THE DAHLMANN CAMPUS INN - ANN ARBOR. *615 E Huron St, Ann Arbor (48104). Phone 734/769-2200; toll-free 800/666-8693; fax 734/769-6222. www.campusinn.com.* This inn is located near the University of Michigan's campus. The property is also near many local shops, galleries, and restaurants. 208 rooms, 15 story. Check-in 4 pm, check-out 11 am. Restaurant, bar. Fitness room. Outdoor pool. **$$**

★ ★ FOUR POINTS BY SHERATON ANN ARBOR. *3200 Boardwalk, Ann Arbor (48108). Phone 734/996-0600; toll-free 800/368-7764; fax 734/996-8136. www.starwood.com.* Savor a breakfast buffet in the morning at this spacious, comfortable hotel, and then head out for a day in the Ann Arbor area. Ideally located 1 mile from downtown Ann Arbor, guests will find no end to nearby events and activities. For NASCAR fans, Michigan International Speedway is only about an hour's drive away. 197 rooms, 6 story. Check-in 3 pm, check-out noon. Restaurant, bar. Fitness room. Indoor pool, outdoor pool, whirlpool. Business center. **$**

★ ★ ★ KENSINGTON COURT ANN ARBOR. *610 Hilton Blvd, Ann Arbor (48108). Phone 734/761-7800; toll-free 800/344-7829; fax 734/761-1040. www.kcourtaa.com.* This hotel is conveniently located 2 miles from the University of Michigan and next to a regional shopping center. Guests will enjoy spacious and handsomely appointed guest rooms and exceptional service. 200 rooms, 3 story. Check-out 11 am. Restaurant, bar. Fitness room. Indoor pool, whirlpool. **$$**

★ ★ ★ WEBER'S INN. *3050 Jackson Ave, Ann Arbor (48103). Phone 734/769-2500; toll-free 800/443-3050; fax 734/769-4743. www.webersinn.com.* This hotel offers 48 poolside guest rooms and suites and is located near the University of Michigan and 30 minutes outside of downtown Detroit. 158 rooms, 4 story. Complimentary continental breakfast. Check-in 4 pm, check-out noon. Restaurant, bar. Fitness room. Indoor pool, whirlpool. Business center. **$**

Restaurants

★ ★ BELLA CIAO. *118 W Liberty St, Ann Arbor (48104). Phone 734/995-2107. www.bellaciao.com.* Italian menu. Dinner. Closed Sun; holidays. Outdoor seating. **$$**

★ ★ EARLE. *121 W Washington, Ann Arbor (48104). Phone 734/994-0211; fax 734/994-3466. www.theearle.com.* In historic brick building (1885). Own sorbet. French, Italian menu. Dinner. Closed holidays; Sun in June-Aug. Bar. Outdoor seating. **$$$**

★ ★ GANDY DANCER. *401 Depot St, Ann Arbor (48104). Phone 734/769-0592; fax 734/769-0415. www.muer.com.* Locals say this is one of the most romantic restaurants in the area. The grand yet intimate atmosphere of this restaurant owes its splendor to the Michigan Central Depot station, from which it was converted in 1969. Seafood is the main focus, but appealing non-fish options are available, such as the Cajun chicken tortellini and London broil. Seafood menu. Lunch, dinner, Sun brunch. Closed Jan 1, Dec 25. Bar. Children's menu. Valet parking. **$$$**

★ PAESANO'S. *3411 Washtenaw Ave, Ann Arbor (48104). Phone 734/971-0484; fax 734/971-0419. www.paesanosannarbor.com.* Lucky for you, this rustic Italian restaurant's entire menu is available for take-out. Each dish combines regional tastes of Italy, resulting in fascinating new flavors. Try the Sicilian skewers of pork tenderloin, served with black grape sauce and sautéed black cabbage, or the fig- and gorgonzola-crusted filet mignon. Enjoy seasonal flavors such as pumpkin and amaretto ravioli and stuffed chicken with fall wild mushrooms and farmer cheese. Prices are reasonable, especially considering the imagination that goes into each dish. Strolling mandolinists on Friday. Italian menu. Lunch, dinner. Closed Jan 1, Thanksgiving, Dec 25. Bar. Children's menu. Outdoor seating. **$$**

★ ZINGERMAN'S DELICATESSEN. *422 Detroit St, Ann Arbor (48104). Phone 734/663-3354; fax 734/769-1235. www.zingermans.com.* Deli menu. Dinner. Closed holidays. Children's menu. **$**

Auburn Hills

Auburn Hills, a 1980s incorporation of the farming communities of Auburn Heights and Avon Township, recently rebuilt its downtown with brick pavers, street lamps, and charming shops. Home of the Chrysler Tech Center and dozens of other high-tech companies, the city is best known for Great Lakes Crossing, a mega-shopping mall with over 200 stores. The Detroit Pistons (NBA) and Shock (WNBA) make their home in the Palace of Auburn Hills.

What to See and Do

Detroit Pistons (NBA). *The Palace of Auburn Hills, 2*

Championship Dr, Auburn Hills (48326). Phone 248/377-0100. www.nba.com/pistons.

Detroit Shock (WNBA). *The Palace of Auburn Hills, 2 Championship Dr, Auburn Hills (48326). Phone 248/377-0100. www.wnba.com/shock.*

Great Lakes Crossing. *4000 Baldwin Rd, Auburn Hills (48326). Phone toll-free 877/746-7452. www.shopgreatlakescrossing.com.* With 1.4 million square feet of shops and other entertainment opportunities, Great Lakes Crossing (GLC) is Michigan's top shopping destination. In addition to over 200 shops, GLC also features a high-tech playland, movie theaters, cafés, and restaurants.

Limited-Service Hotel

★ ★ COURTYARD BY MARRIOTT. *1296 N Opdyke Rd, Auburn Hills (48326). Phone 248/373-4100; toll-free 800/321-2211; fax 248/373-1885. www.courtyard.com.* 148 rooms, 3 story. Check-out noon. Bar. Fitness room. Indoor pool, whirlpool. Business center. **$**

Full-Service Hotel

★ ★ ★ HILTON SUITES AUBURN HILLS. *2300 Featherstone Rd, Auburn Hills (48326). Phone 248/334-2222; toll-free 800/774-1500; fax 248/334-2922. www.hilton.com.* Hotel guests can enjoy complimentary cookies and milk by the lobby fireplace each night. 224 rooms, 5 story, all suites. Pets accepted; fee. Complimentary full breakfast. Check-out noon. Restaurant, bar. Fitness room. Indoor pool, whirlpool. Business center. **$**

Battle Creek (J-4)

See also Jackson, Kalamazoo, Marshall, Three Rivers

Settled 1831
Population 53,540
Elevation 830 ft
Area Code 269
Information Greater Battle Creek/Calhoun County Visitor and Convention Bureau, 77 E Michigan, Suite 80, 49017; phone 269/962-4076 or toll-free 800/397-2240
Web Site www.battlecreek.org

Battle Creek's fame was built by two cereal tycoons, W. K. Kellogg and C. W. Post. The Kellogg and Post cereal plants are the largest of their type anywhere, and Post and Kellogg have influenced more than the economy; signs, streets, parks, and many public institutions also bear their names. The city, now dubbed the "Cereal Capital of the World," takes its name from a small battle that took place on the banks of the creek in 1825 between a native and a land surveyor. Years later, it was a stop on the Underground Railroad; Sojourner Truth lived here for nearly 30 years.

What to See and Do

Binder Park Zoo. *7400 Division Dr, Battle Creek (49014). Phone 269/979-1351. www.binderparkzoo.org.* Exotic, endangered, and domestic animals in natural exhibits. Fifty-acre Wild Africa exhibit including giraffes, zebras, antelope, and African wild dogs; trading village, ranger station, research camp, and working diamond mine alongside a panoramic African savanna. Ride the Wilderness Tram and the Z. O. & O. Railroad (fee). Miller Children's Zoo. Special events during Halloween and Christmas. (Mid-Apr-mid-Oct, daily) **$$**

Fort Custer State Recreation Area. *5163 W Fort Custer Dr, Augusta (49012). 8 miles W via Hwy 96. Phone 269/731-4200.* Swimming beach, fishing, boating (launch); nature, bridle, and bicycle trails, picnic areas, hunting. Improved campgrounds (reservations required). Cross-country skiing, snowmobiling. (Daily) **$$**

Kimball House Museum. *196 Capital Ave NE, Battle Creek (49017). Phone 269/965-2613. www.kimballhouse.org.* (1886). Restored and refurnished Victorian home; displays trace development of use of appliances, tools, medical instruments; herb garden; country store. (Fri 1-4 pm; closed Jan-Apr) **$**

Leila Arboretum. *928 W Michigan Ave, Battle Creek (49017). Phone 269/969-0722. www.leilaarboretumsociety.org.* A 72-acre park containing native trees and shrubs. On the grounds is

> **Kingman Museum of Natural History.** *175 Limit St, Battle Creek (49017). Phone 269/965-5117.* Exhibits include Journey Through the Crust of the Earth, Walk in the Footsteps of the Dinosaurs, Mammals of the Ice Age, Window to the Universe, Planetarium, Wonder of Life, Discovery Room, and others. (Wed-Sun afternoons; closed holidays) **$**

Sojourner Truth Grave. *Oak Hill Cemetery, South Ave and Oak Dr, Battle Creek (49017).* On the cemetery's

Fifth Street is the plain square monument marking the resting place of this remarkable fighter for freedom. Born a slave in the 1790s, Truth gained her freedom in the 1820s and crusaded against slavery until her death in 1883. Although uneducated, she had a brilliant mind as well as an unquenchable devotion to her cause.

Willard Beach. *2 miles S, on shores of Goguac Lake.* Lavishly landscaped; has a wide bathing beach. Supervised swimming; picnicking, pavilion. (Memorial Day-Labor Day, daily) **$**

W. K. Kellogg Bird Sanctuary of Michigan State University. *12685 E C Ave, Battle Creek (49017). 13 miles NW off Hwy 89. Phone 269/671-2510.* Experimental farm and forest nearby. Seven kinds of swans and more than 20 species of ducks and geese inhabit the ponds and Wintergreen Lake. One of the finest bird of prey collections in the Midwest, along with free-roaming upland game birds. Colorful viewing all seasons of the year. Observation deck and educational displays. Grounds and reception center (daily). **$**

Special Event

Cereal City Festival. *171 W Michigan Ave, Battle Creek (49017). Phone toll-free 800/970-7020.* Children's parade, Queen's Pageant, arts and crafts exhibits; also the world's longest breakfast table. Second Sat in June.

Limited-Service Hotel

★ DAYS INN. *4786 Beckley Rd, Battle Creek (49017). Phone 269/979-3561; toll-free 800/329-7466; fax 269/979-1400. www.daysinn.com.* 86 rooms. Pets accepted; fee. Complimentary continental breakfast. Check-in 3 pm, check-out 11 am. Wireless Internet access. **$**

Full-Service Hotels

★ ★ ★ MCCAMLY PLAZA HOTEL. *50 SW Capital Ave, Battle Creek (49017). Phone 269/963-7050; toll-free 888/622-2659; fax 269/963-3880. www.mccamlyplazahotel.com.* This hotel offers well-appointed guest rooms and suites along with a large indoor pool and whirlpool, an exercise room, and more. Golf packages are available for visitors, and the location of the property places it near many attractions. 239 rooms, 16 story. Pets accepted; fee. Check-in 3 pm, check-out 11 am. High-speed Internet access. Restaurants, bar. Fitness room. Indoor pool, whirlpool. Airport transportation available. **$**

★ ★ RAMADA INN AND SUITES. *5050 Beckley Rd, Battle Creek (49015). Phone 269/979-1100; toll-free 800/232-3405; fax 269/979-1899. www.ramada.com.* 132 rooms, 2 story. Pets accepted, some restrictions. Complimentary continental breakfast. Check-in 4 pm, check-out noon. Restaurant, bar. Fitness room. Indoor pool, outdoor pool, whirlpool. **$**

Bay City (G-5)

See also Frankenmuth, Midland, Port Austin, Saginaw

Settled 1831
Population 38,936
Elevation 595 ft
Area Code 989
Information Bay Area Convention & Visitors Bureau, 901 Saginaw St, 48708; phone 989/893-1222 or toll-free 888/229-8696
Web Site www.tourbaycitymi.org

Bay City is a historic port community located on Saginaw Bay, which services Great Lakes freighters as well as seagoing vessels in the handling of millions of tons of products annually. The city is noted for tree-shaded streets and residential areas with new homes and Victorian and Georgian mansions built by the 19th-century lumber barons. Industries include shipbuilding, automobile parts, petrochemicals, and electronics.

Retail, service, specialty dining, and entertainment businesses can be found in the Historic Midland Street area on the west side of Bay City. Summertime roadside stands features melons.

What to See and Do

Bay City State Recreation Area. *3582 State Park Dr, Bay City (48706). 5 miles N on Hwy 247, along Saginaw Bay. Phone 989/684-3020.* Approximately 200 acres. Swimming, bathhouse, fishing, boating; hiking, picnicking, concession, camping. Located here are

Jennison Nature Center. *3582 State Park Dr, Bay City (48706). Phone 989/667-0717.* Displays on the history, geology, wildlife, and general ecology of the area. Hiking trails. (Wed-Sun noon-4 pm; closed holidays) **FREE**

Tobico Marsh. *3582 State Park Dr, Bay City (48706). Phone 989/684-3020.* 1,700 acres of wetland, the largest remaining wildlife refuge on Saginaw Bay's western shore. Two 32-foot towers allow panoramic viewing of deer, beaver, mink, and hundreds of species of waterfowl and song, shore, and marsh birds. Visitor center (Tues-Sun). **FREE**

Bay County Historical Museum. *321 Washington Ave, Bay City (48708). Phone 989/893-5733. www.bchsmuseum.org.* Preserving and displaying the heritage of Bay County. Exhibits interpret life of Native Americans; depict fur trading, lumbering, shipbuilding, industrial development; life of pioneering women; changing exhibits. (Mon-Sat; closed holidays) **DONATION**

City Hall and Bell Tower. *301 Washington Ave, Bay City (48708). Phone 989/893-1222.* (Circa 1895) Meticulously restored Romanesque structure; council chamber has 31-foot-long woven tapestry depicting history of Bay City. View of city and its waterway from bell tower. (Mon-Fri; closed holidays) **FREE**

Deer Acres. *2346 Hwy 13, Pinconning (48650). 17 miles N on Hwy 13. Phone 989/879-2849. www.deeracres.com.* Storybook theme park with petting zoo. Train rides (fee), antique cars, more. (Mid-May-Labor Day: daily; after Labor Day-mid-Oct: Sat-Sun) **$$$**

Scottish Rite Cathedral. *614 Center Ave, Bay City (48707). Phone 989/893-3700.* The only Scottish Rite Cathedral in the state; contains Lord Cornwallis's surrender chair. (Mon-Fri) **FREE**

Special Events

Munger Potato Festival. *Munger Community Park, 1920 S Finn Rd, Munger (48747). SE on Hwy 15, then E on Hwy 138. Phone 989/659-2571.* Potato displays, potato brats, and a Potato King and Queen contest are featured at this fest, along with live music, a parade, and demolition derby. Four days in late July.

St. Stanislaus Polish Festival. *Lincoln Ave S, Bay City (48708). S end of Bay City. Phone 989/893-1749.* Late June.

Limited-Service Hotels

★ ★ BAY VALLEY HOTEL AND RESORT. *2470 Old Bridge Rd, Bay City (48706). Phone 989/686-3500; toll-free 800/241-4653; fax 989/686-6931. www.bayvalley.com.* Located on 470 acres of beautiful landscape, this resort offers its guests tons of recreational activities including biking, tennis, water sports, and great golf. 147 rooms, 3 story. Check-in 3 pm, check-out noon. High-speed Internet access, wireless Internet access. Restaurant, bar. Fitness room. Indoor pool, outdoor pool, whirlpool. Golf, 18 holes. Airport transportation available. Business center. **$**

★ ★ DOUBLETREE HOTEL BAY CITY-RIVERFRONT. *1 Wenonah Park Pl, Bay City (48708). Phone 989/891-6000; fax 989/981-9680. www.doubletree.com.* 150 rooms. Check-in 3 pm, check-out noon. Restaurant, bar. Indoor pool. Business center. **$**

★ ★ HOLIDAY INN. *501 Saginaw St, Bay City (48708). Phone 989/892-3501; toll-free 800/465-4329; fax 989/892-9342. www.holiday-inn.com/baycitymi.* 100 rooms, 4 story. Pets accepted, some restrictions. Check-in 4 pm, check-out noon. Restaurant, bar. Fitness room. Indoor pool, whirlpool. **$**

Restaurant

★ ★ O SOLE MIO. *1005 Saginaw St, Bay City (48708). Phone 989/893-3496; fax 989/893-8393.* Italian menu. Dinner. Closed Sun-Mon; holidays. Bar. Children's menu. Casual attire. **$$**

Bellaire (E-4)

Population 1,104
Elevation 616 ft
Area Code 231
Zip 49615
Information Bellaire Chamber of Commerce, PO Box 205; phone 231/533-6023
Web Site www.bellairemichigan.com/chamber

As Shanty Creek Resort has grown and expanded, so has the tiny town of Bellaire (bell-AIR), which offers several shops and cafés in its downtown area. The main attraction of the city, however, remains Shanty Creek, with its two downhill ski resorts; three world-class golf courses; vast network of trails for cross-country skiing, mountain biking, and hiking; tennis courts, pools, and shopping areas.

What to See and Do

Shanty Creek Resort. *1 Shanty Creek Rd, Bellaire (49615). 2 miles SE off Hwy 88. Phone 231/533-8621; toll-free 800/678-4111. www.shantycreek.com.* Two separate mountains: five quad, two double chairlifts, four surface lifts; patrol, school, rentals; snowmaking; nursery; night skiing; lodge (see FULL-SERVICE RESORT), snowboarding; tubing; restaurant, snack bar, entertainment; indoor/outdoor pool, two whirlpools; health club. Thirty trails on two mountains; longest run approximately 1 mile; vertical drop 450 feet. Cross-country trails (25 miles). (Thanksgiving-Mar, daily) **$$$$**

Full-Service Resort

★ ★ ★ SHANTY CREEK RESORT. *1 Shanty Creek Rd, Bellaire (49615). Phone 231/533-8621; toll-free 800/678-4111; fax 231/533-7001. www.shantycreek.com.* This resort offers three distinct lodges. The Schuss Village offers European style, the Summit Village gives visitors a great view of the snow-covered lakes and forests, while the Cedar River Village overlooks the Tom Weiskopf golf course. 600 rooms, 3 story. Check-in 6 pm, check-out noon. Restaurant, bar. Children's activity center. Fitness room. Indoor pool, outdoor pool, whirlpool. Golf. Tennis. Airport transportation available. Business center. **$**

Beulah (F-3)

See also Frankfort, Traverse City,

Population 421
Elevation 595 ft
Area Code 231
Zip 49617
Information Benzie County Chamber of Commerce, PO Box 204, Benzonia 49616; phone 231/882-5801 or toll-free 800/882-5801
Web Site www.benzie.org

This resort town is at the east end of Crystal Lake, which offers excellent fishing for salmon, trout, perch, bass, and smelt. Skiing, ice fishing, golf, and boating are also popular in Beulah (BEW-la), but if you prefer a quiet afternoon, stroll past the town's quaint shops or visit its wineries.

What to See and Do

Benzie Area Historical Museum. *6941 Traverse Ave, Benzonia (49616). 3 miles S on Hwy 31. Phone 231/882-5539.* Exhibits and artifacts depict area's lumbering, shipping, farming, transportation, homelife; display on Civil War author Bruce Catton. (June-Sept: Tues-Sat; Apr-May and Oct-Nov: Fri-Sat only; special tours by appointment) **$**

Crystal Mountain Resort. *12500 Crystal Mountain Dr, Thompsonville (49683). 3 miles S on Hwy 31, then 7 miles SE on Hwy 115. Phone 231/378-2000; toll-free 800/968-7686. www.crystalmtn.com.* High-speed lift, five chairlifts, two rope tows; night skiing; patrol, school, rentals; snowmaking; nursery; lodge, condominiums, restaurant, cafeteria, bar. 34 trails; longest run 1/2 mile; vertical drop 375 feet. (Thanksgiving-early Apr, daily) Groomed, track-set cross-country trails (14 miles), lighted night trail; rentals, instruction (Dec-Mar, daily). Snowboard half-pipe. Also two golf courses; indoor pool, fitness center; hiking, mountain bike trails; tennis courts. **$$$$**

Gwen Frostic Prints. *5140 River Rd, Benzonia (49616). 3 miles S on Hwy 31, 2 miles W. Phone 231/882-5505. www.gwenfrostic.com.* Original block prints designed by artist and poet Gwen Frostic are featured at this wildlife sanctuary and printing shop. Display room lets visitors observe the printing presses in operation. (Early May-Oct: daily; rest of year: Mon-Sat; closed holidays) **FREE**

Platte River State Anadromous Fish Hatchery. *15120 Hwy 31, Beulah (49617). 10 miles E via Hwy 31. Phone 231/325-4611.* Michigan's largest hatchery annually produces about 9 million anadromous salmon (salmon that live in oceans or lakes and return to the rivers to spawn). This is the birthplace of the coho salmon in the Great Lakes; also produces chinook salmon. Self-guided tours (daily). **FREE**

Limited-Service Hotel

★ BEST WESTERN-SCENIC HILL RESORT. *1400 Beulah Hwy, Beulah (49617). Phone 231/882-0294; fax 231/882-4927.* 43 rooms. Pets accepted; fee. Check-in 3 pm, check-out 11 am. **$**

Restaurants

★ ★ BROOKSIDE INN. *115 Hwy 31, Beulah (49617). Phone 231/882-9688; fax 231/882-4600.*

www.brooksideinn.com. American menu. Dinner. Bar. Children's menu. Casual attire. Outdoor seating. **$$**

★ **CHERRY HUT.** *211 N Michigan Ave (Hwy 31), Beulah (49617). Phone 231/882-4431; fax 231/882-9203. www.cherryhutproducts.com.* American menu. Dinner. Closed late Oct-Memorial Day. Children's menu. Casual attire. Outdoor seating. **$**

★ **SAIL INN.** *Hwy 31, Beulah (49616). Phone 231/882-4971; fax 231/882-7111.* American, Eclectic menu. Dinner. Closed Thanksgiving, Christmas. Bar. Children's menu. **$**

Big Rapids (G-3)

See also Cadillac, Mount Pleasant

Settled 1854
Population 12,603
Elevation 920 ft
Area Code 231
Zip 49307
Information Mecosta County Convention & Visitors Bureau, 246 N State St; phone 231/796-7640 or toll-free 800/833-6697
Web Site www.bigrapids.org

Big Rapids is a town for outdoor lovers, and the activities are nearly endless: hunting, fishing, camping, hiking, biking, canoeing, cross-country skiing, ice skating, snowshoeing, snowmobiling, and more. Fall colors are stunning. Ferris State University and a nearby Amish community offer cultural diversity.

What to See and Do

Mecosta County Parks. *Phone 231/832-3246. www.mecostacountyparks.com.* Parks are open May-October. No pets permitted in Brower and School Section Lake parks. **$$$** Parks include

Brower. *23056 Polk Rd, Stanwood (49346). 6 miles S on Hwy 131 to Stanwood, then 1 mile W to Old State Rd, then 3 miles S on Polk Rd. Phone 231/823-2561.* Swimming, fishing, boating (launch); playgrounds, tennis courts, softball diamond, camping.

Merrill Lake. *3275 Evergreen Rd, Sears (49679). E on Hwy 20 to Hwy 66, then N, 3 miles N of Barryton. Phone 989/382-7158.* Swimming (two beaches), fishing, boating (launch, ramps); picnicking (shelters), playgrounds, camping.

Paris. *22090 Northland Dr, Paris (49338). 6 miles N on Hwy 131. Phone 231/796-3420.* Fishing, canoeing (ramp); wildlife area, picnicking (shelter), camping.

School Section Lake. *9003 90th Ave, Mecosta (49332). Approximately 23 miles E via Hwy 20. Phone 231/972-7450.* Swimming beach, boating (launch); picnicking (shelters), concessions, playgrounds, camping.

Special Event

Labor Day Arts Fair. *Hemlock Park, Warren Ave and Hemlock Dr, Big Rapids (49307). On Muskegon River. Phone 231/796-7649.* More than 150 exhibitors of various arts and crafts; concessions. Labor Day.

Limited-Service Hotels

★ **BEST WESTERN BIG RAPIDS.** *1705 S State St, Big Rapids (49307). Phone 231/592-5150; toll-free 877/592-5150; fax 231/592-5157. www.bestwestern.com.* 96 rooms. Complimentary continental breakfast. Check-in 4 pm, check-out noon. Outdoor pool. **$**

★★ **HOLIDAY INN.** *1005 Perry Ave, Big Rapids (49307). Phone 231/796-4400; toll-free 800/999-9069; fax 231/796-0220. www.hibigrapids.com.* 118 rooms, 4 story. Pets accepted; fee. Check-in 4 pm, check-out noon. High-speed Internet access, wireless Internet access. Restaurant, bar. Children's activity center. Fitness room. Indoor pool, whirlpool. Golf, 18 holes. Business center. **$**

Birch Run (H-5)

See also Flint, Frankenmuth, Saginaw

Population 1,653
Elevation 635 ft
Area Code 989
Zip 48415
Information Birch Run Area Chamber of Commerce, 8070 Main St, 48415; phone 989/624-9193
Web Site www.birchrunchamber.com

Buoyed by the more than 1 million visitors to The Outlets at Birch Run, this town has gone from sleepy to savvy in just a few years. Attractions outside the outlets have sprung up, including golf courses, museums, and a small speedway.

What to See and Do

The Outlets at Birch Run. *12240 S Beyer Rd, Birch Run (48415). Approximately 5 miles S on I-75, exit 136. Phone 989/624-7467.* The Outlets at Birch Run offers outlet shopping at its finest, with 200 stores including Coach, Nike, J. Crew, Eddie Bauer, Ann Taylor, Laura Ashley, and Polo/Ralph Lauren. Additional attractions at the center include indoor golf, a movie theater, an animal zoo, and a skating rink, giving everyone in the family something to enjoy. (Daily)

Birmingham (J-5)

See also Bloomfield Hills, Detroit, Farmington, Royal Oak, Southfield

Population 19,997
Elevation 781 ft
Area Code 248
Information Birmingham-Bloomfield Chamber of Commerce, 124 W Maple, 48009; phone 248/644-1700
Web Site www.bbcc.com

Think of Birmingham and think of shopping: tony, chic, upscale shopping in the boutiques and art galleries of Birmingham's fashionable downtown area. Take a break from shopping at any of the restaurants, cafés, and coffeehouses that are intermingled with city shops. Amtrak stops here with service to Pontiac, Detroit, and Chicago.

Full-Service Hotel

★★★★ THE TOWNSEND HOTEL. *100 Townsend St, Birmingham (48009). Phone 248/642-7900; fax 248/645-9061. www.townsendhotel.com.* The Townsend Hotel brings the refinement of Europe to the heart of Michigan. Tucked away in the quiet community of Birmingham, where tree-lined streets brim with unique stores and bustling cafés, the hotel is conveniently located less than an hour from Detroit. The guest rooms are handsomely furnished with regal décor. Jewel tones add panache, four-poster beds add charm, and full kitchens in the suites and penthouses ensure that guests never need to leave the comforts of home behind. The cherrywood paneling and the warm glow of the fireplace make for a particularly inviting space at the Rugby Grille (see), and its airy gallery filled with the fragrance of fresh flowers is a sunny alternative. The sleek city chic of the Townsend Corner Bar has made it one of the hotspots on the local scene. Its appealing interiors are a perfect match for its Asian-inspired appetizers and creative cocktails. 150 rooms, 4 story. Check-out noon. Restaurant, bar. Business center. **$$$**

Restaurants

★★★ FORTE'. *201 S Old Woodward Ave, Birmingham (48009). Phone 248/594-7300. www.forterestaurant.com.* American menu. Lunch, dinner. Closed Sun; holidays. Business casual attire. Valet parking. **$$$**

★★★ RUGBY GRILLE. *100 Townsend St, Birmingham (48009). Phone 248/642-5999; fax 248/645-9061. www.townsendhotel.com.* Located in the European-style Townsend Hotel (see), this internationally inspired, Continental restaurant's dinner menu features fine steak and chops, fresh seafood, and homemade pastas. Breakfast and lunch, with slightly more standard menu options, are also available in the polished-wood, burgundy-toned space. French menu. Breakfast, lunch, dinner. Bar. Valet parking. **$$$**

Bloomfield Hills (J-5)

See also Birmingham, Detroit, Pontiac, Royal Oak, Southfield, Troy, Warren

Settled 1819
Population 4,288
Elevation 830 ft
Area Code 248
Information Birmingham-Bloomfield Chamber of Commerce, 124 W Maple, Birmingham 48009; phone 248/644-1700
Web Site www.bbcc.com

Amasa Bagley followed a Native American trail and cleared land on what is today the business section of this small residential city. It was known as Bagley's Corners, later as Bloomfield Center, and then as Bloomfield Hills. In 1904, Ellen Scripps Booth and George G. Booth, president of the *Detroit News*, bought 300 acres of farmland here, naming it Cranbrook after the English village in which Mr. Booth's father was born. Since then, they have turned the estate into a vast cultural and educational complex. Today, Bloomfield Hills ranks as the second-wealthiest city in the United States. Plan to drive around residential areas to view the city's Tudor and Georgian mansions that date back to the 1920s, as well as modern mansions built by Detroit's professional athletes, entertainers, and automotive executives.

What to See and Do

Cranbrook Educational Community. *1221 N Woodward Ave, Bloomfield Hills (48304). Phone 248/645-3000. www.cranbrook.edu.* This famous campus is the site of the renowned center for the arts, education, science, and culture. Located on more than 300 acres, Cranbrook is noted for its exceptional architecture, gardens, and sculpture. Cranbrook is composed of

Cranbrook Academy of Art and Museum. *39221 Woodward Ave, Bloomfield Hills (48304). Phone 248/645-3312.* (150 students) Graduate school for design, architecture, and the fine arts. Museum has international arts exhibits and collections. (Wed-Sun afternoons; closed holidays) **$$**

Cranbrook Gardens. *1221 N Woodward Ave, Bloomfield Hills (48304). Phone 248/645-3149.* Forty acres of formal and informal gardens; trails, fountains, outdoor Greek theater. (May-Aug: daily; Sept: afternoons only; Oct: Sat-Sun afternoons) **$$**

Cranbrook House. *380 Lone Pine Rd, Bloomfield Hills (48304). Phone 248/645-3149.* (1908) Tudor-style structure designed by Albert Kahn. Contains exceptional examples of decorative and fine art from the late 19th and early 20th centuries. **$$**

Cranbrook Institute of Science. *39221 Woodward Ave, Bloomfield Hills (48304). Phone 248/645-3200.* Natural history and science museum with exhibits, observatory, nature center; planetarium and laser demonstrations. (Mon-Sat, also Sun afternoons; closed holidays) **$$**

Limited-Service Hotel

★★ RADISSON KINGSLEY. *39475 Woodward Ave, Bloomfield Hills (48304). Phone 248/644-1400; toll-free 800/333-3333; fax 248/644-5449. www.radisson.com.* This quiet hotel offers the friendly service expected from a small inn along with the amenities and facilities of a large hotel. Located near shopping, this hotel offers a pool and Jacuzzi, a seafood restaurant, deli, and much more. 160 rooms, 3 story. Check-out noon. High-speed Internet access. Restaurant, bar. Fitness room. Indoor pool, whirlpool. **$$**

Restaurant

★★★★ THE LARK. *6430 Farmington Rd, West Bloomfield (48322). Phone 248/661-4466; fax 248/661-8891. www.thelark.com.* Quite possibly one of the most elegant dining experiences to be had in the Detroit area, The Lark aims high and makes its mark with ease. The room—a beautiful space with Portuguese-styled tile murals and a trellised terrace—makes settling in for a leisurely evening of delight a no-brainer. (The problem will be leaving.) On the ambitious and delicious menu, you'll find classics like bouillabaisse and lobster Thermidor, as well as heartier dishes like rack of lamb Genghis and Chinese oven-roasted duck with figs, dates, almonds, and brandy. The world-class wine list fits the seasonal, modern French-influenced menu like a glove. The Lark is also known far and wide for its kid-in-a-candy-store-style dessert sampler—a drool-worthy selection of chocolates, tarts, cookies, and pastries to satisfy every sweet tooth. French menu. Dinner. Closed Sun-Mon; Easter, Thanksgiving, Dec 25; also the first week of Jan and the first week of Aug. Bar. Reservations recommended. **$$$**

Boyne City (E-4)

See also Charlevoix, Gaylord, Petoskey

Population 3,400
Elevation 600 ft
Area Code 231
Zip 49712
Information Chamber of Commerce, 28 S Lake St; phone 231/582-6222
Web Site www.boynecity.com

Once an industrial center for both logging and leather tanning, Boyne (BOY-n) City is now a snug resort town located at the southern tip of Lake Charlevoix. Fishing, canoeing, kayaking abound in summer, as does golfing on the two championship courses. Downhill and cross-country skiing, snowshoeing, and snowmobiling keep visitors moving in winter. Nearby Boyne Mountain (6 miles southeast) was northern Michigan's first ski resort and is still one of its best.

What to See and Do

Boyne Mountain. *1 Boyne Mountain Rd, Boyne Falls (49713). SE via Hwy 75 to Boyne Falls, off Hwy*

131. Phone 231/549-6000; toll-free 800/462-6963. www.boynemountain.com. Triple, six-passenger, three quad, three double chairlifts; rope tow; patrol, school, rentals; snowmaking; lodge (see LIMITED-SERVICE HOTELS), cafeteria, restaurant, bar, nursery. Longest run 1 mile; vertical drop 500 feet. Cross-country trails (35 miles), rentals. (Trail ticket; fee) (Late Nov-mid-Apr, daily) **$$$$**

Limited-Service Hotels

★ ★ BOYNE MOUNTAIN RESORT. *1 Boyne Mountain Rd, Boyne Falls (49713). Phone 231/549-6000; toll-free 800/462-6963; fax 231/549-6093. www.boynemountain.com.* Alpine-style décor; fireplace in lobby. Five thousand-foot paved, lighted airstrip. 265 rooms, 3 story. Check-in 5 pm, check-out 1 pm. Restaurant, bar. Fitness room. Indoor pool, outdoor pool, whirlpool. Golf, 45 holes. Tennis. **$**

★ WATER STREET INN. *240 Front St, Boyne City (49712). Phone 231/582-3000; fax 231/582-3001.* 27 rooms, 3 story. Check-out 11 am. Private swimming beach. **$$**

Restaurant

★ PIPPINS. *5 W Main St, Boyne City (49712). Phone 231/582-3311; fax 231/582-3201. www.pippins restaurant.com.* American menu. Dinner. Closed mid-Mar-May, Oct-Dec 25. Bar. Children's menu. Casual attire. **$$**

Brooklyn (K-4)

See also Jackson

Population 1,176
Elevation 992 ft
Area Code 517
Zip 49230
Information 221 N Main St, 49230; phone 517/592-8907
Web Site www.brooklynmi.com

Like many US cities that offer NASCAR racetracks, Brooklyn has gone from relative obscurity to a popular destination for summer race fans.

What to See and Do

Antique Alley. The 50-mile drive west from Saline to Somerset Center with a side trip up Highway 50 to Brooklyn is known locally as Antique Alley, and it makes for a great day of shopping.

Brick Walker Tavern Antiques. *11705 Hwy 12, Brooklyn (49230). Phone 517/467-6961.* Brick Walker Tavern Antiques, in an 1854 building constructed as a three-story inn along the Detroit-Chicago Pike, features collectible glassware, pottery, and china.

Irish Hills Antiques and Outdoor Market. *10600 Hwy 12, Brooklyn (49230). 1 mile E of Hwy 50. Phone 517/467-4646.* Irish Hills Antiques sells antique wood and coal-burning parlor and kitchen stoves, brass cash registers, porcelain signs, and gasoline pumps.

Turn of the Century Lighting Co. *116 W Michigan Ave, Clinton (49236). Phone 517/456-6019.* This shop features gas and electric lighting fixtures from the Victorian era and period lampshades.

Cambridge Junction Historic State Park/Walker Tavern Historic Complex. *13220 Hwy 50, Cambridge Junction (48230). Phone 517/467-4414.* Walker's farmhouse and tavern, a Federal-style white clapboard home and farm, is a museum interpreting Michigan's history as a frontier settlement. The house was a favorite stopping point for stagecoaches making the arduous trip to Chicago from 1836 to 1855. (May-Oct) **FREE**

Fishing. The area is surrounded by 52 lakes and many opportunities for prime fishing. The public-access lakes are the best bet for catching enough to make it fun, according to veteran anglers and the Michigan State Department of Fisheries and Wildlife. **Allen:** *Off Hwy 12, about 2 miles E of Hwy 50.* Largemouth bass, bluegill, and perch. **Deep:** *Off Brix Hwy in Onsted, about 1 1/2 miles S of Hwy 12, W of Hwy 50.* Perch, bluegill, northern pike. **Devils:** *Just S of Hwy 223 in Onsted.* Large- and smallmouth bass, northern pike, bluegill, sunfish. **Iron Lake:** *On Hwy 12 E of Hwy 50, below Wamplers Lake.* Large- and smallmouth bass; good night fishing. **Sand:** *Pentecost Hwy between Hwy 50 and Hwy 12.* Large- and smallmouth bass. Troll slowly for 7-8 pound walleye. Crappies. **Vineyard:** *Along Hwy 124 just E of Hwy 50.* Largemouth bass, walleye, bluegill, sunfish. **Wamplers:** *N of Hwy 12 off M-124; access from Hayes State Park.* Largemouth bass, bluegill, muskie.Two bait and tackle shops around Brooklyn provide updated area fishing conditions and licenses. **Knutson's,** *Hwy 50 and Hwy 124.* Phone toll-free within Michigan 800/292-0857; outside the state, 800/248-9318. **Three Lakes Supply,** *Hwy 50 about 1 mile S of Hwy 12.* Phone 517/467-2468.

Golfing. With 21 public golf courses, Jackson County boasts more public golf holes per person than any other community in the country except Sarasota, Florida. Tee times are relatively easy to get and reasonably priced. **Clark Lake Golf Course,** *5535 Wesch Rd, Brooklyn. Phone 517/592-6259.* Public course with 27 holes. **Greenbriar Golf Course,** *14820 Wellwood Rd, Brooklyn. Phone 517/592-6952.* Public course with 18 holes. **Hills Heart of the Lakes Golf Course,** *500 Case Rd, Brooklyn. Phone 517/592-2110.* Public course with 18 holes. **Silver Lake Golf Course,** *15649 Hwy 12, Brooklyn. Phone 517/592-8036.* Nine-hole, par 3 course.

Hidden Lake Gardens. *6280 Munger Rd (M 50), Tipton (49287). Phone 517/431-2060. www.cpp.msu.edu/hlg.* These "gardens" are spread over nearly 800 acres and feature the Harper collection of dwarf and rare conifers with more than 500 varieties. Hidden Lake also has an 8,000-square-foot tropical plant conservatory and 6 miles of paved roads through the hilly, oak-hickory woods, meadows and landscaped areas that are good for hiking. (Apr-Oct: daily 8 am-dusk; Nov-Mar: daily 9 am-4 pm; closed Jan 1, Thanksgiving, Dec 25) **$**

Irish Hills Fun Center. *5600 Hwy 12, Tipton (49287). Phone 517/431-2217. www.irishhillsgokarts.com.* Go-karts and sprint cars for rent, batting cages, miniature golf and paintball arena. Enough to keep the kids occupied for an afternoon. (June-Aug: daily noon-9 pm; May and Sept: Sat-Sun 1-7 pm; Apr and Oct: Sat-Sun 1-6 pm) **$**

Special Event

Michigan International Speedway. *12626 Hwy 12, Brooklyn (49230). SE on Hwy 50 to I-12, then 1 mile W. Phone toll-free 800/354-1010. www.mispeedway.com.* NASCAR, ARCA, IROC, and Indy Car races on a 2-mile oval track. Mid-June-mid-Aug.

Cadillac (F-3)

See also Big Rapids, Traverse City

Settled 1871
Population 10,104
Elevation 1,328 ft
Area Code 231
Zip 49601
Information Cadillac Area Visitor Bureau, 222 Lake St; phone 231/775-0657 or toll-free 800/225-2537
Web Site www.cadillacmichigan.com

Named for Antoine de la Mothe Cadillac, founder of Detroit, Cadillac was founded as a lumber camp and was once the major lumber center of the area. Lakes Cadillac and Mitchell offer opportunities for swimming, water-skiing, and fishing, while nearby Caberfae is known as one of the best ski resorts in the state.

What to See and Do

Adventure Island. *6083 E Hwy 155, Cadillac (49601). Phone 231/775-5665. www.cadillacmichigan.com/adventureisland.* This family fun park includes mountain miniature golf, go-karts, batting cages, bumper boats, water slides, concessions, an arcade, and a hydro-tube water slide. (Memorial Day-Labor Day, daily 10 am-10 pm) **$$$$**

Caberfae Peaks Ski Resort. *Caberfae Rd, Cadillac (49601). 12 miles W on Hwy 55. Phone 231/862-3000. www.caberfaepeaks.com.* Quad, triple, three double chairlifts, two T-bars, two rope tows; patrol, school, rentals; snowmaking; bar, cafeteria, lodge, motel, nursery, restaurant; snowboard, cross-country, and snowmobile trails. (Late Nov-Mar, daily) **$$$$**

Johnny's Game and Fish Park. *5465 E 46 1/2 Mile Rd, Cadillac (49601). 5 miles SW on Hwy 115, follow signs. Phone 231/775-3700.* Wild and tame animals; 75-foot-long elevated goat walk; fishing for rainbow trout (no license, no limit; fee). (Mid-May-Labor Day, daily) **$$$**

William Mitchell State Park. *6093 E Hwy 115, Cadillac (49601). 2 1/2 miles W via Hwy 55 and 115. Phone 231/775-7911.* Approximately 260 acres between Cadillac and Mitchell lakes. Swimming beach, bathhouse, fishing, boating (launching, rentals); interpretive hiking trail, picnicking, playground, camping (tent and trailer facilities). Visitor center. Nature study area.

Limited-Service Hotels

★★ BEST VALUE INN OF CADILLAC RESORT AND CONFERENCE CENTER. *5676 Hwy 55 E, Cadillac (49601). Phone 231/775-2458; toll-free 888/315-2378; fax 231/775-8383. www.bestvalueinn.com.* 66 rooms. Check-out 11 am. Restaurant. Indoor pool, whirlpool. Tennis. **$**

★ ★ **CADILLAC SANDS RESORT.** *6319 E Hwy 115, Cadillac (49601). Phone 231/775-2407; toll-free 800/647-2637; fax 231/775-6422. www.cadillacsands.com.* 55 rooms, 2 story. Complimentary continental breakfast. Check-out 11 am. Restaurant, bar. Indoor pool. Airport transportation available. Private beach; dockage. **$**

★ **HAMPTON INN.** *1650 S Mitchell, Cadillac (49601). Phone 231/779-2900; toll-free 800/426-7866; fax 231/779-0846. www.hamptoninn.com.* 120 rooms, 4 story. Complimentary continental breakfast. Check-in 2 pm, check-out 11 am. Indoor pool, whirlpool. **$**

Full-Service Resort

★ ★ ★ **MCGUIRE'S RESORT.** *7880 Mackinaw Trail, Cadillac (49601). Phone 231/775-9947; toll-free 800/632-7302; fax 231/775-9621. www.mcguiresresort.com.* This resort is the perfect spot for visitors to relax and enjoy their vacation, with walking and biking trails, two golf courses, a pool, tennis facilities, volleyball and basketball courts, panoramic views of the countryside, and more. It is near shopping, the movie theater, and the lake. 122 rooms, 3 story. Pets accepted, some restrictions; fee. Check-out 11 am. Restaurant, bar. Indoor pool, whirlpool. Golf, 27 holes. Tennis. Airport transportation available. **$**

Restaurants

★ ★ **HERMANN'S EUROPEAN CAFE.** *214 N Mitchell, Cadillac (49601). Phone 231/775-9563. www.chefhermann.com.* French menu. Dinner. Closed Sun; holidays. Bar. Children's menu. Casual attire. Outdoor seating. **$$**

★ ★ **LAKESIDE CHARLIE'S.** *301 S Lake Mitchell, Cadillac (49601). Phone 231/775-5332; fax 231/775-8100.* American menu. Dinner. Closed Mon. Bar. Children's menu. Casual attire. Outdoor seating. **$$**

Calumet (A-6)

See also Copper Harbor, Hancock, Houghton

Population 818
Elevation 1,208 ft
Area Code 906
Zip 49913
Information Keweenaw Peninsula Chamber of Commerce, 326 Shelden, Houghton 49931; phone 906/482-5240 or toll-free 800/338-7982
Web Site www.keweenaw.org

Calumet (cal-you-MET) is a small town today, but it was once a bustling, wealthy copper-mining community of 60,000. Thanks to the red sandstone used to build most of the downtown buildings, Calumet looks much like it did 100 years ago, albeit with far fewer residents. Steeped in history and architectural treasures, Calumet has earned national recognition as part of the Keweenaw National Historic Park.

What to See and Do

Calumet Theatre. *340 6th St, Calumet (49913). Phone 906/337-2610. www.calumettheatre.com.* (1899) Built with boomtown wealth and continually being restored, this ornate theater was host to such great stars as Lillian Russell, Sarah Bernhardt, Lon Chaney, Otis Skinner, James O'Neil, Douglas Fairbanks, and John Philip Sousa. Guided tours (mid-June-Sept, daily). Live performances throughout the year. **$$**

Keweenaw National Historical Park. *100 Red Jacket Rd, Calumet (49913). Phone 906/337-3168. www.nps.gov/kewe.* Established in October 1992, to commemorate the heritage of copper mining on the Keweenaw Peninsula—its mines, machinery, and people. Self-guided walking tour brochures of the historic business and residential districts are available. Fees for cooperating sites include mine tours, museums. Calumet Unit and Quincy Unit. **FREE**

Upper Peninsula Firefighters Memorial Museum. *Red Jacket Fire Station, 327 6th St, Calumet (49913). Phone 906/296-2561.* Housed in the historic Red Jacket Fire Station, this museum features memorabilia and exhibits spanning almost a century of firefighting history. (Mon-Sat) **$**

Charlevoix (E-3)

See also Boyne City, Ellsworth, Petoskey, Traverse City

Population 3,116
Elevation 599 ft
Area Code 231
Zip 49720
Information Charlevoix Area Chamber of Commerce, 408 Bridge St; phone 231/547-2101

Web Site www.charlevoix.org

Known as "Charlevoix the Beautiful" (and pronounced SHAR-la-voy), this harbor town offers gorgeous sandy beaches on both Lake Michigan and Lake Charlevoix, a 17-mile-long inland lake. Every half hour, the drawbridge stops traffic on Charlevoix's main street to allow sailboats and the Beaver Island Ferry to enter Round Lake Harbor. While waiting for the bridge, visitors walk to the pier to view Lake Michigan and the Charlevoix lighthouse, one of the state's most photographed lighthouses. Tourists can also sample freshly made fudge, caramel apples, and ice cream cones while walking a four-block downtown area that features clothing stores, gift shops, art galleries, a bookstore, and eateries. A paved bike trail, suitable for in-line skating, walking, and cycling, links Charlevoix to the city of Petoskey.

What to See and Do

Beaver Island Boat Company. *City Dock, 103 Bridge Park Dr, Charlevoix (49720). Phone 231/547-2311; toll-free 888/446-4095. www.bibco.com.* A 2 1/4-hour trip to Beaver Island, the largest island of the Beaver Archipelago. (June-Sept: daily; mid-Apr-May and Oct-mid-Dec: limited schedule) Advance car reservations necessary. **$$$$**

Swimming, picnicking. *Lake Michigan and Lake Charlevoix beaches.* Depot and Ferry Avenue beaches; charter fishing, boat rentals (power and sail), launching ramp; tennis courts; municipal nine-hole golf course (June-Labor Day).

Special Events

Apple Festival. *408 Bridge St, Charlevoix (49720). Phone 231/547-2101.* Vendors line Charlevoix's main street selling fresh apples, apple pies, cider (with cake-type doughnuts, of course), caramel apples, and apple turnovers. Second weekend in Oct.

Venetian Festival. *408 Bridge St, Charlevoix (49720). Phone 231/547-2101.* Midway, street, and boat parades, fireworks. Fourth full weekend in July.

Waterfront Art Fair. *East Park on Round Lake, Charlevoix (49720). Phone 231/547-2675.* In this juried art show, hundreds of artists display and sell their works in a picturesque setting. Second Sat in Aug.

Limited-Service Hotels

★ ★ EDGEWATER INN. *100 Michigan Ave, Charlevoix (49720). Phone 231/547-6044; toll-free 800/748-0424; fax 231/547-0038. www.edgewater-charlevoix.com.* This inn offers one- and two-bedroom condominium suites that overlook Round Lake. It has both an indoor and an outdoor pool, a Jacuzzi, sauna, and much more. It is also located downtown, close to many local restaurants and attractions. 60 rooms, 3 story, all suites. Check-out 11 am. Restaurant. Fitness room. Indoor pool, outdoor pool, whirlpool. **$$**

★ WEATHERVANE TERRACE INN & SUITES. *111 Pine River Ln, Charlevoix (49720). Phone 231/547-9955; toll-free 800/552-0025; fax 231/547-0070. www.weathervane-chx.com.* 68 rooms, 3 story. Complimentary continental breakfast. Check-in 4 pm, check-out 11 am. High-speed Internet access, wireless Internet access. Outdoor pool, whirlpool. **$**

Restaurants

★ ★ ★ MAHOGANY'S. *9600 Clubhouse Dr, Charlevoix (49720). Phone 231/547-3555.* Located at the Charlevoix Country Club, the fieldstone fireplace and handcrafted mahogany bar set the scene for an elegant experience. Serving casual lunches on the porch and international cuisine in the dining room, this restaurant is the perfect post-game stopping place. American menu. Lunch, dinner. Closed Dec 24-25. Bar. Children's menu. **$$**

★ ★ STAFFORD'S WEATHERVANE. *106 Pine River Ln, Charlevoix (49720). Phone 231/547-4311. www.staffords.com.* American menu. Lunch, dinner. Bar. Children's menu. Casual attire. Reservations recommended (summer). Outdoor seating. **$$$**

Cheboygan (D-4)

See also Harbor Springs, Indian River, Mackinaw City

Founded 1871
Population 4,999
Elevation 600 ft
Area Code 231
Zip 49721
Information Cheboygan Area Chamber of Commerce, 124 N Main St, PO Box 69; phone 231/627-7183 or toll-free 800/968-3302

Web Site www.cheboygan.com

Surrounded by two Great Lakes and large inland lakes, Cheboygan (sha-BOY-gann) has long been famous as a premier boating and fishing area. You also find charming Victorian shops, gorgeous spring blooms, and delightful fall color. And because of heavy snowfall, winter activities abound: snowmobiling, cross-country skiing (hundreds of miles of groomed trails), snowshoeing, ice skating and hockey (skate rentals available), and ice fishing.

What to See and Do

Aloha State Park. *4347 3rd St, Cheboygan (49721). 9 miles S on Hwy 33, then W on Hwy 212, on Mullett Lake. Phone 231/625-2522.* Approximately 95 acres with swimming, sand beach, fishing, boating (launch); picnicking, camping (dump station). (Daily) **$$**

Cheboygan Opera House. *403 N Huron St, Cheboygan (49721). Huron and Backus sts. Phone 231/627-5432; fax 231/627-2643. www.theoperahouse.org.* (1877) Renovated 580-seat auditorium featuring events ranging from bluegrass to ballet. Contact the Chamber of Commerce for show schedule.

Cheboygan State Park. *4490 Beach Rd, Cheboygan (49721). 3 miles NE off Hwy 23, on Lake Huron. Phone 231/627-2811.* More than 1,200 acres with swimming, fishing, boating; hunting, hiking, cross-country skiing, picnicking, camping. Nature study. (Daily) **$$**

Fishing. Locks here lift boats to the Cheboygan River leading to an inland waterway which includes Mullett and Burt lakes, famous for muskie, walleye, salmon, and bass. Cheboygan County is the only place in the state where sturgeon spearing is legal each winter (February). Along the route, marinas supply cruise needs; swimming, boating. Contact the Chamber of Commerce.

The US Coast Guard Cutter *Mackinaw*. One of the world's largest icebreakers, with a complement of 80 officers and crew. When in port, the *Mackinaw* is moored at the turning basin on the east side of the Cheboygan River.

Special Event

Cheboygan County Fair. *Fairgrounds, 204 E Lincoln Ave, Cheboygan (49721). Phone 231/627-7183. www.cheboyganfair.com.* The attractions at this county fair include horse shows, carnival rides, craft displays, and agricultural and animal exhibits. Early Aug.

Limited-Service Hotels

★ BEST WESTERN RIVER TERRACE. *847 S Main St, Cheboygan (49721). Phone 231/627-5688; toll-free 877/627-9552; fax 231/627-2472. www.bestwestern.com.* 53 rooms, 2 story. Check-in 1 pm, check-out 11 am. Fitness room. Indoor pool, whirlpool. **$**

★ FLEETWOOD INN & SUITES. *889 S Main St, Cheboygan (49721). Phone 231/627-3126; toll-free 888/705-4085; fax 231/627-2889.* 42 rooms, 2 story. Complimentary continental breakfast. Check-out 11 am. Airport transportation available. **$**

Specialty Lodging

The following lodging establishment is approved by Mobil Travel Guide, but due to its unique and individualized nature has not been given a traditional Mobil Star rating. Included in this listing you may find bed-and-breakfasts, limited-service inns, guest ranches, and other unique hotel properties.

★ ★ ★ INSEL HAUS B&B RETREAT CENTER. *600 E University, Bois Blanc Island (48307). Phone 231/634-7393; fax 231/634-7163. www.inselhausbandb.com* 13 rooms. Complimentary full breakfast. Check-in 4 pm, check-out 11 am. **$$$**

Restaurant

★ ★ HACK-MA-TACK INN. *8131 Beebe Rd, Cheboygan (49721). Phone 231/625-2919.* Set in wooded area. American menu. Dinner. Closed mid-Oct-mid-Apr. Bar. **$$**

Chesaning (H-5)

See also Flint, Saginaw

Population 2,548
Elevation 644 ft
Area Code 989
Zip 48616
Information Chesaning Chamber of Commerce, 218 N Front St, 48616; phone 989/845-3055 or toll-free 800/255-3055

Web Site www.chesaningchamber.org

Chesaning (CHESS-a-ning), a Native American word for "big rock," is today known as Showboat City, because of the concerts and other events held throughout the summer on the showboat *Shiawassee Queen* that cruises the Shiawassee River. Victorian buildings line the downtown area.

Restaurant

★ ★ ★ **CHESANING HERITAGE HOUSE.** *605 Broad St, Chesaning (48616). Phone 989/845-7700; fax 989/845-4249. www.bonnymillinn.com.* This 1908, Georgian Revival mansion is located across the street from the Bonnymill Inn. It features nine dining areas and has Victorian décor, a crystal chandelier, and a fireplace. American menu. Lunch, dinner. Closed Dec 24-25. Bar. Children's menu. Outdoor seating. **$$**

Clare (G-4)

See also Alma, Harrison, Midland, Mount Pleasant

Population 3,021
Elevation 841 ft
Area Code 989
Zip 48617
Information Chamber of Commerce, 429 McEwan St; phone 989/386-2442 or toll-free 888/282-5273
Web Site www.claremichigan.com

Arriving in Clare—Michigan's "Gateway to the North"—means you're either beginning or ending your Up North vacation. The Welcome Center in Clare features an impressive seven-statue memorial to construction workers.

What to See and Do

Chalet Cross-Country. *5931 Clare Ave, Clare (48617). 6 miles N via Old Hwy 127. Phone 989/386-9697.* Groomed cross-country trails (approximately 8 1/2 miles) graded to skier's experience; patrol, school, rentals; store. (Dec-Mar, daily; closed Dec 25) **$$**

Special Event

Irish Festival. *McEwan St, Clare (48617). Phone 989/386-2442; toll-free 888/282-5273. www.claremichigan.com/irish.* A parade, fish fry, children's carnival, and karaoke contest are among the events at this Irish festival. Mid-Mar.

Limited-Service Hotel

★ ★ **DOHERTY HOTEL & CONFERENCE CENTER.** *604 N McEwan St, Clare (48617). Phone 989/386-3441; toll-free 800/525-4115; fax 989/386-4231. www.dohertyhotel.com.* 157 rooms, 3 story. Pets accepted; fee. Complimentary full breakfast. Check-in 3 pm, check-out noon. Restaurant, bar. Indoor pool, whirlpool. Airport transportation available. **$**

Restaurant

★ ★ **DOHERTY.** *604 N McEwan St, Clare (48617). Phone 989/386-3441; fax 989/386-4231. www.dohertyhotel.com.* Established in 1924. American menu. Breakfast, lunch, dinner, Sun brunch. Bar. Children's menu. Business casual attire. **$$**

Coldwater (K-4)

See also Marshall

Population 9,607
Elevation 969 ft
Area Code 517
Zip 49036
Information Coldwater/Branch County Chamber of Commerce, 20 Division St; phone 517/278-5985 or toll-free 800/968-9333
Web Site www.branch-county.com

Coldwater is renowned for its turn-of-the-century architecture, which has been carefully preserved. Named for the river that runs through town, Coldwater is best know for the Tibbits Opera House, which features numerous concerts, plays, and other events.

What to See and Do

Tibbits Opera House. *14 S Hanchett St, Coldwater (49036). Phone 517/278-6029. www.tibbits.org.* (1882) Renovated 19th-century Victorian opera house. Presently home to professional summer theater series, art exhibits, a winter concert series, children's programs, and community events. Originally owned and operated by businessman Barton S. Tibbits, the house attracted such performers as John Philip Sousa, Ethel Barrymore, P. T. Barnum, John Sullivan, and William Gillette. Tours (Mon-Fri). **FREE**

Wing House Museum. *27 S Jefferson St, Coldwater (49036). Phone 517/278-2871. www.wingmuseum.org.*

(1875) Historical house museum exhibiting Second Empire architectural style. Includes the original kitchen and dining room in the basement, a collection of Oriental rugs, oil paintings, three generations of glassware, Regina music box; furniture from Empire to Eastlake styles. (Wed-Sun 1-5 pm; also by appointment) **$**

Special Events

Branch County 4-H Fair. *31 Division St, Coldwater (49036). Phone 517/279-4313.* Exhibits, animal showing, carnival booths, rides, tractor pulling. Second week in Aug. **$**

Bronson Polish Festival Days. *SW on I-12 in downtown Bronson. Phone toll-free 800/968-9333.* Heritage fest; games, vendors, concessions, dancing. Third week in July. **$**

Car Show Swap Meet. *4-H Fairgrounds, Coldwater (49036). Phone 517/278-5985. carshowswapmeet.com.* Antique and classic car show, arts and crafts, vendors; trophies. Early May. **$**

Quincy Chain of Lakes Tip-Up Festival. *5 miles E via I-12 on Tip-Up Island. Phone 517/639-7355.* Parade, fishing and woodcutting contests; torchlight snowmobile ride; dancing, polar bear splash, pancake breakfast, fish fry. Second weekend in Feb.

Tibbits Professional Summer Theatre Series. *14 S Hanchett St, Coldwater (49036). Phone 517/278-6029. www.tibbits.org/summertheatre.htm.* Resident professional company produces comedies and musicals. Late June-Aug. **$$$$**

Limited-Service Hotel

★ ★ RAMADA INN & SUITES CONVENTION CENTER. *1000 Orleans Blvd, Coldwater (49036). Phone 517/278-2017; toll-free 800/806-8226; fax 517/279-7214. www.ramada.com.* 128 rooms, 2 story. Pets accepted; fee. Complimentary continental breakfast. Check-out 11 am. Restaurant, bar. Indoor pool, whirlpool. **$**

Specialty Lodging

The following lodging establishment is approved by Mobil Travel Guide, but due to its unique and individualized nature has not been given a traditional Mobil Star rating. Included in this listing you may find bed-and-breakfasts, limited-service inns, guest ranches, and other unique hotel properties.

CHICAGO PIKE. *215 E Chicago St, Coldwater (49036). Phone 517/279-8744; toll-free 800/471-0501; fax 517/278-8597. www.chicagopikeinn.com.* Victorian residence (1903); antiques; period furnishings; fireplace in sitting room. 8 rooms, 2 story. Closed Thanksgiving, Dec 24-25. Children over 12 years only. Complimentary full breakfast. Check-in 3 pm, check-out noon. High-speed Internet access. Airport transportation available. **$$**

Copper Harbor (A-6)

See also Calumet, Hancock, Houghton, Isle Royale National Park

Population 55
Elevation 621 ft
Area Code 906
Zip 49918
Information Keweenaw Peninsula Chamber of Commerce, 325 Shelden, Houghton 49913; phone 906/482-5240 or toll-free 800/338-7982
Web Site www.copperharbor.org

Lumps of pure copper studded the lakeshore and attracted the first explorers to this area, but deposits proved thin and unfruitful. A later lumbering boom also ended. Today, this northernmost village in the state is a small but beautiful resort. Streams and inland lakes provide excellent trout, walleye, bass, and northern pike fishing. Lake Superior yields trout, salmon, and other species.

What to See and Do

Astor House Antique Doll & Indian Artifact Museum. *560 Gratiot St (Hwy 41), Copper Harbor (49918). Corner of I-41 and Hwy 26. Phone 906/289-4449; toll-free 800/833-2470.* Early mining boom-days items and hundreds of antique dolls. (June-Oct, daily) **$**

Brockway Mountain Drive. *10 miles; begins 1/4 mile W of junction Hwy 41 and Hwy 26.* Lookouts; views of Lake Superior and forests.

Copper Harbor Lighthouse Tour. *Copper Harbor Marina, 326 Shelden Ave, Houghton (49921). Phone 906/289-4466. www.copperharborlighthouse.com.* Twenty-minute boat ride to one of the oldest lighthouses on Lake Superior; includes guided tour of lighthouse. Trips depart hourly. (Memorial Day-mid-Oct, daily, weather permitting) **$$$$**

Delaware Mine Tour. *7804 Delaware Mine Rd, Copper Harbor (49918). 11 miles W on Hwy-41. Phone 906/289-4688.* Underground guided tour of copper mine dating back to the 1850s. (Mid-May-mid-Oct, daily) **$$$**

Ferry service to Isle Royale National Park. *60 5th St, Houghton (49921). Phone 906/482-0984.* Four ferries and a float plane provide transportation (June-Sept, daily; some trips in May). For fees and schedule contact Park Superintendent.

Fort Wilkins State Park. *Hwy-41, Copper Harbor (49918). 1 mile E. Phone 906/289-4215.* Approximately 200 acres. A historic army post (1844) on Lake Fanny Hooe. The stockade has been restored and the buildings have been preserved to maintain the frontier post atmosphere. Costumed guides demonstrate old army lifestyle. Fishing, boating (launch); cross-country ski trails, picnicking, playground, concession, camping. Museum with relics of early mining days and various exhibits depicting army life in the 1870s. (Daily)

Isle Royale Queen III Evening Cruises. *Copper Harbor (49918). The Isle Royale Line Waterfront Landing. Phone 906/289-4437. www.isleroyale.com.* Narrated 1 1/2-hour cruise on Lake Superior. Reservations advised. (Early July-Labor Day, evenings)

Snowmobiling. *326 Shelden Ave, Houghton (49921). Phone 906/482-2388.* There is a series of interconnecting trails totaling several hundred miles; some overlook Lake Superior from high bluffs. Also 17 miles of cross-country trails. (Dec-Mar)

Special Events

Art in the Park. *Community Center grounds, Main St, Copper Harbor (49918). Phone 906/337-4579.* Juried art show featuring local and regional artists; food; live entertainment. Mid-Aug.

Brockway Mountain Challenge. *Phone 906/337-4579.* A 15-kilometer cross-country ski race. Feb.

Limited-Service Hotel

★ BELLA VISTA MOTEL. *160 6th St, Copper Harbor (49918). Phone 906/289-4213. www.bellavistamotel.com.* 22 rooms, 2 story. Closed mid-Oct-Apr. Check-out 10 am. **$**

Restaurant

★ TAMARACK INN. *512 Gratiot St, Copper Harbor (49918). Phone 906/289-4522.* American menu. Breakfast, lunch, dinner. **$$**

Dearborn (J-5)

See also Ann Arbor, Detroit, Detroit Metropolitan Airport Area, Ypsilanti

Settled 1763
Population 89,286
Elevation 605 ft
Area Code 313
Information Chamber of Commerce, 15544 Michigan Ave, 48126; phone 313/584-6100
Web Site www.dearborn.org

Dearborn is the home of the Ford Motor Company Rouge Assembly Plant, Ford World Headquarters, and The Henry Ford, a complex made up of the Henry Ford Museum, Greenfield Village, and other historical attractions. Although Dearborn has a long and colorful history, its modern eminence is due to Henry Ford, who was born here in 1863.

What to See and Do

The Henry Ford. *20900 Oakwood Blvd, Dearborn (48124). 1/2 mile S of Hwy 12, 1 1/2 miles W of Southfield Rd. Phone 313/271-1620. www.hfmgv.org.* On a 254-acre setting, this indoor-outdoor complex preserves a panorama of American life of the past—an unequaled collection of American historical artifacts. Built by Henry Ford as a tribute to the culture, resourcefulness, and technology of the United States, the museum and village stand as monuments to America's achievements. Dedicated in 1929 to Thomas Edison, they attract millions of visitors from around the world each year. (Mon-Sat 9 am-5 pm, Sun noon-5 pm; closed Thanksgiving, Dec 25)

Greenfield Village. *20900 Oakwood Blvd, Dearborn (48124). Phone 313/271-1620. www.hfmgv.org.* Comprises more than eighty 18th- and 19th-century buildings moved here from all over the country, forming a village that brings history alive. Historic homes, shops, schools, mills, stores, and laboratories that figured in the lives of such historic figures as Lincoln, Webster, Burbank, McGuffey, Carver, the Wright brothers, Firestone, Edison, and

Ford. Among the most interesting are the courthouse where Abraham Lincoln practiced law, the Wright brothers' cycle shop, Henry Ford's birthplace, Edison's Menlo Park laboratory, homes of Noah Webster and Luther Burbank, 19th-century farmstead of Harvey Firestone; steam-operated industries, crafts workers, demonstrations, home activites. (Mon-Sat 9 am-5 pm, Sun noon-5 pm; closed Thanksgiving, Dec 25; interiors also closed Jan-mid-Mar) Also winter sleigh tours. **$$$$**

Henry Ford Museum. *20900 Oakwood Blvd, Dearborn (48124). Phone 313/271-1620. www.hfmgv.org.* Occupies 12 acres and includes major collections in transportation, power and machinery, agriculture, lighting, communications, household furnishings and appliances, ceramics, glass, silver, and pewter. Special exhibits, demonstrations, and hands-on activities. (Mon-Sat 9 am-5 pm, Sun noon-5 pm; closed Thanksgiving, Dec 25) **$$$**

Suwanee Park. Turn-of-the-century amusement center with antique merry-go-round, steamboat, train ride; restaurant, soda fountain. (Mid-May-Sept, some fees). In addition, visitors can take narrated rides in a horse-drawn carriage (fee), on a steam train (fee), or on a riverboat; 1931 Ford bus rides are also available (mid-May-Sept). Varied activities are scheduled throughout the year (see SPECIAL EVENTS). Meals and refreshments are available. Combination ticket for The Henry Ford. **$$$$**

★ **Henry Ford Estate-Fair Lane.** *4901 Evergreen Rd, Dearborn (48128). On the University of Michigan-Dearborn Campus (follow signs). Phone 313/593-5590. www.henryfordestate.com.* (1913-1915) Built by automotive pioneer Henry Ford in 1915, the mansion cost in excess of $2 million and stands on 72 acres of property. The mansion, designed by William Van Tine, reflects Ford's penchant for simplicity and functionalism; its systems for heating, water, electricity, and refrigeration were entirely self-sufficient at that time. The powerhouse, boathouse, and gardens have been restored, and some original furniture and a children's playhouse have been returned to the premises. (Apr-Dec: daily; rest of year: Sun; closed Jan 1, Dec 25) **$$$**

Special Events

Fall Harvest Days. *Greenfield Village, 20900 Oakwood Blvd, Dearborn (48124). Phone 313/271-1620. www.hfmgv.org.* Celebrates turn-of-the-century farm chores, rural home life, and entertainment. Three days in early Oct.

Old Car Festival. *Greenfield Village, 20900 Oakwood Blvd, Dearborn (48124). Phone 313/271-1620. www.hfmgv.org.* More than 500 motorized vehicles from 1932 or earlier are on display. Two days in mid-Sept.

Limited-Service Hotels

★★ BEST WESTERN GREENFIELD INN. *3000 Enterprise Dr, Dearborn (48101). Phone 313/271-1600; toll-free 800/342-5802; fax 313/271-1600. www.bestwestern.com.* 210 rooms, 3 story. Check-in 3 pm, check-out noon. Restaurant, bar. Fitness room. Indoor pool, whirlpool. Airport transportation available. **$**

★★ COURTYARD BY MARRIOTT. *5200 Mercury Dr, Dearborn (48126). Phone 313/271-1400; toll-free 800/321-2211; fax 313/271-1184. www.courtyard.com.* 147 rooms, 3 story. Check-in 3 pm, check-out noon. High-speed Internet access. Bar. Fitness room. Indoor pool, whirlpool. **$**

★ QUALITY INN. *21430 Michigan Ave, Dearborn (48124). Phone 313/565-0800; toll-free 800/221-2222; fax 313/565-2813. www.qualityinn.com.* Near Henry Ford Museum and Greenfield Village. 100 rooms, 2 story. Complimentary continental breakfast. Check-out noon. Outdoor pool. **$**

Full-Service Hotels

★★★ MARRIOTT DETROIT DEARBORN INN. *20301 Oakwood Blvd, Dearborn (48124). Phone 313/271-2700; toll-free 800/228-9290; fax 313/271-7464. www.marriott.com.* Built in 1931, this historic hotel is located on 23 beautifully landscaped acres with gardens. The grounds consist of a Georgian-style inn built by Henry Ford, two Colonial-style lodges, and five Colonial-style houses; Early American décor and furnishings. 222 rooms, 4 story. Check-in 4 pm, check-out noon. Restaurant, bar. Fitness room. Outdoor pool, children's pool. Tennis. **$$**

★★★ THE RITZ-CARLTON, DEARBORN. *300 Town Center Dr, Dearborn (48126). Phone 313/441-2000; toll-free 800/241-3333; fax 313/441-2051. www.ritzcarlton.com.* The Ritz-Carlton is the most prestigious address in the metropolitan Detroit area. Located only 15 minutes from downtown, this hotel is part of a nearly 7-acre complex in historic Dearborn. Its distinguished atmosphere and superior service make it a favorite of socialites and corporate leaders, and the hotel is home to a flurry of charity and business events. The hotel is also a gourmet destination, and reservations at the award-winning The Grille Room (see) are extremely coveted. The guest rooms are a perfect match for demanding travelers, with state-of-the-art technology, oversized bathrooms, and handsome appointments. Fitness is a priority, and the hotel not only provides a gym and indoor pool but also extends privileges to the nearby Fairlane Club & Spa. 308 rooms, 11 story. Check-out noon. Restaurant, bar. Fitness room. Indoor pool, whirlpool. Business center. **$$**

Restaurants

★ ★ ★ **THE GRILLE ROOM.** *300 Town Center Dr, Dearborn (48126). Phone 313/441-2000; toll-free 800/241-3333; fax 313/441-2051. www.ritzcarlton.com.* Any time of day, this Ritz-Carlton, mahogany-clad dining room is a civilized retreat for Chef de cuisine Christian Schmidt's American-Continental cuisine featuring steaks, chops, and seafood. American menu. Breakfast, lunch, dinner, Sun brunch. Bar. Valet parking. **$$$**

★ ★ **KIERNAN'S STEAK HOUSE.** *21931 Michigan Ave (Hwy 12), Dearborn (48124). Phone 313/565-4260; fax 313/565-3712.* Seafood, steak menu. Lunch, dinner. Closed holidays. Bar. Valet parking. **$$$**

★ ★ ★ **MORO'S.** *6535 Allen Rd, Allen Park (48101). Phone 313/382-7152.* Veal is king here, straight from the on-site butcher. Many dishes are prepared tableside. Service and atmosphere are Old World and professional. Italian menu. Lunch, dinner. Closed holidays; also Sun in June-Aug. **$$**

Detroit (J-6)

See also Ann Arbor, Birmingham, Bloomfield Hills, Dearborn, Detroit Metropolitan Airport Area, Farmington, Farmington Hills, Holly, Monroe, Pontiac, Royal Oak, Southfield, St. Clair, Troy, Warren

Founded 1701
Population 1,027,974
Elevation 600 ft
Area Code 313
Information Metropolitan Detroit Convention and Visitors Bureau, 211 W Fort St, Suite 1000, 48226; toll-free 800/338-7648
Web Site www.visitdetroit.com
Suburbs Ann Arbor, Birmingham, Bloomfield Hills, Dearborn, Farmington, Livonia, Mount Clemens, Plymouth, Pontiac, Rochester, Royal Oak, Novi, Southfield, St. Clair, Troy, Warren, Ypsilanti.

Detroit, a high-speed city geared to the tempo of the production line, is the symbol throughout the world of America's productive might. Its name is almost synonymous with the word "automobile." The city that put the world on wheels, Detroit is the birthplace of mass production and the producer of nearly 25 percent of the nation's automobiles, trucks, and tractors. This is the city of Ford, Chrysler, Dodge, the Fishers, and the UAW. Detroit is also a major producer of space propulsion units, automation equipment, plane parts, hardware, rubber tires, office equipment, machine tools, fabricated metal, iron and steel forging, and auto stampings and accessories. Being a port and border city, Detroit puts the Michigan Customs District among the nation's top five customs districts.

Founded by Antoine de la Mothe Cadillac in the name of Louis XIV of France at *le place du détroit*—"the place of the strait"—this strategic frontier trading post was 75 years old when the Revolution began. During the War of Independence, Detroit was ruled by Henry Hamilton, the British governor hated throughout the colonies as "the hair buyer of Detroit" because he encouraged Native Americans to take rebel scalps rather than prisoners. At the end of the war, the British ignored treaty obligations and refused to abandon Detroit. As long as Detroit remained in British hands, it was both a strategic threat and a barrier to westward expansion; however, the settlement was finally wrested away by Major General Anthony Wayne at the Battle of Fallen Timbers. On July 11, 1796, the Stars and Stripes flew over Detroit for the first time.

During the War of 1812, the fortress at Detroit fell mysteriously into British hands again, without a shot fired. It was recaptured by the Americans the following year. In 1815, when the city was incorporated, Detroit was still just a trading post; by 1837, it was a city of 10,000 people. Then, the development of more efficient transportation opened the floodgates of immigration, and the city was on its way as an industrial and shipping hub. Between 1830-1860, population doubled with every decade. At the turn of the century, the auto industry took hold.

Detroit was a quiet city before the automobile—brewing beer and hammering together carriages and stoves. Most people owned their own homes; they called it "the most beautiful city in America." All this swiftly changed when the automobile age burst upon it. Growth became the important concern; production stood as the summit of achievement. The automobile lines produced a new civic personality—there was little time for culture at the end of a day on the line. The city rocketed out beyond its river-hugging confines, developing nearly 100 suburbs. Today growing pains have eased, the automobile worker has more leisure time, and a new Detroit personality is emerging. Civic planning is remodeling the face of the community, particularly downtown and along the riverfront. Five minutes from downtown, twenty separate institutions form Detroit's Cultural Center—all within easy walking distance of one another.

Detroit is one of the few cities in the United States where you can look due south into Canada. The city stretches out along the Detroit River between Lakes Erie and St. Clair, opposite the Canadian city of Windsor, Ontario. Detroit is 143 square miles in size and almost completely flat. The buildings of the Renaissance Center and Civic Center are grouped about the shoreline, and a network of major highways and expressways radiate from this point like the spokes of a wheel. The original city was laid out on the lines of the L'Enfant plan for Washington, DC, with a few major streets radiating from a series of circles. As the city grew, a gridiron pattern was superimposed to handle the maze of subdivisions that had developed into Detroit's 200 neighborhoods.

These main thoroughfares all originate near the Civic Center: Fort Street (Hwy 3); Michigan Avenue (Hwy 12); Grand River Avenue (I-96); John Lodge Freeway (Hwy 10); Woodward Avenue (Hwy 1); Gratiot Avenue (Hwy 3); and Fisher and Chrysler freeways (I-75). Intersecting these and almost parallel with the shoreline are the Edsel Ford Freeway (I-94) and Jefferson Avenue (Hwy 25).

Additional Visitor Information

For additional accommodations, see DETROIT METROPOLITAN AIRPORT AREA, which follows DETROIT.

The Metropolitan Detroit Convention and Visitors Bureau (211 Fort St, Suite 1000, 48226; phone toll-free 800/338-7648) publishes the Visitor's Guide to Greater Detroit, a helpful booklet describing the area. Information is also available from the City of Detroit, Department of Public Information, 608 Coleman A. Young Municipal Center, 48226; phone 313/224-3755. In addition, there are Detroit Visitor and Information Centers located at 100 Renaissance Center, first floor, and at Henry Ford Museum and Greenfield Village in Dearborn (see) that provide booklets and brochures on the city. To receive an information packet on Detroit or to inquire about lodging phone the "Whats Line," 800/338-7648.

Public Transportation

Buses (Suburban Mobility Authority for Regional Transportation), phone 313/962-5515 (Detroit Department of Transportation). Elevated train downtown (the People Mover), phone toll-free 800/541-7245.

What to See and Do

★ **Belle Isle.** *E Jefferson Ave and E Grand Blvd, Detroit (48207). An island park in the middle of the Detroit River, reached by MacArthur Bridge. Phone 313/852-4078.* Between US and Canada, in sight of downtown Detroit, this 1,000-acre island park offers nine-hole golf, a nature center, guided nature walks, swimming, fishing (piers, docks). Picnicking, ball fields, tennis and lighted handball courts. **FREE** Also here are

Belle Isle Zoo. *E Jefferson Ave and E Grand Blvd, Detroit (48207). Phone 313/852-4083.* Animals in natural habitat. (May-Oct, daily) **$$**

Dossin Great Lakes Museum. *100 Strand Dr, Detroit (48207). Phone 313/852-4051.* Scale models of Great Lakes ships; restored "Gothic salon" from Great Lakes liner; marine paintings, reconstructed ship's bridge, and full-scale racing boat, *Miss Pepsi.* (Sat-Sun 11 am-5 pm) **$**

Whitcomb Conservatory. *E Jefferson Ave and E Grand Blvd, Detroit (48207). Phone 313/852-4064.*

Exhibits of ferns, cacti, palms, orchids; special exhibits. (Mon-Sat 10 am-5 pm) **$**

Canada. Windsor, Ontario, is only a five-minute drive through the Detroit-Windsor Tunnel or via the Ambassador Bridge. Tunnel and bridge tolls. Buses run every 12 minutes (fee). For border-crossing regulations, see MAKING THE MOST OF YOUR TRIP.

Charles H. Wright Museum of African-American History. *315 E Warren Ave, Detroit (48201). In the University Cultural Center. Phone 313/494-5800. www.maah-detroit.org.* Exhibits trace 400 years of history and achievements of African Americans. The museums major exhibit, *The African-American Experience*, is an inspiring look at African-American culture. (Tues-Sat 9:30 am-5 pm, Sun 1-5 pm; closed holidays) **$**

Children's Museum. *6134 Second Ave, Detroit (48202). Phone 313/873-8100. www.detroitchildrensmuseum.org.* Exhibits include "America Discovered," Inuit culture, children's art, folk crafts, birds and mammals of Michigan, holiday themes. Participatory activities relate to exhibits. Special workshops and programs and planetarium demonstrations on Saturday and during vacations. (Mon-Fri 9 am-4 pm; closed holidays) **FREE**

Civic Center. *Woodward and Jefferson aves, Detroit (48226).* Dramatic group of buildings in a 95-acre downtown riverfront setting. Included in this group are

Cobo Hall-Cobo Arena. *1 Washington Blvd, Detroit (48226). W Jefferson Ave and Washington Blvd. Phone 313/877-8111; fax 313/877-8577. www.cobocenter.com.* Designed to be the world's finest convention-exposition-recreation building; features an 11,561-seat arena and 720,000 square feet of exhibit area and related facilities. (Daily)

Coleman A. Young Municipal Center. *2 Woodward Ave, Detroit (48226). Phone 313/224-5585.* A $27-million, 13-story white marble office building and 19-story tower housing more than 36 government departments and courtrooms. At the front entrance is the massive bronze sculpture, *Spirit of Detroit.* Building (Mon-Fri; closed holidays). **FREE**

Hart Plaza and Dodge Fountain. *1 Hart Plz, Detroit (48226). Jefferson Ave. Phone 313/877-8077.* A $2 million water display designed by sculptor Isamu Noguchi.

Michigan Consolidated Gas Company Building. *1 Woodward Ave, Detroit (48226).* Glass-walled skyscraper designed by Minoru Yamasaki.

Veterans' Memorial Building. *151 W Jefferson Ave, Detroit (48226).* Rises on site where Cadillac and first French settlers landed in 1701. This $5.75 million monument to the Detroit-area war dead was the first unit of the $180-million Civic Center to be completed. The massive sculptured-marble eagle on the front of the building is by Marshall Fredericks, who also sculpted *Spirit of Detroit* at the City-County Building.

Detroit Historical Museum. *5401 Woodward Ave, Detroit (48202). Phone 313/833-1805. www.detroithistorical.org.* Presents a walk-through history along reconstructed streets of Old Detroit, period alcoves, costumes; changing exhibits portray city life. The museum rotates exhibits that explore Detroit history, from automotive displays to Motown exhibits. (Tues-Fri 9:30 am-5 pm, Sat 10 am-5 pm, Sun 11 am-5 pm; closed holidays) **$$**

Detroit Institute of Arts. *5200 Woodward Ave, Detroit (48202). Between Farnsworth Ave and Kirby St. Phone 313/833-7900. www.dia.org.* (1885) One of the great art museums of the world, tells history of humankind through artistic creations. Every significant art-producing culture is represented. Exhibits include *The Detroit Industry* murals by Diego Rivera, Van Eyck's *St. Jerome*, Bruegel's *Wedding Dance,* and Van Gogh's *Self-Portrait;* African, American, Indian, Dutch, French, Flemish, and Italian collections; medieval arms and armor; an 18th-century American country house reconstructed with period furnishings. Frequent special exhibitions (fee); lectures, films. (Wed-Thurs 10 am-4 pm, Fri 10 am-9 pm, Sat-Sun 10 am-5 pm; closed holidays) **$$**

Detroit Lions (NFL). *Ford Field, 2000 Brush St, Detroit (48226). Phone 313/262-2003 (tickets). www.detroitlions.com.* Located in the heart of downtown Detroit, this is the site of the 2006 Super Bowl.

Detroit Public Library. *5201 Woodward Ave, Detroit (48202). Phone 313/833-1000. www.detroit.lib.mi.us.* Murals by Coppin, Sheets, Melchers, and Blashfield; special collections include National Automotive History, Burton Historical (Old Northwest Territory), Hackley (African Americans in performing arts), Labor, Maps, Rare Books, US Patents Collection from

1790 to present. (Tues-Wed noon-8 pm, Thurs-Sat 10 am-6 pm; closed holidays) **FREE**

Detroit Red Wings (NHL). *Joe Louis Arena, 600 Civic Center Dr, Detroit (48226). Phone 313/396-7444. www.detroitredwings.com.*

Detroit Symphony Orchestra Hall. *3711 Woodward Ave, Detroit (48201). At Parsons. Phone 313/576-5100; fax 313/576-5101. www.detroitsymphony.com.* (1919) Restored public concert hall features classical programs. The Detroit Symphony Orchestra performs here.

Detroit Tigers (MLB). *Comerica Park, 2100 Woodward Ave, Detroit (48201). Woodward Ave and I-75. Phone 313/962-4000. tigers.mlb.com.* Team plays at Comerica Park.

Eastern Market. *2934 Russell St, Detroit (48207). Via I-75 at Gratiot. Phone 313/833-1560.* (1892) Built originally on the site of an early hay and wood market, this and the Chene-Ferry Market are the two remaining produce/wholesale markets. Today the Eastern Market encompasses produce and meat-packing houses, fish markets, and storefronts offering items ranging from spices to paper. It is also recognized as the world's largest bedding flower market. (Mon-Sat; closed holidays) **FREE**

Fisher Building. *3011 W Grand Blvd, Detroit (48202). W Grand and Second blvds. Phone 313/874-4444.* (1928) Designed by architect Albert Kahn, this building was recognized in 1928 as the most beautiful commercial building erected and given a silver medal by the Architectural League of New York. The building consists of a 28-story central tower and two 11-story wings. Housed here are the Fisher Theater, shops, restaurants, art galleries, and offices. Underground pedestrian walkways and skywalk bridges connect to a parking deck and 11 separate structures, including General Motors World Headquarters and New Center One.

Greektown. For well over 100 years, this two-block area of Monroe street has been known as Greektown. Local restaurants specialize in serving large portions of Greek specialties, including souvlaki, mousaka, lamb chops, spinach pie, and gyros. Greektown bars are especially lively on Fridays and Saturdays, with plenty of shouts of "Opa!," while local shops and groceries celebrate Greek culture every day of the week. To complete your tour of Greektown, visit the Annunciation Greek Orthodox Cathedral that anchors the neighborhood.

Greektown Casino. *555 E Lafayette Ave, Detroit (48226). Phone 313/223-2999. www.greektowncasino.net.* Consistently rated the city's top casino by the *Detroit News* and *Detroit Free Press.* Conveniently located in the heart of Greektown and nearby Comerica Park (Detroit Tigers), Ford Field (Detroit Lions), Max M. Fisher Music Center, and the Fox Theater. More than 2,400 slot machines, plus a variety of table games, from craps and roulette to blackjack and seven-card stud. (Daily) **FREE**

Historic Trinity Lutheran Church. *1345 Gratiot Ave, Detroit (48207). Phone 313/567-3100. www.historictrinity.org.* (1931) Third church of congregation founded in 1850; 16th-century-style pier-and-clerestory, neo-Gothic small cathedral. Luther tower is a copy of the tower at a monastery in Erfurt, Germany. Much statuary and stained glass. Bell tower. (Tours by appointment) **DONATION**

International Institute of Metropolitan Detroit. *111 E Kirby Ave, Detroit (48202). Phone 313/871-8600.* Hall of Nations has cultural exhibits from five continents (Mon-Fri; closed holidays). Cultural programs and ethnic festivals throughout the year. **FREE**

Mariners' Church. *170 E Jefferson Ave, Detroit (48226). Phone 313/259-2206.* Oldest stone church in the city, completed in 1849, was moved 800 feet to its present site as part of Civic Center plan. Since that time it has been extensively restored and a bell tower with carillon has been added. Tours (by appointment). **FREE**

Max M. Fisher Music Center. *3711 Woodward Ave, Detroit (48201). Phone 313/576-5111. www.detroitsymphony.com.* The home of the Detroit Symphony Orchestra (DSO), the Max M. Fisher Music Center was built around Orchestra Hall, which is reputed to have the best acoustics in the world. In addition to Orchestra Hall, the Max complex includes the Music Box Theater, which is a smaller concert hall; a large rehearsal hall; and an educational center, among others. (Mon-Fri 10 am-8 pm; Sat on performance days)

MGM Grand Casino. *1300 John C. Lodge, Detroit (48201). Phone toll-free 877/888-2121. detroit.mgmgrand.com.* Over 2,000 slot machines, plus baccarat, blackjack, poker, roulette, and more. All-you-can-eat buffet, sports bar café, restaurant. Live entertainment. (Daily) **FREE**

Motor City Casino. *2901 Grand River Ave, Detroit (48201). Phone toll-free 877/777-0711. www.motorcitycasino.com.* With over 70,000 square feet, the Motor City Casino offers more than 2,500 slot machines, plus blackjack, roulette, craps, and many other games. A variety of cafés and restaurants can be found here as well. On-site entertainment takes place seven days per week. (Daily) **FREE**

Motown Museum. *2648 W Grand Blvd, Detroit (48208). Phone 313/875-2264. www.motownmuseum.com.* "Hitsville USA," the house where legends like Diana Ross and the Supremes, Stevie Wonder, Marvin Gaye, the Jackson Five, and the Temptations recorded their first hits. Motown's original recording Studio A; artifacts, photographs, gold and platinum records, memorabilia. Guided tours. (Tues-Sat 10 am-6 pm) **$$**

Renaissance Center. *100-400 E Jefferson Ave, Detroit (48243). Jefferson Ave at Beaubien. Phone 313/568-5600; fax 313/568-5606.* Seven-tower complex on the riverfront; includes a 73-story hotel (see FULL-SERVICE HOTELS), offices, restaurants, bars, movie theaters, retail shops, and business services.

Wayne State University. *6050 Pass, Detroit (48202). www.wayne.edu.* (1868) (34,950 students) Has 13 professional schools and colleges. The campus has almost 100 buildings, some of the most notable being the award-winning McGregor Memorial Conference Center designed by Minoru Yamasaki; the Walter P. Reuther Library of Labor and Urban Affairs; and the Yamasaki-designed College of Education. Wayne has a medical campus of 16 acres adjacent in the Detroit Medical Center. Three theaters present performances.

Special Events

Detroit Grand Prix. *Belle Isle, 1249 Washington Blvd, Detroit (48207).* Indy car race. Friday is Free Prix Day. June.

Ford International Detroit Jazz Festival. *1 Hart Plz, Detroit (48226). Phone 313/963-7622. www.detroitjazzfest.com.* Five days of free jazz concerts. Labor Day weekend.

Hazel Park. *1650 East Ten Mile Rd, Hazel Park (48030). Phone 248/398-1000.* Harness racing. Mon-Tues, Thurs-Sat. Apr-mid-Oct.

International Auto Show. *Cobo Hall, 1 Washington Blvd, Detroit (48226). Phone 248/643-0250.* Jan.

Michigan State Fair. *Michigan Exposition and Fairgrounds, 8 mile and Woodward Ave, Detroit (48203). Phone 313/369-8250.* Early-late Aug.

Northville Downs. *301 S Center St, Northville (48167). Phone 248/349-1000. www.northvilledowns.com.* Harness racing. Over 12 years only. Mon-Tues, Thurs, Sat. Jan, Oct-Mar.

Riverfront Festivals. *1 Hart Plz, Detroit (48226). Hart Plaza, downtown riverfront. Phone 313/877-8077.* Weekend festivals featuring entertainment, costumes, history, artifacts, and handicrafts of Detroit's diverse ethnic populations. Different country featured most weekends. May-Sept.

The Theatre Company-University of Detroit Mercy. *8200 W Outer Dr, Detroit (48219). Phone 313/993-1130.* Dramas, comedies in university theater. Sept-May.

Woodward Dream Cruise. *Woodward Ave, Detroit. Phone toll-free 800/338-7648. www.woodwarddreamcruise.com.* Each year, more than 1.5 million people watch or ride in 30,000 classic and vintage cars touring Woodward Avenue; the event is billed as the world's largest one-day celebration of car culture. A paradelike atmosphere means you'll find plenty to eat and drink, vendors selling T-shirts and other items commemorating the event, and street entertainers providing music and other events. Third Sat in Aug, 9 am-9 pm, with some events held the preceding Thurs and Fri. **FREE**

Limited-Service Hotels

★ ★ COURTYARD BY MARRIOTT DOWNTOWN. *333 E Jefferson St, Detroit (48226). Phone 313/222-7700; toll-free 800/321-2211; fax 313/222-6509. www.courtyard.com.* Opposite the river, this centrally located hotel is close to the Convention Center and Greektown, as well as Ford Field and Tiger Stadium. The adjacent office complex has shops, restaurants, and a salon. 260 rooms, 21 story. Check-in 3 pm, check-out noon. High-speed Internet access. Restaurant, bar. Fitness room. Indoor pool, whirlpool. Tennis. Business center. **$$**

★ ★ PARKCREST INN. *20000 Harper Ave, Harper Woods (48225). Phone 313/884-8800; fax 313/884-7087.* 49 rooms, 2 story. Pets accepted; fee. Check-out 11 am. Restaurant, bar. Outdoor pool. **$**

Full-Service Hotels

★ ★ ★ ATHENEUM SUITE HOTEL - A SUMMIT HOTEL. *1000 Brush St, Detroit (48226). Phone 313/962-2323; toll-free 800/772-2323; fax 313/*

962-2424. www.atheneumsuites.com. This property is located downtown in Greektown, near many restaurants, shops, and other area attractions. 174 rooms, 10 story, all suites. Check-in 3 pm, check-out noon. Bar. Fitness room. **$$**

★ ★ ★ MARRIOTT DETROIT RENAISSANCE CENTER. *Renaissance Center, Detroit (48243). Phone 313/568-8000; toll-free 800/352-0831; fax 313/568-8146. www.marriott.com.* 1,298 rooms, 72 story. Check-in 3 pm, check-out 1 pm. Restaurant, bar. Fitness room. Indoor pool. Business center. **$$**

★ ★ ★ OMNI DETROIT RIVER PLACE. *1000 River Place Dr, Detroit (48207). Phone 313/259-9500; toll-free 800/843-6664; fax 313/259-3744. www.omnihotels.com.* This elegant hotel is located in downtown Detroit on the historic waterfront. Guest rooms boast views of the river and the Canadian border. The hotel has a championship croquet court which is the only U.S.C.A. sanctioned croquet court in Michigan. 108 rooms, 5 story. Pets accepted, some restrictions; fee. Check-in 3 pm, check-out noon. Restaurant, bar. Fitness room. Indoor pool, whirlpool. **$**

Restaurants

★ ★ ★ BARON'S STEAKHOUSE. *1000 River Place Dr, Detroit (48207). Phone 313/259-4855; fax 313/259-3744. www.omnihotels.com.* The snug dining room and patio in the Omni Detroit River Place (see) overlook the Detroit River. Steak menu. Breakfast, lunch, dinner. Bar. Children's menu. Outdoor seating. **$$$**

★ ★ ★ CAUCUS CLUB. *150 W Congress St, Detroit (48226). Phone 313/965-4970.* One of the city's culinary legends, this English-style dining room serves American cuisine with European accents. The jumbo Dover sole in lemon butter is a signature dish and the cozy, dimly lit bar a popular after-work hangout. American menu. Lunch, dinner. Closed Sun; holidays. **$$**

★ EL ZOCALO. *3400 Bagley, Detroit (48216). Phone 313/841-3700.* Mexican menu. Lunch, dinner. Closed holidays. Bar. **$**

★ ★ FISHBONE'S RHYTHM KITCHEN CAFE. *400 Monroe St, Detroit (48226). Phone 313/965-4600; fax 313/965-1449.* Southern Louisiana, Cajun/Creole menu. Lunch, dinner, Sun brunch. Closed Dec 25. Bar. Valet parking. **$$**

★ ★ ★ OPUS ONE. *565 E Larned, Detroit (48226). Phone 313/961-7766; fax 313/961-9243. www.opus-one.com.* Partners Jim Kokas and Ed Mandziara have overseen this dressy dining room for more than ten years. Executive chef Tim Giznsky creates inventive, American cuisine that can be enjoyed for dinner, weekday power lunches, or pared with local theater tickets. American menu. Lunch, dinner. Closed Sun; holidays. Bar. Valet parking. **$$$**

★ ★ PEGASUS TAVERNA. *558 Monroe St, Detroit (48226). Phone 313/964-6800.* American, Greek menu. Lunch, dinner. Bar. Children's menu. Lattice-worked ceiling; hanging grape vines. **$$**

★ ★ ★ RATTLESNAKE CLUB. *300 River Pl, Detroit (48207). Phone 313/567-4400; fax 313/567-2063.* This Rivertown destination is where well-known chef Jimmy Schmidt offers seasonal, worldly American cuisine, a beautiful riverside dining room, and a superior, well-priced wine list. The flagship restaurant has been open for over ten years, a testament to its popularity. American menu. Lunch, dinner. Closed Sun; holidays. Bar. Valet parking. Outdoor seating. **$$$**

★ TRAFFIC JAM & SNUG. *511 W Canfield St, Detroit (48201). Phone 313/831-9470; fax 313/831-4022. www.traffic-jam.com.* American menu. Lunch, dinner. Closed Sun; holidays. Children's menu. **$$**

★ ★ ★ THE WHITNEY. *4421 Woodward Ave, Detroit (48201). Phone 313/832-5700; fax 313/832-2159. www.thewhitney.com.* Set in the Whitney family home, this mansion with Tiffany windows and crystal chandeliers serves updated versions of traditional favorites. Guests can dine in their choice of rooms including the Music Room, Library, or Oriental Room. American menu. Lunch, dinner, Sun brunch. Closed Mon, holidays. Bar. Valet parking. **$$$**

Detroit Metropolitan Airport Area (J-6)

See also Dearborn, Detroit, Ypsilanti

Airport Information

Airport Detroit Metropolitan Wayne County

Information Phone 734/247-7678

Lost and Found McNamara Terminal phone 734/247-3300, Smith and Berry Terminals 734/942-3669

Web Site www.metroairport.com

Airlines Airlines. Air Canada, American Airlines, American Eagle, American Trans Air, America West, ASA (Delta), British Airways, ComAir, Continental Airlines, Continental Express, Delta Air Lines, Lufthansa, Northwest Airlines, Northwest Airlink (Mesaba), KLM Royal Dutch, Royal Jordanian, Southwest Airlines, Spirit Airlines, United Airlines, United Express, US Airways, US Air Express.

Limited-Service Hotel

★★ **COURTYARD BY MARRIOTT.** *30653 Flynn Dr, Romulus (48174). Phone 734/721-3200; toll-free 800/321-2211; fax 734/721-1304. www.courtyard.com.* 146 rooms, 3 story. Check-in 3 pm, check-out noon. High-speed Internet access. Restaurant, bar. Fitness room. Indoor pool, whirlpool. Airport transportation available. **$**

Full-Service Hotels

★★★ **HILTON SUITES DETROIT METRO AIRPORT.** *8600 Wickham Rd, Romulus (48174). Phone 734/728-9200; toll-free 800/774-1500; fax 734/728-9278. www.hilton.com.* Offering an oasis of comfort and relaxation, and situated just 1 mile from the Detroit Metro Airport, this hotel is guaranteed to provide the perfect home-away-from-home. 151 rooms, 3 story, all suites. Complimentary full breakfast. Check-in 3 pm, check-out noon. Restaurant, bar. Fitness room. Indoor pool, outdoor pool, whirlpool. Airport transportation available. Business center. **$**

★★★ **THE WESTIN DETROIT METRO AIRPORT.** *2501 World Gateway Pl, Romulus (48174). Phone 734/942-6500; toll-free 800/228-3000; fax 734/942-6600. www.westin.com.* 404 rooms. Check-in 3 pm, check-out noon. High-speed Internet access. Restaurant, bar. Fitness room. Indoor pool. Airport transportation available. Business center. **$$**

Dundee (K-5)

See also Ann Arbor, Monroe, Toledo

Population 3,522
Elevation 673 ft
Area Code 734
Zip 48131

Nearly overnight, Dundee (dun-DEE) has grown from a sleepy truck stop on Highway 23 to a major retailing area, the center of which is the largest Cabela's store in the world.

What to See and Do

Cabela's. *110 Cabela Blvd E, Dundee (48131). Phone 734/529-4700; toll-free 800/581-4420. www.cabelas.com.* Cabela's offers the world's largest hunting, fishing, and outdoor store, attracting more than 6 million visitors per year. Cabela's is more than just a store; the 225,000-square-foot center offers museum-quality mounted animals, aquariums, and gun collections; a shooting range; two hotels; three restaurants, including a café that features wild game; and a beef jerky outlet. (Mon-Sat 8 am-9 pm, Sun 10 am-6pm)

East Tawas (F-5)

See also Oscoda, Tawas City

East Tawas (TAO-wass) and its sister-city, Tawas City, are the epitome of Michigan summer resorts, with sandy beaches, charming boutiques, and friendly cafés. Drive just up Highway 23 to Tawas Point State Park, which features a quaint lighthouse. The area is well known among bird-watchers, who watch for migratory stopovers of warblers and other songbirds in spring and fall.

Ellsworth (E-3)

See also Charlevoix

Population 483
Elevation 621 ft
Area Code 231
Zip 49729

Tiny Ellsworth, boasting a population of only 483 residents, sits on both Lake St. Clair and picturesque Ellsworth Lake. Although the town offers few other amenities, it is home to two of the best restaurants in the state.

Restaurants

★ ★ ★ **ROWE INN.** *6303 C-48, Ellsworth (49729). Phone 231/588-7351; fax 231/588-2365. www.roweinn.com.* This elegant fine dining restaurant is located on the lake in Ellsworth. The focus here is on cuisine native to Michigan, and the restaurant boasts an extensive wine list. American, French menu. Dinner. Closed Thanksgiving, Dec 25. Children's menu. Casual attire. Reservations recommended. Outdoor seating. **$$$**

★ ★ ★ ★ **TAPAWINGO.** *9502 Lake St, Ellsworth (49729). Phone 231/588-7971. www.tapawingo.net.* Tapawingo is a magnificent restaurant in every sense of the word: service, food, décor, atmosphere—it's all there. To find Tapawingo (the Indian name for the land on which the restaurant sits), you'll travel about 7 miles on a winding country road. It is an enchanted drive that leads you to this warm, sunny restaurant on Lake Michigan, surrounded by lush gardens. The dining room is equally charming, with a stone fireplace, lots of windows, a stunning wine room (the wine list is a find as well), and an elegant private room with its own veranda. But the best part of Tapawingo is the food, which is simply divine—a pleasure to look at, to eat, and to remember afterwards. Flavors are seasonal, earthy, and spectacular. In short, dinner here is nothing short of dazzling. American menu. Dinner. Closed mid-Nov-mid-Dec. Bar. Reservations recommended. **$$$**

Escanaba (D-2)

See also Gladstone, Manistique

Settled 1830
Population 13,659
Elevation 598 ft
Area Code 906
Zip 49829
Information Delta County Area Chamber of Commerce, 230 Ludington St; phone 906/786-2192 or toll-free 888/335-8264
Web Site www.deltami.org

The first European settlers in this area were lured by the pine timber, which they were quick to log; however, a second growth provides solid forest cover once again. Escanaba (esk-ah-NA-bah) is the only ore-shipping port on Lake Michigan. Sports enthusiasts are attracted by the open water and huge tracts of undeveloped countryside. Fishing is excellent. Escanaba is the headquarters for the Hiawatha National Forest.

What to See and Do

Hiawatha National Forest. *2727 N Lincoln Rd, Escanaba (49829). Phone 906/786-4062.* This 893,000-acre forest offers scenic drives, hunting, camping, picnicking, hiking, horseback riding, cross-country skiing, snowmobiling, winter sports; lake and stream fishing, swimming, sailing, motorboating, and canoeing. It has shoreline on three Great Lakes—Huron, Michigan, and Superior. The eastern section of the forest is close to Sault Ste. Marie, St. Ignace, and the northern foot of the Mackinac Bridge. Fees charged at developed campground sites. (Daily) For further information contact the Supervisor at the above address. **FREE**

Ludington Park. *Lakeshore Dr and Luddington St, Escanaba (49829). On Hwy 35, overlooks Little Bay de Noc. Phone 906/786-4141.* Fishing, boating (launch, marina; fee), swimming, bath house; tennis courts, playground, volleyball court, ball fields, picnic area, tables, stoves, scenic bike path, pavilion, bandshell. (Apr-Nov, daily) **FREE** In the park is

> **Delta County Historical Museum and Sand Point Lighthouse.** *12 Water Plant Rd, Escanaba (49829). Phone 906/786-3763.* Local historical artifacts; lumber, railroad, and maritime industry exhibits; 1867 restored lighthouse (fee). (June-Labor Day, daily) **$**

Pioneer Trail Park and Campground. *6822 Hwy 2/41, Hwy 35, Gladstone (49837). 3 miles N on Hwy 2/41, Hwy 35. Phone 906/786-1020.* A 74-acre park on the Escanaba River. Shoreline fishing; picnicking, nature trails, playground, camping (fee). (May-Sept, daily) **$**

Special Event

Upper Peninsula State Fair. *2401 12th Ave N, Escanaba (49829). Phone 906/786-4011.* Agricultural and 4-H exhibits, midway, entertainment. Six days in mid-Aug.

Limited-Service Hotels

★ ★ **BEST WESTERN PIONEER INN.** *2635 Ludington St, Escanaba (49829). Phone 906/786-0602; toll-free 800/780-7234; fax 906/786-3938. www.bestwestern.com.* 72 rooms, 2 story. Check-in 1 pm, check-out 11 am. Restaurant, bar. Indoor pool. **$**

★ ★ **TERRACE BLUFF BAY INN.** *7146 P Rd, Escanaba (49829). Phone 906/786-7554; toll-free 800/283-4678; fax 906/786-7597.* Overlooks Little Bay de Noc. 71 rooms, 2 story. Check-out 11 am. Restaurant, bar. Fitness room. Indoor pool, whirlpool. Golf. Tennis. **$**

Restaurant

★ ★ **STONEHOUSE.** *2223 Ludington St, Escanaba (49829). Phone 906/786-5003; fax 906/786-5189.* Seafood menu. Lunch, dinner. Closed Sun; holidays. Bar. Children's menu. **$$$**

Farmington (J-5)

See also Birmingham, Detroit, Farmington Hills, Plymouth, Southfield

Population 10,132
Elevation 750 ft
Area Code 248
Information Chamber of Commerce, 30903-B Ten Mile Rd, 48336; phone 248/474-3440
Web Site www.ffhchamber.com

What to See and Do

Kensington Metropark. *2240 W Buno Rd, Milford (48380). 14 miles NW on Hwy-96, Kent Lake Rd or Kensington Rd exits. Phone 248/685-1561.* More than 4,000 acres on Kent Lake. Two swimming beaches (Memorial Day-Labor Day, daily), boating (rentals), ice fishing; biking/hiking trail, tobogganing, skating, picnicking, concessions, 18-hole golf (fee). Also, a 45-minute boat cruises on the *Island Queen* (summer, daily; fee). Nature trails; farm center, nature center. Park (daily). Free admission Tuesday.

Special Event

Farmington Founders Festival. *Grand River and Farmington Rd, Farmington (48336). Phone 248/474-3440.* Ethnic food, arts and crafts, sidewalk sales, carnival, rides, concert, fireworks. Mid-July.

Limited-Service Hotel

★ ★ **DOUBLETREE HOTEL.** *2700 Sheraton Dr, Novi (48377). Phone 248/348-5000; toll-free 800/713-3513; fax 248/348-2315. www.doubletree.com.* 217 rooms, 3 story. Check-in 3 pm, check-out noon. Restaurant, bar. Fitness room. Indoor pool, outdoor pool, whirlpool. **$**

Full-Service Hotel

★ ★ ★ **SHERATON DETROIT NOVI.** *21111 Haggerty Rd, Novi (48375). Phone 248/349-4000; toll-free 800/325-3535; fax 248/349-4066. www.sheraton.com.* Conveniently situated near the intersection to all the major highways, this hotel offers a comfortable stay while being minutes from some of Novi's fun attractions. 239 rooms, 7 story. Check-in 3 pm, check-out noon. Restaurant, bar. Fitness room. Indoor pool, whirlpool. **$**

Restaurants

★ ★ **AH-WOK.** *41563 W Ten Mile Rd, Novi (48375). Phone 248/349-9260.* Chinese menu. Lunch, dinner. **$$$**

★ ★ ★ **FIVE LAKES GRILL.** *424 N Main St, Milford (48381). Phone 248/684-7455; fax 248/684-5935. www.fivelakesgrill.com.* American menu. Dinner. Closed Sun; holidays. Bar. Children's menu. **$$$**

Farmington Hills (J-5)

See also Detroit, Farmington

Web Site www.ffchamber.org

Limited-Service Hotel

★ ★ **RADISSON SUITE HOTEL FARMINGTON HILLS.** *37529 Grand River*

Ave, Farmington Hills (48335). Phone 248/477-7800; toll-free 800/333-3333; fax 248/478-3799. www.radisson.com. 137 rooms, 4 story, all suites. Complimentary continental breakfast. Check-out noon. High-speed Internet access. Restaurant, bar. Fitness room. Indoor pool, whirlpool. **$**

Restaurant

★★★ **TRIBUTE.** *31425 W Twelve Mile Rd, Farmington Hills (48334). Phone 248/848-9393; fax 248/848-1919. www.tributerestaurant.com.* Chef Takashi Yagihashi spent 17 years in some of the most renowned kitchens in Europe and America before settling down to serve his Asian-inspired, contemporary French creations to a moneyed Detroit crowd. The industrial building and luxuriously whimsical dining room are the property of Lawrence Wisne, a Detroit automotive-industry millionaire whose lavish investment has put this restaurant on the nation's culinary map. French menu. Dinner. Closed Sun-Mon; holidays. Valet parking. **$$$**

Flint (H-5)

See also Frankenmuth, Holly, Owosso, Saginaw

Settled 1819
Population 140,761
Elevation 750 ft
Area Code 810
Information Flint Area Convention and Visitors Bureau, 519 S Saginaw St, 48502; phone 810/232-8900 or toll-free 800/253-5468
Web Site www.visitflint.org

Once a small, horse-drawn-carriage-producing town, Flint is now an important automobile manufacturer with the nickname "Buick City." One of the largest cities in the state, it is a blue-collar town that led the 20th-century union movement and retains strong union ties in nearly every aspect of work life. But in spite of its industrial bent, Flint also boasts a rich cultural heritage, including excellent museums, a planetarium, and Crossroads Village, a restored late-1800s small town.

What to See and Do

County recreation areas. *5045 E Stanley Rd, Flint (48502).*

Genesee-C. S. Mott Lake. Approximately 650 acres. Swimming, fishing, boating (launches, fee); snowmobiling. Picnicking with view of Stepping Stone Falls. Riverboat cruises (fee).

Holloway Reservoir. *7240 N Henderson Rd, Davison (48423). 12 miles E on Hwy 21, then 8 miles NE via Hwy 15, Stanley Rd. Phone 810/653-4062.* Approximately 2,000 acres. Swimming, water sports, fishing, boating (launches, fee); snowmobiling, picnicking, camping (fee). (Daily) **FREE**

★ **Crossroads Village/Huckleberry Railroad.** *6140 Bray Rd, Flint (48505). 6 miles NE via I-475, at exit 13. Phone 810/736-7100; toll-free 800/648-7275. www.geneseecountyparks.org.* Restored living community of the 1860-1880 period; 28 buildings and sites including a railroad depot, carousel, Ferris wheel, general store, schoolhouse, and several homes; working sawmill, gristmill, cidermill, blacksmith shop; 8-mile steam train ride; entertainment. Paddlewheel riverboat cruises (fee). Special events most weekends. (Memorial Day-Labor Day: Tues-Sun 10 am-5 pm; Sept: weekends; also special Halloween programs, Dec holiday lighting spectacular) **$$$**

Flint College and Cultural Corporation. *817 E Kearsley St, Flint (48503). Phone 810/237-7330 (Cultural Center).* A complex that includes the University of Michigan-Flint (5,700 students), Mott Community College, Whiting Auditorium, Flint Institute of Music, Bower Theater. Also here are

Flint Institute of Arts. *Cultural Center, 1120 E Kearsley St, Flint (48503). Phone 810/234-1695. www.flintarts.org.* Permanent collections include Renaissance decorative arts, Oriental Gallery, 19th- and 20th-century paintings and sculpture, paperweights; changing exhibits. (Tues-Sat 10 am-5 pm, Sun 1-5 pm; closed holidays) **FREE**

Robert T. Longway Planetarium. *1310 E Kearsley St, Flint (48503). Phone 810/237-3400. www.longwayplanetarium.com.* Ultraviolet, fluorescent murals; Spitz projector. Exhibits. Programs. (Phone for schedule) **$$**

Sloan Museum. *1221 E Kearsley St, Flint (48503). Phone 810/237-3450. www.sloanmuseum.com.* Collection of antique autos and carriages, most manufactured in Flint; exhibitions of Michigan history; health and science exhibits. (Mon-Fri 10 am-5 pm, Sat-Sun noon-5 pm; closed holidays) **$$**

For-Mar Nature Preserve and Arboretum. *2142 N Genesee Rd, Flint (48509). Phone 810/789-8567.* Approximately 380 acres. Nature trails, indoor and outdoor exhibits, two interpretive buildings. Guided hikes available for groups of ten or more (fee). **$**

Special Event

Crim Festival of Races. *100 Mott Foundation Bldg, Flint (48502). Phone 810/235-3396. www.crim.org.* This nationally known annual road race also features a wide range of races, including races for kids. Tens of thousands of people gather to race, including elite athletes from all over the world, while Flint residents line the race course to cheer and encourage. Late Aug. **$$$**

Limited-Service Hotels

★ HOLIDAY INN EXPRESS. *1150 Longway Blvd, Flint (48503). Phone 810/238-7744; toll-free 800/278-1810; fax 810/233-7444. www.holiday-inn.com.* 124 rooms, 5 story. Pets accepted; fee. Complimentary continental breakfast. Check-in 3 pm, check-out 11 am. Airport transportation available. **$**

★ ★ HOLIDAY INN. *5353 Gateway Centre, Flint (48507). Phone 810/232-5300; toll-free 888/570-1770; fax 810/232-9806. www.flintholidayinn.com.* 171 rooms, 4 story. Pets accepted, some restrictions; fee. Check-in 3 pm, check-out noon. High-speed Internet access, wireless Internet access. Restaurant, bar. Children's activity center. Fitness room. Indoor pool, whirlpool. Airport transportation available. Business center. **$**

★ RIVERFRONT CHARACTER INN. *1 W Riverfront Center, Flint (48502). Phone 810/239-1234; fax 810/244-3253. www.characterinns.org.* 250 rooms, 16 story. Check-in 3 pm, check-out noon. Airport transportation available. **$**

Frankenmuth (H-5)

See also Bay City, Flint, Saginaw

Settled 1845
Population 4,408
Elevation 645 ft
Area Code 989
Zip 48734
Information Convention & Visitors Bureau, 635 S Main St; phone 989/652-6106, toll-free 800/386-8696 or 800/386-3378
Web Site www.frankenmuth.org

This city was settled by 15 immigrants from Franconia, Germany, who came here as Lutheran missionaries to spread the faith to the Chippewas. Today, Frankenmuth (FRANK-en-mooth) boasts authentic Bavarian architecture, flower beds, and warm German hospitality. It's known affectionately as Chickenmuth, because the city's two main restaurants, Bavarian Inn and Zehnder's, specialize in chicken dinners.

What to See and Do

Bronner's Christmas Wonderland. *25 Christmas Ln, Frankenmuth (48734). Phone 989/652-9931; toll-free 800/255-9327 (recording). www.bronners.com.* Billing itself as the world's largest Christmas store, Bronner's stocks more than 50,000 trims and gifts from around the world. The store, open since 1945, features a 20-minute multi-image presentation called "World of Bronner's," 260 decorated Christmas trees in varying themes, a Silent Night memorial chapel, and an outdoor display of 100,000 Christmas lights along Christmas Lane (dusk-midnight). It's a great place to snap your Christmas card photo well ahead of the holiday season. (Daily, hours vary by season; closed holidays)

Frankenmuth Historical Museum. *613 S Main St (Hwy 83), Frankenmuth (48734). Phone 989/652-9701.* Local historical exhibits, hands-on displays, audio recordings, and cast-form life figures. Gift shop features folk art. (Jan-Mar: Mon-Thurs noon-4 pm, Fri 10:30 am-5 pm, Sat 10 am-5 pm, Sun noon-5 pm; Apr-Dec: Mon-Thurs 10:30 am-5 pm, Fri 10:30 am-7 pm, Sat 10 am-8 pm, Sun 11 am-7 pm; closed holidays) **$**

Frankenmuth Riverboat Tours. *445 S Main St (Hwy 83), Frankenmuth (48734). Board at dock behind Riverview Cafe. Phone 989/652-8844.* Narrated tours (45 minutes) along Cass River. (May-Oct, daily, weather permitting) **$$**

Glockenspiel. *713 S Main St (Hwy 83), Frankenmuth (48734). Phone 989/652-9941.* This tops the Frankenmuth Bavarian Inn (see RESTAURANT); 35-bell carillon with carved wooden figures moving on a track acting out the story of the Pied Piper of Hamelin.

Michigan's Own Military & Space Museum. *1250 S Weiss St, Frankenmuth (48734). Phone 989/652-8005.*

www.michigansmilitarymuseum.com. Features uniforms, decorations, and photos of men and women from Michigan who served the nation in war and peace; also displays on Medal of Honor recipients, astronauts, former governors. (Mar-Dec: Mon-Sat 10 am-5 pm, Sun 11 am-5 pm; closed Easter, Dec 25) **$$**

Special Events

Bavarian Festival. *Heritage Park, 335 S Main St (Hwy 83), Frankenmuth (48734). Phone 989/652-8155; toll-free 800/228-2742. www.bavarianfestival.com.* Celebration of German heritage. Music, dancing, parades, and other entertainment; food; art demonstrations and agricultural displays. Four days in early June.

Frankenmuth Oktoberfest. *635 S Main St (Hwy 83), Frankenmuth (48734). Phone 989/652-6106.* Serving authentic Munich Oktoberfest and American beer. German food, music, and entertainment. Third weekend in Sept.

Limited-Service Hotels

★ ★ FRANKENMUTH BAVARIAN INN LODGE. *1 Covered Bridge Ln, Frankenmuth (48734). Phone 989/652-7200; toll-free 888/775-6343; fax 989/652-6711. www.bavarianinn.com.* Perched on the banks of the Cass River, this three-generation, family-owned lodge continues to delight guests year after year. Offering a totally unique visit, this impressive lodge sets itself apart from the rest with its five indoor pools, three whirlpools, a Children's Village guaranteed to delight the kid in all of us, plus an 18-hole indoor minature golf center, two lounges and restaurants, and to top off this exciting assortment of amenities, there are four outdoor tennis courts. Guests may come for the relaxation of it all but are guaranteed to leave with the fairy tale of this truly delightful lodge. 354 rooms, 4 story. Check-out 11 am. Restaurant, two bars. Fitness room. Five indoor pools, three whirlpools. Tennis. Airport transportation available. **$**

★ ZEHNDER'S BAVARIAN HAUS. *730 S Main St (Hwy 83), Frankenmuth (48734). Phone 989/652-0400; fax 989/652-9777. www.zehnders.com.* Resembling a cozy chalet in the early European tradition, this inn offers a comfortable stay amidst delightful old-world charm. From the spacious and well-appointed guest rooms, to the beautiful and lush gardens and brick walkway that surrounds a pond and floating fountain, guests are guaranteed to be enchanted by it all. 137 rooms, 2 story. Check-in 4 pm, check-out 11 am. Children's activity center. Fitness room. Indoor pool, outdoor pool, whirlpool. Golf, 18 holes. Airport transportation available. **$**

Restaurant

★ ★ FRANKENMUTH BAVARIAN INN RESTAURANT. *713 S Main St (Hwy 83), Frankenmuth (48734). Phone 989/652-9941; toll-free 888/228-2742; fax 989/652-3481. www.bavarianinn.com.* German menu. Lunch, dinner. Closed also first week in Jan. Bar. Children's menu. Established in 1888. Casual attire. Reservations recommended. Outdoor seating. **$$**

Frankfort (F-2)

See also Beulah, Sleeping Bear Dunes National Lakeshore

Population 1,546
Elevation 585 ft
Area Code 231
Zip 49635
Information Benzie County Chamber of Commerce, PO Box 204, Benzonia 49616; phone 231/882-5801 or toll-free 800/882-5801
Web Site www.benzie.org

An important harbor on Lake Michigan, Frankfort is a popular resort area. Fishing for coho and chinook salmon is excellent here. Frankfort is the burial site of Father Jacques Marquette. Nearby is Sleeping Bear Dunes National Lakeshore.

Limited-Service Hotel

★ ★ CHIMNEY CORNERS RESORT. *1602 Crystal Dr, Frankfort (49635). Phone 231/352-7522; fax 231/352-7252. www.chimneycornersresort.com.* This property features a 1,000-foot beach on Crystal Lake and 300 acres of wooded hills. 27 rooms, 2 story. Closed Dec-Apr. Pets accepted, some restrictions; fee. Check-in 3 pm, check-out 10 am. Restaurant. Tennis. **$**

Restaurants

★ **MANITOU.** *4349 Scenic Hwy (Hwy 22), Frankfort (49635). Phone 231/882-4761.* Vegetarian menu. Dinner. Closed Jan-Apr. Outdoor seating. **$$**

★ ★ **RHONDA'S WHARFSIDE.** *300 Main St, Frankfort (49635). Phone 231/352-5300; fax 231/352-7271.* California menu. Lunch, dinner. Closed Dec 25. Children's menu. **$$**

Gaylord (E-4)

See also Boyne City, Grayling

Settled 1873
Population 3,256
Elevation 1,349 ft
Area Code 989
Zip 49735
Information Gaylord Area Convention & Tourism Bureau, 101 W Main, PO Box 3069; phone 989/732-4000 or toll-free 800/345-8621
Web Site www.gaylordmichigan.net

Known as Michigan's Alpine Village, downtown Gaylord shops give the appearance of charming, Swiss-inspired chalets. The winter theme is fitting, given Gaylord's annual snowfall of over 180 inches. Winter sports abound in Gaylord, and you'll find over 300 miles of groomed snowmobile trails and numerous cross-country ski trails. With nearly 100 small lakes, Gaylord is also home to excellent fishing, both in summer and winter. Gaylord also boasts the best golf experience in Michigan, with two dozen award-winning courses.

What to See and Do

Otsego Lake State Park. *7136 Old Hwy 27 S, Gaylord (49735). 7 miles S off I-75 on Old Hwy 27. Phone 989/732-5485.* Approximately 60 acres. Swimming beach, bathhouse, water-skiing, boating (rentals, launch); fishing for pike, bass, and perch; picnicking, playground, concession, camping. (Mid-Apr-mid-Oct)

Treetops Sylvan Resort. *3962 Wilkinson Rd, Gaylord (49735). 5 miles E via Hwy 32 to Wilkinson Rd. Phone 989/732-6711; toll-free 888/873-3867. www.treetops.com.* Double, two triple chairlifts, four rope tows; patrol, school, rentals; cafeteria, bar. Nineteen runs; longest run 1/2 mile; vertical drop 225 feet. (Dec-mid-Mar, daily) 10 miles of cross-country trails; 3 1/2 miles of lighted trails. **$$$$**

Special Events

Alpenfest. *1535 Opal Lake Rd, Gaylord (49735). Phone 989/732-6333.* Participants dress in costumes of Switzerland; carnival, pageant, grand parade; "world's largest coffee break." Third weekend in July.

Otsego County Fair. *Phone 989/732-4119.* Mid-Aug.

Winterfest. *M South Ct, Gaylord (49735). Phone toll-free 800/345-8621.* Ski racing and slalom, cross-country events, snowmobile events, activities for children, snow sculpting, downhill tubing. Early Feb.

Limited-Service Hotels

★ ★ **BEST WESTERN ALPINE LODGE.** *833 W Main St, Gaylord (49735). Phone 989/732-2431; toll-free 800/684-2233; fax 989/732-9640. www.bestwestern.com.* 137 rooms, 2 story. Pets accepted, some restrictions. Check-in 3 pm, check-out 11 am. Restaurant, bar. Fitness room. Indoor pool, whirlpool. **$**

★ ★ **QUALITY INN.** *137 W Main St, Gaylord (49735). Phone 989/732-7541; toll-free 800/228-5151; fax 989/732-0930. www.qualityinn.com.* 117 rooms, 2 story. Check-in 3 pm, check-out 11 am. Restaurant. Fitness room. Indoor pool, whirlpool. **$**

Full-Service Resorts

★ ★ ★ **GARLAND RESORT & GOLF COURSE.** *4700 N Red Oak Rd, Lewiston (49756). Phone 989/786-2211; fax 989/786-2254. www.garlandusa.com.* Northern Michigan's Garland, located southwest of Gaylord and surrounded by the Mackinaw State Forest, is a first-rate vacation destination. This family-run resort caters to avid golfers with four championship courses surrounded by 3,500 acres of pristine wilderness. Lessons, practice facilities, and a well-stocked pro shop enhance the golfing experience here. Garland is well known for its superb hunting, and during the winter months, miles of cross-country ski trails attract winter sports enthusiasts. You can also rent mountain bikes, fish in the Garland ponds, shoot hoops on the lighted basketball court, or take a guided nature trail hike. Winter brings horse-drawn sleigh rides, sledding, ice skating, and snowmobiling. Four types of lodging await visitors to this full-service resort. From the main lodge to the golf cottages, villas, and condos, the accommodations are comfortable and spacious, and the interiors reflect the rugged setting. The game menu at Hildegard's Dining Room mirrors the hunting lodge setting; Herman's Restaurant, Grill, and Patio all serve American classics; and the Tiki Bar is a casual spot for post-game drinks or snacks. 60 rooms. Closed week of Thanksgiving; also mid-Mar-Apr. Check-in 4 pm, check-out 11 am. Restaurant, bar. Fitness room. Indoor pool, outdoor pool, whirlpool. Golf, 72 holes. Tennis. Airport transportation available. **$**

★ ★ ★ **TREETOPS RESORT.** *3962 Wilkinson Rd, Gaylord (49735). Phone 989/732-6711; fax 989/732-8459. www.treetops.com.* This modern, 4,000-acre hilltop complex offers guest rooms, suites, condominiums, and resort homes, all overlooking the Pigeon River Valley. Facilities include 81 holes of golf, skiing, tennis, indoor and outdoor pools, and much more. 260 rooms, 3 story. Check-in 4 pm, check-out noon. Restaurant, bar. Children's activity center. Fitness room. Indoor pool, outdoor pool, children's pool, whirlpool. Golf, 81 holes. Tennis. Airport transportation available. **$**

Restaurant

★ ★ **SUGAR BOWL.** *216 W Main St (Hwy 32), Gaylord (49734). Phone 989/732-5524; fax 989/732-3448.* Greek, American menu. Dinner. Closed Easter, Thanksgiving, Dec 25; also last week in Mar and first week in Apr. Bar. Children's menu. **$$**

Gladstone (D-2)

See also Escanaba

Population 5,032
Elevation 720 ft
Area Code 906
Zip 49837
Web Site www.gladstonemi.org

With year-round outdoor activities, Gladstone offers something for everyone. The town is located on Little Bay de Noc, a deep harbor that accommodates boats of all sizes. Fishing in summer and winter is quite popular, and the Sports Park offers winter activities including skiing and tubing. Take a picnic lunch to the bay in summer or fall for beautiful sunsets and a stunning show of color.

Restaurant

★ ★ **LOG CABIN SUPPER CLUB.** *7531 Hwy 2, Gladstone (49837). Phone 906/786-5621; fax 906/786-6594.* American menu. Lunch, dinner. Closed holidays. Bar. Children's menu. **$$**

Glen Arbor (E-3)

See also Leland, Sleeping Bear Dunes National Lakeshore, Traverse City

Settled 1848
Population 250
Elevation 591 ft
Area Code 231
Zip 49636
Information Sleeping Bear Area Chamber of Commerce, PO Box 217; phone 231/334-3238
Web Site www.sleepingbeararea.com

This community, situated on Lake Michigan, lies just north of Sleeping Bear Dunes National Lakeshore. Because of its unique location next to one of Michigan's top attractions, Glen Arbor caters to tourists with boutiques, art galleries, and shops selling local crafts. A popular stop is Cherry Republic on Lake Street, which sells only cherry products from the region, from jam to pie to barbeque sauce.

Full-Service Resort

★ ★ ★ **THE HOMESTEAD.** *Wood Ridge Rd, Glen Arbor (49636). Phone 231/334-5000; fax 231/334-5246. www.thehomesteadresort.com.* Visitors can choose to stay in a small hotel, an inn, a lodge, or privately owned guest homes when they stay at this resort. Guests will find beaches, four pools, a small craft harbor, golf, and tennis facilities along with restaurants and shops. 130 rooms, 3 story. Closed mid-Mar-Apr, Nov-late Dec. Check-in 5 pm, check-out 11 am. Restaurant. Children's activity center. Fitness room. Beach. Four outdoor pools, whirlpool. Golf. Tennis. **$$**

Restaurants

★ ★ **LA BECASSE.** *9001 S Dunn's Farm Rd, Maple City (49664). Phone 231/334-3944; fax 231/334-7503.* French menu. Dinner. Closed Mon; holidays; Tues (May-mid-June); also mid-Oct-late

Dec, mid-Feb-early May. Reservations recommended. Outdoor seating. **$$**

★ WESTERN AVENUE GRILL. *6410 Western Ave, Glen Arbor (49636). Phone 231/334-3362; fax 231/334-6378.* American menu. Dinner. Closed Mon-Wed; Thanksgiving, Dec 25. Bar. Children's menu. Casual attire. **$$**

Grand Haven (H-2)

See also Grand Rapids, Holland, Muskegon, Spring Lake

Settled 1834
Population 11,951
Elevation 590 ft
Area Code 616
Zip 49417
Information Grand Haven/Spring Lake Area Visitors Bureau, 1 S Harbor Dr; phone 616/842-4910 or toll-free 800/303-4092
Web Site www.grandhavenchamber.org

Through this port city at the mouth of the Grand River flows a stream of produce for all the Midwest. The port has the largest charter fishing fleet on Lake Michigan and is also used for sportfishing, recreational boating, and as a Coast Guard base. Connecting the pier to downtown shops is a boardwalk and park.

What to See and Do

Grand Haven State Park. *1001 Harbor Ave, Grand Haven (49417). 1 mile SW. Phone 616/798-3711.* Almost 50 acres on Lake Michigan beach. Swimming, bathhouse, fishing; picnicking (shelter), playground, concession, camping. (Daily) **$$**

Harbor Trolleys. *440 N Ferry St, Grand Haven (49417). Transfer point at Chinook Pier. Phone 616/842-3200.* Two different routes: Grand Haven trolley operates between downtown and state park; second trolley goes to Spring Lake. (Mon-Fri 6 am-5:30 pm, Sat 9 am-3:30 pm) **$**

Municipal Marina. *101 N Harbor Dr, Grand Haven (49147). At foot of Washington St, downtown. Phone 616/847-3478.* Contains 57 transient slips; fish cleaning station; stores and restaurants; trolley stop. Also docked here is the

Harbor Steamer. *301 N Harbor, Grand Haven (49417). Phone 616/842-8950.* Stern-wheel paddle-boat cruises to Spring Lake; scenic views, narrated by captain. (Mid-May-Sept, daily)

Musical Fountain. *Dewey Hill, 1 N Harbor St, Grand Haven (49417). Phone 616/842-2550.* Said to be the world's largest electronically controlled musical fountain; water, lights, and music are synchronized. Special Christmas nativity scene in December covering all of Dewey Hill. Programs (Memorial Day-Labor Day, evenings; May and rest of Sept, Fri-Sat only).

Special Events

Coast Guard Festival. *310 S Harbor Dr, Grand Haven (49147). Phone toll-free 888/207-2434.* Includes a parade, carnival, craft exhibit, ship tours, pageant, variety shows, and fireworks. Late July-early Aug.

Great Lakes Kite Festival. *Grand Haven State Park, 106 Washington Ave, Grand Haven (49147). Phone 616/846-7501.* Giant kites fly in the air throughout the day—weather permitting. Various kite demonstrations are held on the main field. May.

On the Waterfront Big Band Concert Series. *Phone 616/842-2550.* Wed evenings. July-Aug.

Polar Ice Cap Golf Tournament. *Spring Lake, 1 S Harbor Dr, Grand Haven (49147). Phone toll-free 800/303-4097.* 18-hole, par-three golf game on ice. Late Jan.

Winterfest. *120 Washington Ave, Grand Haven (49147). Phone 616/842-4499.* Music, dance, parade, children's activities. Late Jan.

Limited-Service Hotel

★ BEST WESTERN BEACON INN. *1525 S Beacon Blvd, Grand Haven (49417). Phone 616/842-4720; toll-free 800/780-7234; fax 616/847-7821. www.bestwestern.com.* 101 rooms. Check-in 3 pm, check-out 11 am. Indoor pool. Airport transportation available. **$**

Specialty Lodgings

The following lodging establishments are approved by Mobil Travel Guide, but due to their unique and individualized nature have not been given a traditional Mobil Star rating. Included in this listing you may find bed-and-breakfasts, limited-service inns, guest ranches, and other unique hotel properties.

HARBOR HOUSE INN. *114 S Harbor Dr, Grand Haven (49417). Phone 616/846-0610; fax 616/846-0530. www.harborhousegh.com.* Early American décor. 17 rooms, 3 story. Closed Dec 24-25. Complimentary continental breakfast. Check-in 2 pm, check-out 11 am. **$$**

HIDEAWAY ACRES BED & BREAKFAST. *1870 Pontaluna Rd, Spring Lake (49456). Phone 231/798-7271; toll-free 800/856-3545; fax 231/798-3352.* 5 rooms, 2 story. Complimentary continental breakfast. Check-in 4 pm, check-out 11 am. Indoor pool, whirlpool. Tennis. **$**

Grand Marais (C-3)

See also Munising, Pictured Rocks National Lakeshore

Population 350
Elevation 640 ft
Area Code 906
Zip 49839
Information Chamber of Commerce, PO Box 139; phone 906/494-2447
Web Site www.grandmaraismichigan.com

On the shore of Lake Superior, Grand Marais (ma-RAY) has a harbor with marina and is surrounded by cool, clear lakes, trout streams, and agate beaches. In the winter, there is snowmobiling and cross-country skiing.

Special Events

500-Miler Snowmobile Run. *Downtown Grand Marais, Grand Marais (49839). Phone 906/494-2447. www.sno-trails.net/GM500Miler.* While not a race, participants must accumulate 500 miles in no less than 14 hours and no more than 24 hours. Mid-Jan.

Music and Arts Festival. *Downtown Grand Marais, Grand Marais (49839). Phone 906/494-2447.* Second weekend in Aug.

Limited-Service Hotel

★ ★ NOAH SHORE LODGE. *E 22020 Coast Guard Pt, Grand Marais (49839). Phone 906/494-2361; fax 906/494-2371.* On Lake Superior; private beach. 41 rooms, 2 story. Pets accepted. Check-out 10 am. Restaurant, bar. Beach. Indoor pool, whirlpool. Tennis. **$**

Grand Rapids (H-3)

See also Grand Haven, Holland, Muskegon

Settled 1826
Population 189,126
Elevation 657 ft
Area Code 616
Information Grand Rapids/Kent County Convention & Visitors Bureau, 140 Monroe Center NW, Suite 300, 49503; phone 616/459-8287 or toll-free 800/678-9859
Web Site www.grcvb.org

Grand Rapids, a widely known furniture center and convention city, is located on the site where Louis Campau established a Native American trading post in 1826. The city derives its name from the rapids in the Grand River, which flows through the heart of the city. There are 50 parks here, totalling 1,270 acres. Calvin College and Calvin Seminary (1876) are located here; several other colleges are in the area.

Thirty-eighth president Gerald R. Ford was raised in Grand Rapids and represented the Fifth Congressional District in Michigan from 1948 to 1973, when he became the nation's vice president.

What to See and Do

Berlin Raceway. *3411 Leonard St NW, Grand Rapids (49504). Phone 616/677-5000. www.berlinraceway.com.* Late-model stock car, sportsman stock car, and super stock car racing. (May-Sept, Fri-Sun) **$$$$**

Blandford Nature Center. *1715 Hillburn Ave NW, Grand Rapids (49504). Phone 616/453-6192. www.grmuseum.org/bnc.* More than 140 acres of woods, fields, and ponds with self-guiding trails; guided tours (fee); interpretive center has exhibits, live animals; furnished pioneer garden; one-room schoolhouse. (Mon-Fri, also Sat-Sun afternoons; closed holidays) **FREE**

Cannonsburg Ski Area. *6800 Cannonsburg Rd, Cannonsburg (49317). 10 miles NE via Hwy-131, W River Dr. Phone 616/874-6711; toll-free 800/253-8748 (IL, IN, OH). www.cannonsburg.com.* Quad, triple, double chairlift; two T-bars, eight rope tows. Longest run approximately 1/3 mile; vertical drop 250 feet. Patrol, school, rentals, snowmaking; nursery, cafeteria, bar. (Late Nov-mid-Mar, Sat-Sun 9 am-10 pm, holidays 9 am-4 pm; closed Thanksgiving, Dec 25) **$$$$**

Fish Ladder. *Sixth St Dam, Grand Rapids.* A unique fish ladder for watching salmon leap the rapids of the Grand River during spawning season.

★ Frederik Meijer Gardens and Sculpture Park. *1000 E Beltline Ave NE, Grand Rapids (49525). Phone 616/957-1580; toll-free 888/957-1580. www.meijergardens.org.* This botanic garden and sculpture park includes a 15,000-square-foot glass conservatory, a desert garden, exotic indoor and outdoor gardens, and more than 60 bronze works. Also outdoor nature trails and tram tour. Gift shop, restaurant. (Mon-Sat 9 am-5 pm, Sun noon-5 pm; closed Jan 1, Dec 25) **$$**

★ Gerald R. Ford Museum. *303 Pearl St NW, Grand Rapids (49504). Phone 616/254-0400.* Exhibits tracing the life and public service of the 38th president of the United States. A 28-minute introductory film on Ford; reproduction of the White House Oval Office; educational exhibits on the US House of Representatives and the presidency; original burglar tools used in the Watergate break-in. (Daily 9 am-5 pm; closed Jan 1, Thanksgiving, Dec 25) **$$**

Grand Rapids Art Museum. *155 Division St N, Grand Rapids (49503). Phone 616/831-1000. www.gramonline.org.* Collections include Renaissance, German Expressionist, French, and American paintings; graphics and a children's gallery augmented by special traveling exhibitions. (Tues-Sun; closed holidays) **$$**

John Ball Zoo. *1300 W Fulton St, Grand Rapids (49504). Phone 616/336-4300.* Located in 100-acre park, zoo features more than 700 animals, Living Shores Aquarium, African Forest exhibit, and children's zoo. (Mid-May-Labor Day: daily 10 am-6 pm; rest of the year: daily 10 am-4 pm; closed Dec 25) **$**

La Grande Vitesse. *County Building, downtown.* This 42-ton stabile was created by Alexander Calder.

Meyer May House. *450 Madison St SE, Grand Rapids (49503). Phone 616/246-4821.* (1908) Frank Lloyd Wright house from the late Prairie period. Authentically restored with all architect-designed furniture, leaded-glass windows, lighting fixtures, rugs, and textiles. Tours begin at visitor center, 442 Madison St SE. (Tues, Thurs, Sun; schedule varies) **FREE**

Pando. *8076 Belding Rd NE, Rockford (49341). 12 miles NE on Hwy 44. Phone 616/874-8343.* Six rope tows, seven lighted runs; patrol, school, rentals, grooming equipment, snowmaking; cafeteria. Vertical drop 125 feet. (Dec-Mar, daily) Seven miles of cross-country trails; 3 miles of lighted trails, track-setting equipment; rentals. Night skiing. **$$$$**

The Public Museum of Grand Rapids. *272 Pearl St NW, Grand Rapids (49504). Phone 616/456-3997.* Located in the Van Andel Museum Center; exhibits of interactive history and natural science, including mammals, birds, furniture, Native American artifacts, re-creation of 1890s Grand Rapids street scene, and 1928 carousel. Chaffee Planetarium offers sky shows and laser light shows (fee). (Tues-Sat 9 am-5 pm; closed Jan 1, Thanksgiving, Dec 25) **$$**

Special Events

Community Circle Theater. *John Ball Park Pavilion, 1300 W Fulton St, Grand Rapids (49504). Phone 616/456-6656.* Mid-May-Sept.

Festival. *Calder Plaza, Grand Rapids (49503). Phone 616/459-2787.* Arts and crafts shows, entertainment, international foods. First full weekend in June.

Limited-Service Hotels

★★ BEST WESTERN MIDWAY HOTEL. *4101 SE 28th St, Grand Rapids (49512). Phone 616/942-2550; toll-free 888/280-0081; fax 616/942-2446. www.bestwestern.com.* 146 rooms, 3 story. Complimentary full breakfast. Check-in 3 pm, check-out noon. Restaurant, bar. Fitness room. Indoor pool, whirlpool. Airport transportation available. **$**

★ COMFORT INN. *4155 SE 28th St, Grand Rapids (49512). Phone 616/957-2080; toll-free 800/638-7949; fax 616/957-9712. www.comfortinn.com.* 109 rooms, 3 story. Complimentary continental breakfast. Check-in 3 pm, check-out noon. **$**

★★ DAYS INN. *310 NW Pearl St, Grand Rapids (49504). Phone 616/235-7611; toll-free 800/329-7466; fax 616/235-1995. www.daysinn.com.* 175 rooms, 8 story. Pets accepted, some restrictions; fee. Check-in 3 pm, check-out 11 am. Restaurant, bar. Fitness room. Indoor pool, whirlpool. **$**

★ HAMPTON INN. *4981 S 28th St, Grand Rapids (49512). Phone 616/956-9304; toll-free 800/426-7866; fax 616/956-6617. www.hamptoninn.com.* 120 rooms, 2 story. Pets accepted, some restrictions. Complimentary continental breakfast. Check-in 3 pm, check-out noon. Fitness room. Outdoor pool. **$**

★★ RADISSON HOTEL GRAND RAPIDS EAST. *3333 SE 28th St, Grand Rapids (49512). Phone 616/949-9222; toll-free 800/333-3333; fax 616/949-3841. www.radisson.com.* 200 rooms, 5 story. Check-out noon. High-speed Internet access, wireless Internet access. Restaurant, bar. Indoor pool, whirlpool. Airport transportation available. **$**

Full-Service Hotels

★★★ AMWAY GRAND PLAZA. *187 Monroe Ave NW, Grand Rapids (49503). Phone 616/774-2000; fax 616/776-6489.* Opened in 1913 as the Pantlind Hotel, this cherished Michigan landmark quickly earned a reputation for providing a distinguished residence for out-of-towners. Fronting the Grand River, the hotel is conveniently located in the heart of Grand Rapids' business and entertainment district. Exuding the elegance of the early 1900s, the lobby is topped by a magnificent gold-leaf ceiling, one of the largest in the world. The guest rooms are beautifully appointed in either classically elegant or delightfully modern décor, with the Tower Rooms featuring sweeping views of the river and city. Fitness and business centers are provided for guests' convenience. From dinner atop the tower at Cygnus to family dining with a river view at Bentham's and casual fare at GP Sports, this hotel has it all. The six restaurants and lounges satisfy demanding appetites, but the 1913 Room, with its fine continental cuisine, is the jewel in the crown. Shops and galleries are located within the hotel, and guests are granted access to the Artistry Beauty Institute. 682 rooms, 29 story. Check-in 4 pm, check-out noon. Restaurant, bar. Fitness room. Indoor pool, whirlpool. Tennis. Airport transportation available. Business center. **$**

★★★ CROWNE PLAZA. *5700 28th St SE, Grand Rapids (49546). Phone 616/957-1770; toll-free 800/957-9575; fax 616/957-0629. www.crowneplaza.com/grr-airport.* Located only 3 miles from the Kent County International Airport and minutes from the largest shopping center in West Michigan, this hotel is very convenient. It offers guests free passes to the nearby country and athletic clubs. 320 rooms, 5 story. Check-out noon. Restaurant, bar. Fitness room. Indoor pool, outdoor pool, whirlpool. Airport transportation available. Business center. **$**

Restaurants

★★ ARNIE'S. *3561 SE 28th St, Grand Rapids (49512). Phone 616/956-7901; fax 616/956-2138.* American menu. Dinner. Closed holidays. Children's menu. **$**

★★ DUBA'S. *420 E Beltline NE, Grand Rapids (49506). Phone 616/949-1011; fax 616/949-4462.* American menu. Dinner. Closed Sun; holidays. Bar. Children's menu. Casual attire. **$**

★★★ GIBSON'S. *1033 Lake Dr, Grand Rapids (49506). Phone 616/774-8535; fax 616/774-9102. www.gibsonsrestaurant.com.* Housed in an old monastery (1860s), this romantic destination sits majestically on a wooded, parklike property. Visitors are attracted with fine food and many uniquely decorated dining spaces. American menu. Dinner. Closed July 4, Thanksgiving, Dec 25; also Sun (June-Aug). Bar. Children's menu. Casual attire. Outdoor seating. **$$**

★★ PIETRO'S BACK DOOR PIZZERIA. *2780 SE Birchcrest St, Grand Rapids (49506). Phone 616/452-3228; fax 616/452-0172. www.rcfc.com.* Italian, American menu. Dinner. Closed Thanksgiving, Dec 25. Bar. Children's menu. Casual attire. Outdoor seating. **$**

★★ SAYFEE'S. *3555 SE Lake Eastbrook Blvd, Grand Rapids (49546). Phone 616/949-5750; fax 616/949-1446.* American menu. Dinner. Closed Sun (except Mother's Day), Easter; holidays. Bar. Children's menu. Casual attire. Valet parking. Outdoor seating. **$$**

★★ SCHNITZELBANK. *342 SE Jefferson Ave, Grand Rapids (49503). Phone 616/459-9527; fax 616/459-9272. www.schnitzelbankgr.com.* German, American menu. Dinner. Closed Sun; holidays. Bar. Children's menu. Casual attire. **$$**

★★ WYOMING CATTLE CO. *1820 44th St SW, Wyoming (49509). Phone 616/534-0704; fax 616/534-1361. www.michiganmenu.com/wcc.html.* American menu. Dinner. Closed Thanksgiving, Dec 24-25. Bar. Children's menu. Casual attire. Outdoor seating. **$$**

Grayling (F-4)

See also Gaylord, Houghton Lake

Population 1,944
Elevation 1,137 ft
Area Code 989

Zip 49738
Information Grayling Area Visitors Council, PO Box 406; phone 989/348-2921 or toll-free 800/937-8837
Web Site www.grayling-mi.com

Named for a fish that was related to both trout and salmon, Grayling has long ties to fishing in its two major rivers, the Au Sable (a-SAAB-uhl) and the Manistee. In fact, fishing was so popular in the area during the late 1800s that the grayling became extinct by 1930. Today, while its most popular fish lives on in name only, Grayling still offers world-class trout fishing. Visitors also take advantage of excellent canoeing opportunities along the Au Sable, and Lake Margarethe offers opportunities for other water sports. Because Grayling's annual snowfall reaches nearly 200 inches, snow sports, including cross-country skiing and snowmobiling, are also popular in the area.

What to See and Do

Canoe trips. There are many canoe liveries in the area, with trip itineraries for the Manistee and Au Sable rivers. Contact Grayling Area Visitors Council for details.

Hartwick Pines State Park. *4216 Ranger Rd, Grayling (49738). 7 miles NE on Hwy 93. Phone 989/348-7068.* Approximately 9,700 acres. Fishing for trout, perch, and largemouth bass; hunting, marked cross-country ski trails, picnicking, playground, concession, camping. Three-dimensional exhibits in interpretive center tell the story of the white pine. Log memorial building, lumberman's museum near virgin pine forest, one of the few remaining stands of virgin white pine in the world; "Chapel in the Pines." Naturalist. (Daily) **$$**

Skyline Ski Area. *4020 Skyline Rd, Grayling (49738). 2 miles S off I-75, exit 251. Phone 989/275-5445. skylineski.com.* Double chairlift, five rope tows; patrol, school, rentals; cafeteria, ski shop. Longest run approximately 1/2 mile; vertical drop 210 feet. Night skiing, cross-country skiing, snowboarding. (Dec-mid-Mar, daily) **$$$$**

Special Events

Au Sable River Festival. *213 N James St, Grayling (49738). Phone toll-free 800/937-8837.* Arts and crafts, parade, car show. Last full weekend in July.

Winter Wolf Festival. *213 N James St, Grayling (49738). Phone toll-free 800/937-8837.* Early Feb.

Limited-Service Hotel

★ ★ HOLIDAY INN. *2650 I-75 Business Loop, Grayling (49738). Phone 989/348-7611; toll-free 800/292-9095; fax 989/348-7984. www.holiday-inn.com.* 151 rooms, 2 story. Pets accepted, some restrictions. Check-out 11 am. Restaurant, bar. Fitness room. Indoor pool, children's pool, whirlpool. Airport transportation available. **$**

Hancock (A-5)

See also Calumet, Copper Harbor, Houghton, Isle Royale National Park

Population 4,547
Elevation 686 ft
Area Code 906
Zip 49930
Information Keweenaw Peninsula Chamber of Commerce, 326 Shelden Ave, PO Box 336, Houghton 49931; phone 906/482-5240 or toll-free 800/338-7982
Web Site www.portup.com/snow

Located across the Portage Waterway from Houghton (see), Hancock is the home of Finlandia University (1896), the only Finnish college in the United States. Hancock's homes are built on 500-foot bluffs that offer a delightful view of the Keeweenau Peninsula and Lake Superior, but the nearly vertical streets can make for treacherous driving.

What to See and Do

Finnish-American Heritage Center. *601 Quincy St, Hancock (49930). Phone 906/487-7347.* Center houses the Finnish-American Historical Archives, a museum, theater, art gallery, and the Finnish-American Family History Center. (Tues-Sat 8 am-4:30 pm; closed holidays) Special events evenings and weekends. Located on the campus of Suomi College. **FREE**

Quincy Mine Steam Hoist, Shafthouse, Tram Rides, and Mine Tours. *201 Royce Rd, Hancock (49930). 1 mile N on Hwy 41. Phone 906/482-3101. www.quincymine.com.* This 790-ton hoist was used at the Quincy Copper Mine between 1920 and 1931; it could raise 10 tons of ore at a speed of 3,200 feet per minute from an inclined depth of more than 9,000 feet. Also available is a guided 45-minute tour of mine shafts. (Mid-May-mid-Oct, daily) **$$$**

Special Event

Houghton County Fair. *Fairgrounds, North Lincoln Rd and 12th Ave N, Hancock (49930). Phone 906/482-6200. www.houghtoncountyfair.com.* The demolition derby, monster truck show, and horse show tournament are among the events at this fair. Late Aug.

Limited-Service Hotel

★ BEST WESTERN COPPER CROWN MOTEL. *235 Hancock Ave, Hancock (49930). Phone 906/482-6111; toll-free 800/780-7234; fax 906/482-0185. www.bestwestern.com.* 47 rooms, 2 story. Check-in 1 pm, check-out 11 am. Indoor pool, whirlpool. **$**

Harbor Springs (E-4)

See also Cheboygan, Petoskey

Settled 1827
Population 1,540
Elevation 600 ft
Area Code 231
Zip 49740
Information Chamber of Commerce, 205 State St; phone 231/526-7999
Web Site www.harborsprings-mi.com

Known as a year-round vacation spot, Harbor Springs is a picturesque town on Little Traverse Bay that boasts sandy beaches in summer and two of Michigan's most popular ski resorts in winter. Downtown Harbor Springs overflows with pricey but quaint shops and eateries. Drive through Wequetonsing, a summer-only community of mansion-size "cottages" nestled in the heart of Harbor Springs. Cycle, walk, or in-line skate to Petoskey on a paved bike trail that links the two cities.

What to See and Do

Andrew J. Blackbird Museum. *368 E Main St, Harbor Springs (49720). Phone 231/526-7731.* Museum of the Ottawa; artifacts. (Memorial Day-Labor Day, daily; Sept-Oct, weekends) Special exhibits (fee). **$**

Boyne Highlands. *600 Highlands Dr, Harbor Springs (49740). 4 1/2 miles NE off Hwy 119. Phone 231/526-3000; toll-free 800/462-6963. www.boynehighlands.com.* Four triple, four quad chairlifts, rope tow; patrol, school, rentals, snowmaking; cafeteria, restaurant, bar, nursery, lodge (see FULL-SERVICE RESORT). (Thanksgiving weekend-mid-Apr, daily) Weekend plan. Cross-country trails (4 miles); rentals. **$$$$**

Nub's Nob. *500 Nub's Nob Rd, Harbor Springs (49740). 5 miles NE. Phone 231/526-2131. www.nubsnob.com.* Two double, three quad, three triple chairlifts; patrol, school, rentals, snowmaking; cafeteria, bar. Longest run 1 mile; vertical drop 427 feet. (Thanksgiving-Easter, daily) Half-day rates. Cross-country trails (same seasons, hours as downhill skiing); night skiing (five nights/week). **$$$$**

Shore Drive. *Along Hwy 119.* One of the most scenic drives in the state. Passes through Devil's Elbow and Springs area, said to be haunted by an evil spirit.

Limited-Service Hotel

★ BEST WESTERN OF HARBOR SPRINGS. *8514 Hwy 119, Harbor Springs (49740). Phone 231/347-9050; toll-free 800/780-7234; fax 231/347-0837. www.bestwestern.com.* 50 rooms. Complimentary continental breakfast. Check-in 3 pm, check-out 10 am. Indoor pool, whirlpool. **$**

Full-Service Resort

★ ★ BOYNE HIGHLANDS RESORT. *600 Highlands Dr, Harbor Springs (49740). Phone 231/526-3000; toll-free 800/462-6963; fax 231/549-6844. www.boynehighlands.com.* On 6,000 acres. European atmosphere. 228 rooms, 3 story. Check-in 5 pm, check-out 1 pm. Restaurant, bar. Children's activity center. Fitness room. Four outdoor pools, children's pool, whirlpool. Golf. Tennis. Business center. **$**

Specialty Lodging

The following lodging establishment is approved by Mobil Travel Guide, but due to its unique and individualized naturc has not been given a traditional Mobil Star rating. Included in this listing you may find bed-and-breakfasts, limited-service inns, guest ranches, and other unique hotel properties.

KIMBERLY COUNTRY ESTATE. *2287 Bester Rd, Harbor Springs (49740). Phone 231/526-7646; fax 231/526-8054. www.kimberlycountryestate.com.* Just four minutes outside town, this colonial plantation home is wrapped in pillared balconies overlooking the swimming pool and Wequetonsing Golf Course. Rooms have English country décor and four-poster beds. Rates include evening wine reception and bedtime sherry and truffles. 6 rooms, 2 story. Children over 12 years only. Complimentary full breakfast. Check-in 2-6 pm, check-out 11 am. High-speed Internet access. **$$$**

Restaurants

★ LEGS INN. *6425 S Lake Shore Dr, Cross Village (49740). Phone 231/526-2281; fax 231/526-2615. www.legsinn.com.* Polish, American menu. Dinner. Closed late Oct-late May. Bar. Children's menu. Outdoor seating. **$$**

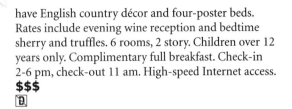

★ ★ THE NEW YORK. *101 State St, Harbor Springs (49740). Phone 231/526-1904; fax 231/526-6286. www.thenewyork.com.* Victorian-style former hotel building. American menu. Dinner. Closed Thanksgiving, Dec 25; also Apr and early Nov. Bar. Children's menu. Casual attire. **$$**

★ ★ STAFFORD'S PIER. *102 Bay St, Harbor Springs (49740). Phone 231/526-6201; fax 231/526-2370. www.staffords.com.* American menu. Dinner. Closed Dec 25. Bar. Children's menu. Casual attire. Outdoor seating. **$$$**

Harrison (G-4)

See also Clare, Houghton Lake

Population 1,835
Elevation 1,186 ft
Area Code 989
Zip 48625
Information Chamber of Commerce, 809 N 1st St, PO Box 682; phone 989/539-6011
Web Site www.harrisonchamber.com

Harrison is a four-season paradise for outdoor lovers. Winter brings opportunities for ice fishing, snowmobiling, cross-country and downhill skiing at Snow Snake (see), and even a frigid golf outing at Wilson State Park (see) in February. Spring and summer mean mushroom hunting, fishing, swimming, and kayaking. Fall may be the busiest and most beautiful, with gorgeous color, hunting, and shopping, especially for Amish-made products.

What to See and Do

Snow Snake Ski & Golf. *3407 Mannsiding Rd, Harrison (48625). 5 miles S on Hwy 27. Phone 989/539-6583. www.snowsnake.com.* Triple chairlift, five rope tows; patrol, school, rentals, snowmaking; snack bar. Longest run is 1/2 mile; vertical drop 210 feet. Night skiing. Snowboarding; tubing; cross-country trails. 18-hole golf course. (Ski area: mid-Dec-mid-Mar, daily; golf: mid-Apr-mid-Oct) **$$$$**

Wilson State Park. *910 First St, Harrison (48625). 1 mile N on Old Hwy 27. Phone 989/539-3021.* Approximately 35 acres on the shore of Budd Lake. Swimming; fishing for largemouth bass, bluegill, perch; picnicking, playground, camping. **$$**

Special Events

Clare County Fair. *Clare County Fairgrounds, 418 Fairlane St, Harrison (48625). Phone 989/539-9011.* Late July-early Aug.

Frostbite Open. *809 N 1st St, Harrison (48625). Phone 989/539-6011.* Winter golf tournament. Feb.

Specialty Lodging

The following lodging establishment is approved by Mobil Travel Guide, but due to its unique and individualized nature has not been given a traditional Mobil Star rating. Included in this listing you may find bed-and-breakfasts, limited-service inns, guest ranches, and other unique hotel properties.

THE CARRIAGE HOUSE INN. *1515 Grant Ave, Harrison (48625). Phone 989/539-1300; fax 989/539-5661. www.carriagehouseinn.com.* 11 rooms. Complimentary full breakfast. Check-in 3 pm, check-out 11 am. **$**

Holland (J-3)

See also Grand Haven, Grand Rapids, Saugatuck

Founded 1847
Population 30,745
Elevation 610 ft
Area Code 616
Information Holland Area Chamber of Commerce, 272 E 8th St, PO Box 1888, 49422-1888; phone 616/392-2389 or Holland Convention and Visitors Bureau, 76 E 8th St; phone 616/394-0000 or toll-free 800/506-1299

Web Site www.holland.org

In 1847, a group of Dutch seeking religious freedom left the Netherlands and settled in this area because its sand dunes and fertile land reminded them of their homeland. Today much of the population is of Dutch descent, as evidenced by the mid-May Tulip Time Festival (see), which features millions of tulips, wooden shoemaking, dancing, and Dutch delicacies. The town prides itself on being the center of Dutch culture in the United States. The city is located at the mouth of the Black River, on the shores of Lake Macatawa, and has developed a resort colony along the shores of Lakes Macatawa and Michigan.

What to See and Do

Cappon House. *228 W 9th St, Holland (49423). Washington Blvd and W 9th St. Phone 616/392-9084; toll-free 888/200-9123.* (1874) Italianate house of first mayor of Holland. Original furnishings, millwork. (June-Oct: Wed-Sat 1-4 pm; Nov-May: Fri-Sat 1-4 pm) **$**

Dutch Village. *12350 James St, Holland (49424). 1 mile NE on Hwy 31. Phone 616/396-1475; fax 616/396-1476. www.dutchvillage.com.* Buildings of Dutch architecture; canals, windmills, tulips, street organs, Dutch dancing; animals, movies, rides; wooden shoe carving and other crafts; museum, tours; restaurant. (Mid-Apr-late Oct, daily) **$$**

Holland Museum. *31 W 10th St, Holland (49423). Phone 616/392-1362; toll-free 888/200-9123. www.hollandmuseum.org.* Features decorative arts from the Netherlands Collection, the Volendam Room. Permanent and changing exhibits pertaining to local history. Gift shop. (Mon, Wed, Fri-Sat 10 am-5 pm, Thurs 10 am-8 pm, Sun 2-5 pm) **$**

Holland State Park. *2215 Ottawa Beach Rd, Holland (49424). 7 miles W off Hwy 31. Phone 616/399-9390.* This 143-acre park includes a 1/4-mile beach on Lake Michigan. Swimming, bathhouse, boating (launch), fishing; picnicking, playground, concessions, camping. **$$**

Hope College. *141 E 12th St, Holland (49423). Between College and Columbia aves. Phone 616/395-7000. www.hope.edu.* (1866) (2,550 students) Liberal arts. Tours of campus. Theater series (July-Aug, fee).

Veldheer's Tulip Gardens and DeKlomp Wooden Shoe & Delftware Factory. *12755 Quincy St, Holland (49424). Phone 616/399-1900.* The only Delftware factory in the United States; factory tours. Visitors can try on wooden shoes and talk to the artisans who made them. (Daily) **$**

Windmill Island. *7th St and Lincoln Ave, Holland (49423). Phone 616/355-1030.* The 225-year-old windmill, "De Zwaan" (the swan), is the only operating imported Dutch windmill in the United States. It was relocated here by special permission of the Dutch government, as the remaining windmills in the Netherlands are considered historic monuments. It is still used today to grind flour. The imported carousel, "Draaimolen," offers free rides. (Apr-May, July-Aug: Mon-Sat 9 am-6 pm, Sun 11:30 am-6 pm; June, Sept-Oct: Mon-Sat 10 am-5 pm, Sun 11:30 am-5 pm) **$$** Includes

> **Little Netherlands.** *7th St and Lincoln Ave, Holland (49423). Phone 616/355-1030.* A miniature reproduction of old Holland; 20-minute film on Dutch windmills in the posthouse; klompen dancing in summer; exhibits, tulips.

Special Event

Tulip Time Festival. *171 Lincoln Ave, Holland (49423). Phone toll-free 800/822-2770. www.tuliptime.org.* A celebration of Dutch heritage: 1,800 klompen dancers, three parades, street scrubbing, Dutch markets, musical and professional entertainment, and millions of tulips. Eight days in mid-May.

Limited-Service Hotels

★ COUNTRY INN BY CARLSON HOLLAND. *12260 James St, Holland (49424). Phone 616/396-6677; toll-free 888/201-1746; fax 616/396-1197. www.countryinns.com.* 116 rooms, 2 story. Complimentary continental breakfast. Check-out noon. Indoor pool. **$**

★ ★ HOLIDAY INN. *650 E 24th St, Holland (49423). Phone 616/394-0111; toll-free 800/279-5286; fax 616/394-4832. www.holiday-inn.com.* 168 rooms, 4 story. Check-out noon. Restaurant, bar. Fitness room. Indoor pool. Airport transportation available. **$**

Specialty Lodging

The following lodging establishment is approved by Mobil Travel Guide, but due to its unique and individualized nature has not been given a traditional Mobil Star rating. Included in this listing you may find bed-and-breakfasts, limited-service inns, guest ranches, and other unique hotel properties.

DUTCH COLONIAL INN. *560 Central Ave, Holland (49423). Phone 616/396-3664; fax 616/396-0461. www.dutchcolonialinn.com.* Built in 1928. 4 rooms, 3 story. Complimentary full breakfast. Check-in 3 pm, check-out 11 am. High-speed Internet access. **$$**

Restaurants

★ **84 EAST PASTA ETC.** *84 E 8th St, Holland (49423). Phone 616/396-8484; fax 616/393-8848. www.84eastpasta.com.* American, Italian menu. Lunch, dinner. Closed Sun; holidays. Bar. Children's menu. Casual attire. **$**

★ ★ ★ **ALPENROSE.** *4 E 8th St, Holland (49423). Phone 616/393-2111; fax 616/393-0027. www.alpenroserestaurant.com.* Austrian menu. Lunch, dinner, Sun brunch. Closed Dec 25. Children's menu. Outdoor seating. **$$**

★ **PEREDDIE'S.** *447 Washington Sq, Holland (49423). Phone 616/394-3061; fax 616/394-9810. www.pereddies.net.* Italian menu. Lunch, dinner. Closed Sun; holidays. Reservations recommended. **$**

★ ★ ★ **PIPER.** *2225 S Shore Dr, Macatawa (49434). Phone 616/335-5866; fax 616/335-6797. www.piperrestaurant.com.* With its light and airy interior overlooking Lake Macatawa, this casually elegant restaurant serves cuisine with professional, friendly service. American menu. Dinner. Closed holidays; also Sun-Mon in winter. Bar. Children's menu. **$$$**

★ ★ **TILL MIDNIGHT.** *208 College Ave, Holland (49423). Phone 616/392-6883; fax 616/392-9638.* Eclectic menu. Lunch, dinner. Closed Sun; holidays. Bar. Children's menu. **$$**

Holly (J-5)

See also Detroit, Flint, Pontiac

Population 5,595
Elevation 937 ft
Area Code 248
Zip 48442
Information Chamber of Commerce, 120 S Saginaw St, PO Box 214; phone 248/634-1900
Web Site www.hollymi.com

Entering the city of Holly is like stepping back in time. At the summer Renaissance Festival, the 16th century comes alive with armor-clad knights on horseback, sword swallowers, and other entertainers, jousting contests, and feasts fit for a king. The 19th-century storefronts beckon at Historic Battle Alley, and Dickens's Victorian novels come alive during the winter Dickens Festival.

What to See and Do

Davisburg Candle Factory. *634 Broadway, Davisburg (48350). 2 miles S, then 3 miles E on Davisburg Rd. Phone 248/634-4214; toll-free 800/748-9440. www.candlefactorymi.com.* Located in a 125-year-old building; produces unique and beautiful handcrafted candles. Unusual taper production line. Showroom and gift shop. Demonstrations by appointment (weekdays). (Mon-Sat 10 am-5 pm, Sun noon-4 pm) **FREE**

DTE Energy Music Center. *7774 Sashabaw Rd, Clarkston (48346). Off I-75 (exit 89). Phone 248/377-0100.* This outdoor ampitheater is considered one of the best in the nation and features summer concerts by top performers. Seats are available close to the stage, but many concertgoers choose to bring blankets for the much cheaper, and more charming, lawn area.

★ **Historic Battle Alley.** *110 Battle Alley, Holly (48442). Downtown, State and National Historic District. Phone 248/634-5208.* Once known for its taverns and brawls, Battle Alley is now a restored 19th-century street featuring antiques, boutiques, specialty shops, crafters; dining at the Historic Holly Hotel (see RESTAURANT). On the Alley is a mosaic of the bicentennial logo made from 1,000 red, white, and blue bricks. (Daily; closed holidays) **FREE**

Mount Holly Ski Area. *13536 S Dixie Hwy, Holly (48442). 7 miles NE off I-75. Phone 248/634-8260; toll-free 800/582-7256. www.skimtholly.com.* Three quad, three triple, double chairlift, six rope tows; patrol, school, rentals, snowmaking; two cafeterias, two bars. Vertical drop 350 feet. Night skiing. (Dec-Mar, daily)

Special Events

Carry Nation Festival. *103 N Saginaw, Holly (48442). Phone 248/634-1900. www.carrynation.com.* Re-creation of Carry Nation's 1908 visit to Holly. The "temperance crusader" charged down Battle Alley with her famed umbrella, smashing bottles and a few heads along the way. Pageant, parade, antique car show, race, games, arts and crafts show, model railroad. Weekend after Labor Day.

Dickens Festival. *Phone 248/634-1900.* Re-creates the Dickensian period with carolers, town crier, strolling characters, skits, bell choirs, street hawkers, carriage rides. Thanksgiving-weekend before Dec 25.

Michigan Renaissance Festival. *12500 Dixie Hwy, Holly (48442). 1 mile N of Mount Holly. Phone 248/634-5552. www.michrenfest.com.* Festivities include jousting tournaments, entertainment, food, and crafts in Renaissance-style village. Eight weekends in Aug-Sept. **$$$**

Restaurant

★ ★ HISTORIC HOLLY HOTEL. *110 Battle Alley, Holly (48442). Phone 248/634-5208; fax 248/634-7977. www.hollyhotel.com.* In restored hotel (1891); Victorian décor. Seafood, steak menu. Lunch, dinner, Sun brunch. Closed holidays. Bar. **$$$**
[D]

Houghton (A-5)

See also Calumet, Copper Harbor, Hancock, Isle Royale National Park, Ontonagon

Settled 1843
Population 7,498
Elevation 607 ft
Area Code 906
Zip 49931
Information Keweenaw Peninsula Chamber of Commerce, 326 Shelden Ave, PO Box 336; phone 906/482-5240 or toll-free 800/338-7982
Web Site www.cityofhoughton.com

Houghton (HO-ton) and its sister city, Hancock (see), face each other across the narrowest part of Portage Lake. This is the area of America's first mining capital, the scene of the first great mineral strike in the Western Hemisphere. The copper-bearing geological formations are believed to be the oldest rock formations in the world. The great mining rush of 1843 and the years following brought people from all over Europe. Two main ethnic groups are identifiable today: Cornishmen, who came from England and made popular the pasties (PAST-ees) available throughout the Upper Peninsula; and Finns, who have made this their cultural center in the United States.

What to See and Do

Ferry service to Isle Royale National Park. *800 E Lakeshore Dr, Houghton (49931). Phone 906/482-0984.* Four ferries and a float plane provide transportation (June-Sept, daily; some trips in May). For fees and schedule contact Park Superintendent.

Maasto Hiihto Ski Trail. *326 Shelden Ave, Houghton (49931). 1/2 mile N via Hwy 41, then 2 miles N on side road. Phone 906/482-2388.* A 9 1/2-mile public cross-country ski trail with beginner-to-expert trails groomed daily. (Dec-Apr, daily) **FREE**

Michigan Technological University. *1400 Townsend Dr, Houghton (49931). Phone 906/487-1885.* (1885) (6,200 students) One of the finest engineering and mining schools in the United States, Michigan Tech also features one of the premier hockey teams in the country. If you get a chance to attend a hockey game, sit on any of the four corners to see up-close checking. Campus tours leave from University Career Center in Administration Building. (See SPECIAL EVENTS) On campus is

> **A. E. Seaman Mineralogical Museum.** *Electrical Energy Resources Center, 1400 Townsend Dr, Houghton (49931). Phone 906/487-2572. www.museum.mtu.edu.* Exhibits one of the nation's best mineral collections. (Mon-Fri 9 am-4:30 pm, Sat noon-4 pm; closed holidays)

Mont Ripley Ski Area. *1400 Townsend Dr, Houghton (49931). 1/2 mile E on Hwy 26. Phone 906/487-2340. www.aux.mtu.edu/ski.* Double chairlift, T-bar; patrol, school, rentals, snowmaking; cafeteria. (Early Dec-late Mar, daily; closed Dec 25) **$$$$**

Special Events

Bridgefest. *326 Shelden Ave, Houghton (49931). On the Houghton and Hancock waterfronts. Phone 906/482-2388.* Parade, arts and crafts show, entertainment, powerboat races, fireworks. Father's Day weekend. Mid June.

Winter Carnival. *Michigan Technological University, 1400 Townsend Dr, Houghton (49931). Phone 906/487-2818.* Snow sculptures and statues; dogsled and snowshoe racing, broomball, skiing, skating; skit contests; Queen Coronation and Snoball Dance. Late Jan-early Feb.

Limited-Service Hotel

★ ★ BEST WESTERN FRANKLIN SQUARE INN. *820 Shelden Ave, Houghton (49931). Phone 906/487-1700; toll-free 888/487-1700; fax 906/487-9432. www.bestwestern.com.* 105 rooms, 7 story. Check-in 2 pm, check-out 11 am. Restaurant, bar. Indoor pool, whirlpool. **$**

Houghton Lake (F-4)

See also Grayling, Harrison

Population 3,353
Elevation 1,162 ft
Area Code 989
Zip 48629
Information Chamber of Commerce, 1625 W Houghton Lake Dr; phone 989/366-5644 or toll-free 800/248-5253
Web Site www.houghtonlakechamber.org

The Houghton (HO-ton) Lake area is the gateway to a popular north country resort area including three of the largest inland lakes in the state and 200,000 acres of state forests. It's best known for fishing, including ice fishing in winter, Houghton Lake has also become popular among snowmobilers, because of the heavy snowfall that accumulates in the middle portion of the Lower Peninsula.

What to See and Do

Higgins Lake. *Between Hwy 27 and I-75.* One of the most beautiful in America, Higgins Lake covers 10,317 acres and has 25 miles of sandy shoreline.

Houghton Lake. *Between Hwy 27 and I-75.* Largest inland lake in Michigan and the source of the Muskegon River. This lake has a 32-mile shoreline and 22,000 acres of water, as well as 200 miles of groomed and marked snowmobile trails. A variety of resorts are in the area.

St. Helen Lake. *E on Hwy 55, then N on Hwy 76.* This pine-bordered lake has 12 miles of shoreline.

Special Event

Tip-Up-Town USA Ice Festival. *1625 W Houghton Lake Dr, Houghton Lake (48629). Phone 989/366-5644.* "Tip-up" is an ice-fishing term for the way anglers set up their gear to signal that a fish is on the line. The Tip-Up-Town USA Ice Festival features ice fishing contests, games, food, parade, fireworks, carnival. Third and fourth weekend in Jan.

Limited-Service Hotel

★ BEST WESTERN BEACHFRONT. *4990 W Houghton Lake Dr, Houghton Lake (48629). Phone 989/366-9126; toll-free 800/780-7234; fax 989/366-1547. www.bestwestern.com.* 60 rooms. Complimentary continental breakfast. Check-in 3 pm, check-out 11 am. **$**

Indian River (E-4)

See also Cheboygan, Petoskey

Population 2,500
Elevation 616 ft
Area Code 231
Zip 49749
Information Chamber of Commerce, 3435 S Straits Hwy, PO Box 57; phone 231/238-9325 or toll-free 800/394-8310
Web Site www.irmi.org

Located on beautiful Burt Lake and the Sturgeon and Pigeon rivers, Indian River is a sportlover's delight: hunting, fishing, canoeing, kayaking, snowmobiling, hiking, snowshoeing, and cross-country skiing. Conveniently located on Interstate 75, Indian River is close to all of northern Michigan's hot spots.

What to See and Do

Burt Lake State Park. *6635 State Park Dr, Indian River (49749). 1/2 mile S off I-75, exit 310. Phone 231/238-9392.* Approximately 400 acres. Beach, beachhouse, water-skiing, fishing for walleyed pike and perch, boating (ramp, rentals); picnicking, playground, concession, camping. (May-Oct, daily) **$$**

Canoeing. *4752 Onaway Rd, Indian River (49749). Phone 231/238-9092.* Trips on Sturgeon and/or Pigeon rivers; difficulty varies with streams. Various trips offered. Reservations advised.

> **Sturgeon & Pigeon River Outfitters.** *4271 S Straits Hwy, Indian River (49749). Phone 231/238-8181.* Canoeing, tubing, kayaking. (May-mid-Sept)
>
> **Tomahawk Trails Canoe Livery.** *6225 Hwy 68, Indian River (49749). Phone 231/238-8703.* (May-Oct, daily)

Cross in the Woods. *7078 Hwy 68, Indian River (49749). 1 mile W of I-75 exit 310, on Hwy 68. Phone 231/238-8973.* Wooden crucifix 55 feet tall. Outdoor shrines. (Mar-Nov, daily) **FREE**

Limited-Service Hotel

★ HOLIDAY INN EXPRESS. *4375 Brudy Rd, Indian River (49749). Phone 231/238-3000; toll-free 888/255-3365; fax 231/238-8992. www.holiday-inn .com.* 50 rooms. Complimentary continental breakfast. Check-in 3 pm, check-out 11 am. Indoor pool, whirlpool. **$**

Interlochen

See also Beulah, Frankfort, Traverse City

Elevation 866 ft
Area Code 231
Zip 49643

This picturesque farming community (pronounced INTER-lock-in) is the cultural and artistic center of northern Michigan. Throughout the year, but especially in summer, you find performances by big-name entertainers that rival those found in the largest cities in the US. The nearby state park offers one of the only virgin white pine forests left in the world.

What to See and Do

Interlochen Center for the Arts. *4000 Hwy 137, Interlochen (49643). 13 miles SW via Hwy 31, then 2 miles S on Hwy 137. Phone 231/276-6230. www.interlochen.org.* The Interlochen Arts Academy, a fine arts boarding high school, is located here (Sept-May). Concerts by students, faculty, and internationally known guests; art exhibits, drama and dance productions (all year). Approximately 2,500 students assemble here every summer to study music, art, drama, and dance (see SPECIAL EVENT).

Interlochen State Park. *S Hwy 137, Interlochen (49643). 15 miles SW via Hwy 31, then S on Hwy 137, adjacent to National Music Camp. Phone 231/276-9511.* A 187-acre park with sand beach on Green and Duck lakes. Swimming, bathhouse, fishing, boating (rentals, launch); picnicking, playground, concession, camping, pavilion. **$$**

Special Event

Interlochen Arts Camp. *Interlochen Center for the Arts, 4000 Hwy 137, Interlochen (49643). Phone 231/276-6230.* www.interlochen.org. A variety of performing arts events by students and visiting professionals. Mid-June-early Sept.

Iron Mountain (D-1)

See also Iron River, Ishpeming

Settled 1878
Population 8,525
Elevation 1,138 ft
Area Code 906
Zip 49801
Information Tourism Association of the Dickinson County Area, 600 S Stephenson Ave, PO Box 672; phone 906/774-2002 or toll-free 800/236-2447
Web Site www.ironmountain.org

After more than a half-century of production, the underground shaft mines of high-grade ore deposits here have closed. Logging, tourism, and wood products are the main economic factors now, and Iron Mountain is the distribution point for the entire Menominee Range area. A nearby bluff heavily striped with iron ore gave the city its name. Abandoned mines, cave-ins, and a huge Cornish mine pump, preserved as tourist attractions, are reminders of mining days.

What to See and Do

Iron Mountain Iron Mine. *W4852 Hwy 2, Vulcan (49892). 8 miles E on Hwy 2. Phone 906/563-8077.* Mine train tours 2,600 feet of underground drifts and tunnels 400 feet below surface. Working machinery, museum. Tours (June-mid-Oct, daily). **$$**

Lake Antoine Park. *N33393 Lake Antoine, Iron Mountain (49801). 2 miles NE. Phone 906/774-8875.* Swimming, boating, water-skiing; nature trail, picnicking, concession, improved county campgrounds (fee); band concerts. (Memorial Day-Labor Day, daily)

Menominee Range Historical Museum. *300 E Ludington St, Iron Mountain (49801). In the Carnegie Public Library. Phone 906/774-4276.* More than 100 exhibits depict life on the Menominee Iron Range in the 1880s and early 1900s; one-room school, Victorian parlor, trapper's cabin, country store. (Mid-May-Sept, daily; rest of year, by appointment) **$$** Combination ticket **$$** includes

Cornish Pumping Engine & Mining Museum. *300 Kent St, Iron Mountain (49801). Phone 906/774-1086.* Features largest steam-driven pumping engine built in United States, with 40-foot-diameter flywheel in engine and weighing 160 tons; also display of underground mining equipment used in Michigan; World War II glider display. (Mid-May-Sept, daily; rest of year, by appointment) **$$**

Pine Mountain Lodge. *N3332 Pine Mountain Rd, Iron Mountain (49801). 2 1/2 miles N off Hwy 2/141. Phone 906/774-2747; toll-free 800/553-7463 (Nov-Apr). www.pinemountainresort.com.* Triple, two double chairlifts, rope tow; snowmaking, patrol, school, rentals; nine-hole golf; two tennis courts; indoor/outdoor pools; restaurant, cafeteria, bar; lodge, condos. Longest run 3/4 mile; vertical drop 500 feet. (Late Nov-early Apr, daily) Cross-country trails.

Special Events

Festival of the Arts. *Phone 906/774-2945.* Crafts demonstrations, antique car show, concerts, square and folk dancing, community theater, international foods. Mid-June-mid-Aug.

Pine Mountain Ski Jumping Tournament. *Pine Mountain Lodge, N3332 Pine Mountain Rd, Iron Mountain (49801). Phone 906/774-2747.* Jan.

Wood-Bee Carvers Show. *Premiere Center, 300 E F St, Iron Mountain (49801). Phone 906/774-2945.* Wood carvers competition and show. Oct.

Limited-Service Hotels

★ **EXECUTIVE INN.** *1518 S Stephenson Ave (Hwy 2), Iron Mountain (49801). Phone 906/774-2040; fax 906/774-0238.* 57 rooms, 2 story. Pets accepted; fee. Complimentary continental breakfast. Check-out 11 am. Indoor pool. **$**

★ **COMFORT INN.** *1555 N Stephenson Ave, Iron Mountain (49801). Phone 906/774-5505; toll-free 800/638-7949; fax 906/774-2631. www.comfortinn.com.* 48 rooms, 2 story. Complimentary continental breakfast. Check-in 3 pm, check-out 11 am. Fitness room. **$**

Iron River (C-5)

See also Iron Mountain

Population 2,095
Elevation 1,510 ft
Area Code 906
Zip 49935
Information Iron County Chamber of Commerce, 50 E Genesee St; phone 906/265-3822 or toll-free 888/879-4766
Web Site www.iron.org

Just north of the Wisconsin-Michigan state line, Iron River was one of the last of the large mining towns to spring up on the Menominee Range. Lumbering has also played a prominent part in the town's past. Ottawa National Forest (see IRONWOOD) lies a few miles to the west, and a Ranger District office is located here.

What to See and Do

Iron County Museum. *100 Museum Dr, Caspian (49915). 2 miles S on County 424. Phone 906/265-2617. www.ironcountymuseum.com.* Indoor/outdoor museum of 22 buildings. Miniature logging exhibit with more than 2,000 pieces; iron mining dioramas; more than 100 major exhibits; log homestead; 1896 one-room schoolhouse; logging camp, home of composer Carrie Jacobs-Bond; Lee LeBlanc Wildlife Art Gallery. Annual ethnic festivals (Scandinavian, Polish, Italian, Yugoslavian; inquire for schedule). (Mid-May-Oct: Mon-Sat 9 am-5 pm, Sun 1-5 pm; rest of year: by appointment) **$$**

Ski Brule. *397 Brule Mountain Rd, Iron River (49935). 3 miles SW off Hwy 189. Phone 906/265-4957; toll-free 800/362-7853. www.skibrule.com.* Four chairlifts, two T-bars, pony lift, rope tow; patrol, school, rentals, snowmaking; chalet and condo lodging, restaurant, cafeteria, bar, nursery. Seventeen runs, longest run 1 mile; vertical drop 500 feet. (Nov-Apr, daily) Cross-country trails. **$$$$**

Special Events

Bass Festival. *Runkle Lake Park, Crystal Falls (49920). Off Hwy 69. Phone 906/265-3822.* Canoe races on the Paint River, softball game, barbecue, music, and events at Runkle Park and Runkle Lake. First weekend in July.

Ferrous Frolics. *Iron County Museum, 100 Museum Dr, Caspian (49915). Phone 906/265-2617.* Arts, crafts, demonstrations, band concert, flea market. Third weekend in July.

Iron County Fair. *Fairgrounds, N 7th Ave and W Franklin St, Iron River (49935). Phone toll-free 888/879-4766. www.ironcountyfair.org.* This down-home county fair features a carnival, rodeo, horse races, and arts and crafts. Four days in late Aug.

Upper Peninsula Championship Rodeo. *Fairgrounds, 50 E Genesee St, Iron River (49935). Phone 906/265-3822.* Late July.

Ironwood (B-4)

See also Hurley, Ontonagon, Wakefield

Settled 1885
Population 6,849
Elevation 1,503 ft
Area Code 906
Zip 49938
Information Ironwood Area Chamber of Commerce, 150 N Lowell; phone 906/932-1122
Web Site www.ironwoodmi.org

Ironwood is a center for summer and winter recreation. The first part of Gogebic County to be settled, the town was linked at first with fur trading. It quickly blossomed into a mining town when a deposit of iron was found in what is now the eastern section of the city. John R. Wood, one of the first mining captains, was known as "Iron" because of his interest in ore—thus, the name Ironwood.

What to See and Do

Big Powderhorn Mountain. *N11375 Powderhorn Rd, Bessemer (49911). Phone 906/932-4838; toll-free 800/501-7669. www.bigpowderhorn.net.* Nine double chairlifts; patrol, school, rentals; three restaurants, cafeteria, three bars, nursery. Twenty-five runs; longest run 1 mile; vertical drop 600 feet. (Thanksgiving-early Apr: daily 9 am-4 pm) **$$$$**

Blackjack. *N11251 Baker Blackjack Rd, Bessemer (49911). 12 miles E of Hwy 51 via Hwy 2, Blackjack exit. Phone 906/229-5115; toll-free 800/848-1125. www.skiblackjack.com.* Four double chairlifts, two rope tows; patrol, school, rentals; cafeteria, restaurant, bar, nursery, lodging. Longest run 1 mile; vertical drop 465 feet. (Nov-Mar, daily) **$$$$**

Black River Harbor. *N15725 Black River Rd, Ironwood (49938). 4 miles E, then 15 miles N on County 513. Phone 906/932-7250.* Deep-sea fishing boats for rent, boat rides, Lake Superior cruises; picnicking, playground, camping.

Copper Peak Ski Flying. *N13870 Copper Peak Rd, Ironwood (49938). 12 miles N on County 513. Phone 906/932-3500.* The only ski flying facility in North America, and one of six in the world, where athletes test their skills in an event that requires more athletic ability than ski jumping. Skiers reach speeds of more than 60 miles per hour and fly farther than 500 feet. International tournament is held every winter. In summer, chairlift and elevator rides take visitors 240 feet above the crest of Copper Peak for a view of three states, Lake Superior, and Canada. (Mid-June-Labor Day: daily; Sept-Oct: weekends) **$$**

Hiawatha–World's Tallest Indian. *Houk St, Ironwood (49938).* Statue of famous Iroquois stands 52 feet high and looks north to the legendary "shining big-sea-water"—Gitchee Gumee, also known as Lake Superior.

Little Girl's Point Park. *104 S Lowell St, Ironwood (49938). County 505 N, 18 miles N, off Hwy 2; on Lake Superior. Phone 906/932-1420.* Notable for the agate pebbles on the beaches. Picnic tables (fee), campsites (fee); Native American burial grounds. (May-Sept)

Mount Zion. *E4946 Jackson Rd, Ironwood (49938). 3/4 mile N of Hwy 2. Phone 906/932-3718.* One of the highest points on the Gogebic Range, with 1,750-foot altitude, 1,150 feet above Lake Superior. Double chairlift, two rope tows; patrol, school, rentals; snack bar. Longest run is 3/4 mile; vertical drop 300 feet. (Mid-Dec-Mar, Tues-Sun; closed Dec 25) Two miles of cross-country ski trails, equipment rentals.

Ottawa National Forest. *2100 E Cloverland Dr, Ironwood (49938). E via Hwy 2, Hwy 28. Phone 906/932-1330.* Wooded hills, picturesque lakes and streams, waterfalls, J. W. Toumey Nursery, Black River Harbor, North Country National Scenic Trail, Watersmeet Visitor Center and Sylvania, Sturgeon River Gorge, and McCormick Wildernesses are all part of this 953,600-acre forest. Fishing for trout, muskie, northern pike, walleye, bass, and panfish; swimming, canoeing, boat landing; hunting for big and small game, hiking, cross-country and downhill skiing, picnicking, camping. (Daily) **FREE**

Special Event

Gogebic County Fair. *Fairgrounds, 104 S Lowell St, Ironwood (49938). Phone 906/932-1420. gogebiccounty fair.homestead.com.* Carnival rides, harness racing, horse shows, and live music and are among the activities at this county fair. Second weekend in Aug.

Limited-Service Hotel

★ COMFORT INN. *210 E Cloverland Dr, Ironwood (49938). Phone 906/932-2224; toll-free 800/572-9412; fax 906/932-9929. www.comfortinn.com.* 63 rooms, 2 story. Complimentary continental breakfast. Check-in 2 pm, check-out 11 am. Indoor pool, whirlpool. **$**

Ishpeming (C-1)

See also Iron Mountain, Marquette

Founded 1844
Population 7,200
Area Code 906
Zip 49849
Information Ishpeming-Negaunee Area Chamber of Commerce, 661 Palms Ave; phone 906/486-4841
Web Site www.marquette.org

Iron mines gave birth to this city and still sustain it. Skiing is the basis of its recreation and tourism business; the national ski jumping championships are held here annually. In 1887, three Norwegians formed a ski club in Ishpeming (ISH-pa-ming), which is a Native American word for "high grounds." That ski club eventually became a US Ski Association, which hosts the National Ski Hall of Fame and Ski Museum, located here.

What to See and Do

★ National Ski Hall of Fame and Ski Museum. *610 Palms Ave, Ishpeming (49849). Between 2nd and 3rd sts, on Hwy 41W. Phone 906/485-6323.* Affiliated with the US Ski Association. Houses national trophies and displays of old skis and ski equipment, includes a replica of the oldest-known ski and ski pole in the world. Roland Palmedo National Ski Library, collection of ski publications for researchers in-house only. (Mon-Sat 10 am-5 pm; closed holidays) **$$**

Suicide Bowl. *On Cliffs Dr at E end of city. Phone 906/485-4242.* Includes five ski-jumping hills from mini-hill to 70-meter hill. There are also four cross-country trails; one is lighted for evening use. **$$**

Van Riper State Park. *1003 AKE Hwy 41, Champion (49814). 17 miles W on Hwy 41. Phone 906/339-4461.* Approximately 1,000 acres on Lake Michigamme. Swimming, water-skiing, bathhouse, fishing, boating (ramp, rentals); hunting, hiking, picnic grounds, concession, playground, camping. (Daily) **$$**

Special Event

Annual Ski Jumping Championships. *National Ski Hall of Fame, 610 Palms Ave, Ishpeming (49849). Between 2nd and 3rd sts, on Hwy 41 W. Phone 906/485-6323.* Paul Bietila Memorial. Also cross-country ski race. Feb.

Limited-Service Hotel

★ ★ BEST WESTERN COUNTRY INN. *850 Hwy 41 W, Ishpeming (49849). Phone 906/485-6345; toll-free 800/780-7234; fax 906/485-6348. www.bestwestern.com.* 60 rooms, 2 story. Pets accepted, some restrictions. Complimentary continental breakfast. Check-in 3 pm, check-out noon. Indoor pool, whirlpool. **$**

Isle Royale National Park (A-3)

See also Copper Harbor, Hancock, Houghton

N of Upper Peninsula, on island in Lake Superior

This unique wilderness area, covering 571,790 acres, is the largest island in Lake Superior, 15 miles from Canada (the nearest mainland), 18 miles from Minnesota, and 45 miles from Michigan. There are no roads, and no automobiles are allowed. The main island, 45 miles long and 8 1/2 miles across at its widest point, is surrounded by more than 400 smaller islands. Isle Royale (ROY-uhl) can be reached by boat from Houghton or Copper Harbor (see both) in Michigan, from Grand Portage (see) in Minnesota, or by seaplane from Houghton. Schedules vary; inquire each year around January 1. Contact the Superintendent, Isle Royale National Park, 800 E Lakeshore Dr, Houghton 49931; phone 906/482-0984.

The only wildlife here are those animals able to fly, swim, drift across the water, or travel on ice. Moose, wolf, fox, and beaver are the dominant mammals; however, before 1900, no moose existed on the island. The current population of 700 evolved from a few moose that swam to the island around 1912. In the winter of 1949, wolves came across on the ice and stayed. More than 200 species of birds have been observed, including loons, bald eagles, and ospreys.

Prehistoric peoples discovered copper on the island 4,000 years ago. Later, white men tried to mine in a number of places. The remains of these mining operations are still visible; some of the ancient mining pits date back 3,800 years.

There are more than 165 miles of foot trails leading to beautiful inland lakes, more than 20 of which have game fish, including pike, perch, walleye, and, in a few, whitefish cisco. There are trout in many streams and lakes. Fishing is under National Park Service and Michigan regulations (see FISHING AND HUNTING in state text). Boat rental and charter fishing are available at Rock Harbor Lodge. Basic supplies are available on the island in limited quantities. Nights are usually cold; bring warm clothing and be prepared to rough it. Group camping is available for parties of seven to ten; inquire for group information. Group campsites must be reserved. The park is open from approximately May to October.

Rock Harbor Lodge is at the east end of the island, about 3 1/2 miles east of Mott Island, which is the Park Service headquarters during the summer. The lodge, open June through Labor Day, offers rooms, cabins, a restaurant, and a camp store. Make room reservations at least three months in advance. For lodge information in summer, write to National Park Concessions, Inc, PO Box 605, Houghton 49931; phone 906/337-4993; in winter, write to National Park Concessions, Inc., PO Box 27, Mammoth Cave, KY 42259; phone 270/773-2191.

Jackson (J-4)

See also Ann Arbor, Battle Creek, Brooklyn, Lansing

Founded 1829
Population 37,446
Elevation 960 ft
Area Code 517
Information Convention & Tourist Bureau, 6007 Ann Arbor Rd, 49201; phone 517/764-4440 or toll-free 800/245-5282
Web Site www.jackson-mich.org

In Jackson on July 6, 1854, the Republican Party was officially born at a convention held "under the green spreading oaks," as there was no hall large enough to accommodate the delegates. Each year, the city attracts thousands of tourists, who use it as a base to explore more than 200 natural lakes in Jackson County.

What to See and Do

Cascades Falls Park. *1992 Warren Ave, Jackson (49203). Brown St via I-94 to exit 138. Phone 517/788-4320.* Approximately 465 acres. Fishing ponds and pier, paddle-boating (rentals); picnicking, playground; 18-hole miniature golf, driving range; fitness and jogging trail; basketball, tennis, and horseshoe courts; restaurant. Also here are

Cascades-Sparks Museum. *Brown St and Denton Rd, Jackson (49203). Phone 517/788-4320.* Depicts early history of falls and its builder, Captain William Sparks; original drawings, models, audio-visual displays. (Memorial Day-Labor Day)

Sparks Illuminated Cascades Waterfalls. *1992 Warren Ave, Jackson (49203). Phone 517/788-4320.* Approximately 500 feet of water cascading over 16 waterfalls and six fountains in continually changing patterns of light, color, and music. (Memorial Day-Labor Day, nightly) **$$**

Dahlem Environmental Education Center. *7117 S Jackson Rd, Jackson (49201). Phone 517/782-3453. www.dahlemcenter.org.* Nature center with 5 miles of trails through forests, fields, marshes; 1/2-mile "special needs" trail for the disabled; visitor center with exhibits, gift shop. (Tues-Sun) **FREE**

Ella Sharp Park. *3225 4th St, Jackson (49203). At S edge of city. Phone 517/788-4040.* Approximately 530 acres with 18-hole golf course, tennis courts, ballfields, swimming pool, miniature golf, picnic facilities, formal gardens. (Daily) **FREE** In park is

Ella Sharp Museum. *3225 4th St, Jackson (49203). Phone 517/787-2320. www.ellasharp.org.* Complex includes Victorian farmhouse, historic farm lane, one-room schoolhouse, log cabin, galleries with rotating art and historic exhibits; studios; planetarium; visitor center. (Tues-Fri 10 am-4 pm, Sat-Sun 11 am-4 pm; closed holidays) **$**

Michigan Space Center. *2111 Emmons Rd, Jackson (49201). Phone 517/787-4425.* US space artifacts and memorabilia displayed in geodesic dome, including *Gemini* trainer, *Apollo 9* Command Module, replica of space shuttle, *Challenger* memorial, space food, space suits, lunar rover, moon rock, satellites, orbiters, landers, giant rocket engines; films and special presentations. Picnicking and children's play areas. Gift shop. (May-Oct: Tues-Sat 10 am-5 pm, Sun noon-5 pm; Nov-Apr: Tues-Sat 10 am-5 pm) **$**

Republican Party founding site. *W Franklin and 2nd sts, Jackson (49203).* Marked with a tablet dedicated by President William Howard Taft.

Waterloo Farm Museum. *9998 Waterloo-Munith Rd, Waterloo Township (49240). 10 miles E via I-94 to exit 150, N on Mount Hope Rd, E on Waterloo-Munith Rd, near Waterloo. Phone 517/596-2254.* Tours of furnished pioneer farmhouse (1855-1885), bakehouse, windmill, farm workshop, barn, milk cellar, log house, granary. (June-Aug: Tues-Sun afternoons; Sept: Sat-Sun; Pioneer Festival second Sun in Oct) **$**

Waterloo State Recreation Area. *16345 McClure Rd, Chelsea (48118). 15 miles E on I-94, then N on unnumbered road. Phone 313/475-8307.* This is the state's largest recreation area, with 20,072 acres. Swimming, beach, bathhouse, water-skiing, fishing, boating (ramp, rentals) on numerous lakes; horseback riding, nature trails, hunting, picnicking, concession, cabins, tent and trailer sites; geology center.

Special Events

Civil War Muster & Battle Reenactment. *Cascade Falls Park, 1992 Warren Ave, Jackson (49203). Phone 517/788-4320.* Thousands of participants re-create a different Civil War battle each year; living history demonstrations, parades, food, entertainment. Third weekend in Aug.

Harness racing. *Jackson Harness Raceway, Jackson County Fairgrounds, 200 W Ganson St, Jackson (49201). Phone 517/788-4500.* Pari-mutuel betting. Spring and fall races.

Hot Air Balloon Jubilee. *Jackson County Airport, 3606 Wildwood Ave, Jackson (49203). Phone 517/782-1515.* Competitive balloon events; skydivers; arts and crafts. Mid-July.

Jackson County Fair. *Jackson County Fairgrounds, 200 W Ganson St, Jackson (49201). Phone 517/788-4405.* Stage shows; displays of produce, handicrafts, farm animals; midway shows; rides. Second week in Aug.

Rose Festival. *Ella Sharp Park, 212 W Michigan Ave, Jackson (49203). Phone 517/787-2065.* Parade, pageant, garden tours, entertainment. Mid-May-mid-June.

Limited-Service Hotels

★ COUNTRY HEARTH INN - JACKSON *1111 Boardman Rd, Jackson (49202). Phone 517/783-6404; toll-free 800/267-5023; fax 517/783-6529. www.countryhearth.com.* 73 rooms, 2 story. Complimentary continental breakfast. Check-in 3 pm, check-out noon. **$**

★★ HOLIDAY INN. *2000 Holiday Inn Dr, Jackson (49202). Phone 517/783-2681; toll-free 800/465-4329; fax 517/783-5744. www.holiday-inn.com.* This family- and budget-friendly hotel features an assortment of activities and amenities to make sure guests are comfortable. With a putting green, game room, ping pong, pool table, and mini golf, the hotel offers an array of fun things to do, while families can dine in the hotel's casual restaurant after a day of area shopping or sightseeing. 184 rooms, 2 story. Pets accepted, some restrictions; fee. Check-in 4 pm, check-out 11 am. Restaurant, bar. Fitness room. Indoor pool, whirlpool. **$**

Restaurant

★★ KNIGHT'S STEAKHOUSE & GRILL. *2125 Horton Rd, Jackson (49203). Phone 517/783-2777.* This steakhouse has a no-frills flair that attracts both locals and out-of-towners. However, consider yourself in the know, because the great selection and value are probably the area's best-kept secret. Steak menu. Dinner. Closed Sun; holidays. Bar. Children's menu. **$$**

Kalamazoo (J-3)

See also Battle Creek, Paw Paw, Three Rivers

Settled 1829
Population 80,277
Elevation 780 ft
Area Code 269
Information Kalamazoo County Convention and Visitors Bureau, 346 W Michigan Ave, 49007; phone 269/381-4003 or toll-free 800/530-9192
Web Site www.kazoofun.com

Yes, there really is a Kalamazoo—a unique name, immortalized in song and verse. The name is derived from the Native American name for the Kalamazoo River, which means "where the water boils in the pot." The concept is noted not only in the community's name but also in its cultural, industrial, and recreational makeup. Diversified industry from bedding plants to pharmaceuticals thrive here. Many recreational activities complete the picture.

What to See and Do

Bittersweet Ski Area. *600 River Rd, Otsego (49078). 18 miles N via Hwy 131, Hwy 89 W to Jefferson Rd exit. Phone 269/694-2820. www.skibittersweet.com.* Quad, four triple chairlifts, double chairlift, five rope tows; school, rentals; lodge, cafeteria, bar. Sixteen trails; longest run 2,300 feet; vertical drop 300 feet. Night skiing. (Dec-Mar: Mon-Thurs noon-10 pm, Fri 10 am-10:30 pm, Sat 9 am-10:30 pm, Sun 9 am-10 pm) **$$$$**

Bronson Park. *200 W South St, Kalamazoo (49007). Extending for two blocks on South St.* A bronze tablet marks the spot where Abraham Lincoln made an antislavery speech in 1856.

Crane Park. *Park St, at the crest of Westnedge Hill overlooking city.* Formal floral gardens, tennis courts.

Echo Valley. *8495 E H Ave, Kalamazoo (49048). Phone 269/349-3291.* 60-mph tobogganing (toboggans furnished), ice skating (rentals). (Dec-Mar, Fri-Sun; closed Dec 25) **$$$**

Gilmore-CCCA Museum. *6865 Hickory Rd, Hickory Corners (49060). 15 miles NE via Hwy 43. Phone 269/671-5089. www.gilmorecarmuseum.org.* More than 120 antique autos tracing the significant technical developments in automotive transportation; on 90 acres of landscaped grounds. (May-Oct: Mon-Fri 9 am-5 pm, Sat-Sun 9 am-6 pm) **$$$**

★ **Kalamazoo Air Zoo.** *3101 E Milham Rd, Kalamazoo (49002). On the grounds of Kalamazoo/Battle Creek Airport. Phone 269/382-6555. www.airzoo.org.* It is home to over 70 beautiful historic and restored aircraft of the World War II period, many in flying condition; exhibits, video theater, flight simulator, observation deck. Tours of Restoration Center (May-Sept). Flight of the Day (May-Sept, afternoons). (Daily; closed holidays) **$$**

Kalamazoo College. *1200 Academy St, Kalamazoo (49006). Phone 269/337-7300. www.kzoo.edu.* (1833) (1,300 students) Private, liberal arts college. Red-brick streets and Georgian architecture characterize this school, one of the 100 oldest colleges in the nation. A 3,023-pipe organ is in Stetson Chapel; Bach Festival (Mar); Festival Playhouse (June-July).

Kalamazoo Institute of Arts. *314 S Park St, Kalamazoo (49007). Phone 269/349-7775. www.kiarts.org.* Galleries, school, shop, library, and auditorium. Collection of 20th-century American art; circulating exhibits. (Tues-Wed, Fri-Sat 10 am-5 pm, Thurs 10 am-8 pm, Sun noon-5 pm; closed holidays) **DONATION**

Kalamazoo Nature Center. *7000 N Westnedge Ave, Kalamazoo (49009). 5 miles N. Phone 269/381-1574. www.naturecenter.org.* Interpretive Center; restored 1860s pioneer homestead; nature trails (tours by appointment); barnyard (May-Labor Day); Public Orientation Room programs, slides, movies, live animals. (Mon-Sat 9 am-5 pm, Sun 1-5 pm; closed holidays) **$$**

Kalamazoo Valley Museum. *230 N Rose St, Kalamazoo (49007). Phone 269/373-7990. kvm.kvcc.edu.* Includes Mary Jane Stryker Interactive Learning Hall with an interactive theater, science gallery, Challenger Learning Center, Egyptian artifacts, and Universe Theater and Planetarium. (Mon-Fri 9 am-5 pm, Sat 9 am-9 pm, Sun 1-5 pm) **FREE**

Timber Ridge Ski Area. *7500 23 1/2 St, Gobles (49055). 5 miles N on Hwy 131, then W at D Ave exit. Phone 269/694-9449; toll-free 800/253-2928. www.timberridgeski.com.* Four chairlifts, Pomalift, three rope tows; patrol, school, snowmaking; snack bar, cafeteria, two bars. Store, repairs, rentals. Fifteen trails; longest run 2/3 mile; vertical drop 250 feet. (Late Nov-mid-Mar: Mon-Fri 11 am-10 pm, Sat 9 am-10 pm, Sun 9 am-8 pm; closed Dec 25) **$$$$**

Western Michigan University. *1903 W Michigan Ave, Kalamazoo (49008). Phone 269/387-1000.* (1903) (28,000 students) Contemporary plays, musical comedies, operas, and melodramas offered in Shaw and York theaters. Touring professional shows, dance programs, and entertainers in Miller Auditorium; dance and music performances are featured in the Irving S. Gilmore University Theatre Complex. Art exhibits in Sangren Hall and East Hall. Inquire for schedules.

Special Events

Kalamazoo County Fair. *2900 Lake St, Kalamazoo (49001). Phone 269/381-4003. www.kalamazoocountyfair.com.* Animal attractions, 4-H exhibits, harness racing, carnival rides, and a laser light show are among the entertainment at this county fair. Aug.

Kalamazoo County Flowerfest. *350 S Burdick St, Kalamazoo (49007). Phone 269/381-3597.* July.

Limited-Service Hotels

★ BEST WESTERN HOSPITALITY INN. *3640 E Cork St, Kalamazoo (49001). Phone 269/381-1900; toll-free 800/780-7234; fax 269/373-6136. www.bestwestern.com.* 124 rooms, 3 story. Complimentary continental breakfast. Check-in 3 pm, check-out noon. Fitness room. Indoor pool, whirlpool. **$**

★ ECONO LODGE. *3750 Easy St, Kalamazoo (49001). Phone 269/388-3551; toll-free 800/687-6667; fax 269/342-9132. www.qualityinn.com.* 116 rooms, 2 story. Pets accepted. Complimentary continental breakfast. Check-in 3 pm, check-out 11 am. Outdoor pool. Airport transportation available. **$**

★ FAIRFIELD INN. *3800 E Cork St, Kalamazoo (49001). Phone 269/344-8300; toll-free 800/228-2800; fax 269/344-8300. www.fairfieldinn.com.* 133 rooms, 3 story. Complimentary continental breakfast. Check-in 3 pm, check-out noon. Outdoor pool. **$**

★ ★ HOLIDAY INN. *2747 S 11th St, Kalamazoo (49009). Phone 269/375-6000; toll-free 800/465-4329; fax 269/375-1220. www.holiday-inn.com.* 186 rooms, 4 story. Check-in 4 pm, check-out 11:30 am. Restaurant, bar. Fitness room. Indoor pool, whirlpool. **$**

★ ★ RADISSON PLAZA HOTEL AT KALAMAZOO CENTER. *100 W Michigan Ave, Kalamazoo (49007). Phone 269/343-3333; toll-free 800/333-3333; fax 269/381-1560. www.radisson.com.* This hotel is located in the heart of Kalamazoo, near the campus of Western Michigan University and the local international airport. 281 rooms, 9 story. Check-out noon. Restaurant, bar. Fitness room. Indoor pool, whirlpool. Airport transportation available. **$$**

Specialty Lodgings

The following lodging establishments are approved by Mobil Travel Guide, but due to their unique and individualized nature have not been given a traditional Mobil Star rating. Included in this listing you may find bed-and-breakfasts, limited-service inns, guest ranches, and other unique hotel properties.

HALL HOUSE BED & BREAKFAST. *106 Thompson St, Kalamazoo (49006). Phone 269/343-2500; toll-free 888/761-2525; fax 269/343-1374. www.hallhouse.com.* Georgian Colonial Revival building (1923). Original artwork. 6 rooms, 3 story. Complimentary full breakfast. Check-in 3 pm, check-out 11 am. **$$**

STUART AVENUE INN BED & BREAKFAST. *229 Stuart Ave, Kalamazoo (49007). Phone 269/342-0230; toll-free 800/461-0621; fax 269/385-3442. www.stuartaveinn.com.* 10 rooms, 3 story. Complimentary continental breakfast. Check-in 3 pm, check-out 11 am. **$$**

Restaurants

★ ★ ★ BLACK SWAN. *3501 Greenleaf Blvd, Kalamazoo (49008). Phone 269/375-2105; fax 269/375-5516. www.millenniumrestaurants.com/swan.* Classic continental cuisine is served in the quiet dining room overlooking beautiful Willow Lake. Caribbean menu. Lunch, dinner, Sun brunch. Closed holidays. Bar. Children's menu. Valet parking. **$$**

★ ★ BRAVO. *5402 Portage Rd, Kalamazoo (49002). Phone 269/344-7700.* American, Italian menu. Lunch, dinner, Sun brunch. Closed holidays. Bar. Children's menu. **$$**

★ ★ ★ WEBSTER'S. *100 W Michigan Ave, Kalamazoo (49007). Phone 269/343-4444; fax 269/381-1560.* The elegant copper and brass display kitchen turns out fresh seafood and grilled steaks as well as tableside Caesar salads and freshly prepared desserts. American menu. Dinner. Closed Sun; holidays. Bar. **$$$**

Lansing (J-4)

See also Jackson, Owosso

Settled 1847
Population 127,321
Elevation 860 ft
Area Code 517
Information Greater Lansing Convention & Visitors Bureau, 1223 Turner St, Suite 200, 48906; phone 517/

487-6800 or toll-free 888/252-6746
Web Site www.lansing.org

When the capital of Michigan moved here in 1847 for lack of agreement on a better place, the "city" consisted of one log house and a sawmill. Today, in addition to state government, Lansing is the headquarters for many trade and professional associations and has much heavy industry. R. E. Olds, who built and marketed one of America's earliest automobiles, started the city's industrial growth. Lansing is the home of the Lansing Automotive Division of General Motors and many allied industries. East Lansing, a neighboring community, is the home of the Michigan State University Spartans and is part of the capital city in all respects except government.

What to See and Do

BoarsHead Theater. *Center for the Arts, 425 S Grand Ave, Lansing (48933). Phone 517/484-7800. www.boarshead.org.* A regional center with a professional resident theater company.

Brenke River Sculpture and Fish Ladder. *300 N Grand Ave, Lansing (48933). 2 miles N via Washington Ave.* Located at North Lansing Dam on the Riverfront Park scenic walk, sculpture encompasses the ladder designed by artist/sculptor Joseph E. Kinnebrew and landscape architect Robert O'Boyle.

Fenner Nature Center. *2020 E Mt Hope Ave, Lansing (48910). At Aurelius Rd. Phone 517/483-4224.* Park features a bald eagle, two waterfowl ponds, replica of a pioneer cabin and garden, 5 miles of nature trails through a variety of habitats; picnicking. Nature center with small animal exhibits (Tues-Sun). Trails (daily 8 am-dusk). **FREE**

Impression 5 Science Center. *200 Museum Dr, Lansing (48933). Phone 517/485-8116. www.impression5.org.* The center has more than 200 interactive, hands-on exhibits, including a computer lab, chemistry experiments; restaurant. (Mon-Sat 10 am-5 pm; closed holidays) **$**

Ledges. *133 Fitzgerald Park Dr, Grand Ledge (48837). 10 miles W via Hwy 43. Phone 517/627-7351.* Edging the Grand River, the Ledges are quartz sandstone 300 million years old. They are considered a good rock climbing area for the experienced. (Daily) **$**

Michigan Historical Museum. *702 W Kalamazoo St, Lansing (48909). Phone 517/373-3559.* (Michigan Library & Historical Center) Exhibits include a copper mine, sawmill, and 54-foot-high relief map of Michigan; audiovisual programs, hands-on exhibits. (Daily; closed holidays) **FREE**

Michigan State University. *1200 E Michigan Ave # 655, Lansing (48912). Phone 517/353-1855. www.msu.edu.* (1855) (42,000 students) Founded as the country's first agricultural college and forerunner of the nationwide land-grant university system, MSU, located on a 5,300-acre landscaped campus with 7,800 different species and varieties of trees, shrubs, and vines, is known for its research, Honors College, and many innovations in education. Among the interesting features of the campus are Abrams Planetarium (shows: Fri-Sun, fee; phone 517/355-4672); Horticultural Gardens; W. J. Beal Botanical Garden; Breslin Student Events Center (box office, phone 517/432-5000); Wharton Center for Performing Arts (box office, phone 517/432-2000); Michigan State University Museum (Mon-Sat, also Sun afternoons, closed holidays); and Kresge Art Museum (daily; closed holidays).

Potter Park Zoo. *1301 S Pennsylvania Ave, Lansing (48912). Phone 517/483-4074. www.potterparkzoo.org.* Zoo on the Red Cedar River; has more than 400 animals. Educational programs, camel and pony rides, playground, concession, and picnic facilities. (Daily) **$$**

★ R. E. Olds Transportation Museum. *240 Museum Dr, Lansing (48933). Phone 517/372-0529. www.reoldsmuseum.org.* Named after Ransom Eli Olds, the museum houses Lansing-built vehicles including Oldsmobile, REO, Star, and Durant autos; REO and Duplex trucks, bicycles, airplanes; period clothing, photographic display of Olds' Victorian home, and a "Wall of Wheels" from the Motor Wheel Corp. Aside from older models, there is also a collection of newer "concept" cars from some of today's top manufacturers and car designers. There is also a gift shop that sells literature on many of the car models displayed within the museum. (Tues-Sat 10 am-5 pm, Sun noon-5 pm; closed Jan 1, Dec 25) **$**

State Capitol Building. *N Capitol and W Michigan aves, Lansing (48906). Phone 517/373-2353.* Dedicated in 1879, this was one of the first state capitol buildings to emulate the dome and wings of the US Capitol in Washington, DC. Interior walls and ceilings reflect the work of many skilled artisans, muralists, and portrait painters. Tours (daily). **FREE**

Woldumar Nature Center. *5739 Old Lansing Rd, Lansing (48917). Phone 517/322-0030. www.woldumar.org.* A 188-acre wildlife preserve; nature walks, interpretive center (Mon-Sat; closed holidays). Trails open for hiking and skiing (daily, dawn-dusk). **DONATION**

Special Events

East Lansing Art Festival. *410 Abbott Rd, East Lansing (48823). Phone 517/319-6884. www.elartfest.com.* Artists' work for sale, continuous performances, ethnic foods, children's activities. Third weekend in May.

Mint Festival. *201 E State St, St. Johns (48879). 18 miles N via Hwy 27. Phone 517/224-7248.* Queen contest, parade, mint farm tours, antiques, arts and crafts, flea market, entertainment. Second weekend in Aug.

Limited-Service Hotels

★ ★ BEST WESTERN MIDWAY. *7111 W Saginaw Hwy, Lansing (48917). Phone 517/627-8471; toll-free 877/772-6100; fax 517/627-8597. www.bestwestern.com.* 149 rooms, 3 story. Pets accepted, some restrictions. Check-in 3 pm, check-out noon. Restaurant, bar. Fitness room. Indoor pool, whirlpool. Airport transportation available. **$**

★ ★ CLARION HOTEL. *3600 Dunckel Dr, Lansing (48910). Phone 517/351-7600; toll-free 877/424-6423; fax 517/351-4640. www.clarionhotel.com.* Located 10 minutes from Michigan State University. A restaurant and lounge are on site for guests' dining pleasure. 150 rooms, 2 story. Pets accepted; fee. Check-in 3 pm, check-out 11 am. High-speed Internet access. Restaurant, bar. Fitness room. Indoor pool, whirlpool. Airport transportation available. **$**

★ COMFORT INN. *2209 University Park Dr, Okemos (48864). Phone 517/349-8700; toll-free 800/349-8701; fax 517/349-5638. www.comfortinn.com.* 160 rooms, 2 story. Complimentary continental breakfast. Check-in 4 pm, check-out 11 am. Fitness room. Indoor pool, whirlpool. **$**

★ ★ COURTYARD BY MARRIOTT. *2710 Lake Lansing Rd, Lansing (48912). Phone 517/482-0500; toll-free 800/321-2211; fax 517/482-0557. www.courtyard.com.* 129 rooms, 2 story. Complimentary full breakfast. Check-in 3 pm, check-out noon. Indoor pool, whirlpool. Business center. **$**

★ FAIRFIELD INN. *2335 Woodlake Dr, Okemos (48864). Phone 517/347-1000; toll-free 800/568-4421; fax 517/347-5092. www.fairfieldinn.com.* 79 rooms, 2 story. Complimentary continental breakfast. Check-in 3 pm, check-out noon. High-speed Internet access. Indoor pool, whirlpool. **$**

★ HAMPTON INN. *525 N Canal Rd, Lansing (48917). Phone 517/627-8381; toll-free 800/426-7866; fax 517/627-5502. www.hamptoninn.com.* 109 rooms, 3 story. Pets accepted. Complimentary continental breakfast. Check-in 3 pm, check-out noon. **$**

★ ★ HOLIDAY INN. *6820 S Cedar St, Lansing (48911). Phone 517/694-8123; toll-free 800/465-4329; fax 517/699-3753. www.holiday-inn.com.* 300 rooms, 5 story. Check-out noon. Restaurant, bar. Fitness room. Indoor pool, whirlpool. Airport transportation available. **$**

★ QUALITY INN. *901 Delta Commerce Dr, Lansing (48917). Phone 517/886-0600; toll-free 800/228-5151; fax 517/886-0103. www.qualityinn.com.* 117 rooms, 4 story. Complimentary full breakfast. Check-in 3 pm, check-out 11 am. Fitness room. Airport transportation available. **$**

★ ★ RADISSON HOTEL LANSING. *111 N Grand Ave, Lansing (48933). Phone 517/482-0188; toll-free 800/333-3333; fax 517/487-6646. www.radisson.com.* The only hotel located in downtown Lansing, it is near many attractions including Oldsmobile Park and the Lansing Convention Center. 260 rooms, 11 story. High-speed Internet access. Check-out noon. Restaurant, bar. Fitness room. Indoor pool, whirlpool. Airport transportation available. **$**

Full-Service Hotels

★ ★ ★ MARRIOTT EAST LANSING AT UNIVERSITY PLACE. *300 M.A.C. Ave, East Lansing (48823). Phone 517/337-4440; toll-free 800/228-9290; fax 517/337-5001. www.marriott.com.* 180 rooms, 7 story. Check-in 3 pm, check-out noon. Restaurant, bar. Fitness room. Indoor pool, whirlpool. Airport transportation available. **$**

★ ★ ★ SHERATON LANSING HOTEL. *925 S Creyts Rd, Lansing (48917). Phone 517/323-7100; toll-free 800/325-3535; fax 517/323-2180. www.sheratonlansing.com.* 219 rooms, 5 story. Check-out noon. Restaurant, bar. Fitness room. Indoor pool. Airport transportation available. **$**

Specialty Lodging

The following lodging establishment is approved by Mobil Travel Guide, but due to its unique and individualized nature has not been given a traditional Mobil Star rating. Included in this listing you may find bed-and-breakfasts, limited-service inns, guest ranches, and other unique hotel properties.

THE ENGLISH INN. *677 S Michigan Rd, Eaton Rapids (48827). Phone 517/663-2500; toll-free 800/858-0598; fax 517/663-2643. www.englishinn.com.* Built in 1927; antiques. 10 rooms, 3 story. Children over 12 years only. Complimentary continental breakfast. Check-in 3 pm, check-out 11 am. Restaurant. Outdoor pool. **$$**

Leland (E-3)

See also Glen Arbor, Sleeping Bear Dunes National Lakeshore, Traverse City

Population 400
Elevation 602 ft
Area Code 231
Zip 49654

Leland (LEE-land), located on the western side of the Leelanau Peninsula, is a fishing town through and through. It was built on a bustling commercial fishing trade, and today, the major attraction is Fishtown, former fishing shacks, now weathered and gray, that are now gift shops, galleries, and a fresh fish store.

What to See and Do

★ Boat trips to Manitou Islands. *Leland Harbor, 207 W River St, Leland (49654). Phone 231/256-9061.* The *Mishe-Mokwa* makes daily trips in summer, including overnight camping excursions, to North and South Manitou islands; also evening cocktail cruise. (June-Aug: daily; May, Sept-Oct: Mon, Wed, Fri-Sun) **$$$$**

Limited-Service Hotel

★ ★ LELAND LODGE. *565 E Pearl St, Leland (49654). Phone 231/256-9848; fax 231/256-8812.* 18 rooms, 2 story. Complimentary continental breakfast. Check-out 11 am. Restaurant, bar. **$**

Specialty Lodging

The following lodging establishment is approved by Mobil Travel Guide, but due to its unique and individualized nature has not been given a traditional Mobil Star rating. Included in this listing you may find bed-and-breakfasts, limited-service inns, guest ranches, and other unique hotel properties.

MANITOU MANOR BED & BREAKFAST. *148 N Manitou Trail, Lake Leelanau (49653). Phone 231/256-7712; fax 231/256-7941.* Historic (1873) farmhouse with 6 acres of cherry trees. 5 rooms. Complimentary full breakfast. Check-in noon, check-out 11 am. High-speed Internet access. **$$**

Restaurants

★ ★ BLUE BIRD. *102 River St, Leland (49654). Phone 231/256-9081; fax 231/256-7052.* Seafood menu. Lunch, dinner, Sun brunch. Closed first three weeks in Nov; also Mon in Apr-mid-June, after Labor Day-Oct. Bar. Children's menu. **$$**

★ ★ COVE. *111 River St, Leland (49654). Phone 231/256-9834; fax 231/256-2704.* Seafood menu. Lunch, dinner. Closed Mid-Oct-mid-May. Bar. Children's menu. Outdoor seating. **$$**

★ ★ LEELANAU COUNTRY INN. *149 E Harbor Hwy, Maple City (49664). Phone 231/228-5060. www.leelanaucountryinn.com.* Converted house (1891). American menu. Dinner. Closed Dec 24-26. Children's menu. **$$**

Ludington (G-2)

See also Manistee, Manitowoc

Settled 1880
Population 8,507
Elevation 610 ft
Area Code 231

Zip 49431
Information Ludington Area Convention & Visitor Bureau, 5300 W Hwy 10; phone 231/845-0324 or toll-free 877/420-6618
Web Site www.ludingtoncvb.com

A large passenger car ferry and freighters keep this important Lake Michigan port busy. First named Father Jacques Marquette, in honor of the missionary explorer who died here in 1675, the community later adopted the name of its more recent founder, James Ludington, a lumber baron. Ludington draws vacationers because of its long stretch of beach on Lake Michigan and miles of forests, lakes, streams, and dunes surrounding the town. The Père Marquette River offers chinook salmon; fishing boats may be chartered.

What to See and Do

Auto Ferry/SS *Badger*. *701 Maritime Dr, Ludington (49431). At the end of Hwy 10. Phone 231/845-5555; toll-free 888/337-7948. www.ssbadger.com.* Instead of driving all the way around Lake Michigan, you can drive right onto the SS *Badger* and ride across. This car ferry takes passengers and vehicles on a four-hour trip to Manitowoc, Wisconsin, and back (if you wish). Amenities include a nautical history display, game room, movie screenings, staterooms, and food service. (May-Oct, daily) **$$$$**

Ludington Pumped Storage Hydroelectric Plant. *3225 S Lakeshore Dr, Ludington (49431). 6 miles S on S Lakeshore Dr. Phone toll-free 800/477-5050.* Scenic overlooks beside Lake Michigan and the plant's 840-acre reservoir. One of the world's largest facilities of this type. (Apr-Nov, daily) **FREE** Footpaths connect to

> **Mason County Campground and Picnic Area.** *5906 W Chauvez Rd, Ludington (49431). S Old Hwy 31 to Chauvez Rd, then 1 1/2 miles S. Phone 231/845-7609.* Picnicking, playground, camping (hookups). (Memorial Day-Labor Day, daily) **$$$**

Ludington State Park. *Hwy 116 N, Ludington (49431). 8 1/2 miles N on Hwy 116. Phone 231/843-8671.* Approximately 4,500 acres on Lakes Michigan and Hamlin and the Sable River. Swimming, bathhouse, water-skiing, fishing, boating (ramp, rentals); hunting, cross-country skiing, picnicking, playground, concession, camping. Visitor center (May-Sept). **$$**

Pere Marquette Memorial Cross. Towers high into the skyline, overlooks the harbor and Lake Michigan.

Stearns Park. Half-mile swimming beach (lifeguard, June-Labor Day), fishing, boating, ramps, launch, 150-slip marina; picnicking, playground, miniature golf, shuffleboard. Fee for some activities.

White Pine Village. *1687 S Lakeshore Dr, Ludington (49431). 3 miles S via Hwy 31 to Iris Rd, follow signs. Phone 231/843-4808.* Historical buildings re-create small-town Michigan life in the late 1800s; general store, trapper's cabin, courthouse/jail, town hall, one-room school, and others. (June-early Sept, Tues-Sun) **$$**

Limited-Service Hotels

★ FOUR SEASONS. *717 E Ludington Ave, Ludington (49431). Phone toll-free 800/968-0180; fax 231/843-2635. www.lodgingandbreakfast.com.* Just a short walk to downtown Ludington, this property has meticulously kept rooms, lobby and dining area. The garden area has an outdoor fireplace and water fountains. 33 rooms. Closed mid-Oct-Apr. Complimentary continental breakfast. Check-in 2 pm, check-out 11 am. **$**

★ ★ RAMADA INN. *4079 W Hwy 10 and Brye Rd, Ludington (49431). Phone 231/845-7311; toll-free 800/707-7475; fax 231/843-8551. www.ramada.com.* 116 rooms, 4 story. Check-out 11 am. Restaurant, bar. Fitness room. Indoor pool, whirlpool. **$**

★ VIKING ARMS INN. *930 E Ludington Ave, Ludington (49431). Phone 231/843-3441; toll-free 800/748-0173; fax 231/845-7703. www.vikingarmsinn.com.* 45 rooms. Complimentary continental breakfast. Check-out 11 am. Outdoor pool, whirlpool. Airport transportation available. **$**

Restaurant

★ ★ SCOTTY'S. *5910 E Ludington Ave (Hwy 10), Ludington (49431). Phone 231/843-4033.* American menu. Dinner. Closed Thanksgiving, Dec 25. Bar. Children's menu. Casual attire. **$$**

Exploring Mackinac Island

Mackinac is truly an island that time forgot: the clippety-clop of horse-drawn wagons echoes in the streets, period-garbed docents stroll among historical reconstructions, and quaint candy shops roll out fudge by the ton. And yet, many tourists manage to go there and only see the two or three square blocks off the tour boat docks and miss all the rest. Mackinac Island is the perfect approximation of living history, tacky tourism, sublime aesthetics, and lovely natural scenery—all contained on an island that can be circumnavigated in one very long but rewarding day hike.

The best option is to take the early-morning ferry. Spend some time lolling around the anachronistic downtown, and make a quick visit to historic Fort Mackinac. Then head a few miles to Arch Rock for stunning views of the sun rising steadily over the Great Lake. From there, head inland to the modest but occasionally daunting central rise of the island, bypassing an old fort and two cemeteries where original settlers and soldiers are buried. Next head south via British Landing Road for a look at the Governor's Residence before returning to the downtown. Or rent a bicycle and ride from the cemeteries all the way to the northwest shoreline, where historic markers indicate the site of the British invasion that occurred over a century ago. If you stay along the main road to the south, you may be lucky enough to witness a most resplendent sunset as you ride back into downtown.

Mackinac Island (D-4)

See also Mackinaw City, St. Ignace

Population 469
Elevation 600-925 ft
Area Code 906
Zip 49757
Information Chamber of Commerce, PO Box 451; phone 906/847-3783 or toll-free 800/454-5227
Web Site www.mackinac.com

Because cars aren't allowed on the island, leaving horse-drawn carriages and bicycles as the chief modes of transportation, Mackinac (MAC-i-naw) Island retains the atmosphere of the 19th century and the imprint of history. In view of the 5-mile-long Mackinac Bridge, the largest expansion bridge in the world, it has been a famous resort for the last century. The island was called "great turtle" by Native Americans who believed that its towering heights and rock formations were shaped by supernatural forces. Later, because of its strategic position, the island became the key to the struggle between England and France for control of the rich fur trade of the great Northwest. Held by the French until 1760, it became British after Wolfe's victory at Québec, was turned over to the United States at the close of the American Revolution, reverted to the British during the War of 1812, and finally was restored to the United States.

With the decline of the fur trade in the 1830s, Mackinac Island began to develop its potential as a resort area. Southern planters and their families summered here prior to the Civil War; wealthy Chicagoans took their place in the years following. Today, the island remains the home of the governor's summer mansion, where a long line of Michigan governors have spent at least a portion of their vacations. Horse and carriages and bicycles can be rented. Passenger ferries make regularly scheduled trips to the island from Mackinaw City and St. Ignace, or visitors can reach the island by air from St. Ignace, Pellston, or Detroit.

What to See and Do

Arnold Mackinac Island Ferry. *Arnold Line Docks, Mackinac Island (49757). Phone 906/847-3351; toll-free 800/542-8528. www.arnoldline.com.* Largest, fastest ferries traveling to Mackinac Island. (May-Dec, daily) **$$$$**

Mackinac Island Carriage Tours, Inc. *Main St, Mackinac Island (49757). Phone 906/847-3307. www.mict.com.* Narrated, historic, and scenic horse-drawn carriage tour (1 3/4 hours) covering 20 sights. (Mid-May-mid-Oct, daily; some tours available rest of year) **$$$$**

★ **Mackinac Island State Park.** *300 S Washington Sq, Mackinac Island (49757). Phone 906/847-3328.* Comprises approximately 80 percent of the island. Michigan's first state park has views of the Straits of

Mackinac, prehistoric geological formations such as Arch Rock, and shoreline and inland trails. Visitor center at Huron Street has informative exhibits, a slide presentation, and guidebooks (mid-May-mid-Oct, daily). British Landing Nature Center (May-Labor Day). Included in the admission price are Mission Church (1830), Biddle House (1780), and McGulpin House. **FREE** Here are

Beaumont Memorial. Monument to Dr. William Beaumont, who charted observations of the human digestive system by viewing this action through an opening in the abdomen of a wounded French-Canadian. (Mid-June-Labor Day, daily)

Benjamin Blacksmith Shop. *Market St, Mackinac Island (49757).* A working forge in replica of blacksmith shop dating from 1880s. (Mid-June-Labor Day, daily)

Fort Mackinac. *Fort St, Mackinac Island (49757). Phone 906/847-3328.* (1780-1895) High on a bluff overlooking the Straits of Mackinac, this 18th-19th-century British and American military outpost is complete with massive limestone ramparts, cannon, guardhouse, blockhouses, barracks; costumed interpreters, reenactments, children's discovery room, crafts demonstrations; rifle and cannon firings; audiovisual presentation. (Mid-May-mid-Oct, daily) **$$$**

Indian Dormitory. (1838) Built as a place for Native Americans to live during annual visits to the Mackinac Island office of the US Indian Agency; interpretive displays, craft demonstrations; murals depicting scenes from Longfellow's "Hiawatha." (Mid-June-Labor Day, daily)

Marquette Park. *401 E Fair Ave, Mackinac Island (49855).* Statue of Father Marquette, historic marker, and 66 varieties of lilacs dominate this park.

Shepler's Mackinac Island Ferry. *556 E Central Ave, Mackinaw City (49701). Phone 231/436-5023. www.sheplersferry.com.* Departs from 556 E Central Ave, Mackinaw City or from downtown St. Ignace. (Early May-early Nov) **$$$$**

Star Line Ferry. *587 N State St, St. Ignace (49781). Phone 906/643-7635; toll-free 800/638-9892. www.mackinacferry.com.* "Hydro Jet" service from Mackinaw City and St. Ignace. (May-Oct) **$$$$**

Special Events

Lilac Festival. *Main St, Mackinac Island (49757). Phone toll-free 800/454-5227.* Second week in June.

Sailing races. *Main St, Mackinac Island (49757). Phone 906/847-3783.* Port Huron to Mackinac and Chicago to Mackinac. Mid-late July.

Limited-Service Hotels

★ ★ ISLAND HOUSE. *50 Lake Shore Dr, Mackinac Island (49757). Phone 906/847-3347; toll-free 800/626-6304; fax 906/847-3819. www.theislandhouse.com.* This hotel, built in 1852, offers a great getaway where visitors can relax and enjoy their time. A short ferry will bring guests to the island. 97 rooms, 4 story. Closed mid-Oct-mid-May. Check-in 3 pm, check-out 11 am. Restaurant, bar. Indoor pool, whirlpool. Airport transportation available. **$$**

★ ★ LAKE VIEW. *1 Huron St, Mackinac Island (49757). Phone 906/847-3384; fax 906/847-6283. www.mackinac.com.* With furnishings reflecting the early Victorian influence on Mackinac Island, this small and unique hotel has cozy guest suites, on-site shops, a restaurant, and a pub. 85 rooms, 4 story. Closed Nov-Apr. Check-out 11 am. Restaurant. Indoor pool, whirlpool. **$**

Full-Service Hotel

★ ★ ★ HOTEL IROQUOIS. *298 Main St, Mackinac Island (49757). Phone 906/847-3321 (Apr-Oct), 616/247-5675 (Nov-mid-Apr); fax 906/847-6274. www.iroquoishotel.com.* This Victorian hotel offers guest rooms and suites at a lakefront location. Guests can enjoy fine dining at the Carriage House (see) or a drink at the Piano Bar. Visitors can rent bicycles from the property to take a tour of the local area. 47 rooms, 3 story. Closed late Oct-mid-May. Check-in 3 pm, check-out noon. Restaurant. **$$**

Full-Service Resorts

★ ★ ★ GRAND HOTEL. *1 Grand Ave, Mackinac Island (49757). Phone 906/847-3331; toll-free 800/334-7263; fax 906/847-3259. www.grandhotel.com.* From the moment one arrives on the island and is delivered to the hotel in a horse-drawn carriage, they are transported back to the 19th-century. The hotel rides regally on a bluff overlooking the straits of Mackinac. Sit in one of the giant rocking chairs on the longest front porch in America and watch the Great Lake freighters glide by while sipping a favorite beverage. Long a popular retreat for the romantic at heart, the hotel offers a variety of accommodations, shops, afternoon tea, and carriage rentals. 385 rooms, 6 story. Closed Dec-mid-May. Check-in 3 pm, check-out noon. Restaurant, bar. Fitness room. Outdoor pool, whirlpool. Golf. Tennis. **$$$**

★ ★ ★ **MISSION POINT RESORT.** *1 Lakeshore Dr, Mackinac Island (49757). Phone 906/847-3312; toll-free 800/833-7711; fax 906/847-3408. www.missionpoint.com.* Mackinac Island offers a slice of Americana with its traditional main street and rugged, natural setting. This historic island in northern Michigan is a seaside playground for adults and children, and the jewel in the crown is the Mission Point Resort. This luxurious getaway looks and feels like a country inn, yet it operates with the amenities and services of a top-notch resort. It's a great choice whether you're looking for a cross-country ski getaway in winter or a destination for an outdoorsy summer wedding. The homey guest rooms are decorated with nautical, lodge, and northern Michigan themes and boast garden, forest, or Lake Huron views. Activities abound here, from an 18-hole putting green to bicycle and in-line skate rentals to hayrides and lawn bowling. In summer, the turn-of-the-20th-century movie theater shows first-run and classic films on Monday evenings. Adults work out in the comprehensive fitness center, while next door the children participate in a series of fun-filled activities at the 3,000-square-foot Discovery Center. After closing for six weeks at the end of high season, the resort reopens at Christmastime, offering horse-drawn sleigh rides, ice skating, and 30 miles of cross-country skiing trails. Downhill skiing is available nearby. The resort's four restaurants attract diners with casual fare and friendly service. 242 rooms, 3 story. Closed Nov-late Dec. Check-in 3 pm, check-out 11 am. Four restaurants, bar. Children's activity center. Fitness room. Outdoor pool, whirlpool. Tennis. Business center. **$$**

Specialty Lodging

The following lodging establishment is approved by Mobil Travel Guide, but due to its unique and individualized nature has not been given a traditional Mobil Star rating. Included in this listing you may find bed-and-breakfasts, limited-service inns, guest ranches, and other unique hotel properties.

BAY VIEW AT MACKINAC. *100 Huron St, Mackinac Island (49757). Phone 906/847-3295; fax 906/847-6219. www.mackinacbayview.com.* Built in 1891 in the Grand Victorian style; on bay. 20 rooms, 3 story. Closed Nov-Apr. No children allowed. Complimentary full breakfast. Check-in 3 pm, check-out 11 am. **$$$$**

Restaurant

★ ★ **CARRIAGE HOUSE.** *298 Main St, Mackinac Island (49757). Phone 906/847-3321; fax 906/847-6274. www.iroquoishotel.com.* American menu. Breakfast, lunch, dinner. Closed mid-Oct-Memorial Day. Bar. Children's menu. Outdoor seating. **$$$**

Mackinaw City (D-4)

See also Cheboygan, Mackinac Island, Pellston, St. Ignace

Settled 1681
Population 875
Elevation 590 ft
Area Code 231
Zip 49701
Information Greater Mackinaw Area Chamber of Commerce, 706 S Huron, PO Box 856, phone 231/436-5574; or the Mackinaw Area Tourist Bureau, 708 S Huron, PO Box 160, phone toll-free 800/666-0160
Web Site www.mackinawcity.com

The only place in America where one can see the sun rise on one Great Lake (Huron) and set on another (Michigan), Mackinaw City sits in the shadow of the 5-mile-long Mackinac Bridge. The French trading post built here became Fort Michilimackinac (mich-ill-i-MAC-i-naw) in about 1715. It was taken over by the British in 1761 and two years later was captured by Native Americans. The British reoccupied the fort in 1764. The fort was rebuilt on Mackinac Island (see) between 1780-1781. Today, the area is not only the gateway to the island, but is a premier shopping destination.

What to See and Do

Arnold Mackinac Island Ferry. *Arnold Line Docks, Mackinac Island (49757). Phone 906/847-3351; toll-free*

800/542-8528. www.arnoldline.com. Largest, fastest ferries traveling to Mackinac Island. **$$$$**

Colonial Michilimackinac. *207 W Sinclair, Mackinaw City (49701). At S end of Mackinac Bridge. Phone 231/436-5563.* Reconstructed French and British outpost and fur-trading village of 1715-1781; costumed interpreters provide music and military demonstrations, pioneer cooking and crafts, children's program, and reenactments of French colonial wedding and arrival of the Voyageurs. Working artisans, musket and cannon firing (mid-June-Labor Day, daily). Murals, dioramas in restored barracks (mid-May-mid-Oct, daily). Re-created Native American encampment (mid-June-Labor Day). Archaeological tunnel "Treasures from the Sand"; visitors can view the longest ongoing archaeological dig in United States (May-early Oct, daily). Visitor Center, audiovisual presentation. **$$** Located here is

> **Mill Creek.** *9001 S Hwy 23, Mackinaw City (49701). 3 miles SE via Hwy-23. Phone 231/436-7301.* Scenic 625-acre park features working water-powered sawmill (1790); nature trails, forest demonstration areas, maple sugar shack, active beaver colony, picnicking. Sawmill demonstrations; archaeological excavations (mid-June-Labor Day, Mon-Fri). Visitor center, audiovisual presentation. (Mid-May-mid-Oct, daily) **$$**

Mackinac Bridge. This imposing structure has reduced crossing time to the Upper Peninsula over the Straits of Mackinac to 10 minutes. Connecting Michigan's upper and lower peninsulas between St. Ignace (see) and Mackinaw City, the 8,344-foot distance between cable anchorages makes it one of the world's longest suspension bridges. (Total length of steel superstructure: 19,243 feet; height above water at midspan: 199 feet; clearance for ships: 155 feet) Fine view from the bridge. Auto toll **$**

Mackinac Bridge Museum. *231 E Central Ave, Mackinaw City (49701). Phone 231/436-5534.* Displays on the construction and maintenance of the bridge. Features original pieces of equipment. (Daily)

Shepler's Mackinac Island Ferry. *556 E Central Ave, Mackinaw City (49701). Phone 231/436-5023. www.sheplersferry.com.* (Early May-early Nov) **$$$$**

Star Line Ferry. *587 N State St, St. Ignace (49781). Phone 906/643-7635. www.mackinacferry.com.* **$$$$**

Wilderness State Park. *903 E Wilderness Park Dr, Carp Lake (49718). 11 miles W of I-75, on Lake Michigan and Straits of Mackinac. Phone 231/436-5381; toll-free 800/447-2757.* Approximately 8,200 acres. Beaches, water-skiing, fishing, boating (launch); hunting in season, snowmobiling, cross-country skiing, picnic areas, playgrounds. Trailside cabins, camping. **$$**

Special Events

Colonial Michilimackinac Pageant. *Phone 231/436-5574.* Pageant and reenactment of Chief Pontiac's capture of the frontier fort in 1763; parade, muzzle-loading contests. Three days during Memorial Day weekend.

Mackinac Bridge Walk. *Phone 517/347-7891; toll-free 800/434-8642.* Michigan's governor leads the walk, which begins in St. Ignace at 7 am, on the north side of the bridge, and ends in Mackinaw City, on the south side. Buses return you to your starting point. Labor Day. **FREE**

Mackinaw Mush Sled Dog Race. *Phone 231/436-5574.* The biggest dog sled race in the contiguous United States. First week in Feb.

Spring/Fall Bike Tours. *Phone 231/436-5574.* Biannual bicycle rides, ranging from 25-100 miles. Mid-June-mid-Sept.

Vesper Cruises. *Arnold's Line Dock, Mackinaw City (49701). Phone 906/847-3351; toll-free 800/542-8528. www.arnoldline.com/Vesper.htm.* Cruises depart on Sunday evenings from the Old State Dock. July-Sept.

Winterfest. *Phone 231/436-5574.* The winter activities at this three-day fest include professional snow sculpting, ice fishing, sleigh rides, and buffalo chip hockey. Mid-Jan.

Limited-Service Hotels

★ BEST WESTERN OF MACKINAW CITY. *112 Old Hwy 31, Mackinaw City (49701). Phone 231/436-5544; toll-free 800/780-7234; fax 231/436-7180. www.bestwestern.com.* 73 rooms, 2 story. Closed Nov-mid-Apr. Complimentary continental breakfast. Check-in 2 pm, check-out 11 am. Indoor pool, whirlpool. **$**

★ COMFORT INN. *611 S Huron St, Mackinaw City (49701). Phone 231/436-5057; toll-free 800/221-2222; fax 231/436-7385. www.comfortinn.com.* 60 rooms, 3 story. Closed Nov-Apr. Check-in 3 pm, check-out

10 am. Indoor pool, whirlpool. **$**

★ **GRAND MACKINAW INN AND SUITES.** *907 S Huron, Mackinaw City (49701). Phone 231/436-8831; toll-free 800/822-8314. www.grandmackinaw.com.* 40 rooms, 2 story. Closed Nov-Apr. Pet accepted, some restrictions; fee. Check-out 11 am. Private sand beach; overlooks Lake Huron. Indoor pool, whirlpool. **$**

★ **HOLIDAY INN EXPRESS.** *364 Lowingney, Mackinaw City (49701). Phone 231/436-7100; toll-free 800/465-4329; fax 231/436-7070. www.holiday-inn.com.* 71 rooms, 3 story. Complimentary continental breakfast. Check-in 4 pm, check-out 11 am. Fitness room. Indoor pool, whirlpool. **$**

★ **QUALITY INN.** *917 S Huron Ave, Mackinaw City (49701). Phone 231/436-5051; toll-free 877/436-5051; fax 231/436-7221. www.qualityinn.com.* 60 rooms, 2 story. Closed Nov-mid-Apr. Check-out 10 am. Private beach on Lake Huron. Indoor pool, whirlpool. Near ferry dock. **$**

★ **RAMADA LIMITED WATERFRONT.** *723 S Huron Ave, Mackinaw City (49721). Phone 231/436-5055; toll-free 888/852-4165; fax 231/436-5921. www.ramada.com.* 42 rooms, 3 story. Closed Nov-mid-Apr. Complimentary continental breakfast. Check-in 4 pm, check-out 11 am. Beach. Indoor pool, whirlpool. **$**

Restaurants

★ ★ **NEATH THE BIRCHES.** *14277 Mackinaw Terrace, Mackinaw City (49701). Phone 231/436-5401; fax 231/436-7178. www.mackinawdining.com/birches.htm.* Steak, seafood menu. Dinner. Closed late Oct-mid-May. Bar. Children's menu. **$$**

★ **PANCAKE CHEF.** *327 Central, Mackinaw City (49701). Phone 231/436-5578; fax 231/436-5579. www.pancakechef.com.* American menu. Breakfast, lunch, dinner. **$**

Manistee (F-2)

See also Ludington

Population 6,734
Elevation 600 ft
Area Code 231
Zip 49660
Information Manistee Area Chamber of Commerce, 11 Cypress St; phone 231/723-2575 or toll-free 800/288-2286
Web Site www.manistee.com

With Lake Michigan on the west and the Manistee National Forest on the east, this site was once the home of 1,000 Native Americans who called it Manistee (man-i-STEE), "spirit of the woods." In the mid-1800s this was a thriving lumber town, serving as headquarters for more than 100 companies. When the timber supply was exhausted, the early settlers found other sources of revenue. Manistee is rich in natural resources including salt, oil, and natural gas. A Ranger District office of the Huron-Manistee National Forest is located in Manistee.

What to See and Do

Huron-Manistee National Forest. *1755 S Mitchell St, Cadillac (49601). E and S of town, via Hwy 31 and Hwy 55. Phone toll-free 800/821-6263.* This 520,968-acre forest is the Manistee section of the Huron-Manistee National Forest (for Huron section see OSCODA). The forest includes the Lake Michigan Recreation Area, which contains trails and panoramic views of the sand dunes and offers beaches; fishing in lakes and in the Pine, Manistee, Little Manistee, White, Little Muskegon, and Père Marquette rivers; boating; hiking, bicycle, and vehicle trails; hunting for deer and small game, camping, and picnicking. Winter sports include downhill and cross-country skiing, snowmobiling, ice fishing, and ice sailing. Fees charged at recreation sites. Contact Forest Supervisor, 412 Red Apple Rd. (Daily) **FREE**

Manistee County Historical Museum. *Russell Memorial Building, 425 River St, Manistee (49660). Phone 231/723-5531.* Fixtures and fittings of 1880 drugstore and early general store; Victorian period rooms, historical photographs; Civil War, marine collections; antique dolls, costumes, housewares. (Tues-Sat 10 am-5 pm; closed holidays) **$**

Old Waterworks Building. *W 1st St, Manistee (49660). Phone 231/723-5531.* Logging wheels, early lumbering, shipping, and railroad exhibits; Victorian parlor, barbershop, shoe shop, kitchen. (Late June-Aug, Tues-Sat) **DONATION**

Orchard Beach State Park. *2064 Lakeshore Rd, Manistee (49660). 2 miles N on Hwy 110. Phone 231/723-7422.* High on a bluff overlooking Lake Michigan; 201 acres. Swimming beach; hiking, picnicking, playground, stone pavilion, camping. **$$**

Ramsdell Theatre and Hall. *101 Maple St, Manistee (49660). At 1st St. Phone 231/723-9948. www.ramsdell-theater.org.* (1903) Constructed by T. J. Ramsdell, pioneer attorney, this opulent building is home to the Manistee Civic Players, who present professional and community productions throughout the year; also art and museum exhibits. Tours (June-Aug: Wed and Sat; rest of year: by appointment). **DONATION**

Special Events

National Forest Festival. *50 Filer St, Manistee (49660). Phone 231/723-2575.* Boat show; car show; US Forestry Service forest tours; parades, athletic events, raft and canoe races, Venetian boat parade, fireworks. Sponsored by the Chamber of Commerce. July 4 week.

Shoot Time in Manistee. *Old Fort Rendezvous, Manistee (49660). Phone 231/723-9006.* Traditional shooting events, costumed participants. Late June.

Victorian Port City Festival. *Phone 231/723-2575.* Musical entertainment, street art fair, antique auto exhibit, food, schooner rides. Early Sept.

Limited-Service Hotel

★ MANISTEE INN & MARINA. *378 River St, Manistee (49660). Phone 231/723-4000; toll-free 800/968-6277; fax 231/723-0007. www.manisteeinn.com.* 25 rooms, 2 story. Complimentary continental breakfast. Check-out 11 am. **$**

Manistique (D-2)

See also Escanaba

Population 3,456
Elevation 600 ft
Area Code 906
Zip 49854
Information Schoolcraft County Chamber of Commerce, 1000 W Lakeshore Dr; phone 906/341-5010
Web Site www.manistique.com

Manistique (man-i-STEEK), the county seat of Schoolcraft County, has a bridge in town named "The Siphon Bridge" that is partially supported by the water that flows underneath it. The roadway is approximately 4 feet below the water level. Fishing for salmon is good in the area. A Ranger District office of the Hiawatha National Forest (see ESCANABA) is located here.

What to See and Do

Fayette. *13700 13.25 Ln, Garden (49835). 15 miles W on Hwy 2, then 17 miles S on Hwy 183 to Fayette on Big Bay de Noc. Phone 906/644-2603.* Approximately 700 acres. Fayette, formerly an industrial town producing charcoal iron (1867-1891), is now a ghost town; self-guided tour of restored remains; interpretive center (May-Oct). Swimming, fishing; picnicking, playground, camping. **$$**

Indian Lake. *Hwy 2, Box 2500, Manistique (49854). 6 miles W on Hwy 2, then 3 miles N on Hwy 149, 1/2 mile E on County Rd 442. Phone 906/341-2355.* Approximately 550 acres. Swimming, sand beach, bathhouse, water-skiing, boating (rentals, launch); fishing for pike, perch, walleye, bass, and bluegill; hiking, picnicking, camping. (Daily)

Palms Book. *Hwy 455 and Hwy 149, Manistique (49854). S on Hwy 2 to Thompson, then 12 miles NW on Hwy 149. Phone 906/341-2355.* Approximately 300 acres. Here is Kitch-iti-kipi, the state's largest spring, 200 feet wide, 40 feet deep; 16,000 gallons of water per minute form a stream to Indian Lake. Observation raft for viewing the spring. Picnicking, concession. No camping allowed. Closed in winter. **$$**

Thompson State Fish Hatchery. *Hwy 149, Manistique. 7 miles SW via Hwy 2, Hwy 149. Phone 906/341-5587.* **FREE**

Special Events

Folkfest. *Phone 906/341-5010.* Mid-July.

Schoolcraft County Snowmobile Poker Run. *Phone 906/341-5010.* Late Jan.

Limited-Service Hotels

★ BEST WESTERN BREAKERS MOTEL. *6770 W Hwy 2, Manistique (49854). Phone 906/341-*

2410; toll-free 888/335-3674; fax 906/341-2207. www.bestwestern.com. 40 rooms. Check-in 3 pm, check-out 11 am. Overlooks Lake Michigan. Private beach opposite. Indoor pool, outdoor pool, whirlpool. **$**

★ **BUDGET HOST INN.** *6031 W Hwy 2, Manistique (49854). Phone 906/341-2552; toll-free 800/283-4678; fax 906/341-2552. www.budgethost.com.* 26 rooms. Check-out 11 am. Outdoor pool. Airport transportation available. **$**

Marquette (C-1)

See also Ishpeming

Settled 1849
Population 21,977
Elevation 628 ft
Area Code 906
Zip 49855
Information Marquette Area Chamber of Commerce, 501 S Front St; phone 906/226-6591
Web Site www.marquette.org

The largest city in the Upper Peninsula, Marquette is the regional center for retailing, government, medicine, and iron ore shipping. Miles of public beaches and picnic areas flank the dock areas on Lake Superior. Rocks rise by the water and bedrock runs just a few feet below the surface. The city is named for the missionary explorer Father Jacques Marquette, who made canoe trips along the shore here between 1669 and 1671. At the rear flank of the city is sand-plain blueberry country, as well as forests and mountains of granite and iron.

What to See and Do

Marquette County Historical Museum. *213 N Front St, Marquette (49855). Phone 906/226-3571. www.marquettecohistory.org.* Exhibits of regional historical interest; J. M. Longyear Research Library. (Mon-Fri; closed holidays) **$**

Marquette Mountain Ski Area. *3 miles SW on County 553. Phone 906/225-1155; toll-free 800/944-7669. www.marquettemountain.com.* Three double chairlifts, rope tow; patrol, school, rentals, snowmaking, night skiing, weekly NASTAR; cafeteria, bar, nursery. Longest run 1 1/4 miles; vertical drop 600 feet. (Late Nov-Apr, daily 9:30 am-5 pm) Cross-country trails (3 miles) nearby.

Mount Marquette Scenic Outlook Area. *1 mile S via Hwy 41.* Provides a lovely view. (May-mid-Oct, daily)

Northern Michigan University. *140 Presque Isle Ave, Marquette (49855). Phone 906/227-1700; toll-free 800/682-9797. www.nmu.edu.* (1899) (8,900 students) The 300-acre campus includes the Superior Dome, the world's largest wooden dome (spans 5.1 acres); Lee Hall Gallery; and a 5-acre technology and applied sciences center. Olson Library has Tyler Collection on Early-American literature. The school has been designated an Olympic Education Center. For information on Olympic Education Center, phone 906/227-2888. Tours available.

Presque Isle Park. *Lakeshore Blvd, Marquette (49855). On the lake in NE part of city. Phone 906/228-0460.* Picnic facilities (four picnic sites for the disabled), swimming, water slide (fees), boating (launch, fee); nature trails, cross-country skiing, tennis courts, playground. A bog walk in Presque Isle (presk-EEL) Park features 4,000-foot trail with plank walkways and observation decks; self-guided with interpretive sign boards at ten conservation points. (May-Oct: daily; rest of year: open only for winter sports) **FREE** Near the park is

> **Upper Harbor ore dock.** Several million tons of ore are shipped annually from this site; the loading of ore freighters is a fascinating sight to watch. Adjacent parking lot for viewing and photography.

Sugar Loaf Mountain. *7 miles N on County 550.* A 3,200-foot trail leads to the summit for a panoramic view of the Lake Superior coastline and forestland.

Tourist Park. *Off County 550. Phone 906/228-0460.* Swimming, fishing; playground, tent and trailer sites (mid-May-mid-Oct, daily; fee). Entrance fee charged during Hiawatha Music Festival (see SPECIAL EVENTS). **FREE**

Upper Peninsula Children's Museum. *123 W Baraga Ave, Marquette (49855). Phone 906/226-3911; toll-free 888/590-8726. www.upcmkids.org.* All exhibits are products of kids' imaginations; regional youth planned their conceptual development. (Tues-Sun; closed holidays) **$$**

Special Events

Art on the Rocks. *Presque Isle Park, Lakeshore Blvd,*

Marquette (49855). Phone 906/225-1952. Nationwide art display and sale. Last full weekend in July.

Hiawatha Music Festival. *Tourist Park, Marquette (49855). Phone 906/226-8575.* Bluegrass, traditional music festival. Third weekend in July.

International Food Festival. *Ellwood Mattson Lower Harbor Park, Marquette (49855). Phone 906/249-1595.* Ethnic foods, crafts, music. July 4 weekend.

Seafood Festival. *Ellwood Mattson Lower Harbor Park, Marquette (49855). Phone 906/226-6591.* Seafood is served at the many booths of this festival, which also features entertainment throughout the day. Weekend before Labor Day.

UP 200 Dog Sled Race. *Phone toll-free 800/544-4321.* Dog sled race; features food, games, entertainment, dog-sledding exhibitions. Mid-late Feb.

Limited-Service Hotel

★★ **NORDIC BAY LODGE.** *1880 Hwy 41 S, Marquette (49855). Phone 906/226-7516; toll-free 800/892-9376; fax 906/226-0699.* 44 rooms, 2 story. Check-out 11 am. Restaurant. **$**

Marshall (J-4)

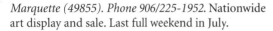

See also Battle Creek, Coldwater

Founded 1830
Population 6,891
Elevation 916 ft
Area Code 269
Zip 49068
Information Chamber of Commerce, 424 E Michigan; phone 269/781-5163 or toll-free 800/877-5163
Web Site www.marshallmi.org

Marshall was, at one time, slated to be Michigan's capital—a grand governor's mansion was built, land was set aside for the capitol, and wealthy and influential people swarmed into the town. In 1847, Marshall lost its capital bid to Lansing. Today, many of the elaborate houses and buildings of the period remain, and more than 30 historical markers dot the city's streets.

What to See and Do

American Museum of Magic. *107 E Michigan Ave, Marshall (49068). Phone 269/781-7674.* Display of vintage magical equipment, rare posters, photographs, and personal effects of some well-known magicians. (By appointment) **$$**

Honolulu House Museum. *107 N Kalamazoo Ave, Marshall (49068). Phone 269/781-8544; toll-free 800/877-5163.* (1860) This exotic structure, blending traditional Italianate architecture with tropical motifs of island plantation houses, was built by the first US Consul to the Sandwich Islands (now Hawaii); period furnishings, artifacts. Also headquarters of Marshall Historical Society, which provides free self-guided walking tour brochures listing town's many interesting 19th-century buildings and more than 30 historical markers. (May-Sept: daily noon-5 pm, rest of year: weekends) **$**

Special Events

Historic Home Tour. *Phone toll-free 800/877-5163.* Informal tours of nine 19th-century homes, including Honolulu House (see), Governor's Mansion, and Capitol Hill School. First weekend after Labor Day.

Welcome to My Garden Tour. *Phone 269/781-5434.* Tour of Marshall's most distinctive gardens. Second weekend in July.

Specialty Lodgings

The following lodging establishments are approved by Mobil Travel Guide, but due to their unique and individualized nature have not been given a traditional Mobil Star rating. Included in this listing you may find bed-and-breakfasts, limited-service inns, guest ranches, and other unique hotel properties.

MCCARTHY'S BEAR CREEK INN. *15230 C Dr N, Marshall (49068). Phone 269/781-8255.* Rooms in renovated house and dairy barn (1948); country décor, antiques. On wooded knoll overlooking Bear Creek; handbuilt fieldstone fencing. 14 rooms, 3 story. Complimentary continental breakfast. Check-in 3 pm, check-out noon. **$**

NATIONAL HOUSE INN. *102 S Parkview St, Marshall (49068). Phone 269/781-7374; fax 269/781-4510. www.nationalhouseinn.com.* Oldest operating inn in state; authentically restored, antique furnishings. Established in 1835. 16 rooms, 2 story. Closed Dec 24-25. Complimentary full breakfast. Check-in after 3 pm, check-out noon. Airport transportation available. **$**

Restaurants

★ CORNWELL'S TURKEYVILLE. *18935 15 1/2 Mile Rd, Marshall (49068). Phone 269/781-4293. www.turkeyville.com.* Take the half-comatose, half-blissful feeling after a Thanksgiving meal and multiply it by about 20 (the number of all-turkey items on the menu), and you're in Turkeyville. With everything from turkey dogs and turkey sandwiches to more elaborate items like old-fashioned turkey dinners and turkey ranch wraps, poultry lovers everywhere will, ahem, flock here. With a gift shop and, of all things, a dinner theater, this restaurant is a destination in itself. American menu. Lunch, dinner. Closed late Dec-mid-Jan. Children's menu. Outdoor seating. **$**

★ ★ SCHULER'S OF MARSHALL. *115 S Eagle St, Marshall (49068). Phone 269/781-0600; fax 269/781-4361. www.schulersrestaurant.com.* In addition to the delicious food and spectacular service, this restaurant has become a local institution since opening in 1909. Schuler's takes on new recipes every week or so and sponsors and organizes local events like the Schuler's Fly-In and Etiquette Day. Beneath all that, though, lies a charming, comfortable atmosphere. American menu. Lunch, dinner, Sun brunch. Closed Dec 25. Bar. Children's menu. Outdoor seating. **$**

Menominee (E-1)

See also Oconto, Peshtigo; also see Marinette, WI

Settled 1796
Population 9,398
Elevation 600 ft
Area Code 906
Zip 49858
Information Menominee Area Chamber of Commerce, 1005 10th Ave, PO Box 427; phone 906/863-2679
Web Site www.cityofmenominee.org

Because of water transportation and water power, many manufacturing industries have located in Menominee. Green Bay and the Menominee river form two sides of the triangle-shaped city. Across the river is the sister city of Marinette, Wisconsin (see). Established as a fur-trading post, later a lumbering center, Menominee County is the largest dairy producer in the state of Michigan. Menominee is a Native American word for "wild rice," which once grew profusely on the riverbanks.

What to See and Do

First Street Historic District. *10th Ave, Menominee (49858). From 10th Ave to 4th Ave.* Variety of specialty shops located in a setting of restored 19th-century buildings. Marina, parks, restaurants, galleries.

Henes Park. *Henes Park Dr and 3rd St, Menominee (49858). NE of city off Hwy 35. Phone 906/863-2656.* Small zoo with deer yards, nature trails, bathing beach, and picnic area. (Memorial Day-mid Oct, daily) **FREE**

J. W. Wells State Park. *N7670 Hwy 35, Cedar River (49813). 23 miles NE on Hwy 35. Phone 906/863-9747.* Approximately 700 acres, including 2 miles along Green Bay and 1,400 feet along Big Cedar River. Swimming, bathhouse, water-skiing, fishing, boating (ramp); hunting, snowmobiling, cross-country skiing, picnicking, playground, camping, cabins and shelters.

Menominee Marina. *Doyle Dr, Menominee (49858). 1st St between 8th and 10th aves. Phone 906/863-8498. www.menomineemarina.com.* One of the best small-craft anchorages on the Great Lakes. Swimming beach, lifeguard. (May-Oct, daily)

Stephenson Island. *In middle of Menominee River.* Reached by bridge that also carries traffic between the sister cities on Highway 41 (see MARINETTE, WI). On island are picnic areas and a historical museum.

Special Event

Waterfront Festival. *Phone 906/863-2679.* Entertainment, music, dancing, footraces, fireworks, food, parade. Four days, first weekend in Aug.

Midland (G-4)

See also Bay City, Clare, Mount Pleasant, Saginaw

Population 38,053
Elevation 629 ft
Area Code 989
Information Midland County Convention & Visitors Bureau, 300 Rodd St, Suite 101, 48640; phone 989/839-9522 or toll-free 888/464-3526
Web Site www.midlandcvb.org

Midland owed its prosperity to the lumber industry until Herbert Henry Dow founded The Dow Chemical Company in 1897. Today, Dow still dominates Midland's attractions, from the Dow Museum to beautiful Dow Gardens. The city also boasts beautiful gardens, parks, and trails.

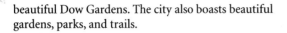

What to See and Do

Architectural tour. *Phone 989/631-5930. www.abdow.org.* Self-guided driving tour of buildings designed by Alden B. Dow, son of Herbert H. Dow. The younger Dow studied under Frank Lloyd Wright at Taliesin. He designed more than 45 buildings in Midland, including the architect's house and studio, churches, Stein House (his Taliesin apprentice project), and the Whitman House, for which he won the 1937 Grand Prix for residential architecture. Many buildings are privately owned and not open to the public. Maps and audiocassettes are available at the Midland Center for the Arts. **$$**

Chippewa Nature Center. *400 S Badour Rd, Midland (48640). Phone 989/631-0830. www.chippewanature center.com.* On more than 1,000 acres; 14 miles of marked and mowed trails; wildflower walkway and pond boardwalk; Homestead Farm; reconstructed 1870s log cabin, barn, sugarhouse, one-room schoolhouse; visitor center; museum depicting evolutionary natural history of the Saginaw Valley; auditorium, library; seasonal programs. (Daily; closed Thanksgiving, Dec 25) **FREE**

★ **Dow Gardens.** *1809 Eastman Ave, Midland (48640). Entrance at Eastman Rd and W St. Andrews. Phone 989/631-2677; toll-free 800/362-4874. www.dowgardens .org.* These gardens, originally the grounds of the residence of Herbert H. Dow, founder of the Dow Chemical Company, include 110 acres of trees, flowers, streams, and waterfalls, as well as a greenhouse and conservatory. Tours by appointment. (Daily 9 am-dusk; closed Jan 1, Thanksgiving, Dec 25) **$**

Herbert H. Dow Historical Museum. *3200 Cook Rd, Midland (48640). 2 miles NW via W Main St. Phone 989/832-5319.* Composed of replicated Evans Flour Mill and adjacent buildings that housed Dow's Midland Chemical Company, predecessor to The Dow Chemical Company. Interpretive galleries include Joseph Dow's workshop, Herbert Dow's office, drillhouse with steam-powered brine pump, laboratory; audiovisual theater. (Wed-Sat 10 am-4 pm, also Sun 1-5 pm; closed holidays) **FREE**

Midland Center for the Arts. *1801 W St. Andrews, Midland (48640). Phone 989/631-5930. www.mcfta.org.* This center houses the Alden B. Dow Museum of Science and Art, which features temporary exhibits and includes the Hall of Ideas, a permanent interactive exhibit. It also hosts concerts and plays. The Dow architectural tour (see) begins here. (Tues-Sat 10 am-6 pm, Sun noon-6 pm; closed holidays) **$**

Special Events

Fall Festival. *Chippewa Nature Center, 400 S Badour Rd, Midland (48640). Phone 989/631-0830.* Second weekend in Oct.

Maple Syrup Festival. *Chippewa Nature Center, 400 S Badour Rd, Midland (48640). Phone 989/631-0830.* Third Sat in Mar.

Matrix: Midland Festival. *Midland Center for the Arts, 1801 W St. Andrews Rd, Midland (48640). Phone 989/631-7980.* Celebration of the arts, sciences, humanities; classical and popular music, theater, dance; lectures by noted professionals. Late June-Sept.

Michigan Antique Festivals. *Midland Michigan Fairgrounds, 2156 N Rudy Ct, Midland (48642). Phone 989/687-9001. www.miantiquefestival.com.* 1,000 vendors inside and outside. Early June, late July, late Sept.

Limited-Service Hotels

★ ★ BEST WESTERN VALLEY PLAZA RESORT. *5221 Bay City Rd, Midland (48642). Phone 989/496-2700; toll-free 800/825-2700; fax 989/496-9233. www.valleyplazaresort.com.* 236 rooms, 2 story. Pets accepted, some restrictions. Complimentary full breakfast. Check-in 4 pm, check-out noon. Two restaurants, bar. Children's activity center. Fitness room, fitness classes available. Three indoor pools, children's pool, whirlpool. Airport transportation available. Movie theater. **$**

★ ★ HOLIDAY INN. *1500 W Wackerly St, Midland (48640). Phone 989/631-4220; toll-free 800/252-7174; fax 989/631-3776. www.holiday-inn.com.* 235 rooms, 2 story. Pets accepted, some restrictions. Complimentary continental breakfast. Check-in 4 pm, check-out 11 am. High-speed Internet access. Restaurant, bar. Children's activity center. Fitness room. Indoor pool, whirlpool. Airport transportation available. Business center. **$**

Monroe (K-5)

See also Detroit

Settled 1780
Population 22,902
Elevation 599 ft
Area Code 734
Zip 48161
Information Monroe County Chamber of Commerce, 106 W Front St, PO Box 1094; phone 734/457-1030
Web Site www.monroeinfo.com

Originally called Frenchtown because of the many French families that settled here, this city on Lake Erie was renamed in 1817 in honor of President James Monroe. The river that flows through the center of the city was named the River Aux Raisin because of the many grapes growing in the area. At one time, Monroe was briefly the home of General George Armstrong Custer of "Little Big Horn" fame.

What to See and Do

Monroe County Historical Museum. *126 S Monroe St, Monroe (48161). Phone 734/243-7137.* Exhibits of General George Custer, Woodland Native Americans, pioneers, War of 1812; trading post, country store museum. (Summer, daily; rest of year, Wed-Sun; closed holidays) **$**

River Raisin Battlefield Visitor Center. *1402 Elm Ave, Monroe (48161). Just off I-75 at Elm Ave exit. Phone 734/243-7136.* Interprets fierce War of 1812 battle of River Raisin (January 1813). Nearly 1,000 US soldiers from Kentucky clashed with British, Native American, and Canadian forces on this site; only 33 Americans escaped death or capture. Exhibits of weapons and uniforms, dioramas; fiber optic audiovisual map program. (Memorial Day-Labor Day, daily; rest of year, weekends; closed holidays) **FREE**

Sterling State Park. *2800 State Park Rd, Monroe (48161). N of city, off I-75. Phone 734/289-2715.* On 1,001 acres. Swimming, water-skiing, fishing, boating (ramp); hiking, picnicking, playground, concession, camping. **$$**

Special Event

Monroe County Fair. *Monroe County Fairgrounds, 3775 S Custer Rd, Monroe (48161). Junction Hwy 50 and Raisinville Rd. Phone 734/241-5775.* Rides, concessions, merchant buildings. Late July-early Aug.

Limited-Service Hotel

★ **HOLIDAY INN EXPRESS.** *1225 N Dixie Hwy, Monroe (48162). Phone 734/242-6000; toll-free 800/242-6008; fax 734/242-0555. www.holiday-inn.com.* 161 rooms, 4 story. Check-out noon. Indoor pool, whirlpool. **$**

Mount Clemens (J-6)

See also St. Clair

Population 18,405
Elevation 614 ft
Area Code 586
Information Central Macomb County Chamber of Commerce, 58 S Gratiot, 48043; phone 586/493-7600
Web Site www.cityofmountclemens.com

What to See and Do

Art Center. *125 Macomb Pl, Mount Clemens (48043). Phone 586/469-8666.* Exhibits and classes, sponsors tours. Sales gallery, gift shop. Holiday Fair (Dec). (Mon-Fri, limited hours Sat; closed July-Aug) **FREE**

Crocker House. *15 Union St, Mount Clemens (48043). Phone 586/465-2488.* (1869) This Italianate building, home of the Macomb County Historical Society, was originally owned by the first two mayors of Mount Clemens; period rooms, changing exhibits. (Mar-Dec, Tues-Thurs; also first Sun in month) **$**

Metro Beach Metropark. *31300 Metropolitan Pkwy, Mount Clemens (48043). 4 miles SE off I-94 on Lake St. Clair, exit 236. Phone 586/463-4581; toll-free 800/234-6534.* Park features 3/4-mile beach (late May-Sept, daily), pool (Memorial Day-Labor Day, daily; fee), bathhouse, boating, marinas, ramps, launch, dock (fee); 18-hole par-three golf course, miniature golf, shuffleboard, tennis, group rental activity center, playgrounds. Picnicking, concessions. Nature center. No pets. Free admission Tuesday. (Daily, hours vary) **$**

Limited-Service Hotel

★ **COMFORT INN.** *11401 Hall Rd, Utica (48317). Phone 586/739-7111; toll-free 877/424-6423; fax 586/739-1041. www.comfortinn.com.* 104 rooms, 3 story. Complimentary continental breakfast. Check-out noon. Airport transportation available. **$**

Mount Pleasant (G-4)

See also Alma, Big Rapids, Clare, Midland

Population 23,285
Elevation 770 ft
Area Code 989
Zip 48858
Information Convention & Visitors Bureau, 114 E Broadway; phone toll-free 800/772-4433
Web Site www.mt-pleasant.net

Home of the aptly named Central Michigan University, Mount Pleasant sits smack in the middle of the state. The city's Soaring Eagle Casino is a major tourist attraction, and Mount Pleasant is also rich in championship golf courses, including the Pohl Cat and Riverwood Golf Club.

What to See and Do

Central Michigan University. *204 W Hall, Mount Pleasant (48858). Phone 989/774-4000. www.cmich.edu.* (1892) (16,300 students) Here are

Center for Cultural & Natural History. *Rowe Hall.* Includes 45 exhibits and dioramas on anthropology, history, and natural science. (Daily; closed holidays) **FREE**

Clarke Historical Library. *409 Park Library, Mount Pleasant (48858). Phone 989/774-3352.* Rare books, manuscripts; historical documents of Northwest Territory; children's library; changing exhibits. (School year, Mon-Fri) **FREE**

Soaring Eagle Casino. *6800 Soaring Eagle Blvd, Mount Pleasant (48858). Phone 989/775-7777; toll-free 888/732-4537. www.soaringeaglecasino.com.* Includes a 2,500-seat Bingo Hall, slot machines, blackjack, craps, and roulette. Saginaw Chippewa Campground is nearby. (Daily) **FREE**

Special Events

Maple Syrup Festival. *Various locations in town. Approximately 5 miles S via Hwy 27.Phone 989/828-6486. www.shepherdmaplesyrupfestival.org.* Pancake and sausage meals, maple syrup and candy sales, arts and crafts, and a parade are among the features of this festival. Last weekend in Apr.

Zonta Apple Fest. *At McIntosh Orchards. Phone 989/772-0114.* Fresh apple cider, home-baked apple desserts, arts and crafts, live music, and children's games are featured at this festival. First weekend in Oct.

Limited-Service Hotels

★ **COMFORT INN.** *2424 S Mission St, Mount Pleasant (48858). Phone 989/772-4000; toll-free 877/424-6423; fax 989/773-6052. www.comfortinn.com.* 138 rooms, 2 story. Complimentary continental breakfast. Check-in 4 pm, check-out noon. Indoor pool. **$**

★ ★ **HOLIDAY INN.** *5665 E Pickard St, Mount Pleasant (48858). Phone 989/772-2905; toll-free 800/292-8891; fax 989/775-9040. www.hiresort.com.* 183 rooms, 3 story. Pets accepted, some restrictions. Check-in 4 pm, check-out 11 am. Wireless Internet access. Restaurant, bar. Children's activity center. Fitness room, fitness classes available. Indoor pool, outdoor pool, whirlpool. Golf, 18 holes. Airport transportation available. **$**

Full-Service Resort

★ ★ ★ **SOARING EAGLE CASINO & RESORT.** *6800 Soaring Eagle Blvd, Mount Pleasant (48858). Phone 989/775-7777; toll-free 888/232-4537; fax 989/775-5383. www.soaringeaglecasino.com.* Native American theme. 512 rooms, 7 story. Check-in 4 pm, check-out 11 am. High-speed Internet access. Three restaurants, bar. Children's activity center. Fitness room, spa. Indoor pool, children's pool, whirlpool. Airport transportation available. Casino. **$**

Restaurants

★ ★ ★ **THE EMBERS.** *1217 S Mission St (Hwy 27 Business), Mount Pleasant (48858). Phone 989/773-5007; fax 989/773-9436. www.theembersdine.com.* The signature "one-pound pork chop" is the main attraction at this elegant restaurant in Mount Pleasant. Smorgasbord first and third Thursdays of each month. Tease, a more casual dining option, is also available within the building. American menu. Dinner. Closed holidays. Bar. Children's menu. Casual attire. **$$$**

★ ★ ★ **WATER LILY.** *6800 Soaring Eagle Blvd, Mount Pleasant (48858). Phone 989/775-5496; toll-free 888/232-4532. www.soaringeaglecasino.com.* American menu. Dinner. Bar. Casual attire. Valet parking. **$$$**

Munising (C-2)

See also Grand Marais, Pictured Rocks National Lakeshore

Population 2,783
Elevation 620 ft
Area Code 906
Zip 49862
Information Alger Chamber of Commerce, 422 E Munising Ave, PO Box 405; phone 906/387-2138
Web Site www.algercounty.org

Colorful sandstone formations, waterfalls, sand dunes, agate beaches, hiking trails, and outdoor recreational facilities are part of the Hiawatha National Forest and the Pictured Rocks National Lakeshore, which stretches eastward from Munising (MEU-niss-ing) along 42 miles of the south shore of Lake Superior. Camping areas are plentiful in the Lakeshore, Hiawatha National Forest, and on Lake Superior. A Ranger District office of the Hiawatha National Forest (see ESCANABA) is located in Munising.

What to See and Do

Pictured Rocks Boat Cruise. *City Pier, 355 Elm Ave, Munising (49862). Phone 906/387-2379. www.picturedrocks.com.* A 37-mile cruise on the *Miners Castle, Pictured Rocks, Grand Island,* or *Miss Superior.* (June-early Oct, daily) **$$$$**

Special Event

Pictured Rocks Road Race. *Alger Centennial Arena, Varnum St, Munising (49862). Phone 906/387-2379. www.algercounty.com/roadrace.* Course runs over wooded, hilly trails, roads passing waterfalls, streams, and Lake Superior. Late June.

Limited-Service Hotels

★ ★ BEST WESTERN. *Hwy 28 E, Munising (49895). Phone 906/387-4864; toll-free 800/780-7234; fax 906/387-2038. www.bestwestern.com.* 80 rooms, 2 story. Pets accepted, some restrictions. Check-in 3 pm, check-out 11 am. Restaurant, bar. Indoor pool, whirlpool. **$**

★ COMFORT INN. *Hwy 28 E, Munising (49862). Phone 906/387-5292; toll-free 877/424-6423; fax 906/387-3753. www.comfortinn.com.* 61 rooms, 2 story. Pets accepted, some restrictions. Complimentary continental breakfast. Check-in 3 pm, check-out 11 am. Fitness room. Indoor pool, whirlpool. **$**

Restaurant

★ SYDNEY'S. *Hwy 28 E, Munising (49862). Phone 906/387-4067.* American menu. Breakfast, lunch, dinner, Sun brunch. Bar. **$**

Muskegon (H-2)

See also Grand Haven, Grand Rapids, Whitehall

Settled 1810
Population 40,283
Elevation 625 ft
Area Code 231
Information Muskegon County Convention & Visitors Bureau, 610 W Western Ave, 49440; phone toll-free 800/235-3866 or 800/250-9283
Web Site www.visitmuskegon.org

Muskegon County is located in the western part of the lower peninsula, along 26 miles of Lake Michigan shoreline. Muskegon Channel, which runs from Lake Michigan through the sand dunes to Muskegon Lake, opens the harbor to world trade. It has 80 miles of waterfront, including 10 miles of public waterfront, and 3,000 acres of public parks—an acre for every 50 persons in the county. The downtown area has been enclosed as a climate-controlled shopping and business mall.

Muskegon Lake, largest of 40 lakes in Muskegon County, is the focal point of the area comprised of Muskegon, Muskegon Heights, North Muskegon, Norton Shores, Roosevelt Park, and surrounding townships. Fishing for coho, chinook salmon, lake trout, perch, walleye, and other fish is good here; ice fishing is popular in the winter months. The first freshwater reef in North America, a natural fish attractant, is located in Lake Michigan, off Père Marquette Park.

What to See and Do

Hackley and Hume Historic Site. *W Webster and Sixth St, Muskegon (49440). Phone 231/722-7578. www.muskegonmuseum.org.* Restored Queen Anne/Victorian mansions (1888-1889) built by two wealthy lumbermen; elaborately carved woodwork; stencilled walls; 15 Renaissance-style, stained-glass windows; tiled fireplaces with carved mantels; period furniture. Tours (mid-May-Sept, Wed, Sat-Sun; also some weekends in Dec). **$**

Michigan's Adventure Amusement Park. *4750 Whitehall Rd, Muskegon (49445). 8 miles N on I-31 via Russell Rd exit. Phone 231/766-3377. www.miadventure.com.* More than 24 amusement rides, including Wolverine Wildcat, the largest wooden roller coaster in the state; Corkscrew roller coaster, Mammoth River water slide, log flume; games, arcade. Also water park with wave pool, lazy river, body flumes, tube slides. Family play areas. (Mid-May-early Sept, daily) **$$$$**

Muskegon Museum of Art. *296 W Webster Ave, Muskegon (49440). Phone 231/720-2570. www.muskegonartmuseum.org.* Permanent collection includes American and European paintings, an extensive print collection, Tiffany and contemporary glass, paintings by Hopper, Inness, Whistler, Homer, Wyeth, and others. (Tues-Wed, Fri-Sat 10 am-4:30 pm, Thurs 10 am-8 pm, Sun noon-4:30 pm; closed holidays) **DONATION**

Muskegon State Park. *3560 Memorial Dr, Muskegon (49445). On Hwy 213. Phone 231/744-3480; toll-free 800/447-2757 (camping). www.muskegonstatepark.com.* A 1,165-acre area with a replica of a frontier blockhouse on one of the park's highest sand dunes, observation point. Swimming, beaches, bathhouse, water-skiing, fishing, boating (ramp, launch); 12 miles of hiking trails, cross-country skiing, skating rink, luge run, picnicking, concession, playground, camping (electrical hook-ups). **$$**

Muskegon Trolley Company. *923 Witham Rd, Muskegon (49445). Phone 231/724-6420.* Two routes cover north side, south side, and downtown; each trolley stops at 11 locations, including Hackley and Hume Historic Site, USS *Silversides*, Muskegon State Park. (Memorial Day-Labor Day, daily; no trips during special events) **$**

P. J. Hoffmaster State Park. *6585 Lake Harbor Rd, Muskegon (49441). S on Henry St to Pontaluna Rd, then W on Lake Harbor Rd. Phone 231/798-3711; toll-free 800/447-2757.* More than 1,000 acres include forest-covered dunes along 2 1/2 miles of Lake Michigan shoreline. Swimming, sandy beach. Ten miles of trails, Dune Climb Stairway to top of one of highest dunes, observation deck. Cross-country ski trails (3 miles), picnicking, concession, camping (electric hook-ups, dump station). Visitor center has displays, exhibits on dune formation (daily). Also here is

> **Gillette Visitor Center.** *6585 Lake Harbor Rd, Muskegon (49441). Phone 231/798-3573.* Sand dune interpretive center. Multi-image slide presentations on the Great Lakes and dune habitats; dune ecology exhibit, hands-on classroom; seasonal animal exhibits. (Daily)

USS *Silversides* and Maritime Museum. *1346 Bluff St, Muskegon (49441). Bluff St at Muskegon Channel. Phone 231/755-1230. www.silversides.org.* Famous World War II submarine that served with Pacific Fleet along Japan's coasts. The *Silverside's* outstanding aggressive war record includes sinking 23 enemy ships, embarking on special minelaying and reconnaisance missions, and rescuing two American aviators downed in air strikes over Japan. Guided tours. No high heels or skirts. (June-Aug: daily; Apr-May and Sept-Oct: Sat-Sun)

Special Events

Blueberry Festival. *Fruitland Township Park, 4545 Nestrom Rd, Muskegon (49445). Phone 231/766-3208.* Late July.

Luge Run. *Muskegon Winter Sports Complex in Muskegon State Park, 462 Scenic Dr, Muskegon (49445). Phone 231/744-9629.* Jan-Mar.

Muskegon Air Fair. *101 Sinclair Dr, Muskegon (49441). Phone 231/798-4596.* More than 100 military and civilian aircraft; displays. Mid-July.

Muskegon Shoreline Spectacular. *Père Marquette Park, 1601 Beach St, Muskegon (49440). Phone 231/737-5791.* Concerts, sporting events, arts and crafts, hot air balloon rides. Labor Day weekend.

Muskegon Summer Celebration. *587 W Western Ave, Muskegon (49440). Phone 231/722-6520.* Family music and entertainment parade, midway, food and beer tents, Venetian boat parade. June-July.

Limited-Service Hotels

★ BEL-AIRE MOTEL. *4240 Airline Rd, Muskegon (49444). Phone 231/733-2196; fax 231/733-2196.* 17 rooms. Check-out 11 am. **$**

★ BEST WESTERN PARK PLAZA HOTEL. *2967 Henry St, Muskegon (49441). Phone 231/733-2651; toll-free 800/780-7234; fax 231/733-5202.*

www.bestwestern.com. 111 rooms, 4 story. Check-in 4 pm, check-out 11 am. Bar. Indoor pool. Airport transportation available. **$**

★ ★ HOLIDAY INN. *939 Third St, Muskegon (49440). Phone 231/722-0100; toll-free 800/846-5253; fax 231/722-5118. www.holiday-inn.com.* 200 rooms, 8 story. Check-in 4 pm, check-out 11 am. Restaurant, bar. Fitness room. Indoor pool, whirlpool. Airport transportation available. **$**

Restaurants

★ ★ RAFFERTY'S DOCKSIDE. *601 Terrace Point Blvd, Muskegon (49440). Phone 231/722-4461; fax 231/722-2422. www.shorelineinn.com.* American menu. Dinner. Closed holidays. Bar. Children's menu. Casual attire. Outdoor seating. **$$$**

★ ★ TONY'S. *785 W Broadway, Muskegon (49441). Phone 231/739-7196; fax 231/739-7056.* Steak menu. Lunch, dinner. Closed Sun; holidays. Bar. Children's menu. **$$**

New Buffalo (K-2)

See also Niles, St. Joseph

Population 2,317
Elevation 630 ft
Area Code 269
Zip 49117
Information Harbor County Chamber of Commerce, 530 S Whittaker, Suite F; phone 269/469-5409
Web Site www.harborcountry.com

Because of its proximity to large Midwestern cities, New Buffalo and the Harbor County area are a popular resort community for year-round vacationers. Sandy Lake Michigan beaches beckon, and numerous shops, galleries, and antiques stores make this a vacationer's paradise.

What to See and Do

Red Arrow Highway. *I-94 and Union Pier, New Buffalo. I-94, exits 4B, 6, or 12.* Many antique stores, inns, galleries, shops, and restaurants can be found along this road that travels from Union Pier to Sawyer, between Lake Michigan and the Interstate.

Warren Dunes State Park. *12032 Red Arrow Hwy, Sawyer (49125). Phone 269/426-4013.* On 1,499 acres on Lake Michigan. Swimming, beach house; hiking, picnicking, playground, concession, camping, cabins. There are 200 acres of virgin forest in Warren Woods. (Daily) **$$**

Specialty Lodging

The following lodging establishment is approved by Mobil Travel Guide, but due to its unique and individualized nature has not been given a traditional Mobil Star rating. Included in this listing you may find bed-and-breakfasts, limited-service inns, guest ranches, and other unique hotel properties.

SANDPIPER INN. *16136 Lakeview Ave, Union Pier (49129). Phone 269/469-1146; toll-free 800/351-2080. www.sandpiperinn.net.* 9 rooms. Complimentary full breakfast. Check-in 4 pm, check-out 11 am. **$$**

Newberry (C-3)

See also Hulbert, Paradise, Soo Junction

Population 1,873
Elevation 788 ft
Area Code 906
Zip 49868
Information Newberry Area Chamber of Commerce, PO Box 308; phone 906/293-5562 or toll-free 800/831-7292
Web Site www.exploringthenorth.com/newberry/home.html

Located in the middle of the eastern Upper Peninsula, Newberry is centrally located to all of the UP's attractions: Lake Superior, Tahquamenon Falls, Paradise and Whitefish Bay, Pictured Rocks, and the Hiawatha National Forest. Enjoy hunting in the fall, a range of sports in winter, and fishing and blueberry picking in summer.

What to See and Do

Luce County Historical Museum. *411 W Harrie St, Newberry (49868). Phone 906/293-5946.* (1894) Restored Queen Anne structure; the stone on the lower portion is Marquette or Jacobsville sandstone, some of the oldest rock in the country. Originally a sheriff's residence and jail, it was saved from razing and is now a museum. The stateroom fireplace is original; many of the rooms have been refurbished to hold records, books, and other artifacts; jail cells are still intact. (Tues-Thurs 2-4 pm) **FREE**

Seney National Wildlife Refuge. *HCR 2 Box 1, Seney (49883). 3 miles S on Hwy 123, then 23 miles W on Hwy 28 to Seney, then 5 miles S on Hwy 77. Phone 906/586-9851. midwest.fws.gov/seney.* On 95,455 acres. Canada geese, bald eagles, sandhill cranes, loons, deer, beaver, otter; several species of ducks. Visitor center has exhibits, films, and information on wildlife observation (mid-May-Sept, daily). Headquarters (Mon-Fri). Self-guided auto tour (mid-May-mid-Oct). Also, 1/2 mile nature trail (daylight hours). Fishing; picnicking, limited hunting. Pets on leash only. **FREE**

Special Events

Lumberjack Days. *Tahquamenon Logging Museum, Hwy 123, Newberry (49868). Phone toll-free 800/831-7292.* Wood carvings, traditional music, logging contests, lumberjack breakfast. Weekend in late Aug.

Michigan Fiddlers' Jamboree. *American Legion, Newberry (49868). Phone 906/293-8711.* Music, dancing, and concessions are featured at this jamboree presented by the original Michigan Fiddler's Association. Weekend in late Sept.

Limited-Service Hotels

★ BEST WESTERN NEWBERRY. *12956 Hwy 28, Newberry (49868). Phone 906/293-4000; toll-free 800/293-3297; fax 906/293-4005. www.bestwestern.com.* 66 rooms, 2 story. Complimentary continental breakfast. Check-in 3 pm, check-out 11 am. Indoor pool, whirlpool. **$**

★ COMFORT INN. *Hwy 28 and 123, Newberry (49868). Phone 906/293-3218; toll-free 800/228-5150; fax 906/293-9375. www.comfortinn.com.* 54 rooms, 2 story. Complimentary continental breakfast. Check-in 2 pm, check-out 10 am. **$**

Niles (K-2)

See also New Buffalo, St. Joseph

Population 12,458
Elevation 658 ft
Area Code 269
Zip 49120
Information Four Flags Area Council on Tourism, 321 E Main, PO Box 1300; phone 269/684-7444
Web Site www.ci.niles.mi.us

Niles calls itself the "city of four flags" because the banners of France, England, Spain, and the United States each have flown over the area. Montgomery Ward and the Dodge brothers are native sons of the town.

What to See and Do

Fernwood Botanic Gardens. *13988 Range Line Rd, Niles (49120). 5 miles NW via I-31/33, Walton Rd exit. Phone 269/695-6491. www.fernwoodbotanical.org.* The scenic grounds comprise 100 acres of woodland trails, spring-fed ponds, a tall grass prairie, and nearly 20 gardens, including rock and fern gardens and a Japanese garden. Nature center features hands-on educational exhibits and panoramic bird observation windows. (Tues-Sun; closed Thanksgiving, Dec 25) **$**

Fort St. Joseph Museum. *508 E Main St, Niles (49120). Phone 269/683-4702.* Contains one of the top five Sioux art collections in the nation. Includes autobiographical pictographs by Sitting Bull and Rain-In-The-Face. Other collections are Fort St. Joseph (1691-1781) and Potawatomi artifacts, local history memorabilia. (Wed-Sat 10 am-4 pm; closed holidays)

Special Events

Four Flags Area Apple Festival. *1740 Lake St, Niles (49120). Lake and 17th sts. Phone 269/683-8870. www.fourflagsapplefestival.org.* This four-day festival offers carnival rides, a parade, arts and crafts, and food vendors. Fourth week in Sept.

Riverfest. *Riverfront Park, Niles (49120). Phone 269/684-5766.* Crafts, games, food, entertainment, raft race. Early Aug.

Northville (J-5)

See also Farmington, Plymouth

Restaurants

★★ LITTLE ITALY. *227 Hutton St, Northville (48167). Phone 248/348-0575; fax 248/347-6204. www.littleitalynorthville.com.* Converted residence; small, intimate dining areas; antiques, original art. Italian menu. Lunch, dinner. Closed holidays. Bar. **$$$**

★ ★ **MACKINNON'S.** *126 E Main St, Northville (48167). Phone 248/348-1991; fax 248/348-9470.* Victorian atmosphere; stained-glass windows. American menu. Lunch, dinner. Bar. Outdoor seating. **$$**

★ **ROCKY'S OF NORTHVILLE.** *41122 W Seven Mile Rd, Northville (48167). Phone 248/349-4434; fax 248/349-8517.* Seafood menu. Lunch, dinner. Closed Jan 1, Dec 25. Bar. Children's menu. **$$**

Ontonagon (B-5)

See also Houghton, Ironwood

Population 2,040
Elevation 620 ft
Area Code 906
Zip 49953
Information Ontonagon County Chamber of Commerce, PO Box 266; phone 906/884-4735
Web Site www.ontonagonmi.com

Ontonagon (on-ten-OG-en) is a beautiful, sleepy town on the shores of Lake Superior that is unspoiled by tourists. Its quaint drawbridge stops traffic every now and then, but the pace of this town is so slow, you'll hardly notice. Nearby Porcupine Mountains and Lake of the Clouds offer rugged hiking trails that reward you with breathtaking mountaintop views.

What to See and Do

Porcupine Mountains Wilderness State Park. *412 S Boundry Rd, Ontonagon (49953). 20 miles W on Hwy 107, on shore of Lake Superior. Phone 906/885-5275. www.exploringthenorth.com/porkiesum/intro.html.* This 63,000-acre forested, mountainous semiwilderness area harbors otters, bears, coyotes, bald eagles, and many other species. There are many streams and lakes with fishing for bass, perch, and trout; boating (launch); hunting in season for grouse, deer, and bear; downhill and cross-country skiing, snowmobiling; hiking trails with overnight rustic cabins (reservations available) and shelters; scenic overlooks, waterfalls, abandoned mine sites. Visitor center. Picnicking, playground, camping. (Daily) **$$** In the park is

Ski area. *412 S Boundary Rd, Ontonagon (49953). Phone 906/885-5275. www.porkies.com.* Triple, double chairlifts, T-bar, rope tow; patrol, school, rentals; snack bar. Longest run 1 mile; vertical drop 641 feet. 25 miles of cross-country trails. (Mid-Dec-Mar, daily; closed Dec 25) **$$$$**

Limited-Service Hotel

★ ★ **AMERICINN.** *120 Lincoln, Ontonagon (49953). Phone 906/885-5311; fax 906/885-5847.* 71 rooms, 3 story. Pets accepted, some restrictions; fee. Complimentary continental breakfast. Check-out 11 am. Restaurant, bar. Indoor pool, whirlpool. Airport transportation available. **$**

Oscoda (F-5)

See also Alpena, East Tawas, Tawas City

Population 1,061
Elevation 590 ft
Area Code 989
Zip 48750
Information Oscoda-Au Sable Chamber of Commerce, 4440 N Hwy 23; phone 989/739-7322 or toll-free 800/235-4625
Web Site www.oscoda.com

This is a resort community where the Au Sable (a-SAAB-uhl) River empties into Lake Huron. Formerly a heavily populated logging town, Oscoda (os-CODE-a) is now an outdoor lover's paradise, with trout and salmon fishing, canoeing, and hunting.

What to See and Do

Huron-Manistee National Forest. *1755 S Mitchell St, Cadillac (49601). W of town on River Rd. Phone 517/739-0728.* This 427,000-acre forest is the Huron section of the Huron-Manistee National Forest (for Manistee section, see MANISTEE). A major attraction of the forest is the Lumberman's Monument overlooking the Au Sable River. A three-figure bronze memorial depicting a timber cruiser, sawyer, and river driver commemorates the loggers who cut the virgin timber in Michigan in the latter part of the 19th century. The visitor center at the monument offers interpretations of this colorful era (Memorial Day-Labor Day). Scenic drives; beaches, swimming, streams, lakes, trout fishing, canoe trips down the Au Sable River; hunting for deer and small game, camping, picnicking, winter sports areas. Contact Huron Shores Ranger Station, US Forest Service, 5761 Skeel Ave. (Daily) **FREE**

Paddle-wheeler boat trips. *Au Sable River Queen, Foote Dam, 1775 Eastside-River Footside, Oscoda (48750). 6 miles W on River Rd. Phone 989/739-7351. www.ausableriverqueen.com.* Boat makes 19-mile (2-hour) round-trips on Au Sable River. (Memorial Day-mid-Oct, daily; schedule may vary, reservations advised) **$$$**

Special Events

Au Sable River International Canoe Marathon. *Phone 989/739-7322.* This 120-mile marathon begins in Grayling (see) and ends in Oscoda. Last weekend in July.

Paul Bunyan Days. *Throughout city, Oscoda (48750). Phone 989/739-7322.* Lumberjack show, chainsaw carving competition, children's events. Third weekend in Sept.

Limited-Service Hotel

★ REDWOOD MOTOR LODGE. *3111 Hwy 23 N, Oscoda (48750). Phone 989/739-2021; toll-free 866/739-3436; fax 989/739-1121. www.redwoodmotorlodge.com.* 45 rooms, 2 story. Closed Dec 23-25. Complimentary continental breakfast. Check-in 2 pm (cottages 4 pm), check-out 11 am. Bar. Children's activity center. Beach. Indoor pool, whirlpool. **$**

Owosso (H-5)

See also Flint, Lansing

Settled 1836
Population 16,322
Elevation 730 ft
Area Code 989
Zip 48867
Information Owosso-Corunna Area Chamber of Commerce, 215 N Water St; phone 989/723-5149
Web Site www.shianet.org

Owosso's most famous sons were James Oliver Curwood, author of many wildlife novels about the Canadian wilderness, and Thomas E. Dewey, governor of New York and twice Republican presidential nominee. The city, rising on the banks of the Shiawassee River, has five parks and many industries.

What to See and Do

Curwood Castle. *224 Curwood Castle Dr, Owosso (48867). Phone 989/725-0597. www.dupontcastle.com/castles/curwood.htm.* This replica of a Norman castle, thought to be architecturally unique in the state, was used as a studio by James Oliver Curwood, author and conservationist. It is maintained as a museum with Curwood memorabilia and local artifacts displayed. (Tues-Sun 1-5 pm; closed holidays) **DONATION**

Special Events

Curwood Festival. *Phone 989/723-2161. curwoodfestival.com.* River raft, bed, and canoe races, juried art show, pioneer displays and demonstrations, fun run, parade, entertainment. First full weekend in June.

Shiawassee County Fair. *County Fairgrounds, 2900 E Hibbard Rd, Corunna (48817). Phone 989/743-3611.* Agricultural and home economics exhibits, rides. First week in Aug.

Paradise (C-4)

See also Newberry, Sault Ste. Marie, Soo Junction

Elevation 407 ft
Area Code 906
Zip 49768
Information Paradise Michigan Chamber of Commerce, PO Box 82, 49768; phone 906/492-3219
Web Site www.paradisemichigan.org

Although residents number only a few hundred, Paradise offers plenty of delights for travelers. With sandy beaches, excellent fishing, bountiful blueberries, gorgeous fall colors, and a wide variety of winter sporting opportunities, Paradise has something for everyone. It is probably best known for its two natural assets: Tahquamenon Falls and Whitefish Bay, the bay the legendary freighter *Edmund Fitzgerald* was attempting to reach before disappearing just 15 miles away.

What to See and Do

Great Lakes Shipwreck Museum and Whitefish Point Light Station. *18335 N Whitefish Point Rd, Paradise (49768). Phone toll-free 888/492-3747. www.shipwreckmuseum.com.* Near Whitefish Bay, where the *Edmund Fitzgerald* and more than 300 other ships sank in the unforgiving waters of Lake

Superior, the Great Lakes Shipwreck Museum pays tribute to these fallen ships. The museum also features a shop featuring brass nautical instruments, miniature lighthouses, artwork and prints, books, and other maritime gifts. To get the most out of your experience, stay overnight at the light station, where you're asked to take on a few simple tasks to keep the lighthouse in operation.

Tahquamenon Falls State Park. *41382 W Hwy 123, Paradise (49768). Phone 906/492-3415. www.exploring thenorth.com/tahqua/tahqua.html.* Approximately 35,000 acres of scenic wilderness; includes Upper (40 feet) and Lower Falls (a series of several scenic falls of lesser height). Swimming, fishing, boating (rentals, launch); snowmobiling, cross-country skiing, hunting in season, playground, picnicking, concession; camping near rapids and near shore of Whitefish Bay, Lake Superior. **$$**

Paw Paw (J-3)

See also Kalamazoo

Population 3,169
Elevation 740 ft
Area Code 269
Zip 49079
Information Chamber of Commerce, 804 S Kalamazoo St; PO Box 105; phone 269/657-5395
Web Site www.pawpaw.net

The center of an important grape-growing area, this town takes its name from the Paw Paw River, so designated by Native Americans for the papaw trees that grew along its banks.

What to See and Do

Maple Lake. Created in 1908 when river waters were dammed for electric power. Boating and swimming on Maple Island; picnicking.

St. Julian Wine Company. *716 S Kalamazoo St, Paw Paw (49079). 2 blocks N of I-94 exit 60. Phone 269/657-5568. www.stjulian.com.* The oldest and largest winery in the state; wine tasting. Tours every 1/2 hour. (Mon-Sat 9 am-5 pm, Sun noon-5 pm; closed holidays)

Warner Vineyards. *706 S Kalamazoo St, Paw Paw (49079). 3 blocks N of I-94. Phone 269/657-3165; toll-free 800/756-5357. www.warnerwines.com.* Produces wine, champagne, and juices. Tours and tasting. (Daily; closed holidays) **FREE**

Special Event

Wine and Harvest Festival. *Michigan Ave at Gremps St, Paw Paw (49079). Phone 269/657-5395.* First weekend in Sept.

Limited-Service Hotel

★ COMFORT INN & SUITES. *153 Ampey Rd, Paw Paw (49079). Phone 269/655-0303; fax 269/657-1015.* 65 rooms. Complimentary continental breakfast. Check-in 3 pm, check-out 11 am. Fitness room. Indoor pool. **$**

Pellston (D-4)

See also Mackinaw City, Petoskey

Population 771
Elevation 702 ft
Area Code 231
Zip 46769

A sign as you enter and leave Pellston advertises this city as the coldest spot in North America, but its real claim to fame is a small international airport that links northern Michigan to Canada and the rest of the United States. With Mackinaw City just 15 miles north, flying into Pellston is the fastest way to get to the Straits of Mackinac and Mackinac Island.

Limited-Service Hotel

★ THE CROOKED RIVER LODGE. *6845 Hwy 31 N, Alanson (49706). Phone 231/548-5000; toll-free 866/548-0700; fax 231/548-1105. www.crookedriver lodge.com.* 40 rooms. Check-in 4 pm, check-out 11 am. Indoor pool. **$**

Pentwater (E-4)

See also Mackinaw City, Petoskey

Population 958
Elevation 689 ft
Area Code 231
Zip 49449
Information Pentwater Chamber of Commerce, phone 231/869-4150
Web Site www.pentwater.org

Located on Lake Michigan, Pentwater is a quiet town that retains much of its Victorian charm from days gone by. Look for unique shops in downtown Pentwater; among the most popular are shops that specialize in antiques from the town's logging heyday, around 1900.

Specialty Lodging

The following lodging establishment is approved by Mobil Travel Guide, but due to its unique and individualized nature has not been given a traditional Mobil Star rating. Included in this listing you may find bed-and-breakfasts, limited-service inns, guest ranches, and other unique hotel properties.

NICKERSON INN. *262 W Lowell St, Pentwater (49449). Phone 231/869-6731; fax 231/869-6151. www.nickersoninn.com.* Built in 1914; antiques. 16 rooms, 3 story. Children over 12 years only. Complimentary full breakfast. Check-in 2 pm, check-out 11 am. Restaurant. **$$**

Restaurant

★ **HISTORIC NICKERSON INN.** *262 W Lowell St, Pentwater (49449). Phone 231/869-6731. www.nickersoninn.com.* International/Fusion menu. Dinner. Closed Sun-Thurs in Apr-May; also Jan-Mar; Dec 25. Children's menu. Casual attire. Outdoor seating. **$$**

Petoskey (E-4)

See also Boyne City, Charlevoix, Harbor Springs, Indian River, Pellston, Pentwater

Settled 1852
Population 6,056
Elevation 786 ft
Area Code 231
Zip 49770
Information Petoskey Regional Chamber of Commerce, 401 E Mitchell St; phone 231/347-4150
Web Site www.petoskey.com

A popular resort nestled in a hillside overlooking Little Traverse Bay, Petoskey (pet-TOSK-ee) is known for its historic Gaslight Shopping District. These downtown shops connect to Waterfront Park, which features a walking path, playground, recreation area, and marina. A bike path connects Petoskey northward to Harbor Springs and southward to Charlevoix, offering opportunities to bike, in-line skate, and walk among these charming cities. Petoskey State Park and numerous local parks offer hiking trails and beaches. Take a drive just north of Petoskey to the lakeside community of Bay View, a summer-only association started by the Methodist church, where homes are passed down within families from generation to generation.

What to See and Do

Little Traverse Historical Museum. *Waterfront Park, 100 Depot Ct, Petoskey (49770). Phone 231/347-2620. www.petoskeymuseum.org.* Housed in a former railroad depot, visitors can see historical exhibits from the area's Native American, pioneer, and Victorian past. (May-Nov, daily)

Petoskey State Park. *2475 Hwy 119, Petoskey (49712). 4 miles NE, on Hwy 119. Phone 231/347-2311.* A 305-acre park with swimming beach, beach house, fishing; hiking, cross-country skiing, picnicking, playground, camping (electrical hook-ups, dump station).

St. Francis Solanus Indian Mission. *W Lake St, Petoskey (49770).* (1859) Built of square hand-cut timbers and held together by dovetailed corners, this church is the oldest structure in Petoskey. Native American burial grounds (not open to public) are adjacent the church. Mass is still held at the church once a year on the feast of St. Francis Solanus, July 14.

Special Event

Art in the Park. *Pennsylvania Park, 401 E Mitchell St, Petoskey (49770). Phone 231/347-4150.* Approximately 125 exhibitors display their artwork at this downtown park location. Third Sat in July.

Limited-Service Hotel

★ ★ **STAFFORD'S PERRY HOTEL.** *Bay and Lewis sts, Petoskey (49770). Phone 231/347-4000; toll-free 800/737-1899; fax 231/347-0636. www.staffords.com.* 81 rooms, 3 story. Check-out 11 am. Restaurant, bar. Fitness room. **$**

Full-Service Resort

★ ★ ★ **RENAISSANCE INN AT BAY HARBOR.** *3600 Village Harbor Dr, Bay Harbor (49770). Phone 231/439-4000; fax 231/439-4094.* The Inn at Bay Harbor seduces guests with its turn-of-the-20th-century glamour. This gracious resort is nestled on 5 acres alongside Lake Michigan in the renowned resort area of northern Michigan. Golf is a major attraction, with 162 holes just outside the hotel, 27 of them part of the property itself. A terrific spa soothes body and soul with a wide variety of pampering procedures, including massages, facials, hydrotherapy, and wellness packages. The inn's suites have a classic appeal with a cheerful spirit, while three-bedroom cottages offer spacious accommodations with views of the Crooked Tree Golf Club. From the photographs of Victorian cruise ships lining the walls at Sagamore's to the dark wood and leather interior at the South American lounge, this resort celebrates its history in its restaurants. 152 rooms, 5 story. Complimentary continental breakfast. Check-out noon. Two restaurants, bar. Children's activity center. Fitness room, spa. Beach. Outdoor pool, whirlpool. Golf, 27 holes. Business center. **$$**

Full-Service Inn

★ ★ ★ **STAFFORD'S BAY VIEW INN.** *2011 Woodland Ave, Petoskey (49770). Phone 231/347-2771; toll-free 800/258-1886; fax 231/347-3413. www.staffords.com.* Built in 1866, this Victorian-style inn features a green mansard roof and overlooks Little Traverse Bay. 31 rooms, 3 story. Complimentary full breakfast. Check-in after 3 pm, check-out 11 am. High-speed Internet access. Restaurant. Airport transportation available. **$$**

Restaurants

★ ★ **ANDANTE.** *321 Bay St, Petoskey (49770). Phone 231/348-3321.* International/Fusion menu. Dinner. Closed Sun-Mon in Oct-May; holidays. **$$$**

★ ★ **STAFFORD'S BAY VIEW INN.** *2011 Woodland Ave, Petoskey (49770). Phone 231/347-2771. www.staffords.com.* American menu. Lunch, dinner, Sun brunch. Children's menu. Casual attire. Outdoor seating. **$$**

Pictured Rocks National Lakeshore (C-2)

See also Munising

On Lake Superior shoreline between Grand Marais and Munising.

Along a 15-mile section of the Lake Superior shoreline are multicolored sandstone cliffs rising to heights of 200 feet. Here the erosive action of the waves, rain, and ice has carved the cliffs to create caves, arches, columns, and promontories. Although many consider the views from a boat superior, most sections are accessible by trails and roads that provide spectacular views of the cliffs and the lake (most roads are closed in winter). The cliffs give way to 12 miles of sand beach followed by the Grand Sable Banks; 5 square miles (3,200 acres) of sand dunes are perched atop the banks. Also here are waterfalls, inland lakes, ponds, streams, hardwood and coniferous forests, and numerous birds and animals. Activities include hiking, swimming, scuba diving, fishing, boating, hunting, and picnicking. Offered in summer are guided historical walks and campfire programs; in winter there is snowmobiling, cross-country skiing on groomed and tracked ski trails, and snowshoeing. Also here are the Grand Marais Maritime Museum (summer) and Munising Falls Interpretive Center (summer, daily). There are three drive-in campgrounds (fee) and numerous hike-in backcountry campsites (permit required, free, obtain from any visitor station). Pets are not permitted in the backcountry; must be on leash in other areas. Visitors can obtain information at Pictured Rocks National Lakeshore-Hiawatha National Forest Visitor Information Station (daily); Munising Headquarters (Mon-Fri); or Grand Sable Visitor Center (summer). For more information, contact thc Superintendent, PO Box 40; phone 906/387-2379.

Plymouth (J-5)

See also Farmington, Northville, Southfield

Population 9,560
Elevation 730 ft
Area Code 734

Zip 48170
Information Chamber of Commerce, 386 S Main St; phone 734/453-1540
Web Site www.plymouthchamber.org

Special Events

Fall Festival. *Phone 734/453-1540.* Antique mart, music, ethnic food. First weekend after Labor Day.

Ice Sculpture Spectacular. *Kellogg Park, Plymouth (48170). Phone 734/453-1540.* Hundreds of ice sculptures line the streets and fill Kellogg Park, as professional and student chefs compete with each other carving huge blocks of ice; the sculptures are lighted at night. Jan.

Limited-Service Hotel

★ **FAIRFIELD INN.** *5700 Haggerty, Canton (48187). Phone 734/981-2440; toll-free 800/228-2800; fax 734/981-2440. www.fairfieldinn.com.* 133 rooms, 3 story. Complimentary continental breakfast. Check-in 3 pm, check-out noon. Outdoor pool. **$**

Restaurants

★ ★ ★ **CAFE BON HOMME.** *844 Penniman, Plymouth (48170). Phone 734/453-6260; fax 734/453-4699.* The modern European cuisine in this very upscale, tranquil restaurant tucked away in the Plymouth boutique shopping district serves such dishes as Southern French lamb pie, and pan-seared breast of duck. French menu. Lunch, dinner. Closed Sun; holidays. **$$$**

★ ★ **ERNESTO'S.** *41661 Plymouth Rd, Plymouth (48170). Phone 734/453-2002; fax 734/453-7490.* Italian menu. Lunch, dinner. Closed Mon; Jan 1, Dec 25. Bar. Outdoor seating. **$$**

Pontiac (J-5)

See also Auburn Hills, Bloomfield Hills, Detroit, Holly, Rochester, Southfield, Troy

Founded 1818
Population 71,166
Elevation 943 ft
Area Code 248
Information Chamber of Commerce, 30 N Saginaw, Suite 404, 48342; phone 248/335-9600
Web Site www.pontiacchamber.com

What was once the summer home of Chief Pontiac of the Ottawas is now the home of the Pontiac division of General Motors. A group of Detroit businessmen established a village here that became a way station on the wagon trail to the West. The Pontiac Spring Wagon Works, in production by the middle 1880s, is the lineal ancestor of the present industry. Today, a revitalized Pontiac is easily accessible by car or train; the *Wolverine* train travels daily between Pontiac and Chicago, making the town convenient for a weekend getaway to the Windy City. Pontiac is surrounded by 11 state parks, and 400 lakes are within a short distance.

What to See and Do

Alpine Valley Ski Resort. *6775 E Highland, White Lake (48383). 12 miles W of Telegraph Rd on Hwy 59 (Highland Rd). Phone 248/887-2180. www.skialpinevalley.com.* Ten chairlifts, ten rope tows; patrol, school, rentals, snowmaking; bar, cafeteria. Longest run 1/3 mile; vertical drop 320 feet. (Nov-Mar, daily; closed Dec 24 afternoon and Dec 25 morning) **$$$$**

Highland. *3500 Wixon Rd, Pontiac (48382). 17 miles W on Hwy 59. Phone 248/685-2433.* On 5,524 wooded acres. Swimming, bathhouse, fishing, boating (launch); hiking, horseback riding, hunting in season, cross-country skiing, picnicking, playground, concession, camping.

Pontiac Lake. *7800 Gale Rd, Waterford (48327). 7 miles W on Hwy 59. Phone 248/666-1020.* Approximately 3,700 acres. Swimming, bathhouse, water-skiing, fishing, boating (launch); horseback riding, riding stable, hunting in season, archery and rifle ranges, winter sports, picnicking, playground, concession, camping. Contact Park Manager, 7800 Gale Rd, Hwy 2, 48327. **$$**

Full-Service Hotel

★ ★ ★ **MARRIOTT PONTIAC AUBURN HILLS.** *3600 Centerpoint Pkwy, Pontiac (48341). Phone 248/253-9800; toll-free 800/228-9290; fax 248/253-9682. www.marriott.com.* 290 rooms, 11 story. Check-out noon. Restaurant. Fitness room. Indoor pool. Business center. **$$**

Port Austin (G-6)

See also Bay City

Population 815
Elevation 600 ft
Area Code 989
Zip 48467
Information Port Austin Chamber of Commerce, 2 W Spring St, PO Box 274; phone 989/738-7600
Web Site www.port-austin.com

Port Austin sits at the tip of Michigan's thumb, an area known for farming sugar beets, melons, blueberries, and potatoes. The city boasts beautiful sunrises and sunsets over Lake Huron, as well as a charming downtown that looks as though time forgot it. Sandy beaches and dunes are perfect for strolling or shell hunting. Nearby Pointe Aux Barques, a small bit of land that extends into Lake Huron, beckons you to drive among its luxurious summer mansions that were built over the last 125 years.

What to See and Do

Albert E. Sleeper State Park. *6573 State Park Rd, Caseville (48725). 13 miles S on Hwy 25, on Saginaw Bay, Lake Huron. Phone 989/856-4411.* On 723 acres. Sand beach, bathhouse, fishing; hunting, hiking, cross-country skiing, picnicking, playground, camping. (Daily) **$$**

Huron City Museum. *7930 Huron City Rd, Port Austin (48467). 8 miles E on Hwy 25. Phone 989/428-4123. huroncitymuseums.com.* Nine preserved buildings from the 1850-1890 Victorian era, including the LaGasse Log Cabin, Phelps Memorial Church, Point Aux Barques US Life Saving Station, Hubbard's General Store, Community House/Inn, Brick Museum, Carriage Shed, and Barn House of Seven Gables, former residence of Langdon Hubbard and later Dr. William Lyon Phelps (additional fee). Buildings house period furnishing and memorabilia. Tours (July-Labor Day, Thurs-Mon) **$$$**

Port Huron (H-6)

See also St. Clair

Population 33,694
Elevation 600 ft
Area Code 810
Zip 48060
Information Greater Port Huron Area Chamber of Commerce, 920 Pine Grove Ave; phone 810/985-7101
Web Site www.porthuron.org

Port Huron is famous for its sandy beaches, and Fort Gratiot Lighthouse, oldest on the Great Lakes, marks the St. Clair Straits. The famous International Blue Water Bridge (toll), south of the lighthouse, crosses to Sarnia, Ontario. (For border-crossing regulations see MAKING THE MOST OF YOUR TRIP.) Port Huron's historic downtown shopping district also offers interesting shops and boutiques.

What to See and Do

Lakeport State Park. *7605 Lakeshore Rd, Lakeport (48059). 10 miles N on Hwy 25. Phone 810/327-6765.* 565 acres on Lake Huron. Beach, bathhouse, waterskiing, fishing for perch, boating (ramp); hiking, picnicking, concession, playground, camping (fee). (Daily) **$$**

Museum of Arts and History. *1115 6th St, Port Huron (48060). Phone 810/982-0891.* Historical and fine arts exhibits; pioneer log home, Native American collections, Thomas Edison's boyhood home archaeological exhibit, marine lore, natural history exhibits, period furniture; also lectures. (Wed-Sun; closed holidays) **DONATION** Also here is

> ***Huron* Lightship Museum.** *1115 6th St, Port Huron (48060). Phone 810/982-0891. www.phmuseum.org.* Lightships were constructed as floating lighthouses, anchored in areas where lighthouse construction was not possible, using their powerful lights and fog horns to guide ships safely past points of danger. Built in 1920, the *Huron* was stationed at various shoals in Lake Michigan and Lake Huron until her retirement in 1971. (June-Sept, Wed-Sun afternoons or by appointment)

Special Events

Feast of the Ste. Claire. *Pine Grove Park, Port Huron (48060). Phone 810/985-7101.* Reenactment of 18th-century crafts, lifestyles, battles; also foods, fife and drum corps. Memorial Day weekend.

Mackinac Race. *Phone 810/985-7101.* Mid-July.

Limited-Service Hotels

★ COMFORT INN. *1700 Yeager St, Port Huron*

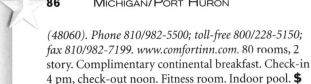

(48060). Phone 810/982-5500; toll-free 800/228-5150; fax 810/982-7199. www.comfortinn.com. 80 rooms, 2 story. Complimentary continental breakfast. Check-in 4 pm, check-out noon. Fitness room. Indoor pool. **$**

★★ **THOMAS EDISON INN.** *500 Thomas Edison Pkwy, Port Huron (48060). Phone 810/984-8000; toll-free 800/451-7991; fax 810/984-3230. www.thomasedisoninn.com.* 149 rooms, 3 story. Pets accepted. Complimentary continental breakfast. Check-in 3 pm, check-out noon. Restaurant, bar. Fitness room. Indoor pool, whirlpool. **$**

Restaurant

★★ **FOGCUTTER.** *511 Fort St, Port Huron (48060). Phone 810/987-3300; fax 810/987-3306. www.fogcutterrestaurant.com.* Seafood, steak menu. Lunch, dinner. Closed holidays. Bar. Children's menu. **$$**

Rochester (J-5)

See also Auburn Hills, Pontiac, Troy

Population 10,467
Elevation 749 ft
Area Code 248
Zip 48309
Information Rochester Regional Chamber of Commerce, 71 Walnut Blvd, Suite 110, 48307; phone 248/651-6700
Web Site www.rochesterregionalchamber.com

Located in the "Heart of the Hills" of Oakland County, as you drive into Rochester, you coast down gentle hills that offer a spectacular view of this charming city. Sandwiched between much-larger Rochester Hills, Auburn Hills, and Troy, Rochester retains its small-town feel. Stroll along the downtown sidewalks and window shop at the extensive array of clothing and shoe stores, home-furnishing shops, and other boutiques. When you're ready to rest your feet, stop in any of the city's cafés and coffeehouses.

What to See and Do

Oakland University. *2200 N Squirrel Rd, Rochester (48309). 3 miles NE off I-75. Phone 248/370-2100. www.oakland.edu.* (1959) (12,500 students) On the grounds of the former Meadow Brook Farms estate of Mr. and Mrs. Alfred G. Wilson. The Eye Research Institute is internationally recognized; Center for Robotics and Advanced Automation promotes education, research, and development in high technology and manufacturing methods. Also on campus are

Meadow Brook Art Gallery. *2200 N Squirrel Rd, Rochester (48309). Phone 248/370-3005.* Series of contemporary, primitive, and Asian art exhibitions, including permanent collection of African art; outdoor sculpture garden adjacent to music festival grounds. (Oct-May, Tues-Sun) **FREE**

Meadow Brook Hall. *2200 N Squirrel Rd, Rochester (48309). Phone 248/370-3140. www.meadowbrookhall.org.* (1926-1929) English Tudor mansion (100 rooms) built by lumber baron Alfred Wilson and his wife, Matilda Dodge Wilson, heir to the automobile family's large fortune. This spectacular mansion, one of the greatest of the early 20th century, has nearly all of its original furnishings and art objects; the library and Wilson's personal office have hand-carved paneling; the dining room has a sculptured ceiling and table that can seat several dozen guests; a two-story ballroom has elaborate stone and woodwork. Outside the mansion is Knole Cottage, Francis Wilson's playhouse featuring pint-sized luxury accommodations. Serves as cultural and conference center of the university. (Daily) **$$$**

Meadow Brook Theatre. *Oakland University, 207 Wilson Hall, Rochester (48309). Phone 248/377-3300; fax 248/370-3343. www.mbtheatre.com.* Professional company. (Early Oct-mid-May, Tues-Sun; matinees Wed, Sat-Sun)

Stony Creek Metropark. *1460 Mead Rd, Rochester (48306). Approximately 6 miles N on Hwy 150 (Rochester Rd) to 26 Mile Rd. Phone 586/781-4242; toll-free 800/477-7756.* More than 4,000 acres. Swimming beaches with bathhouse, lifeguard (Memorial Day-Labor Day, daily), fishing, boating (ramp, rentals); bicycling (rentals, trails), winter sports, picnicking, playground, golf (fee). Nature center with trails, exhibits. Pets on leash only. **$**

Special Event

Meadow Brook Music Festival. *Oakland University Campus, 207 Wilson Hall, Rochester (48309). Phone 248/567-6000.* Concerts featuring popular and classical artists. Dining and picnicking facilities. Mid-June-Aug.

Full-Service Hotel

★ ★ ★ **ROYAL PARK HOTEL.** *600 E University Dr, Rochester (48307). Phone 248/652-2600; fax 248/453-8600. www.royalparkhotel.com.* 143 rooms. Check-in 4 pm, check-out noon. Three restaurants, two bars. Fitness room. **$$$**

Restaurant

★ ★ ★ **BROOKSHIRE.** *600 E University, Rochester (48307). Phone 248/453-8722. www.royalparkhotel.com.* French menu. Breakfast, lunch, dinner, brunch. Bar. Children's menu. Business casual attire. Valet parking. **$$**

Royal Oak (J-6)

See also Birmingham, Bloomfield Hills, Detroit

Population 60,062
Elevation 667 ft
Area Code 248
Zip 48067
Information Greater Royal Oak, Michigan Chamber of Commerce, 301 W 4th St #250, 48067; phone 248/547-4000 or 248/656-0060
Web Site www.royaloakmichigan.com

Just 30 years ago, Royal Oak was just a Detroit bedroom community, with a fading downtown and no personality to speak of. Today, however, a revitalized Royal Oak is one of Michigan's trendiest cities—a place to see and be seen—where stylish shops and chic restaurants line the downtown area. The Detroit Zoo, ranked among the best zoos in the nation, makes its home in the city.

What to See and Do

Detroit Zoo. *8450 W 10 Mile Rd, Royal Oak (48068). Phone 248/398-0900. www.detroitzoo.org.* One of the world's outstanding zoos, with 40 exhibits of more than 1,300 animals in natural habitats. Outstanding chimpanzee, reptile, bear, butterfly, hummingbird, and Arctic animal exhibits. (Daily; closed Jan 1, Thanksgiving, Dec 25) **$$$**

National Shrine of the Little Flower Catholic Church. *2123 Roseland Ave, Royal Oak (48073). Phone 248/541-4122. www.shrinechurch.com.* Built in 1925 in honor of Saint Thérèse of Lisieux, the church—originally located in a largely Protestant area—was torched by the Klan in 1936. Rebuilt out of copper and stone, a dramatic stone tower displays a cross bearing a 28-foot-high figure of Jesus. On the surrounding wall is a carved portrait of Saint Thérèse, who was also known as the Little Flower. The interior of the octagon-shaped national shrine rises 38 feet; a walnut and granite alter stands in the middle of the church, with seats for parishioners surrounding it. Stone angels guard every exterior doorway. Tours available. **FREE**

Restaurant

★ **ATHENS CONEY ISLAND.** *32657 Woodward Ave, Royal Oak (48073). Phone 248/549-1488.* A Woodward tradition since the 1950s, Athens Coney Island is a retro-style diner known for the freshest service in town. On many summer nights, the parking lot is packed with classic cars. American menu. Lunch, dinner. No credit cards accepted. **$**

Saginaw (H-5)

See also Bay City, Flint, Frankenmuth, Midland

Settled 1816
Population 69,512
Elevation 595 ft
Area Code 989
Information Saginaw County Convention and Visitors Bureau, One Tuscola St, Suite 101, 48607; phone 989/752-7164 or toll-free 800/444-9979
Web Site www.saginawcvb.org

When this was the land of the Sauk, the trees grew so thick that it was always night in the swamps on both sides of the Saginaw River. When the loggers "brought daylight to the swamp," the city became the timber capital of the world. When the trees were depleted, Saginaw (SAG-in-awh) turned its attention to industry and agriculture. Today, it is the home of numerous General Motors plants and offers a variety of museums, art galleries, performing art venues, and cultural centers. Saginaw is also home to two sports teams, the Saginaw Spirit minor league hockey team and the Great Lake Storm team that's a part of the Continental Basketball Association (CBA).

What to See and Do

Castle Museum of Saginaw County History. *500 Federal, Saginaw (48607). Phone 989/752-2861. www.castlemuseum.org.* Housed in a replica of a

French chateau; collections pertaining to the history of the Saginaw Valley and central Michigan. (Daily; closed holidays) **$**

Children's Zoo. *1730 S Washington Ave, Saginaw (48601). In Celebration Sq. Phone 989/771-4966. www.saginawzoo.com.* Small animals, including llamas, macaws, swans, snakes, and porcupines. Contact yard featuring goats; train and pony rides (fees); lectures; educational programs. (Mid-May-Labor Day, daily) **$**

Japanese Cultural Center & Tea House. *527 Ezra Rust Dr, Saginaw (48601). Phone 989/759-1648.* Unique showplace on Lake Linton, designed by Yataro Suzue; gift from sister city of Tokushima, Japan. Tea service (fee); garden. (Tues-Sun)

Kokomo's Family Fun Center. *5200 Kokomo Dr, Saginaw (48604). Phone 989/797-5656; fax 989/797-2313. www.kokomos.com.* Go-karts, bumper boats, laser tag, batting cages, miniature golf, indoor driving range. More than 50 arcade games. (Daily) Fee for individual activities.

Marshall M. Fredericks Sculpture Gallery. *Saginaw Valley State University, 2250 Pierce Rd, Saginaw (48710). Phone 989/790-5667. www.svsu.edu/mfsm.* Houses an extraordinary collection of more than 200 works by the world-renowned sculptor. (Tues-Sun) **DONATION**

Saginaw Art Museum. *1126 N Michigan Ave, Saginaw (48602). Phone 989/754-2491. www.saginawartmuseum .org.* Permanent and changing exhibits of paintings, sculpture, fine art; children's gallery; historic formal garden. (Tues-Sun; closed holidays) **$**

Special Events

Great Lakes Rendezvous. *Phone 989/754-2928.* Third weekend in Aug.

Saginaw County Fair. *2701 E Genesee Ave, Saginaw (48601). Phone 989/752-7164.* Late July.

Saginaw Harness Raceway. *2701 E Genesee St, Saginaw (48601). N via I-75, Bridgeport exit. Phone 989/755-3451. www.saginawraceway.com.* Over 12 years only. Racing season May-late Aug.

Limited-Service Hotel

★ HAMPTON INN. *2222 Tittabawassee Rd, Saginaw (48604). Phone 517/792-7666; toll-free 800/426-7866; fax 517/792-3213. www.hampton.com.* 120 rooms, 2 story. Complimentary continental breakfast. Check-in 3 pm, check-out noon. Outdoor pool. **$**

Saugatuck (J-3)

See also Holland, South Haven

Population 954
Elevation 600 ft
Area Code 269
Zip 49453
Information Saugatuck/Douglas Convention & Visitors Bureau, PO Box 28; phone 269/857-1701
Web Site www.saugatuck.com

Long one of the major art colonies in the Midwest, Saugatuck (SAWG-a-tuck) (its sister city is Douglas, just a few miles down the road), is now a year-round resort area. It offers beautiful beaches for swimming and surfing on Lake Michigan, hiking and cross-country skiing in the dunes, canoeing and boating on the Kalamazoo River, yachting from marinas, and a charming shopping area. The northern end of the village covers an ancient Native American burial ground. During the summer months, arts and crafts shows are abundant.

What to See and Do

City of Douglas. *Docked just S of the Douglas-Saugatuck Bridge. Phone 269/857-2107.* Scenic afternoon buffet brunch luncheon, and dinner cruises to Lake Michigan via Kalamazoo River. (Memorial Day weekend-Labor Day, daily)

Fenn Valley Vineyards and Wine Cellar. *6130 122nd Ave, Fennville (49408). 5 miles SE via I-196, exit 34. Phone 269/561-2396. www.fennvalley.com.* Self-guided tour overlooking wine cellar; audiovisual program, wine tasting. (Daily; closed holidays) **FREE**

Harbor Duck Adventures. *Phone 269/857-3825. www.harborduckadventures.com.* This amphibious vehicle, used in World War II, shuttles passengers between Saugatuck and Douglas. Pick up the tour in Saugatuck on Culver Street across from Coughlin Park or in Douglas on Center Street in front of Berry Field. (Daily 10 am-sunset) **$$$$**

Keewatin Maritime Museum. *Harbour Village, 219 Union St, Douglas (49406). Just S of the Saugatuck-Douglas Bridge. Phone 269/857-2464. www.keewatin maritimemuseum.com.* Tours of a restored, turn-of-the-century, passenger steamship of the Canadian

Pacific Railroad, the SS *Keewatin*, maintained as an "in-service" ship; features original, elegant furnishings, carved paneling, and brass fixtures. The quadruple-expansion engine room also is open to tours. (Memorial Day-Labor Day, daily 10 am-4:30 pm) **$$**

Mason Street Warehouse. *Saugatuck Center for the Arts, 400 Culver St, Saugatuck (49453). Phone 269/857-4898. www.masonstreetwarehouse.org.* This theater company stages summertime theater performances in downtown Saugatuck, from comedies to musicals and other lighthearted fare. (June-Sept, Tues-Sun) **$$$$**

Saugatuck Dune Rides. *6495 Washington Rd, Saugatuck (49453). 1/2 mile W of I-196, exit 41 (Blue Star Hwy). Phone 269/857-2253. www.saugatuckdune ride.com.* Buggy rides over the sand dunes near Lake Michigan. Cash and travelers checks only. (Late Apr-Sept: Mon-Sat 10 am-5:30 pm, Sun noon-5:30 pm; Oct: Sat 10 am-5:30 pm, Sun noon-5:30 pm) **$$$**

Star of Saugatuck II. *716 Water St, Saugatuck (49453). At the Fish Dock. Phone 269/857-4261. www.saugatuck boatcruises.com.* This sternwheel paddleboat takes passengers on narrated tours of the Kalamazoo River and Lake Michigan, weather permitting. (Early May-Sept: daily; Oct: weekends only) **$$$**

Special Events

Halloween Harvest Festival. *Village Square, Saugatuck. Phone 269/857-1701.* Events at this festival include country music, storytelling, arts and crafts, and a parade. Late Oct.

Harbor Days. *132 Mason St, Saugatuck (49406). Phone 269/857-1701.* Venetian boat parade, family activities. Last weekend in July.

Taste of Saugatuck. *Phone 269/857-1701.* Enjoy the variety of foods from area restaurants at this street festival. Late Aug.

Limited-Service Hotel

★ TIMBERLINE. *3353 Blue Star Hwy, Saugatuck (49453). Phone 269/857-2147; toll-free 800/257-2147; fax 269/857-2147. www.timberlinemotel.com.* 28 rooms. Check-out 11 am. Outdoor pool, whirlpool. Airport transportation available. **$**

Full-Service Inn

★ ★ ★ WICKWOOD INN. *510 Butler St, Saugatuck (49453). Phone 269/857-1465; fax 269/857-1552. www.wickwoodinn.com.* This romantic inn, adorned with antiques and fireplaces, is located in a resort village near Lake Michigan. Guests will discover intimate and quiet moments here. With a best-selling cookbook author as innkeeper, it's no wonder the food is superb. 11 rooms, 2 story. Closed Dec 24-25. Complimentary full breakfast. Check-in 3 pm, check-out noon. High-speed Internet access. Restaurant. **$$**

Specialty Lodgings

The following lodging establishments are approved by Mobil Travel Guide, but due to their unique and individualized nature have not been given a traditional Mobil Star rating. Included in this listing you may find bed-and-breakfasts, limited-service inns, guest ranches, and other unique hotel properties.

KINGSLEY HOUSE BED & BREAKFAST. *626 W Main St, Fennville (49408). Phone 269/561-6425; fax 269/561-2593. www.kingsleyhouse.com.* Victorian house built in 1886; antiques. 11 rooms, 3 story. Children over 12 years only. Complimentary full breakfast. Check-in 4 pm, check-out 11 am. High-speed Internet access. **$$**

MAPLEWOOD HOTEL. *428 Butler St, Saugatuck (49453). Phone 269/857-1771; toll-free 800/650-9790; fax 269/857-1773. www.maplewoodhotel.com.* Built in 1860; antiques. 15 rooms, 2 story. Complimentary full breakfast. Check-in 3-6 pm, check-out noon. High-speed Internet access. Outdoor pool. **$$**

PARK HOUSE BED & BREAKFAST. *888 Holland St, Saugatuck (49453). Phone 269/857-4535; toll-free 800/321-4535; fax 269/857-1065. www.parkhouseinn.com.* White, clapboard house built for lumberman (1857); oldest house in Saugatuck, once visited by Susan B. Anthony. 9 rooms, 2 story. Complimentary full breakfast. Check-in 3 pm, check-out 11 am. High-speed Internet access. **$$**

ROSEMONT INN RESORT. *83 Lakeshore Dr, Saugatuck (49453). Phone 269/857-2637; toll-free 800/721-2637; fax 269/857-3968. www.rosemontinn.com.* Built in 1901. 14 rooms, 2 story. No children allowed.

Complimentary full breakfast. Check-in 3 pm, check-out noon. Outdoor pool, whirlpool. **$$$**

Restaurants

★ **CHEQUERS.** *220 Culver St, Saugatuck (49453). Phone 269/857-1868; fax 269/857-2298. www.chequersofsaugatuck.com.* English pub menu. Lunch, dinner. Closed Jan 1, Dec 25. Bar. **$$**

★★ **TOULOUSE.** *248 Culver St, Saugatuck (49453). Phone 269/857-1561; fax 269/857-2298. www.restauranttoulouse.com.* French menu. Dinner. Closed Mar. Bar. Outdoor seating. **$$**

Sault Ste. Marie (C-4)

Settled 1668
Population 14,689
Elevation 613 ft
Area Code 906
Zip 49783
Information Sault Convention and Visitors Bureau, 2581 I-75 Business Spur; phone 906/632-3301 or toll-free 800/647-2858
Web Site www.ssmcoc.com

Sault Ste. Marie (SOO-Saint-Marie) is the home of one of the nation's great engineering marvels—the locks of St. Mary's River. Along the river the locks lower or raise lake and ocean vessels 21 feet between Lake Superior and Lake Huron in 6 to 15 minutes. From April to December, about 100 vessels a day pass through with no toll charge. The cascades of the river, which made the locks necessary, give the city its name: the French word for a cascade is *sault* and the name of the patron saint was Mary; combined, the two made Sault de Sainte Marie or "Leap of the Saint Mary's."

The only entrance into Canada for almost 300 miles, the Sault Ste. Marie community began in 1668 when Father Jacques Marquette built the first mission church here. An international bridge spans the St. Mary's River to Sault Ste. Marie, Ontario (toll). (For Border Crossing Regulations see MAKING THE MOST OF YOUR TRIP.) A Ranger District office of the Hiawatha National Forest (see ESCANABA) is located in Sault Ste. Marie.

What to See and Do

Federal Building. *E Portage Ave, Sault Ste. Marie (49783).* Grounds occupy what was the site of Jesuit Fathers' mission and later the original site of Fort Brady (1822) before it was moved. Ground floor houses **River of History Museum,** an interpretive center depicting the history of the St. Mary's River.

Lake Superior State University. *650 W Easterday Ave, Sault Ste. Marie (49783). Phone 906/635-2315. www.lssu.edu.* (1946) (3,000 students) This hillside campus was the second site of historic Fort Brady after it was moved from its original location; many old buildings, including some that were part of the fort, still stand. Library's Marine Collection on Great Lakes Shipping open on request. Carillon concerts (June-Sept, twice daily; free). Headquarters of the famous Unicorn Hunters, official keepers of the Queen's English. Tours.

Museum Ship Valley Camp and Great Lakes Maritime Museum. *Great Lakes Marine Hall of Fame, 501 E Water St, Sault Ste. Marie (49783). 5 blocks E of locks. Phone 906/632-3658.* Ship's store, picnic area, and park. (Mid-May-mid-Oct, daily) **$$**

★ **Soo Locks.** *119 Park Pl, Sault Ste. Marie (49783). Phone 906/632-3311.* The famous locks can be seen from both the upper and lower parks paralleling the locks. The upper park has three observation towers. There is a scale model of the locks at the east end of the MacArthur Lock and a working lock model, photos, and a movie in visitor building in upper park. (Mar-Feb, daily) **FREE**

Soo Locks Boat Tours. *Docks #1 and #2, 515 and 1157 E Portage Ave, Sault Ste. Marie (49783). Phone 906/632-6301. www.soolocks.com.* Two-hour narrated excursions travel through the Soo Locks, focusing on their history. Sunset dinner cruises (approximately 2 3/4 hours; reservations suggested). (Mid-May-mid-Oct, daily) **$$$$**

Tower of History. *326 E Portage Ave, Sault Ste. Marie (49783). Phone 906/632-3658; toll-free 888/744-7867.* A 21-story observation tower with a 20-mile view of Canadian and American cities; show in lobby, displays. (Mid-May-mid-Oct: daily 10 am-6 pm) **$$**

Twin Soo Tour. *315-317 W Portage Ave, Sault Ste. Marie (49783). Phone 906/635-5241.* Guided tour (two to four hours) of both Canadian and American cities of Sault Ste. Marie; provides view of Soo Locks; passen-

gers may disembark in Canada. (June-Oct, daily) **$$**
Also here is

The Haunted Depot. *317 W Portage Ave, Sault Ste. Marie (49783). Phone 906/635-5912.* Guided tours through depot's many unusual chambers; visitors can "fall uphill" in the mystery bedroom, walk through a "storm" in the cemetery, or "lose their heads" at the guillotine. (June-Oct, daily)

Limited-Service Hotels

★ **BEST WESTERN SAULT STE. MARIE.** *4281 I-75 Business Spur, Sault Ste. Marie (49783). Phone 906/632-2170; toll-free 800/297-2858; fax 906/632-7877. www.bestwestern.com.* 110 rooms, 2 story. Complimentary continental breakfast. Check-in 3 pm, check-out 11 am. Indoor pool. **$**

★ ★ **QUALITY INN.** *3290 I-75 Business Spur, Sault Ste. Marie (49783). Phone 906/635-6918; toll-free 877/923-7887; fax 906/635-2941. www.qualityinn.com.* 130 rooms, 2 story. Check-in 4 pm, check-out 11 am. Restaurant, bar. Fitness room. Indoor pool, whirlpool. **$**

★ ★ **RAMADA PLAZA.** *240 W Portage Ave, Sault Ste. Marie (49783). Phone 906/632-4100; toll-free 800/654-2929; fax 906/632-6050. www.ramada.com.* Adjacent to Soo Locks. 71 rooms, 6 story. Check-in 3 pm, check-out noon. Restaurant, bar. Indoor pool, whirlpool. **$**

Restaurants

★ **ANTLER'S.** *804 E Portage Ave, Sault Ste. Marie (49783). Phone 906/632-3571; fax 906/632-6463. www.antlersgiftshop.com.* Historic building (1800s). Family-owned since 1948. Steak menu. Lunch, dinner. Closed Easter, Thanksgiving, Dec 25. Bar. Children's menu. **$$**

★ ★ **FREIGHTERS.** *240 W Portage St, Sault Ste. Marie (49783). Phone 906/632-4211; fax 906/632-6050.* Seafood menu. Breakfast, lunch, dinner, Sun brunch. Closed Dec 25. Bar. Children's menu. **$$$**

Sleeping Bear Dunes National Lakeshore (F-3)

See also Frankfort, Glen Arbor, Leland, Traverse City

On Lake Michigan shoreline between Frankfort and Leland.

In 1970, Congress designated the Manitou Islands and 35 miles of mainland Lake Michigan shoreline, in the vicinity of Empire, as Sleeping Bear Dunes National Lakeshore. Today, the park welcomes more than 1 million visitors per year, and a lighthouse built in 1871 stands guard over the waterways.

An Ojibwa legend tells of a mother bear, who with her two cubs tried to swim across Lake Michigan from Wisconsin to escape from a forest fire. Nearing the Michigan shore, the exhausted cubs fell behind. Mother bear climbed to the top of a bluff to watch and wait for her offspring. They never reached her. Today she can still be seen as the Sleeping Bear, a solitary dune higher than its surroundings. Her cubs are the Manitou Islands, which lie a few miles offshore.

The lakeshore's variety of landforms support a diversity of interrelated plant habitats. Sand dune deserts contrast sharply with hardwood forests. The 71,000-acre lakeshore contains stands of pine, dense cedar swamps, and a few secluded bogs of sphagnum moss. Against this green background are stands of white birch. In addition, the park supports many kinds of animal life, including porcupine, deer, rabbit, squirrel, coyote, and raccoon. More than 200 species of birds may be seen. Fishing and hunting are state-regulated; a Michigan license is required. Bass, bluegill, perch, and pike are plentiful; salmon are numerous in the fall.

Dune Climb takes visitors up 150 feet on foot through the dunes for a panoramic view of Glen Lake and the surrounding countryside. Pierce Stocking Scenic Drive, a 7-mile loop, is a road with a self-guiding brochure available that offers visitors an opportunity to view the high dunes and overlooks from their cars (May-October; park pass required).

Sleeping Bear Point Maritime Museum, 1 mile west of Glen Haven on Highway 209, located in the restored US Coast Guard Station, contains exhibits on the activities of the US Life-Saving Service and the US Coast Guard and the general maritime activities these organizations have aided on the Great Lakes. A restored boat house contains original and replica surf boats and other related rescue equipment. (Memorial Day-Labor Day, daily).

South Manitou Island, an 8-square-mile, 5,260-acre island with 12 miles of shoreline, has a fascinating history. Formed from glacial moraines more than 10,000 years ago, the island slowly grew a covering of forest. European settlers and the US Lighthouse Service, attracted by the forest and the natural harbor, established permanent sites here as early as the 1830s. On the southwest corner is the Valley of the Giants, a grove of white cedar trees more than 500 years old. There are three developed campgrounds on the island, and ranger-guided tours of the 1873 lighthouse.

North Manitou Island, nearby, is a 28-square-mile wilderness with 20 miles of shoreline. There are no facilities for visitors. All travel is by foot and is dependent on weather. Camping is allowed under wilderness regulations; no ground fires are permitted. There is no safe harbor or anchorage on either of the Manitou islands; however, from May-October, the islands are accessible by commercial ferry service from Leland (see).

Camping is available at D. H. Day Campground (May-November; dump station; fee) and Platte River Campground (year-round); camping is limited to 14 days. Pets on leash only. Information may be obtained from the headquarters in Empire (daily; closed off-season holidays). The visitor center there has information on park passes, self-guided trails, hiking, cross-country skiing, evening campfire programs, maritime and natural history exhibits, and other park activities (daily; closed off-season holidays). For further information and fees contact Chief of Interpretation, 9922 Front St, Empire 49630; phone 231/326-5134.

Soo Junction (C-4)

See also Newberry, Paradise

Population 100
Elevation 840 ft
Area Code 906
Zip 49868

Once just an Upper Peninsula railroad stop, Soo Junction grew into a town in its own right in the early 20th century. Tourists visit today because of the city's wide range of outdoor activities, from hiking to snowmobiling. Fall colors are exquisite, and Soo Junction is in close proximity to Hiawatha National Forest, Lake Superior, Whitefish Bay, the city of Paradise, and Tahquamenon Falls.

What to See and Do

Toonerville Trolley and Riverboat Trip to Tahquamenon Falls. *Soo Jct Rd, Soo Junction (49868). Phone 906/876-2311; toll-free 888/778-7246.* Narrated 6 1/2-hour, 53-mile round-trip through Tahquamenon region via narrow-gauge railroad and riverboat, with 1 1/4-hour stop at Upper Tahquamenon Falls. Trolley leaves Soo Junction (mid-June-early Oct, daily). Also 1 3/4-hour train tour (July-Aug, Tues-Sat). **$$$$**

South Haven (J-2)

See also Saugatuck

Population 5,563
Elevation 618 ft
Area Code 269
Zip 49090
Information South Haven/Van Buren County Lakeshore Convention & Visitors Bureau, 415 Phoenix St; phone 269/637-5252 or toll-free 800/764-2836
Web Site www.southhaven.org

A 5-mile beach on Lake Michigan and surrounding lakes make sport fishing a popular summer pastime in South Haven; numerous marinas and charter boat services are available in the area. Views are stunning as the sun sets on Lake Michigan, and South Haven's charming shops and boutiques make shopping an attractive pastime.

What to See and Do

Liberty Hyde Bailey Birthsite Museum. *903 S Bailey Ave, South Haven (49090). Phone 269/637-3251.* The 19th-century house of the famous botanist and horticulturist; family memorabilia, period furnishings, Native American artifacts. (Tues and Fri afternoons; closed holidays) **DONATION**

Michigan Maritime Museum. *260 Dyckman Ave, South Haven (49090). Phone 269/637-8078; toll-free 800/747-3810. www.michiganmaritimemuseum.org.* Exhibits of

Great Lakes maps, photographs, maritime artifacts, historic boats; public boardwalk and park. (Mon, Wed-Sat 10 am-5 pm, Sun noon-5 pm) **$**

Van Buren State Park. *23960 Ruggles Rd, South Haven (49090). 4 miles S off I-196. Phone 269/637-2788; toll-free 800/447-2757.* 326 acres include scenic wooded sand dunes. Swimming, bathhouse; hunting, picnicking, playground, concession, camping. **$$**

Special Events

Blueberry Festival. *300 Broadway St, South Haven (49090). Phone 269/637-0800.* Arts and crafts, entertainment, children's parade, 5K run. Second weekend in Aug.

Harborfest. *Phone 269/637-5252.* Dragon boat races, arts and crafts, musical entertainment, children's activities. Third weekend in June.

Specialty Lodging

The following lodging establishment is approved by Mobil Travel Guide, but due to its unique and individualized nature has not been given a traditional Mobil Star rating. Included in this listing you may find bed-and-breakfasts, limited-service inns, guest ranches, and other unique hotel properties.

YELTON MANOR BED & BREAKFAST. *140 N Shore Dr, South Haven (49090). Phone 269/637-5220; fax 269/637-4957. www.yeltonmanor.com.* Built in 1890; antiques. 17 rooms, 3 story. Complimentary full breakfast. Check-in 3 pm, check-out 11 am. **$**

Restaurant

★ MAGNOLIA GRILLE/IDLER RIVERBOAT. *515 Williams St, #10, South Haven (49090). Phone 269/637-8435.* On historic riverboat (1897), overlooking Black River. American menu. Lunch, dinner. Closed Nov-mid-Apr. Bar. Children's menu. Outdoor seating. **$$**

Southfield (J-6)

See also Birmingham, Bloomfield Hills, Detroit, Farmington, Plymouth, Pontiac

Population 75,728
Elevation 684 ft
Area Code 248
Information Chamber of Commerce, 17515 W 9 Mile Rd, Suite 750; phone 248/557-6661
Web Site www.southfieldchamber.com

Southfield, a northwestern suburb of Detroit, is the largest office center in the Detroit metro area. It is also home to the Lawrence Institute of Technology and has branch campuses of Wayne State University, Central Michigan University, and the University of Phoenix.

Limited-Service Hotels

★★ COURTYARD BY MARRIOTT. *27027 Northwestern Hwy (Hwy 10), Southfield (48034). Phone 248/358-1222; toll-free 800/321-2211; fax 248/354-3820. www.courtyard.com.* 147 rooms, 3 story. Check-in 3 pm, check-out noon. High-speed Internet access. Restaurant. Fitness room. Indoor pool, whirlpool. **$**

★★ HILTON INN SOUTHFIELD. *26000 American Dr, Southfield (48034). Phone 248/357-1100; toll-free 800/774-1500; fax 248/372-2323. www.hilton.com.* 195 rooms, 7 story. Check-in 3 pm, check-out 11 am. High-speed Internet access. Restaurant, bar. Fitness room. Indoor pool, whirlpool. Business center. **$**

Full-Service Hotels

★★★ MARRIOTT DETROIT SOUTHFIELD. *27033 Northwestern Hwy (Hwy 10), Southfield (48034). Phone 248/356-7400; toll-free 800/228-9290; fax 248/356-5501. www.marriott.com.* In the heart of Detroit's business district, visitors will find this hotel near many major corporate companies. 226 rooms, 6 story. Check-in 3 pm, check-out noon. High-speed Internet access. Restaurant, bar. Fitness room. Indoor pool, whirlpool. **$**

★★★ THE WESTIN SOUTHFIELD DETROIT. *1500 Town Center, Southfield (48075). Phone 248/827-4000; toll-free 800/228-3000; fax 248/827-1364. www.westin.com.* 385 rooms, 12 story. Check-in 3 pm, check-out noon. High-speed Internet access. Restaurant, bar. Fitness room. Indoor pool, whirlpool. **$$**

Restaurants

★ ★ ★ **MORTON'S, THE STEAKHOUSE.** *1 Towne Sq, Southfield (48076). Phone 248/354-6006; fax 248/354-6012. www.mortons.com.* The Southfield location of this Chicago-based chain offers the signature tableside presentation of menu favorites, such as steaks and main lobster, along with fresh vegetables, which are presented on a cart by the animated staff. Seafood, steak menu. Dinner. Closed holidays. Bar. Valet parking. **$$$**

★ ★ **SWEET LORRAINE'S CAFE.** *29101 Greenfield Dr, Southfield (48076). Phone 248/559-5985. www.sweetlorraines.com.* Cajun/Creole menu. Lunch, dinner, Sun brunch. Closed holidays. Bar. Modern-style bistro. **$$**

★ ★ **TOM'S OYSTER BAR.** *29106 Franklin Rd, Southfield (48034). Phone 248/356-8881; fax 248/356-6500. www.tomsoysterbar.com.* One of three Detroit locations, the New England chowder house atmosphere complements the fresh seafood here. A variety of fresh raw oysters are offered, which you can order by name. Fish preparation ranges from simple to encrusted, sauced or stuffed. Seafood menu. Lunch, dinner. Closed Jan 1, Dec 25. Bar. Children's menu. Outdoor seating. **$$**

Spring Lake (H-2)

See also Grand Haven

Population 2,514
Elevation 594 ft
Area Code 616
Zip 49456
Web Site www.springlakemi.com

Spring Lake, where "nature smiles for 7 miles," is located just across the Grand River from the town of Grand Haven. Originally named Hopkins Mill, the area's main attraction is Spring Lake, the clear blue lake for which the village is now named. The lake attracts swimmers and boaters, and the town's charm makes them want to linger even longer.

Restaurant

★ **ARBOREAL INN.** *18191 174th Ave, Spring Lake (49417). Phone 616/842-3800; fax 616/842-7429.* American menu. Dinner. Closed Sun; holidays. Bar. **$$$**

St. Clair (H-6)

See also Detroit, Mount Clemens, Port Huron, Warren

Population 5,116
Elevation 600 ft
Area Code 810
Zip 48079
Information St. Clair Chamber of Commerce, 505 N Riverside Ave; phone 810/329-2962
Web Site www.stclairchamber.com

Home to the world's largest freshwater boardwalk and situated along Lake St. Clair, this city is for water lovers. Whether you sail, water-ski, snorkel, or just park your boat at the city's 200-slip marina and stroll through downtown, St. Clair is a charming getaway.

Limited-Service Hotel

★ ★ **ST. CLAIR INN.** *500 N Riverside, St. Clair (48079). Phone 810/329-2222; toll-free 800/482-8327; fax 810/329-7664. www.stclairinn.com.* Overlooks St. Clair River. 78 rooms, 3 story. Check-in 3 pm, check-out noon. Restaurant, bar. Indoor pool, whirlpool. **$**

Restaurants

★ ★ **RIVER CRAB.** *1337 N River Rd (Hwy 29), St. Clair (48079). Phone 810/329-2261; fax 810/329-6056. www.muer.com.* Seafood menu. Lunch, dinner, Sun brunch. Closed Dec 25. Bar. Children's menu. Valet parking. Outdoor seating. **$$$**

★ ★ **ST. CLAIR INN.** *500 N Riverside, St. Clair (48079). Phone 810/329-2222. www.stclairinn.com.* American menu. Breakfast, lunch, dinner. Bar. Children's menu. Valet parking Fri-Sat. Outdoor seating. **$$$**

St. Ignace (D-4)

See also Mackinac Island, Mackinaw City

Population 2,568
Elevation 600 ft
Area Code 906
Zip 49781
Information St. Ignace Area Chamber of Commerce, 560 N State St; phone 906/643-8717 or toll-free 800/338-6660

Web Site www.stignace.com

Located at the north end of the Mackinac Bridge, across the Straits of Mackinac from Mackinaw City (see), St. Ignace (IG-ness) was founded more than 300 years ago by the famous missionary/explorer Jacques Marquette. St. Ignace is the gateway to Michigan's Upper Peninsula, which offers beautiful scenery and vast opportunities for outdoor recreation.

What to See and Do

Arnold Mackinac Island Ferry. *Arnold Line Docks, Mackinac Island (49757). Phone 906/847-3351; toll-free 800/542-8528. www.arnoldline.com.* The largest, fastest ferries traveling to Mackinac Island. **$$$$**

Castle Rock. *Castle Rock Rd, St. Ignace (49781). I-75 exit 348, 5 miles N of Mackinac Bridge. Phone 906/643-8268.* Climb the 170 steps to the top of this 200-foot-high rock to see excellent views of Mackinac Island and Lake Huron. Also features statue of Paul Bunyan and Babe, the blue ox. (Daily)

Father Marquette National Memorial. *Adjacent to Mackinac Bridge Authority Plaza.* This 52-acre memorial pays tribute to the life and work of the famed Jesuit explorer who came to area in the 1600s.

Mackinac Island ferries. Fifteen-minute trips to the island.

Shepler's. *601 N State St, St. Ignace (49781). Phone 906/643-5023. www.sheplersferry.com.* (Early May-early Nov, daily) **$$$$**

Star Line Ferry. *587 N State St, St. Ignace (49781). Phone 906/643-7635; toll-free 800/638-9892. www.mackinacferry.com.*

Marquette Mission Park and Museum of Ojibwa Culture. *500 N State St, St. Ignace (49781). Phone 906/643-9161.* Gravesite of Father Marquette. Museum interprets 17th-century Native American life and the coming of the French. (Memorial Day-Labor Day, daily; after Labor Day-rest of Sept, Tues-Sat) **$**

Statue of Father Marquette. *Marquette Mission Park. Phone 906/228-0460.* On top of a bluff overlooking the site of the first settlement.

Special Events

Arts and Crafts Dockside and St. Ignace Powwow. *Phone 906/643-8717.* Juried show held in conjunction with the Bridge Walk; traditional Native American powwow. Labor Day weekend.

Down Memory Lane Parade and Straits Area Antique Auto Show. *268 Hillcrest Blvd, St. Ignace (49781). Phone 906/643-9402.* Parade features cars, floats, and bands. Vehicles on display and muscle car mania at the auto show. Last Sat in June.

Mackinac Bridge Walk. *Phone 517/347-7891; toll-free 800/434-8642.* The only day each year when walking across the bridge is permitted (some lanes open to motor vehicles). Michigan's governor leads the walk, which begins in St. Ignace at 7 am, on the north side of the bridge, and ends in Mackinaw City, on the south side. Buses return you to your starting point. Labor Day. **FREE**

Limited-Service Hotels

★ BEST WESTERN HARBOUR POINTE LAKEFRONT. *797 N State St, St. Ignace (49781). Phone 906/643-6000; fax 906/643-6946.* 123 rooms, 3 story. Closed Nov-Apr. Complimentary continental breakfast. Check-in 3 pm, check-out 11 am. Indoor pool, outdoor pool, whirlpool. Airport transportation available. **$**

★ DAYS INN. *1067 N State St, St. Ignace (49781). Phone 906/643-8008; toll-free 800/732-9746; fax 906/643-9400. www.daysinn.com.* 119 rooms, 3 story. Complimentary continental breakfast. Check-in 2 pm, check-out 11 am. Indoor pool, whirlpool. Airport transportation available. **$**

★ QUALITY INN. *913 Boulevard Dr, St. Ignace (49781). Phone 906/643-9700; toll-free 800/906-4656; fax 906/643-6762. www.qualityinn.com.* 57 rooms, 2 story. Pets accepted, some restrictions; fee. Complimentary continental breakfast. Check-in 3 pm, check-out 11 am. Indoor pool, whirlpool. **$**

St. Joseph (K-2)

See also New Buffalo, Niles, Stevensville

Population 9,214
Elevation 630 ft
Area Code 269
Zip 49085
Information Cornerstone Chamber Services, 38 W Wall St, PO Box 428, Benton Harbor 49023-0428; phone 269/925-6100
Web Site www.cstonealliance.org

St. Joseph, or "St. Joe," as it's known to locals, was built around the shipping and lumber industries, and many of its 19th-century mansions remain. The well-heeled downtown features fashionable boutiques, art galleries, and cafés. Take a picnic dinner to sandy, beautiful Silver Beach and stay for one of St. Joe's renowned sunsets—prime viewing is at either of the town's two lighthouses.

What to See and Do

Curious Kids' Museum. *415 Lake Blvd, St. Joseph (49085). Phone 269/983-2543. www.curiouskidsmuseum.org.* Interactive museum for children; kids can interact with such exhibits as balloon flying and apple picking and can even run their own TV station. (Wed-Sat 10 am-5 pm, Sun noon-5 pm) **$**

Deer Forest. *6800 Marquette Dr, Coloma (49038). Approximately 12 miles NE via I-94. Phone 269/468-4961; toll-free 800/752-3337.* Approximately 30 acres; more than 500 animals and birds; Story Book Lane, "Santa's Summer Home," train, children's rides, stage events, picnicking. (Memorial Day-Labor Day, daily) **$$**

Krasl Art Center. *707 Lake Blvd, St. Joseph (49085). Phone 269/983-0271. www.krasl.org.* Three galleries house contemporary and traditional works, fine and folk arts, local and major museum collections; art reference library; lectures, tours, films; gift shop. (Mon-Thurs, Sat 10 am-4 pm, Fri 10 am-1 pm, Sun 1-4 pm; closed holidays) **FREE**

Sarett Nature Center. *2300 Benton Center Rd, St. Joseph (49085). Phone 269/927-4832. www.sarett.com.* This bird sanctuary is run by the Michigan Audubon Society and features 350 acres of habitat that birds and people love: beaches, meadows, wooded trails, swamp forests, and marshes. (Tues-Fri 9 am-5 pm, Sat 10 am-5 pm, Sun 1-5 pm)

Warren Dunes State Park. *12032 Red Arrow Hwy, Sawyer (49125). 14 miles S via Hwy 63 and I-94. Phone 269/426-4013.* On 1,499 acres on Lake Michigan. Swimming, beach house; hiking, picnicking, playground, concession, camping, cabins. 200 acres of virgin forest in Warren Woods. (Daily) **$$**

Special Events

Blossomtime Festival. *151 E Napier Ave, St. Joseph (49022). Phone 269/926-7397.* A spring salute to agriculture, industry, and recreation in southwest Michigan; Blessing of the Blossoms; Blossomtime Ball, Grand Floral Parade. Early May.

Krasl Art Fair. *Lake Bluff Park, St. Joseph (49085). Phone 269/983-0271.* One of the major art shows in the state. Second weekend in July.

Sailing Festival. *Phone 269/985-1111.* This family festival features music, horse-drawn trolley rides, food booths, arts and crafts, and more. Labor Day weekend.

Venetian Festival. *305 Lake Blvd, St. Joseph (49085). Phone 269/983-7917.* Boat parades, fireworks, concerts, land and water contests, races, sandcastle sculptures, food booths, photography competition. Mid-July.

Limited-Service Hotels

★ ★ BEST VALUE INN. *2860 Hwy 139 S, Benton Harbor (54547). Phone 269/925-3234; toll-free 888/315-2378; fax 269/925-6131. www.bestvalueinn.com.* 150 rooms, 2 story. Pets accepted. Check-out 11 am. Restaurant, bar. Fitness room. Indoor pool, outdoor pool, whirlpool. **$**

★ BEST WESTERN TWIN CITY INN & SUITES. *1598 Mall Dr, Benton Harbor (49022). Phone 269/925-1880; toll-free 800/780-7234; fax 269/925-0164. www.bestwestern.com.* 52 rooms, 2 story. Pets accepted, some restrictions; fee. Complimentary continental breakfast. Check-in 3 pm, check-out 11 am. Indoor pool, whirlpool. **$**

★ ★ THE BOULEVARD INN. *521 Lake Blvd, St. Joseph (49085). Phone 269/983-6600; toll-free 800/875-6600; fax 269/983-0520. www.theboulevardinn.com.* 85 rooms, 7 story, all suites. Complimentary continental breakfast. Check-out noon. High-speed Internet access. Restaurant, bar. Business center. **$**

Stevensville (K-2)

See also St. Joseph

Population 1,191
Elevation 635 ft
Area Code 269
Zip 49127
Information Village of Stevensville, 5768 St. Joseph Ave; phone 269/429-1802
Web Site www.stevensville.org

Stevensville, located on Lake Michigan south of St. Joseph, is known for its unique shopping and dining, interesting art galleries, and pristine beaches. The town also hosts an annual festival in June that includes a historic walk of approximately three dozen of the town's well-preserved homes.

Tawas City (F-5)

See also East Tawas, Oscoda

Population 2,009
Elevation 587 ft
Area Code 989
Zip 48763
Information Tawas Area Chamber of Commerce, 402 Lake St, PO Box 608, 48764; phone 989/362-8643 or toll-free 800/558-2927
Web Site www.tawas.com

In Tawas (TAO-wass) City and sister-city East Tawas, summer days along Lake Huron are slow and comfortable. Take in quaint shops, grab a bite at a café or ice cream shop, and walk barefoot on the sandy beach. Anglers celebrate their sport with both a winter and a summer festival, while bird-watchers gather in spring and fall to watch the migratory stops of warblers and other songbirds.

Special Events

Perchville USA. *Phone 989/362-8643.* Perch fishing festival featuring parade, fishing contests, softball. First weekend in Feb.

Tawas Bay Waterfront Art Show. *Tawas City Park, 443 W Lake St, Tawas City (48763). Phone 989/362-8643.* More than 200 professional and amateur artists display art and craftwork; juried show. First weekend in Aug.

Limited-Service Hotel

★ ★ TAWAS BAY HOLIDAY INN RESORT. *300 E Bay St, East Tawas (48730). Phone 989/362-8601; toll-free 800/336-8601; fax 989/362-5111. www.tawasholidayinn.com.* 103 rooms, 2 story. Check-in 4 pm, check-out 11 am. Restaurant, two bars. Children's activity center. Fitness room. Beach. Indoor pool, whirlpool. Business center. **$**

Three Rivers (K-3)

See also Battle Creek, Kalamazoo

Population 7,413
Elevation 810 ft
Area Code 269
Zip 49093
Information Three Rivers Area Chamber of Commerce, 57 N Main St; phone 269/278-8193
Web Site www.trchamber.com

The historic, tastefully restored downtown area of Three Rivers is listed on the National Register of Historic Places and features exceptional Victorian architecture. In addition to viewing the buildings themselves, stop in the quaint shops, galleries, and studios located throughout the Three Rivers streetscape.

What to See and Do

Swiss Valley Ski Area. *Patterson Hill Rd, Jones (49061). 10 miles W on Hwy 60, then N on Patterson Hill Rd. Phone 269/244-5635. www.skiswissvalley.com.* Two quad, triple chairlift, four rope tows; patrol, school, rentals, ski shop, snowmaking; NASTAR; restaurant, cafeteria, bar. Vertical drop 225 feet. Night skiing. (Dec-Mar, daily) **$$$$**

Specialty Lodgings

The following lodging establishments are approved by Mobil Travel Guide, but due to their unique and individualized nature have not been given a traditional Mobil Star rating. Included in this listing you may find bed-and-breakfasts, limited-service inns, guest ranches, and other unique hotel properties.

MENDON COUNTRY INN. *440 W Main St, Mendon (49072). Phone 269/496-8132; toll-free 800/304-3366; fax 269/496-8132. www.rivercountry.com/mci.* Built in 1843; antiques. 18 rooms, 2 story. Children over 12 years only. Complimentary continental breakfast. Check-in 3 pm, check-out 11 am. **$**

SANCTUARY AT WILDWOOD. *58138 N Hwy 40, Jones (49061). Phone 269/244-5910; toll-free 800/249-5910. www.sanctuaryatwildwood.com.* 11 rooms, 2 story. Complimentary continental breakfast. Check-in 3 pm, check-out 11 am. High-speed Internet access. **$$**

Traverse City (F-3)

See also Beulah, Cadillac, Charlevoix, Glen Arbor, Interlochen, Leland, Sleeping Bear Dunes National Lakeshore

Settled 1847
Population 15,155
Elevation 600 ft
Area Code 231
Information Traverse City Convention and Visitors Bureau, 101 W Grandview Pkwy, 49684; phone 231/947-1120 or toll-free 800/872-8377
Web Site www.mytraversecity.com

A 1-acre cherry orchard, planted here in the 1880s, has multiplied to such an extent that today the entire region produces more than 75 million pounds of cherries a year. Traverse (TRAV-ers) City is now one of the largest cherry-marketing cities in the country, as well as a year-round resort. The city's beaches are legendary, and the views of Lake Michigan's Grand Traverse Bay are breathtaking. There are six ski areas within 35 miles of town. More than 30 public and private golf courses are also found in the area.

What to See and Do

Clinch Park. *181 E Grandview Pkwy, Traverse City (49684). Grandview Pkwy and Cass St. Phone 231/922-4904 (zoo).* Zoo and aquarium featuring animals native to Michigan (mid-Apr-Nov, daily). Con Foster Museum has exhibits on local history, Native American and pioneer life, and folklore (Memorial Day-Labor Day, daily). Steam train rides; marina (May-Oct). Some fees. Docked in marina is

Schooner *Madeline*. *Phone 231/946-2647.* Full-scale replica of 1850s Great Lakes sailing ship. Original *Madeline* served as first school in Grand Traverse region. Tours (early May-late Sept, Wed-Sun afternoons).

Dennos Art Center. *1701 E Front St, Traverse City (49686). On campus of Northwestern Michigan College. Phone 231/995-1055.* Three galleries; including one of the largest collections of Inuit art in the Midwest. (Daily)

Hickory Hills. *2000 Randolph St, Traverse City (49684). 2 miles W of Division St (Hwy 31) on Randolph Rd. Phone 231/947-8566.* Five rope tows; snowmaking, patrol; snack bar. Vertical drop 250 feet. (Mid-Dec-mid-Mar, daily; closed Jan 1, Dec 25) Lighted cross-country trails (fee). **$$$**

L. Mawby Vineyards/Winery. *4519 S Elm Valley Rd, Sutton Bay (49682). 7 miles N via Hwy 22 toward Suttons Bay, then 1 mile W on Hilltop Rd, 1/4 mile N on Elm Valley Rd. Phone 231/271-3522.* Wine tasting. Guided tours (May-Oct, Thurs-Sat; by appointment only). **FREE**

Scenic drive. *N on Hwy 37.* Extends length of Old Mission Peninsula. At tip is the midway point between the North Pole and the Equator (the 45th parallel). On it stands the Old Mission Lighthouse, one of the first built on the Great Lakes.

Sugar Loaf Resort. *4500 Sugar Loaf Mountain Rd, Cedar (49621). 7 miles W on Hwy 72, then 11 miles NW on County 651, follow signs. Phone 231/228-5461; toll-free 800/952-6390.* Triple, five double chairlifts, three surface lifts; rentals, school, snowmaking; 20 slopes; snowboarding; 17 miles of groomed and tracked cross-country trails. Night skiing. (Dec-Mar, daily) Three restaurants, two bars, entertainment. Vertical drop 500 feet. Kids Klub for children, nursery. 18-hole golf; mountain biking (rentals). **$$$$**

Tall Ship *Malabar*. *13390 S West-Bay Shore Dr, Traverse City (49684). Phone 231/941-2000.* Tours of the classic topsail schooner (late May-early Oct, four times daily). Bed-and-breakfast lodging. **$$$$**

Special Events

Downtown Traverse City Art Fair. *100 E Front St, Traverse City (49684). Phone 231/264-8202.* More than 100 artists participate in this juried art fair featuring painting, jewelry, photography, weaving, pottery, glassworks, and sculpture. Late Aug.

Mesick Mushroom Festival. *10798 Maple Rd, Traverse City (49684). Phone 231/885-2679.* Carnival, rodeo, baseball tournament, flea market, music, parade, mushroom contest, food wagons. Second weekend in May.

National Cherry Festival. *108 W Grandview Pkwy, Traverse City (49684). Phone 231/947-1120. www.cherryfestival.org.* More than 150 activities, including pageants, parades, concerts, road race, fireworks, air show, Native American powwow and crafts, children's contests. Early July.

Limited-Service Hotels

★ BAYSHORE RESORT. *833 E Front St, Traverse City (49686). Phone 231/935-4400; toll-free 800/634-4401; fax 231/935-0262. www.bayshore-resort.com.* 120 rooms, 4 story. Complimentary continental breakfast. Check-out 11 am. High-speed Internet access. Fitness room. Indoor pool, whirlpool. Airport transportation available. **$**

★ DAYS INN. *420 Munson Ave, Traverse City (49686). Phone 231/941-0208; toll-free 800/982-3297; fax 231/941-7521. www.daysinn.com.* 182 rooms, 2 story. Complimentary continental breakfast. Check-out 11 am. Indoor pool, whirlpool. Airport transportation available. **$**

★ GRAND BEACH RESORT HOTEL. *1683 N Hwy 31 N, Traverse City (49686). Phone 231/938-4455; toll-free 800/968-1992; fax 231/938-4435. www.grandbeach.com.* 95 rooms, 3 story. Complimentary continental breakfast. Check-out 11 am. Fitness room. Beach. Indoor pool, whirlpool. **$**

★ ★ HOLIDAY INN. *615 E Front St, Traverse City (49686). Phone 231/947-3700; toll-free 800/888-8020; fax 231/947-0361. www.holiday-inn.com.* 179 rooms, 4 story. Pets accepted, some restrictions; fee. Check-in 4 pm, check-out 11 am. High-speed Internet access. Restaurant. Fitness room. Indoor pool, whirlpool. Airport transportation available. **$$**

★ ★ PARK PLACE HOTEL. *300 E State St, Traverse City (49684). Phone 231/946-5000; toll-free 800/748-0133; fax 231/946-2772. www.park-place-hotel.com.* Restored to 1930s appearance; Victorian décor. 140 rooms, 10 story. Check-out 11 am. Restaurant, bar. Fitness room. Indoor pool, whirlpool. Airport transportation available. **$**

★ SUGAR BEACH RESORT HOTEL. *1773 Hwy 31 N, Traverse City (49686). Phone 231/938-0100; toll-free 800/509-1995; fax 231/938-0200.* 95 rooms, 3 story. Complimentary continental breakfast. Check-out 11 am. Fitness room. Indoor pool, whirlpool. **$**

★ TRAVERSE BAY INN. *2300 Hwy 31 N, Traverse City (49686). Phone 231/938-2646; toll-free 800/968-2646; fax 231/938-5845. www.traversebayinn.com.* 24 rooms, 2 story. Pets accepted, some restrictions; fee. Check-out 11 am. Beach. Outdoor pool, whirlpool. **$**

Full-Service Hotel

★ ★ ★ GREAT WOLF LODGE. *3575 N Hwy 31 S, Traverse City (49684). Phone 231/941-3600; toll-free 866/478-9653. www.greatwolflodge.com.* 300 rooms, all suites. Check-in 4 pm, check-out 11 am. Two restaurants, bar. Fitness room. Indoor pool, outdoor pool, children's pool, whirlpool. **$$$**

Full-Service Resorts

★ ★ CRYSTAL MOUNTAIN RESORT. *12500 Crystal Mountain Dr, Thompsonville (49683). Phone 231/378-2000; toll-free 800/968-9686; fax 231/378-2998. www.crystalmountain.com.* A great vacation spot, this premier resort has plenty to offer in all seasons. Guests can come for great snowskiing in the winter or mountain biking and water recreations in the summer and choose from many luxurious lodging options. 230 rooms, 3 story. Check-in 5 pm, check-out noon. Restaurant, bar. Children's activity center. Fitness room. Indoor pool, outdoor pool, whirlpool. Golf, 36 holes. Tennis. Airport transportation available. Business center. **$**

★ ★ ★ GRAND TRAVERSE RESORT AND SPA. *100 Grand Traverse Village Blvd, Acme (49610). Phone 231/938-2100; toll-free 800/748-0303; fax 231/938-3859. www.grandtraverseresort.com.* The majestic beauty of the area will leave guests relaxed and invigorated, as will the spa. 660 rooms, 17 story. Check-in 11 am, check-out noon. Restaurant, bar. Children's activity center. Fitness room. Indoor pool, outdoor pool. Golf, 54 holes. Tennis. Airport transportation available. Business center. **$$**

Restaurants

★ **AUNTIE PASTA'S.** *2030 S Airport Rd, Traverse City (49684). Phone 231/941-8147; fax 231/941-8301. www.michiganmenu.com.* Italian menu. Lunch, dinner. Bar. Children's menu. Casual attire. Outdoor seating. **$$**

★ ★ ★ **BOWERS HARBOR INN.** *13512 Peninsula Dr, Traverse City (49686). Phone 231/223-4333; fax 231/223-4228.* This historic converted family mansion overlooks Grand Traverse Bay, and serves such favorites as fish in a bag, rack of lamb, lobster tails, steaks, and seafood in a fine dining atmosphere, accompanied by an extensive wine list. American menu. Dinner. Closed Thanksgiving, Dec 24-25. Bar. Children's menu. Casual attire. Valet parking. Outdoor seating. **$$$**

★ ★ **REFLECTIONS.** *2061 Hwy 31 N, Traverse City (49686). Phone 231/938-2321; fax 231/938-9711. www.waterfrontinntc.com.* American menu. Dinner. Closed Thanksgiving, Dec 24-25. Bar. Children's menu. Casual attire. **$$**

★ **SCHELDE'S.** *714 Munson Ave, Traverse City (49686). Phone 231/946-0981; fax 231/946-2807.* American menu. Dinner. Closed Thanksgiving, Dec 24-25. Bar. Children's menu. Casual attire. **$$**

★ ★ ★ **WINDOWS.** *7677 S West Bay Shore Dr, Traverse City (49684). Phone 231/941-0100; fax 231/941-4963.* Just a few miles north of Traverse City, this restaurant, set on Grand Traverse Bay, offers seafood, lamb, and duck, as well as an extensive wine list. Save room for their rich homemade desserts such as truffles and ice cream. American, French menu. Dinner. Closed Dec 25; also Mon (Sept-May) and Sun (Nov-May). Children's menu. Casual attire. Outdoor seating. **$$$**

Troy (J-6)

See also Bloomfield Hills, Detroit, Pontiac, Warren

Settled 1820
Population 72,884
Elevation 670 ft
Area Code 248
Information Chamber of Commerce, 4555 Investment Dr, Suite 300, 48098; phone 248/641-8151
Web Site www.troychamber.com

The year 1819 saw the first land grants in the area that were eventually to become Troy. By 1837, the city was becoming a center for trade between Detroit and Pontiac; today, Troy is the home of many large corporations.

What to See and Do

Troy Museum and Historical Village. *60 W Wattles Rd, Troy (48098). 1 mile NE of I-75, Big Beaver Rd exit. Phone 248/524-3570.* Village museum includes an 1820 log cabin, the 1832 Caswell House, the 1877 Poppleton School, an 1880 general store, an 1890 blacksmith shop, and a 1900 print shop; exhibits, displays. (Tues-Sun; closed holidays) **FREE**

Limited-Service Hotels

★ ★ **COURTYARD BY MARRIOTT.** *1525 E Maple Rd, Troy (48083). Phone 248/528-2800; toll-free 800/321-2211; fax 248/528-0963. www.courtyard.com.* 147 rooms, 3 story. Check-in 3 pm, check-out noon. High-speed Internet access. Fitness room. Indoor pool, whirlpool. Business center. **$**

★ ★ **EMBASSY SUITES.** *850 Tower Dr, Troy (48098). Phone 248/879-7500; toll-free 800/362-2779; fax 248/879-9139. www.embassysuites.com.* 251 rooms, 8 story, all suites. Check-in 3 pm, check-out noon. Restaurant, bar. Fitness room. Indoor pool, whirlpool. **$**

★ **FAIRFIELD INN.** *32800 Stephenson Hwy, Madison Heights (48071). Phone 248/588-3388; toll-free 800/228-2800; fax 248/588-5727. www.fairfieldinn.com.* 121 rooms, 3 story. Complimentary continental breakfast. Check-in 3 pm, check-out noon. High-speed Internet access, wireless Internet access. Outdoor pool. **$**

★ **HAMPTON INN.** *32420 Stephenson Hwy, Madison Heights (48071). Phone 248/585-8881; toll-free 800/426-7866; fax 248/585-9446. www.hamptoninn.com.* 124 rooms, 4 story. Complimentary continental breakfast. Check-in 3 pm, check-out noon. Fitness room. **$**

★★ **SOMERSET INN.** *2601 W Big Beaver Rd, Troy (48084). Phone 248/643-7800; toll-free 800/228-8769; fax 248/643-2220. www.somersetinn.com.* 250 rooms, 13 story. Check-in 3 pm, check-out noon. Restaurant, bar. Fitness room. Outdoor pool. Golf, 9 holes. Business center. **$$**

Full-Service Hotels

★★★ **HILTON NORTHFIELD.** *5500 Crooks Rd, Troy (48098). Phone 248/879-2100; toll-free 800/774-1500; fax 248/879-6054. www.hilton.com.* 185 rooms, 3 story. Pets accepted, some restrictions. Check-in 3 pm, check-out noon. High-speed Internet access. Restaurant, bar. Fitness room. Indoor pool. Business center. **$$**

★★★ **MARRIOTT DETROIT TROY.** *200 W Big Beaver Rd, Troy (48084). Phone 248/680-9797; toll-free 800/228-9290; fax 248/680-9774. www.marriott.com.* 350 rooms, 17 story. Check-in 3 pm, check-out noon. High-speed Internet access. Restaurant, bar. Fitness room. Indoor pool, whirlpool. **$$**

Restaurants

★★ **MON JIN LAU.** *1515 E Maple Rd, Troy (48083). Phone 248/689-2332; fax 248/689-6407. www.monjinlau.com.* American, Asian menu. Lunch, dinner. Closed Thanksgiving, Dec 25. Bar. **$$**

★★ **PICANO'S.** *3775 Rochester Rd, Troy (48083). Phone 248/689-8050; fax 248/689-4360.* Italian menu. Lunch, dinner. Closed holidays. Bar. Valet parking. **$$**

Wakefield (B-4)

See also Ironwood

Population 2,318
Elevation 1,550 ft
Area Code 906
Zip 49968
Web Site www.westernup.com/wakefld.html

Located at the far western tip of the Upper Peninsula, Wakefield is a quintessential UP town, with plenty of winter sports to enjoy, including downhill and cross-country skiing, snowmobiling, snowshoeing, ice fishing, skating, and pick-up hockey. Sunday Lake provides summer fun as well.

What to See and Do

Indianhead Mountain-Bear Creek Ski Resort. *500 Indianhead Rd, Wakefield (49968). 1 mile W on Hwy 2, then 1 mile N. Phone 906/229-5181; toll-free 800/346-3426. www.indianheadmtn.com.* Quad, triple, three double chairlifts; Pomalift, two T-bars; beginner's lift; patrol, school, rentals; NASTAR (daily), snowmaking; lodge, restaurants, cafeterias, bars, nursery. Longest run 1 mile; vertical drop 638 feet. (Nov-mid-Apr, daily) **$$$$**

Warren (J-6)

See also Bloomfield Hills, Detroit, St. Clair, Troy

Population 144,864
Elevation 615 ft
Area Code 586
Information Chamber of Commerce, 30500 Van Dyke Ave, Suite 118, 48093; phone 586/751-3939
Web Site www.wcschamber.com

Warren, a northern suburb of Detroit, is the third-largest city in Michigan. It is home of the General Motors Technical Center, designed by Eero Saarinen, as well as other offices of many large automotive manufacturers. A small farmland community until the 1930s, Warren erupted almost overnight when General Electric's Carboloy Division established a factory in the area. Soon other major manufacturers set up plants in Warren and the city boomed.

Limited-Service Hotels

★★ **BEST WESTERN GEORGIAN INN.** *31327 Gratiot Ave, Roseville (48066). Phone 586/294-0400; toll-free 800/446-1866; fax 586/294-1020. www.bestwestern.com.* 111 rooms, 2 story. Pets accepted, some restrictions; fee. Check-in 3 pm, check-out 11 am. Restaurant, bar. Fitness room. Outdoor pool. **$**

★★ **BEST WESTERN STERLING INN.** *34911 Van Dyke Ave, Sterling Heights (48312). Phone 586/979-1400; toll-free 800/953-1400; fax 586/979-0430. www.sterlinginn.com.* 250 rooms, 3 story. Check-in 3 pm, check-out 11 am. Restaurant, bar. Fitness room. Indoor pool, whirlpool. Business center. **$$**

★★ **COURTYARD BY MARRIOTT.** *30190 Van Dyke Ave, Warren (48093). Phone 586/751-5777; toll-free 800/321-2211; fax 586/751-4463. www.courtyard.com.* 147 rooms, 3 story. Check-in 3 pm, check-out noon. High-speed Internet access. Fitness room. Indoor pool, whirlpool. **$**

★ **HOLIDAY INN EXPRESS.** *11500 E 11 Mile Rd, Warren (48089). Phone 586/754-9700; toll-free 800/465-4329; fax 586/754-0376. www.holiday-inn.com.* 125 rooms, 2 story. Complimentary continental breakfast. Check-in 3 pm, check-out noon. High-speed Internet access. Outdoor pool. **$**

Restaurant

★★ **ANDIAMO ITALIA.** *7096 E 14 Mile Rd, Warren (48092). Phone 586/268-3200; fax 586/268-3224. www.andiamoitalia.com.* Italian menu. Lunch, dinner. Closed holidays. Bar. Valet parking. **$$**

Whitehall (H-2)

See also Muskegon

Population 3,027
Elevation 593 ft
Area Code 231
Zip 49461
Information White Lake Area Chamber of Commerce, 124 W Hanson St; phone 231/893-4585 or toll-free 800/879-9702
Web Site www.whitelake.org

Whitehall and its sister city, Montague, sit about 5 miles off Lake Michigan, on White Lake. Both are unpretentious, slow-paced towns with soda fountains and delightful shops, and both offer excellent opportunities for canoeing and bird-watching on the White River.

What to See and Do

Montague City Museum. *Church and Meade sts, Montague (49461). N on Hwy 31 Business. Phone 231/894-6813.* History of lumbering era, artifacts; displays on Montague resident Nancy Ann Fleming, who was Miss America 1961. (June-Aug, Sat-Sun) **DONATION**

White River Light Station Museum. *6199 Murray Rd, Whitehall (49461). S of the channel on White Lake. Phone 231/894-8265.* The museum is located in an 1875 lighthouse made of Michigan limestone and brick; ship relics and artifacts include binnacle, ship's helm, chronograph, compasses, sextant, charts, models, photographs, paintings. View of Lake Michigan's sand dunes along coastline. (Memorial Day-Labor Day: Tues-Sun; Sept: weekends) **$$**

World's Largest Weather Vane. *Just S of town on Hwy 31 Business, at edge of White Lake.* This 48-foot-tall structure weighs 4,300 pounds and is topped with a model of the lumber schooner *Ella Ellenwood* that once traveled the Great Lakes. Trademark of Whitehall Products Ltd, the company that created it, the vane is mentioned in the *Guinness Book of Records.*

Special Events

Summer Concert Series. *124 W Hanson St, Whitehall (49461). Also, White Lake Music Shell, Launch Ramp Rd, in Montague (49461). Phone 231/893-4585.* Grab a blanket or lawn chair and enjoy the sounds of jazz, folk, country, and swing music. Every Tues in mid-June-late Aug.

White Lake Arts & Crafts Festival. *Funnel Field, Whitehall. Phone 231/893-4585.* 150 exhibitors. Father's Day weekend.

Ypsilanti (J-5)

See also Ann Arbor, Dearborn, Detroit Metropolitan Airport Area

Settled 1823
Population 24,846
Elevation 720 ft
Area Code 734
Zip 48197
Information Ypsilanti Area Visitors and Convention Bureau, 301 W Michigan Ave, Suite 101; phone 734/482-4920
Web Site www.ypsichamber.org

Home to Eastern Michigan University, Ypsilanti (IP-si-lanty) was established as a Native American trading post and later named for a young Greek patriot, Demetrius Ypsilanti. The city had stations on the Underground Railroad before the Civil War and today still demonstrates many fine examples of Greek Revival architecture. A two-block area, known as Depot Town, has renovated 150-year-old houses and storefronts, as well as antique shops and restaurants; in late July, Depot Town hosts the Summer Beer Festival.

What to See and Do

Eastern Michigan University. *202 Welch Hall, Ypsilanti (48197). Phone 734/487-1849. www.emich.edu.* (1849) (25,000 students) The university is home to Quirk/Sponberg Dramatic Arts Theaters, Pease Auditorium, Bowen Field House, Rynearson Stadium, Olds Student Recreation Center; Ford Art Gallery with changing exhibits (Mon-Sat; phone 734/487-1268; free); Intermedia Art Gallery (free). Tours (by appointment) depart from historic Starkweather Hall. (Daily)

Ford Lake Park. *9075 S Huron River Dr, Ypsilanti (48197). Phone 734/485-6880.* This park offers fishing, boating (launch; fee); volleyball, tennis, and handball courts; horseshoes, softball field, four picnic shelters. (Daily; some fees May-Sept) **$$**

Ypsilanti Historical Museum. *220 N Huron St, Ypsilanti (48197). Phone 734/482-4990. www.ypsilantihistoricalmuseum.org.* Victorian house with 11 rooms, including a special children's room and craft room; exhibits. Ypsilanti Historical Archives are located here and are open for research pertaining to local history and genealogy. (Thurs, Sat-Sun 2-4 pm) **DONATION**

Ypsilanti Monument and Water Tower. *Cross and Washtenaw sts, Ypsilanti (48197).* Marble column with a bust of Demetrius Ypsilanti, Greek patriot. Century-old water tower.

Special Events

Summer Beer Festival. *Depot Town, Ypsilanti (48197). Phone 734/483-4444. www.michiganbrewersguild.org.* At this festival, eat, dance, and sample 100 different beers from more than 35 breweries. Local brewers dish the dirt on beer-making techniques. Late July.

Ypsilanti Heritage Festival. *Riverside Park, 106 W Michigan Ave, Ypsilanti (48197). Phone 734/483-4444.* Classic cars, arts and crafts, 18th-century encampment, jazz competition, and continuous entertainment. Third full weekend in Aug.

Restaurant

★★ **HAAB'S.** *18 W Michigan Ave, Ypsilanti (48197). Phone 734/483-8200; fax 734/483-9676.* Building dates from the 19th-century. American menu. Lunch, dinner. Closed Dec 25. Bar. Children's menu. **$$**

Side Trips

From Michigan, it's easy to cross the border to see the possibilities Canada has to offer. Take a few days to explore the cosmopolitan city of Toronto, or spend a few hours taking in the many gardens or casinos in Windsor. Or maybe a dinner cruise in Sault Ste. Marie is more your speed. Whichever activities you enjoy, chances are you can find them in Canada.

Sault Ste. Marie, ON

1 1/2 hours, 88 miles from Mackinaw City, MI

Population 83,300
Elevation 580 ft (177 m)
Area Code 705
Information Chamber of Commerce, 334 Bay St, P6A 1X1; phone 705/949-7152
Web Site www.ssmcoc.com

Founded and built on steel, Sault Ste. Marie is separated from its sister city in Michigan by the St. Mary's River. Lake and ocean freighters traverse the river, which links Lake Huron and Lake Superior—locally known as "the Soo."

What to See and Do

Agawa Canyon Train Excursion. *Phone 705/946-7300; toll-free 800/242-9287. www.agawacanyontourtrain.com.* A scenic day trip by Algoma Central Railway through a wilderness of hills and fjordlike ravines. Two-hour stopover at the canyon. Dining car on train. (June-mid-Oct: daily; Jan-Mar: weekends only) Advance ticket orders available by phone. **$$$$**

Boat cruises. *65 Foster Dr, Sault Ste. Marie (P6A 1X1). Phone 705/253-9850.* Two-hour boat cruises from Norgoma dock, next to Holiday Inn on MV *Chief Shingwauk* and MV *Bon Soo* through American locks; also three-hour dinner cruises. (June-mid-Oct) Contact Lock Tours Canada, PO Box 424, P6A 5M1. **$$$$**

Sault Ste. Marie Museum. *690 Queen St, Sault Ste. Marie (P6A 2A4). Phone 705/759-7278.* Local and national exhibits in a structure originally built as a post office. Skylight Gallery traces history of the region dating back 9,000 years; includes prehistoric artifacts, displays of early industries, re-creation of 1912 Queen Street house interiors. Durham Gallery displays traveling exhibits from the Royal Ontario Museum and locally curated displays. Discovery Gallery for children features hands-on exhibits. (Daily; closed holidays)

Special Events

Algoma Fall Festival. *Algoma Festival Office, 224 Queen St E, Sault Ste. Marie (P6A 1Y8). Phone 705/949-0822. www.algomafallfestival.com.* Visual and performing arts presentations by Canadian and international artists. Late Sept-late Oct. **$$$$**

Ontario Winter Carnival Bon Soo. *269 Queen St E, Sault Ste. Marie (P6A 1Y8). Phone 705/759-3000.* Features more than 100 events: fireworks, fiddle contest, winter sports, polar bear swim, winter playground sculptured from snow. Last weekend in Jan-first weekend in Feb.

Limited-Service Hotels

★ ★ ALGOMAS WATER TOWER INN. *360 Great Northern Rd, Sault Ste. Marie (P6A 5N3). Phone 705/949-8111; toll-free 800/461-0800; fax 705/949-1912. www.watertowerinn.com.* Take a stroll through the waterfall garden and enjoy the beautiful outdoors. 180 rooms, 5 story. Pets accepted. Check-out noon. Restaurant, bar. Fitness room. Indoor pool, children's pool, whirlpool. Airport transportation available. **$**

★ ★ HOLIDAY INN. *208 St. Mary's River Dr, Sault Ste. Marie (P6A 5V4). Phone 705/949-0611; toll-free 888/713-8482; fax 705/945-6972. www.holiday-inn.com.* 195 rooms, 9 story. Pets accepted. Check-out 4 pm. Restaurant, bar. Fitness room. Indoor pool, whirlpool. Airport transportation available. **$**

Restaurants

★ GIOVANNI'S. *516 Great Northern Rd, Sault Ste. Marie (P6B 4Z9). Phone 705/942-3050; fax 705/942-3980. www.giovannisfamilyrestaurant.com.* Italian

Toronto Theater

Theater buffs won't suffer for lack of culture while visiting Toronto. The city has a diverse and lively performing arts scene with something for everyone, from Broadway musicals to stand-up comedy and opera to dance. Toronto has the status of third-largest theater center in the English-speaking world, after London and New York.

There are performance venues throughout the city; however, three areas contain the largest concentration of theater activity. The downtown Entertainment District contains larger venues hosting touring or more lavish productions. Venues include the Canon, Royal Alexandra, Princess of Wales, and Elgin & Winter Garden theaters. Roy Thomson Hall and Massey Hall host symphony and choral events. The East End contains several venues on Front Street, east of Younge Street. Here you'll find the Canadian Stage Company, The Lorraine Kisma Theatre of Young Peoples, the St. Lawrence Centre for the Arts, and the city's largest venue, the Hummingbird Centre, home of the National Ballet of Canada and the Canadian Opera Company. The Annex is devoted to mid-size, alternative, and homegrown theater. This is where the Tarragon Theatre, Theatre Passe Muraille, and the Factory Theatre are located. Today, there are more than 90 theater venues in Toronto, and over 200 professional theater and dance companies, producing more than 10,000 live performances a year.

menu. Lunch, dinner. Closed Jan 1, Labour Day, Dec 25. Bar. Children's menu. **$$**

★ ★ **NEW MARCONI.** *480 Albert St W, Sault Ste. Marie (P6A 1C3). Phone 705/759-8250; fax 705/759-0850.* American, Italian menu. Lunch, dinner. Closed Sun; Jan 1, Dec 25. **$$$**

Toronto, ON

4 hours 15 minutes, 381 miles from Detroit, MI

Founded 1793
Population 3,400,000
Elevation 569 ft (173 m)
Area Code 416
Information Convention & Visitors Association, Queens Quay Terminal at Harbourfront, 207 Queens Quay W, M5J 1A7; phone 416/203-2500 or toll-free 800/363-1990
Web Site www.torontotourism.com

Toronto is one of Canada's leading industrial, commercial, and cultural centers. From its location on the shores of Lake Ontario, it has performed essential communications and transportation services throughout Canadian history. Its name derives from the native word for meeting place, as the area was called by the Hurons who led the first European, Etienne Brule, to the spot. In the mid-1800s, the Grand Trunk and Great Western Railroad and the Northern Railway connected Toronto with the upper St. Lawrence; Portland, Maine; and Chicago, Illinois.

After French fur traders from Québec established Fort Rouille in 1749, Toronto became a base for further Canadian settlement. Its population of Scottish, English, and United States emigrants was subject to frequent armed attacks, especially during the War of 1812 and immediately thereafter. From within the United States, the attackers aimed at annexation; from within Canada, they aimed at emancipation from England. One result of these unsuccessful threats was the protective Confederation of Lower Canada, which later separated again as the province of Québec, and Upper Canada, which still later became the province of Ontario with Toronto as its capital.

Toronto today is a cosmopolitan city with many intriguing features. Once predominantly British, the population is now exceedingly multicultural—the United Nations deemed Toronto the world's most ethnically diverse city in 1989. A major theater center with many professional playhouses, including the Royal Alexandra Theatre, Toronto is also a major banking center, with several architecturally significant banks. Good shopping can be found throughout the city, but Torontonians are most proud of their Underground City, a series of subterranean malls linking more than 300 shops and restaurants in the downtown area. For professional sports fans, Toronto offers the Maple Leafs (hockey), the Blue Jays (baseball), the Raptors (basketball), and the Argonauts (football). A visit to the Harbourfront, a boat tour to the islands, or enjoying an evening on the town should round out your stay in Toronto.

Additional Visitor Information

For further information contact Tourism Toronto, Queens Quay Terminal at Harbourfront, 207 Queens Quay W, M5J 1A7; phone 416/203-2500 or toll-free 800/363-1990 (US and Canada). Toronto's public transportation system is extensive and includes buses, subways, streetcars, and trolley buses; for maps phone 416/393-4636.

Public Transportation

Airport Toronto Pearson International Airport

Information Phone 416/776-3000

Web Site www.lbpia.toronto.on.ca

Airlines Aeroflot Russian, Aeromexico, Aerosvit Airlines, Air Canada, Air Canada Jazz, Air France, Air Jamaica, Air New Zealand, Air Transat, Alaska Airlines, Alitalia, All Nippon Airways, Allegro, American Airlines, American Eagle, America West Airlines, Atlantic Southeast, Austrian Airlines, British Airways, British Midland Airways (BMI), BWIA International, CanJet Airlines, Cathay Pacific, Comair, Continental Airlines, Continental Express, Cubana Airlines, Czech Airlines, Delta Air Lines, EL AL Israel, Finnair, HMY Airlines, Japan Air Lines, Jetsgo, KLM Royal Dutch Airlines, Korean Airlines, LanChile, LOT Polish Airline, LTU International Airways, Lufthansa, Malev Hungarian, Martinair Holland, Mesa Airlines, Mexicana Airlines, Midway Airlines, Midwest Connect, MyTravel Airways, Northwest Airlines, Olympic Airways, Pakistan International, Piedmont PSA Airlines, Qantas, Royal Jordanian, SAS Scandinavian Airlines, SATA Express, Singapore Airlines, Skyservice Airlines, Skyway Airlines, TACA/ Lacsa Thai International Airways, United Airlines, US Airways, Varig Brazil, Westjet, ZOOM Airlines.

What to See and Do

Art Gallery of Ontario. *317 Dundas St W, Toronto (M5T 1G4). Phone 416/977-0414. www.ago.net.* Changing exhibits of paintings, drawings, sculpture, and graphics from the 14th to 20th centuries include the Henry Moore Collection; a permanent Canadian Collection and Contemporary Galleries; films, lectures, concerts. (Thurs-Fri 10 am-9 pm, Sat-Sun 10 am-5:30 pm; closed Jan 1, Dec 25) Free admission Wed evenings. **$$$**

Bata Shoe Museum. *327 Bloor St W, Toronto (M5S 1W7). Phone 416/979-7799. www.batashoemuseum.ca.* When Mrs. Sonja Bata's passion for collecting historical shoes began to surpass her personal storage space, the Bata family established The Bata Shoe Museum Foundation. Architect Raymond Moriyama's award-winning five-story, 3,900-square-foot (362-square-meter) building now holds more than 10,000 shoes, artfully arranged in four galleries to celebrate the style and function of footwear throughout 4,500 years of history. One permanent exhibition, All About Shoes, showcases a collection of 20th-century celebrity shoes; artifacts on exhibit range from Chinese bound-foot shoes and ancient Egyptian sandals to chestnut-crushing clogs and Elton John's platforms. Talk about standing toe-to-toe with history. (Tues-Sat 10 am-5 pm; Thurs to 8 pm, Sun noon-5 pm; June-Aug: Mon 10 am-5 pm) **$$**

Black Creek Pioneer Village. *1000 Murray Ross Pkwy, Downsview (M3J 2P3). 2 miles (3 kilometers) N on Hwy 400, E on Steeles, then 1/2 mile (1 kilometer) to Jane St. Phone 416/736-1733.* Step back in time to a village in 1860s Ontario, when life was much simpler—if you were hearty enough to handle it. In the village of Black Creek, workers wearing period costumes welcome you into 35 authentically restored homes, workshops, public buildings, and farms, and demonstrate skills such as open-hearth cooking, bread-making, looming, milling, blacksmithing, sewing, and printing. (Hours vary by month; call for schedule; closed Dec 25) **$$$**

Bloor/Yorkville area. *Bounded by Bloor St W, Ave Rd, Davenport Rd, and Yonge St. www.toronto.com.* If the last time you visited Toronto was 30 years ago, and you still have images of flower children handing out flowers on Bloor Street, you're in for a surprise. The barefoot girl who gave you a daisy is now a 40-year-old who shops at the very spot where she used to stand. The Bloor/Yorkville area is one of Toronto's most elegant shopping and dining sections, with art galleries, nightclubs, music, designer couture boutiques, and first-rate art galleries. The area itself is fun to walk around, with a cluster of courtyards and alleyways. There's also a contemporary park in the heart of the neighborhood with a huge piece of granite called The Rock. It was brought here from the Canadian Shield, a U-shaped region of ancient rock covering about half of Canada, causing the first part of North America to be permanently elevated above sea level.

Bruce Trail/Toronto Bruce Trail Club. *Phone 416/763-9061.* Canada's first and longest footpath, the Bruce Trail runs 437 miles (703 kilometers) along the Niagara Escarpment from Niagara to the Bruce Peninsula. It provides the only public access to the Escarpment, a UNESCO World Biosphere Reserve. While the Toronto Bruce Trail Club is the largest and, some say, the best organized of the many biking and hiking clubs in the area, you can contact the Toronto Convention and Visitors Bureau (phone 416/203-2600) for Toronto access and the names of organizations that offer activities on the trail. *Note:* Although the Toronto Bruce Trail Club has members, most of its activities can be attended by the general public. (Call for information on meeting places for hikes.)

Canada's Sports Hall of Fame. *160 Princes' Blvd, Toronto (M6K 3C3). Phone 416/260-6789.* Erected to honor the country's greatest athletes in all major sports, Canada's Sports Hall of Fame features exhibit galleries, a theater, a library, archives, and kiosks that show videos of Canada's greatest moments in sports. Don't miss the Heritage Gallery (lower level), which contains artifacts showcasing the development of 125 years of sport. Also, stop in at the 50-seat Red Foster Theatre, which projects highlights from films that highlight Canadian sports, such as *The Terry Fox Story.* (Mon-Fri 10 am-4:30 pm) **FREE**

Canadian Trophy Fishing. *80 The Boardwalk Way, Suite 320, Markham (L6E 1B8). Docked at Bluffers Park in Scarborough; near the corner of Brimley Rd and Kingston Rd. Phone 905/472-8000. www.cdntrophyfishing.com.* Start working out now; you don't want the fish to win. Chinook salmon might weigh as much as 40 pounds. But for the weaker among us, consider coho salmon, Atlantic salmon, rainbow trout, brown trout, lake trout, whitefish...And it doesn't get much easier than this. Canadian Trophy Fishing supplies the equipment and facilities, will arrange for a fishing license (required), brings equipment and lifejackets, and will even pick you up at your hotel. They suggest you bring a large cooler to take home all of your catches, but for an extra fee they will smoke, fillet, freeze, and ship. Ice fishing season is Jan 1-Mar 15. **$$$$**

Casa Loma. *1 Austin Terrace, Toronto (M5R 1X8). 1 1/2 miles (2 kilometers) NW of downtown. Phone 416/923-1171. www.casaloma.org.* Grab an audio cassette and a floor plan and take a self-guided tour of this domestic castle, built in 1911 over three years at a cost of $3.5 million. As romantic as he was a shrewd businessman, Sir Henry Pellatt—who immediately realized the profitability potential when Thomas Edison developed steam-generated electricity, and founded the Toronto Electric Light company—had an architect create this medieval castle. Soaring battlements, secret passageways, flowerbeds warmed by steam pipes, secret doors, servant's rooms, and an 800-foot (244-meter) tunnel are just some of the treats you'll discover. (Daily 9:30 am-5 pm; closed Jan 1, Dec 25) **$$$** Adjacent is

Spadina Historic House and Garden. *285 Spadina Rd, Toronto (M5R 2V5). Phone 416/392-6910.* Built for financier James Austin and his family, this 50-room house has been restored to its 1866 Victorian glory and is open to those who want to see how the upper most of the city's upper crust spent quiet evenings at home. It's filled with the family's art, artifacts, and furniture, and until 1982 it was filled with the family itself; that's when the last generation of Austins left, and the house was turned over to public ownership. Docents tend to the glorious gardens and orchard, which are open to the public in the summer. Tours are given every 15 minutes. (Jan-Mar: Sat-Sun noon-5 pm; Apr-Dec: Mon-Fri noon-4 pm, Sat-Sun to 5 pm; holidays to 5 pm)

City parks around Toronto. *100 Queen St W, Toronto (M5H 2N2). Phone 416/392-1111.* Listed below arc some of Toronto's many parks. Contact the Department of Parks and Recreation.

Allan Gardens. *19 Horticultural Ave, Toronto (M5A 2P2). W side of Sherbourne St to Jarvis St between Carlton St and Gerrard St E. Phone 416/392-7288.* Indoor/outdoor botanical displays, wading pool, picnicking, concerts. (Daily 10 am-5 pm) **FREE**

Edwards Gardens. *777 Lawrence Ave E, Toronto (M5A 2P2). NE of Downtown, at Leslie Ave E and Lawrence St. Phone 416/392-8186.* Civic garden center; rock gardens, pools, pond, rustic bridges. (Daily) **FREE**

Grange Park. *Dundas and Beverly sts, Toronto (M5H 2N2).* Wading pool, playground. Natural ice rink (winter, weather permitting). (Daily) **FREE**

High Park. *Bloor St W and Keele sts, Toronto (M5H 2N2). Between Bloor St W and The Queensway at Parkside Dr, near lakeshore. Phone 416/392-1111.* If you want a low-key adventure after a few days of sightseeing, High Park is your respite. Financier John T. Colborne, who built the mansion next door, also purchased 160 acres (65 hectares) of land intending to develop a "satellite village" for Toronto. But he couldn't sell his before-his-time concept of a subdivision, so he donated the land to the city. Today, High Park is an urban oasis, with expanses of grasses for sports, picnicking, and cycling; a large lake that freezes in the winter; a small zoo, a swimming pool, tennis courts, and bowling greens. (Daily dawn-dusk) **FREE**

Ice Skating at Grenadier Pond. *Phone 416/392-6916.* One of the most romantic ice skating spots you'll find is Grenadier Pond in High Park, one of 25 parks offering free artificial rinks throughout the city. In addition to vendors selling roasted chestnuts, there's a bonfire to keep Jack Frost from nipping at your nose. Other free ice rinks include Nathan Phillips Square in front of City Hall and an area at Harbourfront Centre. Equipment rentals are available on site. **FREE**

Queen's Park. *College and University, Toronto (M7A 1A2). Queen's Park Crescent. Phone 416/325-7500.* Ontario Parliament Buildings are located in this park. (Daily) **FREE**

Riverdale Park. *Broadway Ave, Toronto (M5H 2N2). Between Danforth Ave and Gerrard St E. Phone 416/392-1111.* Summer: swimming, wading pools; tennis, playgrounds, picnicking, band concerts. Winter: skating; 19th-century farm. (Daily)

Toronto Island Park. *9 Queens Quay, Toronto (M5H 2N2). S across Inner Harbour. Phone 416/392-8186.* Just seven minutes by ferry from Toronto lie 14 beautiful islands ripe for exploration. The land was originally a peninsula, but a series of storms in the mid-1800s caused a part of the land to break off into islands. The three major ones are Centre, Ward's, and Algonquin, with Centre being the busiest. This is partly because it's home to Centreville, an old-fashioned amusement park, with an authentic 1890s carousel, flume ride, turn-of-the-century village complete with a Main Street, tiny shops, a firehouse, and even a small working farm. But the best thing to do on Centre Island or any of the 14, is to rent a bike and explore the 612 acres (248 hectares) of park and shaded paths. Try to get lost; that's half the fun. **FREE**

★ **CN Tower.** *301 Front St W, Toronto (M5V 2T6). Phone 416/868-6937. www.cntower.ca.* Is it the Sears Tower in Chicago? The Petronas Towers in Kuala Lumpur? The Ostankino Tower in Moscow? No. The tallest freestanding structure in the world is Toronto's CN Tower. At 1,815 feet (553 meters) from the ground to the tip of its communications aerial, it towers over the rest of the city. If you'd like to see Toronto from a bluejay's view, take the elevator to the top, where on a clear day it's said you can see the spray coming off Niagara Falls 62 miles (100 kilometers) away. But any level provides spectacular views. Don't miss the ground floor's Tour of the Universe, a multimedia voyage set in 2019 with human guides and robots. (Sun-Thurs 9 am-10 pm, Fri-Sat to 10:30 pm; closed Dec 25) **$$$$** Here is

Colborne Lodge. *Colborne Lodge Dr and The Queensway, Toronto (M5H 2N2). Phone 416/392-6916. www.city.toronto.on.ca/culture/colborne.htm.* The successful 19th-century architect John Howard was just 34 when he completed this magnificent manor, named for the architect's first patron, Upper Canada Lieutenant Governor Sir John Colborne. It stands today as an excellent example of Regency-style architecture, with its stately verandas and lovely placement in a beautiful setting. (Jan-Apr: Sat-Sun noon-4 pm; May-Dec: Tues-Sun noon-5 pm; closed Mon; also Jan 1, Good Friday, Dec 25-26) **$**

Dragon City Shopping Mall. *280 Spadina Ave, Toronto (M5T 3A5). Phone 416/596-8885.* Located in the heart of Chinatown, the Dragon City Shopping Mall consists of more than 30 stores and services that allow you to immerse yourself in Chinese culture. Buy Chinese herbs, look at quality Asian jewelry, browse chic Chinese housewares and gifts, or admire Oriental arts and crafts. After your admiration has grown and your wallet has, perhaps, contracted, treat yourself to a meal at Sky Dragon Cuisine in the Dragon City tower, an upscale Chinese restaurant with a beautiful view of the Toronto skyline. (Daily 10 am-8 pm)

Easy and The Fifth. *225 Richmond W, Toronto (M5V 1W2). Phone 416/979-3000. www.easyandthefifth.com.* A dance club for the over-25 crowd, the music is tango to Top 40, the dress code is upscale casual, and the atmosphere is loft-apartment-open, with two bars and several specialty bars (such as The Green Room, where you can shoot pool, play craps, and smoke a cigar to the accompaniment of live jazz). On Thurs from 6-10 pm, enjoy cocktail hour with a complimentary buffet. (Thurs 6 pm-2 am; Fri-Sat from 9 pm) **$$$**

Eaton Centre. *220 Yonge St, Toronto (M5B 2H1). Phone 416/598-8700. www.torontoeatoncentre.com.* Yes, a shopping mall is Toronto's top tourist attraction. And, with due respect to The Sony Store, The Canadian Naturalist, Groucho's Cigars, Sushi-Q, Baskits, London Style Fish & Chips, and the other 285 shops in the mall, it has to do with more than just goods and services. This 3 million-square-foot (278,709-square-meter) building is a masterpiece of architecture and environment. Its glass roof rises 127 feet (39 meters) above the mall's lowest level. The large, open space contains glass-enclosed elevators, dozens of long, graceful escalators, and porthole windows. A flock of fiberglass Canadian geese floats through the air. Even if it usually makes you break out in hives, this is one window-shopping experience worth making. (Mon-Fri 10 am-9 pm; Sat 9:30 am-7 pm; Sun noon-6 pm)

Elgin & Winter Garden Theatre Centre. *189 Yonge St, Toronto (M5B 1M4). Phone 416/872-5555.* The 80-year history of the two theaters speaks more volumes than one of its excellent productions. Built in 1913, it was designed as a double-decker theater complex with the Winter Garden Theatre built seven stories above the Elgin Theatre. Each theater was a masterpiece in its own right: The Elgin was ornate, with gold leaf, plaster cherubs, and elegant opera boxes; the walls of the Winter Garden were hand-painted to resemble a garden, and its ceiling was a mass of beech bows and twinkling lanterns. Through the years, the stages saw the likes of George Burns and Gracie Allen, Edger Bergen and Charlie McCarthy, Milton Berle, and Sophie Tucker before the complex fell into disrepair. A 2 1/2-year, $30 million restoration began in 1987, and included such things as cleaning the walls of the Winter Garden with hundreds of pounds of raw bread dough to avoid damaging the original hand-painted water color art work. The Ontario Heritage Foundation offers year-round guided tours on Thursdays at 5 pm and Saturdays at 11 am.

Exhibition Place. *Lakeshore St, Toronto (M6K 3C3). S off Gardener Expy, on Lakeshore Blvd. Phone 416/393-6000.* Designed to accommodate the Canadian National Exhibition (see SPECIAL EVENTS), this 350-acre (141-hectare) park has events year-round, as well as the Marine Museum of Upper Canada. (Aug-Sept, daily)

First Canadian Place. *100 King St W, 1 First Canadian Pl, Toronto (M5X 1A9). Phone 416/862-8138. www.firstcanadianplace.com.* If only you worked here. You'd have access to a personal shopper to buy your groceries or pick up that asymmetrical slit skirt; and a concierge to plan your business meetings or take care of entertaining out-of-town CEOs. As it is, you can only take advantage of 120 unique shops and boutiques, unusual restaurants, massage or spa services, and ever-interesting on-going art exhibits. Between 10 am and 2 pm there are special promotions, sidewalk sales, and performances as diverse as Opera Atelier's staging of *The Marriage of Figaro* highlights, to the dancing monks of the Tibetan Dikung Monastery. (Mon-Fri 10 am-6 pm; some shops and restaurants open Sat-Sun)

George R. Gardiner Museum of Ceramic Art. *111 Queen's Park, Toronto (M7A 1A2). Phone 416/586-8080.* One of the world's finest collections of Italian majolica, English Delftware, and 18th-century continental porcelain. (Daily; closed Jan 1, Dec 25) **DONATION**

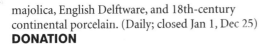

Gibson House. *5172 Yonge St, North York (M2N 5P6). Phone 416/395-7432.* Home of land surveyor and local politician David Gibson; restored and furnished to 1850s style. Costumed interpreters conduct demonstrations. Tours. (Tues-Sun; closed holidays) **$**

Gray Line bus tours. *123 Front St W, Toronto (M5A 4N3). Phone 416/594-3310.*

Harbourfront Centre. *235 Queens Quay W, Toronto (M5J 2G8). Phone 416/973-3000; fax 416/973-6055. www.harbourfront.on.ca.* This 10-acre (4-hectare) waterfront community is alive with theater, dance, films, art shows, music, crafts, and children's programs. Most events are free. (Daily)

Hazelton Lanes. *55 Avenue Rd, Toronto (M5T 3L2). www.hazeltonlanes.com.* Stores that look like movie sets. Stores that sell stunning, $850 gold vermeil, sterling silver, and Swarovski crystal hair clips. Stores that have entire floors devoted to pens. This is Hazelton Lanes, one of Toronto's most exclusive shopping centers, with shops, boutiques, and services designed to turn blood blue. Even if you aren't in the mood (yawn) to buy, take a stroll anyway, and see if you can spot a celeb or two; Whoopi Goldberg, Kate Hudson, Alanis Morrisette, Samuel L. Jackson, and Harrison Ford have all been known to walk by and buy. (Mon-Wed, Fri 10 am-6 pm, Thurs to 7 pm, Sat to 5 pm, Sun noon-5 pm)

Historic Fort York. *100 Garrison Rd, Toronto (M5V 3K9). Phone 416/392-6907. www.city.toronto.on.ca/culture/fort_york.htm.* It may not have seen a lot of action—just one battle during the War of 1812—but Fort York's place in Toronto's history is secure. It is the birthplace of modern Toronto, having played a major role in saving York—now Toronto—from being invaded by 1,700 American soldiers. Today's Fort York has Canada's largest collection of original War of 1812 buildings and is a designated National Historic Site. (Daily; closed Jan 1, last two weeks in Dec) **$$**

Hummingbird Centre for the Performing Arts. *1 Front St E, Toronto (M5E 1B2). Phone 416/393-7469; fax 416/393-7454. www.hummingbirdcentre.com.* Stage presentations of Broadway musicals, dramas, and concerts by international artists. Home of the Canadian Opera Company and National Ballet of Canada. Pre-performance dining; gift shop.

Huronia Historical Parks. *63 miles (101 kilometers) N via Hwy 400, then 34 miles (55 kilometers) N to Midland on Hwy 93. Phone 705/526-7838.* Two living history sites animated by costumed interpreters. (Daily) **$$$** Consists of

Discovery Harbour. *196 Jury St, Penetanguishene (L9M 1G1). Phone 705/549-8064. www.discoveryharbour.on.ca.* Marine heritage center and reconstructed 19th-century British Naval dockyard. Established in 1817, the site includes a 19th-century military base. Now rebuilt, the site features eight furnished buildings and orientation center. Replica of 49-foot (15-meter) British naval schooner, the HMS *Bee;* also HMS *Tecumseth* and *Perseverance.* Costumed interpreters bring the base to life, circa 1830. Sail training and excursions (daily). Audiovisual display; free parking, docking, picnic facilities. Theater; gift shop, restaurant. (Victoria Day-Labor Day: Mon-Fri; after Labor Day-Sept: daily) **$$$**

Ste. Marie among the Hurons. *E of Midland on Hwy 12.* (1639-1649) Reconstruction of 17th-century Jesuit mission that was Ontario's first European community. Twenty-two furnished buildings include native dwellings, workshops, barn, church, cookhouse, hospital. Candlelight tours, canoe excursions. Café features period-inspired meals and snacks. Orientation center, interpretive museum. Free parking and picnic facilities. (Victoria Day weekend-Oct, daily) World-famous Martyrs' Shrine (site of papal visit) is located across the highway. Other area highlights include pioneer museum, replica indigenous village, Wye Marsh Wildlife Centre. **$$$**

Kensington Market. *College St and Spadina Ave, Toronto. Extends from Spadina Ave on the E to Bathurst St to the W, and from Dundas St on the S to College St on the N.* Want to take a trip around the world in a few blocks? It's possible in this maze of narrow streets lined with food shops, vintage clothing stores, restaurants, and jewelry vendors. There are bargain hunters haggling, café owners enticing diners, and little stores brimming with items from Asia, South America, the Middle East, and Europe. Music fills the air, spices scent it, and Toronto's multicultural mix has never been so richly displayed. (Daily)

Kortright Centre for Conservation. *9550 Pine Valley Dr, Woodbridge (L4L 1A6). 12 miles (19.3 kilometers) NW via Hwy 400, Major MacKenzie Dr exit, then 2 miles (3 kilometers) W, then S on Pine Valley Dr. Phone*

905/832-2289. Environmental center with trails, beehouse, maple syrup shack, wildlife pond, and plantings. Naturalist-guided hikes (daily). Cross-country skiing (no rentals); picnic area, cafe; indoor exhibits and theater. (Daily; closed Dec 24-25) **$$**

Little Italy. *W of Bathurst St between Euclid Ave and Shaw St, Toronto. www.torontotourism.com.* After the British, Italians make up the largest cultural group in Toronto. They settled around College Street, just west of Bathurst between Euclid and Shaw, in what became Toronto's first Little Italy. Although the Italian community moved north as it grew, the atmosphere of Little Italy remains. During the day, the coffee shops, billiard halls, and food markets are filled with animated discussions about politics, family, and soccer; when night falls, the area becomes one of the hippest places in Toronto. Restaurants and bars open onto the sidewalks, fashionable cafés are everywhere, color splashes the area, music fills the air—and there's not a bad meal to be had. Two items of note: Café Diplomatico (594 College St), called "The Dip" by locals, is often used as a set by filmmakers. And anyone looking for a little political humor need go just one block south of The Dip, where you'll find the intersection of "Clinton" and "Gore" streets.

Lorraine Kimsa Theatre for Young People. *165 Front St E, Toronto (M5A 3Z4). Phone 416/862-2222; fax 416/363-5136. www.lktyp.ca.* Professional productions for the entire family. (Oct-May: Sat-Sun)

Mackenzie House. *82 Bond St, Toronto (M5B 1X2). Phone 416/392-6915.* Restored 19th-century home of William Lyon Mackenzie, first mayor of Toronto; furnishings and artifacts of the 1850s; 1840s print shop. Group tours (by appointment). (Tues-Sun, afternoons; closed holidays) **$$**

Market Gallery. *95 Front St E, Toronto (M5E 1B4). Phone 416/392-7604.* Exhibition center for Toronto Archives; displays on city's historical, social, and cultural heritage; art, photographs, maps, documents, and artifacts. (Wed-Sat, also Sun afternoons; closed holidays) **FREE**

Martin Goodman Trail. *You can pick up the trail almost anywhere along the waterfront, but it is best to contact Toronto Parks and Recreation for succinct directions. Phone 416/392-8186. www.city.toronto.on.ca/parks.* Leave it to fitness-conscious Toronto not just to have a beautifully maintained waterfront, but to build a trail that takes you from one end to the other. The Martin Goodman Trail is a public jogging, biking, hiking, and in-line skating path that connects all the elements of the waterfront, traversing 13 miles (21 kilometers). It also runs past several spots for bike and skate rentals, so if you start out walking and change your mind, no worries.

McMichael Canadian Art Collection. *10365 Islington Ave, Kleinburg (L0J 1C0). Phone 905/893-1121. www.mcmichael.com.* Works by Canada's most famous artists—the Group of Seven, Tom Thomson, Emily Carr, David Milne, Clarence Gagnon, and others. Also Inuit (Eskimo) and contemporary indigenous art and sculpture. Restaurant; book, gift shop. Constructed from hand-hewn timbers and native stone, the gallery stands in 100 acres (40 hectares) on the crest of Humber Valley; nature trail. (June-early Nov: daily; rest of year: Tues-Sun; closed Dec 25) **$$$**

Medieval Times. *Exhibition Place, Dufferin Gate, Toronto (M6K 3C3). Phone 416/260-1234. www.medievaltimes.com.* If you or anyone in your family would like to play the part of an honored guest of the King of Spain—which means eating a hearty meal with your fingers while watching knights of old joust on hard-charging stallions—you've come to the right place. This 11th-century castle was created to replicate an 11th-century experience, complete with knightly competitions and equestrian displays. As for the eating with your hands part, not to worry—there's not a spaghetti strand in sight. (Wed-Thurs 7 pm, Fri-Sat 7:30 pm, Sun 3:30 pm) **$$$$**

Mount Pleasant Cemetery. *375 Mount Pleasant Rd, Toronto (M4T 2V8). Phone 416/485-9129.* One of the oldest cemeteries in North America, the Mount Pleasant Cemetery is the final resting place of many well-known Canadians, including Sir Frederic Banting and Charles Best, the discoverers of insulin; renowned classical pianist Glenn Gould; and Prime Minister William Lyon Mackenzie King, who led Canada through World War II. The grounds hold rare plants and shrubs as well as a Memorial Peony Garden, and its many paths are used frequently by walkers and cyclists and those who just want a few quiet moments. (Daily 8 am-dusk)

Old City Hall. *100 Queen St W, Toronto (M5H 2N2). www.city.toronto.on.ca/old_cityhall.* The story of Toronto's Old City Hall begins as a story of how an important building begins life as a plan and suddenly becomes a Plan. It took three years to design, ten years to build, and came in at $2 million over budget when it opened in 1889. But everyone agreed it was gorgeous. Over the years it fell into disrepair and was saved from the wrecking ball and declared a National Historic Site by the Historic Sites and Monuments Board of Canada in 1989. It now stands as a majestic, living tribute to 100 years of history and architecture. (Mon-Fri 9 am-5 pm) **FREE**

Ontario Parliament Buildings. *Queen's Park, 111 Wellesley St W, Toronto (M7A 1A2). Phone 416/325-7500.* Guided tours of the Legislature Building and walking tour of grounds. Gardens; art collection; historic displays. (Victoria Day-Labor Day: daily; rest of year: Mon-Fri; closed holidays) **FREE**

Ontario Place. *955 Lakeshore Blvd W, Toronto (M6K 3B9). Phone 416/314-9811; fax 416/314-9993. www.ontarioplace.com.* A 96-acre (39-hectare) cultural, recreational, and entertainment complex on three artificial islands in Lake Ontario. Includes an outdoor amphitheater for concerts, two pavilions with multimedia presentations, Cinesphere theater with IMAX films (year-round; fee); children's village. Three villages of snack bars, restaurants, and pubs; miniature golf; lagoons, canals, two marinas; 370-foot (113-meter) water slide, showboat, pedal and bumper boats; Wilderness Adventure Ride. (Mid-May-early Sept, daily) Parking fee. **$$$$**

Ontario Science Centre. *770 Don Mills Rd, Toronto (M3C 1T3). Phone 416/696-1000. www.ontariosciencecentre.ca.* This is a high-tech playground in Learning Command Central—and it's really for kids. Ten huge exhibition halls in three linked pavilions are filled with exhibits on space and technology. You can stand at the edge of a black hole, watch bees making honey, test your reflexes, your heart rate, or your grip strength, use pedal power to light lights or raise a balloon, hold hands with a robot, or land a spaceship on the moon. Throughout the museum there are slide shows and films that demonstrate various aspects of science, and two Omnimax theaters show larger-than-life films. Plan to spend the whole day. (Daily 10 am-5 pm; closed Dec 25) **$$$**

Parachute School of Toronto. *Baldwin Airport, 5714 Smith Blvd, Baldwin (L0E 1A0). Phone toll-free 800/361-5867. www.parachuteschool.com.* There is growing evidence that learning vacations are gaining in popularity. If this is the sort of learning that makes you feel smarter—jump on it. First, you'll have morning instruction. In the afternoon you'll jump. See how easy? Be sure to call ahead to make sure the school's plane is flying that day. Sometimes they know things about the weather you don't. **$$$$**

Paramount Canada's Wonderland. *9580 Jane St, Vaughan (L6A 1S6). Phone 905/832-7000. www.canadaswonderland.com.* This 300-acre (121-hectare) theme park is situated 30 minutes outside Toronto, and if you ask the locals, they'll tell you it's better than Disneyland. It features more than 140 attractions (with more added every year), including a 20-acre (8-hectare) water park, a participatory play area for the kids, live shows, and more than 50 rides. Specialties among the rides are the park's roller coasters, from creaky old-fashioned wooden ones to "The Fly," a roller coaster designed to make every seat feel as if it's the front car. (June 1-25: Mon-Fri 10 am-8 pm, Fri-Sat to 10 pm; June 26-Labor Day: daily 10 am-10 pm; late May, early Sept-early Oct: Sat-Sun 10 am-8 pm) **$$$$**

Pier: Toronto's Waterfront Museum. *245 Queen's Quay W, Toronto (M5J 2G8).* Original 1930s pier building on Toronto's celebrated waterfront includes two floors of hands-on interactive displays, rare historical artifacts, re-creations of marine history stories, art gallery, boat-building center, narrated walking excursions, children's programs. (Mar-Oct, daily) **$$**

Queen Street West. *A downtown stretch from University Ave to Bathurst St.* If your style is cool and happening, welcome to Mecca. Here you'll find vintage clothing stores, trendy home furnishings, hip styles, and stylish funk that used to be original grunge and street vendor bohemia. You'll also find the handiwork of many up-and-coming fashion designers. In between the boutiques are antique stores, used bookstores, and terrific bistros and cafés. But beware of the heaps of pasta served with heaps of attitude.

Rivoli. *332-334 Queen St W, Toronto (M5V 2A2). Phone 416/596-1908.* This offbeat, artsy performance club opened in 1982 on the site of Toronto's 1920s Rivoli Vaudeville Theatre. The focus is on eclectic and cutting-edge music and performances and includes everything from grunge and rock to poetry readings and comedy. The Indigo Girls, Tori Amos, and Michelle Shocked all made their Toronto debuts here. Don't forget to check out the 5,000-square-foot (465-square-meter) skylit pool hall with its 13 vintage tables, including an 1870s Brunswick Aviator and a 1960s futuristic AMF seen in the Elvis movie *Viva Las Vegas.* (Schedule varies; cover **$-$$$**)

Rogers Centre. *1 Blue Jays Way, Toronto (M5V 1J3). Phone 416/341-2770; fax 416/341-3110. www.rogerscentre.com.* Many people go to see the Toronto Blue Jays play a great game of baseball, others go to see Canada's Argonauts take to the gridiron. But others go to see the place where the two hometown teams play: the Rogers Centre (formerly the SkyDome), the first stadium in the world with a retractable roof. It takes 20 minutes and costs $500 every time somebody wants the sun in. But who wants to watch a baseball game under a roof? (Tours given daily) **$$$**

Royal Ontario Museum. *100 Queen's Park, Toronto (M5S 2C6). Phone 416/586-5549. www.rom.on.ca.* When the ROM opened its doors to the public in 1914, its mission was to "inspire wonder and build understanding of human cultures and the natural world." And its collections—in archaeology, geology, genealogy, paleontology and sociology—have moved in that direction ever since. Today the museum houses 6 million objects, with 67,000 added each year. One of the most-visited galleries is the Nubia Gallery, built in 1998 after a ROM team discovered a new archaeological culture in the Upper Nubia region of Northern Sudan, unearthing the remains of a settlement dating to 1000-800 BCE. The discovery has been officially recognized by UNESCO as "Canada's contribution to the United Nations Decade for Cultural Development." (Mon-Thurs, Sat 10 am-6 pm, Fri to 9:30 pm, Sun 11 am-6 pm; closed Jan 1, Dec 25) **$$$$**

Scarborough Civic Centre. *150 Borough Dr, Scarborough (M1P 4N7). Phone 416/396-7216.* Houses offices of municipal government. Guided tours (daily; closed Dec 25). Concerts Sun afternoons.

Second City. *51 Mercer St, Toronto (M5V 2G3). Phone 416/343-0011. www.secondcity.com.* The Toronto branch of the famous Improv Club has turned out its own respectable list of veterans. Among those who have trained here are Gilda Radner, Mike Meyers, Martin Short, Ryan Stiles, and dozens of others who have set the standards for improvisational comedy. The nightly shows are topical and frequently hilarious, but don't leave; the post-show improv sessions are the ones that will have you trying to keep your sides from splitting. (Mon-Sun 8 pm; Sat 8 and 10:30 pm)

St. Lawrence Centre for the Arts. *27 Front St E, Toronto (M5E 1B4). Phone 416/366-7723 (box office). www.stlc.com.* Performing arts complex features theater, music, dance, films, and other public events.

St. Lawrence Market. *92 Front St E, Toronto (M5E 1B4). Phone 416/392-7219.* In 1803, Governor Peter Hunt designated an area of land to be "market block." Today, the St. Lawrence Market provides a good snippet of the way Toronto used to be, with enough of the character of the original architecture to make you feel as though the old city were alive and well. Some of the wide avenues, too, are reminiscent of European cities. The market itself, Toronto's largest indoor market, sells 14 different categories of foods, which include incredibly fresh seafood, poultry, meat, organic produce, baked goods, gourmet teas and coffees, plus fruit and flowers. And you'll be hard-pressed to find a better selection of cheese in all of Toronto. (Tues-Thurs 8 am-6 pm, Fri 8 am-7 pm, Sat 5 am-5 pm)

Taste of the World Neighbourhood Bicycle Tours and Walks. *Phone 416/966-1550. www.torontowalksbikes .com.* This established tour company offers walking tours that foodies will love. Every Saturday, a group of no more than 12 meets in front of Old City Hall to explore the old and new local traditions of the historic St. Lawrence Farmers' Market. Equal parts fact and food, the tour walks visitors through a forgotten hanging square, a hidden gallery, and a lost pillory site. The eats include East Indian treats with new twists, decadent offerings with Belgian chocolate, sandwich samples at Carousel Bakery, and a spread at St. Urbain Bagel. On Sundays, a different tour focuses on the contributions of 200 years of immigrant activity in the Kensington market, exploring Jewish and East Indian snacks, Lebanese treats, and, of course, chocolate truffles. Different times of the year feature different food-focused themes (fall tours feature harvest traditions; December tours feature holiday festivities of different cultures, etc.). The tour company suggests a light breakfast with the St. Lawrence Tour and no breakfast with the Kensington tour. (Daily 9:30 am-1 pm) **$$$$**

Todmorden Mills Heritage Museum & Arts Centre. *67 Pottery Rd, Toronto (M5E 1C3). 2 1/4 miles (4 kilometers) N, off Don Valley Pkwy in East York between Broadview and Bayview aves. Phone 416/396-2819.* Restored historic houses; Parshall Terry House (1797) and William Helliwell House (1820). Also museum; restored 1899 train station. Picnicking. (Tues-Sun) **$$**

Toronto Blue Jays (MLB). *SkyDome, 1 Blue Jays Way, Toronto (M5V 1J3). Phone 416/341-1000; fax 416/341-1177. www.torontoblue.jays.com.* Professional baseball team.

Toronto Maple Leafs (NHL). *Air Canada Centre, 40 Bay St, Toronto (M5J 2X2). Phone 416/815-5700; fax 416/359-9213. www.mapleleafs.com.* Professional hockey team.

Toronto Music Garden. *475 Queen's Quay W, Toronto (M5J 2G8). Phone 416/973-3000. www.city.toronto.on.ca/parks/music_index.htm.* In the mid-1990s, internationally renowned cellist Yo-Yo Ma worked with several other artists to produce a six-part film series inspired by the work of Johann Sebastian Bach's "Suites for Unaccompanied Cello." The first film was entitled *The Music Garden*, and used nature to interpret the music of Bach's first suite. Toronto was approached to create an actual garden based on *The Music Garden*, and the result—Toronto Music Garden—now graces the waterfront, a symphony of swirls and curves and wandering trails. In the summertime, free concerts are given. Tours are offered, with a guide or self-guided with a hand-held audiotape. The Toronto Music Garden is the only one of its kind in the world. **$**

Toronto Raptors (NBA). *Air Canada Centre, 40 Bay St, Toronto (M5J 2X2). Phone 416/366-3865. www.raptors.com.* Professional basketball team.

Toronto Stock Exchange. *130 King St W, Toronto (M5X 1J2). Phone 416/947-4676. www.tse.com.* The Stock Market Place visitor center has multimedia displays, interactive games, and archival exhibits to aid visitors in understanding the market. **FREE**

Toronto Symphony. *60 Simcoe St, Toronto (M5H 1K5). Phone 416/593-4828; fax 416/598-3375. www.tso.ca.* Classical, pops, and children's programs; Great Performers series. Wheelchair seating, audio enhancement for the hearing impaired.

Toronto Tours Ltd. *145 Queens Quay W, Toronto (M5J 2G8). Phone 416/869-1372. www.torontotours.com.* Four different boat tours of Toronto Harbour. **$$$$**

★ **Toronto Zoo.** *361A Old Finch Ave, Scarborough (M1B 5K7). N of Hwy 401 on Meadowvale Rd. Phone 416/392-5900. www.torontozoo.com.* There are more than 5,000 animals representing just over 450 species at the Toronto Zoo, which was awarded "Best Family Outing" in Toronto.com's first annual poll. Well-designed and laid out, four large tropical indoor pavilions and several smaller indoor viewing areas, plus numerous outdoor exhibits compose 710 acres (287 hectares) of "zoogeographic regions," which can be explored on 6 miles (9.6 kilometers) of walking trails. And when you're tired of walking, sit down for a refreshment, or take a ride on a pony, a camel, or a safari simulator. The Zoo also takes pride in its collection of plants and vegetation, which is valued at $5 million. (Daily; closed Dec 25) **$$$$**

University of Toronto. *25 King's College Cir, Toronto (M5S 1A1). Downtown, W of Queen's Park. Phone 416/978-5000 (tours). www.utoronto.ca.* (1827) (55,000 students) Largest university in Canada. Guided walking tours of magnificent Gothic buildings begin at Hart House and include an account of campus ghost (June-Aug, Mon-Fri; free).

Waddington McLean & Company. *111 Bathurst St, Toronto (M5V 2R1). Phone 416/504-9100.* The largest and oldest auction house in Canada, Waddington's professional services have stayed the same for more than 150 years. They do appraisals, consultation, and valuation. But the real fun comes every Wednesday, when the Canadian-owned house holds weekly estate/household auctions. Twice a year, in spring and fall, they host a fine art auction with catalogued items up for bid. (Mon-Fri 8:30 am-5 pm)

Woodbine Racetrack. *555 Rexdale Blvd, Rexdale (M9W 5L2). 15 miles (24 kilometers) N via Hwy 427. Phone 416/675-7223; fax 416/213-2123. www.woodbineentertainment.com.* The only track in North America that can offer both standardbred and thoroughbred racing on the same day, Woodbine is home to Canada's most important race course events. It hosts the $1 million Queen's Plate, North America's oldest continuously run stakes race; the $1 million ATTO; the $1.5 million Canadian International, and the $1 million North America Cup for Standardbreds. It also has an outstanding grass course; it was here, in 1973, that Secretariat bid farewell to racing with his win of the grass championship. Woodbine has 1,700 slot machines, and many different dining options for those times when you might need intake instead of outgo. **FREE**

Special Events

Beaches International Jazz Festival. *Queen St E, Toronto (M4L 1H8). Phone 416/698-2152. www.beachesjazz.com.* For four days every summer since 1989, the Beaches community of Toronto has resonated with the sound of world-class jazz at the Beaches International Jazz Festival, a musical wonder that attracts nearly a million people to the water's edge. More than 40 bands play nightly, with over 700 musicians casting their spell over a crowd that includes children waving glow sticks, toe-tapping seniors, and just about everyone in between. In addition to international artists (with a focus on Canadians), the Festival also serves as a springboard for talented amateurs. Mid-late July. **FREE**

Bloor Yorkville Wine Festival. *Events held throughout the city. www.santewinefestival.net.* In the late 1990s, three separate organizations, among them the Wine Council of Ontario, began a festival that has grown to include more than 70 wineries from 11 countries. Activities include five days of international wine tastings, dinners, parties, and discussions that are held at various restaurants, bars, and hotels all over town. There is also a strong educational element to the festival, with seminars held throughout the week. If you're truly a wine aficionado you'll definitely want to wait until Saturday, the last day of the festival, which includes eight specially designed wine- and food-related seminars. And if you're a novice, sign up for the Pre-Tasting Seminar to learn how to swish, sip, and savor like the pros.

Canadian International. *Woodbine Racetrack, 555 Rexdale Blvd, Rexdale (M9W 5L2). Phone 416/675-7223. www.woodbineentertainment.com.* World-class thoroughbreds compete in one of Canada's most important races. Mid-late Oct.

Canadian National Exhibition. *Exhibition Place, Lake Shore Blvd and Strachan Ave, Toronto (M6K 3C3). Phone 416/393-6000.* This gala celebration originated in 1879 as the Toronto Industrial Exhibition for the encouragement of agriculture, industry, and the arts, although agricultural events dominated the show. Today sports, industry, labor, and the arts are of equal importance to CNE. The "Ex," as it is locally known, is so inclusive of the nation's activities that it is a condensed Canada. A special 350-acre (141-hectare) park has been built to accommodate the exhibition. Hundreds of events include animal shows, parades, exhibits, a midway, and water and air shows. Virtually every kind of sporting event is represented, from frisbee-throwing to the National Horse Show. Mid-Aug-Labor Day.

Caribana. *Exhibition Place, Lake Shore Blvd and Strachan Ave, Toronto (M6K 3C3).* Caribbean music, grand parade, floating nightclubs, dancing, costumes, and food at various locations throughout city. Late July-early Aug.

Celebrate Toronto Street Festival. *Yonge St, between Lawrence Ave and Dundas St, Toronto (M5H 2N2). Phone 416/395-0490. www.city.toronto.on.ca/special_events/streetfest.* Each July, on the first weekend after Canada Day, Toronto's Yonge Street—the longest street in the world—is transformed into more than 500,000 square feet (46,452 square meters) of free entertainment, with something for people of all ages and tastes. Each of five intersections along Yonge Street runs its own distinctive programming mix; one has nothing but family entertainment, another has world music, a third has classic rock, and so forth. Jugglers, stilt-walkers, and buskers enliven street corners; spectacular thrill shows captivate pedestrians. Opening ceremonies, on Friday night of this weekend event, are usually at the intersection of Yonge and Eglinton; call for schedule. Early July. **FREE**

Chin International Picnic. *Exhibition Place, Lake Shore Blvd and Strachan Ave, Toronto (M6K 3C3). Phone 416/531-9991. www.canadas-wonderland.com.* Contests, sports, picnicking. First weekend in July.

Designs on Ice. *100 Queen St W, Toronto (M5H 2N2). Phone 416/395-0490. www.city.toronto.on.ca.* Not only do you have to be handy with a pick, you have to be awfully quick. This ice sculpture competition gives contestants exactly 48 hours to chisel a block of ice into a winter work of art. Each year brings a different theme. A recent one, for example, was J. R. R. Tolkien's epic *The Lord of the Rings*, which brought forth a wonderland of hobbits, dwarves, trolls, orcs, wizards, and elves. The public chooses the winners, and the awards ceremony is part of a family skating party with live music. The sculptures stay up as long as the weather cooperates. Which, in Toronto, might be a very long time indeed. Last weekend in Dec. **FREE**

Outdoor Art Show. *Nathan Phillips Square, Queen and Bay sts, Toronto (M5H 2N2). Phone 416/408-2754.* Mid-July.

Royal Agricultural Winter Fair. *Coliseum Building, Exhibition Place, Lake Shore Blvd and Strachan Ave, Toronto (M6K 3C3). Phone 416/263-3400.* World's largest indoor agricultural fair exhibits the finest livestock. Food shows. Royal Horse Show features international competitions in several categories. Early Nov.

Sunday Serenades. *5100 Yonge St, Toronto (M3N 5V7). Phone 416/338-0338. www.city.toronto.on.ca.* See if moonlight becomes you, and play Fred and Ginger under the stars at Mel Lastman Square. Each Sunday evening in June and July you can Lindy Hop, Big Apple, and Swing to live big band and swing music from the '30s, '40's and '50s. It's free and easy—and lots of fun. Mid-July-mid-Aug. **FREE**

Toronto International Film Festival. *Eaton Centre, 220 Yonge St, Toronto (M5B 2H1). Phone 416/968-3456.* Celebration of world cinema in downtown theaters;

Canadian and foreign films, international moviemakers, and stars. Early Sept.

Toronto Kids Tuesday. *100 Queen St W, Toronto (MH5 2N1). www.city.toronto.on.ca.* For four consecutive Tuesdays in July and August, Nathan Philips Square is turned into a kids' fantasyland where everyone and everything is devoted to them. There's entertainment, face painting, coloring, chalk art, make-and-take crafts, make your own t-shirts, build-a-kite; it depends on who is entertaining and what the theme of the day is. The Stylamanders brought zany choreography and championship yo-yo tricks for their popular song "Hop, Skip and Jump," which was followed by a high-energy day of play, including interactive games with the Toronto Maple Leafs. No matter who entertains or what the theme, you'll be sure to find a crowd of happy kids. July-Aug. **FREE**

Toronto Wine and Cheese Show. *6900 Airport Rd, Mississauga (L4V 1E8). Phone 416/229-2060. www.towineandcheese.com.* Here's your chance to try award-winning wines without the award-winning price tags. A mainstay since 1983, the Toronto Wine and Cheese Festival brings a world of top-tier wines, beers, lagers, ales, single malt whiskies, cheeses, and specialty food to town. There are also famous chefs sharing their recipes, an exquisite collection of cigars to sample, tips on buying the perfect bottle of wine, and free seminars by well-known food and wine experts presented for both education and enjoyment. It's a great family event, as long as your family is all post-teen; no one under the age of 19 is admitted. Mid-Apr. **$$$$**

Limited-Service Hotels

★ ★ DELTA TORONTO EAST. *2035 Kennedy Rd, Scarborough (M1T 3G2). Phone 416/299-1500; fax 416/299-8959. www.deltahotels.ca.* This property allows its guests to explore the Toronto area from outside the downtown core. 368 rooms, 14 story. Pets accepted; fee. Check-out noon. Restaurant, bar. Children's activity center. Fitness room. Indoor pool, children's pool, whirlpool. **$$**

★ HOLIDAY INN EXPRESS. *50 Estates Dr, Scarborough (M1H 2Z1). Phone 416/439-9666; toll-free 800/465-4329; fax 416/439-4295. www.holiday-inn.com.* 138 rooms, 3 story. Complimentary continental breakfast. Check-in 3 pm, check-out 11 am. **$**

★ ★ INN ON THE PARK. *1100 Eglinton Ave E, Toronto (M3C 1H8). Phone 416/444-2561; toll-free 800/465-4329; fax 416/446-3308. www.innonthepark toronto.com.* This upscale sister of the Holiday Inn Don Valley is perfect for a weekend getaway even if you live in the city. The Inn is a traditional resort-type hotel offering inconspicuous but attentive service; some staff members have been with the inn since it opened in 1963. The rich woods inside echo the 600 acres of woods and parkland outside. You can stroll through the park or choose from several nearby courses if golf is your game. 269 rooms, 23 story. Check-in 3 pm, check-out noon. Restaurant, bar. Children's activity center. Fitness room. Indoor pool, whirlpool. Business center. **$$**

★ ★ QUALITY SUITES TORONTO AIRPORT. *262 Carlingview Dr, Etobicoke (M9W 5G1). Phone 416/674-8442; toll-free 800/424-6423; fax 416/674-3088. www.qualityinn.com.* 254 rooms, 12 story. Pets accepted. Check-in 1 pm, check-out 11 am. Restaurant, bar. Fitness room. **$**

★ ★ RADISSON HOTEL TORONTO EAST. *55 Hallcrown Pl, North York (M2J 4R1). Phone 416/493-7000; toll-free 800/333-3333; fax 416/493-0681. www.radisson.com.* 228 rooms, 9 story. Check-in 3 pm, check-out noon. High-speed Internet access. Restaurant, bar. Indoor pool, whirlpool. **$**

★ ★ RADISSON PLAZA HOTEL ADMIRAL. *249 Queens Quay W, Toronto (M5J 2N5). Phone 416/203-3333; toll-free 800/333-3333; fax 416/203-3100. www.radisson.com.* You can't beat the location of this downtown hotel on Queen's Quay at the heart of the harbor. Choose a room with a view of the city or a view of the lake or go overboard and survey the lake as you bask around the outdoor pool. Situated right on the water, the hotel's nautical theme seems appropriate. The theme is carried out in meeting rooms and public areas and through the restaurants and bar. 157 rooms, 8 story. Check-in 3 pm, check-out noon. High-speed Internet access. Two restaurants, bar. Fitness room. Outdoor pool, whirlpool. Business center. **$$**

Full-Service Hotels

★ ★ ★ DELTA CHELSEA. *33 Gerrard St W, Toronto (M5G 1Z4). Phone 416/595-1975; toll-free 800/*

268-1133; fax 416/585-4375. www.deltachelsea.com. 1,590 rooms, 26 story. Pets accepted, some restrictions. Check-in 3 pm, check-out 11 am. High-speed Internet access. Two restaurants, two bars. Fitness room. Indoor pool, whirlpool. Airport transportation available. Business center. **$$$**

★ ★ ★ FAIRMONT ROYAL YORK. *100 Front St W, Toronto (M5J 1E3). Phone 416/368-2511; toll-free 800/527-4727; fax 416/368-9040. www.fairmont.com.* In 1929, the largest hotel in the British Commonwealth opened on the site of the old Queen's Hotel, which had been an integral part of Toronto's boomtown. It was also rumored to have been the site of Sir John Macdonald's meeting with American Civil War sympathizers who plotted retaliation. The Royal York became known as a city within a city, its 1.5 acres (.6 hectares) of public rooms including a 12-bed hospital, a 12,000-book library, a concert hall with a 50-ton pipe organ, its own bank, and ten ornate passenger elevators. A $100 million project from 1988 to 1993 restored the guest rooms and public spaces to their original elegance and added a health club. Still, many of the hotel's original features are intact, such as the marvelous hand-painted ceilings, travertine pillars, ornate furnishings, and wall hangings. Even if you aren't a guest of the hotel, take a walk through it and think about the illustrious guests who have walked before you. And don't forget to sneak a peak at ornate elevator #9, the designated lift for Her Majesty Queen Elizabeth II. 1,365 rooms, 22 story. Pets accepted, some restrictions; fee. Check-in 3 pm, check-out noon. High-speed Internet access. Five restaurants, four bars. Fitness room. Indoor pool. Business center. **$$$**

★ ★ ★ ★ FOUR SEASONS HOTEL TORONTO. *21 Avenue Rd, Toronto (M5R 2G1). Phone 416/964-0411; toll-free 800/819-5053; fax 416/964-2301. www.fourseasons.com.* The standard-setting Four Seasons Hotel has a stylish home in Toronto. The headquarters is located in the Yorkville District, a fashionable and dynamic neighborhood filled with specialty shops and galleries. The guest rooms are sublimely comfortable and feature fine furnishings and impressive artwork. Guests stay on track with fitness regimes while staying here, with both a fitness center and an indoor-outdoor pool. The spa offers a variety of massages, all of which are also available in the privacy of your guest room. Toronto's dining scene is well represented at the Four Seasons, with four sensational restaurants. The eclectic décor and the striking glass art make the Studio Café a favorite place for casual dining, while the contemporary, sleek style of Avenue attracts the chic. No visit is complete without dining at Truffles (see), where a mouthwatering menu transports diners to the French countryside. 380 rooms, 32 story. Pets accepted, some restrictions. Check-in 3 pm, check-out noon. High-speed Internet access. Two restaurants, two bars. Fitness room. Indoor pool, outdoor pool, whirlpool. Business center. **$$$$**

★ ★ ★ HILTON TORONTO. *145 Richmond St W, Toronto (M5H 2L2). Phone 416/869-3456; toll-free 800/445-8667; fax 416/869-3187. www.toronto.hilton.com.* Guests will enjoy the location of this hotel—it places them in Toronto's financial and entertainment districts. 601 rooms, 32 story. Pets accepted; fee. Check-in 3 pm, check-out noon. High-speed Internet access, wireless Internet access. Two restaurants, two bars. Fitness room. Indoor pool, outdoor pool, whirlpool. Business center. **$$**

★ ★ ★ HOTEL LE GERMAIN. *30 Mercer St, Toronto (M5V 1H3). Phone 416/345-9500; toll-free 800/858-8471; fax 416/345-9501. www.germaintoronto.com.* Sleek lines, modern architecture, and a two-level lobby define this new hotel, located in Toronto's entertainment district. Wood, metal, glass, and ceramics enhance the décor, while facilities such as a massage room, two rooftop terraces, and a library with an open-hearth fireplace enhance guests' stays. Four suites have fireplaces and private terraces. 122 rooms. Pets accepted, some restrictions; fee. Check-in 3 pm, check-out noon. High-speed Internet access. Restaurant, bar. Fitness room. **$$**

★ ★ ★ INTERCONTINENTAL HOTEL TORONTO CENTRE. *225 Front St W, Toronto (M5V 2X3). Phone 416/597-1400; toll-free 800/422-7969; fax 416/597-8128. www.intercontinental.com.* Boasting the ultimate in location and amenities, the downtown outpost of the InterContinental caters to business travelers who need meeting space, business support, and proximity to the adjacent Metro Toronto Convention Centre, as well as to leisure travelers who want to stay in the heart of the city close to theater, dining, and shopping venues. Recent renovations transformed the entrance and lobby into a downtown showpiece. For pampering, indulge in a visit to the Victoria Spa—one of the best in Toronto—for an extensive variety of soothing treatments. 586 rooms, 25 story. Check-in 3 pm, check-out noon. High-speed Internet access. Restaurant, bar. Fitness room, spa. Indoor pool. Business center. **$$$$**

★ ★ ★ INTERCONTINENTAL TORONTO. *220 Bloor St W, Toronto (M5S 1T8). Phone 416/960-5200; toll-free 888/567-8725; fax 416/324-5920. www.ichotelsgroup.com.* A rich, elegant atmosphere permeates this thoroughly up-to-date hotel located in the exclusive Yorkville neighborhood. Rich woods and fresh-cut flowers greet you in the lobby, and well-appointed rooms await upstairs. The guest rooms are designed to be both inviting and efficient, and each has a bay window that actually opens. Catering especially to business travelers, rooms on the two Business Floors include a fax/printer/copier/scanner. In addition, the hotel offers an international newspaper service and will print a copy of any major newspaper you request. 210 rooms, 8 story. Pets accepted; fee. Check-in 3 pm, check-out noon. High-speed Internet access. Restaurant, bar. Fitness room. Indoor pool. Business center. **$$**

★ ★ ★ LE ROYAL MERIDIEN KING EDWARD. *37 King St E, Toronto (M5C 1E9). Phone 416/863-3131; toll-free 800/543-4300; fax 416/367-5515. www.lemeridien-kingedward.com.* Le Royal Meridien King Edward is the grande dame of Toronto. Named in honor of King Edward VII, who also granted the hotel his seal of approval, this historic landmark opened to the public in 1903. It has been hosting the world's elite ever since, and its enviable guest list includes everyone from the Duke of Windsor to the Beatles. Influenced by Edwardian sensibilities, the interiors are luminous. The accommodations are posh, yet comfortable. Guests staying on Le Royal Club floor are entitled to exclusive privileges, making for an exceptional visit. Sharing the hotel's affinity for England in their décor, the Café Victoria and Consort Bar are essential elements of the superb King Edward experience. 292 rooms, 16 story. Pets accepted. Check-in 3 pm, check-out noon. High-speed Internet access. Two restaurants, bar. Fitness room, spa. Business center. **$$$**

★ ★ ★ MARRIOTT BLOOR YORKVILLE. *90 Bloor St E, Toronto (M4W 1A7). Phone 416/961-8000; toll-free 800/859-7180; fax 416/961-4635. www.marriotthotels.com.* Situated in the fashionable Yorkville neighborhood, this hotel's creative and artistic décor makes it fit right in. Although it's located at perhaps the city's busiest intersection, the hotel feels tucked away. The staff offers efficient service to help you make the most of both the hotel's amenities (including valet parking) and the attractions of the tourist-friendly neighborhood. Close to the business district, the hotel draws a faithful business clientele that makes use of the state-of-the-art facilities. 258 rooms, 6 story. Check-in 3 pm, check-out 1 pm. High-speed Internet access. Restaurant, bar. Fitness room. Business center. **$$$**

★ ★ ★ MARRIOTT TORONTO AIRPORT. *901 Dixon Rd, Toronto (M9W 1J5). Phone 416/674-9400; toll-free 800/905-2811; fax 416/674-8292. www.marriott.com/yyzot.* 424 rooms, 9 story. Pets accepted; fee. Check-in 3 pm, check-out noon. Two restaurants, bar. Fitness room. Indoor pool, whirlpool. Airport transportation available. Business center. **$$**

★ ★ ★ MARRIOTT TORONTO EATON CENTRE. *525 Bay St, Toronto (N5G 2L2). Phone 416/597-9200; toll-free 800/905-0667; fax 416/597-9211. www.marriotteatoncentre.com.* In the financial district and near the theater district, this property attracts all types of visitors with its extensive offerings. There is a top-floor pool overlooking the city. 459 rooms, 18 story. Check-in 3 pm, check-out noon. Restaurant, bar. Fitness room, spa. Indoor pool, whirlpool. Business center. **$$**

★ ★ ★ ★ METROPOLITAN HOTEL TORONTO. *108 Chestnut St, Toronto (M5G 1R3). Phone 416/977-5000; toll-free 800/668-6600; fax 416/977-9513. www.metropolitan.com.* All of Toronto is within easy reach from the Metropolitan Hotel, making it an obvious choice for discerning travelers. Not far from the financial district, the hotel also enjoys close proximity to world-renowned shopping, art galleries, and museums. The hotel has the services of a large property and the intimacy of a private residence. Blond woods, earth tones, and simple furnishings deliver a calming sense to guests. The accommodations are a dream, featuring the latest technology, from faxes, laser printers, modems, and multiline telephones to stereo equipment. Fully-staffed fitness and business centers are also on hand to assist all guests with their goals. The beige and black dining room of Lai Wah Heen (see) is a serene setting for its luscious Cantonese cuisine. Considered an excellent example of authentic dim sum, this restaurant is a local sensation. 422 rooms, 26 story. Pets accepted, some restrictions. Check-in 3 pm, check-out noon. Two restaurants, bar. Fitness room. Indoor pool, whirlpool. Business center. **$$$$**

★ ★ **NOVOTEL TORONTO CENTER.** *45 The Esplanade, Toronto (M5E 1W2). Phone 416/367-8900; fax 416/360-8285.* This hotel has a great location near the CN Tower, the Eaton Center, and other attractions, restaurants, and stores. 262 rooms, 9 story. Pets accepted. Check-in 3 pm, check-out 1 pm. High-speed Internet access. Restaurant, bar. Fitness room. Indoor pool, whirlpool. **$$**

★ ★ ★ **PANTAGES SUITES HOTEL AND SPA.** *210 Victoria St, Toronto (M5S 2R3). Phone 416/362-1777; toll-free 866/852-1777; fax 416/214-5618. www.pantageshotel.com.* What distinguishes a boutique hotel? Unique amenities and services such as a complimentary meditation channel, yoga mats, 400-thread-count Egyptian cotton linens, 27-inch flat-screen TVs, and in-room European kitchens. Some rooms have Jacuzzi tubs. Guests are close to The Eaton Centre mall and other Toronto attractions and just two minutes from the subway and Toronto's PATH underground walkway. 111 rooms, all suites. Complimentary continental breakfast. Check-in 3 pm, check-out 11 am. High-speed Internet access, wireless Internet access. Fitness room. Indoor pool, whirlpool. Business center. **$$$**

★ ★ ★ ★ **PARK HYATT TORONTO.** *4 Avenue Rd, Toronto (M5R 2E8). Phone 416/925-1234; toll-free 800/977-4197; fax 416/924-4933. www.parktoronto.hyatt.com.* The Park Hyatt Toronto calls the stylish Yorkville area home. Located at the intersection of Avenue Road and Bloor Street, this hotel has some of the world's leading stores just outside its doors. The hotel echoes its fashionable neighborhood in its interiors. The Art Deco lobby is at once soothing and vibrant with its soft, yellow light and gleaming marble floors. The public and private spaces have a rich feeling completed with handsome furnishings, and a clean, modern look dominates the rooms and suites. The demands of the world dissipate at the Stillwater Spa, where blissful and innovative therapies are offered. Step inside this spa and your cares will be lifted away almost immediately. Overlooking the lobby and the streets of Yorkville, the Mezzanine is a popular gathering place for locals and hotel guests alike. International dishes are the specialty at Annona, while the grilled steaks and seafood of Morton's of Chicago are always a tasty treat. 346 rooms, 18 story. Check-in 3 pm, check-out noon. High-speed Internet access. Restaurant, bar. Fitness room, spa. Business center. **$$$**

★ ★ ★ **RENAISSANCE TORONTO SKYDOME HOTEL.** *1 Blue Jays Way, Toronto (M5V 1J4). Phone 416/341-7100; toll-free 800/237-1512; fax 416/341-5091. www.renaissancehotels.com.* Modern and up-to-date are terms that describe this hotel well. The hotel is designed around ease and comfort, with lively colors and whimsical features. Connected to the SkyDome, where the Toronto Blue Jays play baseball, you can watch a game from your window if you book one of the 70 rooms overlooking the field. If you're into sports other than baseball, the hotel has meeting rooms named for Toronto's Maple Leafs hockey team and Raptors basketball team and offers golf and cruise packages as well as baseball tickets. 348 rooms, 11 story. Check-in 3 pm, check-out noon. High-speed Internet access. Restaurant, bar. Fitness room, fitness classes available. Indoor pool, whirlpool. Business center. **$$$**

★ ★ ★ **SHERATON CENTRE HOTEL.** *123 Queen St W, Toronto (M5H 2M9). Phone 416/361-1000; toll-free 800/325-3535; fax 416/947-4854. www.sheratoncentretoronto.com.* This towering edifice in the heart of downtown does everything on a grand scale. It offers more than 1,300 guest rooms and more than 80,000 square feet of conference and reception rooms. Possibly the most impressive feature, though, would be the waterfall gardens with, yes, an actual waterfall amid 2 1/2 acres of gardens bursting with flowers and greenery. The indoor/outdoor pool bridges the gap between hotel and garden, and decks and terraces give you options in relaxation. 1,382 rooms, 43 story. Pets accepted, some restrictions. Check-in 3 pm, check-out noon. Restaurant, bar. Fitness room, spa. Indoor pool, outdoor pool, whirlpool. Business center. **$$**

★ ★ ★ **SHERATON GATEWAY HOTEL.** *Toronto International Airport, Terminal 3, Toronto (L5P 1C4). Phone 905/672-7000; toll-free 800/325-3535; fax 905/672-7100. www.sheraton.com.* If you want to stay really close to the airport, you can't do better than the Sheraton Gateway. The hotel is connected to Terminal 3 at Toronto International Airport via a climate-controlled walkway. First-class soundproofing and Sheraton Sweet Sleeper beds help ensure a good night's sleep before an early flight. This glass-walled hotel is thoroughly modern, with every imaginable facility for the business traveler and supreme comfort and convenience for the leisure traveler. 474 rooms, 8 story. Pets accepted, some restrictions. Check-in 3 pm, check-out noon. Restaurant, bar. Fitness room. Indoor pool, whirlpool. Business center. **$$**

★ ★ ★ SOHO METROPOLITAN HOTEL. *318 Wellington St W, Toronto (M5V 3T4). Phone 416/599-8800; fax 416/599-8801.* Little black books everywhere have a notation for the Soho Metropolitan Hotel Toronto. This boutique hotel earns high marks for its urban chic interiors, stylish food, central location, and smart technology. The accommodations appeal to design buffs with clean, simple lines and light wood furnishings. The black-and-white photography, and soft beige and cream tones create an atmosphere of pure serenity. Technology adds a luxurious element to the rooms and suites, with heated floors and bedside panels that control lighting and temperature. The Soho Metropolitan's Senses Bakery & Restaurant offers the contemporary gourmet experience to diners with its artfully designed and creatively prepared cuisine. Stop for a drink at the hip Senses Bar and ask for a snack of green tea dried spaghetti with sea salt. From the wireless Internet access available throughout the hotel to the complete fitness center with sun deck, this hotel was designed with modern road warriors in mind. 366 rooms, 26 story. Pets accepted, some restrictions. Check-in 3 pm, check-out noon. Wireless Internet access. Two restaurants, bar. Fitness room. Indoor pool, whirlpool. Airport transportation available. Business center. **$$$**

★ ★ ★ THE SUTTON PLACE HOTEL. *955 Bay St, Toronto (M5S 2A2). Phone 416/924-9221; fax 416/924-1778.* Expect the height of luxury from the time you hand your car over to an exceptionally gracious valet at this centrally located hotel. You get an old Europe feel from the rich surroundings, including mahogany trim in the meeting rooms and crystal chandeliers, and from the detail-oriented service from the staff. Original art and antiques grace the guest rooms and suites. For an extended stay, the hotel offers La Grande Residence, which couples the benefits of living in your own apartment with the amenities of a first-class hotel. 292 rooms, 33 story. Pets accepted; fee. Check-in 3 pm, check-out noon. High-speed Internet access. Restaurant, bar. Fitness room, spa. Indoor pool. Business center. **$$**

★ ★ ★ WESTIN HARBOUR CASTLE. *1 Harbour Sq, Toronto (M5J 1A6). Phone 416/869-1600; toll-free 800/228-3000; fax 416/869-0573. www.westin.com/harbourcastle.* The striking towers of this hotel are among the most recognized landmarks in the city. The glass-walled foyer offers a wide, clear view of Lake Ontario. You can request a room with a harbor view or go for a cityscape instead. Stay here to be near a host of tourist attractions, including the Air Canada Centre, the CN Tower, the Eaton Centre, and the theater district. If you're traveling for business, you're near the financial centers and attached to the Westin Harbour Castle Conference Centre. 977 rooms, 20 story. Pets accepted, some restrictions. Check-in 3 pm, check-out noon. Two restaurants, two bars. Children's activity center. Fitness room, spa. Indoor pool, whirlpool. Tennis. Business center. **$$$$**

★ ★ ★ THE WESTIN PRINCE TORONTO. *900 York Mills Rd, North York (M3B 3H2). Phone 416/444-2511; toll-free 800/228-3000; fax 416/444-9597. www.westin.com.* Located in the center of downtown Toronto, this hotel is just minutes from both the Ontario Science Centre and the Ford Centre for the Performing Arts. 381 rooms, 22 story. Check-in 3 pm, check-out noon. Restaurant, bar. Fitness room. Outdoor pool, whirlpool. Tennis. Business center. **$$**

★ ★ ★ WINDSOR ARMS HOTEL. *18 St. Thomas St, Toronto (M5S 3E7). Phone 416/971-9666; toll-free 877/999-2767; fax 416/921-9121. www.windsorarmshotel.com.* Behind the castlelike façade of the Windsor Arms Hotel is one of Toronto's chicest lodgings. Edgy, yet classic, it is a well-heeled hipster's dream. The accommodations in this intimate and stylish hotel are sleek, modern, and sublime, with mahogany or birch furnishings, frosted glass screens, and Frette linens. Guilty pleasures include the extraordinary 24-hour butler service. This hotel is truly a slice of the good life. The Tea Room serves a traditional tea by day, and at night is transformed into Toronto's only champagne and caviar bar. The stunning décor of the Courtyard Café attracts the fashionable set; Club 22 entertains with piano entertainment and live bands; and the Cigar Lounge offers decadent treats. Guests feeling a bit overindulged head for the fitness center and spa to work off their gastronomical sins and escape the worries of the world. 28 rooms, all suites. Pets accepted. Complimentary continental breakfast. Check-in 3 pm, check-out noon. Restaurant, bar. Fitness room, spa. Indoor pool. **$$$**

★ ★ ★ **WYNDHAM BRISTOL PLACE HOTEL.** *950 Dixon Rd, Etobicoke (M9W 5N4). Phone 416/675-9444; toll-free 877/999-3223; fax 416/675-2037. www.wyndham.com.* 287 rooms, 15 story. Check-in 3 pm, check-out 1 pm. High-speed Internet access. Restaurant. Fitness room. Indoor pool. Airport transportation available. Business center. **$$**

Full-Service Inns

★ ★ ★ **THE INN AT MANITOU.** *Center Rd, McKellar (P0G 1C0). Phone 705/389-2171; toll-free 800/571-8818; fax 705/389-3818. www.manitou-online.com.* World-weary travelers seek the refuge of the serene Inn at Manitou. Nestled on the shores of the Manitouwabing Lake, this intimate hideaway boasts peace and quiet in a picturesque setting. It is paradise for athletic-minded guests, with plentiful physical activities. From golf lessons and water sports to group exercise classes and tennis, this small resort packs a big punch. Guests don jackets for the gourmet meals, while more casual evenings feature bistro-style menus. Twice-weekly wine tastings are held in the lakefront gazebo, and afternoon tea is a daily treat. The inn's dedication to physical well-being is even evident in the kitchen, where a spa menu is provided for those guests watching their waistlines. 35 rooms, 3 story. Check-in 4 pm, check-out noon. Restaurant, bar. Fitness room, spa. Golf. Tennis. **$$**

★ ★ ★ **THE MILLCROFT INN & SPA.** *55 John St, Alton (L0N 1A0). Phone 519/941-8111; toll-free 800/383-3976; fax 519/941-9192. www.millcroft.com.* This former knitting mill (1881) is situated on 100 acres (40 hectares) on the Credit River. 52 rooms, 2 story. Complimentary continental breakfast. Check-in 4 pm, check-out noon. Restaurant, bar. Fitness room, spa. Outdoor pool, whirlpool. Tennis. **$$**

★ ★ ★ **OLD MILL INN AND SPA.** *21 Old Mill Rd, Toronto (M8X 1G5). Phone 416/236-2641; toll-free 866/653-6455; fax 416/232-3709. www.oldmilltoronto.com.* This Tudor-style inn and the adjacent meeting and conference facility exude old-world charm. In summer and winter, the setting is spectacular. The inn sits 15 minutes northwest of downtown Toronto in the Humber River Valley, which offers opportunities for hiking, biking, and in-line skating. Common areas feature dark woods, beamed ceilings, and stone walls, while the guest rooms are light and airy, with fireplaces, 32-inch TVs, separate deep-soaking whirlpool tub and shower, and stereo system. Afternoon tea is served daily, and dinner and dancing are available six nights a week. This is a terrific place for a small wedding or a corporate retreat, with on-site facilities that can accommodate more than 100 people. 60 rooms. Complimentary continental breakfast. Check-in 4 pm, check-out noon. High-speed Internet access. Two restaurants, bar. Fitness room, spa. Business center. **$$$**

Spa

★ ★ ★ ★ **STILLWATER SPA AT PARK HYATT TORONTO.** *4 Avenue Rd, Toronto (M5R 2E8). Phone 416/926-2389. www.stillwaterspa.com.* The Park Hyatt Toronto's sensational Stillwater Spa beckons urban warriors weary of the daily rat race. With its cool, crisp interiors—complete with a fireplace in the Tea Lounge and waterfalls and streams throughout the facility—and fabulous mind and body relaxation therapies, this sanctuary offers you an escape from the hectic pace just outside its doors. Whether you spend a few hours or an entire day here, you will experience tranquility.Among the spa's menu of body treatments is the lavender lush body glow, which includes an exfoliation with sea salts and fragrant lavender oils. Another delicious body buffing therapy is the mandarin-honey body glow, which gently exfoliates skin with honey-infused mandarin juices and French sea salts before moisturizing with a tangerine body crème. If you feel like you're carrying the weight of the world on your shoulders, try an antistress and mental clarity body treatment. A 30-minute massage targets stiff shoulders, back, and neck, and then a warm mud mask purifies your back before a full-body Vichy treatment completely calms your nerves.With an extensive massage therapy menu, Stillwater Spa promises to help you unwind. The signature Stillwater massage customizes an aromatherapy blend to accompany a relaxing bodywork combination of Swedish massage, trigger-points pressure, and stretching techniques. Heated neck and eye pillows and warm booties add luxurious touches. Revel in the warmth of an aroma blanket wrap, where milk and the essential oils of melissa, lavender, and orange are massaged into your skin before you are cocooned in a comfortable blanket. Another signature is the Stillwater aqua therapy, where a therapist stretches, moves, and massages your body while you float in water.Revitalize your skin's appearance with a vitamin C, Q-10, or multivitamin power treatment, or battle the effects of harsh environments and climates with an urban element facial. From men's and express facials to a back treatment and a therapy that incorporates rare yeasts used to produce Champagne, the Stillwater Spa's facials deliver softer, more radiant skin.

Restaurants

★ ★ ★ **360.** *301 Front St W, Toronto (M5V 2T6). Phone 416/362-5411; fax 416/601-4895. www.cntower.ca.* As the name suggests, this restaurant completes a 360-degree rotation, offering a breathtaking view from the CN Tower. The scenery inside is attractive as well, with colorful décor and a fresh, seasonal menu. International menu. Lunch, dinner, Sun brunch. Closed Dec 25. Bar. Business casual attire. Reservations recommended. **$$$**

★ ★ **ARKADIA HOUSE.** *2007 Eglinton Ave E, Scarborough (M1L 2M9). Phone 416/752-5685.* Greek menu. Dinner. Closed Dec 24. Bar. Children's menu. **$$**

★ ★ ★ **AUBERGE DU POMMIER.** *4150 Yonge St, Toronto (M2P 2C6). Phone 416/222-2220; fax 416/222-2580. www.aubergedupommier.com.* Located north of the city, this restaurant in an industrial park manages to feel like it is actually in rural France. The attentive service and comfortable décor are pleasing. French, American menu. Lunch, dinner. Closed Sun; holidays. Bar. Children's menu. Reservations recommended. **$$$**

★ ★ ★ **AVALON.** *270 Adelaide St W, Toronto (M5H 1X6). Phone 416/979-9918; fax 416/599-2006. www.avalonrestaurant.com.* Chef/owner Chris McDonald and executive chef Erik Nowak create a new menu almost daily due to their commitment to providing only what is fresh and seasonal. Guests return again and again to experience the variety and quality of the food. Contemporary Continental menu. Dinner. Closed Sun-Mon; Dec 25-Jan 1, two weeks in July. Casual attire. Reservations recommended. **$$$**

★ ★ **BAROOTES.** *220 King St W, Toronto (M5H 1K4). Phone 416/979-7717; fax 416/979-0292. www.barootes.com.* International menu. Lunch, dinner. Closed Sun. Bar. Children's menu. Casual attire. Reservations recommended. **$$**

★ ★ ★ **BIAGIO.** *155 King St E, Toronto (M5C 1G9). Phone 416/366-4040; fax 416/366-4765.* Located in the historic St. Lawrence Hall near the theater district, this modern Italian restaurant serves specialties from the north. An ornate ceiling and a lovely patio with a fountain add to the ambience. Italian menu. Lunch, dinner. Closed Sun; holidays. Bar. Casual attire. Outdoor seating. **$$$**

★ **BUMPKINS.** *21 Gloucester St, Toronto (M4Y 1L8). Phone 416/922-8655; fax 416/922-0240. www.bumpkinsrestaurant.com.* French menu. Lunch, dinner, brunch. Casual attire. Reservations recommended. Outdoor seating. **$$**

★ ★ ★ ★ **CANOE.** *66 Wellington St W, Toronto (M5K 1H6). Phone 416/364-0054; fax 416/364-4273.* Canoe is a tranquil place to dine. During the day, warm light streams in through the tall windows, filling the elegantly minimalist restaurant with golden tones. At night, a warm glow comes from the room's perfect amber-hued lighting, and the dining room swells with a chic crowd; the sexy cocktail list makes the bar quite popular. Whether you're having lunch or dinner, Canoe, one of restaurateur Oliver Bonacini's many stylish Toronto eateries (others include Jump and Auberge du Pommier), is a stunning venue in which to experience creative, satisfying regional Canadian cuisine. While dazzling ingredients tend to be sourced from wonderful local producers, many organic, the kitchen borrows flavors and techniques from the world at large, including Asia, France, and the American South. The end product is inventive food and an equally original room that take your breath away. Canadian menu. Lunch, dinner. Closed Sat-Sun. Bar. Business casual attire. Reservations recommended. **$$$**

★ ★ **CARMAN'S CLUB.** *26 Alexander St, Toronto (M4Y 1B4). Phone 416/924-8558; fax 416/924-7638.* Steak, seafood menu. Dinner. Closed Sun; Good

Friday, Dec 25. Casual attire. **$$$**

★ ★ ★ CENTRO GRILL & WINE BAR. *2472 Yonge St, Toronto (M4P 2H5). Phone 416/483-2211; fax 416/483-2641. www.centrorestaurant.com.* A lot of tastes are rolled into one destination at this contemporary European restaurant with a downstairs sushi and oyster bar. The wood floors; red, high-backed chairs; white tablecloths; and silver-accented décor create a colorful, New Age-style dining room, and the worldly menu is never a bore with novelties like caribou chop with juniper berry oil, Alsatian spatzle, and Arctic cloudberry sauce. International/Fusion menu. Dinner. Closed Sun; holidays. Bar. Casual attire. Reservations recommended. Valet parking. **$$$**

★ ★ ★ ★ CHIADO. *864 College St, Toronto (M6H 1A3). Phone 416/538-1910; fax 416/588-8383. www.chiadorestaurant.com.* Albino Silva is the chef/owner and loving force behind Chiado, a charming, authentic Portuguese bistro named after the oldest neighborhood in his native Lisbon. Enter the cozy dining room and you are instantly hungry: the air is heavy with the scent of seafood, garlic, and herbs, and a cutting board overflowing with Silva's fresh-baked bread stares you down as you enter the front room. Paying homage to the old seaside town but updating dishes for a more modern sensibility, Chiado features what might best be described as "nouvelle Portuguese cuisine." No matter what title you give it, the food is first-rate and fabulous. You'll find an ocean's worth of fresh fish, simply prepared with olive oil and herbs, as well as innovative takes on pheasant, game, and poultry. To add to the authenticity of the experience, Chiado has the largest collection of fine Portuguese wines in North America and a superb selection of vintage ports. Portuguese menu. Lunch, dinner. Bar. Casual attire. Reservations recommended. Valet parking. **$$$**

★ ★ DAVID DUNCAN HOUSE. *125 Moatfield Dr, North York (M3B 3L6). Phone 416/391-1424; fax 416/391-5302. www.davidduncanhouse.com.* Dark oak, dim lighting, and stained-glass windows help create the luxurious setting of this acclaimed restaurant. But what is most noteworthy is the richness of its cuisine. Dinner. Bar. Jacket required. Valet parking. **$$$**

★ ★ ★ DOCTOR'S HOUSE. *21 Nashville Rd, Kleinberg (L0J 1C0). Phone 905/893-1615; fax 905/893-0660.* American menu. Dinner, Sun brunch. Bar. Children's menu. Outdoor seating. **$$$**

★ ★ DYNASTY CHINESE. *131 Bloor St W, Toronto (M5S 1R1). Phone 416/923-3323; fax 416/923-1826.* Chinese menu. Lunch, dinner. Casual attire. Reservations recommended. **$$$**

★ ★ ★ ★ THE FIFTH. *225 Richmond St W, Toronto (M5V 1W2). Phone 416/979-3005; fax 416/979-9877. www.easyandthefifth.com.* It takes work to make it to The Fifth. First, an alley entrance leads you to The Easy, an upscale nightclub and former speakeasy. Once inside The Easy, you are directed onto a Persian rug-lined vintage freight elevator. There, an old-school attendant takes you to floor number five. Exit, and you have finally arrived at The Fifth, a treasured contemporary French restaurant and supper club. Truly special in every sense, The Fifth is a stunning, intimate, living room—like space with a stone fireplace, blond hardwood floors, picture windows, white linen-draped tables and chairs, and soft candle lighting. The food is of the delicious updated French variety, and the dishes are perfectly prepared, beautifully presented, and easily devoured. In warm weather, retire to the outside deck and enjoy the smooth sounds of live jazz under the stars. French menu. Dinner. Closed Sun-Wed. Bar. Business casual attire. Reservations recommended. Outdoor seating. **$$$$**

★ GRANO. *2035 Yonge St, Toronto (M4S 2A2). Phone 416/440-1986; fax 416/440-1996. www.grano.ca.* Italian menu. Breakfast, lunch, dinner. Closed Sun. Bar. Casual attire. Outdoor seating. **$$**

★ ★ GRAZIE. *2373 Yonge St, Toronto (M4P 2C8). Phone 416/488-0822; fax 416/488-0565. www.grazie.ca.* Italian menu. Lunch, dinner, late-night. Closed holidays. Bar. Casual attire. **$$**

★ ★ ★ ★ HEMISPHERES. *108 Chestnut St, Toronto (M5G 1R3). Phone 416/599-8000; fax 416/977-9513. www.metropolitan.com/hemis.* Hemispheres is a star on the Toronto dining scene. This worldly restaurant elevates hotel dining to a whole new level with its stylish interior design and international fusion cuisine. Located within the hip Metropolitan Hotel Toronto (see), this restaurant is a magnet for a fashionable crowd who frequent this downtown spot for its innovative food and terrific people watching. Its laid-back sophistication is appealing to patrons who want both style and substance. The sexy space is curvy and contemporary, and an exhibition kitchen is the jewel in the crown. Diners may even book the chef's table for an insider's look at the whirlwind behind the scenes. The menu includes European and Continental classics, many with an Asian bent, and seafood accounts for a large part of the selections. The exhaustive dessert list will delight those with a sweet tooth, while wine lovers will appreciate the well-rounded and extensive cellar. International menu. Breakfast, lunch, dinner. Bar. Children's menu. Reservations recommended. Valet parking. **$$**

★ ★ IL POSTO NUOVO. *148 Yorkville Ave, Toronto (M5R 1C2). Phone 416/968-0469; fax 416/968-2329. www.ilposto.ca.* Italian menu. Lunch, dinner. Bar. Casual attire. Reservations recommended. Outdoor seating. **$$$**

★ ★ ★ JOSO'S. *202 Davenport Rd, Toronto (M5R 1J2). Phone 416/925-1903; fax 416/925-6567.* The walls are covered with the chef's racy art and celebrity pictures at this popular restaurant, which offers unique but excellent Mediterranean cuisine. Mediterranean menu. Lunch, dinner. Closed Sun; holidays. Outdoor seating. **$$$**

★ ★ ★ LA FENICE. *319 King St W, Toronto (M5V 1J5). Phone 416/585-2377; fax 416/585-2709. www.lafenice.ca.* The stark, modern dining room of this downtown restaurant recalls the chic design aesthetic of Milan. Italian menu. Lunch, dinner. Closed Sun. Business casual attire. Reservations recommended. **$$$**

★ ★ ★ LAI WAH HEEN. *108 Chestnut St, Toronto (M5G 1R3). Phone 416/977-9899; fax 416/977-8027. www.laiwahheen.com.* Lai Wah Heen, meaning "luxurious meeting place," is truly luxurious with its two-level dining room featuring black granite, 12-foot (3.6-meter) ceilings, and solarium-style glass wall. Exotic herbs and spices, skillful use of tropical fruits, and seafood dishes of exquisite refinement make for a sumptuous Cantonese menu rich with Pacific Rim flair. For an intimate dinner, dim sum, or banquet, Lai Wah Heen delivers a true Hong Kong experience in the heart of Toronto. Cantonese, Chinese menu. Lunch, dinner. Business casual attire. Reservations recommended. Valet parking. **$$**

★ MATIGNON. *51 Ste. Nicholas St, Toronto (M4Y 1W6). Phone 416/921-9226; fax 416/921-2119. www.matignon.ca.* French menu. Dinner. Closed Sun. Business casual attire. Reservations recommended. **$$**

★ ★ MILLCROFT INN. *55 John St, Alton (L0N 1A0). Phone 519/941-8111; fax 519/941-9192. www.millcroft.com.* A restaurant with a substantial reputation for fine dining makes any occasion a time to celebrate, especially during the holidays, when they offer special menus. Be sure to sample their vintage wines. French menu. Dinner, Sun brunch. Bar. Valet parking. **$$$**

★ MILLER'S COUNTRY FARE. *5140 Dundas St W, Etobicoke (M9A 1C2). Phone 416/234-5050; fax 416/233-6747.* Lunch, dinner, brunch. Closed Dec 25. Bar. Children's menu. **$$**

★ ★ ★ MISTURA. *265 Davenport Rd, Toronto (M5R 1J9). Phone 416/515-0009; fax 416/515-7931. www.mistura.ca.* Italian menu. Dinner. Closed Sun; holidays; also Victoria Day. **$$**

★ ★ ★ ★ NORTH 44 DEGREES. *2537 Yonge St, Toronto (M4P 2H9). Phone 416/487-4897; fax 416/487-2179. www.north44restaurant.com.* Style, serenity, and elegance infuse every aspect of North 44 Degrees. From the recently renovated loftlike dining room awash in muted, sandy tones to the world-class New Continental cuisine created nightly by chef/owner Mark McEwan, North 44 Degrees is a sublime and sexy dining experience. A sophisticated crowd fills the restaurant, named for the city's latitude, on most nights, happily gathering in this airy space to dine on inventive and beautiful culinary creations. From behind the stoves, McEwan enlists the finest local produce, fish, poultry, and meats to support his cross-cultural menu, expertly blending the bright flavors of Asia with those of Italy, France, and Canada. The service is smooth, refined, and in perfect harmony with the cool space and stellar cuisine. International/Fusion menu. Dinner. Closed Sun. Bar. Business casual attire. Reservations recommended. Valet parking. **$$$$**

★ ★ ★ OLD MILL. *21 Old Mill Rd, Toronto (M8X 1G5). Phone 416/236-2641; toll-free 866/653-6455; fax 416/236-2749. www.oldmilltoronto.com.* International menu. Breakfast, lunch, dinner, Sun brunch. Bar. Jacket required (weekend dinner). Reservations recommended. Valet parking. Outdoor seating. Cover charge (Fri-Sat from 8 pm). **$$$**

★ ★ ★ OPUS RESTAURANT. *37 Prince Arthur Ave, Toronto (M5R 1B2). Phone 416/921-3105; fax 416/921-9353. www.opusrestaurant.com.* This plush Yorkville restaurant is elegant, romantic, and filled with the energy of Toronto's powerful and moneyed elite. International/Fusion menu. Dinner. Closed

Jan 1, Dec 24-26. Bar. Casual attire. Reservations recommended. Outdoor seating. **$$$**

★ ★ ★ **ORO.** *45 Elm St, Toronto (M5G 1H1). Phone 416/597-0155. www.ororestaurant.com.* This restaurant has changed hands and names many times since it opened in 1922 and is famous for its patrons, who include Ernest Hemingway and Prime Minister Jean Chrétien. The décor is contemporary and elegant, as is the food. International/Fusion menu. Lunch, dinner. Closed Sun; holidays. **$$$**

★ ★ ★ **PANGAEA.** *1221 Bay St, Toronto (M5R 3P5). Phone 416/920-2323; fax 416/920-0002. www.pangaearestaurant.com.* This modern eatery's industrial façade doesn't do its interior space justice. Once guests enter, they'll relish the softer, calming effects of the dining room's vaulted ceiling and exotic floral arrangements. The chef creates sophisticated continental cuisine using the wealth of each season's harvest. Tired Bloor Street shoppers will find this a great place to break for lunch or tea. International/Fusion menu. Lunch, dinner. Closed Sun. Bar. Business casual attire. Reservations recommended. **$$$**

★ ★ **PASTIS.** *1158 Yonge St, Toronto (M4W 2L9). Phone 416/928-2212; fax 416/928-1632.* Skilled preparation and artful presentation characterize this sophisticated bistro environment. This midtown restauant is popular with business professionals and a local favorite among the well-heeled. French menu. Dinner. Closed Sun-Mon. **$$**

★ ★ **PIER 4 STOREHOUSE.** *245 Queen's Quay W, Toronto (M5J 2K9). Phone 416/203-1440; fax 416/203-6292. www.pier4rest.com.* Seafood menu. Dinner. Bar. Children's menu. Casual attire. Reservations recommended. Outdoor seating. **$$$**

★ ★ **PREGO.** *15474 Yonge St, Aurora (L4G 1P2). Phone 905/727-5100; fax 905/727-5103.* Italian menu. Lunch, dinner. Closed Mon; holidays. Bar. Casual attire. **$$**

★ ★ **PROVENCE.** *12 Amelia St, Toronto (M4X 1A1). Phone 416/924-9901; fax 416/924-9680. www.provencerestaurant.com.* French menu. Lunch, dinner, Sat-Sun brunch. Closed Dec 25. Bar. Casual attire. Outdoor seating. **$$$**

★ ★ **QUARTIER.** *2112 Yonge St, Toronto (M4S 2A5). Phone 416/545-0505; fax 416/545-0506.* French menu. Lunch, dinner. Bar. Casual attire. Reservations recommended. Outdoor seating. **$$$**

★ ★ **RODNEY'S OYSTER HOUSE.** *469 King St W, Toronto (M5V 1V4). Phone 416/363-8105; fax 416/363-6638. www.rodneysoysterhouse.com.* Seafood menu. Lunch, dinner. Closed Sun. Bar. Casual attire. Reservations recommended. Outdoor seating. **$$**

★ ★ **ROSEWATER SUPPER CLUB.** *19 Toronto St, Toronto (M5C 2R1). Phone 416/214-5888; fax 416/214-2412. www.libertygroup.com.* This stylishly retro restaurant and nightclub is a three-level extravaganza, complete with Persian carpets, elaborate Victorian crown mouldings, and cathedral-style windows. The food and wine compete with the setting and the beautiful crowd for attention. The main floor and mezzanine both serve lunch and dinner; on the lower level, you'll find a slinky torch singer draped over a baby grand piano, purring the old romantic standards. If you'd prefer just to listen, turn your eyes to the three-story waterfall that flows over the top of the entryway. The club has two lounges: the Front Lounge welcomes casual diners who come for a light bite and to hear live jazz, and the Ember Lounge is where up to 40 people can top off an evening with a cognac or brandy and a cigar from the selection in the Rosewater's well-stocked humidor. French menu. Lunch, dinner. Closed Sun. Bar. Business casual attire. Reservations recommended. Outdoor seating. **$$$**

★ ★ ★ **SASSAFRAZ.** *100 Cumberland St, Toronto (M5R 1A6). Phone 416/964-2222; fax 416/964-2402. www.sassafraz.ca.* California menu. Lunch, dinner, brunch. Bar. Business casual attire. Reservations recommended. Outdoor seating. **$$$**

★ ★ ★ ★ **SCARAMOUCHE.** *1 Benvenuto Pl, Toronto (M4V 2L1). Phone 416/961-8011; fax 416/961-1922. www.scaramoucherestaurant.com.* Up on a hillside overlooking the dazzling downtown lights, Scaramouche is the perfect hideaway for falling in love with food (or your dining companion). This modern, bilevel space is known for its fantastic contemporary French fare and is often jammed with dressed-up, savvy locals. The restaurant is divided between a formal dining room upstairs and a modestly priced pasta bar downstairs. The latter is a casual bistro offering a selection of stunning handmade pastas as well as non-noodle standards like steak frites. The more elegant dining room is where you'll be treated to the restaurant's famed contemporary French fare. While the menu changes seasonally, specialties of the house may include squab, lobster, and filet, plus a coconut cream pie that is as memorable and fantastic as the view. French menu. Dinner. Closed Sun. Bar. Casual attire. Reservations recommended. Valet parking. **$$$$**

★ ★ **SENATOR.** *249 Victoria St, Toronto (M5B 1T8). Phone 416/364-7517; fax 416/364-3784.* Seafood, steak menu. Dinner. Closed Mon; holidays. Bar. Casual attire. **$$$**

★ ★ ★ **SPLENDIDO.** *88 Harbord St, Toronto (M5S 1G5). Phone 416/929-7788; fax 416/929-3501. www.splendidoonline.com.* Located in the middle of the University of Toronto, this restaurant is a popular pick for parents' weekends when kids get a chance to go out for "real food." International/Fusion menu. Dinner. Closed Mon; July-Aug Sun; holidays. Bar. Casual attire. Reservations recommended. Valet parking. **$$$**

★ ★ ★ **SUSUR.** *601 King St W, Toronto. Phone 416/603-2205. www.susur.com.* International/Fusion menu. Dinner. Closed Sun. Business casual attire. Reservations recommended. **$$$**

★ ★ **TA KE SUSHI.** *22 Front St W, Toronto (M5J 1N7). Phone 416/862-1891; fax 416/862-2356.* Japanese, sushi menu. Lunch, dinner. Closed Sun. Bar. Casual attire. Reservations recommended. **$$**

★ **THAI FLAVOUR.** *1554 Avenue Rd, Toronto (M5M 3X5). Phone 416/782-3288.* Thai menu. Lunch, dinner. Closed Jan 1, Dec 25. **$**

★ ★ ★ ★ **TRUFFLES.** *21 Avenue Rd, Toronto (M5R 2G1). Phone 416/964-0411; fax 416/964-8699. www.fourseasons.com.* Filled with light and luxury, Truffles' dining room feels like the parlor room of a fabulous art collector with impeccable taste. Soaring ceilings, rich wood moldings, large bay windows, and deep-chocolate velvet seating set an airy, sophisticated—but minimalist—stage for the works of a talented group of local artisans, sculptors, and artists that are on display. Located in the Four Seasons Hotel Toronto(see), Truffles is known for its distinct, stylized brand of modern Provençal-style cuisine. As the name suggests, the coveted mushrooms do indeed show up on the menu; the restaurant's signature dish is spaghettini with Perigord Black Gold and a light truffle froth. Often the chosen locale for power dinners, Truffles is also ideal for intimate conversation. Smooth service and an extensive wine list make Truffles a truly inspired dining event. French menu. Dinner. Closed Sun. Bar. Jacket required. Reservations recommended. Valet parking. **$$$$**

★ **UNITED BAKER'S DAIRY RESTAURANT.** *506 Lawrence Ave W, Toronto (M6A 1A1). Phone 416/789-0519; fax 416/789-4022.* Jewish menu. Breakfast, lunch, dinner. **$**

★ ★ **VILLA BORGHESE.** *2995 Bloor St W, Etobicoke (M8X 1C1). Phone 416/239-1286; fax 416/245-4870.* Italian menu. Lunch, dinner. Closed Mon; Easter, Dec 25. Bar. **$$**

★ ★ **ZACHARY'S.** *950 Dixon Rd, Toronto (M9W 5N4). Phone 416/675-9444; fax 416/675-4426.* If you're looking for superior dining in refined surroundings, look no further. A stunning room with low ceilings and rich colors, this restaurant provides an original, continually changing menu. International menu. Lunch, dinner, Sun brunch. Bar. Valet parking. **$$$**

Windsor, ON

5 minutes, 4 miles from Detroit, MI

Population 192,083
Elevation 622 ft (190 m)
Area Code 519
Information Convention & Visitors Bureau of Windsor, Essex County and Pelee Island, 333 Riverside Dr W, City Centre Mall, Suite 103, N9A 5K4; phone 519/255-6530 or toll-free 800/265-3633
Web Site www.city.windsor.on.ca/cvb

Windsor is located at the tip of a peninsula and is linked to Detroit, Michigan, by the Ambassador Bridge and the Detroit-Windsor Tunnel. Because of its proximity to the United States, it is often referred to as the Ambassador City. Windsor is also known as the City of Roses for its many beautiful parks. The Sunken Gardens and Rose Gardens in Jackson Park boast more than 500 varieties of roses. Coventry Garden and Peace Fountain has the only fountain floating in international waters. Whatever the nickname, for many people traveling from the United States, Canada begins here.

Windsor is a cosmopolitan city, designated a bilingual-bicultural area because of the French influence so much in evidence. Windsor also has a symphony orchestra, theaters, a light opera company, art galleries, nightlife, and all the amenities of a large city. Within its boundaries are 900 acres (364 hectares) of parks, giving the city the charm of a rural environment. With easy access to lakes Erie and St. Clair and such pleasure troves as Pelee Island, it is also the major city in Canada's "Sun Parlor," Essex County. A mild climate and beautiful beaches make Windsor an excellent place to visit all year.

What to See and Do

Art Gallery of Windsor. *401 Riverside Dr W, Windsor (N9A J71). Phone 519/977-0013. www.artgalleryofwindsor.com.* Collections consist of Canadian art, including Inuit prints and carvings, with emphasis on Canadian artists from the late 18th-century to the present. Children's gallery; gift shop. (Wed-Thurs noon-5 pm; Fri to 9 pm; Sat-Sun 11 am-5 pm; closed Mon, holidays) **$**

Casino Windsor. *377 Riverside Dr, Windsor (N9A 7H7). Phone 519/258-7878; toll-free 800/991-7777. www.casinowindsor.com.* The casino overlooks the Detroit skyline and is easily accessible from a number of hotels. (Daily)

Colasanti Farms, Ltd. *1550 Rd 3 E, Kingsville (N9Y 2X7). 28 miles (45 kilometers) SE, on Hwy 3 near Ruthven. Phone 519/326-3287. www.colasanti.com.* More than 25 greenhouses with acres of exotic plants; large collection of cacti; farm animals, parrots, and tropical birds; crafts; mini-putt; restaurant. (Daily; closed Jan 1, Dec 25) **FREE**

★ **Coventry Gardens and Peace Fountain.** *Riverside Dr E and Pillette Rd, Windsor (N9A 5K4). Phone 519/253-2300.* Riverfront park and floral gardens with a 75-foot-high (23-meter) floating fountain; myriad 3-D water displays with spectacular night illumination (May-Sept, daily). Concessions. (Daily) **FREE**

Fort Malden National Historic Park. *100 Laird Ave, Amherstburg (N9V 2Z2). 18 miles (29 kilometers) S via City Rd 20. Phone 519/736-5416. www.parkscanada.gc.ca/malden.* Ten-acre (4-hectare) park with remains of fortification, original 1838 barracks, and 1851 pensioner's cottage; visitor and interpretation centers with exhibits. (May-Oct: daily 10 am-5 pm; Nov-Apr: contact park for information; closed statutory holidays) **$$**

Heritage Village. *20 miles (32 kilometers) SE via Hwy 3, then 5 miles (8 kilometers) S of Essex on County Rd 23. Phone 519/776-6909.* Historical artifacts and structures on 54 acres (22 hectares). Log cabins (1826 and 1835), railway station (1854), house (1869), church (1885), schoolhouse (1907), barber shop (circa 1920), general store (1847); transportation museum. Special events. Picnic facilities. **$$**

Jack Miner Bird Sanctuary. *332 Rd 3 W, Kingsville (N9Y 2E8). 27 miles (44 kilometers) SE via Hwy 3 and 29S, 2 miles (3 kilometers) N of Kingsville. Phone 519/733-4034; toll-free 877/289-8328. www.jackminer.com.* Canada geese and other migratory waterfowl; ponds; picnicking; museum. Canada geese "air shows" during peak season. (Mon-Sat daily) **FREE**

John Freeman Walls Historic Site and Underground Railroad Museum. *At Puce in Maidstone Township; Hwy 401 E from Windsor to Puce Rd, exit N. Phone 519/258-6253. www.undergroundrailroadmuseum.com.* John Freeman Walls, a fugitive slave from North Carolina, built this log cabin in 1846. It subsequently served as a terminal of the Underground Railroad and the first meeting place of the Puce Baptist Church. It has remained in the possession of Walls's descendants. (May-Oct, by appointment only)

North American Black Historical Museum. *227 King St, Amherstburg (N9V 2C7). 18 miles (29 kilometers) S on City Rd 20, exit Richmond St E. Phone 519/736-5433; toll-free 800/713-6336. www.blackhistoricalmuseum.com.* Chronicles achievements of black North Americans, many of whom fled the United States for freedom in Canada. Permanent exhibits on Underground Railroad; artifacts, archives, genealogical library. (Apr-Nov: Wed-Fri 10 am-5 pm; Sat-Sun 1-5 pm) **$**

Odette Sculpture Park. *Between Church St and Huron along the Detroit River. Phone 519/253-2300; toll-free 888/519-3333. www.windsorsculpturepark.com.* Walk or cycle the paths through this 2-mile (3.5-kilometer) park past large sculptures by Canadian and international artists. Self-guided maps located within the park. Metered parking at three locations. (Daily) **FREE**

Park House Museum. *219 Dalhousie St, Amherstburg (N9V 2C7). 18 miles (29 kilometers) S via City Rd 20, on the King's Naval Yard, near Fort Malden. Phone 519/736-2511.* Solid log, clapboard-sided house (circa 1795), considered to be oldest house in area. Built in Detroit, moved here in 1799. Restored and furnished as in the 1850s. Demonstrations of tinsmithing; pieces for sale. (June-Aug: daily; rest of year: Tues-Fri and Sun) **$**

Point Pelee National Park. *30 miles (48 kilometers) SE via Hwy 3, near Leamington. Phone 519/322-2365. www.parkscanada.gc.ca/pelee.* The park is a 6-square-mile (16-square-kilometer) tip of the Point Pelee peninsula. Combination dry land and marshland, the park also has a deciduous forest and is situated on two major bird migration flyways. More than 350 species have been sighted in the park. A boardwalk winds through the 2,500 acres (1,011 hectares) of marshland. Fishing, swimming, canoeing; picnicking, trails, and interpretive center, biking (rentals), transit ride (free). Contact the Chief of Visitor Services, RR 1, Leamington (N8H 3V4). (Daily) **$$$**

University of Windsor - University Players. *401 Sunset Ave, Windsor (N9B 3P4). Phone 519/253-4232. athena.uwindsor.ca.* (16,000 students) On campus is Essex Hall Theatre, featuring several productions per season (phone 519/253-3000 ext. 2808). (Sept-Mar)

Willistead Manor. *1899 Niagara St, Windsor (N8Y 1K3). Phone 519/253-2365.* (1906) Restored English Tudor mansion built for Edward Chandler Walker, son of famous distiller Hiram Walker, on 15 acres (6 hectares) of wooded parkland; elegant interiors with hand-carved woodwork; furnished in turn-of-the-century style. (July-Aug: Sun and Wed; Sept-June: first and third Sun of each month) **$$**

Windsor's Community Museum. *254 Pitt St W, Windsor (N9A 5L5). Phone 519/253-1812. www.windsorpubliclibrary.com/hours/museum.* Exhibits and collections interpret the history of Windsor and southwestern Ontario. Located in the historic Francois Baby House. (Tues-Sat 10 am-5 pm; also Sun 2-5 pm from May-Sept; closed holidays) **FREE**

Wreck Exploration Tours. *303 Concession 5, Leamington (N8H 3V5). Phone 519/326-1566; toll-free 888/229-7325.* Exploration of a 130-year-old wreck site. Shoreline cruise; artifact orientation. (May-Oct, reservations required)

Special Events

Carrousel of the Nations. *Throughout Windsor. Phone 519/255-1127. www.themcc.com.* This family event features "villages" showcasing food, music traditions, and dancing from all over the world. Three weekends in June.

Festival Epicure: A Celebration of Food, Wine, and Music. *Riverside Festival Plaza, Windsor (N9A 7H7). Phone 519/971-5005. www.festivalepicure.com.* Sample food from local eateries and wine from regional wineries. Performances ranging from pop to bluegrass by Detroit and Windsor musicians. Mid-July.

International Freedom Festival. *Riverside Dr and Ouelette Ave, Windsor (N9A 7H7). Phone 519/252-7264.* Two-week joint celebration by Detroit and Windsor with many events, culminating in fireworks display over the river. Late June-early July.

Leamington Tomato Festival. *Seacliff Park, Sea Cliff Dr and Erie, Leamington (N8H 2L3). Phone 519/326-2878. www.tomatofest.ca.* Mid-Aug.

Limited-Service Hotels

★ ★ BEST WESTERN CONTINENTAL INN. *3345 Huron Church Rd, Windsor (N9E 4H5). Phone 519/966-5541; toll-free 800/780-7234; fax 519/972-3384. www.bestwestern.com.* 71 rooms, 2 story. Check-in 3 pm, check-out 11 am. Restaurant. Outdoor pool. **$**

★ COMFORT INN. *1100 Richmond St, Chatham (N7M 5J5). Phone 519/352-5500; toll-free 800/228-5150; fax 519/352-2520. www.comfortinn.com.* 81 rooms, 2 story. Pets accepted, some restrictions. Check-out 11 am. **$**

★ ★ RADISSON RIVERFRONT HOTEL WINDSOR. *333 Riverside Dr W, Windsor (N9A 5K4). Phone 519/977-9777; toll-free 800/267-9777; fax 519/977-1411. www.radisson.com.* Located on the waterfront, this hotel offers a spectacular view of the Detroit skyline. 207 rooms, 19 story. Pets accepted, some restrictions. Complimentary full breakfast. Check-out noon. Fitness room. Indoor pool, whirlpool. **$**

★ ★ WHEELS INN. *615 Richmond St, Chatham (N7M 1R2). Phone 519/351-1100; fax 519/436-5541. www.wheelsinn.com.* Resort atmosphere; more than 7 acres (2.8 hectares) of indoor facilities. 350 rooms, 10 story. Check-out 11:30 am. Restaurant, bar. Fitness room. Indoor pool, outdoor pool. Business center. **$**

Full-Service Hotels

★ ★ ★ CASINO WINDSOR HOTEL. *377 Riverside Dr E, Windsor (N9A 7H7). Phone 519/258-7878; toll-free 800/991-7777; fax 519/985-5821. www.casinowindsor.com.* An oasis from the frenetic casino activity, this hotel's guest rooms feature views of the Detroit skyline or the city of Windsor. Suites offer perks such as Jacuzzi tubs, dining and living rooms, stereo systems, and towel warmers. The Health Club helps guests stay fit or unwind with a pool, gym, whirlpool, and sauna, while adjacent shops tempt browsers to empty their wallets. 389 rooms. Check-in 4 pm, check-out 11 am. Five restaurants, three bars. Fitness room. Indoor pool. Airport transportation available. Casino. **$$**

★ ★ ★ HILTON WINDSOR. *277 Riverside Dr W, Windsor (N9A 5K4). Phone 519/973-5555; toll-free 800/774-1500; fax 519/973-1600. www.hilton.com.* 305 rooms, 25 story. Check-in 4 pm, check-out noon. Restaurant, bar. Fitness room. Indoor pool, whirlpool. Business center. **$$$**

Restaurants

★ ★ CHATHAM STREET GRILL. *149 Chatham St W, Windsor (N9A 5M7). Phone 519/256-2555; fax 519/256-0346.* Seafood menu. Lunch, dinner. Closed holidays; Good Friday. Bar. **$$**

★ ★ COOK SHOP. *683 Ouellette Ave, Windsor (N9A 4J4). Phone 519/254-3377.* Italian menu. Dinner. Closed Mon; Dec 24-25; also Aug. Reservations recommended. **$$**

★ ★ TOP HAT SUPPER CLUB. *73 University Ave E, Windsor (N9A 2Y6). Phone 519/253-4644; fax 519/253-4646.* Seafood, steak menu. Lunch, dinner. Bar. Children's menu. **$$**

★ TUNNEL BAR-B-Q. *58 Park St E, Windsor (N9A 3A7). Phone 519/258-3663; fax 519/258-2923. www.tunnel-bar-b-q.com.* Barbecue, steak menu. Breakfast, lunch, dinner. Closed Dec 25. Children's menu. **$$**

Minnesota

Mother of the Mississippi and dotted by more than 4,000 square miles of water surface, Minnesota is not the "land of 10,000 lakes" as it so widely advertises—a recount indicates that the figure is closer to 12,000. Natives of the state may tell you that the lakes were stamped out by the hooves of Paul Bunyan's giant blue ox, Babe; geologists say they were created by retreating glaciers during the Ice Age. They are certainly the Minnesota vacationland's prize attraction.

Population: 4,375,099
Area: 79,548 square miles
Elevation: 602-2,301 feet
Peak: Eagle Mountain (Cook County)
Entered Union: May 11, 1858 (32nd state)
Capital: St. Paul
Motto: Star of the North
Nickname: Gopher State, North Star State
Flower: Pink and White Ladyslipper
Bird: Common Loon
Tree: Norway Pine
Fair: August in St. Paul
Time Zone: Central
Web Site: www.exploreminnesota.com
Fun Fact: Minnesota has one recreational boat for every six people, more than any other state.

Although Minnesota borders on Canada and is 1,000 miles from either ocean, it is nevertheless a seaboard state thanks to the St. Lawrence Seaway, which makes Duluth, on Lake Superior, an international port and the world's largest inland freshwater port.

Dense forests, vast grain fields, rich pastures, a large open pit iron mine, wilderness parks, outstanding hospitals and universities, high-technology corporations, and a thriving arts community—these are facets of this richly endowed state.

This is the get-away-from-it-all state: you can fish in a lake, canoe in the Boundary Waters along the Canadian border, or search out the Northwest Angle (near Baudette), which is so isolated that until recently it could be reached only by boat or plane. In winter, you can ice fish, snowmobile, or ski the hundreds of miles of downhill and cross-country areas. If you are not the outdoor type, there are spectator sports, nightlife, shopping, music, theater, and sightseeing in the Twin Cities (Minneapolis/St. Paul).

Explored by Native Americans, fur traders, and missionaries since the dawn of its known history, Minnesota surged ahead on the economic tides of lumber, grain, and ore. Today, the state has 79,000 farms covering 28 million acres; its agricultural production ranks high in sugar beets, butter, turkeys, sweet corn, soybeans, sunflowers, spring wheat, hogs, and peas. Manufacturing is important to Minnesota's economy. It also is a wholesale transportation hub and financial and retailing center of the Upper Midwest—the Mall of America in Bloomington is the country's largest.

The flags of four nations have flown over Minnesota as it passed through Spanish, French, and British rule, finally becoming part of the United States in segments in 1784, 1803, and 1818. A territory in 1849, Minnesota was admitted as a state less than a decade later. The Dakota (Sioux) War was a turning point in the state's history, claiming the lives of 400 settlers and an unknown number of Native Americans in 1862. It marked the end of Sioux control in the domain they called "the land of the sky-tinted waters." The vast forests poured out seemingly unending streams of lumber and the people spun legends of Paul Bunyan, an enduring part of American folklore. With the first

Calendar Highlights

FEBRUARY

John Beargrease Sled Dog Marathon *(Duluth). Phone 218/722-7631. www.beargrease.com.* A 500-mile, five-day marathon from Duluth to Grand Portage and back. About 20 to 25 mushers compete.

Winter Carnival *(St. Paul). Phone 651/223-4700.* Citywide happening, with ice and snow carving, parades, sports events, parties, and pageants.

JUNE

Judy Garland Festival *(Grand Rapids). Judy Garland Birthplace and Museum. Phone 218/327-9276 or toll-free 800/664-5839. www.judygarlandmuseum.com.* Discussions and presentations on the actress and singer's life and accomplishments. Viewing of *The Wizard of Oz*, children's activities, gala dinner.

Vikingland Drum and Bugle Corps Classic *(Alexandria). Phone Chamber of Commerce, 320/763-3161 or toll-free 800/235-9441.* National drum and bugle corps perform in the state's only field show competition.

JULY

Heritagefest *(New Ulm). Phone 507/354-8850.* An Old World-style celebration highlighting German traditions and culture; music, food, arts and crafts. Features entertainers from around the area and from Europe.

Laura Ingalls Wilder Pageant *(Tracy). Phone 507/859-2174.* A celebration of the life of Laura Ingalls Wilder, author of the *Little House* books.

Minneapolis Aquatennial *(Minneapolis). Phone 612/661-4700.* Parades, aquatic events, sports events, entertainment.

Paul Bunyan Water Carnival *(Bemidji). Phone Chamber of Commerce, 218/751-3541 or toll-free 800/458-2223.* Water show, parade, fireworks.

AUGUST

Bayfront Blues Festival *(Duluth). Bayfront Park. Phone 218/722-4011. www.bayfrontblues.com.* Three days of nonstop blues performances.

Minnesota State Fair *(St. Paul). Fairgrounds. Phone 651/642-2200. www.mnstatefair.org.* Horse show, kids' days, all-star revue; agricultural exhibitions and contests; 300 acres of attractions.

WE Country Music Fest *(Detroit Lakes). Soo Pass Ranch. Phone 218/847-1681 or toll-free 800/493-3378. www.wefest.com.* A three-day event featuring top country musicians and groups.

---

shipment of iron ore in 1884, Minnesota was on its way to a mine-farm-factory future.

When to Go/Climate

This state of lakes and prairie land offers warm summers, cool falls (excellent for fall foliage tours), wet springs, and cold winters. In the northernmost portion of the state, even summer temperatures are cool; winters are bitterly cold.

AVERAGE HIGH/LOW TEMPERATURES (° F)

International Falls

Jan 12/-10	**May** 65/40	**Sept** 64/43
Feb 19/-4	**June** 73/55	**Oct** 52/33
Mar 33/11	**July** 79/55	**Nov** 33/17
Apr 50/28	**Aug** 76/52	**Dec** 17/-2

Minneapolis/St. Paul

Jan 21/3	**May** 65/48	**Sept** 71/50
Feb 27/9	**June** 79/63	**Oct** 59/39
Mar 39/23	**July** 84/63	**Nov** 41/25
Apr 57/36	**Aug** 81/60	**Dec** 26/10

Parks and Recreation

Water-related activities, hiking, riding, various other sports, picnicking and visitor centers, as well as camping, are available in many of Minnesota's state parks. A $25 annual permit is required for vehicles entering a state park; it's good for the calendar year. A $7 daily permit is also available. Permits may be purchased at parks. Camping is $11-$15 per night, electric hook-up $3 additional; limited to two weeks in any one park, and reservations are accepted in all parks. In state forests, camping, backpack, or canoe-in sites are $7-$10 per night. There are small fees for other services. Fees are subject to change. Parks are open year-round; however, summer facilities vary in their opening and closing dates. All state parks are game refuges; hunting is prohibited. Pets are allowed on leash only. For further information, contact the Information Center, Minnesota Department of Natural Resources, 500 Lafayette Rd, St. Paul 55155; phone 651/296-6157 or toll-free 888/646-6367; www.dnr.state.mn.us/state_parks.

FISHING AND HUNTING

There's every kind of freshwater fishing here. Many of the lakes have more than 50 pounds of game fish per acre; the total catch in the state is as high as 20 million pounds a year. Dip a line for walleye, large or smallmouth bass, crappie, northern pike, muskellunge, brook, brown, rainbow or lake trout, or panfish. Hunting is equally popular in Minnesota: deer, bears, turkey, small game, and waterfowl are all plentiful.

Nonresident fishing license, $36; nonresident family license, $47; nonresident 24-hour license, $9.50; nonresident three-day license, $21; nonresident seven-day license, $25; trout stamp, $10. Nonresident small game license, $80.50; deer (firearm) $136. Fees are subject to change. For a more complete summary of hunting, fishing, and trapping regulations contact the Department of Natural Resources, 500 Lafayette Rd, St. Paul 55155-4040; phone 651/296-6157; www.dnr.state.mn.us.

Driving Information

Safety belts are mandatory for all persons in the front seat of a vehicle. Children under 12 years must be restrained anywhere in a vehicle; children ages 4-11 must use regulation safety belts; and children under age 4 must be in federally approved safety seats. For more information, phone 651/282-6558.

INTERSTATE HIGHWAY SYSTEM

The following alphabetical listing of Minnesota towns in this book shows that these cities are within 10 miles of the indicated interstate highways. Check a highway map for the nearest exit.

Highway Number	Cities/Towns within 10 Miles
Interstate 35	Albert Lea, Bloomington, Cloquet, Duluth, Faribault, Hinckley, Lakeville, Minneapolis, Northfield, Owatonna, St. Paul.
Interstate 90	Albert Lea, Austin, Blue Earth, Fairmont, Jackson, Luverne, Rochester, Winona.
Interstate 94	Alexandria, Anoka, Bloomington, Elk River, Fergus Falls, Minneapolis, Moorhead, St. Cloud, St. Paul, Sauk Centre.

Additional Visitor Information

Minnesota travel information is available for free from the Minnesota Travel Information Center, 500 Metro Square, 121 7th Pl E, St. Paul 55101. Phone 651/296-5029 or toll-free 800/657-3700 or visit www.exploreminnesota.com for information about special events, recreational activities, and places of interest. Also available is *Minnesota Explorer,* a free seasonal newspaper with events and attraction information, which includes a calendar of events for each season; canoeing, hiking, backpacking, biking, and fishing brochures; a state map and directories to restaurants, accommodations, and campgrounds, as well as regional and community tourism publications.

There are 12 travel information centers at entry points and along several traffic corridors of Minnesota; visitors will find the information provided at these stops helpful in planning a trip through the area. Their locations are as follows: northbound I-35 at the Iowa border; Hwy 53, 10 miles south of Eveleth; I-90 at the South Dakota border near Beaver Creek; I-90 at the Wisconsin border near La Crescent; Hwy 2, 10 miles east of the North Dakota border near Fisher; Hwy 61, 5 miles south of the Canadian border near Grand Portage (May-Oct); Hwy 53 in International Falls; I-94 at the North Dakota border in Moorhead; I-94 at the Wisconsin border near Lakeland; I-35 and Hwy 2 W in Duluth; Hwy 59 and Hwy 60, 5 miles north of the Iowa border near Worthington; Hwy 10 south of St. Cloud.

AVENUE OF THE PINES SCENIC BYWAY

Departing from Grand Rapids, the Avenue of Pines Scenic Byway winds through the Chippewa National Forest, along the shores of innumerable lakes (there are over 1,000 in the national forest alone) and through massive stands of sugar maple, pine, oak, and birch. Historically, the vast forests of northern Minnesota have been home to logging camps and lumbermen; more mythically, these are the woods where the legends of Paul Bunyan took root.

From Grand Rapids, drive west on Highway 2 toward Deer River, a logging and agricultural center. Immediately west of town, take Highway 46 northward, where the route enters the Chippewa National Forest. Wildlife is plentiful throughout the Chippewa National Forest; the highest concentration of breeding eagles in the lower 48 states can be found here. Also watch for black bears, beavers, timber wolves, and white-tailed deer. The lakes are filled with walleye.

Turn at signs for Lake Winnibigoshish and Winnie Dam. The lake—affectionately called Big Winnie—pools the waters of the Mississippi River, and canoeing and rafting the fast-flowing stream are popular activities below Winnie Dam. Campgrounds, swimming beaches, and picnic areas line the lake.

North of Winnie Dam, the route enters the corridor of red pines for which the byway is named. Many of the pines along the highway were planted in the 1930s by the Civilian Conservation Corps (the CCC). Little Cut Foot Sioux Lake is named for a warrior slain in a 1748 battle between the Chippewa and the Sioux. On the shores of the lake are a fish hatchery and a national forest visitor center, with evening naturalist events and exhibits about the flora and fauna of the forest. Adjacent to the center is a historic log ranger station, built in 1908.

Just east of Highway 46, on the shores of Little Cut Foot Sioux Lake, is Turtle Mound, a sacred ritual site for the Native Americans of the area. This turtle-effigy is actually an intaglio, a rare form of "mound" building where the image is sunk in the ground rather than raised above it. The Dakota Sioux constructed the effigy in the 18th century, before the arrival of Europeans to the area. After the Ojibwe people drove the Sioux westward, they adopted the site into their religious observances. A short 1/2-mile trail leads to this curious site, which continues to be used as a place of worship for practitioners of traditional native religion.

North of Squaw Lake, pastures and farms break up the dense forest; at Northome, the byway terminates at Highway 71. Turn west and drive 16 miles to Blackduck, and turn south on Highway 39. In fall this route, locally called the Scenic Highway, is especially beautiful as it cuts through forests of oak, maple, aspen, and birch turned a brilliant mosaic of color by the first frost. Creeks and rivers provide openings in the forest, and you can glimpse black spruce bogs and expansive wetlands occupied by waterfowl, beavers, and songbirds.

Across from Rabideau Lake is Camp Rabideau, a restored CCC camp open to visitors in summer. The camp was built in 1935, and until 1940 it housed hundreds of workers who spent summers planting trees and building roads, ranger stations, fire towers, and other infrastructure projects in Chippewa National Forest. A 1-mile interpretive trail winds through the camp.

The largest lake along this route is Cass Lake. On the lake's south shore is Norway Beach, with a long white sand swimming beach, four campgrounds, and hiking trails. The interpretive center here offers ranger-led activities in summer and also rents boats. A popular boat excursion is Star Island, unusual because the island has another lake at its center. At Highway 2, turn east and return to Grand Rapids. **(Approximately 150 miles)**

MINNESOTA'S RIVER TOWNS: THE GREAT RIVER ROAD

Minnesota's Great River Road is a national scenic byway that follows the mighty Mississippi from its origins in the northern portion of the state down to the Wisconsin border. Along the 575-mile route, the Byway winds through scenic portions of the state, showcasing Minnesota's natural beauty.

The route begins at the headwaters of the Mississippi, Lake Itasca, with its 32,000-acre state park that offers excellent hiking opportunities. The Byway then briefly heads northward toward the Chippewa National Forest, Lake Bemidji State Park, and the quaint town of Bemidji. Stop on the shores of Lake Bemidji for a look at the famous Paul Bunyan and Babe, the Blue Ox. The Byway then winds southward to Grand Rapids–stop by the Forest History Center there. Passing through Aitkin, you're close to the Rice Lake National Wildlife Refuge and Savanna Portage State Park, built around the portage that links the Mississippi with Lake Superior. Less than 10 miles south, in Brainerd, the Paul Bunyan State Trail awaits, along with a variety of recreational areas and a few great stops for lunch. In Little Falls, the Charles A. Lindberg State Park offers bald-eagle viewing, and farther south, the nationally recognized Clemens and Munsinger Gardens in St. Cloud present a variety of breathtaking blooms. Continuing south, two more towns, Elk River and Anoka, overflow with recreational opportunities. From there, the Byway enters the twin cities of Minneapolis and St. Paul.

Drive southeast out of the Twin Cities, tracing the Mississippi River along Minnesota's border with Wisconsin to the southern end of Highway 16. The sights begin in earnest in Hastings, a town started in 1819 and home to well-preserved Hudson River Gothic Revival-style residences. The Byway passes the Cannon River, where travelers can make a pit stop for some fine biking along a multiuse path. Red Wing is a still-thriving old wheat town with excellent bed-and-breakfast inns, hotels, and a theater. Water lovers enjoy little Frontenac State Park, which rests along the shoreline of Lake Pepin, the widest spot on the Mississippi River. Wabasha is one of the state's oldest towns; many of its ornate Victorian buildings have been renovated. South of Wabasha, numerous antebellum structures have been lovingly restored and are open for tours. Finally, Winona finishes the Byway tour, with its excellent fishing opportunities and a national wildlife refuge.

Keep in mind that some portions of the Byway are gravel roads, with low speed limits. You also share the road with cyclists, and although traffic is generally light, in the peak fall-color season, some areas may be crowded. For up-to-date information about this Byway, contact the Mississippi River Parkway Commission of Minnesota at 763/212-2560 or the Byway local Web site at www.mnmississippiriver.com. **(Approximately 125 miles)**

Aitkin (C-3)

See also Brainerd, Deerwood, Onamia

Population 1,698
Elevation 1,201 ft
Area Code 218
Zip 56431
Information Aitkin Area Chamber of Commerce, PO Box 127; phone 218/927-2316
Web Site www.aitkin.com

Once the bed of Lake Aitkin (AY-kin) and since drained by the deep channel of the Mississippi, the city now produces wild rice and other crops. Fishing enthusiasts, bound for one of the hundreds of lakes in Aitkin County, often stop here.

What to See and Do

Mille Lacs Lake. *14 miles S on Hwy 169.* (See ONAMIA)

Rice Lake National Wildlife Refuge. *State Hwy 65, McGregor (55760). 23 miles E on Hwy 210, then 5 miles S, off Hwy 65 near McGregor. Phone 218/768-2402.* An 18,127-acre refuge that includes 4,500-acre Rice Lake; migration and nesting area for ducks and Canada geese along Mississippi Flyway. Walking and auto trails; fishing. Headquarters (Mon-Fri; closed holidays). Area (Daily). **FREE**

Savanna Portage State Park. *County Rd 14 and McGregor, McGregor (55760). 8 miles NE on Hwy 169, then 14 miles E on Hwy 210 to McGregor, then 7 miles N on Hwy 65, 10 miles NE on County 14. Phone 218/426-3271. www.dnr.state.mn.us.* A 15,818-acre wilderness area built around historic portage linking the Mississippi River and Lake Superior. Swimming; fishing; boating (electric motors only; rentals), canoeing; hiking; cross-country skiing, snowmobiling; picnicking; camping.

Special Events

Fish House Parade. *Downtown. Phone 218/927-2316.* This parade features unusual floats, decorated ice-fishing houses, and appearances by celebrity guests. Fri after Thanksgiving.

Riverboat Heritage Days. *Phone 218/927-2316.* Celebrating its ties with the riverboat era, this town's summer festival includes a parade, music, food, children's activities, and historical displays. Mid-July.

Albert Lea (F-3)

See also Austin, Blue Earth, Owatonna

Settled 1855
Population 18,310
Elevation 1,299 ft
Area Code 507
Zip 56007
Information Albert Lea/Freeborn County Convention & Visitors Bureau, 143 W Clark; phone 507/373-3938 or toll-free 800/345-8414
Web Site www.freeborncounty.com/alcvb

An important agriculture, manufacturing, and distribution center, Albert Lea bears the name of the officer who surveyed the area. Known as "the Crossroads of the Upper Midwest" because both I-35 and I-90 cross the city, the town is best known for its two excellent museums.

What to See and Do

Fountain Lake. *Fountain St and Ridge Ave, Albert Lea (56007). Phone 507/377-4370.* Numerous parks offer picnicking, hiking, fishing, swimming, and boating.

Freeborn County Historical Museum, Library, and Village. *1031 N Bridge St, Albert Lea (56007). Phone 507/373-8003. www.smig.net/fchm.* Restored buildings include schoolhouse, general store, sheriff's office and jail, blacksmith and wagon shops, post office, train depot, church and log cabin. Museum has displays of tools, household items, firefighting equipment, toys, musical instruments. Library specializes in Freeborn County history and genealogy. (May-Sept, Tues-Sat)

Myre-Big Island State Park. *3 miles E at junction I-35 and I-90. Phone 507/379-3403.* 1,600 acres. Prairie pothole landscape includes rare white pelicans; hundreds of wildflowers; hiking, cross-country skiing; camping. **$**

Story Lady Doll and Toy Museum. *131 N Broadway Ave, Albert Lea (56007). Phone 507/377-1820.* Collection of 400 storybook dolls on display. Every other month museum exhibits unique dolls from area collectors. Gift shop has collector, designer, and ethnic dolls; puppets; and charms. (Daily; closed holidays).

Special Events

Big Island Rendezvous and Festival. *Bancroft Bay Park, 202 N Broadway Ave, Albert Lea (56007). Phone 507/373-3938; toll-free 800/658-2526.* Reenactment of the fur trade period; bluegrass music; ethnic food. First full weekend in Oct.

Freeborn County Fair. *Fairgrounds, Bridge Ave and Richway Dr, Albert Lea (56007). Just N of city limits on Bridge St. Phone 507/373-6965.* Entertainment; livestock exhibits; midway. Five days in late July or early Aug.

Limited-Service Hotel

★ HOLIDAY INN EXPRESS. *821 Plaza St, Albert Lea (56007). Phone 507/373-4000; toll-free 800/465-4329; fax 507/373-4000. www.holiday-inn.com.* 52 rooms. Complimentary continental breakfast. Check-in 3 pm, check-out 11 am. Indoor pool. **$**

Alexandria (D-2)

See also Fergus Falls, Glenwood, Sauk Centre

Settled 1866
Population 7,838
Elevation 1,400 ft
Area Code 320
Zip 56308
Information Chamber of Commerce, 206 Broadway; phone 320/763-3161 or toll-free 800/245-2539
Web Site www.alexandriamn.org

Easy access to hundreds of fish-filled lakes attracts a steady stream of tourists. The city has a manufacturing and trade industry base. Red River fur traders first explored this area, followed by settlers, one of whom gave the city his name.

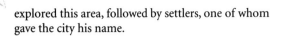

What to See and Do

Lake Carlos State Park. *2601 County Rd 38 NE, Alexandria (56308). 8 miles N on Hwy 29, then 2 miles W on County 38. Phone 320/852-7200.* A 1,236-acre park. Swimming, fishing, boat ramp; hiking, bridle trails; ski trails, snowmobiling; picnicking; camping. Sandy shoreline.

Runestone Museum. *206 Broadway, Alexandria (56308). Phone 320/763-3160. www.runestonemuseum.org.* Runic inscriptions on graywacke stone carry a 1362 date, supporting belief of exploration of North America long before Columbus discovered the New World. Found at the roots of a tree in 1898, authenticity of the stone has been the subject of great controversy. Also restored log cabins, farm artifacts, horse-drawn machinery, schoolhouse. Children with adult only. (Winter: Mon-Fri 10 am-5 pm, Sat 10 am-4 pm; Summer: Mon-Fri 9 am-5 pm, Sat 9 am-4 pm, Sun 11 am-4 pm) **$**

Special Events

Ole Oppe Fest. *Runestone Museum, 206 Broadway, Alexandria (56308). Phone toll-free 800/235-9441.* Dunk tanks, face painting, museum tours, street dance. Memorial Day weekend.

Vikingland Band Festival. *Runestone Museum, 206 Broadway, Alexandria (56308). Phone toll-free 800/235-9441.* Twenty select high school marching bands compete in state's largest summer marching band competition. Last Sun in June.

Vikingland Drum and Bugle Corps Classic. *Runestone Museum, 206 Broadway, Alexandria (56308). Phone toll-free 800/235-9441.* National drum and bugle corps perform in state's only field show competition. June.

Limited-Service Hotels

★★ HOLIDAY INN. *5637 Hwy 29 S, Alexandria (56308). Phone 320/763-6577; toll-free 800/465-4329; fax 320/762-2092. www.holiday-inn.com.* 149 rooms, 2 story. Pets accepted, some restrictions. Check-in 3 pm, check-out noon. High-speed Internet access. Restaurant, bar. Fitness room. Indoor pool, children's pool, whirlpool. **$**

★ RAMADA LIMITED. *507 W 50th Ave, Alexandria (56308). Phone 320/762-5161; toll-free 800/237-1234; fax 320/762-5337. www.ramadaalex.com.* 46 rooms, 2 story. Complimentary continental breakfast. Check-in 3 pm, check-out noon. High-speed Internet access. Indoor pool, whirlpool. **$**

Anoka (D-3)

See also Elk River, Minneapolis, St. Paul

Settled 1844
Population 17,192
Elevation 870 ft
Area Code 763
Information Anoka Area Chamber of Commerce, 12 Bridge Square, 55303; phone 763/421-7130
Web Site www.anokaareachamber.com

Once rivaling Minneapolis as the metropolitan center of the state, Anoka (pronounced a-NOKE-uh) continues as a thriving industrial city at the confluence of the Mississippi and Rum rivers. A city of parks and playgrounds, Anoka is minutes away from ten well-stocked lakes.

What to See and Do

Anoka County History Center. *2136 3rd Ave N, Anoka (55303). Phone 763/421-0600.* Built in 1904 as a home and medical office for two doctors. Now it preserves the history of the county. Photographs, artifacts. Tours (fee). (Tues-Fri, afternoons; first Sat of each month, mornings) **$$**

Father Hennepin Stone. *Near mouth of Rum River.* Inscription reads "Father Louis Hennepin—1680"; possibly carved by the Franciscan explorer.

Jonathan Emerson Monument. *City Cemetery, Anoka (55303).* Old settler inscribed 2,500 words from the Bible and personal philosophy on monument, erected it, and died a year later.

Special Event

Anoka County Suburban Fair. *3203 St. Francis Blvd, Anoka (55303). Phone 763/427-4070.* NTPA Tractor/truck pull, PRCA rodeo, demolition derbies, free entertainment, beer garden. Exhibits and an "old farm place." Last week in July.

Restaurant

★★ THE VINEYARD. *1125 W Main St, Anoka (55303). Phone 763/427-0959.* American menu. Lunch, dinner. Closed Thanksgiving, Dec 25. Bar. Children's menu. Casual attire. **$**

Austin (E-3)

See also Albert Lea, Owatonna, Spring Valley

Founded 1856
Population 21,907
Elevation 1,198 ft
Area Code 507
Zip 55912
Information Convention & Visitors Bureau, 104 11th Ave NW; phone 507/437-4563 or toll-free 800/444-5713
Web Site www.austincvb.com

Named for a pioneer settler, Austin became the county seat after two citizens stole the county records from another contender. The act aroused the voters, who cast their ballots for Austin. The Hormel Institute here, a unit of the Graduate School of the University of Minnesota, does research on fats and oils and their effect on heart disease. Austin's meat and food processing plants are an important industry; livestock, grain, and vegetables from a 100-mile radius are delivered here.

What to See and Do

Austin Fine Arts Center. *Oak Park Mall, 1301 18th Ave NW, Austin (55912). Phone 507/433-8451.* Features local artists. (Fri-Sun) **FREE**

J. C. Hormel Nature Center. *1304 21st St NE, Austin (55912). 1/4 mile N off I-90. Phone 507/437-7519.* Located on the former estate of Jay Hormel, the center includes interpretive building (Mon-Sat, also Sun afternoons; closed holidays); footpaths; woods, pond, streams, meadows; also cross-country skiing in winter, canoeing in summer. (Daily) **FREE**

Mower County Historical Center. *Mower County Fairgrounds, 12th St and 6th Ave SW, Austin (55912). Phone 507/437-6082.* Restored buildings include original Hormel building, log cabin, church, depot, country school; also steam locomotive, firefighting equipment and horse-drawn carriages; Native American artifacts; telephone museum; guide service (summer only). (June-Aug: daily; rest of year: by appointment) **$$**

SPAM Museum. *1937 Spam Blvd, Austin (55912). Phone 507/437-5100; toll-free 800/588-7726. www.spam.com.* The museum's love affair with America's favorite canned meat does not detract from its excellence as a museum, and even if you're not a SPAM fan, you'll enjoy the historic, hilarious, and slightly eccentric exhibits about the product. If you're looking for a unique gift to take home, the SPAM Museum gift shop offers up SPAM-labeled goods of every kind. (Mon-Sat 10 am-5 pm, Sun noon-4 pm) **FREE**

Special Events

Mower County Fair. *Mower County Fairgrounds, 700 12th St SW, Austin (55912). Phone 507/433-1868. www.mowercountyfair.com.* A Midwest steer show, tractor pull, 4-H fair, carnival, and old-time fiddlers contest are among the events at this county fair. Mid-Aug.

National Barrow Show. *Mower County Fairgrounds, 700 12th St SW, Austin (55912). Phone 507/433-1868.* This event, also known as the "World Series of Swine Shows," is a premier purebred hog show. Second week in Sept.

SpamTown USA Festival/Spam Jam. *329 N Main St, Austin (55912). Phone 507/437-4561.* Activities, which are held in various locations throughout the city, include a parade, concerts, street dance, canoe sprint, watermelon-eating contest, and fireworks. First weekend in July.

Limited-Service Hotel

★★ HOLIDAY INN. *1701 4th St NW, Austin (55912). Phone 507/433-1000; toll-free 800/985-8850; fax 507/433-8749. www.holiday-inn.com.* 121 rooms, 2 story. Pets accepted, some restrictions; fee. Complimentary continental breakfast. Check-in 3 pm, check-out 11 am. High-speed Internet access. Restaurant, two bars. Fitness room. Indoor pool, children's pool, whirlpool. Business center. **$**

Baudette (A-2)

See also International Falls, Roseau

Population 1,146
Elevation 1,086 ft

Area Code 218
Zip 56623
Information Lake of the Woods Area Tourism Bureau, PO Box 518; phone 218/634-1174 or toll-free 800/382-3474
Web Site www.lakeofthewoodsmn.com

On the Rainy River, Baudette (buh-DETT) is the gateway to the waters and thousands of islands of the Lake of the Woods area. Across the border from Ontario, it is an important trade and commerce center for a farm area producing seed potatoes, flax, alfalfa, clover, and small grain crops. It is also a 24-hour port of entry, with a toll-free bridge to Canada. (For border-crossing regulations, see MAKING THE MOST OF YOUR TRIP.)

What to See and Do

Lake of the Woods. *12 miles N on Hwy 172. Phone 218/634-1174; toll-free 800/382-3474. www.lakeofthewoods.com.* This lake is partly in the United States, partly in Canada. More than 2,000 square miles in area, with 14,000 charted islands and 65,000 miles of shoreline, it's known for its fishing, sandy beaches, and scenic beauty. It's especially famous for walleyed pike. Maps of driving tours through lush forests and wildlife areas are available from the Tourism Bureau. Also here is

> **Zippel Bay State Park.** *1 mile W on Hwy 11 to Hwy 172, 12 miles N to County 8, then 9 miles W. Phone 218/783-6252.* A 2,946-acre park. Swimming; fishing; boating (ramps). Hiking, snowmobiling. Picnicking. Camping. Beach area.

Lake of the Woods County Museum. *119 8th Ave SE, Baudette (56623). Phone 218/634-1200.* Museum of local history. (Late May-Sept, Tues-Sat) **FREE**

Northwest Angle/Islands. A Minnesota peninsula connected to Canada and separated by Lake of the Woods. Fishing. Lodging.

Rainy River. *70 miles from Rainy Lake, flows NW into Lake of the Woods.* Fishing, boating.

Red Lake Wildlife Management Area and Norris Camp. *Phone 218/783-6861.* 285,000 acres. Songbirds, bald eagles, moose, wolves, bears, grouse, deer, and waterfowl; hunting permitted in season; blueberry picking; camping (permit required). Norris Camp is a historic CCC camp from the 1930s. **FREE**

Limited-Service Hotel

★ AMERICINN *Hwy 11 W, Baudette (56623). Phone 218/634-3200; fax 218/634-3200. www.americinn.com.* 45 rooms. Complimentary continental breakfast. Check-in 3 pm, check-out 11 am. Indoor pool, whirlpool. **$**

Bemidji (B-2)

See also Itasca State Park, Walker

Settled 1894
Population 11,245
Elevation 1,350 ft
Area Code 218
Information Convention & Visitors Bureau, PO Box 66, 56619; phone 218/759-0164 or toll-free 800/458-2223
Web Site www.visitbemidji.com

Northland vacations support this city in a lake and forest area at the foot of Lake Bemidji (beh-MID-jee). Logging and Native American trails, wooded shorelines, and scenic rivers are just a few minutes away. Bemidji started as a trading post, became a lumber boomtown, a dairy and farming center, and is now enjoying the bounty of a new cycle of forest harvests. Once strictly a summer vacation area, Bemidji is host to winter sports enthusiasts, spring anglers, fall hunters, and nature lovers.

What to See and Do

Bemidji State University. *1500 Birchmont Dr NE, Bemidji (56601). Overlooking Diamond Point and Lake Bemidji. Phone 218/755-2040 (for appointment and calendar of campus events). www.bemidjistate.edu.* (1919) (5,400 students) Renowned for peat research, music programs, environmental studies, accounting, industrial technology. Guided tours.

Bemidji Tourist Information Center. *Hwy 197 (Paul Bunyan Dr), Bemidji (56619).* Houses collection of Paul Bunyan tools and artifacts with amusing descriptions. Fireplace of the States has stones from every state (except Alaska and Hawaii) and most Canadian provinces. (Memorial Day-Labor Day: daily; rest of year: Mon-Fri) **FREE** Adjacent is

Paul Bunyan and Babe. Giant replicas of Paul Bunyan and Babe, the Blue Ox; one of the most photographed statues in America.

Lake Bemidji State Park. *3401 State Park Rd NE, Bemidji (56601). 6 miles NE off Hwy 71. Phone 218/755-3843. www.dnr.state.mn.us.* A 1,688-acre park. Swimming, picnicking, fishing, hiking in a virgin pine forest. Boating (ramp, rentals); cross-country skiing; camping; biking. Naturalist programs. Visitor center.

Special Events

Annual 4th of July Water Carnival. *Phone 218/444-4401.* Water show, parade, fireworks. July 4 weekend.

Beltrami County Fair. *Phone 218/759-1425.* Agricultural exhibits, carnival rides, nightly entertainment. Early Aug.

Paul Bunyan Playhouse. *314 Beltrami Ave, Bemidji (56601). Downtown. Phone 218/751-7270. www.paulbunyanplayhouse.com.* Plays and musicals; professional casts. Wed-Sun. Reservations advised. Mid-June-mid-Aug.

Limited-Service Hotel

★ BEST WESTERN BEMIDJI INN. *2420 Paul Bunyan Dr NW, Bemidji (56601). Phone 218/751-0390; toll-free 800/780-7234; fax 218/751-2887. www.bestwestern.com.* 60 rooms, 2 story. Complimentary continental breakfast. Check-in 3 pm, check-out 11 am. High-speed Internet access. Indoor pool, whirlpool. **$**

Full-Service Resort

★ ★ RUTTGER'S BIRCHMONT LODGE. *530 Birchmont Beach Rd NE, Bemidji (56601). Phone 218/751-1630; toll-free 888/788-8437; fax 218/751-9519. www.ruttger.com.* This resort is a great vacation spot for all seasons. With sandy beaches, sailing, tennis, snowmobile trails, and more, this family-owned paradise has played host to some very high-profile guests including Woodrow Wilson and Malcolm Forbes. 28 rooms, 3 story. Check-in 4:30 pm, check-out 11:30 am. Restaurant, bar. Children's activity center. Fitness room. Beach. Indoor pool, outdoor pool, whirlpool. Tennis. Airport transportation available. **$**

Bloomington (D-3)

See also Minneapolis, St. Paul

Population 86,335
Elevation 830 ft
Area Code 952
Information Convention and Visitors Bureau, 7900 International Dr, Suite 990, 55425; phone 952/858-8500 or toll-free 800/346-4289
Web Site www.bloomingtonmn.org

Bloomington, located south of Minneapolis, is the state's fifth-largest city. The Mall of America, the largest shopping mall in the United States, draws an astounding 2.5 millions visitors each year, more than Walt Disney World, the Grand Canyon, and Graceland combined! But Bloomington is more than stores: a 10,000-acre wildlife refuge offers opportunities to view bald eagles and other wildlife, hike, cycle, and horseback ride, while the city's zoo is considered on the finest in the nation.

Bloomington Fun Fact:

- The Mall of America in Bloomington is the size of 78 football fields–9.5 million square feet.

What to See and Do

Hyland Ski & Snowboard Area. *8800 Chalet Rd, Bloomington (55438). 2 miles SW off I-494. Phone 952/835-4250. www.hylandski.com.* Three triple chairlifts, rope tow; cross-country trails; patrol, school, rentals; snowmaking; food court; nursery. Longest run is 2,000 feet; vertical drop 175 feet. (Thanksgiving-mid-Mar: Mon-Thurs 10 am-9 pm, Sat 9 am-10 pm, Sun 9 am-9 pm; closed Dec 25) **$$$$**

Mall of America. *60 E Broadway, Bloomington (55425). I-494 exit 24th Ave S; bounded by 81st St, Killebrew Dr, Hwy 77, and 24th Ave S. Phone 952/883-8800. www.mallofamerica.com.* A retail/family entertainment complex with more than 600 stores and restaurants. The fact that there is no sales tax on clothing makes shopping especially appealing here. The mall also features plenty of non-shopping activities for kids, such as Knott's Camp Snoopy, a 7-acre indoor theme park with rides and entertainment; the LEGO Imagination Center, with giant LEGO models and play areas; Golf Mountain miniature golf course; a 14-screen movie complex; and Underwater World, a walk-through aquarium. (Daily) Separate fees for activities. (Mon-Sat 10 am-9:30 pm, Sun 11 am-7 pm; closed Thanksgiving, Dec 25)

Minnesota Valley National Wildlife Refuge. *3815 American Blvd, Bloomington (55425). Phone 952/854-5900.* One of the only urban wildlife refuges in the nation. A 34-mile corridor of marsh and forest that is home to coyotes, badgers, and bald eagles; the refuge offers miles of trails for hiking, biking, horseback riding, and skiing. (Daily)

Minnesota Zoo. *13000 Zoo Blvd, Apple Valley (55124). E on I-494, then S on Hwy 77. Phone 952/431-9200; toll-free 800/366-7811. www.mnzoo.com.* Simulated natural habitats house 450 species of animals and 2,000 varieties of plants. Includes Discovery Bay, IMAX theater, Minnesota tropics, Ocean and Discovery Trails sections; 1 1/4-mile monorail. (Daily; closed Thanksgiving, Dec 25) **$$$**

Valleyfair. *1 Valleyfair Dr, Shakopee (55379). 7 miles S on I-35 W, then 9 miles W on Hwy 101. Phone 952/445-6500. www.valleyfair.com.* A 68-acre family amusement park bordering the Minnesota River. More than 75 rides and attractions, including four roller coasters, three water rides, antique carousel, and special rides for children. Entertainment includes an IMAX Theater plus musical shows. (Memorial Day-Labor Day, daily; May and Sept, some weekends) **$$$$**

Special Event

Renaissance Festival. *Hwy 169 S and Hwy 41, Shakopee (55379). Phone 952/445-7361.* Re-creation of 16th-century Renaissance village celebrating a harvest holiday. Entertainment, ethnic foods, 250 arts and crafts shops, games, equestrian events. Seven weekends beginning mid-Aug.

Limited-Service Hotels

★ ★ COUNTRY INN & SUITES BY CARLSON BLOOMINGTON AT MALL OF AMERICA. *2221 Killebrew Dr, Bloomington (55425). Phone 952/854-5555; toll-free 888/201-1746; fax 952/854-5564. www.countryinns.com.* 234 rooms, 6 story. Complimentary continental breakfast. Check-in 3 pm, check-out noon. Restaurant, bar. Fitness room. Indoor pool, whirlpool. Airport transportation available. **$**

★ ★ EMBASSY SUITES. *7901 34th Ave S, Bloomington (55425). Phone 952/854-1000; toll-free 800/362-2779; fax 952/854-6557. www.embassysuites.com.* Visitors here will appreciate the beauty of the garden atrium, which features bubbling brooks and waterfalls. Located at the airport, this hotel is a nice retreat for the business traveler. It offers two-room suites and a host of convenient amenities. 219 rooms, 10 story, all suites. Check-in 3 pm, check-out noon. Restaurant, bar. Fitness room. Indoor pool, whirlpool. Airport transportation available. Business center. **$$**

★ RAMADA INN. *250 N River Ridge Cir, Burnsville (55337). Phone 952/890-9550; toll-free 800/272-6232; fax 952/890-5161. www.ramada.com.* With 28 themed suites such as Casino Royale and Arabian Nights, this hotel is the perfect escape for leisure travelers. 60 rooms, 2 story. Complimentary continental breakfast. Check-in 4 pm, check-out 11 am. Bar. Fitness room. Indoor/outdoor pool, whirlpool. **$**

Full-Service Hotels

★ ★ ★ MALL OF AMERICA GRAND HOTEL. *7901 24th Ave S, Bloomington (55425). Phone 952/854-2244; toll-free 888/624-7263; fax 952/854-4421. www.moagrandhotel.com.* 300 rooms. Check-in 3 pm, check-out noon. Restaurant, bar. Fitness room. Indoor pool, whirlpool. Airport transportation available. Business center. **$**

★ ★ ★ MARRIOTT MINNEAPOLIS AIRPORT BLOOMINGTON. *2020 E 79th St, Bloomington (55425). Phone 952/854-7441; toll-free 800/228-9290; fax 952/854-7671. www.marriott.com.* Located just five minutes from the airport, guests will also appreciate that this hotel is adjacent to the famous Mall of America, the largest shopping mall in the country. Guests can also enjoy nearby restaurants, and much more. 473 rooms, 5 story. Check-in 4 pm, check-out noon. Restaurant, bar. Fitness room. Indoor pool. Airport transportation available. Business center. **$$**

Restaurants

★ ★ CIAO BELLA. *3501 Minnesota Dr, Bloomington (55435). Phone 952/841-1000; fax 952/841-9141.* The service, the food (portions are serious), and the bustling bar scene are all draws at this Italian-influenced

American restaurant. It's hard to resist the glamorous interior, especially when owner Rick Webb makes certain the philosophy is good, solid fun. Italian menu. Lunch, dinner. Closed Sun; holidays. Bar. Casual attire. Outdoor seating. **$$$**

★ **DA AFGHAN.** *929 W 80th St, Bloomington (55420). Phone 952/888-5824. www.daafghan.com.* Middle Eastern menu. Lunch, dinner. Closed Mon; Dec 24-25. Children's menu. Casual attire. **$**

★ **DAVID FONG'S.** *9329 Lyndale Ave S, Bloomington (55420). Phone 952/888-9294. www.davidfongs.com.* Chinese menu. Lunch, dinner. Closed Sun; holidays. Bar. Children's menu. Casual attire. **$$**

★ ★ ★ **KINCAID'S.** *8400 Normandale Lake Blvd, Bloomington (55437). Phone 952/921-2255; fax 952/921-2252. www.r-u-i.com/kin.* Touted as a fish, chop, and steak house, this restaurant delivers with a menu of well-portioned dishes, such as rock salt-roasted prime rib. The décor is reminiscent of a turn-of-the-century saloon, and the service carries on this relaxed social-center style. Steak menu. Lunch, dinner. Closed Thanksgiving, Dec 25. Bar. Children's menu. Casual attire. Outdoor seating. **$$**

★ ★ **LA FOUGASSE.** *5601 W 78th St, Bloomington (55439). Phone 952/835-1900. www.sofitel.com.* Mediterranean menu. Lunch, dinner, Sun brunch. Bar. Casual attire. Valet parking. Outdoor seating. **$$**

★ **LEEANN CHIN.** *14023 Aldrich Ave S, Burnsville (55337). Phone 952/898-3303. www.leeannchin.com.* Chinese menu. Lunch, dinner. Closed Memorial Day, Thanksgiving, Dec 25. Children's menu. Casual attire. Outdoor seating. **$$**

Blue Earth (F-3)

See also Albert Lea, Fairmont

Population 3,745
Elevation 1,093 ft
Area Code 507
Zip 56013
Information Chamber of Commerce, 118 E Sixth St; phone 507/526-2916
Web Site www.chamber.blue-earth.mn.us

The city gets its name from the Blue Earth River, which circles the town. The river was given the Native American name "Mahkota" (meaning blue earth) for a blue-black clay found in the high river banks. The town is the birthplace of the ice cream sandwich, and a 55 1/2-foot statue of the Jolly Green Giant stands in Green Giant Park.

What to See and Do

Faribault County Historical Society. *405 E Sixth St, Blue Earth (56013). Phone 507/526-5421.* (Wakefield House) Maintained as a pioneer home with furnishings depicting life between 1875 and 1900 (Tues-Sat 2-5 pm; also by appointment). Also 1870 rural school, an original log house, an Episcopal Church (1872), the Etta C. Ross Museum (limited hours), and an antique museum. **FREE**

Woodland School and Krosch Log House. *Faribault County Fairgrounds, N Main St and I-90, Blue Earth (56013). Phone 507/526-5421.* The Woodland School (circa 1870) is furnished as were one-room schools in the early 20th century. The Krosch Log House (circa 1860) was once home to a family of 11 children. Inquire for tours.

Special Events

Citywide Garage Sales. *118 E Sixth St, Blue Earth (56013). Phone 507/526-2916.* Late Apr.

Faribault County Fair. *Faribault County Fairgrounds, Giant Dr and Blue Earth, Blue Earth (56013). Phone 507/893-3704.* Carnival, 4-H exhibits, entertainment. Fourth week in July.

Upper Midwest Woodcarvers and Quilters Expo. *405 E Sixth St, Blue Earth (56013). Phone 507/526-2916.* Creative quilters and skilled carvers display their crafts. Visitors can watch as exhibitors demonstrate how to carve a piece of wood into a work of art. Mid-Aug.

Limited-Service Hotel

★ **SUPER 8.** *1420 Giant Dr, Blue Earth (56013). Phone 507/526-7376; toll-free 800/800-8000; fax 507/526-2246. www.super8.com.* 42 rooms. Check-out 11 am. **$**

Boundary Waters Canoe Area Wilderness (B-5)

Information Phone toll-free 800/745-3399
Web Site www.bwcaw.org

The Boundary Waters Canoe Area Wilderness, part of the Superior National Forest, is perhaps the finest canoe country in the United States. Extending 150 miles along the border with Canada, this 1 million-acre wilderness area welcomes nearly a quarter-million canoes enthusiasts each year, yet the area retains its wilderness feel and a rich plant and animal life, including bears, wolves, mountain lions, bald eagles, hawks — over 200 species altogether. To canoe along the 1,200 miles of various canoe routes, you must apply for a travel permit ($12) by early January, which is processed by a lottery; notifications are generally given in late January. Additional fees are $10 for adults; $5 for senior citizens and children under 18. Camping and cabins are also available for overnight stays, and hiking trails are plentiful in the area.

Brainerd (C-2)

See also Aitkin, Deerwood, Little Falls, Onamia, Pine River

Founded 1870
Population 12,353
Elevation 1,231 ft
Area Code 218
Zip 56401
Information Brainerd Lakes Area Chamber of Commerce, 124 N 6th St, PO Box 356; phone 218/829-2838 or toll-free 800/450-2838
Web Site www.explorebrainerdlakes.com

Brainerd calls itself the "hometown of Paul Bunyan" and is the center of lore and legend about the giant lumberjack and his blue ox, Babe. On the Mississippi River at the geographical center of the state, the city was once part of a dense forest used by the Chippewa as a hunting ground and blueberry field. Created by the Northern Pacific Railroad, Brainerd was named for the wife of a railroad official. There are 465 pine-studded, sandy-bottomed lakes within a 25-mile radius and over 180 lodging choices. Golfing, fishing, canoeing, swimming, and water sports are available in the summer; skiing and snowmobiling in the winter.

What to See and Do

Crow Wing County Historical Society Museum. *320 Laurel St, Brainerd (56401). Adjacent to Courthouse. Phone 218/829-3268.* Restored sheriff's residence and remodeled jail features exhibits on domestic life, logging, mining, and the railroad. Research library. (Mon-Sat; closed holidays) **$$**

Paul Bunyan State Trail. *Hwy 371 and Excelsior Rd, Brainerd (56401). www.paulbunyantrail.com.* 100-mile recreational trail for joggers, walkers, bikers, hikers, and snowmobilers (rentals available). Trail passes by six communities, nine rivers, and 21 lakes.

Recreational Areas. Swimming at hundreds of lakes in the area. Also boating, canoe routes, fishing, water-skiing, playground, golf courses, picnicking, hiking, biking, camping; snowmobile and ski trails. Phone Chamber of Commerce at 218/829-2838 or at toll-free 800/450-2838.

Special Events

Brainerd International Raceway. *5523 Birchdale Rd, Brainerd (56401). 7 miles N on Hwy 371. Phone 218/824-7220. www.brainerdraceway.com.* Motor racing events. Early May-mid-Aug.

Crow Wing County Fair. *2000 13th St, Brainerd (56401). Phone 218/824-1065.* Amusement rides; livestock; entertainment. Five days in early Aug.

Ice Fest. *Breezy Point Resort, Brainerd (56401). Phone 218/829-2838.* Ice sculptures, carving. Bands, races, dance, golf. Second weekend in Jan.

Limited-Service Hotels

★★ CRAGUN'S PINE BEACH LODGE AND CONFERENCE CENTER. *11000 Cragun's Rd, Brainerd (56401). Phone 218/829-3591; toll-free 800/272-4867; fax 218/829-9188.* 285 rooms, 2 story. Check-in 5 pm, check-out noon. Restaurant, bar. Children's activity center. Fitness room. Beach. Indoor pool, outdoor pool, whirlpools. Tennis. Airport transportation available. **$**

★★ GRAND VIEW LODGE. *23521 Nokomis Ave, Nisswa (56468). Phone 218/963-2234; toll-free 800/*

432-3788; *fax 218/963-0261. www.grandviewlodge.com.* Overlooks Gull Lake. 77 rooms, 2 story. Check-in 4:30 pm, check-out 12:30 pm. Restaurant, bar. Children's activity center. Beach. Indoor pool, whirlpool. Golf. Tennis. Airport transportation available. **$$**

★ ★ **MADDEN'S ON GULL LAKE.** *11266 Pine Beach Peninsula, Brainerd (56401). Phone 218/829-2811; toll-free 800/642-5363; fax 218/829-6583. www.maddens.com.* As Minnesota's largest resort, it encompasses over 1,000 acres of land. 293 rooms, 3 story. Closed mid-Oct-mid-Apr. Check-in 4:30 pm, check-out 11 am. Restaurant, bar. Children's activity center. Fitness room. Beach. Three indoor pools, two outdoor pools, whirlpools. Golf. Tennis. Airport transportation available. **$**

★ ★ **RAMADA INN.** *2115 S 6th St, Brainerd (56401). Phone 218/829-1441; toll-free 800/272-6232; fax 218/829-1444. www.ramada.com.* 150 rooms, 2 story. Pets accepted; fee. Check-in 3 pm, check-out 11 am. High-speed Internet access. Restaurant, bar. Indoor pool, whirlpool. Tennis. Airport transportation available. **$**

Restaurants

★ **BAR HARBOR SUPPER CLUB.** *8164 Interlachen Rd, Lake Shore (56468). Phone 218/963-2568; fax 218/963-2841.* American menu. Lunch, dinner. Closed Dec 24-25. Bar. Children's menu. Outdoor seating. **$$**

★ **IVEN'S ON THE BAY.** *5195 N Hwy 371, Brainerd (56401). Phone 218/829-9872; fax 218/829-6666. www.ivensonthebay.com.* Seafood menu. Dinner. Closed holidays. Bar. Children's menu. **$$**

Cloquet (C-4)

See also Duluth

Population 10,885
Elevation 1,204 ft
Area Code 218
Zip 55720
Information Cloquet Area Chamber of Commerce, 225 Sunnyside Dr, PO Box 426; phone 218/879-1551 or toll-free 800/554-4350

Formerly known as Knife Falls, Cloquet (clo-KAY) is a largely a lumber and mill town. A treasure in the town is the Lindholm Service Station, a gas station and tire store designed by Frank Lloyd Wright in 1956.

Limited-Service Hotel

★ **AMERICINN.** *111 Big Lake Rd, Cloquet (55720). Phone 218/879-1231; fax 218/879-2237.* 51 rooms, 2 story. Pets accepted, some restrictions; fee. Complimentary continental breakfast. Check-out 11 am. Indoor pool, whirlpool. **$**

Cook (B-3)

See also Boundary Waters Canoe Area Wilderness, Crane Lake, Eveleth, Hibbing, Superior National Forest, Tower, Virginia

Population 680
Elevation 1,306 ft
Area Code 218
Zip 55723
Information Cook Area Chamber of Commerce, PO Box 296; phone toll-free 800/648-5897
Web Site www.cookminnesota.com

Almost at the center of the "arrowhead country," Cook provides access to outdoor vacations, serves the logging industry, and is the western gateway to Superior National Forest (see). A Ranger District office of the forest is located here.

What to See and Do

Lakes. In this area, fishing for northern pike, panfish, crappie, and walleye is excellent.

Elbow Lake. *26 Central Ave S, Cook (55723). 10 miles N on County 24.* 2,000 acres, 12 islands.

Lake Vermilion. *3068 Vermilion Dr, Cook (55723). 5 1/2 miles NE via County 24 or County 78. Phone 218/666-2627.*

Pelican Lake. *21 miles N on Hwy 53.* 54 miles of shoreline, 50 islands, sandy beaches; fishing for northern pike and panfish.

Limited-Service Hotel

★ **NORTH COUNTRY INN.** *4483 Hwy 53, Orr (55771). Phone 218/757-3778; fax 218/757-3116.*

www.northcountryinn.com. 12 rooms. Pets accepted, some restrictions; fee. Check-out 11 am. **$**

Crane Lake (B-4)

See also Cook, Superior National Forest, Tower

Population 350
Elevation 1160 ft
Area Code 218
Zip 55725
Information Visitor & Tourism Bureau, 7238 Handberg Rd; phone 218/993-2901 or toll-free 800/362-7405
Web Site www.visitcranelake.com

A natural entry to the Voyageur Country, Crane Lake, in Superior National Forest (see), is bounded on the north by the Canadian Quetico Provincial Park. (For border-crossing regulations, see MAKING THE MOST OF YOUR TRIP.)

Crookston (B-1)

See also Minnetonka, Thief River Falls

Settled 1872
Population 8,119
Elevation 890 ft
Area Code 218
Zip 56716
Information Convention & Visitors Bureau, 118 Fletcher St, PO Box 115; phone 218/281-4320 or toll-free 800/809-5997
Web Site www.visitcrookston.com

Crookston is the major city of the broad and level Red River Valley, carved by glacial Lake Agassiz; the area is known for the huge catfish that make their home by the dam on Red Lake River, which is also an excellent canoeing route. For a taste of old-fashioned, homemade candy and drinks from a soda fountain, visit Widman's Candy Store on South Broadway.

What to See and Do

Central Park. *Ash and Robert sts, Crookston (56716). N Ash St, on Red Lake River. Phone 218/281-1232.* Playground, picnicking, boat ramp, fishing, canoeing; tent, trailer and RV camping (Mid-May-early Oct, fee), showers. Indoor swimming pool adjacent. Civic arena, roller skating (May-Oct), ice skating (Nov-Mar), indoor tennis (Apr-Oct). **$$$**

Polk County Historical Museum. *719 E Robert St, Crookston (56716). Hwy 2 E. Phone 218/281-1038.* Houses several rooms depicting early days of America including an original log cabin, one-room schoolhouse, and a building with antique machinery. Also on the premises are a chapel and miniature train exhibit. (Mid-May-mid-Sept: daily; rest of year: by appointment) **DONATION**

Special Event

Ox Cart Days. *Phone toll-free 800/809-5997.* Held in the city's Central Park, this festival includes ox cart races, battle of the bands, pageants, parades, and fireworks. Third weekend in Aug.

Deer River (B-3)

See also Grand Rapids, Hibbing

Population 838
Elevation 1,291 ft
Area Code 218
Zip 56636
Information Chamber of Commerce, PO Box 505; phone 218/246-8055 or toll-free 888/701-2226
Web Site www.deerriver.org

A harvesting point for lumber products of Chippewa National Forest, Deer River also serves nearby farms as well as hunting and fishing camps. A Ranger District office of the Chippewa National Forest (see GRAND RAPIDS) is located here.

What to See and Do

Chippewa National Forest. *200 Ash Ave NW, Cass Lake (56633). At W edge of city, access on Hwy 46. Phone 218/335-8600.* (See GRAND RAPIDS)

Cut Foot Sioux Lakes. *15 miles NW on both sides of Hwy 46.* Fishing, hunting, camping. Turtle and snake Indian mounds along shore.

Deerwood

See also Aitkin, Brainerd

Population 524
Elevation 1,079 ft

Area Code 218
Zip 56444

The area surrounding Deerwood is dotted with small lakes, making fishing, canoeing, and boating-related water sports top attractions here. Winter recreational activities, including snowmobiling and cross-country skiing, also abound.

Limited-Service Hotels

★ COUNTRY INN BY CARLSON DEERWOOD. *23884 Front St, Deerwood (56444). Phone 218/534-3101; toll-free 888/201-1746; fax 218/534-3685. www.countryinns.com.* 38 rooms, 2 story. Pets accepted, some restrictions; fee. Complimentary continental breakfast. Check-out 11 am. High-speed Internet access, wireless Internet access. Indoor pool, whirlpool. **$**

★ ★ RUTTGER'S BAY LAKE LODGE. *25039 Tame Fish Lake Rd, Deerwood (56444). Phone 218/678-2885; toll-free 800/450-4545; fax 218/678-2864. www.ruttgers.com.* Founded in 1898, this rustic lodge is rich with family pride and history and overlooks the lake. 30 rooms, 2 story. Check-in 5 pm, check-out noon. Restaurant, bar. Children's activity center. Fitness room. Beach. Indoor pool, two outdoor pools, whirlpools. Golf. **$**

Detroit Lakes (C-1)

See also Fergus Falls, Itasca State Park, Moorhead, Park Rapids

Population 6,635
Elevation 1,365 ft
Area Code 218
Zip 56501
Information Detroit Lakes Regional Chamber of Commerce, PO Box 348, 56502; phone 218/847-9202 or toll-free 800/542-3992
Web Site www.visitdetroitlakes.com

A French missionary visiting this spot more than 200 years ago commented on the beautiful *détroit* (strait), and this came to be the name of the town. "Lakes" was added to promote the 412 lakes found within 25 miles. Tourism and agriculture are major sources of income.

What to See and Do

Becker County Historical Society Museum. *714 Summit Ave, Detroit Lakes (56502). Corner of Summit and W Front, two blocks off Hwy 10. Phone 218/847-2938. www.beckercountyhistory.org.* Exhibits pertaining to the history of the county. (Memorial Day-Labor Day: Tues-Sat; rest of year: Sat-Sun; closed holidays) **FREE**

Detroit Lakes City Park. *Washington Ave and W Lake Dr, Detroit Lakes (56502).* Picnic tables, grills, shelters; tennis courts, lifeguard (Mid-June-Aug), shuffleboard, ball diamonds; playground, boat rentals, fishing. One mile-long beach, bathhouse. Motorboat sightseeing services nearby. Shops. (June-Labor Day, daily) **FREE**

Tamarac National Wildlife Refuge. *35704 County Hwy 26, Rochert (56578). 8 miles E on Hwy 34, then 9 miles N on County 29. Phone 218/847-2641.* On 43,000 acres. Twenty-one lakes, abundant wild rice; trumpeter swans, grouse, beaver, deer; flyway sanctuary for thousands of songbirds, ducks, geese; picnicking, fishing. (Daily) Visitor center (Memorial Day-Labor Day: daily; rest of year: Mon-Fri; closed holidays). **FREE**

Thousand Pines Resort. *2 miles E, off Hwy 34. Phone 218/847-1661.* Double and triple chairlifts, two T-bars, four rope tows; patrol, school, rentals, snowmaking; cafeteria. Vertical drop 235 feet. (Mid-Nov-Mar, Fri-Sun) **$$$$**

Special Events

Becker County Fair. *Becker County Fairgrounds, West Lake Dr and Rossman Ave, Detroit Lakes (56501). Phone 218/847-8407.* This county fair has been held for more than 100 years and features musical entertainment, 4-H show, pony rides, demo derby, and arts and crafts. Late July.

Festival of Birds. *Phone 218/847-9202.* Three-day migration celebration. Workshop, speakers, displays and guided field trips. Mid-May.

Northwest Water Carnival. *Detroit Lake, throughout city. Phone 218/847-3081.* Includes water show, races, fishing derby, parade, flea markets. Mid-July.

Polar Fest. *Phone 218/817-9202.* Weekend filled with sports, entertainment, polar plunge. Mid-Feb.

WE Country Music Fest. *Soo Pass Ranch, 3 miles S on Hwy 59. Phone 218/847-1681; toll-free 800/493-3378. www.wefest.com.* Three-day event featuring many top country musicians and groups. First weekend in Aug.

White Earth Powwow. *Phone 218/935-0417; toll-free 800/542-3992.* Celebrates the treaty between the Sioux and Chippewa. Mid-June.

Limited-Service Hotel

★ ★ **HOLIDAY INN.** *1155 Hwy 10 E, Detroit Lakes (56501). Phone 218/847-2121; toll-free 800/465-4329; fax 218/847-2121. www.holiday-inn.com.* 98 rooms, 4 story. Check-in 3 pm, check-out noon. High-speed Internet access. Restaurant, bar. Beach. Indoor pool, whirlpool. **$**

Restaurants

★ ★ **FIRESIDE.** *1462 E Shore Dr, Detroit Lakes (56501). Phone 218/847-8192.* American menu. Dinner. Closed late Nov-Mar. Children's menu. **$$**

★ **LAKESIDE 1891.** *200 W Lake Dr, Detroit Lakes (56501). Phone 218/847-7887; fax 215/847-7887.* Former hotel built in 1891. American menu. Dinner, Sun brunch. Closed holidays. Bar. Children's menu. Outdoor seating. **$$**

Duluth (C-4)

See also Cloquet, Two Harbors, Virginia

Founded 1856
Population 85,493
Elevation 620 ft
Area Code 218
Information Convention & Visitors Bureau, 100 Lake Place Dr, 55802; phone 218/722-4011 or toll-free 800/438-5884
Web Site www.visitduluth.com

At the western tip of Lake Superior, Duluth is a world port thanks to the St. Lawrence Seaway. Ships of many countries fly their flags at its 49 miles of docks. This gives the products of Minnesota and the Northwestern states better access to markets of the world and stimulates development of new industries converting raw materials to finished goods. One of the foremost grain exporting ports in the nation, Duluth-Superior Harbor also handles iron ore, coal, limestone, petroleum products, cement, molasses, salt, grain, soybean oil, soybeans, wood pulp, paper, and chemicals. The twin ports are the westernmost water terminus for goods consigned to the Northwest.

High bluffs rise from the lakeshore, protecting the harbor from the elements. Minnesota Point, a sandbar extending 7 miles from Minnesota to the Wisconsin shore, protects the inner harbor.

There are two ways for ships to enter the Duluth-Superior Harbor: one by way of the Superior side, called the Superior Entry; and the other, the Duluth Ship Canal, with an aerial lift bridge located a few blocks south of downtown Duluth. The distance between the two is about 8 miles.

As the state's gateway to the sea, Duluth is a business, industrial, cultural, recreational, and vacation center. The great Minnesota northwoods begin almost at the city's boundaries. From here the North Shore Drive (see GRAND MARAIS) follows Lake Superior into Canada; other highways fan out to the lake country, the great forests, and south to the Twin Cities. The headquarters of the Superior National Forest is located here.

Long a fur trading post, Duluth is the city of early voyageurs, Chippewa, and French and British explorers. The first major shipment from the twin ports of Duluth and Superior was 60 canoe loads of furs in 1660. Modern commerce started in 1855 following construction of the lock at Sault Ste. Marie, Michigan, the eastern entrance to Lake Superior. The French explorer Daniel Greysolon, Sieur du Lhut, landed here in 1679. The city takes its name from him.

What to See and Do

Aerial Lift Bridge. *525 Lake Ave S, Duluth (55802). Foot of Lake Ave. Phone 218/722-3119.* (138-foot high, 336-foot long, 900 tons in weight). Connects mainland with Minnesota Point, lifting 138 feet in less than a minute to let ships through.

Clayton Jackson McGhie Memorial. *First St and Second Ave E, Duluth (55807). Phone 218/591-0729. www.claytonjacksonmcghie.org.* In 1920, three African-American circus workers, held in the Duluth City Jail on false charges of raping a white woman, were dragged by a mob of thousands to First Street and Second Avenue and lynched, much to the delight of the cheering crowd. The entire event was recorded in photographs, but with a few years, forgotten. Today, the Clayton Jackson McGhie Memorial pays tribute to the three men killed—their likenesses are carved in a 7-foot bronze relief on the monument—and reminds visitors and citizens alike of this painful event in Duluth's history, so that it can never be repeated.

The Depot, St. Louis County Heritage and Arts Center. *506 W Michigan St, Duluth (55802). Phone 218/727-8025.* Building was originally Union Depot (1890); houses three museums, a visual arts institute, and four performing arts organizations. (Daily; closed holidays) **$$$** Admission includes

Depot Square. (Lower level). Reproduction of 1910 Duluth street scene with ice cream parlor, storefronts, gift shops, trolley rides.

Duluth Children's Museum. *506 W Michigan St, Duluth (55802). Phone 218/733-7543.* Natural, world, and cultural history; featuring giant walk-through tree in habitat exhibit.

Lake Superior Railroad Museum. *506 W Michigan St, Duluth (55802).* Extensive displays of historic railroad equipment and memorabilia. Trolley car rides and periodical excursions, some using steam locomotives.

St. Louis County Historical Society. *506 W Michigan St, Duluth (55802). Phone 218/733-7580.* Settlement of northern Minnesota; logging, mining, railroading, and pioneer life exhibits.

Duluth-Superior Excursions. *323 Harbor Dr, Duluth (55802). Foot of 5th Ave W and waterfront. Phone 218/722-6218.* Two-hour tour of Duluth-Superior Harbor and Lake Superior on the *Vista King* and *Star.* (Mid-May-mid-Oct, daily) Also dinner and dance cruises. **$$$**

Enger Tower. *Skyline Dr and 18th Ave W, Duluth (55802).* Tower providing the best view of Duluth-Superior; dedicated in 1939 by Norway's King Olav V, then Crown Prince; dwarf conifer and Japanese gardens, picnic tables on grounds. **FREE**

Fitger's Brewery Complex. *600 E Superior St, Duluth (55802). Phone 218/722-8826.* Historic renovated brewery transformed into more than 25 specialty shops and restaurants on the shore of Lake Superior. Summer courtyard activities. (Daily; closed holidays) **FREE** From here take

Duluth Lakewalk. *600 E Superior St, Duluth (55802). Phone toll-free 800/438-5884.* Walk along Lake Superior to the Aerial Lift Bridge; statues, kiosks; horse and buggy rides.

Glensheen. *3300 London Rd, Duluth (55804). Phone 218/726-8910 (recording).* (Circa 1905-1908). Historic 22-acre Great Lake estate on west shore of Lake Superior; owned by University of Minnesota. Tours. Grounds (Daily). Mansion (May-Oct: daily; rest of year: weekends; closed holidays). **$$$**

Jay Cooke State Park. *500 Hwy 210 E, Carlton (55718). SW via Hwy 23, 210, adjoining gorge of St. Louis River. Phone 218/384-4610.* Located on 8,813 acres of rugged country; fishing; cross-country skiing, snowmobiling; picnicking; camping (electric hook-ups, dump station); visitor center.

Karpeles Manuscript Library Museum. *902 E First St, Duluth (55805). Phone 218/727-3967.* Holds original drafts of *US Bill of Rights, Emancipation Proclamation,* Handel's *Messiah,* and others. (June-Aug: daily noon-4 pm; rest of year: Tues-Sun) **FREE**

Lake Superior Maritime Visitors Center. *600 Lake Ave S, Duluth (55802). Canal Park Dr next to Aerial Bridge. Phone 218/727-2497.* Ship models, relics of shipwrecks, reconstructed ship cabins; exhibits related to maritime history of Lake Superior and Duluth Harbor and the Corps of Engineers. Vessel schedules and close-up views of passing ship traffic. (Apr-mid-Dec: daily; rest of year: Fri-Sun; closed Jan 1, Thanksgiving, Dec 25) **FREE**

Lake Superior Zoological Gardens. *7210 Fremont St, Duluth (55802). Phone 218/723-3748.* This is a 12-acre zoo with more than 80 exhibits; picnicking. (Daily) **$$$**

Leif Erikson Park. *11th Ave E and London Rd, Duluth (55802). Phone 218/723-3347.* Statue of Norwegian explorer and half-size replica of boat he sailed to America in AD 997. Rose Garden. (May-mid-Sept, daily) **FREE**

North Shore Scenic Railroad. *506 W Michigan St, Duluth (55802). Departs from the Depot. Phone 218/722-1273; toll-free 800/423-1273.* Narrated sightseeing trips along 28 miles of Lake Superior's scenic North Shore, from Duluth to Two Harbors. Other excursions available: Duluth to Lester River, Pizza Train. Trips range from 1 1/2 to 6 hours. (Apr-Oct, daily) **$$$**

Park Point Recreation Center. *At tip of Minnesota Point.* 200-acre playground; picnicking; boat ramp; swimming facilities, lifeguard. (June-Labor Day, daily) **FREE**

S/S *William A. Irvin*. *350 Harbor Dr, Duluth (55802). On the waterfront, adjacent to Duluth Convention Center. Phone 218/722-5573.* Guided tours of former flagship of United States Steel's Great Lakes fleet that journeyed inland waters from 1938 to 1978. Explore decks and compartments of restored 610-foot ore carrier, including the engine room, elaborate guest staterooms, galley, pilothouse, observation lounge, elegant dining room. Free parking. (May-mid-Oct) **$$$**

Scenic North Shore Drive. *Hwy 61 from Duluth to Canada along Lake Superior.*

Site of Fond du Lac. *On St. Louis River.* Originally a Native American village, later a trading post; school, mission established here in 1834.

Skyline Parkway Drive. A 27-mile scenic road along bluffs of city constructed during 1930s; view from 600 feet overlooks harbor, lake, bay, and river.

Spirit Mountain Ski Area. *9500 Spirit Mountain Pl, Duluth (55810). 10 miles S on I-35, exit 249. Phone 218/628-2891; toll-free 800/642-6377. www.spirirmt.com.* Two quad, two triple, double chairlifts; patrol, school, rentals, snowmaking; bar, cafeteria; children's center. Twenty-four runs, longest run 5,400 feet; vertical drop 700 feet. (Nov-Mar, daily) Half-day rates. Snowboarding; tubing. Cross-country trails (Dec-Apr, daily). **$$$$**

University of Minnesota, Duluth. *10 University Dr, Duluth (55812). Phone 218/726-8000. www.d.umn.edu.* (1902) (7,800 students) On campus are

> **Marshall W. Alworth Planetarium.** *10 University Dr, Duluth (55812). Phone 218/726-7129.* Shows (Wed; closed holidays). **FREE**
>
> **Tweed Museum of Art.** *1201 Ordean Ct, 10 University Dr, Duluth (55812). Phone 218/726-8222.* Exhibits of 19th- and 20th-century paintings; contemporary works. (Tues-Sun; closed holidays) **DONATION**

Special Events

Bayfront Blues Festival. *Bayfront Park, Commerce St and Canal Park Dr, Duluth (55802). Phone 218/722-4011. www.bayfrontblues.com.* This music festival features a variety of blues artists performing on three stages. Mid-Aug.

Grandma's Marathon. *PO Box 16234, Duluth (55816). Phone 218/727-0947. www.grandmasmarathon.com.* Held each year in mid-June, Grandma's Marathon is one of the largest marathons in the United States, with 9,000 participants. The beautiful course runs along Lake Superior, beginning in Two Harbors and ending in Duluth. Registration usually begins early in the year and closes by March. Mid-June.

International Folk Festival. *Leif Erikson Park, 11th Ave E and London Rd, Duluth (55802). Phone 218/722-7425.* Folk music, dancing, crafts, foods. First Sat in Aug.

John Beargrease Sled Dog Marathon. *218 W Superior St, Duluth (55801). Phone 218/722-7631. www.beargrease.com.* Late Feb.

Limited-Service Hotels

★ BEST WESTERN EDGEWATER. *2400 London Rd, Duluth (55812). Phone 218/728-3601; toll-free 800/777-7925; fax 218/728-3727. www.bestwestern.com.* 282 rooms, 5 story. Pets accepted, some restrictions; fee. Complimentary continental breakfast. Check-in 3 pm, check-out noon. High-speed Internet access. Fitness room. Indoor pool, whirlpool. Business center. **$**

★ COMFORT INN. *408 Canal Park Dr, Duluth (55802). Phone 218/727-1378; fax 218/727-1947.* 82 rooms, 3 story, all suites. Complimentary continental breakfast. Check-in 3 pm, check-out 11 am. Indoor pool, whirlpools. **$**

★ DAYS INN. *909 Cottonwood Ave, Duluth (55811). Phone 218/727-3110; toll-free 800/329-7466; fax 218/727-3110. www.daysinn.com.* 86 rooms, 3 story. Pets accepted. Complimentary continental breakfast. Check-in 2 pm, check-out noon. **$**

★ FITGER'S INN. *600 E Superior St, Duluth (55802). Phone 218/722-8826; toll-free 888/348-4377; fax 218/722-8826. www.fitgers.com.* Housed in what was once a thriving brewery, this historic hotel has a European style with modern facilities. 62 rooms, 3 story. Complimentary continental breakfast. High-speed Internet access. Check-out noon. Bar. Fitness room. **$**

★ ★ RADISSON HOTEL DULUTH. *505 W Superior St, Duluth (55802). Phone 218/727-8981; toll-free 800/333-3333; fax 218/727-0162. www.radisson.com.* Located downtown and connected to the indoor skyway system. 268 rooms, 16 story. Check-in 2 pm, check-out noon. High-speed Internet access, wireless Internet access. Restaurant, bar. Fitness room. Indoor pool, whirlpool. Business center. **$**

Restaurants

★★★ **BELLISIO'S.** *405 Lake Ave S, Duluth (55802). Phone 218/727-4921; fax 215/720-3804. www.grandmasrestaurants.com.* The restaurant features floor-to-ceiling wine racks and white tablecloths with full table settings to help guests enjoy a true Italian experience. Italian menu. Lunch, dinner. Bar. **$$**

★★ **BENNETT'S ON THE LAKE.** *600 E Superior St, Duluth (55802). Phone 218/722-2829. www.bennettsonthelake.com.* Situated in a turn of the century factory building with views of Lake Superior and displays of local artwork. American menu. Breakfast, lunch, dinner. **$$**

★ **FITGER'S BREWHOUSE.** *600 E Superior St, Duluth (55802). Phone 218/726-1392. www.brewhouse.net.* Duluth's oldest operating brewery and pub established in 1857. Bar Food. Lunch, dinner. **$**

★ **GRANDMA'S CANAL PARK.** *522 Lake Ave S, Duluth (55802). Phone 218/727-4192; fax 218/723-1986.* Under Aerial Lift Bridge at entrance to harbor. American menu. Lunch, dinner. Closed holidays. Bar. Children's menu. **$**

★★ **PICKWICK.** *508 E Superior St, Duluth (55802). Phone 218/727-8901; fax 218/786-0228.* The wood-paneled dining area and antique-filled rooms of this historic bar and restaurant offer incredible views of Lake Superior. The international menu is an eclectic mix of regional and internationally influenced dishes from smoked white fish to Grecian lamb chops. International/Fusion menu. Lunch, dinner. Closed Sun; holidays. Bar. Children's menu. **$$**

★ **SCENIC CAFE.** *5461 N Shore Dr, Duluth (55804). Phone 218/525-2286. www.sceniccafe.com.* Creative, worldly cuisine with excellent desserts and an extensive beer and wine selections. International menu. Lunch, dinner. **$**

★ **TOP OF THE HARBOR.** *505 W Superior St, Duluth (55802). Phone 218/727-8981. www.radisson.com/duluthmn.* This 16th-floor revolving restaurant offers panoramic views of the city, Duluth Harbor, and Lake Superior. American menu. Breakfast, lunch, dinner. Children's menu. **$$**

Elk River (D-3)

See also Anoka, Minneapolis, St. Cloud, St. Paul

Population 11,143
Elevation 924 ft
Area Code 763
Zip 55330
Information Elk River Area Chamber of Commerce, 509 Hwy 10; phone 763/441-3110
Web Site www.elkriverchamber.org

Although it's just 35 miles from Minneapolis and St. Paul, Elk River is a peaceful, simple community located on the banks of the Mississippi River. Famous son Oliver Kelley started The Grange, an almost unionlike organization of farmers that quickly spread across the country and had more than 1 million members at its peak.

What to See and Do

Oliver H. Kelley Farm. *15788 Kelley Farm Rd, Elk River (55330). 2 miles SE on Hwy 10, 52. Phone 763/441-6896.* Birthplace of National Grange and organized agriculture. Now a living history farm of the mid-19th century. Visitor center. (May and Sept-Oct: Sat-Sun, holidays; June-Aug: Thurs-Mon) **$$$**

Sherburne National Wildlife Refuge. *17076 293rd Ave, Zimmerman (55398). 13 miles N on Hwy 169, then 5 miles W on County 9. Phone 763/389-3323.* Wildlife observation; interpretive hiking and cross-country skiing trails in season; hunting, fishing; canoeing. Includes a self-guided auto tour route (weekends and holidays). **FREE**

Limited-Service Hotel

★ **AMERICINN ELK RIVER.** *17432 Hwy 10, Elk River (55330). Phone 763/441-8554; fax 763/441-5057.* 40 rooms, 2 story. Pets accepted; fee. Complimentary continental breakfast. Check-in 3 pm, check-out 11 am. Indoor pool, whirlpool. **$**

Ely (B-4)

See also Boundary Waters Canoe Area Wilderness, Grand Marais, Superior National Forest, Tower

Settled 1883

Population 3,968
Elevation 1,473 ft
Area Code 218
Zip 55731
Information Chamber of Commerce, 1600 E Sheridan St; phone 218/365-6123 or toll-free 800/777-7281
Web Site www.ely.org

A vacation and resort community, Ely is also the gateway to one of the finest canoeing areas, Boundary Waters Canoe Area Wilderness, and is in the heart of the Superior National Forest. A Ranger District office of this forest is located here. From the Laurentian Divide, south of here, all waters flow north to the Arctic.

What to See and Do

Canoe trips. Canoes, equipment, supplies. Guides available. Phone Chamber of Commerce for information.

Canoe Country Outfitters. *629 E Sheridan St, Ely (55731). Phone 218/365-4046.* Offers complete and partial ultra-light outfitting for trips to BWCAW and Quetico Park. Boat fishing trips and fly-in canoe trips; also camping, cabins on Moose Lake. (May-Oct, daily)

Tom and Woods' Moose Lake Wilderness Canoe Trips. *5855 Moose Lake Rd, Ely (55731). 20 miles NE on Moose Lake. Phone toll-free 800/322-5837.* Family, weekly rates. Specializes in ultra-lightweight canoe trips. (May-Sept)

Dorothy Molter Museum. *2002 E Sheridan, Ely (55731). Phone 218/365-4451.* Last living resident of the Boundary Waters Canoe Area Wilderness who passed away December 1986. Museum has two of her furnished cabins as they were in the wilderness. (Memorial Day-Sept, daily) **$$**

Greenstone outcropping. *13th Ave E and Main St, Ely (55731).* Only surface of ellipsoidal greenstone in the United States, judged to be more than 2 billion years old.

International Wolf Center. *E on Hwy 169. Phone toll-free 800/359-9653.* Houses a wolf pack; exhibits. Animal tracking, hikes and tours of abandoned wolf dens, wolf communication mini-classes (howling optional). (May-mid-Oct: daily; rest of year: Sat-Sun)

Native American Pictographs. *7 miles N via Hwy 88 and 116 (Echo Trail).* Cliff paintings can be seen on Hegman Lake. These are simple exhibits of art painted by tribes who inhabited the region long ago.

Superior-Quetico Wilderness. Superior in the United States, Quetico in Canada.

Vermilion Interpretive Center. *1900 E Camp St, Ely (55731). Phone 218/365-3226.* Presentation of local history through photos, tapes, film, artifacts, and displays; focuses on heritage of local people and land. (Apr-Oct, daily) **$**

Special Events

Blueberry Arts Festival. *Whiteside Park, E Sheridan St, Ely. Between 7th and 8th aves. Phone 218/365-6123.* Last full weekend in July.

Harvest Moon Festival. *Whiteside Park, Ely. Phone 218/365-6123.* More than 120 arts and crafts exhibitors are featured at this festival, along with food and entertainment. Weaving, chainsaw carving, and snowshoe making are among the demonstrations offered here. Weekend after Labor Day.

Voyageur Winter Festival. *1600 E Sheridan St, Ely (55731). Phone 218/365-6123. www.voyageurwinterfestival.com.* Snow sculptures by local, state, and international artists are the highlight at this festival celebrating the area's culture, history, and art. Early Feb.

Limited-Service Hotel

★ SUPER 8. *1605 E Sheridan St, Ely (55731). Phone 218/365-2873; toll-free 800/800-8000; fax 218/365-5632. www.super8.com.* 30 rooms, 2 story. Check-in 4 pm, check-out 11 am. **$**

Eveleth (B-4)

See also Cook, Hibbing, Tower, Virginia

Founded 1893
Population 4,064
Elevation 1,610 ft
Area Code 218
Zip 55734
Information Eveleth Area Chamber of Commerce, 122 Grant Ave; phone 218/744-1940
Web Site www.evelethchamber.org

Site of a large taconite operation, mines within a 50-mile radius produce a large amount of the nation's requirements of iron ore. Located about 1 mile west of town on County Highway 101, Leonidas Overlook provides a panoramic view of the taconite operations and Minntac Mine.

What to See and Do

US Hockey Hall of Fame. *801 Hat Trick Ave (Hwy 53), Eveleth (55734). Phone 218/744-5167; toll-free 800/443-7825.* Museum honoring American players and the sport; theater. (Daily; closed holidays) **$$**

Limited-Service Hotels

★★ **DAYS INN.** *701 Hat Trick Ave, Eveleth (55734). Phone 218/744-2703; toll-free 800/329-7466; fax 218/744-5865. www.daysinn.com.* Hockey fans unite in Eveleth where the largest hockey stick in the world is located. This inn offers guests a kid-friendly environment with an Olympic-sized pool, mini golf course, volleyball court, and on-site restaurant. 145 rooms, 2 story. Pets accepted, some restrictions; fee. Check-in 3 pm, check-out noon. Restaurant, bar. Indoor pool. **$**

★ **SUPER 8.** *1080 Industrial Park Dr (Hwy 53), Eveleth (55734). Phone 218/744-1661; toll-free 888/800-8000; fax 218/744-4343. www.super8.com.* 54 rooms, 2 story. Complimentary continental breakfast. Check-in 2 pm, check-out 11 am. Indoor pool, whirlpool. **$**

Fairmont (F-2)

See also Blue Earth, Jackson

Population 11,265
Elevation 1,185 ft
Area Code 507
Zip 56031
Information Convention & Visitors Bureau, 1201 Torgerson Dr; phone 507/235-5547
Web Site www.fairmontcvb.com

Fairmont, the seat of Martin County, is 10 miles north of the Iowa line at the junction of Interstate 90 and Highway 15. Situated on a north-south chain of lakes, fishing and water sports are popular pastimes. A group of English farmers who arrived in the 1870s and were known as the "Fairmont sportsmen" introduced fox hunting into southern Minnesota.

What to See and Do

Fairmont Opera House. *45 Downtown Plz, Fairmont (56031). Phone 507/238-4900; toll-free 800/657-3280.* Built in 1901, this historic theater has been completely restored. Guided tours. Fees for productions vary. (Mon-Fri, also by appointment; closed holidays) **FREE**

Martin County Historical Society and Pioneer Museum. *304 E Blue Earth Ave, Fairmont (56031). Phone 507/235-5178.* Operated by Martin County Historical Society; pioneer memorabilia, Native American artifacts. Under 12 years with adult only. (Mon-Sat) **FREE**

Limited-Service Hotel

★★ **HOLIDAY INN.** *I-90 and Hwy 15, Fairmont (56031). Phone 507/238-4771; toll-free 800/465-4329; fax 507/238-9371. www.holidayinnfairmont.com.* 105 rooms, 2 story. Check-in 2 pm, check-out noon. High-speed Internet access. Restaurant, bar. Indoor pool, children's pool, whirlpool. Airport transportation available. **$**

Restaurant

★ **THE RANCH FAMILY RESTAURANT.** *1330 N State St, Fairmont (56031). Phone 507/235-3044. www.theranchrestaurant.com.* American menu. Breakfast, lunch, dinner. Closed Dec 25. Bar. Children's menu. **$**

Faribault (E-3)

See also Lakeville, Le Sueur, Mankato, Northfield, Owatonna, St. Peter

Settled 1826
Population 17,085
Elevation 971 ft
Area Code 507
Zip 55021
Information Faribault Area Chamber of Commerce, 530 Wilson Ave; phone 507/334-4381 or toll-free 800/658-2354
Web Site www.faribaultmn.org

In 1826, Alexander Faribault, a French-Canadian fur trader, built the largest of his six trading posts here. Faribault (pronounced FAIR-ih-boe) now is known for Faribo wool blankets and Tilt-A-Whirl amusement rides. The town, seat of Rice County, is surrounded by 20 area lakes and 3,000 acres of parkland. Faribault is also home to several historic landmarks, including the Cathedral of Our Merciful Saviour, built in 1869, and the limestone buildings of Shattuck-St. Mary's Schools, founded in 1858.

What to See and Do

Alexander Faribault House. *12 NE 1st Ave, Faribault (55021). Phone 507/334-7913.* (1853) House of the fur trader for whom the town was named. Period furnishings; museum of Native American artifacts and historical items. (May-Sept: Mon-Fri; rest of year: by appointment) **$**

Faribault Woolen Mill Company. *1500 NW 2nd Ave, Faribault (55021). Phone 507/334-1644.* Wool blankets, items made in century-old mill on the Cannon River. Factory store, mill seconds. Check in at store for 45-minute guided tour (Mon-Fri; closed first two weeks in July). Store (Daily; closed holidays). **FREE**

Rice County Historical Society Museum. *1814 NW 2nd Ave, Faribault (55021). Adjacent to county fairgrounds. Phone 507/332-2121.* Slide show; video presentation; Native American and pioneer artifacts; turn-of-the-century Main Street; works of local artists. Nearby are log cabin, church, one-room schoolhouse, and two steel annexes. (June-Aug: weekends; rest of year: Mon-Fri) **$$**

River Bend Nature Center. *1000 Rustad Rd, Faribault (55021). SE via Hwy 60, on Rustad Rd. Phone 507/332-7151.* More than 700 acres of mixed habitat including woodlands, prairie, ponds, and rivers. Ten miles of trails (cross-country in winter) meander through the area. (Daily) **FREE**

Special Event

Tree Frog Music Festival. *122 1st Ave NE, Faribault (55021). Phone 507/334-4381.* Two-day event featuring headliner concert each day. Arts and crafts. Mid-Sept.

Fergus Falls (C-1)

See also Alexandria, Detroit Lakes, Moorhead, Morris

Settled 1857
Population 12,362
Elevation 1,196 ft
Area Code 218
Zip 56537
Information Chamber of Commerce, 202 S Court St; phone 218/736-6951
Web Site www.fergusfalls.com

Fergus Falls was named in honor of James Fergus, who financed Joseph Whitford, a frontiersman who led an expedition here in 1857. The town is the seat of Otter Tail County, which has 1,029 lakes. The city has a remarkable park and recreation system.

What to See and Do

Glendalough State Park. *25287 Whitetail Ln, Battle Lake (56515). 25 miles from Fergus Falls. 1.5 miles N of Battle Lake on State Hwy 78, then 1.8 miles E on County Hwy 16 to the park entrance. Phone 218/864-0110.* Voted the state's favorite park by readers of *Minnesota Monthly* magazine, this largely undeveloped, 1,900-acre state park includes six lakes and more than 9 miles of shoreline. The largest at 335 acres, Annie Battle Lake is a designated Heritage Fishery, which means that it offers plenty of bass, panfish, and walleye but also imposes restrictions that ensure fishing levels will remain stable. Bird-watching, hiking, picnicking, observation areas. Camping sites; cabins. (Daily 9 am-4 pm)

Otter Tail County Historical Society Museum. *1110 W Lincoln Ave, Fergus Falls (56537). Phone 218/736-6038.* Modern facility featuring dioramas and changing exhibits interpreting regional history; also library, archives, and genealogical materials. (Daily; closed holidays) **$$**

Pebble Lake City Park. *205 S Peck St, Fergus Falls (56537). SE on Hwy 59. Phone 218/739-3205.* Picnicking, swimming, beach. Also, 18-hole golf (Apr-Sept, daily; fee). Park open early June-late Aug, daily.

Limited-Service Hotel

★ DAYS INN. *610 Western Ave, Fergus Falls (56537). Phone 218/739-3311; toll-free 800/329-7466; fax 218/736-6576. www.daysinn.com.* 57 rooms, 2 story. Pets accepted, some restrictions; fee. Complimentary continental breakfast. Check-out 11 am. Indoor pool, whirlpool. **$**

Restaurant

★ ★ MABEL MURPHY'S EATING LTD. *Hwy 210 W, Fergus Falls (56537). Phone 218/739-4406. www.mabelmurphysmn.com.* American menu. Lunch, dinner. Bar. Children's menu. **$$**

Glenwood (D-2)

See also Alexandria, Morris, Sauk Centre

Population 2,573
Elevation 1,350 ft
Area Code 320
Zip 56334
Information Chamber of Commerce, 202 N Franklin St; phone 320/634-3636 or toll-free 800/304-5666

Located on the banks of Lake Minnewaska, the 13th largest lake in Minnesota, Glenwood's identity is intertwined with fishing. Be sure to visit the state fish hatchery, just a mile from town.

What to See and Do

Chalet Campsite. *956 S Hwy 104, Glenwood (56334). 1/2 mile S on Hwy 104. Phone 320/634-5433.* Boating (launch), swimming beach, bicycling, picnicking, playground, tennis court, camping (fee), restrooms, showers. (Mid-May-Sept, daily)

Department of Natural Resources, Area Fisheries Headquarters. *1 1/2 miles W on N Lakeshore Dr, Hwy 28, 29. Phone 320/634-4573.* Trout in display ponds (Mon-Fri; closed holidays). Grounds (daily). **FREE**

Pope County Historical Museum. *809 S Hwy 104, Glenwood (56334). 1/2 mile S on Hwy 104. Phone 320/634-3293.* Helbing Gallery of Native American arts and crafts; country store, school and church; exhibits of local history, farm machinery and artifacts; furnished log cabin (1880). (Memorial Day-Labor Day: Tues-Sun; rest of year: Tues-Sat) **$$**

Special Events

Pope County Fair. *Phone 320/634-3636.* First week in Aug.

Scout Fishing Derby. *Phone 320/634-3636.* First weekend in Feb.

Terrence Mill Fiddlers' Contest. *Phone 320/278-3289.* Late Sept.

Waterama. *Phone 320/634-3636.* Water carnival; contests, parade. Last full weekend in July.

Limited-Service Hotel

★ ★ PETERS' SUNSET BEACH RESORT. *20000 S Lakeshore Dr, Glenwood (56334). Phone 320/634-4501; toll-free 800/356-8654. www.petersresort.com.* Located on beautiful Lake Minnewaska, this golf resort has breathtaking views and lush landscaping. With golf, a swimming beach, boating, fishing, and much more, the whole family will enjoy the fun-filled adventures here. 51 rooms. Closed Nov-Apr. Check-in 4:30 pm, check-out 12:30 pm. Restaurant. Beach. Golf. Tennis. **$$**

Restaurant

★ ★ MINNEWASKA HOUSE SUPPER CLUB. *24895 Hwy 28, Glenwood (56334). Phone 320/634-4566; toll-free 800/828-0882.* American menu. Lunch, dinner. Closed holidays. Bar. **$$**

Grand Marais (B-5)

See also Boundary Waters Canoe Area Wilderness, Ely, Grand Portage, Lutsen, Superior National Forest

Population 1,171
Elevation 688 ft
Area Code 218
Zip 55604
Information Grand Marais Information Center, 13 N Broadway, PO Box 1048; phone 218/387-2524 or toll-free 888/922-5000
Web Site www.grandmarais.com

This municipality on the rocky north shore of Lake Superior (pronounced GRAND ma-RAY) is the major community in the northeast point of Minnesota. The area resembles the tip of an arrow and is known as the "arrowhead country." The cool climate and pollen-free air, as well as lake and stream fishing, abundant wildlife, water sports, camping, and stretches of wilderness, make this a leading resort area. A Ranger District office of the Superior National Forest is located here.

What to See and Do

Canoe trips. Canoes, equipment, guides. For map, folder, and names of outfitters, contact Grand Marais Information Center.

Gunflint Trail. *Starting at NW edge of town, the road goes N and W 58 miles to Saganaga Lake on the*

Canadian border. The trail penetrates into an area of hundreds of lakes where camping, picnicking, fishing, and canoeing are available.

North Shore Drive. *Hwy 61 along Lake Superior from Duluth to Pigeon River (150 miles).* Considered one of the most scenic shore drives in the United States.

Special Events

Cook County Fair. *Five blocks N on Hwy 61. Phone 218/387-2524.* Late Aug.

Fisherman's Picnic. *Phone 218/387-2524.* Parade, rides, dancing, queen's coronation; food. First week in Aug.

Limited-Service Hotels

★ ★ BEARSKIN LODGE. *124 E Bearskin Rd, Grand Marais (55604). Phone 218/388-2292; toll-free 800/338-4170; fax 218/388-4410. www.bearskin.com.* 15 rooms. Check-in 4 pm, check-out 10 am. Restaurant. Children's activity center. Private docks. Nature program. **$**

★ BEST WESTERN SUPERIOR INN AND SUITES. *Hwy 61 E, Grand Marais (55604). Phone 218/387-2240; toll-free 800/842-8439; fax 218/387-2244. www.bestwestern.com.* Views of Lake Superior. 66 rooms, 3 story. Pets accepted, some restrictions. Complimentary continental breakfast. Check-in 2 pm, check-out 11 am. Beach. Whirlpool. **$**

Specialty Lodgings

The following lodging establishments are approved by Mobil Travel Guide, but due to their unique and individualized nature have not been given a traditional Mobil Star rating. Included in this listing you may find bed-and-breakfasts, limited-service inns, guest ranches, and other unique hotel properties.

DREAM CATCHER BED & BREAKFAST. *2614 Hwy 7, Grand Marais (55604). Phone 218/387-2876; toll-free 800/682-3119. www.dreamcatcherbb.com.* This bed-and-breakfast is situated in the woods of Northeastern Minnesota, high above Lake Superior's rugged North Shore. 3 rooms, 2 story. Complimentary continental breakfast. Check-in 2 pm, check-out 11 am. **$**

STONE HEARTH INN BED & BREAKFAST. *6598 Lakeside Estates Rd, Little Marais (55614). Phone 218/226-3020; toll-free 888/206-3020. www.stonehearthinn.com.* Romantic 1920s inn on Lake Superior. Old-fashioned porch, large stone fireplace in living room. Guest rooms furnished with antiques; some have whirlpools, gas fireplaces, kitchens. All rooms have private baths. 8 rooms, 2 story. Complimentary full breakfast. Check-in 4 pm, check-out noon. **$$**

Restaurant

★ BIRCH TERRACE. *601 W Hwy 61, Grand Marais (55604). Phone 218/387-2215; fax 218/387-2215.* This Northwoods mansion was built in 1898. Two fireplaces warm the interior dining room during the winter, and a deck overlooking the marina provides pleasant summertime views. American menu. Dinner. Bar. Children's menu. **$$**

Grand Portage (B-5)

See also Grand Marais, Superior National Forest; also see Isle Royale National Park, MI

Population 557
Elevation 610 ft
Area Code 218
Zip 55605
Web Site www.grandportage.com

The Ojibwas (oh-JIB-ways) named this area "gitche onigaming," meaning "great carrying place" or "great portage", because canoers took a trail through the area to avoid the steep and dangerous falls on the Pigeon River. With so much traffic carrying canoes around the falls—Ojibwes, voyageurs and other fur traders, and traveling merchants—the savvy North West Company established a post, making Grand Portage (PORT-ihj) a commercial center for more than 30 years. Today, the Grand Portage National Monument reenacts the history of the region.

What to See and Do

Ferry Service to Isle Royale National Park. *Phone 715/392-2100.* From Grand Portage there is passenger ferry service to Isle Royale National Park within Michigan state waters (Mid-May-late Oct).

Grand Portage National Monument. *315 S Broadway, Grand Portage (55604). S of Hwy 61, 5 miles* from the Canadian border. Phone 218/387-2788. This area was once a rendezvous point and central supply depot for fur traders operating between Montreal and Lake Athabasca. The partially reconstructed summer headquarters of the North West Company include a stockade, great hall, kitchen, and warehouse.The Grand Portage begins at the stockade and runs 8 1/2 miles northwest from Lake Superior to the Pigeon River. Primitive camping is available at Fort Charlotte (accessible only by hiking the Grand Portage or by canoe). Buildings and grounds (mid-May-mid-Oct, daily). Trail (all year). **$$**

Grand Rapids (B-3)

See also Deer River, Hibbing

Settled 1877
Population 7,976
Elevation 1,290 ft
Area Code 218
Zip 55744
Information Grand Rapids Area Chamber of Commerce, The Depot, 1 NW 3rd St; phone 218/326-6619 or toll-free 800/472-6366
Web Site www.grandmn.com

At the head of navigation on the Mississippi River, Grand Rapids was named for nearby waters. For years it served as a center for logging. Paper production and tourism are the principal industries today. Seat of Itasca County, Grand Rapids serves as a diverse regional center at the western end of the Mesabi Iron Range. A number of open pit mines nearby have observation stands for the public. The forested area surrounding the town includes more than a thousand lakes. Four of them—Crystal, Hale, Forest, and McKinney—are within the city limits.

What to See and Do

Canoeing. On Mississippi River, north on Bigfork waters to Rainy Lake, Lake of the Woods; also to Lake Itasca and on many nearby rivers.

Central School. *10 NW 5th St, Grand Rapids (55744). Phone 218/326-6431.* Heritage center housing historical museum, Judy Garland display, antiques, shops, and a restaurant. (Daily)

Chippewa National Forest. *200 Ash Ave NW, Cass Lake (56633). Between Grand Rapids and Bemidji on Hwy 2. Phone 218/335-8600.* Has 661,400 acres of timbered land; 1,321 lakes, with 699 larger than 10 acres; swimming, boating, canoeing, hiking, hunting, fishing, picnicking, camping (fee); winter sports. Bald eagle viewing; several historic sites.

Forest History Center. *2609 County Rd 76, Grand Rapids (55744). 3 miles SW via S Hwy 169. Phone 218/327-4482.* Center includes a museum building, re-created 1900 logging camp and log drive wanigan maintained by Minnesota Historical Society as part of an interpretive program. Early Forest Service cabin and fire tower, modern pine plantation, living history exhibits; nature trails. (Early June-Labor Day, daily). **$$$**

Judy Garland Birthplace and Museum. *2727 Hwy 169 S, Grand Rapids (55744). Phone 218/327-9276; toll-free 800/664-5839. www.judygarlandmuseum.com.* The childhood home of the actress serves as a museum honoring her life and work. The 1-acre memorial garden on the grounds includes 50 Judy Garland rose bushes. (Daily 10 am-5 pm; closed holidays) **$**

Pokegama Dam. *34385 S Hwy 2, Grand Rapids (55744). Phone 218/326-6128.* Camping on 21 trailer sites (hook-ups, dump station; 14-day maximum); picnicking, fishing. **$$$$**

Quadna Mountain Resort Area Convention Center. *100 Quadna Rd, Hill City (55748). 18 miles S on Hwy 169, 1 mile S of Hill City. Phone 218/697-8444. www.quadna-resort.com.* Quad chairlift, two T-bars, rope tow; patrol, school, rentals, snowmaking; motel, lodge and restaurant. Cross-country trails. Includes 16 runs, longest run 26,430 feet, vertical drop 350 feet. (Thanksgiving-mid-Mar, Fri-Tues) Also golf, outdoor tennis, horseback riding, lake activities in summer. **$$$$**

Scenic State Park. *56956 Scenic Hwy # 7, Bigfork (56628). 12 miles N on Hwy 169, then 32 miles N on County 7. Phone 218/743-3362.* Primitive area of 3,000 acres with seven lakes. Swimming; fishing; boating (ramp, rentals), hiking; cross-country skiing, snowmobiling; picnicking; camping (electrical hook-ups); lodging; interpretive programs.

Special Events

Itasca County Fair. *Fairgrounds, 1336 NE 3rd Ave, Grand Rapids (55744). Phone 218/326-6619.* This old-fashioned county fair features cattle barns, 4-H competitions, food, and fun. Mid-Aug.

Judy Garland Festival. *2727 Hwy 169 S, Grand Rapids (55744). Phone 218/327-9276; toll-free 800/664-5839. www.judygarlandmuseum.com.* Showings of Garland movies; *Wizard of Oz* souvenirs for sale. Late June.

***Mississippi Melodie* Showboat.** *16th Ave W, on Mississippi River. Phone 218/259-0814.* Amateur musical variety show. Three weekends in July.

North Star Stampede. *Phone 218/743-3893.* Three-day rodeo. Late July.

Northern Minnesota Vintage Car Show and Swap Meet. *Itasca County Fairgrounds, Grand Rapids (55744). Phone 218/326-0234.* This large car show features classic antique cars and roaring street rods, along with a giant swap meet for some outdoor shopping. Late July.

Tall Timber Days Festival. *Downtown. Phone toll-free 800/472-6366.* This downtown celebration features chainsaw carving, an arts and crafts fair, canoe races, a parade, and lumberjacks climbing 40-foot logs. First weekend in Aug.

Limited-Service Hotels

★★ **SAWMILL INN.** *2301 S Pokegama Ave, Grand Rapids (55744). Phone 218/326-8501; toll-free 800/235-6455; fax 218/326-1039. www.sawmillinn.com.* 124 rooms, 2 story. Pets accepted, some restrictions. Check-out noon. Restaurant, bar. Indoor pool, whirlpool. Airport transportation available. **$**

★ **SUPER 8.** *1702 S Pokegama Ave, Grand Rapids (55744). Phone 218/327-1108; toll-free 800/800-8000; fax 218/327-1108. www.super8.com.* 58 rooms, 2 story. Complimentary continental breakfast. Check-in 1 pm, check-out 11 am. **$**

Restaurant

★★ **SAWMILL INN.** *2301 Pokegama Ave, Grand Rapids (55744). Phone 218/326-8501. www.sawmillin.com.* Known for choice prime rib. American menu. Lunch, dinner. **$$**

Granite Falls (D-2)

See also Marshall, Redwood Falls, Willmar

Population 3,083
Elevation 920 ft
Area Code 320
Zip 56241
Information Chamber of Commerce, 155 7th Ave, PO Box 220; phone 320/564-4039
Web Site www.granitefalls.com

The falls for which this city is named still power the town's energy needs through its hydroelectric plant. Founded by mill workers, the town today is known for its outdoor adventure areas; two state parks are nearby.

What to See and Do

Lac qui Parle State Park. *County Rd 33 and Hwy 7, Montevideo (56265). 14 miles NW on Hwy 212, 8 miles NW on Hwy 59, then 4 1/2 miles W on County 13. Phone 320/752-4736.* Approximately 529 acres. On Lac qui Parle and Minnesota rivers. Dense timber. Swimming, fishing; boating (ramps); hiking, riding; cross-country skiing; picnicking; camping. (Daily)

Olof Swensson Farm Museum. *151 Pioneer Dr, Montevideo (56265). 4 miles N on County 5, then 2 1/2 miles W on County 15. Phone 320/269-7636.* A 22-room, brick family-built farmhouse, barn, and family burial plot on a 17-acre plot. Olof Swensson ran unsuccessfully for governor of Minnesota, but the title was given to him by the community out of respect and admiration. (Memorial Day-Labor Day, Sun) **$$**

Upper Sioux Agency State Park. *9805 Hwy 67, Granite Falls (56241). 8 miles SE on Hwy 67. Phone 320/564-4777.* 1,280 acres. Boating (ramps, canoe campsites). Bridle trails. Snowmobiling. Picnicking. Semi-modern campsite; rustic horserider campground. Visitor center.

Yellow Medicine County Museum. *726 Prentice St, Granite Falls (56241). 1/2 mile from center of town via Hwy 67. Phone 320/564-4479.* Depicts life in the county and state dating from the 1800s. Two authentic log cabins and bandstand on site. Also here is an exposed rock outcropping estimated to be 3.8 billion years old. (Mid-May-mid-Oct: Tues-Sun; mid-Apr-mid-May: Tues-Fri) **FREE**

Special Event

Western Fest Stampede Rodeo. *155 7th Ave, Granite Falls (56241). Phone 320/564-4039.* Rodeo, street dances, parade. Weekend after Father's Day.

Limited-Service Hotel

★ SUPER 8. *845 W Hwy 212, Granite Falls (56241). Phone 320/564-4075; toll-free 800/800-8000; fax 320/564-4038. www.super8.com.* 62 rooms. Check-in 3 pm, check-out 11 am. Indoor pool, whirlpool. **$**

Restaurant

★ ★ JAVA RIVER CAFE. *210 S 1st St, Montevideo (56265). Phone 320/269-7106. www.javarivercafe.com.* Featuring homemade specialty coffee and related foods with an emphasis on sustainable agriculture and land preservation. American menu. Breakfast, lunch, dinner. Closed Sun. **$**

Hastings (E-3)

See also Lakeville, Minneapolis, Northfield, Red Wing, St. Paul

Settled 1850
Population 15,445
Elevation 726 ft
Area Code 651
Zip 55033
Information Hastings Area Chamber of Commerce & Tourism Bureau, 111 E 3rd St; phone 651/437-6775 or toll-free 888/612-6122
Web Site www.hastingsmn.org

Diversified farming and industry are the mainstays of this community, founded by a trader who felt the area was a good town site.

What to See and Do

Afton Alps. *6600 Peller Ave S, Hastings (55033). 10 miles N via Hwy 61, 95. Phone 651/436-5245. www.aftonalps.com.* Three triple, 15 double chairlifts, two rope tows; patrol, school, rentals; snowmaking; store, cafeteria, snack bar; bar. Longest run 3,000 feet; vertical drop 330 feet. (Nov-Mar, daily) **$$$$**

Alexis Bailly Vineyard. *18200 Kirby Ave, Hastings (55033). Phone 651/437-1413.* First vineyard to make wine with 100 percent Minnesota-grown grapes. Wine tastings (June-Oct, Fri-Sun). Group tours (by appointment).

Carpenter St. Croix Valley Nature Center. *12805 St. Croix Trail, Hastings (55033). 2 miles N via Hwy 61, then 3 miles E via Hwy 10. Phone 651/437-4359.* Environmental education center with more than 15 miles of hiking trails and 1 mile of shoreline on the St. Croix River. Various seasonal programs and activities (some fees). (Daily; closed holidays)

Historic Walking Tour. A self-guided tour featuring the historic buildings of Hastings, including the exterior of the LeDuc-Simmons Mansion and Norrish "Octagon House." Tour booklets with background detail and map are available at the Chamber of Commerce. Guided tours by appointment.

Ramsey Mill. *E 18th St and McNamara, Hastings (55033). On Hwy 291 on the Vermillion River. Phone toll-free 800/222-7077.* Remains of first flour mill in state, built by Governor Alexander Ramsey in 1857.

Treasure Island Resort and Casino. *5734 Sturgeon Lake Rd, Hastings (55033). S on Hwy 61, 316 to Welch, follow signs. Phone toll-free 800/222-7077.* This 24-hour casino offers blackjack, slots, bingo, and pull-tabs. Buffet, sports bar. Marina. National local entertainment. (Daily).

Special Event

Rivertown Days. *Phone 651/437-6775.* Gala community-wide festival. Riverfront activities; exhibits and tours; sporting events; fireworks. Mid-July.

Specialty Lodgings

The following lodging establishments are approved by Mobil Travel Guide, but due to their unique and individualized nature have not been given a traditional Mobil Star rating. Included in this listing you may find bed-and-breakfasts, limited-service inns, guest ranches, and other unique hotel properties.

ROSEWOOD HISTORIC INN. *620 Ramsey St, Hastings (55033). Phone 651/437-3297; toll-free 888/846-7966; fax 651/437-4129. www.thorwoodinn.com.* 8 rooms. Complimentary full breakfast. Check-in 4 pm, check-out noon. Whirlpool. **$$**

THORWOOD HISTORIC INN. *315 Pine St, Hastings (55033). Phone 651/437-3297; toll-free 888/846-7966; fax 651/437-4129. www.thorwoodinn.com.* 6 rooms. Complimentary full breakfast. Check-in 4 pm, check-out noon. Whirlpool. **$$**

Restaurant

★ ★ **MISSISSIPPI BELLE.** *101 E 2nd St, Hastings (55033). Phone 651/437-4814; fax 651/437-2403.* Dining in the tradition of the riverboat era (1855-1875); riverboat steel engravings. Italian menu. Lunch, dinner. Closed Mon. Bar. Children's menu. Casual attire. **$$**

Hibbing (B-3)

See also Cook, Deer River, Eveleth, Grand Rapids, Virginia

Founded 1893
Population 18,046
Elevation 1,489 ft
Area Code 218
Zip 55746
Information Chamber of Commerce, 211 E Howard St, PO Box 727; phone 218/262-3895 or toll-free 800/444-2246
Web Site www.hibbing.org

Here is the world's largest open-pit iron mine, which produced one-quarter of the ore mined in the country during World War II. Hibbing calls itself the "iron ore capital of the world." On the Mesabi (Native American for "sleeping giant") Iron Range, Hibbing mines and processes taconite, yielding a rich iron concentrate. Frank Hibbing, the town's founder, built the first hotel, sawmill, and bank building. In 1918, when the Hull-Rust pit encroached on the heart of town, the community was moved on wheels 2 miles south. The move was not completed until 1957. A local bus line, begun here in 1914 with an open touring car, is now the nationwide Greyhound Bus system. Hibbing was the boyhood home of singer-guitarist Bob Dylan.

What to See and Do

Bus Tour. *211 E Howard St, Hibbing (55746). Phone 218/262-3895.* Three-hour bus tour of town and nearby taconite plant. Includes stops at Paulucci Space Theatre, high school. (Mid-June-mid-Aug, Mon-Fri) **$$**

Hull-Rust Mahoning Mine. *1200 E Howard St, Hibbing (55746). N of town. Phone 218/262-3895.* Observation building provides view of "Grand Canyon of Minnesota," with the mining area extending 3 miles. Individual mines have merged through the years into a single pit producing hundreds of millions of tons. Deepest part of pit, on east side, dips 535 feet into earth. Observation building; self-guided walking tours. (Mid-May-Sept, daily) Contact the Chamber of Commerce for further information. **FREE**

Ironworld Discovery Center. *Hwy 169 W, Chisholm (55719). 5 miles NE on Hwy 169. Phone toll-free 800/372-6437. www.ironworld.com.* Displays and audio-visual presentations interpret culture and history of the iron mining industry and its people. Ethnic craft demonstrations and food specialties; entertainment; scenic train rides; outdoor amphitheater. (May-Sept, daily) (See SPECIAL EVENTS) **$$$**

McCarthy Beach State Park. *7622 McCarthy Beach Rd, Side Lake (55781). 20 miles NW on County 5. Phone 218/254-7979.* Approximately 2,566 acres. Virgin pine, two lakes. Swimming, fishing, boating (ramp, rentals); cross-country skiing; hiking; snowmobiling; camping; naturalist (summer). **$$**

Minnesota Museum of Mining. *Memorial Park Complex, Hwy 169, Chisholm (55719). 6 miles NE via Hwy 73, on W Lake St. Phone 218/254-5543.* Records the past 70 years of iron mining; equipment, exhibits, models; jet and rotary drills, steam engine, ore cars, and railroad caboose, 120-ton Euclid and fire trucks; first Greyhound bus, and steam railroad diorama. (Mid-May-mid-Sept, daily) Self-guided tours. Picnicking. **$$**

Paulucci Space Theatre. *1502 E 23rd St, Hibbing (55746). Phone 218/262-6720.* General interest programs from astronomy to dinosaurs, using stars, slides, special effects, and hemispheric film projection; multimedia theater with tilted-dome screen; display area; gift shop. Shows (June-Aug: daily; Sept-May: Sat-Sun). **$$**

Special Events

Last Chance Curling Bonspiel. *Memorial Building, Hibbing (55746). Phone 218/263-4379.* International curling competition on 14 sheets of ice. Early Apr.

Minnesota Ethnic Days. *Ironworld Discovery Center, Hwy 169 W, Hibbing (55746). Phone 218/254-7959.* A series of celebrations of ethnic heritage. Entertainment, history, crafts and food. Each day devoted to different nationality. July.

St. Louis County Fair. *Fairgrounds, 12th Ave, Hibbing (55746). Phone 218/254-7959.* Cattle and rock exhibits, auto races, carnival midway. Early Aug.

Hinckley (C-3)

See also Mora

Population 946
Elevation 1,030 ft
Area Code 320
Zip 55037

Located at a convenient stop between the Twin Cities and Duluth, Hinckley's major attraction is the Fire Museum, which describes the worst single-day disaster in Minnesota, the Hinckley Fire of September 1, 1894. The museum is housed in an old train depot because of the connection between the fire and the St. Paul & Duluth train line, which Hinckley residents hoped would save them from the approaching fire. When the train finally arrived, long after the town was engulfed by flames, the train, too, was overwhelmed by fire. In all, the fire claimed 400 square miles of land and more than 400 victims.

What to See and Do

Hinckley Fire Museum. *106 Hwy 61, Hinckley (55037). Phone 320/384-7338.* Old Northern Pacific Railroad Depot houses museum that depicts the disastrous forest fire that swept across Hinckley in 1894. Mural, video tape, diorama, reconstructed living quarters. (May-Oct, Tues-Sun) **$$**

North West Company Fur Post. *County Rd 7, Pine City (55063). Phone 320/629-6356.* A reconstruction of an 1800 fur trade outpost, based on archaeological findings and other research; picnic area. (May-Labor Day: Mon-Sat 10 am-5 pm, Sun noon-5 pm; early Sept-Oct: Fri-Sat 10 am-5 pm, Sun noon-5 pm) **FREE**

St. Croix State Park. *30065 St. Croix Rd, Hinckley (55037). 15 miles E on Hwy 48, then S. Phone 320/384-6591.* A 34,037-acre park. Swimming (lake), fishing, canoeing (Memorial Day-Labor Day, rentals); hiking, riding trails, cross-country skiing, snowmobiling; picnicking, 6-mile blacktop wooded bike trail, camping (electric, dump station).

Limited-Service Hotel

★ DAYS INN. *104 Grindstone Ct, Hinckley (55037). Phone 320/384-7751; toll-free 800/559-8951; fax 320/384-6403. www.daysinn.com.* 69 rooms, 2 story. Pets accepted; fee. Complimentary continental breakfast. Check-in 3 pm, check-out 11 am. Indoor pool, whirlpool. **$**

Restaurants

★★ CASSSIDY'S. *I-35 and Hwy 48, Hinckley (55037). Phone 320/384-6129.* American menu. Breakfast, lunch, dinner. Children's menu. **$**

★ TOBIE'S. *504 Fire Monument Rd, Hinckley (55037). Phone 320/384-6174. www.tobies.com.* American menu. Breakfast, lunch, dinner. Closed Dec 25. Bar. **$**

International Falls (A-3)

See also Baudette, Boundary Waters Canoe Area Wilderness, Kabetogama, Lake Elmo, Superior National Forest, Voyageurs National Park

Population 8,325
Elevation 1,124 ft
Area Code 218
Zip 56649
Information International Falls Area Chamber of Commerce, 301 2nd Ave; phone 218/283-9400 or toll-free 800/325-5766
Web Site www.intlfalls.org

In addition to tourism, converting trees and wood chips into paper is big business here. The town takes its name from a 35-foot drop of the Rainy River, now concealed by a reservoir above a dam that harnesses the water power. International Falls is a port of entry to Canada by way of Fort Frances, Ontario. (For border-crossing regulations, see MAKING THE MOST OF YOUR TRIP.)

What to See and Do

Boise Cascade Paper Mill. *2nd St and 4th Ave, International Falls (56649). Phone 218/285-5511.* No cameras allowed. No children under ten years. Proper footwear required. Tours (June-Aug, Mon-Fri; closed holidays). Reservations advised. **FREE**

Fishing. Rainy Lake. East along the international boundary. Walleye, sand pike, muskie, crappie, perch, bass. **Rainy River.** West along the international boundary. Walleye, sand pike, sturgeon, northern pike.

International Falls City Beach. *3 1/2 miles E on Hwy 11.* Sandy beach for swimming; picnic grounds, play equipment.

Smokey the Bear Statue. *Municipal Park. NW edge of business district.* Giant symbol of the campaign against forest fires. In park is a giant thermometer, standing 22 feet tall; it electronically records the temperature. Also in the park is

Bronko Nagurski Museum. Highlighting the life and career of football hero Bronko Nagurski; features exhibits, diorama, audiovisual program, photographs, and archives.

Koochiching Museums. *214 6th Ave, International Falls (56649). Phone 218/283-4316.* Exhibits, manuscripts, pictures, articles used by early settlers in area. (Mon-Fri) **$$**

Limited-Service Hotel

★★ HOLIDAY INN. *1500 Hwy 71, International Falls (56649). Phone 218/283-8000; toll-free 800/331-4443; fax 218/283-3774. www.holiday-inn.com.* View of Rainy River. 127 rooms, 2 story. Pets accepted, some restrictions. Check-in 3 pm, check-out noon. High-speed Internet access. Restaurant, bar. Indoor pool, children's pool, whirlpool. Airport transportation available. **$**

Itasca State Park (B-2)

See also Bemidji, Detroit Lakes

28 miles N on Hwy 71.

In the deep forests that cover most of the 32,000 acres of this park, there is a small stream just 15 steps across; this is the headwaters of the Mississippi River at its source, Lake Itasca (eye-TASK-uh). The name of the park and the lake itself is a contraction of the Latin *veritas caput*, meaning "true head." The lake is the largest of more than 100 that sparkle amid the virgin woodlands. The park offers swimming, fishing, boating (ramp, rentals); snowmobiling, cross-country skiing, biking (rentals), and hiking. There are cabins, camping and picnic grounds, and a lodge that offers food service. In the summer, there are daily boat cruises aboard the *Chester Charles*, from Douglas Lodge Pier to the headwaters of the Mississippi River (fee). A lookout tower, Aiton Heights, in the southeastern part of the park just off the 10-mile wilderness drive, provides a bird's-eye view of the park. American Indian burial mounds and a pioneer cabin are some of the many historic sites preserved at Itasca. The University of Minnesota's forestry school and biological station operate here during the summer.

Naturalist program provides self-guided and guided hikes, auto tours, boat launch tours, campfire programs, and evening movies on history and features of the area. Exhibits show many animals and plants native to the state, as well as park history. Inquire at the entrance gates for details. (For further information, contact Itasca State Park, HC05, Box 4, Lake Itasca, 56470-9702.)

Jackson (F-2)

See also Fairmont

Founded 1856
Population 3,559
Elevation 1,312 ft
Area Code 507
Zip 56143
Information Chamber of Commerce, 82 W Ashley St; phone 507/847-3867
Web Site www.jacksonmn.com

A peaceful community on the banks of the Des Moines River, Jackson processes the farm produce of the fertile river valley and also manufactures industrial farm equipment. Thirteen blocks of Jackson's business district are on the National Register of Historic Places.

What to See and Do

Fort Belmont. *Phone 507/847-3867.* Blacksmith shop, 19th-century farmhouse, historic church, sodhouse and other buildings; Native American artifacts. (Memorial Day-Labor Day, daily). **$$**

Kilen Woods State Park. *4 miles N on Hwy 71, then 5 miles W. Phone 507/662-6258.* 219 acres of forested hills in Des Moines Valley. Fishing, hiking, snowmobiling, picnicking, camping (hook-ups, dump station); visitor center.

Monument to Slain Settlers. *Ashley Park, State St and Riverside Dr, Jackson (56143).* Marks scene of attack by the Sioux in 1857.

Special Events

Jackson County Fair. *Fairgrounds. Phone 507/847-3867.* This county fair has taken place since 1868 and features a 4-H show, carnival, demolition derby, food, and music. Late July-early Aug.

Town and Country Day Celebration. *Main St, Jackson (56143). Phone 507/847-3867.* Third Sat in July.

Limited-Service Hotel

★ ★ ECONO LODGE COUNTRY MANOR INN. *2007 Hwy 71 N, Jackson (56143). Phone 507/847-3110; toll-free 800/424-6423; fax 507/847-3110. www.econolodge.com.* 41 rooms. Pets accepted; fee. Complimentary continental breakfast. Check-in 3 pm, check-out 11 am. Restaurant, bar. Indoor pool, whirlpool. **$**

Kabetogama (A-3)

See also International Falls, Lake Elmo, Voyageurs National Park

Population 60
Elevation 1,155 ft
Area Code 218
Zip 56669
Information Kabetogama Lake Assn, Inc, 9903 Gamma Rd; phone 218/875-2621 or toll-free 800/524-9085
Web Site www.kabetogama.com

The tiny town of Kabetogama (CAB-uh-TOE-guh-ma) sits on the shores of deep-blue Kabetogama Lake, which offers more than 500 miles of shoreline and over 200 small islands. Fishing here is solitary and peaceful, and the waters hold bass, crappies, perch, northern pike, sauger, and walleye. In fall, the colors surrounding the lake are spectacular, making the lake a popular spot for canoeing and kayaking. All year round, the area teems with wildlife, including deer, black bears, moose, and wolves. Be sure to visit the Kabetogama Lake Visitors Center—not only for the brochures and other resources available but also for the spectacular view of the lake. Just a few miles from the town of Kabetogama is the central entrance to Voyageurs National Park (see).

What to See and Do

Ellsworth Rock Gardens. *North shore of Kabetogama Lake.* Located within Voyageurs National Park, the Ellsworth Rock Gardens were created over a span of 20 years by Jack E. Ellsworth, a retired Chicago building contractor. With Kabetogama Lake as a background, large stones and granite mix with flowers, trees, and other plantings to create a rich, stunning setting. Picnic area. Park entrance fee required.

Kabetogama Lake. *7 miles NE off Hwy 53.* This lake is 22 miles long, 6 miles wide, with hundreds of miles of rugged shoreline, numerous islands, and secluded bays for fishing, sand beaches, woodland trails, snowmobiling, cross-country skiing, hunting for partridge, deer, bear; many resorts.

Voyageurs National Park. *Hwy 53 and County Rd 122, Lake Kabetogama (56649). Off Hwy 53 on County Roads 122 and 123. Phone 218/283-9821.* (see)

Lake Elmo (A-3)

See also International Falls, Kabetogama, Voyageurs National Park

Population 6,863
Elevation 639 ft
Area Code 612, 651
Zip 55042
Information City of Lake Elmo, 3800 Laverne Ave N
Web Site www.lakeelmo.com

For well over 100 years, visitors have sought out Lake Elmo for the excellent fishing opportunities in its five lakes: Horseshoe Lake and Lakes Demontreville, Elmo, Jane, and Olson. Anglers catch bluegill, crappie, largemouth bass, northern pike, panfish, sunfish, and walleye. In winter, snowmobiling and ice fishing are popular, and the four golf courses in Lake Elmo offer summertime fun.

What to See and Do

Lake Elmo Park Reserve. *1515 Keat Ave N, Lake Elmo (55042). Phone 651/430-8370.* The reserve offers a range of outdoor activities, including archery, canoeing, fishing, and swimming (pool and lake). You'll also find trails for cross-country skiing, hiking, horseback riding, and mountain biking. The park offers several orienteering courses, ranging from easy to difficult. Playground, picnicking. Boat launch. (Daily)

Restaurant

★ ★ ★ LAKE ELMO INN. *3442 Lake Elmo Ave, Lake Elmo (55042). Phone 651/777-8495.* Guests enjoy the hearty portions of rich, creative cuisine, charming outdoor seating, and a stellar Sunday brunch at this restored inn (1881). American menu.

Lunch, dinner, Sun brunch. Closed holidays. Bar. Children's menu. Casual attire. Outdoor seating. **$$**

Lakeville (E-3)

See also Faribault, Hastings, Minneapolis, Northfield, Red Wing, St. Paul

Population 24,854
Elevation 974 ft
Area Code 952
Zip 55044
Information Lakeville Area Chamber of Commerce & Visitors Bureau, PO Box 12; phone 952/469-2020 or toll-free 888/525-3845
Web Site www.visitlakeville.org

Lakeville is a convenient stop when visiting the Twin Cities or Bloomington—it offers a quiet place to stay and eat and an abundance of outdoor activities in the town's many small parks and recreation area. Year-round ice skating is also available in the Lakeville Ames Arena.

Limited-Service Hotel

★ **MOTEL 6.** *11274 210th St, Lakeville (55044). Phone 952/469-1900; toll-free 800/466-8356; fax 952/469-5359. www.motel6.com.* 85 rooms, 2 story. Pets accepted, some restrictions. Check-out noon. **$**

Full-Service Inn

★ ★ ★ **SCHUMACHER'S HOTEL.** *212 W Main St, New Prague (56071). Phone 952/758-2133; toll-free 800/283-2049; fax 952/758-2400. www.schumachershotel.com.* Built in 1898. Décor resembles country inns, hotels in Bavaria, southern Bohemia and Austria. 16 rooms, 2 story. Check-in 3 pm, check-out 11:30 am. Restaurant, bar. **$$$**

Restaurant

★ ★ **SCHUMACHER'S.** *212 W Main St, New Prague (56071). Phone 952/758-2133; toll-free 800/283-2049. www.schumachershotel.com.* Fifty miles outside the Twin Cities, the German-style cuisine is worth the trip, especially if you can arrange a stay at the inn. Sample sauerbraten with stuffing and Czech dumplings, elk steaks with cranberry relish, and banana cream pie. German menu. Breakfast, lunch, dinner. Bar. **$$$**

Le Sueur (E-3)

See also Faribault, Mankato, St. Peter

Population 3,714
Elevation 800 ft
Area Code 507
Zip 56058
Information Chamber of Commerce, 500 N Main St, Suite 106; phone 507/665-2501
Web Site www.lesueurchamber.org

This town on the Minnesota River was named for Pierre Charles le Sueur (luh-SOOR), who explored the river valley at the end of the 17th century. The Green Giant Company, one of the world's largest packers of peas and corn, was founded here and merged with Pillsbury in 1980. Home office of Le Sueur Inc, and plant sites for ADC Telcommunications, UNIMIN, and Le Sueur Cheese are located here.

What to See and Do

W. W. Mayo House. *118 N Main St, Le Sueur (56058). Phone 507/665-3250.* (1859). Home of Mayo Clinic founder; restored to 1859-1864 period when Dr. Mayo carried on a typical frontier medical practice from his office on the second floor. Adjacent park is location of Paul Granland's bronze sculpture *The Mothers Louise.* (June-Aug: Tues-Sat; May and Sept-Oct: Sat only) **$**

Litchfield (D-2)

See also Minneapolis, St. Cloud, Willmar

Population 6,041
Elevation 1,132 ft
Area Code 320
Zip 55355
Information Chamber of Commerce, 219 N Sibley Ave; phone 320/693-8184
Web Site www.litch.com

Litchfield is best known for its central building, the Grand Army of the Republic Hall, which was built by Union Veterans of the Civil War, a political organization of the late 1800s. As a result, the town is steeped in Civil War history, which is unexpected in Minnesota.

What to See and Do

Meeker County Historical Society Museum. *308 Marshall Ave N, Litchfield (55355). Phone 320/693-8911.* The museum stands behind the Grand Army of the Republic Hall. Includes a log cabin, old barn display, blacksmith shop, general store, and Native American display. Original newspapers, furniture, and uniforms are also exhibited. (Tues-Sun afternoons, also by appointment; closed holidays except Memorial Day) **DONATION**

Grand Army of the Republic Hall. *308 Marshall Ave N, Litchfield (55355).* Built in 1885, the hall has two rooms in original condition. Commemorates the members of the GAR (Grand Army of the Republic).

Limited-Service Hotel

★ SCOTWOOD. *1017 E Hwy 12, Litchfield (55355). Phone 320/693-2496; toll-free 800/225-5489; fax 320/693-2496.* 35 rooms, 2 story. Pets accepted, some restrictions. Complimentary continental breakfast. Check-out 11 am. **$**

Little Falls (C-2)

See also Brainerd, Onamia, Sauk Centre, St. Cloud

Population 7,232
Elevation 1,120 ft
Area Code 320
Zip 56345
Information Convention & Visitors Bureau, 606 First St SE; phone 320/616-4959 or toll-free 800/325-5916
Web Site www.littlefallsmn.com

This town gets its name from the rapids of the Mississippi River, which flows next to the city and provides opportunities for canoeing and fishing. Little Falls was the hometown of Charles Lindbergh, Jr., the first person to fly solo across the Atlantic. The state park in the area bears Lindbergh's name, and his house is open for tours.

What to See and Do

Charles A. Lindbergh House and History Center. *1200 Lindbergh Dr S, Little Falls (56345). S edge of town, on W bank of Mississippi River. Phone 320/632-3154.* Home of C. A. Lindbergh, former US congressman, and Charles A. Lindbergh, famous aviator. Homestead restored to its 1906-1920 appearance with much original furniture; visitor center has exhibits, audiovisual program, gift shop. (May-Labor Day: daily; Sept-Oct: weekends) **$$** Adjacent is

Charles A. Lindbergh State Park. *1201 Lindbergh Dr S, Little Falls (56345). Phone 320/616-2525.* 436 acres. Hiking; cross-country skiing; picnicking; camping (hook-ups, dump station).

Charles A. Weyerhaeuser Memorial Museum. *2151 Lindbergh Dr S, Little Falls (56345). Phone 320/632-4007.* Museum and resource center for Morrison County and regional history. (Tues-Sun; closed holidays) **FREE**

Minnesota Military Museum. *15000 Hwy 115, Little Falls (56345). Camp Ripley, 7 miles N on Hwy 371, W on Hwy 115. Phone 320/632-7374.* Located in a former regimental headquarters, the museum documents US military history as experienced by Minnesotans, from frontier garrisons to the Persian Gulf. Exhibits; military decorations; tanks and aircraft. (Sept-May: Thurs-Fri; late May-late Aug: Wed-Sun) **FREE**

Primeval Pine Grove Municipal Park. *Broadway Ave and NW 10 St, Little Falls (56345). Phone 320/616-5500.* Picnicking, playground, zoo with native animals (all year); stand of virgin pine. (May-Sept, daily) **FREE**

Limited-Service Hotel

★ SUPER 8. *300 12th St NE, Little Falls (56345). Phone 320/632-2351; toll-free 800/800-8000; fax 320/632-2351. www.super8.com.* 51 rooms, 2 story. Check-out 11 am. **$**

Lutsen (B-5)

See also Boundary Waters Canoe Area Wilderness, Grand Marais

Population 290
Elevation 671 ft
Area Code 218
Zip 55612
Information Lutsen-Tofte Tourism Association, PO Box 2248, Tofte, 55615; phone toll-free 888/616-6784
Web Site www.61north.com

Lutsen, situated on Lake Superior and next to Lutsen Mountain, is an outdoor lover's paradise. Whether you want to downhill ski, cross-country ski, hike, mountain bike, canoe or kayak, play golf, or watch fall colors, Lutsen's variety of outdoor opportunities are endless.

What to See and Do

Lutsen Mountains Ski Area. *468 Ski Hill Rd, Lutsen (55612). 1 1/2 miles SW on Hwy 61, then 1 1/2 miles N. Phone 218/663-7281. www.lutsen.com.* Seven double chairlifts, surface lift; school, rentals; snowmaking; lodge, cafeteria, bar. Longest run 2 miles; vertical drop 1,088 feet. Gondola. Cross-country trails. (Mid-Nov-mid-Apr, daily) **$$$$** Also here are

> **Alpine Slide.** *467 Ski Hole Rd, Lutsen (55612). Phone 218/663-7281.* Chairlift takes riders up mountain to slide; riders control sled on 1/2-mile track down mountain. Concession and picnic area. (May-mid-Oct) **$$$$**

> **Mountain Tram.** *467 Ski Hole Rd, Lutsen (55612). Phone 218/663-7281.* A 2-mile round trip sightseeing ride to the highest point on the North Shore. Particularly scenic view in fall. (May-mid-Oct). Horseback riding. (Mid-May-mid-Oct, fee) **$$$**

Limited-Service Hotels

★ BEST WESTERN CLIFF DWELLER. *Hwy 61, Lutsen (55612). Phone 218/663-7273; toll-free 800/780-7234; fax 218/663-7273.* 22 rooms, 2 story. Check-in 2 pm, check-out 11 am. Restaurant. **$**

★ ★ CARIBOU HIGHLANDS LODGE. *371 Ski Hill Rd, Lutsen (55612). Phone 218/663-7241; toll-free 800/642-6036; fax 218/663-7920. www.cariboughighlands.com.* This lodge is located in the Lutsen Mountains on the north shore of Lake Superior. 110 rooms, 3 story. Check-in 4:30 pm, check-out 11 am. Restaurant, bar. Children's activity center. Fitness room. Indoor pool, outdoor pool. Tennis. **$**

Full-Service Resort

★ ★ CASCADE LODGE. *3719 W Hwy 61, Lutsen (55612). Phone 218/387-1112; toll-free 800/322-9543. www.cascadelodgemn.com.* 23 rooms. Check-in 1 pm, check-out 11 am. Restaurant. **$**

Luverne (E-1)

See also Pipestone, Pipestone National Monument, Sioux Falls

Population 4,382
Elevation 1,450 ft
Area Code 507
Zip 56156
Information Luverne Area Chamber of Commerce, 102 E Main St; phone 507/283-4061 or toll-free 888/283-4061
Web Site www.luvernemn.com

Called the "Garden of Eden" by the man who founded the city, Luverne still evokes such praise for its beautiful natural resources. Craggy cliffs overlook native prairie land where buffalo still roam. Downtown, a walking tour allows visitors to amble among historic buildings.

What to See and Do

Blue Mounds State Park. *5 miles N of I-90 on Hwy 75, 1 mile E on County 20. Phone 507/283-1307.* A 2,028-acre park. Main feature is Blue Mound, a 1 1/2-mile-long quartzite bluff. Buffalo can be observed in park. Swimming, fishing, boating; snowmobiling; picnicking; camping; visitor center. **$$**

Limited-Service Hotel

★ SUPER 8. *I-90 and Hwy 75, Luverne (56156). Phone 507/283-9541; toll-free 800/800-8000. www.super8.com.* 36 rooms, 2 story. Pets accepted, some restrictions; fee. Check-in 2 pm, check-out 11 am. **$**

Mankato (E-3)

See also Faribault, Le Sueur, New Ulm, St. Peter

Founded 1852
Population 31,477
Elevation 785 ft
Area Code 507
Information Chamber & Convention Bureau, 112 Riverfront Dr, PO Box 999, 56002; phone 507/345-4519 or toll-free 800/657-4733
Web Site www.mankato.com

In a wooded valley where the Minnesota and Blue Earth rivers join, Mankato (Native American for "blue earth") takes its name from the blue clay that lines the riverbanks. Settled by Eastern professional men, farmers, and Scandinavian and German immigrants, Mankato (man-KAY-toe) today enjoys an economy based on farming, retailing, manufacturing, and distributing.

What to See and Do

Hubbard House. *606 S Broad St, Mankato (56001). Phone 507/345-4154.* (1871) Historic Victorian home with cherry woodwork, three marble fireplaces, silk wall coverings, signed Tiffany lampshade; carriage house; Victorian gardens. **$$**

Land of Memories. *S via Hwy 169, then E at municipal campground sign. Phone 507/387-8649.* Picnicking, camping (hook-ups, dump station, rest rooms), fishing, boating (launch), nature trails. **$$$**

Minneopa State Park. *54497 Gadwall Rd, Mankato (56001). 3 miles W off Hwy 60. Phone 507/389-5464.* A 1,145-acre park. Scenic falls and gorge; historic mill site; fishing, hiking, picnicking, camping. Adjacent is

Minneopa-Williams Outdoor Learning Center. *Phone 507/625-3281.* Wide variety of native animals and vegetation; information stations; outdoor classroom. (Daily) **FREE**

Mount Kato Ski Area. *20461 Hwy 66, Mankato (56001). 1 mile S on Hwy 66. Phone 507/625-3363. www.mountkato.com.* Five quad, three double chairlifts; patrol, school, rental; snowmaking; cafeteria; bar. (Nov-Apr, daily) **$$$$**

Sibley Park. *End of Park Lane, Mankato (56001).* Fishing, picnicking; river walk, playground, zoo (daily); rest rooms; beautiful gardens, scenic view of rivers. **FREE**

Tourtelotte Park. *N Broad and Mabel sts, Mankato (56001). Phone 507/387-8649.* Picnicking, playground. Swimming pool (early June-Labor Day, daily; fee), wading pool. **$**

Limited-Service Hotels

★ DAYS INN. *1285 Range St, Mankato (56001). Phone 507/387-3332; toll-free 800/329-7466; fax 507/387-6279. www.daysinn.com.* 50 rooms, 2 story. Pets accepted, some restrictions; fee. Complimentary continental breakfast. Check-in 3 pm, check-out 11 am. Wireless Internet access. Indoor pool, whirlpool. **$**

★ ★ HOLIDAY INN. *101 E Main St, Mankato (56001). Phone 507/345-1234; toll-free 800/465-4329; fax 507/345-1248. www.holiday-inn.com.* Civic Center nearby. 151 rooms, 4 story. Check-in 3 pm, check-out noon. Restaurant, bar. Fitness room. Indoor pool, whirlpool. **$**

Specialty Lodging

The following lodging establishment is approved by Mobil Travel Guide, but due to its unique and individualized nature has not been given a traditional Mobil Star rating. Included in this listing you may find bed-and-breakfasts, limited-service inns, guest ranches, and other unique hotel properties.

THE BUTLER HOUSE. *704 S Broad St, Mankato (56001). Phone 507/387-5055. www.butlerhouse.com.* Offering turn-of-the-century elegance and regional cuisine in a restored Victorian mansion. 5 rooms, 3 story. Complimentary full breakfast. Check-in 4 pm, check-out noon. **$**

Mantorville (E-3)

See also Owatonna, Rochester

Founded 1853
Population 1,054
Elevation 1,150 ft
Area Code 507
Zip 55955
Web Site www.mantorville.com

Downtown Mantorville is a nationally recognized historic place, where historic buildings dating back to the mid- and late 1800s are well preserved. Take the downtown historic walking tour, and you can visit a former stagecoach stop, the 1865 courthouse, an opera house, a log cabin, and some mansions. The excellent condition of the buildings is due partially to the Mantorville limestone that was used to build most of the town. The limestone quarries here kept the town employed, and the limestone was used both in local structures and as exports to other areas.

Marshall (E-1)

See also Granite Falls, Redwood Falls, Tracy

Population 12,023
Elevation 1,170 ft
Area Code 507
Zip 56258
Information Marshall Area Chamber of Commerce, 1210 E College Dr, PO Box 352B; phone 507/532-4484
Web Site www.marshall-mn.org

At the crossroads of five highways, Marshall is a major industrial and retail center for the southwestern part of Minnesota. Thanks to Southwest State University, the town also boasts a fine anthropological museum and, next door, a planetarium.

What to See and Do

Camden State Park. *1897 County Rd 68, Lynd (56157). 10 miles S, off Hwy 23. Phone 507/865-4530.* More than 2,200 acres in forested Redwood River Valley. Swimming, fishing; hiking, riding, cross-country skiing, snowmobiling; picnicking, camping.

Southwest State University. *1501 State St, Marshall (56258). Phone 507/537-6255. www.southwestmsu.edu.* (1963) (5,000 students) Liberal arts and technical programs. Planetarium (fee), museum, and greenhouse (daily; closed holidays; free). **FREE**

Special Events

International Rolle Bolle Tournament. *Phone 507/532-4484.* 150 teams compete for prize money. Mid-Aug.

Shades of the Past '50s Revival Weekend. *Phone 507/532-4484.* Over 500 classic and collector cars. Flea market, swap meet, street dance. First weekend in June.

Limited-Service Hotel

★★ BEST WESTERN MARSHALL INN.
1500 E College Dr, Marshall (56258). Phone 507/532-3221; toll-free 800/780-7234; fax 507/532-4089. www.bestwestern.com. 100 rooms, 2 story. Pets accepted; fee. Check-in 3 pm, check-out noon. Restaurant, bar. Indoor pool, whirlpool. Airport transportation available. **$**

Minneapolis (D-3)

See also Anoka, Bloomington, Elk River, Hastings, Lakeville, Litchfield, Northfield, St. Cloud, St. Paul, St. Peter

Settled 1847
Population 368,383
Elevation 687-980 ft
Area Code 612
Information Greater Minneapolis Convention & Visitors Assn, 4000 Multifoods Tower, 33 S 6th St, 55402; phone 612/661-4700 or toll-free 888/676-6757
Web Site www.minneapolis.org

Across the Mississippi from Minnesota's capital, St. Paul, is this handsome city with skyscrapers, lovely parks, and teeming industries. Minneapolis still has a frontier vigor; it is growing and brimming with confidence in itself and its future. Clean and modern, a north country fountainhead of culture, Minneapolis is also a university town, a river town, and a lake town.

A surprising array of nightlife, a revitalized downtown with many fine stores, a rich, year-round sports program, a symphony orchestra, and theaters provide an excellent opportunity to enjoy the niceties of city life. Minneapolis has one of the largest one-campus universities in the country and more than 400 churches and synagogues. Hunting and fishing, which are among the state's major tourist attractions, are easily accessible. The Minneapolis park system, with over a hundred parks, has been judged one of the best in the country. The city has also been a consistent winner of traffic safety awards.

Capital of Upper Midwest agriculture, with one of the largest cash grain markets in the world, Minneapolis is the processing and distribution center for a large sector of America's cattle lands and grainfields. Several of the largest milling companies in the world have their headquarters here. Graphic arts, electronics, medical technology, machinery, lumber, paper, and chemicals are also major industries.

Minneapolis was born when two mills were built to cut lumber and grind flour for the men of a nearby fort. Despite the fact that these were reservation lands and that cabins were torn down by army troops almost as soon as settlers built them, the community of St. Anthony developed at St. Anthony Falls around the twin mills. In 1885, the boundaries of the reservation were changed, and the squatters' claims became valid. The swiftly growing community took the new name of Minneapolis (*Minne,* a Sioux word for water, and *polis,* Greek for city).

Additional Visitor Information

For further information contact the Greater Minneapolis Convention & Visitors Association, 4000 Multifoods Tower, 33 S 6th St, 55402, phone 612/661-4700 or toll-free 800/445-7412. The Minneapolis Park and Recreation Board, 400 4th Ave S, 55415, phone 612/661-4800, provides city park information.

Public Transportation

Buses (Metropolitan Transit Commission), phone 612/349-7000

Airport Minneapolis-St. Paul International Airport; weather phone 952/361-6680; cash machines Main Terminal, between entrances to Blue & Green Concourses

Information Humphrey Terminal (Minneapolis) phone 612/726-5800, Lindbergh Terminal (St. Paul) phone 612/726-5555

Lost and Found Phone 612/726-5141

Web site www.mspairport.com/msp

Airlines At Humphrey Terminal (Minneapolis): Casino Express, Champion Air, Miami Air International, Omni Air, Ryan International, Sun Country Airlines, Transmeridian Airlines; at Lindbergh Terminal (St. Paul): Air Canada, Air Tran Airways, America West, American Airlines, American Trans Air, Comair, Continental, Delta Air Lines, Frontier Airlines, Icelandair, KLM Royal Dutch, Mesaba Airlines, Northwest Airlines, Midwest Connect, SkyWest, United Airlines, Great Lakes Aviation, US Airways

What to See and Do

American Swedish Institute. *2600 Park Ave, Minneapolis (55407). Phone 612/871-4907. www.americanswedishinst.org.* This museum is housed in a turn-of-the-century, 33-room mansion and features hand-carved woodwork, porcelainized tile stoves, and sculpted ceilings, plus Swedish fine art and artifacts. (Tues, Thurs-Sat noon-4 pm; Wed noon-8 pm; Sun 1-5 pm; closed Mon, holidays) **$**

Basilica of St. Mary. *88 N 17th St, Minneapolis (55403). Hennepin Ave between 16th and 17th sts. Phone 612/333-1381. www.mary.org.* Renaissance architecture patterned after Basilica of St. John Lateran in Rome. (Daily)

Buck Hill Ski Area. *15400 Buck Hill Rd, Burnsville (55306). 14 miles S on I-35 W or I-35 E. Phone 952/435-7174. www.buckhill.com.* Quad, three double chairlifts; J-bar; three rope tows; snowmaking; patrol, school, rentals; restaurant, bar, cafeteria. (Late Nov-Mar, daily) BMX racing, mountain biking, and mountain boarding (May-Aug, daily). **$$$$**

Eloise Butler Wildflower Garden and Bird Sanctuary. *Theodore Wirth Pkwy and Glenwood Ave, Minneapolis (55422). Phone 612/370-4903. www.minneapolisparks.org.* Horseshoe-shaped glen contains natural bog, swamp; habitat for prairie and woodland flowers and birds. Guided tours. (Early Apr-mid-Oct: daily 7:30 am-30 minutes before sunset) **FREE**

Gray Line Twin Cities Tour. *21160 Holyoke Ave, Lakeville (55044). Phone 952/469-5020. www.grayline-mpls.com.* This 3 1/2-hour bus tour of the Twin Cities area departs from the Mall of America and includes Minnehaha Falls, Fort Snelling, and the St. Paul Cathedral. (Daily at 10:15 am; late May-late Aug, Sat-Sun; no tours on July 4) **$$$$**

Guthrie Theater. *725 Vineland Pl, Minneapolis (55403). 1 block S of junction I-94 and I-394. Phone 612/377-2224. www.guthrietheater.org.* Produces classic plays in repertory, as well as new works. (Nightly Tues-Sun; matinees Wed, Sat-Sun)

Hennepin History Museum. *2303 Third Ave S, Minneapolis (55404). Phone 612/870-1329. www.hhmuseum.org.* Permanent and temporary exhibits on the history of Minneapolis and Hennepin County. Includes collection of textiles, costumes, toys, and material unique to central Minnesota. Research library and archive. (Sun, Wed, Fri-Sat 10 am-5 pm; Tues 10 am-2 pm; Thurs 1-8 pm; closed Mon, holidays) **$**

Hubert H. Humphrey Metrodome. *900 S Fifth St, Minneapolis (55415). Phone 612/332-0386.* Home of Minnesota Twins (baseball), Minnesota Vikings (football), and University of Minnesota football. Seats up to 63,000. (Mon-Fri and special events) **$$**

James Sewell Ballet. *528 Hennepin Avenue, Suite 205, Minneapolis (55403). Phone 507/287-2222. www.jsballet.org.* The James Sewell Ballet company performs beautiful and uniquely choreographed ballets with a small ensemble of eight dancers. Two ballets are created each year by critically acclaimed choreographer James Sewell, the company's namesake. Many of the company's performances have a contemporary, creative, and bold bent. (Mid-Aug-mid-May) **$$$$**

Lakewood Cemetery Memorial Chapel. *3600 Hennepin Ave, Minneapolis (55408). Phone 612/822-2171.* Going to a cemetery may not be your idea of a vacation, but the chapel at Lakewood Cemetery is an architectural wonder worth visiting. Stained-glass windows reflect brilliant light off the more than 10 million 1/2-inch tiles that line the walls. If the door is locked, stop by the cemetery administration building. (Daily) **FREE**

Lyndale Park Gardens. *1500 E Lake Harriet Parkway, Minneapolis (55409). Off E Lake Harriet Pkwy and Roseway Rd, on the NE shore of Lake Harriet. Phone 612/230-6400. www.minneapolisparks.org.* Four distinctive gardens: one for roses, two for perennials, and the Peace (rock) Garden. Displays of roses, bulbs, other annuals and perennials; exotic and native trees; rock garden; two decorative fountains; adjacent to bird sanctuary. April to September is the best time to visit. (Daily 7:30 am-10 pm) **FREE**

MetroConnections. *1219 Marquette Ave, Minneapolis (55403). Phone 612/333-8687; toll-free 800/747-8687.* Motorcoach tours include Twin Cities Highlights (Jan-Nov); Stillwater, a historic river town (June-Oct); and Lake Minnetonka (June-Aug). **$$$$**

Minneapolis City Hall. *350 S 5th St, Minneapolis (55415). Phone 612/673-2491.* (1891) *Father of Waters* statue in rotunda, carved of largest single block of marble produced from quarries of Carrara, Italy. Self-guided tours. Guided tours first Wednesday of the month. (Mon-Fri; closed holidays) **FREE**

Minneapolis College of Art and Design. *2501 Stevens Ave S, Minneapolis (55404). Phone 612/874-3700. www.mcad.edu.* (1886) (560 students) Four-year college of fine arts, media arts, and design. MCAD Gallery (daily; closed holidays). **FREE**

Minneapolis Grain Exchange. *400 S 4th St, Minneapolis (55415). Phone 612/321-7101. www.mgex.com.* Visit cash grain market and futures market. Tours (Tues-Thurs). Visitors' balcony; reservations required (mornings; closed holidays). **FREE**

Minneapolis Institute of Arts. *2400 Third Ave S, Minneapolis (55404). Phone 612/870-3131. www.artsmia.org.* Masterpieces from every age and culture. Collection of more than 80,000 objects covers American and European painting, sculpture, decorative arts; period rooms, prints and drawings, textiles, photography; American, African, Oceanic, Asian, and ancient Asian objects. Lectures, classes, films (fee), special events (fee); restaurants. (Tues-Wed, Fri-Sat 10 am-5 pm; Thurs 10 am-9 pm; Sun 11 am-5 pm; closed July 4, Thanksgiving, Dec 25) **FREE**

Minnesota Lynx (WNBA). *Target Center, 600 First Ave N, Minneapolis (55403). Phone 612/673-8400. www.wnba.com/lnyx.* Team plays at the Target Center.

Minnesota Timberwolves (NBA). *Target Center, 600 First Ave N, Minneapolis (55403). Phone 612/337-3865. www.nba.com/timberwolves.* Team plays at the Target Center.

Minnesota Twins (MLB). *Metrodome, 900 S Fifth Ave, Minneapolis (55415). Phone 612/375-1366. twins.mlb.com.* Team plays at the Metrodome.

Minnesota Vikings (NFL). *Metrodome, 900 S Fifth Ave, Minneapolis (55415). Phone 612/338-4537. www.vikings.com.* Team plays at the Metrodome.

★ **Nicollet Mall.** *700 Nicollet Mall, Minneapolis (55402). Downtown. Phone 612/332-3101.* A world-famous shopping promenade with a variety of shops, restaurants, museums, and art galleries as well as entertainment ranging from an art show to symphony orchestra performances (see SPECIAL EVENTS). No traffic is allowed on this avenue except for buses and cabs. Beautifully designed with spacious walkways, fountains, shade trees, flowers, and a skyway system, it is certainly worth a visit. Also here is

> **IDS Tower.** *80 S 8th St, Minneapolis (55403).* 775 feet, 57 stories; one of the tallest buildings between Chicago and the West Coast.

River City Trolley. *Minneapolis Convention Center, 1301 Second Ave S, Minneapolis (55403). Phone 612/378-7833. www.rivercitytrolley.com.* A 40-minute loop traverses the core of downtown, passing through the Mississippi Mile, St. Anthony Falls, and the warehouse district. A Chain of Lakes tour is also available. Onboard narration; tours run approximately every 20 minutes. (May-Oct, daily, also Fri-Sat evenings) **$**

St. Anthony Falls. *Main St SE and Central Ave, Minneapolis (55403).* Head of the navigable Mississippi, site of village of St. Anthony. A public vantage point at the upper locks and dam provides a view of the falls and of the operation of the locks. Also includes a renovated warehouse with shops and restaurants.

University of Minnesota. *Admissions Building, 77 Pleasant St SE, Minneapolis (55455). On the E and W banks of Mississippi River on University Ave SE. Phone 612/624-6888. www1.umn.edu.* Founded in 1851. More than 46,000 students populate one of the largest single campuses in the United States. Several art galleries and museums on campus. Tours. On campus are

Bell Museum of Natural History. *University Ave and 17th Ave, Minneapolis (55455). 17th and University Ave SE. Phone 612/624-7083. www.bellmuseum.org.* Dioramas show Minnesota birds and mammals in natural settings; special traveling exhibits; exhibits on art, photography, and natural history research change frequently. The Touch and See Room encourages hands-on exploration and comparison of natural objects. Free admission Sunday. (Tues-Fri 9 am-5 pm, Sat 10 am-5 pm, Sun noon-5 pm; closed Mon, holidays) **$**

Frederick R. Weisman Art Museum. *333 E River Rd, Minneapolis (55455). Phone 612/625-9494. hudson.acad.umn.edu.* Striking stainless steel exterior is oddly shaped and was designed by Frank Gehry. Inside are collections of early 20th-century and contemporary American art, Asian ceramics, and Native American Mimbres pottery. Special exhibits. Group tours (by appointment, phone 612/625-9656 three weeks in advance). (Tues-Wed, Fri 10 am-5 pm; Thurs 10 am-8 pm; Sat-Sun 11 am-5 pm; closed Mon, holidays) **FREE**

Walker Art Center. *1750 Hennepin Ave, Minneapolis (55403). Phone 612/375-7622. www.walkerart.org.* Permanent collection of 20th-century painting, sculpture, prints, and photographs; also changing exhibits, performances, concerts, films, lectures. Free admission on the first Thurs and Sat of each month. (Gallery open Tues-Wed, Fri-Sat 10 am-5 pm; Thurs 10 am-9 pm; Sun 11 am-5 pm; closed Mon) **$$** Opposite is

Minneapolis Sculpture Garden. *Vineland Pl and Lyndale Ave S, Minneapolis (55403). Phone 612/375-7577. www.minneapolisparks.org.* Ten-acre urban garden features more than 40 sculptures by leading American and international artists; glass conservatory. (Daily 6 am-midnight) **FREE**

Special Events

Minnesota Orchestra. *Orchestra Hall, 1111 Nicollet Mall, Minneapolis (55403). Phone 612/371-5656.* Mid-Sept-June.

Showboat. *Phone 612/625-4001.* On University of Minnesota campus, on Mississippi River. During the 1800s, melodramas, comedies, and light opera were presented on riverboats; University Theater productions preserve this tradition aboard an authentic, air-conditioned sternwheeler moored on the river. July-Aug.

Sommerfest. *Orchestra Hall, 1111 Nicollet Mall, Minneapolis (55403). Phone 612/371-5656.* Summer concert series of Minnesota Orchestra with Viennese flavor; food booths. Mid-July-late Aug.

University Theatre. *120 Rarig Center, Minneapolis (55455). On University of Minnesota campus. Phone 612/625-4001.* Student-professional productions of musicals, comedies, and dramas in four-theater complex. Early Oct-late May.

Limited-Service Hotels

★★ COURTYARD BY MARRIOTT - DEPOT. *225 S Third Ave, Minneapolis (55401). Phone 612/375-1700; toll-free 800/627-7468; fax 612/375-1300. www.courtyard.com.* 227 rooms. Check-in 3 pm, check-out noon. High-speed Internet access. Restaurant, bar. Fitness room. Indoor pool. Airport transportation available. Business center. **$**

★★ DOUBLETREE HOTEL. *1101 LaSalle Ave, Minneapolis (55403). Phone 612/332-6800; toll-free 800/662-3232; fax 612/332-8246. www.doubletree.com.* Located only one block from the Nicollet Mall in downtown Minneapolis's shopping and theater district. 230 rooms, 12 story, all suites. Check-in 3 pm, check-out noon. Restaurant, bar. Fitness room. **$$**

★★ EMBASSY SUITES. *425 S 7th St, Minneapolis (55415). Phone 612/333-3111; toll-free 800/362-2779; fax 612/333-7984. www.embassysuites.com.* A six-story atrium filled with tropical plants will greet visitors as they enter the hotel. Located in the business and financial district, the property is near the Target Center, Orpheum Theatre, fine shops, and entertainment. 216 rooms, 6 story, all suites. Check-in 3 pm, check-out noon. Restaurant, bar. Fitness room. Indoor pool, whirlpool. **$**

★★ RADISSON HOTEL METRODOME. *615 Washington Ave SE, Minneapolis (55414). Phone 612/379-8888; toll-free 800/822-6757; fax 612/379-8682.*

www.radisson.com. Conveniently located between downtown Minneapolis and St. Paul, this hotel is near the University of Minnesota's campus, museums, sporting events, family attractions, and a busy night life. 304 rooms, 8 story. Check-in 3 pm, check-out noon. Restaurant, bar. Fitness room. **$$**

★ ★ RADISSON PLAZA HOTEL MINNEAPOLIS. *35 S 7th St, Minneapolis (55402). Phone 612/339-4900; toll-free 800/333-3333; fax 612/337-9766. www.radisson.com.* 357 rooms, 17 story. Pets accepted; fee. Check-in 3 pm, check-out noon. Fitness room. **$$**

Full-Service Hotels

★ ★ ★ CROWNE PLAZA. *618 Second Ave S, Minneapolis (55402). Phone 612/338-2288; toll-free 800/556-7827; fax 612/673-1157. www.crowneplaza.com.* Located in downtown Minneapolis, this hotel is connected to the city's skywalk system making for easy access to shopping, dining, sports, and entertainment. A fitness and business center is offered along with the Rosewood Room Restaurant. 223 rooms, 11 story. Check-in 3 pm, check-out 1 pm. Restaurant, bar. Fitness room. Business center. **$$**

★ ★ ★ HILTON MINNEAPOLIS. *1001 Marquette Ave S, Minneapolis (55403). Phone 612/376-1000; toll-free 800/774-1500; fax 612/397-4875. www.hilton.com.* Found in the heart of downtown, this hotel is connected by skyway to the Minneapolis Convention Center and is near Orchestra Hall, Guthrie Theater, great shopping, dining, and more. 821 rooms, 25 story. Pets accepted. Check-in 3 pm, check-out noon. Restaurant, bar. Fitness room. Indoor pool, whirlpool. **$$**

★ ★ ★ HYATT REGENCY MINNEAPOLIS. *1300 Nicollet Mall, Minneapolis (55403). Phone 612/370-1234; toll-free 800/633-7313; fax 612/370-1463. www.hyatt.com.* Located in the heart of the downtown business and financial district, this hotel offers access to the Minneapolis Convention Center via the city's skywalk. It is near the Guthrie Theatre, Walker Art Center, and much more. 533 rooms, 24 story. Check-in 3 pm, check-out noon. Restaurant, bar. Fitness room. Indoor pool, whirlpool. Airport transportation available. **$$**

★ ★ ★ LE MERIDIEN MINNEAPOLIS. *601 First Ave N, Minneapolis (55403). Phone 612/677-1100; toll-free 888/451-2076; fax 612/677-1200. www.lemeridien.com.* Calling downtown Minneapolis home, Le Meridien brings cutting-edge design to this Midwestern capital city. It may be cold outside, but this hotel is decidedly hot with its 1950s-meets-2010 appeal, where geometric designs, Indonesian wood walls, marble floors, and striking glass walls create a unique space. The guest rooms and suites are modern in both look and feel. Tech-savvy, the accommodations feature an artistic ambience with backlit photographs, glass-etched headboards, and plasma screen televisions, and the bathrooms appear to be straight from the pages of a home design magazine with rain showers, etched-glass sinks, and serene limestone. Le Meridien's signature cool extends to its Cosmos Restaurant and hip Infiniti Room club. 255 rooms. Pets accepted, some restrictions; fee. Check-in 3 pm, check-out noon. High-speed Internet access. Restaurant, bar. Fitness room. Airport transportation available. Business center. **$$**

★ ★ ★ THE MARQUETTE. *7th St and Marquette Ave, Minneapolis (55402). Phone 612/333-4545; fax 612/376-7419. www.marquette.hilton.com.* Located in the downtown area, this hotel is connected to shops, restaurants, and entertainment by the city's skywalk system. 277 rooms, 19 story. Pets accepted, some restrictions; fee. Check-in 3 pm, check-out noon. Restaurant, bar. Fitness room. Business center. **$$$**

★ ★ ★ MARRIOTT MINNEAPOLIS CITY CENTER. *30 S 7th St, Minneapolis (55402). Phone 612/349-4000; toll-free 800/228-9290; fax 612/332-7165. www.marriott.com.* Linked by the enclosed skywalk to many of the city's offices and shopping complexes in the downtown area, this hotel is very convenient. Golf courses and tennis facilities are nearby. 583 rooms, 31 story. Pets accepted; fee. Check-in 3 pm, check-out noon. Restaurant, bar. Fitness room. Business center. **$$**

★ ★ ★ MINNEAPOLIS GRAND HOTEL. *615 Second Ave S, Minneapolis (55402). Phone 612/339-3655; fax 612/339-7923.* The Grand Hotel is Minneapolis's finest lodging. Its downtown location with access to the city's climate-controlled skyway, professionally staffed business center, and in-room technology make it a business traveler's dream, but this elegant hotel is also a favorite of vacationers to the Twin Cities. The guest rooms and suites are tastefully appointed with Tuscan-style furnishings and stylish artwork. Egyptian cotton linens, plush towels, Aveda bath products, limousine service, complimentary shoeshine, and nightly turndown service with Godiva chocolates are among the amenities that win rave reviews from discerning travelers. The Grand's Martini Blu restaurant enjoys a thriving scene, while the sushi bar and spa deli are convenient stops for quick pick-me-ups. Guests receive complimentary access to the 58,000-square-foot LifeTime Fitness facility, which has an indoor pool, racquetball and squash courts, and an aerobics studio in addition to the expected cardiovascular and weight-training equipment, and the LifeSpa Aveda Concept Salon. 140 rooms, 12 story. Check-in 3 pm, check-out noon. High-speed Internet access. Two restaurants, bar. Fitness room, spa. Indoor pool. Business center. **$$**

Specialty Lodgings

The following lodging establishments are approved by Mobil Travel Guide, but due to their unique and individualized nature have not been given a traditional Mobil Star rating. Included in this listing you may find bed-and-breakfasts, limited-service inns, guest ranches, and other unique hotel properties.

ELMWOOD HOUSE. *1 E Elmwood Pl, Minneapolis (55419). Phone 612/822-4558; toll-free 888/822-4558. www.elmwoodhouse.us.* This 1887 Norman chateau is listed on the National Register of Historic Homes. 4 rooms, 3 story. **$**

NICOLLET ISLAND INN. *95 Merriam St, Minneapolis (55401). Phone 612/331-1800; toll-free 800/331-6528; fax 612/331-6528. www.nicolletisland inn.com.* 24 rooms, 2 story. Check-in 3 pm, check-out noon. Restaurant, bar. **$$**

Restaurants

★★ **510 RESTAURANT.** *510 Groveland Ave, Minneapolis (55403). Phone 612/874-6440. www.510restaurant.com.* Originally a glittery 1920s-era hotel, this restaurant's grand opulence is a step back in time. The food is wonderfully inventive and artistic. French menu. Dinner. Closed Sun and Mon. Bar. Casual attire. **$$**

★ **BLACK FOREST INN.** *1 E 26th St, Minneapolis (55404). Phone 612/872-0812; fax 612/872-0423. www. blackforestinnmpls.com.* German menu. Breakfast, lunch, dinner, late-night. Bar. Casual attire. Outdoor seating. **$$**

★★ **CAFE BRENDA.** *300 First Ave N, Minneapolis (55401). Phone 612/342-9230; fax 612/342-0155. www.cafebrenda.com.* Vegetarian menu. Lunch, dinner. Closed Sun; holidays. Casual attire. **$$**

★★ **CAMPIELLO.** *1320 W Lake St, Minneapolis (55408). Phone 612/825-2222; fax 612/825-2162. www.damico.com.* Italian menu. Dinner, Sun brunch. Closed Dec 25. Bar. Children's menu. Casual attire. Valet parking. Outdoor seating. **$$$**

★★★ **CHIANG MAI THAI.** *3001 Hennepin Ave S, Minneapolis (55408). Phone 612/827-1606. www.chiangmaithai.com.* Authentic Thai cuisine in the heart of uptown Minneapolis. Thai menu. Lunch, dinner. Closed holidays. **$**

★★ **CHRISTOS.** *2632 Nicollet Ave S, Minneapolis (55408). Phone 612/871-2111. www.christos.com.* Greek menu. Lunch, dinner. Closed holidays. Casual attire. **$$**

★★★ **D'AMICO CUCINA.** *100 N 6th St, Minneapolis (55403). Phone 612/338-2401; fax 612/337-5130. www.damico.com.* Only dinner is served at this elegant Italian fine-dining restaurant, offering pasta dishes and an exceptional Italian wine list, including many fine reserve selections. Try the gnocchi. Italian menu. Dinner. Closed Sun; holidays. Bar. Children's menu. Casual attire. **$$$**

★ **EMILY'S LEBANESE DELI.** *641 University Ave NE, Minneapolis (55413). Phone 612/379-4069.* Lebanes menu. Lunch, dinner. Closed Tues; Easter, Thanksgiving, Dec 25. Casual attire. **$**

★★ **FIGLIO.** *3001 Hennepin Ave S, Minneapolis (55408). Phone 612/822-1688; fax 612/822-0433. www.figlio.com.* Italian menu. Lunch, dinner, late-night. Bar. Casual attire. Outdoor seating. **$$**

★★ **GARDENS - SALONICA.** *19 5th St NE, Minneapolis (55413). Phone 612/378-0611; fax 612/378-2300.* Greek menu. Lunch, dinner. Closed Sun-Mon; Thanksgiving, Dec 25. Bar. Casual attire. **$$**

★★ **GIORGIO.** *2451 Hennepin Ave, Minneapolis (55405). Phone 612/374-5131.* Italian menu. Dinner. Closed Thanksgiving, Dec 24-25. Casual attire. Outdoor seating. **$$**

★ ★ ★ **GOODFELLOW'S.** *40 S 7th St, Minneapolis (55402). Phone 612/332-4800. www.goodfellowsrestaurant.com.* This former Forum-Cafeteria space feels like a trip back to the 1930s, albeit a luxurious trip, with a décor of polished wood, Art Deco fixtures, and jade accents. Executive chef Kevin Cullen's regional American offerings highlight local, seasonal ingredients and may include a lamb trio of grilled chop, sweet-onion strudel, and seared leg with marjoram sauce. The Forum space offers four private dining/meeting rooms. American menu. Lunch, dinner. Closed Sun; holidays. Bar. **$$$**

★ **ICHIBAN JAPANESE STEAK HOUSE.** *1333 Nicollet Mall Ave, Minneapolis (55403). Phone 612/339-0540. www.ichiban.ca.* Japanese menu. Dinner. Closed Easter, Thanksgiving, Dec 24. Bar. Children's menu. **$$**

★ **IT'S GREEK TO ME.** *626 W Lake St, Minneapolis (55408). Phone 612/825-9922.* Greek menu. Lunch, dinner. Closed Mon; holidays. Bar. Casual attire. Outdoor seating. **$$**

★ **J. D. HOYT'S.** *301 Washington Ave N, Minneapolis (55401). Phone 612/338-3499; fax 612/338-1560. www.jdhoyts.com.* Cajun/Creole menu. Breakfast, lunch, dinner, Sun brunch. Closed holidays. Bar. Casual attire. Valet parking. Outdoor seating. **$**

★ ★ ★ **JAX CAFE.** *1928 University Ave NE, Minneapolis (55418). Phone 612/789-7297. www.jaxcafe.com.* The bar is adorned with stained-glass windows of the seven dwarfs at this restaurant specializing in steaks. There is a fireplace in the dining room for cozy winter dining and a patio for the summer. American menu. Lunch, dinner, Sun brunch. Bar. Children's menu. Casual attire. Outdoor seating. **$$$**

★ ★ **KIKUGAWA.** *43 SE Main St, Minneapolis (55414). Phone 612/378-3006; fax 612/378-0819.* Japanese menu. Lunch, dinner. Closed Jan 1, Thanksgiving, Dec 25. Bar. Casual attire. **$$$**

★ **THE KING AND I THAI.** *1346 LaSalle Ave, Minneapolis (55403). Phone 612/332-6928; fax 612/338-4293. www.kingandithai.com.* Thai menu. Dinner. Closed Sun. Bar. Casual attire. Outdoor seating. **$$**

★ ★ **LA BODEGA TAPAS BAR.** *3005 Lyndale Ave S, Minneapolis (55408). Phone 612/823-2661.* Italian, Spanish menu. Lunch, dinner, late-night. Bar. Casual attire. Outdoor seating. **$$**

★ ★ ★ **LUCIA'S.** *1432 W 31st St, Minneapolis (55408). Phone 612/825-1572; fax 612/824-4553. www.lucias.com.* This lively bistro offers a weekly changing menu that focuses on seasonal dishes, and a complementary wine list. Chef Lucia Watson was recently recognized by the James Beard Award as one of the top five chefs in the Midwest. The adjacent wine bar allows diners to choose from an ever-evolving wine list, with many options by the glass. American menu. Lunch, dinner, Sat and Sun brunch. Closed Mon; holidays. Bar. Casual attire. Outdoor seating. **$$**

★ ★ ★ **MANNY'S.** *1300 Nicollet Mall, Minneapolis (55403). Phone 612/339-9900. www.mannyssteakhouse.com.* This Manhattan-style steakhouse offers traditional meat entrées with à la carte sides served family style. Hardwood floors and a bustling atmosphere make this an active dining space. Steak menu. Dinner. Closed holidays. Bar. Casual attire. Reservations recommended. **$$$**

★ ★ ★ **MORTON'S, THE STEAKHOUSE.** *555 Nicollet Mall, Minneapolis (55402). Phone 612/673-9700. www.mortons.com.* Consistent with expectations, this outlet serves famed steaks and seafood. A knowledgeable staff explains the menu in a fun tableside presentation. A warm, clublike atmosphere welcomes a martini-sipping, steak-eating crowd. Steak menu. Lunch, dinner. Closed Jan 1, Dec 25. Bar. Casual attire. **$$$**

★ ★ **NYE'S POLONAISE.** *112 E Hennepin Ave, Minneapolis (55414). Phone 612/379-2021. www.nyespolonaise.com.* American menu. Lunch, dinner, late-night. Closed Dec 25. Bar. Casual attire. Polka Thurs-Sat. **$$**

★ ★ ★ **OCEANAIRE SEAFOOD INN.** *1300 Nicollet Mall, Minneapolis (55403). Phone 612/333-2277; fax 612/305-1923. www.theoceanaire.com.* A stunning oyster bar displaying eight varieties glistens with shaved ice at the entrance of this retro-style seafood room. Reminiscent of a 1930s ocean liner, the Hyatt Regency restaurant serves both simple preparations and more involved specialties. The all-American childhood dessert favorites, including root beer floats and Dixie cups, are a fun touch. Seafood menu. Dinner. Closed holidays. Bar. Casual attire. **$$$**

★ ★ **ORIGAMI.** *30 N 1st St, Minneapolis (55401). Phone 612/333-8430. www.origamirestaurant.com.* Japanese menu. Lunch, dinner. Closed Jan 1, Dec 25. Bar. Casual attire. **$$$**

★ ★ ★ **PALOMINO.** *825 Hennepin Ave, Minneapolis (55402). Phone 612/339-3800; fax 612/339-1628. www.r-u-i.com.* One of the trendiest concepts in the country, this European bistro-style restaurant offers an unusual combination of rustic, hardwood-fired Mediterranean cooking and a chic, bustling ambience. The oft-changing menu offers the season's best, prepared in distinctive style. Mediterranean menu. Lunch, dinner. Closed Thanksgiving, Dec 25. Bar. Children's menu. Casual attire. **$$$**

★ **PHO 79 RESTAURANT.** *2529 Nicollet Ave S, Minneapolis (55404). Phone 612/871-3226.* Chinese, Vietnamese menu. Lunch, dinner. Closed July 4, Thanksgiving, Dec 25. Casual attire. **$**

★ ★ **PING'S SZECHUAN BAR AND GRILL.** *1401 Nicollet Ave S, Minneapolis (55403). Phone 612/874-9404; fax 612/874-0647. www.pingsmpls.com.* Chinese menu. Lunch, dinner. Closed Thanksgiving. Bar. Casual attire. Valet parking. **$$**

★ **PRACNA ON MAIN.** *117 Main St SE, Minneapolis (55414). Phone 612/379-3200.* American menu. Lunch, dinner, late-night. Bar. Casual attire. Outdoor seating. **$**

★ ★ **THE RESTAURANT AT THE LOUNGE.** *411 2nd Ave N, Minneapolis (55401). Phone 612/333-8800; fax 612/333-5800. www.theloungempls.com.* International/Fusion menu. Dinner. Closed Sun-Tues. Bar. Casual attire. Outdoor seating. **$$$**

★ ★ ★ **RUTH'S CHRIS STEAK HOUSE.** *920 Second Ave S, Minneapolis (55402). Phone 612/672-9000; fax 612/672-9102. www.ruthschris.com.* This classic steakhouse serves the fast-paced business crowd at its central downtown location. Steak menu. Dinner. Closed Thanksgiving, Dec 25. Bar. Casual attire. Valet parking. **$$$**

★ **SAWATDEE.** *607 Washington Ave S, Minneapolis (55415). Phone 612/338-6451; fax 612/338-6498. www.sawatdee.com.* Thai menu. Lunch, dinner. Bar. Casual attire. **$$**

★ ★ **SOPHIA.** *65 SE Main St, Minneapolis (55414). Phone 612/379-1111; fax 612/379-2507.* American menu. Lunch, dinner, late-night. Closed Jan 1, Dec 25. Bar. Casual attire. Outdoor seating. **$$**

★ ★ **TEJAS.** *3910 W 50th St, Edina (55424). Phone 952/926-0800; fax 952/926-8444. www.tejasrestaurant.com.* Southwestern menu. Lunch, dinner. Closed Sun. Bar. Children's menu. Casual attire. **$$**

Minnetonka (B-1)

See also Crookston, Thief River Falls

Population 51,301
Elevation 812 ft
Area Code 612, 952
Zip 55345
Information Minnetonka Chamber of Commerce, 10550 Wayzata Blvd (55305); phone 612/540-0234

Minnetonka, the Ojibwe (oh-JIB-way) name for big water, sits on the shores of Lake Minnetonka, a prime tourist attraction that's only 10 miles from Minneapolis. Tonka Trucks were first manufactured near here in 1947—the toy truck's name stems from the name of the lake and city—and Tonka Toy Group, a division of Hasbro, has its world headquarters in the nearby city of Mound.

Restaurants

★ **MARSH.** *15000 Minnetonka Blvd, Minnetonka (55345). Phone 952/935-2202; fax 952/935-9685. www.themarsh.com.* American menu. Breakfast, lunch, dinner, Sun brunch. Closed Dec 25. Bar. Children's menu. Casual attire. Outdoor seating. **$$**

★ ★ ★ **OLD LAKE LODGE.** *3746 Sunset Dr, Spring Park (55384). Phone 952/471-8513; fax 952/471-8937. www.lordfletchers.com.* This popular nautical respite about 14 miles west of Minnetonka resembles an old lodge, with cozy fireplaces for cooler days. Local ingredients and unusual flavors come together in the kitchen's inventive dishes. American, International menu. Lunch, dinner, Sun brunch. Closed Jan 1, Dec 24-25. Bar. Casual attire. Outdoor seating. **$$**

Moorhead (C-1)

See also Detroit Lakes, Fargo, Fergus Falls

Founded 1871
Population 32,295
Elevation 903 ft
Area Code 218
Information Chamber of Commerce of Fargo Moorhead, 321 N 4th St, PO Box 2443, Fargo, ND, 58108-2443; phone 701/237-5678

Web Site www.moreheadrowan.com

Along with the neighboring city to the west, Fargo, North Dakota, Moorhead is considered an agricultural capital. A shipping and processing center for agricultural products, the town is also a retailing and distribution point. The biggest industries are sugar refining and grain malting. Millions of pounds of sugar are produced annually from beets raised in and near Clay County. Moorhead is the home of Moorhead State University, Concordia College, and Northwest Technical College-Moorhead.

What to See and Do

Comstock Historic House. *506 8th St S, Moorhead (56560). Phone 218/233-0848.* (1882). Eleven-room home of Solomon Comstock, the founder of Moorhead State University, and his daughter Ada Louise Comstock, who was the first full-time president of Radcliffe College (1923-1943). The house has period furniture and historical artifacts. Guided tours. (June-Sept, Sat-Sun) **$**

Heritage-Hjemkomst Interpretive Center. *202 1st Ave N, Moorhead (56560). Phone 218/299-5511.* Home of the *Hjemkomst,* a Viking ship that sailed to Norway in 1982, the Stave Church and the Red River Valley Heritage exhibit. Also major traveling exhibits. (Mon-Sat, also Sun afternoons; closed Jan 1, Easter, Dec 25) **$$**

Regional Science Center-Planetarium. *1104 7th Ave S, Moorhead (56560). Phone 218/236-3982.* Offers variety of astronomy programs. Minnesota State University Moorhead campus. (Sept-May: Sun-Mon; summer: Thurs) **$$**

Special Event

Scandinavian Hjemkomst Festival. *Phone 218/299-5452. www.scandinavianhjemkomstfestival.org.* The Scandinavian Hjemkomst (meaning homecoming in Norwegian) Festival features ethnic foods, folk dancing, storytellers, art exhibits, and more. Late June.

Limited-Service Hotel

★ SUPER 8. *3621 S 8th St, Moorhead (56560). Phone 218/233-8880; toll-free 800/800-8000. www.super8.com.* 61 rooms, 2 story. Complimentary continental breakfast. Check-in 2 pm, check-out 11 am. **$**

Mora (D-3)

See also Hinckley, Onamia

Population 3,193
Elevation 1,010 ft
Area Code 320
Zip 55051
Information Mora Area Chamber of Commerce, Tourist Information Center, 105 S Union St S; phone 320/679-5792 or toll-free 800/291-5792
Web Site www.moramn.com

Rich in Swedish heritage, Mora's name led to its sister city affiliation with Mora, Sweden. Mora is the place for outdoor enthusiasts, whether you play golf, fish, canoe or kayak, cross-country ski, snowmobile, or bird-watch. The downtown area also offers opportunities to stroll past charming boutiques and shops.

What to See and Do

Fishing. Snake River. *Runs along N, S, and W perimeters of city.* Canoeing. **Fish Lake.** *5 miles S off Hwy 65.* **Ann Lake.** *8 miles NW, off Hwy 47.* **Knife Lake.** *8 miles N on Hwy 65.*

Kanabec History Center. *805 Forest Ave W, Mora (55051). Phone 320/679-1665.* Exhibits, gift shop, picnic area, hiking and ski trails; research information. (Daily; closed Jan 1, Thanksgiving, Dec 24-25) **$$**

Special Events

Bike Tour. *Phone 320/679-1677. www.morabiketour.org.* This bike tour, which starts and finishes on 9th Street, offers tours of 30, 60, and 100 miles. Third Sat in Sept.

Half-Marathon. *Phone 320/679-1838. www.morahalfmarathon.org.* Starting on Union Street in downtown Mora, this 13.1-mile run goes through the Kanabec County countryside. Third Sat in Aug.

Snake River Canoe Race. *Phone 320/679-1081.* This 25-kilometer course runs down the Snake River from the Hinckley Road Bridge to the landing in Mora below the Kanabec History Center. First Sat in May.

Vasaloppet Cross-Country Ski Race. *Phone toll-free 800/368-6672. www.vasaloppet.org.* This race has separate 58K and 35K courses, wooded trails, and an exciting finish line in downtown Mora. Second Sun in Feb.

Morris (D-1)

See also Fergus Falls, Glenwood, Willmar

Population 5,613
Area Code 320
Zip 56267
Information Morris Area Chamber of Commerce & Agriculture, 507 Atlantic Ave; phone 320/589-1242
Web Site www.morrischamber.org

Morris is the county seat of Stevens County and provides a regional shopping center for west central Minnesota. The surrounding area offers good fishing and hunting and is known for wildfowl, especially pheasants. The Wetland Management office is located here and manages seven counties along with 43,000 acres of waterfowl protection areas.

What to See and Do

Pomme de Terre City Park. *2 3/4 miles E on County 10.* A 363-acre public recreational area along Pomme de Terre River; picnicking, canoeing, fishing; camping (hook-ups; fee), nature and bicycle trail; swimming beach; sand volleyball court; concession. (Apr-Oct, daily) **FREE**

University of Minnesota, Morris. *600 E 4th St, Morris (56267). 4th and College sts. Phone 320/589-6050.* (1960) (2,000 students) Humanities Fine Arts Center Gallery presents changing contemporary exhibits (Oct-mid-June, Mon-Fri) and performing arts series (Oct-Apr). Tours.

Special Event

Prairie Pioneer Days. *Phone 320/589-1242.* Arts and crafts, parade, games, and activities. Second weekend in July.

Limited-Service Hotel

★ ★ BEST WESTERN PRAIRIE INN. *200 E Hwy 28, Morris (56267). Phone 320/589-3030; toll-free 800/565-3035; fax 320/589-3030. www.bestwestern.com.* 78 rooms, 2 story. Pets accepted, some restrictions. Complimentary continental breakfast. Check-in 2 pm, check-out 11 am. Restaurant, bar. Indoor pool, children's pool, whirlpool. **$**

New Ulm (E-2)

See also Mankato, Redwood Falls, St. Peter

Founded 1854
Population 13,132
Elevation 896 ft
Area Code 507
Zip 56073
Information New Ulm Convention & Visitors Bureau, 1 N Minnesota, Box 862; phone 507/233-4300 or toll-free 888/463-9856
Web Site www.ic.new-ulm.mn.us

Settled by German immigrants who borrowed the name of their home city, New Ulm is one of the few planned communities in the state. After more than a century, it still retains the order and cleanliness of the original settlement. The city today is in the center of a prosperous agricultural and dairy area and has developed a substantial business community. There is a visitor center at 1 North Minnesota Street (May-Oct: daily; Nov-Apr: Mon-Sat).

What to See and Do

Brown County Historical Museum. *2 N Broadway St, New Ulm (56073). Center St and Broadway. Phone 507/354-2016.* Former post office. Historical exhibits on Native Americans and pioneers; artwork; research library with 5,000 family files. (Mon-Fri, also Sat-Sun afternoons; closed holidays) **$**

Flandrau. *1300 Summit Ave, New Ulm (56073). Located at the city limits, on S Summit Ave; 1 mile S on Hwy 15, then W. Phone 507/233-9800.* Comprised of 801 acres on Cottonwood River. Swimming; cross-country skiing (rentals); camping; hiking.

Fort Ridgely. *14 miles W on Hwy 14, then 12 miles N on Hwy 4. Phone 507/426-7840.* A 584-acre park. Fort partly restored; interpretive center (May-Labor Day, daily). Nine-hole golf course (fee); cross-country skiing; camping; hiking; annual historical festival.

Glockenspiel. *4th N and Minnesota sts, New Ulm (56073). Phone 507/354-4217.* A 45-foot-high musical clock tower with performing animated figures; carillon with 37 bells. Performances (three times daily; noon, 3 pm, and 5 pm).

Harkin Store. *2 N Broadway St, New Ulm (56073). 8 miles NW of town via County 21. Phone 507/354-8666.* General store built by Alexander Harkin in 1870 in the small town of West Newton. The town died when it was bypassed by the railroad, but the store stayed open as a convenience until 1901, when rural free delivery closed the post office. The store has been restored to its original appearance and still has many original items on the shelves. Special programs in summer months. (Summer: Tues-Sun; May-Sept: weekends) **$**

Hermann's Monument. *Hermann Heights Park, Center and Monument sts, New Ulm (56073). On the bluff W of city. Phone 507/354-4217.* Erected by a fraternal order, monument recalls Hermann the Cheruscan, a German hero of AD 9. Towering 102 feet, monument has winding stairway to platform with view of city and Minnesota Valley. (June-Labor Day, daily) Picnic area. **$**

Schell Garden and Deer Park. *Schells Park, New Ulm. S on Hwy 15, then W on 18th St; on Schell Brewery grounds. Phone 507/354-5528.* Garden with deer and peacocks (all year). Brewery tours, museum, gift shop. (Memorial Day-Labor Day: daily; rest of year: Sat) **$**

Special Events

Brown County Fair. *Fairgrounds, 1200 N State St, New Ulm (56073). Phone 507/354-2223. www.browncountyfreefair.com.* This county fair, which has been held for more than 130 years, features chain saw carving, 4-H exhibits, carnival rides, pony rides, music, and more. Mid-Aug.

Fasching. *118 N Minnesota St, New Ulm (56073). Phone 507/354-8850.* Traditional German winter festival. Includes German food, music; costume ball. Late Feb.

Heritagefest. *118 N Minnesota St, New Ulm (56073). Phone 507/354-8850.* Old World-style celebration highlighting German traditions and culture through music, food, arts and crafts. Features entertainers from around the area and from Europe. Two weekends in mid-July.

Limited-Service Hotel

★ ★ HOLIDAY INN. *21015 S Broadway St, New Ulm (56073). Phone 507/359-2941; toll-free 877/359-2941; fax 507/354-7147. www.holiday-inn.com.* 120 rooms, 2 story. Check-out noon. Restaurant, bar. Indoor pool, whirlpool. Business center. **$**

Specialty Lodgings

The following lodging establishments are approved by Mobil Travel Guide, but due to their unique and individualized nature have not been given a traditional Mobil Star rating. Included in this listing you may find bed-and-breakfasts, limited-service inns, guest ranches, and other unique hotel properties.

THE BOHEMIAN. *304 S German St, New Ulm (56073). Phone 507/354-2268; toll-free 866/499-6870. www.the-bohemian.com.* A Grand Eastern Stick Style Victorian with seven rooms, all with private bath. Romantic whirlpool and fireplace suites available. 7 rooms, 3 story. Check-in 11 am, check-out 11 am. **$$**

DEUTSCHE STRASSE BED & BREAKFAST. *404 S German St, New Ulm (56073). Phone toll-free 866/226-9856.* Located in the historic district of New Ulm within blocks from unique German and antique shops. 5 rooms, 3 story. **$**

Restaurants

★ VEIGEL'S KAISERHOF. *221 N Minnesota St, New Ulm (56073). Phone 507/359-2071; fax 507/354-2006.* New Ulm's oldest and most venerable dining establishment. German menu. Lunch, dinner. Closed Dec 25. Bar. Children's menu. **$$**

Northfield (E-3)

See also Faribault, Hastings, Lakeville, Minneapolis, Owatonna, Red Wing, St. Paul

Founded 1855
Population 14,684
Elevation 919 ft
Area Code 507
Zip 55057
Information Northfield Area Chamber of Commerce, 500 Water St S, PO Box 198; phone 507/645-5604 or toll-free 800/658-2548
Web Site www.northfieldchamber.com

This bustling, historic river town, located 30 miles south of the Twin Cities, offers a captivating blend of the old and new. Its history is one of the most dramatic of any Midwestern community. Each year on the weekend after Labor Day, thousands flock here to share in the retelling of the defeat of Jesse James and his gang who, on September 7, 1876, were foiled in their attempt to raid the Northfield Bank in what proved to be one of the last chapters in the brutal saga of the Old West.

This history has been preserved in the Northfield Bank Museum at 408 Division Street, keystone of the city's unique historical downtown district. The well-preserved storefronts house boutiques, antique stores, and other interesting shops.

What to See and Do

Carleton College. *1 N College St, Northfield (55507). NE edge of town on Hwy 19. Phone 507/646-4000.* (1866) (1,800 students) Liberal arts. Arboretum (455 acres) has hiking and jogging trails along Cannon River. Also here is a 35-acre prairie maintained by college. Tours of arboretum and prairie with advance notice. Summer theater programs.

Nerstrand Woods State Park. *9700 170th St E, Nerstrand (55053). 12 miles SE, off Hwy 246. Phone 507/334-8848.* More than 1,280 acres, heavily wooded; hiking, cross-country skiing, snowmobiling; picnicking, camping (dump station).

Northfield Arts Guild. *304 Division St S, Northfield (55057). Downtown. Phone 507/645-8877.* Exhibits of local and regional fine arts housed in historic YMCA Building (1885); juried handcrafted items. (Mon-Sat; closed holidays) **FREE**

St. Olaf College. *1520 St. Olaf Ave, Northfield (55057). 1 mile W of business district. Phone 507/646-2222.* (1874) (3,000 students) Famous for its choir, band, and orchestra, which tour nationally and abroad. Steensland Art Gallery (daily). Home of national offices and archives of Norwegian-American Historical Association.

Special Event

Defeat of Jesse James Days. *Phone 507/645-5604.* Raid reenactment, parade, outdoor arts fair, rodeo. Four days beginning weekend after Labor Day.

Limited-Service Hotel

★ COUNTRY INN BY CARLSON NORTHFIELD. *300 S Hwy 3, Northfield (55057). Phone 507/645-2286; toll-free 800/456-4000; fax 507/645-2958.* 54 rooms, 2 story. Complimentary continental breakfast. Check-out noon. Indoor pool, whirlpool. **$**

Specialty Lodging

The following lodging establishment is approved by Mobil Travel Guide, but due to its unique and individualized nature has not been given a traditional Mobil Star rating. Included in this listing you may find bed-and-breakfasts, limited-service inns, guest ranches, and other unique hotel properties.

ARCHER HOUSE HOTEL. *212 Division St, Northfield (55057). Phone 507/645-5661; toll-free 800/247-2235; fax 507/645-4295. www.archerhouse.com.* Built in 1877; antiques, country décor. On river. 34 rooms, 3 story. Check-in 11 am, check-out 11 am. High-speed Internet access. Restaurant. **$**

Onamia (C-3)

See also Aitkin, Brainerd, Little Falls, Mora

Population 847
Elevation 1,264 ft
Area Code 320
Zip 56359
Web Site www.millelacs.com

Tourists tend to visit Onamia (oh-NAY-mee-ah) because of Mille Lacs (mill-LAX) Lake, situated just north of town. The largest city in the Mille Lacs area, Onamia is a good place to stop for groceries and supplies or to browse a few boutiques and gift shops.

What to See and Do

Mille Lacs Kathio State Park. *15066 Kathio Park Rd, Onamia (56359). 8 miles NW on Hwy 169, then 1 mile S on County Rd 26. Phone 320/532-3523.* Comprises 10,577 acres surrounding main outlet of Mille Lacs Lake. Evidence of Native American habitation and culture dating back over 4,000 years. Here in 1679, Daniel Greysolon, Sieur du Lhut, claimed the upper Mississippi region for France. Swimming, fishing, boating (rentals); hiking, riding trails; cross-country skiing (rentals), snowmobiling; picnicking; camping (dump station). Interpretive center. **$$**

Mille Lacs Lake. *4 miles N on Hwy 169. Phone toll-free 888/350-2692. www.millelacs.com.* Has 150 miles of shoreline; one of the largest and loveliest in the state.

Near lakeshore are nearly 9,000 Native American mounds. Fishing, boating, camping.

Full-Service Resort

★ ★ IZATY'S GOLF AND YACHT CLUB. *40005 85th Ave, Onamia (56359). Phone 320/532-3101; toll-free 800/533-1728; fax 320/532-3208. www.izatys.com.* Offering both hotel rooms and two-, three-, and four-bedroom townhomes, this resort has something for every vacationer. Two golf courses are found at the resort along with a full marina and indoor and outdoor pools. 28 rooms, 2 story. Check-in 4 pm, check-out noon. Restaurant, bar. Children's activity center. Indoor pool, outdoor pool, whirlpool. Golf. **$**

Owatonna (E-3)

See also Albert Lea, Austin, Faribault, Mantorville, Northfield, Rochester

Settled 1854
Population 19,386
Elevation 1,154 ft
Area Code 507
Zip 55060
Information Chamber of Commerce and Tourism, 320 Hoffman Dr; phone 507/451-7970 or toll-free 800/423-6466
Web Site www.owatonna.org

Legend has it that the city was named after a beautiful but frail Native American princess named Owatonna (oh-wah-TUN-na). It is said that her father, Chief Wabena, had heard about the healing water called "minnewaucan." When the waters' curing powers restored his daughter's health, he moved his entire village to the site now known as Mineral Springs Park. A statue of Princess Owatonna stands in the park and watches over the springs that are still providing cold, fresh mineral water.

What to See and Do

Minnesota State Public School Orphanage Museum. *540 West Hills Cir, Owatonna (55060). Phone 507/451-2149.* This museum is on the site of a former orphanage that housed nearly 13,000 children from 1866 to 1945. The main building is on the National Registry of Historic Places. (Daily) **FREE**

Norwest Bank Owatonna, NA Building. *101 N Cedar Ave, Owatonna (55060). At Broadway. Phone 507/451-7970.* Completed in 1908 as the National Farmers Bank, this nationally acclaimed architectural treasure was designed by one of America's outstanding architects, Louis H. Sullivan. The cubelike exterior with huge arched stained-glass windows by Louis Millet quickly earned the building widespread recognition as, according to one historian, "a jewel box set down in a prairie town."

Owatonna Arts Center. *West Hills Complex, 435 Garden View Ln, Owatonna (55060). Phone 507/451-0533.* Housed in a historic Romanesque structure. Permanent collection includes 100-piece collection of garments from around the world, and 14-foot stained-glass panels featured in the Performing Arts Hall. Outdoor sculpture garden has works by Minnesota artists John Rood, Richard and Donald Hammel, Paul Grandlund, and Charles Gagnon. Changing gallery shows every month. (Tues-Sun; closed holidays) **DONATION**

Village of Yesteryear. *1448 Austin Rd, Owatonna (55060). Phone 507/451-1420.* Eleven restored pioneer buildings from mid-1800s include church, two log cabins, schoolhouse, large family home, old fire department, and country store; depot, farm machinery building, blacksmith shop; museum; period furnishings, memorabilia and a C-52 locomotive caboose (1905). (May-Sept, afternoons except Mon) **$$**

Limited-Service Hotels

★ ★ HOLIDAY INN HOTEL & SUITES. *2365 43rd St NW, Owatonna (55060). Phone 507/446-8900; toll-free 800/465-4329; fax 507/446-8999. www.holiday-inn.com.* 130 rooms. Check-in 4 pm, check-out 11 am. Restaurant, bar. Indoor pool, whirlpool. Airport transportation available. **$**

★ SUPER 8. *1150 W Frontage Rd, Owatonna (55060). Phone 507/451-0380; toll-free 800/800-8000; fax 507/451-0380. www.super8.com.* 60 rooms, 2 story. Pets accepted; fee. Complimentary continental breakfast. Check-in 2 pm, check-out 11 am. **$**

Park Rapids (C-2)

See also Detroit Lakes, Walker

Founded 1880
Population 2,863
Elevation 1,440 ft
Area Code 218
Zip 56470
Information Chamber of Commerce, PO Box 249; phone 218/732-4111 or toll-free 800/247-0054
Web Site www.parkrapids.com

This resort center is surrounded by 400 lakes, nearly as many streams, and beautiful woods. There are more than 200 resorts within 20 miles. Fishing is excellent for bass, walleye, northern pike, muskie, and trout.

What to See and Do

Hubbard County Historical Museum/North Country Museum of Arts. *Court Ave and Third St, Park Rapids (56470). Phone 218/732-5237.* Historical museum has displays on pioneer life, including pioneer farm implements, one-room schoolhouse, and foreign wars. Museum of arts has five galleries of contemporary art and also features a section on 15th- to 18th-century European art. (May-Sept: Tues-Sat; Feb-Apr: Tues-Sun)

Rapid River Logging Camp. *3 miles N via Hwy 71, 2 1/2 miles E on County 18 and follow signs. Phone 218/732-3444.* Authentic logging camp with nature trail; antiques; serves lumberjack meals; logging demonstrations (Tues and Fri). See sluiceway in the river. (Memorial Day weekend-Labor Day weekend, daily) **FREE**

Limited-Service Hotel

★ **SUPER 8.** *1020 E 1st St, Park Rapids (56470). Phone 218/732-9704; toll-free 800/800-8000; fax 218/732-9704. www.super8.com.* 62 rooms, 2 story. Complimentary continental breakfast. Check-out 11 am. **$**

Pine River (C-2)

See also Brainerd, Walker

Population 871
Elevation 1,290 ft
Area Code 218
Zip 56474
Web Site www.pinerivermn.com

The city and the river for which it is named are inseparable; tourists visit Pine River primarily to fish bass, northern pike, and walleye and to canoe down the river, a 19-mile paddle to the mighty Mississippi. Snowmobiling, hiking, and cycling are also popular activities in the area.

Full-Service Resort

★★ **PINEY RIDGE LODGE.** *6023 Wildamere Dr, Pine River (56474). Phone 218/587-2296; toll-free 800/450-3333; fax 218/587-4323. www.pineyridge.com.* 26 rooms. Closed late Sept-Apr. Check-in 4 pm, check-out 10 am. Restaurant. Children's activity center. **$**

Pipestone (E-1)

See also Luverne, Pipestone National Monument, Tracy

Settled 1874
Population 4,554
Elevation 1,738 ft
Area Code 507
Zip 56164
Information Chamber of Commerce, 117 8th Ave SE, PO Box 8; phone 507/825-3316 or toll-free 800/336-6125
Web Site www.pipestoneminnesota.com

County seat and center of a fertile farming area, Pipestone is host to visitors en route to Pipestone National Monument. Some of the red Sioux quartzite from the quarries shows up in Pipestone's public buildings. George Catlin, famous painter of Native Americans, was the first white man to report on the area.

What to See and Do

Pipestone County Museum. *113 S Hiawatha Ave, Pipestone (56164). Phone 507/825-2563.* Prehistory, early settlement, Native American, pioneer exhibits; research library, gift shop. Tours. (Daily, closed holidays) **$$**

Split Rock Creek State Park. *6 miles SW on Hwy 23, then 1 mile S on County 20. Phone 507/348-7908; toll-free 800/766-6000.* On 1,300 acres. Swimming; fishing (accessible to the disabled); boating (rentals). Hiking;

cross-country skiing; picnicking; camping (dump station).

Special Events

Hiawatha Pageant. *117 8th Ave SE, Pipestone (56164). Just S of Pipestone National Monument entrance. Phone 507/825-3316.* Outdoor performance. All seats reserved; ticket office opens 1 pm on show dates. Last two weekends in July and first weekend in Aug.

Watertower Festival. *Courthouse lawn. Phone 507/825-3316.* Large arts and crafts show; parade. Last Fri and Sat in June.

Limited-Service Hotels

★★ HISTORIC CALUMET INN. *104 W Main St, Pipestone (56164). Phone 507/825-5871; toll-free 800/535-7610; fax 507/825-4578. www.calumetinn.com.* This historic inn, which features rooms full of antiques, was built from Sioux Quartzite in 1888. Guests will be awed by the two-story lobby with its tin ceiling and will enjoy a nightcap at the large antique oak bar in Cally's Lounge, which was once the bank. 40 rooms, 4 story. Pets accepted; some restrictions. Complimentary full breakfast. Check-in 2 pm, check-out 11 am. Restaurant, bar. **$**

★ SUPER 8. *605 8th Ave SE, Pipestone (56164). Phone 507/825-4217; toll-free 800/800-8000; fax 507/825-4219. www.super8.com.* 39 rooms, 2 story. Check-in 2 pm, check-out 11 am. **$**

Restaurant

★ LANGE'S CAFE. *110 8th Ave SE, Pipestone (56164). Phone 507/825-4488.* American menu. Breakfast, lunch, dinner, late-night. Casual attire. **$$**

Pipestone National Monument (E-1)

See also Luverne, Pipestone

On Hwy 75, Hwy 23, 30, adjacent to N boundary of Pipestone.

The ancient pipestone in the quarries of this 283-acre area is found in few other places. The Native Americans quarried this reddish stone and carved it into ceremonial pipes. Pipestone deposits, named catlinite for George Catlin, who first described the stone, run about a foot thick, though most usable sections are about two inches thick. Principal features of the monument are **Winnewissa Falls,** flowing over quartzite outcroppings; **Three Maidens,** group of glacial boulders near quarries; **Leaping Rock,** used by Native Americans as a test of strength of young men who attemped to leap from the top of quartzite ridge to its crest, 11 feet away; **Nicollet Marker,** inscription on boulder recalls visit here in 1838 of Joseph Nicollet's exploring party. He carved his name and initials of members of his party, including Lieutenant John C. Frémont.

Established as a national monument in 1937, Pipestone protects the remaining red stone and preserves it for use by Native Americans of all tribes. The visitor center has exhibits, slides, pipe-making demonstrations, and a self-guided tour booklet for the circle trail and other information; also here is Upper Midwest Indian Cultural Center with craft displays. (Daily; visitor center closed Jan 1, Dec 25) Phone 507/825-5464.

Red Wing (E-4)

See also Hastings, Lakeville, Northfield, St. Paul

Founded 1836
Population 15,134
Elevation 720 ft
Area Code 651
Zip 55066
Information Visitors and Convention Bureau, 418 Levee St; phone 651/385-5934 or toll-free 800/498-3444
Web Site www.redwing.org

Established as a missionary society outpost, this community bears the name of one of the great Dakota chiefs, Koo-Poo-Hoo-Sha (wing of the wild swan dyed scarlet). Red Wing industries produce leather, shoes, precision instruments, malt, flour, linseed oil, diplomas, rubber, and wood products.

What to See and Do

Biking. *306 Mills St W, Cannon Falls (55009). Phone 507/263-0508.* Wheel passes needed for biking. For further information, contact the Cannon Valley Trail office. (18 years and over only)

Cannon Valley Trail. *Hwy 19, Cannon Falls (55009). Phone 651/263-0508. www.cannonvalleytrail.com.*

Twenty-mile cross-country skiing trail connects Cannon Falls, Welch, and Red Wing. **$$**

Goodhue County Historical Museum. *1166 Oak St, Red Wing (55066). Phone 651/388-6024.* This is one of the state's most comprehensive museums. Permanent exhibits relate local and regional history from glacial age to present. Extensive collection of Red Wing pottery; artifacts from Prairie Island Native American community. (Tues-Sun; closed holidays) **FREE**

Hiking. A 1 1/2-mile hiking trail to top of Mount LaGrange (Barn Bluff) with scenic overlook of Mississippi River. Cannon Valley Trail provides 25 miles of improved trail following Cannon Bottom River to Cannon Falls. **FREE**

Mount Frontenac. *32420 Ski Rd, Frontenac (55026). 9 miles S on Hwy 61. Phone 651/388-5826. www.ski-frontenac.com.* Three double chairlifts, three rope tows; patrol, school, rentals; snowmaking; cafeteria. Vertical drop 420 feet. (Nov-mid-Mar, Wed-Sun; closed Dec 25) Also 18-hole golf course (Mid-Apr-Oct; fee). **$$$$**

Red Wing Stoneware. *4909 Moundview Dr, Red Wing (55066). 4 miles W on Hwy 61. Phone 651/388-4610.* Popular stoneware facility; visitors can watch artisans create various types of pottery. Call for hours.

Sheldon Theatre. *443 W Third St, Red Wing (55066). At East Ave. Phone 651/385-3667.* The United States' first municipal theater, opened in 1904. Performances available regularly. Group tours available. (June-Oct: Fri-Sat; Nov-May: Sat).

Soldiers' Memorial Park/East End Recreation Area. *Skyline Dr, Red Wing (55066). www.redwingchamber.com.* On plateau overlooking city and river; 476 acres; 5 miles of hiking trails. **Colvill Park.** On Mississippi. Also waterpark (June-Aug, fee), playground; boat launching, marina. **Bay Point Park.** On Mississippi. Showers, boat launching, marina, picnicking, playground, walking trail. (May-Oct, daily)

Welch Village. *26685 County 7 Blvd, Welch (55089). 12 miles NW on Hwy 61, then 3 miles S on County 7 to Welch. Phone 651/258-4567. www.welchvillage.com.* Three quad, five double, triple chairlifts, Mitey-mite; patrol, rentals; snowmaking; cafeteria. Longest run 4,000 feet; vertical drop 350 feet. (Nov-Mar, daily; closed Dec 25) **$$$$**

Special Events

Fall Festival of the Arts. *Historic downtown. Phone 651/385-5934.* This fine arts show features more than 80 artists, live music, food, and children's activities. First weekend in Oct.

River City Days. *Phone 651/385-5934.* A lumberjack show, carnival, parade, concession stands, and an arts and crafts fair are among the activities at this annual celebration. First weekend in Aug.

Limited-Service Hotels

★ BEST WESTERN QUIET HOUSE & SUITES. *752 Withers Harbor Dr, Red Wing (55066). Phone 651/388-1577; toll-free 800/780-7234; fax 651/388-1150. www.quiethouse.com.* 51 rooms, 2 story. Pets accepted, some restrictions; fee. Check-out 11 am. Fitness room. Indoor pool, outdoor pool, whirlpool. **$**

★ ★ ST. JAMES HOTEL. *406 Main St, Red Wing (55066). Phone 651/388-2846; toll-free 800/252-1875; fax 651/388-5226. www.st-james-hotel.com.* Built in 1875, this hotel offers 19th-century Victorian style along with modern amenities. It is located on the bank of the Mississippi River in the heart of Red Wing, near many local attractions, restaurants, and shops. 60 rooms, 5 story. Restaurant, bar. Airport transportation available. **$**

Specialty Lodging

The following lodging establishment is approved by Mobil Travel Guide, but due to its unique and individualized nature has not been given a traditional Mobil Star rating. Included in this listing you may find bed-and-breakfasts, limited-service inns, guest ranches, and other unique hotel properties.

GOLDEN LANTERN INN. *721 East Ave, Red Wing (55066). Phone 651/388-3315; toll-free 888/288-3315; fax 651/385-9178. www.goldenlantern.com.* Tudor brick house built in 1932. 5 rooms, 2 story. Accepts children by arrangement. Complimentary full breakfast. Check-in 4-5 pm, check-out 11 am. **$**

Redwood Falls (E-2)

See also Granite Falls, Marshall, New Ulm, Tracy

Population 4,859

Elevation 1,044 ft
Area Code 507
Zip 56283
Information Redwood Area Chamber and Tourism, 200 S Mill St, PO Box 21; phone 507/637-2828 or toll-free 800/657-7070
Web Site www.redwoodfalls.org

The main attraction in the town of Redwood Falls is Ramsey Park, which highlights both the falls for which the city is named and Ramsey Falls, which are equally beautiful.

What to See and Do

Lower Sioux Agency and Historic Site. *32469 Redwood County Hwy 2, Morton (56270). 7 miles E of Redwood Falls. Phone 507/697-6321.* Exhibits, trail system, and restored 1861 warehouse trace history of the Dakota in Minnesota from the mid-17th century through the present. (May-Sept: daily; rest of year: by appointment)

Ramsey Park. *W edge of town, off Hwy 19.* A 200-acre park of rugged woodland carved by Redwood River and Ramsey Creek. Includes picnicking, trail riding, cross-country ski trail, hiking; golf; camping. Small zoo, playground shelters, 30-foot waterfall.

Special Event

Minnesota Inventors Congress. *Redwood Valley School, 805 E Bridge St, Redwood Falls (56283). Phone 507/637-2344.* Exhibit of inventions by adult and student inventors; seminars. Food; arts and crafts; parade; also resource center. Three days of the second full weekend in June.

Rochester (E-4)

See also Mantorville, Owatonna, Spring Valley, Winona

Settled 1854
Population 70,745
Elevation 1,297 ft
Area Code 507
Information Convention & Visitors Bureau, 150 S Broadway, Suite A, 55904; phone 507/288-4331 or toll-free 800/634-8277
Web Site www.rochestercvb.org

The world-famous Mayo Clinic has made what was once a crossroads campground for immigrant wagon trains a city of doctors, hospitals, and lodging places. Each year thousands of people come here in search of medical aid. One of the first dairy farms in the state began here, and Rochester still remains a central point for this industry. Canned goods, fabricated metals, and electronic data processing equipment are among its industrial products.

What to See and Do

Mayo Clinic. *200 1st St SW, Rochester (55905). Phone 507/284-9258. www.mayo.edu.* Over 30 buildings now accommodate the famous group practice of medicine that grew from the work of Dr. William Worrall Mayo and his sons, Dr. William James Mayo and Dr. Charles Horace Mayo. There are now 1,041 doctors at the clinic as well as 935 residents in training in virtually every medical and surgical specialty. The 14-story Plummer Building (1928) includes a medical library and historical exhibit. The Conrad N. Hilton and Guggenheim buildings (1974) house clinical and research laboratories. The 19-story Mayo Building (1955, 1967) covers an entire block. It houses facilities for diagnosis and treatment. Clinic tours (Mon-Fri; closed holidays). **FREE** Also here is

> **The Rochester Carillon.** In the tower of the Plummer Building. Concerts (schedule varies). **FREE**

Mayowood. *1195 W Circle Dr SW, Rochester (55906). Phone 507/282-9447.* Home of Doctors C. H. and C. W. Mayo, historic 38-room country mansion on 15 acres; period antiques, works of art. **$$$**

Olmsted County History Center and Museum. *1195 W Circle Dr SW, Rochester (55906). Corner of County rds 22 and 25. Phone 507/282-9447.* Changing historical exhibits (Daily; closed holidays); research library (Mon-Fri; closed holidays). **$**

Plummer House of the Arts. *1091 Plummber Ln SW, Rochester (55902). 12th Ave and 9th St. Phone 507/281-6160.* Former estate of Dr. Henry S. Plummer, a 35-year member of the Mayo Clinic. Today, 11 acres remain, with formal gardens, quarry, water tower. The five-story house is an English Tudor mansion (circa 1920) with original furnishings and a slate roof. Tours (June-Aug, Wed afternoons, also first and third Sun afternoons). **$$**

Whitewater State Park. *20 miles E on Hwy 14, then 7 miles N on Hwy 74. Phone 507/932-3007.* A 1,822-acre park. Limestone formations in a hardwood forest.

Swimming, fishing; hiking, cross-country skiing; picnicking; primitive camping. Interpretive center.

Limited-Service Hotels

★ ★ BEST WESTERN SOLDIERS FIELD TOWER & SUITES. *401 6th St SW, Rochester (55902). Phone 507/288-2677; toll-free 800/780-7234; fax 507/282-2042. www.bestwestern.com.* 218 rooms, 8 story. Complimentary continental breakfast. Check-in 4 pm, check-out noon. Restaurant, bar. Fitness room. Indoor pool, children's pool, whirlpool. Airport transportation available. **$**

★ HAMPTON INN. *1755 S Broadway, Rochester (55904). Phone 507/287-9050; toll-free 800/426-7866; fax 507/287-9139. www.hamptoninn.com.* 105 rooms, 3 story. Complimentary continental breakfast. Check-in 3 pm, check-out noon. Fitness room. Indoor pool, whirlpool. **$**

★ ★ HOLIDAY INN. *220 S Broadway, Rochester (55903). Phone 507/288-1844; toll-free 800/465-4329; fax 507/288-1844. www.holiday-inn.com.* 195 rooms, 2 story. Pets accepted. Check-in 4 pm, check-out noon. Restaurant, bar. Indoor pool. Airport transportation available. **$**

★ ★ RADISSON PLAZA HOTEL ROCHESTER. *150 S Broadway, Rochester (55904). Phone 507/281-8000; toll-free 800/333-3333; fax 507/281-4280. www.radisson.com.* Guest rooms and five suites with whirlpool tubs are offered by this downtown hotel with skyway access to the Mayo Clinic, Government Center, shopping, dining, and entertainment. The property is only 8 miles from the Rochester Airport. 212 rooms, 11 story. Check-out noon. High-speed Internet access. Restaurant, bar. Fitness room. Indoor pool, whirlpool. **$**

★ ★ RAMADA HOTEL & CONFERENCE CENTER. *1517 16th St SW, Rochester (55902). Phone 507/289-8866; fax 507/292-0000.* 149 rooms, 3 story. Complimentary continental breakfast. Check-in 3 pm, check-out noon. High-speed Internet access. Restaurant, bar. Indoor pool, children's pool, whirlpool. Airport transportation available. **$**

Full-Service Hotels

★ ★ ★ KAHLER GRAND. *20 2nd Ave SW, Rochester (55902). Phone 507/280-6200; toll-free 800/533-1655; fax 507/285-2701. www.kahler.com.* Original section English Tudor; vaulted ceilings, paneling. Walkway to Mayo Clinic. Located across from the Mayo Clininc in the downtown area. 700 rooms, 11 story. Pets accepted, some restrictions; fee. Check-out 2 pm. Restaurant, bar. Fitness room. Indoor pool, whirlpool. Airport transportation available. **$**

★ ★ ★ MARRIOTT ROCHESTER MAYO CLINIC. *101 1st Ave SW, Rochester (55902). Phone 507/280-6000; toll-free 877/623-7775; fax 507/280-8531. www.rochestermarriott.com.* Near the Galleria Mall, Miracle Mile Shopping Complex, tennis facilities, and many golf courses. 203 rooms, 9 story. Pets accepted, some restrictions. Check-in 3 pm, check-out noon. High-speed Internet access. Restaurant, bar. Fitness room. Indoor pool, whirlpool. Business center. **$$**

Restaurants

★ ★ BROADSTREET CAFE AND BAR. *300 1st Ave NW, Rochester (55901). Phone 507/281-2451; fax 507/278-9804. www.broadstreet-cafe.com.* Former warehouse. American menu. Lunch, dinner. Closed July 4, Thanksgiving, Dec 25. Bar. Children's menu. Casual attire. Reservations recommended. **$$$**

★ ★ CHARDONNAY. *723 2nd St SW, Rochester (55902). Phone 507/252-1310.* International/Fusion menu. Dinner. Closed Sun. Casual attire. Reservations recommended. Four dining rooms in remodeled house. **$$$**

★ JOHN BARLEYCORN. *2780 S Broadway, Rochester (55904). Phone 507/285-0178; fax 507/280-9165.* American menu. Lunch, dinner. Bar. Children's menu. Casual attire. **$$$**

★ ★ MICHAEL'S FINE DINING. *15 S Broadway, Rochester (55904). Phone 507/288-2020. www.michaelsfinedining.com.* Seafood, steak menu. Lunch, dinner. Closed Sun; holidays. Bar. Children's menu. Casual attire. Reservations recommended. **$$**

★ SANDY POINT. *18 Sandy Point Ct NE, Rochester (55906). Phone 507/367-4983.* American menu. Lunch, dinner. Bar. Children's menu. Casual attire. Reservations recommended. **$**

Roseau (A-2)

See also Baudette, Thief River Falls

Population 2,396
Elevation 1,048 ft
Area Code 218
Zip 56751

Over 150 years ago, Roseau (ROE-zoe) was the site of a busy Hudson's Bay Company fur-trading post. Today, the city is a snowmobiler's dream, with a number of snowmobile trails. Polaris Industries, the first mass producer of snowmobiles and today a leading snowmobile manufacturer, is located here and offers tours at its facility.

What to See and Do

Hayes Lake State Park. *48990 County Rd 4, Roseau (56751). 15 miles S on Hwy 89, then 9 miles E on County 4. Phone 218/425-7504.* A 2,950-acre park. Swimming, fishing, hiking, cross-country skiing, snowmobiling, picnicking, camping (dump station).

Pioneer Farm and Village. *2 1/2 miles W via Hwy 11. Phone 218/463-2187.* Restored buildings include log barn, museum, church, parish hall, equipped printery, log house, school, store, blacksmith shop, and post office. Picnicking. (Mid-May-mid-Sept; schedule varies) **FREE**

Polaris Experience Center. *205 5th Ave SW, Roseau (56751). In the Reed River Trading Co. building just N of the Polaris plant. Phone 218/463-4999. www.polarisindustries.com.* In essence a snowmobile museum, the center mixes exhibits of snowmobile designs throughout history with photographs and videos that you view on a self-guided tour. (Mon-Sat noon-8 pm, Sun noon-6 pm) The main Polaris manufacturing plant is also open for tours. (Daily 4 pm) **FREE**

Roseau City Park. *11th Ave SE, Roseau (56751).* This 40-acre park offers canoeing, hiking, and picnicking. Camping (electric and water hook-ups, dump station).

Roseau County Historical Museum and Interpretive Center. *110 2nd Ave NE, Roseau (56751). Phone 218/463-1918.* Natural history, collection of mounted birds and eggs; Native American artifacts and pioneer history. (Tues-Sat; closed holidays) **$**

Roseau River Wildlife Management Area. *27952 400th St, Roseau (56751). 20 miles W and N via Hwy 11, 89 and County Rd 3. Phone 218/463-1557.* More than 2,000 ducks raised here annually on 65,000 acres. Bird-watching area, canoeing on river, hunting during season, with license. **FREE**

Sauk Centre (D-2)

See also Alexandria, Glenwood, Little Falls

Population 3,581
Elevation 1,246 ft
Area Code 320
Zip 56378
Information Sauk Centre Area Chamber of Commerce, PO Box 222; phone 320/352-5201
Web Site www.saukcentrechamber.com

Sauk Centre (SAWK CEN-ter) is "Gopher Prairie," the boyhood home of Nobel Prize-winning novelist Sinclair Lewis. Sauk Centre was the setting for his best-known novel, *Main Street,* as well as many of his other works. The town is at the southern tip of Big Sauk Lake.

What to See and Do

Sinclair Lewis Boyhood Home. *812 Sinclair Lewis Ave, Sauk Centre (56378). Phone 320/352-5201.* Restored home of America's first Nobel Prize-winning novelist. Original furnishings; family memorabilia. (Memorial Day-Labor Day: Tues-Sun; rest of year: by appointment) **$$**

Sinclair Lewis Interpretive Center. *1220 Main St S, Sauk Centre (56378). At jct I-94, Hwy 71. Phone 320/352-5201.* Exhibits include original manuscripts, photographs, letters; 15-minute video on the author's life; research library. (Labor Day-Memorial Day: Mon-Fri; Memorial Day-Labor Day: daily) **FREE**

Special Event

Sinclair Lewis Days. *Phone 320/352-5201.* Activities at this event include the battle of the bands, concert in the park, a parade, craft show, and fireworks. Mid-July.

Spring Valley (E-4)

See also Austin, Rochester

Population 2,461

Elevation 1,279 ft
Area Code 507
Zip 55975
Information Spring Valley Chamber of Commerce, PO Box 13; phone 507/346-7367

As the name suggests, there are many large springs in this area, and the underground rivers, caves, and limestone outcroppings here are of particular interest. This was the hometown of Almanzo Wilder, and he and wife Laura Ingalls Wilder briefly attended church here.

What to See and Do

Forestville/Mystery Cave State Park. *6 miles E on Hwy 16, 4 miles S on County 5, then 2 miles E on County 12. Phone 507/352-5111.* A 3,075-acre park in the Root River Valley with a historic townsite. Fishing; hiking; bridle trails. Cross-country skiing, snowmobiling; picnicking; camping. **$$** Also in park is

> **Mystery Cave.** *Rte 2, Preston (55965). Phone 507/352-5111.* 60-minute guided tours; 48° F in cave. (Memorial Day-Labor Day: daily; mid-Apr-Memorial Day: weekends) Picnicking. Vehicle permit required (additional fee). **$$$**

Methodist Church. *221 W Courtland St, Spring Valley (55975). Phone 507/346-7659.* (1876) Victorian Gothic architecture; 23 stained-glass windows. Laura Ingalls Wilder site. Lower-level displays include country store, history room; military and business displays. (June-Aug: daily; Sept-Oct: weekends; also by appointment) **$$**

Washburn-Zittleman House. *220 W Courtland St, Spring Valley (55975). Phone 507/346-7659.* (1866) Two-story frame house with period furnishings, quilts; farm equipment, one-room school, toys. (Memorial Day-Labor Day: daily; Sept-Oct: weekends; also by appointment) **$$**

St. Cloud (D-3)

See also Elk River, Litchfield, Little Falls, Minneapolis

Founded 1856
Population 48,812
Elevation 1,041 ft
Area Code 320
Information St. Cloud Area Covention & Visitors Bureau, 30 S 6th Ave, PO Box 487, 56302; phone 320/251-2940 or toll-free 800/264-2940
Web Site www.stcloudcvb.com

Its central location makes St. Cloud a convention hub and retail center for the area. The granite quarried here is prized throughout the United States. This Mississippi River community's architecture reflects the German and New England roots of its early settlers.

What to See and Do

City Recreation Areas. Riverside Park. *1725 Kilian Blvd, St. Cloud (56303). Phone 320/255-7256.* Monument to Zebulon Pike who discovered and named the nearby Beaver Islands in 1805 during exploration of the Mississippi. Shelter; flower gardens; wading pool, tennis, picnicking, lighted cross-country skiing. **Wilson Park,** 625 Riverside Dr NE. Picnicking; boat landing, tennis, disc golf course. **Lake George Eastman Park,** 9th Ave and Division. Swimming (Early June-mid-Aug, daily; fee); skating (Late Dec-early Feb, daily; free); paddleboats (fee), fishing, picnicking. **Municipal Athletic Complex,** 5001 8th St N. Indoor ice skating (Mid-June-mid-May, phone 320/255-7223 for fee and schedule information). **Whitney Memorial Park,** Northway Dr. Walking trails, playground, picnicking, softball and soccer. **Heritage Park,** 33rd Ave S. Nature trails, skating, cross-country skiing, earth-covered shelter; nearby is an interpretive heritage museum (Memorial Day-Labor Day, daily; rest of year, Tues-Sun; closed holidays; fee) with replica of working granite quarry and historical scenes of central Minnesota.

Clemens Gardens & Munsinger Gardens. *13th St and Kilian Blvd, St. Cloud (56301). 13th St. S, along the Mississippi River. Phone toll-free 800/264-2940.* Clemens Gardens features, among other gardens, the White Garden, based upon Kent, England's White Garden at Sissinghurst Garden. Munsinger Gardens is surrounded by pine and hemlock trees. (Memorial Day-Labor Day) **FREE**

College of St. Benedict. *7 miles W on I-94. Phone 320/363-5777.* (1887) (1,742 women) On campus is the $6 million Ardolf Science Center. Guided tours. Art exhibits, concerts, plays, lectures, and films in Benedicta Arts Center. Also here is

> **St. Benedict's Convent.** *104 Chapel Ln, St. Joseph (56374). NW via I-94. Phone 320/363-7100.* (1857) Community of more than 400 Benedictine women. Tours of historic Sacred Heart Chapel (1913), and archives. Gift and crafts shop; Monastic Gardens.

Minnesota Baseball Hall of Fame. *St. Cloud Civic Center, second floor, 10 4th Ave S, St. Cloud (56301).*

Phone 320/255-7272. Features great moments from amateur and professional baseball. (Mon-Fri) **FREE**

Powder Ridge Ski Area. *15015 93rd Ave, Kimball (55353). 16 miles S on Hwy 15. Phone 320/398-7200; toll-free 800/348-7734.* Quad, two double chairlifts, J-bar, rope tow; patrol, school, rentals; snowmaking; bar, cafeteria. (Mid-Nov-Mar, daily) Fifteen runs. **$$$$**

St. Cloud State University. *4th Ave S, St. Cloud (56301). Overlooks Mississippi River. Phone 320/255-3151.* (1869) (15,600 students) Marked historical sites; anthropology museum, planetarium, art gallery (Mon-Fri; closed holidays and school breaks).

St. John's University and Abbey, Preparatory School. *1857 Watertower Rd, Collegeville (56321). 13 miles W on I-94. Phone 320/363-3321; toll-free 800/525-7737. www.sjprep.net.* (1857) (1,900 university students) Impressive modern abbey, university, church, and Hill Monastic manuscript library, other buildings designed by the late Marcel Breuer; 2,450 acres of woodlands and lakes.

Stearns History Museum. *235 S 33rd Ave, St. Cloud (56301). Phone 320/253-8424.* Located in a 100-acre park, the center showcases cultural and historical aspects of past and present life in central Minnesota; contains replica of working granite quarry; agricultural and automobile displays; research center and archives. (Daily; closed holidays) **$$**

Special Events

Mississippi Music Fest. *Riverside Park, St. Cloud (56301). Phone 320/255-2205.* Strolling artisans, musicians, and craftspeople are featured at this annual festival highlighted by a variety of modern music. Late Apr.

Wheels, Wings & Water Festival. *Phone 320/251-0083.* June.

Limited-Service Hotels

★ FAIRFIELD INN. *4120 2nd St S, St. Cloud (56301). Phone 320/654-1881; toll-free 800/828-2800; fax 320/654-1881. www.fairfieldinn.com.* 57 rooms, 3 story. Complimentary continental breakfast. Check-in 3 pm, check-out noon. High-speed Internet access. Indoor pool, whirlpool. **$**

★★ HOLIDAY INN. *75 37th Ave S, St. Cloud (56301). Phone 320/253-9000; toll-free 800/465-4329; fax 320/253-5998. www.holiday-inn.com.* 257 rooms, 3 story. Pets accepted. Check-in 4 pm, check-out 11 am. High-speed Internet access. Restaurant, bar. Children's activity center. Fitness room. Two indoor pools, children's pool, two whirlpools. **$**

Restaurant

★ D. B. SEARLE'S. *18 5th Ave S, St. Cloud (56301). Phone 320/253-0655.* Built in 1886. American menu. Lunch, dinner. Closed holidays. **$$**

St. Paul (D-3)

See also Anoka, Bloomington, Elk River, Hastings, Lakeville, Minneapolis, Northfield, Red Wing, St. Peter, Stillwater, Taylors Falls

Settled 1840
Population 272,235
Elevation 874 ft
Area Code 651
Information Convention and Visitors Bureau, 175 W Kellogg Blvd, Suite 502, 55102; phone 651/265-4900 or toll-free 800/627-6101
Web Site www.stpaulcvb.org

The distribution center for the great Northwest and dignified capital of Minnesota, stately St. Paul had its humble beginnings in a settlement known as "Pig's Eye." At the great bend of the Mississippi and tangent to the point where the waters of the Mississippi and Minnesota rivers meet, St. Paul and its twin city, Minneapolis, form a mighty northern metropolis. Together, they are a center for computers, electronics, medical technology, printing, and publishing. In many ways they complement each other, yet they are also friendly rivals. Fiercely proud of their professional sports teams (baseball's Minnesota Twins, football's Minnesota Vikings, and basketball's Minnesota Timberwolves), the partisans of both cities troop to the Hubert H. Humphrey Metrodome Stadium in Minneapolis (see), as well as other arenas in the area, to watch their heroes in action.

A terraced city of diversified industry and lovely homes, St. Paul boasts 30 lakes within a 30-minute drive, as well as more than 90 parks. St. Paul is home to 3M Companies and other major corporations.

Historic St. Paul

The center of St. Paul contains a number of historic structures and cultural institutions, as well as the Minnesota state capitol. A morning or afternoon stroll easily links all of the following sites.

Begin at Rice Park, located at 5th and Market streets. Established 150 years ago, this park, with its vast old trees, manicured lawns, flowers, and fountains, is an oasis of nature in the midst of urban St. Paul. Surrounding the park are some of the city's most noted landmarks. Facing the park to the east is the St. Paul Hotel (350 Market St), built in 1910 as the city's finest. After a loving refurbishment, it is once again one of the city's premier luxury hotels. Step inside to wander the lobby, which is filled with chandeliers, oriental carpets, and fine furniture.

Facing Rice Park from the south is the handsome turn-of-the-20th-century St. Paul Public Library. To the west, the Ordway Music Theatre (345 Washington St) is an elegant concert hall where the St. Paul Chamber Orchestra and the Minnesota Orchestra frequently perform. The Landmark Center, facing Rice Park to the north (75 W 5th St), is a castlelike federal courthouse built in 1902. A number of galleries and arts organizations are now housed in the structure, including the Minnesota Museum of American Art.

Cross St. Peter Street and continue east on East 6th Street. At Cedar Street is Town Center Park, the world's largest indoor park, complete with trees, fountains, flowers, and a carousel. From the north side of the park there are good views of the state capitol. Exit the north end of the park onto 7th Street, walk one block east to Wabasha Street, and turn north. At the corner of Wabasha and Exchange streets is the World Theater (10 Exchange St), where Garrison Keillor frequently broadcasts *The Prairie Home Companion,* the acclaimed public radio show.

One block north is the Science Museum of Minnesota (30 E 10th St) with exhibits on geology, paleontology, and the sciences, and the William L. McKnight-3M Omnitheater, with a 76-foot-wide domed screen. From the main entrance of the Science Museum, walk up Cedar Street toward the capitol building, passing through the parklike Capitol Mall. The magnificent Minnesota Capitol sits on a hill overlooking the city and is crowned by the world's largest unsupported dome. Wander the marble-clad hallways, or join a free tour of the legislative chambers.

From the capitol, follow John Ireland Boulevard south to the Cathedral of St. Paul. Modeled after St. Peter's Basilica in Rome, this 3,000-seat church occupies the highest point in St. Paul. Just south of the cathedral is the James J. Hill House at 240 Summit Avenue. This late 19th-century, five-story mansion was built by James Hill, founder of the Great Northern Railroad. When built, this mansion was the largest and most expensive private home in the upper Midwest. Tours are offered. Return to downtown St. Paul along Kellogg Boulevard.

The junction of the Mississippi and Minnesota rivers was chosen in 1807 as the site for a fort that later became known as Fort Snelling. Squatters soon settled on the reservation lands nearby, only to be expelled in 1840 with one group moving a few miles east and a French-Canadian trader, Pierre Parrant, settling at the landing near Fort Snelling. Parrant was nicknamed "Pig's Eye," and the settlement that developed at the landing took this name.

When Father Lucien Galtier built a log cabin chapel there in 1841, he prevailed on the settlers to rename their community for St. Paul. A Mississippi steamboat terminus since 1823, St. Paul prospered on river trade, furs, pioneer traffic, and agricultural commerce. Incorporated as a town in 1849, it was host to the first legislature of the Minnesota Territory and has been the capital ever since.

A number of institutions of higher education are located in St. Paul, including the University of Minnesota—Twin Cities Campus, University of St. Thomas, College of St. Catherine, Macalester College, Hamline University, Concordia University, Bethel College, and William Mitchell College of Law.

Public Transportation

Buses (Metropolitan Council Transit Operations)

Airport **Minneapolis-St. Paul International Airport;** weather phone 952/361/6680, cash machines, Main Terminal, between entrances to Blue and Green Concourses

Information Humphrey Terminal (Minneapolis) phone 612/726-5800, Lindbergh Terminal (St. Paul) phone 612/726-5555

Lost and Found 612/726-5141

Web Site www.mspairport.com/msp

Airlines At Humphrey Terminal (Minneapolis): Casino Express, Champion Air, Miami Air International, Omni Air, Ryan International, Sun Country Airlines, Transmeridian Airlines; at Lindbergh Terminal (St. Paul): Air Canada, Air Tran Airways, America West, American Airlines, American Trans Air, Comair, Continental, Delta Air Lines, Frontier Airlines, Icelandair, KLM Royal Dutch, Mesaba Airlines, Northwest Airlines, Midwest Connect, SkyWest, United Airlines, Great Lakes Aviation, US Airways

What to See and Do

6th Street Center Skyway. *56 E 6th St, St. Paul (55102). In the center of downtown.* Created out of the second level of 6th Street Center's five-story parking garage. The center includes shops and restaurants. (Daily; closed holidays)

Alexander Ramsey House. *265 S Exchange St, St. Paul (55102). Phone 651/296-0100. www.mnhs.org/places/sites/arh.* (1872) This was the home of Minnesota's first territorial governor and his wife, Anne. The house is full of original Victorian furnishings and features carved walnut woodwork, marble fireplaces, and crystal chandeliers. Guided tours show visitors what family and servant life was like in the 1870s; reservations are suggested. (Fri-Sat 10 am-3 pm; expanded holiday hours) **$$**

Capital City Trolley. *525 Farwell Avenue, St. Paul (55106). Phone 651/223-5600. www.capitalcitytrolleys.com.* This hour-long narrated tour takes visitors through the downtown area and along the Mississippi riverfront, stopping at historical sites like the mansion of railroad magnate James J. Hill on Summit Avenue. Reservations are required. (May-Oct, Thurs) **$$**

Cathedral of St. Paul. *239 Selby Ave, St. Paul (55102). Phone 651/228-1766.* The dome of this Classical Renaissance-style Roman Catholic cathedral, in which services began in 1915, is 175 feet high; the central rose window is a dominant feature. (Daily)

City Hall and Courthouse. *15 W Kellogg Blvd, St. Paul (55102). Phone 651/266-8023.* This 1932 building, listed on the National Register of Historic Places, is a prominent example of Art Deco. Carl Milles's 60-ton, 36-foot-tall onyx *Vision of Peace* statue graces the lobby.

Como Park. *Midway and Lexington pkwys, St. Paul (55102). Phone 651/266-6400.* A 448-acre park with a 70-acre lake. You can fish, hike, picnic, swim in the pool, play the 18-hole golf course (fee), or enjoy outdoor concerts and plays in the summer. The glass-domed conservatory ($) features an authentic Japanese garden (May-Sept) and the Enchanted Garden and Frog Pond. The Como Zoo includes bison, lions, and other big cats, and Galapagos tortoises. There is also an amusement area (Memorial Day-Labor Day) with a carousel and other children's rides ($) and a miniature golf course. (Daily 10 am-4 pm; Apr-Sept until 6 pm)

Fort Snelling State Park. *1 Post Rd, St. Paul (55111). At the junction of Hwy 5 and Post Rd, just S of Main Terminal exit. Phone 612/725-2389. www.dnr.state.mn.us/state_parks/fort_snelling.* A 4,000-acre park at the confluence of the Minnesota and Mississippi rivers. Swimming, fishing, boating; hiking, biking, cross-country skiing; picnicking; visitor center. (Daily 8 am-4 pm) Includes

> **Historic Fort Snelling.** *Hwy 55, Saint Paul (55111). Phone 612/726-1171.* Stone frontier fortress restored to its appearance of the 1820s; daily drills and cannon firings; craft demonstrations (June-Aug, daily; May and Sept-Oct, weekends only). Visitor center with films, exhibits. (May-Oct, daily) **$$**

Gray Line Twin Cities Tour. *21160 Holyoke Ave, Lakeville (55044). Phone 952/469-5020. www.grayline-mpls.com.* This 3 1/2-hour bus tour of the Twin Cities area departs from the Mall of America and includes Minnehaha Falls, Fort Snelling, and the St. Paul Cathedral. (Daily at 10:15 am; late May-late Aug, Sat-Sun; no tours on July 4) **$$$$**

Great American History Theatre. *30 10th St E, St. Paul (55101). Phone 651/292-4323. www.historytheatre.com.*

Original plays and musicals with American and Midwestern themes. (Year-round, Thurs-Sun) **$$$$**

Indian Mounds Park. *Earl St and Mounds Blvd, St. Paul (55102). Atop Dayton's Bluff. Phone 651/266-6400. www.nps.gov/miss/maps/model/mounds.html.* This park, one of the oldest in the region, is made up of more than 25 acres and contains prehistoric Native American burial mounds built 1,500 to 2,000 years ago. Eighteen mounds existed on this site in 1856, but only six remain. The park also has picnic facilities, paved trails, and outstanding views of the Mississippi River and the city skyline. (Daily, half an hour before sunrise until half an hour after sunset)

James J. Hill House. *240 Summit Ave, St. Paul (55102). Phone 651/297-2555. www.mnhs.org/places/sites/jjhh.* This 1891 house, made of red sandstone, was the showplace of the city when it was built for the famous railroad magnate. Reservations are recommended for the guided tours, which depart every 30 minutes. (Wed-Sat 10 am-3:30 pm, Sun 1-3:30 pm; closed holidays) **$$**

Landmark Center. *75 W 5th St, St. Paul (55102). Phone 651/292-3228. www.landmarkcenter.org.* This restored Federal Courts Building was constructed in 1902; it's currently the center for cultural programs and gangster history tours. It houses four courtrooms and a four-story indoor courtyard, the Musser Cortile. You'll also find a restaurant, an archive gallery, an auditorium, the Schubert Club Keyboard Instrument Collection (Mon-Fri), and the Minnesota Museum of American Art (see). Visitors can take 45-minute guided tours (Thurs and Sun; also by appointment) and self-guided tours (daily). (Building open daily; closed holidays) **FREE**

Luther Seminary. *2481 Como Ave, St. Paul (55108). Phone 651/641-3456. www.luthersem.edu.* (1869) (780 students) On campus is the Old Muskego Church (1844), the first church built by Norse immigrants in America; it was moved to present site in 1904. Tours.

Minnesota Children's Museum. *10 W 7th St, St. Paul (55102). Phone 651/225-6000. www.mcm.org.* This museum features hands-on learning exhibits in seven galleries for children up to 10 years old and their adult companions. The museum store is stocked with unique puzzles, maps, toys, games, and books. (Memorial Day-Labor Day: daily; rest of year: Tues-Sun; closed holidays) **$$**

Minnesota Historical Society Center. *345 Kellogg Blvd W, St. Paul (55102). Phone 651/296-6126; toll-free 800/657-3773 (except in the Twin Cities). www.mnhs.org.* Home to the Historical Society, the center houses a museum with interactive exhibits and an extensive genealogical and research library, as well as special events, two museum shops, and a café. (Museum: Memorial Day-Labor Day, daily; rest of the year,Tues-Sun; library, Tues-Sat) **FREE**

Minnesota Museum of American Art–Landmark Center. *Kellogg Boulevard at Market Street, St. Paul (55102). Phone 651/292-4355. www.mmaa.org.* This museum includes changing exhibits and a permanent collection of American art from the 19th century to the present. Artists such as Thomas Hart Benton are featured, as are new art forms. There's also a Museum School and store. (Tues-Sun, hours vary; closed holidays) **FREE**

Minnesota Transportation Museum. *193 Pennsylvania Ave E, St. Paul (55101). W 42nd St and Queen Ave S. Phone 651/228-0263. www.mtmuseum.org.* Display museum and restoration shop; 2-mile rides in early 1900s electric streetcars along reconstructed Como-Harriet line (Memorial Day weekend-Labor Day: daily; after Labor Day-Oct: weekends). **$**

Minnesota Wild (NHL). *Xcel Energy Center, 175 W Kellogg Blvd, St. Paul (55102). Phone 651/222-9453. www.wild.com.* Professional hockey team. **$$$$**

Science Museum of Minnesota. *120 W Kellogg Blvd, St. Paul (55102). Phone 651/221-9444. www.smm.org.* This 8-acre museum showcases technology, anthropology, paleontology, geography, and biology exhibits and a 3-D cinema. The William L. McKnight 3M Omnitheater shows IMAX films, and there's a new Mississippi River Visitor Center. (Daily, hours vary) **$$**

Sibley Historic Site. *1357 Sibley Memorial Hwy (Hwy 13), Mendota (55150). Phone 651/452-1596. www.mnhs.org/places/sites/shs.* On this site sits the 1838 home of General Henry Sibley, Minnesota's first governor, now preserved as a museum. Also on the grounds are three other restored limestone buildings, including the Faribault House Museum (1840), the home of pioneer fur trader Jean Baptiste Faribault, now a museum of the Native American and fur trade era. (May-Oct, Tues-Sun, hours vary) **$**

★ **Sightseeing cruises.** *Harriet Island Park, W of Wabasha bridge and Boom Island in Minneapolis. Phone 651/227-1100.* Authentic Mississippi River sternwheelers *Harriet Bishop, Betsy Northrop,* and *Jonathan Padelford* make 1 3/4-hour narrated trips to

Historic Fort Snelling (see). The sidewheeler *Anson Northrup* makes trips through the lock at St. Anthony Falls, departing from Boom Island at noon and 2 pm. Dinner and brunch cruises and showboat tours are also available. (Memorial Day-Labor Day: daily; May and Sept: weekends)

State Capitol. *75 Constitution Ave, St. Paul (55101). Phone 651/296-2881. www.mnhs.org/places/sites/msc.* (1896-1905) Designed in the Italian Renaissance style by Cass Gilbert and decorated with murals, sculptures, stencils, and marble, the capitol opened in 1905. Guided 45-minute tours leave on the hour; the last tour leaves one hour before closing (group reservations required). (Daily; closed holidays) **FREE**

University of Minnesota, Twin Cities Campus. *56 Delaware SE, St. Paul (55445). Phone 612/625-5000. www.umn.edu.* (1851) (39,315 students) Campus tours; animal barn tours for small children. Near campus is

Gibbs Museum of Pioneer & Dakotah Life. *323 Landmark Center, St. Paul (55113). Phone 651/646-8629. www.rchs.com/gbbsfm2.htm.* This restored furnished farmhouse dating to 1854 depicts the lives of pioneers and Dakotahs at the turn of the 20th century. The site includes two barns, two Dakotah-style tipis, and a one-room schoolhouse. Interpretations, demonstrations, and a summer schoolhouse program round out the offerings. (Mid-Apr-mid-Nov: Tues-Fri 10 am-4 pm, Sat and Sun noon-4 pm) **$**

Special Events

Minnesota State Fair. *Fairgrounds, 1265 Snelling Ave N, St. Paul (55108). www.mnstatefair.org.* Midway, thrill show, horse show, kids' days, all-star revue; more than 1 million visitors each year; 300 acres of attractions. Late Aug-early Sept.

Winter Carnival. *75 5th St W, St. Paul (55102). Throughout the city. Phone 651/223-4700.* One of the leading winter festivals in America; ice and snow carving; parades, sports events, parties, pageants. The highlight of the festival is a remarkable ice palace that rivals traditionally built mansions and castles in terms of scale and grandeur; visitors can walk through the palace's rooms and hallways ($$). Last weekend in Jan-first weekend in Feb.

Limited-Service Hotels

★★ EMBASSY SUITES. *175 E 10th St, St. Paul (55101). Phone 651/224-5400; toll-free 800/362-2779; fax 651/224-0957. www.embassystpaul.com.* This hotel is located near the Science Museum of Minneapolis, Galtier Plaza, the Mall of America, and much more. 210 rooms, 8 story. Check-in 3 pm, check-out noon. Restaurant, bar. Fitness room. Indoor pool, whirlpool. Airport transportation available. **$$**

★★ FOUR POINTS BY SHERATON. *400 Hamline Ave N, St. Paul (55104). Phone 651/642-1234; toll-free 800/535-2339; fax 651/642-1126. www.sheraton.com.* 197 rooms, 4 story. Pets accepted, some restrictions. Check-in 3 pm, check-out noon. Restaurant, bar. Fitness room. Beach. Indoor pool, whirlpool. **$**

★★ RADISSON RIVERFRONT. *11 E Kellogg Blvd, St. Paul (55101). Phone 651/292-1900; toll-free 800/333-3333; fax 651/605-0189. www.radisson.com.* This hotel is located in downtown near many attractions, shopping, and dining. It offers spacious guest rooms, a pool and Jacuzzi, 24-hour workout facilities, and a restaurant found on the 22nd floor with a great view of the river. 475 rooms, 22 story. Check-in 3 pm, check-out noon. Restaurant, bar. Fitness room. Indoor pool, whirlpool. **$$**

Full-Service Hotel

★★★ THE SAINT PAUL HOTEL. *350 Market St, St. Paul (55102). Phone 651/292-9292; toll-free 800/292-9292; fax 651/228-9506. www.stpaulhotel.com.* A Historic Hotel of America, this beautifully restored property was founded in 1910 by wealthy businessman Lucius P. Ordway and still maintains an old-style, European charm. Connected to the downtown skyway system, the hotel has hosted many famous individuals, including presidents Herbert Hoover, Woodrow Wilson, and George W. Bush. Most of the guest rooms have splendid views of downtown, Rice Park, or the St. Paul Cathedral. 254 rooms, 12 story. Check-in 4 pm, check-out noon. Two restaurants, bar. Fitness room. Airport transportation available. Business center. **$$**

Specialty Lodging

The following lodging establishment is approved by Mobil Travel Guide, but due to its unique and individualized nature has not been given a traditional Mobil Star rating. Included in this listing you may find bed-and-breakfasts, limited-service inns, guest ranches, and other unique hotel properties.

ROSE ARBOR INN. *341 Dayton Ave, St. Paul (55102). Phone 651/222-0243; toll-free 866/324-9067; fax 651/222-0243. www.rosearborinn.com.* 4 rooms. Complimentary continental breakfast. Check-in 4-6 pm, check-out 11 am. **$**

Restaurants

★ **CECIL'S DELI.** *651 S Cleveland, St Paul (55116). Phone 651/698-0334. www.cecilsdeli.com.* American menu. Breakfast, lunch, dinner. **$**

★ **CIATTI'S.** *850 Grand Ave, St. Paul (55105). Phone 651/292-9942; fax 651/292-0195.* Italian menu. Lunch, dinner, Sun brunch. Closed Dec 24-25. Bar. Children's menu. Casual attire. **$**

★ ★ **DAKOTA BAR AND GRILL.** *1021 E Bandana Blvd, St. Paul (55108). Phone 651/642-1442.* Jazz fans will enjoy this modern restaurant in Bandana Square. Regional ingredients are used in such eclectic dishes as pheasant fritters. Along with the extensive wine list, guests can enjoy dining on the outdoor patio in the summer. American menu. Dinner. Closed Sun. Bar. Casual attire. Outdoor seating. **$$**

★ **DIXIE'S.** *695 Grand Ave, St. Paul (55105). Phone 651/222-7345; fax 651/225-8248. www.dixiesrestaurants.com.* Southern, Cajun menu. Lunch, dinner, Sun brunch. Closed Thanksgiving, Dec 25. Bar. Children's menu. Casual attire. Outdoor seating. **$**

★ ★ ★ **FOREPAUGH'S.** *276 S Exchange St, St. Paul (55102). Phone 651/224-5606; fax 651/224-5607. www.forepaughs.com.* Some say the ghost of the former owner haunts this romantic three-story home (1870) in St. Paul with nine dining rooms complete with lace curtains. The French menu has English "subtitles," and the restaurant offers shuttle service to nearby theaters. French menu. Lunch, dinner, Sun brunch. Closed holidays. Bar. Children's menu. Casual attire. Valet parking. Outdoor seating. **$$**

★ **GALLIVAN'S.** *354 Wabasha St, St. Paul (55102). Phone 651/227-6688; fax 651/292-9700.* American menu. Lunch, dinner. Closed Sun; holidays. Bar. Casual attire. **$**

★ ★ ★ **KOZLAKS ROYAL OAK.** *4785 Hodgson Rd, Shoreview (55126). Phone 651/484-8484; fax 651/484-7753.* Guests receive the royal treatment here, beginning with personalized note pads or matchbooks left on the table. Mood-enhancing colored lights reflect beauty, from the dozens of flowers and etched-glass windows to the scenic garden seating. American menu. Lunch, dinner, Sun brunch. Closed holidays. Bar. Children's menu. Casual attire. Outdoor seating. **$$$**

★ **LEEANN CHIN.** *214 E 4th St, St. Paul (55101). Phone 651/224-8814; fax 651/224-8746. www.leeannchin.com.* Chinese menu. Lunch, dinner. Closed holidays. Bar. Children's menu. Casual attire. **$$**

★ ★ **LEXINGTON.** *1096 Grand Ave, St. Paul (55105). Phone 651/222-5878; fax 651/222-8230. www.the-lexington.com.* The comfortable, clubby dining room is chandelier-lit and boasts a curving mahogany bar. Since 1935, the restaurant has prepared such traditional favorites as chateaubriand and prime rib in a simple and straightforward manner. American menu. Lunch, dinner, Sun brunch. Closed Dec 25. Bar. Children's menu. Casual attire. **$$$**

★ **LINDEY'S PRIME STEAKHOUSE.** *3600 Snelling Ave N, Arden Hills (55112). Phone 651/633-9813. www.lindey.com.* Steak menu. Dinner. Closed Sun; holidays. Bar. Children's menu. Casual attire. **$$**

★ **MANCINI'S CHAR HOUSE.** *531 W 7th St, St. Paul (55102). Phone 651/224-7345.* Steak menu. Dinner. Closed holidays. Bar. Children's menu. Casual attire. **$$$**

★ ★ **MUFFULETTA IN THE PARK.** *2260 Como Ave, St. Paul (55108). Phone 651/644-9116; fax 651/644-5329.* International/Fusion menu. Lunch, dinner, Sun brunch. Closed holidays. Casual attire. Outdoor seating. **$$**

★ ★ **RISTORANTE LUCI.** *470 Cleveland Ave S, St. Paul (55105). Phone 651/699-8258. www.ristoranteluci.com.* No surprises, just the kind of food everyone wants to eat all the time; simple and satisfying. Italian menu. Dinner. Closed Sun-Mon; holidays, children's menu. Casual attire. **$$**

★ ★ **SAKURA.** *350 St. Peter St #338, St. Paul (55102). Phone 651/224-0185; fax 651/225-9350.*

www.sakurastpaul.com. Japanese menu. Lunch, dinner. Closed Jan 1, Thanksgiving, Dec 25. Bar. Casual attire. **$$**

★ **SAWATDEE.** *289 E 5th St, St. Paul (55101). Phone 651/222-5859; fax 651/222-7524. www.sawatdee.com.* Thai menu. Lunch, dinner. Closed Sun; holidays. Bar. Casual attire. **$**

★ ★ **THE ST. PAUL GRILL.** *350 Market St, St. Paul (55102). Phone 651/224-7455. www.stpaulhotel.com.* American menu. Lunch, dinner, late-night, Sun brunch. Bar. Casual attire. Valet parking. **$**

★ ★ **TOBY'S ON THE LAKE.** *249 Geneva Ave N, St. Paul (55128). Phone 651/739-1600. www.tobysonthelake.com.* American menu. Lunch, dinner, Sun brunch. Closed Dec 25. Bar. Children's menu. Casual attire. Outdoor seating. **$$**

★ ★ ★ **W. A. FROST AND COMPANY.** *374 Selby Ave, St. Paul (55201). Phone 651/224-5715; fax 651/224-7945. www.wafrost.com.* Located in the historic Dakotah Building (1887), the four dining rooms of this restaurant are decorated with Victorian-style wallpaper, furnishings, and oil paintings. American menu. Lunch, dinner, late-night, Sun brunch. Closed holidays. Bar. Children's menu. Casual attire. Valet parking Fri-Sat. Outdoor seating. **$$$**

St. Peter (E-3)

See also Faribault, Le Sueur, Mankato, Minneapolis, New Ulm, St. Paul

Founded 1853
Population 9,421
Elevation 770 ft
Area Code 507
Zip 56082
Information St. Peter Area Chamber of Commerce, 101 S Front St; phone 507/931-3400 or toll-free 800/473-3404

What to See and Do

Eugene Saint Julien Cox House. *500 N Washington Ave, St. Peter (56082). Phone 507/931-2160.* (1871) Fully restored home is best example of Gothic Italianate architecture in the state. Built by town's first mayor; late Victorian furnishings. Guided tours. (June-Aug: Wed-Sun; May and Sept: Sat-Sun afternoons) **$$**

Gustavus Adolphus College. *800 W College Ave, St. Peter (56082). Phone 507/933-8000.* (1862) (2,300 students) On campus are Old Main (dedicated 1876); Alfred Nobel Hall of Science and Gallery; Lund Center for Physical Education; Folke Bernadotte Memorial Library; Linnaeus Arboretum; Schaefer Fine Arts Gallery; Christ Chapel, featuring door and narthex art by noted sculptor Paul Granlund. At various other locations on campus are sculptures by Granlund, sculptor-in-residence, including one depicting Joseph Nicollét, mid-19th-century French explorer and cartographer of the Minnesota River Valley. Campus tours. In October, the college hosts the nationally known Nobel Conference, which has been held annually since 1965.

Treaty Site History Center. *1851 N Minnesota Ave, St. Peter (56082). Phone 507/931-2160.* County historical items relating to Dakota people, explorers, settlers, traders, and cartographers and their impact on the 1851 Treaty of Traverse des Sioux. Archives. Museum shop. (Daily; closed holidays) **$$**

Restaurant

★ ★ **THE COUNTRY PUB.** *1179 E Pearl St, Kasota (56050). Phone 507/931-5888. www.countrypubmn.com.* Located in beautiful downtown Kasota, the Country Pub features dry aged meats and elegant white tablecloth dining. American menu. Dinner. **$$**

Stillwater (D-3)

See also St. Paul, Taylors Falls

Settled 1839
Population 13,882
Elevation 700 ft
Area Code 651
Zip 55082
Information Chamber of Commerce, 423 S Main St, Brick Alley Building; phone 651/439-4001
Web Site www.ilovestillwater.com

Center of the logging industry in pioneer days, Stillwater became a busy river town, host to the men who rode the logs downriver and the lumbermen who cleared the forests. Some buildings from that era remain today. An 1848 convention in Stillwater led to the creation of the Minnesota Territory, leading to the town's nickname of the "birthplace of Minnesota." The charming downtown area is filled with antique shops, clothing boutiques, and crafts stores.

What to See and Do

St. Croix Scenic Highway. Hwy 95 runs 50 miles from Afton to Taylors Falls along the "Rhine of America," the St. Croix River.

Washington County Historical Museum. *602 Main St N, Stillwater (55082). Phone 651/439-5956.* Former warden's house at old prison site; mementos of lumbering days (1846-1910); pioneer kitchen, furniture. (May-Oct, Thurs-Sun; also by appointment) **$$**

William O'Brien State Park. *16 miles N on Hwy 95. Phone 651/433-0500.* A 1,273-acre park. Swimming, fishing, boating (ramp); hiking, cross-country skiing, picnicking, camping (hook-ups, dump station).

Special Events

Lumberjack Days. *423 Main St S, Stillwater (55082). Phone 651/430-2306. www.lumberjackdays.com.* Lumberjack shows, a parade, and musically choreographed fireworks are among the activities at this annual summer celebration. Most of the festivities are held in Lowell Park. Late July.

Rivertown Art Fair. *Lowell Park, 201 Main St, Stillwater (55082). Phone 651/430-2306.* Hundreds of area artisans and craftspeople participate in this annual two-day event along the banks of the St. Croix River. Third weekend in May.

Limited-Service Hotel

★ COUNTRY INN & SUITES BY CARLSON STILLWATER. *2200 W Frontage Rd, Stillwater (55082). Phone 651/430-2699; toll-free 800/456-4000; fax 651/430-1233.* 66 rooms, 2 story. Complimentary continental breakfast. Check-in 3 pm, check-out 11 am. Indoor pool, whirlpool. **$**

Full-Service Inns

★★★ AFTON HOUSE INN. *3291 S St. Croix Trail, Afton (55001). Phone 651/436-8883; toll-free 877/436-8883; fax 651/436-6859. www.aftonhouseinn.com.* For a great escape, this romantic country inn is the perfect answer. Whether curling up with a book in the pine loft or taking a cruise on the St. Croix River, guests will find uninterrupted peace and relaxation here. 25 rooms, 2 story. Check-in 2 pm, check-out 11 am. High-speed Internet access. Restaurant, bar. Airport transportation available. **$**

★★★ LOWELL INN. *102 2nd St N, Stillwater (55082). Phone 651/439-1100; toll-free 888/569-3554; fax 651/439-4686. www.lowellinn.com.* Located in the historic area of Stillwater, on the banks of the beautifull St. Croix River, this hotel is a convenient getaway spot from the Twin Cities. Each of the hotel's rooms are individually decorated with fine furnishings. 23 rooms, 3 story. Complimentary full breakfast. Check-in 3 pm, check-out 11 am. Restaurant, bar. **$$**

★★★ WATER STREET INN. *101 S Water St, Stillwater (55082). Phone 651/439-6000; fax 651/430-9393. www.waterstreetinn.us.* This intimate Victorian-style hotel offers guest rooms that overlook the scenic St. Croix River. The property is located in the historic downtown of Stillwater. 41 rooms, 3 story. Complimentary full breakfast. Check-in 4 pm, check-out 11 am. Restaurant, bar. **$**

Specialty Lodgings

The following lodging establishments are approved by Mobil Travel Guide, but due to their unique and individualized nature have not been given a traditional Mobil Star rating. Included in this listing you may find bed-and-breakfasts, limited-service inns, guest ranches, and other unique hotel properties.

AURORA STAPLES INN. *303 N 4th St, Stillwater (55082). Phone 651/351-1187; toll-free 800/580-3092. www.aurorastaplesinn.com.* 5 rooms. Complimentary full breakfast. Check-in 4-6 pm, check-out 11 am. **$$**

COVER PARK MANOR BED AND BREAKFAST. *15330 58th St N, Stillwater (55082). Phone 651/430-9292; toll-free 877/430-9292; fax 651/430-0034. www.coverpark.com.* 4 rooms, 2 story. Complimentary full breakfast. Check-in 4 pm, check-out 11:30 am. **$$**

RIVERTOWN INN. *306 W Olive St, Stillwater (55082). Phone 651/430-2955; fax 651/430-2206. www.rivertowninn.com.* 8 rooms. Complimentary full breakfast. Check-in 3 pm, check-out 11 am. **$$**

Restaurants

★★ AFTON HOUSE. *3291 S St. Croix Trail, Afton (55001). Phone 651/436-8883. www.aftonhouseinn.com.* Tableside presentations, complete with the traditional flame effects, are featured at this renovated historic inn (1867), with such dishes as Caesar salad, steak Diane, and dessert items like cherries jubilee, bananas Foster and strawberries Victoria. Seafood menu.

Breakfast, lunch, dinner, Sun brunch. Closed Dec 25; also Mon, Jan-Apr. Bar. Children's menu. Casual attire. **$$$**

★★★ **BAYPORT COOKERY.** *328 5th Ave N, Bayport (55003). Phone 651/430-1066. www.bayportcookery.com.* With only one nightly seating, diners can plan on an adventure of innovative cuisine at this St. Croix River Valley destination. Even city dwellers travel to experience the daily changing dinners featuring artistic presentations of local ingredients. American menu. Dinner. Closed Mon; holidays. Casual attire. Reservations recommended. Outdoor seating. **$$$**

★ **GASTHAUS BAVARIAN HUNTER.** *8390 Lofton Ave N, Stillwater (55082). Phone 651/439-7128; fax 651/439-0562. www.gasthausbavarianhunter.com.* German menu. Lunch, dinner, brunch. Closed holidays. Bar. Children's menu. Casual attire. Outdoor seating. Accordianist Fri evening, Sun afternoon. **$**

★★ **LOWELL INN RESTAURANT.** *102 N 2nd St, Stillwater (55082). Phone 651/439-1100; toll-free 888/569-3554. www.lowellinn.com.* Journey back to colonial times at this "Mount Vernon of the West". Along with traditional preparations, complete palate-cleansing sorbets and finger bowls recall the past. For something a bit different, try the fondue room. American, Swiss menu. Breakfast, lunch, dinner. Closed Thanksgiving, Dec 24-25. Bar. Children's menu. Casual attire. **$$$**

Superior National Forest (B-4)

See also Boundary Waters Canoe Area Wilderness, Cook, Crane Lake, Ely, Grand Marais, Grand Portage, International Falls, Tower, Virginia, Voyageurs National Park

On the N side of Lake Superior, W to Virginia, N to the Canadian border, and E to Grand Marais.

With more than 2,000 beautiful clear lakes, rugged shorelines, picturesque islands, and deep woods, this is a magnificent portion of Minnesota's famous northern area.

Scenic water routes through the Boundary Waters Canoe Area Wilderness and near the international border offer opportunities for adventure. The adjacent Quetico Provincial Park is similar, but guns are prohibited. Entry through Canadian Customs (see Border-Crossing Regulations in MAKING THE MOST OF YOUR TRIP) and Park Rangers' Ports of Entry.

Boating, swimming, water sports; fishing and hunting under Minnesota game and fish regulations; winter sports; camping (fee), picnicking, and scenic drives along Honeymoon, Gunflint, Echo, and Sawbill trails.

For further information, contact the Forest Supervisor, 8901 Grand Avenue Pl, Duluth 55808; phone 218/626-4300.

Taylors Falls (D-3)

See also St. Paul, Stillwater

Settled 1838
Population 694
Elevation 900 ft
Area Code 612
Zip 55084
Information Taylors Falls Chamber of Commerce, PO Box 235; phone 612/465-6315, 612/257-3550 (Twin Cities), or toll-free 800/447-4958 (outside the 612 area code)
Web Site www.wildmountain.com

Located on the Wisconsin border and just 40 miles from the Twin Cities, Taylors Falls is named for a series of rapids on the St. Croix River. The falls have now been dammed, but the name remains. The downtown area, which reminds tourists of a quaint New England town, has preserved its historic buildings, which include the oldest schoolhouse in the state, a number of churches, and several houses from the mid-1800s.

What to See and Do

Boat Excursions. Taylors Falls Scenic Boat Tour. *37350 Wild Mountain Rd, Taylors Falls (55084). Base of bridge, downtown, off Hwy 8. Phone 612/465-6315; toll-free 800/447-4958.* (Early May-mid-Oct, daily); 30-minute, 3-mile trip through St. Croix Dalles; also 1 1/3-hour, 7-mile trip on *Taylors Falls Queen* or *Princess.* Scenic, brunch, luncheon, and dinner cruises; fall color cruises. Also Taylors Falls one-way canoe rentals to Osceola or Williams O'Brien State Park, trips (with shuttle) (May-mid-Oct, daily).

Interstate. *1 mile S on Hwy 8. Phone 612/465-5711.* A 295-acre park. Geologic formations. Boating (ramp), canoe rentals, fishing, hiking, picnicking, camping (electric hook-ups, dump station). Excursion boat (fee).

St. Croix and Lower St. Croix National Scenic Riverway. *Phone 715/483-3284.* From its origins in northern Wisconsin the St. Croix flows southward to form part of the Minnesota-Wisconsin border before joining the Mississippi near Point Douglas. Two segments of the river totaling more than 250 miles have been designated National Scenic Riverways and are administered by the National Park Service. Information headquarters (mid-May-Oct: daily; rest of year: Mon-Fri); two information stations (Memorial Day-Labor Day, daily).

W. H. C. Folsom House. *120 Government Rd, Taylors Falls (55084). Phone 612/465-3125.* (1855) Federal/Greek Revival mansion reflects New England heritage of early settlers; many original furnishings. (Memorial Day weekend-mid-Oct, daily) **$$**

Wild Mountain Ski Area. *County Rd 16, Taylors Falls (55084). 7 miles N on County 16. Phone 651/257-3550; toll-free 800/447-4958. www.wildmountain.com.* Four quad chairlifts, two rope tows; patrol, school, rentals; snowmaking; cafeteria. Twenty-three runs, longest run 5,000 feet; vertical drop 300 feet. (Nov-Mar, daily) **$$$$** Also here is

> **Water Park.** *37200 Wild Mountain Rd, Taylors Falls (55084). Phone 651/465-6315; toll-free 800/447-4958. www.wildmountain.com.* The water slides at this park include a speed slide, an inner tube adventure, a fully enclosed hydrotube, and kiddie slides. The park also has a lazy river, two 1,700-foot alpine slides, and adult and kiddie go-karts. (Early May-early Sept, daily) **$$$$**

Wild River. *10 miles NW via Hwy 95, then 3 miles N on County 12. Phone 612/583-2125.* On 6,706 acres in the St. Croix River Valley. Fishing, canoeing (rentals); 35 miles of trails for hiking and cross-country skiing and 20 miles of horseback riding trails; picnicking; primitive and modern camping (electric hook-ups, dump station). Interpretive center and Trail Center (Daily).

Thief River Falls (B-1)

See also Crookston, Minnetonka, Roseau

Population 8,010
Elevation 1,133 ft
Area Code 218
Zip 56701
Information Chamber of Commerce, 2017 Hwy 59 SE; phone 218/681-3720 or toll-free 800/827-1629
Web Site www.ci.thief-river-falls.mn.us

The town of Thief River Falls—sitting at the confluence of the Thief and Red Lake rivers—claims more residents of Norwegian descent than any other city in the United States. Both Dakotas (Sioux) and Ojibwes (oh-JIB-ways) lived in small villages here before the Norwegian settlers arrived. Today, the area's biggest attraction is the Agassiz National Wildlife Refuge, which teems with migratory birds and other wildlife.

What to See and Do

Agassiz National Wildlife Refuge. *Marshall County Rd 7 E, Thief River Falls (56701). 23 miles NE via Hwy 32 to County 7 E. Phone 218/449-4115.* Approximately 61,500 acres of forest, water, and marshland. A haven for 280 species of migratory and upland game birds; 41 species of resident mammals. Refuge headquarters (Mon-Fri; closed holidays); auto tour route (daily, except winter). No camping. **FREE**

Peder Engelstad Pioneer Village. *Hwy 32 S and Oakland Park Blvd, Thief River Falls (56701). Phone 218/681-5767.* A reconstructed village features 19 turn-of-the-century buildings, including a one-room schoolhouse, general store, candy shop, blacksmith shop, barber shop, and church, along with two railroad depots and several homes and cabins. Museum houses historic vehicles and farm equipment and Norwegian and Native American artifacts, reflecting the town's history. (Summer, daily 1-5 pm) **$**

Limited-Service Hotels

★ ★ BEST WESTERN INN OF THIEF RIVER FALLS. *1060 Hwy 32 S, Thief River Falls (56701). Phone 218/681-7555; toll-free 800/780-7234; fax 218/681-7721. www.bestwestern.com.* 78 rooms. Check-in 2 pm, check-out noon. Restaurant, bar. Fitness room. Indoor pool, whirlpool. Airport transportation available. **$**

★ C'MON INN. *1586 Hwy 59 S, Thief River Falls (56701). Phone 218/681-3000; toll-free 800/950-8111; fax 218/681-3060.* 44 rooms, 2 story. Pets accepted, some restrictions. Complimentary continental breakfast. Check-out noon. Indoor pool, whirlpool. **$**

Tower (B-4)

See also Boundary Waters Canoe Area Wilderness, Cook, Crane Lake, Ely, Eveleth, Superior National Forest, Virginia

Founded 1882
Population 502
Elevation 1,400 ft
Area Code 218
Zip 55790

Although today it's a tiny town that offers spectacular natural resources, Tower was a flourishing mining and lumber town in its early days. You can tour the state's first underground mine at the state park close by. Tower sits just off Lake Vermillion, the state's fifth-largest lake, which harbors bald eagles and loons, as well as a wealth of fish: bass, northern pike, and walleye.

What to See and Do

Arrowhead Snowmobile/Bike Trail. *Trailhead 2 miles W of Hwy 169 on Hwy 1. www.dnr.state.mn.us/state_trails/arrowhead.* This 135-mile footpath, which extends approximately from Tower to International Falls, is used by hikers, mountain bikers, horseback riders, and snowmobilers. Fall colors are especially spectacular. Adjoining seven other state trails along its route, the Arrowhead Trail passes near the Boundary Waters Canoe Area Wilderness, Superior National Forest, and Voyageurs National Park. The trail ranges from flat and easy sections to hilly and strenuous areas.

Lake Vermilion. *515 Main St, Tower (55790). Phone 218/753-2301.* This lake is 40 miles long, with 1,250 miles of wooded shoreline, and 365 islands varying in size from specklike rocks to Pine Island, which is 9 miles long and has its own lake in its interior. Fishing for walleye, northern pike, bass, and panfish. Swimming, boating, water sports; hunting for duck, deer, and small game in fall; snowmobiling and cross-country skiing; camping and lodging. Primarily located in Superior National Forest.

Soudan Underground Mine State Park. *1379 Stuntz Bay Rd, Soudan (55782). 2 miles E on Hwy 169. Phone 218/753-2245.* Has 1,300 acres including site of the Soudan Mine, the state's first underground iron mine (52° F; 2,400 feet) in operation from 1882 to 1962. Self-guided tour of open pits, engine house, crusher building, drill shop, interpretive center; one-hour guided underground mine tour includes train ride (fees). Hiking trails. Picnic area. (Memorial Day-Labor Day, daily) **$$$**

Steam Locomotive and Coach. *515 Main St, Tower (55790). W end Main St, near junction Hwy 135, 169. Phone 218/753-2301.* Locomotive (1910) served Duluth & Iron Range Railroad. Coach is now a museum housing early logging, mining, and Native American displays. (Memorial Day-Labor Day, daily; early spring and late fall, by appointment) On grounds is a tourist information center and gift shop. **DONATION**

Tracy (E-2)

See also Marshall, Pipestone, Redwood Falls

Population 2,059
Elevation 1,395 ft
Area Code 507
Zip 56175
Information Chamber of Commerce, Prairie Pavilion, 372 Morgan St; phone 507/629-4021
Web Site www.tracymn.com/chamber

The town of Tracy could well be called Laura Ingalls Wilder town, because it is forever linked to the author of numerous children's books. Laura's first train ride was from her home in Walnut Grove to the train depot in Tracy, 8 miles away; a passage in *By the Shores of Silver Lake* describes the adventure. The town celebrates the Laura Ingalls Wilder Pageant each year, and the museum and tourist center named for the novelist is just 7 miles away.

What to See and Do

Lake Shetek State Park. *163 State Park Rd, Currie (56123). 14 miles S on County 11 and 38. Phone 507/763-3256.* Comprises 1,011 acres on one of largest lakes in Southwest Minnesota. Monument to settlers who were victims of the Dakota Conflict in 1862; restored pioneer cabin. Swimming, fishing, boating (ramp, rentals); hiking, snowmobiling, picnicking, camping. Naturalist (late May-early Sept).

★ Laura Ingalls Wilder Museum and Tourist Center. *330 8th St, Walnut Grove (56180). 7 miles E on Hwy 14. Phone 507/859-2358.* This tribute to Laura Ingalls Wilder is five buildings of museums. The depression in the ground where the dugout used to be, and the rock and spring mentioned in *On the Banks of Plum Creek* are all 1 1/2 miles north of Walnut Grove; fee per vehicle at farm site. (May-Oct: daily; rest of year: by appointment) **$$**

Special Event

Laura Ingalls Wilder Pageant. *313 Main St, Tracy (56175). 7 miles E on Hwy 14, 1 mile W of Walnut Grove.Phone 507/859-2174.* Story of the Ingalls family of Walnut Grove in the 1870s. Daughter was Laura Ingalls Wilder, author of the *Little House* books. July.

Two Harbors (C-4)

See also Duluth

Founded 1884
Population 3,651
Elevation 699 ft
Area Code 218
Zip 55616
Information Two Harbors Area Chamber of Commerce, 1026 7th Ave; phone 218/834-2600 or toll-free 800/777-7384
Web Site www.twoharbors.com/chamber

Two Harbors was given its start when the Duluth & Iron Range Railroad reached Lake Superior at Agate Bay. Ore docks were constructed immediately and the city became an important ore shipping terminal. Today, it is a bustling harbor community nestled between the twin harbors of Agate Bay and Burlington Bay.

What to See and Do

Depot Museum. *520 South Ave, Two Harbors (55616). In depot of Duluth & Iron Range Railroad, foot of Waterfront Dr. Phone 218/834-4898.* Historic depot (1907) highlights the geological history and the discovery and mining of iron ore. Mallet locomotive (1941), world's most powerful steam engine, on display. (May: weekends; Memorial Day-Oct: daily) **$**

The *Edna G.* *Waterfront Dr, Two Harbors (55616). Phone 218/834-4898.* The *Edna G.* served Two Harbors from 1896 to1981. It was designated a National Historic Site in 1974 as the only steam-powered tug still operating on the Great Lakes. Now retired, the *Edna G.* features seasonal tours where visitors can see her beautiful interior décor of wood paneling and brass fittings. Visitors get a look at the captain's quarters, the engine room, the crew's quarters, and the pilot house.

Gooseberry Falls State Park. *3206 Hwy 61, Two Harbors (55616). 14 miles NE on Hwy 61. Phone 218/834-3855.* A 1,662-acre park. Fishing, hiking, cross-country skiing, snowmobiling, picnicking, camping (dump station). State park vehicle permit required.

Lighthouse Point and Harbor Museum. *520 South Ave, Two Harbors (55616). Off Hwy 61, on Waterfront Dr at Lighthouse Point. Phone 218/834-4898.* Displays tell the story of iron ore shipping and the development of the first iron ore port in the state. A renovated pilot house from an ore boat is located on the site. Shipwreck display. Tours of operating lighthouse. (May-early Nov, daily) **$$**

Split Rock Lighthouse State Park. *3755 Split Rock Lighthouse, Two Harbors (55616). 20 miles NE on Hwy 61. Phone 218/226-6377 (park).* 1,987 acres. The lighthouse served as the guiding sentinel for the north shore of Lake Superior from 1910 to 1969. Also in the park is a historic complex (fee) that includes a fog-signal building, keeper's dwellings, several outbuildings, and the ruins of a tramway (mid-May-mid-Oct, daily). The Gitchi-Gami State Trail, a 10-foot-wide paved walking trail, stretches 7 miles from Beaver Bay to the Split Rock River and will eventually run 86 miles from Two Harbors to Grand Marais. Waterfalls. Picnicking. Cart-in camping (fee) on Lake Superior, access to Superior Hiking Trail. State park vehicle permit required. (Daily) **$$**

Superior Hiking Trail. *Phone 218/834-2700. www.shta.org.* This 205-mile footpath extends from Two Harbors to the Canadian border, following the rocky hills and ridgeline along Lake Superior. Thirty trailheads and parking areas make the trail ideal for day-hiking; 75 rustic campsites are available for thru-hikes. New sections of the trail open periodically; get a copy of *The Guide to the Superior Hiking Trail* from the SHTA for more information (Superior Hiking Trail Association, PO Box 4, Two Harbors, 55616).

Full-Service Resort

★ ★ SUPERIOR SHORES RESORT. *1521 Superior Shores Dr, Two Harbors (55616). Phone 218/834-5671; toll-free 800/242-1988; fax 218/834-*

5677. *www.superiorshores.com.* 104 rooms, 3 story. Pets accepted, some restrictions; fee. Check-in by arrangement, check-out 11 am. Restaurant, bar. Indoor pool, two outdoor pools, whirlpool. **$**

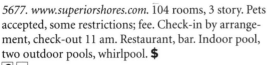

Specialty Lodging

The following lodging establishment is approved by Mobil Travel Guide, but due to its unique and individualized nature has not been given a traditional Mobil Star rating. Included in this listing you may find bed-and-breakfasts, limited-service inns, guest ranches, and other unique hotel properties.

LIGHTHOUSE BED & BREAKFAST. *1 Lighthouse Point, Two Harbors (55616). Phone 218/834-4898; toll-free 888/532-5606; fax 218/834-7198. www.lighthousebb.org.* 3 rooms, 2 story. Complimentary full breakfast. Check-in 3 pm, check-out 11 am. **$**

Virginia (B-4)

See also Cook, Duluth, Eveleth, Hibbing, Superior National Forest, Tower

Founded 1892
Population 9,410
Elevation 1,437 ft
Area Code 218
Zip 55792
Information Virginia Area Chamber of Commerce, 403 1st St N, PO Box 1072; phone 218/741-2717
Web Site www.virginiachamber.com

Born of lumbering, Virginia is nurtured by mining and vacationing. Great open iron ore pits mark the surrounding green countryside—man-made canyons are right at the city limits. Vacationers come to Virginia en route to the Boundary Waters Canoe Area Wilderness, Superior National Forest, and Voyageurs National Park. A Ranger District office of the Superior National Forest is located nearby.

What to See and Do

Mine View in the Sky. *403 1st St N, Virginia (55792). S edge of town on Hwy 53. Phone 218/741-2717.* Observation building (and visitors information center) gives view of a Mesabi Range open-pit mine 650 feet below. (May-Sept, daily) **FREE**

World's Largest Floating Loon. *1409 N Broadway, Virginia (55906). Phone 218/741-2717.* Listed in the *Guinness Book of World Records,* this 20-foot-long, 10-foot-high, 7 1/2-foot-wide, fiberglass loon swims on Silver Lake (located in the heart of the city) during the summer months.

Limited-Service Hotel

★ **AMERICINN VIRGINIA.** *5480 Mountain Iron Dr, Virginia (55792). Phone 218/741-7839; fax 218/741-9050.* 45 rooms. Check-in 3 pm, check-out 11 am. **$**

Voyageurs National Park (A-3)

See also International Falls, Kabetogama, Superior National Forest

Web Site www.nps.gov/voya

Off Hwy 53 on country roads 122 and 123 or E on Hwy 11.

Voyageurs (voy-ah-ZHERZ) National Park is on Minnesota's northern border and lies in the southern part of the Canadian Shield, representing some of the oldest rock formations in the world. Over 1/3 water, the park is water-based and rugged, but varied, with most trails and campsites accessible by boat. Rolling hills, bogs, beaver ponds, swamps, islands, and large and small lakes make up the vast scenery. Voyageurs has a cool climate with short, warm summers and long winters. Common summer activities include boating, swimming, fishing (with some of the best bass and walleye water in the United States), hiking, and camping, while outdoor enthusiasts enjoy skiing, snowmobiling, and snowshoeing during the colder months. A rich location for wildlife viewing, Voyagers is located in black bear country, and designated campsites are equipped with bear lockers for food storage. If a locker is not available, be prepared to hang your food, as bear-proofing food storage is required. In the summer, park-sponsored programs include interpretive walks, children's activities, and canoe trips. In the winter, activities include candlelight skiing and snowshoe hikes. Also in the park, Kettle Falls Dam, built by the Minnesota and Ontario Paper Company, converted 20-foot falls to a 12-foot dam; a damkeepers cabin was built in 1910. Lodging is available in the park during the summer months at Kettle Falls Hotel (listed on the National Register of Historic Places), and houseboats are available for rent. (Closed Jan 1, Thanksgiving, Dec 25)

Walker (B-2)

See also Bemidji, Park Rapids, Pine River

Population 950
Elevation 1,336 ft
Area Code 218
Zip 56484
Information Chamber of Commerce, PO Box 1089; phone 218/547-1313 or toll-free 800/833-1118
Web Site www.leech-lake.com

At the foot of Chippewa National Forest and Leech Lake, Walker serves tourists heading for adventures among woods and waters. Snowmobiling and cross-country skiing are popular sports here. The town is named for a pioneer lumberman and landowner. A Ranger District office of the Chippewa National Forest (see GRAND RAPIDS) is located here.

What to See and Do

Leech Lake. *Hwy 200/371.* Third-largest lake in the state; fishing and swimming.

Limited-Service Hotel

★ **AMERICINN.** *Hwys 371 and 34, Walker (56484). Phone 218/547-2200; fax 218/547-2176.* 37 rooms, 2 story. Complimentary continental breakfast. Check-out 11 am. Indoor pool, whirlpool. **$**

Willmar (D-2)

See also Granite Falls, Litchfield, Morris

Founded 1869
Population 17,531
Elevation 1,130 ft
Area Code 320
Zip 56201
Information Willmar Area Chamber of Commerce, 2104 E Hwy 12; phone 320/235-0300 or toll-free 800/845-8747
Web Site www.willmarareachamber.com

Founded as a railroad town, Willmar (WILL-mer) is still linked to the train industry today. This area's rich farmland and peaceful scenery make it one of the fastest growing cities in Minnesota.

What to See and Do

Kandiyohi County Historical Society Museum. *610 Hwy 71 NE, Willmar (56201). 1 mile N on Hwy 71 Business. Phone 320/235-1881.* Steam locomotive, country schoolhouse, restored house (1893); historical exhibits, agriculture building, research library. (Memorial Day-Labor Day: daily; rest of year: Mon-Fri; also by appointment; closed holidays) **DONATION**

Sibley State Park. *800 Sibley Park Rd, New London (56273). 15 miles N on Hwy 71. Phone 320/354-2055.* A 2,600-acre park; was a favorite hunting ground of first governor of state, for whom park is named. Swimming, fishing, boating (ramps, rentals); horseback riding, hiking; cross-country skiing, snowmobiling; camping (dump station); nature center.

Limited-Service Hotels

★ **DAYS INN.** *225 28th St SE, Willmar (56201). Phone 320/231-1275; toll-free 877/241-5235; fax 320/214-7552. www.daysinn.com.* 59 rooms, 2 story. Pets accepted. Complimentary continental breakfast. Check-in 3 pm, check-out 11 am. High-speed Internet access, wireless Internet access. Fitness room. **$**

★ ★ **HOLIDAY INN.** *2100 E Hwy 12, Willmar (56201). Phone 320/235-6060; toll-free 877/405-4466; fax 320/235-4231. www.holiday-inn.com.* 98 rooms, 2 story. Pets accepted, some restrictions. Check-in 3 pm, check-out noon. High-speed Internet access. Restaurant, bar. Indoor pool, children's pool, whirlpool. **$**

Winona (E-4)

See also Rochester

Settled 1851
Population 25,399
Elevation 666 ft
Area Code 507
Zip 55987
Information Convention & Visitors Bureau, 67 Main

St, PO Box 870; phone 507/452-2272
Web Site www.visitwinona.com

New Englanders and Germans came to this site on the west bank of the Mississippi and built an industrial city graced with three colleges. An early lumbering town, Winona today is one of the state's leading business and industrial centers and home of Winona State University.

What to See and Do

Fishing. Whitman Dam and Locks #5. *Lake Winona. 12 miles N on Hwy 61.* Dresbach Dam and Locks #7. *15 miles S on Hwy 61. S side of town.* Float and boat fishing.

Garvin Heights. *Huff St and Garvin Heights Rd, Winona (55987). Accessible via Huff St.* Park with 575-foot bluff, offering majestic views of the Mississippi River Valley. Picnic area. (Dawn-dusk)

Julius C. Wilkie Steamboat Center. *Levee Park, Winona (55987). Phone 507/454-1254.* Replica and exhibits. (June-Oct, Tues-Sun) **$**

Prairie Island Park. *Winona (55987). Prairie Island Rd, 3 miles N off Hwy 61.* Camping (Apr-Oct), picnicking, water, rest rooms, fireplaces. Fishing (all-year). Some fees.

Upper Mississippi River National Wildlife and Fish Refuge. *51 E 4th St, Winona (55987). Phone 507/452-4232 (Mon-Fri).* From Wabasha, Minnesota, extending 261 miles to Rock Island, Illinois, the refuge encompasses 200,000 acres of wooded islands, marshes, sloughs, and backwaters. Abounds in fish, wildlife, and plants. (Daily) Twenty percent of the refuge is closed for hunting and trapping until after duck hunting season. Boat required for access to most parts of refuge.

Winona County Historical Society Museum. *160 Johnson St, Winona (55987). Phone 507/454-2723.* Country store; blacksmith, barber shops; Native American artifacts; logging and lumbering exhibits; early vehicles and fire fighting equipment, award-winning children's exhibit, gift shop, library. (Daily; closed holidays) **$$** The society also maintains

> **Bunnell House.** *710 Johnson St, Homer (55942). 5 miles S on Hwy 14, 61. Phone 507/452-7575.* (Circa 1850) Unusual mid-19th-century Steamboat Gothic architecture; period furnishings. (Memorial Day-Labor Day, Wed-Sun; Labor Day-second weekend in Oct, weekends only; rest of year, by appointment) Also here is Carriage House Museum Shop (same schedule). **$$**

Special Events

Victorian Fair. *160 Johnson St, Winona (55987). Phone 507/452-2272.* Living history; costumed guides; boat rides. Late Sept.

Winona Steamboat Days. *Phone 507/452-2272. www.winonasteamboatdays.com.* Activities at this annual celebration include a lumberjack show, craft fair, water-ski show, food court and arcade, and boat rides. Mid-June.

Limited-Service Hotel

★ ★ BEST WESTERN RIVERPORT INN & SUITES. *900 Bruski Dr, Winona (55987). Phone 507/452-0606; toll-free 800/595-0606; fax 507/452-6489. www.bestwestern.com.* 106 rooms, 3 story. Pets accepted, some restrictions; fee. Complimentary continental breakfast. Check-in 3 pm, check-out 11 am. High-speed Internet access. Restaurant, bar. Indoor pool, whirlpool. **$**

Side Trips

Winnipeg, the provincial capital of Manitoba, is roughly 100 miles north of the Minnesota border. While visiting Minnesota, take advantage of the proximity and take a few days to visit our neighbor to the north. Whether you're a sports fan, a ballet aficionado, a shop-aholic, or a foodie, Winnipeg has activities to suit all interests.

Winnipeg, MB

2 hours 45 minutes, 70 miles from St. Vincent, MN

Population 650,000
Elevation 915 ft (279 m)
Area Code 204
Information Tourism Winnipeg, 279 Portage Rd, R3B 2B4; phone 204/943-1970 or toll-free 800/665-0204
Web Site www.tourism.winnipeg.mb.ca

Winnipeg, the provincial capital, is situated in the heart of the continent and combines the sophistication and friendliness of east and west. This formerly prairie-covered landscape was inhabited by Assiniboine, Cree, and Ojibwa tribes over 6,000 years ago. These tribes met at the junction of the Assiniboine and Red rivers to trade. Today, Winnipeg, derived from the Cree word for "muddy waters," is home to Canada's largest city-dwelling aboriginal community. A historic gathering place, it is still a destination that foreigners and Canadians alike visit to enjoy a wide range of attractions and cultural offerings. The city offers much for any visitor, including relaxing cruises on the Assiniboine and Red rivers, Rainbow Stage summer theater in Kildonan Park, the Manitoba Theatre Centre, the Winnipeg Symphony, the Manitoba Opera, and the renowned Royal Winnipeg Ballet. Sports fans will enjoy the Blue Bombers football team and the Manitoba Moose hockey team. Shopping, nightlife, gourmet restaurants—Winnipeg has it all.

Public Transportation

Airport Winnipeg International Airport

Information Phone 204/987-9402

Website www.waa.ca

Airlines Air Canada, Air Canada Jazz, Air Canada Tango, Calm Air, Bearskin Airlines, First Air, Northwest Airlines, SkyService, United Airlines, United Express, WestJet, Zip

What to See and Do

Assiniboine Forest Nature Park. *2355 Corydon Ave, Winnipeg (R3P 2K7). Phone 204/986-3989 (park).* This park features colorful English and formal gardens, the Leo Mol Sculpture Garden, a conservatory with floral displays, a duck pond, playgrounds, picnic sites, a cricket and field hockey area, a refreshment pavilion, a miniature train, bike paths, and a fitness trail. Cycle or hike on trails through 700 acres of aspen and oak in one of the largest urban natural parks in Canada. Search the surroundings for more than 39 species of mammals and more than 80 species of birds. The **Assiniboine Park Zoo** has a collection of rare and endangered species, tropical mammals, birds, and reptiles; the children's discovery area features a variety of young animals. (Daily) **FREE**

Assiniboine Park Conservatory. *Assiniboine Park, Winnipeg (R3P 2K7). Phone 204/986-5537.* The longest established conservatory in western Canada gives visitors a chance to view tropical trees and plants, exotic flowers, and foliage not indigenous to the country. Gallery, gift shop, coffee shop. (Apr-mid-Sept: daily 9 am-8 pm; Sept-Mar: daily 9 am-4:30 pm) **FREE**

Leo Mol Sculpture Garden. *Assiniboine Park, Winnipeg (R3P 2K7). Phone 204/986-6531.* Garden and gallery to view the bronze sculptures and other artwork by this acclaimed local artist. The sculpture garden is the only one in North America dedicated entirely to the work of a single artist. An on-site studio allows visitors to see how bronze sculptures are created. (Grounds open daily at 7 am; studio and gallery Tues-Sun 10 am-8 pm) **FREE**

Lyric Theatre. *Assiniboine Park, Winnipeg (R3P 2K7). Phone 204/888-5466.* View performances by the Royal Winnipeg Ballet, the Winnipeg Symphony Orchestra, and during assorted festivals.

Birds Hill Provincial Park. *8 miles (13 kilometers) N on Hwy 59. Phone 204/222-9151.* A 8,275-acre (3,350-hectare) park situated on a glacial formation called an eskar. The park has a large population of white-tailed deer and many orchid species. Interpretive, hiking, bridle, and bicycle trails; in-line skating path; snowshoe, snowmobile, and cross-country skiing trails (winter). Interpretive programs. Swimming, camping, and picnicking at an 81 1/2-acre (33-hectare) lake (seasonal). Riding stables (phone 204/222-1137). Per vehicle (May-Sept) **$$**

★ **Centennial Centre.** *555 Main St, Winnipeg (R3B 1C3). Phone 204/956-1360 (free tours of concert hall).* Complex includes concert hall and Manitoba Theatre Centre Building. Here are

Manitoba Museum of Man and Nature. *190 Rupert Ave, Winnipeg (R3B 1C3). Phone 204/956-2830. www.manitobamuseum.ca.* Galleries interpret Manitoba's human and natural history: Orientation; Earth History (geological background); Grasslands (prairie); Arctic-Subarctic; Boreal Forest; *Nonsuch* (full-size replica of a 17th-century ship); and Urban. (Late May-early Sept: daily 10 am-6 pm; rest of year: Tues-Fri 10 am-5 pm, closed holidays) **$$$**

Planetarium. *Phone 204/943-3142 (recording).* Circular, multipurpose audiovisual theater. Wide variety of shows; subjects include cosmic catastrophes and the edge of the universe. In the Science Gallery, visitors can learn about science through hands-on exhibits (separate admission fee). (Victoria Day-Labor Day: daily; rest of year: Tues-Sun) **$$**

Dalnavert Museum. *61 Carlton St, Winnipeg (R3C 1N7). Phone 204/943-2835.* Restored Victorian residence (1895) of Sir Hugh John Macdonald, premier of Manitoba, depicts the lifestyle and furnishings of the period. Gift shop. Guided tours (June-Aug: Tues-Thurs, Sat-Sun 10 am-4:30 pm; Sept-Dec and Mar-May: noon-4 pm; Jan-Feb: Sat-Sun noon-4 pm; closed holidays. Last tour 30 minutes before closing.) **$**

Forks. *Downtown, at the junction of the Red and Assinibione rivers. Phone 204/943-7752. www.theforks.com.* Several key Winnipeg attractions are centered in the general location of what has been a gathering place for people for thousands of years. Come here to shop, dine, explore museums and historic sites, or simply stroll along the Riverwalk.

The Forks Market. *Winnipeg. Phone 204/942-6302.* In between browsing through the more than 50 specialty shops for handicrafts, toys, gift items, and more, dine on cuisine from around the world and on local specialties.

The Forks National Historic Site of Canada. *401-25 Forks Market Rd, Winnipeg (R3C 0A2). Downtown, at the junction of the Red and Assinibione rivers. Phone 204/983-6757. www.parkscanada.gc.ca/forks.* Situated on 13.6 acres (5.5 hectares). Riverside promenade; walkways throughout. Historical exhibits, playground; evening performances. Special events. (May-Sept) Grounds (daily). Adjacent area open in winter for skating, cross-country skiing. **FREE**

The Manitoba Children's Museum. *Phone 204/924-4000. www.childrensmuseum.com.* Children explore and create in seven galleries, such as one that enables preschoolers to learn about the habitats of different animal species and to climb on a 17-foot (5.2-meter) oak tree, while older children can surf the Internet. Travel into the past on a 1952 diesel locomotive and passenger coach, or into a fairytale wonderland. (Daily)

The Splash Dash Water Bus. *Phone 204/783-6633. www.icenter.net/~gordcart.* Explore the river on a half-hour boat tour, rent a canoe, or use the water taxi service to get to downtown locations. (May-Oct: daily 11 am-sunset)

Fort Whyte Centre for Family Adventure and Recreation. *1961 McCreary Rd, Winnipeg (R3P 2K9). Phone 204/989-8355. www.fortwhyte.org.* Hike on self-guided trails through 400 acres (162 hectares)of marshes, lakes, and forests that are home to 27 species of birds and mammals. Year-round fishing; canoe and boat rentals. Dine at Buffalo Stone Café and shop for souvenirs at The Nature Shop. A 10,000-square-foot (920-square-meter) interpretive center showcases a variety of exhibits. Don't miss the Bison Prairie, with the largest urban-based herd of Plains bison in the country, or the Prairie Dog Exhibit. (Daily)

Legislative Building. *450 Broadway, Winnipeg (R3C 0V8). Phone 204/945-5813.* Example of neoclassical architecture. Grounds contain statues of Queen Victoria, Lord Selkirk, George Cartier. Tours (early July-early Sept: 9 am-6 pm; off-season: Mon-Thurs by appointment). **FREE**

Manitoba Opera Association. *Portage Place, 380 Graham Ave, Winnipeg (R3C 4K2). Phone 204/942-7479.* (Nov-May)

Oak Hammock Marsh Wildlife Management Area. *14 miles (23 kilometers) N via Hwy 7 or 8, then 5 miles (8 kilometers) to Hwy 67. Phone 204/467-3300.* More than 8,000 acres (3,238 hectares) of marshland and grassland wildlife habitat. Attracts up to 300,000 ducks and geese during spring (Apr-mid-May) and fall migration (Sept-Oct). Nature trails; picnic sites, marsh boardwalk, viewing mounds, drinking water. Conservation center with displays, interpretive programs (daily; fee). **FREE**

Paddlewheel/River Rouge boat and bus tours. *The Provencher Dock, Winnipeg (R2C 0A1). Phone 204/942-4500. www.paddlewheelcruises.com.* Floating restaurant, moonlight dance, and sightseeing cruises; also guided tours on double-decker buses. Bus/cruise combinations available. Boat cruises (May-Sept, 1-3 pm, 7-10 pm; also Fri-Sat 10 pm-1 am). Contact PO Box 3930, Postal Station B, R2W 5H9. **$$$$**

Ross House. *Joe Zuken Heritage Park, 140 Meade St N, Winnipeg (R2W 3K5). Between Euclid and Sutherland aves. Phone 204/943-3958.* (1854) Oldest building in the original city of Winnipeg; first post office in western Canada. Displays and period-furnished rooms depict daily life in the Red River Settlement. (June-Aug: Wed-Sun 10 am-5 pm) **FREE**

Royal Canadian Mint. *520 Lagimodière Blvd, Winnipeg (R2C 0A1). Phone 204/257-3359.* (1976) One of the world's most modern mints; striking glass tower, landscaped interior courtyard. Tour allows viewing of coining process; coin museum. (May-Aug: Mon-Fri 9 am-4 pm; Sept-Apr: Mon-Fri 10 am-2 pm; closed holidays) Tours by appointment only. **$**

Royal Winnipeg Ballet. *Centennial Concert Hall, 555 Main St, Winnipeg (R3B 1C3). Phone 204/956-0183; toll-free 800/667-4792. www.rwb.org.* This nationally acclaimed company performs throughout the year in Winnipeg and also presents Ballet in the Park during the summer.

Seven Oaks House Museum. *115 Rupertsland Ave E, Winnipeg (R2C 0A1). In West Kildonan area. Phone 204/339-7429.* Oldest habitable house in Manitoba (1851). Log construction, original furnishings, housewares. Adjoining buildings include general store, post office. (Late May-Labor Day, daily 9 am-5 pm) **$**

St. Boniface Museum. *494 ave Taché, Winnipeg (R2H 2B2). Phone 204/237-4500.* (1846) Located in the largest French-Canadian community west of Québec, where Louis Riel, a founder of Manitoba, was born, this museum is housed in the oldest structure in the city, dating to the days of the Red River Colony; it's the largest oak-log construction in North America. (Daily 9 am-5 pm; no weekend hours in winter)

Winnipeg Art Gallery. *300 Memorial Blvd, Winnipeg (R3C 1V1). Phone 204/786-6641. www.wag.mb.ca.* Canada's first civic gallery (1912). Eight galleries present changing exhibitions of contemporary, historical, and decorative art, plus world's largest public collection of Inuit Art. Free admission charge Wednesday evening and all day Saturday. Programming includes tours, lectures, films, concerts. Restaurant. (Mid-June-early Sept: daily from 10 am; rest of year: Tues-Sun 11 am-5 pm, open until 9 pm Wed) **$$**

Winnipeg Symphony Orchestra. *Centennial Concert Hall, 555 Main St, Winnipeg (R3B 1C3). Phone 204/949-3950. www.wso.mb.ca.* Performances ranging from classical to pop to family-oriented music at Centennial Concert Hall. (May-Sept)

Special Events

Festival du Voyageur. *Voyageur Park, St. Joseph and Messager sts, Winnipeg (R2H 2C4). Phone 204/237-7692. www.festivalvoyageur.mb.ca.* In St. Boniface, Winnipeg's "French Quarter." Winter festival celebrating the French-Canadian voyageur and the fur trade era. Ten days in mid-Feb.

Folklorama. *183 Kennedy St, Winnipeg (R3C 1S6). Pavilions throughout city. Phone 204/982-6210; toll-free 800/665-0234. www.folklorama.com.* Multicultural festival featuring more than 40 pavilions. Singing, dancing, food, cultural displays. Aug.

Red River Exhibition. *3977 Portage Ave, Winnipeg (R3K 2E8). Phone 204/888-6990. www.redriverex.com.* Large event encompassing grandstand shows, band competitions, displays, agricultural exhibits, parade, entertainment, midway, petting zoo, shows, food. Late June-early July.

Winnipeg Folk Festival. *Birds Hill Provincial Park, 264 ave Taché, Winnipeg (R2H 1Z9). 8 miles (13 kilometers) N on Hwy 59. Phone 204/231-0096. www.winnipegfolkfestival.ca.* More than 60 regional, national, and international artists perform; nine stages; children's village; evening concerts. Juried crafts exhibit and sale; international food village. Early July.

Winnipeg Fringe Theatre Festival. *Old Market Square, 174 Market Ave, Winnipeg (R3B 0P8). Phone 204/943-7464. www.mtc.mb.ca.* More than 100 theater companies perform during North America's second-largest Fringe Festival. July.

Limited-Service Hotels

★ ★ BEST WESTERN CHARTER HOUSE HOTEL. *330 York Ave, Winnipeg (R3C 0N9). Phone 204/942-0101; toll-free 800/780-7234; fax 204/956-0665.* 90 rooms, 5 story. Check-in 3 pm, check-out 11 am. Restaurant, bar. **$**

★ COMFORT INN. *1770 Sargent Ave, Winnipeg (R3H 0C8). Phone 204/783-5627; toll-free 800/228-5150; fax 204/783-5661. www.comfortinn.com.* 81 rooms, 2 story. Pets accepted, some restrictions. Check-out 11 am. **$**

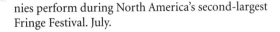

★ ★ DELTA WINNIPEG. *350 St. Mary Ave, Winnipeg (R3C 3J2). Phone 877/814-7706; toll-free 877/814-7706; fax 204/942-6491. www.deltahotels.com.* 392 rooms, 18 story. Check-out noon. Restaurant. Fitness room. Indoor pool, outdoor pool, children's pool, whirlpool. Airport transportation available. **$$**

★ ★ HOLIDAY INN. *2520 Portage Ave, Winnipeg (R3J 3T6). Phone 204/885-4478; toll-free 800/465-4329; fax 204/831-5734. www.holiday-inn.com/winnipeg-arpt.* 226 rooms, 15 story. Check-out 1 pm. Restaurant, bar. Children's activity center. Fitness room. Indoor pool, children's pool, whirlpool. Business center. **$$**

★ ★ RADISSON HOTEL DOWNTOWN. *288 Portage Ave, Winnipeg (R3C 0B8). Phone 204/956-0410; toll-free 800/333-3333; fax 204/947-1129. www.radisson.com.* 272 rooms, 29 story. Pets accepted. Check-out 1 pm. Restaurant, bar. Fitness room. Indoor pool. Business center. **$**

★ ★ VICTORIA INN HOTEL CONVENTION. *1808 Wellington Ave, Winnipeg (R3H 0G3). Phone 204/786-4801; fax 204/786-1329.* 288 rooms, 5 story. Pets accepted, some restrictions; fee. Check-out noon. Restaurant, bar. Indoor pool, whirlpool. Airport transportation available. **$**

Full-Service Hotels

★ ★ ★ THE FAIRMONT WINNIPEG. *2 Lombard Pl, Winnipeg (R3B 0Y3). Phone 204/957-1350; toll-free 800/257-7544; fax 204/956-1791. www.fairmont.com.* The Fairmont Winnipeg's stylish interiors and central location have earned it a loyal following among leisure and business travelers. The city's large historic district, cultural attractions, restaurants, shops, and businesses are all within walking distance from this hotel, located in the heart of downtown. The rooms and suites show off an unmistakable panache while remaining exceedingly comfortable. This hotel is perfectly poised to cater to business travelers, with spacious quarters, in-room technical amenities, and a professionally-staffed business center. The 21st-floor fitness center frames inspiring city views, while the spa helps visitors forget their urban warrior status. The Velvet Glove restaurant is an ideal place for business meetings or tête-à-têtes with inspired Canadian cuisine and an exceptional wine list. 340 rooms, 20 story. Check-out noon. Restaurant. Fitness room. Business center. **$$**

★ ★ ★ SHERATON WINNIPEG HOTEL. *161 Donald St, Winnipeg (R3C 1M3). Phone 204/942-5300; toll-free 800/463-6400; fax 204/943-7975. www.sheraton.com.* This hotel is conveniently located three blocks from the convention center. 271 rooms, 21 story. Pets accepted, some restrictions; fee. Check-out noon. Restaurant, bar. Indoor pool, whirlpool. **$$**

Restaurants

★ ★ AMICI. *326 Broadway, Winnipeg (R3C 0S5). Phone 204/943-4997. www.amiciwpg.com.* Italian menu. Dinner. Closed Sun; holidays. Bar. Children's menu. **$$$**

★ ★ HY'S STEAK LOFT. *216 Kennedy, Winnipeg (R3C 1T1). Phone 204/942-1000. www.hyssteakhouse.com.* Steak menu. Dinner. Closed holidays. Bar. **$$$**

★ ★ ICHIBAN JAPANESE STEAKHOUSE AND SUSHI BAR. *189 Carlton St, Winnipeg (R3C 3H7). Phone 204/925-7400.* Teppanyaki cooking. Japanese menu. Dinner. Closed holidays. Bar. **$$$**

Wisconsin

Virgin forests blotted out the sky over Wisconsin when the first French voyageurs arrived more than three centuries ago. Rich in natural resources, modern conservation concepts took strong root here; Wisconsin's 15,000 lakes and 2,200 streams are teeming with fish, and millions of acres of its publicly owned forest are abundant with game.

Population: 4,891,769
Area: 54,424 square miles
Elevation: 581-1,951 feet
Peak: Timms Hill (Price County)
Entered Union: May 29, 1848 (30th state)
Capital: Madison
Motto: Forward
Nickname: Badger State
Flower: Wood Violet
Bird: Robin
Tree: Sugar Maple
Fair: August in Milwaukee
Time Zone: Central
Web Site: www.travelwisconsin.com
Fun Fact: Wisconsin produces more milk than any other state.

People of many heritages have contributed to the state's colorful past, busy industries, and productive farms. Wisconsin is famous for the breweries of Milwaukee, great universities, forests, paper mills, dairy products, and diverse vacation attractions.

Wisconsin is the birthplace of the statewide primary election law, worker's compensation law, unemployment compensation, and many other reforms that have since been widely adopted. It produced Senator Robert M. La Follette, one of the 20th century's foremost progressives, and many other honored citizens.

The Badger State acquired its nickname during the lead rush of 1827, when miners built their homes by digging into the hillsides like badgers. It is "America's dairyland," producing much of the nation's milk and over 30 percent of all cheese consumed in the United States. It is a leader in the production of hay, cranberries, and ginseng, and harvests huge crops of peas, beans, carrots, corn, and oats. It is the leading canner of fresh vegetables and an important source of cherries, apples, maple syrup, and wood pulp. A great part of the nation's paper products, agricultural implements, and nonferrous metal products and alloys are manufactured here.

The Wisconsin summer is balmy, and the winter offers an abundance of activities, making the state a year-round vacationland that lures millions of visitors annually. They find a land of many contrasts: rounded hills and narrow valleys to the southwest, a huge central plain, rolling prairie in the southeast, and the north, majestic with forests, marshes, and lakes.

Native Americans called this land *Ouisconsin* ("where the waters gather"). French explorer Jean Nicolet, seeking the Northwest Passage to the Orient, landed near Green Bay in 1634 and greeted what he thought were Asians. These Winnebago made a treaty of alliance with the French, and for the next 125 years a brisk trade in furs developed. The British won Wisconsin from the French in 1760 and lost it to the United States after the American Revolution.

Shortly before Wisconsin became a state it was a battleground in the Black Hawk War. After the campaign, word spread of the state's beauty and fertile land in the East, and opened the doors to a flood of settlers.

Calendar Highlights

JANUARY

World Championship Snowmobile Derby *(Eagle River). Phone 715/479-4424 or toll-free 800/359-6315.* More than 300 professional racers fight for the championship.

FEBRUARY

American Birkebeiner *(Hayward). Phone 715/634-5025 or toll-free 800/872-2753.* Cross-country ski race (337 miles). More than 6,000 participants from 40 states and 15 countries.

Winter Festival *(Cedarburg). Phone 262/377-9620 or toll-free 800/827-8020.* Ice carving and snow sculpture contests, bed and barrel races across ice, winter softball and volleyball, Alaskan malamute weight pull, snow goose egg hunt; torchlight parade, horse-drawn sleigh rides.

MAY

Festival of Blossoms *(Door County). Phone 920/743-4456 or toll-free 800/527-3529.* Month-long celebration of spring, with a million daffodils and blooming cherry and apple trees.

Great Wisconsin Dells Balloon Rally *(Wisconsin Dells). Phone toll-free 800/223-3557.* More than 90 hot air balloons participate in contests and mass liftoffs.

JUNE

Summerfest *(Milwaukee). Henry Maier Festival Grounds. Phone toll-free 800/273-3378. www.summerfest.com.* Eleven different music stages; food.

Walleye Weekend Festival and Mercury Marine National Walleye Tournament *(Fond du Lac). Lakeside Park. Phone 920/923-6555 or toll-free 800/937-9123.* Fish fry, food, entertainment, sports competitions.

JULY

Art Fair on the Square *(Madison). Capitol Concourse. Phone 608/257-0158.* Exhibits by 500 artists and craftspersons; food, entertainment.

AUGUST

EAA (Experimental Aircraft Association) International Fly-In Convention *(Oshkosh). Wittman Regional Airport. Phone 920/235-3007 (air show lodging info) or 920/426-4800 (general information). www.wittmanairport.com.* One of the nation's largest aviation events. More than 500 educational forums, workshops, and seminars; daily air shows; exhibits; more than 12,000 aircraft.

Wisconsin State Fair *(Milwaukee). State Fair Park in West Allis. Phone 414/266-7000.* Entertainment, 12 stages, auto races, exhibits, contests, demonstrations, fireworks.

The rich lead mines brought another wave of settlers, and the forests attracted lumbermen—both groups remained to till the soil or work in the factories.

Diversified industry, enhanced recreational facilities, the trade opportunities opened by the St. Lawrence Seaway, and enlightened agricultural techniques promise continuing prosperity for Wisconsin.

When to Go/Climate

Cool forests and lake breezes make northern Wisconsin summers pleasant and comfortable, while the southern farmland is often hot. Temperatures from northern to southern Wisconsin can vary as much as 20° F. Winters are often snowy and harsh statewide. Fall is the best time to visit, with brilliant foliage, harvests, and festivals.

AVERAGE HIGH/LOW TEMPERATURES (° F)

Green Bay

Jan 23/6	**May** 67/44	**Sept** 69/49
Feb 27/10	**June** 76/54	**Oct** 57/39
Mar 39/21	**July** 81/59	**Nov** 42/27
Apr 54/34	**Aug** 78/57	**Dec** 28/13

Milwaukee

Jan 26/12	**May** 64/45	**Sept** 71/53
Feb 30/16	**June** 75/55	**Oct** 59/42
Mar 40/26	**July** 80/62	**Nov** 45/31
Apr 53/36	**Aug** 78/61	**Dec** 31/18

Parks and Recreation

Water-related activities, hiking, bicycling, riding, various other sports, picnicking and visitor centers, as well as camping, are available in many of these areas. From May-October, camping is limited to three weeks; fee is $10-$12/unit/night; electricity $5. Camps can be taken down or set up between 6 am and 11 pm. Motor vehicle sticker for nonresidents: daily $10; annual $30; residents: daily $5; annual $20. For additional information contact Wisconsin Department of Natural Resources, Bureau of Parks & Recreation, PO Box 7921, Madison 53707. Phone 608/266-2181.

FISHING AND HUNTING

Wisconsin waters boast trout, muskellunge, northern pike, walleye, large and smallmouth bass, and panfish throughout the state; salmon is primarily found in the Lake Superior/Michigan area; lake sturgeon in Winnebago Waters/St. Croix/Wisconsin, Chippewa, Flambeau, and Menominee rivers; and catfish in Wolf, Mississippi, and Wisconsin rivers. Inquire for seasons and bag limits.

Wisconsin, eager to have visitors share the abundance of fish in the lakes and streams, posts few barriers. The state is very conservation-minded; regulations have been developed to ensure equally good fishing in the future. Fishing licenses: nonresident over 16, four-day $18; 15-day $24; annual $40; family 15-day, $40; annual family $65; licenses expire March 31. Two-day Great Lakes, $14. A trout stamp must be purchased by all licensed anglers in order to fish for trout in inland waters, $7.25. A salmon and trout stamp is required, except those having a two-day license, to fish the Great Lakes, $10. For further information, contact the Wisconsin Department of Natural Resources, Customer Service and Licensing, PO Box 7921, Madison 53707; phone 608/266-2621; www.dnr.state.wi.us.

Wisconsin is a premier state in which to hunt deer, bears, waterfowl, pheasants, turkeys, geese, and other small game. The Department of Natural Resources issues separate pamphlets on trapping big game, pheasant, and waterfowl hunting regulations. Hunting licenses: nonresident, furbearer $160; small game $80; deer (archery or gun) $160; five-day small game $50. Hunting migratory birds requires a special federal stamp ($15), obtainable at any post office, as well as a state stamp ($7). A pheasant stamp ($7.25) is also required. Special hunting regulations apply to minors; contact Department of Natural Resources for further information. *Note:* License fees are subject to change.

Driving Information

Safety belts are mandatory for all persons in designated seating spaces within a vehicle. Children under 4 years of age must be in an approved safety seat anywhere in a vehicle. Children ages 4-8 may use regulation safety belts. For more information, phone 608/266-3212.

INTERSTATE HIGHWAY SYSTEM

The following alphabetical listing of Wisconsin towns in this book shows that these cities are within 10 miles of the indicated interstate highways. Check a highway map for the nearest exit.

Highway Number	Cities/Towns within 10 Miles
Interstate 43	Cedarburg, Green Bay, Manitowoc, Milwaukee, Port Washington, Sheboygan.
Interstate 90	Baraboo, Beloit, Janesville, La Crosse, Madison, Mauston, Portage, Sparta, Tomah, Wisconsin Dells.
Interstate 94	Baraboo, Black River Falls, Eau Claire, Hudson, Kenosha, Madison, Milwaukee, Oconomowoc, Portage, Racine, Tomah, Watertown, Waukesha, Wauwatosa, Wisconsin Dells.

Additional Visitor Information

The Wisconsin Department of Tourism, PO Box 7976, Madison 53707; phone 608/266-2161, toll-

THE CRANBERRY HIGHWAY

Cranberries are the big money crop around Wisconsin Rapids. In the fall, mechanical harvesters sweep across 13,000 acres of cranberry marshes, dislodging the bright red berries that then float to the surface, creating a crimson sea of fruit. Although fall is an ideal time to visit, you can travel "the Cranberry Highway" year-round, stopping perhaps for a cranberry shake or a cranberry muffin or to visit a cheese factory for "cran-jack" cheese, studded with dried fruit. The full route runs approximately 40 miles and includes visits to numerous marsh areas, historic sites, museums, markets, shops, and restaurants. A south loop covers about 70 miles and is described here.

Begin in downtown Wisconsin Rapids at Paul Gross Jewelers (241 Oak St), where you can pick up a gold cranberry rake necklace complete with ruby cranberry. Then stop at South Wood County Historical Museum (3rd St between E Grand Ave and Riverview Expy) for a look at local history and changing displays, including a cranberry exhibit.

Continue on 3rd Street to Highway 54, which traces the Wisconsin River through Port Edwards. Stop at Alexander House Art & History Center (1131 Wisconsin River Dr), a combination art gallery and historical museum that is located in a stately colonial home along the banks of the river. Continue on Highway 54 and take County D south. Along the way, visit Glacial Lake Cranberries for a thorough introduction to Wisconsin's cranberry industry, which produces about 150 million pounds of fruit annually. Operated by third-generation cranberry farmers, it offers Marsh Tours year-round. A gift shop carries fresh fruit in season, and the Stone Cottage accommodates up to four guests. From here, continue south on County D, then east on Highway 173 to County Z south. At the intersection of County Z and Wakely Road in Nekoosa, find Historic Point Basse, an 1837 living history site that stages events throughout the year. It protects an endangered historic site placed on the National Register of Historic Places in 2001.

Golfers tired of shelling out outrageous green fees enjoy the lower costs at the region's championship courses. Lake Arrowhead at Nekoosa (1 mile off Hwy 13), with two challenging 18-hole courses, is ranked by Golf Digest as one of the nation's best golf values. It charges only $60 per round (with cart). Another golfing bargain awaits at The Ridges (east on County Z), where greens fees are only $56 (with cart) for 18 holes featuring challenging elevations and plenty of water and woods–white birch, green willows, and towering pines. From the clubhouse restaurant, watch golfers tee off on the back nine with a shot from an 80-foot-high ridge into a valley flanked by tall pines and a twisting creek.

A shopping find is Studio of Good Earth, located on 52nd Street, just 1/2 mile north of Highway 73. Operated by William and Annette Gudim, the studio offers the work of more than 45 artists and crafters, ranging from paintings, calligraphy, and baskets to weavings, handmade paper, and stained glass. Included are Annette's pottery and William's woodwork. Find lots of bird feeders and birdbaths among quality traditional and contemporary arts and crafts at prices based on the local economy–remarkably lower than those at well-traveled resorts. Take time to enjoy the Gudims' beautiful flower gardens.

For an aerial view of cranberry marshes, head for Wings Air Charter (at Alexander Field). Short flights cost $10 per person ($55 for a 30-minute flight for three persons). From Airport Avenue, head north on Lincoln Street to Grand Avenue to find lodgings at the Hotel Mead and Conference Center (451 E Grand Ave), where a $9 million expansion added an 89-room, four-story tower, bringing the total number of rooms to 157. All new guest rooms have refrigerators, coffee makers, hair dryers, and desks with dataports. The Mead has an indoor swimming pool and sauna, a fitness center, two restaurants, and a lively bar with entertainment. Breakfast in the Grand Avenue Grill features cranberry French toast.

Local eateries in Wisconsin Rapids include Harriet's Kitchen Nook (9041 Hwy 13 S), which, contrary to its blue-painted tables and cutesy motif, has true diner lineage. It's a good spot to find breakfast: pancakes, eggs, and superb hash browns (this is also a potato-growing country). It is derigueur to include a glass of cranberry juice with breakfast. Another local time-warp eatery is Herschleb's (640 16th St N), where carhops serve burgers, homemade soups (try chicken with dumplings), and their own brand of ice cream (which in cranberry harvest season includes cranberry swirl flavor). This is an excellent spot for shakes, malts, and floats. Prices are retro, too. **(Approximately 40 miles)** free 800/372-2737 (northern IL, IA, MI, MN, and WI only) or toll-free 800/432-8747 (anywhere in US); www.travelwisconsin.com. You can order, free of charge, a variety of publications covering sports, attractions, events, and recreation. When requesting information, ask for *Wisconsin Travel Guide, Events/Recreation Guide, Heritage Traveler, Attractions Guide and Highway Map, Golf Guide, Lodging Directory,* or *Campground Directory.*

There are several tourist information centers in Wisconsin. Visitors who stop will find helpful information and brochures. They are located in Beloit (I-90); Genoa City (Hwy 12), (seasonal); Grant County (Hwy 151/61), (seasonal); Hudson (I-94); Hurley (Hwy 51); Kenosha (I-94); La Crosse (I-90); Madison (201 W Washington Ave); Prairie du Chien (211 Main St), (seasonal); Superior (305 E 2nd St), (seasonal). There is also an information center in Chicago, Illinois (140 S Dearborn St, Room 104).

Wisconsin offers a fabulous system of bicycle routes. To order a free guide to bicycling in Wisconsin, contact the Department of Tourism, PO Box 7976, Madison 53707; phone 608/266-2161, toll-free 800/432-8747, or toll-free 800/372-2737; www.travelwisconsin.com.

Algoma (C-5)

See also Green Bay, Sturgeon Bay

Settled 1818
Population 3,353
Elevation 600 ft
Area Code 920
Zip 54201
Information Algoma Area Chamber of Commerce, 1226 Lake St; phone 920/487-2041 or toll-free 800/498-4888
Web Site www.algoma.org

What to See and Do

Ahnapee State Trail. *Hwy S and Hwy M, Algoma (54201). Phone 920/487-2041; toll-free 800/498-4888.* More than 15 miles of hiking and biking along the Ahnapee River; snowmobiling. (Daily) **FREE**

Kewaunee County Historical Museum. *Court House Sq, 613 Dodge St, Kewaunee (54216). 10 miles S via Hwy 42. Phone 920/388-4410.* Century-old building; displays include a letter written by George Washington, wood carvings, child's playroom with toys of 1890-1910 period, sheriff's office, ship models, old farm tools, and artifacts. (Memorial Day-Labor Day: daily; rest of year: by appointment) **DONATION**

Von Stiehl Winery. *115 Navarino St, Algoma (54201). Phone 920/487-5208; toll-free 800/955-5208. www.vonstiehl.com.* Housed in a 140-year-old brewery. Wine, cheese, and jelly tasting at the end of tour. Under 21 only with adult (wine tasting); no smoking. Gift shop; candy shop features homemade fudge. (May-Oct: daily; rest of year: Fri-Sun) **$**

Limited-Service Hotel

★ RIVER HILLS MOTEL. *820 N Water St, Algoma (54201). Phone 920/487-3451; toll-free 800/236-3451; fax 920/487-2031.* 30 rooms. Pets accepted; fee. Check-out 11 am. **$**

Restaurant

★ CAPTAIN'S TABLE. *133 N Water St (Hwy 42 N), Algoma (54201). Phone 920/487-5304.* American menu. Breakfast, lunch, dinner, brunch. Bar. Children's menu. Casual attire. **$**

Antigo (C-4)

See also Wausau

Settled 1876
Population 8,276
Elevation 1,498 ft
Area Code 715
Zip 54409
Information Chamber of Commerce, 329 Superior St, PO Box 339; phone 715/623-4134 or toll-free 888/526-4523
Web Site www.antigo-city.org

What to See and Do

F. A. Deleglise Cabin. *404 Superior St, Antigo (54409). 7th and Superior sts, on grounds of public library. Phone 715/627-4464.* (1878) First home of city's founder. (May-Sept, Wed-Mon) **DONATION**

Restaurant

★ BLACKJACK STEAK HOUSE. *800 S Superior St, Antigo (54409). Phone 715/623-2514.* Seafood, steak menu. Dinner. Closed Tues; Dec 24-25. Bar. Children's menu. **$$**

Appleton (D-4)

See also Green Bay, Neenah-Menasha, Oshkosh

Settled 1848
Population 65,695
Elevation 780 ft
Area Code 920
Information Fox Cities Convention & Visitors Bureau, 3433 W College Ave, 54914; phone 920/734-3358 or toll-free 800/236-6673
Web Site www.appleton.org

Located astride the Fox River, Appleton's economy centers around the manufacture of paper and paper products and insurance and service industries.

What to See and Do

★ Charles A. Grignon Mansion. *1313 Augustine St, Kaukauna (54130). 8 miles E off Hwy 41. Phone 920/766-3122.* (1837) First deeded property in Wisconsin (1793); restored Greek Revival house of one of the area's early French-Canadian settlers; period furnishings, displays; summer events. Picnic area. Tours. (June-Aug: daily; rest of year: by appointment) **$$**

Fox Cities Children's Museum. *100 W College Ave, Appleton (54911). In Avenue Mall. Phone 920/734-3226. www.kidmuseum.org.* Hands-on exhibits; climb through a human heart, play in the New Happy Baby Garden, or visit Grandma's Attic. (Tues-Thurs 9 am-5 pm; Fri 9 am-8 pm; Sat 10 am-5 pm; Sun noon-5 pm; closed Mon) **$**

Lawrence University. *706 E College Ave, Appleton (54912). At Lawe St. Phone 920/832-6500. www.lawrence.edu.* (1847) (1,400 students) Merged in 1964 with Milwaukee-Downer College. Main Hall (1854), College Avenue. For campus tours contact Admissions Office. On campus is

Music-Drama Center. *420 E College Ave, Appleton (54912). Phone 920/832-6611.* (1959) Quarters for Conservatory of Music, concert hall, practice rooms, classrooms; Cloak Theater, an experimental arena playhouse; Stansbury Theater. Concerts and plays (academic year). Summer theater (mid-June-Aug), phone 920/734-8797.

Wriston Art Center. *613 E College Ave, Appleton (54912). 1/2 block S of College Ave on Lawe St. Phone 920/832-6621.* Traveling exhibits, lectures, and art shows. (Sept-May, Tues-Sun; schedule may vary; closed holidays) **FREE**

Outagamie Museum. *330 E College Ave, Appleton (54911). Phone 920/735-9370.* Features local technology and industrial accomplishments. Major exhibit themes include electricity, papermaking, agriculture, transportation, communications. Also an extensive exhibit devoted to Appleton native Harry Houdini. (Sept-May: Tues-Sun; rest of year: daily; closed holidays) **$$**

Limited-Service Hotels

★★ BEST WESTERN MIDWAY HOTEL. *3033 W College Ave, Appleton (54914). Phone 920/731-4141; toll-free 800/482-3879; fax 920/731-6343. www.bestwestern.com.* 105 rooms, 2 story. Pets accepted; fee. Complimentary continental breakfast. Check-in 3 pm, check-out 11 am. High-speed Internet access, wireless Internet access. Restaurant, bar. Fitness room. Indoor pool, whirlpool. Airport transportation available. Business center. **$**

★★ HOLIDAY INN. *150 S Nicolet Rd, Appleton (54914). Phone 920/735-9955; toll-free 800/465-4329; fax 920/735-0309. www.holiday-inn.com.* 228 rooms, 8 story. Check-in 4 pm, check-out noon. High-speed Internet access, wireless Internet access. Restaurant, bar. Fitness room, fitness classes available. Indoor pool, whirlpool. Airport transportation available. Business center. **$**

★★ RADISSON PAPER VALLEY HOTEL. *333 W College Ave, Appleton (54913). Phone 920/733-8000; toll-free 800/333-3333; fax 920/733-9220. www.radisson.com.* 390 rooms, 7 story. Check-in 3 pm, check-out noon. High-speed Internet access. Four restaurants, two bars. Fitness room. Indoor pool, whirlpool. Airport transportation available. Business center. **$**

★ WOODFIELD SUITES. *3730 W College Ave, Appleton (54914). Phone 920/734-7777; fax 920/734-0049.* 98 rooms, 2 story, all suites. Pets accepted; fee.

Complimentary continental breakfast. Check-in 2 pm, check-out noon. High-speed Internet access, wireless Internet access. Fitness room. Indoor pool, whirlpool. Airport transportation available. **$**

Restaurant

★ ★ GEORGE'S STEAK HOUSE. *2208 S Memorial Dr, Appleton (54915). Phone 920/733-4939; fax 920/733-3731. www.foodspot.com/georges.* Steak menu. Lunch, dinner. Closed Sun; holidays. Bar. Children's menu. Casual attire. Reservations recommended. **$$**

Ashland (A-2)

See also Bayfield

Founded 1854
Population 8,695
Elevation 671 ft
Area Code 715
Zip 54806
Information Ashland Area Chamber of Commerce, 320 4th Ave W, PO Box 746; phone 715/682-2500 or toll-free 800/284-9484
Web Site www.visitashland.com

Located on Chequamegon Bay, which legend says is the "shining big sea water" of Longfellow's *Hiawatha,* Ashland is a port for Great Lakes ships delivering coal for the Midwest. It is also a gateway to the Apostle Islands. Papermaking machinery, fabricated steel, and other industrial products provide a diversified economy.

What to See and Do

Copper Falls State Park. *Hwy 169 and Copper Falls Rd, Mellen (54546). S off Hwy 13, 169. Phone 715/274-5123.* This 2,500-acre park has more than 8 miles of river; nature and hiking trails provide spectacular views of the river gorge and thc falls. Swimming, fishing, canoeing; backpacking, cross-country skiing, picnicking, playground, concession, primitive and improved camping (hook-ups, dump station). (Daily) **$$$**

Fishing. In Chequamegon Bay and in 65 trout streams and inland lakes (license and stamp required). Ice fishing is a popular winter sport. Also spring smelting and deep sea trolling in Lake Superior. Public boat landing at Sunset Park; RV park adjacent to Sunset Park (hook-ups, dump station).

Northland College. *1411 Ellis Ave, Ashland (54806). Phone 715/682-1699.* (1892) (750 students) Founded to bring higher education to the people of the isolated logging camps and farm communities of northern Wisconsin. On campus are Sigurd Olson Environmental Institute, in an earth-sheltered, solar-heated building; and historic Wheeler Hall (1892), constructed of brownstone from the nearby Apostle Islands.

Special Event

Bay Days Festival. *101 Lake Shore Dr W, Ashland (54806). Phone toll-free 800/284-9484.* Sailboat regatta, art fair, bicycle and foot races, ethnic food booths, entertainment, dancing. Third weekend in July.

Limited-Service Hotels

★ ★ BEST WESTERN LAKE SUPERIOR INN. *30600 Hwy 2, Ashland (54806). Phone 715/682-5235; toll-free 800/452-7749; fax 715/682-4730. www.bestwestern.com.* 64 rooms, 2 story. Check-in 2 pm, check-out 11 am. Restaurant, bar. Indoor pool, whirlpool. **$**

★ ★ HOTEL CHEQUAMEGON. *101 W Lakeshore Dr, Ashland (54806). Phone 715/682-9095; toll-free 800/946-5555; fax 715/682-9410.* At this hotel on the shores of Lake Superior, guests will find a gracious home with refined air, a classic setting, and elegant dining. 65 rooms, 3 story. Check-out 11 am. Restaurant, bar. Indoor pool, whirlpool. **$**

Baileys Harbor (Door County) (C-5)

Settled 1851
Population 780
Elevation 595 ft
Area Code 920
Zip 54202
Information Door County Chamber of Commerce, 1015 Green Bay Rd, PO Box 406, Sturgeon Bay 54235; phone 920/743-4456 or toll-free 800/527-3529
Web Site www.doorcountyvacations.com

Baileys Harbor is the oldest village in Door County, with one of the best harbors on the east shore. Range lights, built in 1870 to guide ships into the harbor, still operate. Its waters feature charter fishing for trout and salmon.

What to See and Do

Bjorklunden. *7603 Chapel Ln, Baileys Harbor (54202). Hwy 57, 1 mile S of Baileys Harbor. Phone 920/839-2216.* A 425-acre estate, owned by Lawrence University (Appleton), with a replica of a Norwegian wooden chapel (stavkirke). The chapel was handcrafted by the original owners, the Boynton family, during the summers of 1939-1947. Seminars in the humanities are held on the estate each summer. Tours of chapel. (Mid-June-Aug, Mon, Wed) **$$**

Kangaroo Lake. *2799 N Kangaroo Lake Dr, Baileys Harbor (54202). S on Hwy 57.* Swimming, fishing, boating; picnicking.

Special Event

Baileys Harbor Brown Trout Tournament. *Phone 920/743-4456.* This event has developed into one of the premier fishing contests on Lake Michigan, and many Great Lakes anglers view it as the "kick off" to their season of fishing. Late Apr.

Limited-Service Hotel

★ ★ GORDON LODGE. *1420 Pine Dr, Baileys Harbor (54202). Phone 920/839-2331; toll-free 800/830-6235; fax 920/839-2450. www.gordonlodge.com.* Resting among an evergreen forest surrounded by Lake Michigan, this hotel is a nature enthusiast's home away from home. 40 rooms. Closed mid-Oct-mid-May. Complimentary full breakfast. Check-in 4 pm, check-out 11 am. Restaurant, bar. Beach. Indoor pool, whirlpool. Tennis. **$$**

Restaurants

★ ★ COMMON HOUSE. *8041 Hwy 57, Baileys Harbor (54202). Phone 920/839-2708; fax 920/839-2708.* Old-fashioned wood stove in dining room. American menu. Dinner. Bar. Children's menu. **$$$**

★ SANDPIPER. *8166 Hwy 57, Baileys Harbor (54202). Phone 920/839-2528.* American menu. Breakfast, lunch, dinner. Closed Nov-Apr. Children's menu. Casual attire. Outdoor seating. **$$**

Baraboo (E-3)

See also Devil's Lake State Park, Portage, Prairie du Sac, Reedsburg, Wisconsin Dells

Founded 1830
Population 9,203
Elevation 894 ft
Area Code 608
Zip 53913
Information Chamber of Commerce, PO Box 442; phone 608/356-8333 or toll-free 800/227-2266
Web Site www.baraboo.com/chamber

A center for the distribution of dairy products, Baraboo is a neatly ordered town of lawns, gardens, parks, homes, and factories. The city is the original home of the Ringling Brothers and Gollmar circuses and still holds memories of its circus-town days. It was founded by Jean Baribeau as a trading post for the Hudson's Bay Company. Beautiful spring-fed Devil's Lake is 3 miles south of town.

What to See and Do

Circus World Museum. *550 Water St, Baraboo (53913). Phone 608/356-8341. www.circusworldmuseum.com.* Has 50 acres and eight buildings of circus lore; original winter quarters of Ringling Brothers Circus. Live circus acts under "Big Top," daily circus parade, display of circus parade wagons, steam calliope concerts, P. T. Barnum sideshow, wild animal menagerie; carousel, band organ. Unloading circus train with Percheron horses; picnic facilities. (Early May-mid-Sept, daily) Exhibit Hall (Daily). **$$$$**

Devil's Head Resort. *S-6330 Bluff Rd, Merrimac (53561). 12 miles SE via Hwy 113, 78. Phone 608/493-2251. www.devils-head.com.* The area has triple, six double, three quad chairlifts; four rope tows; patrol, school, rentals, snowmaking; lodge, restaurants, cafeteria, and bars. Longest run 1 3/4 miles; vertical drop 500 feet. (Dec-Mar, daily) Night skiing; cross-country trails. Golf, 18 holes. Swimming pool, whirlpool. Tennis courts. Mountain biking. **$$$$**

Ho-Chunk Casino & Bingo. *S3214A Hwy 12, Baraboo (53913). Phone toll-free 800/746-2486. www.ho-chunk.com.* Gaming casino featuring 48 blackjack tables, 1,200 slot machines, video poker, and keno. (Daily, 24 hours)

International Crane Foundation. *E11376 Shady Lane Rd, Baraboo (53913). Phone 608/356-9462.* A nonprofit organization promoting the study and preservation of cranes. Features cranes and their chicks from all over the world. Movies, displays, nature trails. (May-Oct, daily) Guided tours (Memorial Day-Labor Day: daily; Sept-Oct: weekends) **$$$**

Mid-Continent Railway Museum. *E8948 Diamond Hill Rd, North Freedom (53951). 5 miles W via Hwy 136, then 2 miles S. Phone 608/522-4261.* Restored 1894 depot, complete 1900 rail environment; steam locomotives, coaches, steam wrecker, snowplows; artifacts and historical exhibits. Picnic area, gift shop. (Mid-May-Labor Day: daily; after Labor Day-mid-Oct: weekends only) One-hour steam train round-trip on a branch of C & NW Railroad line, which once served early iron mines and rock quarries. Leaves North Freedom (same dates as museum; four departures daily). **$$$**

Mirror Lake State Park. *E10320 Fern Dell Rd, Baraboo (53913). 2 miles W off Hwy 12. Phone 608/254-2333.* A 2,050-acre park with swimming, fishing, boating, canoeing; hiking, cross-country skiing, picnicking, playground, camping (fee; electric hook-ups, dump station). (Daily) **$**

Sauk County Historical Museum. *531 4th Ave, Baraboo (53913). Phone 608/356-1001.* Houses 19th-century household goods, textiles, toys, china, military items, pioneer collection, Native American artifacts, circus memorabilia, natural history display, photos; research library. (May-Oct, Tues-Sun) **$**

Limited-Service Hotel

★ BEST WESTERN. *725 W Pine (Hwy 12), West Baraboo (53913). Phone 608/356-1100; toll-free 800/831-3881; fax 608/356-4585. www.bestwestern.com.* 82 rooms. Check-in 3 pm, check-out 11 am. Whirlpool. **$**

Full-Service Hotel

★ ★ HO-CHUNK HOTEL & CASINO. *S3214 Hwy 12, Baraboo (53913). Phone 608/356-6210; toll-free 800/746-2486; fax 608/355-4035. www.ho-chunk.com.* 315 rooms. Check-in 3 pm, check-out noon. Five restaurants, three bars. Children's activity center. Fitness room. Airport transportation available. Casino. **$$**

Bayfield (A-2)

See also Ashland

Population 686
Elevation 700 ft
Area Code 715
Zip 54814
Information Chamber of Commerce, 42 S Broad St, PO Box 138; phone 715/779-3335 or toll-free 800/447-4094
Web Site www.bayfield.org

What to See and Do

Apostle Islands National Lakeshore. *415 Washington Ave, Bayfield (54814). N and E off Bayfield Peninsula. Phone 715/779-3397.* Eleven miles of mainland shoreline and 21 islands of varying size. The lakeshore area features hiking, boating, fishing; primitive campsites on 18 islands. Two visitor centers, in Bayfield (daily) and at Little Sand Bay (Memorial Day-Sept), 13 miles NW of Bayfield. National Lakeshore Headquarters/Visitor Center (daily; free). Boat trips provided by

Apostle Islands Cruise Service. *City Dock, Rittenhouse Ave, Bayfield (54814). Phone 715/779-3925.* Lake Superior cruises to Apostle Islands on the *Island Princess* (May-early Oct, departures daily); also Stockton Island shuttle with Raspberry Island Lighthouse Adventure: two-hour layover and naturalist hike. Reservations advised, inquire for schedule. **$$$$**

Lake Superior Big Top Chautauqua. *3 miles S on Hwy 13, then W on Ski Hill Rd. Phone 715/373-5552; toll-free 888/244-8368.* This outdoor theater features folk and bluegrass performances, musicals, and theater pieces. (June-Labor Day, Wed-Sat evenings; some Tues, Sun, and matinee performances)

Madeline Island. Part of island group but not under federal jurisdiction. 14 miles long, has 45 miles of roads. Off the dock at La Pointe is

Madeline Island Ferry Line. *1 Washington Ave, Bayfield (54814). Phone 715/747-2051.* The *Island Queen, Nichevo II,* and the *Madeline Bayfield* make frequent trips. (Apr-Jan, daily) **$$**

Madeline Island Historical Museum. *Col. Wood Ave and Main St, Bayfield (54814). Phone 715/747-2415.* Located near the site of an American Fur Company post and housed in a single building combining four pioneer log structures. (Late May-early Oct, daily; fee) There are motels, housekeeping cottages, and restaurants on the island. Guided bus tours. Marina; camping in two parks, cross-country skiing.

Mount Ashwabay Ski Area. *3 miles S on Hwy 13. Phone 715/779-3227.* T-bar, four rope tows; patrol, school, rentals; snow-making machine; restaurant, cafeteria, concession, bar. Longest run 1,500 feet; vertical drop 317 feet. (Dec-Mar, Wed, Sat-Sun; Christmas week, daily) Half-day rates; night skiing (Wed, Sat); cross-country skiing (Tues-Sun), 24 miles of trails.

Special Events

Apple Festival. *42 S Broad St, Bayfield (54814). Phone toll-free 800/447-4094.* For three days, orchard owners, artists, musicians, street entertainers, crafters and festival food vendors line the historic streets of this quaint fishing village. First full weekend in Oct.

Bayfield Festival of Arts. *Memorial Park, 2 E Front St, Bayfield (54814). Phone toll-free 800/447-4094.* The Bayfield Festival of Arts has been held for over 40 years on Lake Superior. Artists and crafters from across the Midwest gather in Bayfield's picturesque waterfront park to display their work. Last full weekend in July.

Great Schooner Race. *Memorial Park, 2 E Front St, Bayfield (54814). Phone toll-free 800/447-4094.* Last weekend in Sept.

Run on Water. *Bayfield Lakeside Pavilion, 2 E Front St, Bayfield (54814). Phone toll-free 800/447-4094.* When Lake Superior freezes there is no better way to celebrate the winter or the road between Bayfield and Madeline Island than to run across. First Sat in Feb.

Sailboat Race Week. *Bayfield Lakeside Pavilion, 2 E Front St, Bayfield (54814). Phone toll-free 800/447-4094. www.bayfieldraceweek.org.* As Lake Superior's premier sailboat regatta, this is the high point of sailboat racing on Lake Superior. About 40 boats and over 400 sailors from throughout the upper Midwest and Canada participate in this event. First week in July.

Limited-Service Hotel

★ ★ BAYFIELD INN. *20 Rittenhouse Ave, Bayfield (54814). Phone 715/779-3363; toll-free 800/382-0995; fax 715/779-9810. www.bayfieldinn.com.* 21 rooms, 2 story. Complimentary continental breakfast. Check-in 3 pm, check-out 11 am. Restaurant. **$**

Full-Service Inn

★ ★ ★ OLD RITTENHOUSE INN. *301 Rittenhouse Ave, Bayfield (54814). Phone 715/779-5111; toll-free 800/779-2129; fax 715/779-5887. www.rittenhouseinn.com.* Travelers looking for something a little different can find it in the whimsical romance of this charming inn. Considered by many as the preferred lodging for romance and weekend getaways, this inn consists of two extraordinary Victorian homes and one charming cottage, all located just blocks from the historic district of downtown Bayfield. Guests will delight in the comfortably appointed guest rooms, with lovely antiques. 19 rooms, 3 story. Complimentary continental breakfast. Check-in 3:30 pm, check-out noon. Restaurant. **$**

Restaurant

★ ★ OLD RITTENHOUSE. *301 Rittenhouse Ave, Bayfield (54814). Phone 715/779-5111; toll-free 800/779-2129. www.rittenhouseinn.com.* Romantic and elegant dining at its finest. American menu. Breakfast, lunch, dinner. Children's menu. Casual attire. **$$$**

Beaver Dam (E-4)

See also Watertown, Waupun

Settled 1841
Population 14,196
Elevation 879 ft
Area Code 920
Zip 53916
Information Chamber of Commerce, 127 S Spring St; phone 920/887-8879
Web Site www.beaverdamchamber.com

What to See and Do

Beaver Dam Lake. *Hwy 33 and County B, Beaver Dam (53916). Phone 920/885-6766.* 14 miles long. Fishing for bullhead, perch, crappie, walleye, and northern pike; ice fishing, boating (docks, ramps), water-skiing; waterfowl hunting. (Daily) **FREE**

Dodge County Historical Museum. *105 Park Ave, Beaver Dam (53916). Phone 920/887-1266.* In 1890 Romanesque building; Chinese and Native American artifacts, spinning wheels, dolls. (Tues-Sat, afternoons; closed holidays) **FREE**

Special Events

Dodge County Fair. *Fairgrounds, W7435 Hwy 33 E, Beaver Dam (53916). 3 miles E on Hwy 33. Phone 920/885-3586.* Country artists, demo derby, pig races, and chain saw carver are some of the activities found at this county fair. Five days in mid-late Aug.

Swan City Car Show. *Swan City Park, S University and Mill St, Beaver Dam (53916). Phone 920/887-7000.* Antique and classic vehicles on display with over 100 trophies are awarded. Musical entertainment and food are part of the show. Father's Day.

Limited-Service Hotels

★ ★ **BEST WESTERN CAMPUS INN MOTOR LODGE.** *815 Park Ave, Beaver Dam (53916). Phone 920/887-7171; toll-free 800/572-4891; fax 920/887-7171. www.bestwestern.com.* 94 rooms, 4 story. Check-in 2 pm, check-out 11 am. Restaurant, bar. Indoor pool, whirlpool. **$**

★ **MAYVILLE INN.** *Hwy 28 W, Mayville (53050). Phone 920/387-1234; fax 920/387-1234. www.mayvilleinn.com.* 29 rooms, 2 story. Complimentary continental breakfast. Check-out 11 am. Bar. Whirlpool. **$**

Beloit (E-4)

See also Delavan, Fontana, Janesville; also see Rockford, IL

Settled 1836
Population 35,573
Elevation 750 ft
Area Code 608
Zip 53511
Information Convention and Visitors Bureau, 1003 Pleasant St; phone 608/365-4838 or toll-free 800/423-5648
Web Site www.visitbeloit.com

In 1837, the town of Colebrook, New Hampshire, moved almost en masse to this point at the confluence of Turtle Creek and Rock River. The community, successively known as Turtle, Blodgett's Settlement, and New Albany, was finally named Beloit in 1857. The New Englanders, determined to sustain standards of Eastern culture and education, founded Beloit Seminary soon after settling; this small coeducational school became Beloit College. Today, the city's economy centers around the college, food processing, and the production of heavy machinery.

What to See and Do

Angel Museum. *656 Pleasant St, Beloit (53511). Phone 608/362-9099.* Collection of 11,000 angels made from everything from leather to china. Oprah Winfrey has donated over 500 angels from her private collection. (Mon-Sat 10 am-5 pm; Sun afternoons; closed holidays) **$$**

Beloit College. *700 College St, Beloit (53511). On Hwy 51. Phone 608/363-2000.* (1846) (1,100 students) Noted for Theodore Lyman Wright Museum of Art (academic year, daily). Logan Museum of Anthropology has changing displays of Native American and Stone Age artifacts. Campus contains prehistoric mounds. Campus tours (by appointment).

Hanchett-Bartlett Homestead. *2149 St. Lawrence Ave, Beloit (53511). Phone 608/365-7835.* (1857) Restored historic limestone homestead on 15 acres is built in the transitional Greek Revival style, with Italianate details; restored in period colors. House contains furnishings of the mid-19th century; limestone barn houses collection of farm implements. On the grounds is a one-room schoolhouse (1880); picnic area. (June-Sept, Wed-Sun afternoons; also by appointment) **$**

Special Event

Riverfest. *Riverside Park, Hwys 81 and 51, Beloit (53511). Phone 608/365-4838.* Music festival with top-name performers; more than 50 bands featuring a variety of music. Food, carnival rides, children's entertainment. Mid-July.

Limited-Service Hotels

★ **HOLIDAY INN EXPRESS.** *2790 Milwaukee Rd, Beloit (53511). Phone 608/365-6000; toll-free 800/465-4329; fax 608/365-1974. www.holiday-inn.com.* Adjacent to a movie theater, this motel is easily accessible from I-90 and I-43. 73 rooms, 2 story. Complimentary continental breakfast. Check-in 2 pm, check-out noon. Fitness room. Indoor pool, whirlpool. **$**

★ ★ **RAMADA INN.** *200 Dearborn Ave, South Beloit (61080). Phone 815/389-3481; toll-free 800/272-6232; fax 815/389-1812. www.ramada.com.* 166 rooms, 2 story. Check-in 4 pm, check-out noon. Restaurant, bar. Fitness room. Indoor pool, whirlpool. Business center. **$**

Restaurant

★ ★ **BUTTERFLY CLUB.** *5246 E County Rd X, Beloit (53511). Phone 608/362-8577; fax 608/362-8277.* American menu. Dinner. Closed Mon; Jan 1, Dec 24-25. Bar. Children's menu. Outdoor seating. **$$**

Black River Falls (D-2)

See also Sparta, Tomah

Population 3,490
Elevation 796 ft
Area Code 715
Zip 54615
Information Black River Area Chamber of Commerce, 120 N Water St; phone 715/284-4658 or toll-free 800/404-4008
Web Site www.blackrivercountry.com

In 1819, when the Black River countryside was a wilderness of pine, one of the first sawmills in Wisconsin was built here. Among the early settlers were a group of Mormons from Nauvoo, Illinois. Conflict developed with local landowners, and the Mormons soon returned to Nauvoo. The seat of Jackson County, Black River Falls is situated on the Black River, which offers boating and canoeing. The area is also noted for deer hunting and winter sports.

What to See and Do

Black River Falls State Forest. *910 Hwy 54 E, Black River Falls (54615). 6 miles E on Hwy 54. Phone 715/284-1400.* A 66,000-acre forest. Swimming, fishing, boating, canoeing; hiking, cross-country skiing, snowmobiling, bridle trail, picnicking, playground, camping (fee). Lookout tower; abundant wildlife. Self-guided auto trail. All motor vehicles must have parking sticker. (Daily) **$$**

Thunderbird Museum. *N9517 Thunderbird Ln, Merrillan (54754). 10 miles NE via Hwy 12, County K exit at Merrillan. Phone 715/333-5841.* Exhibits include Native American artifacts dating back to paleolithic man, weapons, minerals, dolls, coins, stamps, art. (May-Sept, weekends or by appointment) **$$**

Special Event

Winnebago Powwow. *3 miles NE via Hwy 54, at Red Cloud Memorial Powwow Grounds. Phone 715/284-4658.* Dancing. Held twice annually: Sun-Mon, Memorial Day and Labor Day weekends.

Limited-Service Hotels

★ ★ **BEST WESTERN ARROWHEAD LODGE & SUITES.** *600 Oasis Rd, Black River Falls (54615). Phone 715/284-9471; toll-free 800/284-9471; fax 715/284-9664. www.bestwestern.com.* 143 rooms, 3 story. Pets accepted. Complimentary continental breakfast. Check-in 3 pm, check-out noon. Wireless Internet access. Restaurant, bar. Indoor pool, whirlpool. **$**

★ **DAYS INN.** *919 Hwy 54 E, Black River Falls (54615). Phone 715/284-4333; toll-free 800/356-8018; fax 715/284-9068. www.daysinn.com.* 86 rooms, 2 story. Pets accepted, some restrictions; fee. Complimentary continental breakfast. Check-in 3 pm, check-out noon. Indoor pool, whirlpool. **$**

Boulder Junction (B-3)

See also Eagle River, Land O Lakes, Manitowish Waters, Minocqua, Sayner, Woodruff

Population 1,000
Elevation 1,640 ft
Area Code 715
Zip 54512
Information Chamber of Commerce, PO Box 286; phone 715/385-2400 or toll-free 800/466-8759
Web Site www.boulderjet.org

This secluded little village within the Northern Highland-American Legion State Forest is the gateway to a vast recreational area with woodlands, scenic drives, streams, and several hundred lakes where fishing for muskellunge is excellent. Indeed, "Musky Capital of the World" is its registered trademark. Boulder Junction also offers various winter activities, including snowmobiling, cross-country skiing, and ice fishing. In nearby state nurseries, millions of young pine trees are raised and shipped all over the state for forest planting.

What to See and Do

Northern Highland-American Legion State Forest. *4125 CTH M, Boulder Junction (54512). Phone 715/385-3521.* A 225,000-acre forest with swimming beaches, water-skiing, fishing, boating, canoeing; hiking, cross-country skiing, snowmobiling, picnicking, improved and primitive camping (896 sites on lakes; dump station; fee), sites also along water trails. (Daily) **$$**

Special Event

Musky Jamboree/Arts and Crafts Fair. *W7435 Hwy 33 E, Boulder Junction (54512). Phone 715/385-2400.* Second Sun in Aug.

Restaurant

★★ **GUIDE'S INN.** *County Hwy M, Boulder Junction (54512). Phone 715/385-2233.* American menu. Dinner. Closed Sun; Easter, Thanksgiving, Dec 25. Bar. Children's menu. **$$**

Burlington (E-4)

See also Delavan, Elkhorn, Fontana, Lake Geneva, Racine

Settled 1835
Population 8,855
Elevation 766 ft
Area Code 262
Zip 53105
Information Chamber of Commerce, 112 E Chesnut St, PO Box 156; phone 262/763-6044
Web Site www.burlingtonareachamber.com

Originally called Foxville, Burlington was renamed for the city in Vermont by a group of settlers arriving in 1835. It is the home of the Liar's Club, an organization dedicated to the preservation of the art of telling tall tales. A prize is awarded each year to the contributor who submits the most incredible "stretcher."

What to See and Do

Green Meadows Farm. *33603 High Dr, Burlington (53105). 5 miles N via Hwy 36, 3 miles W of Waterford on Hwy 20. Phone 262/534-2891.* Operating farm offers daily guided tours; pony rides, tractor-drawn hayrides; more than 20 "hands-on" animal areas; picnic areas. (May-June: Tues-Sat; July-Labor Day: Oct, daily; closed Sept) Pumpkin picking in Oct. **$$$**

Historic Burlington. Visit 22 historic spots in the city, including the Lincoln Monument and the Meinhardt Homestead.

Spinning Top Exploratory Museum. *533 Milwaukee Ave, Burlington (53105). Phone 262/763-3946.* Exhibits and displays dealing with tops, yo-yos, gyroscopes; top games, demonstrations; 35 tops for hands-on experiments. Video presentations.

Tall Tales Trail. This 17-stop walking tour features tall tales preserved on plaques and mounted on public buildings and storefronts.

Special Events

Aquaducks Water Ski Show. *Fischer Park on Browns Lake, Burlington (53105). Phone 262/763-6044.* Performance each Sat evening; rain date Sun. June-Labor Day.

Chocolate City Festival. *112 E Chestnut St, Burlington (53105). Phone 262/763-3300.* Two-day, citywide celebration including arts and crafts fair (fee), parade, entertainment. Weekend after Mother's Day.

Limited-Service Hotel

★ **AMERICINN.** *2709 Brown's Lake Rd, Burlington (53813). Phone 262/534-2125; fax 262/534-5221. www.americinn.com.* 50 rooms, 2 story. Complimentary continental breakfast. Check-in 3 pm, check-out 11 am. Indoor pool, whirlpool. **$**

Cable (B-2)

See also Hayward

Population 817
Elevation 1,370 ft
Area Code 715
Zip 54821
Information Cable Area Chamber of Commerce, PO Box 217; phone 715/798-3833 or toll-free 800/533-7454
Web Site www.cable4fun.com

What to See and Do

Mount Telemark Ski Area. *3 miles E on County M. Phone 715/798-3999.* Area has two chairlifts, two T-bars, rope tow; alpine and nordic ski schools, rentals, patrol, snowmaking; nursery, restaurants, cafeteria, bar, lodge. Longest run 1/2 mile; vertical drop 370 feet. (Thanksgiving-Mar, daily) Cross-country trails (Dec-Mar, daily; rentals), more than 40 miles of trails. Hiking, bridle, and bicycle trails rest of year; also 18-hole golf, eight tennis courts (four indoor).

Cedarburg (E-5)

See also Milwaukee, Port Washington

Population 9,895
Elevation 780 ft
Area Code 262
Zip 53012
Information Chamber of Commerce, PO Box 104; phone 262/377-9620 or toll-free 800/237-2874
Web Site www.cedarburg.org

Cedarburg, surrounded by rich farmlands and protected forests and wetlands, has many beautiful old homes that were built in the 1800s. Many buildings in the historic downtown area have been restored.

What to See and Do

Cedar Creek Settlement and Winery. *N70W6340 Bridge Rd, Cedarburg (53012). Bridge Rd at N Washington. Phone 262/377-8020; toll-free 800/827-8020.* Stone woolen mill (1864) converted into a winery and houses shops, art studios, and restaurants. The winery makes strawberry, cranberry, and grape wines; museum of antique wine-making tools. (Daily; closed holidays) **$**

Special Events

Ozaukee County Fair. *Firemen's Park and County Grounds, W65N796 Washington Ave, Cedarburg (53012). Phone 262/377-9620.* Educational and commercial exhibits, carnival, entertainment. Late July-early Aug.

Stone and Century House Tour. *Cedarburg Cultural Center, W62N546 Washington, Cedarburg (53012). Phone 262/375-3676.* Tour of historic homes in the area. First full weekend in June.

Strawberry Festival. *W63N641 Washington Ave, Cedarburg (53012). Phone 262/377-9620.* Strawberry foods, contests, craft fair, entertainment. Fourth full weekend in June.

Wine and Harvest Festival. *Cedar Creek Winery, N70W6340 Bridge Rd #21, Cedarburg (53012). Phone 262/377-9620.* Grape-stomping contests, farmers' market, arts and crafts fair, scarecrow contest; entertainment, food. Third weekend in Sept.

Winter Festival. *W63N641 Washington Ave, Cedarburg (53012). Phone 262/377-9620; toll-free 800/827-8020.* Ice carving and snow sculpture contests, bed and barrel races across ice, winter softball and volleyball, Alaskan malamute weight pull, snow goose egg hunt; torchlight parade, horse-drawn sleigh rides. First full weekend in Feb.

Limited-Service Hotel

★ BEST WESTERN QUIET HOUSE & SUITES. *10330 N Port Washington Rd, Mequon (53092). Phone 262/241-3677; toll-free 800/780-7234; fax 262/241-3707. www.bestwestern.com.* 54 rooms, 2 story. Pets accepted, some restrictions; fee. Complimentary continental breakfast. Check-in 2 pm, check-out 11 am. High-speed Internet access. Fitness room. Indoor pool, outdoor pool, whirlpool. Airport transportation available. **$**

Specialty Lodging

The following lodging establishment is approved by Mobil Travel Guide, but due to its unique and individualized nature has not been given a traditional Mobil Star rating. Included in this listing you may find bed-and-breakfasts, limited-service inns, guest ranches, and other unique hotel properties.

WASHINGTON HOUSE INN. *W62N573 Washington Ave, Cedarburg (53012). Phone 262/375-3550; toll-free 800/554-4717; fax 262/375-9422. www.washingtonhouseinn.com.* Experience all the personal touches added to make this Victorian inn (1886) feel like home. Each of the rooms is furnished with antique appointments and down comforters and is named after one of the city's pioneers. 34 rooms, 3 story. Complimentary continental breakfast. Check-in 3 pm, check-out noon. Business center. **$**

Restaurants

★ KOWLOON. *W63N145 Washington Ave, Cedarburg (53012). Phone 262/375-3030; fax 262/375-3051.* Chinese menu. Lunch, dinner. Closed Mon. Bar. **$**

★ ★ **RIVERSITE.** *11120 N Cedarburg Rd, Mequon (53092). Phone 262/242-6050.* Seafood menu. Dinner. Closed Sun; holidays. Bar. **$$**

Chippewa Falls (C-2)

See also Eau Claire, Menomonie

Settled 1836
Population 12,727
Elevation 902 ft
Area Code 715
Zip 54729
Information Chamber of Commerce, 10 S Bridge St; phone 715/723-0331
Web Site www.chippewachamber.org

Water has replaced lumber as the prime natural resource of this city on the Chippewa River. Jean Brunet, a pioneer settler, built a sawmill and then a dam here. Soon the area was populated by lumberjacks. Today, hydroelectric power is channeled to the industries of Chippewa Falls, which has water noted for its purity.

What to See and Do

Brunet Island State Park. *23125 255th St, Cornell (54732). N via Hwy 53, then E on Hwy 64. Phone 715/239-6888.* A 1,032-acre river island park. Swimming, fishing (pier), boating, canoeing; nature and hiking trails, cross-country skiing, picnicking, playground, camping (electric hook-ups, dump station). (Daily) **$$$**

Chippewa Falls Zoo. *Irvine Park, 109 E Spruce St, Chippewa Falls (54729). N on Hwy 124. Phone 715/723-3890.* Concentrates on native animals. Also picnic tables, playground, tennis courts, pool. Fee for some activities. (May-Oct, daily) **FREE**

Cook-Rutledge Mansion. *505 W Grand Ave, Chippewa Falls (54729). Phone 715/723-7181.* (1870s) Restored Victorian mansion. Guided tours (June-Aug: Thurs-Sun; rest of year: by appointment). **$$$**

Lake Wissota State Park. *18127 County Hwy O, Chippewa Falls (54729). 8 miles E on Hwy 29. Phone 715/382-4574.* A 1,062-acre park with swimming, water-skiing, fishing, boating, canoeing; hiking, cross-country skiing, picnicking, playground, concession, camping (dump station, electro-hook-ups; reservations accepted). Observation points. (Daily) **$$$**

Special Events

Northern Wisconsin State Fair. *Fairgrounds, 330 Jefferson Ave, Chippewa Falls (54729). Phone 715/723-2861.* Early or mid-July.

Pure Water Days. *10 S Bridge St, Chippewa Falls (54729). Downtown. Phone 715/723-0331.* Canoe paddling, sport competitions, contests, parade, dances, beer garden, food. Second weekend in Aug.

Limited-Service Hotels

★ **COUNTRY INN & SUITES BY CARLSON CHIPPEWA FALLS.** *1021 W Park Ave, Chippewa Falls (54729). Phone 715/720-1414; toll-free 888/201-1746; fax 715/720-1122. www.countryinns.com.* 62 rooms, 2 story. Complimentary continental breakfast. Check-out 11 am. Indoor pool, whirlpool. **$**

★ ★ **PARK AVENUE INN CHIPPEWA.** *1009 W Park Ave, Chippewa Falls (54729). Phone 715/723-2281; fax 715/723-2283.* 67 rooms. Pets accepted, some restrictions; fee. Check-out noon. Restaurant, bar. Indoor pool, whirlpool. **$**

Restaurant

★ **LINDSAY'S ON GRAND.** *24 W Grand Ave, Chippewa Falls (54729). Phone 715/723-4025.* American menu. Breakfast, lunch, dinner. Children's menu. Casual attire. **$**

Crandon (B-4)

See also Rhinelander, Three Lakes

Population 1,958
Elevation 1,629 ft
Area Code 715
Zip 54520
Information Chamber of Commerce, 201 S Lake Ave, PO Box 88; phone 715/478-3450 or toll-free 800/334-3387
Web Site www.crandonwi.com

What to See and Do

Camp Five Museum and "Lumberjack Special" Steam Train Tour. *5480 Connor Farm Rd, Laona (54541). 11 miles E on Hwy 8 and Hwy 32. Phone 715/674-3414 or 800/774-3414.* Old steam train ride to Camp Five

Museum complex; harness and an active blacksmith shop, 1900 country store, logging museum with audiovisual presentation, nature center with diorama featuring area wildlife, 30-minute guided forest tour, hayrack/pontoon boat trip (fee); children's playground, concession. (Mid-June-late Aug, four departures daily; closed Sun) **$$$$**

Limited-Service Hotel

★ FOUR SEASONS MOTEL. *304 W Glen St, Crandon (54520). Phone 715/478-3377; toll-free 888/816-6835; fax 715/478-3785.* 20 rooms. Check-out 11 am. **$**

Delavan (E-4)

See also Beloit, Burlington, Elkhorn, Fontana, Lake Geneva

Settled 1836
Population 6,073
Elevation 940 ft
Area Code 262
Zip 53115
Information Delavan Chamber of Commerce, 52 E Walworth Ave; phone 262/728-5095 or toll-free 800/624-0052
Web Site www.delavanwi.org

Between 1847 and 1894, Delavan was the headquarters of 28 different circuses. The original P. T. Barnum circus was organized here during the winter of 1870-1871 by William C. Coup. Spring Grove and St. Andrew's cemeteries are "last lot" resting places for more than 100 members of the 19th-century circus colony. Today, many flowering crabapple trees grace the town, blooming usually in mid-May.

Restaurant

★ ★ MILLIE'S. *N2484 County O, Delavan (53115). Phone 262/728-2434.* On 80-acre farm; English gardens, gazebo. American menu. Breakfast, lunch, dinner. Closed Mon (except July-Aug); Thanksgiving, Dec 25; also Tues-Fri in Jan-Feb. Bar. **$$**

Devil's Lake State Park (E-3)

See also Baraboo

3 miles S of Baraboo on Hwy 123.

These 11,050 acres, with spring-fed Devil's Lake as the greatest single attraction, form Wisconsin's most beautiful state park. Remnants of an ancient mountain range surround the lake, providing unique scenery. The lake, 1 1/4 miles long, is in the midst of sheer cliffs of quartzite that rise as high as 500 feet above the water. Unusual rock formations may be found at the top of the bluffs. The park has a naturalist in residence who may be contacted for information concerning year-round nature hikes and programs. Sandy swimming beaches with bathhouses, concessions, and boat landings are at either end. No motorboats are permitted. The park provides hiking and cross-country skiing trails, picnic grounds, improved tent and trailer facilities (electric hook-ups, dump station), and a nature center. The lake is restocked yearly. Native American mounds include the Eagle, Bear, and Lynx mounds. General tourist supplies are available at the north and south shores. (Daily) Contact the Park Superintendent, S5975 Park Rd, Baraboo 53913. Phone 608/356-8301. $$

What to See amd Do

Ice Age National Scientific Reserve. Naturalists explain evidence of Wisconsin glaciation; exhibits of local Ice Age features; trails; under development. Also included in the reserve are Northern Unit Kettle Moraine State Forest (see FOND DU LAC) and two state parks, Mill Bluff (see TOMAH) and Interstate (see ST. CROIX FALLS). Per vehicle **$$**

Dodgeville (E-3)

See also Mineral Point, Mount Horeb, New Glarus, Platteville, Spring Green

Settled 1827
Population 3,882
Elevation 1,222 ft
Area Code 608
Zip 53533
Information Dodgeville Chamber of Commerce, 178

1/2 N Iowa St, Suite 201; phone 608/935-5993
Web Site www.dodgeville.com

What to See and Do

Governor Dodge State Park. *4175 Hwy 23, Dodgeville (53533). 3 miles N via Hwy 151, Hwy 23. Phone 608/935-2315.* A 5,029-acre park with 95-acre and 150-acre lakes. Rock formations, white pine. Swimming, bathhouse, fishing, boating (electric motors only; ramps), canoeing (rentals); bicycle, hiking, and bridle trails; cross-country skiing, snowmobiling, picnicking, playgrounds, concession, camping (electric hook-ups, dump station), backpack campsites, horse campground. Nature programs (June-Aug). (Daily)

Limited-Service Hotels

★ ★ DON Q INN. *3656 Hwy 23, Dodgeville (53533). Phone 608/935-2321; toll-free 800/666-7848; fax 608/935-2416.* 61 rooms, 3 story. Complimentary continental breakfast. Check-out noon. Restaurant. Indoor pool, outdoor pool, whirlpool. **$**

★ THE HOUSE ON THE ROCK INN. *3591 Hwy 23, Dodgeville (53533). Phone 608/935-3711; toll-free 888/935-3960. www.concordinn.com.* 114 rooms. Check-in 3 pm, check-out noon. Children's activity center. Indoor pool, whirlpool. **$$**

Door County (C-5)

Famous for its fish boils, foliage, and 250 miles of shoreline, Door County is a peninsula with Green Bay on the west and Lake Michigan on the east. Its picturesque villages, rolling woodlands, limestone bluffs, and beautiful vistas are the reason the area is often referred to as the Cape Cod of the Midwest.

Door County offers year-round recreational opportunitics. Spring and summer bring fishing, sailing, beachcombing, camping, hiking, biking, and horseback riding. Thousands of acres of apple and cherry blossoms color the landscape in late May. There is excellent scuba diving in the *Portes des Mortes* (Death's Door) Straits at the tip of the peninsula, where hundreds of shipwrecks lie in the shifting freshwater sands. Fall colors can be viewed from the endless miles of trails and country roads, which become cross-country ski routes in winter.

Many artists reside here, as is evidenced by the towns' shops, galleries, and boutiques. Summertime theater and concerts also attract tourists.

The taste of the peninsula is unquestionably the legendary fish boil. Trout or whitefish and potatoes and onions are cooked in a cauldron over an open fire. When the fish has almost finished cooking, kerosene is thrown onto the fire, creating a huge flame and causing the unwanted oils to boil out and over the pot. (See the restaurant listings in individual towns.)

The Door County Chamber of Commerce has winter and summer schedules of events, maps, and details on recreational facilities. Contact 1015 Green Bay Rd, PO Box 406, Sturgeon Bay, 54235; phone 920/743-4456 or toll-free 800/527-3529. For a free vacation guide, phone 800/527-3529.

The following towns in Door County are included in the Mobil Travel Guide (for information about any one of them, see the individual alphabetical listing): Baileys Harbor, Egg Harbor, Ellison Bay, Ephraim, Fish Creek, Sister Bay, Sturgeon Bay, and Washington Island.

Special Event

Festival of Blossoms. *Countywide. Phone 920/743-4456.* Month of May.

Eagle River (B-3)

See also Boulder Junction, Land O Lakes, Minocqua, Rhinelander, Sayner, St. Germain, Three Lakes, Woodruff

Population 1,374
Elevation 1,647 ft
Area Code 715
Zip 54521
Information Eagle River Area Chamber of Commerce, PO Box 1917; phone 715/479-6400 or toll-free 800/359-6315
Web Site www.eagle-river.com

The bald eagles that gave this town its name are still occasionally seen, and the Eagle chain of 28 lakes, the largest inland chain of freshwater lakes in the world, is an outstanding tourist attraction. Eagle River has developed as a center of winter sports. The result is lake vacationers in summer and ski fans, both cross-country and downhill, and snowmobilers in winter. There are more than 11 miles of cross-country ski trails on Anvil Lake trail, and 600 miles of snowmobile trails and several hiking areas are in the Nicolet National Forest. A Ranger District office of the Nicolet National Forest (see THREE LAKES) is located here.

What to See and Do

Trees For Tomorrow Natural Resources Education Center. *519 Sheridan St, Eagle River (54521). Phone 715/479-6456.* Demonstration forests, nature trail; "talking tree." (Daily) Outdoor skills and natural resource programs with emphasis on forest ecology and conservation. Cross-country skiing. Orienteering. Natural resources workshops (fee). Guided tours (Tues, Thurs in summer). **FREE**

Special Events

Cranberry Fest. *Vilas County Fairgrounds, 164 Forest, Eagle River (54521). Phone toll-free 800/359-6315.* Cranberry bog tours, events. First weekend in Oct.

Klondike Days. *1311 Hwy 45 N, Eagle River (54521). Phone 715/479-4456.* Oval sled dog races, winter events. Mid-Feb.

National Championship Musky Open. *Vilas County Fairgrounds, 164 Forest, Eagle River (54521). Phone 715/479-6400.* Third weekend in Aug.

World Championship Snowmobile Derby. *1311 Hwy 45 N, Eagle River (54521). 1 1/2 miles N on Hwy 45. Phone 715/479-4424; toll-free 800/359-6315.* Third weekend in Jan.

Limited-Service Hotels

★ ★ CHANTICLEER INN. *1458 E Dollar Lake Rd, Eagle River (54521). Phone 715/479-4486; toll-free 800/752-9193; fax 715/479-0004. www.chanticleerinn.com.* 71 rooms, 2 story. Check-in 3 pm, check-out 10:30 am. Restaurant, bar. Tennis. Airport transportation available. **$**

★ DAYS INN. *844 Railroad St N, Eagle River (54521). Phone 715/479-5151; toll-free 800/356-8018; fax 715/479-8259. www.daysinn.com.* 93 rooms, 2 story. Pets accepted, some restrictions; fee. Complimentary continental breakfast. Check-in 3 pm, check-out 11 am. Indoor pool, whirlpool. **$**

★ ★ EAGLE RIVER INN AND RESORT. *5260 Hwy 70 W, Eagle River (54521). Phone 715/479-2000; toll-free 877/479-2051; fax 715/479-9198. www.eriver-inn.com.* 36 rooms, 2 story. Check-out 11 am. Restaurant, bar. Fitness room. Indoor pool, whirlpool. **$**

Restaurant

★ BAERTSCHY'S PINE GABLES SUPPER CLUB. *5009 Hwy 70 W, Eagle River (54521). Phone 715/479-7689.* German menu. Dinner. Closed Tues. Bar. **$**

Eau Claire (C-2)

See also Chippewa Falls, Menomonie

Settled 1844
Population 56,856
Elevation 796 ft
Area Code 715
Information Eau Claire Convention Bureau, 3625 Gateway Dr, Suite F, 54701; phone 715/831-2345 or toll-free 800/344-3866
Web Site www.eauclaire-info.com

Once a wild and robust lumber camp and sawmill on the shores of the Eau Claire and Chippewa rivers, the city has turned to diversified industry. The name is French for "clear water."

What to See and Do

Chippewa Valley Museum. *Carson Park, 1204 Carson Park Dr, Eau Claire (54703). Phone 715/834-7871. www.cvmuseum.com.* "Paths of the People" Ojibwe exhibit, "Settlement and Survival" 1850-1925 history of Chippewa Valley. Street scene, 21-room doll house, agricultural wing, old-fashioned ice cream parlor, research library. Log house (1860); Sunnyview School (1880). Gift shop. (Tues-Sun) **$$**

Dells Mills Museum. *E 18855 County V, Augusta (54722). 20 miles SE via Hwy 12, 3 miles N of Augusta via Hwy 27 on County V. Phone 715/286-2714.* (1864) Historic five-story water-powered flour and grist mill built of hand-hewn timbers; wooden pegged. One-room schoolhouse museum. Gun shop, antique shop. (May-Oct, daily) **$$$**

Paul Bunyan Logging Camp. *Carson Park, 1110 Carson Park Dr, Eau Claire (54703). Clairemont Ave to Menomonie St, E to Carson Park Dr. Phone 715/835-6200.* Restored 1890s logging camp with bunkhouse, cook shack, blacksmith shop, dingle, filers shack, barn; heavy equipment display. Artifacts, film at interpretive center. (First Mon in Apr-first Mon in Oct) **$$**

University of Wisconsin-Eau Claire. *105 Garfield Ave, Eau Claire (54701). Park and Garfield aves. Phone 715/836-2637.* (1916) (10,500 students) Planetarium, bird museum, greenhouses; dramatic productions, musical events, art gallery (free). Putnam Park arboretum, a 230-acre tract of forest land kept in its natural state, has self-guided nature trails.

Limited-Service Hotels

★ BEST WESTERN WHITE HOUSE INN. *1828 S Hastings Way, Eau Claire (54701). Phone 715/832-8356; toll-free 877/213-1600; fax 715/836-9686. www.bestwestern.com.* 66 rooms, 2 story. Pets accepted; fee. Complimentary continental breakfast. Check-in 3 pm, check-out 11 am. Indoor pool, whirlpool. **$**

★ HAMPTON INN. *2622 Craig Rd, Eau Claire (54701). Phone 715/833-0003; toll-free 800/426-7866; fax 715/833-0915. www.hamptoninn.com.* 106 rooms, 3 story. Complimentary continental breakfast. Check-in 3 pm, check-out noon. Wireless Internet access. Fitness room. Indoor pool, whirlpool. **$**

★ HEARTLAND INN EAU CLAIRE. *4075 Commonwealth Ave, Eau Claire (54701). Phone 715/839-7100; toll-free 800/334-3277; fax 715/839-7050. www.heartlandinns.com.* 87 rooms, 2 story. Pets accepted; fee. Complimentary full breakfast. Check-in 3 pm, check-out noon. Wireless Internet access. Indoor pool. Business center. **$**

★ ★ PLAZA HOTEL AND SUITES EAU CLAIRE. *1202 W Clairemont Ave, Eau Claire (54701). Phone 715/834-3181; fax 715/834-1630.* 233 rooms, 5 story. Check-out 11 am. Restaurant, bar. Indoor pool. Airport transportation available. **$**

Full-Service Inn

★ ★ ★ FANNY HILL VICTORIAN INN & DINNER THEATRE. *3919 Crescent Ave, Eau Claire (54703). Phone 715/836-8184; toll-free 800/292-8026; fax 715/836-8180. www.fannyhill.com.* A beautiful river view is the claim to fame in this elegant inn with a classic air. Each room is appointed with Victorian touches to cap off the true romantic sense in the air. There is a Victorian garden overlooking the Chippewa River and a dinner theater is on the premises. 11 rooms. Complimentary full breakfast. Check-in 2:30 pm, check-out 11 am. High-speed Internet access. Bar. **$$**

Egg Harbor (Door County) (C-5)

Population 183
Elevation 600 feet
Area Code 920
Zip 54209
Information Door County Chamber of Commerce, 1015 Green Bay Rd, PO Box 406, Sturgeon Bay 54235; phone 920/743-4456 or toll-free 800/527-3529
Web Site www.doorcountyvacations.com

This town in Door County is on the shores of Green Bay.

Special Event

Birch Creek Music Center. *3821 Hwy E, Egg Harbor (54209). 3 miles E via County E. Phone 920/868-3763. www.birchcreek.org.* Concert series in unique barn concert hall. Early-mid-July: percussion series; mid-July-mid-Aug: big band series. Other concerts and events through Labor Day.

Limited-Service Hotels

★ ★ ALPINE INN. *7715 Alpine Rd, Egg Harbor (54209). Phone 920/868-3000.* 52 rooms, 3 story. Closed Nov-Memorial Day. Pets accepted, some restrictions; fee. Check-out 10 am. Restaurant, bar. Children's activity center. Beach. Outdoor pool. Golf, 27 holes. Tennis. **$**

★ THE ASHBROOKE. *7942 Egg Harbor Rd, Egg Harbor (54209). Phone 920/868-3113; toll-free*

877/868-3113; fax 920/868-2837. 36 rooms, 2 story. Closed Mar; also weekdays Nov-Apr. Children over 16 years only. Complimentary continental breakfast. Check-in 3 pm, check-out 11 am. Fitness room. Indoor pool, whirlpool. **$**

Specialty Lodging

The following lodging establishment is approved by Mobil Travel Guide, but due to its unique and individualized nature has not been given a traditional Mobil Star rating. Included in this listing you may find bed-and-breakfasts, limited-service inns, guest ranches, and other unique hotel properties.

BAY POINT INN. *7933 Hwy 42, Egg Harbor (54209). Phone 920/868-3297; toll-free 800/707-6660; fax 920/868-2876. www.baypointinn.com.* This all-suite property overlooks Door County's beautiful, wooded shoreline. 10 rooms, 2 story, all suites. Complimentary full breakfast. Check-in 3 pm, check-out 11 am. Outdoor pool, whirlpool. **$$**

Restaurants

★ GRANT'S OLDE STAGE STATION TAVERN. *7778 Egg Harbor Rd, Egg Harbor (54209). Phone 920/868-3247. www.oldestagestation.com.* Former stagecoach stop (1889). American menu. Lunch, dinner, brunch. Bar. Children's menu. Casual attire. Outdoor seating. **$$**

★ VILLAGE CAFE. *7918 Egg Harbor Rd, Egg Harbor (54209). Phone 920/868-3342.* American menu. Breakfast, lunch. Closed Tues-Thurs Nov-Apr. Children's menu. Casual attire. **$**

Elkhart Lake (D-4)

See also Fond du Lac, Sheboygan

Population 1,019
Elevation 945 ft
Area Code 920
Zip 53020
Information Chamber of Commerce, 41 E Rhine St, PO Box 425; phone 920/876-2922
Web Site www.elkhartlake.com

This lake resort, famous for its good beaches, is one of the state's oldest vacation spots.

What to See and Do

Broughton-Sheboygan County Marsh. *W7039 County SR, Elkhart Lake (53020). 1 mile NE on County J. Phone 920/876-2535.* A 14,000-acre wildlife area. Fishing, boating, canoeing; duck hunting, camping (53 sites; hook-ups), lodge, restaurant. **FREE**

Little Elkhart Lake. A 131-acre lake with heavy concentrations of pike, walleye, bass, and panfish.

Old Wade House Historic Site. *W7824 Center Rd, Greenbush (53026). 2 miles N on County P, then SW via County P and A. Phone 920/526-3271.* Restored Old Wade House (1850), early stagecoach inn. Nearby are smokehouse, blacksmith shop, mill dam site; and Jung Carriage Museum housing more than 100 restored horse and hand-drawn vehicles. Picnicking, concession. Horse-drawn carriage rides. (May-Oct, call for schedule) **$$$**

Timm House. *1600 Wisconsin Ave, New Holstein (53061). Approximately 15 miles N via Hwy 32, NW via Hwy 57. Phone 920/898-9006.* (1892) Ten-room, Victorian-style house contains period furniture; guided tours. (June-Sept: Sun; rest of year: by appointment) **$** Admission includes

Pioneer Corner Museum. *2103 Main St, New Holstein (53061). Phone 920/898-9006.* Exhibits of early German immigrant furniture; extensive button collection; general store and post office; Panama Canal memorabilia. (June-Sept: Sun; rest of year: by appointment)

Special Event

Road America. *N7390 Hwy 67, Elkhart Lake (53020). 1 1/2 miles S on Hwy 67. Phone toll-free 800/365-7223.* Located on 525 rolling, wooded acres; a closed-circuit 4-mile sports car racecourse with 14 turns. One of the most popular events of the season is the CART Indy race, which draws top-name race teams. June-Sept.

Limited-Service Hotel

★ ★ VICTORIAN VILLAGE ON ELKHART LAKE. *279 Lake St, Elkhart Lake (53020). Phone 920/876-3323; toll-free 877/860-9988; fax 920/876-3484. www.vicvill.com.* 120 rooms. Check-in 4 pm, check-out 11:30 am. Restaurant, bar. Children's activity center. Beach. Indoor pool, outdoor pool. **$**

Full-Service Resort

★ ★ ★ THE OSTHOFF RESORT. *101 Osthoff Ave, Elkhart Lake (53020). Phone 920/876-3366; toll-free 800/876-3399; fax 920/876-3228. www.osthoff.com.* 145 rooms, 4 story. Check-in 3 pm, check-out noon. Restaurant, bar. Children's activity center. Fitness room, spa. Indoor pool, two outdoor pools, whirlpool. Tennis. **$$**

Full-Service Inn

★ ★ ★ 52 STAFFORD. *52 S Stafford St, Plymouth (53073). Phone 920/893-0552; fax 920/893-1800. www.classicinnsofwisconsin.com.* Remodeled to be reminiscent of a fine Irish manor home, the luxurious furnishings and atmosphere of this restored 1892 home make guests feel more like they're on the Emerald Isle than in Wisconsin. 23 rooms, 3 story. Complimentary continental breakfast. Check-in 3 pm, check-out 10:30 am. Restaurant. **$**

Specialty Lodging

The following lodging establishment is approved by Mobil Travel Guide, but due to its unique and individualized nature has not been given a traditional Mobil Star rating. Included in this listing you may find bed-and-breakfasts, limited-service inns, guest ranches, and other unique hotel properties.

YANKEE HILL INN BED AND BREAKFAST. *405 Collins St, Plymouth (53073). Phone 920/892-2222; fax 920/892-6228. www.yankeehillinn.com.* Huson house built in 1870; Gothic Italianate home. 12 rooms, 2 story. Complimentary full breakfast. Check-in 3 pm, check-out 11 am. High-speed Internet access. **$$**

Elkhorn (E-4)

See also Burlington, Delavan, Fontana, Fort Atkinson, Janesville, Lake Geneva, Waukesha

Settled 1837
Population 5,337
Elevation 1,033 feet
Area Code 262
Zip 53121
Information Chamber of Commerce, 114 W Court St; phone 262/723-5788
Web Site www.elkhorn-wi.org

What to See and Do

Alpine Valley Ski Resort. *W2501 County Rd D, Elkhorn (53121). 1 1/2 miles S off I-43 on County D and Townline Rd near East Troy. Phone 262/642-7374. www.alpinevalleyresort.com.* Resort has quad, five triple, three double chairlifts; four rope tows; patrol, school, rentals; snowmaking; restaurant, cafeteria, bar. Longest run 3,000 feet; vertical drop 388 feet. (Dec-mid-Mar, daily; closed Dec 24 afternoon) Night skiing. Also motel; indoor/outdoor pools, whirlpool; golf, tennis. **$$$$**

Watson's Wild West Museum. *W4865 Potter Rd, Elkhorn (53121). Phone 262/723-7505.* Re-creation of general store, storytelling, western-style barbecues. (May-Oct, Tues-Sun) **$**

Webster House. *9 E Rockwell St, Elkhorn (53121). Phone 262/723-4248.* Restored 19th-century home of Joseph Philbrick Webster, composer of *Sweet Bye and Bye* and *Lorena.* Mounted game bird collection. (Memorial Day-mid-Oct: Wed-Sat afternoons; Apr: by appointment) **$$**

Special Events

Festival of Summer. *100 W Walworth St, Elkhorn (53121). Phone 262/723-5788.* Town Square Arts and crafts fair; custom car show. First weekend in Aug.

Walworth County Fair. *411 E Court St, Elkhorn (53121). NE via Hwy 11 E to city limits. Phone 262/723-3228.* Agricultural fair, grandstand entertainment, and harness racing. Six days ending on Labor Day.

Ellison Bay (Door County) (C-5)

Population 250
Elevation 610 feet
Area Code 920
Zip 54210
Information Door County Chamber of Commerce, 1015 Green Bay Rd, PO Box 406, Sturgeon Bay 54235; phone 920/743-4456 or toll-free 800/527-3529
Web Site www.doorcountyvacations.com

This resort area is near the northern end of Door County. Fishing and boating are popular here; public launching ramps and charter boats are available. This is also considered a good area for scuba diving.

What to See and Do

Death's Door Bluff. Near the top of the peninsula between the mainland and Washington Island. According to legend, 300 Native Americans, attempting a surprise attack, were betrayed and dashed to death against the rocks. Also named because of the large number of ships lost here.

Ferry to Washington Island. *Northport Pier, Detroit Harbor Rd, Gills Rock (54235). 8 miles E and N on Hwy 42 to Northport Pier. Phone 920/847-2546.* Enclosed cabin plus open deck seating. Trips are 30-minutes. (Year-round) Also accommodates cars and bicycles (fees vary). Contact Washington Island Ferry Line. (Daily) **$$$**

Newport State Park. *475 County Rd NP, Ellison Bay (54210). NE of town on County Rd NP. Phone 920/854-2500.* A 2,370-acre wilderness park with 11 miles of Lake Michigan shoreline. Beach. Hiking, cross-country ski trails; picnicking, backpack and winter camping.

Special Event

Old Ellison Bay Days. *Community Center, Hwy 42, Ellison Bay (54210). Phone 920/743-4456.* Parade, fishing contests, fish boil, bazaars, fireworks. Late June.

Limited-Service Hotel

★ ★ WAGON TRAIL. *1041 County Rd ZZ, Ellison Bay (54210). Phone 920/854-2385; toll-free 800/999-2466; fax 920/854-5278. www.wagontrail.com.* On shores of Rowley's Bay; extensive wooded grounds. 72 rooms, 2 story. Check-in 3 pm, check-out 11 am. Restaurant. Fitness room. Beach. Indoor pool, whirlpool. Tennis. **$**

Specialty Lodging

The following lodging establishment is approved by Mobil Travel Guide, but due to its unique and individualized nature has not been given a traditional Mobil Star rating. Included in this listing you may find bed-and-breakfasts, limited-service inns, guest ranches, and other unique hotel properties.

HARBOR HOUSE INN. *12666 Hwy 42, Ellison Bay (54210). Phone 920/854-5196; fax 920/854-9917. www.door-county-inn.com.* This Victorian-style house built in 1904 features many antiques. 15 rooms, 2 story. Closed Nov-Apr. Pets accepted; fee. Complimentary continental breakfast. Check-in 3 pm, check-out 10 am. Whirlpool. **$**

Restaurant

★ VIKING GRILL. *12029 Hwy 42, Ellison Bay (54210). Phone 920/854-2998; fax 920/854-9281. www.doorcountyfishboil.com.* American menu. Breakfast, lunch, dinner. Closed holidays; also early Feb-late Mar. Bar. Children's menu. Casual attire. Outdoor seating. **$$**

Ephraim (Door County) (C-5)

Founded 1853
Population 261
Elevation 600 feet
Area Code 920
Zip 54211
Information Door County Chamber of Commerce, 1015 Green Bay Rd, PO Box 406, Sturgeon Bay 54235; phone 920/743-4456 or toll-free 800/527-3529
Web Site www.doorcountyvacations.com

Moravian colonists founded the second Ephraim here after leaving the first town of that name, now a part of Green Bay; a monument at the harbor commemorates the landing of Moravians in 1853. The village is now a quaint resort community and a center for exploration of the north and west shores of Door County.

Special Event

Fyr-Bal Fest. *Ephraim Village Hall, Hwy 42, Ephraim (54211). Phone 920/854-4989.* Scandinavian welcome to summer. Fish boil, Blessing of the Fleet, art fair, lighting of the bonfires on the beach at dusk, coronation of Viking Chieftain. Three days in mid-June.

Limited-Service Hotels

★ ★ EDGEWATER RESORT MOTEL. *10040 Water St, Ephraim (54211). Phone 920/854-2734;*

fax 920/854-4127. On Green Bay. 38 rooms, 2 story. Closed Nov-Apr. Check-out 11 am. Restaurant. Outdoor pool. **$**

★ ★ EPHRAIM SHORES MOTEL. *10018 Water St, Ephraim (54211). Phone 920/854-2371; fax 920/854-4926. www.ephraimshores.com.* On Green Bay, overlooking Eagle Harbor. 46 rooms, 2 story. Check-out 10:30 am. Restaurant. Fitness room. Indoor pool, whirlpool. **$**

★ EVERGREEN BEACH. *9944 Water St, Ephraim (54211). Phone 920/854-2831; toll-free 800/420-8130; fax 920/854-9222. www.evergreenbeach.com.* On Eagle Harbor. 30 rooms, 2 story. Closed late Oct-late May. Complimentary continental breakfast. Check-out 10:30 am. Beach. Outdoor pool. **$**

★ TROLLHAUGEN LODGE. *10176 Hwy 42, Ephraim (54211). Phone 920/854-2713; toll-free 800/854-4118. trollhaugenlodge.com.* 13 rooms. Closed Sept-June. Complimentary continental breakfast. Check-out 10 am. **$**

Specialty Lodgings

The following lodging establishments are approved by Mobil Travel Guide, but due to their unique and individualized nature have not been given a traditional Mobil Star rating. Included in this listing you may find bed-and-breakfasts, limited-service inns, guest ranches, and other unique hotel properties.

EAGLE HARBOR INN. *9914 Water St, Ephraim (54211). Phone 920/854-2121; toll-free 800/324-5427; fax 920/854-2121. www.eagleharbor.com.* Guests get a warm feeling when approaching this classic inn. Enjoy the serenity of the wooded areas surrounding the hotel, or take a stroll down to the beach nearby. 41 rooms, 2 story. Complimentary full breakfast. Check-in 3 pm, check-out 10 am. Fitness room. Indoor pool. **$**

EPHRAIM INN. *9994 Pioneer Ln, Ephraim (54211). Phone 920/854-4515; fax 920/854-1859. www.theephraiminn.com.* Overlooks Green Bay. Each room has a different theme. 16 rooms, 2 story. Closed Nov-Apr (Mon-Thurs). Children over 12 years only. Check-in 3 pm, check-out 11 am. High-speed Internet access. **$**

Restaurant

★ OLD POST OFFICE RESTAURANT. *10040 Water St, Ephraim (54211). Phone 920/854-4034.* American menu. Breakfast, dinner. Closed Nov-Apr. Casual attire. Outdoor seating. **$$**

Fish Creek (Door County) (C-5)

Population 200
Elevation 583 ft
Area Code 920
Zip 54212
Information Door County Chamber of Commerce, 1015 Green Bay Rd, PO Box 406, Sturgeon Bay 54235; phone 920/743-4456 or toll-free 800/527-3529
Web Site www.doorcountyvacations.com

This picturesque Green Bay resort village, with its many interesting shops, is in Door County.

What to See and Do

Peninsula State Park. *9462 Shore Rd, Fish Creek (54212). N off Hwy 42. Phone 920/868-3258.* A 3,763-acre park with 9 miles of waterfront including sandy and cobblestone beaches; caves, cliffs; observation tower. Swimming, fishing, boating, water-skiing; hiking, bicycle trails; cross-country skiing, snowmobiling, picnic grounds, playground, concession, camping (471 sites, hook-ups, dump station). Naturalist programs. Eighteen-hole golf course (mid-May-mid-Oct). **$$$**

Special Event

American Folklore Theatre. *Peninsula State Park Amphitheater, 9462 Shore Rd, Fish Creek (54212). Phone 920/868-1100.* Original folk musical productions based on American lore and literature. Limited fall season. July-Aug.

Limited-Service Hotel

★ HOMESTEAD SUITES. *4006 Hwy 42, Fish Creek (54212). Phone 920/868-3748; toll-free 800/686-6621; fax 920/868-2874. www.homesteadsuites.com.* Adjacent to Peninsula State Park. 48 rooms, 2 story, all suites. Complimentary continental breakfast. Check-in 3 pm, check-out 11 am. Fitness room. Indoor pool, outdoor pool, whirlpool. **$$**

Full-Service Inn

★ ★ ★ **WHITE GULL INN.** *4225 Main St, Fish Creek (54212). Phone 920/868-3517; fax 920/868-2367. www.whitegullinn.com.* Built in 1896; library, antiques. 17 rooms, 2 story. Complimentary full breakfast. Check-in 3 pm, check-out 11 am. Restaurant, bar. Airport transportation available. **$$**

Specialty Lodgings

The following lodging establishments are approved by Mobil Travel Guide, but due to their unique and individualized nature have not been given a traditional Mobil Star rating. Included in this listing you may find bed-and-breakfasts, limited-service inns, guest ranches, and other unique hotel properties.

CEDAR COURT. *9429 Cedar St, Fish Creek (54212). Phone 920/868-3361; fax 920/868-2541. www.cedarcourt.com.* 16 rooms, 2 story. Pets accepted, some restrictions. Check-in 2 pm, check-out 11 am. Outdoor pool. **$**

THE WHISTLING SWAN INN. *4192 Main St, Fish Creek (54212). Phone 920/868-3442; toll-free 888/277-4289; fax 920/868-1703.* This quaint, renovated country-style inn (1887) has a lot to offer in addition to a comfortable stay. The boutiques on the lobby level draw many people looking for fine clothing and more for the whole family. 7 rooms, 2 story. Complimentary continental breakfast. Check-in 3 pm, check-out 11 am. Restaurant. **$$**

Restaurants

★ ★ **C AND C SUPPER CLUB.** *Hwy 42, Fish Creek (54212). Phone 920/868-3412; fax 920/854-2627. www.ccsupperclub.com.* American menu. Lunch, dinner. Closed three weeks in Mar. Bar. Children's menu. Business casual attire. Reservations recommended. **$$**

★ **THE COOKERY.** *Hwy 42, Fish Creek (54212). Phone 920/868-3634; fax 920/868-2831. www.cookeryfishcreek.com.* American menu. Breakfast, lunch, dinner. Closed Mon-Thurs Nov-Mar. Children's menu. Casual attire. **$$**

★ **PELLETIER'S.** *4199 Main St, Fish Creek (54212). Phone 920/868-3313; fax 920/868-3931. www.doorcountyfishboil.com.* American menu. Breakfast, lunch, dinner. Closed late Oct-mid-May. Children's menu. Casual attire. Reservations recommended. Outdoor seating. **$$**

★ ★ **SUMMERTIME.** *1 N Spruce St, Fish Creek (54212). Phone 920/868-3738; fax 920/868-2683. www.thesummertime.com.* American menu. Breakfast, lunch, dinner. Closed Nov-Apr. Children's menu. Casual attire. Outdoor seating. **$$**

★ ★ **WHITE GULL INN.** *4225 Main St, Fish Creek (54212). Phone 920/868-3517. www.whitegullinn.com.* Turn-of-the-century décor. American menu. Breakfast, lunch, dinner. Closed Thanksgiving, Dec 25. Children's menu. Casual attire. Reservations recommended. Outdoor seating. **$$**

Fond du Lac (D-4)

See also Elkhart Lake, Green Lake, Oshkosh, Waupun

Settled 1835
Population 42,000
Elevation 760 ft
Area Code 920
Information Convention & Visitors Bureau, 171 S Pioneer Rd St; phone 920/923-3010 or toll-free 800/937-9123, ext 71
Web Site www.fdl.com

Located at the foot of Lake Winnebago and named by French explorers in the 1600s, Fond du Lac, "foot of the lake," was an early outpost for fur trading, later achieving prominence as a lumbering center and railroad city.

What to See and Do

Galloway House and Village. *336 Old Pioneer Rd, Fond du Lac (54935). Phone 920/922-6390.* Restored 30-room Victorian mansion with four fireplaces, carved woodwork, and stenciled ceilings; village of late 1800s; 24 buildings including one-room schoolhouse, print shop, general store, operating gristmill, museum with collection of Native American artifacts; war displays; other area artifacts. (Memorial Day-Labor Day: daily; rest of Sept: Sat-Sun) **$$$**

Kettle Moraine State Forest, Northern Unit. *N1765 Hwy G, Campbellsport (53010). 17 miles SE on Hwy 45 to Waucousta, then E on County F. Phone 262/626-*

2116. The forest is being developed as part of Ice Age National Scientific Reserve (see DEVIL'S LAKE STATE PARK). The forest's 30,000 acres include Long and Mauthe Lake Recreation Areas and scenic Kettle Moraine Drive. Swimming, water-skiing, fishing, boating, canoeing; 58 miles of hiking and bridle trails. Snowmobiling, cross-country skiing, picnicking, camping available (338 sites, hook-ups, dump station), including primitive and winter camping. Observation tower. The Forest Supervisor is in Campbellsport. (Daily) **$$$** Also here is

> **Ice Age Visitor Center.** *N2875 Hwy 67, Campbellsport (53010). Phone 920/533-8322.* Films, slides, and panoramas show visitors how glaciers molded Wisconsin's terrain; naturalists answer questions. (Daily; closed Jan 1, Dec 25) **FREE**

Lakeside Park. *555 N Park Ave, Fond du Lac (54935). N end of Main St. Phone 920/989-6846.* A 400-acre park on Lake Winnebago. Boating (ramps, canoe rentals); petting zoo, playground, rides, picnic area; lighthouse. (June-Aug, daily) (See SPECIAL EVENT) **FREE**

Lake Winnebago. *Hwy 41 and N Main, Fond du Lac (54935). Phone toll-free 800/937-9123, ext 35.* Boating, sailing, windsurfing, water-skiing, fishing, ice-fishing, sturgeon spearing (last two weeks in Feb), ice-boating, snowmobiling.

★ **Octagon House.** *276 Linden St, Fond du Lac (54935). Phone 920/922-1608.* A 12-room octagonal house built in 1856 by Isaac Brown and designed by Orson Fowler has a hidden room, secret passageways, and an underground tunnel. Period antiques, dolls, clothing; native American display, ship collection, spinning wheel demonstrations. Carriage house has pony carriages. Also, 90-minute guided tours Mon, Wed, Fri, afternoons. **$$$**

Silver Wheel Manor. *N6221 County K, Fond Du Lac (54935). E on Hwy 23, S on County K. Phone 920/922-1608.* A 30-room mansion that was once part of a 400-acre farm established in 1860; antique furnishings; collection of more than 1,200 dolls and accessories; model trains; circus room, photography room. (Mon, Wed, Fri-Sat, mornings) **$$$**

St. Paul's Cathedral. *51 W Division, Fond du Lac (54935). Phone 920/921-3363.* Episcopal. English Gothic limestone structure with wood carvings from Oberammergau, Germany, rare ecclesiastical artifacts, and a variety of stained-glass windows; cloister garden. Self-guided tours (by appointment).

Special Event

Walleye Weekend Festival and Mercury Marine National Walleye Tournament. *Lakeside Park, 555 N Park Ave, Fond du Lac (54935). Phone 920/923-6555; toll-free 800/937-9123.* Fish fry, food, entertainment, sports competions. Second weekend in June.

Limited-Service Hotels

★ **DAYS INN.** *107 N Pioneer Rd, Fond du Lac (54935). Phone 920/923-6790; toll-free 800/329-7466; fax 920/923-6790. www.daysinn.com.* 59 rooms, 2 story. Pets accepted, some restrictions; fee. Complimentary continental breakfast. Check-out 11 am. **$**

★★ **HOLIDAY INN.** *625 W Rolling Meadows Dr, Fond du Lac (54937). Phone 920/923-1440; toll-free 800/465-4329; fax 920/923-1366. www.holiday-inn.com.* 141 rooms, 2 story. Pets accepted, some restrictions. Check-out 11 am. Restaurant, bar. Fitness room. Indoor pool, whirlpool. Airport transportation available. **$**

Restaurants

★ **SALTY'S SEAFOOD AND SPIRITS.** *503 N Park Ave, Fond du Lac (54935). Phone 920/922-9940.* Seafood menu. Lunch, dinner. Closed holidays. Bar. Children's menu. Casual attire. **$$**

★★ **SCHREINER'S.** *168 N Pioneer Rd, Fond du Lac (54935). Phone 920/922-0590; fax 920/922-1922. www.fdlchowder.com.* American menu. Breakfast, lunch, dinner. Closed Easter, Thanksgiving, Dec 25. Bar. Children's menu. Casual attire. **$**

Fontana (E-4)

See also Beloit, Burlington, Delavan, Elkhorn, Lake Geneva

Population 1,635
Elevation 900 ft
Area Code 262
Zip 53125

Located on the western shore of Lake Geneva in territory once occupied by the Potawatomi, this town was named for its many springs.

Full-Service Resort

★★★ ABBEY RESORT & FONTANA SPA. *269 Fontana Blvd, Fontana (53125). Phone 262/275-6811; toll-free 800/558-2405; fax 262/275-3264. www.theabbeyresort.com.* Situated on 90 lush acres and set on the water's edge, this elegant resort and spa delights guests with its restaurants, exquisitely prepared dishes, crisp linens, and wonderful selection of wines to complement any meal. The atmosphere of quiet elegance make for a very enjoyable stay. 334 rooms, 2 story. Check-in 4 pm, check-out noon. Restaurant, bar. Children's activity center. Fitness room, spa. Two indoor pools, three outdoor pools, whirlpool. Tennis. Airport transportation available. Business center. **$**

Fort Atkinson (E-4)

See also Elkhorn, Janesville, Madison, Watertown

Settled 1836
Population 10,227
Elevation 790 ft
Area Code 920
Zip 53538
Information Chamber of Commerce, 244 N Main St; phone 920/563-3210 or toll-free 888/733-3678
Web Site www.fortchamber.com

In 1872, William Dempster Hoard, later governor of Wisconsin, organized the Wisconsin State Dairyman's Association here. He toured the area, drumming up support by preaching the virtues of the cow, "the foster mother of the human race." More than any other man, Hoard was responsible for Wisconsin's development as a leading dairy state. Nearby are Lake Koshkonong, a popular recreation area, and Lake Ripley, where Ole Evinrude invented the outboard motor in 1908.

What to See and Do

Hoard Historical Museum. *407 Merchants Ave, Fort Atkinson (53538). Phone 920/563-7769.* Housed in a historic home (1864), the museum features pioneer history and archaeology of the area; period rooms, antique quilt, bird room, old costumes and clothing, antique firearms; reference library; permanent and changing displays. (June-Aug: Tues-Sun; rest of year: Tues-Sat; closed Thanksgiving, Dec 25) **FREE** Also here are

Dwight Foster House. *407 Merchants Ave, Fort Atkinson (53538). Phone 920/563-7769.* (1841) Historic home of city's founder; five-room, two-story Greek Revival frame house is furnished in the period, with many original pieces. (June-Aug: Tues-Sun; rest of year: Tues-Sat; closed Thanksgiving, Dec 25) **FREE**

National Dairy Shrine Museum. *407 Merchants Ave, Fort Atkinson (53538). Phone 920/563-7769.* Traces the development of the dairy industry for the past 100 years. Collection of memorabilia; exhibits include old creamery, replica of early dairy farm kitchen, old barn, and milk-hauling equipment. Multimedia presentation. (June-Aug: Tues-Sun; rest of year: Tues-Sat; closed Thanksgiving, Dec 25) **FREE**

Panther Intaglio. *1236 Riverside Dr, Fort Atkinson (53538).* Panther-shaped prehistoric earthwork; dates to AD 1000. Discovered by Increase Lapham in 1850.

Limited-Service Hotel

★ SUPER 8. *225 S Water St E, Fort Atkinson (53538). Phone 920/563-8444; toll-free 800/800-8000; fax 920/563-8444. www.super8.com.* Overlooks Rock River. 40 rooms, 3 story. Pets accepted; fee. Complimentary continental breakfast. Check-out 11 am. Bar. **$**

Fox Point

Restaurant

★★★ MANIACI'S CAFE SICILIANO. *6904 N Santa Monica Blvd, Fox Point (53217). Phone 414/352-5757.* After nearly 25 years under the watchful eyes of Arthur and Rose Maniaci, chef Anthony Mandella is now at the helm of this intimate Italian-Sicilian restaurant known for caring service. Italian menu. Dinner. Closed Sun; holidays; also week of July 4. Children's menu. **$$$**

Galesville (D-2)

See also La Crosse

Population 1,278
Elevation 712 ft

Area Code 608
Zip 54630

What to See and Do

State parks. Fishing, boating, canoeing; hiking, picnicking, playgrounds, camping (electric hook-ups, dump stations).

Merrick State Park. *S2965 Hwy 35, Fountain City (54629). 22 miles NW on Hwy 35. Phone 608/687-4936.* A 324-acre park along Mississippi River. Canoeing; camping. (Daily)

Perrot State Park. *W26247 Sullivan Rd, Trempealeau (54661). 2 miles W on Trempealeau. Phone 608/534-6409.* Trempealeau Mountain, a beacon for voyageurs for more than 300 years, is in this 1,425-acre park. Nicolas Perrot set up winter quarters here in 1686; a French fort was built on the site in 1731. Cross-country skiing. Vistas, bluffs. (Daily)

Germantown

Limited-Service Hotel

★ SUPER 8. *N96W17490 County Line Rd, Germantown (53022). Phone 262/255-0880; toll-free 800/800-8000; fax 262/255-7741. www.super8.com.* 81 rooms, 2 story. Pets accepted, some restrictions. Complimentary continental breakfast. Check-out 11 am. **$**

Restaurants

★ ★ JERY'S OLD TOWN INN. *N116W15841 Main St, Germantown (53022). Phone 262/251-4455; fax 262/250-2282.* Barbecue menu. Dinner. Bar. Children's menu. Casual attire. **$**

★ ★ LOHMANN'S STEAK HOUSE. *W183N9609 Appleton Ave, Germantown (53051). Phone 262/251-8430; fax 262/251-8432. www.foodspot.com/lohmanns.* Steak menu. Lunch, dinner. Closed Sun; holidays. Bar. Children's menu. **$$$**

Green Bay (C-5)

See also Algoma, Appleton, Manitowoc, Neenah-Menasha, Oconto, Sturgeon Bay, Two Rivers

Population 96,466
Elevation 594 ft
Area Code 920
Information Visitor & Convention Bureau, 1901 S Oneida St, 54307-0596; phone 920/494-9507 or toll-free 888/867-3342
Web Site www.greenbay.org

The strategic location that made Green Bay a trading center as far back as 1669 today enables this port city to handle nearly 1.8 million tons of cargo a year. The region was claimed for the King of France in 1634, and was named La Baye in 1669 when it became the site of the mission of St. Francis. It then saw the rise of fur trading, a series of Native American wars, and French, British, and US conflicts. Although it became part of the United States in 1783, Green Bay did not yield to American influence until after the War of 1812, when agents of John Jacob Astor gained control of the fur trade. The oldest settlement in the state, Green Bay is a paper and cheese producing center as well as a hub for health care and insurance. It is also famous for its professional football team, the Green Bay Packers.

What to See and Do

Children's Museum of Green Bay. *320 N Adams St, Green Bay (54301). Upper Level Washington Commons Mall. Phone 920/432-4397. www.thechildrensmuseumofgreenbay.org.* Hands-on exhibits and interactive programs. Areas include the Hospital, Submarine, Fire Truck, Police Station, Bank, and Grocery Store. (Daily; closed holidays) **$**

Green Bay Botanical Gardens. *2600 Larsen Rd, Green Bay (54307). Phone 920/490-9457. www.gbbg.org.* Educational and recreational facility. Formal rose garden; children's garden; four-season garden; gift shop. (Tues-Sun, daily) **$**

Green Bay Packers (NFL). *Lambeau Field, 1265 Lombardi Ave, Green Bay (54304). Phone 920/496-5700. www.packers.com.* Probably the most storied football venue in the NFL is Green Bay's Curly Lambeau Field. Site of the famous Ice Bowl, the stadium is known for its harsh weather (it's commonly referred to as the frozen tundra of Lambeau Field), as well as for the "Lambeau Leaps" that Packer players take into the waiting arms of fans in the front row of the end zone. Tailgating is a must, as the beer and the bratwurst are always plentiful before home games. Just be sure to bring your warmest clothes for gametime. **$$$$**

Green Bay Packers Hall of Fame. *Brown County Expo Centre, 855 Lombardi Ave, Green Bay (54304). Across from Lambeau Field. Phone 920/499-4281; toll-free 888/442-7225.* History of team from 1919 to present; a unique collection of multimedia presentations, memorabilia, hands-on activites, NFL films. (Daily; closed holidays) **$$$**

Hazelwood Historic Home Museum. *1008 S Monroe Ave, Green Bay (54301). Phone 920/437-1840.* (1837-1838) Greek Revival house where state constitution was drafted. (Memorial Day-Labor Day: Mon-Fri; rest of year: by appointment) **$$**

Heritage Hill State Park. *2640 S Webster, Green Bay (54301). Phone 920/448-5150.* The park includes a 40-acre living history museum and a complex of 26 historical buildings that illustrate the development of northeast Wisconsin. (Memorial Day-Labor Day: Tues-Sun; Dec: Sat-Sun) Christmas festival (Fri-Sun in Dec). **$$$**

★ **National Railroad Museum.** *2285 S Broadway, Green Bay (54304). Phone 920/437-7623. www.nationalrrmuseum.org.* Seventy-five steam locomotives, diesels, and cars; train rides; exhibit building; theater; gift shop. (May-mid-Oct: daily; rest of year: weekdays)

Neville Public Museum. *210 Museum Pl, Green Bay (54303). Phone 920/448-4460.* Science, history, and art collections and exhibits. (Daily; closed Mon, holidays) **DONATION**

Northeastern Wisconsin Zoo. *4378 Reforestation Rd, Green Bay (54313). Phone 920/434-7841.* Over 43 acres of animals in natural settings. Children's zoo. Exhibits include Wisconsin Trail, International and Northern trail. (Daily) **$**

Oneida Nation Museum. *W892 County Rd EE, De Pere (54115). 7 miles SW on Hwy 41 to County Rd EE. Phone 920/869-2768.* Permanent and hands-on exhibits tell the story of the Oneida Nation. (Tues-Fri; closed holidays) **$**

University of Wisconsin-Green Bay. *2420 Nicolet Dr, Green Bay (54311). Phone 920/465-2000. www.uwgb.edu.* (1965) (5,000 students) Campus built on 700 acres. Weidner Center for the Performing Arts. Also here is Cofrin Memorial Arboretum; nine-hole golf course (fee); Bayshore picnic area. Tours of campus (by appointment).

Special Event

Waterboard Warriors. *Brown County Park, Green Bay (54301). Phone 920/448-4466.* Water-ski shows performed by skiers from the area. Tues and Thurs (evenings). June-Aug.

Limited-Service Hotels

★ **BAYMONT INN.** *2840 S Oneida St, Green Bay (54304). Phone 920/494-7887; toll-free 877/229-6668; fax 920/494-3370. www.baymontinns.com.* 77 rooms, 2 story. Pets accepted, some restrictions. Complimentary continental breakfast. Check-in 3 pm, check-out noon. High-speed Internet access, wireless Internet access. Business center. **$**

★★ **BEST WESTERN MIDWAY HOTEL.** *780 Packer Dr, Green Bay (54304). Phone 920/499-3161; toll-free 800/780-7234; fax 920/499-9401. www.bestwestern.com.* 145 rooms, 2 story. Check-in 3 pm, check-out 11 am. Restaurant, bar. Fitness room. Indoor pool, whirlpool. Airport transportation available. **$**

★ **FAIRFIELD INN.** *2850 S Oneida St, Green Bay (54304). Phone 920/497-1010; toll-free 800/228-2800; fax 920/497-3098. www.fairfieldinn.com.* 63 rooms, 3 story. Complimentary continental breakfast. Check-out noon. Indoor pool, whirlpool. **$**

★★ **HOLIDAY INN.** *200 Main St, Green Bay (54301). Phone 920/437-5900; toll-free 800/457-2929; fax 920/437-1199. www.holiday-inn.com.* 149 rooms, 7 story. Pets accepted, some restrictions. Check-out noon. Restaurant, bar. Indoor pool, whirlpool. **$**

★★ **RADISSON HOTEL & CONFERENCE CENTER GREEN BAY.** *2040 Airport Dr, Green Bay (54313). Phone 920/494-7300; toll-free 800/333-3333; fax 920/494-9599. www.radisson.com.* This hotel is located on the west side of town adjacent to Oneida Bingo and Casino, making it a great choice for gamblers. Interior corridors linked to the casino mean that you don't have to face the Wisconsin winter in order to hit the slots or the gaming tables. Jacuzzi and fireplace suites are available, as are executive tower rooms with complimentary high-speed Internet access. 409 rooms, 6 story. Two restaurants, bar. Fitness room. Indoor pool, whirlpool. Airport transportation available. Business center. **$**

★ **SUPER 8.** *2868 S Oneida St, Green Bay (54304). Phone 920/494-2042; toll-free 800/800-8000; fax 920/494-6959. www.super8.com.* 84 rooms, 2 story. Pets accepted; fee. Complimentary continental breakfast. Check-out 11 am. Whirlpool. **$**

Specialty Lodgings

The following lodging establishments are approved by Mobil Travel Guide, but due to their unique and individualized nature have not been given a traditional Mobil Star rating. Included in this listing you may find bed-and-breakfasts, limited-service inns, guest ranches, and other unique hotel properties.

ASTOR HOUSE. *637 S Monroe Ave, Green Bay (54301). Phone 920/432-3585; toll-free 888/303-6370; fax 920/436-3145. www.astorhouse.com.* The only bed-and-breakfast in Green Bay, this charming 1880s Victorian house serves up intimate home-style hospitality. 5 rooms, 3 story. Complimentary continental breakfast. Check-in 4-6 pm, check-out 11 am. **$**

JAMES STREET INN. *201 James St, De Pere (54115). Phone 920/337-0111; toll-free 800/897-8483; fax 920/337-6135.* Upon entering this enchanting inn (an old flour mill built in 1858), guests are lured to relaxation by the simple elegance and romantic lobby with all of its charming furnishings, including the magnificent antique mahogany and cherry fireplace. Guests will appreciate the elegant accommodations, personal and attentive service, and classically appointed guest rooms, some featuring private waterfront decks and panoramic views of the Fox River. 36 rooms, 4 story. Complimentary continental breakfast. Check-in 3 pm, check-out noon. **$$**

Restaurants

★ ★ **EVE'S SUPPER CLUB.** *2020 Riverside Dr, Green Bay (54301). Phone 920/435-1571; fax 920/435-2899.* American menu. Lunch, dinner. Closed Sun; holidays. Bar. Casual attire. Reservations recommended. **$$$**

★ ★ **RIVER'S BEND.** *792 Riverview Dr, Howard (54303). Phone 920/434-1383.* American menu. Dinner. Closed Mon; holidays. Bar. Children's menu. Casual attire. **$$**

★ ★ **WELLINGTON.** *1060 Hansen Rd, Green Bay (54304). Phone 920/499-2000; fax 920/499-7894.* American menu. Lunch, dinner. Closed Sun; holidays. Children's menu. Outdoor seating. **$$**

Green Lake (D-4)

See also Fond du Lac, Waupun, Wautoma

Population 1,064
Elevation 828 ft
Area Code 920
Zip 54941
Information Chamber of Commerce, 550 Mill St, PO Box 386; phone 920/294-3231 or toll-free 800/253-7354

This county seat, known as the oldest resort community west of Niagara Falls, is a popular four-season recreational area. Green Lake, at 7,325 acres, is the deepest natural lake in the state and affords good fishing (including lake trout), swimming, sailing, powerboating, and iceboating.

What to See and Do

Green Lake Conference Center/American Baptist Assembly. *W2511 Hwy 23, Green Lake (54941). Phone 920/294-3323.* A 1,000-acre all-year vacation-conference center. Activities include indoor swimming; fishing; cross-country skiing (rentals), tobogganing, ice skating, camping (fee), hiking, biking, tennis, 36-hole golf. (Daily) **$**

Lake cruises. *Heidel House, 643 Illinois Ave, Green Lake (54941). Phone 920/294-3344; toll-free 800/444-2812.* A 1 1/4-hour narrated cruise. Also dinner, brunch cruises; private charters. (June-Aug: daily; May and Sept-Oct: Sat-Sun) **$$$**

Limited-Service Hotel

★ **AMERICINN.** *1219 W Fond du Lac St, Ripon (54971). Phone 920/748-7578; fax 920/748-7897.* 42 rooms, 2 story. Complimentary continental breakfast. Indoor pool, whirlpool. **$**

Full-Service Resort

★ ★ ★ HEIDEL HOUSE RESORT & CONFERENCE CENTER. *643 Illinois Ave, Green Lake (54941). Phone 920/294-3344; fax 920/294-6128. www.heidelhouse.com.* 205 rooms, 4 story. Check-out noon. Restaurant. Fitness room. Indoor pool, outdoor pool. Business center. **$$**

Specialty Lodging

The following lodging establishment is approved by Mobil Travel Guide, but due to its unique and individualized nature has not been given a traditional Mobil Star rating. Included in this listing you may find bed-and-breakfasts, limited-service inns, guest ranches, and other unique hotel properties.

CARVER'S ON THE LAKE. *N5529 County Rd A, Green Lake (54941). Phone 920/294-6931. www.carversonthelake.com.* Built in 1925; antiques. 9 rooms, 2 story. Complimentary continental breakfast. Check-in 3 pm, check-out 11 am. Restaurant. **$$**

Restaurants

★ ★ ★ CARVER'S ON THE LAKE. *N5529 County Rd A, Green Lake (54941). Phone 920/294-6931. www.carversonthelake.com.* The English country décor and cozy atmosphere of this inn and restaurant draw visitors for New American cuisine along the lake's eastern shore. Linger over a drink fireside at the Great Room bar. American menu. Dinner. Closed Mon; holidays. Bar. Children's menu. Business casual attire. Reservations recommended. **$$**

★ ★ NORTON'S MARINE DINING ROOM. *380 S Lawson Dr, Green Lake (54941). Phone 920/294-6577; fax 920/294-6922. www.nortonsdining.com.* American menu. Lunch, dinner. Closed holidays. Bar. Children's menu. Casual attire. Reservations recommended. Outdoor seating. **$$**

Hartford

What to See and Do

Little Switzerland Ski Area. *105 Hwy AA, Slinger (53086). One block off of State Hwy 41; exit on Hwy 144 and then go S to Hwy AA. Phone 262/644-5020. www.littleswitz.com.* 15 runs; 30 percent beginner, 40 percent intermediate, 30 percent advanced. Longest run 1,800 feet; vertical drop 200 feet. Quad, four double chairlifts; two rope tows; school, rentals, snowmaking; bar, snack bar. (Fri-Mon, holidays 10 am-4 pm, 4:30-10 pm) **$$$$**

Hayward (B-2)

See also Cable, Spooner

Settled 1881
Population 1,897
Elevation 1,198 ft
Area Code 715
Zip 54843
Information Hayward Area Chamber of Commerce, 101 W 1st St; phone 715/634-8662
Web Site www.haywardlakes.com

A Ranger District office of the Chequamegon National Forest is located here.

What to See and Do

National Freshwater Fishing Hall of Fame. *10360 Hall of Fame Dr, Hayward (54843). Jct Hwy B and Hwy 27. Phone 715/634-4440.* A 143-foot long and 4 1/2-story high walk-thru "muskie"; the mouth serves as an observation deck. Museum and educational complex contains more than 400 mounts representing many world species; world records and record photo gallery and library; thousands of angling artifacts; 350 outboard motor relics. Project covers 6 acres and includes five other museum display buildings. (Mid-Apr-Nov, daily) Snack shop, gift shop, playground with fish theme. **$$**

Special Events

American Birkebeiner. *11 Main St, Hayward (54843). Phone 715/634-5025; toll-free 800/872-2753.* Cross-country ski race (337 miles). More than 6,000 participants from 40 states and 15 countries. Late Feb.

Lumberjack World Championship. *County B, Hayward (54843). Phone 715/634-2484.* Logrolling, tree chopping, climbing, and sawing. Late July.

Scheer's Lumberjack Show. *15648 County Rd B, Hayward (54843). Hwy 51, 2 miles N of Minocqua to Hwy 47. Phone 715/634-6923.* World champion lumberjacks provide entertainment, live music. June-Aug.

Limited-Service Hotel

★ **AMERICINN HAYWARD.** *15601 Hwy 63 N, Hayward (54843). Phone 715/634-2700; toll-free 800/634-3444; fax 715/634-3958. www.americinn.com.* 42 rooms, 2 story. Pets accepted; fee. Complimentary continental breakfast. Check-in 3 pm, check-out 11 am. High-speed Internet access. Indoor pool, whirlpool. Business center. **$**

Restaurant

★ **KARIBALIS.** *10564 Main St, Hayward (54843). Phone 715/634-2462.* American menu. Lunch, dinner. Bar. Children's menu. Casual attire. Outdoor seating. **$$**

Hudson (C-1)

Population 6,378
Elevation 780 ft
Area Code 715
Zip 54016
Information Hudson Area Chamber of Commerce, 502 2nd St; phone 715/386-8411 or toll-free 800/657-6775
Web Site www.hudsonwi.org

What to See and Do

Octagon House. *1004 3rd St, Hudson (54016). Phone 715/386-2654.* (1855) Octagonal home furnished in the style of gracious living of the 1800s; garden house museum with country store and lumbering and farming implements; carriage house museum with special display areas. (May-Oct, Tues-Sun; first three weeks in Dec; closed holidays) **$$**

Willow River State Park. *1034 County Trunk A, Hudson (54016). 5 miles N on County A. Phone 715/386-5931.* A 2,800-acre park with swimming, fishing, boating, canoeing; cross-country skiing, picnicking, camping (hook-ups, dump station). Naturalist programs (summer only). River scenery with two dams. (Daily) **$$**

Limited-Service Hotel

★★ **BEST WESTERN HUDSON HOUSE INN.** *1616 Crest View Dr, Hudson (54016). Phone 715/386-2394; toll-free 800/780-7234; fax 715/386-3167. www.bestwestern.com.* 102 rooms, 2 story. Check-in 3 pm, check-out 11 am. Restaurant, bar. Indoor pool. **$**

Specialty Lodging

The following lodging establishment is approved by Mobil Travel Guide, but due to its unique and individualized nature has not been given a traditional Mobil Star rating. Included in this listing you may find bed-and-breakfasts, limited-service inns, guest ranches, and other unique hotel properties.

PHIPPS INN. *1005 3rd St, Hudson (54016). Phone 715/386-0800; toll-free 888/865-9388. www.phippsinn.com.* Nestled in scenic St. Croix Valley, this Queen Anne-style inn (1884) offers a quiet retreat in a lavish setting. 9 rooms, 3 story. Complimentary full breakfast. Check-in 4:30-6 pm, check-out 11 am. **$$**

Hurley (A-3)

See also Ironwood, Manitowish Waters

Founded 1885
Population 1,782
Elevation 1,493 ft
Area Code 715
Zip 54534
Information Chamber of Commerce, 316 Silver St; phone 715/561-4334
Web Site www.hurleywi.com

Originally a lumber and mining town, Hurley is now a winter sports center.

What to See and Do

Iron County Historical Museum. *303 Iron St, Hurley (54534). Iron St at 3rd Ave S. Phone 715/561-2244.* Exhibits of county's iron mining past; local artifacts, photo gallery. (Daily; closed Dec 25) **FREE**

Whitecap Mountain Ski Area. *County Rd E, Hurley (54534). 8 miles W on Hwy 77 to Iron Belt, then 3 miles W on County E. Phone 715/561-2776; toll-free 800/933-7669. www.skiwhitecap.com.* Area has six chairlifts, rope tow; patrol, school, rentals; nursery; restaurant, cafeteria, concession area. Longest run 1 1/2 mile; vertical drop 450 feet. (Nov-Mar, daily) Half-day rates. **$$$$**

Special Events

Iron County Heritage Festival. *316 Silver St, Hurley (54534). Phone 715/561-4334.* Various heritage themes and costumed cast of characters. Last Sat in July.

Paavo Nurmi Marathon. *316 Silver St, Hurley (54534). Begins in Upson, SW via Hwy 77. Phone 715/561-3290.* Oldest marathon in the state. Related activities Fri-Sat. Second weekend in Aug.

Red Light Snowmobile Rally. *316 Silver St, Hurley (54534). Phone 715/561-4334.* Second weekend in Dec.

Janesville (E-4)

See also Beloit, Elkhorn, Fort Atkinson, Madison, Monroe

Founded 1836
Population 52,133
Elevation 858 ft
Area Code 608
Information Janesville Area Convention & Visitors Bureau, 51 S Jackson St, 53545; phone 608/757-3171 or toll-free 800/487-2757
Web Site www.janesville.com

In 1836, pioneer Henry F. Janes carved his initials into a tree on the bank of the Rock River. The site is now the intersection of the two main streets of industrial Janesville. Janes went on to found other Janesvilles in Iowa and Minnesota. Wisconsin's Janesville has a truck and bus assembly plant that offers tours. Because of its 1,900 acres of parkland, Janesville has been called "Wisconsin's Park Place."

What to See and Do

General Motors Corporation. *1000 Industrial Ave, Janesville (53545). Phone 608/756-7681.* Guided tours. No cameras. Reservations required. (Mon-Thurs; closed holidays) **FREE**

Lincoln-Tallman Restorations. *440 N Jackson St, Janesville (53548). 4 blocks N on Hwy 14 Business. Phone 608/752-4519.* Tallman House (1855-1857), 26-room antebellum mansion of Italianate design considered among the top ten mid-19th-century structures for the study of American culture at the time of the Civil War. Restored Greek Revival Stone House (1842). Horse Barn (1855-1857) serves as visitor center and museum shop. Tours (daily). **$$$**

Milton House Museum. *18 N Janesville St, Milton (53563). 8 miles NE at junction Hwy 26, 59. Phone 608/868-7772.* (1844) Hexagonal building constructed of grout; underground railroad tunnel connects it with original log cabin; country store; guided tours. (Memorial Day-Labor Day: daily; May and Sept-mid-Oct: weekends, also Mon-Fri by appointment) **$$**

Municipal parks. *2200 Parkside Dr, Janesville (53547). Phone 608/755-3025.* Wading pool, fishing, boat launch; picnicking, hiking, cross-country skiing, tennis courts, 18-hole golf, concession. N Washington St, N on Hwy 14 Business. **Palmer.** Wading pool, swimming beach; picnicking, tennis courts, exercise course, nine-hole golf, concession. E Racine St, E on Hwy 14 Business, exit Hwy 11. **Traxler.** Boat launching ramps for Rock River, fishing, children's fishing pond; picnicking, ice skating; water-ski shows, rose gardens. (Daily, May-Sept) N Parker Dr, 1/2 mile N on Hwy 51. **Rockport.** Swimming pool, bathhouse; cross-country skiing, hiking. 2800 Rockport Rd. **FREE**

Rotary Gardens. *1455 Palmer Dr, Janesville (53545). Phone 608/752-3885.* 15-acre botanical garden (daily). Gift shop.

Special Event

Rock County 4-H Fair. *Rock County 4-H Fairgrounds, 100 Craig Ave, Janesville (53545). Phone 608/754-1470.* One of the largest 4-H fairs in country. Exhibits, competitions, carnival, grandstand shows, concerts. Last week in July.

Limited-Service Hotels

★ ★ BEST WESTERN JANESVILLE. *3900 Milton Ave, Janesville (53545). Phone 608/756-4511; toll-free 800/334-4271; fax 608/756-0025. www.bestwestern.com.* 105 rooms, 3 story. Pets accepted, some restrictions; fee. Complimentary continental breakfast. Check-in 3 pm, check-out 11 am. Restaurant, bar. Fitness room. Indoor pool, whirlpool. Airport transportation available. **$**

★ ★ RAMADA INN. *3431 Milton Ave, Janesville (53545). Phone 608/756-2341; toll-free 800/433-7787; fax 608/756-4183. www.ramada.com.* 189 rooms, 2 story. Complimentary continental breakfast. Check-in 3 pm, check-out noon. Restaurant, bar. Fitness room. Indoor pool, whirlpool. **$**

Restaurant

★ ★ COACHMAN'S GOLF RESORT. *984 County Trunk A, Edgerton (53534). Phone 608/884-8484. www.coachman.com.* American menu. Lunch, dinner, Sun brunch. Closed Jan 1, Dec 25; Mon in Nov-Apr. Bar. Children's menu. **$$**

Kenosha (F-5)

See also Lake Geneva, Milwaukee, Racine; also see Waukegan, IL

Settled 1835
Population 80,352
Elevation 610 ft
Area Code 262
Information Kenosha Area Convention & Visitors Bureau, 812 56th St, 53140; phone 262/654-7307 or toll-free 800/654-7309
Web Site www.kenoshacvb.com

A major industrial city, port, and transportation center, Kenosha was settled by New Englanders. The city owns 84 percent of its Lake Michigan frontage, most of it developed as parks.

What to See and Do

Bong State Recreation Area. *26313 Burlington Rd, Kansasville (53139). 17 miles W via Hwy 142; 9 miles W of I-94. Phone 262/878-5600.* A 4,515-acre area. Swimming, fishing, boating; hiking, bridle, and off-road motorcycle trails; cross-country skiing, snowmobiling, picnicking, guided nature hikes, nature center, special events area; family, group camping (fee). **$$$**

Carthage College. *2001 Alford Park Dr, Kenosha (53140). Hwy 32, N edge of city on lakeside. Phone 262/551-8500.* (1847) (2,100 students) Civil War Museum in Johnson Art Center (Mon-Fri; closed holidays). **FREE**

Factory outlet stores. *Original Outlet Mall, 7700 120th Ave, Kenosha (53142). Phone 262/857-7961.* More than 170 outlet stores can be found at Original Outlet Mall, 7700 120th Ave; phone 262/857-7961. **Prime Outlets at Pleasant Prairie,** 11211 120th Ave; phone 262/857-2101. (Daily)

Kemper Center. *6501 3rd Ave, Kenosha (53143). Phone 262/657-6005. www.kempercenter.com.* Approximately 11 acres. Several buildings including an Italianate Victorian mansion (1860); complex has more than 100 different trees, rose collection; mosiac mural; outdoor tennis courts, picnic area; also Anderson Art Gallery (Thurs-Sun afternoons). Guided tours by appointment. Office (Mon-Fri). Grounds (daily). **FREE**

Kenosha County Historical Society and Museum. *220 51st Pl, Kenosha (53140). Phone 262/654-5770.* Items and settings of local and Wisconsin history, Native American material, folk and decorative art. Research library. (Tues-Sun afternoons; closed holidays) **FREE**

Rambler Legacy Gallery. *Civic Center, 5500 1st Ave, Kenosha (53140). Phone 262/653-4140.* Lorado Taft dioramas of famous art studios; Native American, Oceanic, and African arts; Asian ivory and porcelain, Wisconsin folk pottery; mammals exhibit, dinosaur exhibit. Changing art, natural history exhibits. (Daily; closed holidays) **DONATION**

Southport Marina. *97 57th St, Kenosha (53140). 97th to 57th sts. Phone 262/657-5565.* 2-mile walkway on Lake Michigan; playground. (Daily) **FREE**

University of Wisconsin-Parkside. *940 Wood Rd, Kenosha (53144). Phone 262/595-2355.* (1968) (5,100 students) A 700-acre campus. Buildings are connected by glass-walled interior corridors that radiate from $8-million trilevel Wyllie Library Learning Center. Nature, cross-country ski trails. Tours.

Special Event

Bristol Renaissance Faire. *12550 120th Ave, Kenosha (53142). 6 miles SW via I-94, Russell Rd exit, just N of the IL/WI state line.Phone 847/395-7773; toll-free 800/523-2473. www.renfair.com/bristol.* Step back into a 16th-century European marketplace filled with richly gowned ladies, tattered beggars, and soldiers at the Bristol Renaissance Fair. As you stroll the grounds, stop in at a comedy show, swordfight, or thrilling jousting competition. Open nine weekends beginning July 9, plus Labor Day. (Sat-Sun 10 am-7 pm) **$$$$**

Limited-Service Hotels

★ BAYMONT INN. *7540 118th Ave, Pleasant Prairie (53158). Phone 262/857-7911; toll-free 877/229-6668; fax 262/857-2370. www.baymontinns.com.* 93 rooms, 2 story. Pets accepted, some restrictions. Complimentary continental breakfast. Check-in 2 pm, check-out noon. **$**

★ HOLIDAY INN EXPRESS. *5125 6th Ave, Kenosha (53140). Phone 262/658-3281; toll-free*

800/465-4329; fax 262/658-3420. www.hiexpress.com/kenoshawi. 111 rooms, 5 story. Pets accepted. Complimentary continental breakfast. Check-in 3 pm, check-out 11 am. Indoor pool, whirlpool. **$**

Restaurants

★ ★ HOUSE OF GERHARD. *3927 75th St, Kenosha (53142). Phone 262/694-5212; fax 262/694-5201. www.foodspot.com/gerhards.* German menu. Lunch, dinner. Closed Sun; holidays; also one week in early July. Bar. Children's menu. Casual attire. Reservations recommended. **$$**

★ ★ MANGIA TRATTORIA. *5717 Sheridan Rd, Kenosha (53140). Phone 262/652-4285; fax 262/652-9313.* Italian menu. Lunch, dinner. Closed holidays. Bar. Children's menu. Casual attire. Reservations recommended. Outdoor seating. **$$$**

★ ★ ★ RAY RADIGAN'S. *11712 S Sheridan Rd, Pleasant Prairie (53158). Phone 262/694-0455; fax 262/694-0798. www.foodspot.com/rayradigans.* Just 3 miles from town, this popular stop has been a local standby since 1933. American menu. Lunch, dinner. Closed Mon; holidays. Bar. Children's menu. Casual attire. Reservations recommended. **$$**

Kohler (D-5)

See also Sheboygan

Population 1,989
Area Code 920
Zip 53044
Information Sheboygan County Chamber of Commerce, 712 Riverfront Dr, Suite 101, Sheboygan 53081; phone 920/457-9495 or toll-free 800/457-9497
Web Site www.destinationkohler.com

Kohler, a small town near Sheboygan, has gained a reputation as one of the region's top resort destinations. One of the nation's first planned communities, designed with the help of the Olmstead Brothers firm of Boston, Massachusetts, Kohler began as a "garden at the factory gate and headquarters for the country's largest plumbing manufacturer. Running through Kohler is 7 miles of the Sheboygan River and a 500-acre wildlife sanctuary.

What to See and Do

John Michael Kohler Arts Center. *608 New York Ave, Kohler (53044). Phone 920/458-6144.* Changing contemporary art exhibitions, galleries, shop, historic house; theater, dance, and concert series. Center's exhibitions emphasize craft-related forms, installation works, photography, new genres, ongoing cultural traditions, and the work of self-taught artists. (Daily; closed holidays) **FREE**

Kohler Design Center. *101 Upper Rd, Kohler (53044). Phone 920/457-3699. www.us.kohler.com/designkb/designcenter/designcenter.jsp.* A 36,000-square-foot, three-story exhibition center of kitchen and bath design ideas and the newest Kohler plumbing products. Although you can't purchase products here, it's a great place to come if you're looking for kitchen and bathroom remodeling ideas. Three-hour Industry in Action tours of the massive Kohler Company pottery, brass works, and cast-iron foundry are given weekdays at 8:30 am (reservations required). Also here is the Museum of Kohler Company, depicting the history of the village and housing the Kohler Company Art Collection gallery. (Mon-Fri 8 am-5 pm, Sat-Sun 10 am-4 pm; closed Thanksgiving, Dec 25) **FREE**

Shops at Woodlake. *Phone 920/459-1713. www.destinationkohler.com/shops/shops.html.* Pick up clothing, fly-fishing supplies, furniture, home accessories, and other specialty goods at this small shopping center in Kohler village. (Mon-Fri 10 am-6 pm, Sat 10 am-5 pm, Sun noon-5 pm)

Waelderhaus. *1100 W Riverside Dr, Kohler (53044). 1 mile S off County Rd PP. Phone 920/452-4079.* A reproduction of the Kohler family chalet and furnishings in the Austrian Alps. (Guided tours daily at 2, 3, and 4 pm; closed holidays) **FREE**

Special Events

Great Gingerbread Holiday Festival. *Waelderhaus, 1100 W Riverside Dr, Kohler (53044). Phone 920/452-4079.* Gingerbread house creations designed and executed by area school children at the Waelderhaus. Dec.

Kohler Food & Wine Experience. *Phone toll-free 800/344-2838. www.destinationkohler.com/food/food.html.* This annual event features cooking demonstrations, food and wine tastings, and seminars. Varied admission fees are charged for individual sessions. Three days in late Oct.

Traditional Holiday Illumination. *Highland Dr, Kohler (53044). Phone 920/457-8000.* More than 200,000 lights on trees surrounding Kohler hospitality facilities create a winter fanstasyland in the Kohler Village. Thanksgiving-Feb.

Limited-Service Hotel

★ ★ **INN ON WOODLAKE.** *705 Woodlake Rd, Kohler (53044). Phone 920/452-7800; toll-free 800/919-3600; fax 920/457-7011. www.innonwoodlake.com.* Situated between the meadows and the Southern shore of Wood Lake, this property gives guests the choice of a prairie view or a lake view from their room. 121 rooms, 3 story. Complimentary continental breakfast. Check-out noon. Fitness room. Indoor pool, whirlpool. **$$**

Full-Service Resort

★ ★ ★ ★ **THE AMERICAN CLUB.** *444 Highland Dr, Kohler (53044). Phone 920/457-8000; toll-free 800/344-2838; fax 920/457-0299. www.destinationkohler.com.* Located in the charming village of Kohler, The American Club offers a country getaway only one hour north of Milwaukee. Travelers stay and play here, and with the wide variety of available activities, visitors are never at a loss for something to do. Avid golfers wax poetic about the resort's four 18-hole courses sculpted out of the rugged terrain by renowned course architect Pete Dye. Whistling Straits calls to mind the natural beauty of Scotland and Ireland in its design, while Blackwolf Run is often considered the top public course in America. After a competitive round of golf, a tennis match, or a workout at the fitness center, guests succumb to the relaxing wonders of the Kohler Waters Spa. Everyone finds a favorite among ten distinctive dining establishments, and after a delicious meal, guests find the comfort of their tastefully appointed accommodations just right for a restful end to a wonderful day. 237 rooms, 3 story. Check-in 4 pm, check-out noon. High-speed Internet access, wireless Internet access. Ten restaurants, seven bars. Children's activity center. Fitness room, fitness classes available, spa. Indoor pool, children's pool, whirlpool. Golf, 72 holes. Tennis. Airport transportation available. Business center. **$$$**

Restaurants

★ ★ ★ **THE IMMIGRANT RESTAURANT & WINERY BAR.** *444 Highland Dr, Kohler (53044). Phone 920/457-8888; toll-free 800/344-2838; fax 920/457-0299. www.destinationkohler.com.* Exquisite food and exceptional service radiates through the six rooms decorated to salute the European ethnic mix of early Wisconsin settlers. American menu. Dinner. Closed Sun. Bar. Jacket required. Reservations recommended. Valet parking. **$$$**

★ ★ **RICHARD'S.** *501 Monroe St, Sheboygan Falls (53085). Phone 920/467-6401. www.richardsoffalls.com.* Former stagecoach inn (circa 1840s). American menu. Dinner. Closed Mon; holidays. Bar. Business casual attire. Reservations recommended. **$$**

La Crosse (D-2)

See also Galesville, Sparta

Settled 1842
Population 51,003
Elevation 669 ft
Area Code 608
Information La Crosse Area Convention and Visitor Bureau, 410 E Veterans Memorial Dr, 54601; phone 608/782-2366 or toll-free 800/658-9424
Web Site www.explorelacrosse.com

An agricultural, commercial, and industrial city, La Crosse is washed by the waters of the Mississippi, Black, and La Crosse rivers. Once a trading post, it was named by the French for the native game the French called lacrosse. More than 200 businesses and industries operate here today.

What to See and Do

City Brewery Tour. *City Brewery, 925 3rd St S, La Crosse (54601). Phone 608/785-4200; toll-free 800/433-2337.* One-hour guided tours. Gift shop. (Mon-Sat; closed holidays) **FREE**

Goose Island County Park. *W6488 County Rd GI, Stoddard (54658). 3 miles S on Hwy 35, then 2 miles W on County GI. Phone 608/788-7018.* Beach, fishing, boat ramps; hiking trails, picnicking, camping (electric hook-ups). (Mid-Apr-mid-Oct, daily) **$$$**

Granddad Bluff. *400 La Crosse St, La Crosse (54601). Phone 608/789-7533.* Tallest (1,172 feet) of the crags that overlook the city; it provides a panoramic view of the winding Mississippi, the tree-shaded city, and the Minnesota and Iowa bluffs. Picnic area. (May-late Oct, daily) Surfaced path to shelter house and top of bluff for the disabled. **FREE**

Hixon House. *429 N 7th St, La Crosse (54601). Phone 608/782-1980.* (Circa 1860) 15-room home; Victorian and Asian furnishings. A visitor information center and gift shop are located in the building that once served as a wash house. (Memorial Day-Labor Day, daily) **$$**

***La Crosse Queen* Cruises.** *Boat Dock, Riverside Park, W end of State St. Phone 608/784-2893.* Sightseeing cruise on the Mississippi River aboard 150-passenger, double-deck paddlewheeler (early May-mid-Oct, daily). Also dinner cruise (Fri night, Sat-Sun). Charters (approximately Apr-Oct).

Mount La Crosse Ski Area. *2 miles S on Hwy 35. Phone 608/788-0044; toll-free 800/426-3665. www.mtlacrosse.com.* Area has three chairlifts, rope tow; patrol, rentals, school; snowmaking; night skiing; cafeteria, bar. Longest run 1 mile; vertical drop 516 feet. (Thanksgiving-mid-Mar, daily; closed Dec 25) Half-day rates on weekends, holidays. Cross-country trails (Dec-mid-Mar, daily).

Pump House Regional Arts Center. *119 King St, La Crosse. Phone 608/785-1434.* (Western Wisconsin Regional Arts) Regional art exhibits; performing arts (weekends). (Tues-Sat; closed holidays) **DONATION**

Swarthout Museum. *112 9th St N, La Crosse (54601). Phone 608/782-1980.* Changing historical exhibits ranging from prehistoric times to the 20th century. (Memorial Day-Labor Day: Tues-Sat; rest of year: Tues-Sun; closed holidays) **FREE**

Special Events

La Crosse Interstate Fair. *La Crosse Fairgrounds Speedway, W4985 County Hwy M, West Salem (54669). 11 miles E on I-90. Phone 608/786-1525; toll-free 800/658-9424. www.lacrossespeedway.com.* Stock car racing, farm exhibits; carnival, entertainment. Mid-July.

Oktoberfest. *1 Oktoberfest Dr, La Crosse (54601). S side of town. Phone toll-free 800/658-9424.* Six days beginning last weekend in Sept or first weekend in Oct.

Riverfest. *Riverside Park, 410 Veteran's Memorial Dr, La Crosse (54601). Phone 608/782-6000. www.riverfest.org.* Five-day festival with river events, music, food, entertainment, fireworks, children's events. Late June-early July.**$$**

Limited-Service Hotels

★ ★ BEST WESTERN MIDWAY HOTEL. *1835 Rose St, La Crosse (54603). Phone 608/781-7000; toll-free 877/688-9260; fax 608/781-3195. www.midwayhotels.com.* 121 rooms, 2 story. Pets accepted; fee. Check-in 3 pm, check-out noon. High-speed Internet access, wireless Internet access. Restaurant, bar. Fitness room. Indoor pool, whirlpool. Airport transportation available. Business center. **$**

★ HAMPTON INN. *2110 Rose St, La Crosse (54603). Phone 608/781-5100; toll-free 800/426-7866; fax 608/781-3574. www.hamptoninnlacrosse.com.* 101 rooms, 2 story. Complimentary full breakfast. Check-in 2 pm, check-out noon. Wireless Internet access. Fitness room. Indoor pool, whirlpool. **$**

★ ★ RADISSON HOTEL LA CROSSE. *200 Harborview Plz, La Crosse (54601). Phone 608/784-6680; toll-free 800/333-3333; fax 608/784-6694. www.radisson.com.* Providing a lovely view of the river, the spacious accommodations at this hotel are designed to make guests feel at home. 169 rooms, 8 story. Pets accepted. Check-in 3 pm, check-out noon. High-speed Internet access. Restaurant, bar. Fitness room. Indoor pool, whirlpool. **$**

★ SUPER 8. *1625 Rose St, La Crosse (54603). Phone 608/781-8880; toll-free 800/800-8000; fax 608/781-4366. www.super8.com.* 82 rooms, 2 story. Complimentary continental breakfast. Check-in 3 pm, check-out 11 am. Fitness room. Indoor pool, whirlpool. **$**

Restaurants

★ ★ FREIGHTHOUSE. *107 Vine St, La Crosse (54601). Phone 608/784-6211; fax 608/784-6280. www.freighthouserestaurant.com.* Former freight house of the Chicago, Milwaukee, and St. Paul Railroad (1880). Steak menu. Dinner. Bar. Casual attire. **$$$**

★ PICASSO'S CAFE. *600 N 3rd St, La Crosse (54601). Phone 608/784-4485.* Located in beautiful downtown La Crosse, this restaurant serves California-inspired Mediterranean cuisine in a hip, sophisticated atmosphere. Mediterranean menu. Lunch, dinner. Closed Sun. **$**

★★ PIGGY'S. *328 S Front St, La Crosse (54601). Phone 608/784-4877; toll-free 888/865-9632; fax 608/784-5756. www.piggys.com.* American menu. Dinner. Closed holidays. Bar. Children's menu. Casual attire. Reservations recommended. **$$**

Lac du Flambeau (B-3)

See also Manitowish Waters, Minocqua, Park Falls, Woodruff

Population 1,423
Elevation 1,635 ft
Area Code 715
Zip 54538
Information Chamber of Commerce, PO Box 158; phone 715/588-3346 or toll-free 877/588-3346
Web Site www.lacduflambeauchamber.com

The French gave this village the name "Lake of the Torch" because of the Chippewa practice of fishing and canoeing at night by the light of birch bark torches. Located in the center of the Lac du Flambeau Reservation, the village is tribal headquarters for more than 1,200 Chippewa still living in the area. It is also the center for a popular, lake-filled north woods recreation area. The reservation boasts 126 spring-fed lakes and its own fish hatchery.

What to See and Do

Lac du Flambeau Chippewa Museum and Cultural Center. *603 Peace Pipe Rd, Lac du Flambeau (54538). Downtown. Phone 715/588-3333.* Displays of Native American artifacts, fur trading, and historical items. Chippewa craft workshops (May-Oct). (Mon-Sat; also by appointment) **$$**

Waswagoning Ojibwe Village. *2750 County Rd H, Lac du Flambeau (54538). 1 mile N on County H. Phone 715/588-3560.* Twenty acres of Ojibwe culture with guided tours. (Memorial Day-Labor Day). **$$$**

Special Events

Colorama. *622 Peace Pipe Rd, Lac du Flambeau (54538). Downtown. Phone 715/588-3346.* Last Sat in Sept.

Powwows. *603 Peace Pipe Rd, Lac du Flambeau (54538). Phone 715/588-3333.* At Indian Bowl, fronting on Lake Interlaken. Dancing by Wa-swa-gon Dancers. July-mid-Aug.

Ladysmith (B-2)

Population 3,938
Elevation 1,144 ft
Area Code 715
Zip 54848
Information Rusk County Visitor Center, 205 W 9th St; phone 715/532-2642 or toll-free 800/535-7875
Web Site www.ruskcounty.org

Ladysmith, county seat of Rusk County, is located along the Flambeau River. The economy is based on processing lumber and marketing dairy and farm produce. There are fishing and canoeing facilities in the area.

What to See and Do

Flambeau River State Forest. *W1613 County Rd W, Winter (54896). E on Hwy 8 to Hawkins, then N on County M to County W. Phone 715/332-5271.* A 91,000-acre forest. Canoeing river, swimming, fishing, boating; backpacking, nature and hiking trails, mountain biking, cross-country skiing, snowmobiling, picnicking, camping (dump station). (Daily)

Special Events

Leaf it to Rusk Fall Festival. *Phone 715/532-2642.* Countywide events. Last weekend in Sept.

Northland Mardi Gras. *Parade starts at Middle School, 115 E 6th St S, Ladysmith (54848). Events at Memorial Park, Ladysmith (54848). Phone 715/532-2642.* Third weekend in July.

Rusk County Fair. *Fairgrounds, E 3rd St, Ladysmith (54848). Phone 715/532-2639.* Four days in mid-Aug.

Limited-Service Hotel

★★ BEST WESTERN EL RANCHO. *8500 W Flambeau Ave, Ladysmith (54848). Phone 715/532-6666; toll-free 800/780-7234; fax 715/532-7551. www.bestwestern.com.* 27 rooms. Pets accepted; fee. Check-in 1 pm, check-out 11 am. Restaurant, bar. **$**

Lake Geneva (F-4)

See also Burlington, Delavan, Elkhorn, Fontana, Kenosha

Settled 1840
Population 5,979
Elevation 880 ft
Area Code 262
Zip 53147
Information Geneva Lake Area Chamber of Commerce, 201 Wrigley Dr; phone 262/248-4416 or toll-free 800/345-1020
Web Site www.lakegenevawi.com

This is a popular and attractive four-season resort area. Recreational activities include boating, fishing, swimming, horseback riding, camping, hiking, biking, golf, tennis, skiing, cross-country skiing, ice fishing, snowmobiling, and ice boating.

What to See and Do

Big Foot Beach State Park. *1452 Hwy H, Lake Geneva (53147). 1 mile S on Hwy 120. Phone 262/248-2528.* A 272-acre beach park on Geneva Lake. Swimming (lifeguard on duty mid-June-Labor Day, weekends only), fishing; picnicking, playground, winter sports, camping. (Daily) **$$$**

Excursion boats. *Riviera Docks, 812 Wrigley Dr, Lake Geneva (53147). Phone 262/248-6206; toll-free 800/558-5911.* Two-hour round-trip and one-hour rides; also lunch, Sun brunch, dinner cruises. (May-Oct, daily) Reservations required. Mail boat (mid-June-mid-Sept, once daily). **$$$$**

Geneva Lake. This 5,230-acre lake provides a variety of game fish in clear waters. The surrounding hills are heavily wooded with elm, maple, and oak trees.

Grand Geneva Resort. *7036 Grand Geneva Way, Lake Geneva (53147). 2 miles E at jct Hwy 12 and Hwy 50. Phone toll-free 800/558-3417. www.grandgeneva.com.* Area has three chairlifts, two rope tows; patrol, school, rentals; snowmaking; lodging (see FULL-SERVICE RESORTS); restaurant, cafeteria, concession, bar. Longest run 1/4 mile; vertical drop 211 feet (Dec-Mar, daily) Cross-country trails, night skiing. **$$$$**

Wilmot Mountain. *3 miles N of Antioch, IL, on Hwy 83, then W on Hwy C; 1 mile S of Wilmot, WI, Hwy W on the IL state line. Phone 262/862-2301. www.wilmotmountain.com.* Quad, three triple, four double chairlifts, three rope tows; patrol, school, rentals, snowmaking; restaurant, cafeteria, bar. Snowboarding. Longest run 2,500 feet; vertical drop 230 feet. Night skiing. (Mid-Nov-Mar, daily; closed Dec 24 evening)

Special Events

Venetian Festival. *Flatiron Park, 201 Wrigley Dr, Lake Geneva (53147). Phone 262/248-4416.* Rides, games, food; lighted boat parade and fireworks. Third weekend in Aug.

Winterfest. *Riviera Park, 201 Wrigley Dr, Lake Geneva (53147). At the lakefront.Phone 262/248-4416.* Host of the US Snow Sculpting Championships. Early Feb.

Limited-Service Hotel

★ ★ BEST WESTERN HARBOR SHORES. *300 Wrigley Dr, Lake Geneva (53147). Phone 262/248-9181; toll-free 888/746-7371; fax 262/248-1885. www.bestwestern.com.* 108 rooms. Complimentary continental breakfast. Check-in 4 pm, check-out 11 am. Restaurant, bar. Indoor pool, outdoor pool, whirlpool. **$**

Full-Service Resorts

★ ★ ★ GRAND GENEVA RESORT & SPA. *7036 Grand Geneva Way, Lake Geneva (53147). Phone 262/248-8811; toll-free 800/558-3417; fax 262/249-4763. www.grandgeneva.com.* 1,300 acres of wooded meadowland with private lake. 355 rooms, 3 story. Check-in 4 pm, check-out noon. Restaurant, bar. Children's activity center. Fitness room. Two indoor pools, outdoor pool, whirlpool. Golf. Tennis. Airport transportation available. Business center. **$$**

★ ★ ★ INTERLAKEN RESORT AND COUNTRY SPA. *W4240 Hwy 50, Lake Geneva (53147). Phone 262/248-9121; toll-free 800/225-5558; fax 262/245-5016. www.interlakenresort.com.* This serene resort promotes an air of pure relaxation and hosts several wonderful views. 144 rooms, 3 story. Check-out noon. Restaurant, bar. Children's activity center. Fitness room. Indoor pool, outdoor pool, children's pool, whirlpool. Tennis. **$**

★ ★ ★ TIMBER RIDGE LODGE & WATERPARK. *7020 Grand Geneva Way, Lake*

Geneva (53147). Phone 262/249-0375; toll-free 866/636-4502; fax 262/249-3410. www.timberridgeresort.com. 225 rooms, all suites. Check-in 4 pm, check-out 11 am. High-speed Internet access. Two restaurants, two bars. Children's activity center. Fitness room. Indoor pool, outdoor pool, children's pool, whirlpool. Business center. **$$**

Specialty Lodging

The following lodging establishment is approved by Mobil Travel Guide, but due to its unique and individualized nature has not been given a traditional Mobil Star rating. Included in this listing you may find bed-and-breakfasts, limited-service inns, guest ranches, and other unique hotel properties.

FRENCH COUNTRY INN. *W4190 West End Rd, Lake Geneva (53147). Phone 262/245-5220; fax 262/245-9060. www.frenchcountryinn.com.* Portions of the guest house were built in Denmark and shipped to the United States for the Danish exhibit at the 1893 Columbian Exposition in Chicago. 24 rooms, 2 story. Check-in 4 pm, check-out 11 am. Restaurant. Beach. Outdoor pool. **$$$**

Restaurants

★ CACTUS CLUB. *430 Broad St, Lake Geneva (53147). Phone 262/248-1999; fax 262/248-7114.* American, Mexican menu. Lunch, dinner. Bar. Children's menu. Casual attire. **$$**

★ POPEYE'S GALLEY AND GROG. *811 Wrigley Dr, Lake Geneva (53147). Phone 262/248-4381.* American menu. Lunch, dinner. Closed Dec 25. Bar. Children's menu. **$$**

★★★ RISTORANTE BRISSAGO. *7036 Grand Geneva Way, Lake Geneva (53147). Phone 262/248-8811. www.grandgeneva.com.* Named after a town on Lake Maggiore in the Italian-Swiss countryside, this restaurant enjoys a Midwestern, countryside home all its own. The dining room is just one of the options at the Grand Geneva Resort & Spa (see). Italian menu. Dinner. Closed Mon. Bar. Valet parking. **$$$**

Land O Lakes (B-3)

See also Boulder Junction, Eagle River

Population 700
Elevation 1,700 ft
Area Code 715
Zip 54540
Information Chamber of Commerce, Hwy 45, PO Box 599; phone 715/547-3432 or toll-free 800/236-3432
Web Site www.ci.land-o-lakes.wi.us

This lovely village, on the Michigan border amid more than 100 lakes, serves as a center for tourist traffic. Fishing and boating in the area are exceptional. East of town is Lac Vieux Desert, source of the Wisconsin River.

Madison (E-3)

See also Fort Atkinson, Janesville, Mount Horeb, New Glarus, Prairie du Sac

Settled 1837
Population 191,262
Elevation 863 ft
Area Code 608
Information Greater Madison Convention & Visitors Bureau, 615 E Washington Ave, 53703; phone 608/255-2537 or toll-free 800/373-6376
Web Site www.visitmadison.com

Madison was a virgin wilderness in 1836 when the territorial legislature selected the spot for the capital and the state university. Today, this "City of Four Lakes," located on an isthmus between Lake Mendota and Lake Monona, is a recreational, cultural, and manufacturing center. Both the university and state government play important roles in the community.

Madison has a rich architectural heritage left by Frank Lloyd Wright and the Prairie School movement. There are a number of Wright buildings here; many are private homes and not open to the public but may be viewed from the outside.

Airport Information

Airport Dane County Regional Airport

Information 608/246-3380.

Airlines American Eagle, American Trans Air/Chicago Express, Comair, Continental, Midwest Express Skyway, Northwest Airlines, United Express, US Airways Express

What to See and Do

Dane County Farmers' Market. *200 Martin Luther King Jr. Blvd, Madison (53703). (Two locations) Capitol Sq and 200 Martin Luther King Jr. Blvd. Phone 608/424-6714.* Festive open-air market selling Wisconsin produce and agricultural products. Capitol Square (May-Oct, Sat); Martin Luther King Jr. Boulevard (May-Oct, Wed).

Edgewood College. *1000 Edgewood College Dr, Madison (53711). Phone 608/257-4861. www.edgewood.edu.* (1927) (1,725 students) A 55-acre campus on Lake Wingra; Native American burial mounds.

First Unitarian Society. *900 University Bay Dr, Madison (53705). Phone 608/233-9774.* A classic example of Wright's Prairie School work. (May-Sept, Mon-Fri afternoons, also Sat mornings; closed holidays and two weeks in Aug) **$$**

Henry Vilas Park Zoo. *702 S Randall Ave, Madison (53715). On Lake Wingra. Phone 608/258-9490. www.vilaszoo.org.* World famous for successful orangutan, Siberian tiger, spectacle bear, penguin, and camel breeding programs. Zoo exhibits include 600 specimens consisting of 140 species. Petting zoo, picnic area on an island in Lake Wingra's lagoon, bathing beach, tennis courts. (Daily) **FREE**

Lake Kegonsa State Park. *2405 Door Creek Rd, Stoughton (53589). 13 miles SE via I-90, then S on County N. Phone 608/873-9695.* A 343-acre park. Swimming, water-skiing, fishing, boating; hiking and nature trails, picnicking, playground, camping (May-mid-Oct, dump station). (Daily)

Madison Art Center. *Civic Center, 211 State St, Madison (53703). Phone 608/257-0158. www.madisonartcenter.org.* Features modern and contemporary art by international, national, regional, and local artists; permanent collection. Tours (by appointment, fee). (Tues-Sun; closed holidays) **FREE**

Madison Children's Museum. *100 State St, Madison (53703). Phone 608/256-6445. www.madisonchildrensmuseum.com.* Hands-on museum. Special craft and activity programs every weekend. (Tues-Sun, daily; closed holidays) **$**

Olbrich Botanical Gardens. *3330 Atwood Ave, Madison (53704). Phone 608/246-4551. www.olbrich.org.* Contains 14 acres of horticultural displays featuring annuals, perennials, shrubs, hybrid roses, lilies, dahlias, spring bulbs, and rock and herb gardens. All-American Rose Selection Demonstration Garden. Garden building has a tropical conservatory housed inside a 50-foot high glass pyramid; tropical ferns, palms, flowering plants; waterfall, stream. (Daily; closed Dec 25) **$**

Self-driving tour. These are private homes and not open to the public. However, they may be viewed from the outside. **Airplane House** (1908), 120 Ely Place; **Dr. Arnold Jackson House** (1957), 3515 W Beltline Hwy; **Lamp House** (1899), 22 N Butler St; **J. C. Pew House** (1939), 3650 Lake Mendota Dr; **Louis Sullivan's Bradley House,** 106 N Prospect; **"Jacobs I" House** (1937), 441 Toepfer Ave.

State Capitol. *Capital Sq, 2 E Main St, Madison (53702). Phone 608/266-0382.* Dominates the center of the city. The white granite building has a classic dome topped by Daniel Chester French's gilded bronze statue *Wisconsin.* Tours (daily; closed holidays). **FREE**

State Historical Museum. *30 N Carroll St, Madison (53702). Located on Capitol Sq, junction State, Mifflin, and Carroll sts. Phone 608/264-6555.* Permanent exhibits explore the history of Native American life in Wisconsin; gallery with changing Wisconsin, US history exhibits. Theater. (Tues-Sat) **FREE**

University of Wisconsin-Madison. *716 Langdon St, Madison (53706). 7 blocks W of Capitol. Maps and general information at Visitor and Information Place, N Park and Langdon sts; or at Campus Assistance Center, 420 N Lake St. Phone 608/263-2400.* (1849) (41,948 students) The 929-acre campus extends for more than 2 miles along south shore of Lake Mendota. On campus are

Carillon Tower. *1160 Observatory Dr, Madison (53706). Phone 608/263-1900.* Features 56 bells; afternoon concerts (Sun).

Elvehjem Museum of Art. *800 University Ave, Madison (53706). Phone 608/263-2246.* Paintings, sculpture, decorative arts, prints, Japanese woodcuts, other artwork from 2300 BC to present day; changing exhibits; 80,000-volume Kohler Art Library. (Tues-Sun; closed Jan 1, Thanksgiving, Dec 25) **FREE**

Geology Museum. *1215 W Dayton St, Madison (53706). At Charter St. Phone 608/262-2399.* Exhibits include a 6-foot rotating globe, rocks, minerals, a black light display, a walk-through cave, meteorites, and fossils including the skeletons of a giant mastodon and dinosaurs. (Mon-Fri, daily, also Sat mornings; closed holidays) **FREE**

Memorial Library. *728 State St, Madison (53706). Langdon and Lake sts. Phone 608/262-3193.* More than 5 million volumes; collection of rare books.

Observatory and Willow drives. Scenic drives along shore of Lake Mendota.

Washburn Observatory. *1401 Observatory Dr, Madison (53706). Phone 608/262-9274.* Public viewing first and third Wed evenings of each month (weather permitting). **FREE**

USDA Forest Products Laboratory. *1 Gifford Pinchot Dr, Madison. Off N Walnut St. Phone 608/231-9200.* Devoted to scientific and technical research on properties, processing, and uses of wood and wood products. Guided tour (one departure, Mon-Thurs afternoons; closed hols). **FREE**

Wisconsin Veterans Museum. *30 W Mifflin St, Madison (53703). Phone 608/267-1799.* Dioramas, exhibits of events from Civil War to Persian Gulf War. (June-Sept: daily; rest of year: Mon-Sat; closed holidays) **FREE**

Special Events

Art Fair on the Square. *Capitol Concourse, 2 E Main, Madison (53703). Phone 608/257-0158.* Exhibits by 500 artists and craftspersons; food, entertainment. Contact Madison Art Center. Mid-July.

Concerts on the Square. *Capitol Concourse, 2 E Main, Madison (53703). Phone 608/257-0638.* Six-week series; Wed evenings. Late June-early Aug.

Dane County Fair. *Alliant Energy Center, 1919 Alliant Energy Center Way, Madison (53703). Phone 608/224-0500.* Mid-July.

Paddle & Portage Canoe Race. *Gorham and Blair sts, Madison (53703). Phone 608/255-1008.* July.

Limited-Service Hotels

★ ★ BEST WESTERN INN ON THE PARK. *22 S Carroll St, Madison (53703). Phone 608/257-8811; toll-free 800/279-8811; fax 608/257-5995. www.innonthepark.net.* 212 rooms, 9 story. Check-in 3 pm, check-out noon. Restaurant, bar. Fitness room. Indoor pool, whirlpool. Airport transportation available. **$**

★ ★ ★ EDGEWATER HOTEL. *666 Wisconsin Ave, Madison (53703). Phone 608/256-9071; toll-free 800/922-5512; fax 608/256-0910. www.theedgewater.com.* Lakeview rooms loaded with the latest in modern features await guests at this getaway on Lake Mendota. 108 rooms, 8 story. Pets accepted. Check-in 3 pm, check-out 11 am. Restaurant, bar. Beach. Airport transportation available. **$**

★ HAMPTON INN. *4820 Hayes Rd, Madison (53704). Phone 608/244-9400; toll-free 800/426-7866; fax 608/244-7177. www.hamptoninn.com.* 116 rooms, 4 story. Complimentary continental breakfast. Check-in 3 pm, check-out noon. Fitness room. Indoor pool, whirlpool. **$**

★ ★ HOWARD JOHNSON. *525 W Johnson St, Madison (53705). Phone 608/251-5511; toll-free 800/446-4656; fax 608/251-4824. www.hjplazamadison.com.* 163 rooms, 7 story. Check-in 4 pm, check-out noon. Restaurant, bar. Fitness room. Indoor pool, whirlpool. Airport transportation available. **$**

Full-Service Hotels

★ ★ ★ MADISON CONCOURSE HOTEL & GOVERNOR'S CLUB. *1 W Dayton St, Madison (53703). Phone 608/257-6000; toll-free 800/356-8293; fax 608/257-5280. www.concoursehotel.com.* Stylish and warm are often used to describe this inn. 356 rooms, 13 story. Check-in 3 pm, check-out 11 am. Two restaurants, bar. Fitness room. Indoor pool, whirlpool. Airport transportation available. Business center. **$**

★ ★ ★ SHERATON MADISON HOTEL. *706 John Nolen Dr, Madison (53713). Phone 608/251-2300; toll-free 800/325-3535; fax 608/251-1189. www.sheraton.com.* 237 rooms, 7 story. Pets accepted; fee. Check-in 3 pm, check-out noon. Restaurant, bar. Fitness room. Indoor pool, whirlpool. **$**

Restaurants

★ ★ ★ ADMIRALTY. *666 Wisconsin Ave, Madison (53703). Phone 608/256-9071. www.theedgewater.com.* This dining room boasts spectacular sunset views over Lake Mendota and a classic, international menu. The space carries old-world charm with its leather chairs, framed photographs, and tableside preparations of dishes. International/Fusion menu. Breakfast, lunch, dinner, Sun brunch. Bar. Outdoor seating. **$$**

★ AMY'S CAFE. *414 W Gilman St, Madison (53703). Phone 608/255-8172.* American menu. Lunch, dinner. Bar. Outdoor seating. **$**

★ ELLA'S DELI. *2902 E Washington Ave, Madison (53704). Phone 608/241-5291.* Outdoor carousel. American menu. Lunch, dinner. Closed Thanksgiving, Dec 24-25. Children's menu. **$**

★ ESSEN HAUS. *514 E Wilson St, Madison (53703). Phone 608/255-4674; fax 608/258-8632. www.essenhaus.com.* German menu. Dinner. Closed Mon; Dec 24-25. Bar. Childrens's menu. Outdoor seating. **$$**

★ ★ ★ L'ETOILE. *25 N Pinckney, Madison (53703). Phone 608/251-0500; fax 608/251-7577. www.letoile-restaurant.com.* This second-floor dining room may be hard to find, but it's worth the search for some of this university town's best dining. Chef/owner Odessa Piper changes her menu weekly to highlight the wares of local markets and organic farms. French menu. Dinner. Closed Sun-Mon; holidays. Bar. **$$$**

★ ★ NAU-TI-GAL. *5360 Westport Rd, Madison (53704). Phone 608/246-3130. www.nautigal.com.* American menu. Lunch, dinner, Sun brunch. Closed holidays. Bar. Children's menu. Outdoor seating. **$$**

★ ★ QUIVEY'S GROVE. *6261 Nesbitt Rd, Madison (53719). Phone 608/273-4900. www.quiveysgrove.com.* Converted historic mansion and stables (1855); many antiques. American menu. Lunch, dinner. Closed holidays. Bar. Children's menu. Outdoor seating. **$$**

★ SA-BAI THONG. *2840 University Ave, Madison (53705). Phone 608/238-3100. www.sabaithong.com.* Thai menu. Lunch, dinner. Closed Thanksgiving, Dec 25. **$$**

Manitowish Waters (B-3)

See also Boulder Junction, Hurley, Lac du Flambeau, Minocqua, Park Falls, Woodruff

Population 686
Elevation 1,611 ft
Area Code 715
Zip 54545
Information Chamber of Commerce, PO Box 251, 54545; phone 715/543-8488 or toll-free 888/626-9877
Web Site www.manitowishwaters.org

Manitowish Waters is in Northern Highland-American Legion State Forest, which abounds in small- and medium-size lakes linked by streams. Ten of the fourteen lakes are navigable without portaging, making them ideal for canoeing. There are 16 campgrounds on lakes in the forest (standard fees) and 135 overnight campsites on water trails. Canoe trips, fishing, swimming, boating, water-skiing, and snowmobiling are popular here.

What to See and Do

Cranberry bog tours. *Community Center, Hwy 51 Airport Rd, Manitowish Waters (54545). Phone 715/543-8488.* Tours begin with a video and samples, then follow guides in own vehicle. (Late July-early Oct, Fri)

Limited-Service Hotel

★ ★ GREAT NORTHERN. *Hwy 51 S, Mercer (54547). Phone 715/476-2440; fax 715/476-2205.* 80 rooms, 2 story. Pets accepted, some restrictions; fee. Complimentary continental breakfast. Check-out 11 am. Restaurant, bar. Indoor pool, whirlpool. **$**

Restaurants

★ ★ LITTLE BOHEMIA. *County W, Manitowish Waters (54545). Phone 715/543-8433. www.littlebohemia.net.* Site of a 1930s shoot-out between John Dillinger and the FBI; musuem. Steak menu. Dinner. Closed Wed; also Feb-Mar. Bar. Children's menu. **$$**

★ ★ SWANBERG'S BAVARIAN INN. *W140 County W, Manitowish Waters (54545). Phone 715/543-2122; fax 715/543-2047.* German menu. Lunch, dinner. Closed Sun. Bar. Children's menu. **$$**

Manitowoc (D-5)

See also Green Bay, Ludington, Sheboygan, Two Rivers

Settled 1836
Population 32,520
Elevation 606 ft
Area Code 920
Zip 54220
Information Manitowoc-Two Rivers Area Chamber of

Commerce, 1515 Memorial Dr, PO Box 903, 54221-0903; phone 920/684-5575 or toll-free 800/262-7892
Web Site www.mtvcchamber.com

A shipping, shopping, and industrial center, Manitowoc has an excellent harbor and a geographical position improved by the completion of the St. Lawrence Seaway. Shipbuilding has been an important industry since the earliest days. During World War II, Manitowoc shipyards produced nearly 100 vessels for the United States Navy including landing craft, wooden minesweepers, sub chasers, and 28 submarines. Manitowoc is the home of one of the largest manufacturers of aluminum ware and is a leader in the state's canning industry. Nearby lakes and streams provide excellent fishing.

What to See and Do

Hidden Valley Ski Area. *1815 Maple St, Manitowoc (54220). 13 miles N via I-43, exit 164, 1/2 mile S on County R to E Hidden Valley Rd. Phone 920/683-2713 (snow report).* Area has double chairlift, two surface lifts; patrol, school, rentals; snowmaking; snack bar, bar. Longest run is 2,600 feet; vertical drop 200 feet. (Dec-Mar, Fri-Sun; night skiing Tues-Fri) **$$$$**

Lake Michigan car ferry. *900 S Lakeview Dr, Manitowoc (54220). Trips to Ludington, MI. Phone 920/684-0888; toll-free 800/841-4243.* Departs from dock at South Lakeview Drive. (Early May-Oct, daily; advance reservations strongly recommended)

Lincoln Park Zoo. *1215 N 8th St, Manitowoc (54220). Phone 920/683-4537.* Array of animals in attractive settings; picnic, recreational facilities. (Daily) **FREE**

Pine Crest Historical Village. *924 Pine Crest Ln, Manitowoc (54220). I-43 exit 152, then 3 miles W on County JJ, then left on Pine Crest Lane. Phone 920/684-5110.* Site of 22 historic buildings depicting a typical turn-of-the-century Manitowoc county village. (May-Labor Day: daily; Sept-mid-Oct: Fri-Sun; also two weekends in late Nov-early Dec) **$$$**

Rahr-West Art Museum. *610 N 8th St, Manitowoc (54220). At Park St. Phone 920/683-4501.* Victorian house with period rooms; American art; collection of Chinese ivory carvings. Modern art wing featuring changing exhibits. (Daily; closed holidays) **DONATION**

Wisconsin Maritime Museum. *75 Maritime Dr, Manitowoc (54220). Phone 920/684-0218. www.wimaritimemuseum.org.* Exhibits depict 150 years of maritime history including model ship gallery; narrated tours through the USS *Cobia*, a 312-foot World War II submarine. (Daily; closed holidays) **$$$**

Marinette (C-5)

See also Menominee, Oconto, Peshtigo

Settled 1795
Population 11,843
Elevation 598 ft
Area Code 715
Zip 54143
Information Chamber of Commerce, 601 Marinette Ave, PO Box 512; phone 715/735-6681 or toll-free 800/236-6681
Web Site www.cybrzn.com/chamber

Located along the south bank of the Menominee River, Marinette is named for Queen Marinette, daughter of a Menominee chief. An industrial and port city, it is also the retail trade center for the surrounding recreational area.

What to See and Do

City Park. *2000 Alice Ln, Marinette (54143). Between Carney Ave and Mary St. Phone 715/732-0558.* Picnicking, camping (electric hook-ups, dump station; May-Sept). **$$$**

Fishing, whitewater rafting, canoeing. Trout streams, lakes, and the Peshtigo River nearby. Inquire at Chamber of Commerce.

Marinette County Historical Museum. *Stephenson Island, Hwy 41 at state border, Marinette (54143). Phone 715/732-0831.* Features logging history of area; miniature wood carvings of logging camp; Native American artifacts. Tours by appointment. (Memorial Day-Sept, daily) **DONATION**

Special Event

Theatre on the Bay. *University of Wisconsin Center/Marinette County, 750 W Bay Shore St, Marinette (54143). Phone 715/735-4300.* Comedies, dramas, musicals. June-Aug.

Limited-Service Hotel

★ ★ BEST WESTERN RIVERFRONT INN. *1821 Riverside Ave, Marinette (54143). Phone 715/732-1000; toll-free 800/338-3305; fax 715/732-0800.*

www.bestwestern.com. 120 rooms, 6 story. Check-in 3 pm, check-out 11 am. Restaurant, bar. Indoor pool. **$**

Specialty Lodging

The following lodging establishment is approved by Mobil Travel Guide, but due to its unique and individualized nature has not been given a traditional Mobil Star rating. Included in this listing you may find bed-and-breakfasts, limited-service inns, guest ranches, and other unique hotel properties.

LAUERMAN GUEST HOUSE INN. *1975 Riverside Ave, Marinette (54143). Phone 715/732-7800. www.explorewisconsin.com/lauermanguesthouseinn.* 7 rooms, 3 story. Complimentary full breakfast. Check-in 2 pm, check-out 11 am. Airport transportation available. **$$**

Marshfield (C-3)

See also Stevens Point, Wisconsin Rapids

Settled 1872
Population 19,291
Elevation 1,262 ft
Area Code 715
Zip 54449
Information Visitors & Promotion Bureau, 700 S Central St, PO Box 868; phone 715/384-3454 or toll-free 800/422-4541
Web Site www.mtecnserv.com/macci

Marshfield, a city that once boasted one sawmill and 19 taverns, was almost destroyed by fire in 1887. It was rebuilt on a more substantial structural and industrial basis. This is a busy northern dairy center, noted for its large medical clinic, manufactured housing wood products, and steel fabrication industries.

What to See and Do

Upham Mansion. *212 W 3rd St, Marshfield (54449). Phone 715/387-3322; toll-free 800/422-4541.* (1880) Italianate, mid-Victorian house built entirely of wood. Some original furniture, custom-made in the factory of the owner. (Wed and Sun afternoons) **FREE**

Wildwood Park and Zoo. *630 S Central Ave, Marshfield (54449). Off Hwy 13 (Roddis Ave), S of business district or off 17th St from Central Ave S. Phone 715/384-4642; toll-free 800/422-4541.* Zoo houses a variety of animals and birds, mostly native to Wisconsin. (Mid-May-late Sept: daily; rest of year: Mon-Fri) **FREE**

Special Events

Central Wisconsin State Fair. *Fair Park, Vine Ave and 14th St, Marshfield (54449). Phone 715/387-1261.* Six days ending on Labor Day.

Dairyfest. *Vetrans Park, 7th and Central, Marshfield (54449). Phone toll-free 800/422-4541.* Salute to the dairy industry. First weekend in June.

Fall Festival. *Wildwood Park, 17th and Central, Marshfield (54449). Phone toll-free 800/422-4541.* Mid-Sept.

Mauston (D-3)

See also Wisconsin Dells

Settled 1840
Population 3,439
Elevation 883 ft
Area Code 608
Zip 53948
Information Greater Mauston Area Chamber of Commerce, 503 Hwy 82, PO Box 171; phone 608/847-4142

What to See and Do

Buckhorn State Park. *W8450 Buckhorn Park Ave, Necedah (54646). 11 miles N via County rds 58 and G, near Necedah. Phone 608/565-2789.* A 2,504-acre park with facilities for swimming, water-skiing, fishing, boating, canoeing; hunting, hiking, nature trails, picnicking, playground, backpack and canoe camping. (Daily) **$$**

Limited-Service Hotel

★★ WOODSIDE RANCH RESORT & CONFERENCE CENTER. *W 4015 WI 82, Mauston (53948). Phone 608/847-4275; toll-free 800/626-4275; fax 608/848-2630. www.woodsideranch.com.* 37 rooms, 2 story. Pets accepted. Check-in 1:30 pm, check-out 10 am. Wireless Internet access. Restaurant, bar. Fitness room. Outdoor pool. Tennis. Ski in/ski out. **$$**

Menomonee Falls (E-4)

See also Milwaukee, Wauwatosa

Settled 1843
Population 26,840
Elevation 840 ft
Area Code 262
Zip 53051
Information Menomonee Falls Chamber of Commerce, N88W16621 Appleton Ave, PO Box 73, 53052; phone 262/251-6565 or toll-free 800/801-6565

What to See and Do

Bugline Recreation Trail. *Appleton Ave, Menomonee Falls (53051).* A 12.2-mile trail located on the former Chicago, Milwaukee, St. Paul, and Pacific Railroad right-of-way. Bicycling, hiking, jogging, horseback riding (some areas), cross-country skiing, snowmobiling. Dogs allowed (on leash).

Old Falls Village. *N96W15791 County Line Rd, Menomonee Falls (53051). 1/2 mile N on County Line Rd. Phone 262/255-8346.* Miller-Davidson farmhouse (1858) of Greek Revival style, decorative arts museum, 1851 schoolhouse, carriage house, barn museum, 1890 railroad depot, two restored log cabins,1873 Victorian cottage; extensive grounds, picnic area. (May-Sept, Sun; also by appointment) **$**

Sub-Continental Divide. *Main St, 1 block W of Town Line Rd. Phone 262/251-6565; toll-free 800/801-6565.* Water falling west of this crest of land goes into the Fox River Watershed and eventually into the Gulf of Mexico via the Mississippi River. Water falling on the east side goes into the Menomonee River watershed and enters the St. Lawrence Seaway by flowing through the Great Lakes.

Limited-Service Hotel

★ ★ FOUR POINTS BY SHERATON. *8900 N Kildeer Ct, Brown Deer (53209). Phone 414/355-8585; toll-free 800/368-7764; fax 414/355-3566. www.fourpoints.com.* 149 rooms, 6 story. Check-in 3 pm, check-out noon. Restaurant, bar. Indoor pool, whirlpool. Airport transportation available. **$**

Restaurants

★ ★ ★ FOX AND HOUNDS. *1298 Freiss Lake Rd, Hubertus (53033). Phone 262/628-1111. www.ratzsch.com.* This renowned spot, located a few miles west of Milwaukee, is set in an authentic-feeling, 1845 log cabin. It's worth thinking ahead for a reservation at the Friday fish fry. American menu. Dinner. Closed Mon; Jan 1, Dec 24-25. Bar. Children's menu. **$$$**

★ ★ RIVER LANE INN. *4313 W River Ln, Brown Deer (53223). Phone 414/354-1995.* Seafood menu. Lunch, dinner. Closed Sun; Thanksgiving, Dec 25. Bar. **$$$**

Menomonie (C-1)

See also Chippewa Falls, Eau Claire

Settled 1859
Population 13,547
Elevation 877 ft
Area Code 715
Zip 54751
Information Chamber of Commerce, 700 Wolske Bay Rd, Suite 200; phone 715/235-9087 or toll-free 800/283-1862

Located on the banks of the Red Cedar River, Menomonie is home of the University of Wisconsin-Stout and was once headquarters for one of the largest lumber corporations in the country. The decline of the lumber industry diverted the economy to dairy products. Recently several new industries have located here, giving the city a more diversified economic base.

What to See and Do

Caddie Woodlawn Park. *Hwys 25 and C, Downsville (54735). 10 miles S on Hwy 25. Phone 715/235-2070.* Two century-old houses and log smokehouse in 5-acre park; memorial to pioneer girl Caddie Woodlawn. Picnicking. (Daily) **FREE**

Empire in Pine Lumber Museum. *E4541 County Rd C, Downsville (54751). 7 miles S on Hwy 25. Phone 715/664-8690.* Lumbering artifacts, slides of life in lumber camps; primitive furniture, displays include original pay office. (Early May-Oct: daily; mid-Apr-early May: by appointment) **FREE**

Mabel Tainter Memorial Building. *205 Main St E, Menomonie (54751). Phone 715/235-9726; toll-free*

800/236-7675. Hand-stenciled and ornately carved cultural center constructed in 1889 by lumber baron Andrew Tainter in memory of his daughter Mabel. Theater with performing arts season; reading room, pipe organ. Gift shop. Guided tours (daily). **$$**

Wilson Place Museum. *Wilson Place Museum, 101 Wilson Ct, Menomonie (54751). Phone 715/235-2283.* Victorian mansion (1846); former residence of Senator James H. Stout, founder of University of Wisconsin. Almost all original furnishings. Guided tours (Memorial Day-Labor Day, daily; closed Jan 1, Thanksgiving, Dec 25) **$$**

Special Events

Victorian Christmas. *Wilson Place Museum, 101 Wilson Ct, Menomonie (54751). Phone 715/235-2283.* Mid-Nov-Dec.

Winter Carnival. *Wakanda Park, Pine Ave and Broadway, Menomonie (54751). Phone 715/235-9087.* Second weekend in Feb.

Limited-Service Hotel

★ BEST WESTERN INN OF MENOMONIE. *1815 N Broadway, Menomonie (54751). Phone 715/235-9651; toll-free 800/622-0504; fax 715/235-6568. www.bestwestern.com.* 102 rooms. Pets accepted; fee. Complimentary full breakfast. Check-in 3 pm, check-out 11 am. Wireless Internet access. Indoor pool, whirlpool. Business center. **$**

Milwaukee (E-5)

See also Cedarburg, Kenosha, Menomonee Falls, Oconomowoc, Port Washington, Racine, Waukesha, Wauwatosa

Settled 1822
Population 628,088
Elevation 634 ft
Area Code 414
Information Greater Milwaukee Convention & Visitors Bureau, 101 W Wisconsin Ave, 53203; phone 414/273-3950 or toll-free 800/231-0903
Web Site www.officialmilwaukee.com
Suburbs Menomonee Falls, Port Washington, Waukesha, Wauwatosa.

Thriving and progressive, Milwaukee has retained its *Gemütlichkeit*—though today's lively conviviality is as likely to be expressed at a soccer game or at a symphony concert as at the beer garden. This is not to say that raising beer steins has noticeably declined as a popular local form of exercise. While Milwaukee is still the beer capital of the nation, its leading single industry is not brewing but the manufacture of X-ray apparatus and tubes.

Long a French trading post and an early campsite between Chicago and Green Bay, the city was founded by Solomon Juneau, who settled on the east side of the Milwaukee River. English settlement began in significant numbers in 1833 and was followed by an influx of Germans, Scandinavians, Dutch, Bohemians, Irish, Austrians, and large numbers of Poles. By 1846, Milwaukee was big and prosperous enough to be incorporated as a city. In its recent history, perhaps the most colorful period was from 1916 to 1940 when Daniel Webster Hoan, its Socialist mayor, held the reins of government.

The city's Teutonic personality has dimmed, becoming only a part of the local color of a city long famous for good government, a low crime rate, and high standards of civic performance.

With a history going back to the days when the Native Americans called this area Millioki, "gathering place by the waters," Milwaukee has undergone tremendous development since World War II. The skyline changed with new building, an expressway system was constructed, the St. Lawrence Seaway opened new markets, new cultural activities were introduced, and 44 square miles were tacked onto the city's girth.

Today, a city of 96.5 square miles on the west shore of Lake Michigan, where the Milwaukee, Menomonee, and Kinnickinnic rivers meet, Milwaukee is the metropolitan center of five counties. "The machine shop of America" ranks among the nation's top industrial cities and is a leader in the output of diesel and gasoline engines, outboard motors, motorcycles, tractors, wheelbarrows, padlocks, and, of course, beer.

As a result of the St. Lawrence Seaway, Milwaukee has become a major seaport on America's new fourth seacoast. Docks and piers handle traffic of ten lines of oceangoing ships.

The city provides abundant tourist attractions including professional and college basketball, hockey, and football, major league baseball, top-rated polo, soccer, and auto racing. There is also golf, tennis, swimming, sailing, fishing, hiking, skiing, tobogganing, and skating. For the less athletic, Milwaukee has art exhibits, museums, music programs, ballet, and theater including the Marcus Center for Performing Arts. Its many beautiful churches include St. Josaphat's Basilica, St. John Cathedral, and the Gesu Church.

Additional Visitor Information

The Greater Milwaukee Convention & Visitors Bureau, 101 W Wisconsin Ave, 53203; phone 414/273-3950 or toll-free 800/231-0903 and a visitor center at 400 Wisconsin Ave (daily).

Public Transportation

Buses, Subway, and elevated trains (Milwaukee County Transit System), phone 414/344-6711.

Airport **General Mitchell International Airport;** weather phone 414/936-1212

Information Phone 414/747-5300

Lost and Found Phone 414/747-5245

What to See and Do

Annunciation Greek Orthodox Church. *9400 W Congress St, Milwaukee (53225). Phone 414/461-9400.* Domed structure designed by Frank Lloyd Wright.

Betty Brinn Children's Museum. *O'Donnell Park, 929 E Wisconsin Ave, Milwaukee (53202). Near the lakefront. Phone 414/390-5437. www.bbcmkids.org.* Kids ten and under will have a blast at this interactive museum, where they can enter a digestion tunnel and hear what their body sounds like as its's digesting food or create their own racetrack and test drive golf ball-shaped push carts on different road surfaces. (Tues-Sat 9 am-5 pm, Sun noon-5 pm, also Mon in June-Aug 9 am-5 pm) **$**

Bradford Beach. The city's finest bathing beach, with bathhouse, concessions. **FREE**

The Brew City Queen. *1137 N Old World Third St, Milwaukee (53203). Pere Marquette Park on Third St between State and Kilbourn sts. Phone 414/283-9999. www.riverwalkboats.com.* In Milwaukee, brewery tours are a must. Hit three at once by hopping on *The Brew City Queen* pontoon boat, which motors up and down the Milwaukee River with pit stops at Lakefront Brewery (1872 N Commerce), the Milwaukee Ale House (233 N Water), and Rock Bottom Brewery (740 N Plankinton) for tours and tastings. The three-hour trip is available Saturdays and Sundays from mid-May through August and Saturdays only in September, depending on the weather. Board at one of the three breweries. Riverwalk Boat Rentals, which operates the tours, also rents pontoons and paddleboats by the hour, half-day, and full day. **$$$$**

Captain Frederick Pabst Mansion. *2000 W Wisconsin Ave, Milwaukee (53233). Downtown. Phone 414/931-0808. www.pabstmansion.com.* (1893) Magnificent house of the beer baron; exquisite woodwork, wrought iron, and stained glass; restored interior. Guided tours. (Daily; closed holidays) **$$$**

Charles Allis Art Museum. *1801 N Prospect Ave, Milwaukee (53202). Near the lakefront. Phone 414/278-8295. www.charlesallismuseum.org.* Art treasures from the United States, Near East, Far East, and Europe dating from 600 BC to the 1900s; personal collection of Charles Allis in his preserved Tudor-style mansion. (Wed-Sun afternoons) **$$**

City Hall. *200 E Wells St, Milwaukee (53202). Downtown. Phone 414/286-3285.* (1895) Milwaukee landmark of Flemish Renaissance design. Common Council Chamber and Anteroom retain their turn-of-the-century character; ornately carved woodwork, leaded glass, stenciled ceilings, and two large stained-glass windows; ironwork balconies surround eight-story atrium. (Mon-Fri; closed holidays) **FREE**

Court of Honor. Three-block area serving as a monument to the city's Civil War heros. Bounded by Marquette University on the west and the downtown business district on the east, it contains the Public Library, many towering churches, and statues of historic figures.

Discovery World: The James Lovell Museum of Science, Economics, and Technology. *815 N James Lovell St, Milwaukee (53233). Downtown, at Wells St. Phone 414/765-9966. www.discoveryworld.org.* Discovery World, aimed at kids 14 and under, is filled with 150 interactive exhibits. At the 4Cast Center, try your hand at weather forecasting with live Doppler Radar, the Lightning Track, and a seismograph. In the Gears & Linkages section, figure out the simple mechanics behind pulleys and other tools. (Daily 9 am-5 pm; closed July 4, Thanksgiving, Dec 25) **$$**

Iroquois Boat Line Tours. *445 W Oklahoma Ave, Milwaukee (53207). Board at Clybourn St Bridge on W bank of Milwaukee River. Phone 414/294-9450.* View the lakefront, harbor, lighthouse, breakwater, and foreign ships in port. (Early June-Aug, daily) **$$$$**

Kilbourntown House. *Estabrook Park, 4400 W Estabrook Dr, Milwaukee (52303). 5 miles N on I-43, Capitol Dr E exit. Phone 414/273-8288.* (1844) Excellent example of Greek Revival architecture; restored and furnished in the 1844-1864 period. (Late June-Labor Day, Tues, Thurs, Sat-Sun) **FREE**

Marcus Center for the Performing Arts. *929 N Water St, Milwaukee (53202). Downtown. Phone 414/273-7206.* Strikingly beautiful structure, overlooking the Milwaukee River, with four theaters, reception areas, and parking facility connected by a skywalk. Outdoor riverfront Peck Pavilion. Also here is

Milwaukee Ballet. *405 W National, Milwaukee (53202). Phone 414/643-7677.* Classical and contemporary ballet presentations. (Late Oct-early May)

Marquette University. *1217 W Wisconsin Ave, Milwaukee (53233). Wisconsin Ave and 9th-17th sts, downtown. Phone 414/288-3178. www.mu.edu.* (1881) (11,000 students) On campus are

Haggerty Museum of Art. *530 N 13th St, Milwaukee (53233). Phone 414/288-7290.* Paintings, prints, drawings, sculpture, and decorative arts; changing exhibits. (Daily) **FREE**

Marquette Hall's 48-bell carillon. *1217 W Wisconsin Ave, Milwaukee (53233).* One of the largest in the country. Occasional concerts. **FREE**

St. Joan of Arc Chapel. *14th St and Wisconsin Ave, Milwaukee (53233). Phone 414/288-6873.* (15th century) Brought from France and reconstructed on Long Island, New York, in 1927 and here in 1964. Tours (daily).

Miller Brewery Tour. *4251 W State St, Milwaukee (53208). Phone 414/931-2337; toll-free 800/944-5483. www.millerbrewing.com.* Milwaukee is synonymous with beer, so you've got to take the one-hour guided tour of Miller Brewing Company, Milwaukee's sole remaining large-scale brewery and the nation's second largest. Most of what you see is through windows. But you do get to see some equipment up close in the brew house, and the Caves Museum, a small showcase of brewery memorabilia housed in hand-dug tunnels once used to store beer, is cool. At the end, adults receive free beer samples while kids get root beer. Everyone also gets a packet of pretzels and a postcard. (Labor Day-Memorial Day: Mon-Sat 10 am-5 pm; rest of year: 10 am-5:30 pm; last tour at 3:30 pm; closed holidays) **FREE**

Miller Park Tour. *One Brewers Way, Milwaukee (53214). Phone 414/902-4005. www.brewers.mlb.com.* Home of the Milwaukee Brewers, Miller Park is the only ballpark in North America with a fan-shaped, convertible roof and natural grass playing field. Seventy-minute tours showcase the dugout, luxury suites, clubhouse, press box, Bob Uecker's broadcast booth, and more. Tours meet in the Brewers Fan Zone Store in Miller Park's Hot Corner down the left field line; tickets can be purchased in the ticket booth just outside the store. Wheelchair accessible. General parking (fee). (Daily 10:30 am, noon, 1:30 pm and 3 pm during baseball session; no tours on home game days; closed holidays) **$$**

Milwaukee Art Museum. *700 N Art Museum Dr, Milwaukee (53202). Near the lakefront. Phone 414/224-3200. www.mam.org.* Permanent collection of American and European masters; folk, decorative, and contemporary art. Special exhibits; films and tours. (Daily; closed Jan 1, Thanksgiving, Dec 25) **$$$**

Milwaukee Brewers (MLB). *Miller Park, 1 Brewers Way, Milwaukee (53202). Phone 414/902-4400. www.milwaukeebrewers.com.*

Milwaukee Bucks (NBA). *Bradley Center, 1001 N Fourth St, Milwaukee (53203). Phone 414/227-0500. www.nba.com/bucks.*

Milwaukee County Historical Center. *910 N Old World 3rd St, Milwaukee (53203). 3rd St at Pere Marquette Park. Downtown. Phone 414/273-8288.* Milwaukee history and children's exhibits; archive library housed in bank building (1913). (Daily; closed holidays) **FREE**

Milwaukee County Zoo. *10001 W Blue Mound Rd, Milwaukee (53226). 6 miles W. Phone 414/771-3040. www.milwaukeezoo.org.* See 2,500 mammals, birds, reptiles, and fish at the Milwaukee County Zoo, renowned for displaying predators next to their normal prey. The zoo features an animal health center with a public viewing area; make sure to catch a treatment procedure or surgery (mornings are best). Sea lion show, minature zoo train, zoomobile with guided tours, and carousel are available for a fee. Parking (fee). Stroller rental available. (May-Sept: Mon-Sat 9 am-5 pm, Sun and holidays 9 am-6 pm; rest of year: daily 9 am-4:30 pm) **$$**

Milwaukee Public Museum. *800 W Wells St, Milwaukee (53233). Downtown. Phone 414/278-2700. www.mpm.edu.* Natural and human history museum; unique "walk-through" dioramas and exhibits; life-size replicas of dinosaurs. Rain forest, Native American, and special exhibits. Shops; restaurant. (Daily 9 am-5 pm; closed July 4, Thanksgiving, Dec 25) **$$$**

Humphrey IMAX Dome Theater. *800 W Wells St, Milwaukee (53233). Phone 414/319-4629.* A 275-seat theater; giant wraparound domed screen. **$$$**

Mitchell Park Horticultural Conservatory. *S 27th St, Milwaukee (53202). Phone 414/649-9800.* Superb modern design, three self-supporting domes (tropical, arid, and show dome) feature outstanding seasonal shows and beautiful exhibits all year. Each dome is almost half the length of a football field in diameter and nearly as tall as a seven-story building. Also gift shop, picnic area; parking (free). (Daily) **$$**

Old World 3rd Street. *Old World 3rd and W Wells sts, Milwaukee (53202). Between W Wells St and W Highland Blvd.* Downtown walking tour for gourmets, historians, and lovers of antiques and atmosphere. Includes the *Milwaukee Journal* company's history of the newspaper. Most shops (Mon-Sat).

Pabst Theater. *144 E Wells St, Milwaukee (53202). Downtown. Phone 414/286-3663.* (1895) Center of Milwaukee's earlier cultural life; restored to its original elegance. Lavish décor and excellent acoustics enhance the charm of the theater. Musical and dramatic events. Tours (Sat).

Park system. *9480 W Watertown Plank Rd, Milwaukee (53226). Phone 414/257-6100.* One of the largest in the nation, with 14,681 acres; 137 parks and parkways, community centers, five beaches, 19 pools, 16 golf courses, 134 tennis courts, and winter activities including cross-country skiing, skating, and sledding. Fees vary. Of special interest is

Whitnall Park. *5879 S 92nd St, Franklin (53132). Phone 414/425-1130.* A 640-acre park with Boerner Botanical Gardens (parking fee) featuring the Rose Garden, one of the All-American Selection Gardens; also nature trails, woodlands, formal gardens, wildflowers, shrubs, test gardens, fruit trees, rock, and herb gardens; Wehr Nature Center. Also, 18-hole golf (fee). (Early Apr-mid-Oct, daily) **FREE**

Port of Milwaukee. *2323 S Lincoln Memorial Dr, Milwaukee (53207). Phone 414/286-3511.* Includes Inner Harbor, formed by the Milwaukee, Menomonee, and Kinnickinnic rivers, and the commercial municipal port development in the Outer Harbor on the lakefront. Ships flying foreign flags may be seen at Jones Island on Milwaukee's south side.(Mon-Fri)

Schlitz Audubon Center. *1111 E Brown Deer Rd, Milwaukee (53217). Phone 414/352-2880.* Center has 225 acres of shoreline, grassland, bluff, ravine, and woodland habitats with a variety of plants and wildlife including fox, deer, skunk, and opossum; self-guided trails; some guided programs. (Daily). **$$**

University of Wisconsin-Milwaukee. *2200 E Kenwood Blvd, Milwaukee (53201). Phone 414/229-1122.* (1956) (25,400 students) The Manfred Olson Planetarium (fee) offers programs Friday and Saturday evenings during academic year. There is also an art museum and three art galleries that are open to the public (3203 N Downer Ave).

Villa Terrace Decorative Arts Museum. *2220 N Terrace Ave, Milwaukee (53202). Phone 414/271-3656. www.villaterracemuseum.org.* (1923) This Italian Renaissance-style house serves as a museum for decorative arts. Guided tours (reservations required). (Wed-Sun afternoons; closed Jan 1, Dec 25) **$$**

★ **War Memorial Center.** *750 N Lincoln Memorial Dr, Milwaukee (53202). Phone 414/273-5533.* An imposing modern monument to honor the dead by serving the living; designed by Eero Saarinen.

Wisconsin Lake Schooner. *2500 N Lincoln Memorial Dr, Milwaukee (53202). Phone 414/276-7700. www.pierwisconsin.org.* Three-masted schooners aren't just the province of the oceans. Here on Lake Michigan, you can sail on the 137-foot SN *Denis Sullivan,* the first tall ship built in Wisconsin in more than 100 years. The ship is a recreation of a typical 19th-century Great Lakes schooner. Two-and-a-half-hour tours are typically held on select dates from May through September. **$$$$**

Special Events

Ethnic Festivals. *Henry Maier Festival Grounds, 200 N Harbor Dr, Milwaukee (53203). Phone 414/273-3950.* African, Arabian, German, Italian, Irish, Asian, Mexican, and Polish festivals take place throughout the summer. Convention and Visitors Bureau has information. Mid-June-Sept.

Great Circus Parade. *Fairgrounds, Lincoln Memorial Dr and Mason, Milwaukee (53913). Downtown. Phone 608/356-8341.* This re-creation of an old-time circus parade includes bands, costumed units, animals, and an unusual collection of horsedrawn wagons from the Circus World Museum. Late June.

Holiday Folk Fair. *Henry Maier Festival Grounds, 200 N Harbor Dr, Milwaukee (53203). Phone 414/225-6225.* Continuous ethnic entertainment, 300 types of food from around the world, cultural exhibits, workshops. Weekend before Thanksgiving.

Summerfest. *Henry Maier Festival Grounds, 200 N Harbor Dr, Milwaukee (53203). Phone toll-free 800/273-3378. www.summerfest.com.* Eleven different music stages; food. Late June-early July.

Wisconsin State Fair. *State Fair Park, 8100 W Greenfield Ave, West Allis (53214). Bounded by I-94, Greenfield Ave, 76th and 84th sts.Phone 414/266-7000; toll-free 800/884-3247. www.wistatefair.com.* Entertainment, 12 stages, auto races, exhibits, contests, demonstrations, fireworks. Aug.

Limited-Service Hotels

★ ★ COURTYARD BY MARRIOTT. *300 W Michigan St, Milwaukee (53203). Phone 414/291-4122; toll-free 800/321-2211; fax 414/291-4188. www.courtyard.com.* Guests will find no shortage of things to see and do near this pleasant, comfortable hotel, which is connected to downtown Milwaukee's impressive Grand Avenue Mall and within walking distance to the river and many dining options. 169 rooms, 6 story. Check-in 3 pm, check-out noon. High-speed Internet access. Restaurant. Fitness room. Indoor pool, whirlpool. Airport transportation available. Business center. **$**

★ ★ EMBASSY SUITES. *1200 S Moorland Rd, Brookfield (53008). Phone 262/782-2900; toll-free 800/362-2779; fax 262/796-9159. www.embassysuites.com.* 203 rooms, 5 story, all suites. Complimentary full breakfast. Check-in 4 pm, check-out noon. Restaurant, bar. Fitness room. Indoor pool, whirlpool. Airport transportation available. Business center. **$**

★ ★ HOLIDAY INN. *611 W Wisconsin Ave, Milwaukee (53203). Phone 414/273-2950; toll-free 800/465-4329; fax 414/273-7662. www.holiday-inn.com.* Located right across from Milwaukee's massive Midwest Express Center, this ten-story hotel features a rooftop pool and sundeck on its second level. Families will enjoy the restaurant on the ground floor and the option of adjoining rooms, while business travelers can take advantage of the hotel's business services and downtown location. 247 rooms, 10 story. Check-in 3 pm, check-out noon. Restaurant, bar. Fitness room. Outdoor pool. Business center. **$**

Full-Service Hotels

★ ★ ★ HILTON MILWAUKEE CITY CENTER. *509 W Wisconsin Ave, Milwaukee (53203). Phone 414/271-7250; toll-free 800/774-1500; fax 414/271-1039. www.hilton.com.* Those looking to stay in the downtown area will enjoy all this hotel has to offer, with its location near local theaters, museums, and major businesses. 730 rooms, 25 story. Check-in 4 pm, check-out 11 am. Three restaurants, bar. Fitness room. Indoor pool, children's pool, whirlpool. **$**

★ ★ ★ HILTON MILWAUKEE RIVER. *4700 N Port Washington Rd, Milwaukee (53212). Phone 414/962-6040; toll-free 800/445-8667; fax 414/962-6166. www.milwaukeeriver.hilton.com.* This hotel provides a modern and convenient environment for guests. It is minutes away from many attractions, including sports arenas, museums, the zoo, and a brewery. 163 rooms, 5 story. Check-in 3 pm, check-out 11 am. Wireless Internet access. Restaurant, bar. Fitness room. Indoor pool. Airport transportation available. Business center. **$$**

★ ★ ★ HOTEL METRO. *411 Mason Ave, Milwaukee (53203). Phone 414/272-1937; fax 414/223-1158.* 65 rooms, all suites. Pets accepted, some restrictions. Check-in 3 pm, check-out noon. High-speed Internet access. Restaurant, bar. Airport transportation available. **$$**

★ ★ ★ HYATT REGENCY MILWAUKEE. *333 W Kilbourn Ave, Milwaukee (53203). Phone 414/276-1234; toll-free 800/233-1234; fax 414/276-6338. www.milwaukee.hyatt.com.* This hotel delights guests with spacious and elegantly appointed guest rooms and offers Milwaukee's only revolving rooftop restaurant, which affords guests panoramic views of the city's skyline. 484 rooms, 22 story. Check-in 3 pm, check-out noon. High-speed Internet access, wireless

Internet access. Three restaurants, two bars. Fitness room. Airport transportation available. Business center. **$$**

★ ★ ★ **THE PFISTER HOTEL.** *424 E Wisconsin Ave, Milwaukee (53202). Phone 414/273-8222; toll-free 800/558-8222; fax 414/390-3839. www.thepfisterhotel.com.* The Pfister, in the heart of downtown Milwaukee, has been a perennial favorite of discerning travelers since 1893. All of the city's treasures, from businesses and restaurants to shops and attractions, are within walking distance of this historic landmark. The hotel embraces its past with a museum-quality collection of Victorian artwork. The views of the city and Lake Michigan are particularly alluring, and the restaurants and lounges are the places to see and be seen in the city. Sunday brunch at Café Rouge is popular with guests and locals, while Blu spices up the scene with special martinis and flights of wine. 307 rooms, 23 story. Check-in 3 pm, check-out noon. High-speed Internet access, wireless Internet access. Three restaurants, two bars. Fitness room. Indoor pool. Airport transportation available. **$$**

★ ★ ★ **SHERATON MILWAUKEE BROOKFIELD HOTEL.** *375 S Moorland Rd, Brookfield (53005). Phone 262/364-1100; toll-free 800/325-3535; fax 262/786-5210. www.sheraton.com.* 389 rooms, 12 story. Pets accepted, some restrictions. Check-out noon. Restaurant. Fitness room. Indoor pool, outdoor pool, whirlpool. Business center. **$$**

★ ★ ★ **WYNDHAM MILWAUKEE CENTER.** *139 E Kilbourn Ave, Milwaukee (53202). Phone 414/276-8686; toll-free 800/996-3426; fax 414/276-8007. www.wyndham.com.* Nestled in Milwaukee's charming theater district, this elegant hotel is actually located within the same building complex as the Milwaukee Repertory and Pabst Theaters. Well-appointed rooms overlook the Milwaukee River and guests are within walking distance of the Marcus Center, City Hall, and plenty of shopping and dining. 220 rooms, 10 story. Check-in 3 pm, check-out noon. High-speed Internet access. Restaurant, two bars. Fitness room. Whirlpool. Airport transportation available. **$**

Specialty Lodgings

The following lodging establishments are approved by Mobil Travel Guide, but due to their unique and individualized nature have not been given a traditional Mobil Star rating. Included in this listing you may find bed-and-breakfasts, limited-service inns, guest ranches, and other unique hotel properties.

ACANTHUS INN B&B. *3009 W Highland Blvd, Milwaukee (53208). Phone 414/342-9788; fax 414/342-3460.* 6 rooms. Pets accepted, some restrictions. Complimentary full breakfast. Check-in 3 pm, check-out 11 am. **$$**

BRUMDER MANSION. *3046 W Wisconsin Ave, Milwaukee (53208). Phone 414/342-9767; toll-free 866/793-3676; fax 414/342-4772. www.brumdermansion.com.* 5 rooms. Complimentary full breakfast. Check-in 4-6 pm, check-out 11 am. **$$**

COUNTY CLARE IRISH INN & PUB. *1234 N Astor St, Milwaukee (53202). Phone 414/272-5273; toll-free 888/942-5273; fax 414/290-6300. www.countyclare-inn.com.* 30 rooms. Check-in 3 pm, check-out 11 am. Restaurant, bar. **$$**

THE KILBOURN GUEST HOUSE. *2825 W Kilbourn Ave, Milwaukee (53208). Phone 414/344-3167. www.kilbournguesthouse.com.* 4 rooms. Complimentary full breakfast. Check-in 3 pm, check-out 11 am. **$**

Restaurants

★ **AU BON APPETIT.** *1016 E Brady St, Milwaukee (53202). Phone 414/278-1233; fax 414/223-3202. www.aubonappetit.com.* Mediterranean menu. Dinner. Closed Sun-Mon; holidays. Casual attire. Reservations recommended. **$$**

★ **BALISTRERI'S BLUE MOUND INN.** *6501 W Bluemound Rd, Milwaukee (53213). Phone 414/258-9881. www.balistreris.com.* Italian, American menu. Lunch Mon-Fri, dinner daily. Closed Thanksgiving, Dec 24-25. Bar. **$$**

★ ★ ★ **BARTOLOTTA'S LAKE PARK BISTRO.** *3133 E Newberry Blvd, Milwaukee (53211). Phone 414/962-6300; fax 414/962-4248. www.lakeparkbistro.com.* Restaurateur Joe Bartolotta, who also owns Bartolotta Ristorante (see) in Wauwatosa, serves authentic dishes and many wood-fired oven specialties in this lovely,

Paris-like dining room. The second-story location in the Lake Park Pavilion affords beautiful Lake Michigan views. French menu. Lunch, dinner, Sun brunch. Closed holidays. Bar. Children's menu. **$$**

★ **COUNTY CLARE.** *1234 N Astor St, Milwaukee (53202). Phone 414/272-5273; fax 414/290-6300. www.countyclare-inn.com.* Irish menu. Lunch, dinner. Closed holidays. Bar. Children's menu. Casual attire. Outdoor seating. **$$**

★ **DOS BANDIDOS.** *5932 N Green Bay Ave, Milwaukee (53209). Phone 414/228-1911; fax 414/431-1532. www.whgonline.com/dosbandidos.php.* American, Mexican menu. Lunch, dinner. Closed holidays. Bar. Outdoor seating. **$$**

★ ★ **EAGAN'S.** *1030 N Water St, Milwaukee (53202). Phone 414/271-6900; fax 414/226-3225. www.eagansonwater.com.* Seafood menu. Lunch, dinner, Sun brunch. Closed holidays. Bar. Business casual attire. Outdoor seating. **$$**

★ **FRIDAY'S FRONT ROW SPORTS GRILL.** *1 Brewers Way, Milwaukee (53214). Phone 414/902-4201; fax 414/902-4202.* American menu. Lunch, dinner. Bar. Casual attire. **$$**

★ **IZUMI'S.** *2150 N Prospect Ave, Milwaukee (53209). Phone 414/271-5278; fax 414/287-0196. www.izumisrestaurant.com.* Japanese menu. Lunch, dinner. Closed holidays. **$$**

★ ★ **JACK PANDL'S WHITEFISH BAY INN.** *1319 E Henry Clay St, Whitefish Bay (53217). Phone 414/964-3800.* Established in 1915; antique beer stein collection. German menu. Lunch, dinner. Bar. Children's menu. **$$$**

★ ★ **KARL RATZSCH'S.** *320 E Mason St, Milwaukee (53202). Phone 414/276-2720; fax 414/276-3534. www.karlratzsch.com.* This restaurant features a collection of rare steins and glassware. German menu. Lunch Wed-Sat, dinner Mon-Sat. Closed Sun; holidays. Bar. Children's menu. Casual attire. Valet parking. **$$$**

★ ★ **THE KING AND I.** *823 N 2nd St, Milwaukee (53203). Phone 414/276-4181; fax 414/276-4387. www.kingandirestaurant.com.* Thai menu. Lunch Mon-Fri, dinner daily. Bar. Casual attire. Reservations recommended. **$$**

★ **THE KNICK.** *1030 E Juneau Ave, Milwaukee (53202). Phone 414/272-0011; fax 414/272-0702. www.theknickrestaurant.com.* American menu. Breakfast, lunch, dinner, brunch. Closed holidays. Bar. Casual attire. Valet parking. Outdoor seating. **$$**

★ ★ **MADER'S.** *1037 N Old World 3rd St, Milwaukee (53203). Phone 414/271-3377; fax 414/271-7914. www.maders.com.* German menu. Lunch, dinner, Sun brunch. Bar. Children's menu. Valet parking. **$$**

★ ★ ★ **MIMMA'S CAFE.** *1307 E Brady St, Milwaukee (53202). Phone 414/271-7337. www.mimmas.com.* This family-run establishment has grown from an eight-seat eatery to a 150-seat, fine Italian restaurant with impressive faux-marble walls, paintings, chandeliers, and polished-tile flooring. Italian menu. Dinner. Closed holidays. Bar. Business casual attire. Reservations recommended. Outdoor seating. **$$**

★ **OLD TOWN SERBIAN GOURMET HOUSE.** *522 W Lincoln Ave, Milwaukee (53207). Phone 414/672-0206; fax 414/672-0209. www.wwbci.com/oldtown.* American, Serbian menu. Lunch, dinner. Closed Mon; holidays. Bar. Children's menu. **$$**

★ ★ ★ **OSTERIA DEL MONDO.** *1028 E Juneau Ave, Milwaukee (53202). Phone 414/291-3770. www.osteria.com.* Chef/owner Marc Bianchini enhances the German landscape of Wisconsin with this authentic Italian café. The wine, food, and desserts transport guests into an Italian province, and the wine bar adds an exquisite touch to this casual yet intimate restaurant. Italian menu. Dinner. Closed holidays. Bar. Business casual attire. Reservations recommended. Valet parking. Outdoor seating. **$$**

★ ★ ★ **PANDL'S BAYSIDE.** *8825 N Lake Dr, Milwaukee (53217). Phone 414/352-7300. www.pandls.com.* This restaurant serves up a wonderfully cozy atmosphere in an attractive parklike setting with an elaborate salad bar, family-friendly brunches, and good value. Enjoy fresh fish, steaks, and the ever-popular duckling with raspberry sauce. Private rooms are available. American menu. Lunch, dinner. Closed Labor Day, Dec 25. Bar. Children's menu. **$$$**

★ **PLEASANT VALLEY INN.** *9801 W Dakota St, Milwaukee (53227). Phone 414/321-4321; fax 414/543-3197. www.foodspot.com/pleasantvalleyinn.* American menu. Dinner. Closed Mon; holidays. Bar. Children's menu. **$$**

★ ★ **POLARIS.** *333 W Kilbourn Ave, Milwaukee (53203). Phone 414/276-1234; fax 414/276-6338.* American menu. Dinner, brunch. Bar. Children's menu. Casual attire. Reservations recommended. **$$**

★ ★ **PORTERHOUSE.** *800 W Layton Ave, Milwaukee (53221). Phone 414/744-1750; fax 414/744-7804. www.foodspot.com/porterhouse.* Steak menu. Dinner. Bar. Children's menu. **$$$**

★ **RED ROCK CAFE.** *4022 N Oakland Ave, Shorewood (53211). Phone 414/962-4545; fax 414/962-6671. www.theredrockcafe.com.* Seafood menu. Lunch, dinner, Sun brunch. Closed Mon; holidays. Bar. Children's menu. **$$**

★ **ROYAL INDIA.** *3400 S 27th St, Milwaukee (53215). Phone 414/647-9600.* Indian menu. Lunch, dinner. Casual attire. **$$**

★ ★ **SAFE HOUSE.** *779 N Front St, Milwaukee (53202). Phone 414/271-2007; fax 414/271-2676. www.safe-house.com/mainmenu.cfm.* It can be a bit tricky to get into the Safe House, a spy-themed restaurant and bar in downtown Milwaukee. But don't let that stop you, because the joint is worth the hassle. A few tips: the establishment is in a building marked International Exports, Ltd., and you need a password to get inside. (Ask a local before you go.) If you don't know it, you'll have to perform a silly trick to get in. Once in, feast on the tasty grub—burgers, salads, sandwiches, steak, and killer chicken tortilla soup—then wander around the Safe House to discover all of its spy gadgets: secret mirrors, surveillance equipment, and even a CIA "cover" phone booth with 99 background sounds to provide you with an instant alibi as you your whereabouts. When you're ready to leave, pay 25 cents to use the secret exit. American menu. Lunch Mon-Sat, dinner daily. Closed holidays. Bar. Children's menu. **$$**

★ ★ ★ **SANFORD.** *1547 N Jackson St, Milwaukee (53202). Phone 414/276-9608; fax 414/278-8509. www.sanfordrestaurant.com.* The site, once a grocery store owned by Sanford's family, houses a modern, sophisticated dining room offering internationally flavored, New American cuisine from an à la carte menu. An additional, five-course ethnic tasting menu is offered on weeknights. American menu. Dinner. Closed Sun; holidays. Business casual attire. Reservations recommended. Valet parking. **$$$**

★ **SARAPHINO'S ITALIAN RESTAURANT.** *3074 E Layton Ave, St. Francis (53235). Phone 414/744-0303; fax 414/431-1329.* Italian menu. Breakfast, lunch, dinner. Children's menu. Casual attire. **$$**

★ **SAZ'S STATE HOUSE.** *5539 W State St, Milwaukee (53208). Phone 414/453-2410; fax 414/256-8778. www.sazs.com.* This uber-popular rib joint, located in a 1905 roadhouse, is consistently rated Milwaukee's best. Try the sour cream and chive fries, a local favorite. American, barbecue menu. Lunch, dinner, Sun brunch. Closed Dec 24-25. Bar. Outdoor seating. **$$**

★ **SINGHA THAI.** *2237 S 108th St, West Allis (53227). Phone 414/541-1234; fax 414/541-0683. www.singha-thai.com.* Thai menu. Lunch, dinner. Closed holidays. Casual attire. Reservations recommended. **$$**

★ ★ **THIRD STREET PIER.** *1110 N Old World 3rd St, Milwaukee (53203). Phone 414/272-0330; fax 414/272-6463. www.weissgerbers.com.* In restored landmark building on Milwaukee River. American menu. Dinner, brunch. Closed holidays. Bar. Children's menu. Valet parking. Outdoor seating. **$$**

★ **THREE BROTHERS.** *2414 S St. Clair St, Milwaukee (53207). Phone 414/481-7530; fax 414/481-8652.* Serbian menu. Dinner. Closed Mon; holidays. **$$**

★ ★ **WEST BANK CAFE.** *732 E Burleigh St, Milwaukee (5321v2). Phone 414/562-5555.* Chinese, Vietnamese menu. Dinner. Closed holidays. **$$**

★ **YEN CHING.** *7630 W Good Hope Rd, Milwaukee (53223). Phone 414/353-6677. www.yenchingchinese.com/index.html.* Chinese menu. Lunch, dinner. **$$**

Mineral Point (E-3)

See also Dodgeville, New Glarus, Platteville, Spring Green

Settled 1827
Population 2,428
Elevation 1,135 ft
Area Code 608
Zip 53565
Information Chamber of Commerce, 225 High St; phone 608/987-3201 or toll-free 888/764-6894
Web Site www.mineralpoint.com

The first settlers were New Englanders and Southerners attracted by the lead (galena) deposits. In the 1830s, miners from Cornwall, England, settled here. These "Cousin Jacks," as they were called, introduced superior mining methods and also built the first permanent homes, duplicating the rock houses they had left in Cornwall. Since the mines were in sight of their homes their wives called them to meals by stepping to the door and shaking a rag—so the town was first called "Shake Rag."

Visitors to Mineral Point can experience the way small towns used to be. The city offers a wide variety of shopping opportunities, including artisan galleries and working studios, antique shops, and specialty shops.

What to See and Do

Mineral Point Toy Museum. *215 Commerce, Mineral Point (53565). Phone 608/987-3160.* Antique and collectible doll houses, toys, and trains. (May-Oct, Fri-Sun) **$$**

Pendarvis, Cornish Restoration. *114 Shake Rag St, Mineral Point (53565). Phone 608/987-2122.* Guided tour of six restored log and limestone homes of Cornish miners (circa 1845). Also 40-acre nature walk in old mining area (free), which has mine shafts, wildflowers, and abandoned "badger holes." (May-Oct, daily) **$$$**

Minocqua (B-3)

See also Boulder Junction, Eagle River, Lac du Flambeau, Manitowish Waters, Rhinelander, Sayner, St. Germain, Woodruff

Population 3,522
Elevation 1,603 ft
Area Code 715
Zip 54548
Information Minocqua-Arbor Vitae-Woodruff Area Chamber of Commerce, 8216 Hwy 51, PO Box 1006; phone 715/356-5266 or toll-free 800/446-6784
Web Site www.minocqua.org

Minocqua is a four-season resort area known for its thousands of acres of lakes. The area contains one of the largest concentrations of freshwater bodies in America. Minocqua, the "Island City," was once completely surrounded by Lake Minocqua. Now youth camps and resorts are along the lakeshore.

What to See and Do

Area lakes, streams, and ponds. Contain every major type of freshwater fish found in Wisconsin. Also clear water for diving. Min-Aqua-Bat water-ski shows (mid-June-mid-Aug, Wed, Fri, and also Sun evening). For winter sports enthusiasts there are thousands of miles of groomed snowmobile and hundreds of miles of cross-country ski trails. Inquire at Chamber of Commerce.

Circle M Corral Family Fun Park. *10295 Hwy 70, Minocqua (54548). 2 1/2 miles W of Hwy 51 on Hwy 70 W. Phone 715/356-4441.* Horseback riding, bumper boats, go-carts; train ride with robbery aboard replica *C. P. Huntington*; water slide; miniature golf; children's rides. Picnic area, snack bar. (Mid-May-mid-Oct, daily) **$$$**

Jim Peck's Wildwood. *10094 State Hwy 70, Minocqua (54548). Hwy 51 to Hwy 70, then 2 miles W. Phone 715/356-5588.* A wildlife park featuring hundreds of tame animals and birds native to the area; many can be pet at baby animal nursery; walk among tame deer; trout and musky ponds. Picnic area; nature walk; adventure boat rides; gift shop, snack wagon. (May-mid-Oct, daily) **$$$**

Minocqua Museum. *416 Chicago Ave, Minocqua (54548). Hwy 51 to Chicago Ave. Downtown. Phone 715/356-7666.* Ongoing display of Island City's unique history. Main gallery exhibits change annually; some permanent exhibits. (June-Sept, daily; or by appointment) **DONATION**

Minocqua Winter Park Nordic Center. *12375 Scotchman Lake Rd, Minocqua (54548). 6 miles W on Hwy 70 to Squirrel Lake Rd, then approximately 6 miles S, follow the signs. Phone 715/356-3309. www.skimwp.org.* Center has over 35 miles of groomed and tracked cross-country trails; two groomed telemarking slopes; more than 1 mile of lighted trails for night skiing (Thurs-Fri only). School, shop, rentals. Heated chalet, concessions. (Dec-Mar, Thurs-Tues) **$$$$**

Northwoods Wildlife Center. *8683 Blumstein Rd, Minocqua (54548). Hwy 51 to Hwy 70, then 1 mile W. Phone 715/356-7400.* Wildlife hospital, wildlife educational center with tours and scheduled programs. (Mon-Sat, daily) **DONATION**

Wilderness Cruise. *4973 Willow Dam Rd, Hazelhurst (54531). 7 miles S on Hwy 51, then 7 miles on County Y to Willow Dam Rd. Phone 715/453-3310; toll-free 800/*

472-1516. Two-hour cruise on the Willow Flowage aboard the *Wilderness Queen.* Also brunch, dinner, and sightseeing cruises. (Mid-May-Oct, call for hours; reservations required) **$$$$**

Special Event

Northern Lights Playhouse. *5611 Hwy 51, Hazelhurst (54531). 10 miles S of Minocqua on Hwy 51.Phone 715/356-7173.* Professional repertory theater presents Broadway plays, musicals, and comedies; also Children's Theatre. Memorial Day-early Oct. **$$$$**

Limited-Service Hotels

★ LAKEVIEW MOTOR LODGE. *311 E Park Ave, Minocqua (54548). Phone 715/356-5208; fax 715/356-1412.* On Lake Minocqua; dock. 41 rooms, 2 story. Pets accepted, some restrictions; fee. Complimentary continental breakfast. Check-out 11 am. Whirlpool. **$**

★ NEW CONCORD INN. *320 Front St, Minocqua (54548). Phone 715/356-1800; toll-free 800/356-8888; fax 715/356-6955. www.newconcordinn.com.* 53 rooms, 3 story. Complimentary continental breakfast. Check-out 11 am. Beach. Indoor pool, whirlpool. **$**

Restaurants

★★ NORWOOD PINES. *10171 Hwy 70 W, Minocqua (54548). Phone 715/356-3666.* Steak menu. Dinner. Closed Sun; Dec 24-25. Children's menu. **$$$**

★ PAUL BUNYAN'S. *8653 Hwy 51 N, Minocqua (54548). Phone 715/356-6270; fax 715/356-2780. www.paulbunyans.com.* Replica of typical 1890 logging camp. American menu. Breakfast, lunch, dinner. Closed Oct-Apr. Bar. Children's menu. **$$**

★ RED STEER. *8230 Hwy 51 S, Minocqua (54548). Phone 715/356-6332. www.theredsteer.com.* Seafood, steak menu. Dinner. Closed Thanksgiving, Dec 24-25. Bar. Children's menu. **$$**

★ SPANG'S. *318 Milwaukee St, Minocqua (54548). Phone 715/356-4401.* Italian menu. Dinner. Closed Easter, Thanksgiving, Dec 24-25. Bar. Children's menu. **$$**

Monroe (F-3)

See also Janesville, New Glarus

Population 10,241
Elevation 1,099 ft
Area Code 608
Zip 53566
Information Chamber of Commerce, 1505 9th St; phone 608/325-7648
Web Site www.monroechamber.org

A well-known community of Swiss heritage in an area of abundant dairy production, Monroe is the site of a unique courthouse with a 120-foot tall clock tower.

What to See and Do

Alp and Dell Cheesery, Deli, and Country Cafe. *657 2nd St, Monroe (53566). Phone 608/328-3355.* Watch cheesemaking process (Mon-Fri). Self-guided tours. Retail store (daily).

Yellowstone Lake State Park. *8495 Lake Rd, Blanchardville (53516). 16 miles NW on Hwy 81 to Argyle, then N on County N, then W on Lake Rd. Phone 608/523-4427; toll-free 800/947-8757.* A 968-acre park on Yellowstone Lake. Swimming, water-skiing, fishing, boating (rentals); hiking, cross-country skiing, snowmobiling, picnicking, playground, concession, camping (electric, dump station; reservations accepted through reserve America), winter camping. (Daily) **$$**

Special Event

Balloon Rally. *Green County Fairgrounds, 2600 10th St, Monroe (53566). Phone 608/325-7648.* Mid-June.

Limited-Service Hotel

★ AMERICINN MONROE. *424 Fourth Ave, Monroe (53566). Phone 608/328-3444; fax 608/328-3454.* 54 rooms. Check-in 3 pm, check-out 11 am. Indoor pool, whirlpool. **$**

Mount Horeb (E-3)

See also Dodgeville, Madison, New Glarus

Population 4,182
Elevation 1,230 ft

Area Code 608
Zip 53572
Information Chamber of Commerce, PO Box 84; phone 608/437-5914 or toll-free 888/765-5929

What to See and Do

Blue Mound State Park. *4350 Mounds Park Rd, Blue Mounds (53517). W on Hwy 18, 1 mile NW of Blue Mounds. Phone 608/437-5711.* A 1,150-acre park with scenic views and lookout towers. Swimming pool; nature, mountain bike trails, hiking, and cross-country ski trails; picnicking, playgrounds, camping (dump station). (Daily) **$$$**

Cave of the Mounds. *2975 Cave of the Mounds Rd, Blue Mounds (53517). 4 miles W on Hwy 18/151, then follow signs to Cave of the Mounds. Phone 608/437-3038.* Colorful onyx formations in limestone cavern, rooms on two levels. Registered National Natural Landmark. One-hour guided tours. (Year-round, call for hours) Also picnic grounds, gardens, snack bar, and gift shops. **$$$**

★ **Little Norway.** *3576 Hwy JG Larth, Mount Horeb (53517). W via Hwy 18/151 to Cave of the Mounds Rd, then follow signs to County JG. Phone 608/437-8211.* Norwegian pioneer farmstead built in 1856; museum of Norse antiques. Guided tours (45 minutes). (May-late Oct, daily) **$$$**

Mount Horeb Mustard Museum. *100 W Main St, Mount Horeb (53517). Phone 608/437-3986; toll-free 800/438-6878.* Large collection of mustards, mustard memorabilia, and samplings. (Daily)

Limited-Service Hotel

★★ **KARAKAHL COUNTRY INN.** *1405 Hwy 18/151 E, Mount Horeb (53572). Phone 608/437-5545; toll-free 888/621-1884; fax 608/437-5908. www.karakahl.com.* 76 rooms, 2 story. Pets accepted, some restrictions; fee. Complimentary continental breakfast. Check-out noon. Restaurant, bar. Indoor pool. **$**

Neenah-Menasha (D-4)

See also Appleton, Green Bay, Oshkosh

Settled 1843
Population 23,219
Elevation 750 ft
Area Code 920
Zip Neenah, 54956; Menasha, 54952
Information Fox Cities Convention & Visitor Bureau, 3433 W College Ave, Appleton, 54914; phone 920/734-3358 or toll-free 800/236-6673
Web Site www.foxcities.org

Wisconsin's great paper industry started in Neenah and its twin city, Menasha. The two cities, located on Lake Winnebago, are still among the nation's leaders in dollar volume of paper products. Many paper product factories are located here in addition to large wood product plants, printing and publishing houses, foundries, and machine shops.

What to See and Do

Barlow Planetarium. *1478 Midway Rd, Menasha (54952). Phone 920/832-2848.* 3-D projections explain the stars. (Thurs-Fri evening; Sat-Sun) **$$**

Bergstrom-Mahler Museum. *165 N Park Ave, Neenah (54956). Phone 920/751-4658.* More than 1,800 glass paperweights; antique German glass; American regional paintings; changing exhibits. Museum shop, specializing in glass. (Tues-Sun; closed holidays) **DONATION**

Doty Cabin. *Doty Park, 701 Lincoln St, Neenah (54956). Webster and Lincoln sts. Phone 920/751-4614.* Home of Wisconsin's second territorial governor, James Duane Doty. Boating (ramp); tennis courts, picnic facilities, playgrounds; park (daily), cabin (June-mid-Aug, daily). **DONATION**

High Cliff State Park. *N7630 State Park Rd, Sherwood (54169). 9 miles E, off Hwy 114, on opposite shore of Lake Winnebago. Phone 920/989-1106.* A 1,139-acre park with beautiful wooded bluffs. Swimming, bathhouse, water-skiing, fishing, boating (marina); nature, hiking, snowmobile, and cross-country ski trails; picnicking, playgrounds, concession, camping (dump station). Naturalist program. (Daily) **$$** In the park is

High Cliff General Store Museum. *N7630 State Park Rd, Sherwood (54169). Phone 920/989-1106.* Museum depicts life in the area from 1850 to the early 1900s. Store was once the center of activity of the lime kiln community and housed the post and telegraph offices. Relic of old lime kiln oven nearby. (Mid-May-Sept: Sat-Sun, holidays) **FREE**

Smith Park. *140 Main St, Menasha (54952). Phone 920/967-5106.* Monument to Jean Nicolet, who came in 1634 to arrange peace between Native American tribes. Tennis courts, cross-country skiing, picnic areas, pavilion, playground. Native American effigy mounds; formal gardens; historic railroad caboose representing birthplace of Central Wisconsin Railroad. (Daily) **FREE**

New Glarus (E-3)

See also Dodgeville, Madison, Mineral Point, Monroe, Mount Horeb

Settled 1845
Population 1,899
Elevation 900 ft
Area Code 608
Zip 53574
Information New Glarus Tourism, PO Box 713; phone 608/527-2095 or toll-free 800/527-6838

When bad times struck the Swiss canton of Glarus in 1845, a group of 108 set out for the New World and settled New Glarus. Their knowledge of dairying brought prosperity. The town is still predominantly Swiss in character and ancestry.

What to See and Do

Chalet of the Golden Fleece. *618 2nd St, New Glarus (53574). Phone 608/527-2614.* Replica of Swiss chalet, with more than 3,000 Swiss items. Guided tours. (May-Oct, daily) **$$**

New Glarus Woods State Park. *W5446 County Rd NN, New Glarus (53574). 1 mile S on Hwy 69. Phone 608/527-2335.* Park has 38 campsites in 425 acres of wooded valleys. Picnicking, playgrounds. (Daily) **$$**

Sugar River State Trail. *418 Railroad St, New Glarus (53574). Phone 608/527-2334.* A 24-mile trail follows abandoned railroad bed between New Glarus and Brodhead to the southeast. Hiking, biking, snowmobiling, and cross-country skiing. (Daily) **$$**

Swiss Historical Village. *612 7th Ave, New Glarus (53574). Phone 608/527-2317. www.swisshistoricalvillage.com.* Replicas of first buildings erected by settlers, includes blacksmith shops, cheese factory, schoolhouse, and print shop; original furnishings and tools; guided tours. (May-Oct, daily) **$$$**

Special Events

Heidi Festival. *New Glarus High School, 1701 2nd St, New Glarus (53574). Phone 608/527-2095.* Mid-June.

Swiss Volksfest. *Wilhelm Tell Shooting Park, County O, New Glarus (53574). 1/2 mile N on County O. Phone 608/527-2095.* Singing, yodeling, dancing. Honors birth of Swiss confederation in 1291. First Sun in Aug.

Wilhelm Tell Festival. *Tell Amphitheater, Wilhelm Tell Grounds, County W, New Glarus (53574). 1 mile E on County W. Phone 608/527-2095.* Alpine Festival, Swiss entertainment (Sat). Schiller's drama, *Wilhelm Tell,* in German (Sun); in English (Sat-Mon). Also fine arts show, Village Park (Sun). Labor Day weekend.

Limited-Service Hotel

★ SWISS-AIRE MOTEL. *1200 Hwy 69, New Glarus (53574). Phone 608/527-2138; toll-free 800/798-4391; fax 608/527-5818. www.swissaire.com.* 26 rooms. Pets accepted, some restrictions; fee. Complimentary continental breakfast. Check-out 11 am. Outdoor pool. **$**

Full-Service Resort

★★★ CHALET LANDHAUS INN. *801 Hwy 69, New Glarus (53574). Phone 608/527-5234; toll-free 800/944-1716; fax 608/527-2365. www.chaletlandhaus.com.* 67 rooms, 4 story. Check-out 11 am. Restaurant. Spa. **$$**

Specialty Lodging

The following lodging establishment is approved by Mobil Travel Guide, but due to its unique and individualized nature has not been given a traditional Mobil Star rating. Included in this listing you may find bed-and-breakfasts, limited-service inns, guest ranches, and other unique hotel properties.

COUNTRY HOUSE. *180 Hwy 69, New Glarus (53574). Phone 608/527-5399.* Built in 1892; antiques. 4 rooms, 2 story. Complimentary full breakfast. Check-in 4-7 pm, check-out 11 am. Restaurant. **$$**

Restaurant

★★ NEW GLARUS HOTEL. *100 6th Ave, New Glarus (53574). Phone 608/527-5244; fax 608/527-5055. www.newglarushotel.com.* American, Swiss menu. Lunch, dinner, Sun brunch. Closed Thanksgiving, Dec 24-25; also Tues in Nov-Apr. Bar. Children's menu. Polka Fri-Sat; yodeling (summer). **$$**

A Stroll through a Swiss Mountain Village (In Wisconsin!)

Snuggled in the Little Sugar River Valley, tiny New Glarus resembles a Swiss mountain village. And with good reason. The town was founded in 1845 by 108 immigrants from the Swiss canton of Glarus who traveled to America to escape poverty and unemployment. Today, it not unusual to see dairy herds grazing among the pretty hills, nor is it startling to hear a yodel echo across the valley. In fact, every year on the first Sunday in August, yodelers, alphornists, and folk dancers gather here to celebrate Swiss Independence Day.

Gather brochures at the New Glarus Information Center at Railroad Street and Sixth Avenue, then walk one block east to First Street, the town's main business thoroughfare. On the corner is the New Glarus Hotel, built in 1853 by Swiss settlers. Its main dining room occupies an old opera house (where talking movies were introduced in 1930). On an enclosed upper balcony, picture windows look out onto picturesque shops and over rooftops to surrounding green hills. Veal dishes include geschetzlets (thin slices lightly browned and served with a white wine sauce). Don't miss the baked-on-the-premises rhubarb-custard torte. The hotel has lodging in six guest rooms. Across the street are three god "foodie" stops. Chalet-style Scholo-Laden is a retail outlet for imported chocolates, home-made fudge, ice cream, and locally made cheeses. Ruef's Meat Market offers a variety of wurst, including fresh and smoked brats and landjaeger (dried sausage that makes a great munchie) sausages favored by Swiss hunters. New Glarus Bakery and Tea Room is the spot for an afternoon respite or to buy tempting baked goods that include rich, dense stolen (German sweet bread).

Wandering downtown's few short blocks, visitors quickly realize just how much the village resembles a Swiss mountain town. Chalet-style buildings feature carved balconies decorated by colorful coats of arms, Swiss flags and banners, and window boxes spilling with bright red geraniums. Many businesses bear Swiss-German inscriptions proclaiming the nature of the commerce conducted within. The clank of cowbells welcomes you to shops selling lace, embroidery, and raclette grills. Just east of First Street on Seventh Avenue, the Chalet of the Golden Fleece Museum replicates a Swiss Bernese mountain chalet. Rocks and logs on the roof reflect a Swiss practice designed to protect slate shingles from strong mountain winds. The museum houses a collection of more than 3,000 Swiss items, from dolls to kitchenware, as well as artifacts collected from around the world (such as a jeweled watch once owned by King Louis XVI, 2,000-year-old Etruscan earrings, and Gregorian chants on parchment dating from 1485). Continue east on Seventh Avenue to the Swiss Historical Village Museum, a replica pioneer village with log cabins, a log church, and a one-room schoolhouse. Operated by the local historical society, the museum preserves the history and records of New Glarus and tells the story of Swiss immigration and colonization. Its 14 buildings include a traditional Swiss bee house, a replica cheese factory, a blacksmith's shop, a general store, and a print shop that displays equipment used to print the *New Glarus Post* from 1897 to 1967.

Oconomowoc (E-4)

See also Milwaukee, Watertown

Population 10,993
Elevation 873 ft
Area Code 262
Zip 53066
Information Greater Oconomowoc Area Chamber of Commerce, 152 E Wisconsin Ave; phone 262/567-2666
Web Site www.oconomowoc.com

Native Americans called this place "the gathering of waters," because of its location between Fowler Lake and Lake Lac La Belle.

What to See and Do

Highlands Ski Hill. *965 Cannon Gate Rd, Oconomowoc (53066). Hwy 67 and I-94. Phone 262/567-2577.* Area has two chairlifts, rope tow; patrol, school, rentals; snowmaking; bar. Longest run is 2,200 feet; vertical drop 196 feet. (Nov-Mar, daily) **$$$$**

Honey of a Museum. *Honey Acres, N1557 Hwy 67, Ashippun (53003). 10 miles N on Hwy 67. Phone 920/*

474-4411; toll-free 800/558-7745. www.honeyacres.com. Less than 10 miles from downtown Oconomowoc is Honey Acres's Honey of a Museum, dedicated to the making of honey through the age-old practice of beekeeping. Situated on 40 acres, the business has been run by the Diehnelt family for five generations. Although visitors to the museum cannot tour the adjoining honey factory, they can still take home several varieties of the sweetened bee pollen, along with honey candies, honey mustards, and other honey products. The Bee Tree provides a close-up view of bee activities. (Mon-Fri 9 am-3:30 pm, weekends noon-4 pm) **FREE**

Limited-Service Hotel

★ ★ **OLYMPIA RESORT.** *1350 Royale Mile Rd, Oconomowoc (53066). Phone 800/558-9573; toll-free 800/558-9573; fax 262/369-4998. www.olympiaresort.com.* The goal of this resort is to recreate a European-style spa. 256 rooms, 4 story. Check-in 4 pm, check-out noon. Restaurant, bar. Fitness room. Indoor pool, outdoor pool, whirlpool. Golf, 18 holes. Tennis. **$**

Specialty Lodging

The following lodging establishment is approved by Mobil Travel Guide, but due to its unique and individualized nature has not been given a traditional Mobil Star rating. Included in this listing you may find bed-and-breakfasts, limited-service inns, guest ranches, and other unique hotel properties.

INN AT PINE TERRACE. *351 E Lisbon Rd, Oconomowoc (53066). Phone 262/893-0552; toll-free 800/421-4667; fax 262/567-7532. www.innatpineterrace.com.* Restored mansion (1879); antique furnishings. 13 rooms, 3 story. Pets accepted; fee. Complimentary continental breakfast. Check-in 3 pm, check-out 10:30 am. Restaurant. Outdoor pool. **$$**

Restaurants

★ ★ ★ **GOLDEN MAST INN.** *1270 Lacy Ln, Okauchee (53066). Phone 262/567-7047. www.weissgerbers.com.* This favorite local restaurant offers a wide array of entrées with a German flair. American menu. Dinner, brunch. Closed Mon; Dec 24-25. Bar. Children's menu. Business casual attire. Reservations recommended. Outdoor seating. **$$$**

★ **RED CIRCLE INN.** *33013 Watertown Plank Rd, Nashotah (53058). Phone 262/367-4883. www.foodspot.com/redcircleinn.* Former stagecoach stop; one of oldest restaurants in state (established in 1848). French menu. Dinner. Closed Sun-Mon; holidays. Bar. Business casual attire. Reservations recommended. **$$$**

★ ★ **SEVEN SEAS.** *1807 Nagawicka Rd, Hartland (53029). Phone 262/367-3903; fax 262/367-6877. www.weissgerbers.com.* Seafood menu. Dinner, brunch. Closed Jan 1, Dec 24-25. Bar. Children's menu. Business casual attire. Reservations recommended. Outdoor seating. **$$$**

Oconto (C-5)

See also Green Bay, Marinette, Menominee, Peshtigo

Population 4,474
Elevation 591 ft
Area Code 920
Zip 54153

On Green Bay at the mouth of the Oconto River, Oconto was the home of Copper Culture people 4,500 years ago.

What to See and Do

Beyer Home. *917 Park Ave, Oconto (54153). Phone 920/834-6206.* (Circa 1868) Victorian house with furnishings of 1880-1890s. Adjacent museum annex has exhibits of Copper Culture people and antique vehicles. (June-Labor Day, Mon-Sat, also Sun afternoons) **$$**

North Bay Shore County Park. *500 Bay Rd, Oconto (54153). 9 miles N on County Y. Phone 920/834-6825.* Swimming, fishing, boating; tent and trailer sites, camping (late May-late Sept; fee). Fall Salmon Run. (Daily) **FREE**

Oshkosh (D-4)

See also Appleton, Fond du Lac, Neenah-Menasha

Settled 1836
Population 55,006
Elevation 767 ft
Area Code 920
Information Oshkosh Convention & Visitors Bureau, 2 N Main St, 54901; phone 920/236-5250 or toll-free 800/876-5250

Web Site www.oshkoshcvb.org

Named for the Chief of the Menominee, Oshkosh is located on the west shore of Lake Winnebago, the largest freshwater lake within the state. The city is known for the many recreational activities offered by its lakes and rivers. This is the original home of the company that produces the famous overalls that help make Oshkosh a household word. The economy of the town, once called "Sawdust City," is centered on transportation equipment manufacturing, tourism, and candle making.

What to See and Do

EAA Air Adventure Museum. *3000 Poberezny Rd, Oshkosh (54902). Phone 920/426-4818.* More than 90 aircraft on display including home-built aircraft, antiques, classics, ultralights, aerobatic, and rotary-winged planes. Special World War II collection. Extensive collections of aviation art and photography; special displays of engines, propellers, and scale models. Five theaters. Antique airplanes fly on weekends (May-Oct). (Daily; closed holidays) **$$$**

Grand Opera House. *100 High Ave, Oshkosh (54901). Phone 920/424-2350 (box office).* A restored 1883 Victorian Theater, offers a variety of performing arts.

Menominee Park. *1200 E Irving, Oshkosh (54901). On Lake Winnebago, enter off Hazel or Merritt sts. Phone 920/236-5080.* Swimming beach (lifeguard), fishing, sailing, paddleboats; tennis courts, picnic shelters, concession. Train rides, children's zoo (late May-early Sept, daily). Fee for some activities. (Daily)

Oshkosh Public Museum. *1331 Algoma Blvd, Oshkosh (54901). Phone 920/424-4731.* Housed in a turn-of-the-century, Tudor-style mansion with Tiffany stained-glass windows and interior; also occupies adjacent addition. Apostles Clock, china and glassware collection; life-sized dioramas depicting French exploration, British occupation, pioneer settlement, and native wildlife; antique fire and train equipment; meteorites; Native American exhibits; fine and decorative art; 1913 Harley-Davidson; miniature lumber company. (Tues-Sun; closed holidays) **FREE**

Paine Art Center and Arboretum. *1410 Algoma Blvd, Oshkosh (54901). At jct Hwy 21, 110. Phone 920/235-6903.* Tudor Revival house; period rooms, European and American paintings and sculpture, Asian rugs, furniture, and decorative arts; changing art exhibitions. Arboretum and display gardens. (Tues-Sun afternoons; closed holidays) **$$**

Rebel Alliance Theater. *445 N Main St, Oshkosh (54901). Phone 920/426-8580 (box office).* Non-profit organization dedicated to bringing the live theater experience to Fox Valley.

University of Wisconsin-Oshkosh. *800 Algoma Blvd, Oshkosh (54901). Phone 920/424-0202; toll-free 800/624-1466. www.uwosh.edu.* (1871) (11,000 students) Priebe Art Gallery, Reeve Memorial Union, Kolf Sports and Recreation Center. Campus tours (Mon-Fri; Sat by appointment).

Special Events

EAA Air Venture. *Wittman Regional Airport, 525 W 20th Ave, Oshkosh (54902). Phone 920/426-0092. www.wittmanairport.com.* (Experimental Aircraft Association). Held at Wittman Regional Airport. One of the nation's largest aviation events. More than 500 educational forums, workshops, and seminars; daily air shows; exhibits; more than 12,000 aircraft. Late July-early Aug.

Oshkosh Public Museum Art Fair. *1331 Algoma Blvd, Oshkosh (54901). Phone 920/424-4731.* On Oshkosh Public Museum grounds. Featuring original fine art by over 200 quality artists from around the country. Music, entertainment, concessions. Early July.

Sawdust Days. *Menominee Park, Hazel St and E Irving Ave, Oshkosh (54901). Phone 920/235-5584.* Commemorates lumbering era. Early July.

Limited-Service Hotels

★ **BAYMONT INN.** *1950 Omro Rd, Oshkosh (54901). Phone 920/233-4190; toll-free 800/428-3438; fax 920/233-8197. www.baymontinns.com.* 97 rooms, 2 story. Pets accepted; fee. Complimentary continental breakfast. Check-in 3 pm, check-out noon. **$**

★ **HOLIDAY INN EXPRESS.** *2251 Westowne Ave, Oshkosh (54904). Phone 920/303-1300; toll-free 888/522-9472; fax 920/303-9330. www.hiexpress.com.* 69 rooms, 3 story. Pets accepted. Check-in 3 pm, check-out 11 am. High-speed Internet access. Fitness room. Indoor pool, whirlpool. Airport transportation available. **$**

★ ★ **PARK PLAZA OSHKOSH.** *1 N Main St, Oshkosh (54901). Phone 920/231-5000; toll-free 800/365-4458; fax 920/231-8383. www.parkplazaoshkosh.com.* Convenient to the convention center. 179 rooms, 8 story. Pets accepted; fee. Check-in 3 pm, check-out noon. High-speed Internet access. Restaurant, bar. Fitness room. Indoor pool, whirlpool. Airport transportation available. Business center. **$**

★ ★ **PIONEER RESORT & MARINA.** *1000 Pioneer Dr, Oshkosh (54902). Phone 920/233-1980; toll-free 800/683-1980; fax 920/426-2115. www.pioneerresort.com.* Enjoy the height of relaxation at this island resort. On lake; boat rentals, marina, sailing. 192 rooms, 3 story. Check-in 3 pm, check-out noon. Three restaurants, two bars. Fitness room. Indoor pool, outdoor pool, children's pool, whirlpool. Airport transportation available. **$**

Restaurants

★ **FIN 'N FEATHER SHOWBOATS.** *22 W Main St, Winneconne (54986). Phone 920/582-4305. www.fin-n-feathershowboats.com.* Replica of riverboat; excursions available on *Showboat II*. Steak menu. Breakfast, lunch, dinner, Sun brunch. Closed Dec 25. Bar. **$$**

★ ★ **ROBBINS.** *1810 Omro Rd, Oshkosh (54902). Phone 920/235-2840; fax 920/235-2906.* Seafood menu. Lunch, dinner. Closed Dec 25. Bar. Children's menu. **$$**

★ **WISCONSIN FARMS.** *2450 Washburn, Oshkosh (54904). Phone 920/233-7555; fax 920/233-7520.* American menu. Breakfast, lunch, dinner. Closed Mon; holidays. Children's menu. Casual attire. Reservations recommended. Outdoor seating. **$$**

Park Falls (B-3)

See also Lac du Flambeau, Manitowish Waters

Population 3,104
Elevation 1,490 ft
Area Code 715
Zip 54552
Information Park Falls Area Chamber of Commerce, 400 S 4th Ave S, Suite 8; phone 715/762-2703 or toll-free 800/762-2709
Web Site www.parkfalls.com

Park Falls has been proclaimed "ruffed grouse capital of the world," since more than 5,000 acres within this area have been used to create a natural habitat for the bird.

What to See and Do

Chequamegon National Forest. *1170 4th Ave S, Park Falls (54552). E on Hwy 29, 70, or Hwy 8 and 2; also NW on Hwy 13 and 63. Phone 715/762-2461.* Aspen, maple, pine, spruce, balsam, and birch on 855,000 acres. Rainbow Lake and Porcupine Lake Wildernes areas; Great Divide National Scenic Byway. Canoeing on south fork of Flambeau River, the north and south forks of the Chippewa River and Namekagon River; muskellunge, northern pike, walleye, and bass fishing; hunting for deer, bear, and small game; archery. Blueberry and raspberry picking. Swimming, boat launching; Ice Age and North Country national scenic trails; hiking, motorcycle, cross-country skiing, and snowmobile trails; camping (May-Sept; some sites to Dec) on a first-come basis (fee). Pets must be leashed. Resorts and cabins are located in and near the forest. A District Ranger office is located here. (Daily) **FREE**

Concrete Park. *82 36th St, Phillips (54555). 22 miles S via Hwy 13. Phone toll-free 800/762-2709.* Fred Smith's concrete and glass statues include northwoods people, folklore, fantasies, historic personages, Native Americans, angels, and animals. (Daily) **FREE**

Old Town Hall Museum. *W7213 Pine St, Park Falls (54552). Phone 715/762-4571.* Artifacts of logging era (1876-1930); replica of turn-of-the-century living room and kitchen; county historic display; old opera house. (June-Labor Day, Fri and Sun afternoons) **FREE**

Post Office Lumberjack Mural. *109 N 1st St, Park Falls (54552). Phone 715/762-4575.* In 1938, the US Government provided artists the opportunity to submit artwork to be displayed in local post offices throughout the country. The Park Falls Post Office features one of the 2,200 that were finally selected. The restored mural, covering one entire wall, depicts the history of logging. (Mon-Sat)

Special Event

Flambeau Rama. *400 4th Ave S, Park Falls (54552). Downtown. Phone 715/762-2703.* A four-day event includes parades, arts and crafts show, Evergreen Road Run, games. Early Aug.

Peshtigo (C-5)

See also Marinette, Menominee, Oconto

Population 3,154
Elevation 600 ft
Area Code 715
Zip 54157
Information City Clerk, City Hall, 331 French St, PO Box 100; phone 715/582-3041

On October 8, 1871, the same day that the Chicago fire claimed 250 lives, 800 people died in Peshtigo, virtually unpublicized, when the entire town burned to the ground in a disastrous forest fire. A monument to those who died in the fire is located in the Peshtigo Fire Cemetery on Oconto Avenue. The city is now a manufacturing center.

What to See and Do

Badger Park. *N Emery Ave, Peshtigo (54157). On Peshtigo River. Phone 715/582-4321.* Swimming, fishing (northern, bass, coho salmon); tent and trailer sites (electric hook-ups), playground. (May-Oct, daily) **$$$$**

Peshtigo Fire Museum. *400 Oconto Ave, Peshtigo (54157). Phone 715/582-3244.* Local historical items. (Memorial Day-early Oct, daily) **FREE**

Platteville (E-2)

See also Dodgeville, Mineral Point

Population 9,708
Elevation 994 ft
Area Code 608
Zip 53818
Information Chamber of Commerce, 275 Hwy 151 W, PO Box 16; phone 608/348-8888
Web Site www.platteville.com

Sport fishing is very popular in the many streams in the area as are ice fishing on the Mississippi River and hunting for upland game, waterfowl, and deer. The world's largest letter "M" was built on Platteville Mound in 1936 by mining engineering students; it is lit twice each year for the University of Wisconsin-Platteville's homecoming and Miner's Ball.

What to See and Do

Mining Museum. *385 E Main St, Platteville (53818). Phone 608/348-3301.* Traces the development of lead and zinc mining in the area. Guided tour includes a walk down into Bevans Lead Mine and a mine train ride (May-Oct, daily). Changing exhibits (Nov-Apr, Mon-Fri). **$$$** Admission includes

> **Rollo Jamison Museum.** *405 Main St, Platteville (53818). Phone 608/348-3301.* Museum contains a large collection of everyday items collected by Jamison during his lifetime, including horse-drawn vehicles, tools, and musical instruments.

Stone Cottage. *W Madison and Lancaster, Platteville (53818). West, Madison, and Hwy 81. Phone 608/348-8888.* (1837) Much of the interior is the original furnishing of the home; 2-foot-thick walls of dolomite Galena limestone. Was private residence until 1960s. **$**

Special Events

Dairy Days Celebration. *Legion Field, Pitt and Water sts, Platteville (53818). Phone 608/348-8888.* Carnival, parade, food, live music, tractor and truck pulls, car show, 4-H exhibits. First weekend after Labor Day.

Wisconsin Shakespeare Festival. *198 Ullsvik Center, Platteville (53818). Phone 608/342-1398.* In Center for the Arts on campus of University of Wisconsin-Platteville. Nightly Tues-Sun; matinees Wed, Sat-Sun. Early July-early Aug.

Limited-Service Hotels

★★ GOVERNOR DODGE HOTEL. *300 W Hwy 151, Platteville (53818). Phone 608/348-2301; fax 608/348-8579.* State university five blocks. 74 rooms, 2 story. Pets accepted, some restrictions. Check-out noon. Restaurant. Fitness room. Indoor pool, whirlpool. **$**

★ SUPER 8. *100 Hwy 80/81 S, Platteville (53818). Phone 608/348-8800; toll-free 800/800-8000; www.super8.com.* 73 rooms, 2 story. Pets accepted; fee. Complimentary continental breakfast. Check-in 3 pm, check-out 11 am. Whirlpool. **$**

Restaurant

★★ TIMBERS. *670 Ellen St, Platteville (53818). Phone 608/348-2406; fax 608/348-4995.* Large custom-built electronic theater pipe organ. American menu. Lunch, dinner, Sun brunch. Bar. Children's menu. **$$**

Port Washington (E-5)

See also Cedarburg, Milwaukee, Sheboygan

Settled 1830
Population 9,338
Elevation 612 ft
Area Code 262
Zip 53074
Information Tourist Center located in the Pebble House, 126 E Grand Ave, PO Box 153; phone 262/284-0900 or toll-free 800/719-4881
Web Site www.discoverusa.com/wi/ptwash

Located along the shore of Lake Michigan, Port Washington has many pre-Civil War homes. The Port Washington Marina, one of the finest on Lake Michigan, provides exceptional facilities for boating and fishing.

What to See and Do

Eghart House. *316 Grand Ave, Port Washington (53074). Phone 262/284-2875.* Built in 1872; Victorian furnishings from 1850 to 1900 in hall, parlor, dining-living room, bedroom, kitchen, and pantry. Tours. (Late May-Labor Day, Sun afternoons; weekdays by appointment) **$**

Limited-Service Hotels

★ ★ HOLIDAY INN PORT WASHINGTON. *135 E Grand Ave, Port Washington (53074). Phone 262/284-9461; fax 262/284-3169.* 96 rooms, 5 story. Pets accepted, some restrictions; fee. Check-out 11 am. Restaurant, bar. Fitness room. Indoor pool, whirlpool. **$**

★ WEST BEND FANTASUITES. *2520 W Washington St, West Bend (53095). Phone 262/338-0636; toll-free 800/727-9727; fax 262/338-4290.* Uniquely decorated suites with varying themes. 86 rooms, 2 story, all suites. Complimentary continental breakfast. Check-out noon. Bar. Indoor pool, outdoor pool, whirlpool. **$**

Restaurants

★ ★ BUCHEL'S COLONIAL HOUSE. *1000 S Spring St, Port Washington (53074). Phone 262/284-2212.* American, German menu. Dinner. Closed Sun-Mon; holidays. Bar. Children's menu. Casual attire. Reservations recommended. **$$**

★ ★ SMITH BROTHERS' FISH SHANTY. *100 N Franklin St, Port Washington (53074). Phone 262/284-5592; fax 262/377-7923.* Seafood menu. Lunch, dinner. Closed holidays. Bar. Children's menu. Casual attire. Outdoor seating. **$$**

Portage (D-3)

See also Baraboo, Prairie du Sac, Reedsburg, Wisconsin Dells

Settled 1835
Population 8,640
Elevation 800 ft
Area Code 608
Zip 53901
Information Chamber of Commerce, 301 W Wisconsin St; phone 608/742-6242 or toll-free 800/474-2525

Portage is built on a narrow strip of land separating the Fox and Wisconsin rivers. In the early flow of traffic, goods were hauled from one river to another, providing the name for the city. Before permanent settlement, Fort Winnebago occupied this site; several historic buildings remain. Modern Portage is the business center of Columbia County.

What to See and Do

Cascade Mountain Ski Area. *W10441 Cascade Mountain Rd, Portage (53901). NW on I-90/94, then 1/4 mile W on Hwy 33 to Cascade Mtn Rd. Phone 608/742-5588; toll-free 800/992-2754. www.cascademountain.com.* Two double, three quad, three triple chairlifts, rope tow; patrol, school, snowmaking; snack bar, cafeteria, dining room, bar. 27 runs; longest run 1 mile; vertical drop 460 feet. Night skiing. (Mid-Nov-Mar, daily)

Fort Winnebago Surgeons' Quarters. *W8687 State Rd 33, Portage (53901). 1 mile E on Hwy 33. Phone 608/742-2949.* Original log house (1828), surviving from Old Fort Winnebago, used by medical officers stationed at the fort. Restored; many original furnishings. Garrison school (1850-1960). (Mid-May-mid-Oct, daily) **$$**

Home of Zona Gale. *506 W Edgewater St, Portage (53901). Phone 608/742-7744.* Greek Revival house built in 1906 for the Pulitzer Prize-winning novelist; some original furnishings. (Mon-Fri, by appointment) **$**

Old Indian Agency House. *RR 1, Portage (53901). 1 mile E on Hwy 33 to Agency House Rd. Phone 608/742-6362.* (1832) Restored house of John Kinzie, US Indian Agent to the Winnebago and an important pioneer; his wife Juliette wrote *Wau-bun,* an early history of their voyages to Fort Winnebago. Period furnishings. (May-Oct: daily; rest of year: by appointment) **$$**

Silver Lake. *N side of town. Phone 608/742-2176.* Swimming, beach, lifeguards, water-skiing, fishing (rainbow trout, largemouth bass, northern pike, panfish, muskie, walleye), boating (public landing); picnic area (shelter), playground. Parking. (Early June-Labor Day, daily) **FREE**

Limited-Service Hotel

★ ★ RIDGE MOTOR INN. *2900 New Pinery Rd, Portage (53901). Phone 608/742-5306; toll-free 877/742-5306. www.theridgemotorinn.com.* 100 rooms, 3 story. Check-in 3 pm, check-out 11 am. High-speed Internet access. Restaurant, bar. Fitness room. Indoor pool, whirlpool. **$**

Prairie du Chien (E-2)

Settled 1736
Population 5,659
Elevation 642 ft
Area Code 608
Zip 53821
Information Chamber of Commerce, 211 S Main St, PO Box 326; phone 608/326-2032 or toll-free 800/732-1673
Web Site www.prairieduchien.org

Dating back to 1673, this is the second-oldest European settlement in Wisconsin. Marquette and Jolliet discovered the Mississippi River just south of the prairie that the French adventurers then named Prairie du Chien ("prairie of the dog") for Chief Alim, whose name meant "dog." The site became a popular gathering place and trading post. The War of 1812 led to the construction of Fort Shelby and Fort Crawford on an ancient Native American burial ground in the village. Stationed here were Jefferson Davis, later president of the Confederacy, and Zachary Taylor, later president of the United States. In 1826, Hercules Dousman, an agent for John Jacob Astor's American Fur Company, came and built a personal fortune, becoming Wisconsin's first millionaire. When Fort Crawford was moved, Dousman bought the site and erected Villa Louis, the "House of the Mound," a palatial mansion.

What to See and Do

Fort Crawford Museum. *717 S Beaumont Rd, Prairie du Chien (53821). Phone 608/326-6960.* Relics of 19th-century medicine, Native American herbal remedies, drugstore, dentist and physicians' offices. Educational health exhibits; Dessloch Theater displays "transparent twins." Dedicated to Dr. William Beaumont, who did some of his famous digestive system studies at Fort Crawford. (May-Oct, daily) **$$**

★ Kickapoo Indian Caverns and Native American Museum. *W200 Rhein Hollow, Wauzeka (53826). 6 miles S on Hwy 18, then 9 miles E on Hwy 60. Phone 608/875-7723. www.kickapooindiancaverns.com.* Largest caverns in Wisconsin, used by Native Americans for centuries as a shelter. Sights include subterranean lake, Cathedral Room, Turquoise Room, Stalactite Chamber, and Chamber of the Lost Waters. Guided tours. (Mid-May-Oct, daily) **$$$**

Nelson Dewey State Park. *12190 County Rd VV, Cassville (53806). 35 miles S via Hwy 18, Hwy 35, and 133. Phone 608/725-5374.* This 756-acre park offers nature, hiking trails; camping (hook-ups). (Daily) Also here is

Stonefield. *12195 County Rd VV, Cassville (53806). Phone 608/725-5210.* Named for a rock-studded, 2,000-acre farm that Dewey (first elected governor of Wisconsin) established on the bluffs of the Mississippi River. State Agricultural Museum contains display of farm machinery. Site also features re-creation of an 1890 Stonefield Village including blacksmith, general store, print shop, school, church, and 26 other buildings. Horse-drawn wagon rides (limited hours; fee). (Memorial Day-early Oct, Wed-Sun) **$$$**

★ Villa Louis. *521 N Villa Louis Rd, Prairie du Chien (53821). Off Hwy 18. Phone 608/326-2721.* (1870) Built on site of Fort Crawford. Restored to its 19th-century splendor. Contains original furnishings, collection of Victorian decorative arts. Surrounded by extensive grounds, bounded by the Mississippi River. Tours include Fur Trade Museum. (May-Oct: daily 10 am-5 pm) **$$$**

Wyalusing State Park. *13081 State Park Ln, Bagley (53801). 7 miles SE on Hwy 18, then W on County C, X. Phone 608/996-2261.* A 2,654-acre park at the confluence of the Mississippi and Wisconsin rivers. Sentinel Ridge (500 feet) provides a commanding view of the area; valleys, caves, waterfalls, springs; Native American effigy mounds. Swimming beach nearby, fishing, boating (landing), canoeing; 18 miles of nature, hiking, and cross-country ski trails; picnicking, playground, concession, camping (electric hook-ups, dump station). Nature center; naturalist programs (summer). (Daily) **$$**

Limited-Service Hotel

★ BEST WESTERN QUIET HOUSE & SUITES. *Hwys 18 and 35 S, Prairie du Chien (53821). Phone 608/326-4777; toll-free 800/780-7234; fax 608/326-4787. www.bestwestern.com.* 42 rooms, 2 story. Pets accepted, some restrictions; fee. Check-in 2 pm, check-out 11 am. Fitness room. Indoor pool, whirlpool. **$**

Prairie du Sac (E-3)

See also Baraboo, Madison, Portage, Reedsburg, Spring Green, Wisconsin Dells

Population 2,380
Elevation 780 ft
Area Code 608
Zip 53578
Information Sauk Prairie Area Chamber of Commerce, 207 Water St, Sauk City 53583; phone 608/643-4168

A favorite launching area for canoeists on the Wisconsin River. It is possible to see bald eagles south of the village at Ferry Bluff, where many of them winter. Watching them feed on fish in the open water is a favorite winter pastime.

What to See and Do

Wollersheim Winery. *7876 Hwy 188, Prairie du Sac (53578). Phone 608/643-6515; toll-free 800/847-9463.* (1857) Guided tours, wine tasting, cheese, gift shop. (Daily; closed holidays) **$$**

Special Event

Harvest Festival. *Wollersheim Winery, 7876 Hwy 188, Prairie du Sac (53578). Phone 608/643-6515; toll-free 800/847-9463.* Grape stompers competition; music; cork toss; grape spitting contest; foods. First full weekend in Oct.

Racine (E-5)

See also Burlington, Kenosha, Milwaukee

Founded 1834
Population 84,298
Elevation 626 ft
Area Code 262
Information Racine County Convention and Visitors Bureau, 345 Main St, 53403; phone 262/634-3293 or toll-free 800/272-2463
Web Site www.racine.org

Racine is situated on a thumb of land jutting into Lake Michigan. The largest concentration of people of Danish descent in the United States can be found here; in fact, West Racine is known as "Kringleville" because of its Danish pastry. There are more than 300 manufacturing firms located here.

What to See and Do

Architectural tour. *1525 Howe St, Racine (53403). Phone 262/260-2154.* A 45-minute tour of SC Johnson Wax world headquarters designed by Frank Lloyd Wright. Reservations required. (Fri; closed holidays) **FREE**

Charles A. Wustum Museum of Fine Arts. *2519 Northwestern Ave, Racine (53404). Phone 262/636-9177.* Painting, photography, graphics, crafts, and sculpture displays; works of local, regional, and nationally known artists are featured. Permanent and changing exhibits. Also park and formal gardens. (Daily; closed holidays) **FREE**

Racine Heritage Museum. *701 S Main St, Racine (53403). Phone 262/636-3926.* Cultural history of Racine includes permanent and temporary exhibits, archive, and photographic collection. (Tues-Sat; closed holidays) **FREE**

Racine Zoological Gardens. *2131 N Main, Racine (53402). Phone 262/636-9189.* Extensive animal collection, picnic area, swimming (beach). (Daily; closed Dec 25) **FREE**

Special Event

Salmon-A-Rama. *5 Fifth St, Racine (53402). Lakefront. Phone 262/636-9229.* Fishing contest. Two weekends. Mid-July.

Limited-Service Hotel

★★ DAYS INN. *3700 Northwestern Ave, Racine (53405). Phone 262/637-9311; toll-free 888/242-6494; fax 262/637-4575. www.daysinn.com.* On Root River. 110 rooms, 2 story. Pets accepted. Complimentary continental breakfast. Check-in 4 pm, check-out 11 am. Restaurant, bar. Fitness room. Outdoor pool. **$**

Full-Service Hotel

★★★ MARRIOTT RACINE. *7111 Washington Ave, Racine (53406). Phone 262/886-6100; toll-free 800/228-9290; fax 262/886-1048. www.marriott.com.* 222 rooms, 5 story. Pets accepted. Check-in 3 pm, check-out noon. High-speed Internet access, wireless Internet access. Restaurant, bar. Fitness room. Indoor pool, whirlpool. Airport transportation available. Business center. **$**

Restaurants

★ GREAT WALL. *6214 Washington Ave, Racine (53406). Phone 262/886-9700.* Chinese menu. Lunch, dinner. Closed Mon; holidays. Children's menu. Casual attire. Reservations recommended. **$**

★★ HOB NOB. *277 S Sheridan Rd, Racine (53403). Phone 262/552-8008; fax 262/552-8009. www.thehobnob.com.* American menu. Dinner. Closed holidays. Bar. Children's menu. Business casual attire. Reservations recommended. **$$**

Reedsburg (E-3)

See also Baraboo, Portage, Prairie du Sac, Richland Center, Wisconsin Dells

Population 5,834
Elevation 926 ft
Area Code 608
Zip 53959
Information Chamber of Commerce, 240 Railroad St, PO Box 142; phone 608/524-2850 or toll-free 800/844-3507

Self-proclaimed "butter capital of America," Reedsburg is the home of one of the largest butter producing plants in the world. The Wisconsin Dairies plant produces more than 50,000,000 pounds of butter here each year.

What to See and Do

Carr Valley Cheese Factory. *S3797 County Rd G, La Valle (53941). 9 miles W on County K, G. Phone 608/986-2781.* Observation area for viewing production of cheddar cheese. (Mon-Sat; closed Jan 1, Dec 25) **FREE**

Foremost Farms. *501 S Pine, Reedsburg (53959). Phone 608/524-2351.* Viewing window for butter-making process. (Mon-Fri) **FREE**

Historical Society Log Village and Museum. *3 miles E via Hwy 33. Phone 608/524-2807.* Log cabin with loft, Oetzman log house (1876), log church and library, one-room schoolhouse, blacksmith shop; completely furnished kitchen, living room, and bedroom; apothecary shop; Native American and army memorabilia. Located on 52 acres of pine forest and farm fields. (June-Sept, Sat-Sun) **DONATION**

Museum of Norman Rockwell Art. *227 S Park, Reedsburg (53959). Phone 608/524-2123.* One of the largest collections of Norman Rockwell memorabilia spans the artist's 65-year career. Video. Gift shop. (Mid-May-Oct: daily; rest of year: Tues-Sun; closed holidays) **$$$**

Park Lane Model Railroad Museum. *S2083 Herwig Rd, Reedsburg (53959). 8 miles E on Hwy 23 at Herwig Rd. Phone 608/254-8050.* Features working model railroad layouts; hundreds of individual cars on display. (Mid-May-mid-Sept, daily) **$$**

Special Event

Butter Festival. *Nishan Park, County H and 8th St, Reedsburg (53959). Phone 608/524-2850.* A four-day festival with parade, tractor and horse pulls, carnival rides, events, arts and crafts, food. Six days in mid-June.

Rhinelander (B-3)

See also Chequamegon National Forest, Crandon, Eagle River, Minocqua, Three Lakes, Woodruff

Settled 1880
Population 7,427
Elevation 1,560 ft
Area Code 715
Zip 54501
Information Rhinelander Area Chamber of Commerce, 450 W Kemp St, PO Box 795; phone 715/365-7464 or toll-free 800/236-4386
Web Site www.ci.rhinelander.wi.us

Rhinelander is the gateway to the "world's most concentrated lake region." It lies at the junction of the Wisconsin and Pelican rivers. The 232 lakes, 11 trout streams, and 2 rivers within a 12-mile radius make the city a thriving resort center. Fishing is good in lakes and streams, and there is hunting for upland game and deer. The logging industry, which built this area, still thrives and the many miles of old logging roads are excellent for hiking and mountain biking. Paved bicycle trails, cross-country skiing, and snowmobiling are also popular in this northwoods area.

Rhinelander is headquarters for the Chequamegon-Nicolet National Forest (see THREE LAKES); phone 715/362-3415.

What to See and Do

★ **Rhinelander Logging Museum.** *810 Keenan St, Rhinelander (54501). In Pioneer Park, on Hwy 8, Hwy 47. Phone 715/369-5004.* Most complete displays of old-time lumbering in Midwest. On grounds are Five Spot, last narrow-gauge railroad locomotive to work Wisconsin's northwoods, and a restored depot dating from late 1800s. Also on premises is a one-room schoolhouse. Museum houses the "hodag," called "the strangest animal known to man." Created as a hoax, it has become the symbol of the city. (Memorial Day-Labor Day, daily) **DONATION** Also on the grounds is

Civilian Conservation Corps Museum. *Kemp and Oneida Ave, Rhinelander (54501). Phone toll-free 800/236-4386.* Houses photographs, memorabilia, artifacts, tools, and papers that record much of the history of the CCC. The manner of clothing worn, how the enrollee was housed and fed, and the tools used in project work are on the display. (Late May-early Sept, daily) **FREE**

Special Events

Art Fair. *Courthouse lawn, 1 Courthouse Sq, Rhinelander (54501). Phone 715/365-7464.* Second Sat in June.

Hodag Country Festival. *5476 River Rd, Rhinelander (54501). Phone 715/369-1300; toll-free 800/762-3803. www.hodag.com.* Three-day country music festival featuring top-name entertainment. Mid-July. **$$$$**

Oktoberfest. *156 Courtney on the Green, Rhinelander (54501). Downtown. Phone 715/365-7464; toll-free 800/236-4386.* German music, food. Mid-Oct.

Limited-Service Hotels

★★ BEST WESTERN CLARIDGE MOTOR INN. *70 N Stevens St, Rhinelander (54501). Phone 715/362-7100; toll-free 800/427-1377; fax 715/362-3883. www.bestwestern.com.* 81 rooms, 4 story. Pets accepted, some restrictions; fee. Check-in 2 pm, check-out 11 am. Restaurant, bar. Fitness room. Indoor pool, whirlpool. Airport transportation available. **$**

★★ HOLIDAY INN EXPRESS. *668 W Kemp St, Rhinelander (54501). Phone 715/369-3600; toll-free 800/465-4329; fax 715/369-3601. www.holiday-inn.com.* 101 rooms, 2 story. Pets accepted. Check-in 3 pm, check-out noon. Restaurant, bar. Fitness room. Indoor pool, whirlpool. Airport transportation available. **$**

Restaurants

★★ RHINELANDER CAFE AND PUB. *33 N Brown St, Rhinelander (54501). Phone 715/362-2424; fax 715/362-6062.* American menu. Breakfast, lunch, dinner. Closed Thanksgiving, Dec 25. Bar. Children's menu. **$$**

★ TULA'S FAMILY RESTAURANT. *232 S Courtney, Rhinelander (54501). Phone 715/369-5248; fax 715/369-5802.* American menu. Breakfast, lunch, dinner. Closed Dec 25. Bar. Children's menu. Outdoor seating. **$$**

Rice Lake (B-1)

See also Spooner

Population 7,998
Elevation 1,140 ft
Area Code 715
Zip 54868
Information Rice Lake Area Chamber of Commerce, 37 S Main St; phone 715/234-2126 or toll-free 800/523-6318
Web Site www.chamber.rice-lake.wi.us

Formerly headquarters for the world's largest hardwood mills, Rice Lake has an economy based on industry and retail trade. The city and lake were named for nearby wild rice sloughs, which were an important Sioux and Chippewa food source. Surrounded by 84 lakes, the city is in a major recreation area.

Special Events

Aquafest. *37 S Main, Rice Lake (54868). Phone toll-free 800/523-6318.* June.

County Fair. *Barron County Fairgrounds, 101 Short St, Rice Lake (54868). Phone toll-free 800/523-6318.* July.

Limited-Service Hotel

★ AMERICINN. *2906 Pioneer Ave, Rice Lake (54868). Phone 715/234-9060; fax 715/736-9060.* 43 rooms, 2 story. Complimentary continental breakfast. Check-in 3 pm, check-out 11 am. Indoor pool, whirlpool. **$**

Full-Service Inn

★★★★ CANOE BAY. *Off Hwy 53, Rice Lake (54728). Phone 715/924-4594; fax 715/924-4594. www.canoebay.com.* Canoe Bay is rather like a luxurious camp for adults, with gourmet dining, an award winning wine cellar, and extensive amenities. Situated on 280 acres in northwestern Wisconsin, the resort's three private, spring-fed lakes are perfect for a multitude of recreational opportunities. The wilderness trails are ideal for hiking in summer months, while snowshoeing and cross-country skiing are popular during the winter. Embodying the definition of a getaway, this resort has no telephones or televisions to distract from the peaceful setting. Guests enjoy plucking books off the shelves at the Great Room's library or working out in the fitness center. The guest rooms and cottages are characterized by regional décor and offer great privacy. Couples linger over romantic evenings at the candlelit Dining Room, where an extensive wine list and a nightly tasting menu make for terrific memories. 19 rooms. No children allowed. Complimentary full breakfast. Check-in 3 pm, check-out 11 am. Restaurant. Fitness room. **$$$**

Restaurant

★★ NORSKE NOOK. *2900 Pioneer Ave, Rice Lake (54868). Phone 715/234-1733; fax 715/234-1733. www.norskenook.com.* Old-style family restaurant. American menu. Breakfast, lunch, dinner. Closed holidays. Children's menu. Casual attire. **$**

Richland Center (E-3)

See also Reedsburg, Spring Green

Settled 1849
Population 5,018
Elevation 731 ft
Area Code 608
Zip 53581
Information Richland Chamber of Commerce, 174 S Central, PO Box 128; phone 608/647-6205 or toll-free 800/422-1318
Web Site www.richlandcounty.com

This is the birthplace of famed architect Frank Lloyd Wright (1867).

What to See and Do

Eagle Cave. *16320 Cavern Ln, Blue River (53518). 12 miles SW via Hwy 80 and 60. Phone 608/537-2988.* Large onyx cavern contains stalactites, stalagmites, fossils. Camping (hook-ups; fee); marked trails, picnicking, deer farm; fishing, swimming, horseback riding; hay rides; game room. 220 acres. Guided cave tours (Memorial Day-Labor Day, daily) **$$**

Special Events

Richland County Fair. *Fairgrounds, 1/2 mile S Hwy AA and Industrial Park Dr, Richland Center (53581). Phone 608/647-6859.* Early-Sept.

Wisconsin High School State Rodeo Finals. *Fairgrounds, 1/2 mile S Hwy AA and Industrial Park*

Dr, Richland Center (53581). Phone 608/647-6859. Late June.

Sayner (B-3)

See also Boulder Junction, Eagle River, Minocqua, Woodruff

Population 450
Elevation 1,675 ft
Area Code 715
Zip 54560

Centrally located in the Northern Highland-American Legion State Forest and boasting 42 sparkling lakes, the Sayner-Star Lake area offers camping, water-skiing, and excellent year-round fishing. Considered the birthplace of the snowmobile, Sayner is near miles of scenic well-groomed trails.

Limited-Service Hotel

★ ★ FROELICH'S SAYNER LODGE. *3221 Plum Lake Dr, Sayner (54560). Phone 715/542-3261. www.saynerlodge.com.* 36 rooms, 2 story. Closed Nov-late-May. Complimentary continental breakfast. Check-in 2 pm, check-out 10 am. Bar. Outdoor pool. Tennis. Airport transportation available. **$**

Shawano (C-4)

Settled 1843
Population 7,598
Elevation 821 ft
Area Code 715
Zip 54166
Information Chamber of Commerce, 1404 E Green Bay St, PO Box 38; phone 715/524-2139 or toll-free 800/235-8528
Web Site www.shawano.com

A city born of the lumber boom, Shawano is now a retail trade center for the small surrounding farms and produces dairy and wood products.

What to See and Do

Shawano Lake. *Hwy 22 and Lake Dr, Shawano (54166). 2 miles E on Hwy 22. Phone toll-free 800/235-8528.* Lake is 4 miles wide and 7 miles long. Fishing, boating (ramps); ice fishing, hunting. 300 miles of snowmobile trails, 8 miles of cross-country ski trails. Camping (fee).

Special Event

Flea Market. *Shawano County Fairgrounds, 211 W Green Bay St, Shawano (54166). Phone 715/526-9769.* Sun in Apr-Oct.

Limited-Service Hotels

★ AMERICINN. *1330 E Green Bay St, Shawano (54166). Phone 715/524-5111; fax 715/526-3626.* 47 rooms, 2 story. Complimentary continental breakfast. Check-out 11 am. Indoor pool, whirlpool. **$**

★ ★ BEST WESTERN VILLAGE HAUS MOTOR LODGE. *201 N Airport Dr, Shawano (54166). Phone 715/526-9595; toll-free 800/553-4479; fax 715/526-9826. www.bestwestern.com.* 89 rooms, 2 story. Check-in 1 pm, check-out 11 am. Restaurant, bar. Indoor pool, whirlpool. **$**

Restaurant

★ ANELLO'S TORCHLIGHT. *1276 E Green Bay St, Shawano (54166). Phone 715/526-5680; fax 715/524-5368.* American, Italian menu. Dinner. Closed Thanksgiving, Dec 24. Bar. **$$**

Sheboygan (D-5)

See also Elkhart Lake, Kohler, Manitowoc, Port Washington, Two Rivers

Settled 1818
Population 49,676
Elevation 633 ft
Area Code 262, 920
Information Sheboygan County Convention & Visitors Bureau, 712 Riverfront Dr, 53081; phone 920/457-9495, ext 900 or toll-free 800/457-9497, ext 900
Web Site www.sheboygan.org

A harbor city on the west shore of Lake Michigan, Sheboygan is a major industrial city and a popular fishing port.

What to See and Do

Kohler Andrae State Park. *1020 Beach Park Ln, Sheboygan (53081). S on I-43 exit 120, on Lake Michigan. Phone 920/451-4080.* Includes 1,000 acres of woods and sand dunes. Swimming, bathhouse; nature and cross-country ski trails, picnicking, playgrounds, concession, camping (105 sites, electric hook-ups), winter camping. Nature center (closed winter). (Daily)

Lakeland College. *10 miles NW on County M off County A (access to County A from Hwy 42 and 57). Phone 262/565-2111.* (1862) (2,500 students) On campus are Lakeland College Museum (Wed-Thurs, also by appointment; free) and Bradley Fine Arts Gallery (Mon-Fri afternoon during school year; free).

Scenic drives. Along lakeshore on Broughton Drive, Riverfront Drive, Lakeshore Drive.

Sheboygan County Historical Museum. *3110 Erie Ave, Sheboygan (53081). Phone 920/458-1103.* Exhibit center plus Judge David Taylor home (1850); two-story log house (1864) furnished with pioneer items; restored barn; 1867 cheese factory. (Apr-Oct, Tues-Sat; closed Good Friday, Easter, July 4) **$$**

Special Events

Brat Days. *Kiwanis Park, 17th and New Jersey sts, Sheboygan (53081). Phone 920/457-9491. www.sheboyganjaycees.com.* Don't mistake this festival for a day filled with poorly behaved children. It's really a celebration of the area's German heritage and its famous bratwurst. Begun in 1953, the gathering is the biggest festival in the city each year and features more than 50 stands selling the namesake sausage, as well as a contest to see who can down the most bratwurst in ten minutes. There is also the Brat Trot, a 4-mile run with all the proceeds going to find a cure for diabetes. As incentive to register for the race, every participant gets a brat-on-a-stick. Early Aug.

Great Cardboard Boat Regatta. *Rotary Riverview Park, Pennsylvania and 6th sts, Sheboygan (53081). Phone 920/458-6144.* Human-powered cardboard craft compete in various classes for fun and prizes. Part of citywide Independence Day festivities. July 4.

Holland Fest. *118 Main St, Cedar Grove (53013). 1 mile W off I-43 via exit 113. Phone 920/457-9491. www.hollandfest.com.* Dutch traditions: wooden-shoe dancing, street scrubbing, folk fair, food, music, art fair, parade. Last Fri-Sat in July.

Outdoor Arts Festival. *608 New York Ave, Sheboygan (53081). Phone 920/458-6144.* On the grounds of John Michael Kohler Arts Center. Multi-arts event features works by 125 juried artists; demonstrations, entertainment, refreshments. Third full weekend in July.

Polar Bear Swim. *Deland Park, Niagra St and Broughton Dr, Sheboygan (53081). Phone 920/457-9491.* More than 350 swimmers brave Lake Michigan's icy winter waters. Jan 1.

Limited-Service Hotels

★ BAYMONT INN. *2932 Kohler Memorial Dr, Sheboygan (53081). Phone 920/457-2321; toll-free 800/301-0200; fax 920/457-0827. www.baymontinn.com.* 98 rooms, 2 story. Pets accepted, some restrictions. Complimentary continental breakfast. High-speed Internet access. Check-out noon. **$**

★ BEST VALUE INN. *3900 Motel Rd, Sheboygan (53081). Phone 920/458-8338; toll-free 888/315-2378; fax 920/459-7470. www.bestvalueinn.com.* 32 rooms. Pets accepted, some restrictions; fee. Check-out 11 am. **$**

Full-Service Resort

★★★ BLUE HARBOR RESORT & CONFERENCE CENTER. *725 Blue Harbor Dr, Sheboygan (53081). Phone 920/452-2900; toll-free 866/701-2583; fax 920/452-2909. www.blueharborresort.com.* 183 rooms, all suites. Check-in 3 pm, check-out noon. High-speed Internet access. Three restaurants, two bars. Children's activity center. Fitness room. Indoor pool, children's pool, whirlpool. Airport transportation available. **$$**

Restaurant

★★ CITY STREETS RIVERSIDE. *712 Riverfront Dr, Sheboygan (53081). Phone 920/457-9050; fax 920/457-9541.* American menu. Lunch, dinner. Closed Sun; holidays. Bar. Children's menu. Casual attire. **$$**

Sister Bay (Door County) (C-5)

Population 675
Elevation 587 ft
Area Code 920
Zip 54234
Information Door County Chamber of Commerce, 1015 Green Bay Rd, PO Box 406, Sturgeon Bay 54235; phone 920/743-4456 or toll-free 800/527-3529
Web Site www.doorcountyvacations.com

This town is near the northern tip of Door County. Sister Bay was settled in 1857 by Norwegian immigrants. Today it's known for its shopping, dining, and boating opportunities, but still retains a distinct Scandinavian flavor.

Special Event

Sister Bay Fall Festival. *700 Bay Shore Dr, Sister Bay (54234). Phone 920/743-4456.* Fish boil, fireworks, parade, street auction. Mid-Oct.

Limited-Service Hotels

★ BLUFFSIDE MOTEL. *403 Bluffside Ln, Sister Bay (54234). Phone 920/854-2530; toll-free 877/854-2530. www.bluffside.com.* 17 rooms, 2 story. Closed Nov-Mar. Complimentary continental breakfast. Check-in 3 pm, check-out 10 am. Airport transportation available. **$**

★ ★ COUNTRY HOUSE RESORT. *715 Highland Rd, Sister Bay (54234). Phone 920/854-4551; toll-free 800/424-0041; fax 920/854-9809. www.countryhouseresort.com.* This 16-acre resort is an ideal romantic retreat along the Green Bay shoreline. Enjoy beautiful rooms at night and a variety of recreational options during the day. 46 rooms, 2 story. Children over 13 years only. Complimentary continental breakfast. Check-in 3 pm, check-out 11 am. Wireless Internet access. Outdoor pool, whirlpool. Tennis. **$**

★ ★ HOTEL DU NORD. *11000 Bayshore Dr, Sister Bay (54234). Phone 920/854-4221; toll-free 800/582-6667; fax 920/854-2710. www.hoteldunord.com.* On Green Bay. 56 rooms, 2 story. Check-in 3 pm, check-out 11 am. Restaurant. Outdoor pool. **$**

★ OPEN HEARTH LODGE. *1109 S Bayshore Dr, Sister Bay (54234). Phone 920/854-4890; fax 920/854-7486. www.openhearthlodge.com.* 32 rooms, 2 story. Complimentary continental breakfast. Check-in 3 pm, check-out 11 am. Indoor pool, whirlpool. **$**

Specialty Lodging

The following lodging establishment is approved by Mobil Travel Guide, but due to its unique and individualized nature has not been given a traditional Mobil Star rating. Included in this listing you may find bed-and-breakfasts, limited-service inns, guest ranches, and other unique hotel properties.

THE CHURCH HILL INN. *425 Gateway Dr, Sister Bay (54234). Phone 920/854-4885; toll-free 800/422-4906; fax 920/854-4634. www.churchhillinn.com.* This inn features beautiful English country décor. The private parlors are ideal for relaxing. 34 rooms, 2 story. Closed Dec 24-25. Children over 10 years only. Complimentary full breakfast. Check-in 3 pm, check-out 10:30 am. Fitness room. Outdoor pool, whirlpool. Business center. **$**

Restaurant

★ AL JOHNSON'S SWEDISH RESTAURANT. *702 Bay Shore Dr, Sister Bay (54234). Phone 920/854-2626; fax 920/854-9650.* Goats graze on grass-covered roof. American menu. Breakfast, lunch, dinner. Closed Dec 25. Children's menu. Casual attire. **$$**

Sparta (D-2)

See also Black River Falls, La Crosse, Tomah

Settled 1849
Population 7,788
Elevation 793 ft
Area Code 608
Zip 54656
Information Chamber of Commerce, 111 Milwaukee St; 608/269-4123 or 608/269-2453

Sparta is the home of several small industries manufacturing, among other items, dairy products, brushes, and automobile parts. The area is also well known for its biking trails. Fort McCoy, a US Army base, is 5 miles northeast on Highway 21.

What to See and Do

Elroy-Sparta State Trail. *113 White St, Kendall (54638). Phone 608/337-4775.* Built on an old railroad bed, this 32-mile hard-surfaced (limestone screenings) trail passes through three tunnels and over 23 trestles. Biking (fee). (Apr-Oct, daily) **$$**

Limited-Service Hotel

★ COUNTRY INN & SUITES BY CARLSON SPARTA. *737 Avon Rd, Sparta (54656). Phone 608/269-3110; toll-free 888/201-1746; fax 608/269-6726. www.countryinns.com.* 61 rooms, 2 story. Pets accepted; fee. Complimentary continental breakfast. Check-in 3 pm, check-out noon. Bar. Indoor pool, whirlpool. **$**

Specialty Lodging

The following lodging establishment is approved by Mobil Travel Guide, but due to its unique and individualized nature has not been given a traditional Mobil Star rating. Included in this listing you may find bed-and-breakfasts, limited-service inns, guest ranches, and other unique hotel properties.

JUSTIN TRAILS RESORT. *7452 Kathryn Ave, Sparta (54656). Phone 608/269-4522; toll-free 800/488-4521; fax 608/269-3280. www.justintrails.com.* Restored 1920s farmhouse; log cabins. 6 rooms, 2 story. Pets accepted; fee. Complimentary full breakfast. Check-in 3 pm, check-out noon. Restaurant. Children's activity center. **$$**

Restaurant

★ BACK DOOR CAFE. *1223 Front St, Cashton (54619). Phone toll-free 888/322-5494.* Inside a beautifully restored Victorian home with an elegant dining room and antique furnishings with family-oriented home-style cuisine. American menu. Lunch, dinner. Closed Sun. **$**

Spooner (B-1)

See also Hayward, Rice Lake

Settled 1883
Population 2,464
Elevation 1,065 ft
Area Code 715
Zip 54801
Information Spooner Area Chamber of Commerce, 122 N River St; phone 715/635-2168 or toll-free 800/367-3306
Web Site www.spoonerwisconsin.com

Once a busy railroad town, Spooner is now a popular destination for fishermen and nature lovers.

What to See and Do

Railroad Memories Museum. *424 Front St, Spooner (54801). Phone 715/635-3325.* Memorabilia, model railroad in old Chicago & Northwestern depot. (Mid-May-mid-Oct, daily) **$$**

St. Croix National Scenic Riverway. *Phone 715/635-8346.* One of two in the United States; excellent canoeing (Class #1 rapids) and tubing. Contact Chamber of Commerce or National Park Service Information Station in Trego.

Trego Lake Park. *W5665 Trego Park Rd, Trego (54888). 1/4 mile N, junction Hwy 53, 63. Phone 715/635-9931.* Heavily wooded area on the Namekagon River (Wild River). Fishing, boating, canoeing, inner tubing; hiking, picnicking, camping (electric hook-ups). (May-Sept) **$$$**

Special Events

Spooner Car Show. *Washburn County Fairgrounds, W Beaver Brook Ave and Hwy 63, Spooner (54801). Phone 715/635-3740.* Early June.

Spooner Rodeo. *Washburn County Fairgrounds, W Beaver Brook Ave and Hwy 63, Spooner (54801). Phone toll-free 800/367-3306.* PRCA approved. Country music. Mid-July.

Limited-Service Hotel

★ BEST WESTERN AMERICAN HERITAGE INN. *101 Maple St, Spooner (54801). Phone 715/635-9770; toll-free 800/780-7234; fax 715/635-9774. www.bestwestern.com.* 45 rooms. Check-in 3 pm, check-out noon. Indoor pool, whirlpool. **$**

Spring Green (E-3)

See also Dodgeville, Mineral Point, Prairie du Sac, Richland Center

Population 1,283
Elevation 729 ft
Area Code 608
Zip 53588
Information Chamber of Commerce, PO Box 3; phone 608/588-2042 or toll-free 800/588-2042
Web Site www.springgreen.com

This is where Frank Lloyd Wright grew up, built his home (Taliesin East), and established the Taliesin Fellowship for the training of apprentice architects.

What to See and Do

★ **House on the Rock.** *5754 Hwy 23, Spring Green (53588). 9 miles S on Hwy 23. Phone 608/935-3639. www.thehouseontherock.com.* Designed and built by Alexander J. Jordan atop a chimneylike rock, 450 feet above a valley. Waterfalls, trees throughout house; collections of antiques, Asian objets d'art, and automated music machines (many of the musical exhibits require additional money to activate the automation mechanism). Restaurant. (Mid-March-late Oct, daily) **$$$$**

★ **Taliesin East.** *5607 County Hwy C, Spring Green (53588). 3 miles S on Hwy 23. Phone 608/588-7948.* Features Frank Lloyd Wright's home, studio, farm, and school. (May-Oct, daily) **$$$$**

Tower Hill State Park. *5808 County Hwy C, Spring Green (53588). 3 miles E on Hwy 14, then S on County Hwy C. Phone 608/588-2116.* The park has 77 acres of wooded hills and bluffs overlooking the Wisconsin River. It was the site of a pre-Civil War shot tower and the early lead-mining village of Helena. Fishing, canoeing; picnicking (shelter), playgrounds, camping. (Daily) **$**

Special Event

American Players Theatre. *E2930 Golf Course Rd, Spring Green (53588). Phone 608/588-2361.* Theater arts center for the classics. Summer performances in outdoor amphitheater (Tues-Sun; also matinees Tues-Fri in Sept-Oct) Mid-June-early Oct.

Limited-Service Hotels

★ ★ HOUSE ON THE ROCK RESORT. *5754 Hwy 23, Spring Green (53588). Phone 608/935-3639. www.concordinn.com.* 80 rooms, all suites. Check-in 3 pm, check-out noon. Restaurant, bar. Indoor pool, outdoor pool, children's pool, whirlpool. Golf, 27 holes. Tennis. **$$**

★ ★ ROUND BARN LODGE. *Hwy 14, Spring Green (53588). Phone 608/588-2568; fax 608/588-2100. www.roundbarn.com.* 44 rooms, 2 story. Check-in 3 pm, check-out 11 am. Restaurant, bar. Indoor pool, whirlpool. **$**

St. Croix Falls (B-1)

Settled 1837
Population 1,640
Elevation 900 ft
Area Code 715
Zip 54024

Headquarters for the Interstate State Park, St. Croix Falls has become a summer and winter resort area. The oldest community in Polk County, it depends on farming, industry, dairying, and the tourist trade. Lions Park north of town has picnicking and boat launching, and there are many miles of groomed snowmobile trails in Polk County. Fishing for catfish, walleye, sturgeon, and panfish is excellent in the St. Croix River and the many area lakes.

What to See and Do

Crex Meadows Wildlife Area. *325 Hwy 70, St. Croix Falls (54840). N via Hwy 87, 1 mile N of Grantsburg. Phone 715/463-2896.* This 30,000-acre state-owned wildlife area is a prairie-wetlands habitat; breeding wildlife species include giant Canada geese, 11 species of ducks, sharp-tailed grouse, sandhill cranes, bald eagles, ospreys, trumpeter swans, and loons. Wildlife observation and photography; guided (by appointment) and self-guided tours. Canoeing; hunting, trapping (fall); hiking, picnicking, camping (Sept-Dec). (Daily) **FREE**

Governor Knowles State Forest. *325 Hwy 70, Grantsburg (54840). Headquarters 27 miles N via Hwy 87, just N of Grantsburg on Hwy 70. Phone 715/463-2898.* A 33,000-acre forest extending north and south along the St. Croix River. Fishing, boating, canoeing; hiking, bridle, snowmobile (fee), and cross-country ski trails; picnicking, group camping. (Daily)

Interstate State Park. *Hwy 35, St. Croix Falls (54024). 2 blocks S of Hwy 8 on Hwy 35. Phone 715/483-3747.* A 1,325-acre park; Wisconsin's oldest state park. Swimming, fishing, boating, canoeing; nature, hiking, and cross-country ski trails; picnicking, camping (dump station). Permanent naturalist; naturalist programs. Part of the Ice Age National Scientific Reserve. The Reserve operates a visitor center here. (Daily) **$$$** In the park is

The Gorge of the St. Croix River. Forms the Dalles of the St. Croix, with volcanic rock formation and sheer rock walls, some over 200 feet tall; series of potholes, wooded hills and valley; state trout hatchery is located just north of Interstate Park (daily).

St. Croix National Scenic Riverway. *Phone 715/483-3284.* Northern unit, 200 miles of scenic riverway in a mixed pine and hardwood forest. Southern unit, 52 miles of scenic riverway in mixed pine and hardwood forests, high rocky bluffs. National Park visitor centers (daily).

Trollhaugen Ski Resort. *2232 100th Ave, Dresser (54009). 3 miles S on Hwy 35 to Dresser, then 3/4 mile E on County F. Phone 715/755-2955; toll-free 800/826-7166 (WI). www.trollhaugen.com.* Resort has three chairlifts, seven rope tows; patrol, school, rentals; snowmaking; bars, cafeterias, restaurant. 22 runs. (Early Nov-Mar, daily) **$$$$**

Limited-Service Hotel

★ **DALLES HOUSE MOTEL.** *Hwy 35 S, St. Croix Falls (54024). Phone 205/702-2700; fax 205/702-2700.* Interstate State Park adjacent. 47 rooms, 2 story. Pets accepted. Complimentary continental breakfast. Check-in 2 pm, check-out 11 am. Indoor pool. **$**

St. Germain (B-3)

See also Eagle River, Minocqua, Three Lakes, Woodruff

Population 1,100
Elevation 1,627 ft
Area Code 715
Zip 54558

Restaurants

★ **ELIASON'S SOME PLACE ELSE.** *438 Hwy 70, St. Germain (54558). Phone 715/542-3779.* American menu. Dinner. Closed Mon; Dec 24-25; also Nov. Bar. **$$**

★ **SPANG'S.** *6229 Hwy 70, East St. Germain (54558). Phone 715/479-9400; fax 715/477-2173.* Garden lounge. American, Italian menu. Dinner. Closed Easter, Thanksgiving, Dec 24-25. Bar. Children's menu. **$$**

Stevens Point (C-3)

See also Marshfield, Waupaca, Wausau, Wisconsin Rapids

Settled 1838
Population 23,006
Elevation 1,093 ft
Area Code 715
Zip 54481
Information Stevens Point Area Convention and Visitors Bureau, 23 Park Ridge Dr; phone 715/344-2556 or toll-free 800/236-4636
Web Site www.easy-axcess.com/spacvb

A diversified community on the Wisconsin River near the middle of the state, Stevens Point was established as a trading post by George Stevens, who bartered with the Potawatomi. Incorporated as a city in 1858, today it has a number of industries and markets the dairy produce and vegetable crops of Portage County.

What to See and Do

George W. Mead Wildlife Area. *2148 County Rd S, Milladore (54454). 15 miles NW on Hwy 10 to Milladore, then 5 miles N on County S. Phone 715/457-6771.* Preserved and managed for waterfowl, fur bearers, deer, prairie chickens, ruffed grouse, and other game and nongame species. Limited fishing; hunting, bird-watching, hiking. (Mon-Fri) **FREE**

Stevens Point Brewery. *2617 Water St, Stevens Point (54481). Beer and Water sts. Phone 715/344-9310.* (1857) The brewery tour has been described as one of the most interesting in the country. (Mon-Sat, reservations suggested). **$**

University of Wisconsin-Stevens Point. *2100 Main St, Stevens Point (54481). Phone 715/346-4242.*

www.uwsp.edu. (1894) (8,500 students) Across the entire front of the four-story Natural Resources Building is the world's largest computer-assisted mosaic mural. The Museum of Natural History has one of the most complete collections of preserved birds and bird eggs in the country (academic year, daily). Planetarium show in Science Hall (academic year, Sun). Fine Arts Center houses 1,300 American Pattern glass goblets.

Limited-Service Hotel

★ COMFORT SUITES. *300 N Division St, Stevens Point (54481). Phone 715/341-6000; fax 715/341-8908.* 105 rooms, 3 story. Complimentary continental breakfast. Check-out noon. Fitness room. Indoor pool, whirlpool. **$**

Restaurant

★ ★ ★ THE RESTAURANT AND PAGLIACCI'S. *1800 N Point Dr, Stevens Point (54481). Phone 715/346-6010; fax 715/346-6608.* There are actually two restaurants in one at this small town destination. Italian menu. Dinner. Closed Sun; holidays. Bar. Outdoor seating. **$$**

Sturgeon Bay (Door County) (C-5)

See also Algoma, Door County, Green Bay

Settled 1870
Population 9,176
Elevation 588 ft
Area Code 920
Zip 54235
Information Door County Chamber of Commerce, 1015 Green Bay Rd, PO Box 406; phone 920/743-4456 or toll-free 800/527-3529
Web Site www.doorcountyvacations.com

Sturgeon Bay, in Door County (see), sits at the farthest inland point of a bay where swarms of sturgeon were once caught and piled like cordwood along the shore. The historic portage from the bay to Lake Michigan, used for centuries by Native Americans and early explorers, began here. The Sturgeon Bay ship canal now makes the route a waterway used by lake freighters and pleasure craft. The city is the county seat and trading center. Two shipyards and a number of other industries are located here. Ten million pounds of cherries are processed every year in Door County.

What to See and Do

Cave Point County Park. *3701 Clark Lake Rd, Sturgeon Bay (54235). 10 miles NE via Hwy 57, County Hwy D. Phone 920/823-2400.* Wave-worn grottoes and caves in limestone bluffs. Sand dunes, beautiful landscapes nearby.

Door County Maritime Museum. *120 N Madison Ave, Sturgeon Bay (54235). 5 miles E and N on Hwy 42. Phone 920/854-2860.* Artifacts of fishing and shipbuilding industries; fishing tug open to public; Great Lakes sailing and US Coast Guard; nautical painting; also film on history of commercial fishing. (July-mid-Oct: days vary; Memorial Day-June: Fri-Sun; closed rest of year) **$**

Door County Museum. *18 N 4th Ave, Sturgeon Bay (54235). 4th Ave and Michigan St. Phone 920/743-5809.* Old-time stores; fire department with antique trucks; county memorabilia and photographs. Video presentation. Gift shop. (May-Oct, daily) **DONATION**

The Farm. *4285 State Hwy 57, Sturgeon Bay (54235). 4 miles N on Hwy 57. Phone 920/743-6666.* Farm animals and fowl in natural surroundings; pioneer farmstead; wildlife display. (Memorial Day-Mid-Oct, daily) **$$$**

Potawatomi State Park. *3740 Park Dr, Sturgeon Bay (54235). 2 miles NW. Phone 920/746-2890.* 1,200-acre woodland along the shores of Sturgeon Bay. Limestone bluffs. Water-skiing, fishing, boating, canoeing; nature, hiking, snowmobile, cross-country ski, and bicycle trails; downhill skiing. Picnicking, playgrounds, camping (125 sites, 23 hook-ups), winter camping.

Robert La Salle County Park. *County J and County U, Sturgeon Bay (54235). SE on Lake Michigan. Phone toll-free 800/527-3529.* Site where La Salle and his band of explorers were rescued from starvation by friendly Native Americans. Monument marks location of La Salle's fortified camp. Picnicking.

US Coast Guard Canal Station. *2501 Canal Rd, Sturgeon Bay (54235). Phone 920/743-3367.* At entrance to ship canal on Lake Michigan. Coast Guard provides maritime law enforcement patrols, search and rescue duties, weather reports; lighthouse. Tours (by appointment). **FREE**

Special Events

Annual Sturgeon Bay Harvest Fest. *23 N 5th St, S turgeon Bay (54235). Along 3rd Ave. Phone toll-free 800/301-6695.* Art show, huge craft show, farmers' market, food booths, music and entertainment. Late Sept.

Shipyards Tour. *Palmer Johnson's Inc, 61 Michigan St, Sturgeon Bay (54235). Phone 920/746-2286.* Early May.

Limited-Service Hotels

★ BAY SHORE INN. *4205 N Bay Shore Dr, Sturgeon Bay (54235). Phone 920/743-4551; toll-free 800/556-4551; fax 920/743-3299. www.bayshoreinn.net.* 30 rooms, 3 story. Check-out 11 am. Beach. Indoor pool, whirlpool. Tennis. **$**

★ BEST WESTERN MARITIME INN. *1001 N 14th Ave, Sturgeon Bay (54235). Phone 920/743-7231; toll-free 800/780-7234; fax 920/743-9341. www.bestwestern.com.* 91 rooms, 2 story. Pets accepted, some restrictions. Complimentary continental breakfast. Check-in 3 pm, check-out 11 am. Indoor pool, whirlpool. **$**

★ CHAL-A MOTEL. *3910 Hwy 42 and 57, Sturgeon Bay (54235). Phone 920/743-6788.* Museum on premises; features collections of cars, toys, and dolls. 20 rooms. Check-out 10:30 am. **$**

★ ★ CHERRY HILLS LODGE. *5905 Dunn Rd, Sturgeon Bay (54235). Phone 920/743-4222; toll-free 800/545-2307; fax 920/743-4222. www.golfdoorcounty.com.* 31 rooms, 2 story. Check-out 11 am. Restaurant, bar. Outdoor pool, whirlpool. Golf, 18 holes. **$**

Full-Service Resort

★ ★ LEATHEM SMITH LODGE AND MARINA. *1640 Memorial Dr, Sturgeon Bay (54235). Phone 920/743-5555; toll-free 800/366-7947; fax 920/743-5355. www.leathemsmithlodge.com.* 63 rooms, 2 story. Complimentary continental breakfast. Check-in 2 pm, check-out 11 am. Restaurant, two bars. Outdoor pool. Golf, 9 holes. Tennis. **$**

Specialty Lodgings

The following lodging establishments are approved by Mobil Travel Guide, but due to their unique and individualized nature have not been given a traditional Mobil Star rating. Included in this listing you may find bed-and-breakfasts, limited-service inns, guest ranches, and other unique hotel properties.

BARBICAN INN. *132 N 2nd Ave, Sturgeon Bay (54235). Phone 920/743-4854; toll-free 877/427-8491; fax 920/743-1961. www.barbicanbandb.com.* This beautiful Victorian inn (1873) close to historic Sturgeon Bay features comfortable suites, each appointed with unique themes. 17 rooms, 2 story, all suites. Closed Dec 24-25. Complimentary continental breakfast. Check-in 2 pm, check-out 11 am. **$**

CHADWICK INN. *25 N 8th Ave, Sturgeon Bay (54235). Phone 920/743-2771; fax 920/743-4386. www.thechadwickinn.com.* Built in 1895; original woodwork, antique glassware, Chickering piano (1823). 3 rooms, 3 story. Complimentary continental breakfast. Check-in 2 pm, check-out noon. **$**

CHANTICLEER GUEST HOUSE. *4072 Cherry Rd (County HH), Sturgeon Bay (54235). Phone 920/746-0334; fax 920/746-1368. www.chanticleerguesthouse.com.* Romance, serenity, peace, and relaxation are just a few words that can describe the guest experience here. Nestled among the orchards of Door County, this 30-acre bed-and-breakfast (1916) is truly one of the finest and most unique. 10 rooms, 3 story. No children allowed. Complimentary continental breakfast. Check-in 2 pm, check-out 11 am. Outdoor pool. **$$**

SCOFIELD HOUSE BED AND BREAKFAST. *908 Michigan St, Sturgeon Bay (54235). Phone 920/743-7727; toll-free 888/463-0204; fax 920/743-7727. www.scofieldhouse.com.* Built in 1901, this elegant inn welcomes guests to enjoy a very delightful stay in appointed guest rooms filled with lovely antiques. This desirable inn is able to charmingly combine the comforts of modern amenities while maintaining all the charm and ambience of a turn-of-the-century mansion. 6 rooms, 3 story. Complimentary full breakfast. Check-in 3-7 pm, check-out 11 am. **$$**

WHITE LACE INN. *16 N 5th Ave, Sturgeon Bay (54235). Phone 920/743-1105; toll-free 877/948-5223; fax 920/743-8180. www.whitelaceinn.com.* Four buildings built in 1880 and 1900. 18 rooms, 2 story. Children over 12 years only. Complimentary full breakfast. Check-in 3 pm, check-out 11 am. **$**

Restaurants

★★ **INN AT CEDAR CROSSING.** *336 Louisiana St, Sturgeon Bay (54235). Phone 920/743-4249. www.innatcedarcrossing.com.* Victorian storefront (1884); antique furnishings, fireplaces. American menu. Breakfast, lunch, dinner. Closed Dec 24-25. Bar. Children's menu. Casual attire. Reservations recommended. **$$**

★★ **MILL SUPPER CLUB.** *4128 Hwy 42/57, Sturgeon Bay (54235). Phone 920/743-5044.* Seafood menu. Dinner. Closed Mon; holidays. Bar. Children's menu. Casual attire. **$$**

Superior (A-1)

See also Duluth

Founded 1852
Population 27,134
Elevation 642 ft
Area Code 715
Zip 54880
Information Tourist Information Center, 305 Harborview Parkway; phone toll-free 800/942-5313
Web Site www.visitsuperior.com

At the head of Lake Superior, with the finest natural harbor on the Great Lakes, Superior-Duluth has been one of the leading ports in the country in volume of tonnage for many years. The Burlington Northern Docks and taconite pellet handling complex are the largest in the United States. More than 200 million bushels of grain are shipped in and out of the area's elevators each year. Here is the largest coal-loading terminal in the United States with 12 coal docks in the Superior-Duluth area, also a briquet plant, a shipyard, a refinery, and a flour mill. Production of dairy products is also a major industry. Long before its founding date, the city was the site of a series of trading posts. The University of Wisconsin-Superior is located here.

What to See and Do

Amnicon Falls State Park. *4279 S County Rd U, South Range (54874). 10 miles E on Hwy 2. Phone 715/398-3000.* An 825-acre park with many small waterfalls and interesting rock formations. Hiking, picnicking, camping. (Daily) **$$**

Barker's Island. *Marina Dr and Hwy 2 (53), Superior (54880). From E 2nd St and 6th Ave E, off Hwy 2, Hwy 53, Hwy 13. Phone toll-free 800/942-5313.* Boating (launching ramps, marina); picnic facilities, lodging, dining. Also here are

Duluth-Superior Excursions. *250 Marina Dr, Superior (54880). Phone 218/722-6218.* A 1 3/4-hour narrated tour of Superior-Duluth Harbor and Lake Superior on excursion boats. Also lunch and dinner cruises. (mid-May-mid-Oct, daily) **$$$$**

The SS *Meteor*. *Phone 715/392-5712.* (1896) Last remaining whaleback freighter, the *Meteor* is moored here and is open to visitors as a maritime museum. (May-Sept, daily) **$$**

Brule River State Forest. *6250 S Ranger Rd, Brule (54820). 30 miles SE via Hwy 2. Phone 715/372-4866.* On 40,218 acres. Fishing, boating, canoeing; nature, hiking, snowmobile, and cross-country ski trails; picnicking, camping. (Daily) **$$$$**

Fairlawn Mansion and Museum. *906 E 2nd St, Superior (54880). Phone 715/394-5712.* Restored 42-room Victorian mansion overlooking Lake Superior. First floor and exterior fully restored and furnished. (Daily; closed holidays) **$$$**

Old Fire House and Police Museum. *23rd Ave E and 4th St, Superior (54880). Phone 715/398-7558.* Firehouse (1898) serving as a museum devoted to the history of police and fire fighting. Historical vehicles, artifacts. (June-Aug; daily) **$$**

Pattison State Park. *6294 Hwy 35 S, Superior (54880). 15 miles S on Hwy 35. Phone 715/399-3111.* Has 1,476 acres of sand beach and woodlands. Swimming, fishing, canoeing; nature, hiking, and cross-country ski trails; picnic grove, playgrounds, primitive and improved camping (electric hook-ups, dump station). Nature center. Outstanding park attraction is Big Manitou Falls (165-foot drop), the highest waterfall in the state. Little Manitou Falls (31-foot drop) is located upstream of the main falls. (Daily)

Superior Municipal Forest. *N 28th St and Billings Dr, Superior (54880).* Has 4,500 acres of scenic woods bordering the shores of the St. Louis River. Fishing, boating; hiking, jogging, cross-country skiing, archery. **FREE**

Wisconsin Point. *Moccasin Mike Rd and Wisconsin Point Rd, Superior (54880). On shores of Lake Superior. Phone toll-free 800/942-5313.* Popular for picnicking by light of driftwood fires. Swimming, fishing; bird-watching. **FREE**

Special Events

Head-of-the-Lakes Fair. *4700 Tower Ave, Superior (54880). Phone 715/394-7848.* July.

Miller Lite Northern Nationals Stock Car Races. *Superior Speedway, 4700 Tower Ave, Superior (54880). Phone 715/394-7848.* Sept.

Limited-Service Hotels

★ BEST WESTERN BAY WALK INN. *1405 Susquehanna Ave, Superior (54880). Phone 715/392-7600; toll-free 800/780-7234; fax 715/392-7680. www.bestwestern.com.* 50 rooms, 2 story. Pets accepted. Complimentary continental breakfast. Check-in 3 pm, check-out 11 am. High-speed Internet access. Indoor pool, whirlpool. **$**

★ BEST WESTERN BRIDGEVIEW MOTOR INN. *415 Hammond Ave, Superior (54880). Phone 715/392-8174; toll-free 800/777-5572; fax 715/392-8487. www.bestwestern.com.* 96 rooms, 2 story. Pets accepted. Complimentary continental breakfast. Check-in 2 pm, check-out noon. High-speed Internet access. Indoor pool, whirlpool. **$**

★ ★ DAYS INN. *110 Harbor View Pkwy, Superior (54880). Phone 715/392-4783; toll-free 888/515-5040; fax 715/392-4787. www.daysinnsuperior.com.* 111 rooms, 2 story. Pets accepted; fee. Complimentary continental breakfast. Check-in 3 pm, check-out 11 am. Restaurant, bar. Indoor pool, whirlpool. **$**

Restaurant

★ ★ SHACK SMOKEHOUSE AND GRILLE. *3301 Belknap St, Superior (54880). Phone 715/392-9836; fax 715/392-4831. www.shackonline.com.* American menu. Lunch, dinner. Bar. Children's menu. Casual attire. Reservations recommended. **$$**

Three Lakes (B-3)

See also Crandon, Eagle River, Rhinelander, St. Germain

Population 1,900
Elevation 1,637 ft
Area Code 715
Zip 54562
Information Three Lakes Information Bureau, 1704 Superior St, PO Box 268; phone 715/546-3344 or toll-free 800/972-6103
Web Site www.threelakes.com

Between Thunder Lake and the interlocking series of 28 lakes on the west boundary of Nicolet National Forest, Three Lakes is a provisioning point for parties exploring the forest and lake country.

What to See and Do

Chequamegon-Nicolet National Forest. *4364 Wall St, Eagle River (54521). N on Hwy 32. Phone 715/479-2827.* Forest has 661,000 acres, and is 62 miles long and 36 miles wide; elevation ranges from 860 feet to 1,880 feet. Noted for scenic drives through pine, spruce, fir, sugar maple, oak, and birch trees. More than 1,200 lakes and 1,100 miles of trout streams. Fishing for trout, pike, bass, muskellunge and walleye, and hunting for deer, bear, grouse, and waterfowl. Swimming, canoeing, boating, rafting; interpretive nature trails, hiking. More than 122 miles of cross-country ski trails, 520 miles of snowmobile trails, snowshoeing. Three wilderness areas and several non-motorized walk-in areas provide more than 33,000 acres for backpacking and primitive camping. Picnicking, camping, and other outdoor recreational activities in general forest zone are unrestricted and no permits are required. Within developed areas, camping and picnicking are restricted to designated sites and most are on a first-come basis; reservations are available for selected campgrounds. Fees are charged at most developed campgrounds. (Daily) **FREE**

Three Lakes Winery. *6971 Gogebic St, Three Lakes (54562). Corner of Hwy 45 and County A. Phone 715/546-3080.* Produces fruit wines. Winery tours (late May-mid-Oct, daily); wine tasting (daily; must be 21 or over to taste wine). **FREE**

Tomah (D-2)

See also Black River Falls, Sparta

Population 7,570
Elevation 960 ft
Area Code 608
Zip 54660
Information Greater Tomah Area Chamber of Commerce, 306 Arthur St, PO Box 625; phone 608/372-2166 or toll-free 800/948-6624
Web Site www.tomahwisconsin.com

Tomah is Wisconsin's "Gateway to Cranberry Country." This was also the home of Frank King, the creator of the comic strip "Gasoline Alley"; the main street was named after him. Lake Tomah, on the west edge of town, has boating, water-skiing, fishing, ice-fishing, and snowmobiling.

What to See and Do

Little Red Schoolhouse Museum. *Gillett Park, Superior Ave, Tomah (54660). Phone 608/372-2166.* Built in 1864, and in use until 1965; many original furnishings, books. (Memorial Day-Labor Day, afternoons) **FREE**

Mill Bluff State Park. *15819 Funnel Rd, Camp Douglas (54618). 7 miles E, off Hwy 12, 16. Phone 608/427-6692.* Has 1,258 acres with rock bluffs. Swimming; picnicking, camping. Being developed as part of Ice Age National Scientific Reserve. (Daily) **$$**

Necedah National Wildlife Refuge. *W7996 20th St W, Necedah (54646). 6 miles E via Hwy 21. Phone 608/565-2551.* Water birds may be seen during seasonal migrations; lesser numbers present during the summer. Resident wildlife include deer, wild turkey, ruffed grouse, wolf, and bear. Viewing via 11-mile self-guided auto tour or 1-mile self-guided foot trail. (Daily; office, Mon-Fri; foot trail, mid-Mar-mid-Nov only; auto tour is along township roads, which may close due to inclement weather) **FREE**

Wildcat Mountain State Park. *Hwy 33 E, Ontario (54651). 25 miles S via Hwy 131, 33. Phone 608/337-4775.* Has 3,470 acres of hills and valleys. Trout fishing in Kickapoo River, Billings and Cheyenne creeks. Canoeing; nature, hiking, bridle, and cross-country ski trails; picnicking, playgrounds, camping. Observation points provide panoramic view of countryside. (Daily)

Special Event

Cranberry Festival. *402 Pine St, Warrens (54666). Phone 608/378-4200.* Late Sept.

Limited-Service Hotels

★ COMFORT INN. *305 Wittig Rd, Tomah (54660). Phone 608/372-6600; toll-free 800/228-5150; fax 608/372-6600. www.comfortinn.com.* 52 rooms, 2 story. Pets accepted, some restrictions. Complimentary continental breakfast. Check-in 2 pm, check-out 11 am. Indoor pool, whirlpool. **$**

★ ★ HOLIDAY INN. *Hwy 21, Tomah (54660). Phone 608/372-3211; toll-free 866/372-3211; fax 608/372-3243. www.holiday-inn.com.* 100 rooms, 2 story. Pets accepted. Check-in 2 pm, check-out noon. High-speed Internet access. Restaurant, bar. Fitness room. Indoor pool, whirlpool. Business center. **$**

Restaurant

★ ★ BURNSTAD'S EUROPEAN CAFE. *Hwys 12 and 16 E, Tomah (54660). Phone 608/372-4040; fax 608/372-4062. www.burnstads.com.* American menu. Breakfast, lunch, dinner. Bar. Casual attire. Outdoor seating. **$$**

Two Rivers (D-5)

See also Green Bay, Manitowoc, Sheboygan

Population 13,030
Elevation 595 ft
Area Code 920
Zip 54241
Information Manitowoc-Two Rivers Area Chamber of Commerce, 1515 Memorial Dr, PO Box 903, Manitowoc 54221-0903; phone 920/684-5575 or toll-free 800/262-7892
Web Site www.manitowoc.com

A fishing fleet in Lake Michigan and light industry support Two Rivers.

What to See and Do

Point Beach State Forest. *9400 County Trunk O, Two Rivers (54241). 5 miles N on County Trunk Hwy 0. Phone 920/794-7480.* A 2,900-acre park with heavily wooded areas, sand dunes, and beach along Lake Michigan. Nature, hiking, snowmobile, and cross-country ski trails; ice skating. Picnicking, playgrounds, concession, improved camping, winter camping. Nature center. (Daily) **$$**

Rogers Street Fishing Village Museum. *2102 Jackson St, Two Rivers (54241). Phone 920/793-5905.* Artifacts of commercial fishing industry; 60-year-old diesel engine; artifacts from sunken vessels; 1886 lighthouse; life-size woodcarvings. Art and craft galleries feature local area artists. (June-Aug, daily) **$**

Washington Island (Door County) (B-5)

Settled 1869
Population 623
Elevation 600 ft
Area Code 920
Zip 54246
Information Door County Chamber of Commerce, 1015 Green Bay Rd, PO Box 406, Sturgeon Bay 54235; phone 920/743-4456 or toll-free 800/527-3529
Web Site www.doorcountyvacations.com

Washington Island, 6 miles off the coast of Door County (see) is one of the oldest Icelandic settlements in the United States. Many Scandinavian festivals are still celebrated. Surrounding waters offer excellent fishing. The island may be reached by ferry.

What to See and Do

Rock Island State Park. *Washington Island (54246). Little Lake Rd, NW corner of island. Phone 920/847-2235 (mid-Apr-mid-Nov).* Reached by privately-operated ferry (June-Oct, daily; fee) from Jackson Harbor located at the northeast corner of island. This 912-acre park was the summer home of electric tycoon C. H. Thordarson. Buildings in Icelandic architectural style. Potawatomi Lighthouse (1836) on northern point. Swimming, fishing, boating; nature trail, more than 9 miles of hiking and snowmobile trails, picnicking, primitive camping (no supplies available). No vehicles permitted. (Daily)

Washington Island Museum. *Little Lake Rd, Washington Island (54246). NW corner of island. Phone 920/847-2522.* Native American artifacts; antiques; rocks and fossils. (May-mid-Oct, daily)

Special Event

Scandinavian Dance Festival. *Community Center, Main Rd RR 1, Box 3, Washington Island (54246). Phone 920/847-2179.* Dance festival and Viking Games. Early Aug.

Limited-Service Hotel

★★ FINDLAY'S HOLIDAY INN AND VIKING VILLAGE. *1 Main Rd, Washington Island (54246). Phone 920/847-2526; toll-free 800/522-5469; fax 920/847-2752. www.holidayinn.net.* 16 rooms. Closed Nov-Apr. Check-in 2 pm, check-out 10 am. Restaurant. Beach. **$**

Restaurant

★★ FINDLAY'S HOLIDAY INN. *1 Main Rd, Washington Island (54246). Phone 920/847-2526; toll-free 800/522-5469; fax 920/847-2752. www.holidayinn.net.* American menu. Breakfast, lunch, dinner. Closed Nov-Apr. Casual attire. **$$**

Watertown (E-4)

See also Beaver Dam, Fort Atkinson, Oconomowoc

Settled 1836
Population 19,142
Elevation 823 ft
Area Code 920
Zip 53094
Information Chamber of Commerce, 519 E Main St; phone 920/261-6320

Waterpower, created where the Rock River falls 20 feet in 2 miles, attracted the first New England settlers. A vast number of German immigrants followed, including Carl Schurz, who became Lincoln's minister to Spain and Secretary of the Interior under President Hayes. His wife, Margarethe Meyer Schurz, established the first kindergarten in the United States. Watertown, with diversified industries, is in the center of an important farming and dairy community.

What to See and Do

★ Octagon House and First Kindergarten in USA. *919 Charles St, Watertown (53094). Phone 920/261-2796.* Completed in 1854 by John Richards, the 57-room mansion has a 40-foot spiral cantilever hanging staircase; Victorian-style furnishings throughout, many original pieces. On grounds are restored kindergarten founded by Margarethe Meyer Schurz in 1856 and 100-year-old barn with early farm implements. (May-Oct, daily) **$$**

Special Event

Riverfest. *Riverside Park, Labaree and Division, Watertown (53094). Phone 920/261-6320.* Four-day event; craft show, carnival, raft race, entertainment. Early Aug.

Waukesha (E-4)

See also Elkhorn, Milwaukee

Settled 1834
Population 56,958
Elevation 821 ft
Area Code 262
Information Waukesha Area Convention & Visitors Bureau, 223 Wisconsin Ave, 53186; phone 262/542-0330 or toll-free 800/366-8474
Web Site www.wauknet.com/visit

Mineral springs found here by pioneer settlers made Waukesha famous as a health resort; in the latter half of the 19th century, it was one of the nation's most fashionable. Before that it was an important point on the Underground Railroad. The *American Freeman* (1844-1848) was published here. Today the city is enjoying important industrial growth. Carroll College lends the city a gracious academic atmosphere. The name Waukesha (*by the little fox*) comes from the river that runs through it. The river, along with the city's many parks and wooded areas, adds to a beautiful atmosphere for leisure activities.

What to See and Do

Kettle Moraine State Forest, Southern Unit. *S91W39091 Hwy 59, Eagle (53119). 17 miles SW on Hwy 59. Phone 262/594-2135.* The forest contains 20,000 acres of rough, wooded country as well as Ottawa and Whitewater lakes. Swimming, waterskiing, fishing, boating, canoeing. Trails: hiking, 74 miles; bridle, 50 miles; snowmobile, 52 miles; cross-country skiing, 40 miles; nature, 3 miles. Picnicking, playground, primitive and improved camping (electric hook-ups, dump station), winter camping. (Daily) **$$**

★ **Old World Wisconsin.** *S103W37890 Hwy 67, Eagle (53119). 14 miles SW on Hwy 67; 1 1/2 miles S of Eagle. Phone 262/594-6300.* A 576-acre outdoor museum with more than 65 historic structures (1840-1915) reflecting various ethnic backgrounds of Wisconsin history. Restored buildings include church, town hall, schoolhouse, stagecoach inn, blacksmith shop, and ten complete 19th-century farmsteads. All buildings are furnished with period artifacts; staffed by costumed interpreters. Tram system; restaurant. (May-Oct, daily) **$$$$**

Waukesha County Museum. *101 W Main St, Waukesha (53186). At East Ave. Phone 262/548-7186.* Historical exhibits (Tues-Sat, also Sun afternoons; closed holidays). Research library (Tues-Sat; closed holidays; fee). **FREE**

Special Events

Fiesta Waukesha. *Frame Park, 1120 Baxter St, Waukesha (53186). On Fox River banks.Phone 262/547-0887.* Music, folklore, dance, diverse food, and cultural activities. Mid-June.

Holiday Fair, Christmas Walk, and Annual Parade. *Downtown Waukesha (53186). Phone 262/549-6154.* Merchants offer special bargains, festive treats. Mid-Nov.

Waukesha County Fair. *2417 Silvernail Rd, Pewaukee (53072). Phone 262/544-5922.* Includes performances by top-name Country and Western and rock artists. Mid-July.

Waukesha JanBoree. *Frame Park, 1120 Baxter St, Waukesha (53186). Phone 262/524-3737.* Three days of winter activities. Late Jan.

Limited-Service Hotel

★★ WYNDHAM BROOKFIELD GARDEN. *18155 Bluemound Rd, Brookfield (53045). Phone 262/792-1212; toll-free 800/822-4200; fax 262/792-1201. www.wyndham.com.* 178 rooms, 3 story. Check-out noon. Restaurant, bar. Fitness room. Indoor pool, whirlpool. Airport transportation available. **$**

Full-Service Hotel

★★★ MARRIOTT MILWAUKEE WEST. *W231N1600, Waukesha (53186). Phone 262/574-0888; toll-free 800/228-9290; fax 262/574-7599. www.marriott.com.* Twenty miles west of Milwaukee, in the peaceful suburb of Waukesha, this modern, comfortable hotel overlooks a small pond and features a plush, upscale lobby. With convenient access to highways and area activities, and an indoor pool and whirlpool, guests are sure to enjoy their stay. 283 rooms, 6 story. Check-in 3 pm, check-out noon. High-speed Internet access. Restaurant, bar. Fitness room. Indoor pool, whirlpool. Airport transportation available. Business center. **$**

Restaurants

★ THE CHOCOLATE SWAN. *13320 Watertown Plank Rd, Elm Grove (53122). Phone 262/784-7926; fax 262/784-7161.* Dessert menu only. Closed Sun; holidays. Tea room ambience. **$**

★★ ELM GROVE INN. *13275 Watertone Plank Rd, Elm Grove (53122). Phone 262/782-7090. www.elmgroveinn.com.* American menu. Lunch, dinner. Closed Sun; Jan 1, Thanksgiving, Dec 25. Bar. **$$$**

★★ WEISSGERBER'S GASTHAUS INN. *2720 N Grandview Blvd, Waukesha (53188). Phone 262/544-4460; fax 262/544-9315. www.weissgerbers.com.* Milwaukee's traditional German restaurant and beer garden. Original German entrées provide a gourmet tour through the Old World. The warm woodwork, fieldstone fireplaces, and colorful stained-glass windows provide a comfortable and intimate atmosphere in all our rooms and lounge. German menu. Lunch, dinner. Closed Sun; holidays. Bar. Children's menu. Casual attire. Reservations recommended. Outdoor seating. **$$**

Waupaca (D-4)

See also Stevens Point, Wautoma

Population 4,957
Elevation 870 ft
Area Code 715
Zip 54981
Information Waupaca Area Chamber of Commerce, 221 S Main; phone 715/258-7343 or toll-free 888/417-4040
Web Site www.waupacaareachamber.com

This community, near a chain of 22 lakes to the southwest, is a boating, fishing, and tourist recreation area.

What to See and Do

Canoeing and tubing. *N2498 W Columbia Lake Dr, Waupaca (54981). On the Crystal and Little Wolf rivers. Phone 715/258-7343.* Two-three-hour trips. (May-Labor Day) Contact Chamber of Commerce.

Covered Bridge. *Fulton (54W) and Joann Ln, Waupaca (54981). 3 miles S on Hwy K near the Red Mill Colonial Shop. Phone 715/258-7343.* A 40-foot lattice design with 400 handmade oak pegs used in its construction.

Hartman Creek State Park. *N2480 Hartman Creek Rd, Waupaca (54981). 6 miles W via Hwy 54, then 1 1/2 miles S on Hartman Creek Rd. Phone 715/258-2372.* A 1,400-acre park with 300-foot sand beach on Hartman Lake. Swimming, fishing, boating (no gasoline motors), canoeing; nature, hiking, snowmobile, and cross-country ski trails; picnicking, camping (dump station), winter camping. (Daily) **$$$**

Scenic cruises. *N2757 County Rd QQ, Waupaca (54981). 4 miles SW via Hwy 54 and County QQ at Clear Water Harbor. Phone 715/258-2866.* Sternwheeler *Chief Waupaca* offers 1 1/2-hour cruises on eight lakes of the Chain O' Lakes. Also cruises aboard motor yacht *Lady of the Lakes.* (Memorial Day-Sept, daily) Private evening charters arranged. **$$$**

South Park. *921 S Main St, Waupaca (54981). Mirror and Shadow lakes, S end of Main St. Phone 715/258-7343.* Offers swimming beach, bathhouse, fishing dock, boat landing; picnicking. Also in park is

> **Hutchinson House Museum.** *921 S Main St, Waupaca (54981). End of Main St in South Park. Phone 715/258-7343.* Restored 12-room Victorian pioneer home (1854); furnishings, artifacts; herb garden; Heritage House. Contact the Chamber of Commerce. **$**

Special Events

Fall-O-Rama. *South Park, 921 S Main St, Waupaca (54981). Phone 715/258-7343.* Arts and crafts fair, entertainment, food. Third Sat in Sept.

Strawberry Fest. *Downtown Square, 111 S Main, Waupaca (54981). Phone 715/258-7343.* Arts and crafts, entertainment, fresh strawberries. Third Sat in June.

Limited-Service Hotel

★★ BEST WESTERN GRAND SEASONS HOTEL. *110 Grand Seasons Dr, Waupaca (54981).*

Phone 715/258-9212; fax 715/258-4294. 90 rooms, 3 story. Pets accepted. Complimentary continental breakfast. Check-out 11 am. Restaurant, bar. Fitness room. Indoor pool, whirlpool. **$**

Waupun (D-4)

See also Beaver Dam, Fond du Lac, Green Lake

Founded 1839
Population 8,207
Elevation 904 ft
Area Code 920
Zip 53963
Information Chamber of Commerce, 434 E Main; phone 920/324-3491

The city's Native American name means "Early Dawn of Day." Diversified crops, light industry, and three state institutions contribute to this small city's economy.

What to See and Do

City of Sculpture. *Madison St and Shaler Park, Waupun (53963).* First bronze casting of famous sculpture by James Earl Frazer, designer of Indian head nickel. Also six other historical bronze statues.

Fond du Lac County Park. *N2825 County Rd MMM, Waupun (53963). W on Hwy 49 to County Trunk MMM. Phone 920/324-2769.* Park has 100 acres of virgin timber on Rock River. Swimming pool (mid-June-Aug, daily; fee); picnic area (tables, fireplaces), playgrounds, camping (mid-May-Nov, daily). Park (daily). **$$$$**

Horicon National Wildlife Refuge. *W4279 Headquarters Rd, Mayville (53050). Visitor Center, 6 1/2 miles E on Hwy 49, then 4 miles S on Dodge County Z. Phone 920/387-2658.* Large flocks of Canada geese and various species of ducks can be seen October, November, March, April. Many visitors stop during migratory seasons to watch the birds resting and feeding on the Horicon Marsh (daylight hours). Limited hunting and fishing (inquire for dates); canoeing. Hiking trails. (Daily) **FREE**

Limited-Service Hotel

★ INN TOWN. *27 S State St, Waupun (53963). Phone 920/324-4211; toll-free 800/433-6231; fax 920/324-6921.* 16 rooms. Pets accepted, some restrictions; fee. Check-out 10 am. **$**

Wausau (C-3)

See also Antigo, Stevens Point

Settled 1839
Population 37,060
Elevation 1,195 ft
Area Code 715
Zip 54401
Information Wausau Area Convention and Visitors Bureau, 300 3rd St, Suite 200, PO Box 6190, 54402-6190; phone 715/845-6231, ext 324 or toll-free 800/236-9728
Web Site www.wausauchamber.com

Known as Big Bull Falls when it was settled as a lumber camp, the town was renamed Wausau, Native American for "Faraway Place." When the big timber was gone, the lumber barons started paper mills; paper products are still one of the city's many industries.

What to See and Do

Leigh Yawkey Woodson Art Museum. *700 N 12th St, Wausau (54401). Phone 715/845-7010.* Collection of wildlife art, porcelain, and glass; changing exhibits. (Tues-Sun; closed holidays) **FREE**

Marathon County Historical Museum. *403 McIndoe St, Wausau (54401). Phone 715/848-6143.* Former home of early lumberman Cyrus C. Yawkey. Victorian period rooms; model railroad display; changing theme exhibits. (Tues-Thurs, Sat-Sun; closed holidays) **FREE**

Rib Mountain State Park. *5301 Rib Mountain Dr, Wausau (54401). 4 miles SW on County N. Phone 715/842-2522 (summer months).* An 860-acre park; summit of Rib Mountain is one of the highest points (1,940 feet) in the state; 60-foot observation tower. Hiking trails that wind past rocky ridges and natural oddities in quartzite rocks. View of miles of Wisconsin River Valley, the city and countryside. Picnicking, playgrounds, concession, camping. (Daily) **$$** In park is

Granite Peak Ski Area. *3605 N Mountain Rd, Wausau (54402). 2 miles SW via Hwy 51 and 29, NN exit. Phone 715/849-5959. www.skigranitepeak.com.* The area has three chairlifts, rope tow; patrol, school, rentals; snowmaking; cafeteria, bar. Longest run 3,800 feet; vertical drop 624 feet. (Late Nov-mid-Apr, daily) **$$$$**

Special Events

Big Bull Falls Blues Festival. *Fern Island Park, Stewart Ave and River Dr, Wausau (54401). Phone 715/355-8788.* Mid-Aug.

Wisconsin Valley Fair. *Marathon Park, 17th and Stewart, Wausau (54401). Phone 715/355-8788.* Early Aug.

Limited-Service Hotels

★ BAYMONT INN. *1910 Stewart Ave, Wausau (54401). Phone 715/842-0421; toll-free 800/428-3438; fax 715/845-5096. www.baymontinns.com.* 96 rooms, 2 story. Pets accepted, some restrictions. High-speed Internet access. Check-out noon. Indoor pool. **$**

★ ★ BEST WESTERN MIDWAY HOTEL. *2901 Martin Ave, Wausau (54401). Phone 715/842-1616; toll-free 800/780-7234; fax 715/845-3726. www.bestwestern.com.* 98 rooms, 2 story. Pets accepted, some restrictions; fee. Check-in 3 pm, check-out noon. Restaurant, bar. Fitness room. Indoor pool, whirlpool. Airport transportation available. **$**

★ RIB MOUNTAIN INN. *2900 Rib Mountain Way, Wausau (54401). Phone 715/848-2802; toll-free 877/960-8900; fax 715/848-1908.* On Rib Mountain. Adjacent to state park. 16 rooms, 2 story. Pets accepted; fee. Complimentary continental breakfast. Check-out 11 am. **$**

Specialty Lodging

The following lodging establishment is approved by Mobil Travel Guide, but due to its unique and individualized nature has not been given a traditional Mobil Star rating. Included in this listing you may find bed-and-breakfasts, limited-service inns, guest ranches, and other unique hotel properties.

ROSENBERRY INN. *511 Franklin St, Wausau (54403). Phone 715/842-5733; fax 715/843-5659. www.rosenberryinn.com.* Two historic homes built in 1908; Prairie school-style architecture. 8 rooms, 3 story. Complimentary full breakfast. Check-in 3 pm, check-out 11 am. **$**

Restaurants

★ CARMELO'S. *3607 N Mountain Rd, Wausau (54401). Phone 715/845-5570.* Italian menu. Dinner. Closed holidays. Bar. **$$**

★ ★ GULLIVER'S LANDING. *1701 Mallard Ln, Wausau (54401). Phone 715/849-8409; fax 715/843-0915. www.gulliverslanding.com.* Dockage. Seafood menu. Lunch, dinner. Closed holidays. Bar. Children's menu. Outdoor seating. **$$$**

★ ★ MICHAEL'S. *2901 Rib Mountain Dr, Wausau (54401). Phone 715/842-9856.* Wildlife pictures on walls. German, American menu. Dinner. Closed Sun; holidays. Bar. Children's menu. **$$$**

★ ★ WAGON WHEEL SUPPER CLUB. *3901 N 6th St, Wausau (54403). Phone 715/675-2263.* Seafood, steak menu. Dinner. Closed Sun. Bar. **$$$**

★ WAUSAU MINE CO. *3904 W Stewart Ave, Wausau (54401). Phone 715/845-7304; fax 715/842-1575. www.wausaumine.com.* American menu. Dinner. Closed Easter, Thanksgiving, Dec 24-25. Bar. Children's menu. **$$**

Wautoma (D-3)

See also Green Lake, Waupaca

Population 1,784
Elevation 867 ft
Area Code 920
Zip 54982

What to See and Do

Nordic Mountain Ski Area. *W5806 County Rd W, Wautoma (54982). 8 miles N via Hwy 152. Phone 920/787-3324; toll-free 800/253-7266. www.nordicmountain.com.* Triple, double chairlifts, T-bar, pomalift, two rope tows; patrol, school, rentals; snowmaking; restaurant, cafeteria, concession, bar. Longest run 1 mile; vertical drop 265 feet. Night skiing. (Dec-mid-Mar, Thurs-Tues; closed Dec 25); 13 miles of cross-country trails (weekends only; free). **$$$$**

Wild Rose Pioneer Museum. *Main St, Wild Rose (54984). 8 miles N on Hwy 22. Phone 920/622-3364.* Historical complex of buildings including Elisha Stewart House, containing furniture of the late 19th century; pioneer hall; outbuildings; carriage house; blacksmith shop, cobbler shop, replica of general store, one-room schoolhouse, apothecary; weaving room; gift shop. Tours. (Mid-June-Labor Day, Wed and Sat afternoons; also by appointment during summer) **$**

Wauwatosa (E-4)

See also Menomonee Falls, Milwaukee

Settled 1835
Population 49,366
Elevation 634 ft
Area Code 414
Information Chamber of Commerce, 7707 W State St, 53213; phone 414/453-2330

What to See and Do

Harley-Davidson Tour. *11700 W Capitol Dr, Wauwatosa (53222). Phone 414/343-7850; toll-free 877/883-1450. www.harleydavidson.com.* Milwaukee is Hog Heaven, so it's only fitting to tour the propeller-factory-turned-Harley-facility and see transmission and engine assembly from start to finish, plus some engine remanufacturing. The one-hour tour also features a video on company history and a peek at the assembly line. Tickets are handed out a 9 am on a first-come, first-served basis; it's strongly recommended to arrive early. To be eligible for the tour, you must be 12 years old; wear fully enclosed, low-heeled shoes; show a valid government-issued photo ID or passport (age 18 and over); complete a registration card; and pass through a metal detector. Backpacks, camera bags, camcorders, and pocketknives are prohibited on the factory floor. (Mon-Fri 9:30 am-1 pm; closed holidays) **FREE**

Lowell Damon House. *2107 Wauwatosa Ave, Wauwatosa (53213). Phone 414/273-8288.* (1844) Community's oldest home is a classic example of colonial architecture; period furnishings. Tours (Sun, Wed; closed holidays). **FREE**

Limited-Service Hotel

★ HOLIDAY INN EXPRESS. *11111 W North Ave, Wauwatosa (53226). Phone 414/778-0333; toll-free 800/465-4329; fax 414/778-0331. www.holiday-inn.com.* 122 rooms, 3 story. Complimentary continental breakfast. Check-out noon. Wireless Internet access. **$**

Restaurants

★ ★ ★ BARTOLOTTA'S. *7616 W State St, Wauwatosa (53213). Phone 414/771-7910; fax 414/771-1589. www.bartolottas.com.* A classic representation of trattoria-style dining. The menu highlights fresh and authentic ingredients. This is a family-owned restaurant that has a wonderful following and promises a casual, yet rewarding dining experience. Italian menu. Dinner. Closed holidays. Bar. Children's menu. Casual attire. Reservations recommended. Outdoor seating. **$$**

★ BJONDA. *7754 Harwood Ave, Wauwatosa (53213). Phone 414/431-1444.* French menu. Lunch, dinner. Bar. Children's menu. **$$**

Wisconsin Dells (D-3)

See also Baraboo, Mauston, Portage, Prairie du Sac, Reedsburg

Settled 1856
Population 2,393
Elevation 912 ft
Area Code 608
Zip 53965
Information Wisconsin Dells Visitor & Convention Bureau, 701 Superior St, PO Box 390; phone 608/254-4636 or toll-free 800/223-3557
Web Site www.wisdells.com

Until 1931, this city was called Kilbourn, but it changed its name in the hope of attracting tourists to the nearby Dells. It seems to have worked—the Wisconsin Dells has become the state's prime tourist attraction. This burgeoning destination quickly became one of the top spots for family travel in the Midwest. Walk through downtown or visit some of the area attractions and there will be no mistaking the focus on tourism. Although some aspects of the Dells lean toward the tacky side, the overall feel is good, clean fun.

The Wisconsin Dells are well equipped for the throngs of tourists who stop through here every summer. The region offers a wide selection of campgrounds, bed-and-breakfasts, hotels, motels, resorts, condos, and cottages; of these, more than 40 welcome guests with pets, and 17 house indoor water parks. Man-made and natural attractions keep visitors from lingering too long at area accommodations.

Families can explore the Upper and Lower Dells on a Dells Boat Tour or the water- and land-based environs on an original *World War II Duck.* Take to the water in the largest indoor water park in the United States at Kalahari Resort & Convention Center, or at Noah's Ark, America's largest water park, housing 5 million gallons of water and 3 miles of water slides. Uncover the enchantment under the Big Top at Circus World Museum in nearby Baraboo, take a wagon tour through a working elk ranch (Nanchas Elk Ranch Tours, phone 608/524-4355), or ride the rails through the Baraboo Hills at the Mid-Continent Railway Museum (phone 608/522-4261).

Spectators flock to the Tommy Bartlett show, where entertainers amaze through daring feats in the water, on stage, and in the sky. Fast-paced action circles the track at the Dells Motor Speedway—the place to head for stock car racing (phone 608/345-7274). Those in search of quieter pursuits can stroll along the new RiverWalk in the downtown Dells River District. The 1,100-foot walkway is equipped with a bicycle path, benches, and game tables. Mirror Lake State Park and Rocky Arbor State Park are two other places to commune with nature, or tour the vineyards at Prairie du Sac's Wollersheim Winery, the largest producer of wine in Wisconsin.

Sports-minded visitors will find five horseback riding stables, several championship golf courses, and ample space to reel in the catch of the day. Fish for walleye, trout, bass, catfish, northern pike, and muskellunge—all are plentiful in the area.

What to See and Do

Beaver Springs Fishing Park and Riding Stables. *600 Trout Rd, Wisconsin Dells (53965). 1/2 mile S on Hwy 13. Phone 608/254-2735 (fishing).* Guided one-hour rides. Spring-fed ponds stocked with trout, catfish, bass, and other fish. Pay for fish caught. Pole rental. (Apr-Oct, daily) **$$**

Christmas Mountain Village. *S944 Christmas Mountain Rd, Wisconsin Dells (53965). 4 miles W on County H. Phone 608/254-3971. www.christmasmountainvillage.com.* Area has two double chairlifts, rope tow; patrol, school, rentals; snowmaking; restaurant, bar, snack bar. Lodge. Seven power-tilled runs; longest run 1/2 mile; vertical drop 250 feet. Cross-country trails; night skiing. (Mid-Dec-mid-Mar, daily; closed Dec 24 evening) **$$$$**

Dells Boat Tours. *11 Broadway, Wisconsin Dells (53965). Phone 608/254-8555.* Guided sightseeing tours through the Dells Scenic Riverway. View of towering sandstone cliffs, narrow fern-filled canyons, and unique rock formations. Upper Dells tour is two hours with scenic shore landings at Stand Rock and Witches Gulch; Lower Dells tour is one hour and features the Rocky Island region, caverns and cliffs; complete tour is Upper and Lower Dells combined. (Mid-Apr-Oct, daily; departures every 30 minutes in July-Aug) **$$$$**

★ **Dells Ducks.** *1550 Wisconsin Dells Pkwy, Wisconsin Dells (53965). 1 1/2 miles S on Hwy 12. Phone 608/254-6080.* One-hour land/water tour of scenic rock formations along the Wisconsin River. (Late May-late Oct, daily) **$$$$**

H. H. Bennett Studio and History Center. *215 Broadway, Wisconsin Dells (53965). Phone 608/253-3523. www.hhbennett.com.* (1865) Oldest photographic studio in the United States. The landscape and nature photography of H. H. Bennett helped make the Dells area famous. The studio is still in operation and it is possible to purchase enlargements made from Bennett's original glass negatives. (Memorial Day-Labor Day: daily; rest of year: by appointment)

Original Wisconsin Ducks. *1890 Wisconsin Dells Pkwy, Wisconsin Dells (53965). 1 mile S on Hwy 12. Phone 608/254-8751.* One-hour, 8 1/2-mile land and water tours on the Original Wisconsin Ducks. (Apr-Oct, daily) **$$$$**

Riverview Park & Waterworld. *Hwy 12, Wisconsin Dells (53965). 1/4 mile S on Hwy 12. Phone 608/254-2608.* Wave pool, speed slides, tube rides, and kids' pools. Grand Prix, go-carts, dune cat track. Park (late May-early Sept); admission free; fee for activities. Waterworld (late May-early Sept, daily). **$$$$**

Tommy Bartlett's Robot World & Exploratory. *560 Wisconsin Dells Pkwy, Wisconsin Dells (53965). Lake Delton, 3 miles S on Hwy 12. Phone 608/254-2525.* More than 150 hands-on exhibits, including the world's only Russian Mir Space Station core module. Principles of light, sound, and motion are explored. Features robot-guided tour. (Daily) **$$$** Also here is

> **Tommy Bartlett's Thrill Show.** *560 Wisconsin Dells Pkwy, Wisconsin Dells (53965). Lake Delton, 3 miles S on Hwy 12. Phone 608/254-2525.* Water-ski theme, "Hooray for Hollywood," features juggling jokester, the Nerveless Knocks, "Mr. Sound Effects" Wes Harrison, and colorful entrancing waters; also

laser light show (evening performances only). (Late May-early Sept, daily) **$$$$**

Wisconsin Deer Park. *583 Wisconsin Dells Pkwy, Wisconsin Dells (53965). 1/2 mile S on Hwy 12. Phone 608/253-2041.* A 28-acre wildlife exhibit. (May-mid-Oct, daily) **$$$**

Limited-Service Hotels

★ BEST WESTERN AMBASSADOR INN & SUITES. *610 Frontage Rd S, Wisconsin Dells (53965). Phone 608/254-4477; toll-free 800/828-6888; fax 608/253-6662. www.bestwestern-dells.com.* 181 rooms, 3 story. Check-in 4 pm, check-out 11 am. High-speed Internet access. Indoor pool, outdoor pool, children's pool, whirlpool. **$**

★ COMFORT INN. *703 Frontage Rd N, Wisconsin Dells (53965). Phone 608/253-3711; toll-free 800/424-6423; fax 608/254-2164. www.comfortinn.com.* 75 rooms, 3 story. Complimentary full breakfast. Check-in 4 pm, check-out 11 am. Wireless Internet access. Indoor pool, whirlpool. **$**

★ ★ RIVERWALK HOTEL. *1015 River Rd, Wisconsin Dells (53965). Phone 608/253-1231; toll-free 800/659-5395; fax 608/253-6145.* 54 rooms, 5 story. Check-in 2 pm, check-out 11 am. Restaurant, bar. Indoor pool, outdoor pool, whirlpool. **$**

★ ★ WINTERGREEN RESORT AND CONFERENCE CENTER. *60 Gasser Rd, Wisconsin Dells (53965). Phone 608/254-2285; toll-free 800/648-4765; fax 608/253-6235. www.wintergreen-resort.com.* 111 rooms, 3 story. Check-in 4 pm, check-out 11 am. High-speed Internet access, wireless Internet access. Restaurant, bar. Fitness room. Indoor pool, outdoor pool, children's pool, whirlpool. Indoor/outdoor water park. **$**

Full-Service Hotels

★ ★ ★ GREAT WOLF LODGE. *1400 Great Wolf Dr, Wisconsin Dells (53965). Phone 608/253-2222; toll-free 800/559-9653; fax 608/253-2224. www.greatwolflodge.com.* 300 rooms. Check-in 3 pm, check-out noon. Restaurant, bar. Children's activity center. Fitness room. Indoor pool, children's pool, whirlpool. Airport transportation available. **$$**

★ ★ HOWARD JOHNSON. *655 N Frontage Rd, Wisconsin Dells (53965). Phone 608/254-8306; toll-free 800/543-3557; fax 608/253-2829. www.howardjohnson.com.* The Antigua Bay Waterpark is what makes this hotel special. With indoor and outdoor water slides, a beach-entry pool, and 13,000 square feet of heated indoor pools, this Howard Johnson is a water-lover's dream and a terrific choice for families with young children. It also offers ample meeting and exhibit space. 228 rooms, 2 story. Pets accepted, some restrictions. Check-in 4 pm, check-out 10:30 am. Wireless Internet access. Restaurant, bar. Fitness room. Indoor pool, outdoor pool, children's pool, whirlpool. **$$**

★ ★ ★ RAINTREE RESORT & CONFERENCE CENTER. *1435 Wisconsin Dells Pkwy, Wisconsin Dells (53965). Phone 608/253-4386; toll-free 888/253-4386; fax 608/253-3192. www.dellsraintree.com.* 158 rooms. Check-in 3:30 pm, check-out 10:30 am. High-speed Internet access. Two restaurants, bar. Fitness room. Indoor pool, outdoor pool, whirlpool. Business center. **$$**

Full-Service Resorts

★ ★ ★ KALAHARI RESORT. *1305 Kalahari Dr, Wisconsin Dells (53965). Phone 608/254-5466; toll-free 877/254-5466; fax 608/254-2381. www.kalahariresort.com.* 738 rooms, 4 story. Check-in 4 pm, check-out 11 am. High-speed Internet access, wireless Internet access. Six restaurants, five bars. Children's activity center. Two fitness rooms, spa. Indoor pools, outdoor pools, children's pool, whirlpool. Business center. **$$**

★ ★ ★ WILDERNESS HOTEL & GOLF RESORT. *511 E Adams St, Wisconsin Dells (53965). Phone 608/253-9729; toll-free 800/867-9453; fax 608/254-4982. www.wildernessresort.com.* 483 rooms. Check-in 4 pm, check-out 11 am. High-speed Internet access. Four restaurants, two bars. Fitness room. Indoor pool, outdoor pool, children's pool, whirlpool. Golf, 18 holes. Airport transportation available. Business center. **$$**

Restaurants

★ ★ DEL-BAR. *800 Wisconsin Dells Pkwy, Lake Delton (53940). Phone 608/253-1861; fax 608/258-1871. www.del-bar.com.* American menu. Dinner. Closed Thanksgiving, Dec 24-25. Bar. Children's menu. Casual attire. Reservations recommended. Outdoor seating. **$$$**

★ MESA GRILLE CHULA VISTA RESORT. *N 4031 River Rd, Wisconsin Dells (53965). Phone 608/254-8366.* Mexican menu. Breakfast, lunch, dinner. Bar. Children's menu. Reservations recommended. **$$**

★ ★ WALLY'S HOUSE OF EMBERS. *935 Wisconsin Dells Pkwy, Lake Delton (53940). Phone 608/253-6411; fax 608/253-2433. www.houseofembers.com.* American menu. Dinner. Bar. Children's menu. Casual attire. Reservations recommended. Outdoor seating. **$$**

Wisconsin Rapids (D-3)

See also Marshfield, Stevens Point

Population 18,245
Elevation 1,028 ft
Area Code 715
Zip 54494
Information Wisconsin Rapids Area Convention & Visitors Bureau, 1120 Lincoln St; phone 715/422-4856 or toll-free 800/554-4484
Web Site www.wctc.net/chamber

A paper manufacturing and cranberry center, Wisconsin Rapids was formed in 1900 by consolidating the two towns of Grand Rapids and Centralia after the Wisconsin River had devastated large sections of both communities. At first the combined town was called Grand Rapids, but the name was changed when confusion with the Michigan city developed. Cranberry marshes here produce the largest inland cranberry crop in the world.

What to See and Do

Forest tour. *5 miles NE on County U, on banks of Wisconsin River. Phone 715/422-3789.* Self-guided walking or cross-country skiing tour of site of Consolidated Papers' first tree nursery, now planted with various types of hard and soft woods; 27 marked points of special interest on 60 acres. (Daily) **FREE**

Grotto Gardens. *6975 Grotto Ave, Rudolph (54475). 7 miles N via Hwy 34, County C. Phone 715/435-3120.* A 6-acre garden park with series of religious tableaux, statues, and grottoes (daily). Picnic grounds. Gift shop/information center (Memorial Day-Labor Day, daily). **$**

South Wood County Historical Corporation Museum. *540 3rd St S, Wisconsin Rapids (54494). Phone 715/423-1580.* Historical museum in town mansion. (June-Aug, Sun-Thurs, afternoons) **FREE**

Special Event

River Cities Fun Fest. *W Grand Ave and 2nd St N, Wisconsin Rapids (54494). Phone 715/423-1830.* Tours, car show, arts and crafts fair, water-ski shows. First weekend in Aug.

Limited-Service Hotels

★ BEST WESTERN RAPIDS MOTOR INN. *911 Huntington Ave, Wisconsin Rapids (54494). Phone 715/423-3211; toll-free 800/780-7234; fax 715/423-2875. www.bestwestern.com.* 43 rooms, 2 story. Pets accepted. Check-out 11 am. **$**

★ QUALITY INN. *3120 8th St, Wisconsin Rapids (54494). Phone 715/423-5506; toll-free 800/755-1336; fax 715/423-7150. www.qualityinn.com.* 36 rooms, 2 story. Complimentary continental breakfast. Check-out 11 am. **$**

Full-Service Hotel

★ ★ ★ HOTEL MEAD. *451 E Grand Ave, Wisconsin Rapids (54494). Phone 715/423-1500; toll-free 800/843-6323; fax 715/422-7064. www.hotelmead.com.* Centrally located and considered by many as the hospitality center of central Wisconsin, this hotel caters to business, leisure, and adventure travelers. 157 rooms, 5 story. Pets accepted, some restrictions; fee. Check-out noon. Restaurant, bar. Fitness room. Indoor pool, whirlpool. **$**

Woodruff

See also Boulder Junction, Eagle River, Lac du Flambeau, Manitowish Waters, Minocqua, Rhinelander, Sayner, St. Germain

Population 2,000

Elevation 1,610 ft
Area Code 715
Zip 54568
Information Minocqua-Arbor Vitae-Woodruff Area Chamber of Commerce, 8216 Hwy 51 S, Minocqua, 54548; phone 715/356-5266 or toll-free 800/446-6784
Web Site www.minocqua.org

Woodruff is a four-seasons playground for families and outdoor recreationalists alike. The area has one of the largest concentrations of freshwater bodies in America, providing unlimited fishing and water activities.

What to See and Do

Kastle Rock. *9438 County Hwy J, Woodruff (54568). Hwy 51 to County Trunk J, 2 blocks E. Phone 715/356-6865.* 18-hole miniature golf with 500-foot train track. (May-Aug, daily) **$$$**

Woodruff State Fish Hatchery. *8770 Country Rd J, Woodruff (54568). 2 1/2 miles SE on County Trunk J. Phone 715/356-5211.* Hatchery (mid-Apr-mid-June). Tours (Memorial Day-Labor Day, Mon-Fri) **FREE**

Side Trips

While visiting Milwaukee, plan to take a day or two and drive south an hour and a half to Chicago—you won't be disappointed. Gaze at the breathtaking skyline, stroll along the awe-inspiring lakefront, indulge in the world-famous deep-dish pizza, soak up authentic blues music, and then plan for day two of your excursion.

Chicago

1 1/2 hours, 95 miles from Milwaukee, WI

Settled 1803
Population 2,896,016
Elevation 596 feet
Area Code 312, 773
Information Chicago Office of Tourism, Chicago Cultural Center, 78 E Washington St, 60602; phone 312/744-2400 or toll-free 800/226-6632
Web Site www.choosechicago.com

Suburbs *North:* Evanston, Glenview, Gurnee, Highland Park, Highwood, Northbrook, Skokie, and Wilmette; *Northwest:* Arlington Heights, Itasca, Schaumburg, and Wheeling; *South:* Homewood and Oak Lawn; *West:* Brookfield, Cicero, Downers Grove, Elmhurst, Geneva, Glen Ellyn, Hillside, Hinsdale, La Grange, Naperville, Oak Brook, Oak Park, St. Charles, and Wheaton.

Rudyard Kipling wrote of Chicago, "I have struck a city—a real city—and they call it Chicago." For poet Carl Sandburg, it was the "City of the Big Shoulders"; for writer A. J. Liebling, a New Yorker, it was the "Second City." Songwriters have dubbed it a "toddlin' town" and "my kind of town." Boosters say it's "the city that works"; and to most people, it is "the Windy City." But over and above all the words and slogans is the city itself and the people who helped make it what it is today.

The people of Chicago represent a varied ethnic and racial mix: Native Americans gave the city its name—Checagou; restless Easterners traveled here in search of land and opportunity; hundreds of thousands of venturesome immigrants from Europe, Asia, and Latin America came here and brought the foods and customs of the Old World; and Southern blacks and Appalachians came with hopes of finding better jobs and housing. All of these unique groups have contributed to the strength, vitality, and cosmopolitan ambience that make Chicago a distinctive and special experience for visitors.

Chicago's past is equally distinctive, built on adversity and contradiction. The first permanent settler was a black man, Jean Baptiste Point du Sable. The city's worst tragedy, the Great Chicago Fire of 1871, was the basis for its physical and cultural renaissance. In the heart of one of the poorest ethnic neighborhoods, two young women of means, Jane Addams and Ellen Gates Starr, created Hull House, a social service institution that has been copied throughout the world. A city of neat frame cottages and bulky stone mansions, it produced the geniuses of the Chicago school of architecture (Louis Sullivan, Daniel Burnham, Dankmar Adler, William LeBaron Jenney, and John Willborn Root), whose innovative tradition was carried on by Frank Lloyd Wright and Ludwig Mies van der Rohe. Even its most famous crooks provide a study in contrasts: Al Capone, the Prohibition gangster, and Samuel Insull, the financial finagler whose stock manipulations left thousands of small investors penniless in the late 1920s.

Chicago's early merchants resisted the intrusion of the railroad, yet the city became the rail center of the nation. Although Chicago no longer boasts a stockyard, its widely diversified economy makes it one of the most stable cities in the country. Metropolitan Chicago has more than 12,000 factories with a $20 billion annual payroll and ranks first in the United States in the production of canned and frozen foods, metal products, machinery, railroad equipment, letterpress printing, office equipment, musical instruments, telephones, housewares, candy, and lampshades. It has one of the world's busiest airports, the largest grain exchange, and the biggest mail-order business. It is a great educational center (58 institutions of higher learning); one of the world's largest convention and trade show cities; a showplace, marketplace, shopping, and financial center; and a city of skyscrapers, museums, parks, and churches, with more than 2,700 places of worship.

Art Deco the Chicago Way

Chicago is a textbook of Art Deco design. Look up at the façades of historic high rises, peek into the lobbies of landmark office buildings, ride an elevator or two. Begin at the Chicago Board of Trade (141 W Jackson Blvd), home to the world's oldest and largest futures exchange, formed in 1848. Ceres, the Roman goddess of grain and harvest, receives due homage with a 31-foot-tall statue atop the original 1930 building and a monumental mural in the atrium, added in the 1980s. A massive clock is ornamented with a distinctive agrarian motif. The three-story lobby, a dazzling Art Deco masterpiece, gleams with contrasting black- and buff-colored marble trimmed with silver; the elevator doors are silver and black. Light fixtures behind translucent panels throw out a diffused glow, and stylized figures are abundant.

Walk a couple of blocks west for breakfast at Lou Mitchell's (565 W Jackson Blvd), known for egg dishes served in sizzling skillets. The restaurant presents boxes of Milk Duds to waiting female patrons. Then head north to the American National Bank Building (1 N LaSalle St). This 49-story limestone building, with typical Art Deco setbacks and dominant vertical lines, occupies an entire block of Chicago's financial district. A stunning Art Deco lobby features dark marble contrasted by gleaming metalwork and exquisite carved wood sconces. Outside, at the fifth-floor level, relief panels chronicle the 17th-century explorations of René-Robert Cavelier, Sieur de La Salle (Vitzhum & Burns, 1930).

Turn east to the former Chicago Daily News Building (400 W Madison St). The careers of Horace Greeley, Joseph Pulitzer, and other famous journalists, as well as events from Chicago's rich newspaper history, are chronicled with stylized bas-relief figures carved by Alvin Meyer. Originally, the limestone building with dramatic setbacks and an open riverfront plaza was designed to house the newspaper's offices and plant. Inside are ornate metal elevator doors, grillwork, and terrazzo floors in a geometric pattern. Travel north to the Carbide and Carbon Building (230 N Michigan Ave). This Art Deco skyscraper is as dramatically dark as its eponymous minerals. Offsetting piles of black polished granite are dark green masonry and gold terra-cotta trim. The stunning two-story lobby features marble walls, elegant bronze grillwork, gold-and-white plaster, and recessed lights of frosted glass. Just a block or two southwest, Heaven on Seven is tucked away on the seventh floor of the Garland Building (111 N Wabash St). Notable Cajun and Creole cooking includes gumbo, po' boy sandwiches, spicy jambalaya, sweet potato pie, and bread pudding.

Divert your attention to the fifth floor of the limestone building at 343 North Michigan Avenue. Seven-foot-high carved panels depicting settlers and Native Americans commemorate the site of Fort Dearborn, which overlooked the Chicago River at this spot. The lobby has terrazzo floors of black, russet, and green and brass elevator doors decorated with stylized figures. Farther north on the Magnificent Mile, look up above chic storefronts at the former Palmolive/Playboy Building (919 N Michigan Ave). Notice the dark bas-relief designs between the windows of this massive, stepped building. Turn the corner onto Walton and check out the lobby. It features Art Deco lights and handsome walnut elevator doors sculpted with bas-relief figures. If you ride an elevator, you'll see that the ornate carvings continue inside. Saloon Steakhouse (200 E Chestnut) is a warm, cheery steakhouse with high-quality, flavorful meat, suitably marbled and dry-aged. Be sure to try a side of bacon-scallion mashed potatoes. Décor features stenciled earth-tone walls, parchment sconces, and Native American murals.

Chicago turns its best face toward Lake Michigan, where a green fringe of parks forms an arc from Evanston to the Indiana border. The Loop is a city within a city, with many corporate headquarters, banks, stores, and other enterprises. To the far south are the docks along the Calumet River, used by ocean vessels since the opening of the St. Lawrence Seaway and servicing a belt of factories, steel mills, and warehouses. Behind these lies a maze of industrial and shopping areas, schools, and houses.

Although Louis Jolliet mapped the area as early as 1673 and du Sable and a compatriot, Antoine Ouilmette, had established a trading post by 1796, the real growth of the city did not begin until the 19th century and the onset of the Industrial Revolution. In 1803, the fledging US government took possession of the area and sent a small military contingent from Detroit to select the site for a fort. Fort Dearborn was built at a strategic spot on the mouth of the Chicago River; on the opposite bank, a settlement slowly grew. Fort and settlement were abandoned when the British threatened them during the War of 1812. On their way to Fort Wayne, soldiers and settlers were attacked and killed or held captive by Native Americans who had been armed by the British. The fort was rebuilt in 1816; a few survivors returned and new settlers arrived, but there was little activity until Chicago was selected as the terminal site of the proposed Illinois and Michigan Canal. This started a land boom.

Twenty thousand Easterners swept through on their way to the riches of the West. Merchants opened stores; land speculation was rampant. Although 1837—the year Chicago was incorporated as a city—was marked by financial panic, the pace of expansion and building did not falter. In 1841, grain destined for world ports began to pour into the city; almost immediately, Chicago became the largest grain market in the world. In the wake of the grain came herds of hogs and cattle for the Chicago slaughterhouses. Tanneries, packing plants, mills, and factories soon sprang up.

The Illinois and Michigan Canal, completed in 1848, quadrupled imports and exports. Railroads fanned out from the city, transporting merchandise throughout the nation and bringing new produce to Chicago. During the slump that followed the panic of 1857, Chicago built a huge wooden shed (the Wigwam) at the southeast corner of Wacker and Lake to house the Republican National Convention. Abraham Lincoln was nominated Republican candidate for president here in 1860. The Civil War doubled grain shipments from Chicago. In 1865, the mile-square Union Stock Yards were established. Chicago was riotously prosperous; its population skyrocketed. Then, on October 8, 1871, fire erupted in a cow barn and roared through the city, destroying 15,768 buildings, killing almost 300 people, and leaving a third of the population homeless. But temporary and permanent rebuilding started at once, and Chicago emerged from the ashes to take advantage of the rise of industrialization. The labor unrest of the period produced the Haymarket bombing and the Pullman and other strikes. The 1890s were noteworthy for cultural achievements: orchestras, libraries, universities, and the new urban architectural form for which the term "skyscraper" was coined. The Columbian Exposition of 1893, a magnificent success, was followed by depression and municipal corruption.

Chicago's fantastic rate of growth continued into the 20th century. Industries boomed during World War I, and, in the 1920s, the city prospered as never before—unruffled by dizzying financial speculation and notorious gang warfare, an outgrowth of Prohibition. The stock market crash of 1929 brought down the shakier financial pyramids; the repeal of Prohibition virtually ended the rackets; and a more sober Chicago produced the Century of Progress Exposition in 1933. Chicago's granaries and steel mills helped carry the country through World War II. The past several decades have seen a reduction of manufacturing jobs in the area and an increase of jobs in service industries and in the fields of finance, law, advertising, and insurance. The 1996 relocation of Lake Shore Drive made it possible to create the Museum Campus. This 57-acre extension of Burnham Park provides an easier and more scenic route to the Adler Planetarium, Field Museum of Natural History, and Shedd Aquarium and surrounds them with one continuous park featuring terraced gardens and broad walkways.

Although, in the eyes of some, Chicago evokes the image of an industrial giant, it is also a city in which the arts flourish. Chicagoans are proud of their world-famous symphony orchestra, their Lyric Opera, and their numerous and diverse dance companies. Since 1912, Chicago has been the home of *Poetry* magazine. Chicago's theater community is vibrant, with more than 100 off-Loop theaters presenting quality drama. The collections at the Art Institute of Chicago, Museum of Contemporary Art, and many galleries along Michigan Avenue and in the River North area are among the best in the country.

Other museums are equally renowned: the Museum of Science and Industry, the Field Museum of Natural History, the Chicago Children's Museum at Navy Pier, and the various specialty museums that reflect the ethnic and civic interests of the city.

The zoos, planetarium, and aquarium, as well as many parks and beaches along the lakefront, afford pleasure for visitors of all ages. Chicago's attractions are many,

Did Somebody Say "Second City"?

In any given week, in any given season, you can walk into the Steppenwolf Theatre (1650 N Halsted St) and probably see the award-winning actor Gary Sinese on stage. He may work all over the world, but he has said that his heart is here in Chicago at the company he helped found. Over at the Goodman Theatre (170 N Dearborn St), you might see a pre-Broadway tryout on its way to becoming a multiple Tony Award winner, such as the acclaimed revival of Arthur Miller's *Death of a Salesman*, starring Brian Dennehy. Besides terrific performances with superb performers and solid production values in a city of outstanding theater, what do these companies have in common? Both have received Tony Awards for the best regional theater in America, making Chicago the only city in the country with three theaters that have won that prestigious award.

Chicago is "second city" to none when it comes to theater. A place of multiple companies, it has mainstream stages and storefront theaters, front-page attention-getters and neighborhood gems. And there are names galore. When he graduated from Northwestern University, long before he became a "Friend", actor David Schwimmer co-founded Lookingglass Theatre (806 N Michigan Ave), a company known for its sometimes acrobatic, always colorful, and highly creative performances. Pegasus Players (1145 W Wilson Ave) has a knack for getting the rights to Stephen Sondheim's works. Sometimes the productions are smaller and less frequently produced, like *Anyone Can Whistle*; sometimes they are coups, like the American premiere of Sondheim's first effort, *Saturday Night*.

Actor John Malkovich got his start here. He began his career at the Steppenwolf alongside Sinese and still comes back to perform from time to time. So do Laurie Metcalf (of television's *Roseanne* fame) and stage actor Jeff Perry. Joan Cusack lives here, as does John Mahoney, formerly of *Frasier*. He, too, appears at the Steppenwolf, as well as at other venues around town.

And there are plenty of venues—enough for both the famous and the becoming-famous. Chicago-style entertainment comes in dozens of styles and sizes. The adventurous Bailiwick Repertory Theatre (1229 W Belmont Ave) frequently puts on performances for the deaf; its production of *Our Town* featured both hearing and hearing-impaired actors. ETA Creative Arts Foundation (7558 S Chicago Ave) puts on original or seldom-seen dramatic works by African-American writers. While presenting full-length plays on its main stage, Noble Fool Theater (16 W Randolph St) uses its studio for *Flanagan's Wake*, its signature "interactive Irish wake." Roadworks (1239 N Ashland Ave) is a young company, a strong ensemble cast that focuses on Midwest and world premieres.

Each week from June through August, a different independent theater company puts on a production at Theatre on the Lake, a screened-in Prairie school-style building in Lincoln Park on the shore of Lake Michigan. The relaxed atmosphere, lake breezes, and smart performances are accentuated by a bonus: walking out of the theater at intermission and gazing south at the city's gorgeous skyline.

and sightseeing tours can be taken by boat, bus, car, bicycle, or foot.

Buses and rapid transit lines are integrated into one system—the most extensive in the nation—with interchangeable transfers. Elevated lines run through the Loop. Subway trains run under State and Dearborn streets and run on elevated structures to both the north and south. Rapid transit lines also serve the West Side, as well as O'Hare and Midway airports. Commuter trains stretch out to the far western and southern suburbs and near the Wisconsin and Indiana borders.

Driving and parking in Chicago are no more or less difficult than in any other major city. There are indoor and outdoor parking areas near and in the Loop; some provide shuttle bus service to the Loop or to the Merchandise Mart.

Additional Visitor Information

When available, half-price, day-of-performance tickets are offered, with a slight service charge, at Hot Tix ticket booths, Chicago Place at 700 N Michigan Avenue, 108 N State Street; 1616 Sherman Avenue in Evanston; and Oak Park Visitor Center at 158 Forest Avenue in Oak Park. (Tues-Sat; Sun tickets sold on Sat) For available tickets, phone 312/977-1755.

Chicago magazine is helpful for anyone visiting Chicago; it's available at most newsstands. *Key-This Week in Chicago* and *Where,* at major hotels, provide up-to-date information. For additional information, see any of the daily newspapers; special sections to look at are *Friday* in the Friday *Chicago Tribune,* the *Arts & Entertainment* section in the Sunday *Chicago Tribune,* and the *Weekend Plus* section of the Friday *Sun-Times.* A free weekly newspaper, *The Reader,* provides information about local events, art, and entertainment.

There are five Illinois Travel Information centers, located at 310 South Michigan Avenue, at the Sears Tower, at the James R. Thompson Center (100 W Randolph St), and at Midway and O'Hare airports. (Mon-Fri)

The Pumping Station, at the corner of Chicago and Michigan avenues, houses a visitor information center that provides brochures and information about points of interest and transportation. (Daily)

Contact the Chicago Office of Tourism, Chicago Cultural Center, 78 East Washington Street, 60602; phone 312/744-2400 or toll-free 800/226-6632. The Office of Tourism distributes an event calendar, maps and museum guides, and hotel and restaurant guides, plus other information about the Chicago area. (Mon-Sat, also Sun afternoons)

Public Transportation

Buses, subways and elevated trains Chicago Transit Authority (CTA)/Regional Transit Authority (RTA), phone 312/836-7000.

Chicago Fun Facts

- The world's first skyscraper was built in Chicago in 1885.
- Chicago is home to the world's longest street: Western Avenue.
- The Hostess Twinkie was first produced in Chicago in 1930.
- Chicago is home to the world's largest food festival–the Taste of Chicago (see SPECIAL EVENTS)–every summer in Grant Park.
- The Chicago Public Library is the world's largest public library with a collection of more than 2 million books.
- The abbreviation ORD for Chicago's O'Hare Airport comes from its old name, Orchard Field.

What to See and Do

Adler Planetarium & Astronomy Museum. *1300 S Lake Shore Dr, Chicago (60605). On a peninsula in Lake Michigan. Phone 312/322-0300. www.adlerplanetarium.org.* One of the oldest observatories in the Western Hemisphere, the Adler Planetarium offers a high-tech look at the night sky. In May 2003, schoolchildren were able to videoconference with astronauts and cosmonauts aboard the International Space Station, and astronomers are studying meteorite fragments that landed in Chicago's suburbs that same month. The planetarium works closely with scientists at the University of Chicago (see) and is linked via computer with the Apache Point observatory in New Mexico. Exhibits commemorate the Space Race of the 1960s, as well as new techniques to learn more about the Milky Way. Tours of the facility are available, and shows are included with the price of admission. If you want a bargain, go between September and December on Mondays and Tuesdays, when admission is free. (Mon-Fri 9:30 am-4:30 pm, Sat-Sun 9 am-4:30 pm; Memorial Day-Labor Day: daily until 6 pm; closed Thanksgiving, Dec 25) **$$$**

American Girl Place. *111 E Chicago Ave, Chicago (60611). Phone 312/943-9400; toll-free 877/247-5223. www.americangirlplace.com.* If you're strolling around downtown Chicago, you're bound to see legions of girls toting red shopping bags from American Girl

Place. Dolls are the major draw here, but the store also sells clothing and accessories (for dolls and their owners) and doll furniture and toys. American Girl Place also features a café (reservations recommended), various special events, and a Broadway-style show ($$$$), *Circle of Friends: An American Girls Musical,* at the on-site theater. (Sun 9 am-7 pm, Mon-Thurs 10 am-7 pm, Fri 10 am-9 pm, Sat 9 am-9 pm) **FREE**

American Sightseeing Chicago. *27 E Monroe St, Chicago (60603). Phone 312/251-3100; toll-free 800/621-4153. www.americansightseeing.org/chicago.htm.* Tours depart from the Palmer House hotel (see) and range from two to eight hours. Options include a historic Oak Park and Frank Lloyd Wright tour and a dinner tour of Chinatown. **$$$$**

Apollo Theatre. *2540 N Lincoln Ave, Chicago (60614). Phone 773/935-6100; fax 773/935-6214. www.apollochicago.com.* An intimate theater in Chicago's Lincoln Park neighborhood, the Apollo has been home to both famous and infamous productions over the years. The year 2003 saw a run of Eve Ensler's *The Vagina Monologues,* and previous years have included productions of the plays of Neil Simon, Clifford Odets, and many others. Built in 1978, the theater saw many productions by the Steppenwolf Theater Company (including *Balm in Gilead* with Gary Sinise and John Malkovich), as well as native Chicagoan Jim Belushi starring in David Mamet's *Sexual Perversity in Chicago.* It is a great setting in which to see a show, with small crowds filling the seats and big names on the stage.

Arie Crown Theater. *2301 S Lake Shore Dr, Chicago (60616). Phone 312/791-6000. www.ariecrown.com.* This theater near McCormick Place (see) hosts an irregular lineup of plays, concerts, and conferences. It seats 5,000.

★ **Art Institute of Chicago.** *111 S Michigan Ave, Chicago (60603). Phone 312/443-3600. www.artic.edu.* No visit to Chicago is complete without a stop at the Art Institute of Chicago, a local treasure with an international reputation. Adjacent to Millennium Park on South Michigan Avenue, this 1879 Beaux Arts building, originally part of the Columbian Exposition, houses more than 300,000 works of art within its ten curatorial departments. The museum has what's considered the finest and most comprehensive modern and contemporary art collection in the world, one of the largest arms collections in America, and one of the two finest collections of Japanese woodblock prints. Highlights include Georges Seurat's *A Sunday on La Grande Jatte—1884,* Grant Wood's *American Gothic,* Edward Hopper's *Nighthawks,* 33 Monet paintings, Marc Chagall stained-glass windows, a reconstructed Adler and Sullivan Chicago Stock Exchange trading room, and significant photo and architectural drawing collections. You can also attend free daily lectures, visit the well-stocked gift shop, dine at one of three restaurants, including a summertime garden, and take a special tour for the visually impaired. Free admission Tues. (Mon-Wed, Fri 10:30 am-4:30 pm; Thurs 10:30 am-8 pm; Sat-Sun 10 am-5 pm; closed Thanksgiving, Dec 25) **$$**

Auditorium Building. *430 S Michigan Ave, Chicago (60605).* (1889) Landmark structure designed by World-renowned architects Louis Sullivan and Dankmar Adler. The interior is noted for its intricate system of iron framing, breathtaking ornamentation, and near-perfect acoustics. Now houses Roosevelt University (see).

Auditorium Theatre. *50 E Congress Pkwy, Chicago (60605). Phone 312/922-2110; fax 312/431-2360. www.auditoriumtheatre.org.* The Auditorium Theatre building, designed by world-renowned architects Louis Sullivan and Dankmar Adler, underwent a facelift in 2003, getting a new state-of-the-art stage and orchestra pit. The stage was returned to its original height, as designed in the 1880s. The building has been host to many different types of performances in its history, from large-scale musical productions like *Les Misérables* to its function in the 1960s and 1970s as the premier concert venue in Chicago, hosting names like Jimi Hendrix and Janis Joplin. The Joffrey Ballet opened the new stage in late 2003, and the historic building begins yet another era as one of the premier places to watch a show of any kind in the City of Big Shoulders.

Balmoral Park Race Track. *26435 S Dixie Hwy, Crete (60417). 25 miles S on I-94 to Hwy 394, continue S to Elmscourt Ln. Phone 708/672-1414; fax 708/672-5932. www.balmoralpark.com.* Harness racing. (All year, days vary)

Balzekas Museum of Lithuanian Culture. *6500 S Pulaski Rd, Chicago (60629). South Side. Phone 773/582-6500.* Antiques, art, children's museum, memorabilia, and literature spanning 1,000 years of Lithuanian history. Exhibits include amber, armor and antique weapons, rare maps, textiles, dolls, stamps, coins; research library. (Daily; closed Jan 1, Thanksgiving, Dec 25) Free admission Mon. **$$**

Bloomingdale's Home + Furniture Store. *600 N Wabash Ave, Chicago (60611). Phone 312/324-7500.* Set in the historic Medinah Temple, formerly the home of Chicago's Shriners, this four-level wonder is filled with both architectural and commercial treasures. If the store's ample selection of high-end kitchenware, linens, and home furnishings doesn't grab your attention, the magnificently restored stained-glass windows, soaring dome, and shining façade are sure to have you oohing and aahing. (Mon-Sat 10 am-8 pm, Sun 11 am-7 pm)

Briar Street Theatre. *3133 N Halsted St, Chicago (60657). Phone 773/348-4000; fax 773/348-7365.* The Briar Street Theatre has been the Chicago home of the national sensation Blue Man Group, which incorporates everyday objects like metal drums and pipes into a musical experience rife with color and comedy. Prior to men in blue body paint entertaining the crowds, the 625-seat venue hosted long-running renditions of *Driving Miss Daisy* and Steve Martin's *Picasso at the Lapin Agile.* It's easily accessible by CTA rapid transit, and tickets are less pricey than at many other theaters in the city. The theater sits on the old site of the horse stables of Marshall Field's department store, having been used as a theater only since 1985.

Blue Man Group. *3133 N Halsted St, Chicago (60657). In the Briar Street Theatre. Phone 773/348-4000. www.blueman.com.* Blue Man Group is a percussion (drums) band and performance group that's literally blue—all three members cover themselves in blue body paint. The group performs by thumping on drums, banging on barrels, and pounding on pipes. The heart-pounding, entertaining, dramatic performance includes audience members (although no one is forced to participate against his will); if you so choose, you may even get painted, too! Performances last just over two hours. **$$$$**

Cadillac-Palace Theater. *151 W Randolph St, Chicago (60601). Phone 312/977-1700.* This theater is a Chicago landmark inspired by the decadence of the palace at Versailles in France. It originally played first-run movies during the 1920s and 1930s and was converted to a live theater in the 1950s. It was purchased by the Bismarck hotel in the 1970s and turned into a banquet hall. In 1999, the theater reopened in its origial role and hosted performances of Giuseppe Verdi's *Aida* (as adapted by Elton John and Tim Rice), as well as the hit theatrical production of Disney's *The Lion King.*

Carson Pirie Scott. *1 S State St, Chicago (60603). At Madison St. In the Loop. Phone 312/641-7000. www.carsons.com.* (1899) This landmark department store building is considered architect Louis Sullivan's masterpiece. Extraordinary cast-iron ornamentation on the first and second floors frames display windows like paintings. (Daily; closed holidays)

★ **Chicago Architecture Foundation tours.** *224 S Michigan Ave, Chicago (60604). Phone 312/922-3432. www.architecture.org.* For an interesting and informative introduction to Chicago, sign up for a Chicago Architecture Foundation tour. This not-for-profit organization dedicated to raising public awareness of architecture features 65 different tours given by more than 450 volunteer (but extraordinarily well trained and knowledgeable) docents. The two-hour Loop and Historic Skyscraper walking tours give an excellent general history of the city and how it grew, while other tours cater to more specialized interests, such as Art Deco buildings, the Theater District, modern skyscrapers, and Loop sculpture, as well as individual city neighborhoods like Old Town, River North, Printers Row, the Gold Coast, and the Sheffield Historic District. One of the most popular tours is the 90-minute Architecture River Cruise that passes more than 50 architecturally significant sights. Bus tours, bike tours, and even 'L' train tours are also available (on specific dates only). You can purchase tickets and meet for tours at one of two tour centers on Michigan Avenue. **$$$$** Among the tours offered are

Chicago Highlights Bus Tour. *224 S Michigan Ave, Chicago (60604). Phone 312/922-3432. www.architecture.org.* This four-hour bus tour covers the Loop, the Gold Coast, Hyde Park, three historic districts, and three university campuses; includes interior of Frank Lloyd Wright's Robie House (see). Reservations required. (April-Nov: Wed, Fri, Sat and Sun at 9:30 am; Dec-March: Sat at 9:30 am) **$$$$**

Chicago River Boat Tour. *455 E Illinois St, Chicago (60611). Phone 312/922-3432. www.architecture.org.* This 1 1/2-hour tour covers the north and south branches of the Chicago River, with views of the city's celebrated riverfront architecture; historic 19th-century railroad bridges and warehouses, 20th-century bridgehouses, and magnificent Loop skyscrapers. Reservations required. (May-Sept, daily; Oct Tues, Thurs, Sat-Sun; no tours Labor Day) **$$$$**

Singin' the Blues

It all started in a small, lopsided former automobile parts factory at 2120 S Michigan Ave, an address immortalized by the Rolling Stones in their bluesy instrumental of the same name. The building was purchased by the Chess brothers, and, from 1957 to 1967, it operated as the home of Chess Records, the recording studio that gave the world the sad, edgy sound of the "Chicago blues."

They all recorded here, or wanted to: the great Muddy Waters, Koko Taylor, and Etta James. Willie Dixon, who, with Magic Sam, Otis Rush, and Luther Allison, helped define Chicago's West Side scene. Junior Wells, whose harmonica playing—"harps," as it was called—influenced countless blues greats, including Junior's longtime friend and partner, Chicago legend Buddy Guy. Junior met Buddy at a Battle of the Blues event, which Buddy won. They hit it off and collaborated for years, taking the sound of the Chicago blues a step further.

What exactly were the Chicago blues? When blacks migrating from the Mississippi Delta came through Memphis and settled in Chicago, their soulful music took on a tougher edge, mandated by the rhythms of the city and the noise of the clubs. Chicago blues were the Southern blues gone edgier and amplified.

In the early days, Buddy was a red-hot backup musician. But as the years wore on, he became a showman, a flamboyant stylist who would hit his guitar against a microphone to get an acoustic sound, pluck its strings with his tongue, or hit the strings with a belt or drumstick to get a tone. He could coax any sound he wanted out of that thing, they said. Buddy made his guitar talk to you, they said. They said other things, too. Eric Clapton called him the greatest blues guitar player in the world and asked Buddy to play with him at Royal Albert Hall. The accolades inspired Guy's ironically titled album, *Damn Right I've Got the Blues,* the first of his four albums to win Grammys. Clapton wasn't the only rock star influenced by Guy, nor was he the first. The Rolling Stones asked Buddy and Junior Wells to open for them on their 1970 tour.

In 1989, Buddy opened a club on Chicago's South Side, Buddy Guy's Legends, so that blues artists would have a home in the Windy City. At Legends, blues fans eat from a Cajun-inspired menu while listening to a jam on Mondays, an acoustic blues artist on Fridays and Saturdays, and a consistently high level of talent the other four nights of the week. You never know when Mick Jagger and Ron Wood will drop in for an impromptu jam of "Little Red Rooster," as they did when the Stones were last in town for a gig. And you know it's January because that's when Buddy's in town, stunning the crowd, plucking the guitar with his tongue, as great as he ever was—even greater, richer, more soulful. Damn right, he's still got the blues.

Buddy Guy's Legends is open Sunday 6 pm-2 am, Monday-Thursday 5 pm-2 am, Friday 4 pm-2 am, and Saturday 5 pm-3 am. Tickets are available for general admission; you can buy them through Ticketmaster, but plan to arrive at the small, 120-seat club early for a decent seat. For general information, phone 312/427-0333 or visit the Web site www.buddyguys.com.

Graceland Cemetery Tour. *4001 N Clark St, Chicago (60613). Phone 773/525-1105.* Walking through Graceland Cemetery on the city's north side is like taking a step back into Chicago's early history. Not only will you recognize the names of the movers and shakers who put Chicago on the map—Philip Armour, Mayor Joseph Medill, Cyrus McCormick, George Pullman, Potter Palmer, and Marshall Field, to name a few—but you'll also find memorials to the people who helped build it: architects Louis Sullivan, Daniel Burnham, John Root, and Mies van der Rohe. Established in 1860, Graceland, with its winding pathways and gorgeous old trees, is perfect for solo exploration any time of the year. Throughout the cemetery, you'll discover varied and artistic memorials, from Greek temples and Egyptian pyramids to Celtic crosses and ethereal angels. Highlights include Louis Sullivan's tomb for Carrie Eliza Getty, a landmark described as the beginning of modern architecture in America; Daniel Burnham's island resting place in the middle of the lake; and Mies van der Rohe's elegantly understated grave marker. (Daily 8 am-4:30 pm) **FREE**

Loop Walking Tours. *224 S Michigan Ave, Chicago (60604). Depart from Tour Center. Phone 312/922-3432. www.architecture.org.* Each tour is two hours long. *Early Skyscrapers* traces the origins of the Chicago school of architecture and the skyscrapers built from 1880 to 1940. The tour includes the Monadnock and Rookery buildings. *Modern & Beyond* reviews important newer buildings, including the Federal Center, the IBM Building, and the James R. Thompson Center; also public murals and sculptures by Calder, Chagall, Miro, Picasso, Henry Moore, and Dubuffet. (Daily) **$$$**

Chicago Cultural Center. *78 E Washington St, Chicago (60602). In the Loop. Phone 312/744-6630; fax 312/744-2089. www.ci.chi.il.us/tourism/culturalcenter.* If you have a couple of hours free, you may want to wander into the Chicago Cultural Center on Michigan Avenue between Randolph and Washington, a gem of a building that offers a wealth of free daily programming and ongoing exhibits. The landmark building, formerly a library, features Tiffany glass domes, mosaics, and marble walls and stairs. The center itself often offers exhibitions of groundbreaking art, as well as frequent performances by renowned poets and musicians. On weekdays during the summer, you can catch "Lunchbreak," a program designed to infuse lunch in the bustling city with good music in a great setting. (Mon-Thurs 10 am-7 pm; Fri until 6 pm; Sat until 5 pm; Sun 11 am-5 pm; archives closed Sun; closed holidays) **FREE**

Chicago Fire Academy. *558 W DeKoven St, Chicago (60607). West Side. Phone 312/747-8151.* Built on the site where the Great Chicago Fire of 1871 is believed to have started. Legend has it that it was a cow in Mrs. O'Leary's barn knocking over a lantern that began the fire, but recent investigations suggest this story may be fictitious. The fire academy pays tribute to those who serve the Windy City and donate their lives to the safety of Chicago's citizens. **FREE**

Chicago Historical Society. *1601 N Clark St, Chicago (60614). Clark St at North Ave. Phone 312/642-4600. www.chicagohs.org.* Changing exhibits focus on the history and development of Chicago. Selected aspects of Illinois and US history, including galleries devoted to costumes, decorative arts, and architecture. Pioneer craft demonstrations; hands-on gallery. Free admission Mon. Additional charges for special exhibits. (Daily; closed Jan 1, Thanksgiving, Dec 25) **$$**

Chicago Loop Synagogue. *16 S Clark St, Chicago (60603). In the Loop. Phone 312/346-7370. www.chicagoloopsynagogue.org.* (1957) The eastern wall of this building is a unique example of contemporary stained glass, depicting ancient Hebraic symbols whirling through the cosmos.

Chicago Motor Coach Company. *1 N Water Tower, Chicago. Phone 312/666-1000.* Double-decker tours depart from the Sears Tower at Jackson and Wacker, the Field Museum of Natural History, Michigan and Pearson, and Michigan and Wacker.

Chicago Neighborhood Tours. *77 E Randolph St, Chicago (60602). Phone 312/742-1190. www.chgocitytours.com.* Tours depart at 10 am from the Chicago Cultural Center and last approximately four hours. Narrated tours visit 11 different neighborhoods via motor coach. Tours are held on Saturday only, spotlighting a different area each week. Reservations are strongly recommended. **$$$$**

Chicago Temple. *77 W Washington St, Chicago (60602). In the Loop. Phone 312/236-4548. www.chicagotemple.org.* (First Methodist Episcopal Church, 1923) At 568 feet from street level to the tip of its Gothic tower, this is the highest church spire in the world. Tours (Mon-Sat 2 pm, Sun after 8:30 am and 11 am services; no tours holidays).

Chicago Theatre. *175 N State St, Chicago (60601). Phone 312/443-1130; fax 312/263-9505.* The Chicago Theatre may be best known for the flashy sign spelling out CHICAGO vertically above its marquee, but visitors to the theater likely will be more impressed by its magnificent French baroque design. Proceed through the front doors, passing underneath a miniature replica of the Arc de Triomphe, and enter an opulent five-story lobby modeled after the Mansarts Chapel at the Palace of Versailles. The extravagant and ornate interior features bronze light fixtures with Steuben glass shades, crystal chandeliers, polished marble, and soaring murals hand-painted on the auditorium's ceiling. Opened in 1921 as the city's first movie palace, the Chicago Theatre today hosts live performances by internationally renowned musicians, comedians, and actors. The theater's original Wurlitzer pipe organ has been restored and still produces a lush, powerful sound.

Chicago Tribune Tower. *435 N Michigan Ave, Chicago (60611). Phone 312/222-3994.* (1925) Essentially, this 36-story tower is a *moderne* building with a Gothic-detailed base and crown. It does exactly what publisher Joseph Medill intended: it "thames" the Chicago River. The tower's once strong foundation has been loosening in recent years, and structural engineers have noted that the edifice has been slowly sinking at the rate of almost a foot a year due to seepage from a sublevel bog just west along the riverbank. Bits and pieces of historic structures from around the world are embedded in the exterior walls of the lower floors.

Chicago Trolley Company. *233 S Wacker Dr, Chicago (60606). Phone 773/648-5000. www.chicagotrolley.com.* One-fee, all-day ride on a trolley or double-decker bus, with the ability to hop on and off at major sites. The tour goes as far north as the John Hancock Center, as far south as the Field Museum of Natural History, as far west as the Sears Tower, and as far east as Navy Pier. **$$$$**

Chicago Water Works. *163 E Pearson, Chicago (60611). Phone 312/744-8783.* The pumping station, opened in 1869, is responsible for pumping water to the central Chicago district. Walk through to see how the station works and visit the other attractions inside. Visitor information booth (7:30 am-7 pm). City of Chicago store (Daily 9 am-6 pm). Hot Tix booth (Tues-Sat 10 am-6 pm, Sun noon-5 pm).

Chicago White Sox (MLB). *US Cellular Field, 333 W 35th St, Chicago (60616). Phone 312/674-1000; toll-free 866/769-4263; fax 312/674-5500. www.whitesox.com.* On paper, it might look like the White Sox changed stadiums to begin the 2003 season, but really it was just the moniker of the building that switched from historic Comiskey Park (honoring former owner Charles) to US Cellular Field. **$$$$**

Chinatown. *Cermak Rd and Wentworth Ave, Chicago (60616). Phone 312/326-5320 (Chinatown Chamber of Commerce). www.chicagochinatown.org.* Though not as large as New York's or San Francisco's Chinatowns, Chicago's Chinatown is a vibrant and lively cultural center that makes for a fascinating visit. Located south of the Loop at Cermak and Wentworth, Chinatown's boundary is marked by a tiled gateway and traditional architecture that is reflected in the smallest details, such as the rooftops, lampposts, and phone booths. Within a ten-block radius are 10,000 community members, more than 40 restaurants, 20 gifts shops, herbal and tea stores, and bakeries. Locals tend to visit on Sunday mornings for dim sum, but it's also fun to be in the neighborhood during any of the traditional festivals, including Chinese New Year, the Dragon Boat Festival, and the mid-autumn Moon Festival. Chinatown is a 10- to 15-minute cab ride from the Loop. During summer weekends, it is also accessible via a free trolley that departs from the Field Museum of Natural History and from the intersection of State Street and Roosevelt Road. **FREE**

Civic Opera Building. *20 N Wacker Dr, Chicago (60606). In the Loop. Phone 312/332-2244.* (1929) On the lower levels, under 45 floors of commercial office space, is the richly Art Deco, 3,400-seat Civic Opera House, home of the Lyric Opera of Chicago.

Civic Opera House. *20 N Wacker Dr, Chicago (60606). Phone 312/419-0033. www.civicoperahouse.com.* Owned and operated by the Lyric Opera of Chicago.

Lyric Opera of Chicago. *20 N Wacker Dr, Chicago (60606). Phone 312/419-0033. www.lyricopera.org.* Chicago's Lyric Opera performs some of the biggest names in operatic theater. Each year offers recognizable stories, as well as a few to broaden the horizons of even the most seasoned opera connoisseur. Often, the operas are done in the language in which they were written, but with English subtitles projected above the stage so that all can follow the story. Each season begins with a new 12-person repertory cast chosen in March and given additional professional training to make Chicago's performances among the finest anywhere. **$$$$**

DePaul University. *Loop Campus, 1 E Jackson Blvd, Chicago (60604). Lincoln Park campus, Fullerton and Sheffield aves. Phone 312/362-8300. www.depaul.edu.* (20,500 students) The Lincoln Park campus, with its blend of modern and Gothic architecture, is an integral part of Chicago's historic Lincoln Park neighborhood. The Blue Demons, DePaul's basketball team, play home games at the Allstate Arena. Tours (by appointment).

DuSable Museum of African-American History. *740 E 56th Pl, Chicago (60637). South Side. Phone 773/947-0600. www.dusablemuseum.org.* African and African American art objects; displays of black history in Africa and the United States. Extensive collection includes paintings, sculptures, artifacts, textiles, books, and photographs. Free admission Sun. (Tues-Sun, Jan-May: Mon; closed Jan 1, Thanksgiving, Dec 25) **$$**

Eli's Cheesecake World. *6701 W Forest Preserve Dr, Chicago (60634). Phone 773/736-3417; toll-free 800/354-2253. www.elicheesecake.com.* Watch bakers create Eli's claim-to-fame cheesecakes while visiting the 62,000-square-foot bakery, taste the end result, and shop for a take-home supply. (Walk-in tours Mon-Fri at 1 pm; tours by reservation Mon-Fri 10 am-3 pm) **$**

Elks National Veterans Memorial. *2750 N Lakeview Ave, Chicago (60614). Phone 773/755-4876. www.elks.org/memorial.* The Elks Fraternal Order, founded in 1868, erected this memorial designed by New York architect Egerton Swarthout in 1926 to honor Americans' profound sacrifices in World War I. The memorial has since become a tribute to Americans who lost their lives in World War II, the Korean War, and the Vietnam War. Visitors are welcome to walk inside the domed structure to view the 100-foot rotunda made of marble and adorned with murals, art-glass windows, and bronze sculptures. The rotunda opens into an ornate reception room, also available for public viewing. (Mon-Fri 9 am-5 pm; Apr-Nov, also Sat-Sun 10 am-5 pm)

ESPN Zone. *43 E Ohio St, Chicago (60611). Phone 312/644-3776. espn.go.com/espninc/zone/chicago.html.* Sports fans flock here to view events on big-screen TVs, play an array of video and simulated games, dine, drink, and purchase ESPN-related merchandise. (Sun-Thurs 11:30 am-11 pm, Fri 11:30 am-12 am, Sat 11 am-12 am)

Federal Reserve Bank of Chicago. *230 S LaSalle St, Chicago (60604). Phone 312/322-5322. www.chicagofed.org.* Tour the visitor center of one of the 12 regional Reserve Banks across the United States and learn about money and banking—everything from counterfeit currency to interest rates. (Mon-Fri 9 am-4:15 pm, except bank holidays; tours at 1 pm) **FREE**

★ Field Museum of Natural History. *1400 S Lake Shore Dr, Chicago (60605). Phone 312/922-9410. www.fmnh.org.* The Field Museum, dedicated to the world's natural history, has made great strides to improve its already vast collection in recent years, with the biggest addition (literally!) being Sue, the largest and most complete tyrannosaurus Rex skeleton ever unearthed. Sue adds to a fine collection of artifacts from bygone civilizations like those in Egypt and Mesopotamia. Past exhibits have included a look at how chocolate has influenced the world and "Baseball As America," which detailed how America's pastime follows closely the threads of history that surround it. Be sure to look for the museum's collections from China, Japan, and the rest of the Orient. A list of touchables for the visually impaired is available. Discounted admission in Jan-Feb, mid-Sept-late Dec on Mon-Tues. (Daily 9 am-5 pm; closed Dec 25) **$$**

Ford Center for the Performing Arts Oriental Theater. *24 W Randolph St, Chicago (60602). Phone 312/977-1700.* The Oriental Theater was originally a movie house that doubled as an entertainment venue for musicians like Duke Ellington during the early 20th century. The theater closed its doors to moviegoers in the 1980s but came back with a flourish. Re-opening in 1998, it was converted into a place to see live shows, sharing the Theater District with places like the Chicago and Shubert theaters. Recent productions have included *The Producers, Mamma Mia, Ragtime,* and *Miss Saigon.*

Fourth Presbyterian Church. *126 E Chestnut St, Chicago (60611). Phone 312/787-4570. www.fourthchurch.org.* Completed in 1914, this beautiful church is a fine example of Gothic design. One of its architects, Ralph A. Cram, was a leader of the Gothic Revival in the United States. Tours are available by appointment or after Sun services. (Daily)

Garfield Park and Conservatory. *300 N Central Park Ave, Chicago (60624). Phone 312/746-5100. www.garfield-conservatory.org.* Outdoor formal gardens. Conservatory has eight houses and propagating houses on more than 5 acres. Permanent exhibits. Four major shows annually at Horticultural Hall and Show House. (Fri-Wed 9 am-5 pm, Thurs to 8 pm) **FREE**

Goodman Theatre. *170 N Dearborn St, Chicago (60601). Phone 312/443-3800. www.goodman-theatre.org.* The Goodman Theatre can be considered a breeding ground for up-and-coming actors and productions. A good example is its production of Eugene O'Neill's *A Long Day's Journey into Night,* which took star Brian Dennehy with it to Broadway and captured several Tony Awards. Actors of Dennehy's caliber are not uncommon at the Goodman, as other theater dignitaries like Charles S. Dutton regularly perform works by such noted playwrights as August Wilson and Steven Sondheim. Tickets can be pricey, but not as expensive as a Broadway show, and there are discounts for students and groups. Most shows are adult oriented, but the Goodman does make a point of providing family-friendly fare, including its annual production of Charles Dickens's *A Christmas Carol.*

Grant Park. *331 E Randolph St, Chicago (60601). Stretches from Randolph St to McFetridge Dr. In the Loop. Phone 312/742-7648. www.chicagoparkdistrict.com.* Grant Park was built on a landfill created by debris from the Great Chicago Fire of 1871. Now it stands as one of the great landmarks of the city, with majestic Buckingham Fountain as its centerpiece. The fountain is one piece of the original design that has survived and looks as though it's right out of Louis XIV's Palace at Versailles. Each year, the Taste of Chicago (see SPECIAL EVENTS) is held here, as are many picnics and smaller festivals. Grant Park borders the Art Institute of Chicago (see) and runs parallel with Michigan Avenue. You can enjoy concerts at the Petrillo Music Shell or relax on the lawn on summer evenings to watch outdoor movies during the yearly Chicago Outdoor Film Festival (see SPECIAL EVENTS). A beautiful green centerpiece to the Windy City, the park also includes fragrant rose gardens that frame the north and south end of Buckingham Fountain. (Daily 6 am-11 pm)

Buckingham Fountain. *Grant Park, Columbus Dr and Congress Pkwy, Chicago (60611). Phone 312/742-7529. www.chicagoparkdistrict.com.* When the World Cup was held in Chicago in 1994, foreign visitors identified the Buckingham Fountain as the "Bundy fountain" because of its prominent place in the opening credits of the TV show *Married with Children.* That notoriety aside, Buckingham Fountain is an integral part of the city and one of the largest fountains in the world. The fountain was given to the city by Kate Buckingham in 1927 in honor of her brother. Every minute, 133 jets spray approximately 14,000 gallons of water as high as 150 feet. Every hour on the hour, there's a 20-minute water display (accompanied, at dusk, by lights and music). For locals, the fountain marks the changing seasons; when it's turned on—to much fanfare—it heralds the beginning of summer, and, when it's turned off, it signals that the dreaded Chicago winter will soon follow. (May-early Oct, daily 10 am-11 pm) **FREE**

Gray Line Bus Tours. *17 E Monroe St, Chicago (60603). Phone 312/251-3107; toll-free 800/621-4153. www.grayline.com.* Tours range from 1 1/2 to 7 hours. **$$$$**

Green Mill. *4802 N Broadway St, Chicago (60640). Phone 773/878-5552.* The oldest jazz club in America, the Green Mill is located in the still-dicey Uptown neighborhood. It's more than a great place to hear jazz; it's also a chance to step back in time. With a vintage sign out front and a gorgeous carved bar inside, this former speakeasy of the Capone gang reeks of atmosphere (and cigarettes) of a bygone era. The jazz, however, is strictly contemporary, showcasing some of the most acclaimed musicians working today, from international performers to local luminaries such as Patricia Barber, Kurt Elling, and Von Freeman. On weeknights, you might find swing or a big band; on weekend nights, several acts pack in aficionados until the wee hours; and on Sundays, you can experience the Poetry Slam (the nation's first, hosted by Marc Smith, the "godfather" of poetry slams), where area poets test their mettle against audience reaction. (Daily) **$$$**

Harborside International Golf Center. *11001 S Doty Ave E, Chicago (60628). Phone 312/782-7837. www.harborsidegolf.com.* Located just south of downtown Chicago, Harborside was manufactured by architect Dick Nugent out of a converted landfill into one of the most renowned municipal courses in America. The center has two courses, the Starboard and the Port layouts, and features four tee boxes on each hole to accommodate almost every golfer. The center's practice facility is also top-notch, with driving ranges of longer than 400 yards and many opportunities to practice middle irons and short games—even at night, as the 58-acre practice facility is fully lit. **$$$$**

Haymarket Riot Monument. *1300 W Jackson Blvd, Chicago (60607).* Erected in 1893, the monument commemorates the riot that killed seven policemen when a bomb exploded during a labor strike on May 4, 1886. The statue still stirs passions over labor issues; labor organizations gather at the statue every year on the Sunday closest to May 4, as well as November 11, the anniversary of Black Friday.

Holy Name Cathedral. *735 N State St, Chicago (60610). Phone 312/787-8040. www.holynamecathedral.org.* The home to the Chicago archdiocese and Francis Cardinal George, Holy Name is a good example of Gothic Revival architecture in Chicago. Thousands of parishoners attend services at Holy Name each week, many of them to hear Cardinal George on Sunday morning. The church is also affiliated with the Francis Xavier Warde School.

Illinois Institute of Technology (IIT). *3300 S Federal St, Chicago (60616). South Side. Phone 312/567-3000. www.iit.edu.* (1892) (6,000 students) Students from more than 100 countries converge on this campus to engage themselves in IIT's Interprofessional Project, which aims to teach students the skills they'll need to fit in wherever they choose in a job market that is constantly expanding technologically. Ninety-eight percent of the faculty (who teach almost all the classes, rather than teaching assistants) hold doctorate or other terminal degrees. The campus was designed by architect Mies van de Rohe.

International Museum of Surgical Science. *1524 N Lake Shore Dr, Chicago (60610). Phone 312/642-6502. www.imss.org.* Covering the advancement of surgical medicine across more than four millennia of history, this four-story museum housed in an old mansion organizes its exhibits into categories like radiology, orthopedics, and "A Day in the Life of a Turn-of-the-Century Apothecary." Located on scenic Lake Shore Drive in the heart of the Windy City, the museum offers free admission on Tuesday. There are permanent exhibits, like the optical history exhibit and displays of Victorian-era surgical implements, as well as rotating features covering subjects like art's depiction of anatomy. (Sept-Apr, Tues-Sat; May-Aug, Tues-Sun; 10 am-4 pm) **$$**

Jackson Park Golf Club. *6400 Richards Dr, Chicago (60645). 63rd St and Lake Shore Dr. Phone 312/245-0909.* On Chicago's near south side is this short, but still tough, course. Several par-fours measure less than 300 yards, but they're all deceptively difficult. The course's two par-fives are situated next to one another on the back nine and can easily ruin a good round of golf. The greens fee is always reasonable, with 18 holes and a cart available for just $25 at most times. For twilight golfers, the rate is just $17. **$$$$**

John Hancock Center. *875 N Michigan Ave, Chicago (60611). Phone 312/751-3681; toll-free 888/875-8439 (observatory). www.hancock-observatory.com.* Anchoring North Michigan Avenue is yet another undeniable Chicago landmark, the John Hancock Center, which at 1,127 feet and 100 floors is the world's 13th tallest building. Since completion in 1969, this innovative office/residential building with its distinctive exterior X bracing—which eliminated the need for inner support beams, thus increasing usable space—has won numerous architectural awards. It also claims many notables, including the world's highest residence and the world's highest indoor swimming pool. The 94th-floor observatory features an open-air skywalk, a history wall chronicling Chicago's growth, multi lingual "sky tours," and a 360-degree view that spans 80 miles and four states (Michigan, Indiana, Wisconsin, and Illinois). The best viewing is from sunset onward, when the sun shimmers on the skyline and lake. Visitors who want to extend the experience can dine at the Signature Room (see), an upscale restaurant located on the building's 95th floor. (Daily 9 am-11 pm) **$$**

★ **Lake Michigan.** *Phone 312/742-7529. www.chicagoparkdistrict.com.* Chicago's lakefront reflects the vision of architect Daniel Burnham, whose 1909 Plan for Chicago specified that the shoreline remain publicly owned and enjoyed by all. It is also one of the things that make this city sparkle. After all, how many major cities have bathing beaches—31 in total—within the city limits? In addition to beaches, the lakefront sports 18 miles of bicycle, jogging, and in-line skating paths, several golf courses and driving ranges, skating rinks, tennis courts, field houses, theaters, and more, all easily accessible and open to the public. Chicagoans rich and poor flock to the lakefront year-round to exercise, sunbathe, picnic, and simply enjoy the view. If you have the opportunity and the weather cooperates, rent a bicycle at Navy Pier and spend a few hours following the well-marked path north. Look for the chess players at North Avenue Beach and the skyline views from Montrose Harbor. (Daily sunrise-11 pm)

Lincoln Park. *2400 N Stockton Dr, Chicago (60614). Near North Side. Phone 312/742-7529.* The largest in Chicago, Lincoln Park stretches almost the entire length of the north end of the city along the lake. It contains statues of Lincoln, Hans Christian Andersen, Shakespeare, and others; nine-hole golf course, driving range, miniature golf, bike and jogging paths, obstacle course, protected beaches. In the park are

Lincoln Park Conservatory. *2391 N Stockton Dr, Chicago (60614). Near Fullerton Ave. Phone 312/742-7736.* Has four glass buildings, 18 propagating houses, and 3 acres of cold frames; formal and rock gardens; an extensive collection of orchids. Four major flower shows annually at the Show House. (Daily 9 am-5 pm) **FREE**

Lincoln Park Zoo. *2200 N Cannon Dr, Chicago (60614). W entrance, Webster Ave and Stockton Dr; E entrance, Cannon Dr off Fullerton Pkwy. Phone 312/742-2000. www.lpzoo.com.* The Lincoln Park Zoo may be small (just 35 acres), but it has so much going for it—it's free, it's open 365 days a year, and it's a leader in education and conservation—that this gem of a zoo is a big part of the Chicago experience. Not only can visitors enjoy seeing animals from around the world, including gorillas, big cats, polar bears, exotic birds, and reptiles, but they can do so in style among architecturally significant structures, beautiful gardens, and modern visitor facilities, all in a prime location in the heart of Chicago's famed Lincoln Park. Families can double their fun at the Farm in the Zoo, where children can milk cows, churn butter, groom goats, and experience a working farmhouse kitchen. Also available are paddleboat rentals on the adjacent lagoon, a restaurant, and special events like family sleepovers, trick-or-treating on Halloween, and caroling to the animals during Christmas. (Daily; hours vary by season) **FREE**

Lori's Designer Shoes. *824 W Armitage Ave, Chicago (60614). Phone 773/281-5655. www.lorisshoes.com.* Women all over Chicago know that *the* place to go for shoes is Lori's. Truly a shoe lover's mecca, you can find everything here from summer sandals to knee-high leather boots from such designers as Kenneth Cole, Fruit, and Via Spiga. Owner Lori Andre, a self-proclaimed shoe addict, makes frequent trips abroad so that she can keep her fashion-conscious clientele up-to-date on the latest trends and cutting-edge styles. And if you happen to find that pair of shoes you just can't do without, but—gasp!—your size is nowhere to be found, no need to worry. The helpful salespeople will be glad to call their other stores in west suburban Naperville (27 W Jefferson, phone 630/416-3663) and north suburban Highland Park (585 Central Ave, phone 847/681-1532) and Northfield (311 Happ Rd, phone 847/446-3818) to check for your size and have them delivered to the store. Because Lori's is so popular, weekends are usually packed, and the 5,000-square-foot space can become tight. Your best bet is to go on weekdays, when crowds are more subdued. This is especially true during end-of-season sales, when shoes (not to mention accessories like handbags, scarves, hats, and hosiery) are reduced by more than 50 percent. (Mon-Thurs 11 am-7 pm, Fri to 6 pm, Sat 10 am-6 pm, Sun noon-5 pm)

Loyola University. *Lake Shore campus, 6525 N Sheridan Rd, Chicago (60626). Downtown campus, 820 N Michigan Ave. Phone 773/274-3000 (Lake Shore campus). www.luc.edu.* (1870) (14,300 students) Four campuses in Chicago. One of the biggest Jesuit universities in the United States. Excellent law and nursing programs. Martin d'Arcy Museum of Art (phonc 773/508-2679; Tues-Sat; closed holidays, semester breaks). Fine Arts Gallery of the Edward Crown Center; exhibits (Mon-Fri; closed holidays).

Marina City. *300 N State St, Chicago (60610). N of Chicago River.* (1959-1967) Condominium and commercial building complex with marina and boat storage. Includes two 550-foot-tall cylindrical buildings; home of House of Blues club and hotel (see). Designed by Bertrand Goldberg Associates; one of the most unusual downtown living-working complexes in the United States.

★ **The Magnificent Mile.** *N Michigan Ave, Chicago (60611). Between Oak St and the Chicago River. www.themagnificentmile.com.* Although often compared to Rodeo Drive in Beverly Hills and Fifth Avenue in New York because of the quality and quantity of its stores, Chicago's Michigan Avenue has a vibe all its own. Known as the Magnificent Mile, this 1-mile flower-lined stretch between Oak Street and the Chicago River boasts 3.1 million square feet of retail space, 460 stores, 275 restaurants, 51 hotels, numerous art galleries, and two museums, all set among some of Chicago's most architecturally significant buildings. In addition, there are four vertical malls, including the granddaddy of them all, Water Tower Place; high-end department stores like Neiman Marcus, Saks Fifth Avenue, and Marshall Field's; and international retailers like Hermes, Cartier, Armani, Tiffany, and Burberry. (Daily; closed holidays) Also on the Magnificent Mile are

900 North Michigan Shops. *900 N Michigan Ave, Chicago (60611). Phone 312/915-3916. www.shop900.com.* More than 70 shops and restaurants, including Bloomingdale's and Gucci, surround a marble atrium in this mall that's adjacent to the Four Seasons (see). (Mon-Sat 10 am-7 pm, Sun noon-6 pm; closed holidays)

Chicago Place. *700 N Michigan Ave, Chicago (60611). Phone 312/642-4811. www.chicago-place.com.* This eight-story vertical mall has more than 45 stores and several restaurants. (Mon-Fri 10 am-7:30 pm, Sat 10 am-6:30 pm, Sun noon-5:30 pm; closed Jan 1, Easter, Dec 25)

Crate & Barrel. *646 N Michigan Ave, Chicago (60611). Phone 312/787-5900. www.crateandbarrel.com.* This housewares and home furnishings chain got its start in Chicago in 1962 and has since grown to more than 100 stores nationwide. Its large flagship store on Michigan Avenue brings in hordes of visitors drawn in by its clean designs, eye-catching colors, and reasonable prices. (Mon-Thurs 10 am-8 pm, Fri 10 am-9 pm, Sat 10 am-7 pm and Sun 11 am-6 pm)

Niketown. *669 N Michigan Ave, Chicago (60611). Phone 312/642-6363. www.niketown.com.* Since opening in 1993, this five-story sports store has become a major tourist attraction. It includes the

Nike Museum, a video theater, a display of athletic gear worn by Michael Jordan, and a basketball court with a 28-foot likeness of "His Airness." (Mon-Sat 10 am-9 pm, Sun to 6 pm; closed holidays)

Water Tower Place. *835 N Michigan Ave, Chicago (60611). Phone 312/440-3165. www.shopwatertower.com.* This atrium mall connected to the Ritz-Carlton (see) has more than 100 shops, including Chicago favorite Marshall Field's, plus restaurants and a movie theater complex. (Mon-Sat 10 am-7 pm, Sun noon-6 pm; closed holidays)

Marshall Field's. *111 N State St, Chicago (60602). In the Loop. Phone 312/781-4483. www.marshallfields.com.* A Chicago landmark for more than a century and one of the most famous stores in the country. A traditional Chicago meeting place is under its clock, which projects over the sidewalk. On one side is an inner court rising 13 stories, and on the other is a six-story rotunda topped by a Tiffany dome made of 1.6 million pieces of glass. (Mon-Sat 9 am-8 pm, Sun 11 am-6 pm; closed Thanksgiving, Dec 25)

Maywood Park Race Track. *8600 W North Ave, Maywood. I-290, exit 1st Ave N. Phone 708/343-4800; fax 708/348-2564. www.maywoodpark.com.* Pari-mutuel harness racing. Nightly Mon, Wed, Fri. Also TV simulcast thoroughbred racing (daily).

McCormick Place Convention Complex. *2301 S Lake Shore Dr, Chicago (60616). E 23rd St and S Lake Shore Dr. Phone 312/791-7000; fax 312/791-6543. www.mccormickplace.com.* McCormick Place, the largest convention and meeting space in the world, underwent an almost complete overhaul in the late 1990s to make it one of the most modern facilities imaginable. With over 2.2 million square feet of exhibition space and more than 110 meeting rooms, McCormick Place can accommodate any gathering. Annual outdoor and auto shows happen every year, and the facility also includes the newly renovated Arie Crown Theatre (see). Shops and restaurants are located inside the campus's four buildings (with a fifth—the west wing—in design), and a Hyatt Regency hotel (see) is attached to the convention center for easy access for presenters and visitors.

Merchandise Mart. *222 Merchandise Mart Plz, Chicago (60654). On Wells St just N of the Chicago River. Phone 312/527-7600. www.merchandisemart.com.* The world's largest commercial building, built in 1930; restaurants, shopping, and special events.

Mercury Skyline Cruiseline. *Wacker Dr and Michigan Ave, Chicago (60601). S side of Michigan Ave Bridge. Phone 312/332-1353. www.mercuryskylinecruiseline.com.* Offers 1 1/2-hour and 2-hour lake and river cruises. (May-Oct) **$$$$**

Mexican Fine Arts Center Museum. *1852 W 19th St, Chicago (60608). Phone 312/738-1503.* Showcase of Mexican art and heritage; museum features revolving exhibits of contemporary and classical works by renowned Mexican artists. (Tues-Sun 10 am-5 pm; closed Mon; also holidays) **FREE**

Michigan Avenue Bridge. *At the Chicago River between Michigan and Wabash aves.* This well-known Chicago landmark offers stunning views of the city as it crosses the Chicago River. The bridge was completed in 1920, designed by Edward Burnnett based on the Alexander III Bridge over the Seine River in Paris. Four 40-foot limestone bridge houses (two on either end) were added in 1928. Each contains a sculptured relief depicting historic Chicago events.

Millennium Park. *Michigan Ave and Randolph St, Chicago (60602). Phone 312/742-1168. www.millenniumpark.org.* This 24.5-acre park is the center of world-class art, music, architecture and landscape design. Don't miss the 50-foot-high water-spewing towers of the Crown Fountain, with their constantly changing human faces, or the Frank Gehry-designed band shell and bridge. The giant silver reflective *Cloud Gate* sculpture, known in common parlance as "the bean," is also a sight to check out. (Daily; 6 am-11 pm)

Monadnock Building. *53 W Jackson Blvd, Chicago (60604). In the Loop.* (1889-1891) Highest wall-bearing building in Chicago was, at the time of its construction, the tallest and largest office building in the world. It is now considered one of the masterworks of the Chicago school of architecture. Designed by Burnham & Root; south addition by Holabird & Roche (1893).

Museum of Contemporary Art. *220 E Chicago Ave, Chicago (60611). Near North Side. Phone 312/280-2660. www.mcachicago.org.* Just a half a block east of Michigan Avenue in the tiny Streeterville neighborhood lies Chicago's Museum of Contemporary Art, one of the nation's largest facilities dedicated to post-1945 works. With a large, rotating permanent collection and a reputation for cutting-edge exhibits, the museum showcases some of the finest artists working today, whether in painting, sculpture, video and film, photography, or performance. The museum—in a new building since 1995—also positions itself as a cultural center, and its 300-seat theater hosts a variety of programming, from lectures and films to experimental theater and music festivals. An annual highlight is the 24-hour summer solstice celebration, which attracts art lovers and partygoers in droves. The museum also has a stellar gift shop and bookstore, a restaurant run by Wolfgang Puck, and a terraced sculpture garden with views of Lake Michigan that serves as a peaceful urban sanctuary just steps from the heart of Chicago. Free admission Tues. (Tues-Sun; closed Jan 1, Thanksgiving, Dec 25) **$$**

Museum of Contemporary Photography. *600 S Michigan Ave, Chicago (60605). Phone 312/663-5554. www.mocp.org.* This museum, affiliated with Columbia College, focuses on photography from 1950 to the present. View a wide range of exhibits at one of only two fully accredited photography museums in the United States. (Mon-Fri 10 am-5 pm, Thurs until 8 pm, Sun noon-5 pm) **FREE**

Museum of Holography. *1134 W Washington Blvd, Chicago (60607). Phone 312/226-1007. holographic center.com.* Permanent collection of 150 holograms (three-dimensional images made with lasers) featuring pieces from the United States and many European and Asian countries. (Wed-Sun 12:30-4:30 pm; closed holidays) **$**

★ **Museum of Science and Industry.** *5700 S Lake Shore Dr, Chicago (60637). South Side. Phone 773/684-1414; toll-free 800/468-6674. www.msichicago.org.* Chicago's Museum of Science and Industry is one of the preeminent museums in the entire country. Constantly improving, the museum seems to always have new hands-on exhibits that interest adults and children alike. The museum includes a free tour of a German U-Boat captured during World War II, a re-creation of a coal mine that visitors can tour, and a model train layout that encapsulates almost the entire country. The museum also includes an exhibit on genetics and the improvements made to medicine through the Human Genome Project, as well as several rooms dedicated to the telling of time, with more than 500 unique instruments for doing so. An Omnimax theater can be found inside the giant space exploration exhibit. If you visit one museum in Chicago, visit this one. Free admission varies by season; see Web site for details. (Daily; hours vary by season; closed Dec 25) **$$** Also here is

Henry Crown Space Center. *5700 S Lake Shore Dr, Chicago (60637). Phone 773/684-1414; toll-free 800/468-6674. www.msichicago.org/exhibit/apollo.* This 35,000-square-foot space center houses the latest in space exhibitions; 334-seat Omnimax theater in a 76-foot-diameter projection dome. **$$**

Music Box Theatre. *3733 N Southport Ave, Chicago (60613). Phone 773/871-6604. www.musicbox theatre.com.* Those raised on multiplex cinemas are in for a treat at the Music Box Theatre, a neighborhood art house that attracts a loyal following—and not just because it's one of the few places in town devoted to independent, foreign, cult, documentary, and classic films. The Music Box is one of the last surviving old-time movie palaces. Built in 1929 and restored in 1983, its style is what one architectural critic called "an eclectic mélange of Italian, Spanish, and Pardon-My-Fantasy put together with passion," including a ceiling replete with "twinkling stars" and moving cloud formations, plus a genuine organ, still played on Saturday nights and at special events. The theater is also home to periodic productions of *The Rocky Horror Picture Show*; sing-alongs to classics (for example, The Sound of Music); and screenings for the Chicago International Film Festival (see SPECIAL EVENTS), held for three weeks each October. The theater is located in trendy Lakeview, a neighborhood of small shops and diverse restaurants. (Daily) **$$**

National Vietnam Veterans Art Museum. *1801 S Indiana Ave, Chicago (60616). Phone 312/326-0270. www.nvvam.org.* This museum houses more than 1,000 works of fine art created by artists who served in the Vietnam War. Interactive dioramas, artifacts; museum store, café. (Tues-Fri 11 am-6 pm, Sat 10 am-5 pm, Memorial Day-Labor Day:, Sun noon-5 pm; closed holidays) **$$**

Navy Pier. *600 E Grand Ave, Chicago (60611). Phone 312/595-7437. www.navypier.com.* Known as one of the city's top venues for families, Navy Pier—an old naval station renovated during the 1990s and converted into an urban playground—seems to offer something for everyone. Its most visible attraction, the 150-foot-high Ferris wheel, offers spectacular views of the lake and skyline and is modeled after the world's first, built in Chicago in 1893. During the summer, families flock to the pier for boat cruises, free outdoor concerts, and fireworks; during the winter, they can ice skate (free). Year-round, visitors can enjoy an

IMAX theater, a Shakespeare theater, a stained-glass museum, a children's museum, shops and kiosks, a food court, and six restaurants catering to tastes from casual "street food" to formal—and pricey—fare (see also RIVA). Many of the pier's attractions are free, but parking can be expensive; instead, take advantage of the city's free trolley service from downtown hotels and other locations. (Daily) **FREE** Also here is

Chicago Children's Museum. *700 E Grand Ave, Chicago (60611). Phone 312/527-1000. www.chichildrensmuseum.org.* Chock full of interesting and interactive activities, the Chicago Children's Museum at Navy Pier strikes a near-perfect balance between fun and learning. Plus, with an ever-changing slate of exhibits and activities, it's the kind of place that children can return to again and again. Overall, the exhibits encourage imagination, exploration, curiosity, and learning through experience; there's a play maze, an inventing lab where kids can perform experiments, and Treehouse Trails for children under 5 to explore the great outdoors. A recent exhibit called "Face to Face" dealt with prejudice and discrimination, and an Afghan children's art exhibit made the realities of life during wartime real for American kids. The programming is stellar, and, in any given week, the museum may have programs such as trilingual storytelling (English, Spanish, and American Sign Language), sing-alongs, art shows, ethnic festivals and celebrations, theater shows, art classes, and even a clown college for kids. (Daily 10 am-8 pm) **$$**

Newberry Library. *60 W Walton St, Chicago (60610). Phone 312/943-9090. www.newberry.org.* (1887) Houses more than 1.4 million volumes and several million manuscripts. Internationally famous collections on the Renaissance, Native Americans, the Chicago Renaissance, the American West, local and family history, music history, the history of printing, calligraphy, cartography, and others. Exhibits open to the public. Admission to reading rooms by registration. (Tues-Sat; closed holidays) Tours (Thurs, Sat). **FREE**

New Maxwell Street. *Canal St and Roosevelt Rd, Chicago. Phone 312/922-3100.* Soak up the colorful atmosphere at the city's oldest outdoor market in its new location near downtown Chicago. Hone your bargaining skills on everything from food and clothing to antiques and imported goods sold by more than 480 local and international vendors year-round. Entertainment (varies). (Sun 7 am-4 pm) **FREE**

Northwestern University Chicago Campus. *357 E Chicago Ave, Chicago (60611). At Lake Shore Dr. Phone 312/503-8649. www.northwestern.edu.* (1920) (5,400 students) Schools of Medicine, Law, Dentistry, and University College.

Oak Street. *Michigan Ave and Oak St, Chicago (60611).* The block between Michigan Avenue and North Rush Street is lined with small shops that specialize in high fashion and the avant-garde from around the world.

Old Chicago Water Tower and Pumping Station. *806 N Michigan Ave, Chicago (60611). Phone 312/742-0808 (City Gallery).* One of the few buildings to survive the Great Chicago Fire of 1871 that ravaged the city, the old Water Tower and the Chicago Avenue Pumping Station are rare monuments to Chicago's early history. Built in 1869 by W. W. Boyington and granted city landmark status in 1972, these gingerbready, castlelike Gothic Revival buildings house a visitor center and City Gallery, presenting photography exhibits with a Chicago theme. They recently became the new home of the acclaimed Lookingglass Theater Company. For first-time visitors to Chicago, the old Water Tower, located at North Michigan and Chicago avenues in the heart of the Magnificent Mile, makes a good starting point for getting oriented. The visitor center is stocked with information about city attractions and tours and is just steps away from shopping, restaurants, hotels, museums, entertainment, and Lake Michigan beaches. (Mon-Sat 10 am-6:30 pm, Sun 10 am-5 pm; closed Thanksgiving, Dec 25) **FREE**

The Oprah Winfrey Show. *1058 W Washington Blvd, Chicago (60607). Phone 312/591-9222 (reservations). www.oprah.com.* One of the most coveted tickets in town is for *The Oprah Winfrey Show*, taped at Harpo Studios in the West Loop area. It may be tough to plan a visit to Chicago around the show, because it generally tapes only on Tuesdays, Wednesdays, and Thursdays from September through early December and from January to June. The only way to get tickets is to call the studio's Audience Department in advance. Note that security for the show is tight and that you must be over 18 to attend (although teens ages 16 and 17 can attend with a parent or legal guardian if they bring a copy of their birth certificate for check-in). If you do get to a taping, allow yourself extra time to explore the surrounding neighborhood. Amid loft condos and meatpacking plants, you'll find some of the hottest restaurants and bars in the city (see BLACKBIRD and REDLIGHT, for example). **FREE**

Osaka Garden. *Jackson Park, 6401 S Stony Island Ave, Chicago (60637). Phone 312/744-8074.* This tranquil Japanese strolling garden was established in 1934 as a thank you to Japan for a building given to Chicago for the 1893 World Columbian Exposition. Visitors can tour the garden with its pavilion, moon bridge, Shinto gate, and typical Japanese foliage and participate in assorted Japanese cultural activities.

Our Lady of Sorrows Basilica. *3121 W Jackson Blvd, Chicago (60612). Phone 773/638-0159. www.ols-chicago.org.* (1890-1902) Worth seeing are the Shrine Altar of the Seven Holy Founders of the Servites (main altar of Carrara marble) and the beautiful English baroque steeple, chapels, paintings, and other architectural ornamentations (daily). Tours (by reservation).

Outdoor art.

Batcolumn. *Harold Washington Social Security Administration Building plaza, 600 W Madison St, Chicago (60661). In the Loop.* (1977) Designed by artist Claes Oldenburg. This 100-foot-tall, 20-ton welded steel sculpture resembles a baseball bat, set in a concrete base.

Flamingo. *Federal Center Plaza, Adams and Dearborn sts, Chicago (60603). In the Loop.* (1974) Sculptor Alexander Calder's famous red stabile, a Chicago landmark, is 53 feet high and weighs 50 tons.

The Four Seasons. *First National Plaza, Monroe and Dearborn sts, Chicago (60603). In the Loop.* (1974) This 3,000-square-foot mosaic designed by Marc Chagall contains more than 320 different shades and hues of marble, stone, granite, and glass.

Miro's *Chicago*. *Brunswick Building, 69 W Washington, Chicago (60602). In the Loop.* (1981) The structure, made of steel, wire mesh, concrete, bronze, and ceramic tile, is 39 feet tall.

Picasso Sculpture. *50 W Washington Blvd, Chicago (60602).* No one's really sure what it is—perhaps a horse, a bird, or a woman—but people around the world know that the Picasso sculpture outside Daley Plaza represents Chicago. Since its unveiling in 1967, this 50-foot-tall, 162-ton steel work of art has become an unofficial logo and an unlikely icon for the city. Some consider it a miracle that the city's famously conservative mayor, Richard J. Daley (aka "the Boss"), would commission a work of cubist abstract expressionism from the bad boy of modern art, but with one of Chicago's leading architectural firms as liaison, the project came to fruition. It led the way for other major public art projects, including the Miro statue (69 W Washington Blvd), the Chagall mosaic (First National Plaza), Calder's Flamingo (Federal Center Plaza), and the Dubuffet outside the James R. Thompson Center (100 W Randolph St), that give the Loop its distinctive and accessible feel.

Untitled Sounding Sculpture. *Amoco Building, 200 E Randolph St, Chicago (60601). In the Loop.* (1975) Unique "sounding sculpture" set in a reflecting pool. Designed by Harry Bertoia.

Peace Museum. *Garfield Park Dome, 100 N Central Park Ave, Chicago (60624). One block E and four blocks N of Independence St exit of Eisenhower Expy. Phone 773/638-6450. www.peacemuseum.org.* Exhibits focusing on the role of the arts, the sciences, labor, women, minorities, and religious institutions on issues of war and peace and on the contributions of individual peacemakers. (Wed-Fri 10 am-4 pm, Sat 11 am-3 pm; closed Jan 1, Dec 24-25 and 31) **$$**

Peggy Notebaert Nature Museum. *2430 N Cannon Dr, Chicago (60614). At Lake Shore Dr and Fullerton Pkwy. Phone 773/755-5100. www.naturemuseum.org.* Hands-on exploration of nature is the mission of the Peggy Notebaert Nature Museum. Built in 1999 as an off-shoot of the Chicago Academy of Sciences (Chicago's first museum), it takes its mission seriously. Here, visitors and city dwellers alike can connect with the natural world via indoor exhibits and outdoor adventures. Children can dress up like animals, adults can explore the Midwestern landscape, and urbanites can forget their cares while surrounded by wildflowers. Permanent exhibits include a 28-foot-high butterfly haven, a city science interactive display, a family water lab, a wilderness walk, and a children's gallery designed for kids ages 3 to 8. Special exhibits are real kiddie-pleasers, judging by two recent ones: "Grossology: The Impolite Science of the Human Body" and "Monster Creepy Crawlies." The museum is beautifully situated in Lincoln Park (see) and is within walking distance of the Lincoln Park Zoo (see), the lagoon, and Fullerton Avenue Beach. Free admission Thurs. (Mon-Fri 9 am-4:30 pm, Sat-Sun 10 am-5 pm) **$$**

Pistachios. *55 E Grand Ave, Chicago (60611). Phone 312/595-9437. www.pistachiosonline.com.* This gem of a jewelry store (actually, "gallery" is more appropriate) features contemporary, one-of-a-kind items crafted by artists from the United States and Europe. Selections include silver and platinum rings, earrings, cufflinks, knitted bracelets, hand-blown glass items, and metal items for the home (including oh-so-chic salt and pepper shakers). And, with your purchase, you receive a little gift: a bag of—what else?—pistachios. (Mon-Fri 10:30 am-7 pm, Sat 10:30 am-6 pm, Sun noon-5 pm)

Polish Museum of America. *984 N Milwaukee Ave, Chicago (60611). Phone 773/384-3352. www.prcua.org.* Exhibits on Polish culture, folklore, and immigration; art gallery, archives, and library; Paderewski and Kosciuszko rooms. The museum has one of the best collections of Polish music and literature outside of Warsaw, catering to Chicago's large Polish population. Founded in 1935, many Polish scholars attend the museum to complete research on projects they produce. (Fri-Wed 11 am-4 pm; closed Thurs; also Jan 1, Good Friday, Dec 25) **DONATION**

Prairie Avenue Historic District. *1800 S Prairie Ave, Chicago (60616). Between 18th and Cullerton sts. South Side. Phone 312/326-1480.* This is the area where millionaires lived during the 1800s. The Clarke House (circa 1835), the oldest house still standing in the city, has been restored and now stands at a site near its original location. The Glessner House (1886), 1800 South Prairie Avenue, is owned and maintained by the Chicago Architecture Foundation. Designed by architect Henry Hobson Richardson, the house has 35 rooms, many of which are restored with original furnishings; interior courtyard. Two-hour guided tour of both houses (Wed-Sun). Other houses on the cobblestone street are Kimball House (1890), 1801 South Prairie Avenue, replica of a French château; Coleman House (circa 1885), 1811 South Prairie Avenue; and Keith House (circa 1870), 1900 South Prairie Avenue. Architectural tours. Free admission Wed. **$$$**

★ **Pullman Historic District Walking Tours.** *614 E 113th St, Chicago (60628). Phone 773/785-8901. www.pullmanil.org.* Built in 1880-1884 to house the workers at George M. Pullman's Palace Car Company, the original town was a complete model community with many civic and recreational facilities. Unlike in most historic districts, nine-tenths of the original buildings are still standing. The 1 1/2-hour tour starts at the Historic Pullman Center. Tours (May-Oct, first Sun of the month, two departures). **$$**

Richard J. Daley Center and Plaza. *50 W Washington Blvd, Chicago (60602). Randolph and Clark Sts. In the Loop. Phone 312/603-7980.* This 31-story, 648-foot building houses county and city courts and administrative offices. In the plaza is the Chicago Picasso sculpture; across Washington Street is Miro's *Chicago* sculpture.

River North Gallery District. With the highest concentration of art galleries outside Manhattan, Chicago's River North Gallery District, just a short walk from Michigan Avenue and the Loop, offers world-class art in a stylish setting of renovated warehouses and upscale restaurants. Although the district is loosely bordered by the Chicago River, Orleans Street, Chicago Avenue, and State Street, you'll find the majority of galleries on Superior and Franklin streets. If you happen to be in town on the second Friday of the month, wander over to the opening-night receptions (5-7 pm) for a glass of wine and a glimpse of Chicago's black-clad art scenesters. Serious collectors may want to visit Carl Hammer and Judy Saslow for outsider art, Ann Nathan for contemporary art, Douglas Dawson and Primitive Artworks for tribal art, Manifesto for high-end furniture, Aldo Castillo for global art, and Douglas Rosin for 20th-century modern art. (Tues-Sat) **FREE**

Rookery. *209 S LaSalle St, Chicago (60604). In the Loop.* (1886) Oldest remaining steel-skeleton skyscraper in the world. Designed by Burnham & Root, the remarkable glass-encased lobby was remodeled in 1905 by Frank Lloyd Wright.

Roosevelt University. *430 S Michigan Ave, Chicago (60605). In the Loop. Phone 312/341-3500; toll-free www.roosevelt.edu.* (1945) (6,400 students) Campuses in Chicago and northwest suburban Schaumburg. Auditorium Building designed by Louis Sullivan and engineered by Dankmar Adler in 1889.

Royal George Theatre. *1641 N Halsted St, Chicago (60614). Phone 312/988-9000.* Located in Chicago's Lincoln Park neighborhood, this theater features seats that are sparse in number but well spaced, enabling a relaxing theater experience. The stage has hosted such shows as Tony Kushner's acclaimed *Angels in America* and the review *Forever Plaid.*

★ **Sears Tower.** *233 S Wacker Dr, Chicago (60660). In the Loop. Phone 312/875-9696 (skydeck). www.searstower.com or www.theskydeck.com.* It seems fitting that the town that gave birth to the skyscraper should lay claim to North America's tallest building (and the world's tallest until 1996). Built in 1974 by Skidmore, Owings & Merrill, the 110-story Sears Tower soars

1/4 mile (1,450 feet) above the city, making it the most prominent building in the skyline. The building, which houses 10,000 office workers and hosts 25,000 visitors daily, was constructed of black anodized aluminum in nine bundled square tubes, an innovation that provides both wind protection and the necessary support for its extraordinary height. The elevators that whisk visitors to the 103rd-floor observatory are among the world's fastest—and well worth the ride. The observatory offers panoramic views of the city; on a clear day, you can easily see 35 miles away. During the height of tourist season—the summer—expect long waits. (May-Sept, daily 10 am-10 pm; Oct-Apr, daily 10 am-8 pm) **$$$**

The Second City. *1616 N Wells St, Chicago (60614). Phone 312/337-3992. www.secondcity.com.* The Second City is known worldwide as the home to smart, cutting-edge comedy. Opened in 1959 by a group of University of Chicago students, The Second City has launched the careers of many successful comics, the likes of which include John Belushi, Bill Murray, Gilda Radner, John Candy, and Mike Myers. Resident troupes perform original comedy revues nightly on two stages: The Second City Mainstage, seating 340, and The Second City e.t.c., which seats 180. The Second City also operates a comedy training center, with student productions held at Donny's Skybox Studio Theatre (1608 N Wells St).

★ **Shedd Aquarium.** *1200 S Lake Shore Dr, Chicago (60605). At Roosevelt Rd. Phone 312/939-2438. www.sheddnet.org.* Not all the best aquariums are on the ocean. Shedd, the world's largest indoor aquarium, features more than 8,000 freshwater and marine animals displayed in 200 naturalistic habitats; divers hand-feed fish, sharks, eels, and turtles several times daily in the 90,000-gallon Caribbean Reef exhibit. The Oceanarium re-creates a Pacific Northwest ecosystem with whales, dolphins, sea otters, and seals. A colony of penguins inhabits a Falkland Islands exhibit; while the Seahorse Symphony exhibit takes a look at some of the ocean's smaller creatures. In the summer, Chicago's music scene invades the aquarium for "Jazzin' at the Shedd," with live performances weekly. Free admission Mon-Tues (Sept-Feb only). (Summer: daily 9 am-6 pm; winter: daily 9 am-5 pm; closed Dec 25) **$$$$**

Shoreline Marine Company. *474 N Lake Shore Dr, Chicago (60611). Phone 312/222-9328. www.shorelinesightseeing.com.* Thirty-minute tours of the lakefront. Departs from Navy Pier. (May-Sept, daily) **$$$**

Soldier Field. *Gate 14, 1410 S. Museum Campus Dr, Chicago (60605). Phone 847/295-6600. www.soldierfield.net.* Soldier Field opened in 1924 as Municipal Grant Park Stadium, and the first game played there saw Notre Dame down Northwestern 13-6. The Chicago Bears didn't play home games at the stadium until 1971, when they moved from baseball's Wrigley Field (see). The stadium was part of a recent lakefront improvement project costing more than $500 million, with benefits including the addition of more seats and better amenities to the historic building. Soldier Field also plays host to the Chicago Fire of Major League Soccer, as well as several larger concert events each summer.

Chicago Bears (NFL). *Soldier Field, 1410 S Museum Campus Dr, Chicago (60605). Phone 847/295-6600. www.chicagobears.com.* After playing the 2002 season at the University of Illinois's Memorial Field, the Bears moved back into Chicago's storied Soldier Field in 2003 following a multimillion-dollar renovation. The stadium now sports a more modern look, but it still retains the feel of an early 20th-century arena. Whatever the team's performance, season-ticket holders are seemingly immune to the lakefront weather and loyal to the orange and blue. Don't miss taking in a game here if you're a true football fan.

Chicago Fire (MLS). *Soldier Field, 1410 S Museum Campus Dr, Chicago (60605). Phone toll-free 888/657-3473. www.chicago-fire.com.* The Fire won one of the first Major League Soccer Cups and have consistently been a playoff team since the league's inception. The team has replaced the veterans who garnered it early success with a recent youth movement and continues to be one of the better-drawing clubs in the league. Like the Bears, the Fire moved back into Soldier Field after millions of dollars were spent to revive and renovate the old structure.

Spertus Museum. *618 S Michigan Ave, Chicago (60605). At the Spertus Institute of Jewish Studies. In the Loop. Phone 312/322-1747. www.spertus.edu/museum.html.* Permanent collection of ceremonial objects from many parts of the world; sculpture, graphic arts, and paintings; ethnic materials spanning centuries; changing exhibits in fine arts; documentary films and photographs. Rosenbaum Artifact Center has hands-on exhibits on ancient Near East archaeology. Free admission Fri. (Mon-Fri, Sun; closed holidays and Jewish holidays) **$**

***Spirit of Chicago* Cruises.** *Navy Pier, 455 E Illinois St, Chicago (60611). Phone 312/836-7899; toll-free 866/211-3804. www.spiritcruises.com.* Take a cruise leaving year-round from Chicago's Navy Pier (see) out onto Lake Michigan for a couple hours away from the hustle and bustle of the mainland. Tickets can be purchased individually, or groups can rent the ship for gatherings and celebrations. **$$$$**

State Street Shopping District. *State and Madison sts, Chicago (60602). Between Lake St and Jackson Blvd. In the Loop.* Yes, State Street is "that great street" alluded to in song. Once dubbed the busiest intersection in the world, State Street today is a Loop shopping mecca anchored by Chicago's two most famous department retailers: Marshall Field's (see) and Carson Pirie Scott (see). These flagship stores have been joined by national chains, discount stores, and specialty shops. More interesting than the merchandise available for purchase, however, may be the street's architecture. Check out the graceful Louis Sullivan grillwork at Carson's main entrance, the Tiffany dome inside Field's, and the exterior of the Burnham Hotel (see), a masterful renovation and restoration of the former Reliance Building, once termed "the crown jewel of Chicago architecture." For lunch, try Marshall Field's venerable Walnut Room or the Atwood Café (see) in the Burnham Hotel. And if you need to meet up with someone, do so under the Marshall Field's clock at Washington Boulevard and State Street, as Chicagoans have done for generations. (Daily)

Steppenwolf Theater Company. *1650 N Halsted St, Chicago (60614). At North Ave and Halsted St; accessible by red line trains. Phone 312/335-1650. www.steppenwolf.org.* One of the most acclaimed theater groups in the country, Steppenwolf not only helped put Chicago theater on the map, but also gave many famous actors, including John Malkovich, Joan Allen, Gary Sinise, Laurie Metcalf, and John Mahoney, their start. The dozens of awards its shows and performers have won, including Tonys, Emmys, and Obies, belie its humble founding in a suburban church basement in 1974 by Sinise, Terry Kinney, and Jeff Perry. Steppenwolf quickly became known for its risky choices and edgy performances, an approach critics aptly termed "rock-and-roll theater." Today, the company has its own state-of-the-art building in the Lincoln Park neighborhood (just a short cab or "L" train ride from downtown), which includes a studio space and a school and hosts several specialty series. Steppenwolf performances are almost uniformly excellent, with stunning sets, strong acting, and plenty of original material; theater lovers should try to reserve tickets as far in advance of their Chicago visit as possible.

Sur La Table. *52-54 E Walton St, Chicago (60611). Phone 312/337-0600. www.surlatable.com.* In the 1970s, Seattle spawned this clearinghouse for hard-to-find kitchen gear, and it soon became known as a source for cookware, small appliances, cutlery, kitchen tools, linens, tableware, gadgets, and specialty foods. Sur La Table has since expanded to include cooking classes ($$$$), chef demonstrations, and cookbook author signings, as well as a catalog and online presence. Cooking connoisseurs discover such finds as cool oven mitts, zest graters, copper whisks, onion soup bowls, and inspired TV dinner trays. (Daily)

Swedish-American Museum Center. *5211 N Clark St, Chicago (60640). Phone 773/728-8111. www.samac.org.* Pays tribute to Swedish heritage and history. Exhibits on Swedish memorabilia. The museum features a children's museum dedicated to immigration, as well as several exhibits detailing how Swedes came to reside in Chicago over the years. Museum also includes periodic performances of traditional Swedish music and dance to enhance the sense of Scandinavian folklore. (Tues-Fri 10 am-4 pm, Sat-Sun 11 am-4 pm) **$**

Symphony Center. *220 S Michigan Ave, Chicago (60604). In the Loop. Phone 312/294-3000 (tickets). www.cso.org.* (1904) The historic Symphony Center is the home of the Chicago Symphony Orchestra and the stage for the Civic Orchestra of Chicago, chamber music groups, diverse musical attractions, and children's programs. Includes Buntrock Hall, a ballroom, rehearsal space, and restaurant.

Chicago Symphony Orchestra (CSO). *220 S Michigan Ave, Chicago (60604). Phone 312/294-3333. www.cso.org.* Long considered one of the great orchestras of the world, the CSO has been a fixture on the Chicago cultural scene for more than 100 years. It may have reached its highest acclaim under the late, great Sir Georg Solti, when so many of its recordings were virtual shoe-ins for Grammy awards, but today, with three conductors and an award-winning composer in residence, the orchestra continues to produce innovative and inspiring music in a classically beautiful setting at the Symphony Center across from the Art Institute of Chicago. While the big-name shows may sell out in advance, it is often possible to get day-of-show or single-seat tickets at the box office—especially for weeknight and Friday afternoon performances—at a reasonable price.

Theatre Building. *1225 W Belmont Ave, Chicago (60657). Phone 773/327-5252. www.theatrebuilding chicago.org.* The Theatre Building serves as the impromptu home for traveling companies to show their wares. More often than not, these shows are a little more "off the beaten path" and do not include names or plays that may be recognizable, but this does not take away from the enjoyment of the experience. Shows are generally cheaper than at other area theaters, but may not be for the entire family.

United Center. *1901 W Madison St, Chicago (60612). Phone 312/455-4500; fax 312/455-4511. www.unitedcenter.com.* Affectionately known as "the house that Michael built," the United Center replaced the cavernous Chicago Stadium in the mid-1990s as the home of Chicago Bulls professional basketball team. Even though the Blackhawks professional hockey team skates here and numerous concerts and special events are held here, the giant statue of Michael Jordan in front of the building's north entrance attests to the building's true provenance. Inside is a shrine to the glory years of Chicago sports: hanging from the rafters are banners from the Bulls' six championship seasons, the Blackhawks' Stanley Cup wins, and a variety of retired jerseys, including Jordan's number 23. Although the Bulls aren't packing in the crowds the way they did when "His Airness," as the local sportswriters called him, ruled the courts, a visit to the United Center enables you to see where history took place. Tours of the arena are available through the Guest Relations office. The United Center is accessible via public transportation, but because the neighborhood is in transition, it's probably safer to take a cab or to drive (there is ample parking close by).

Chicago Blackhawks (NHL). *United Center, 1901 W Madison St, Chicago (60612). Phone 312/455-7000. www.chicagoblackhawks.com.* The Chicago Blackhawks are one of the oldest NHL teams in the league. Although their last Stanley Cup victory was in 1961, the Hawks have a loyal (and raucous) fan base that can contest the game as hotly in their seats as the players do on the ice. And although, like all professional sports contests, Blackhawks games are marketed as family events, you still get a sense that within the plush confines of the United Center lies the same rough-and-tumble crowd that rocked the old Chicago Stadium.

Chicago Bulls (NBA). *United Center, 1901 W Madison St, Chicago (60612). Phone 312/455-4500. www.nba.com/bulls.* Although the team has not enjoyed much success since the second retirement of Michael Jordan, the Bulls continue to rebuild around young players, as well as veterans. Tickets are relatively easy to come by, although still on the expensive side. **$$$$**

United States Post Office. *433 W Harrison, Chicago (60607). In the Loop. Phone 312/983-7550.* (1933) Largest in the world under one roof. Individuals may join 1 1/2-hour guided group tours (Mon-Fri, three tours daily; no tours holidays and Dec). No cameras, packages, or purses. Reservations required. **FREE**

University of Chicago. *5801 S Ellis Ave, Chicago (60637). South Side. Phone 773/702-8374. www.uchicago.edu.* (1892) (12,750 students) On this campus, Enrico Fermi produced the first sustained nuclear reaction. The University of Chicago also has had one of the highest numbers of Nobel Prize winners of any institution. The campus includes the Oriental Institute, Robie House, Rockefeller Memorial Chapel, and David and Alfred Smart Museum of Art (5550 S Greenwood Ave) (Tues-Sun; free; phone 773/702-0200). On campus are

Oriental Institute. *1155 E 58th St, Chicago (60637). On the University of Chicago campus. South Side. Phone 773/702-9514. www.oi.uchicago.edu.* Outstanding collection of archaeological material illustrating the art, architecture, religion, and literature from the ancient Near East. Lectures, workshops, free films (Sun; limited hours). Museum (Tues-Sun; closed Jan 1, Thanksgiving, Dec 25). **FREE**

Robie House. *5757 S Woodlawn Ave, Chicago (60637). Near the University of Chicago campus. South Side. Phone 773/834-1847. www.wrightplus .org/robiehouse/robiehouse.* (1909) Designed by Frank Lloyd Wright, this may be the ultimate example of a Prairie house. Designed and built for Excelsior sewing machine magnate Frederick Robie, the house was nearly torn down in the 1960s after having been used as a dormitory by the University of Chicago. However, it was saved and is in the middle of an ambitious ten-year restoration plan to bring it back to the splendor of almost a century ago. Tours. (Daily 10 am-3 pm; closed holidays) **$$$**

Rockefeller Memorial Chapel. *5850 S Woodlawn Ave, Chicago (60637). On the University of Chicago campus. South Side. Phone 773/702-2100.* Designed by Bertram Grosvenor Goodhue Associates; noted for its Gothic construction, vaulted ceiling, 8,600-pipe organ, and 72-bell carillon. Guided tours by appointment. (Daily 8 am-4 pm).

University of Illinois at Chicago. *1200 W Harrison, Chicago (60607). Near I-94 and I-290. Phone 312/996-4350. www.uic.edu.* (1965) (25,000 students) Comprehensive urban university. On campus is Jane Addams's Hull-House Museum (see). The Flames plays NCAA Division I athletics, and basketball games are usually well attended. Easy access to the campus from Eisenhower Expressway. UIC Medical Center is one of the leading teaching and research hospitals in the city of Chicago.

Jane Addams Hull-House Museum. *800 S Halsted St, Chicago (60607). On the campus of the University of Illinois at Chicago. Phone 312/413-5353. www.uic.edu/jaddams/hull/hull_house.html.* Two original Hull-House buildings, the restored Hull Mansion (1856) and dining hall (1905), which formed the nucleus of the 13-building settlement complex founded in 1889 by Jane Addams and Ellen Gates Starr, social welfare pioneers. Exhibits and presentations on the history of Hull-House, the surrounding neighborhood, ethnic groups, and women's history. (Tues-Fri 10 am-4 pm, Sun noon-4 pm; closed holidays) **FREE**

Untouchable Tours. *600 N Clark St, Chicago (60610). Phone 773/881-1195. www.gangstertour.com.* Guided tour of gangster hotspots of the 1920s and 1930s. (Daily; reservations strongly recommended) **$$$$**

Victory Gardens Theater. *2257 N Lincoln Ave, Chicago (60614). Phone 773/549-5788. www.victorygardens.org.* Although it often produces plays by lesser-known authors, the Victory Gardens did win the Regional Theatre Tony Award in 2001. Some better-known playwrights and plays have been produced here as well, such as Neil Simon's *Lost in Yonkers.*

Wabash Avenue. *Wabash Ave and Congress Pkwy, Chicago (60604). S of the river to Congress Ave. In the Loop.* This unique street, always in the shadow of the elevated train tracks, is known for its many specialty stores—books, music, musical instruments, records, men's clothing, tobacco, etc.—as well as being the center of the wholesale and retail jewelry trade.

Wendella boat tours. *400 N Michigan Ave, Chicago (60611). At the Wrigley Building (NW side of Michigan Ave Bridge). Phone 312/337-1446. www.wendellaboats.com.* Lake and river cruises (1, 1 1/2, and 2 hours) on the RiverBus, featuring live narration. (Apr-mid-Nov, daily) **$$$$**

Westfield North Bridge. *520 N Michigan Ave, Chicago (60611). Phone 312/327-2300. www.northbridgechicago.com.* Deplete the contents of your wallet at 50 upscale shops, including Nordstrom, Swatch, and Vosges Haut-Chocolat. Replenish your energy while dining at eateries in a casual food court on the fourth level, or over a more leisurely meal at one of several restaurants. (Mon-Sat 10 am-8 pm, Sun 11 am-6 pm; closed Thanksgiving, Dec 25)

Wicker Park/Bucktown neighborhood. *1608 N Milwaukee Ave, Chicago (60647). Neighborhood starts at the intersection of North, Milwaukee, and Damen aves. Blue line "L" train-Damen stop. Phone 773/384-2672. www.wickerparkbucktown.com.* Just a short cab or "L" train ride northwest of downtown Chicago is one of the city's liveliest and most diverse areas, the Wicker Park/Bucktown neighborhood. You may recognize it from the film *High Fidelity,* shot on location here. The area is home to artists and musicians, urban pioneers and hipsters, plus a wealth of trendy stores and restaurants. Start at the neighborhood's epicenter, the intersection of North, Milwaukee, and Damen avenues. Within a several block radius, you'll find antique stores and thrift shops, art galleries, boutiques, design studios, day spas, nightclubs, coffeehouses, bars, and restaurants. Be sure to walk down Pierce and Hoyne streets, where the beer barons lived, as well as around the park itself for a glimpse of the grand homes from this historic neighborhood's past—a combination of German, Polish, Ukrainian, and, more recently, Latino roots.

Wrigley Building. *410 N Michigan Ave, Chicago (60611). Phone 312/923-8080. www.wrigley.com.* Perched on the north bank of the Chicago River on Michigan Avenue, the sparkling white Wrigley Building has been one of Chicago's most recognized skyscrapers since its completion in 1924 by prominent architects Graham, Anderson, Probst, and White. The building's triangular shape is patterned after the Seville Cathedral's Giralda Tower in Spain, and its ornamental design is an adaptation of French Renaissance style. Note that the building is actually two towers linked by an open walkway at street level and two enclosed walkways on the third and 14th floors. Today, the building remains the headquarters of the Wrigley family of chewing gum fame, although other firms also rent office space. At night, the exterior, clad with more than 250,000 glazed terra-cotta tiles, is floodlit, making it one of the nation's major commercial lighting displays and one of the most highly visible symbols of the city. Unfortunately, no tours of the building's interior are available.

Wrigley Field. *1060 W Addison St, Chicago (60613). Phone 773/404-2827. www.cubs.com.* America's second-oldest National League ballpark is also one of its most unique, located within a vibrant city neighborhood where residents often watch games from their roof decks. While the Cubs' perpetual losing streak is a running joke in Chicago, it never keeps people away from the ballpark; during the summer, it's one of the hottest tickets in town, mostly because "the Friendly Confines," as it is known, offers the ultimate old-time baseball experience. The best place to sit is in the box seats just past first or third base, where the players in their bull pens will talk to the fans. If you want to catch a home run, try the left field bleachers, especially during batting practice. Be sure to walk to the upper deck at sunset for spectacular views of the city. After the game, you can continue the party at one of the dozens of bars and restaurants within walking distance of the park.

Chicago Cubs (MLB). *1060 W Addison St, Chicago (60613). Phone 773/404-2827. www.cubs.com.* Although Hall of Fame players like Ernie Banks and Billy Williams have come and gone, the team still remains the favorite among Chicago fans. Fans come from miles around just to watch a baseball game in Wrigley Field, one of the oldest ballparks anywhere.

Special Events

57th Street Art Fair. *57th St between Kenwood and Dorchester, Chicago (60637). Phone 773/493-3247. www.57thstreetartfair.org.* Every year, the 57th Street Art Fair shuts down a city block between Kenwood and Dorchester to vend the wares of more than 300 artists from around the country. Participants are chosen by a panel of professional artists and curators in March for the early June celebration. There is no corporate sponsorship for the fair, which includes painting, sculpture, photography and ceramics, among other media. Early June. **FREE**

Air and Water Show. *1600 N Lake Shore Dr, Chicago (60614). Phone 312/744-2400 (Chicago Office of Tourism). egov.cityofchicago.org.* The nation's largest two-day air show, attracting more than 2 million people every August, is a free event and a favorite of kids and adults alike. There are daredevil pilots, parachute teams, and jets flying in formation, as well as a water-skiing and boat-jumping component for additional thrills. The great thing about this festival is that it's visible from almost everywhere along the Chicago lakefront. Grandstand seats for the water show are located at North Avenue Beach, but some of the best viewing points are farther north, at Montrose Harbor and between Belmont and Addison. Mid-Aug. **FREE**

Around the Coyote Arts Festival. *Wicker Park, Chicago (60622). At the intersection of Milwaukee, North, and Damen aves (Blue Line "L" train-Damen stop). Phone 773/342-6777. www.aroundthecoyote.org.* With one of the highest concentrations of artists in the country residing in the Wicker Park/Bucktown neighborhood, it made sense to find a way to showcase their work. That's exactly what Paris art dealer Jim Happy-Delpesh did when he came back to Chicago in 1989. Although the festival revolves around visual artists, it also encompasses cutting-edge dance, theater, poetry, film and video, fashion, and furniture design. Typically, the timing of the festival—held the second weekend in September—results in glorious early fall weather, and tens of thousands of people walk through the neighborhood visiting galleries, group shows, the Flat Iron Arts Building, and artists' homes and studios. And because the neighborhood is spilling over with hip boutiques and dozens of trendy restaurants and outdoor cafés, many people make a day of it. A smaller winter version of the festival is held in February. Second weekend in Sept, Feb. **FREE**

Art Chicago. *Butler Field, Columbus Dr, Chicago (60611). Phone 312/587-3300.* In conjunction with Chicago's Museum of Contemporary Art (see), this festival gives collectors and admirers of fine art a chance to see some of the newest and hippest pieces in the art world. Art Chicago takes place at Butler Field in mid-May each year and attracts hundreds of dealers from around the globe. Before the show opens, serious collectors can attend the Vernissage party for $125 a ticket and preview the art before the general public is admitted the following day. Mid-May. **$$$**

Chicago Auto Show. *McCormick Place, 2301 S Lake Shore Dr, Chicago (60616). Phone 312/744-3370.* The world's largest auto show takes up all of the south wing of Chicago's enormous McCormick Place (see).

It is often here that domestic and international automakers first put their latest models on public display. The show has been an annual Chicago staple since 1901 and has grown right along with the industry itself. It's a good opportunity to see celebrities, as well as the expected concept cars and latest models of old favorites. Feb. **$$**

Chicago Blues Fest. *Grant Park, 331 E Randolph St, Chicago (60602). Phone 312/744-2400 (Chicago Office of Tourism). egov.cityofchicago.org.* In a city virtually synonymous with the blues, Chicago's annual Blues Fest, held in late May-early June, is the crème de la crème of blues festivals, attracting local stars such as Buddy Guy, Koko Taylor, Otis Rush, Sugar Blue, and Son Seals, as well as national names like Bo Diddley, Ruth Brown, Howlin' Wolf, Muddy Waters, Honeyboy Edwards, and the North Mississippi Allstars. With such a wealth of local talent, even the small stages and daytime shows rival the best blues clubs in the United States. Low-key and racially diverse, this free outdoor festival attracts more than 600,000 visitors over its four-day run. It's a great place to experience a true cross-section of the city while enjoying barbecue, the start of summer, and the best in traditional and contemporary blues music. Early-mid-June. **FREE**

Chicago Humanities Festival. *500 N Dearborn St, Suite 1028, Chicago (60610). Phone 312/661-1028. www.chfestival.org.* For years, this festival was one of the best-kept secrets in Chicago: world-renowned authors, scholars, poets, policymakers, artists, and performers would gather for a weekend in November to celebrate the power of ideas in human culture and the role of the humanities in our daily lives. Dozens of lectures, performances, panels, and seminars, featuring names like Gore Vidal, Mira Nair, V. S. Naipul, Arthur Miller, Germaine Greer, Stephen Sondheim, and Robert Pinsky—were available to the public for just $5. Now, in its 15th year, the festival lasts for two weeks, features hundreds of events, and takes on a particular theme. Past themes have included Saving + Spending, Brains + Beauty, Crime & Punishment, Work & Play, Love & Marriage, and He/She. Tickets are still only $5 per event, yet now it's better to purchase them in advance since the secret is out. Two weeks in fall. **$**

Chicago International Film Festival. *32 W Randolph St, Chicago (60601). Phone 312/683-0121. www.chicagofilmfestival.com.* The oldest international film festival in North America. For three weeks each October, Chicagoans are introduced to some of the best cinema from around the world, as well as from those creating great work in the United States. Over the years, the festival has helped introduce innovative filmmakers like Martin Scorsese and John Carpenter. There are categories for feature films, first- and second-time directors, documentaries, and short films (including animation and student productions), all judged by The International Feature Film Jury, which is comprised of professional actors, directors, and critics. Oct.

Chicago Jazz Fest. *Grant Park, 331 E Randolph St, Chicago (60602). Phone 312/744-2400 (Chicago Office of Tourism). egov.cityofchicago.org.* Held each Labor Day weekend for the past 25 years, this event is worth planning a trip to Chicago around. During the four days of this most prestigious of US jazz festivals, Grant Park becomes a giant outdoor jazz café with more than 300,000 people in attendance. Lesser-known and local artists perform during the day on the small stages near the food concession area, but the main headliners—world-class jazz musicians such as Herbie Hancock, Cassandra Wilson, Betty Carter, Wayne Shorter, and Roy Hargrove—take the main stage at the Petrillo Music Shell after 5 pm. You need to arrive early to get a seat near the stage, but most folks prefer to picnic on the lawn, enjoying the perfect skyline views and listening to the strategically placed speakers. Labor Day weekend. **FREE**

Chicago Outdoor Film Festival. *Grant Park, 331 E Randolph St, Chicago (60602). Phone 312/744-2400 (Chicago Office of Tourism). egov.cityofchicago.org.* What started out as a small twice-a-month event at Grant Park a few years ago has become a real phenomenon—the urban equivalent of an old-fashioned drive-in movie. Once a week in July and August, couples, families, and groups of friends flock to the park to see free classic movies, from *Casablanca* and *Vertigo* to *West Side Story* and *Singin' in the Rain.* With the city skyline as the backdrop, the lake breeze for air-conditioning, and homemade picnics instead of overpriced movie concessions, it's a near-perfect outing. Movies start at dusk, but go early because it gets crowded. Mid-July-late Aug. **FREE**

Chicago to Mackinac Races. *400 E Monroe St, Chicago (60603). Phone 312/744-3370. www.chicagomackinac.com.* For more than a century, yacht racers have taken on mighty Lake Michigan in a race from the Windy City to Mackinac Island in Michigan's Upper Peninsula. Run by the Chicago Yacht Club, the race attracts around 300 vessels every year to take advantage of brisk northerly winds the third weekend in July. Participation is by invitation only and usually takes between 40 and 60 hours to complete. There are several different levels of competition, depending on the type of boat making the 333-mile trip. It is a great spectacle to watch as the boats leave Chicago. July.

Grant Park July 3 Concert. *Petrillo Music Shell, 235 S Columbus Dr, Chicago (60601). Phone 312/744-3370.* The lakefront blazes with cannon flashes as the Grant Park Symphony welcomes Independence Day with Tchaikovsky's *1812 Overture*;fireworks. July 3. **FREE**

Grant Park Music Festival. *Pritzker Pavillion, N Columbus Dr, Chicago (60601). Phone 312/742-4763.* Concerts Wed, Fri-Sat, late June-Sept. **FREE**

Magnificent Mile Lights Festival. *N Michigan Ave, Chicago (60611). Phone 312/409-5560. www.themagnificentmile.com.* As a kickoff to the holiday season, for the last 13 years the North Michigan Avenue Association has sponsored the Magnificent Lights Festival, during which the avenue's trademark tiny white lights get turned on to much fanfare. Generally held the weekend before Thanksgiving, the festival has grown to become a family day, starting with carolers, gingerbread decorating, ice-carving displays, Disney character stage shows, and a lively procession down Michigan Avenue, culminating in the lighting and fireworks spectacular. Attendance is usually high; of course, all depends on Chicago's unpredictable winter weather. Late Nov. **FREE**

Marshall Field's holiday window displays. *111 N State St, Chicago (60602). Phone 312/781-1000. www.marshallfields.com.* Every holiday season, children and adults alike flock to Marshall Field's State Street store (see) to gaze in wonder at the elaborate and magical window displays. It's a Chicago ritual to line up outside the windows, three, four, and five deep, the day after Thanksgiving for the unveiling of the new season's displays. Although Field's has been delighting Chicagoans for more than a century with its innovative decorations, not until 1946 did its stores feature "stories"—from a reenactment of "'Twas the Night Before Christmas" to recent tales of Harry Potter—that progress from window to window. To avoid the crowds, visit right after Christmas. When you've stood out in the cold long enough, treat yourself to lunch in the store's elegant Walnut Room—another Chicago holiday tradition—where every table offers a view of its famous 40-plus-foot Christmas tree. Mid-Nov-mid-Jan.

Navy Pier Art Fair. *Navy Pier, 331 E Randolph St, Chicago (60601). Phone 312/744-3370.* Month-long exhibit of local artists' work. Jan. **FREE**

Spring Flower Show. *Garfield Park Conservatory, 300 N Central Ave, Chicago (60624). Phone 312/746-5100. www.garfield-conservatory.org.* Apr. **FREE**

St. Patrick's Day Parade. *Columbus Dr, Chicago. Downtown. Phone 312/744-3370. www.chicagostpatsparade.com.* Chicago's St. Patrick's Day parade is famous around the world, not because of its size (although it is one of the largest) or its spirit (it is one of the rowdiest), but for the fact that on the day of the parade, the city dyes the Chicago River green, a tradition started during the early 1960s. If nothing else, this tells you how seriously Chicago takes the holiday. Held annually on the Saturday closest to St. Patrick's Day, the parade features dozens of bands, thousands of Irish step dancers, a multitude of floats, representatives of unions and local organizations, politicians, dignitaries, and many a surprise guest—often famous people with Chicago roots—all "wearin' the green." Mostly, however, the parade is one big party for hundreds of thousands of Chicagoans and visitors alike, where everyone gets to be Irish, at least for an afternoon. Weekend closest to St. Patrick's Day. **FREE**

Taste of Chicago. *Michigan Ave, Chicago. In Grant Park. Phone 312/744-2400 (Chicago Office of Tourism). egov.cityofchicago.org.* What started out in 1980 as a way to sample cuisines from some of the city's best-known restaurants has become an all-out food fest and Fourth of July celebration that attracts more than 3.5 million visitors a year. At this ten-day event, which features booths from more than 50 area vendors, you can stick to Taste favorites—Lou Malnati's pizza, Eli's cheesecake, Robinson's ribs and giant turkey drumsticks, and sautéed goat meat and plantains from Vee-Vee's African restaurant—or indulge in more refined specialties, like coconut lime sorbet, duck with lingonberries, grilled lobster tail, and alligator on a stick. In addition to food, you'll find free live music by big-name headliners, amusement park rides, and even a parent helper tent with free diapers. The crowds can get oppressive, so the earlier in the day you go, the better; don't forget to bring water, sunscreen, patience, and, perhaps, some wetnaps. Also try to buy food tickets in advance to avoid long lines. Late June-early July. **FREE**

Venetian Night. *Monroe Harbor, 100 S Lake Shore Dr, Chicago (60603). Phone 773/256-0949.* Venetian aquatic parade, fireworks. Late July. **FREE**

Winter Delights. *Mayor's Office of Special Events, Room 703, 121 N LaSalle St, Chicago (60602). Citywide. Phone 312/744-3315. www.winterdelights.com.* Includes snow-carving contests. First two weeks in Feb.

Limited-Service Hotels

★ ★ COURTYARD BY MARRIOTT. *30 E Hubbard St, Chicago (60611). Phone 312/329-2500; toll-free 800/321-2211; fax 312/329-0293. www.courtyard.com.* 337 rooms, 15 story. Check-in 4 pm, check-out noon. Restaurant, bar. Fitness room. Indoor pool, whirlpool. **$$**

★ ★ EMBASSY SUITES DOWNTOWN/ LAKEFRONT. *511 N Columbus Dr, Chicago (60611). Phone 312/836-5900; fax 312/836-5901. www.embassysuites.com.* 455 rooms, all suites. Check-in 4 pm, check-out 11 am. Restaurant, bar. Fitness room. Indoor pool, whirlpool. Airport transportation available. Business center. **$**

★ FAIRFIELD INN. *216 E Ontario St, Chicago (60611). Phone 312/787-3777; fax 312/787-8714. www.fairfieldsuiteschicago.com.* Just a block off the Magnificent Mile and three blocks from the lake, this clean, well-maintained hotel is a great choice for budget-minded travelers who don't want to give up on location to save money. Although the property doesn't have much in the way of extra amenities, it has an attractive and inviting lobby, and the staff is very accommodating. If you'd prefer to spend the bulk of your vacation dollars on shopping and fine dining rather than on accommodations, this is THE choice in downtown Chicago. 185 rooms. Complimentary continental breakfast. Check-in 3 pm, check-out noon. Fitness room. **$**

★ HAMPTON INN CHICAGO & SUITES. *33 W Illinois St, Chicago (60610). Phone 312/832-0330; fax 312/832-0333.* With a convenient location, reasonable rates, a large number of suites and ample meeting space, the hotel welcomes families and business travelers. Ruth's Chris Steak House is connected to the hotel by a second-floor skywalk, and guests have plenty of other restaurants to choose from in the surrounding area. 230 rooms, all suites. Complimentary continental breakfast. Check-in 3 pm, check-out noon. Fitness room. Indoor pool. Business center. **$**

★ ★ TREMONT HOTEL. *100 E Chestnut St, Chicago (60611). Phone 312/751-1900; toll-free 800/621-8133; fax 312/751-8691. www.tremontchicago.com.* Located just off North Michigan Avenue, not far from the John Hancock Building, this 130-room hotel is popular with business travelers. Amenities are limited and guest rooms are on the small side, making the hotel not especially convenient for families, but the cozy rooms are attractively furnished in soothing shades of yellow, green, and cream and retain some of the building's historical character. The hotel's restaurant, Mike Ditka's (see), serves steaks and chops in a clubby setting. 130 rooms, 16 story. Pets accepted. Check-in 3 pm, check-out noon. Restaurant. Fitness room. **$$**

Full-Service Hotels

★ ★ ★ ALLERTON CROWNE PLAZA HOTEL. *701 N Michigan Ave, Chicago (60611). Phone 312/440-1500; toll-free 800/621-8311; fax 312/440-1819. www.allertonchi.crowneplaza.com.* The Gold Coast's long-standing Allerton Crowne Plaza boasts both Historic Landmark Hotel status, designated by the city of Chicago, and a $60 million renovation that brought the hotel up to today's standards. It was built in 1924 and has served as a men's hotel for Northwestern University; at the time of its construction, it was the tallest building on Michigan Avenue. Today, business and leisure travelers are attracted to the ideal location on Chicago's Magnificent Mile, as well as to all-day dining at Taps on Two restaurant and a 25th-floor health club where guests gasp for breath over both exercise and the view of the city spread out beneath them. The hotel maintains its ties with its history; arched doorways, original elevators and crown molding, and old photos are found throughout, and no two guest rooms have the same layout or design. Wireless Internet access is available in the third-floor lobby. 443 rooms, 25 story. Pets accepted; fee. Check-in 3 pm, check-out noon. High-speed Internet access. Restaurant, bar. Fitness room. Airport transportation available. Business center. **$$**

★ ★ ★ AMALFI HOTEL CHICAGO. *20 W Kinzie, Chicago (60610). Phone 312/395-9000; fax 312/395-9001. www.amalfihotelchicago.com.* Ultra-modern, luxurious, unique, and presented with an Italian flair, a place where guest rooms are referred to as "Spaces" and doormen are called "Impressionists," the Amalfi is a hotel like no other. It is a place where the experience of providing comfort is as important as the comfort itself. You will have not a just a conversation, but a relationship with your Experience Designer (concierge), who will give you individual attention 24/7. Your Comfort Stylist (housekeeper), who normally turns down your bed on the right, will pay attention to whether or not you sleep on the left, and will thereafter turn down your bed accordingly. A Libation and Leisure Artist (bartender) will pour champagne, wine, or the cocktail of your choice during the manager's complimentary cocktail hour every evening in the hotel's intimate 6th-floor lounge. In your Space (room), you'll find a pillow-top mattress and 316-thread-count Egyptian cotton linens, a CD library, and a multihead shower. "How can I enhance your experience?" asks each employee you pass in the hall. An experience indeed—but try not to let the expectations extend to the driver of the taxi who takes you to your first museum or appointment. 215 rooms. Pets accepted, some restrictions. Check-in 3 pm, check-out noon. High-speed Internet access. Restaurant, bar. Fitness room. Whirlpool. Airport transportation available. Business center. **$$**

★ ★ ★ **BURNHAM HOTEL.** *1 W Washington Blvd, Chicago (60602). Phone 312/782-1111; toll-free 877/294-9712; fax 312/782-0899. www.burnhamhotel.com.* Reviving the historic Reliance Building (predecessor of the modern skyscraper and early 1900s home of department store Carson Pirie Scott), the Burnham retains the integrity of the landmark architecture, integrating it with a whimsically elegant, clubby ambience. In the Loop near the downtown theater district, major museums, and parks, the hotel is appropriate for business or leisure travel. Rooms and suites offer dramatic views of the Chicago cityscape. The in-house Atwood Café (see) serves upscale American comfort food (including breakfast, lunch, dinner, Sunday brunch, and pre-theater options). The hotel offers 24-hour room service, as well as pampering pet treatments. 122 rooms, 15 story. Pets accepted. Check-in 3 pm, check-out noon. Restaurant, bar. Fitness room. **$$**

★ ★ ★ **CROWNE PLAZA.** *10 S Wabash Ave, Chicago (60603). Phone 312/372-7696; fax 312/372-7320. www.crowneplaza.com.* This historic hotel features unusual characteristics, such as rooms with 12-foot ceilings, 10-foot windows, and oversized bathrooms. Guests are within walking distance of the Art Institute and Symphony Center, local theaters, and the heart of the financial district. 206 rooms, 10 story. Check-in 3 pm, check-out noon. Restaurant, bar. Fitness room. Business center. **$$**

★ ★ ★ **DOUBLETREE GUEST SUITES.** *198 E Delaware Pl, Chicago (60611). Phone 312/664-1100; toll-free 800/222-8733; fax 312/664-9881. www.doubletree.com.* In an ideal location one block east of Michigan Avenue, guests won't know where to head first when heading offsite—to the John Hancock Center across the street, to the Mag Mile and Oak Street shops, to the beach and the park, or to nearby restaurants. All the guest accommodations are two-room suites with a living room and separate bedroom. Sleeper sofas, two televisions, and in-suite refreshment centers make this a good choice for families or extended stays. 345 rooms, 30 story, all suites. Check-in 3 pm, check-out noon. Restaurant, bar. Fitness room. Indoor pool, whirlpool. Business center. **$$**

★ ★ ★ **THE DRAKE HOTEL CHICAGO.** *140 E Walton Pl, Chicago (60611). Phone 312/787-2200; fax 312/787-1431. www.thedrakehotel.com.* A favorite landmark in the Michigan Avenue skyline, The Drake is a luxury lakefront hotel offering both spectacular views and a prime Gold Coast location. Built in 1920 as a summer resort, extensive renovations have preserved the ornate, elegant charm of this venerable classic. Amenities include executive floors, luxurious bathrooms, an exercise facility, a shopping arcade, and multiple dining options. The clubby Cape Cod Room (see) is famous for its oyster bar and seafood, the Oak Terrace for its lakefront views, and the Coq d'Or for its piano bar. Afternoon tea in the lobby's Palm Court and 24-hour room service are also offered. 537 rooms, 10 story. Pets accepted, some restrictions, fee. Check-in 3 pm, check-out noon. Restaurants, bar. Fitness room. Business center. **$$**

★ ★ ★ **EMBASSY SUITES.** *600 N State St, Chicago (60610). Phone 312/943-3800; toll-free 800/362-2779; fax 312/943-7629. www.embassysuiteschicago.com.* Both business- and family-friendly, this all-suite hotel boasts a prime River North location, just a short walk to a multitude of galleries and dining and entertainment venues, as well as to Michigan Avenue shopping. Beautifully appointed two-room suites are modern and spacious and include kitchen appliances and sleeper sofas. Lush with greenery and fountains, the inviting lobby leads to an 11-story atrium. Immediately adjacent are both a Starbucks and the quaint Papagus Greek Taverna (see). Other amenities include VIP rooms; complimentary breakfast; on-site car rental; business, meeting, and conference facilities; and fitness facilities with sauna and pool. 358 rooms, 11 story, all suites. Complimentary full breakfast. Check-in 3 pm, check-out noon. High-speed Internet access. Restaurant, bar. Fitness room. Indoor pool, whirlpool. Airport transportation available. **$$**

★ ★ ★ **THE FAIRMONT CHICAGO.** *200 N Columbus Dr, Chicago (60601). Phone 312/565-8000; toll-free 800/866-5577; fax 312/856-1032. www.fairmont.com.* The Fairmont hotel is at once traditional and contemporary. Just a short distance from the lake and near the renowned shopping of the Magnificent Mile, its sleek tower rests on the edge of leafy Grant Park. The interiors are refined, with rich colors and antique reproductions, and spectacular lakefront views define many of the elegant accommodations. Diners and critics alike are singing the praises of the American dishes at Aria restaurant (see), and afternoon tea is a special event at the Lobby Lounge. The comprehensive business center keeps travelers in touch with the office, while fitness-minded visitors appreciate the guest privileges at the adjoining Lakeshore Athletic Club and Waves day spa. Noteworthy for its indoor rock-climbing wall, this establishment is often considered the city's top exercise facility. 692 rooms, 41 story. Pets accepted, some restrictions; fee. Check-in 3 pm, check-out 1 pm. Restaurant, bar. Fitness room, spa. Indoor pool, outdoor pool, whirlpool. Business center. **$$**

★ ★ ★ ★ ★ **FOUR SEASONS HOTEL CHICAGO.** *120 E Delaware Pl, Chicago (60611). Phone 312/280-8800; fax 312/280-1748. www.fourseasons.com/chicagofs.* Located in a 66-story building atop the world-renowned shops of 900 North Michigan, the Four Seasons Hotel Chicago is a well-heeled shopper's paradise. More than 100 world-class stores, including Gucci and Bloomingdale's, await only steps from your door. This palatial skytop hotel exudes glamour, from its gleaming marble lobby with grand staircase to its regal accommodations. Even exercise is refined here, with a marvelous Roman-columned indoor pool. Occupying the 30th through 46th floors of the tower, the guest rooms afford jaw-dropping views of the magnificent skyline and Lake Michigan. From this vantage point, guests truly feel on top of the world. The accommodations have an opulent character enhanced by jewel tones, rich fabrics, and timeless furnishings. Body and mind are calmed at the spa (see), where a whimsical element inspires the decadent champagne cocktail and caviar facials. Edible indulgences include American and French dishes at Seasons restaurant (see) and continental favorites at The Café. 343 rooms, 66 story. Pets accepted, some restrictions. Check-in 3 pm, check-out noon. High-speed Internet access. Two restaurants, bar. Fitness room, spa. Indoor pool, whirlpool. Airport transportation available. Business center. **$$$$**

★ ★ ★ **HARD ROCK HOTEL CHICAGO.** *230 N Michigan Ave, Chicago (60601). Phone 312/345-1000; toll-free 877/762-5468; fax 312/345-1012.* This hip and happening hotel is located in Chicago's historic Carbon and Carbide building, an Art Deco skyscraper on the Chicago River. Inside, the lobby gives you a taste of what's to come with its piped-in music, rock-and-roll memorabilia, and special exhibits (such as the famous Space Suit, Space Boots, and guitar of Styx's James Young). The theme extends through the hallways up to your room, where zebra-wood furnishings are accented by artwork like a Beatles mural in the bathroom, a Kiss mirror above the desk, and a David Bowie print above the bed. But there's plenty of comfort, too. The beds have down comforters and pillows, and each room has high-speed Internet access, a laptop safe, and an entertainment center with a 27-inch flat-screen TV and DVD/CD player with five-disc changer. And when you come back hungry at 3 am after having spent an evening at one of Chicago's famed jazz or blues clubs, no worries: the Hard Rock offers 24-hour room service. 381 rooms. Pets accepted; fee. Check-in 3 pm, check-out noon. High-speed Internet access. Restaurant, bar. Fitness room. Airport transportation available. Business center. **$$**

★ ★ ★ **HILTON CHICAGO.** *720 S Michigan Ave, Chicago (60605). Phone 312/922-4400; fax 312/922-5240. www.hilton.com.* Built in 1927 as the world's largest hotel, this grande dame of Michigan Avenue overlooks Grant Park and Lake Michigan. Its central location and rich history make it a popular stop, even with those who elect to stay elsewhere. Pay a visit to the lobby's Great Hall and take in the ceiling mural 40 feet overhead, framed by imposing Italian marble columns. Even more spectacular, the Versailles-inspired Grand Ballroom, with its gold leaf molding, mirrors, and crystal chandeliers, has played host to kings and queens, presidents, diginitaries, and celebrities. Tower rooms on the top floors offer slightly more luxurious accommodations. Amenities include three restaurants and a 28,000-square-foot athletic club with a 20-yard swimming pool and sun deck. 1,544 rooms, 25 story. Pets accepted, some restrictions. Check-in 3 pm, check-out 11 am. Restaurants, bar. Fitness room. Indoor pool, whirlpools. Business center. **$$**

★ ★ ★ HOTEL INTERCONTINENTAL CHICAGO. *505 N Michigan Ave, Chicago (60611). Phone 312/944-4100; fax 312/944-3050. www.chicago .intercontinental.com.* Built in 1929 as a luxury men's club (the original swimming pool remains in the fitness center), the InterContinental has undergone extensive renovations in recent years. Uniting the modern main tower and the historic north tower, the dramatic lobby is open and airy, with mosaic tile flooring, a four-story rotunda, and a grand staircase. The Magnificent Mile location, ornate and richly appointed guest rooms with Michigan Avenue or Lake Michigan views, numerous ballrooms, and unique meeting spaces are among the draws. Room service is available 24 hours, and the hotel's restaurant, Zest, serves contemporary Mediterranean fare. High tea is also offered in the Salon. 807 rooms, 42 story. Pets accepted, some restrictions; fee. Check-in 3 pm, check-out noon. High-speed Internet access. Restaurant, two bars. Fitness room (fee). Indoor pool. Airport transportation available. Business center. **$$**

★ ★ ★ HOTEL MONACO CHICAGO. *225 N Wabash Ave, Chicago (60601). Phone 312/960-8500; fax 312/960-1883. www.monaco-chicago.com.* In the heart of downtown, between the Loop and the Magnificent Mile, the Monaco's stylishly eclectic, Euro aesthetic is equally suited to business or pleasure travel. The front desk recalls a vintage steamer trunk; the lobby has the feel of a posh living room, with a grand limestone fireplace. Colorful rooms are retreats of creature comfort, with plush furnishings, distinctive bath products (and Fuji tubs in the suites), and even a companion goldfish on request. Enjoy round-the-clock room service or visit the South Water Kitchen, the hotel's restaurant, for breakfast, lunch, or dinner. Pets also are accommodated with aplomb. 192 rooms, 14 story. Pets accepted. Check-in 3 pm, check-out noon. Restaurant. Fitness room. Business center. **$$**

★ ★ ★ HOUSE OF BLUES, A LOEWS HOTEL. *333 N Dearborn, Chicago (60610). Phone 312/245-0333; fax 312/923-2444. www.loewshotels.com.* With its exotic Gothic-Moroccan-East Indian décor, eye-popping art collection, and adjacent live concert venue, the hip House of Blues Hotel appeals to a new generation of travelers. Guest rooms are spacious and well appointed; vast meeting space and related services cater to business travelers. The namesake restaurant serves Southern American fare and hosts a popular Sunday gospel brunch. In the same complex are the chic, wine-themed bistro Bin 36 (see) and Smith & Wollensky Steak House. The location puts guests in the heart of the River North gallery, dining, and entertainment district and close to the Loop and Michigan Avenue. 367 rooms, 15 story. Pets accepted. Check-in 3 pm, check-out noon. Restaurant, bar. Fitness room, spa. Business center. **$$**

★ ★ ★ HYATT ON PRINTERS ROW. *500 S Dearborn St, Chicago (60605). Phone 312/986-1234; toll-free 800/233-1234; fax 312/939-2468. www.hyatt.com.* Although the location is convenient to downtown and the area pulses with urban energy, the residential buildings that surround this hotel give it a neighborhood feel. The guest rooms in this National Historic Landmark feature 12-foot vaulted ceilings. Bright corner rooms offer views of the South Loop, while west-side rooms are quiet and private. Another key attraction, Prairie restaurant, serves up cuisine from America's heartland in a setting inspired by Frank Lloyd Wright's Prairie school of architecture. 161 rooms, 12 story. Pets accepted; fee. Check-in 3 pm, check-out noon. Restaurant, bar. Fitness room. Airport transportation available. **$$$**

★ ★ ★ HYATT REGENCY MCCORMICK PLACE. *2233 S Martin Luther King Dr, Chicago (60616). Phone 312/567-1234; fax 312/528-4000. www. mccormickplace.hyatt.com.* Conveniently connected by the enclosed Grand Concourse walkway to three exposition buildings, this hotel offers a splendid stay for the busy executive or the guest who just needs to unwind. Providing guests with spacious and well-furnished accommodations and just steps from downtown Chicago, State Street shopping, and Michigan Avenue, this hotel has something for everyone and guarantees return visits by even the most discriminating traveler. 800 rooms, 33 story. Check-in 3 pm, check-out noon. Restaurant, bar. Fitness room. Indoor pool. Business center. **$$**

★★★ **LE MERIDIEN CHICAGO.** *521 N Rush St, Chicago (60611). Phone 312/645-1500; fax 312/645-1550. www.lemeridien.com.* Perched atop The Shops at North Bridge and Nordstrom, with a main entrance on Rush Street and an entrance on Michigan Avenue, this hotel has an ideal location—close to the Loop, the Merchandise Mart, and Navy Pier. Cerise restaurant (see) offers exceptional cuisine in a casual setting, while Lerendezvous bar provides an intimate place to mingle and sample the signature chocolate martini. Work off the indulgence in the 24-hour fitness center. Rooms offer high-tech accoutrements such as CD player/clock radios, cordless phones, and electronic safes with charging capabilities. 311 rooms, 12 story. Pets accepted, some restrictions. Check-in 3 pm, check-out noon. High-speed Internet access. Restaurant, bar. Fitness room. Business center. **$$$**

★★★ **MARRIOTT CHICAGO DOWNTOWN.** *540 N Michigan Ave, Chicago (60611). Phone 312/836-0100; fax 312/836-6139. www.marriott.com.* Business travelers appreciate this hotel's convenient location along the Magnificent Mile and near many Loop corporate offices. Leisure travelers walk steps from the lobby to area attractions and a wealth of shops, including the nearby Shops at North Bridge containing Nordstrom. Guest rooms are designed for working travelers, with data ports, voice mail, lamp-lit work areas, and high-speed Internet access. 1,192 rooms, 46 story. Check-in 4 pm, check-out noon. Two restaurants, bars. Fitness room, spa. Indoor pool, whirlpool. Business center. **$$$**

★★★ **MARRIOTT CHICAGO DOWNTOWN MEDICAL DISTRICT UIC.** *625 S Ashland Ave, Chicago (60607). Phone 312/491-1234; toll-free 800/228-9290; fax 312/529-6095. www.marriott.com/chidm.* Tucked within a half-mile radius of John H. Stroger Hospital, Rush Presbyterian/St. Luke's Hospital, and the University of Illinois at Chicago Medical Center, this comfortable, 114-room hotel provides a relaxing place to stay for business or personal reasons. In addition to the standard amenities, the hotel has a computer and printer available, as well as fax and copier services; a car rental desk and airline desk are also on-site. Even if you aren't in town to visit one of the medical facilities, what makes this Marriott especially attractive is its proximity to so much of what Chicago has to offer. You'll be within 5 miles of a large number the city's best sights, but you won't have to stay amid the congestion of the major tourist areas. Enjoy a fireside dinner at Jaxx Restaurant and then a nightcap at Jaxx Lounge, both located in the hotel. 114 rooms, 4 story. Check-in 1 pm, check-out noon. High-speed Internet access, wireless Internet access. Restaurant, bar. Fitness room. Airport transportation available. Business center. **$$**

★★★ **OMNI AMBASSADOR EAST.** *1301 N State Pkwy, Chicago (60610). Phone 312/787-7200; toll-free 800/843-6664; fax 312/787-4760. www.omnihotels.com.* A prime Gold Coast location and the world-famous Pump Room restaurant (see) are two reasons to stay at this grand hotel, designated a Historic Hotel of America. The 14 Celebrity Suites honor some of the many notable guests who have stayed or eaten on-site. Enjoy French-inspired American cuisine and live jazz music in the Pump Room, which has served a steady stream of patrons since 1926. 285 rooms, 17 story. Pets accepted, some restrictions; fee. Check-in 3 pm, check-out noon. High-speed Internet access, wireless Internet access. Restaurant, bar. Fitness room. Airport transportation available. Business center. **$$**

★★★ **OMNI CHICAGO HOTEL.** *676 N Michigan Ave, Chicago (60611). Phone 312/944-6664; toll-free 800/788-6664; fax 312/266-3015. www.omnihotels.com.* In the center of Michigan Avenue within a mixed-use building sits this 347-suite property, host to many famous guests of *The Oprah Winfrey Show.* All accommodations offer spacious sitting rooms with bedrooms hidden behind French doors, great for corporate clientele needing their room to double as an office. The fourth floor Cielo restaurant provides fantastic views of the street excitement below. 347 rooms, 25 story. Pets accepted, some restrictions; fee. Check-in 3 pm, check-out noon. Restaurant, bar. Children's activity center. Fitness room. Indoor pool, whirlpool. Business center. **$$**

★★★ **PALMER HOUSE HILTON.** *17 E Monroe St, Chicago (60603). Phone 312/726-7500; fax 312/917-1707. www.hilton.com.* Grand and gilded, the Palmer House Hilton has harbored visitors to the Windy City for 130 years, making it America's longest-operating hotel. This Loop landmark has undergone a full renovation to restore designer-builder Potter Palmer's original French Empire opulence, including the breathtaking Beaux Arts ceiling in the palatial lobby. Amenities include an 11-room penthouse suite, executive levels with private elevator, an entire floor of "deluxe-tech" conference and meeting facilities, a fitness club, and a shopping arcade. Four restaurants and bars include the 1940s-themed Big Downtown restaurant and bar and the retro Polynesian favorite, Trader Vic's. 1,639 rooms, 25 story. Pets accepted, some restrictions. Check-in 3 pm, check-out 11 am. Restaurants, bar. Fitness room. Indoor pool, whirlpool. Airport transportation available. Business center. **$$**

★★★★ PARK HYATT CHICAGO. *800 N Michigan Ave, Chicago (60611). Phone 312/335-1234; toll-free 800/335-1234; fax 312/239-4000. www.parkhyattchicago.com.* From its stylish interiors to its historic Water Tower Square location, the Park Hyatt is intrinsically tied to the history of Chicago. Occupying a landmark building in the heart of the Magnificent Mile shopping area, the hotel has a sleek, modern attitude. The public and private spaces celebrate the city's long-lasting love affair with architecture and its artists. Mies van der Rohe, Eames, and Noguchi furnishings are showcased throughout the guest rooms, while photography commissioned by the Art Institute of Chicago graces the walls. A health club, spa, and salon are the perfect antidotes to stress, and the flawless service always ensures a carefree visit. The nouvelle cuisine at NoMI (see) is a standout, although the dramatic seventh-floor views from the floor-to-ceiling windows are not for the faint of heart. To escape the urban pace, visitors head to the NoMI Garden for American barbecue favorites. 202 rooms, 18 story. Pets accepted, some restrictions; fee. Check-in 3 pm, check-out noon. High-speed Internet access. Restaurant, bar. Fitness room. Indoor pool, whirlpool. Airport transportation available. Business center. **$$$$**

★★★★★ THE PENINSULA CHICAGO. *108 E Superior St, Chicago (60611). Phone 312/337-2888; fax 312/751-2888. www.peninsula.com.* Reigning over Chicago's famed Magnificent Mile, The Peninsula Chicago hotel basks in a golden aura. From the sun-filled lobby to the gleaming, gilded details, this hotel simply sparkles. With Tiffany and Ralph Lauren downstairs and Saks and Neiman Marcus across the street, the gracious bellmen outfitted in crisp white uniforms are a shopper's savior. Asian sensibilities are expertly blended with details highlighting the city's Art Deco heritage in the public spaces. Soft lighting, polished woods, and golden hues create glorious shelters in the guest rooms. Proving the point that modern amenities are a hallmark of this property, all rooms are fitted with bedside electronic control panels and flat-screen televisions. Guests escape the pressures of the everyday at the state-of-the-art exercise facility and spa, complete with an outdoor sundeck. Whether taking tea, nibbling flammekuchen, sampling Asian specialties, or savoring seafood, guests traverse the world at five distinctive dining venues. 339 rooms, 20 story. Pets accepted, some restrictions. Check-in 3 pm, check-out noon. Wireless Internet access. Four restaurants, bar. Fitness room, fitness classes available, spa. Indoor pool, whirlpool. Airport transportation available. Business center. **$$$$**

★★★ RENAISSANCE CHICAGO HOTEL. *1 W Wacker Dr, Chicago (60601). Phone 312/372-7200; toll-free 888/236-2427; fax 312/372-0093. www.renaissancehotels.com.* This Marriott-owned Loop high-rise features stone and glass exterior towers that rise above the intersection of State and Wacker. The Renaissance is a welcome haven to its audience of business travelers and vacationers looking for a central location accessible to theaters and museums. The handsome lobby sets a posh, executive tone; comfortable rooms boast spectacular views (especially on the higher floors). The Great Street Restaurant in the hotel's atrium serves American breakfast, lunch, and dinner (and has a bargain theater menu) with a view of the river. Additional amenities include 24-hour room service, expanded club-level rooms, a fitness club and pool, a lobby bar, and a 24-hour Kinko's business center. 553 rooms, 27 story. Pets accepted, some restrictions; fee. Check-in 3 pm, check-out 1 pm. Restaurant, bar. Fitness room. Indoor pool, whirlpool. Business center. **$$$**

★★★★★ THE RITZ-CARLTON, A FOUR SEASONS HOTEL. *160 E Pearson St, Chicago (60611). Phone 312/266-1000; toll-free 800/621-6906; fax 312/266-1194. www.fourseasons.com.* Guests of the esteemed Ritz-Carlton Chicago often wonder if heaven could get any better than this. The unparalleled levels of service, commitment to excellence, and meticulous attention to detail make this one of the country's finest hotels. Gracing the upper levels of prestigious Water Tower Place on the Magnificent Mile, the hotel's guest rooms afford picture-perfect views through large windows. Rich tones and dignified furnishings define the accommodations. Managed by the Four Seasons, The Ritz-Carlton offers guests a taste of the luxe life, from the resplendent décor and seamless service to the superlative cuisine at the four restaurants and lounges. The sublime contemporary French menu and sensational ambience at The Dining Room (see) make it one of the most coveted tables in town. Human guests, however, are not the only ones to be spoiled—furry visitors feast in-room on filet mignon and salmon! 435 rooms, 31 story. Pets accepted, some restrictions. Check-in 3 pm, check-out noon. High-speed Internet access. Three restaurants, bar. Fitness room, fitness classes available, spa. Indoor pool, whirlpool. Airport transportation available. Business center. **$$$$**

★ ★ ★ SHERATON CHICAGO HOTEL AND TOWERS. *301 E North Water St, Chicago (60611). Phone 312/464-1000; toll-free 800/233-4100; fax 312/464-9140. www.sheratonchicago.com.* Contemporary yet comfortable, every room of the handsomely appointed Sheraton Chicago Hotel & Towers promises a sweeping view of the cityscape, the Chicago River, or Lake Michigan. The central location is just minutes from the Magnificent Mile, the Loop, Navy Pier, and McCormick Place. The spacious lobby is appointed in imported marble and rich woods, and luxurious fitness facilities feature a pool and sauna. Close to numerous fine restaurants, the Sheraton's five in-house dining options include Shula's Steak House and an indoor-outdoor café overlooking the river. Extensive and elegant meeting facilities, a full-service business center, and club-level rooms cater to business travelers. 1,200 rooms, 34 story. Pets accepted, some restrictions. Check-in 3 pm, check-out noon. Restaurant, bar. Fitness room. Indoor pool. Business center. **$$**

★ ★ ★ SOFITEL CHICAGO WATER TOWER. *20 E Chestnut St, Chicago (60611). Phone 312/324-4000; fax 312/324-4026.* A stunning design created by French architect Jean-Paul Viguier gives this hotel an unmistakable presence on the Gold Coast, just off the Magnificent Mile. Le Bar is a popular after-work place to meet and mingle, while Café des Architectes serves up French cuisine in a contemporary setting. 415 rooms, 32 story. Pets accepted, some restrictions. Check-in 3 pm, check-out noon. Restaurant, bar. Fitness room. **$$**

★ ★ ★ THE SUTTON PLACE HOTEL – CHICAGO. *21 E Bellevue Pl, Chicago (60611). Phone 312/266-2100; fax 312/266-2103.* Stylish understatement is the mantra of this luxurious 23-story hotel, an Art Deco-inspired building housing a handsome, modern interior. The prime Gold Coast location offers immediate access to such attractions as Magnificent Mile shopping, Rush Street nightlife, and some of the city's finest restaurants. Soundproofed rooms feature deep-soaking tubs, separate glass-enclosed showers, plush robes, and lavish bath accessories. Room service is 24/7, and destination dining and people-watching are available at the Whiskey Bar & Grill. Popular with corporate travelers, Sutton Place is equally suited to private getaways—even with your pet (with some restrictions). 246 rooms, 23 story. Pets accepted, some restrictions; fee. Check-in 3 pm, check-out noon. Restaurant, bar. Fitness room. Airport transportation available. Business center. **$$**

★ ★ ★ SWISSOTEL CHICAGO. *323 E Wacker Dr, Chicago (60601). Phone 312/565-0565; fax 312/565-0540. www.swissotel-chicago.com.* High ceilings, dark woods, and a well-lit lobby dominate the first glimpse into the tastefully decorated and operated Swissôtel Chicago. Stunning views of Lake Michigan and Grant Park lend a tranquil feel and help guests forget the hustle and bustle outside, despite the central location near Navy Pier and Michigan Avenue. With oversized rooms and cheerful service, this hotel is a solid choice for even the most discerning traveler. 632 rooms, 43 story. Check-in 3 pm, check-out noon. Two restaurants. Fitness room. Indoor pool, whirlpool. Business center. **$$**

★ ★ ★ THE WESTIN CHICAGO RIVER NORTH. *320 Dearborn St, Chicago (60610). Phone 312/744-1900; toll-free 800/937-8461; fax 312/527-2650. www.westin.com/rivernorth.* The Westin Chicago River North enjoys a wonderful location overlooking the Chicago River in the heart of the city's financial and theater districts. This luxury hotel is an impressive sight and offers a welcoming home for business or leisure travelers visiting the Windy City. Attractive and comfortable, the rooms use a blend of brass, black, and caramel tones to create a soothing atmosphere, the furnishings a contemporary interpretation of classic design. Westin's signature Heavenly Beds make for luxurious slumber, and the Heavenly Baths ensure aquatic therapy. Athletic-minded guests reap the rewards of the full-service fitness center. The Kamehachi Sushi Bar delights fish lovers; the Celebrity Café features all-day dining with a focus on American dishes; and the Hana Lounge entertains nightly with hors d'oeuvres and live music. 424 rooms, 20 story. Pets accepted, some restrictions. Check-in 3 pm, check-out noon. High-speed Internet access. Two restaurants, two bars. Fitness room. Airport transportation available. Business center. **$$**

★★★ **THE WHITEHALL HOTEL.** *105 E Delaware Pl, Chicago (60611). Phone 312/944-6300; toll-free 800/948-4255; fax 312/944-8552. www.thewhitehallhotel.com.* A historic Gold Coast landmark, this venerable hotel is just off the Magnificent Mile and steps from Water Tower Place. Built in 1927 and extensively renovated in recent years, the independent Whitehall retains its stature as a small sanctuary with personal service and sedate, old-world charm. Rooms combine traditional décor (including some four-poster beds) and modern technology. The California-Mediterranean restaurant, Molive, offers an excellent wine program, a bar, and outdoor dining. Additional highlights include club floors and complimentary sedan service (within 2 miles). 221 rooms, 21 story. Pets accepted, some restrictions; fee. Check-in 3 pm, check-out noon. Restaurant, bar. Fitness room. **$$**

★★★ **W CHICAGO CITY CENTER.** *172 W Adams St, Chicago (60603). Phone 312/332-1200; toll-free 888/625-5144; fax 312/917-5771. www.whotels.com.* Blending in perfectly in a decidedly urban setting in the city's financial district, this hotel provides a much-needed, hip hotspot for locals and tourists alike. Old architecture of the former Midland Hotel mixes with modern accents in the W Living Room, where an after-work crowd mingles with drinks beneath the vaulted ceiling while listening to tunes spun by the DJ from a balcony above. Guest rooms are modern but comfortable, providing a respite from the commotion below. Grab a light bite at the W Café or dine on more substantial Italian fare at Wë. Rande Gerber's adjacent Whiskey Blue bar gives guests a choice Chicago nightspot just steps from the hotel elevators. 390 rooms, 20 story. Pets accepted, some restrictions; fee. Check-in 3 pm, check-out noon. High-speed Internet access. Restaurant, bar. Fitness room. **$$$**

★★★ **WYNDHAM CHICAGO DOWNTOWN HOTEL.** *633 N St. Clair St, Chicago (60611). Phone 312/573-0300; toll-free 800/996-3426; fax 312/274-0164. www.wyndham.com.* Escape the stresses of city life without venturing too far from the hub of activity at this hotel, just blocks from Chicago's Magnificent Mile. Attractions, restaurants, and shops are an easy walk or a quick cab ride away, including the Museum of Contemporary Art and the John Hancock Building. Caliterra Bar & Grill (see) offers a convenient dining option, serving Californian and Italian cuisine, with live jazz in the evenings. The comfortable guest rooms feature pillowtop mattresses, Herman Miller work chairs, and Golden Door bath products. 417 rooms, 17 story. Check-in 4 pm, check-out 11 am. High-speed Internet access, wireless Internet access. Restaurant, bar. Fitness room. Indoor pool, whirlpool. Airport transportation available. Business center. **$$**

Specialty Lodgings

The following lodging establishments are approved by Mobil Travel Guide, but due to their unique and individualized nature have not been given a traditional Mobil Star rating. Included in this listing you may find bed-and-breakfasts, limited-service inns, guest ranches, and other unique hotel properties.

GOLD COAST GUEST HOUSE. *113 W Elm St, Chicago (60610). Phone 312/337-0361; fax 312/337-0362. www.bbchicago.com.* Tucked into the heart of the lively Gold Coast neighborhood, within walking distance of the Magnificent Mile, this bed-and-breakfast provides an unlikely oasis of calm. Guests stay in one of four cozily furnished rooms, all individually air-conditioned and with private baths. This 1873 brick townhome features a 20-foot glass window off the living room, overlooking a small two-level garden out back. Guests enjoy health club privileges (for a fee) at a nearby multiplex as well as access to the house kitchen for snacks. 4 rooms, 3 story. Children over 12 years only. Complimentary continental breakfast. Check-in by arrangement, check-out 11 am. **$**

OLD TOWN CHICAGO BED AND BREAKFAST. *1442 N North Park Ave, Chicago (60610). Phone 312/440-9268. www.oldtownchicago.com.* Guests staying in this modern, four-suite bed-and-breakfast (an Art Deco mansion) are afforded amenities such as a private bathroom, walk-in closet with a wall safe, television, VCR, and private-line telephone. Situated on a residential, tree-lined street, accommodations are close to restaurants, theaters, and an eclectic array of shops. 4 rooms, 4 story. Complimentary continental breakfast. Check-out 11 am. Fitness room. **$$**

THE WHEELER MANSION. *2020 S Calumet Ave, Chicago (60616). Phone 312/945-2020; fax 312/945-2021. www.wheelermansion.com.* 11 rooms. Complimentary full breakfast. Check-in 3 pm, check-out noon. **$$$**

Spas

★ ★ ★ ★ THE SPA AT FOUR SEASONS HOTEL CHICAGO. *120 E Delaware Pl, Chicago (60611).Phone 312/280-8800; toll-free 800/819-5053. www.fourseasons.com/chicagofs.* The Four Seasons Hotel Chicago redefines luxury from its perch above the city's Magnificent Mile. Stressed-out urbanites can work off anxiety in the fitness center, where the elliptical trainers, stationary bicycles, and treadmills come complete with views of the Magnificent Mile. Individual fitness consultations are available, and for those who prefer to exercise outside, jogging routes are mapped out based on personal preferences. Swimming laps takes on a grander element at this Four Seasons, where the indoor pool is capped off by a glass-domed ceiling with Roman columns.

Once you are safely ensconced inside The Spa, the hectic pace and noise of city living become distant memories. Five soundproofed treatment rooms are available to coax the tension from your muscles and let your body unwind. Decadent and luxurious, this spa wants you to spoil yourself. Drink a toast to your skin with the champagne cocktail facial or savor the splendid benefits of the perle de caviar facial. Melt away with a Swedish, hot stone, sports conditioning, or scalp rejuvenator massage. The elixir paraffin wrap combines olive stones, lavender, juniper berries, and grapefruit to produce baby-soft skin. Your body will thank you after receiving a crushed pearls and lavender body polish, a citrus refresher body scrub, or a green tea and ginger mud body mask. Enjoy an aroma blend massage, which uses different scents and types of massage to celebrate the season of your choice, or take a journey through all four with the Four Seasons In One treatment. A variety of therapies, including manicures and pedicures, pamper and primp hands and feet.

★ ★ ★ THE SPA AT THE CARLTON CLUB, *160 E Pearson St, Chicago (60611).Phone 312/266-1000; toll-free 800/621-6906. www.fourseasons.com.* Escape from the rat race at The Spa at The Carlton Club. The state-of-the-art fitness center is a boon for those who want to keep in shape while on the road. Treadmills, stair climbers, elliptical trainers, and stationary bicycles are equipped with televisions and VCRs to entertain you while you work up a sweat. The center also offers terrific group fitness classes, including Pilates, yoga, cardio boxing, aerobics, water aerobics, and even salsa dancing. After an intense workout, relax in the whirlpool or unwind in the sauna or steam room. The lap pool provides a refreshing fitness alternative, and with dazzling views of the city and lake, the sundeck is a perfect spot to unwind before or after you exercise.

At the spa, relish your quiet time away from the hustle and bustle of the city. If you prefer to enjoy the spa life in the privacy of your own room, many facials, massages, and nail care services can be booked as in-room treatments. Deep tissue, Swedish, healing stone, and aromatherapy massages are wonderful ways to reward yourself, and The Carlton Club signature massage blends components of deep tissue and aromatherapy for total relaxation. The herbal body wrap is a spa signature, while the seaweed mud body wrap envelops you in seaweed, minerals, botanical extracts, fruit enzymes, and customized aromatherapy oils to soften and soothe your skin.

From The Carlton Club signature facial that includes hand and foot reflexology massages as well as a hand paraffin treatment to the deep-cleansing facial aux Champagne that concludes with a glass of Louis Roederer Champagne in the lounge, the spa's skin care services are decadent. Even the manicures and pedicures—with tea tree paraffin treatments that heal dry skin, citrus C treatments that revitalize your hands and feet, and aromatherapy or reflexology therapies that calm sore muscles—pamper in style.

Restaurants

★ ★ 312 CHICAGO. *136 N La Salle St, Chicago (60602). Phone 312/696-2420; fax 312/236-0153. www.312chicago.com.* Named for Chicago's urban area code, 312 Chicago is adjacent to the Hotel Allegro in the heart of the Loop's business, shopping, and theater district. The tempting menu marries fresh, contemporary Italian fare with more rustic options. The bilevel setting is clubby yet airy, with a bustling open kitchen and an aromatic rotisserie. The restaurant also serves upscale breakfast and lunch, and the chic bar is a great spot for cocktails. American, Italian menu. Breakfast, lunch, dinner, Sun brunch. Closed holidays. Bar. Children's menu. Business casual attire. Reservations recommended. Valet parking. Outdoor seating. **$$**

★ A LA TURKA. *3134 N Lincoln Ave, Chicago (60657). Phone 773/935-6101; fax 773/935-8894.*

www.turkishkitchen.us. Belly dancing shows and sunken tables surrounded by pillow seats lend exotic allure to this north side Turkish eatery. Sharable starters are ideally suited to grazing. For a complete culinary journey, progress from bread spreads and salads to grilled meats, concluding with muddy Turkish coffee. Make like the Turks who frequent A La Turka and bring the late-night gang to its weekend dances. Turkish menu. Lunch, dinner. Closed Dec 25. Bar. Business casual attire. Reservations recommended. Outdoor seating. **$$**

★ **ABU NAWAS.** *2411 N Clark St, Chicago (60614). Phone 773/529-1705.* For good, cheap, and plentiful portions of savory Middle Eastern fare, it's hard to beat Abu Nawas. This cheerful, smoke-free Lincoln Parker serves heaping plates of hummus and the eggplant spread baba ghanoush with pita bread, falafel with mango sauce, and grilled lamb kebab skewers. Wash it down with juice, tea, a yogurt drink, or Turkish coffee (alcohol is BYOB). Its prime location near Clark and Fullerton streets makes Abu Nawas a great lunchtime shopping stop. Indian menu. Lunch, dinner. Casual attire. **$**

★ ★ **ADOBO GRILL.** *1610 N Wells St, Chicago (60614). Phone 312/266-7999; fax 312/266-9299. www.adobogrill.com.* Fans of beyond-the-taco Mexican food will appreciate this upscale, up-tempo Old Towner known for its extensive tequila list, tableside guacamole preparation, and intriguing (and extensive) menu offerings—with some equally intriguing cocktails. The scene at night can be raucous; brunch-time is quieter. Mexican menu. Dinner. Closed holidays. Two vintage bars. Children's menu. Casual attire. Reservations recommended. Valet parking. **$$**

★ **AMARIND'S.** *6822 W North Ave, Chicago (60607). Phone 773/889-9999.* Amarind's creative and inexpensive fare may well warrant a drive out to the western edge of the city (Amarind's is closer to suburban River Forest than to downtown). The chef/owner hails from Arun's (see), the north side gourmet eatery consistently ranked as one of the country's best Thai restaurants. His experience shows in offerings such as spicy curry pork, ginger scallop salad, and spinach noodles with shrimp and crab. With the exception of a couple of "market price" items, nothing tops $11 here. Thai menu. Lunch, dinner. Closed Mon. Casual attire. Reservations recommended. **$**

★ ★ ★ ★ **AMBRIA.** *2300 N Lincoln Park W, Chicago (60614). Phone 773/472-5959; toll-free 888/538-8823; fax 773/472-9077. www.leye.com.* Ambria is located at the base of Lincoln Park in The Belden-Stratford, a 1922 architectural landmark turned residential hotel on Chicago's romantic lakefront. With dark mahogany walls and luxuriously appointed tabletops set with tiny shaded votive lamps, this beautiful, graceful space is filled with radiant women and striking men, who glow in the room's creamy amber light. Ambria is a civilized spot, ideal for business or pleasure. The menu is as elegant as the room, with Mediterranean accents from Italy, Spain, and beyond (saffron, piquillo peppers, olives, and polenta) turning up the flavor on the kitchen's top-quality selection of fish, game, lamb, and beef. In addition to the enticing á la carte menu, the kitchen offers the Ambria Classic menu, a decadent five-course prix fixe option that should be ordered if a big enough appetite presents itself. The service is helpful, efficient, and warm, making dining here a delight on every level. French menu. Dinner. Closed Sun; holidays. Bar. Children's menu. Jacket required. Reservations recommended. Valet parking. **$$$$**

★ **ANN SATHER.** *929 W Belmont Ave, Chicago (60657). Phone 773/348-2378; fax 773/348-1731. www.annsather.com.* Open since 1945, this Swedish family of comfy, come-as-you-are restaurants may be best known for its sinful cinnamon rolls, but fans of all ages also appreciate the hearty Swedish and American classics (for example, Swedish pancakes with lingonberries or roast turkey dinner), the no-nonsense service, and the reasonable prices. The breakfast menu is available all day. Four additional locations can be found on the city's North Side: 5207 N Clark, 1448 N Milwaukee, 3416 N Southport, and 3411 N Broadway. Swedish, American menu. Breakfast, lunch, dinner. Bar. Casual attire. Reservations recommended. **$$**

★ ★ **ARCO DE CUCHILLEROS.** *3445 N Halsted St, Chicago (60657). Phone 773/296-6046; fax 773/296-6091.* Located in a storefront in the bustling Lakeview neighborhood, this charming eatery features more than 40 different selections of soups, hot and cold tapas, and larger entrées, as well as what has been said to be the best sangria in the city. Enjoy the authentic Spanish cuisine at one of the cozy tables tucked away in the dining room or, in warmer months, dine on the outdoor backyard patio, aglow with torches and candles. Spanish, tapas menu. Dinner. Closed Mon; holidays. Bar. Casual attire. Reservations recommended. Valet parking. Outdoor seating. **$$**

★★★ **ARIA.** *200 N Columbus Dr, Chicago (60601). Phone 312/565-8000; fax 312/946-7953. www.ariachicago.com.* Globe-trotting food in a trendy setting make Aria one of the city's more fashionable eateries. Although it is lodged in the Fairmont Chicago (see), Aria distances itself from the bland stereotype of hotel restaurants by maintaining a street entrance to encourage local patrons to visit. Aria's Asian-inspired décor features Tibetan artwork, orchids, and plush upholstery, underscoring the menu's Eastern orientation. Chef James Wierzelewski formerly worked in Thailand and Malaysia, influences that show up in steamed black bass and crispy duck leg confit, although Indian, Italian, and French notes also flavor the fare. The bar serves a small-bites menu to the cocktail crowd. International/Fusion menu. Breakfast, lunch, dinner. Bar. Children's menu. Business casual attire. Reservations recommended. Valet parking. **$$$**

★★★ **ARUN'S.** *4156 N Kedzie Ave, Chicago (60618). Phone 773/539-1909; fax 773/539-2125. www.arunsthai.com.* Arun's version of Thai food is as similar to neighborhood take-out as caviar is to peanut butter. Regarded as the best Thai interpreter in the city, if not the country, Arun's takes a fine-dining turn with the complex cooking of Thailand, but without the attendant snobbery of many serious restaurants. A phalanx of eager, well-informed servers cheerfully work the alcove-lodged tables in the tranquil, Asian-art-filled rooms. Chef Arun Sampanthavivat prepares an original prix fixe menu nightly, proffering 12 courses, half of them small appetizers, served family style. You won't know what's on until you arrive, but the kitchen easily adapts to food and spice sensitivities. Thai menu. Dinner. Closed Mon; holidays, the first week in Jan. Bar. Business casual attire. Reservations recommended. **$$$$**

★★ **ATWOOD CAFE.** *1 W Washington Blvd, Chicago (60602). Phone 312/368-1900; fax 312/357-2875. www.atwoodcafe.com.* The whimsical ground-floor occupant of the Burnham Hotel (see), Atwood draws a cross-section of travelers, desk jockeys, theatergoers, and shoppers in for chef Heather Terhune's café menu. Modern dishes like grilled calamari and tuna carpaccio balance such comfort food classics as grilled pork chops with spaetzle. Soak up the Loop scene through floor-to-ceiling windows framing the downtown bustle at lunch and romantic, marquee-lit streetscapes at dinner. Cozy velvet banquettes and settees encourage lingering. American menu. Breakfast, lunch, dinner, Sun brunch. Closed holidays. Bar. Children's menu. Casual attire. Outdoor seating. **$$**

★★ **AVEC.** *615 W Randolph St, Chicago (60661). Phone 312/377-2002; fax 312/377-2008. www.avecrestaurant.com.* Thinking man's Mediterranean comfort food is served in a chic sliver of space next to parent restaurant Blackbird (see). An ultra-hip power crowd mingles with restaurant industry insiders; the wood walls, floor, and long communal seating area blend together to create the illusion of an upscale mess hall-cum-sauna. The wine bar concept is fulfilled by a daring list of lesser-known and small-production bottles (40 by the mini carafe). Mediterranean menu. Dinner, late-night. Bar. Casual attire. Valet parking. **$$**

★★★ **AVENUES.** *508 E Superior, Chicago (60611). Phone 312/573-6754. www.chicago.peninsula.com.* Set in an elegant space on the fifth floor of the Peninsula hotel (see), Avenues offers creative contemporary fare with an emphasis on seafood, served by polished professionals in a refined ambience. The wine list is expertly chosen to harmonize with the food. Hushed tones and a discreet, old-world service attitude bespeak this modern restaurant's spot in the upper echelon of fine urban hotel dining. American, Seafood menu. Dinner. Bar. Business casual attire. **$$$$**

★★ **BANDERA.** *535 N Michigan Ave, Chicago (60611). Phone 312/644-3524. www.banderarestaurants.com.* A shopper's delight one story above Michigan Avenue, Bandera boosts its Mag Mile views with a crowd-pleasing American menu. The emphasis is on Western (think baby-back ribs) and rotisserie fare (spit-roasted chicken), but the restaurant offers enough variety to please most tastes. Vintage photographs of Chicago localize this link in the Houston's restaurant chain. American menu. Lunch, dinner. Closed holidays. Bar. Children's menu. Business casual attire. **$$**

★ **BASTA PASTA.** *6733 Olmstead St, Chicago (60631). Phone 773/763-0667; fax 773/763-1114. www.bastapastachicago.com.* Homemade Italian food like "mama" used to make is the order of the day at this restaurant, located in a former bank in the Edison Park neighborhood (the rest rooms are the former vaults). Favorites like spaghetti, linguini, and rigatoni are served in gargantuan portions that, when you're done eating, may feel as if they were the size of the giant bowl of pasta that marks the restaurant's exterior. But despite its name, pasta isn't the only reason to visit—the menu also offers a good selection of home-style seafood and chicken dishes, pizzas, and salads. Italian menu. Dinner. Closed holidays. Bar. Children's menu. Casual attire. Reservations recommended. Valet parking. Outdoor seating. **$$**

★ **THE BERGHOFF.** *17 W Adams St, Chicago (60603). Phone 312/427-3170; fax 312/427-6549. www.berghoff.com.* The Loop's beloved Berghoff, a landmark of 100-plus years, mingles tourists and locals alike. Out-of-towners line up for the German restaurant's lavishly trimmed dining room, where warm potato salad accompanies oversized weiner schnitzel and smoky sausages. Office workers pack the long, wood-paneled barroom slugging mugs of the house beer and munching carved roast beef sandwiches. The bar proudly displays the city's first post-Prohibition liquor license. American, German menu. Lunch, dinner. Closed Sun; holidays. Bar. Children's menu. Casual attire. Reservations recommended. **$$**

★ ★ ★ **BICE.** *158 E Ontario St, Chicago (60611). Phone 312/664-1474; fax 312/664-9008. www.bice ristorante.com.* A chain that grew out of Milan, Bice stays true to its northern Italian roots at its Chicago link. The Art Deco-inspired design provides a glamorous backdrop in sync with the chic Streeterville neighborhood in which it resides. While the menu changes monthly, expect hits including veal Milanese and beef carpaccio. For a cheaper, more casual version of Bice food, try its sibling next door, Bice Café, a lunchtime favorite of Michigan Avenue shoppers. Italian menu. Lunch, dinner. Closed Jan 1, Dec 25. Bar. Children's menu. Casual attire. Valet parking. Outdoor seating. **$$$**

★ ★ **BIN 36.** *339 N Dearborn St, Chicago (60610). Phone 312/755-9463; fax 312/755-9410. www.bin36 .com.* This wine-centric River North restaurant and bar pairs 50 wines with moderately priced, creative American food. There's an environment for every occasion, from an after-work cocktail at the bar to a light bite in the lounge to a full meal in the dining room. A retail section sells wine and related goodies. American menu. Breakfast, lunch, dinner, brunch. Bar. Children's menu. Business casual attire. Reservations recommended. Valet parking. **$$**

★ ★ ★ **BLACKBIRD.** *619 W Randolph St, Chicago (60606). Phone 312/715-0708; fax 312/715-0774. www.blackbirdrestaurant.com.* The minimalist chic Blackbird girds style with substance. Aluminum chairs and pale mohair banquettes seat guests at tables within easy eavesdropping distance of one another. But instead of the boring details of someone's career, what you're likely to hear are raves for chef Paul Kahan's French-influenced cooking. Like the décor, his style is spare, hitting just the right contemporary notes without drowning in too many flavors. The market-driven menu changes frequently, with seasonal favorites such as homemade charcuterie, quail with foie gras, and braised veal cheeks. Noise levels are high but the elegantly attired fans who flock here consider it simply good buzz. American menu. Lunch, dinner. Closed Sun; Jan 1, Thanksgiving, Dec 25. Bar. Casual attire. Valet parking. Outdoor seating. **$$$**

★ ★ **BLUE FIN.** *1952 W North Ave, Chicago (60622). Phone 773/394-7373.* A good choice for sushi in the Wicker Park/Bucktown area, Blue Fin manages to engender romance in a neighborhood that parties hardy. But its modern sensibility—lots of candlelight and low-key techno music—make it at home in the 'hood. In addition to a good range of raw-based sushi, sashimi, and maki rolls, Blue Fin entertains fans of cooked food with tempura and fish choices on the nicely priced menu. Expect crowds on weekends. Japanese, sushi menu. Dinner. Closed Sun. Casual attire. Outdoor seating. **$$**

★ ★ **BLUEPOINT OYSTER BAR.** *741 W Randolph St, Chicago (60661). Phone 312/207-1222; fax 312/207-1222. www.rdgchicago.com.* A clubby setting for seafood in the Randolph Market District, upscale Bluepoint is known for its extensive selection of fresh fish and shellfish. The wine list includes a generous array of wines by the glass and the half-bottle. Budget-minded diners might want to consider a lunchtime visit. Seafood menu. Lunch, dinner. Closed holidays. Bar. Children's menu. Business casual attire. Reservations recommended. Valet parking. Outdoor seating. **$$**

★ ★ ★ **BOB SAN.** *1805-07 W Division, Chicago (60622). Phone 773/235-8888. www.bob-san.com.* Sushi-savvy urban diners will appreciate this comfortably hip Wicker Park Japanese entry with a long list of fresh fish offerings that includes a multitude of maki—and entrées are no afterthought. A sequel to Naniwa (see), Bob San maintains the pace with a contemporary, loftlike space; centralized sushi bar; fashionable servers; and a generous sake selection (plus specialty martinis). Sushi chefs will go off the menu for you if they're not too busy. Japanese, sushi menu. Dinner. Bar. Casual attire. Outdoor seating. **$$$**

★ ★ **BONGO ROOM.** *1470 N Milwaukee Ave, Chicago (60622). Phone 773/489-0690.* Sleepyheads, mother-daughter duos, and Wicker Park locals of all ages crowd into this funky favorite for bohemian breakfast, Bongo style. Known for long weekend waits, decadent pancakes, and other inventive, seasonal brunch-lunch fare, this is an eclectically decorated, come-as-you-are destination for daytime dining only (no dinner service). American menu. Breakfast, lunch. Bar. Casual attire. **$$**

★ ★ **BRASSERIE JO.** *59 W Hubbard St, Chicago (60610). Phone 312/595-0800; fax 312/595-0808. www.leye.com.* In the brasserie tradition, Jean Joho's spacious, lively River North spot welcomes café society for a quick bite with a glass of moderately priced French wine or handcrafted beer, iced fruits de mer at the zinc bar, or a leisurely meal of robust, reasonably priced Alsatian-French fare. Menu classics include salad Niçoise, choucroute, coq au vin, and bouillabaisse. Light floods in from the street-level windows; vast murals, woven café chairs, and tile floors create a chic, vintage Parisian atmosphere. To finish your meal, request a visit from the "cheese chariot." French bistro menu. Dinner. Closed Thanksgiving, Dec 24-25. Bar. Valet parking. Outdoor seating. **$$**

★ ★ **BRETT'S.** *2011 W Roscoe St, Chicago (60618). Phone 773/248-0999.* Although Brett's is a popular spot for weekend brunch, the dim lighting, understated décor, and soft background music make it an ideal destination for a romantic dinner as well. But don't be afraid to bring the whole family—a children's menu offers the little ones a variety of pastas and sandwiches, and, although the dining experience is relatively upscale, the atmosphere remains casual. You can even bring along the family dog in good weather, when man's best friend is allowed at outdoor tables. American menu. Lunch, dinner, Sat-Sun brunch. Closed Mon-Tues; Dec 25. Bar. Children's menu. Casual attire. Reservations recommended. Outdoor seating. **$$**

★ ★ **BRICKS.** *1909 N Lincoln Ave, Chicago (60614). Phone 312/255-0851.* If you're craving gourmet pizza (and maybe a nice cold beer to accompany it), head to this restaurant and pub, a favorite with locals. Build your own pizza from a list of toppings that includes Maytag blue, gouda, and goat cheeses; banana peppers; and barbecue sauce. Or you may want to enjoy one of Bricks's own creations, like the Ditka, a pizza tribute to the former Chicago Bears coach. An impressive selection of craft brews and imports is on hand, as are a number of wines by the glass, half-bottle, and bottle. Pizza. Dinner. Closed holidays. Bar. Casual attire. Reservations recommended. **$$**

★ ★ **CAFE ABSINTHE.** *1954 W North Ave, Chicago (60622). Phone 773/278-4488; fax 773/278-5291.* You'd never know what lies behind the walls of this Wicker Park restaurant from the looks of the unassuming façade (and the entrance off an alley behind the building): an intimate and elegant bistro with some of most innovative cuisine in the city. Take note, however, that it is definitely an "urban" experience—the restaurant can become crowded and, at times, very noisy. American menu. Dinner. Closed holidays. Bar. Casual attire. Reservations recommended. Valet parking. **$$$**

★ ★ **CAFE BA-BA-REEBA!.** *2024 N Halsted St, Chicago (60614). Phone 773/935-5000; toll-free 888/538-8823; fax 773/935-0660. www.cafebabareeba.com.* The granddaddy of Chicago tapas spots, Cafe Ba-Ba-Reeba! was serving up those small plates long before "tapas" and "sangria" became household words. The colorful Mediterranean décor is the perfect complement to the lively Spanish cuisine. The authentic atmosphere is noisy and fun, and seating in the outdoor dining area is highly coveted in warm weather. You may find yourself waiting for a table, especially on weekends. Too hungry to wait? Take a seat at the front or back bar, where the full menu is available. Tapas menu. Lunch, dinner. Closed holidays. Bar. Children's menu. Casual attire. Reservations recommended. Valet parking. Outdoor seating. **$$**

★ ★ **CAFE IBERICO.** *739 N LaSalle Dr, Chicago (60610). Phone 312/573-1510; fax 312/751-0098. www.cafe-iberico.com.* Elbow your way into this River North tapas hotspot for small plates of hot and cold Spanish fare, refreshing sangria, and casual camaraderie. The food is great for sharing—whether in a group or on a date—and the atmosphere, while boisterous during prime time, creates a festive mood. Spanish, tapas menu. Lunch, dinner. Closed July 4, Thanksgiving, Dec 24-25. Bar. Casual attire. Reservations recommended. Valet parking. **$$**

★ ★ **CAFE BERNARD.** *2100 N Halsted St, Chicago (60614). Phone 773/871-2100. www.cafebernard.com.* If you're looking for a no-frills country French meal, you'll find it here. This intimate little café is sometimes overlooked for its flashier competition, but Café Bernard has been serving moderately priced fare in a cozy setting for more than 30 years. The kitchen offers dishes such as mussels, escargots, and steak au poivre that are simply yet elegantly presented. The menu is somewhat limited, but daily specials on the blackboard keep regulars returning. The low-lit, homey dining room, decorated with French posters, etchings, and dried flowers, serves as the perfect backdrop to the restaurant's cuisine and is a great spot for an intimate dinner for two. French menu. Dinner. Closed Dec 25. Bar. Casual attire. Reservations recommended. Valet parking. Outdoor seating. **$$**

★ ★ ★ **CALITERRA.** *633 N St. Clair St, Chicago (60611). Phone 312/274-4444; fax 312/274-0164. www.wyndham.com.* Aptly named considering its Cal-Ital culinary concept (Tuscany meets northern California), this handsome—and somewhat hidden—oasis in the Wyndham Chicago hotel (see) draws a well-heeled Gold Coast business and shopping crowd. Innovative seasonal fare emphasizes organic produce and non-hormone-treated meats; additional monthly specialty menus showcase a particular ingredient in various preparations. The dining room is dressed in wood and textiles, with a display kitchen and a glass mural of a grape arbor as focal points. The gracious cocktail lounge, noteworthy cheese cart, and Italian-American wine list are additional highlights. Italian menu. Breakfast, lunch, dinner, Sun brunch. Bar. Children's menu. Business casual attire. Reservations recommended. Valet parking. **$$$**

★ ★ **CALLIOPE CAFE.** *2826 N Lincoln Ave, Chicago (60657). Phone 773/528-8055.* Lakeview's Calliope Cafe, popular with the neighborhood lunch crowd, distinguishes itself from the average deli with upscale sandwiches, splashes of colorful paint, and funky mismatched tables and chairs. Popular options include the salmon club, steak and avocado wrap, and pesto chicken sandwich, plus addictive homemade potato chips. You're unlikely to walk by this stretch of Lincoln Avenue, but the café offers an adjacent parking lot to encourage mealtime commuters. Deli menu. Lunch, dinner. Children's menu. Casual attire. Outdoor seating. **$**

★ ★ **CAPE COD ROOM.** *140 E Walton Pl, Chicago (60611). Phone 312/440-8486; toll-free 800/553-7253; fax 312/787-0256. www.thedrakehotel.com.* Escape to a New England fishing town without leaving the city at this nautically themed seafood restaurant in the Drake Hotel (see). Decorated with dark wood walls, low-beamed ceilings, and red-and-white-checked tablecloths, the Cape Cod Room offers a comfortable place to dine, along with an extensive selection of seafood. From Dover sole and tuna to oysters and clams, seafood lovers will find everything their hearts desire here. Seafood menu. Lunch, dinner. Closed Dec 25. Bar. Casual attire. Valet parking. Outdoor seating. **$$$**

★ ★ ★ **THE CAPITAL GRILLE.** *633 N St. Clair St, Chicago (60611). Phone 312/337-9400; fax 312/337-1259. www.thecapitalgrille.com.* This Washington, DC-based chain deliberately cultivates the old boys' network vibe. The clubby, masculine décor features dark woods and original oil paintings of fox hunts, cattle drives, and the like. But even if cigars and cell phones aren't your thing, you'll find it hard to resist the top-notch steakhouse fare served up here. Sizable à la carte entrées like porterhouse steak, filet mignon, and broiled fresh lobster, along with traditional sides that serve three, tempt the taste buds and ensure that you'll leave feeling quite full. Beef is dry-aged on the premises for 14 days and hand-cut daily. The restaurant sits just off the Magnificent Mile in the same building that houses the Wyndham Chicago hotel (see). Steak menu. Lunch, dinner. Closed holidays. Bar. Business casual attire. Reservations recommended. Valet parking. **$$$**

★ ★ **CARMINE'S.** *1043 N Rush St, Chicago (60611). Phone 312/988-7676; fax 312/988-7957. www.rosebudrestaurants.com.* This Italian steak and seafood house, located in the ritzy Gold Coast area, has been a Chicago favorite since opening in 1995. Generously sized chops and steaks and hearty portions of seafood and pasta are served in the dim—and usually packed—dining room, where politicians, sports personalities, and celebrities have been known to turn up. Italian, seafood menu. Lunch, dinner. **$$**

★ ★ **CERISE.** *521 N Rush St, Chicago (60611). Phone 312/327-0564.* The fine dining room of the French-owned Le Meridien Chicago (see), Cerise hews to the hotel's nationality with a French menu. There are plenty of haut classics like foie gras and duck consommé, but the greatest applause here comes for the fish dishes and French comfort foods like chicken "gran mere." Finish with the chocolate and cherry crepes before heading next door to the convivial Le Rendezvous lounge for a digestif. French menu. Breakfast, lunch, dinner. Bar. Children's menu. Casual attire. Outdoor seating. **$$**

★ ★ ★ ★ ★ **CHARLIE TROTTER'S.** *816 W Armitage Ave, Chicago (60614). Phone 773/248-6228; fax 773/248-6088. www.charlietrotters.com.* Charlie Trotter's is a place for people who equate food with the highest form of art. It is also a restaurant for those who value a chef's masterful ability to transform sustenance into culinary wonder. But even those who doubt these two tenets will leave Charlie Trotter's understanding that food is not just for eating. It is for savoring, honoring, marveling at, and, most of all, thoroughly enjoying. Set inside a two-story brick brownstone, Charlie Trotter's is an intimate, peaceful temple of cuisine of the most refined and innovative variety. Trotter is the Nobel laureate of the kitchen—a mad maestro of gastronomy, if you will—and you must experience his talent for yourself to understand the hype. Charlie Trotter's offers several magnificent menus, including The Grand Tasting, The Vegetable Menu, and The Kitchen Table Degustation. Each combines pristine seasonal products (Trotter has a network of more than 90 purveyors, many of them local small farms) with impeccable French techniques and slight Asian influences. Trotter prefers saucing with vegetable juice-based vinaigrettes, light emulsified stocks, and purees as well as delicate broths and herb-infused meat and fish essences. The result is that flavors are remarkably intense, yet dishes stay light. Dining at Charlie Trotter's is an astonishing and extraordinary dining journey. French menu. Dinner. Closed Sun-Mon; holidays. Bar. Jacket required. Reservations recommended. Valet parking. **$$$$**

★ ★ ★ **CHEZ JOEL.** *1119 W Taylor St, Chicago (60607). Phone 312/226-6479; fax 312/226-6589.* Just a few minutes from the Loop, tiny Chez Joel dares to be French within the friendly confines of Little Italy. Classic bistro fare (paté, escargots, coquilles St. Jacques, coq au vin, steak frites) is seasoned with more adventurous specials and an appealing sandwich selection at lunch. The cozy room invites with a buttery glow, courtesy of soft yellow walls accented with French prints and posters; in warm weather, the outdoor garden is a charming oasis. The wine list is moderately priced, and a limited reserve list is offered. Make reservations; the secret is out. French bistro menu. Lunch, dinner. Closed holidays. Bar. Business casual attire. Reservations recommended. Valet parking. Outdoor seating. **$$**

★ ★ **CHICAGO CHOP HOUSE.** *60 W Ontario St, Chicago (60610). Phone 312/787-7100; toll-free 800/229-2356; fax 312/787-3219. www.chicagochophouse.com.* Choosing a steakhouse among the many in Chicago is no easy task, but independently owned Chicago Chop House stands out for its affinity for the metropolis. Papered in 1,400 photos of the city, its meat packers and mayors, most taken before 1930, the Chop House provides a history lesson as a side dish to meals centered on steaks and chops. Steak menu. Lunch, dinner. Closed holidays. Bar. Business casual attire. Reservations recommended. Valet parking. **$$$**

★ **CHICAGO DINER.** *3411 N Halsted St, Chicago (60657). Phone 773/935-6696. www.veggiediner.com.* If you think that vegetarian cuisine is nothing but lettuce leaves and sprouts, think again. Since 1983, this Lakeview diner has been serving hearty meatless fare that has won over the taste buds of vegetarians and meat lovers alike. Craving a hot dog? Try the "No Dog." How about Mexican food? They offer a "No Meata Fajita." Using products like seitan (wheat gluten), tofu (soybean curd), and tempeh (fermented soybean cake) along with grains, beans, and fresh vegetables, the Chicago Diner creates healthy alternatives to traditional meat dishes. A second location has opened in Highland Park at 581 Elm Place. Vegetarian menu. Lunch, dinner. Closed Jan 1, Dec 25. Bar. Casual attire. **$**

★ ★ **CHILPANCINGO.** *358 W Ontario St, Chicago (60610). Phone 312/266-9525; fax 312/266-6428. www.chilpancingorestaurant.com.* Chef Geno Bahena cooked at Frontera Grill (see) before breaking out on his own with Ixcapuzalco (see) in Logan Square and the follow-up Chilpancingo downtown. Festooned in colorful folk art and murals, Chilpancingo creates a lively setting where authentic Mexican market fare, including quail and rabbit, merge with more familiar standards, such as enchiladas and ceviche, on the menu. Mexican menu. Lunch, dinner, Sun brunch. Closed Dec 25. Bar. Business casual attire. Reservations recommended. Valet parking. Outdoor seating. **$$$**

★ ★ **CLUB LUCKY.** *1824 W Wabansia Ave, Chicago (60622). Phone 773/227-2300; fax 773/227-2236. www.clubluckychicago.com.* In the 1920s, it was a hardware store. In the 1930s, it was a banquet hall. Throughout the 1980s, it was a bar. Today, the building tucked away on the corner of Honore and Wabansia—smack-dab in the middle of one of the city's hottest neighborhoods, Wicker Park/Bucktown—is Club Lucky, a 1940s-style restaurant and lounge. It's a place to bring a group of friends and enjoy heaping portions of traditional Italian favorites, as well as a martini or two. Italian menu. Lunch, dinner. Closed Thanksgiving, Dec 25. Bar. Casual attire. Reservations recommended. Valet parking. Outdoor seating. **$$**

★★ COCO PAZZO. *300 W Hubbard St, Chicago (60610). Phone 312/836-0900; fax 312/836-0257.* A renovated loft with velvet swagged curtains and rustic wood floors sets an aptly dramatic stage for the robust Italian cooking on offer at Coco Pazzo. Chef Tony Priolo mans the stoves, turning out recipes that range from the sophisticated but uncomplicated beef carpaccio with black truffle oil to the crowd-pleasing rigatoni with sausage and cream. Pastas come in appetizer portions, allowing you to save room for the traditional Italian "second plate" of Florentine steak or wood-fired salmon. A longtime River North resident, Coco Pazzo draws dealmakers among the ad and art world types working nearby. Italian menu. Lunch, dinner. Closed Thanksgiving, Dec 25. Bar. Casual attire. Valet parking. Outdoor seating. **$$**

★ COMO. *695 N Milwaukee Ave, Chicago (60622). Phone 312/733-7400.* Longtime Chicago restaurateurs the Marchetti brothers cashed in on the beloved and enormous Como Inn in River West to make room for residential development. They resurfaced with the downscaled Como nearby, trading in their Italian murals and rambling rooms for a contemporary space with soaring headroom. The menu sticks to Italian classics in chicken Vesuvio and pasta Bolognese, the very thing that keeps old Como Inn fans coming around to Como. Italian menu. Dinner. Closed Mon. Bar. Casual attire. Outdoor seating. **$$**

★★★ COOBAH. *3423 N Southport Ave, Chicago (60657). Phone 773/528-2220.* Latin eats and lots of drinks make hip Coobah a restaurant that crosses over into a late-night hangout. The kitchen puts in long hours, beginning with a creative weekend brunch that includes a Spanish-style granola and chorizo gravy with biscuits, plus sandwiches such as the Cuban reuben. Dinner is the main event; you can get it until 1 am nightly, 2 am on Saturday. Tamales, lamb adobo, and fish with Spanish olives testify to the range of dishes offered here. Freely flowing mojitos, sangria, and "Coobah libres" encourage diners to stick around this swinging Southport stop. International/Fusion menu. Lunch, dinner, late-night, Sun brunch. Bar. Casual attire. Outdoor seating. **$$**

★★★★ CROFTON ON WELLS. *535 N Wells St, Chicago (60610). Phone 312/755-1790; fax 312/755-1890. www.croftononwells.com.* Chicago chef Suzy Crofton flies well below the see-and-be-seen radar and that's just the way aficionados—and the proprietor herself—like it. Rather than trendy, Crofton turns out elegant meals in an understated setting warmed by candlelight in River North, a region rife with look-at-me eateries. The French-trained Crofton specializes in refined American cooking that marries style and substance with attention to detail and presentation. Flavor combinations are both harmonious and exciting as typified by the sweet/savory grilled foie gras with peppered pineapple and pan-seared scallops with blood orange salad. Her signature smoked apple chutney, also sold by the bottle, tops barbecued pork tenderloin and roast quail. Crofton thoughtfully caters to special interests with both a vegetarian menu and an extensive list of loose-leaf teas. Dine before 6:30 (think pre-theater) to take advantage of Crofton on Wells' bargain four-course prix fixe for $45. American menu. Dinner, late-night. Closed Sun. Bar. Business casual attire. Reservations recommended. Valet parking. **$$$**

★★ CYRANO'S BISTROT AND WINE BAR. *546 N Wells St, Chicago (60610). Phone 312/467-0546; fax 312/467-1850. www.cyranosbistrot.com.* Cozy and unpretentious, Cyrano's is a country French getaway in Chicago's frenzied River North area. The rustic, un-Americanized menu encompasses bistro classics (including game and offal dishes), with a specialty in rotisserie meats. The décor is all sunny yellow walls, gilded mirrors, and provincial French accoutrements. The regional French wine list and bargain four-course lunch are added attractions, and an outdoor café makes diners part of the neighborhood scene in warm weather. Live cabaret and jazz entertainment is featured Fridays and Saturdays. French bistro menu. Lunch, dinner. Closed Sun; holidays. Bar. Casual attire. Reservations recommended. Valet parking. Outdoor seating. **$$**

★★★★ THE DINING ROOM. *160 E Pearson St, Chicago (60611). Phone 312/266-1000; fax 312/266-1194. www.fourseasons.com.* Innovative contemporary French cuisine is served in quiet luxury at The Dining Room, the opulent restaurant of The Ritz-Carlton (see). The décor of this striking, clubby room is rich and luxurious, from the fabrics to the breathtaking fresh flowers updated weekly. In addition to the superb à la carte choices—a signature dish is a succulent Maine lobster served with wild mushrooms over a crisp golden lobster cake—the chef offers an adventurous, personalized eight-course tasting menu, a five-course degustation menu, and a five-course vegetarian menu. To complement the fantastic fare, the award-winning wine list emphasizes boutique wines from Bordeaux, Burgundy, and California. The service at The Dining Room is in keeping with the décor.

Waiters are tuxedoed and formal, and each presentation detail matches the classic atmosphere that The Dining Room strives to represent. American menu. Dinner, Sun brunch. Closed Mon. Children's menu. Business casual attire. Reservations recommended. Valet parking. **$$$$**

★ ★ DINOTTO RISTORANTE. *215 W North Ave, Chicago (60610). Phone 312/202-0302.* With caring service, a warm atmosphere, and substantial, rustic Italian fare, Dinotto endears itself to Old Town residents and tourists passing through. Chili-spiced grilled calamari and goat cheese ravioli rank among the standouts on the menu, which offers plenty of chicken and veal options to succeed its pastas. In addition to the bustling dining room, in season, seating spills onto a charming brick-walled outdoor patio. Italian menu. Lunch, dinner. Bar. Casual attire. Outdoor seating. **$$**

★ ED DEBEVIC'S. *640 N Wells St, Chicago (60610). Phone 312/664-1707; fax 312/664-7444. www.eddebevics.com.* Treat your tweens and teens to Ed Debevic's, a retro 1950s diner where sassy, gum-snapping servers in period uniforms delight in giving diners a hard time. It's all in good fun, as is the lighthearted menu of burgers, hot dogs, and shakes, plus hearty Middle American staples like meat loaf and pot roast. American menu. Lunch, dinner. Closed holidays. Bar. Children's menu. Casual attire. Valet parking. **$**

★ ★ ELI'S THE PLACE FOR STEAK. *215 E Chicago Ave, Chicago (60611). Phone 312/642-1393; fax 312/642-4089. www.eliplaceforsteak.com.* When Chicagoans hear the name Eli's, one thing comes to mind: cheesecake. But Eli's The Place for Steak was around long before the now-famous dessert was; the late Eli Schulman opened his restaurant in 1966, and his cheesecake made its debut in 1980. Over the years, the restaurant has attracted many famous faces, from Frank Sinatra and Sean Connery to Chicago politicians and sports figures, and has also expanded its menu. No longer just "the place for steak," it's also the place for chops, seafood, and "Liver Eli." Steak menu. Lunch, dinner. Closed holidays. Bar. Children's menu. Business casual attire. Reservations recommended. **$$$**

★ ★ ERWIN. *2925 N Halsted St, Chicago (60657). Phone 773/528-7200; fax 773/528-1931. www.erwincafe.com.* Low on contrivance, high on flavor, chef/owner Erwin Dreschler's "urban heartland" cuisine is right at home in his comfy and convivial North Side restaurant. This is the thinking man's contemporary American comfort food, served amid a nature-inspired scheme of warm woods, forest green walls, and white tablecloths. The well-chosen wines, including extensive by-the-glass options, are central to the concept of the ever-changing seasonal menu (Dreschler is a champion of local foodstuffs and leads tours of area farmers' markets). With choices like banana-cinnamon French toast, eggs Benedict, and rainbow trout, erwin is also a popular brunch destination. American menu. Dinner, Sun brunch. Closed Mon; holidays. Bar. Casual attire. Reservations recommended. Valet parking. **$$**

★ ★ ★ ★ EVEREST. *440 S LaSalle St, Chicago (60605). Phone 312/663-8920; fax 312/663-8802.* Perched high atop the city on the 40th floor of the Chicago Stock Exchange building, Everest affords spectacular views and equally fabulous contemporary French cuisine. Chef/owner Jean Joho blends European influences with local, seasonal American ingredients; he is not afraid to pair noble ingredients like caviar and foie gras with humbler fruits of American soil such as potatoes and turnips. The à la carte menu offers several signature dishes, including the Fantasy of Chocolate—five different riffs on the decadent cocoa theme artfully piled onto one glorious plate. Everest's dining room is luxuriously decorated with polished gold railings, vaulted draped ceilings, mirrored walls, and, of course, floor-to-ceiling windows for fabulous unobstructed views. French menu. Dinner. Closed Sun-Mon; Jan 1, Dec 25. Bar. Reservations recommended. Valet parking. **$$$$**

★ ★ FLO. *1434 W Chicago Ave, Chicago (60622). Phone 312/243-0477; fax 312/243-0655.* A storefront hidden away on a strip of Chicago Avenue teeming with secondhand shops and bargain stores, Flo is a diamond in the rough. A friendly staff serves fresh and flavorful dishes from the mostly Southwestern-inspired menu in two bright and cozy dining rooms, which are decorated with vibrant pieces of art. Weekend brunch packs in crowds who wait in line for scrumptious dishes like huevos rancheros, chilaquiles, and blueberry and strawberry pancakes with homemade syrup. Southwestern menu. Breakfast, lunch, dinner, Sat-Sun brunch. Closed Mon. Bar. Children's menu. Casual attire. Reservations recommended. **$$**

★ ★ FOGO DE CHÃO. *661 N LaSalle St, Chicago (60610). Phone 312/932-9330; fax 312/932-9388. www.fogodechao.com.* If you're in a carnivorous mood, this upscale, aromatic Brazilian churrascaria is the place to indulge. Fifteen all-you-can-eat grilled and roasted meats waft through the room on spits, borne by efficient "gauchos" who descend upon you at your whim. The massive salad bar and side dishes represent the other food groups—but at this price, save room for plenty of meat. Brazilian Steak menu. Lunch, dinner. Bar. Casual attire. Reservations recommended. Valet parking. **$$$**

★ ★ **FRONTERA GRILL.** *445 N Clark St, Chicago (60610). Phone 312/661-1434; fax 312/661-1830. www.fronterakitchens.com.* Born of chef/owner Rick Bayless's genius for, and scholarly pursuit of, regional Mexican cuisine, this River North superstar's brand has become a name to reckon with. The casual, more accessible of Bayless's side-by-side duo (see also TOPOLOBAMPO), Frontera introduces a wealth of deceptively simple Mexican dishes—and a world of flavors—that you won't find at your neighborhood taco stand. An exhaustive tequila list for sipping or for shaken-to-order margaritas and a fine wine list stand up to the food. A seat here is a coveted one, as reservations are for parties of five to ten only. Mexican menu. Lunch, dinner, Sat brunch. Closed Sun-Mon; holidays, early July, early Jan. Bar. Children's menu. Business casual attire. Reservations recommended. Valet parking. Outdoor seating. **$$$**

★ ★ **GEJA'S CAFE.** *340 W Armitage Ave, Chicago (60614). Phone 773/281-9101; fax 773/281-0849. www.gejascafe.com.* The fondue craze never ended at this venerable Lincoln Park classic, always at or near the top of all those "most romantic" lists. It's dark and cozy inside, and after all, there is something flirtatious about swirling your food around in a pot and occasionally crossing forks with your tablemate to the stylings of live flamenco guitar music. Fondue menu. Dinner. Closed holidays. Casual attire. Reservations recommended. Valet parking. **$$$**

★ ★ ★ **GENE & GEORGETTI.** *500 N Franklin St, Chicago (60610). Phone 312/527-3718; fax 312/527-2039. www.geneandgeorgetti.com.* A veteran steakhouse with a masculine, insider's ambience and a past (it opened in 1941, long before River North was a hip 'hood), Gene & Georgetti is an old-school Chicago carnivore's haunt. Prime steaks, gigantic "garbage salad," and gruff service are among the draws. Italian, American menu. Lunch, dinner. Closed Sun; holidays; also the first week in July. Bar. Casual attire. Valet parking. **$$$**

★ ★ ★ **GIBSON'S STEAKHOUSE.** *1028 N Rush St, Chicago (60611). Phone 312/266-8999; fax 312/787-5649. www.gibsonssteakhouse.com.* The theme at Gibson's is outsized, from the massive steaks on the plate to the stogie-puffing personalities—a blend of politicians, sports figures, celebrities, and conventioneers—who energize the room. Carnivores crave the generous porterhouses here, but the kitchen also manages to issue some of the sea's biggest lobster tails and desserts that easily feed a four-top. Do call for a reservation, but don't be surprised if you still have to wait. In that case, squeeze into the smoky, convivial bar, order a martini, and prepare to make new friends. Steak, seafood menu. Lunch, dinner. Closed holidays. Bar. Business casual attire. Reservations recommended. Valet parking. Outdoor seating. **$$$**

★ ★ **GIOCO.** *1312 S Wabash Ave, Chicago (60605). Phone 312/939-3870; fax 312/939-3858. www.giocochicago.com.* A riot of earthy flavors is in store at this chic former speakeasy in the South Loop. The simply sophisticated Italian food is offered up in a comfortable setting that's simultaneously rustic and clubby—and the seasonal outdoor patio is a rare treat in this up-and-coming neighborhood. Italian menu. Lunch, dinner. Closed holidays. Bar. Children's menu. Reservations recommended. Valet parking. Outdoor seating. **$$$**

★ ★ **GREEK ISLANDS.** *200 S Halsted St, Chicago (60661). Phone 312/782-9855; fax 312/454-0937. www.greekislands.net.* The largest of the Greektown restaurants, with a seating capacity of 400, Greek Islands offers a menu brimming with moderately priced Greek favorites like moussaka and dolmades, as well as a number of fresh seafood selections. Mediterranean tones of coral and blue, white stucco walls, traditional Greek music, and shouts of "Opaa!" capture the spirit of Greece and create a casual and festive atmosphere. Greek menu. Lunch, dinner. Closed Thanksgiving, Dec 25. Bar. Children's menu. Business casual attire. Reservations recommended. Valet parking. Outdoor seating. **$$**

★ ★ **HARRY CARAY'S.** *33 W Kinzie St, Chicago (60610). Phone 312/828-0966; fax 312/828-0962. www.harrycarays.com.* Although the legendary Cubs announcer died in 1998, his boisterous spirit thrives at this restaurant in River North, a vintage brick building emblazoned with Caray's signature expression, "Holy cow!" Inside, choose from the casual saloon with numerous sports-tuned TVs or the white-tablecloth dining room specializing in Harry's favorite food,

Italian. Wherever you sit, you'll find a casual vibe and walls plastered with baseball memorabilia. Steak menu. Lunch, dinner. Closed Jan 1, Thanksgiving, Dec 25. Bar. Children's menu. Business casual attire. Reservations recommended. Valet parking. **$$$**

★ ★ ★ HEAT. *1507 N Sedgwick, Chicago (60610). Phone 312/397-9818; toll-free 866/230-6387. www.heatsushi.com.* Top-tier, ultra-fresh sushi—some of which is still swimming in tanks under the bar—is the draw at this upscale spot in an up-and-coming stretch of Old Town. The menu changes daily, with occasional esoteric offerings that have earned Heat a loyal following of sushi purists. The multicourse, prix fixe omakase and kaiseki menus are beautifully presented culinary adventures. The minimal modern décor, gracious service, and fine selections of sake and wine complete the elevated experience. Japanese, sushi menu. Dinner. Closed Sun. Bar. Casual attire. **$$$$**

★ ★ HEAVEN ON SEVEN ON RUSH. *600 N Michigan Ave, Chicago (60611). Phone 312/280-7774. www.heavenonseven.com.* Chef Jimmy Bannos is Chicago's answer to New Orleans, cooking up Cajun and Creole dishes in this just-off-Michigan Avenue outpost. Grab a seat under the shelved hot sauce collection known as the Wall of Fire and order up red beans and rice, gumbo, and po' boy sandwiches. In addition to such standards, the dinner menu elaborates on the theme with gussied-up entrées like grilled salmon on andouille sausage and a multicourse tasting menu. Cajun/Creole menu. Lunch, dinner. Bar. Casual attire. **$$**

★ HEMA'S KITCHEN. *2111 N Clark St, Chicago (60645). Phone 773/338-1627.* Chef Hema Potla runs this no-frills restaurant off the main Devon Avenue drag, where diners can choose from plenty of delicious and inexpensive traditional Indian dishes. You'll probably see Hema herself circling the room as she makes menu suggestions to her customers. Indian menu. Lunch, dinner. Casual attire. **$**

★ ★ INDIAN GARDEN. *2546 W Devon Ave, Chicago (60659). Phone 773/338-2929; fax 773/338-3930.* A trip to the strip of Devon Street's Little India is worth the ride for lovers of Indian food. This classic is more upscale than some, with a bright interior and the requisite aromatic ambience. The generous buffet is a great deal, and there are plenty of vegetarian offerings. Indian menu. Lunch, dinner. Bar. Casual attire. Reservations recommended. Valet parking. **$$**

★ ★ IXCAPUZALCO. *2919 N Milwaukee Ave, Chicago (60618). Phone 773/486-7340; fax 773/486-7348.* Authentic, regional Mexican fare is the draw at this unpretentious neighborhood storefront. While a few dishes are recognizable renditions, Ixcapuzalco presents an opportunity to savor more intriguing, less familiar preparations for lunch, dinner, or Sunday brunch. There's also a traditional mole of the day, paired with a variety of meats. Dozens of premium tequilas may be sipped or shaken into margaritas. Candlelight and white tablecloths, rustic hand-carved wood chairs, and brilliant-hued artwork warm the small, smoke-free main dining room (which can be noisy due to the presence of the small, open kitchen; the back room is quieter). Mexican menu. Lunch, dinner, Sun brunch. Closed Tues. Bar. Casual attire. Reservations recommended. **$$**

★ ★ JANE'S. *1655 W Cortland St, Chicago (60622). Phone 773/862-5263. www.janesresaurant.com.* Befitting the Bucktown location, this eclectic American girl is something of a funky flower child. The quaint setting and creative menu offerings (including some vegetarian choices) make it a favorite of neighborhood denizens and dating couples. American menu. Dinner, brunch. Closed holidays. Bar. Casual attire. Reservations recommended. Outdoor seating. **$$**

★ ★ ★ JAPONAIS. *600 W Chicago Ave, Chicago (60610). Phone 312/822-9600; fax 312/822-9623. www.japonaischicago.com.* This spacious River North restaurant is a sensuous, hip setting for contemporary Japanese fare that includes, but goes far beyond, traditional sushi. The creative menu inspires sharing and ordering in phases while enjoying the exotic cocktails or selections from the extensive sake and wine lists. Four dazzling environments set different moods; in warm weather, the subterranean riverfront terrace is an exotic escape. Japanese menu. Lunch, dinner, late-night. Bar. Business casual attire. Reservations recommended. Valet parking. Outdoor seating. **$$$**

★ ★ JIN JU. *5203 N Clark St, Chicago (60640). Phone 773/334-6377.* Korean food gets the hipster treatment at Jin Ju. What emerges is a polished neighborhood ethnic with enough flair to entice newcomers to the exotic fare. By juicing the scene with techno beats and sleek décor, the Andersonville restaurant boosts the atmosphere missing at most Korean barbecue eateries. Despite the Western trappings, the food remains fairly traditional, including bi bim bop, kimchee soup, and barbecued short ribs. Don't miss the martinis made with the Korean liquor soju. Korean menu. Dinner. Closed Mon. Bar. Casual attire. **$$**

★ JOE'S BE-BOP CAFE. *600 E Grand Ave, Chicago (60611). Phone 312/595-5299; fax 312/832-6986. www.joesbebop.com.* On tourist-centric Navy Pier, Joe's unites two Chicago favorites, ribs and jazz. Cajun jambalaya and lighter salads supplement the tangy, slow-cooked ribs on the menu. Entertainment runs the jazz gamut from swing to Latin, with acts performing atop a raised stage that ensures good sightlines from around the expansive restaurant. Sunday brunch serves up a Bloody Mary bar and a big band. Barbecue menu. Lunch, dinner. Closed Thanksgiving, Dec 25. Bar. Children's menu. Casual attire. Outdoor seating. **$$**

★ JOHN'S PLACE. *1200 W Webster Ave, Chicago (60614). Phone 773/525-6670; fax 773/525-6804.* A solid neighborhood café in an unlikely residential locale—at the corner of Racine and Webster in the DePaul University area—guarantees John's a steady clientele. The food is comforting but conscientious. John's touts organic produce and line-caught fish in a menu that includes roast chicken, baked whitefish, and several vegetarian options. Families in particular crowd John's; expect to climb over strollers at lunch and the popular weekend brunch. American menu. Lunch, dinner, Sat-Sun brunch. Closed Mon; holidays. Bar. Children's menu. Casual attire. Outdoor seating. **$$**

★ ★ ★ KEEFER'S. *20 W Kinzie, Chicago (60610). Phone 312/467-9525. www.keefersrestaurant.com.* In bustling River North, stylish Keefer's offers prime steaks, chops, seafood, and some bistro dishes served up in a handsome round dining room with a contemporary Arts and Crafts feel. Soups, salads, and sides are predominantly steakhouse classics (lobster bisque, Caesar salad, creamed spinach), along with some updated but not fussy alternatives. They also serve a somewhat pared-down lunch menu, plus there's the adjacent "Keefer's Kaffe" with a menu of soups, salads, and simple sandwiches, great for quick take-out. Seafood, Steak menu. Lunch, dinner. Closed Sun. Bar. Casual attire. Outdoor seating. **$$$**

★ ★ ★ KEVIN. *9 W Hubbard, Chicago (60610). Phone 312/595-0055. www.kevinrestaurant.com.* Chicago fans of chef Kevin Shikami chased him from kitchen to kitchen around town for years. But in Kevin, his eponymous restaurant, they finally know where to find the talented chef each night. From delicate fish to juicy meats, Shikami brings an Asian flair to contemporary dishes that include tuna tartare, sesame-crusted opakapaka (a Hawaiian fish), and sautéed buffalo strip steak. The smart but warm River North room and polished servers make Kevin a good choice for shoppers and business lunches. American, French, Asian menu. Lunch, dinner. Closed Sun. Bar. Outdoor seating. **$$$**

★ ★ ★ KIKI'S BISTRO. *900 N Franklin St, Chicago (60610). Phone 312/335-5454; fax 312/335-0614. www.kikisbistro.com.* Long before bistros were blossoming all over town, this little charmer on an out-of-the-way corner in River North was pleasing patrons with its traditional bistro fare and regional specials. The softly lit dining rooms are appointed in wood, rose-pink draping and upholstery, and lace curtains. A somewhat older crowd frequents cozy, casual Kiki's for its romantic, country inn ambience, reliable kitchen, and free valet parking (a real boon in this bustling neighborhood). It's also fun to dine at the bar here. French bistro menu. Lunch, dinner. Closed Sun; holidays. Bar. Business casual attire. Reservations recommended. Valet parking. **$$**

★ ★ KLAY OVEN. *414 N Orleans St, Chicago (60610). Phone 312/527-3999; fax 312/527-1563.* White tablecloths, exotic textiles, and tasteful serving carts set the tone for fine Indian dining at Klay Oven. Offerings include several tandoori options, plenty of vegetarian choices, and eight varieties of fresh-baked bread. Wine and beer options exceed expectations, and the lunch buffet is a great deal for the quality. Indian menu. Lunch, dinner. Closed holidays. Bar. Business casual attire. Reservations recommended. Valet parking. **$$**

★ ★ LA BOCCA DELLA VERITA. *4618 N Lincoln Ave, Chicago (60618). Phone 773/784-6222; fax 773/784-6272. www.laboccachicago.com.* Lincoln Square's long-standing Italian storefront La Bocca Della Verita was here and popular before the neighborhood took off (witness the restaurant's wall of fame featuring old headshots of past stars who have dined here). Ample portions of well-priced northern Italian dishes cooked with the flair of a downtown café bring guests back for more. Raves go to the duck breast ravioli and sea bass baked in salt. Neighboring the Davis Theatre, Bocca makes a great pre- or post-movie dinner date. Italian menu. Lunch, dinner. Closed holidays. Casual attire. Outdoor seating. **$$**

★ LA CREPERIE. *2845 N Clark St, Chicago (60657). Phone 773/528-9050.* A Clark Street staple since 1971, La Creperie is Chicago's sole source for eat-out French crepes. Everything from coq au vin to curry gets wrapped in thin, pastry-style pancakes. That goes for dessert, too: the options here include the classic flaming crepes Suzette. French posters and candlelight create café romance in the storefront locale. French menu. Breakfast, lunch, dinner. Closed Mon. Bar. Casual attire. Reservations recommended. Outdoor seating. **$$**

★ ★ ★ **LA SARDINE.** *111 N Carpenter St, Chicago (60607). Phone 312/421-2800; fax 312/421-2318. www.lasardine.com.* Perhaps a bit large for a bistro, La Sardine nevertheless delivers the requisite aromas, creature comforts, and menu classics. Warm and bustling (and sometimes noisy) despite a fairly industrial location, La Sardine draws both hip and mature urbanites for the likes of escargots, brandade, bouillabaisse, roast chicken, and profiteroles. Servers wear butcher aprons; the walls are buttery yellow; and those scents waft from an open kitchen and rotisserie. The impressive wine list includes some hard-to-find French selections. French menu. Lunch, dinner. Closed Sun; holidays. Bar. Casual attire. Reservations recommended. Valet parking. **$$**

★ ★ **LA TACHE.** *1475 W Balmoral Ave, Chicago (60640). Phone 773/334-7168.* La Tache—French for "the spot"—looks and eats like a downtown restaurant. But to the good fortune of North Siders, it's located in Andersonville and priced accordingly. The smart French bistro offers comforting classics like sautéed escargot, duck à l'orange, and steak frites with enough creative spin to pique your palate. The service is far more professional than you'd expect in a neighborhood joint, and the owners invested La Tache with warm good looks courtesy of wood paneling and ceiling-suspended lamp shades. The busy bar traffics in wine and appetizers. French menu. Dinner, late-night, Sun brunch. Bar. Casual attire. Outdoor seating. **$$**

★ ★ **LAWRY'S THE PRIME RIB.** *100 E Ontario St, Chicago (60611). Phone 312/787-5000; fax 312/787-1264. www.lawrysonline.com.* As the name suggests, prime rib is the star at Lawry's The Prime Rib. At this unpretentious dining spot, it is offered in a variety of cuts for different tastes and appetites, from the smaller California cut to the extra-thick "Diamond Jim Brady" cut. Housed in the 1896 English manor-style McCormick Mansion, the restaurant exudes a stately feel, with hardwood furnishings, opulent chandeliers, a grand staircase, and a pair of brass lions outside the main dining area. Steak menu. Lunch, dinner. Closed holidays. Bar. Business casual attire. Reservations recommended. Valet parking. **$$$**

★ ★ **LE BOUCHON.** *1958 N Damen Ave, Chicago (60647). Phone 773/862-6600; fax 773/524-1208. www.lebouchonofchicago.com.* Tiny Le Bouchon is known almost as much for its cozy, oh-so-Parisian space with crowded tables, lace curtains, and a pressed tin ceiling as it is for its authentic French bistro cuisine at reasonable prices. A regular following of Bucktown locals and foodies is willing to wait for a table here. French menu. Dinner. Closed Sun; holidays. Bar. Casual attire. Reservations recommended. **$$**

★ ★ **LE COLONIAL.** *937 N Rush St, Chicago (60611). Phone 312/255-0088. www.lecolonialchicago.com.* While other, more daring Asian fusion concepts have come along, this Gold Coast link in an upscale chain holds its own with refined Vietnamese cuisine and elegant, escapist décor circa French-colonial Vietnam. This is a great place for a date or a Magnificent Mile shopping break. In warm weather, try to snag one of the much-coveted second-floor terrace tables. Vietnamese menu. Lunch, dinner. Bar. Outdoor seating. **$$**

★ ★ ★ ★ **LES NOMADES.** *222 E Ontario St, Chicago (60611). Phone 312/649-9010; fax 312/649-0608. www.lesnomades.net.* Les Nomades is a serene little spot tucked away from the bustle of Michigan Avenue in an elegant turn-of-the-century townhouse. Romantic and intimate, with a fireplace; hardwood floors; deep, cozy banquettes; and gorgeous flower arrangements, Les Nomades was originally opened as a private club. It is now open to the public, and what a lucky public we are. While many of Chicago's hottest dining rooms are filled with as much noise as they are with wonderful food, Les Nomades is a peaceful, reserved restaurant that offers perfect service and a magnificent menu of French fare flecked with Asian accents. Excessive noise is not present to distract you from the task at hand. Any spontaneous exclamations of love directed toward the delicious dishes you are consuming (game, foie gras, scallops, lamb, and fish among them) should be kept to a quiet roar, as the tables are closely spaced and exclamations of wonder are often shared. Dining here is a wonderful gastronomic experience, thus this is not a place for a casual dinner. Men are required to dine in jackets and ties, and women are comparably fitted for the occasion. Even children who are rightfully pampered by the attentive staff dress in their holiday best for a memorable evening. French menu. Dinner. Closed

Sun-Mon; holidays. Bar. Jacket required. Reservations recommended. Valet parking. **$$$$**

★ **MAGGIANO'S.** *516 N Clark St, Chicago (60610). Phone 312/644-7700; fax 312/644-1077. www.maggianos.com.* From this River North location, Maggiano's ode to classic Italian-American neighborhoods has spawned spin-offs around the country. Fans love it for its big-hearted spirit as expressed in huge portions of familiar red-sauced pastas and the genuine warmth of servers and staff. But be forewarned: it's loud and crowded, better suited to convivial groups than to intimacy-seeking couples. Italian menu. Lunch, dinner. Closed Dec 25. Bar. Casual attire. Reservations recommended. Valet parking. Outdoor seating. **$$**

★ ★ **MARCHE.** *833 W Randolph St, Chicago (60607). Phone 312/226-8399; fax 312/226-4169. www.marche-chicago.com.* Located along restaurant row in the West Loop, Marche serves imaginative versions of brasserie-style French fare in a nightclub-like setting. Numerous chef changes over the years have done nothing to diminish the popularity of this Randolph Market District mainstay. Vibrant paintings and ultra-modern furnishings give the restaurant a funky-chic feel and may make you feel as if you have stepped onto the set of *Moulin Rouge*. Sit back with a glass of Veuve and enjoy the theatrical surroundings of this hip hangout and its bustling bar. French bistro menu. Dinner. Closed holidays. Bar. Business casual attire. Reservations recommended. Valet parking. Outdoor seating. **$$$**

★ ★ **MAS.** *1670 W Division St, Chicago (60622). Phone 773/276-8700.* This Wicker Park favorite is a good place for a Nuevo Latino feast, a wonderful alternative to more familiar cuisines. The fresh, spicy, and creative fare is best paired with a caipirinha, batida, or mojito to get, literally, in the spirit. Exposed brick and tile and an open kitchen set a hip yet earthy mood. Latin menu. Dinner. Bar. Casual attire. Outdoor seating. **$$$**

★ ★ **MAZA.** *2748 N Lincoln Ave, Chicago (60657). Phone 773/929-9600; fax 773/929-9394.* Chicago's not strong on Middle Eastern eats, but it hardly needs to be with a standout like Maza. This unassuming Lincoln Park spot specializes in small-plate appetizers that could constitute a grazer's meal. When you're ready to commit to something more substantial, try the shawirma or the rack of lamb. Complete your thematic meal with a bottle of Lebanese red wine. Lebanese menu. Dinner. Bar. Business casual attire. Reservations recommended. Valet parking. **$$**

★ ★ **MENAGERIE.** *1232 W Belmont, Chicago (60657). Phone 773/404-8333.* Across the street from the Theatre Building in Lakeview, Menagerie aims to please audiences with creative modern American meals. The co-chefs—whose résumés include past stints at such high-profile restaurants as Bistro 110, Spring (see), and Green Dolphin Street—do best when they dare the most. Fish-and-chips are reinvented here in an Asian style, and duck confit is paired with macaroni and cheese. For-sale works of local artists decorate the walls. Expect a sizable bar crowd for drinks and nibbles post-curtain. International/Fusion menu. Dinner. Closed Tues. Bar. Casual attire. Outdoor seating. **$$**

★ ★ ★ **MERITAGE.** *2118 N Damen Ave, Chicago (60647). Phone 773/235-6434; fax 773/235-6318. www.meritagecafe.com.* For a storefront Bucktown restaurant, Meritage aims high, dishing seafood-focused fare inspired by the cuisine and wines of the Pacific Northwest. Pacific Rim influences edge into seared salmon with taro pancake and Japanese spiced roast scallops. Meat lovers and red wine drinkers are ably served with seared lamb and duck confit. Though the spacious outdoor patio is enclosed and heated in winter, only a canopy cloisters the space in summer, making Meritage one of the city's best open-air eateries. American menu. Dinner, Sun brunch. Closed holidays. Bar. Business casual attire. Reservations recommended. Valet parking. Outdoor seating. **$$$** [B]

★ ★ **MIA FRANCESCA.** *3311 N Clark St, Chicago (60657). Phone 773/281-3310; fax 773/281-6671. www.miafrancesca.com.* The original of an ever-expanding family of restaurants, still-trendy (and loud) Mia Francesca packs 'em in for the earthy, ever-changing, moderately priced northern Italian fare. The casually stylish, colorful crowd is comprised of all ages and persuasions; the décor manages to be simultaneously sleek and warm. The second floor is a bit calmer; the outdoor tables are a lucky score for summer dining. Long waits at the vintage bar or in the coach house are often part of the dining experience here, as Mia takes no reservations. Italian menu. Dinner. Closed Thanksgiving, Dec 25. Bar. Casual attire. Reservations recommended. Valet parking. Outdoor seating. **$$**

★ ★ **MIKE DITKA'S.** *100 E Chestnut St, Chicago (60611). Phone 312/587-8989. www.mikeditkaschicago.*

com. Former Chicago Bears coach Mike Ditka's namesake restaurant is manly, naturally, yet surprisingly civilized. While a museum installation quality sports memorabilia display decorates the clubby restaurant, the patrons exhibit more steakhouse than stadium behavior. Conveniently located near the Magnificent Mile and its many hotels and shopping destinations, Ditka's dishes up generous portions of quality meats (including a massive signature pork chop and "training table" pot roast), as well as seafood, pastas, and salads. The cigar-friendly bar is a louder, more casual destination for snacks and televised sports; upstairs, the cigar lounge features live piano music. American menu. Lunch, dinner, Sat-Sun brunch. Closed Dec 25. Bar. Children's menu. Casual attire. Outdoor seating. **$$$**

★★★ **MIRAI SUSHI.** *2020 W Division St, Chicago (60622). Phone 773/862-8500; fax 773/862-8510.* Wicker Park's funky, hip sushi hotspot is serious about sushi. Offering more than just your everyday maki and nigiri, Mirai ups the ante on sushi (fish is flown in daily, and some selections are still swimming), sake (a generous list), and Japanese culinary creativity (with an intriguing menu items and specials). The bilevel restaurant boasts a bright, smoke-free main-floor dining area and sushi bar, your best bet for experiencing the sushi chef's specials; the upstairs sake bar is dark and seductive, with a choice of barstools, tables, or sleek lounge furniture, with DJ music on weekends. Japanese, sushi menu. Dinner. Closed holidays. Bar. Casual attire. Reservations recommended. Valet parking. Outdoor seating. **$$$**

★★★ **MK.** *868 N Franklin St, Chicago (60610). Phone 312/482-9179; fax 312/482-9171. www.mkchicago.com.* Style meets substance at Michael Kornick's mk, where refined yet real contemporary cuisine is offered in a perfectly compatible setting. The seasonal American food is clean and uncontrived, the multitiered architectural space linear and neutral without severity. Mergers (stylish couples) and acquisitions (salt-and-pepper-haired types in fashionable eyewear) are all a part of the mk dining experience—as are knowledgeable service, a fine wine list (including private-label selections), and excellent desserts. Degustation menus are available, and the chic lounge area is perfect for a before-or-after glass of bubbly. American menu. Dinner. Closed holidays; also the week of July 4. Bar. **$$$**

★★★ **MON AMI GABI.** *2300 N Lincoln Park W, Chicago (60614). Phone 773/348-8886. www.monamigabi.com.* This charming (and aromatic) setting in Lincoln Park's Belden Stratford is so French, you may start speaking with an accent. Solid bistro fare, including a juicy selection of steak preparations and fresh fruits de mer, is a big draw, as are the cozy ambience and rolling wine cart. A second location is in west-suburban Oak Brook, in Oakbrook Center (phone 630/472-1900). Steak menu. Dinner. Closed holidays. Bar. Business casual attire. Reservations recommended. Valet parking. Outdoor seating. **$$**

★★ **MONSOON.** *2813 N Broadway, Chicago (60657). Phone 773/665-9463.* A fascinating menu of contemporary Indian-Asian fusion is presented in an exotic, erotic setting. It's easy to give yourself over to your senses in this upscale opium den dining room; between courses of intriguing food and creative cocktails, you can catch the action in the open kitchen (with tandoor oven) or study the *Kama Sutra* artwork in the rest rooms. Indian menu. Dinner. Closed Mon. Bar. Casual attire. Outdoor seating. **$$$**

★★★ **MORTON'S, THE STEAKHOUSE.** *1050 N State St, Chicago (60610). Phone 312/266-4820; fax 312/266-4852. www.mortons.com.* This steakhouse chain, which originated in Chicago in 1978, appeals to serious meat lovers. With a selection of belt-busting carnivorous delights (like the house specialty, a 24-ounce porterhouse), as well as fresh fish, lobster, and chicken entrées, Morton's rarely disappoints. If you just aren't sure what you're in the mood for, the tableside menu presentation may help you decide. Here, main course selections are placed on a cart that's rolled to your table, where servers describe each item in detail. Steak menu. Dinner. Closed holidays. Bar. Casual attire. Valet parking. **$$$**

★★★ **NACIONAL 27.** *325 W Huron, Chicago (60610). Phone 312/664-2727. www.leye.com.* The name hints at the 27 Latin countries informing the menu at this stylish, even sexy, River North restaurant. Exotic ingredients and creative preparations (including some refreshingly different desserts) lend an escapist feel to a meal here; an array of tapas is one dining option. The ambience is upscale, contemporary supper club, with a posh lounge that's a popular gathering place for after-work or date drinks. Things really heat up on weekends with late-night DJ dancing (with a cover charge for nondiners). Latin American menu. Dinner, late-night. Closed Sun. Bar. Casual attire. Outdoor seating. **$$$**

★★★ **NAHA.** *500 N Clark St, Chicago (60610). Phone 312/321-6242; fax 312/321-7561. www.naha-*

chicago.com. Chef Carrie Nahabadian cooked at the Four Seasons Beverly Hills before opening her own River North spot, Naha, where she merges her Armenian background with her California training. The result is a luscious Mediterranean-like blend of flavors in creative dishes such as sea scallops with grapefruit, bass with olive oil-poached tomatoes, and roast pheasant with grilled asparagus. The sleek, sophisticated décor and attentive service vault Naha above area competitors. American menu. Lunch, dinner. Closed Sun; holidays. Bar. Children's menu. Business casual attire. Reservations recommended. Valet parking. **$$$**

★ ★ **NANIWA.** *607 N Wells St, Chicago (60610). Phone 312/255-8555. www.sushinaniwa.com.* You don't expect an overlooked gem of a restaurant to be housed on busy Wells Street in River North. But Naniwa is hidden in plain sight. Distinct from the many trendy sushi joints that double as lounges, Naniwa plays it straight with good, fresh fish and deluxe maki rolls. Indoor tables are close together, but in season the patio offers prime viewing of the passing parades of people on Wells. Open for lunch, Naniwa does a big to-go business with area office workers. Japanese menu. Lunch, dinner. Bar. Children's menu. Casual attire. Reservations recommended. Outdoor seating. **$$**

★ ★ ★ **NICK'S FISHMARKET.** *51 S Clark St, Chicago (60603). Phone 312/621-0200; fax 312/621-1118. www.nicksfishmarketchicago.com.* Although Nick's specializes in seafood, it acts in every other way like a steakhouse. Consider the dark, subterranean room with low ceilings and attentive tuxedoed waiters. Traditional preparations like lobster bisque and lobster thermador encourage the simile. But in the kitchen, Nick is all about fish. An operation born in Hawaii in the mid-1960s, Nick's reveals its roots in Hawaiian fish specials and the "Maui Wowie" salad. Appetizers feature shellfish, sashimi, and caviar, followed by sole, salmon, and lobster entrées. The street-level bar serves casual versions. Seafood menu. Lunch, dinner. Closed Sun; holidays. Bar. Business casual attire. Reservations recommended. Valet parking. **$$$**

★ ★ ★ **NINE.** *440 W Randolph St, Chicago (60606). Phone 312/575-9900; fax 312/575-9901. www.n9ne.com.* A scene-setter in the West Loop, this Vegas-worthy spot blends sophistication and sizzle and backs it up with serious American steakhouse fare, a central champagne and caviar bar, and great people-watching. Equally suited to business and social dining, Nine is a one-stop evening out, with a large bar/lounge area and another late-night upstairs lounge, the Ghost Bar. Seafood, Steak menu. Lunch, dinner. Closed Sun; holidays. Bar. Business casual attire. Reservations recommended. Valet parking. **$$$**

★ ★ **NIX.** *163 E Walton Pl, Chicago (60611). Phone 312/867-7575; toll-free 866/866-8086; fax 312/751-9205. www.milleniumhotels.com.* This stylishly modern, eclectic offering in the Millennium Knickerbocker Hotel serves a breakfast buffet, lunch, and dinner, with selections running the gamut from upscale comfort food to global fusion. The crowd is a mix of business types and traveling families. Don't miss the 44-strong martini list. American menu. Breakfast, lunch, dinner. Closed holidays. Bar. Business casual attire. Reservations recommended. Valet parking. **$$$**

★ ★ ★ **NOMI.** *800 N Michigan Ave, Chicago (60611). Phone 312/239-4030; fax 312/239-4000. www.nomirestaurant.com.* A posh perch over Chicago's famed Magnificent Mile, NoMI (an acronym for North Michigan) is the Park Hyatt's (see) stylish, civilized destination for critically acclaimed contemporary French cuisine. Asian influences are evident in sushi and sashimi selections on the sophisticated menu. Luxurious materials combine in the streamlined décor, highlighted by an eye-catching art collection, glittering open kitchen, and scintillating view from floor-to-ceiling windows. The wine list is both impressive and extensive, with 3,000 or so bottles. NoMI also serves breakfast and lunch and offers outdoor terrace dining in fair weather. French menu. Breakfast, lunch, dinner, Sun brunch. Bar. Children's menu. Business casual attire. Reservations recommended. Valet parking. Outdoor seating. **$$$$**

★ ★ ★ **NORTH POND.** *2610 N Cannon Dr, Chicago (60614). Phone 773/477-5845; fax 773/477-3234. www.northpondrestaurant.com.* North Pond delivers a dining experience like no other. Seasonal, contemporary American food emphasizing regional ingredients is paired with an all-American wine list and served in a one-of-a-kind location on the Lincoln Park lagoon. The handsome Arts and Crafts décor gives the feeling that Frank Lloyd Wright had a hand in the proceedings. No roads lead here; cab it or look for parking along Cannon Drive and then follow the garden path to the restaurant. Sunday brunch is a refined indulgence, and outdoor dining is a special treat in seasonable weather. French menu. Lunch, dinner, Sun brunch. Closed Mon; holidays. Bar.

Business casual attire. Reservations recommended. Valet parking. **$$$**

★ NORTHSIDE CAFE. *1635 N Damen Ave, Chicago (60647). Phone 773/384-3555; fax 773/384-6337. www.northsidechicago.com.* Northside Cafe is a popular local spot for casual, concept-free dining. A great place for people-watching or for a late-night snack (the kitchen is open until 2 am), it's a local favorite for standard—but tasty—bar food, such as burgers, salads, and sandwiches. Summer is especially popular here, when the patio opens up and patrons can enjoy the great weather while sipping on one of Northside's famous frozen margaritas. Bar Food. Lunch, dinner, late-night, Sat-Sun brunch. Closed holidays. Bar. Casual attire. Valet parking. Outdoor seating. **$$**

★ OAK TREE. *900 N Michigan Ave, Chicago (60611). Phone 312/751-1988.* With its location on the sixth floor of the busy indoor mall at 900 North Michigan (known to locals as the Bloomingdale's Building), Oak Tree is a popular spot with shoppers and tourists who need a break from the hustle and bustle of the Magnificent Mile. The varied menu features everything from Americanized versions of Asian, Mexican, and Italian dishes to dressed-up breakfast items (served all day) such as pancakes, omelets, and eggs Benedict. If you can't snag a window seat to enjoy the views of Michigan Avenue, don't worry—the bright, nature-inspired dining room makes for a pleasurable experience nonetheless. American menu. Breakfast, lunch, dinner, brunch. Closed holidays. Casual attire. **$**

★★★ ONE SIXTYBLUE. *1400 W Randolph, Chicago (60607). Phone 312/850-0303; fax 312/829-3046. www.onesixtyblue.com.* Award-winning, haute contemporary cuisine and sleek, high-styled décor by famed designer Adam Tihany define this adult, urban dining experience in the West Loop. Bold American fare with French roots is at home in the contemporary yet comfortable dining room, done in dark wood and citrus hues with discreet lighting and great sightlines. The open kitchen and dramatic wine storage are focal points. A cocoa bar offers sinful chocolate creations; the chic lounge is a hot cocktail spot. The buzz over former Chicago Bull Michael Jordan's partnership is a mere whisper now that his limelight has dimmed. American menu. Dinner. Closed Sun; holidays. Bar. Casual attire. **$$$**

★★★ OPERA. *1301 S Wabash Ave, Chicago (60605). Phone 312/461-0161; fax 312/461-0181. www.opera-chicago.com.* Helping to position the gentrifying South Loop as a foodie destination, Opera updates Chinese fare by banning gummy sauces and upping the presentation appeal. Top picks include five-spice squid and slow-roasted pork shoulder. The lively, art-filled interior—don't miss the Asian girlie collages—encourages lingering over cocktails. Romantics are served by tables set within a series of narrow vaults in this former film storage warehouse. Chinese menu. Dinner. Closed holidays. Bar. Casual attire. Reservations recommended. Valet parking. **$$$**

★ ORANGE. *3231 N Clark St, Chicago (60657). Phone 773/549-4400; fax 773/549-4413.* This Wrigleyville breakfast and lunch spot made its mark in the restaurant-mad neighborhood with inventive fare like "green eggs and ham" (pesto eggs and pancetta), jelly donut pancakes, and steak sandwiches with Spanish blue cheese. The juice bar will squeeze anything garden-grown, from oranges to cucumbers to beets. The colorful interior, family-friendly vibe, and budget-minded menu spread good cheer here. American menu. Breakfast, lunch, brunch. Children's menu. Casual attire. Outdoor seating. **$**

★★★ THE PALM. *323 E Wacker Dr, Chicago (60601). Phone 312/616-1000; fax 312/616-3717. www.thepalm.com.* While some people feel that this classic concept has become watered down, The Palm in the Swissôtel (see) still delivers on its promise of giant steaks and lobsters in a business-casual steakhouse atmosphere, complete with a caricature wall of fame and platinum-card prices. Seasonal outdoor seating offers great views. American, steak menu. Lunch, dinner. Bar. Casual attire. Valet parking. Outdoor seating. **$$$**

★★★ PANE CALDO. *72 E Walton St, Chicago (60611). Phone 312/649-0055; fax 312/274-0540. www.pane-caldo.com.* This little gem off the Magnificent Mile is home to some of the best Italian food this side of Piedmont. It's easy to miss this tiny restaurant—look for the ultra-posh shoppers enjoying a midday respite and the suit-coated businessmen having power lunches over risotto Milanese. An extensive wine list complements the kitchen's lovely creations, made with organic meats and locally grown organic produce. Italian menu. Lunch, dinner. Closed holidays. Bar. Business casual attire. Reservations recommended. **$$$**

★★ PAPRIKASH. *5210 W Diversey, Chicago (60639). Phone 773/736-4949; fax 773/736-4982. www.*

paprikashrestaurant.com. Hungarian menu. Lunch, dinner. Closed Mon. Bar. Casual attire. Reservations recommended. **$$**

★ PARTHENON. *314 S Halsted St, Chicago (60661). Phone 312/726-2407; fax 312/726-3203. www.theparthenon.com.* A Greektown landmark, this long-standing, family-run favorite is known for its convivial taverna atmosphere and solid renditions of moderately priced, classic Greek fare (flaming cheese and lamb dishes are standouts) and the free valet parking is a bonus. Greek menu. Lunch, dinner. Closed Thanksgiving, Dec 25. Bar. Casual attire. Reservations recommended. Valet parking. **$$**

★ PENNY'S NOODLE SHOP. *3400 N Sheffield Ave, Chicago (60657). Phone 773/281-8222.* Hungry bargain-hunters have been slurping up Penny's namesake noodles by the carload ever since this convenient (and expanding) concept opened its doors a few years ago. Draws include the healthful fare, low prices, and low-key atmosphere. Thai menu. Lunch, dinner. Closed Mon; holidays. Casual attire. Outdoor seating. **$**

★ ★ PETTERINO'S. *150 N Dearborn, Chicago (60601). Phone 312/422-0150. www.leye.com.* Named after Arturo Petterino, the longtime maitre d' of Chicago's famed Pump Room, this theater-district restaurant packs in a crowd that loves the 1940s supper club feel. Classic Italian-American dishes like chicken cacciatore, spaghetti and meatballs, and veal marsala are served nightly in this darkly lit, wood-paneled dining room with welcoming red booths. American, steak menu. Lunch, dinner. Bar. Valet parking. **$$**

★ PIECE. *1927 W North Ave, Chicago (60622). Phone 773/772-4422.* Chicago may be the home of deep-dish pizza, but you'll never find it on the menu at *this* Wicker Park pizzeria. The only pizza served here is the East Coast-style thin-crust variety (one of the co-owners hails from Connecticut). Diners can order one of Piece's specialty pizzas or create their own using one of the bases—red, white, or plain—and a variety of ingredients ranging from the traditional tomatoes and mushrooms to the more adventurous clams and bacon. And what's pizza without beer? Ten regional microbrews and seven house-brewed beers are on hand to wash it all down. Pizza. Lunch, dinner, late-night. Bar. Casual attire. **$**

★ PIZZA D. O. C. *2251 W Lawrence, Chicago (60625). Phone 773/784-8777.* Italian menu. Dinner. Closed holidays. **$**

★ PIZZERIA UNO. *29 E Ohio St, Chicago (60611). Phone 312/321-1000. www.unos.com.* Surely you've heard about Chicago-style pizza: the kind made of a flaky, pie-like crust and stuffed with generous amounts of meats, cheeses, vegetables, and spices. This legendary deep-dish pizza originated at Pizzeria Uno, a casual eatery decorated with hardwood booths and pictures of famous Chicagoans. Because these pizzas take up to 45 minutes to prepare, your order is taken while you wait for your table. Not willing to wait for a seat? Head across the street to Pizzeria Due, which was opened to handle the overflow of crowds at Pizzeria Uno. Pizza. Lunch, dinner, late-night. Closed holidays. Bar. Children's menu. Casual attire. Outdoor seating. **$$**

★ POT PAN. *1750 W North Ave, Chicago (60622). Phone 773/862-6990; fax 773/862-6993.* This simple noodle house is a favorite with Wicker Park/Bucktown locals, who enjoy the homey décor and inexpensive Thai food. Pot Pan is known for its outstanding Panang curry as well as its great spring rolls. Thai menu. Lunch, dinner. **$**

★ ★ ★ PUMP ROOM. *1301 N State Pkwy, Chicago (60610). Phone 312/266-0360; fax 312/266-1798. www.pumproom.com.* This revered Chicago classic combines the grand, gracious hotel dining of yesteryear with contemporary French-American fare. Having undergone several chef changes in recent years (and a major renovation a few years ago), the Pump Room remains popular with tourists and special-occasion celebrants. Booth One lives on, complete with vintage telephone; the bar could have been transported from a *Thin Man* set. The photo wall is a sentimental journey down the memory lane of film, music, and politics. Highlights include live music with a small dance floor and Sunday champagne brunch. The "upscale casual" dress code attests to the times. American menu. Breakfast, lunch, dinner, Sun brunch. Bar. Valet parking. **$$$**

★ ★ RAS DASHEN. *5846 N Broadway, Chicago (60660). Phone 773/506-9601; fax 773/506-9685. www.rasdashenchicago.com.* Feel free to eat with your hands at Ras Dashen, an Ethiopian eatery that provides an authentic taste of the North African nation. In native style, diners tear hunks of the spongy inerja bread that forms a plate for chicken and lamb dishes and use it to scoop up tasty bites. Ethiopian art and artifacts, including imported straw tables and chairs, fill the tidy

Uptown storefront. Ethiopian menu. Lunch, dinner. Bar. Casual attire. Reservations recommended. **$$**

★ ★ RED LIGHT. *820 W Randolph St, Chicago (60607). Phone 312/733-8880; fax 312/733-8571. www.redlight-chicago.com.* Asian fusion in an avant-garde, fantasy atmosphere defines this restaurant row favorite. Renowned chef Jackie Shen has taken over the kitchen, which produces fresh, creative combinations of Chinese, Thai, Japanese, and American ingredients and preparations. This hotspot can be very noisy during prime time. Pan-Asian menu. Lunch, dinner. Closed Jan 1, Thanksgiving, Dec 25. Bar. Business casual attire. Reservations recommended. Valet parking. Outdoor seating. **$$$**

★ REDFISH. *400 N State St, Chicago (60610). Phone 312/467-1600; fax 312/467-0325. www.redfishamerica.com.* This thematic Cajun spot goes all out with "N'awlins" décor, a catch-all of voodoo dolls, Mardis Gras masks, and hot sauces. The namesake redfish leads the menu (have it blackened) along with crab-stuffed salmon and pastas. In keeping with its Big Easy affinity, drinking is a sport here. To encourage late-night guzzling, the restaurant brings in zydeco and R & B bands on the weekends. Cajun/Creole menu. Lunch, dinner. Closed holidays. Bar. Children's menu. Casual attire. Reservations recommended. Valet parking. **$$**

★ ★ RIVA. *700 E Grand Ave, Chicago (60611). Phone 312/644-7482; fax 312/644-4377. www.stefanirestaurants.com.* Bustling with Navy Pier tourists and locals alike, this elegant restaurant is popular for its fresh seafood, as well as its spectacular views of the Chicago skyline. Along with a 40-foot-long open kitchen, the dining room features nautical décor that re-creates the atmosphere of the Italian Riviera. On Wednesdays (9:30 pm) and Saturdays (10:15 pm) from Memorial Day to Labor Day, enjoy Navy Pier's dazzling evening fireworks displays while you dine. Seafood menu. Lunch, dinner. Closed Thanksgiving, Dec 24-25. Bar. Children's menu. Business casual attire. Reservations recommended. Valet parking. Outdoor seating. **$$$**

★ ★ ★ RL RESTAURANT. *115 E Chicago Ave, Chicago (60611). Phone 312/475-1100; fax 312/266-9853.* American menu. Lunch, dinner, Sun brunch. Bar. Children's menu. Casual attire. Reservations recommended. Valet parking. Outdoor seating. **$$$**

★ ★ ★ RODAN. *1530 N Milwaukee Ave, Chicago (60622). Phone 773/276-7036.* A funky, globe-trotting Wicker Parker, Rodan unites the foods of South America and Asia on its menu. Graze from gingered swordfish and shrimp rolls back West to adobo Cornish hen and fish tacos with mango salsa. Somewhere in between lie the tasty wasabi tempura fries. Go casual to Rodan, and go late-night if you're looking for a hip lounge. As the night progresses, the lights come down, the music comes up, and the bar fills with revelers. South American, Southeast Asian menu. Dinner, late-night. Bar. Casual attire. **$$**

★ ★ ROSEBUD. *1500 W Taylor St, Chicago (60607). Phone 312/942-1117. www.rosebudrestaurants.com.* The Taylor Street original of this expanding family of old-school Italian restaurants is a Little Italy tradition, revered for its boisterous Sinatra-swagger ambience; clubby, carved wood décor; and giant portions with inevitable doggie bags. There's a large bar area for waiting during peak periods. Italian menu. Lunch, dinner. Closed Thanksgiving, Dec 25. Bar. Business casual attire. Reservations recommended. Valet parking. Outdoor seating. **$$**

★ ★ ROY'S. *720 N State St, Chicago (60610). Phone 312/787-7599. roysrestaurant.com.* Don't expect luau fare—and don't wear your Hawaiian shirt—at this sleek, contemporary Hawaiian chain member. Lots of creative seafood dishes populate the menu, with several unusual fish varieties offered; French and Asian fusion elements are evident throughout. There are also several meat dishes for the seafood squeamish. Menu selections are listed with suggested wine pairings (the restaurant has its own wine label produced by various houses—plus its own range of sake, which partners nicely with much of the food). Hawaiian menu. Dinner. Closed Thanksgiving, Dec 25. Bar. Children's menu. Casual attire. Outdoor seating. **$$$**

★ ★ RUMBA. *351 W Hubbard St, Chicago (60610). Phone 312/222-1226; fax 312/222-1822. www.rumba351.com.* Nuevo Latino menu. Lunch, dinner. Closed Sun-Mon; Jan 1, Dec 24-25. Bar. Casual attire. **$$$**

★ ★ RUSHMORE. *1023 W Lake St, Chicago (60607). Phone 312/421-8845; fax 312/421-8860. www.rushmore-chicago.com.* American regional food shines at Rushmore in the trendy West Loop. The kitchen plucks comfort food classics from around the country to include smoked cheddar macaroni and cheese, cornmeal-crusted fried chicken, and fish-and-chips fancied up to include trout and matchstick potatoes. In contrast to the homey food, the atmosphere leans toward the contemporary, providing a window to the front line cooks. American menu. Dinner.

Closed Sun. Bar. Children's menu. Casual attire. Reservations recommended. **$$**

★ ★ RUSSIAN TEA TIME. *77 E Adams St, Chicago (60603). Phone 312/360-0000; fax 312/360-0575. www.russianteatime.com.* Despite the name, the emphasis here is on Russian food rather than tea. Traditional caviar service and classics like borscht, salmon blinis, and stuffed cabbage wave the old-world torch, as does the time-warp look of red booths, brass chandeliers, and waiters in tuxedos. Neighboring both the Art Institute of Chicago and Symphony Center, Russian Tea Time draws a cultured crowd. Russian menu. Lunch, dinner. Closed holidays. Bar. Business casual attire. Reservations recommended. **$$**

★ ★ SAI CAFE. *2010 N Sheffield Ave, Chicago (60614). Phone 773/472-8080. www.saicafe.com.* This old-guard Lincoln Park neighborhood standby for sushi and classic Japanese cuisine was crowded long before the wave of hip sushi spots hit town. It's a comfortable, low-attitude place for reliable fare and friendly service—and the selection of both sushi and maki rolls is extensive. Sushi menu. Dinner. Bar. Casual attire. Reservations recommended. **$$**

★ ★ SALOON STEAKHOUSE. *200 E Chestnut St, Chicago (60611). Phone 312/280-5454; fax 312/280-6986. www.saloonsteakhouse.com.* Don't expect swinging doors and cowpokes at this refined, modern "saloon," a masculine steaks-and-cigars carnivore haven. If you're looking for a light bite, The Saloon is *not* the place to go; this steakhouse offers mega-sized portions, like the 2-pound porterhouse and the 14-ounce strip loin. Located on a somewhat secluded strip just off of busy Michigan Avenue, the swanky Saloon is the perfect place to escape the crowds of power shoppers on the Magnificent Mile. Steak menu. Lunch, dinner. Closed holidays. Bar. Casual attire. **$$$**

★ ★ ★ SALPIÇON. *1252 N Wells St, Chicago (60610). Phone 312/988-7811; fax 312/988-7715. www.salpicon.com.* In a town where chef Rick Bayless and his Frontera Grill (see) rule the gourmet Mexican roost, Salpicon remains an in-the-know treasure. Chef Priscilla Satkoff grew up in Mexico City and honors her native cuisine here with rich moles, tender-roasted meats, and upscale twists on both, such as ancho chile quail. The extensive wine list, managed by the chef's husband, has won numerous awards. But it's hard to get past the 50-some tequilas on offer to mix in margaritas (knowing servers ably steer agave gringos). Salpicon's boldly colored interiors generate a spirit of fiesta. Mexican menu. Dinner, Sun brunch. Closed Thanksgiving, Dec 25. Bar. Valet parking. Outdoor seating. **$$**

★ ★ SANTORINI. *800 W Adams St, Chicago (60607). Phone 312/829-8820; fax 312/829-6263. www.santorinichicago.com.* This Greektown seafood specialist represents an oasis of calm amid its more boisterous companions on the neighborhood's busy strip. Authentic, fresh fish (especially the whole-grilled offerings) and the airy, Mediterranean seaside atmosphere with whitewashed walls transport patrons to the island of the same name. Greek menu. Lunch, dinner. Closed Thanksgiving, Dec 25. Bar. Casual attire. Reservations recommended. Valet parking. Outdoor seating. **$$**

★ SAUCE. *1750 N Clark St, Chicago (60614). Phone 312/932-1750; fax 312/932-0056. www.saucechicago.com.* Opposite Lincoln Park on the fringe of Old Town, Sauce intends to be a restaurant. But a pack of young, martini-swilling regulars have claimed it as a hangout. The menu ranges far and wide to include bar fare (artichoke dip, quesadillas, pizza), comfort food (lasagna), and trendy options (seared tuna). If you're only after the food, come early. But if it's eye candy you crave, drop by late. American, Cajun menu. Dinner, late-night. Closed Sun; Jan 1, Dec 25. Bar. Casual attire. Outdoor seating. **$$**

★ SAYAT NOVA. *157 E Ohio St, Chicago (60611). Phone 312/644-9159; fax 312/644-9715.* For something completely different, try this family-run Armenian spot for a touch of foreign intrigue and bargain-priced kebabs, lamb dishes, stuffed grape leaves, and other traditional Middle Eastern fare. Opened in 1969, Sayat Nova is now a pleasant anachronism in its chichi off-the Magn Mile location. Armenian menu. Lunch, dinner. Closed holidays. Bar. Casual attire. Reservations recommended. **$$**

★ ★ SCOOZI. *410 W Huron, Chicago (60610). Phone 312/943-5900; fax 312/943-8969.* An early pioneer of now-booming River North, this Lettuce Entertain You Italian concept—once hip, now comfortable—is a convivial place to gather for cocktails in the large bar area, cracker-crust pizzas, goodies from the generous antipasto bar, or full-blown Italian dining. The cavernous space gets warmth and gravitas from the faux-antiqued décor. Italian menu. Dinner. Closed holidays. Bar. Children's menu. Casual attire. Reservations recommended. Valet parking. Outdoor seating. **$$**

★ ★ ★ ★ **SEASONS.** *120 E Delaware Pl, Chicago (60611). Phone 312/649-2349; fax 312/280-9184. www.fourseasons.com/chicagofs.* Dining at Seasons, the upscale and elegant restaurant of the Four Seasons Hotel Chicago (see), is the sort of experience that may cause whiplash. Your head will whip back and forth as you watch stunning plates pass by in the rich and refined dining room. Each dish looks better than the next. On a nightly basis, the dining room is filled with food envy. Perhaps this is because the kitchen prepares every plate with a deep respect for ingredients, making every inventive dish on the menu of New American fare a delight to admire from afar and devour from up close. The chef offers five-course and eight-course tasting menus. What's more, while a restaurant of this stature could easily feel pretentious, the staff's warmth and charm makes dining here easy and comfortable—a pleasure from start to finish. American, French menu. Breakfast, lunch, dinner, Sun brunch. Bar. Children's menu. Valet parking. Business casual attire. Reservations recommended. **$$$$**

★ ★ ★ **SHANGHAI TERRACE.** *108 E Superior, Chicago (60610). Phone 312/573-6744. www.chicago.peninsula.com.* Fittingly, the Asian-run Peninsula hotel (see) gives Chicago its best Chinese restaurant. Intimate and trimmed in rich hues of ruby red and lacquer black, Shanghai Terrace is the best looking of its category, too. Start with the eatery's refined three-bite dim sum dishes. Save room for flavorful entrées like spicy Sichuan beef and wok-fried lobster. You'll find Shanghai Terrace one level below the ornate hotel lobby. The restaurant adjoins an expansive terrace offering alfresco dining in the summer six stories above Michigan Avenue. Chinese menu. Lunch, dinner. Closed Sun. Bar. Casual attire. Outdoor seating. **$$$**

★ ★ **SHAW'S CRAB HOUSE.** *21 E Hubbard St, Chicago (60611). Phone 312/527-2722; fax 312/527-4740. www.shawscrabhouse.com.* A longtime seafood standard bearer, popular Shaw's in River North goes the extra mile to fly in an extensive variety of fresh seafood, served in a choice of environments—upscale clubby dining room or East Coast style oyster bar ambience in the Blue Crab Lounge. Seafood menu. Lunch, dinner. Closed holidays. Bar. Business casual attire. Reservations recommended. Valet parking. **$$$**

★ ★ **SHE SHE.** *4539 N Lincoln Ave, Chicago (60625). Phone 773/293-3690.* Fine dining-caliber food in funky digs endears She She to residents of the Lincoln Square neighborhood. Although the menu changes seasonally, expect chef Nicole Parthemore's signature coconut-crusted shrimp, salmon maki rolls, and contemporized entrées like duck confit linguine. While the food is serious, the scene—from the leopard print seats to the RuPaul martini—is anything but. American menu. Dinner, Sun brunch. Closed Mon; Thanksgiving, Dec 25. Bar. Children's menu. Casual attire. Reservations recommended. Outdoor seating. **$$**

★ ★ **SIGNATURE ROOM AT THE 95TH.** *875 N Michigan Ave, Chicago (60611). Phone 312/787-9596; fax 312/280-9448. www.signatureroom.com.* Situated atop one of the world's tallest buildings, the John Hancock Center, and towering 1,000 feet above the Magnificent Mile, the Signature Room is deservedly famous for its breathtaking vistas. It affords spectacular views from every part of its dining room. Sumptuous Art Deco surroundings complement picture-perfect scenes of the city and Lake Michigan, visible through the floor-to-ceiling windows that circle the room. The food is contemporary American (consider the reasonably priced lunch buffet or the Sunday brunch). Convenient to downtown hotels and shopping, the Signature Lounge is also a popular spot for a romantic rendezvous or business cocktails. American menu. Lunch, dinner, Sun brunch. Closed Jan 1, Dec 25. Bar. Children's menu. Business casual attire. Reservations recommended. **$$$**

★ ★ **SOUK.** *1552 N Milwaukee Ave, Chicago (60622). Phone 773/227-1818; fax 773/278-1455. www.soukrestaurant.com.* Stepping into the exotic surroundings of Souk (Arabic for "marketplace") is like entering another world—tile artwork, beads, candles, leather-topped tables, and long, plush banquettes decorate the cozy dining room. It is the perfect atmosphere in which to dine on a menu that reflects all cultures of the Mediterranean, including Turkey, Greece, Morocco, and Egypt. Familiar dishes like hummus and baba ghanoush are among the selections, as are some not-so-familiar dishes like toshka and keba. Entertainment, which includes jazz and belly dancing, is offered weekly and perfect to watch while enjoying a post-dinner shisha (water pipe) filled with fruit tobacco. Mediterranean menu. Dinner. Closed Sun-Mon; holidays. Bar. Casual attire. Reservations recommended. Valet parking. **$$**

★ ★ ★ **SPIAGGIA.** *980 N Michigan Ave, Chicago (60611). Phone 312/280-2750; fax 312/943-8560. www.spiaggiarestaurant.com.* Next to Spiaggia, you'd have to fly to Milan to get a dose of the sort of contemporary, sophisticated Italian cuisine served here. Chef Tony Mantuano has a light, refined touch, working with artisanal and exotic ingredients like Piemontese beef and seasonal white truffles. Expect frequent menu changes, but typical dishes include wood-roasted scallops with porcini mushrooms and Parmesan shavings, pumpkin risotto with seared foie gras, and lamb chops with slow-cooked lamb shoulder. Favored by both expense accounts and special occasion affairs, the opulent trilevel room completes the seduction, offering each table a view over Lake Michigan. Italian menu. Dinner. Closed holidays. Bar. Jacket required. Reservations recommended. Valet parking. **$$$**

★ ★ ★ ★ SPRING. *2039 W North Ave, Chicago (60647). Phone 773/395-7100; fax 773/394-3360. www.springrestaurant.net.* Although you can't always count on the fickle Chicago weather, you can always expect Spring to deliver freshness in food, service, and style. The upscale restaurant showcases chef Shawn McClain's talent with seafood, a light approach often inflected with an Asian accent. Though they change to reflect the seasons, dishes such as tuna tartare with quail egg, cod in crab and sweet pea sauce, and diver scallops with braised oxtail are artistic but unfussy. In a nod to carnivores, the menu also lists several meat options. Lodged in a former Russian bathhouse and still sporting vintage white ceramic tile walls from the 1920s, Spring faces east for inspiration, drawing on Zen principles of design in a foyer rock garden, cleverly angled banquettes, warm lighting, and minimalist flower arrangements. Chicago's bohemian Wicker Park area is an unlikely host for a restaurant of such acclaim, but the neighborhood locale helps defrost any potential fine dining chill. American menu. Dinner. Closed Mon; holidays. Bar. Business casual attire. Reservations recommended. Valet parking. **$$$**

★ STANLEY'S. *1970 N Lincoln Ave, Chicago (60614). Phone 312/642-0007.* As you enter through the front door, Stanley's looks like a typical Lincoln Park bar. But walk a little farther into the dining area and you'll feel like you've entered someone's home; this family-friendly space is decorated with photos, children's drawings, and knickknacks. And the food will make you feel at home, too. Large portions of American comfort food like mac and cheese, meat loaf, and mashed potatoes and gravy are sure to bring back memories of the way Mom used to cook. American menu. Breakfast, lunch, dinner. Bar. Casual attire. Outdoor seating. **$$**

★ SU CASA. *49 E Ontario St, Chicago (60611). Phone 312/943-4041; fax 312/943-6480.* A River North staple for Tex-Mex, Su Casa has been dishing its brand of south-of-the-border hospitality since 1963. Founded by the same golden-touch restaurateur who established Pizzeria Uno (see), Su Casa sticks to crowd-pleasing favorites like fajitas, chimichangas, and burritos. Colorful Mexican piñatas and murals help generate a fiesta feel. Mexican menu. Lunch, dinner. Closed Thanksgiving, Dec 25. Bar. Children's menu. Casual attire. Outdoor seating. **$$**

★ ★ SUSHI SAMBA RIO. *504 N Wells St, Chicago (60610). Phone 312/595-2300; fax 312/595-0532. www.sushisamba.com.* Flashy and splashy, this New York/Miami import serves up a wild fusion menu of sushi with Japanese and Brazilian dishes—and cocktails to match. The high-concept contemporary décor offers multiple environments (including a crowded bar area), plenty of people-watching, and a nightclub-like ambience when busy. The all-weather rooftop dining area is exposed in summer, enclosed in winter. Sushi menu. Lunch, dinner. Bar. Business casual attire. Reservations recommended. Valet parking. Outdoor seating. **$$**

★ ★ SUSHI WABI. *842 W Randolph St, Chicago (60607). Phone 312/563-1224; fax 312/563-9579. www.sushiwabi.com.* Chicago's first in a wave of hipster sushi bars draws a fashionable crowd to the West Loop market district for the fresh fish, industrial-chic atmosphere, and late-night DJ music. The clubby (noisy) scene is secondary to the seafood, and savvy sushi lovers know that reservations are a must. Japanese, sushi menu. Lunch, dinner. Closed holidays. Bar. Casual attire. Reservations recommended. Valet parking. **$$**

★ ★ SZECHWAN EAST. *340 E Ohio St, Chicago (60611). ; fax 312/642-3902. www.szechwaneast.com.* The refined atmosphere at Szechwan East makes it a fitting resident of the tony Streeterville area. The Chinese restaurant rounds up an appreciative lunch crowd of office workers eager to sample its value-priced lunch buffet. Off-the-menu favorites include hot and sour soup and sesame chicken. Szechwan fare tends to be spicy, but the kitchen will tone it down upon request. Dine after 9 pm on weekends to catch live pop music acts along with your meal. Chinese menu. Lunch, dinner. Bar. Casual attire. Outdoor seating. **$$**

★ ★ TIZI MELLOUL. *531 N Wells St, Chicago (60610). Phone 312/670-4338; fax 312/670-4254.*

www.tizimelloul.com. A hipster version of Morocco is as close as a cab ride to River North's Tizi Melloul. Filtered through a modern design sensibility, Tizi references North Africa in its spice market color palette and circular communal dining room lit by lanterns. Grilled octopus, tabbouleh salad, and coriander-roasted duck complete the culinary tour. Come on a Sunday for cocktail hour belly dancing. Mediterranean menu. Dinner. Closed holidays. Bar. Business casual attire. Reservations recommended. Valet parking. **$$**

★ **TOAST.** *2046 N Damen Ave, Chicago (60647). Phone 773/772-5600.* This popular breakfast and lunch spot gives classic favorites a trendy twist: eggs Benedict are served with a decadent white truffle hollandaise, and a mountain of French toast is stuffed with strawberries and mascarpone cheese. Prices are reasonable, and the atmosphere is fun, with vintage toasters decorating the small, colorful dining room. American menu. Breakfast, lunch. Closed holidays. Children's menu. Casual attire. Outdoor seating. **$**

★ ★ **TOPO GIGIO RISTORANTE.** *1516 N Wells St, Chicago (60610). Phone 312/266-9355; fax 312/266-8531.* Old Town favorite Topo Gigio draws diners from near and far for crowd-pleasing Italian dishes in a bustling café setting featuring exposed-brick walls and paper-topped tables. The friendly owner also does the cooking and draws up a slate of daily specials to supplement his menu of salads, pastas, and meats. Table waits can be lengthy. For best results, come in summer—early—and snag a table on the outdoor patio or have a drink at the outdoor bar. Italian menu. Lunch, dinner. Bar. Casual attire. Reservations recommended. Valet parking. Outdoor seating. **$$**

★ ★ ★ **TOPOLOBAMPO.** *445 N Clark St, Chicago (60610). Phone 312/661-1434; fax 312/661-1830. www.fronterakitchens.com.* Pioneering chef/owner Rick Bayless is a cookbook author, television personality, and perennial culinary award winner with a devoted following. His celebration of the regional cuisines of Mexico is realized at Topolobampo, the upscale counterpart to his famed Frontera Grill (see)—and the shrine where the faithful gather to revel in the bright, earthy flavors of his fine-dining Mexican fare. The seasonal menu is paired with a tome of premium tequilas and an excellent wine list. White tablecloths and colorful folk art help set the tone for a memorable Mexican meal. Mexican menu. Lunch, dinner. Closed Sun-Mon; holidays, early Jan, early July. Bar. Children's menu. Business casual attire. Reservations recommended. Valet parking. **$$$**

★ ★ **TRATTORIA NO. 10.** *10 N Dearborn St, Chicago (60602). Phone 312/984-1718; fax 312/984-1525. www.trattoriaten.com.* A rustic yet elegant respite from the hectic rush of the Loop business district, Trattoria No. 10 welcomes diners with arched ceilings, murals, and ceramic tile floors. House-made ravioli is a specialty, as are pastas, risottos, and fresh seafood selections on the menu of updated Italian classics. A popular lunch and dinner spot for downtown denizens, Trattoria No. 10 is perhaps best known for its bountiful, bargain-priced cocktail hour buffet—a great pre-theater option or a pick-me-up after museums and shopping. Italian menu. Lunch, dinner. Closed Sun; holidays. Bar. Business casual attire. Reservations recommended. Valet parking. **$$**

★ **TRE KRONOR.** *3258 W Foster Ave, Chicago (60625). Phone 773/267-9888; fax 773/478-3058.* Although it's out of the way, Tre Kronor warrants a trip to the North Park neighborhood for its sincere welcome and delicious Scandinavian comfort food. The family-run storefront serves meals all day, from muesli and Danish blue cheese omelets at breakfast to Swedish meatball sandwiches at lunch and roast pork with figs at dinner. The servers are cheerful, as is the folk-art décor. Scandanavian menu. Breakfast, lunch, dinner, Sun brunch. Closed holidays. Casual attire. Outdoor seating. **$$**

★ ★ ★ ★ **TRU.** *676 N St. Clair St, Chicago (60611). Phone 312/202-0001; fax 312/202-0003. www.trurestaurant.com.* Awash in white and set in a chic, lofty space, TRU's modern, airy dining room is a stunning stage for chef and co-owner Rick Tramonto's savory, progressive French creations and co-owner pastry chef Gale Gand's incredible, one-of-a-kind sweet and savory endings. Tramonto offers plates filled with flawless ingredients that are treated to his unmatched creativity and artistic flair. The result is food that is precious and, some say, overdone. Indeed, many of the plates are so beautiful and complicated that you may not want to dig in and ruin the presentation, or you may be unable to decipher the appropriate way to consume the dish. TRU offers three- to eight-course "Collections" (prix fixe menus) and a unique and extraordinary four-course dessert and champagne dessert tasting. Like the savory side of the menu, the desserts have a distinctive sense of ingredient choice, style, and humor. French menu. Dinner.

Closed Sun. Bar. Jacket required. Reservations recommended. Valet parking. **$$$$**

★ ★ **TSUNAMI.** *1160 N Dearborn St, Chicago (60610). Phone 312/642-9911.* Just a stone's throw from the rowdy Division Street bars, Tsunami keeps it playful, serving up sushi in a style that suits the party-time locale. Piped-in dance tunes, low-slung couches, and dim lighting keep it casual in the upstairs lounge, where you can nosh from the Japanese menu while sipping cocktails. To get the full attention of the creative chefs, sit at the sushi bar and let them concoct unique rolls tailored to your tastes. Sushi menu. Dinner. Bar. Casual attire. Outdoor seating. **$$$**

★ ★ **TUSCANY.** *1014 W Taylor St, Chicago (60612). Phone 312/829-1990; fax 312/829-8023. www.stefanirestaurants.com.* With its cozy dining area, wood-burning ovens, and rustic atmosphere, this upscale Little Italy eatery is reminiscent of an Italian trattoria. The northern Italian menu features homemade pastas and gourmet pizzas, as well as a selection of grilled items like pork, chicken, duck, veal, and steak. And who can forget dessert? Classic Italian sweets like gelato, tiramisu, and cannoli are among the ways to end your meal. Italian menu. Lunch, dinner. Closed holidays. Bar. Business casual attire. Reservations recommended. Valet parking. **$$**

★ **TWIN ANCHORS RESTAURANT AND TAVERN.** *1655 N Sedgwick St, Chicago (60614). Phone 312/266-1616. www.twinanchorsribs.com.* Make no bones about it: Chicago is a meat-and-potatoes kind of town, and there are few things that native Chicagoans like more than a great slab of ribs. Choices abound, but a local favorite is Twin Anchors Restaurant and Tavern in the Old Town neighborhood just north of downtown (and a fairly short cab ride away). Although this former speakeasy was reincarnated as a restaurant in 1932, it maintains its hole-in-the-wall appeal, complete with diner-style booths, linoleum tabletops, a jukebox stocked with an eclectic mix of tunes, and an extensive collection of beers. The real attraction, however, is the ribs; rumor has it that they were Frank Sinatra's favorites. Order them zesty, like a local, and then let the feast begin. The menu may be limited, but the portions are generous. If ribs aren't your style, the hamburgers and filet mignon are also excellent. Be prepared for a long wait, though; this 60-seat restaurant fills up fast. American menu. Lunch, dinner. Closed holidays. Bar. Children's menu. Casual attire. Valet parking. Outdoor seating. **$$**

★ ★ **VIVERE.** *71 W Monroe St, Chicago (60603). Phone 312/332-4040; fax 312/332-2656. www.italianvillage-chicago.com.* The high end of a trio of restaurants that comprises the Loop's long-standing Italian Village, Vivere plays it cool with showy décor and luxurious meals. The warmly lit dining room with decorative scrolls and swirls aims to distract, but the food stands its ground with riffs on the familiar, such as squid ink tortellini stuffed with bass. The Italian wine list rates among the country's best, making this a solid special-occasion choice. Italian menu. Lunch, dinner. Closed Sun; holidays. Bar. Casual attire. Reservations recommended. Valet parking. **$$**

★ ★ **VIVO.** *838 W Randolph St, Chicago (60607). Phone 312/733-3379; fax 312/733-4436. www.vivo-chicago.com.* With the distinction of having pioneered the now-booming Randolph Street restaurant row, Vivo continues to draw a hip crowd for its groovy, contemporary grotto atmosphere (exposed brick, candlelight, and piles of wine bottles) and straightforward Italian fare. The antipasti spread near the entrance is a welcoming, authentic touch. Italian menu. Lunch, dinner. Closed Jan 1, Dec 25. Bar. Business casual attire. Reservations recommended. Valet parking. Outdoor seating. **$$**

★ ★ **VONG'S THAI KITCHEN.** *6 W Hubbard, Chicago (60610). Phone 312/644-8664. www.vongsthaikitchen.com.* This toned-down version of renowned chef Jean-Georges Vongerichten's original, pricier Vong remains a stylish destination for well-crafted Thai-French fusion cuisine. The posh ambience is a bit more casual now, with hip background music, but retains a refined air thanks to rich appointments and polished service. Exotic cocktails enhance the escapist mood; booths in the lounge are a plush place to stop for a sip and a snack. Thai menu. Lunch, dinner. Bar. Children's menu (lunch). Casual attire. Outdoor seating. **$$**

★ ★ **WAVE.** *644 N Lake Shore Dr, Chicago (60611). Phone 312/255-4460. www.whotels.com.* Located in the W hotel across from Lake Michigan, Wave delivers ultra-stylish dining in a chic, modern space. The creative, contemporary seafood menu is laced with exotic spices; "tasting plates" are great for grazing with drinks. The loungy bar also offers elaborate cold seafood concoctions from the "ice bar" paired with high-concept cocktails. American, Mediterranean menu. Breakfast, lunch, dinner. Bar. Casual attire. Outdoor seating. **$$**

★ ★ ★ WEST TOWN TAVERN. *1329 W Chicago Ave, Chicago (60622). Phone 312/666-6175. www.westtowntavern.com.* Beloved Chicago chef Susan Goss and her wine-knowing husband Drew Goss run West Town Tavern, an upscale comfort foodie in a handsome brick-walled storefront that encourages repeats with genuine warmth. If it's on the menu, start with the beer cheese ball, the kind of spreadable cheddar last seen on New Year's Eve in the late 1960s. Entrées include maple-cured pork chops, steak in zinfandel sauce, and duck confit. Desserts finish charmingly via the classed-up s'mores with homemade marshmallows. West Town's wine selection roams far and wide on the interesting and largely affordable list. American menu. Dinner. Closed Sun. Bar. Casual attire. Outdoor seating. **$$**

★ WISHBONE. *1001 W Washington Blvd, Chicago (60607). Phone 312/850-2663; fax 312/850-4332. www.wishbonechicago.com.* Casual Southern dishes at reasonable prices in colorful settings filled with faux-outdoor art comprise the winning combination at Wishbone. Lunches and dinners serve up bean-based hoppin' John, blackened catfish, and shrimp and grits. Breakfast offers plenty of unusual choices, such as crab cakes, to round out the egg offerings. Be an early bird at any meal to expect to dine here on a weekend; throngs of diners are drawn to both this location in the West Loop and in Lakeview (3300 N Lincoln). American menu. Breakfast, lunch, dinner, brunch. Closed holidays. Bar. Children's menu. Casual attire. Reservations recommended. Valet parking. Outdoor seating. **$$**

★ ★ XIPPO. *3759 N Damen, Chicago (60618). Phone 773/529-9135.* Velvet chairs, swagged curtains, exposed-brick walls, and a DJ booth transformed a former North Center corner bar into the lounge eatery Xippo. The menu outclasses the average neighborhood saloon in Chicago, with ambitious dishes like pretzel-crusted pork chops and pan-seared duck breast. On weekends, don't be surprised if the young crowd is more likely to have a cake shot than a slice of cake for dessert. American menu. Dinner. Bar. Casual attire. **$$**

★ ★ ★ YOSHI'S CAFE. *3257 N Halsted St, Chicago (60657). Phone 773/248-6160.* Namesake chef Yoshi Katsumura comes from a fine-dining background, which accounts for the quality and sophistication of his French-Japanese fusion cuisine. But the long-standing Lakeview café stays dear to its neighbors by keeping the atmosphere relaxed—with good service and even a children's menu—the kind of casual shop that invites repeat dining. Although the menu changes frequently, it maintains the chef's high standards as it meanders from shrimp cappuccino soup all the way to sirloin steak. Eclectic/International menu. Lunch, dinner. Closed Mon. Bar. Casual attire. Outdoor seating. **$$**

★ ★ ★ ZEALOUS. *419 W Superior St, Chicago (60610). Phone 312/475-9112; fax 312/475-0165. www.zealousrestaurant.com.* Charlie Trotter protégé Michael Taus runs Zealous with a Trotter-like attention to detail and innovation. Menus change constantly, but you can expect the daring, like veal sweetbread-topped beignets, taro root and mushroom ravioli with sea-urchin sauce, and star-anise braised veal cheeks. Put yourself in the chef's hands with a five- or seven-course degustation menu. This is event dining, amplified by the thoughtful Asian-influenced décor. Bamboo planters, skylit 18-foot ceilings, and a glass-clad wine room make Zealous a fitting resident of the River North gallery district. American menu. Dinner. Closed Sun-Mon; holidays. Bar. Business casual attire. Reservations recommended. Valet parking. **$$$**

Index

B

C

D

E

F

H

M

N

O

P

Q

R

T

X

Y

Z

Notes

Notes

Notes

Notes

Notes

Notes

Notes

Notes

Notes

Notes

Notes

Notes

Notes

Notes

Notes

Notes

Notes

Notes